Lecture Notes in Computer Science 2195
Edited by G. Goos, J. Hartmanis and J. van Leeuwen

Springer-Verlag Berlin Heidelberg GmbH

Heung-Yeung Shum Mark Liao
Shih-Fu Chang (Eds.)

Advances in Multimedia Information Processing – PCM 2001

Second IEEE Pacific Rim Conference on Multimedia
Beijing, China, October 24-26, 2001
Proceedings

Volume 1

Volume Editors

Heung-Yeung Shum
Microsoft Research China
5/F Beijing Sigma Center
49 Zhichung Road, Haidian District, Beijing 100080, China
E-mail: hshum@microsoft.com

Mark Liao
Institute of Information Science, Academia Sinica, Taiwan
E-mail: liao@iis.sinica.edu.tw

Shih-Fu Chang
Columbia University, Department of Electrical Engineering
New York, NY 10027, USA
E-mail: sfchang@ctr.columbia.edu

Cataloging-in-Publication Data applied for

Die Deutsche Bibliothek - CIP-Einheitsaufnahme

Advances in multimedia information processing : proceedings / PCM 2001, Second IEEE Pacific Rim Conference on Multimedia, Beijing, China, October 24 - 26, 2001. Heung-Yeung Shum ... (ed.). - Berlin ; Heidelberg ; New York ; Barcelona ; Hong Kong ; London ; Milan ; Paris ; Tokyo : Springer, 2001
(Lecture notes in computer science ; Vol. 2195)

CR Subject Classification (1998): H.5.1, H.3, H.5, C.2, K.6, H.4

ISSN 0302-9743

ISBN 978-3-540-42680-6 ISBN 978-3-540-45453-3 (eBook)
DOI 10.1007/978-3-540-45453-3

http://www.springer.de

Originally published by Springer-Verlag Berlin Heidelberg New York in 2001.

Typesetting: Camera-ready by author
Printed on acid-free paper SPIN 10840648 06/3142 5 4 3 2 1 0

Preface

Welcome to the second IEEE Pacific-Rim Conference on Multimedia (IEEE-PCM 2001) held in Zhongguanchun, Beijing, China, October 22-24, 2001. Building upon the success of the inaugural IEEE-PCM 2000 in Sydney in December 2000, the second PCM again brought together the researchers, developers, practitioners, and educators of multimedia in the Pacific area. Theoretical breakthroughs and practical systems were presented at this conference, thanks to the sponsorship by the IEEE Circuit and Systems Society, IEEE Signal Processing Society, China Computer Foundation, China Society of Image and Graphics, National Natural Science Foundation of China, Tsinghua University, and Microsoft Research, China.

IEEE-PCM 2001 featured a comprehensive program including keynote talks, regular paper presentations, posters, demos, and special sessions. We received 244 papers and accepted only 104 of them as regular papers, and 53 as poster papers. Our special session chairs, Shin'ichi Satoh and Mohan Kankanhalli, organized 6 special sessions. We acknowledge the great contribution from our program committee members and paper reviewers who spent many hours reviewing submitted papers and providing valuable comments for the authors.

The conference would not have been successful without the help of so many people. We greatly appreciated the support of our honorary chairs: Prof. Sun-Yuan Kung of Princeton University, Dr. Ya-Qin Zhang of Microsoft Research China, and Prof. Chao-huan Hou of the National Science Foundation of China. A number of people deserve special thanks for helping with the logistics. Yuan-chun Shi smoothly handled publication of these proceedings with Springer-Verlag. Feng Wu and Zhong Su did a wonderful job as web masters. Timely help from Le Guo and Ling Huang was tremendous. Financial sponsorships from industrial research and development labs (Intel, GE, Legend, and Microsoft) in China are gratefully acknowledged.

July 2001

Heung-Yeung Shum
Mark Liao
Shih-Fu Chang

Hong-Jiang Zhang
P.C. Ching
Xing-Gang Lin

The Second IEEE Pacific-Rim Conference on Multimedia

Advisory Committee Chairs:
Chao-Huan Hou National Science Foundation, China
Sun-Yuan Kung Princeton University, USA
Ya-Qin Zhang Microsoft Research, China

General Co-chairs:
P.C. Ching Chinese University of Hong Kong, China
Xing-Gang Lin Tsinghua University, China
Hong-Jiang Zhang Microsoft Research, China

Program Co-chairs:
Shih-Fu Chang Columbia University, USA
Mark Liao Academy Sinica, China
Heung-Yeung Shum Microsoft Research, China

Poster Chair:
Yu-Jin Zhang Tsinghua University, China

Tutorial and Special Session Chairs:
Mohan Kankanhalli National University of Singapore, Singapore
Shin'ichi Satoh Japan National Institute of Informatics, Japan

Demo Chair:
Yun He Tsinghua University, China

Publicity Chair:
Ching-Yung Lin IBM T. J. Watson Research Center, USA

Proceedings Chair:
Yuanchun Shi Tsinghua University, China

Local Arrangement Chair:
Shipeng Li Microsoft Research, China

Japan Liaison:
Kiyoharu Aizawa University of Tokyo, Japan

Australia Liaison:
Svetha Venkatesh Curtin University of Technology, Australia

Treasurer:
Wen-Yin Liu Microsoft Research, China

Web Masters:
Feng Wu/Zhong Su Microsoft Research, China

Reviewers:

Kiyo Aizawa
Mahesh Balakrishnan
Eric Chang
Chang Wen Chen
Jinlin Chen
Xiangrong Chen
Zheng Chen
Ti-hao Chiang
L.F. Chien
Tat-Seng Chua
Wen Gao
Lie Gu
Guodong Guo
Hsueh-Ming Hang
Yuwen He
Yo Sung Ho
J.W. Hsieh
Xiansheng Hua
Chao Huang
Qiang Huo
Horace Ip
Yunde Jia
Jesse Jin
Mohan Kankanhalli
C.-C. Jay Kuo
Chuen-Chien Lee
Sang Wan Lee
Chung-Sheng Li
Jiang Li
Mingjing Li
Shipeng Li
Stan Li
Zeyu Li
Zhen Li
Steve Lin
Wenyin Liu
Alexander C Loui
C.S. Lu
Le Lu
Lie Lu
Daniel Lun
Weiying Ma
Yufei Ma
Antonio Ortega
Shinji Ozawa
Jong Beom Ra
Takahiro Saito
Yoichi Sato
Shin'ichi Satoh
Jacky Shen
Timothy Shih
Peter-Pike Sloan
Uma Srinivasan
Zhong Su
Sang Hoon Sull
Huifang Sun
Xiaoyan Sun
Qi Tian
Xin Tong
Svetha Venkatesh
Guijin Wang
Hao Wang
Minghui Wang
Tianshu Wang
Chi Sun Won
Hong Wu
Lide Wu
Ze Xiang
Guangyou Xu
Jizheng Xu
Yingqing Xu
Rong Yan
Jie Yang
Shiqiang Yang
Hong You
Bing Zeng
Aidong Zhang
Dong Zhang
Hongjiang Zhang
Qian Zhang
Hua Zhong
Jianlai Zhou
Wenwu Zhu
Yueting Zhuang

Organized by

Microsoft Research, China
Tsinghua University, China
National Natural Science Foundation of China

Sponsored by

IEEE Circuits and Systems Society
IEEE Signal Processing Society
China Computer Foundation
China Society of Image and Graphics

Table of Contents

Wearable Computing

Retrieval Techniques

Coding Techniques

Systems

Vision and Graphics

Face

Multimedia Retrieval

Multimedia Education

Multimedia Presentation and Databases

Data Hiding

Image and Video Coding

Retrieval

Speech and Sound

Networking

Spoken Dialog

Multimedia Security

Systems

Multimedia Networking

Learning and Recognition

Watermarking

Poster 1: Retrieval

Poster 2: Coding/Systems/Data Hiding

Poster 3: Vision/Graphics/Speech/Learning

Linux Watch: Hardware Platform for Wearable Computing Research

Noboru Kamijoh, Tadanobu Inoue, Kohichiroh Kishimoto, Ken Tamagawa

IBM Tokyo Research Laboratory
1623-14, Shimotsuruma, Yamato, Kanagawa 242-8502, Japan
{kamijo, inouet, kishimo, keny}@jp.ibm.com

Abstract. The Linux Watch is a wearable information access device that is worn on the wrist. It is an ARM7-based low-power Linux system with short-range wireless communications and a multi-modal (voice and image) user interface with a watch shape and is used as a hardware platform for wearable computing research. The Hands-free Mobile System is a kind of speech-oriented client-server system using the Linux Watch. The Linux Watch acts as a front-end user interface device but appears to have all the functions and intelligence of the server including voice-recognition and synthetic speech capability via its multi-modal user interface. This paper describes The Linux Watch hardware platform and the concept of the Hands-free Mobile System.

1. Introduction

For the practical use of wearable computers, it is important that end-users feel comfortable wearing them. Wristwatches have been used and accepted by many people for a long time. They have the advantage of always being there and instantly viewable with a flick of the wrist without taking it out of a pocket or bag.

We focused on this ergonomic advantage and have prototyped a wearable computer, called the Linux Watch, in this form factor as a hardware platform for wearable computing research in areas such as user interfaces [1], high resolution displays [2], system software, wireless communications, and power management.

We chose the Linux operating system for the watch, because it is suitable for a research platform with high programmability. Linux makes it very easy for many researchers to start developing programs on this new platform, because there is a lot of source code and a wide variety of software tools available.

The screen size of a wristwatch is relatively limited because of its small size overall and the requirements for elegance fashion do not allow many buttons on the device. Voice can be used as an additional user interface method to supplement image information and virtual buttons [3][4] and users find it very satisfactory when it is well integrated into a multi-modal user interface with images [5]. The extra audio information can effectively compensate for the limited display size. But it is quite difficult for the Linux Watch to recognize and synthesize human voices by itself, given its available processor power and power consumption at present. We suggested using the capabilities of another machine nearby or somewhere on the network via wireless communications to compensate for its computing limitations. In other words, we recommend load balancing using wireless communications between the Linux Watch and a server on a network.

In the following sections we introduce the system hardware and the Hands-free Mobile System concept.

2. Hardware of the Linux Watch

We made the hardware design modular to allow the use of various shells. The Linux Watch system has two types of shells now as shown in Figure 1. One is smaller and fancier and is called the "basic shell", and the other, intended to be more functional with an accessory card, called the "enhanced shell".

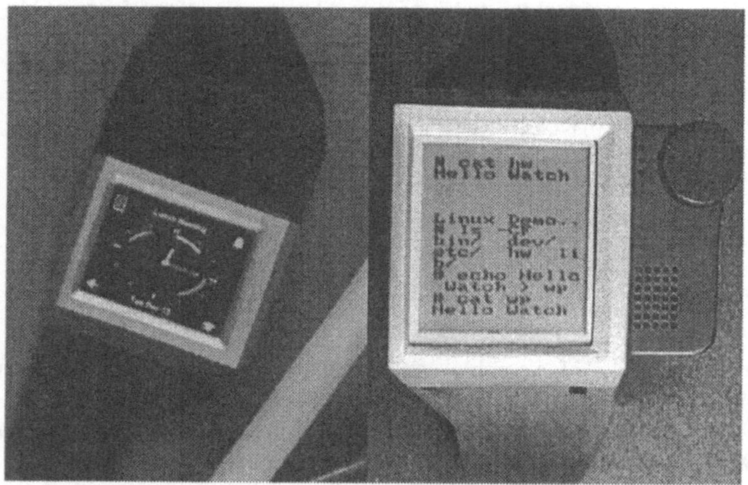

Fig. 1. Linux Watch Shells (Left: Basic Shell, Right: Enhanced Shell)

The Linux Watch uses an ARM7 core system LSI as its MPU. A touch panel and a roller wheel are employed as the primary input devices. A tilt switch is used to detect arm motions for gesture input. The enhanced shell has an accessory bay for various additional functions. A Bluetooth card and a RF-modem card are now available, along with PCM audio functions including a speaker and a microphone for a multi-modal (voice and image) user interface. As a display device, a self emitting organic LED display (OLED) with VGA resolution or a 96 x 120 pixels B/W LCD display is used. A rechargeable lithium-polymer was selected to resolve the problem of supplying peak current in a small form factor, though its capacity is smaller than the primary battery. Table 1 summrizes the specifications.

The main circuit card was designed using the off-the-shelf parts, but using the state-of-the-art packaging technology called Surface Luminar Circuit (SLC). It is packaged in a small stamp sized board, only 35.3 x 27.5 x 3.0 mm as shown in Figure 2. Accessory cards are connected to the main board using an ultra low-profile elastomer connection method.

Table 1. System Specifications

Size / Weight	56 (W) x 48 (L) x 12 (T) mm, 44 g
CPU	ARM7 core (18 – 74 MHz)
Memory	DRAM 8MB / Flash ROM 8MB
Display	VGA OLED (740 dpi) / 96 x 120 LCD
Communication	IrDA v1.2, RS232C (Cradle), Bluetooth (Accessory card), RF modem (Accessory card)
Input Device	Touch Panel, Roller Wheel, Tilt Switch
Power Source	Li-Polymer Battery
OS / Window System	Linux 2.2.1 / X11R6.4
Bluetooth Protocol Stack	IBM BlueDrekar

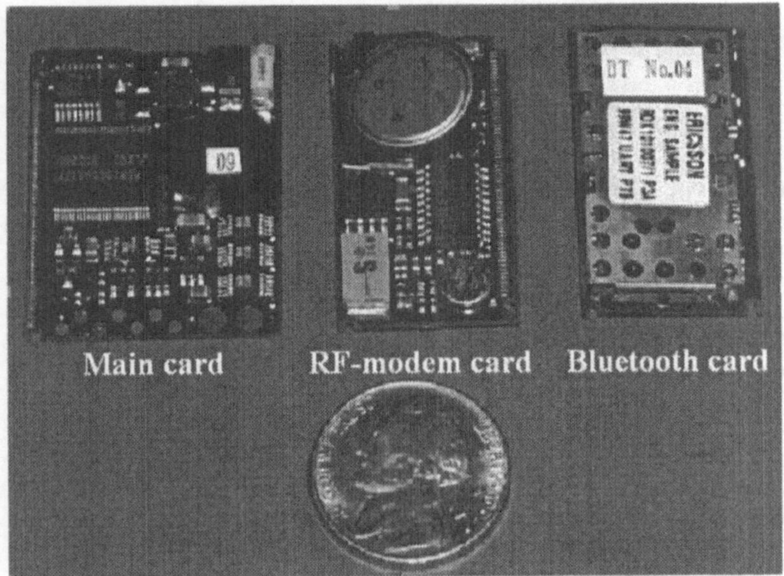

Fig. 2. Linux Watch Main Card and Accessory Cards

The interface between the accessory card and the main card is designed to support various additional functions using the interfaces of a Compact Flash (CF) and a Serial Peripheral Interface (SPI), as well as a Universal Asynchronous Receiver Transmitter (UART) and Pulse Code Modulation (PCM), which is actually used for the Bluetooth card and the RF-modem card. For example, a Peripheral Interface Controller (PIC) controlling sensors on an accessory card can be easily interfaced with the main card through the SPI.

The Linux Watch system is designed based on the modular concept shown in Figure 3. The basic device, which is composed of the main card and Linux, is very small to easily fit in larger devices, and can be used as a pervasive computing platform in the future.

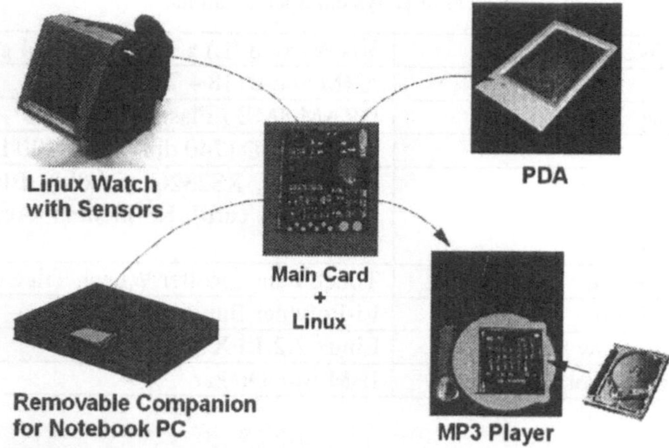

Fig. 3. Modular Concept: Design Variety for other form factors

3. Hands-free Mobile System

3.1. Hands-free Mobile System Concept

The Hands-free Mobile System is a kind of speech-oriented client-server system based on short-range wireless communications as shown in Figure 4.

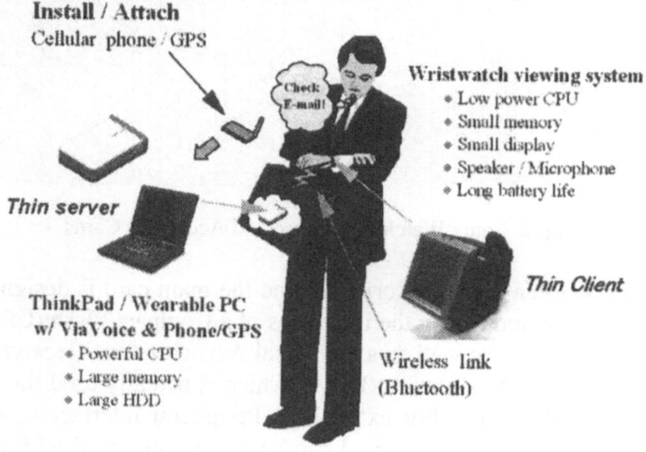

Fig. 4. Hands-free Mobile System Concept

This concept is based on a thin server and a wristwatch type thin client. The thin server has capabilities of handling voice, short-range wireless communications, and some application programs. We think the Linux Watch can be the thin client and a

ThinkPad or a wearable PC prototyped by IBM can act as the thin server. The thin client is a low power device for long battery life and has capabilities for short range wireless communications and to support a multi-modal (voice and image) user interface. In this system, a thin client transfers voice or user input to the thin server. The thin server receives this data and replies with an image or voice data sent to the thin client using wireless communications. Data processing should be handled, especially voice recognition and speech synthesis, in the thin server or in some cases the thin server can act as a relay to a more powerful remote system using long-range wireless communications.

Relying mostly on the computing power of the thin server, the thin client needs to have little more than I/O capabilities. Its form factor and the battery life become the important design constraints, rather than its computing power. When the thin client is a simple I/O system, developers can concentrate their application program development on the thin server side.

The short range wireless communications sytem will not be expected to connect every time and the thin client should have a cache mechanism for the information from the thin server and have some processing power, not only I/O capabilities. The progress of technology will lead the voice recognition with low power consumption even on a wristwatch type computer. Distributing various functions between the thin server and client will be an important design tradeoff. However, we think the Hands-free Mobile System concept system can be the first step for exploring how to get contextual information at the point of need in a ubiquitous computing world using the Linux Watch.

At the next stage, when short-range wireless communications such as Bluetooth becomes commonplace, it will be possible for information to be obtained from various hosts--ThinkPads, desktop PCs, or even devices like household appliances and the Linux Watch can be a general purpose browser or a controller.

3.2. Experiment Using Prototypes

We have prototyped an experimental system using a Linux Watch, including an RF modem card and a wearable PC produced by IBM to experiment with this concept as shown in Figure 5. Since the RF modem card cannot handle voice data to the wearable PC, a bone conduction microphone with an earphone is used for providing the voice input and output.

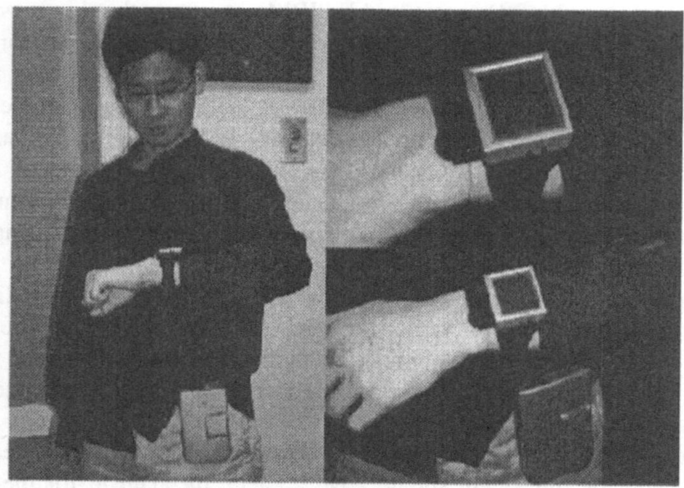

Fig. 5. Experimental System

Using this system, we studied the usability of personal information management applications such as a scheduler, mailer, car navigator, and a cellular telephone. All these applications are executed in the wearable PC and the Linux Watch acted only as an I/O device to transmit the user input from the touch panel and the roller wheel and to receive the image data from the PC with the assistance of voice-activated functions using the bone conduction microphone and voice the earphone.

We sometimes had difficulty in verifying whether the voice-activated functions worked correctly or not. We adopted a dialogue-based operation method to increase the tolerance for mistakes in voice recognition in the noisy environment. For example, when a user wanted to execute mailer application, he or she said "Mailer" and then the system would answer "Mailer" and change the image to the mailer for the verification by the user.

3.3. Feasibility Study Using Bluetooth

Bluetooth is expected to spread rapidly and widely in small gadgets like the Linux Watch and cellular phones and even to PCs and we anticipate good interoperability among them. This will be a good fit for our hands-free mobile system concept, because it can communicate not only text and binary data but also voice information. We used a bone conduction microphone in the above experimental system, but we believe we will be able to eliminate it when using a Bluetooth-based voice link.

Once the Bluetooth environment matures, any third generation cellular phone system (IMT-2000) might act as a relay device, and any computer connected to the Internet can act as a host for such a system. The Linux Watch will seem to have intelligence and many functions with the assistance of these powerful background computers.

We have prototyped another system in which we could control a presentation package made with PowerPoint and Freelance on a laptop PC from the Linux Watch via Bluetooth like a remote control. Using this prototype system, we verified that we can control presentations easily without standing near the laptop PC.

We tried a feasibility study of voice commands via a voice link using Bluetooth with this sytem and we succeeded in achieving the recognition in a quiet laboratory. However, it was still impractical in noisy real world environments.

4. Conclusions and Future Work

We are prototyping a Linux Watch as a research platform which has a capability of short-range wireless communications and multi-modal user interfaces. The Hands-free Mobile System concept has been tested and the usability of the prototype using a multi-modal user interface on the Linux Watch was verified.

As the next stage of this research, we will continue to study the multi-modal user interface using the Bluetooth-based voice link and would like to study other sensors for recognition of the user's context and for a new user interface. Other research areas will be involved such as developing suitable applications for such the Hands-free Mobile System, balancing functions between the thin server and client, and studying the power-consumption and local-function tradeoffs for the Linux Watch itself.

5. Acknowledgements

We would like to thank Dr. Chandra Narayanaswami, Dr. Mandayam Raghunath, Mr. Kazuhiko Yamazaki, Mr. Toshihiko Nishio, Mr. Seiji Kodama, Dr. John Karidis and Mr. Tom Cippolla.

References

1. Chandra Narayanaswami, Mandayam Raghunath: Application Design for a Smart Watch with a High Resolution Display. Proceedings of the International Symposium on Wearable Computing, (2000) 7-14
2. James L. Sanford and Eugene S. Schlig: Direct View Active Matrix VGA OLED-on-Crystalline-Sillicon Display. 2001 SID International Symposium Digest of Technical Papers, Vol. 32 (2001) 376-379
3. Nitin Sawhney, Chris Schmandt: Nomadic Radio: Scaleable and Contextual Notification for Wearable Audio Messaging. ACM SIGCHI Conference on Human Factors in Computing Systems (1999) 96-103
4. Asim Smailagic, Dan Siewiorek, Richard Martin, Denis Reilly: CMU Wearable Computers for Real-Time Speech Translation. The 3rd International Symposium on Wearable Computers (1999) 187-190
5. Jonny Farringdon, Vanessa Oni, Chi Ming Kan, Leo Poll: Co-Modal Browser – An Interface for Wearable Computers. The 3rd International Symposium on Wearable Computers (1999) 45-51

Wearable Computer Application for Open Air Exhibition in EXPO 2005

Ryoko Ueoka[1], Michitaka Hirose[1], Kengo Kuma[2], Michie Sone[3], Kenji Kohiyama[4], Tomohiro Kawamura[4], Kenichiro Hiroto[1]

1 University of Tokyo, Research Center for Advanced Science and Technology, 4-6-1 Komaba Meguro-Ku Tokyo 153-8904, Japan
{yogurt, hirose, hiroto}@cyber.rcast.u-tokyo.ac.jp
2 Keio University, Department of Science and Technology, 3-14-1 Hiyoshi Kouhoku-Ku Yokohama Kanagawa-Ken 223-0061, Japan
kuma@ba2.so-net.ne.jp
3 Media Fashion Laboratory, 5-2-16-202 Minami Aoyama Minato-Ku Tokyo 107-0062, Japan
Sonemichie@aol.com
4 Keio University, Shonan Fujisawa Campus, 5322 Endo Fujisawa-Shi Kanagawa-Ken 252-0816, Japan
{kohiyama,pyanko}@sfc.keio.ac.jp

Abstract. Wearable computers have been receiving a great deal of attention as a new computer device. The Open Air Exhibition research group for the World Exposition 2005 (EXPO 2005) is focusing on this new device as a means of making effective use of the outdoor exhibition. Since the year 2000, we have performed annual experiments to evaluate the possibilities of the wearable computer. Also, in order to increase the popularity, the experimental system was constructed for targeting to the general, not to the laboratory use. Therefore the weight of prototype device is restricted to enable any person to carry it and it is designed to be less obtrusive. In this paper, we discuss the basic requirements of the system for the Open Air Exhibition which is acceptable to the general.

1 Introduction

The recent trend toward the downsizing of computer devices has tremendously changed the way information technologies are used in everyday life.[1] The greatest difference is that computers have become mobile. On the other hand, people used to have to go to the specific location in order to access information. Mobile technology has eliminated the restriction of space but the human-computer interface has remained the same. This means that the input interface is a keypad or a pen pad similar to those of conventional desktop computers and the information is still accessed using a rectangular display monitor. In this paper, we discuss the wearable computer which has the potential to change many aspects of using computer devices. To be able to wear computers will bring qualitative changes comparable to the changes brought about by the advent of mobile devices.

2 Definition of Wearable Computer

We divide wearable computers into two broad categories according to their characteristic functions. One is information gathering and the other is information display. As a wearable computer fits the human body closely, it holds great potential for scanning and recording real-time information regarding the immediate surroundings and ambience around the user. Figure 1 shows the prototype system for recording experience. This prototype system records visual, audio, heartbeat and walking pitch data automatically; to the best of our knowledge, these have not been simultaneously recorded before.[2] Also, the wearable computer has great potential for displaying information regardless of location because the wearable computer is always close to an individual. Figure 2 shows the information display prototype system. The information projected on the display attached to the glass switches according to the user's facial expression measured by piezo sensor.[3]

Fig. 1. Information gathering prototype

Fig. 2. Information display prototype

3 Wearable Computer for EXPO 2005

The Open Air Exhibition research group is mainly focused on displaying the use of the wearable computer and is studying outdoor exhibition methods as an advanced

exhibition style because the floor area of the pavilions in EXPO 2005 will be reduced for environmental reasons. Thus the EXPO organization is very interested in using the wearable computer as an exhibition method as it provides an alternative infrastructure. The conventional exhibition style is to display artwork inside a building and have people go there to appreciate the work. In that case, a structure has to be built for displaying the artwork. In contrast, the Open Air Exhibition doesn't require any building. A person with a wearable computer can walk outside and experience the overall artwork through the interaction of the virtual and the real without modifying the actual environment.
Since the year 2000, we have performed annual experiments. The main purpose of these experiments is to learn the unique characteristics of the Open Air Exhibition. Initially, we set location determination as a fundamental function for the Open Air Exhibition because location variables could be applied as a trigger to change the exhibition content. We adapted different types of technologies to realize location determination with different exhibition styles in two experiments.

4 Experiment

4.1 Experiment I

In the year 2000, we performed the experiment in public. We used a microwave system for the location driven content changer. A participant wearing a coat called a "site scanner" took walks around the venue and a small vibration motor embedded in a binocular-type head mounted display (HMD) beeped when the content changed. Upon this signal, the participant looked into the HMD and enjoyed still images or audio content related to the location at which he/she stood.
From this experiment, we learned that the microwave system is not suitable for covering wide area positioning although its performance was quite good in relatively small areas, because it is necessary to place all the transmitters beforehand in order to make the system work. This is unrealistic in the case of covering a wide area. Moreover, we learned that the Open Air Exhibition has great potential to realize a participatory style of exhibition which varies according to the wearer's interaction. In that case, because it appears strange for one wearer who is attending an exhibition to be alone outside, real time communication among participants must be enabled.

Fig. 3. Site scanner wearers looking into HMD

4.2 Experiment II

Putting the findings of the previous experiment to use, we performed an experiment this year. The purpose of the experiment is to include a location free positioning system and enable a high degree of interaction among participants. It was carried out at EXPO location. As elementary school students were selected as participants, the contents of this experiment were planned as a real world role-playing game, the style of which is familiar to children who are used to playing computer games but it is not common as exhibition material. Our goal is to have participants understand the importance of nature through the experience of this game type outdoor exhibition, in cooperation with other participants.

4.2.1 Application

The experiment was performed at Aichi Youth State Park on March 4th 2001. Each team consisted of four persons. Half of them become field players and the others become backyard players who stayed in the center to take a role as a commander. This is a treasure hunt type game. Two teams compete to reach the goal in the shortest time. The field and backyard players cooperate with one another to answer quiz questions to reach the goal. Quiz questions are sent via e-mail. By providing correct answer, the team can move forward to each game area, where one of the members plays an enemy hunting game. Upon winning this game, they can open a virtual treasure box which has a key number inside that enables them to open a real treasure box in the area. In the box, a piece of a map is hidden. By collecting all of the pieces hidden in the play field, they can fill in the missing parts of the map which then reveals the goal of the game. The game can't be accomplished without cooperation between field and backyard member, because there are some questions which can't be answered without an encyclopedia and some of the enemies in the game area can be seen only from a backyard screen.

4.2.2 System Configuration

The overall system configuration is shown in Figure 4. The dotted line in the figure indicates the wireless network path. As an Internet line was not available in the outdoor environment, a digital satellite car was set up to provide a temporary connection to the Internet.

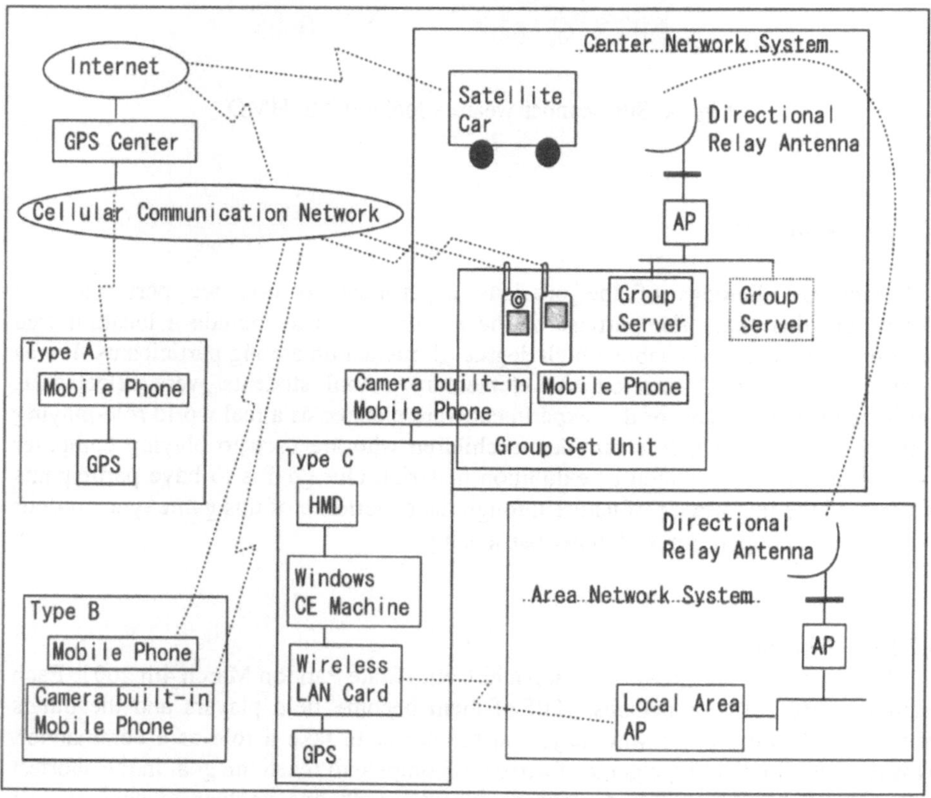

Fig. 4. System configuration

The basic hardware is divided into three types. Type A is a combination of a mobile phone and a small global positioning system (GPS) which transmits a wearer's position instantly to the GPS center. We can trace the position of the wearer as a dotted line on the map via the Internet. Type B combines an i - Mode type mobile phone and mobile phone with a built-in camera. A wearer with the type B system is a communicator between field players and backyard players. With this system, e-mail, video and voice communication is possible. The Type B system wearer has to use the three communication methods creatively as well as to check out the e-mail constantly since there is sometimes a surprise e-mail which provides a great hint for reaching the goal. Type C combines a HMD, Windows CE machine, GPS and wireless LAN card. The type C system wearer is a player who catches virtual enemy projected on the HMD when it enters the game area.

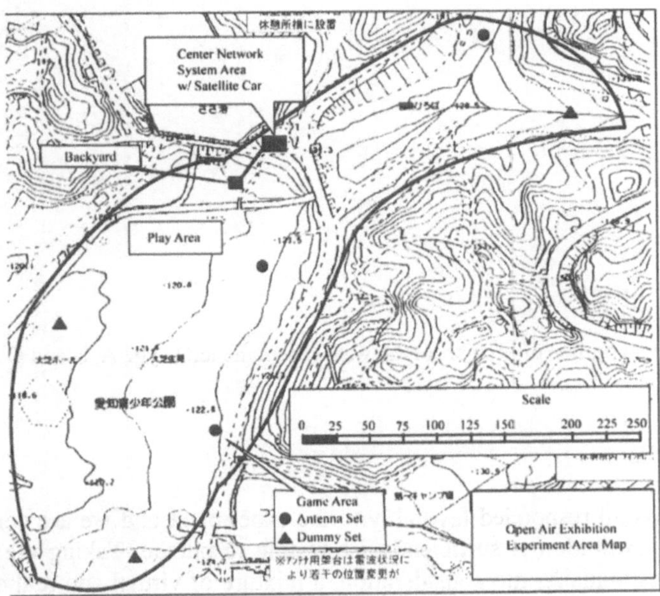

Fig. 5. Location map of the experiment

There are some enemies which are invisible on the HMD but visible on the backyard screen. Thus, backyard members instruct a field member the relative position of the enemy and the field member moves his/her body according to the instructions in order to catch an enemy. For the realization of this cooperative system, a dual LAN system is constructed to send the positioning data of the player to the group server. There are three area network systems set in the field along with three dummy sets to cheat on players not to go to the right direction. Figure 5 shows the scale map of the venue and locations of each system. And Figure 6 shows the system outline of each set of the wear. The wears are originally designed and devices are built with consideration given to keeping the weight of devices reasonable and avoiding the restriction of body movement. In addition, the wiring as well as the computer interface is considered to realize unification of a wear and devices. For example, the mouse click interface for the type C system is embedded on the front of the shoulders for the outdoor adapted interface.

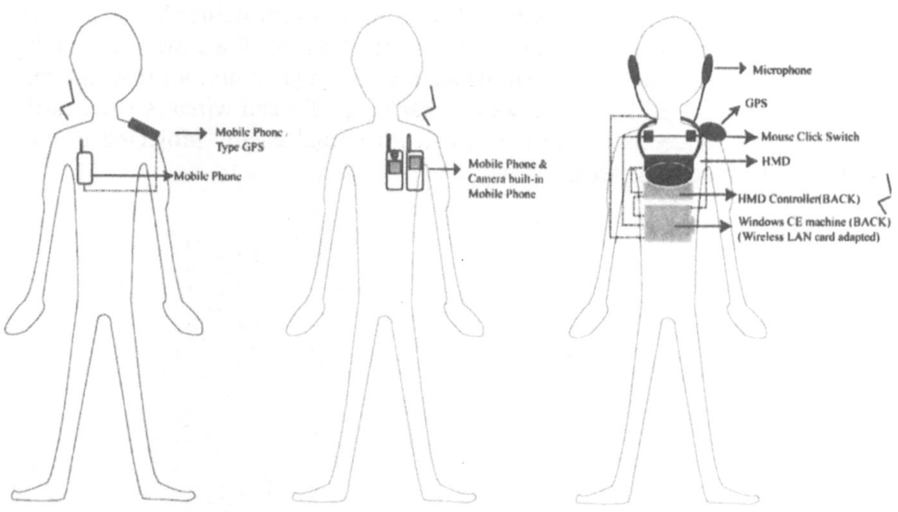

Fig. 6. System outline of each set of the wear (From the left, Type A, B and C system)

4.2.3 Results

The participants all responded favorably to the experiment and we are confident that the Open Air Exhibition is sufficiently interesting to pursue. Taking the result of a participant questionnaire into consideration, a mixture of virtual and real experiences enjoyed via computer devices seems to make the experience more favorable. In terms of negative response, participants pointed out the low quality of the current device.
On the day of the experiment, the morning experiment was cancelled because of heavy rain due to the risk of electric leak of the wearable computers. Creating a system that is stable under all weather conditions is critical for an outdoor exhibition.

Table 1. Result of questionnaire

Participants	8 elementary school students from local school
Which Player do you want to play next?	Type C player: 4 persons Type B player: 2 persons Backyard player: 2 persons
What is like of game?	a virtual charcter control by physical movement cooperative work to get an invisible enemy a real time monitoring of member's location a search for a real treasure box or hint in the field
What is dislike of the game?	difficulty to see HMD monitor due to the optical reflection delay of the reflection of positioning on the screen burred picture quality of a mobile phone w/ a built-in camera

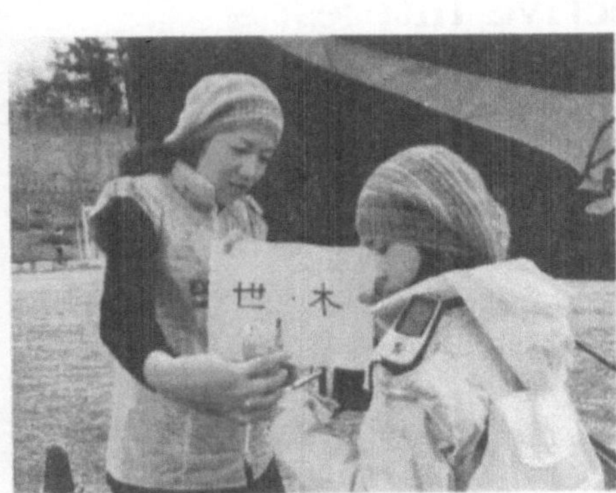

Fig. 7. Experiment scene (Communicating with the backyard members (Left), Playing enemy hunting game (Right))

5 Conclusion

On the basis of our two experiments, we are now confident that a wearable computer is a practical means of realizing the Open Air Exhibition.

In order to make this type of exhibition more lively and interesting, technical improvement in order to realize highly real virtual interaction is required. This involves unifying the function of wearable computers both information gathering and display to realize a dynamic flow of virtual information according to the physical and environmental changes that possibly draw a participant deeply into the world of the exhibition.

Reference

1. Steve Mann: Wearable Computing: A First Step Toward Personal Imaging. Proc. IEEE, (1997) 25-32
2. Michitaka H., Ryoko U.,Atsushi,H.,Akiyoshi,Y: The Study of Personal Experience Record for Wearable Computer Application. Proc. of the Virtual Reality Society of Japan Fifth Annual Conference, (2000) 389-392 (Japanese)
3. Atsushi H., Ryoko U., Koichi H., Michitaka H.: Hands-Free Input Interface for Wearable Computing. Correspondences on Human Interface, (2001) 61-64 (Japanese)

Automatic Summarization of Wearable Video - Indexing Subjective Interest -

Kiyoharu Aizawa[1],, Kenichiro Ishijima[1], and Makoto Shiina[1]

University of Tokyo, Dept. of Elec. Eng.,
7-3-1 Hongo, Bunkyo, Tokyo, 113-8656, Japan
{aizawa, ken-i}@hal.t.u-tokyo.ac.jp
http://www.hal.t.u-tokyo.ac.jp

Abstract. "We want to keep our entire life by video" is the motivation of this research. Recent development of wearable devices and huge storage devices will make it possible to keep entire life by video. We could capture 70 years of our life, however, the problem is how to handle such a huge data. Automatic summarization based on personal interest should be indispensable. In this paper we propose an approach to automatic structuring and summarization of wearable video. (Wearable video is our abbreviation of "video captured by a wearable camera".) In our approach, we make use of a wearable camera and a sensor of brain waves. Video is firstly structured by objective features of video, and the shots are rated by subjective measures based on brain waves. The approach was very successful for real world experiments and it automatically extracted all the events that the subjects reported they had felt interesting.

1 Introduction

Personal experiences are usually maintained by such media as diaries, pictures and movies. For example, we memorize our daily experiences in a diary, and we use photos and movies to keep our special events such as travels etc. However, those existing media, so far, keep records of only a small part of our life. Even though we make use of photos and movies, we always miss the best moments because the camera is not always ready.

Significant progress has been being made in digital imaging technologies: cameras, displays, compression, storage etc. Small size integration also advances so that computational devices and imaging devices become intimate as wearable computers and wearable cameras [1, 2]. These small wearable devices will provide fully personal information gathering and processing environments. We believe that by using such wearable devices, an entire personal life will be able to be imaged and reproduced as video. Then, we will never miss the moment that we want to maintain forever.

Such a long-term imaging requires automatic summarization. Imagine we have a year-long or much longer video recording, how do we handle such a huge volume of data in order to watch the scene that we felt interesting when it was captured? Manual handling is nonsense because manual operation takes longer than the length of recording. We would like to extract the scenes that we felt something at the moment. Then, summarization should be based on our subjective sensation.

In the previous works, automatic summarization has been applied to broadcasting TV programs (ex. [3]). Their summarization methods were based on objective visual features of video and audio. Then, methodology of summarization of wearable video has to differ because it needs to take into account subjective feeling of the person.

In this paper, we first discuss the potentials and the feasibility of life-long imaging, and propose our approach to automatic summarization that segments video based on the visual objective features and evaluates the shots by making use of brain wave.

Use of physiological signals was also attempted for wearable cameras. Healey et al. [4] used skin conductivity and heart rate for turning on and off the wearable camera. We use brain waves that show clearly the status of the person whether he pays attention or not.

2 Feasibility and potential of life long imaging

Imagine we wear a single camera and constantly record what we would see, how huge would be the amount of images that we could capture during 70 years? (The captured video would be first stored in the wearable device and then occasionally moved to a huge storage.) Video quality depends on the compression. Assuming 16 hours per day is captured for 70 years, the amount of video data is listed below.

quality	rate (bits/second)	data size for 70 years
TV phone quality	64kbps	11 Tbytes
VCR quality	1Mbps	183 Tbytes
Broadcasting quality	4Mbps	736 Tbytes

Lets take a look at the TV phone quality, it needs only 11 Tbytes for recoding 70 years. Even today, we have a small lunch box size of 10GB HDD available with less than $100. Thus, if we have 1000 of them, their capacity is almost enough for 70 years! The progress of capacity improvement of HDD is very fast. it will be in the not too distant future feasible to contain 70 years of video in a few of HDDs.

As for sensing devices, CCD or CMOS cameras are getting smaller, too. A glass-type wearable CCD camera is already introduced in the market. (In Fig.1, the glass-type CCD camera is shown, that is used in our experiments.) The progress of wearable computers will further drive the imaging devices smaller.

Then, from the hardware point of view, storage and sensing, we believe in not too remote future, life long video will be able to be captured and maintained in personal environments. Let's take a look at potential advantages and disadvantages of such systems. They are listed below.

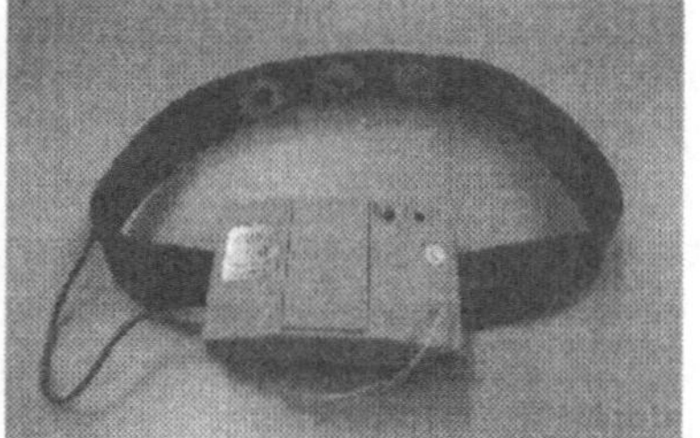

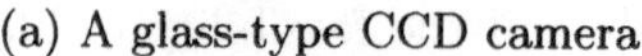

(a) A glass-type CCD camera A sensor to capture brain waves

Fig. 1. A glass type CCD camera with microphone(left) and A sensor to capture brain waves(right)

* **Advantages**
- we can catch the best moment that we want to keep forever.
- we can vividly reproduce and recollect our experiences by video.
- we can remember what we have forgotten.
- we can see what we did not see.
- we can prove what we did not do.

* **Disadvantages**
- we may see what we do not want to remember.
- we may violate privacy of other person.

3 Summarization of wearable video

As described in the previous sections, constantly recording will be feasible from the hardware point of view. The most difficult issue is how to extract and reproduce what we want to see. The data size is too huge, then its automatic summarization is the most critical problem.

Almost all the previous works dealt with TV programs and motion films [3, 5]. They make use of objective visual and audio features of the video. In our wearable application, we also take into account the degree of subjective interest of the person, that he felt at the very moment when the scene was captured. Then, the video should be rated by the subjective measure too.

In order to measure the point of interest of the person, we make use of physiological signals, that is brain waves captured simultaneously. The sensor is also wearable enough. As shown in Fig. 1, the sensor we use is head-band size. (It is still noticeable, but it could be much smaller.) The data from the sensor is recorded using one of the audio channels of the VCR of the wearable camera. We utilize α wave of the brain waves.

The framework of our approach to automatic summarization, thus, comprises two major steps: In the first step, the video stream is analyzed and segmented based on the objective visual features, and in the next step, video segment is evaluated based on the subjective signals.

The whole framework is shown in Fig.2. First, the video stream is segmented into shots, using motion information. Shots are integrated into scenes using color information. Then, the scenes are evaluated based on the status of α waves. The summary is finally produced by using the rated segments.

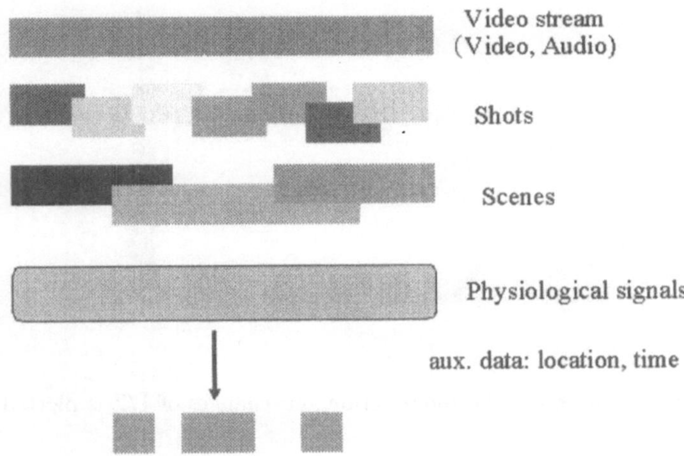

Fig. 2. The framework of summarization of wearable video.

4 Video segmentation into shots

Video segmentation using visual features rather differs from the ordinary segmentation applied to the TV programs because contents of the video stream captured by the wearable camera is continuous and it does not have explicit shot changes.

However, the motion information reflects the users movement in the environment. Color information also reflects the environment information. Thus, we first estimate the global motion of the images which shows the person's movement; whether he stands still, moving forward/backward, turing left/right.

The global motion model comprises zoom Z, pan H and tilt V. They are estimated using motion vectors (u, v) determined for the blocks of the image by the block matching. The estimation of the global motion parameter is done by two steps: in the first step, the global motion parameters are estimated by using the model of eq.(1) by the least squares using all the motion vectors. In the second step, excluding the motion vectors that differs too much from that caused by the estimated global motion parameters, the global motion parameters are estimated again using the remaining motion vectors. The estimated parameters are also filtered by median filtering over 50 frames to smooth the variation.

$$\begin{pmatrix} u \\ v \end{pmatrix} = Z \begin{pmatrix} x - x_0 \\ y - y_0 \end{pmatrix} + \begin{pmatrix} H \\ V \end{pmatrix} \tag{1}$$

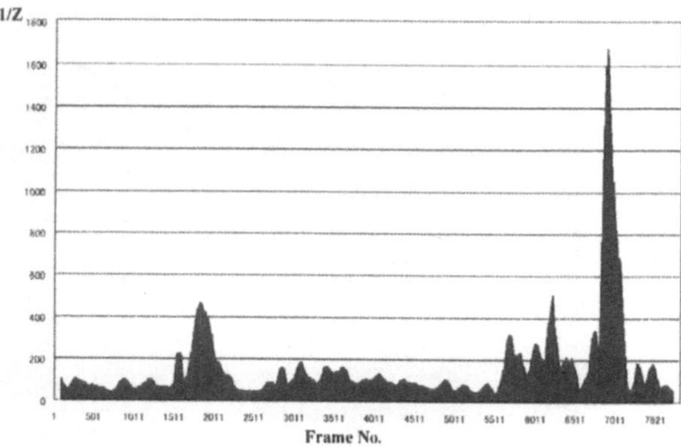

Fig. 3. Estimation of the zoom parameter: changes of 1/Z is plotted.

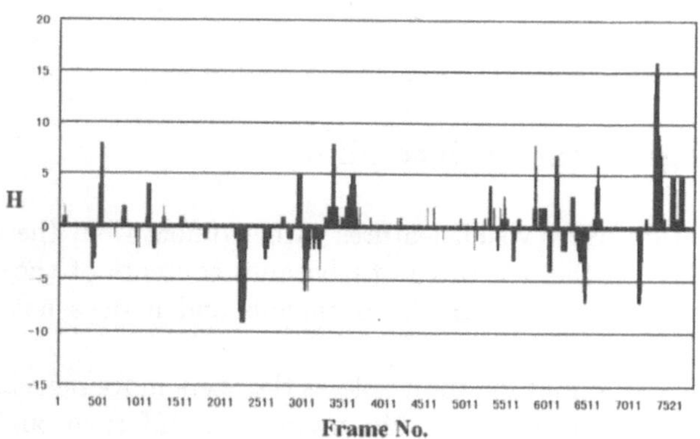

Fig. 4. Estimation of the pan parameter

The zoom factor is changing as shown in the Fig.3. Note inverse of Z is plotted in the figure. Then the peaks show when the person stands almost still. Pan and tilt parameters show horizontal and vertical change of the direction of the person's head. Because the person often looks up and down, tilt parameter changes too often. Then, excluding tilt parameters we make use of the zoom and pan parameters to segment the video into shots. An example of the shot

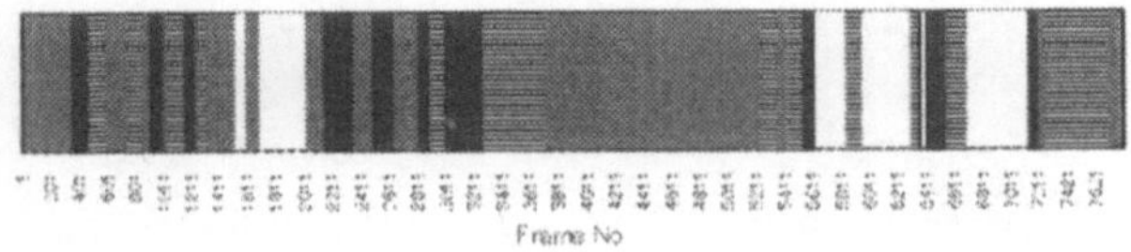

Fig. 5. Segmentation Results: video is captured by a wearable camera while the person is walking around in the University

segmentation is shown in Fig.5. In Fig.5, white, gray, stripe and black areas corresponds to 'still', 'move forward', 'turn right' and 'turn left', respectively.

The shots will be finally grouped into scenes using color information. Shot grouping is not described in this paper. In the next section, the shots are rated by the status of brain waves. Use of additional signals such as audio is now under investigation.

5 Subjective rating of the shots: use of brain waves

The goal of this research is to extract video shots which are supposed to be paid much interest when the person has seen the scene. Brain waves can very effectively show his status. According to the literatures of psychology, brain waves has a feature such that α wave attenuation (α blocking) occurs when the person feel awake, interested, excited etc. The status of α wave is a good index for the arousal of the subject.

In our experiment, the power of α wave is simply thresholded. The length of the attenuation is also taken into account in order to reduce artifacts. The system we developed is shown in the Fig.6. Our system shows the video and the brain waves on the screen. The top left is the image window and the plots shows the brain waves. The bottom one is α wave (7.5 Hz) and the other are β waves (15, 22.5 and 30 Hz). The Fig.6 shows the moment when the person arrived at the paddock in the race track. α wave (bottom) shows quick attenuation (changes high to low), and it is very visible that the subject paid high attention to the scene.

In the experiments, persons wore the camera (Fig.1) and the simple brain wave sensor (Fig.1). In the experiment, the subjects walked around the university and visited an amusement park and a horse race track, etc. The subjects reported what were interesting, impressive to them during the experiments.

In the first experiment, group of frames are extracted only by using brain waves. One example of the experiments in the amusement park: The original video stream is about an hour. On the basis of α wave, the number of groups of frames extracted are 347. The summarized video were about 8min long. The scene that the subjects had reported interesting were all extracted.

In second experments, the video stream is first segmented into shots based on the global motion as described earlier. Then, the α wave is averaged in each shot and the shots are rated five levels according to the value of the averaged α

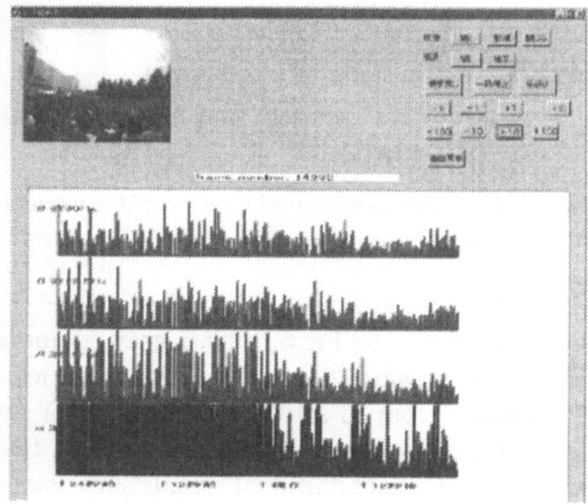

Fig. 6. The system shows video and brain waves.

waves, that reflects the degree of interest the person felt. Smaller value means more interest.

The result for the race track experiment is shown in Fig.7. It displays the shots with five levels of degree of interest of the subject. Darker color shows more interest, and lighter color shows less interest. In the Fig.7 the length of the shots are normalized so that they have a same width. Roughly speaking, darker region appears four times in Fig.7: The first one is when the experiment started and he was not pleasant. He got gradually accustomed to the devices he was wearing. The second one is when he bought a ticket. The third one is when he was at the paddock. The forth one is when the races started. It appears that the evaluation well reflects subjective status. The extracted shots which are rated as level three or higher are extracted and displayed in Fig.8. Among 175 shots of an hour-long video, only 35 shots are extracted.

Fig. 7. The shots rated by α wave. Darker means more interest and whiter means less interest.

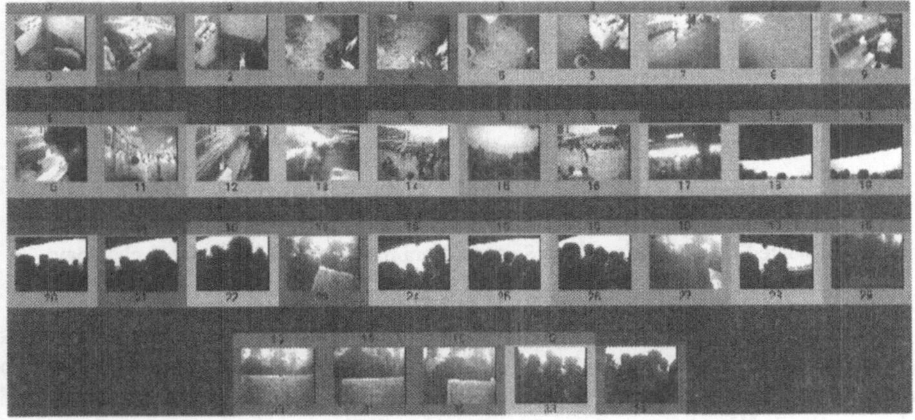

Fig. 8. The shots extracted: level three or higher

6 Conclusion

In this paper, we proposed a novel approach of summarizing video captured by a wearable camera. We discussed potential and feasibility of wearable imaging for life long time. Our summarization proceeds in two steps: in the first step, the video stream is segmented by using objective visual features such as motion, and in the second step the shots are evaluated by physiological signal that is brain waves. In the experiments, we have observed that the proposed method works well for wearable video.

References

1. S.Mann, WearCam (The Wearable Camera), ISWC, pp.124-131, 1998
2. The PC goes ready-to-wear, IEEE Spectrum, pp.34-39, Oct. 2000
3. M.A.Smith, T.Kanade, Video skimming and characterization through the combination of image and language understanding techniques, CVPR97, pp.775-781, 1997
4. J.Healey, R. W. Picard, StartleCam: A Cybernetic Wearable Camera, ISWC, pp.42-49, 1998
5. A.W.M Smeulders etc., Content-based image retrieval at the end of the early years, Vol.22, No.12, pp.1349-1380, Dec. 2000

A Novel Video Retrieval Method to Support a User's Recollection of Past Events Aiming for Wearable Information Playing

Tatsuyuki Kawamura, Yasuyuki Kono, and Masatsugu Kidode

Graduate School of Information Science, Nara Institute of Science and Technology
8916-5, Takayama-Cho, Ikoma, Nara 630-0101, Japan
{tatsu-k,kono,kidode}@is.aist-nara.ac.jp

Abstract. Our system supports a user's location-based recollection of past events with direct input such as in always 'gazing' video data, which allows the user to associate by simply looking at a viewpoint, and providing stable online and real-time video retrieval. We propose three functional methods: image retrieval with motion information, video scene segmentation, and real-time video retrieval. Our experimental results have shown that these functions are effective enough to perform wearable information playing.

1 Introduction

This paper suggests a novel application of wearable computers for location-based recollections of past events. Our aim is to realize a framework that supports a direct, intensive, and automatic extension of human memory. Since a wearable information player [1] in the near future should be available for a daily uses, it must be portable and independently usable at any time/place. Our System can retrieve an associable video in previous recorded video data set, which is stored in the wearable computer, triggered by current video data, which is captured by a head-mounted camera. Users do not have to know that they are storing video data of their daily lives, but do not plan on utilizing such video data in the future.

Our intelligent framework should understand locations that are recorded in video data as scenes to be searched for in the future. If the user tracks a moving object, its video scene might look as if the object has stopped and its background is moving. In order to retrieve a video even in this kind of moving objects, we introduce effective functions to detect the movement of the user's camera and compensate its effect. We suggest three functional methods that use a retrieval method of location-based similar images of past events using motion information, a method of segmenting video scenes, and a method of dividing video data for real-time process.

2 Our Approach

Our system provides associable video retrieval in a previous data set triggered by current video data. The similar images of associable video images are shown in Figure 1. To achieve high speed and an appropriate location-based video retrieval method, our system must efficiently pick up location information from the video data achieved by a face-on wearable camera placed at the center of a head-mounted display (depicted in Fig.1.). Tracking the user's head movements and moving objects in a scene and avoiding above two motion on the video retrieval process.

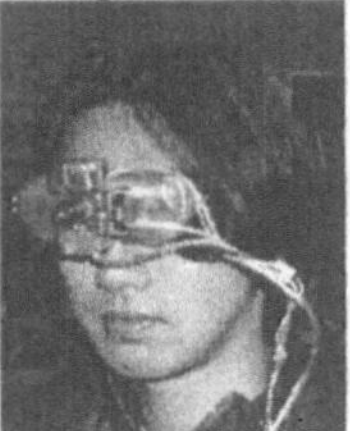

Fig. 1. Similar images in terms of location (left) and our wearable camera (right)

Motion information exclusion from video data is performed using the wearable camera by:

- tracking of yaw and pitch head movements with two mono-axis gyro sensors,
- tracking of moving objects in a scene using a block matching method, and
- excluding motion information by masking moving areas in the scene.

Video scene segmentation from continuous input video data is changed by:

- detecting scene changes continuously from current video data and two gyro data, and
- indexing each scene for easy viewing.

Real-time video retrieval from large sequential video data is retrieved by:

- dividing small segments from video data for stable and high-speed video retrieval, and
- retrieving a associable scene from a segment similar to the current video data.

2.1 Location-based Video Retrieval

Our aim is to achieve a support level for user's memories with a wearable computer. This support system retrieves an associable video data set with current video data from approximately the same viewpoint. This approach retrieves video scenes that trigger user's memory such as about persons, objects, actions, reasons, and time, which relate to a location.

The user's ideal recollection support system must include several functions. The "Forget-me-not" system [2] can detect the person whom a user met, or the time when the user give/take the person a document. The remembrance agent system [3] supports the editing of documents related to a particular time/place from the history of editing by the user. The use of these two studies is limited to an indoor environment, because sensors placed on the sides of the room. In contrast to the above two studies, the following studies use a video and stand-alone type wearable system. Clarkson's system [4], however, cannot directly retrieve previous associable video data for a user who wants to know detailed location information. Aoki's system [5] also cannot select similar video of approximately the same place/viewpoint quickly from continuously recorded video because an offline training sequence is used.

2.2 Image Retrieval using Motion Information

Wearable computers must treat motion information. We divided motion information into two types. The first type is the user's head motion information. The second type is moving object information. Each type of information must be removed to retrieve location-based images.

In the image retrieval method, we adopt three processes. The first process is to exclude head motion information from merged motion information. Motion information is made from two sequential images. We attached perceptual sensors near the wearable camera to recognize the user's head motion. These sensors are two mono-axis gyro sensors, which detect both yaw and pitch axis head rotation information. The second process is to recognize moving objects in a scene using a block matching method. This method divides an image into small blocks. The third process calculates the similarity of images using motion information detected by the prior processes. Location-based image similarity in this paper is defined as follows:

- an image recorded from approximately the same viewpoint, and
- moving objects that do not influence the similarity of an image.

Tracking Head Movements

User's head movements directly influence video data from the wearable camera. This head motion information must be removed from video data for recognizing moving objects. We adopt two mono-axis gyro sensors and place these sensors at the center of the wearable camera as shown in Fig. 1 (right). In order to remove the user's head motion information, an examination of the relationship between the amount of value transition with the gyro sensor and the amount of shift with images is necessary. Fig.2 show both relationships (left: yaw, right: pitch). These results can remove the user's head motion information from video data.

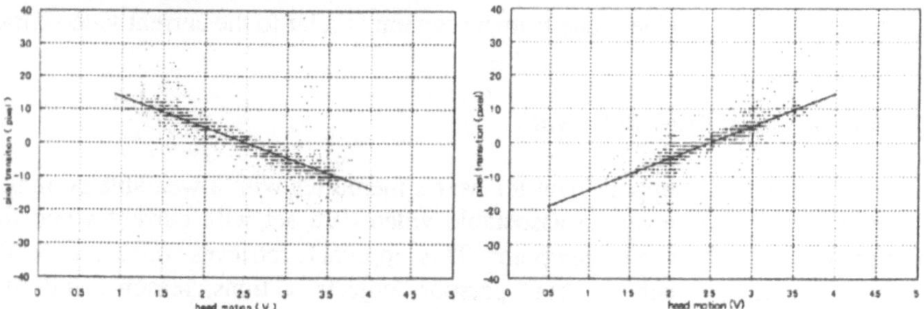

Fig. 2. A gyro sensor value and the amount of image shift value (yaw and pitch)

Tracking Moving Objects

We adopted a block matching method that detects areas, each of which includes moving objects in a scene. The method divides an image into small blocks. The matching process compares divided blocks and an area of the same size. The method is normally limited in calculation amount. The pixel data to recognize moving objects in a scene is the (r,g,b) pixel. The system selects the ($I=r+g+b$, $I_r=r/I$, $I_g=g/I$, $I_b=b/I$) data obtained from the (r,g,b). Our method is defined in the following formulae:

$$Mr_{i,j}(u,v,t)=\sum(Ir(i_0,j_0,t)-Ir(i_u,j_v,t))^2\ , \tag{1}$$

$$Mg_{i,j}(u,v,t)=\sum(Ig(i_0,j_0,t)-Ig(i_u,j_v,t))^2\ , \tag{2}$$

$$Mb_{i,j}(u,v,t)=\sum(Ib(i_0,j_0,t)-Ib(i_u,j_v,t))^2\ , \tag{3}$$

$$M_{i,j}=Mr_{i,j}+Mg_{i,j}+Mb_{i,j}\ . \tag{4}$$

The calculated minimum value of comparisons in a limited area shows an estimated block motion vector $(u_{\min},v_{\min})$. The block motion vectors calculated by the above method are redefined into five simple states (up, down, left, right, and non-movement). If a motion vector is adequately small, this block is named as "non-movement."

Exclusion of Motion Information

The current query image and the previous images each have specific motion information. In order to remove mutual motion blocks in each image from target searching blocks, a motion block mask should be made. First, the image matching process compares the same address block in two images with blocks called "non-movement" states. The block matching method uses the same method mentioned in the section "Tracking Moving Objects." The second process divides a value, from the summed values calculated by the previous process, by the number of "non-movement" blocks. We adopt the divided value for an evaluation of image similarity. This value is derived from the value calculated by using the block matching method.

2.3 Video Scene Segmentation

We construct scene changes using color differences appearing on the entire screen and a moving average method with two mono-axis gyro sensors. Unlike a video data used in television, there are no clear scene changes in the wearable video data we use in our research. If the difference and the amount of the value transition of gyro sensors are large, we choose the point to divide the scene. We then merge some sequential short scenes into one scene for easy viewing.

In the moving average method, continuously input gyro sensor values are added from the past value in T frames prior to the current value and T divides added value. This method can obtain a meta-trend of captured data. The moving average method equation is as follows:

$$MA_T(t)=\frac{\sum_{i=t-T}^{t}f(i)}{T}\ . \tag{5}$$

In this paper, four values are calculated by the moving average method: Two values are calculated with yaw-axis gyro value, and other two values are calculated with pitch-axis gyro value. The following three states are defined to detect scene changes:

- Stable state: Both the moving average value of a short interval (e.g. T=30) and that of a long interval (e.g. T=300) are under a certain range
- Side1 state: The moving average of the short interval is higher than the long interval.
- Side2 state: The moving average of the long interval is higher than the short interval.

By using the parameter, $MA_T(t)$, a scene change is detected by a state transition. The minimum length of a segmented scene is limited to 30 frames. If the color difference between adjacent images is under a threshold, this frame does not make a new scene.

2.4 Real-time Video Retrieval

The proposed video retrieval method is based on similarity predictions, which divide video data into small segments and retrieves the associable video data, because the cost of the retrieval process increases as the video data set becomes large. In this retrieval method process, all images in a segment l are compared with a current query image from the wearable camera. The next process for video retrieval is changed from l to the next segment $l+1$, when the maximum image similarity, $HM(l)$, is under a threshold th. We consider the following hypothesis: Similar images form clusters in a sequential video set.

$$l = \begin{cases} l, & \text{for } HM(l) \geq th, \\ l+1, & \text{for } HM(l) < th. \end{cases} \tag{6}$$

3. Experimental Results

We use an IBM ThinkPad X20 (Intel Pentium III 600MHz, 320 MB Memory). The wearable camera has an I-O DATA USB-CCD 320x240 triad resolution. We selected a video see-through head-mounted display, the OLYMPUS EYE-TREK FMD700. The motion detection sensor, which has two mono-axis gyro sensors, is from Silicon Sensing Systems (max 100deg/s).

3.1 Video Retrieval with Motion Information

The experiment took place during the daytime, outdoors, in a hall, and in a room. The experimental tasks were recorded four times in each place. The first frame image in the recorded video data is defined as the retrieval query. The experimental task consists of two parts. One task was for the subject to wave his/her hand several times.

The other task required that the subject turn his/her head to the left. The "normal" method, which does not consider motion information, was performed to compare with our proposed method. The result is shown in Fig.3. In the figure, a higher location-based image similarity corresponds to a lower evaluation value. Our method clearly shows a higher similarity than the normal method in the hand waving task. Our method removes larger distance from the evaluation values in the hand waving task to the evaluation values in the head turning task than in the normal method.

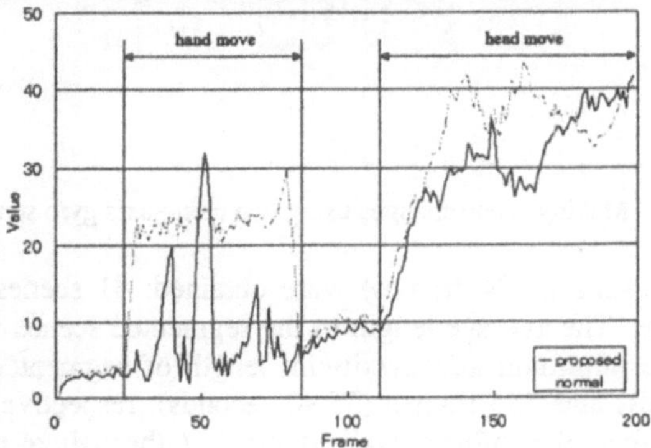

Fig. 3. Evaluation and targeting of video similarity between base images

Table 1 illustrates the relevance and recall rates of both methods. The relevance rate is the rate of retrieved data for all correct data. The recall rate is the rate of correct data for all retrieval data. Our method is well suited to retrieve location-based similar images, because the relevance rate of the proposed method performed 1.3 times as well as the normal method.

Table 1. Relevance and recall rate

	relevance		recall	
	proposed	normal	proposed	normal
outdoor	0.90	0.54	0.98	0.96
hall	0.97	0.56	0.92	0.90
room	0.88	0.57	0.97	0.96
average	0.92	0.56	0.96	0.94

3.2 Video Scene Segmentation

Both image and gyro data, which consist of 5584 frames (191.36 seconds, 29.19 frame/second), were recorded for evaluation. A subject walked two times around a specified route in our laboratory. We set intervals of the moving average as 30 frames (about 1 second) and 300 frames (about 10 seconds). The process limited the minimum scene length to 30 frames. The remarkable result of the experiment is shown in Fig.4. Upper lines in the figure are the moving average values. The lower line shows the scene changes. The scene changes took place 9 times in the figure.

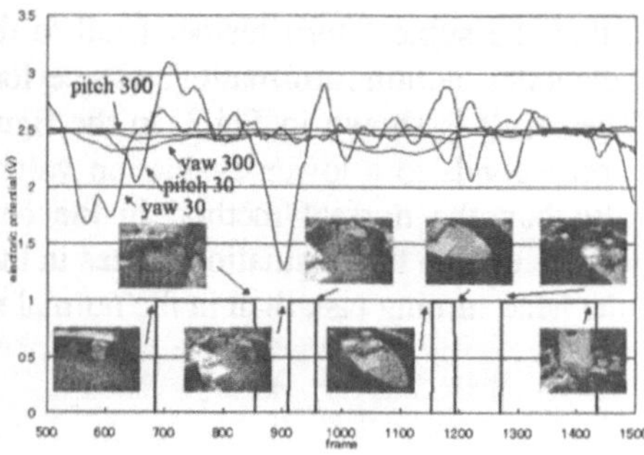

Fig. 4. Making scene changes using two mono-axis gyro sensors

The following results (5584 frames) ware obtained: 41 scenes were segmented from a video data set. The average length of the segmented scenes was 119.51frames (4.09 seconds). The minimum and maximum length of segmented scenes were 31 frames (1.06 seconds) and 756 frames (25.90 seconds), respectively. The minimum scene was made when the subject walked quickly through a narrow path. The maximum scene change was segmented on a long straight and un-diversified hallway. From the experimental results, we conclude that a user's motion information can be used to segment scene changes on a wearable computer environment.

3.3 Real-time Video Retrieval

We compared our method and the normal method. The data set is the same as that for the scene segmentation. We used the first half of the recorded data set as an associable data set, and the latter half as a query of one. We divided the associable data set into 30 small segments. We set a process condition that retrieves location-based similar images from the same segment when the evaluation value is over or equal to 0.2.

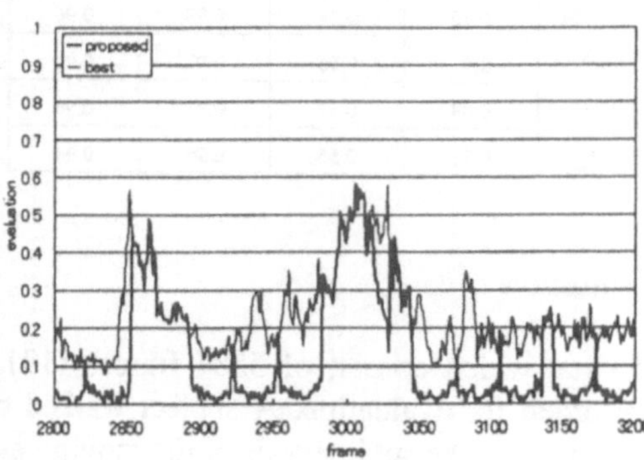

Fig. 5. Proposed and full data sequence search

The remarkable part of the results of the experiment is shown in Figure. 5. In the figure, a higher similarity of location-based images corresponds to a higher evaluation value. The thick line shows the experimental results of our method, and the other line to the normal method. The calculation time of the process per frame reduced searching for full data sequence to 1/30. The best evaluation value of all data sets is tracked by comparing the same segment of divided video data to the query image when the evaluation value is maintained over or equal to 0.2. We conclude that the hypothesis regarding the clusters of similar images is correct.

4. Concluding Remarks

We have proposed three functions to support a user's location-based recollection of past events. First, we have realized the associable image retrieval method with head movements and moving objects in a scene. We adopted two mono-axis gyro sensors for tracking two-axis head movement. In the future, we are planning to implement other axes or the parallel movement, such as roll axis head movement or walking by various sensors. Second, we proposed a video scene segmentation method to make comprehensible video scenes for users. We adopted the moving average method using two mono-axis gyro sensors to recognize the user's action history. Finally, we proposed a real-time video retrieval method that divides a large video data set into small segments and selects the segment to search an associable video scene with a continuous input image. A future direction of this study will be to develop a faster, stabilized, and efficient video retrieval method to cope with longer continuous video memory.

Acknowledgements

This research is supported by CREST of JST (Japan Science and Technology).

References

1. M. Kidode: Advanced Computing and Communication Techniques for Wearable Information Playing (in Japanese). IEICE, SIG-PRMU2000-159, pp. 93-94, 2001.
2. M. Lamming, and M. Flynn: Forget-me-not: Intimate computing in support of human memory. In FRIENDS21: International Symposium on Next Generation Human Interface, pp. 125-128, 1994.
3. B.J. Rhodes: The Wearable Remembrance Agent: a System for Augmented Memory. Proc. ISWC'97, pp. 123-128, 1997.
4. B. Clarkson, and A. Pentland: Unsupervised Clustering of Ambulatory Audio and Videol. Proc. ICASSP99, 1999.
5. H. Aoki, B. Schiele, and A. Pentland: Realtime Personal Positioning System for Wearable Computers. Proc. ISWC'99, pp. 37-43, 1999.

Experience of Immersive Virtual World Using Cellular Phone Interface

Tetsuro Ogi[1, 2, 3], Koji Yamamoto[3], Toshio Yamada[1], Michitaka Hirose[2]

[1] Gifu MVL Research Center, TAO
Iutelligent Modeling Laboratory, The University of Tokyo
2-11-16, Yayoi, Bunkyo-ku, Tokyo 113-8656, Japan
{tetsu, yamada}@iml.u-tokyo.ac.jp
[2] Research Center for Advanced Science and Technology
The University of Tokyo
4-6-1, Komaba, Meguro-ku, Tokyo 153-8904, Japan
hirose@cyber.rcast.u-tokyo.ac.jp
[3] Mitsubishi Research Institute
2-3-6, Otemachi, Chiyoda-ku, Tokyo 100-8141, Japan
koji@mri.co.jp

Abstract. The cellular phone has become a popular portable information device. In this study, the i-mode of the cellular phone was applied to the interface with the immersive virtual world. By using the cellular phone interface, the user can experience the immersive virtual world easily using his own device. The interaction using the i-mode was experimentally evaluated in the walk-through application. In addition, by integrating the cellular phone interface with the transparent immersive projection display, an invisible immersive interface that enables the user to experience the virtual environment in the real work place was constructed. This system was applied to several fields of application such as the visualization of data and the telecommunication.

1. Introduction

Recently, mobile media such as the cellular phone and the PDA (Personal Digital Assistance) have become very popular, and they are used as personal devices being carried everyday. By using these devices, the user can easily access information everywhere and at any time in the daily life. However, in these devices, the displayed information is restricted because only the small LCD (Liquid Crystal Display) is equipped.

On the other hand, immersive projection display such as the CAVE or the CABIN can generate a high presence information space around the user [1][2]. However, in order to use this kind of display system, the user must operate the graphics workstation to run the application program and interact with the virtual world using a special device such as the wand or the wanda [3]. Therefore, it is difficult that the ordinary people experience the high presence virtual world in the immersive projection display.

In this study, an interface technology with the immersive virtual world using the personal device of the cellular phone was developed in order to experience the high presence virtual world easily. In this system, the user can also experience the immersive environment in the real world, by integrating the transparent display system with the cellular phone interface. This paper describes the system construction, the features and several applications of the immersive environment using the cellular phone interface.

2. Cellular Phone Interface

2.1 Features of Cellular Phone Device

In order to experience the high presence virtual world using the immersive projection display, the user must operate the graphics workstation to run the application program and interact with the virtual world using the special interface devices. For example, in the CAVE developed at the University of Illinois, the wand and the wanda are used for the interface devices. In the case of the CABIN developed at the University of Tokyo, the Nintendo64 Controller, the VibroPointer, and the Twiddler are used for the joystick, the haptic pointer and the character input devices respectively [4][5]. In particular, it is difficult to input characters in the three-dimensional immersive virtual environment. Although the practiced user is able to input characters rapidly using the Twiddler by one hand, it is hard for the unfamiliar user to use this kind of device efficiently. Therefore, it is desired that the everyday device that is carried in the daily life should be used for the interaction so that a large number of people can experience the immersive information space easily.

On the other hand, the recent cellular phone has been used to access Internet, and the cellular phone device itself has several functions. For example, the dial button can be used to input characters as well as to dial telephone numbers, and the LCD is used to display information. The pager motor is often installed to inform the phone call using the vibration sensation, and it can be used to display haptic information. In addition, the cellular phone device that is equipped with the Internet access function such as the i-mode or the WAP (Wireless Application) can be used to transmit data to the computer as a kind of computer terminal. Therefore, we can consider that the cellular phone that is used in the daily life can be used as an interface device with the virtual world effectively.

2.2 i-mode Interface

In this study, an interface technology using the i-mode was developed to interact with the immersive virtual world. The i-mode is an Internet access service for the cellular phone provided by the NTT DoCoMo Inc., and the user can access web information using the dial button and the LCD [6]. Currently, in Japan, about twenty-three million people are using this service, and it has become a popular portable information device.

The i-mode was applied to realize the interactions such as the walk-through and character input in the virtual world. In these interactions, the dial button of the cellular phone is used for the button and the keyboard functions. Since the LCD is also equipped on it, the user can perform the input operation in the local feedback, without displaying the three-dimensional input window or the menu in the virtual world.

In addition, the cellular phone device can also be used as a pointing device by attaching the position tracker to it. In this system, a Polhemus electromagnetic sensor was used to

Fig. 1. Cellular Phone Interface with Position Tracker

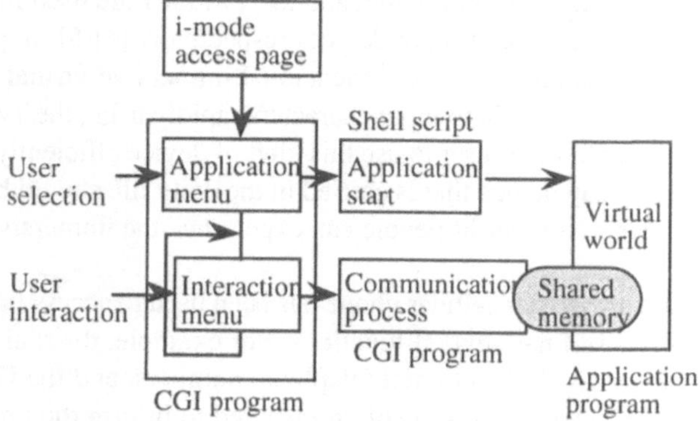

Fig. 2. Software Construction of the i-mode Interface

track the position of the cellular phone. In this case, when the cellular phone communicates with the Internet, it generates an electromagnetic wave that causes a tracking error. Therefore, the position tracker was attached about 8 cm away from the body of the cellular phone to reduce the influence of the electromagnetic wave as shown in figure 1.

2.3 Software Construction

The i-mode interface is used both as a computer terminal to start the virtual reality application and as an interface device to interact with the virtual world in the application program. Figure 2 shows the software construction of the i-mode interface.

In order to start the virtual reality application program, the user first accesses the graphics workstation through the DoCoMo i-mode Center. The application program runs when the user selects the menu item or inputs the name of the application in the i-mode web page. This i-mode page is written in CGI (Common Gateway Interface), and it runs the shell script to start the application program. By using this method, the user can start the virtual reality application without using a computer terminal.

After starting the application program, the CGI program moves to the interaction i-mode page. When the user inputs characters or selects menu item in the interaction i-

Fig. 3. Interaction i-mode Page for the Walk-through

Fig. 4. Walk-through Using the i-mode Interface in the CABIN

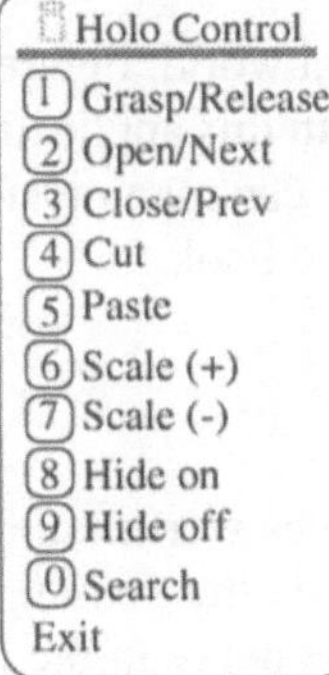

Fig. 5. Interaction i-mode Page for the Data Manipulation

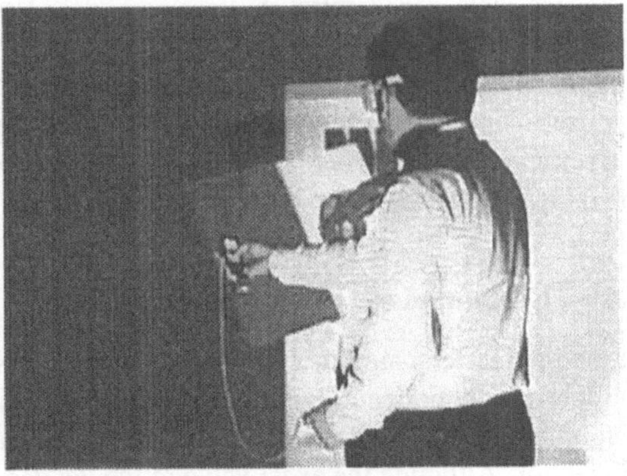

Fig. 6. Data Manipulation Using the i-mode Interface in the CABIN

mode page, the CGI program generates a communication process that transmits the interaction command to the application program. This communication process is generated every time the user interacts with the virtual world, and this interaction command is transmitted to the application through the shared memory.

For example, figure 3 shows the interaction i-mode page to walk through the virtual world. In this example, the dial buttons are assigned to several moving functions such as "go ahead", "stop", "turn right", "turn left", "go up" and "go down", and the user can walk through the virtual world freely by operating these dial buttons. Figure 4 shows the user walking thorough the virtual town by using the i-mode interface in the immersive projection display CABIN.

Figure 5 shows the other example of the interaction i-mode page to retrieve data and manipulate it in the virtual world. When the user selects the "search" button and input keywords, the data is retrieved from the database system and is visualized in the virtual world. And when the user reaches his hand for the visualized data and pushes the "grasp"

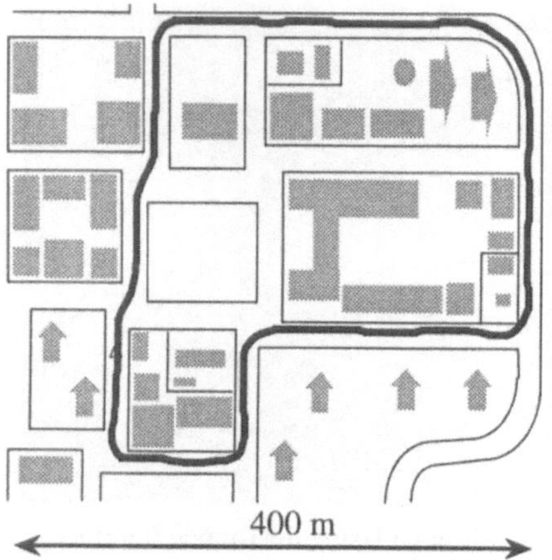

Fig. 7. Typical Track of the Walk-through Using the Nintendo64 Controller

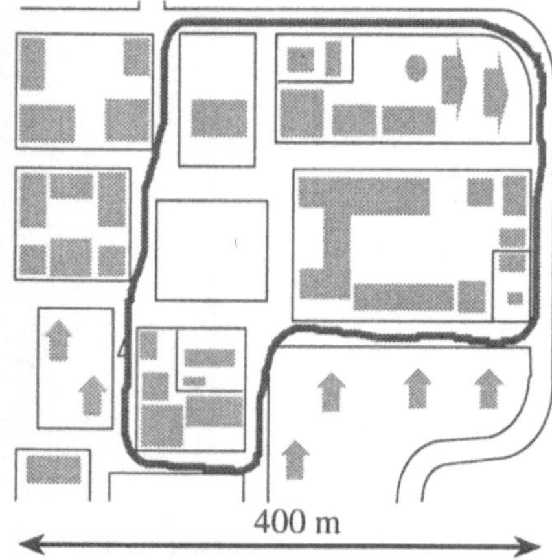

Fig. 8. Typical Track of the Walk-through Using the i-mode Interface

button, he can grasp and manipulate it as an object in the virtual world. Figure 6 shows the user manipulating the visualized data in the virtual office. In this application, since the retrieved data is visualized being filed in the book, the user can manipulate data by grasping it or browse data by turning the pages of the visualized book.

2.4 Evaluation of i-mode Interaction

In the interaction using the i-mode, the user accesses the graphics workstation through the Internet by connecting with the DoCoMo i-mode Center via the 9600 bps packet communication. Then, we cannot avoid a problem of the time delay in the real-time interaction. Although the exact value of the lag depends on the network condition, in the ordinary use, the average lag between the command input and the change of the displayed image was about 0.48 sec.

The influence the time delay has on the interaction with the virtual world must be fully investigated. In the case of the command type interaction such as selecting a menu item or grasping the virtual object, a small lag would be an insignificant problem. However, in the continuous interaction such as walking through the virtual world, we are afraid that the time delay has a severe influence on the real-time interaction.

In this study, we conducted an experiment to investigate whether the user can walk through the virtual town smoothly using the i-mode interaction. In this experiment, the subjects were asked to move along the indicated way, and the tracks were compared between using the Nintendo64 Controller which was directly connected to the serial port of the graphics workstation and using the i-mode interface. In the case of using the i-mode interface, the interaction method shown in figure 3 was used, and then the user moved the virtual town using the dial button operation.

Figure 7 and figure 8 show the typical results of the tracks along which the subject moved by using the Nintendo64 Controller and the i-mode interface respectively. In both cases, the maximum speed of the movement was about 35 km/h. When the subject

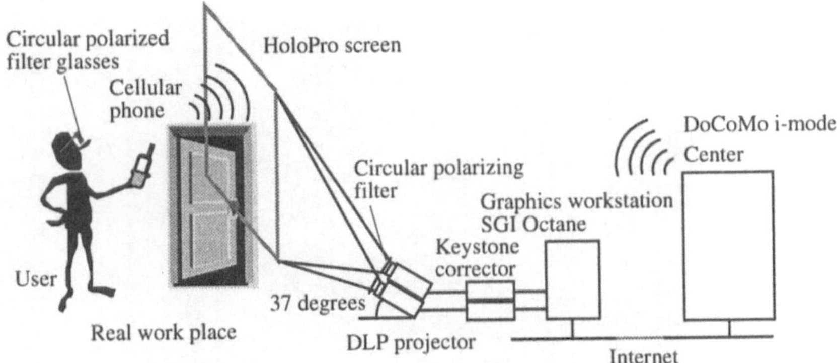

Fig. 9. Invisible Immersive Interface System Using HoloPro Screen and i-mode Interface

turned a corner using the i-mode interface, he occasionally strayed off the course being caused by the time delay and the difficulty of the dial button operation. However, on the whole, the subjects could walk through the virtual town smoothly by using the i-mode interaction.

3 Invisible Immersive Interface

3.1 Transparent Display

Although the user can easily interact with the virtual world using the cellular phone interface, the display system also should be equipped in the real world so that he can experience it everywhere. However, if the immersive projection display such as the CAVE was equipped in the real work place, it would obstruct the working space of the user. In this study, a transparent immersive projection display that can present a high presence virtual world in the air without disturbing the user's view was introduced. By using this display system, the user can experience the three-dimensional immersive virtual world in the real work place only when it is necessary.

As for the transparent screen, HoloPro screen made by G+B Pronova was used [7]. This screen is constructed by laminating a gelatin light directing film inside the multi-layer glass. Since the image projected from the specific angle between 35 degrees and 40 degrees is redirected in the direction of the viewer, the projector can be placed on the floor or on the ceiling behind from the user's view. Moreover, since the polarization of the light is preserved when it goes through the screen, the polarizing filter method can be used to generate a three-dimensional stereo image. This screen can also be used outdoors in daylight, because the projected image is hardly affected by the ambient light. Therefore, this system can be used in the real work place as a real world oriented virtual reality system.

In this study, the invisible immersive interface system was constructed by combining the HoloPro screen and the cellular phone interface technologies as shown in figure 9. The diagonal size of the HoloPro screen is 50 inches, and the SGI Octane graphics

Fig. 10. Visualization of Design Model Using the Invisible Immersive Interface

Fig. 11. Telecommunication Using the Invisible Immersive Interface

workstation is used to generate parallax images for the left and right eyes. These two images are transmitted to the NEC LT140J DLP (Digital Light Processing) projectors, and are projected from the angle of 37 degrees through the Analog Way Keystonix KC-100 keystone correctors. When the user accesses the graphics workstation using the cellular phone, he can see the stereo image in the real world by wearing the circular polarizing filter glasses.

3.2 Applications

By using the invisible immersive interface, the user can easily experience the immersive virtual environment in the real work place. In this study, this system was introduced into the meeting room in the Intelligent Modeling Laboratory at the University of Tokyo. The designers often discuss the design data looking at the drawing. When this system is used, they can visualize the three-dimensional design model in the meeting room by accessing the data using the cellular phone. Figure 10 shows the example in which the designers are discussing the design model in the real meeting room.

This system was also applied to the high presence telecommunication between remote places. The authors have been studying the communication technology using the video avatar in the networked shared virtual world [8]. The video avatar is a three-dimensional video image that is constructed using the depth data calculated from the stereo video images. In this system, the video avatar was applied to the communication between the real worlds as shown in figure 11. When the user calls the remote user using the cellular phone, the video avatar of the remote user appears in the real space projected onto the transparent screen, and they can communicate with each other with a high quality of presence.

4 Conclusions

In this study, the interaction technology using the i-mode of the cellular phone was developed to experience the virtual world easily. In this method, the user can run the virtual reality application program without using the computer terminal and interact with the virtual world using the cellular phone. In addition, by integrating the cellular phone interface with the transparent immersive projection display, the invisible immersive interface was constructed which enables the user to experience the immersive virtual world in the real work place. This system was introduced into the meeting room and was applied to the visualization of the design model and the telecommunication between remote places. In this method, the user can interact with the virtual world easily by using his own cellular phone that is carried in the daily life. Future work will include applying this technology to the more practical fields of application and evaluating the effectiveness of this technology.

References

1. Cruz-Neira, C., Sandin, D.J., DeFanti, T.A.: Surround-Screen Projection-Based Virtual Reality: The Design and Implementation of the CAVE, Proceedings of SIGGRAPH'93 (1993) 135-142
2. Hirose, M., Ogi, T., Yamada, T.: Integrating Live Video for Immersive Environments, IEEE Multimedia, Vol.6, No.3, July-September (1999) 14-22
3. Browning, D.R., Cruz-Neira, C., Sandin, D.J., DeFanti, T.A., Edel, J.G.: Input Interfacing to the CAVE by Persons with Disabilities, Virtual Reality and People with Disabilities (1994)
4. Ogi, T., Watanabe, H., Hirose, M.: Interactive Scientific Visualization in Immersive Virtual Environment, 3rd International Immersive Projection Technology Workshop (IPT99) (1999) 223-230
5. Ogi, T., Yamada, T., Kano, M., Yamamoto, K., Hirota, K., Hirose, M.: Multimedia Virtual Laboratory on the Gigabit Network, The Tenth International Conference on Artificial Reality and Telexistence (ICAT2000) (2000) 98-103
6. http://www.nttdocomo.com/i/index.html
7. http://www.holopro.com/
8. Ogi, T., Yamada, T., Tamagawa, K., Hirose, M.: Video Avatar Communication in Networked Virtual Environment, INET 2000 The Internet Global Summit Proceedings (2000)

VizWear: Toward Human-Centered Interaction through Wearable Vision and Visualization

Takeshi Kurata, Takashi Okuma, Masakatsu Kourogi,
Takekazu Kato, and Katsuhiko Sakaue

Intelligent Systems Institute,
National Institute of Advanced Industrial Science and Technology (AIST),
1-1-1 Umezono, Tsukuba, Ibaraki, 305-8568 JAPAN
kurata@ieee.org
http://www.aist.go.jp/ETL/~7234/vizwear/

Abstract. In this paper, we discuss the development of wearable systems which we collectively term *VizWear*. Vision plays an important role in both people's and computers' understanding of contextual information, and the use of augmented reality (AR) techniques is a good way to show information intuitively. This is the basis of our research on wearable computer vision and visualization systems. Our wearable systems enable us to run different vision tasks in real-time. We describe a novel approach not only to sensing the wearer's position and direction, but also to displaying video frames overlaid with 2-D annotations related to the wearer's view. We have also developed a method for 3-D graphical overlay by applying object recognition techniques and the *Hand Mouse*, which enables the wearer to interact directly with an AR environment. We also describe an efficient method of face registration using wearable active vision.

1 Introduction

Wearable computing has attracted more attention with the progress made in miniaturizing the hardware required. One of the advantages of wearing computers, sensors, and displays is that they have the potential to assist the wearers by continually sharing the same experiences with them [10], by understand their situation, and by giving them immediate feedback [11, 15]. Key issues in wearable context-aware applications is therefore how to collect real-world data, derive the context of the wearers' situation from the data, and present information relevant to those results. Vision plays an important role in both people's and computers' understanding of contextual information, and visualization based on AR techniques is a good way to show information intuitively. This is the basis of our research on the concept of human-centered wearable systems and services, which we call *VizWear*.

Here, we discuss the results we have achieved since 1999. First, we describe our wearable vision systems. Although many vision algorithms are computationally heavy for existing stand-alone wearable computers, our systems enable us to run different vision tasks in real-time, in both a parallel and cooperative manner. Next, we describe a method for 2-D annotation overlay, which is based on sensing the wearer's position and direction by using image registration, and a method for 3-D graphical overlay, which is based on object-recognition techniques. We also discuss an intuitive input interface for wearable systems, *the Hand Mouse*, and our recent work on efficient face registration using a wearable active vision system.

2 Wearable Vision Systems

We constructed prototype wearable systems as the basis for exploring applications that will be put into practice when users continually wear video cameras and take live video. The systems all consist of a wearable client, a vision server (a PC cluster or multi-processor), and wireless LAN, as shown in Figure 1. A mobile PC in the wearable client captures and compresses each image taken by the wearable camera, using JPEG encoding, and transmits it to the vision server. The wearable client then receives and displays the output from the server.

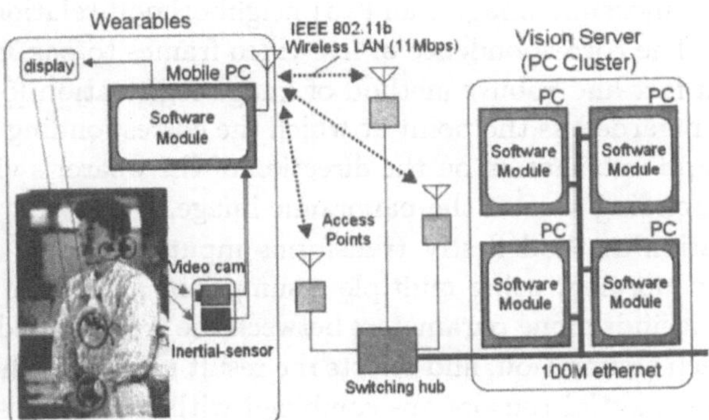

Fig. 1. Wearable client and vision server.

Although many vision algorithms are computationally heavy for existing stand-alone wearable computers, we have experimentally used our systems to run different vision tasks in (near) real-time in both a parallel and cooperative manner. Figure 2 shows the wearable apparatus that we have developed. At present, they weigh about 2.4 kg with a two-hour battery. However, soon, we will be able to install our systems in fourth generation (4G) mobile-phone network. The bandwidth of the 4G network will be equal to or higher than that of our systems and 4G appliances are expected to have sufficient video-processing capability to compress and decompress high quality video in real-time.

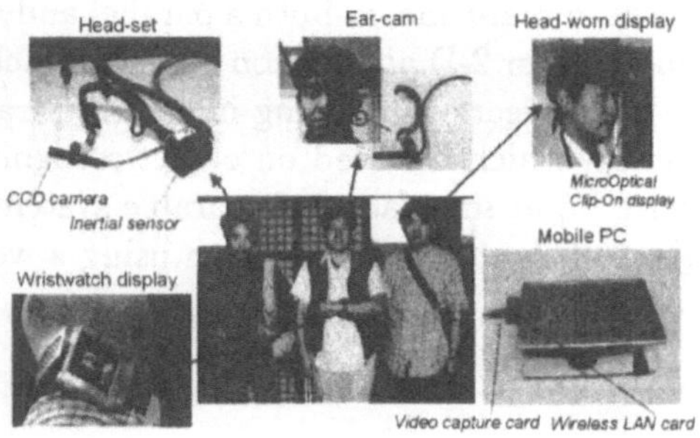

Fig. 2. Apparatus for wearable clients.

3 Panorama-Based Annotation

Panorama-based-annotation [5, 7] is a novel approach to sensing the wearer's position and direction, and to displaying video frames overlaid with 2-D annotations related to the wearer's view. An overview of this method is shown in Figure 3. As sources of information on the environment, the method uses (1) a set of panoramic images captured by omnidirectional vision sensors or panning cameras at various points, (2) annotations interactively linked to specific position on the panoramic images, and (3) neighborhood relationships between each panorama. The correspondence of live video frames to panoramic images is established by a fast and robust method of image registration [5]. The location of the wearer is regarded as the point at which the corresponding panoramic image was taken, and information on the direction of the wearer's view is obtained from the corresponding area of the panoramic image.

The registration method firstly transforms input frames to the cylindrical surface of each panorama, using multiple assumptions about the view angles of elevation. Next, it finds affine parameters between the transformed frame and the panorama for each assumption, and selects the result that gives the largest cross-correlation value. Inertial sensors are combined with this vision-based method not only to compensate for measurement errors made by the method, but to improve throughput and overcome delaying annotation overlay [6]. This approach can be applied to visual remembrance agents, personal navigation systems, etc (Figure 4).

4 3-D Annotation on Recognized Objects

In addition to 2-D annotation, we have developed a method for annotating input images with 3-D annotations and virtual objects [13, 14]. Displaying 3-D annotations enables the system to show the wearer detailed information, for example,

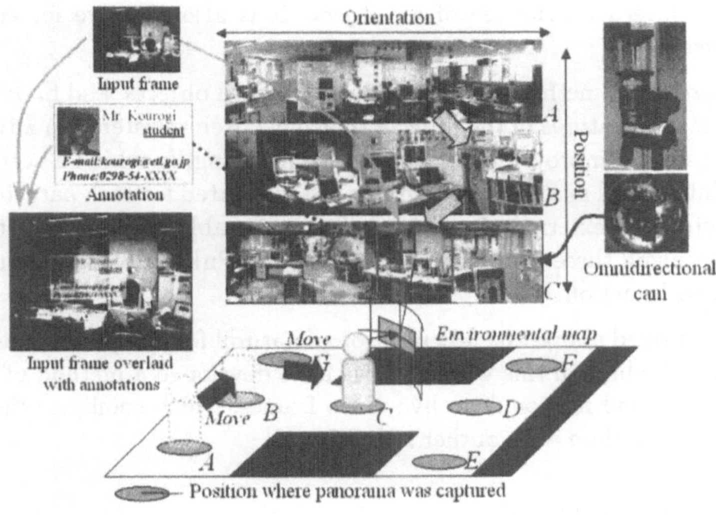

Fig. 3. Overview of panorama-based annotation.

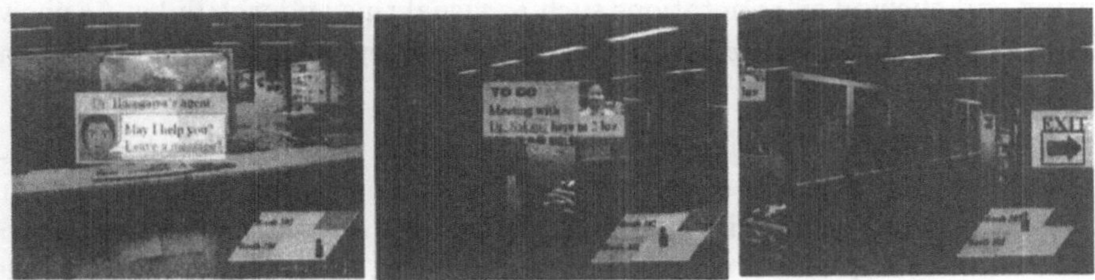

Fig. 4. Examples of output frames overlaid with annotations and environmental map.

Fig. 5. Example application of 3-D annotation: interactive pop-up poster.

about the internal structure of an object. It is also effective for emphasizing visual effects.

The proposed method recognizes the annotated objects, and finds and tracks known natural features of the objects that have been registered in advance. This method uses an improved color histogram matching, in which a scene image is divided into plural parts and histograms are calculated for each part, to recognize the objects. The external parameters of the wearable camera are estimated by selectively using three algorithms for calculating PnP problems. Figure 5 shows the method in action.

As mentioned above, the 3-D position of natural feature points must be input in advance. To lighten this workload, we have developed a method of recovering 3-D structure and motion from live video frames, which combines the recursive factorization method with outlier reduction [8].

5 The Hand Mouse

Visual context awareness can be regarded as an autonomous input interface that is needed for the adaptive construction of augmented environment. Explicit input interfaces are also essential for interaction with the environment, for example, pointing and clicking on annotations such as visual tips and web links. As shown in Figure 6, *the Hand Mouse* interface we have developed uses the wearer's hand as a pointing device [9].

In this interface, we primarily use color information to detect and track the hand. Instead of using predefined skin-color models, we dynamically construct hand- and background-color models based on the hand-color-segmentation method described by Zhu et al. [17]. The method uses a Gaussian Mixture Model (GMM) to approximate the color histogram of each input image (the GMM is estimated by a restricted Expectation-Maximization (EM) algorithm). This method uses a static spatial-probability distribution of hand pixels to detect hands. However, static distribution is inadequate for *the Hand Mouse* because the hand location is not fixed. Our method therefore translates the distribution into the appropriate position based on *the mean shift algorithm* [3]. This method is both effective and computationally inexpensive.

In Figure 7 (a), (GMM HAND), (GMM BACKGROUND), and (INPUT) indicate estimated hand-color distribution, estimated background-color distribution, and the input histogram, respectively. In (b), the dark area around the hand, which is blue in the color image, indicates the translated spatial-probability distribution of hand pixels; the green area in the color image indicates estimated hand pixels. An example of a GUI for a wearable display is shown in (c).

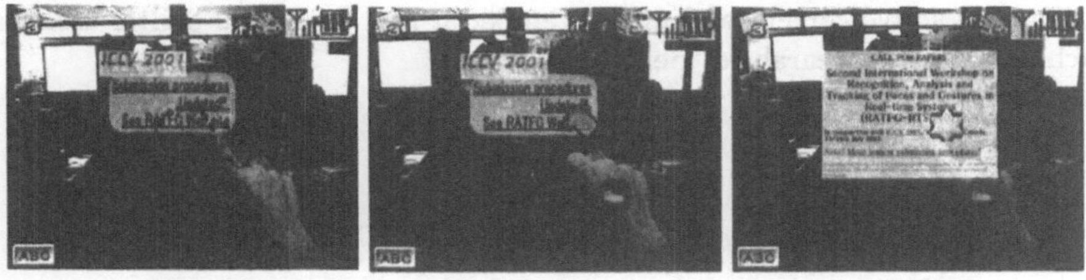

Fig. 6. Results of wearer clicking on annotation associated with poster on front wall.

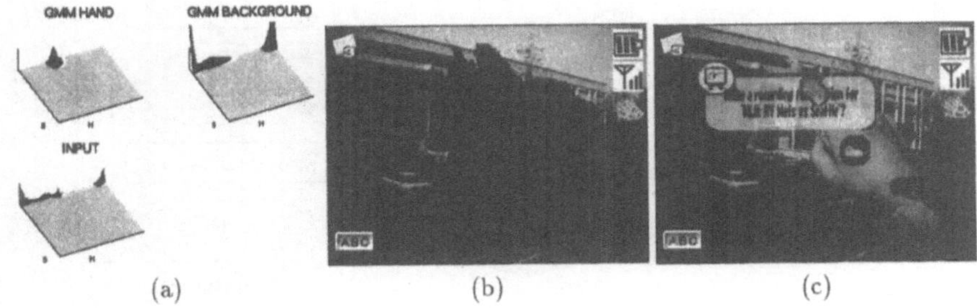

(a) (b) (c)

Fig. 7. Experimental results obtained in outdoor environment.

6 Efficient Face Registration with Wearable Active Vision

Recently, we have been developing augmented-memory applications and wearable active vision systems. To give wearers visual cues for recalling past events and situations relating to the person in front of them [2, 15], the system must be capable of autonomously detecting and identifying faces. To achieve robust face recognition in a real-world environment, the face dictionary should contain a variety of facial appearances. Kato et al. [4] described a framework for updating a face dictionary automatically and efficiently. The framework was designed for a cooperative distributed vision system, but we have used it for wearable augmented-memory applications with a wearable active vision system [12].

Figure 8 illustrates our prototype of the system with an active camera which stabilizes input images using inertial sensors. The system finds candidates for face images from the input images by fitting an elliptic head model [1]. It then extracts a face image from one of the candidates using the eigenface method [16]. The system then controls the direction of the active camera to keep the face in the center of the images. When different facial appearances are observed, they are registered in the face dictionary. The dictionary can be used to search video logs indexed with the face dictionary.

We have been using an off-the-shelf pan-tilt camera to study the feasibility of the process. However, it is not small enough to wear. We have therefore developed a wearable active camera and plan to embed it in a "personal digital assistant" such as a mobile/wearables "pet".

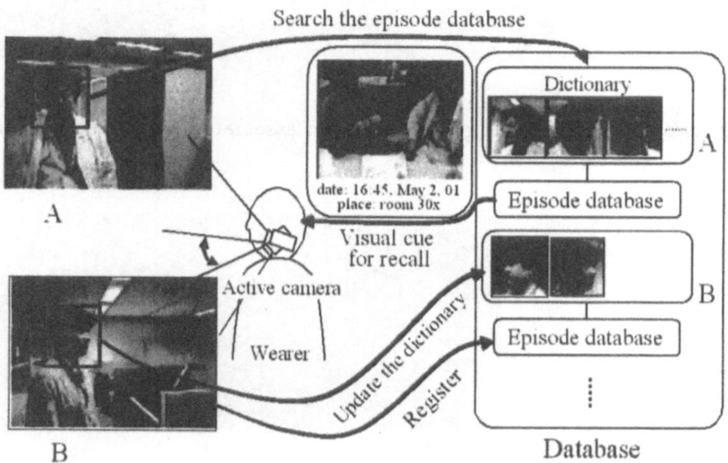

Fig. 8. Efficient face registration using wearable active vision system for visual augmented memory.

7 Conclusions

We have discussed our research on the *VizWear* concept. We expect that technologies based on the concepts we have described, such as human-centered sensing and interaction, will play essential roles in the development of wearable context-aware systems/applications. Our work focuses on the use of computer vision and AR to sense real-world situations around the wearer and present relevant information. To develop practical context-aware applications we need to consider how to deal with the vast quantity of data generated, such as sensor outputs and daily video logs, how to select appropriate information from the data, and how to present helpful and timely information without annoying them. In future work we will address combining our results with user modeling and data mining technologies.

Acknowledgments

This work is supported in part by the Real World Computing (RWC) Program of METI and also by Special Coordination Funds for Promoting Science and Technology of MEXT of the Japanese Government.

References

1. S. Birchfield. Elliptical head tracking using intensity gradients and color histograms. In *Proc. IEEE Comp. Soc. Conf. on Computer Vision and Pattern Recognition (CVPR98)*, pages 232–237, 1998.
2. J. Farringdon and V. Oni. Visual augmented memory (VAM). In *Proc. 4th Int'l Symp. on Wearable Computers (ISWC2000)*, pages 167–168, 2000.
3. K. Fukunaga. *Introduction to Statistical Pattern Recognition*. Academic Press, Boston, 1990.
4. T. Kato, Y. Mukaigawa, and T. Shakunaga. Cooperative distributed registration for face recognition in natural environment. In *Proc. 4th Asian Conference on Computer Vision (ACCV2000)*, pages 729–735, 2000.
5. M. Kourogi, T. Kurata, and K. Sakaue. A panorama-based method of personal positioning and orientation and its rea-time applications for wearable computers. In *Proc. 5th Int'l Symp. on Wearable Computers (ISWC2001)*, 2001.
6. M. Kourogi, T. Kurata, K. Sakaue, and Y. Muraoka. Improvement of panorama-based annotation overlay using omnidirectional vision and inertial sensors. In *Proc. 4th Int'l Symp. on Wearable Computers (ISWC2000)*, pages 183–184, 2000.
7. M. Kourogi, T. Kurata, K. Sakaue, and Y. Muraoka. A panorama-based technique for annotation overlay and its real-time implementation. In *Proc. Int'l Conf. on Multimedia and Expo (ICME2000)*, TA2.05, 2000.
8. T. Kurata, J. Fujiki, M. Kourogi, and K. Sakaue. A fast and robust approach to recovering structure and motion from live video frames. In *Proc. IEEE Comp. Soc. Conf. on Computer Vision and Pattern Recognition (CVPR2000)*, volume 2, pages 528–535, 2000.
9. T. Kurata, T. Okuma, M. Kourogi, and K. Sakaue. The hand-mouse: Gmm hand color classification and mean shift tracking. In *Proc. 2nd Int'l Workshop on Recognition, Analysis and Tracking of Faces and Gestures in Real-time Systems (RATFG-RTS2001) in conjunction with ICCV2001*, 2001.
10. M. Lamming and M. Flynn. "forget-me-not" intimate computing in support of human memory. Technical Report EPC-1994-103, RXRC Cambridge Laboratory, 1994.
11. S. Mann. Wearable computing: A first step toward personal imaging. *Computer*, 30(2):25–32, 1997.
12. W.W. Mayol, B. Tordoff, and D.W. Murray. Wearable visual robots. In *Proc. 4nd Int'l Symp. on Wearable Computers (ISWC2000)*, pages 95–102, 2000.
13. T. Okuma, T. Kurata, and K. Sakaue. Real-time camera parameter estimation from images for a wearable vision system. In *Proc. IAPR Workshop on Machine Vision Applications (MVA2000)*, pages 83–86, 2000.
14. T. Okuma, T. Kurata, and K. Sakaue. 3-D annotation of images captured from a wearer's camera based on object recognition. In *Proc. 2nd Int'l Symp. on Mixed Reality (ISMR2001)*, pages 184–185, 2001.
15. T. Starner, S. Mann, B. Rhodes, J. Levine, J. Healey, D. Kirsch, W. R. Picard, and A. Pentland. Augmented reality through wearable computing. Technical Report 397, M.I.T Media Lab. Perceptual Computing Section, 1997.
16. M. Turk and A. Pentland. Eigenfaces for recognition. *Journal of Cognitive Neuroscience*, 3(1):71–86, 1991.
17. X. Zhu, J. Yang, and A. Waibel. Segmenting hands of arbitrary color. In *Proc. 4th Int'l Conf. on Automatic Face and Gesture Recognition (FG2000)*, pages 446–453, 2000.

Face Indexing and Retrieval in Personal Digital Album

Haizhou Ai, Luhong Liang, Xipan Xiao, Guangyou Xu

Computer Science and Technology Department, Tsinghua University,
State Key Laboratory of Intelligent Technology and Systems,
Beijing 100084, PR China
ahz@mail.tsinghua.edu.cn

Abstract. In this paper a face indexing and retrieval scheme based on face detection and face identification techniques is presented. We developed a face detection algorithm based on SVM classifier in template matching filtered subspace for face indexing in personal digital album. For face retrieval of a particular person a classifier is learned on samples using SVM technique. Experimental results show its feasibility.

1 Introduction

Face indexing and retrieval is becoming an interesting problem as digital album appears more and more popular due to widely spread of digital cameras. In the near future, digital personal album will grow quickly in its capacity so that automatic or pseudo-automatic face indexing and retrieval tools are necessary facilities as a particular case of content-based retrieval.

Two important techniques are involved in face indexing and retrieval, that is, face detection and face identification which have been both intensively researched for decades and resulted in some effective techniques including Moghaddam and Pentland [1] based on eigenfaces, Rowley, Baluja and Kanade [2] based on neural networks, Osuna, Freund and Girosi [3] and Kumar and Poggio [4] based on SVM (Support Vector Machines), Schneiderman and Kanade [5] based on probabilistic modeling, Garcia and Tziritas [6] based on color and wavelet packet analysis. In this paper we use a SVM classifier in template matching filtered subspace for face detection, and SVM classifiers learned on samples for face retrieval. Important applications of those techniques on video parsing and image database retrieving have been attracting attentions recently, such as image annotation [7] and Name-It [8]. In this paper, we approach the feasibility of face indexing and retrieval in personal digital album based on face detection and face identification techniques.

2 Face Indexing and Retrieval Framework

As illustrated in Figure 1, the proposed face indexing and retrieval scheme consists of mainly two procedures, face detection and face identification both of which are based on SVM classification techniques. For color pictures, skin color segmentation is used as preprocessing to reduce searching space.

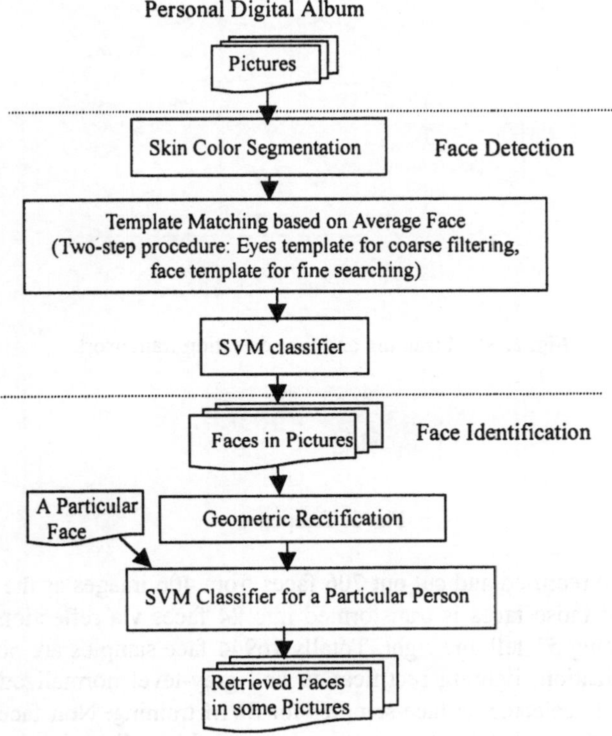

Fig. 1. Face Indexing and Retrieval Framework.

For skin color segmentation, a lookup table of 256×256×16 of binary value 0 or 1 in HSV color space is set up over a training color face samples in which 1 corresponds to skin color and 0 non-skin color. After skin color classification, pixels of skin color will be grouped into rectangle regions according to color uniformity and pixel connectivity, and then rectangle regions will be merged according to color and position nearness and some heuristic rules about permitted scale difference and area changing bounds after merging [9].

2.1 Face Detection

As shown in Figure 2, template matching filters are used to produce a subspace in which a SVM classifier is trained to detect faces. Two templates (Figure 3): eyes-in-whole and face itself of an average face, are used one by one in template matching. SVM is trained via bootstrap procedures similar to Osuna's [3]. In this way, we can develop an effective face detection algorithm on a much smaller training set compared with Osuna's [3].

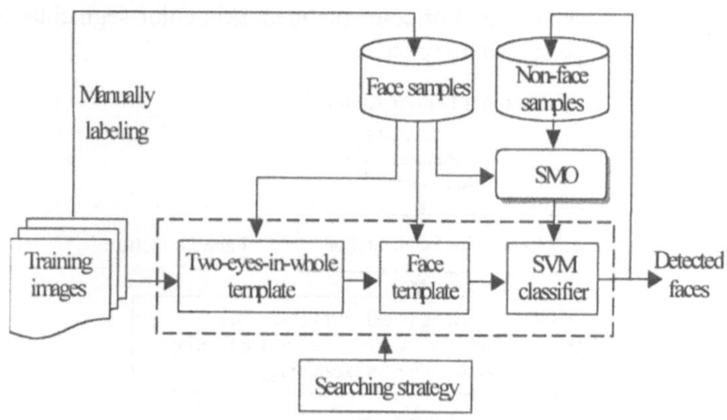

Fig. 2. SVM training and face detection framework

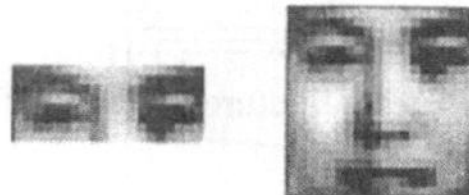

Fig. 3. Templates

In practice, we rectified and cut out 706 faces from 406 images as the original face samples. Each of those faces is transformed into 24 faces via reflection, stretch 1.1, enlarge 1.1, rotating 5° left and right. Totally 16944 face samples are normalized via histogram equalization, lighting rectification and gray-level normalization of which 5125 are randomly selected as face samples for SVM training. Non-face samples are collected via bootstrapping method in template matching filtered subspace. In this way, not only training becomes much easier but also results 20 times speedup in the final detection procedure via template matching filtering. A fast algorithm called SMO (Sequential Minimal Optimization) proposed by Plat [10] is used for training SVM, in which Gaussian radial basis function is selected as the kernel and constrained by C=200. Input vectors are 374 in dimension excluding some corner points of 20×20 window. At the final loop 5047 non-face samples are used together with 5125 face samples in training SVM, which resulted in 2207 support vectors.

In order to detect faces in different scale, each image is repeatedly subsampled via a ratio 1.2 and results in a pyramid of images. Faces are located under a similar strategy proposed by Rowley [2] in the filtered pyramid.

2.2 Face Identification

As a case study, here we discuss the problem retrieving faces of a particular person in the personal digital album. We suppose a face sub-set of that particular person is known which can be used in training. In practice, that can be collected over a training subset of the digital album containing that person. Similarly a face set of other persons can also be collected by means of face detection assisted by user interference. A SVM identifier of that person is trained over the above two sets. Figure 4 illustrates the training procedure.

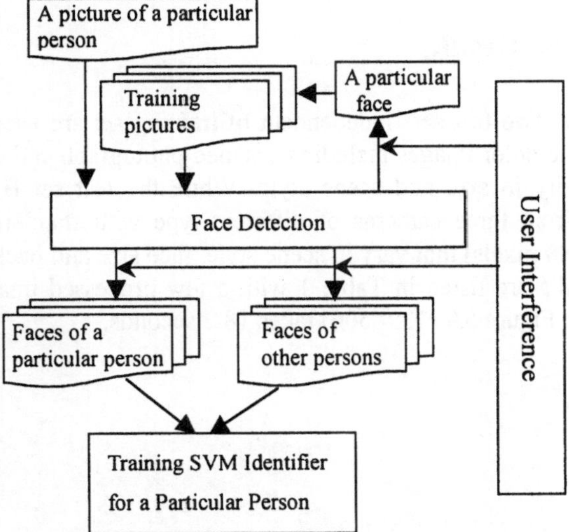

Fig. 4. Training a SVM Face Identifier

In practice, all training faces are normalized both in geometry by warping based on four facial points of which two center points of pupils and two corner points of mouth, and in intensity by transforming to the same average and standard deviation with the same size 32×32. Each face is finally transformed into 96 faces before used for SVM training with Gaussian radial basis kernel function and C=200.

Given a SVM face identifier of a particular person is learnt on the initial training set of the digital album, the face retrieval of that person can be processed over the rest of digital album. User can edit those retrieval results in the way that deleting wrong ones, adding missed ones and adjusting their sizes and positions if necessary. In this way, both training sets of that person and others can be added with more samples so that an update SVM identifier can be learnt. This above procedure can be iteratively processed to guarantee more and more effective searching engine of that particular person be learnt as the personal digital album grows in size.

2.3 Face Retrieval

Face retrieval consists of three procedures: face detection/manually labeling if necessary, geometric rectification and face identification.

For each detected face or labeled face, its rectified form is selected according to the outputs of the SVM face detector corresponding to its transformations including rotations ([-4°, 4°], 2° in spacing), stretching (0.9~1.1, 0.1 in spacing), and translation (in X and Y, maximum 2 pixels), of which with the maximum is used as the rectified face.

Each rectified face is fed into the face identifier, pictures that have positive output of its contained face are retrieved out together with the location of that face.

3 Experimental Results

For face detection, two test sets independent of training set are used. The test set A consists of 120 true-color images including scanned photograph and download images with much diversity in size and scene style. While the test set B consists of 110 grabbed images from three cameras of different type with standard size (320×240 pixels and 352×288 pixels) that vary in scene style, face size and background too. The experimental results are listed in Table 1 with a few processed images are given in Figure 5, of which Figure 5A (739×506) takes 18.2 seconds.

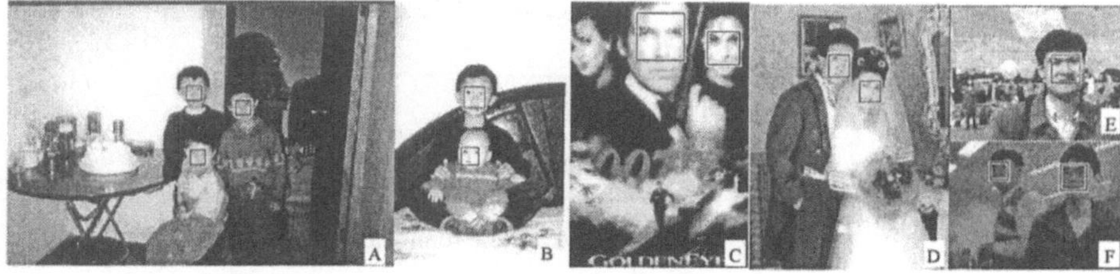

Fig. 5. Face Detection Results

For face retrieval, we particularly asked a friend to provide his photos. We get 75 pictures and scanned them to get digital forms. Face detection results on this album are listed in Table 1. This photo album is separated into two parts, one with 22 pictures as the training set, of which two are shown in Figure 6 with a particular person marked for training and the remained 53 pictures as test set for retrieval use. The training data are listed in Table 2. It should be mentioned that even in the training set, face retrieving may not certainly reach 100% since face samples are normalized before training in order to achieve better performance on non-training set. The face retrieval results on test set are given in Table 3 with three retrieved images shown in Figure 7. The one corresponding to person *Xxp* is the worst due to fewer faces existed in the training set that do not cover the diversity of his face existed in the test set. Results will be improved when training set grows due to the learning nature of this scheme.

Table 1. Face Detection Results

Test Sets	Number of Images	Number of Faces	Faces Detected	Detect Rate	False Alarms
Set A	120	420	370	88.1%	118
Set B	110	122	118	96.7%	27
Album	75	220	178	80.9%	59

Table 2. Training Set (22 images with 62 faces) and Face Retrieval on that Set

Person	Number of Images Having that Person	Support Vectors	Correctly Re-trieved	Retrieved Rate	False Re-trieval
Bigface	3	100	3	100.0%	0
Fatboy	7	219	3	42.9%	1
Hellen	9	115	8	88.9%	2
Xxp	4	71	4	100.0%	2

Table 3. Face Retrieval on Test Set (53 images with 158 faces)

Person	Number of Images Having that Person	Correctly Re-trieved	Retrieved Rate	False Re-trieval
Bigface	5	5	100.0%	4
Fatboy	6	6	100.0%	4
Hellen	12	9	75.0%	4
Xxp	13	4	30.8%	1

Fig. 6. Two Images in the Training Set with a Particular Person (Hellen) for Training Marked

Fig. 7. Retrieval Results of a Particular Person (Hellen)

4 Summary

This paper has demonstrated the feasibility of face indexing and retrieval in personal digital album by means of SVM techniques used both in face detection and face identification procedures. The SVM classifier for face detection is trained in template matching filtered subspace, which greatly reduced the complexity of training SVM and resulted in a much faster speed in detection via template matching preprocessing. Face retrieval based on SVM face identification technique trained over face set of a particular person against that of other persons demonstrates a feasible scheme for further research which may have promising potentials considering the learning nature it involved.

Although at present our experiments are aimed at approximately upright frontal faces, the techniques developed in this paper can be generalize to more general cases such as tilted faces, or even profile faces.

References

1. Moghaddam B and Pentland A. Beyond Linear Eigenspaces: Bayesian Matching for Face Recognition", *in Face Recognition from Theory to Applications, edited by H. Wechsler et al.*, Springer 1998, pages 230-243.
2. Rowley H. A., Baluja S. and Kanade T. Neural Network-Based Face Detection", *IEEE Trans. Pattern Analysis and Machine Intelligence*, 20(1):23-38, 1998.
3. Osuna E., Freund R. and Girosi F. Training Support Vector Machines: an application to face detection", *in Proc. of CVPR*, Puerto Rico, 1997.
4. Kumar V. P. and Poggio T. Learning-Based Approach to Real Time Tracking and Analysis of Faces", *MIT A.I. Memo* No.1672, Sept, 1999.
5. Schneiderman H. and Kanade T. Probabilistic Modeling of Local Appearance and Spatial Relationships for Object", *in Proc. CVPR*, 1998.
6. Garcia C. and Tziritas G. Face Detection Using Quantized Skin Color Regions Merging and Wavelet Packet Analysis", *IEEE Trans. Multimedia*, 1(3):264-277, 1999.
7. Wei G. and Sethi I.K. Face Detection for Image Annotation", *Pattern Recognition Letters* 20:1313-1321, 1999.
8. Satoh S., Nakamura Y. and Kanade T. Name-It: Naming and Detecting Faces in News Videos", *IEEE MultiMedia*, 6(1):22-35, 1999.
9. Ai H., Liang L. and Xu G. A General Framework for Face Detection", *Lecture Notes in Computer Science*, Springer-Verlag Berlin Heidelberg New York, 1948:119-126, 2000.
10. Platt J. C. Sequential Minimal Optimization: A Fast Algorithm for Training Support Vector Machines", *Technical Report* MSR-TR-98-14, 1998

An Image Retrieval System Based on Local and Global Color Descriptors

K. Idrissi, J. Ricard, A Anwander[1] and A. Baskurt

LIGIM (Computer Graphics, Image and Modeling Laboratory)
EA 1899, University Claude Bernard, Lyon 1 France
[1]Max Plank Institue, Bennewitz, Germany

Abstract. This paper presents a new approach for visual-based image retrieval method with respect to the MPEG-7 still image description scheme. A segmentation method based on a multivariate minimum cross entropy is used hierarchically for partitioning the color image in classes and regions. Local and global descriptors are defined in order to characterize the color feature of these regions. The local descriptors provide information about the local activity in the image, and the global ones evaluate the qualitative image content. Their combination increases significantly the performances of the image retrieval system IMALBUM presented in this paper . The retrieved images are presented in a description space allowing the user to better understand and interact with the search engine results.

1. General Context

With the rapid growing of the number and the size of digital image databases, the research communities working on the image retrieval have recently focused their activity on visual-based approaches. A complete survey of existing techniques and systems can be found in [1],[2]. The color feature has been widely used in image retrieval systems [3]. Especially low level descriptors are proposed to describe this feature in local and homogeneous regions. In this study, we introduce two global color descriptors in order to take into account the global spatial aspect of the color feature. These descriptors allow us to quantify the impression one has when a color image is visualized. This impression can be related for example to the sharpness or smoothness of the color or to the spatial distribution or global business of the color.

The use of both local and global descriptors leads to a real improvement of the performances of the image retrieval scheme.

This paper proposes a visual-based image retrieval scheme for still color images (IMALBUM) respecting MPEG-7 standardization studies [4]. Section 2 details our approach.

Results obtained on MPEG-7 data set are presented in section 3.

2. Method

A- Color Image Segmentation

In image retrieval context, the key image segmentation as well as the extraction of key image regions descriptors are real time procedures. For this purpose, we privilege the use of a fast and simple segmentation. The proposed method is based on Minimum Cross Entropy (MCE) segmentation which allows a hierarchical partitioning of the image in classes and regions, similar to the tree structure of the areas proposed in MPEG-7 [5]. Each class is formed with a set of similar separate regions of the original image. The Cross Entropy expression is proportional to [6][7]:

$$mce(l) = \sum_{i=1}^{l-1} ih_i \log_2\left(\frac{i}{N_1(l)}\right) + \sum_{i=l}^{L} ih_i \log_2\left(\frac{i}{N_2(l)}\right) \tag{1}$$

Where h_i is the number of pixels with gray level i, L is the number of gray levels in the image, N_k represents the mean value of class k in the segmentation map and l is a possible threshold value. The optimal threshold is given by the value l_{opt} that minimizes $mce(l)$. l_{opt} can be viewed as the optimal value that divides a 1D histogram into 2 parts.

A generalized multivariate MCE method is proposed by [8] where a new variable M is defined as a combination of a set of image local features (gray level, local entropy, color...):

$$M = f(x_1, x_2, ..., x_N) \tag{2}$$

and the equation (1) can then be applied on a new image I associated to M. In our approach, we use $M = f(L,a,b)$ considering the (L,a,b) color space. This procedure lead to N final classes and can be seen as a hierarchical adaptive partitioning of (L,a,b) space. The segmentation method proposed in this study is equivalent to a (L,a,b) color space quantization.

We use the generalized form of the MCE, with a variable M function of (L,a,b). We suppose that the dominant color D_k of a class k, is given by the maximum of (L,a,b) histogram called "centroid of class k" and noted with its coordinates $(O_{k,1}, O_{k,2}, O_{k,3})$. We define a new image I_k expressed by :

$$I_k(m,n) = \sqrt{\sum_{i=1}^{3} [(C_i - O_{k,i})]^2} \tag{3}$$

where $I_k(m,n)$ represents the color distance between the pixel (m,n) and the centroid $(O_{k,1}, O_{k,2}, O_{k,3})$ and C_i is the ith component color of the pixel (m,n).

The choice of the uniform space color (L,a,b) enables us to use the Euclidean distance. The segmentation of $I_k(m,n)$ by MCE provides the optimal value l_{opt} which separates the (L,a,b) histogram in 2 classes: colors close to the centroid and the other colors. The segmentation is then applied in an iterative way to each new class in order to obtain N final classes. At each level of this hierarchical segmentation, this method privileges the selection of a new local maxima (new class) far (in (L,a,b) space) from the current dominant color. In this study, the number of final classes N (dominant colors) is fixed to 16.

B- Color Description

Among the features used for description, the color feature plays a very significant role. Two types of colors descriptors are considered: classical local descriptors and two new global ones.

B-1. Local Color Description

An image is represented by the most characteristic color classes issued from segmentation and described by three classical descriptors:

- Dominant color (Centroid) considered as Dominant Color, the maximum of color histogram of each class.
- Compactness and Directivity of the color histogram (eigenvalues and eigenvectors of the histogram of the dominant color in the (L,a,b) color space).
- Percentage of each class in the image space.

B-2. Global Color Description

In order to quantify the qualitative aspects related to the impression given by the image, two new global descriptors are considered:

- Maximum probability of multiscale color gradient $p_{\max}[\nabla(L,a,b)]$: which gives an indication of the importance of the color contour content of an image. Easy to implement, this descriptor is related to the amount of color changes in the image. The contour image is computed from the multiscale color gradient image $\nabla(L,a,b)$ defined in [9][10]. The analysis of gradient histogram (near to Gaussian distribution) shows that this simple parameter is quite discriminant. For images with poor content for color contours, the probability density function remains compact, this leads to high values for $p_{\max}[\nabla(L,a,b)]$. When the image is characterized with an important activity of color contours, the probability density function is shifted and spread to higher gradients. In this case, low values of $p_{\max}[\nabla(L,a,b)]$ is obtained.

- Spatial Coherency of the first dominant color: a new spatial histogram H_s is introduced to quantify the spatial coherency. A $(2W+1)*(2W+1)$ window is defined representing the level of the required compactness. H_s is computed as follow:

$$H_s(c)=\sum_{i=0}^{Y-1}\sum_{j=0}^{X-1}\delta(I(i,j),c).\alpha(i,j) \tag{4}$$

where I is a segmented color image of (X,Y) size, c is the color at the location (i,j), δ is the Kronecker function and $\alpha(i,j)$ is defined as:

$$\alpha(i,j)=\begin{cases}1 \ \text{if} & \forall k,k' \in [-W,W] \\ & I(i+k,j+k')=I(i,j) \\ 0 \ \text{if not} & \end{cases}$$

The Spatial Coherency Ratio SCR for a given color c, is then defined as $SCR(c)=\dfrac{H_s(c)}{H(c)}$, where H represents the classical color histogram. A low value of $SCR(c)$ indicates a low compactness of the color c in the image. $SCR(c)$ is near to 1 when the color c is homogeneous in the image.

We introduce these global descriptors in order to take into account the global visual impression that a human being perceived in terms of contour sharpness and the spatial distribution of the color.

C- Search Engine

The search is a two steps procedure. For a given key image, we first calculate global descriptors to reduce the search to images that are globally similar to the key image. The second step consists on comparing the local descriptors of the key image and those of images issued from the first step. The selection is done by minimization of a similarity criterion, calculated between the descriptors of the key image and those of the images of the database. This hierarchical approach allows to reduce the search time, the calculation of distance being done only with the images belonging to the families closest to the key image.

In order to mix the descriptors of different nature, we carry out a normalization of the distance [11] :

$$d_n(X_i,Y_i)=\frac{d(X_i,Y_i)-(\mu_i-3\sigma_i)}{6\sigma_i} \tag{5}$$

where d_n represents the normalized distance, d the distance between the descriptors X_i and Y_i for the descriptor i and μ_i, σ_i respectively the average and the standard deviation of d. We obtain a distance taking the majority of its values in the interval [0,1]. The final distance combining all the descriptors is then expressed by:

$$D = \sum_{i=1}^{Nd} w_i d_n(X_i, Y_i) \tag{6}$$

where Nd is the number of descriptors of the image. The weights w_i are fixed interactively by the user.

A feedback mechanism is used to allow the user to refine the search, by indicating the relevance of the retrieved images [12].

3. Results and Discussion

Our experiments were conducted on MPEG7 database with 5 classes and on an other database composed of images rich and heterogeneous in term of color content with 9 classes.

A- Quantitative Evaluation

For the evaluation of the retrieval process, two criteria are considered [13]:

The Recall: $$R_k = \frac{A_k}{A_k + C_k} = \frac{A_k}{A_N}$$

The Precision: $$P_k = \frac{A_k}{A_k + B_k} = \frac{A_k}{k}$$

where:

$$A_k = \sum_{n=0}^{k-1} V_n, \quad B_k = \sum_{n=0}^{k-1}(1 - V_n) \text{ and } C_k = \sum_{n=0}^{N-1} V_n - A_k$$

$V_n \in \{0,1\}$ is the relevance of the retrieved image, k is the rank order (number of images to be retrieved) and N is the number of images in the database.

Fig. 1 presents Recall and Precision curves function of k. Combining global&local descriptors increases the performances of IMALBUM for these two criteria. This means that for a given k, the detection of similar images is improved, i.e. for $k = 7$, near to 20% of gain is obtained for R_k and the precision P_k remains about 15% higher.

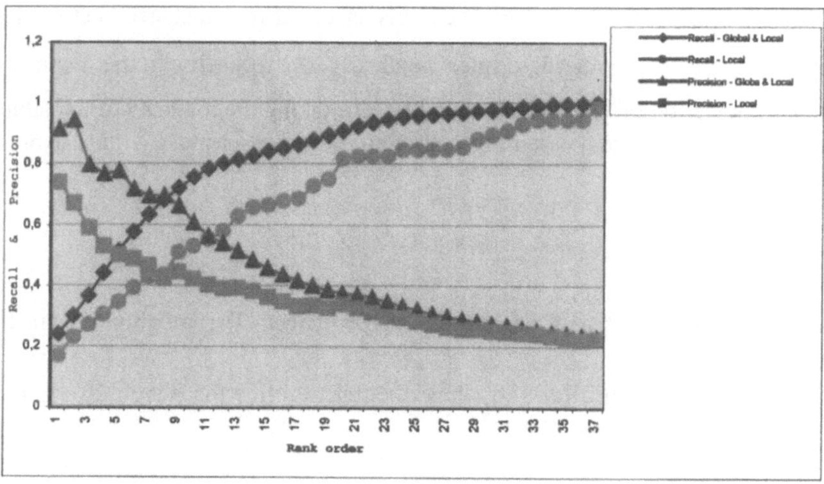

Fig. 1. Recall and Precision results comparing local and global&local descriptors

B- Representation of Retrieved Images

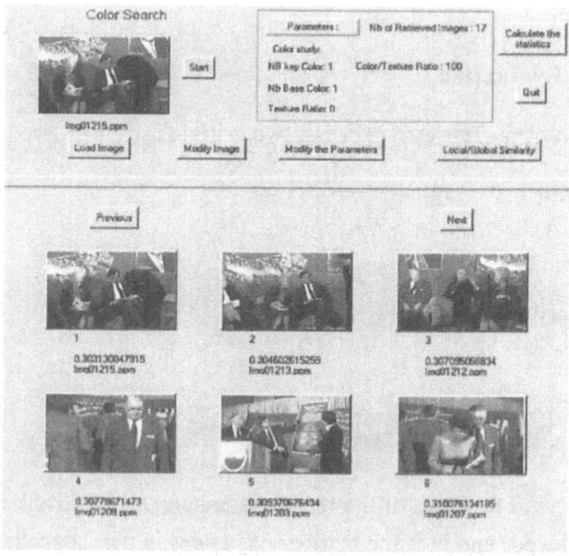

Fig. 2. IMALBUM Interface

Figure 2 depicts IMALBUM interface. The user can interactively choose the search parameters, and determine the weight associated to each parameter.

Our approach allows an other type of representation of retrieved images in a "description space" (Fig.4). In this example, this space is reduced to a plane where X axis corresponds to the dominant color (centroid) distance while Y one represents the spatial coherency descriptor distance. Thus, any selected image issued from the search process, corresponds to a point in this space. This point represents the similarity between this image and the key image. After the search process, the most similar images can be displayed in a user-defined description space.

In Fig.3, the key image is located at the origin. It has an homogeneous red dominant color. If the retrieved images are projected on Y axis, the homogeneity of the dominant color decreases. Analyzing only X axis, high differences for the dominant color are detected. When these two descriptors are combined, the resulting description plane offers an other vision of the similarity between color images. The user can then visually refine the search by choosing a new key image from the displayed ones, privileging for example one of two descriptors.

It can also be interesting to define an other descriptor plane with two other descriptors.

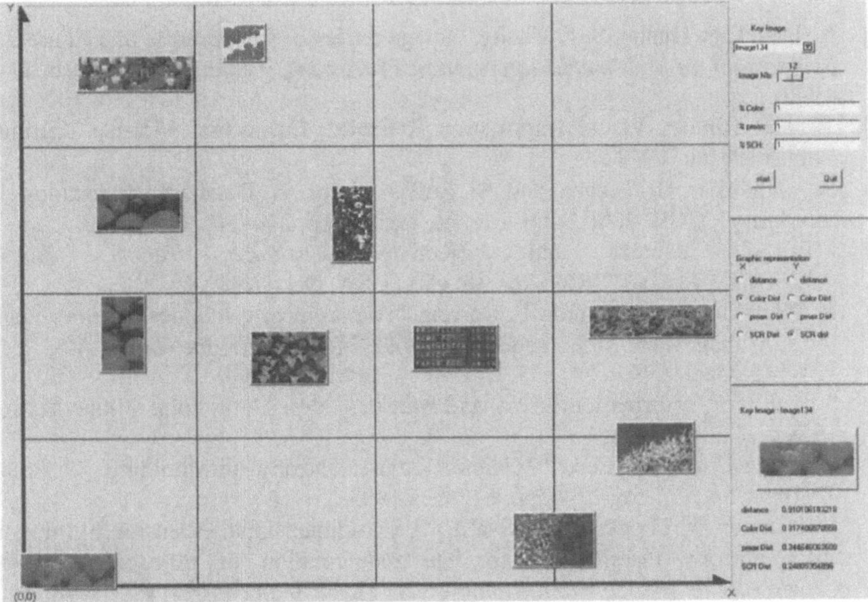

Fig. 3. Example of user-defined description space. X axis represents the Dominant Color distance and Y axis represents the distance of the Spatial Coherency Ration of The Dominant Color.

4. Conclusion

An image retrieval system (IMALBUM) was presented. The main idea was to combine low level and well known color descriptors with new ones which provide us with global aspect of the color feature. Two descriptors were introduced: the maximum probability of multiscale color gradient $p_{\max}[\nabla(L,a,b)]$ related to the amount of color changes in the image; the Spatial Coherency Ratio SCR which measures the spatial distribution (compactness or disparity) of the color content. To evaluate the performance improvement of IMALBUM due to these attributes, Recall and Precision criteria were evaluated on MPEG7 data set and an other database composed of images rich and heterogeneous in term of color content. The results are satisfactory.

The second idea was to present the retrieved images in a description space providing the user with a more explicit visualization in order to facilitate the feedback mechanism. Further research will include shape and context descriptors in the existing image retrieval system.

5. References

[1] Y. Rui, T. S. Huang, S. F. Chang, "Image retrieval: past, present and future", *Int. Symposium on Multimedia Information Processing*, Taipei, Taiwan, Dec. 11-13, 1997.

[2] A. Del Bimbo, Visual Information Retrieval, California: Morgan Kaufmann Publishers Inc. 1999

[3] R. Schettini, G. Ciocca and S. Zuffi, "Color in Database: Indexation and Similarity", CGIP 2000 Saint-Etienne, France, pp. 244-249, Oct. 2000.

[4] MPEG-7: context and objectives, *Technical report, ISO/IEC JTC1/SC29/WG11/W2460*, Atlantic City, USA, Oct. 1998.

[5] P. Salembier, N. O'Connor, P. Correia, "Hierarchical visual description schemes for still images and video sequences", *IEEE ICIP'99*, Kobe, Japan, Vol. 2, pp. 121-125, Oct. 1999.

[6] S. Kullback, Information theory and statistics. New York: John Winley & Sons, 1959.

[7] C. H. Li, C. K. Lee, "Minimum cross entropy thresholding", *Pattern Recognition*, Vol. 26, N° 4, pp. 617-625,1993.

[8] Y. Zimmer, R. Tepper, S. Akselrod, "A two-dimensional extension of minimum cross entropy thresholding for the segmentation of ultrasound images", *Ultrasound in Medicine and Biology*, Vol. 22, N° 9, pp. 1183-1190, 1996.

[9] H. C. Lee, D. R. Cok, "Detecting boundaries in a Vector Field", *IEEE Trans. on Signal Processing,* Vol. 39, N°5, pp.1181-1194, 1991.

[10] A. Anwander, B. Neyran, A. Baskurt, "Segmentation of Crystals in Microscopic Images using Multiscale Color Gradient (MCG)", *CGIP 2000*, Saint-Etienne, France, pp. 311-316, Oct. 2000.

[11] C. Nastar, N. Boujemaa, M. Mitschke, C. Meilhac, Surfimage : Un système flexible d'indexation et de recherche d'images. In CORESA'98, Lannion, France, June 1998.

[12] R. Schettini, G. Ciocca, I. Gagliardi, "Content Based Color Image Retrieval with Relevance Feedback", *IEEE ICIP'99*, Kobe, Japan, Vol. 2, pp. 75-79, Oct. 1999.

[13] J. R. Smith, "Image Retrieval Evaluation", *IEEE CBAIVL'98*, June 1998.

A New Shot Boundary Detection Algorithm

Dong Zhang, Wei Qi, Hong Jiang Zhang

Microsoft Research, China
hjzhang@microsoft.com

Abstract. Shot is often used as basic unit for both analyzing and indexing video. In this paper, we present an algorithm for automatic shot detection. In our algorithm, we use a 'flash model' and a 'cut model' to deal with the false detection due to flashing lights. A technique for determining the threshold that uses the local window based method combined with reliability verify process is also developed. The experimental results of our method are very promising, improving the performance of shot detection.

1 Introduction

There are many shot detection methods already proposed in past decades [1-6]. The common way for shot detection is to evaluate the difference between consecutive frames represented by a given feature. Although reasonable accuracy can be achieved, there are still problems that limit the robustness of these algorithms.

One of the common problems in robust shot detection results from the fact that there are many flashlights in news video, which often introduce false detection of shot boundaries. Only some simple solutions to this problem have been proposed in [2]. Their main limitations are that they assume the flashlight just occur during one frame. In real world, such as news video, there will be many flashlights occur during a period of time and influence multiple consecutive frames.

Another problem that has not been solved very effectively well is threshold selection when comparing changes between two frames. Most of the existing methods use global pre-defined thresholds, or simple local window based adaptive threshold. Global threshold is definitely not efficient since the video property could change dramatically when content changes, and it is often impossible to find a universal optimal threshold across any video segments. The local window based adaptive threshold selection method also has its limitation because in some situation the local statistic are 'polluted' by strong noises such as big motions and flashlights

To address these two practical problems, we developed two new techniques: a robust flashlight detection technique and a new adaptive threshold selection technique. In the flashlight detection technique, we distinguish flashlights from real shot cut by applying a 'cut model' and a 'flashlight model' which are defined based on the temporal property of average intensity value across a frame sequence in a local window. For threshold detection, we proposed a strategy on whether to recalculate the threshold from the current local window or use the existing threshold based on the local shot activity statistic. In this way, our shot detection algorithm incorporates certain safeguards that ensure that thresholds are set in accordance with the received video content only if the content is relatively stable.

The rest of this paper is organized as follows. Section 2 gives a detail description of the two new algorithms. Section 3 presents experimental results, and we conclude this paper and discuss the future work in Section 4.

2 Proposed Algorithm

Our new algorithm is based on the framework of the twin-threshold method proposed by Zhang [3] that is able to detect both abrupt and gradual transition, such as dissolve and wipe, in video. We integrate our two methods for flashlight detection and threshold selection into this framework. A brief diagram of the framework is shown in Fig. 1. Our proposed two techniques are integrated into to the true cut decision and threshold selection functional blocks.

2.1 Metrics in Shot Detection

To partition the video, we should first define suitable metrics, so that a shot boundary is declared whenever that metric exceeds a given threshold. We use histogram difference as the first metric in our algorithm because histogram is less sensitive to object motion than other metrics, shown in equation (1). Another metric adopted in our algorithm is average intensity difference, shown in equation (4). We define the two metrics as bellow:

$$D_i = \sum_{j=1}^{Bins} | H_i(j) - H_{i-1}(j) | \tag{1}$$

$$AI_i = \frac{\sum_{j=1}^{Bins} j * H_i(j)}{\sum_{j=1}^{Bins} H_i(j)} \tag{2}$$

$$AI_{i-1} = \frac{\sum_{j=1}^{Bins} j * H_{i-1}(j)}{\sum_{j=1}^{Bins} H_{i-1}(j)} \tag{3}$$

$$AID_i = AI_i - AI_{i-1} \tag{4}$$

Where $H_i(j)$ indicates j-th bin of the gray-value histogram belonging to frame i. Generally, we choose 256 bins for gray level histogram. D_i denotes the histogram difference between frame i and its preceding frame (i-1). AI_i is the average intensity value of the frame i, and AID_i is the average intensity difference between frame i and $(i\text{-}1)$.

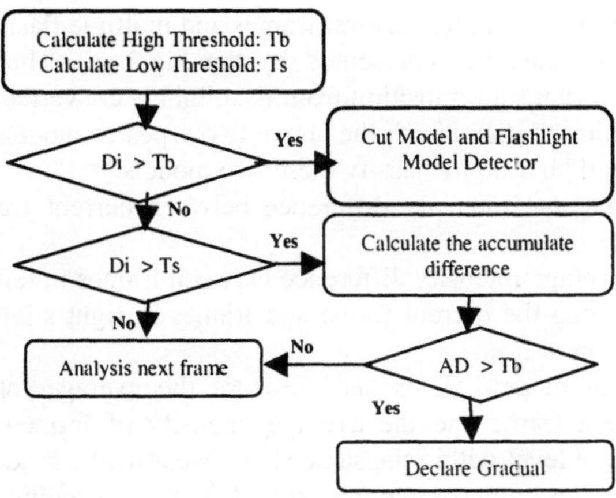

Fig. 1. Overview of the algorithm

2.2 Cut Model and Flash Model

Both the real shot cut and flashlight could cause a great change in histogram difference. So by only using the histogram difference to detect shot boundaries may cause a lot of false alarms because of flashlights. If the histogram difference of consecutive frames is larger than a particular threshold, shot boundary detector invokes an instance of flashlight detector to distinguish a potential flashlight condition from an actual shot cut boundary. In flashlight detector, we define two models based on the temporal property of flashlight and cut. If the histogram difference of adjacent frames is larger than an adaptive higher threshold: T_b, we can use either the histogram difference or average intensity difference as input of our models that are illustrated in Figure 2.

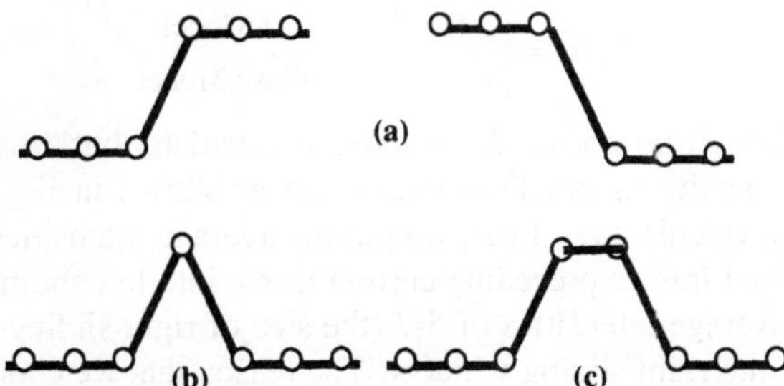

Fig. 2. "Flash Model" and "Cut Model"

Next, we use average intensity difference to describe our ideas. The ideal models for shot cut and flashlight based on average intensity are shown respectively in Fig. 2(a) and Fig. 2(b). Where the lines indicate the average intensity curve of a frame sequence. When a true abrupt transition occurs, the average intensity changes from one level to another, then the change will sustain in the next whole shot. When a flashlight occurs, the average intensity changes from one level to another, and then fall back to the original level after one frame. This is the ideal model for flashlight. In real world, the flashlight could last several frames and multiple flashlights could occur consequently, which could be represented by the Fig.2 (c). Then the problem of distinguishing true abrupt shot transition from flashlight is converted to the problem of designing an algorithm to distinguish the above two types of models. First, we define two 'heights' that will be used to classify these two models.

- *H1*: the average intensity difference between current frame and previous frame
- *H2*: the average intensity difference between frames in left sliding windows preceding the current frame and frames in right sliding windows after the current frame.

In ideal flashlight model, *H2* is zero because the average intensity of frames preceding the current frame and the average intensity of frames after the current frames are at the same level within the same shot. Meanwhile, in ideal cut model, *H2* is identical to *H1* because the average intensity of frames preceding the current frame is not at the same level with that of frames after the current frames. Thus, we use the ratio of H_1 and H_2 as the metric to distinguish these two models. We define the ratio as:

$$Ratio = \frac{H2}{H1}$$

Then we have the following rule:

$$Ratio = \begin{cases} 1 & \text{Cut Model} \\ 0 & \text{Flash Model} \end{cases}$$

As Ratio goes to a value of 1, flashlight detector concludes that the intensity change is due to a shot cut event and is, therefore indicative of a shot boundary. Deviations from a Ratio value of 1 are determined to be indicative of a flashlight event. Actually, we use a threshold *T* to make the decision. Threshold *T* should be larger than zero and less than one, we set it 0.5 in our experiment, and then the above rule is converted to:

$$Ratio = \begin{cases} > T & \text{Cut Model} \\ < T & \text{Flash Model} \end{cases}$$

When we calculate *Ratio* above, H_1 is easy to calculate, but H_2 is hard to define because of the complexity of practical video data as shown in Fig. 4. We use the following method to calculate H_2. First, we put the average intensities of 5-7 (the size of left sliding window) frames preceding current frame into left sliding window, at the same time put the average intensities of 5-7 (the size of right sliding window) frames after current frame into right sliding window. The reason that we choose 5-7 frames is based on the fact flashlight events do not, generally, last longer than 5-7 frames. Then, we use the average intensity of all frames within right and left sliding window to calculate *H2*. The advantages of using average intensity of all frames within right and left sliding windows as representative frames lie in two facts: One is that the flashlights always make the average intensity of frame larger. The other reason is that there are often several frames whose change is unstable within right or left sliding windows. The flow char is shown in Fig. 3.

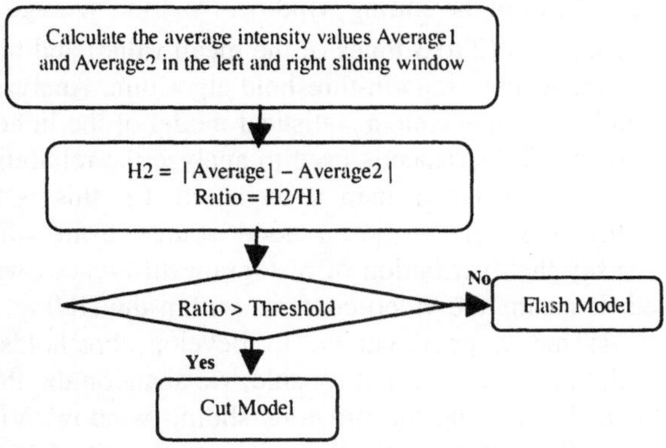

Fig. 3. Flow char of the Flashlight detector

According to one example implementation, this algorithm is applied to sequence 'CNN news', a segment with a lot of flashlight. The average intensity of frames from 277 to 700 is shown in Fig. 4. From left to right, there are a true cut and six occurrences of flashlight. We can observe that: in the average intensity diagram, a single or multiple pulses usually represent a flashlight. However, when a true cut occurs, the average intensity of frame is changed from one level to another.

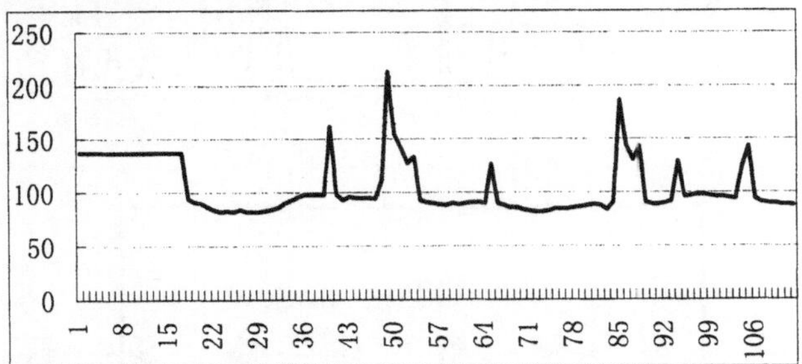

Fig. 4. **Average intensity diagram**

We can also use histogram difference in our 'flash model' and 'cut model' detector, where average intensity of all frames within sliding windows is replaced by the average histogram of all frames within sliding windows. The average intensity difference is replaced by histogram difference.

2.3 Threshold Selection

The problem of choosing the appropriate threshold is a key issue in applying the shot detection algorithms. Heuristically chosen global thresholds is inappropriate because experiments have shown that the threshold for determining a segment boundary varies from one shot to another which must be based on the distribution of the frame-to-frame differences of shots. So adaptive threshold is more reasonable than global threshold. In our algorithm, we proposed the local window based threshold calculation method combined with reliability verify process. We build a sliding window preceding the current frame. Then we calculate the mean value: μ and the variance of histogram differences: σ within the sliding window. Next the average value is used to calculate the low threshold Ts (2 to 3 times of the mean value) and high threshold *Tb* (3 to 5 times of mean value) used in twin-threshold algorithm. Analyzing the variance within the sliding window can generate a statistical model of the light intensity of the frames within the window. So variance is used to analyze the reliability of calculated thresholds. If the variance is larger than a threshold T2, this is an indicator to threshold selection that the data is not a good source from which to develop thresholds. That is to say the distribution of histogram differences within the sliding window is dispersed. It means the video contents within the sliding window change dramatically, which is not a good source to develop thresholds. So threshold calculated using the sliding window is not reliable, we abandon the threshold and use previous threshold calculated using the previous sliding window. Vice verse, if the variance is smaller than the threshold *T2*, that is to say the distribution of histogram differences within the sliding window is concentrated. So threshold calculated using the sliding window is reliable, we adopt the threshold to judge whether current frame is shot boundary or not. Fig. 5 shows the illustration of the sliding window threshold selection.

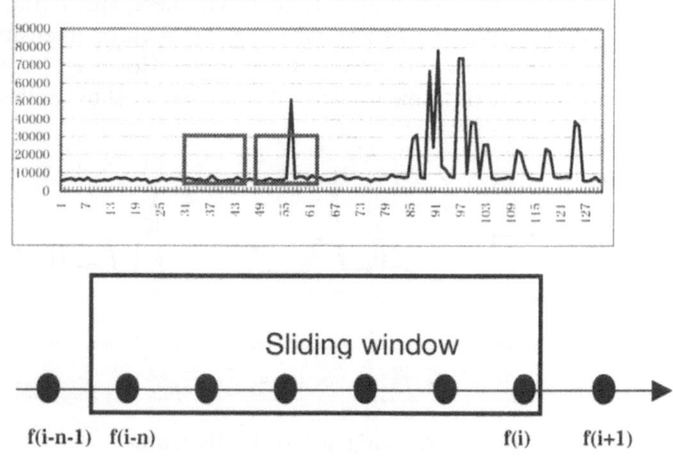

Fig. 5. Histogram difference diagram and illustration of sliding window

As shown in Fig. 5, the diagram is the histogram difference of consecutive frames in sequence 'CNN news'. In the left sliding window, there is little variation of histogram difference, we regard the thresholds calculated using the window is reliable; while in the right sliding window, the histogram difference has large variance due to camera motion and flashlight, and then we abandon the thresholds calculated using the window and adopt pre-determined thresholds for use until the frames within the sliding window do not result in such a high variance.

3 Experimental Results

The algorithms described in this paper have been tested on a number of video sequences, especially news video in which a lot of flash occurs. The parameters used in our algorithm are fixed to all test video. We summarize all parameters in the following table.

Table 1. Parameters in experiment

Parameters	Size	Tb	Ts	T1	T2
Value	15	3.5	2.0	0.5	500

In table1, 'Size' is the frame number within the sliding window. In threshold selection, we put 15 frames preceding current frame into sliding window; and in flashlight detector we put 7 frames preceding current frame into left sliding window and 7 frames after current frame into right sliding window. It will be noticed that sliding windows of more or less frames could well be used, the size of 5-7 frames is chosen because flashlight events do not, generally, last longer than 5-7 frames. *Tb* and *Ts* are the high and low thresholds used in twin-threshold algorithm. *T1* is the threshold in flashlight detector. *T2* is the threshold used in adaptive thresholds selection. In table 2, we present the results of shot detection of 5-min "CNN" news and two10-min "SPORTS" news and a 2-min MPEG-7 test sequence "CUT15". They are representative material for testing our algorithm.

Table 2. Experiment Results. D: correct detections; M: missed detections; F: false alarms

Tested Video	Cut			Flash			Gradual Tran.		
	D	M	F	D	M	F	D	M	F
CNN	32	3	4	45	4	2	5	1	1
SPORT1	30	6	3	36	3	4	8	2	3
SPORT2	70	9	5	0	0	0	7	2	2
CUT15	4	0	1	0	0	0	16	2	2

Table 2 indicates that our algorithm can detect not only camera transition but also flashing lights with satisfactory accuracy. Approximately 87% of camera transitions and flashlight is detected. The miss camera transition mainly results from the fact that the differences between consecutive frames across a camera transition are lower than the given threshold because the histograms of the two frames are similar. Object movement is the source of false detection of camera transition, especially for gradual transitions. Flashlight detection fails are due to two main reasons. One reason is that some flash may be too weak to detect. The other reason is that the flash may sustain too many frames exceeding the size of the sliding window, so the detector mistake 'Flash Model' as 'Cut Model'.

4 Conclusion and Future Work

This paper has presented an effective shot detection algorithm, which focus on two difficult problems solutions: false detection of shot transition due to flashing light and threshold selection. The main contributions of the presented work are to build two models and an adaptive threshold selection algorithm that uses the local window combined with reliability verify process. Experiments show that the proposed algorithm is promising.

However the automatic video partition is still a very challenging research problem especially for detecting gradual transitions. Further work is still needed.

5 References

[1] A. Nagasaka and Y.Tanaka, Automatic Video Indexing and Full-Video Search for Object Appearances, Visual Database Systems, II, pp.113-127, Elsevier Science Publishers, 1992.

[2] F. Arman, A. Hsu, and M.Y. Chiu, Image processing on compressed data for large video databases, Proceedings of 1st ACM International Conference on Multimedia, Anaheim, CA, pp.267-272, 1993.

[3] H. J. Zhang, A. Kankanhalli, S. W. Smoliar, Automatic Partitioning of Full-motion Video, ACM Multimedia System, Vol. 1, No.1, pp. 10-28, 1993.

[4] Hampapur, A., Jain, R., and Weymouth, T., Digital Video Segmentation, Proc. ACM Multimedia 94, San Francisco, CA, October, 1994, pp.357-364.

[5] B.L. Yeo and B. Liu, Rapid scene analysis on compressed video, IEEE Transactions on Circuits and Systems For Video Technology, 5,6, pp.533-544, 1995.

[6] Ishwar K. Sethi, Nilesh Patel. A Statistical Approach to Scene Change Detection. SPIE vol.2420, 329-338. San Jose, California: 1995.

An Adaptive Index Structure for High-Dimensional Similarity Search

P. Wu, B. S. Manjunath and S. Chandrasekaran
Department of Electrical and Computer Engineering
University of California, Santa Barbara, CA 93106-9560
{peng, manj, shiv}@ece.ucsb.edu

Abstract: A practical method for creating a high dimensional index structure that adapts to the data distribution and scales well with the database size, is presented. Typical media descriptors are high dimensional and are not uniformly distributed in the feature space. The performance of many existing methods degrade if the data is not uniformly distributed. The proposed method offers an efficient solution to this problem. First, the data's marginal distribution along each dimension is characterized using a Gaussian mixture model. The parameters of this model are estimated using the well known Expectation-Maximization (EM) method. These model parameters can also be estimated sequentially for on-line updating. Using the marginal distribution information, each of the data dimensions can be partitioned such that each bin contains approximately an equal number of objects. Experimental results on a real image texture data set are presented. Comparisons with existing techniques, such as the VA-File, demonstrate a significant overall improvement.

1 Introduction

Typical audio-visual descriptors are high dimensional vectors and not uniformly distributed [6]. These descriptors are useful in content based image/video retrieval, data mining and knowledge discovery. To index high dimensional feature vectors, various index structures such as R*-tree, X-tree, TV-tree, etc., have been proposed. A good overview and analysis of these techniques can be found from [5]. The study in [5] also argued that typical tree based index methods are outperformed by a linear search when the search dimensions exceed 10. This has motivated the introduction of approximation methods [2, 5] to speed up the linear search.

Approximation based methods have certain advantages. First, they support different distance measures. This is an important property especially for learning and concept mining related applications. Secondly, the construction of approximation can be made adaptive to the dimensionality of data. However, the approximation method [5] is sensitive to data's distribution. does not perform well when feature vectors are not uniformly distributed.

In [5], the approximation is constructed by partitioning the feature space into hyper rectangles. The grids on each dimension are equally spaced. We refer to such uniform partitioning as "regular approximation" in the following discussion. In [2], the feature space is first transformed using the KL-transform to reduce the correlation of data at different dimensions. Secondly, in the transformed space, the data in each dimension is clustered into a pre-assigned number of grids using the Lloyd's algorithm. But in [3], it is reported that for high dimensional data, transforming the data space by rotation does not result in a significant decorrelation of the data. This implies that global statistics, such as the second order statistics used in [2], may not be able to characterize the data distribution effectively for high dimensional spaces.

In this work, we propose an effective and practical solution to adapt the design of the approximation based index structure to the data's distribution. The main idea of the proposed method is to model the marginal distribution of the data using a mixture of Gaussians and use the estimated parameters of the model to partition the data space. By adapting the construction of approximations to data's marginal distribution, the proposed method overcomes the sensitivity of index performance to data's distribution, thus resulting in a significant improvement compared with regular the VA-File [2, 5].

In the next section, we summarize the construction of regular approximation and its associated indexing. We also discuss the limitations of using regular approximation. Our proposed method is presented in Section 3. Experimental results are provided in Section 4.

2 Regular Approximation

2.1 Construction of regular approximation [5]

In regular approximation methods, such as the VA-File approach [5], the range of the feature vectors in each dimension is uniformly partitioned. Let D denote the total number of dimensions of data space, and let B_i bits ($i = 1, \ldots, D$) be allocated to each of the dimensions. Then the range of feature values on dimension i is segmented to 2^{B_i} partitions by a set of boundary points, denoted as $c^i[k]$ ($k = 0, \ldots, 2^{B_i}$) with equal length, each partition is uniquely identified by a binary string of length B_i. The high dimensional space is in turn segmented into D dimensional hyper cells. Each of them can be uniquely identified by a binary string of length B ($B = \sum B_i$). For a feature vector $v[i][j]$, $j = 0, \ldots, N$, wherein N is the total number of object in a database, its approximation is such a binary string of length B to indicate which hyper cell it is contained in. If $v[i][j]$ falls into a partition bounded by $[c^i[k-1], c^i[k]]$, it satisfies

$$c^i[k-1] \le v[i][j] < c^i[k] \tag{1}$$

So the boundary points provide an approximation of the value of $v[i][j]$. As in [5], a lower bound and a upper bound of the distance between any vector with a query vector can be computed using this property.

Figure 1 gives an illustrative example of constructing the regular approximation for two dimension data. The 1856 image objects are collected from the Brodatz album [4]. Figure 1 shows the first two components of the 60 dimensional feature vectors computed in [4]. The feature distribution is clearly not uniform.

2.2 Indexing based on regular approximation

Approximation based nearest neighbor search can be considered as a two phase filtering process. In the first phase, the set of all approximations is scanned sequentially and lower and upper bounds on the distances of each object in the database to the query object are computed. In this phase, if an approximation is encountered such that its lower bound is larger than the k-th smallest upper bound found so far, the corresponding feature vector can be skipped since at least k better candidates exist. At the end of the first phase filtering, the set of vectors that are not skipped are collected as candidates for the second phase filtering. Denote the number of candidates to be N_1.

In the second phase filtering, the actual N_1 feature vectors are examined. The feature vectors are visited in increasing order of their lower bounds and then exact distances to the query vector are computed. If a lower bound is reached that is larger than the k-th actual nearest neighbor distance encountered so far, there is no need to visit the remaining candidates. Let N_2 denote the number of feature vectors visited before the thresholding lower bound is encountered.

For approximation based methods, the index performance is measured by N_1 and N_2 (see [5]). Smaller values of N_1 and N_2 indicate a better performance.

2.3 Limitations

The effectiveness of using VA-File based indexing structure is sensitive to data's distribution. For the example given in Figure 1, the data on each dimension is not uniformly distributed. As a result, if a query vector happens to be one that falls into the cell "A" in Figure 1, in which approximately 30% of elements are contained, we will have $N_1 > 0.3N$ and $N_2 > 0.3N$, which indicates a poor block selectivity and a high I/O cost, see [5].

This example illustrates one of the shortcomings of the regular approximation. In such cases, the first phase filtering still results in a large number of items to search. Our proposed method specifically addresses this problem.

3 Approximation Based on Marginal Distribution

Densely populated cells can potentially degrade the indexing performance. For this reason, we propose an approach to adaptively construct the approximation of feature vectors. The general idea is to first estimate data's marginal distribution in each dimension. Secondly, individual axes are partitioned such that the data has equal probability of falling into any partition. The approximation such constructed reduces the possibility of having densely populated cells, which in turn improves the indexing performance.

3.1 pdf modeling using mixture of Gaussians

Denote $p_i(x)$ to be the pdf of data on dimension i. The algorithm introduced below is applied to data in each dimension independently. For notation simplicity, we denote $p(x)$

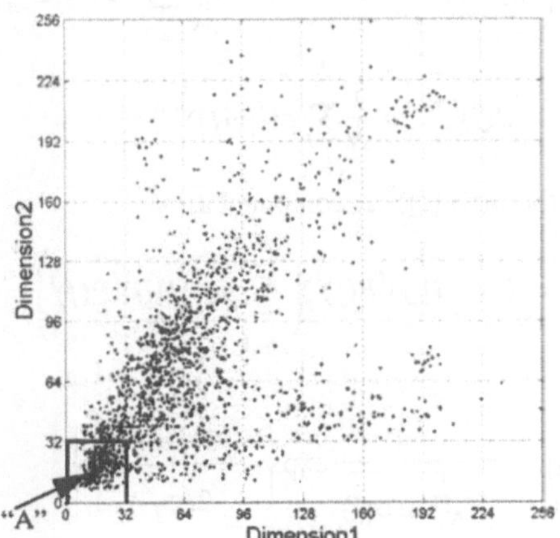

Fig 1. Using regular approximation to uniformly partition a two dimensional space. $N = 1856$, $B_1 = B_2 = 3$.

to be the pdf of an one dimensional signal. The one-dimensional pdf is modeled using a mixture of Gaussians, represented as

$$p(x) = \sum_{j=1}^{M} p(x|j)P(j) \tag{2}$$

where

$$p(x|j) = \frac{1}{\sqrt{2\pi\sigma_j^2}}\exp\left\{-\frac{(x-\mu_j)^2}{2\sigma_j^2}\right\} \tag{3}$$

The coefficients $P(j)$ are called the mixing parameters, which satisfies $\sum_{j=1,\ldots,M} P(j) = 1$ and $0 \le P(j) \le 1$.

The task of estimating the pdf is then converted to be a problem of parameter estimation. The parameters we need to estimate are $\phi_j = \{P(j), \mu_j, \sigma_j^2\}$, for $j = 1, \ldots, M$.

3.2 Parameter estimation using the EM algorithm

The classical maximum likelihood (ML) approach is used to estimate the parameters. The task is to find ϕ_j, $j = 1, \ldots, M$, to maximize

$$\Phi(\phi_1, \ldots, \phi_M) = \prod_{l=1}^{N} p(v[l]|(\phi_1, \ldots, \phi_M)) \tag{4}$$

where $v[l]$, $l = 1, \ldots, N$, are the given data set.

A simple and practical method of solving this optimization problem is to use the Expectation-Maximization algorithm [1]. Given N data $v[l]$ available as the input for the estimation, EM algorithm estimates the parameters iteratively using all the N data in each iteration. Let t denote the iteration number. Then the following equations are used to update the parameters

$$\mu_j^{t+1} = \left(\sum_{l=1}^{N} p(j|v[l])^t v[l]\right)\left(\sum_{l=1}^{N} p(j|v[l])^t\right)^{-1} \tag{5}$$

$$(\sigma_j^2)^{t+1} = \left(\sum_{l=1}^{N} p(j|v[l])^t (v[l]-\mu_j^t)^2\right)\left(\sum_{l=1}^{N} p(j|v[l])^t\right)^{-1} \tag{6}$$

$$P(j)^{t+1} = \frac{1}{N}\sum_{l=1}^{N} p(j|v[l])^t \tag{7}$$

Using Bayes' theorem [1], the $p(j|v[l])^t$ is computed as

$$p(j|v[l])^t = (p(v[l]|j)^t P(j)^t)\left(\sum_{j=1}^{M} p(v[l]|j)^t P(j)^t\right)^{-1} \tag{8}$$

where

$$p(v[l]|j)^t = \frac{1}{\sqrt{2\pi(\sigma_j^2)^t}}\exp\left\{-\frac{(v[l]-\mu_j^t)^2}{2(\sigma_j^2)^t}\right\} \tag{9}$$

3.3 Sequential updating of parameters

For a large database, N is usually only a small portion of the total number of elements in the database. In practice, it is desirable to have an incremental pdf update scheme that can track the changes of the data distribution. The EM algorithm can be modified for sequential updating [1]. Given that $\{P(j)^N, \mu_j^N, (\sigma_j^2)^N\}$ is the parameter set estimated form using the N data $v[l]$, the updated parameter set, when there is a new data $v[N+1]$ coming in, can be computed as

$$\mu_j^{N+1} = \mu_j^N + \theta_j^{N+1}(v[N+1] - \mu_j^N) \quad (10)$$

$$(\sigma_j^2)^{N+1} = (\sigma_j^2)^N + \theta_j^{N+1}[(v[N+1] - \mu_j^N)^2 - (\sigma_j^2)^N] \quad (11)$$

$$P(j)^{N+1} = P(j)^N + \frac{1}{N+1}(p(j|v[N+1]) - P(j)^N) \quad (12)$$

where

$$(\theta_j^{N+1})^{-1} = \frac{p(j|v[N])}{p(j|v[N+1])}(\theta_j^N)^{-1} + 1 \quad (13)$$

The conditional probability $p(j|v[N+1])$ is computed as in (8) and (9).

3.4 Bit allocation

Denote the estimated pdf to be $\hat{p}(x)$ as the approximation of $p(x)$. The objective of nonlinear quantization is to segment the pdf into grids of equal area. If the boundary points are denoted by $c[l]$, $l = 0, \ldots, 2^b$, b is the number of bits allocated, the boundary points should satisfy

$$\int_{c[l]}^{c[l+1]} \hat{p}(x)dx = \frac{1}{2^b}\int_{c[0]}^{c[2^b]} \hat{p}(x)dx \quad (14)$$

Using this criterion, the boundary points can be determined efficiently from a single scan of the estimated pdf.

3.5 Approximation updating

For dynamic databases, the pdf estimates are to be updated periodically. In our implementation, we update the estimates whenever a certain number of new data items are added. The approximation and pdf quantization are updated only when the new pdf, denoted as $\hat{p}_{new}(x)$, differs significantly from the current pdf, denoted as $\hat{p}_{old}(x)$. We use the following measure to quantify this change

$$\rho = \left(\int (\hat{p}_{old}(x) - \hat{p}_{new}(x))^2 dx\right)\left(\int \hat{p}_{old}(x)^2 dx\right)^{-1} \quad (15)$$

The approximation on that dimension is updated when ρ is larger than a certain threshold.

4 Experiments and Discussions

Our evaluation is performed on a database containing 275,465 aerial photo images. For each image, the method developed in [4] is used to extract a 60 dimensional texture feature descriptor. Initially, around 10% of total number of image objects are used to initialize the pdf estimation using the algorithms proposed in Section 3.2. Based on the estimated pdf, the approximation is constructed to support nearest neighbor search of the whole database. Meanwhile, an updating strategy is developed to take the rest of the data as input to the on-line estimation. For each dimension, when the change of the estimated pdf, which is measured by (15), is beyond the threshold $\rho > 0.15$, the approximation is adjusted accordingly.

The approach that uses the regular approximation, VA-File, is also implemented for comparison purpose. The number of candidate N_1 and the number of visited feature vectors N_2 are used to evaluate the performance. We tested using 3, 4, 5 and 6 bits for each dimension to construct the approximation. For each approximation, we consider the queries to be all image items in the database. For each query, the 10 nearest neighbor search is performed and results in a N_1 and a N_2. The average performances of N_1 and N_2 are computed by averaging N_1 and N_2 from all queries. The results are shown in Figure 2(a) and (b) for N_1 and N_2, respectively. Note that the figures are plotted on a logarithmic Y-axis. To normalize the results into the same range for displaying, the maximum value of N_1 (N_2) of VA-File is used to normalize all the values of N_1 (N_2). As observed, N_1 for the VA-File is about 3 to 20 times more than the proposed adaptive method (Figure 2(a)). After the second phase filtering, the VA-File visits 16 to 60 times more feature vectors

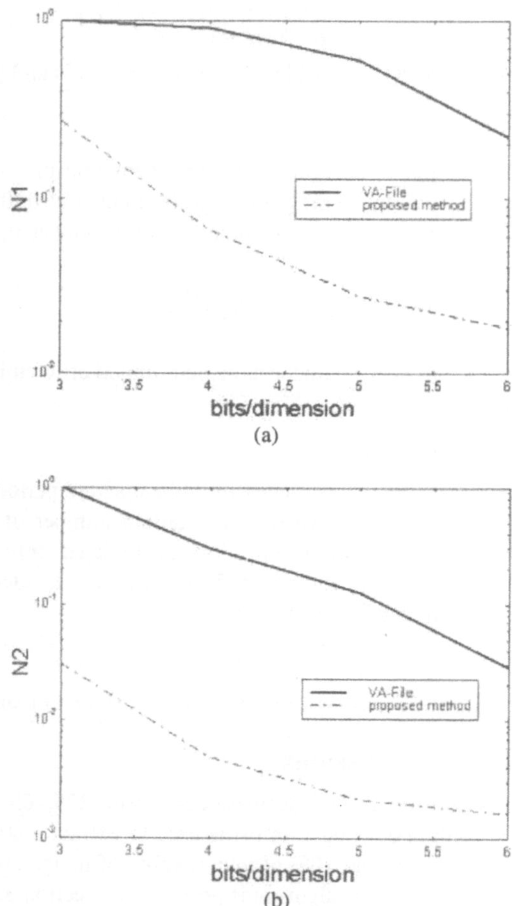

Fig 2. Comparison between VA-File and the proposed method: (a) Number of candidates (N1); (b) Number of visited feature vectors (N2) after the second phase filtering.The proposed methods offers a significant reduction in N1 and N2 compared to the VA files.

than the proposed method (Figure 2(b). One can conclude that the adaptive pdf quantization results in an order of magnitude performance improvement over the regular VA-File.

We have also investigated the indexing performance as the size of the database grows. For this purpose, we construct 4 databases, including 10%, 25%, 50% and 100% percent of the total 275,645 image objects. For each dimension, 6 bits are assigned to construct the approximation. In measuring the scalability, we are mainly concerned with N_1 as this relates directly to the I/O cost of the index structure. Figure 3 illustrates that as the size of the database grows, how fast the number of candidates N_1 increase for the VA-File and

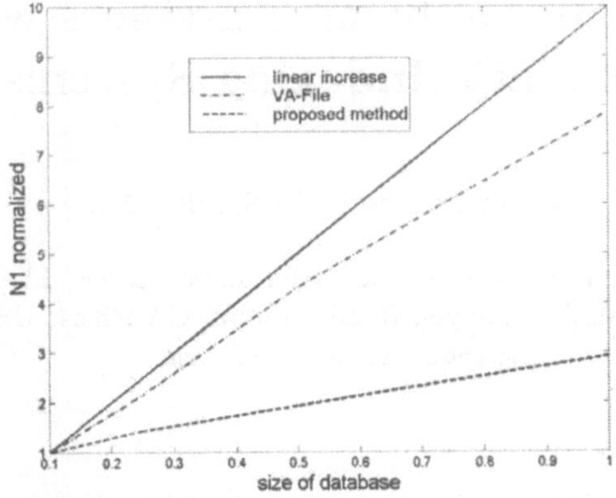

Fig 3. The increase of the number of candidates (N1) vs. the size of databases, the solid line is plotted to illustrate a linear increase of N1 as the database grows.

the proposed approach. As can be observed, in terms of the scalability with the size of databases, the proposed method tends to maintain a much better sub-linear behavior as the database grows.

We have presented a novel adaptive indexing scheme for high-dimensional feature vectors. The method is adaptive to the data distribution. The indexing performance scales well with the size of the database. Experiments demonstrate a significant improvement over the VA-file data structures for high dimensional datasets.

Ackowledgements: This research was in part supported by the following grants/awards: LLNL/ISCR award #0108, NSF-IRI 9704785, NSF Instrumentation #EIA-9986057, NSF Infrastructure NSF#EIA-0080134, and by Samsung Electronics.

References

[1] C. M. Bishop, *Neural networks for pattern recognition*, Oxford: Clarendon Press, 1995.

[2] H. Ferhatosmanoglu, E. Tuncel, D. Agrawal, A. E. Abbadi, "Vector approximation based indexing for non-uniform high dimensional data sets," Proc. Int'l Conf. Information and Knowledge Management (CIKM), pp. 202-209, Washington, DC, USA. November 2000.

[3] S. Kaski, "Dimensionality reduction by random mapping: Fast similarity computation for clustering," Proc. Int'l Joint Conference on Neural Networks, volume 1, pages 413-418. IEEE Service Center, Piscataway, NJ, 1998.

[4] B. S. Manjunath and W. Y. Ma, "Texture features for browsing and retrieval of image data," IEEE Trans. on Pattern Analysis and Machine Intelligence, 18(8), pp. 837-842, 1996.

[5] R. Webber, J.-J. Schek and S. Blott, "A quantitative analysis and performance study for similarity-search methods in high-dimensional space," Proc. Int'l Conf. Very Large Databases, pp. 194-205, New York City, New York, August 1998.

[6] ISO/IEC JTC1/SC29/WG11, "MPEG-7 Working Draft 4.0," Beijing, July, 2000.

Combining Hierarchical Classifiers with Video Semantic Indexing Systems

Wensheng Zhou and Son K. Dao

Information Sciences Lab, HRL Laboratories, LLC.,
3011 Malibu Canyon Road, Malibu, CA 90264, USA
{wzhou, skdao}@hrl.com

Abstract. This paper proposes a mechanism to integrate hierarchical video classification into video indexing systems seamlessly using video mixed media cues. Our approach centers on novel techniques that semi-automatically generate a media concept hierarchy using hierarchical classifiers to represent relevant video, audio and closed-caption text features for each video concept. Video classification functions, which directly connect low-level features with high-level semantic meanings for various applications, are first learned from training data using supervised learning algorithms for the hierarchical video concepts. The text classifier and video/audio classifier are constructed using independent learning algorithms and independent media streams of video. The joint classification fusion strategy is derived from Bayesian Theory and provides consistent and optimized classification results.

1 Introduction

With the current high growth rate in the amount of digital information, especially for information-rich multimedia streams, query results are growing incomprehensibly large and manual classification/annotation in topic hierarchies such as is provided by Yahoo![1], a text-only search engine, is creating an immense information bottle-neck and therefore inadequate for addressing users' information needs. Creating and organizing a semantic description of the un-constructed multimedia data is an important step in achieving efficient discovery of and access to relevant media data. However, the natural alternative – efficient multimedia management and manipulation, which often requires automatic understanding of semantic content – has been severely hampered by the gap that exists between the low-level media features and the semantics. In this paper we show an efficient and hierarchical video classification mechanism which can bridge the gap between visual low-level features and high-level semantic meanings, and thus facilitate video database indexing and querying.

Given that much of the video information is multi-stream media in nature, much research has been done for video understanding using multi-model analysis of all possible sources in video, including visual, audio and text information. But

[1] http://www.yahoo.com

most of the work still focuses on video semantic segmentation [1] and classifying videos into static video semantic categories such as news video, sports video, and so on, which belong to the same level of meanings[2]. While Huang *et al.* [3] used mixed cues of video, audio and text to automatically segment news videos into different hierarchical levels, such as commercial break, news anchor person, news summary and news story sequences, these semantics are still at a very high level of abstraction of the video, and thus often fail when people want to do more specific and sophisticated queries, such as about some sub-topics of a certain topic. Furthermore, very few researchers have tried to give a presentation on how the low-level features differentiate video classes which have various semantic relationships, such as being a subset or a superset of certain semantic concepts.

Accordingly, we propose in this paper a general hierarchical semantic concept tree to model and abstract the semantics of videos, using sports videos as an example. Multimedia classification and understanding at different levels of meaning are also addressed based on this hierarchical video concept modeling. Since all the media in video data, such as image, audio and text signals, display different characteristics, and express information at different levels and in different degrees of detail, we also incorporate a uniform representation of the low-level features from the mixed media cues in video, audio and captioned text into each concept classifier by means of a set of classification functions. Unlike the existing video semantic indexing systems, our proposed hierarchical classifier is a part of the indexing system and thus it not only allows queries on different granularities of video semantic meaning, but also allows queries based on low-level feature matching from different views and different media.

2 System Architecture

Figure 1 shows our proposed video indexing and querying system, which incorporates the video semantic concept modeling and classifiers. The system is composed of four major modules: Media Browser and Query Interface, Media Classification/Inference and Matching Module, Media Repository, and Media Planner for Query and Filtering. This paper will focus on the Media Classification Module used to support efficient hierarchical video indexing and retrieval in the Media Repository. Our main contributions are

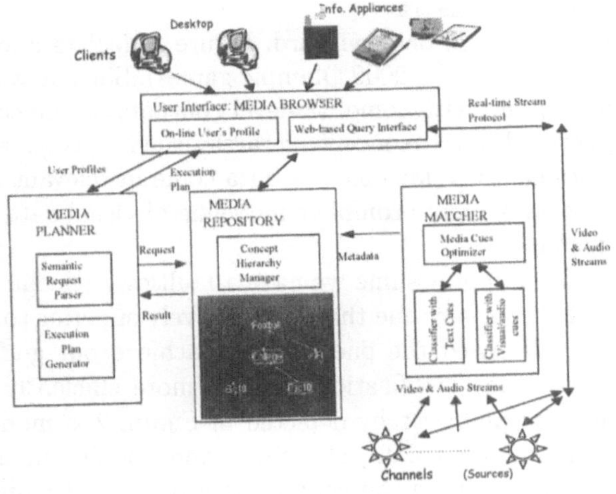

Fig. 1. Video indexing system architecture.

twofold. First we propose and construct a unique architecture to integrate data indexing and querying with classifiers. Each node in the hierarchical concept tree is not only an indexing label of a video, but also a video classifier which supports both indexing and query processes. Second, we propose a fusing strategy which solves any decision ambiguity, or issues of competence and confidence of multiple classifiers using different mixed media cues from multiple sources and modalities.

2.1 Media Concept Hierarchy

The Media Repository in Figure 1 is created based on the media concept hierarchy. A concept hierarchy consists of a set of nodes where each node represents a specific topic. A topic is represented by a node in level n which has subtopics in level $n+1$; that is, the topics become more general or more specific as the hierarchy is traversed upward or downward. Figure 2 depicts a simple concept hierarchy of a sports video (the 2000 Olympic games). Since it is usually very easy for humans to come up with some top-level concepts as the schema, we propose a human-generated initial concept hierarchy such as is shown in Figure 2. New concept nodes can be added as new data come in relevant to significantly different concepts, and a more complete modeling of visual data can become a big ontological lexicon.

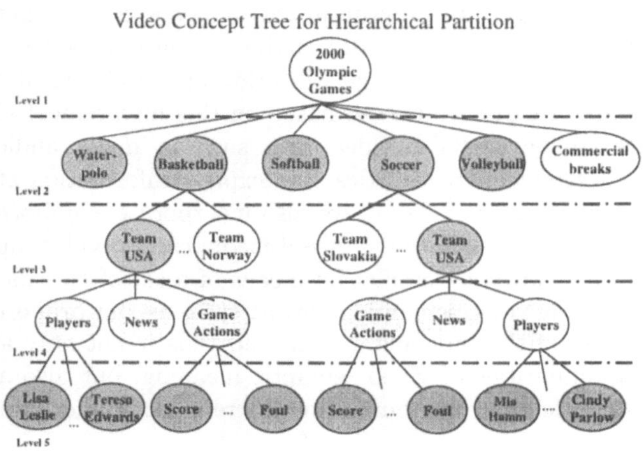

Fig. 2. Sports video concept tree hierarchy.

We do not assume we have a faultless concept hierarchy. In fact, we should not look for any one that is exclusively superior to any other even for the same data. We need the one that can achieve our goals, such as on arrangement, search, and classification of data, more efficiently and more accurately. Since the concept hierarchy depicted in Figure 2 is modeled based on the semantics of Sports News data, and since, additionally, many team sports share similar scenarios such as the concept of scoring and team names, we can use almost 80% of the concept hierarchy for different team sports such as football, baseball, hockey, etc. This semantic description provides a flexible and open-ended framework that explicitly accounts for the dependency, relationship and co-occurrence between video semantic concepts at various hierarchical levels. Thus, querying with respect to a concept hierarchy is more efficient and reliable than searching for specific keywords or matching certain low-level features, since the views of the collected documents are refined as we go down in the concept hierarchy. Also this concept hierarchy can serve as a browsing and guiding tool for users.

2.2 Video Decomposition and Feature Extraction

Much research has studied video/image retrieval based on content descriptors such as color, shape, motion, and other low-level features. We also use such features of multimedia cues in video, but we want to go beyond that by connecting the low-level features with the video concepts to enhance query process performance and flexibility. First of all, video, audio and text signals are partitioned in our system. Secondly, video shot detection is pursued to parse video into basic units, i.e. shots, scenes and events based on visual and audio features. Captioned texts for each segmented video clip and documents for each node are also segmented and analyzed. Finally, rule-based classifier functions map low-level features into each concept for later video classification. The mapping function of low-level features can serve both classification and query processes. Features are collected for each node from the bottom up; features from child nodes are all passed up to the parent node. The low-level features we used for this research include the following:

1. Visual features are extracted for key frames of each scene. They include color histogram, regional color value and location, dominant color value and location, and edge patterns.
2. Audio features include statistics such as the mean and variance of the distribution parameters of the zero-crossing rate, volume, short-time fundamental frequency, controid frequency, peak, and sub-band energies in [0-400 Hz], [400-1720Hz], [1800-3500Hz] and [3500-4500Hz] for each segmented audio clip.
3. We also calculate the mean and variance of MPEG-1 frame bit-rates, motion directions and the motion magnitudes of the segmented video clips.
4. For each video document, we collect its corresponding captioned text. Text features are presented as $TFIDF$ vectors which are calculated as follows: The text document is first processed using stemming and stopping procedures [5, 6] to obtain a bag-of-words for document d. The term frequency $TF(w_i, d)$ of the ith word w_i is the number of times w_i occurs in document d. The document frequency $DF(w_i)$ with the word w_i is the number of documents in which w_i occurs at least once. The inverse document frequency $IDF(w_i)$ of the word w_i is defined as $IDF(w_i) = log(|D|/DF(w_i))$, where $|D|$ is the total number of documents below the parent of the current node under consideration. Then, the term frequency-inverse document frequency $TFIDF(w_i)$ of the word w_i is given by $TF(w_i, d) \times IDF(w_i)$ [5, 6]. The vector representation of a captioned text document d is represented by $[TFIDF(w_1, d), TFIDF(w_2, d), \ldots, TFIDF(w_{|v|}, d)]$.

3 Combined Video Classifiers

Two independent classifiers, video/audio and text classifiers, are first constructed.

3.1 Video / Audio Classifier

Contrary to the bottom-up collection procedure of feature aggregation for each concept node, we start to construct all classification functions with video/audio features from the top down. Classification functions of parent nodes are passed to all children under them. The procedure is as follows:

1. We treat the nodes S which are in the same level of the video concept tree and have the same parent node as a set of unclassified data.
2. If S contains one or more tuples *all* labeled class C_i, then the decision tree is labeled as a leaf identifying class C_i and the procedure goes to Step 5.
3. Otherwise, S contains tuples with mixed concept classes. We split S into subgroups S_1, S_2, ... , S_m that "tend to belong" to the same class upon a variable feature $< f_k >$ that maximizes the entropy gain [4]. The split is executed according to possible outcomes(feature values) $\{\theta_1, \theta_2, \dots, \theta_m\}$ of a certain feature attribute f_k. Thus, S_i contains all $f \in S$ such that $< f_k, \theta_i >$. In this case, the tree for S is a node with m children. The operators $<>$ are the Boolean comparison operators $(=, >, >=, <, <=)$. The decision tree node is labeled with feature attribute f_k and the function $F(f_k, \theta) =< f_k, \theta_i >$.
4. Perform Step 2 and Step 3 recursively for each S_1, S_2, ..., S_m.
5. Check if the nodes are in the bottom of the video semantic concept tree or not (in our experiment, check if the nodes are at level 5). If yes, stop. Otherwise, for each concept node in S, pass the classification functions of the concept to all its children, go to the next level of video concept nodes with the same parent node and repeat Step 1.

3.2 Text Classifier

A *TFIDF*-based text classifier is constructed as follows: Let C be a collection of document classes of interest which includes all its children node documents. A prototype vector (c) (for each node in the concept hierarchy) is generated for each class in C by adding up the entire document vectors in the class. To admit a new text document into a concept, we have to let the projection value, which is a *cosine* function, of the $TFIDF$ vector ($\boldsymbol{n}$) and the prototype vector ($\boldsymbol{c}$) of the class (see Fig. 3) be larger than a threshold θ that is trained to be the best value to include all the trained text documents under that concept node. After training, we obtain a classifier for each

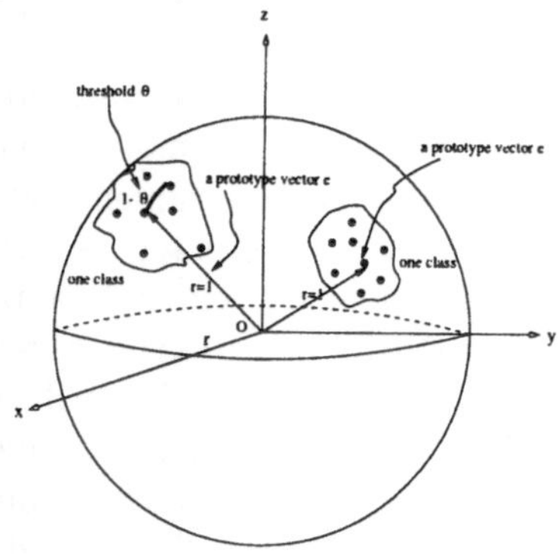

Fig. 3. Learning the threshold for each concept's text classifier.

node with a text classification function $cos(\boldsymbol{n}, \boldsymbol{c}) = \frac{\boldsymbol{n} \cdot \boldsymbol{c}}{\|\boldsymbol{n}\| \cdot \|\boldsymbol{c}\|} \geq \theta$, together with the visual/audio differentiate functions described in the previous subsection.

3.3 Schema for Indexing, not Just a Classifier

Figure 4 depicts the final constructed video classification system to be integrated into the video indexing system as shown in Figure 1: A hierarchical classifier consists of a video classifier and a text classifier; both can be used to classify a video clip into a topic or subtopics in the concept hierarchy. Within each node of the concept hierarchy index, we also store classification functions related to each semantic segment of video mapped to that index, such as the relevant features and their threshold for the classifier to admit a new document into the concept. A classification function $< F_i(x, f_i), \theta_i >$ is represented as a function of media feature f_i from either text or video or audio cues and a threshold θ_i for that feature. This suggests that each node in the concept hierarchy is not only a concept label for video indexing, but also a classifier and query plan generator. A simplified illustration for node C_3 in Figure 4 is as follows: if $F_{visual}(x, f_{32}) >= \theta_{32}$ and $F_{audio}(x, f_{33}) >= \theta_{33}$, then $x \in C_3$. Here, f_{32} and f_{33} are visual/audio feature descriptors and x is an unclassified audio/video clip. Of course, a real node concept classifier will contain more functions of feature and threshold pairs.

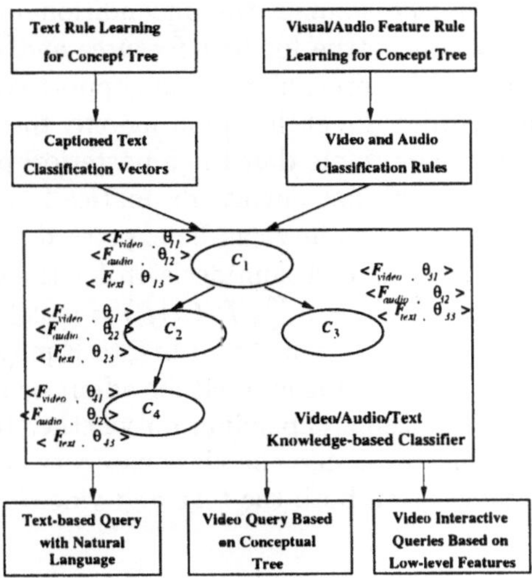

Fig. 4. The classifier with mixed media cues for indexing.

In the query procedures, a user can use the Media Browser to specify queries using either free text or the concept hierarchy and/or identifying relevant low-level features. The Media Planner (MP) parses and matches the user specific queries with the concept hierarchy, and extracts relevant functions describing the data sources that have the contents matched with the user's request.

3.4 Classifier Synthesis Strategy

To solve any conflict of the classification results between the two classifiers, we need to fuse final classification results based on a combined judgment from both classifiers. The two main reasons for combining classifier results are to increase the efficiency and to improve the accuracy. We established our classifier fusion strategy based on the work of Kittler et al. [7] which shows that the sum rule of the Bayesian decision rule outperforms other classifier combination schemes.

According to the Bayesian theory, given m classifiers, each with a distinct measurement feature vector f_i, the pattern function of the final classification F, should be assigned to class C_i, where $C \in \{C_1, ..., C_n\}$, provided the a posteriori probability of that interpretation is maximum. In other words, assign $F \to C_i$ if $P(C_j|f_1, f_2, \ldots, f_m) = \sum_k P(C_k|f_1, f_2, \ldots, f_m)$ (1). To simplify the procedure, the sum rule assumes the unconditional measurement of feature vectors f_1, ..., f_m , which is true for text features and video/audio features. Then (1) can be reiterated in terms of decision support computations performed by the individual classifiers F_i, each exploiting only the information conveyed by the vector f_i. We further assume that the a posteriori probability computed by the respective classifiers will not deviate dramatically from the prior probabilities and thus a posteriori probability can be expressed as $P(C_j|f_1) = P(C_j)(1 + \delta_{ki})$. where δ_{ki} satisfies $\delta_{ki} \ll 1$. A sum decision for the combined classifiers is: Assign $F \to C_i$ if $(1-m)P(C_j) + \sum_{i=1}^{m} P(C_j|f_i) = \max_{k=1}^{n}[(1-m)P(C_k) + \sum_{i=1}^{m} P(C_k|f_i)]$ (2). In our system $m = 2$. According to Eqn.(2), the final decision of our synthesized video classifier rule is to either admit or reject an entrance for a new video into certain concepts depending on whether both classifiers get the same class category; if not, assign the class category which maximizes the probability in the training, given both the text and video/audio feature patterns.

4 Experimental Results

In our experiment, we recorded many hours of the Sydney 2000 Olympic Games, including basketball, soccer, volleyball, water polo and softball games. For each sport, we used the video data of games played by one pairs of teams as a training set, and then used another set of videos of the same type of game played by one of the original teams against some other teams as test data. We manually placed two sets of video documents at each concept node in the hierarchy (Figure 2) to serve as training and test data for ***supervised learning*** and ***video classification evaluation*** respectively. The performance of the classifiers at each node is measured by their accuracy, which is defined by the percentage of documents which are correctly classified into the class.

Figure 5 shows the average accuracy for each concept level in the concept hierarchy. Classification evaluation starts from level 2 nodes. Both the text classifier and the video/audio classifier gives above 84% average accurarcy at level 2. For the nodes from levels 3 to 5, we only evaluated basketball and soccer; we found the text and the video/audio classifier performed quite differently in these three levels because of the different nature of the

		Sample #		Average Accuracy of Classifiers		
		Train	Test	Text	Video/Audio	Combined
d	1					
e	2	265	200	84.5%	86.0%	89.0%
p	3	225	170	81.3%	N/A	81.3%
t	4	185	135	63.0%	71.1%	74.1%
h	5	177	130	56.2%	68.5%	69.2%

Fig. 5. Average accuracy for classifiers at each depth of the video concept hierarchy.

two independent classifiers. Certainly, it is very difficult to detect a team's and players' names by using most visual/audio features. More sophisticated image/audio processing techniques, such as object tracking, face detection or speech recognition, which are often not available for on-line analysis or for fast analyses, are required to detect team players with higher accuracy. On the other hand, the last level of sports video semantics is more related to visual/motional effects, such as fastbreaks and dunks in basketball games. Therefore, unless reporters specifically comment on these events, it is difficult to detect sports events purely from captioned text streams, which justifies the performance difference of text and video/audio classifiers in this level of concepts. From Figure 5, we can also see that the combined classifier performs better than, or at least as well as, any independent classifier for all concept nodes.

5 Conclusion

We have described an integrated hierarchical video classification and indexing system with mixed media cues as applied to sports video. Using a pre-defined video concept tree, we have enforced the domain knowledge by supervised learning so that the proposed system can pick up classification functions automatically for future intelligent video analysis. Each independent classifier becomes essentially unique but with similar representation for the classifier at each concept node. Moreover, by allowing indexing and querying based on either the text classifier or the visual/audio classifier, any inadequacy or limitation of using a classifier based on a single type of signal is compensated for. The system prototype is suitable for both on-line and off-line information access applications due to its integrated representation of video semantic concepts and their corresponding low-level functions.

References

1. Maybury, M., Merilino, A., Rayson, J.: Segmentation, Content Extraction and Visualization of Broadcast News Video Using Multistream Analysis. Proceedings of the 1997 AAAI Spring Symposium on Intelligent Integration and Use of Text, Image, Video, and Audio Corpora, (1997) 102–112
2. Liu, Z., Huang, Q., Wang, Y.: Classification of TV programs Based on Audio Information Using Hidden Markov Model. IEEE Signal Processing Society 1998 Workshop on Multimedia Signal Processing. (1998)
3. Huang, Q., Liu, Z., Rosenberg, A., Gibbon, D., Shahraray, B.: Automated Generation of News Content Hierarchy by Integrating Audio, Video and Text Information. International Conference on Acoustics, Speech and Signal Processing. (1999)
4. Quinlan, J.R.: C4.5: Programs for machine learning. Morgan Kaufmann, 1993.
5. Salton, G.: Automatic Text Processing: the Transformation, Analysis, and Retrieval of Information by Computer, Reading, Massachusetts: Addison-Wesley, 1989.
6. Korfhage, R.: Information Storage and Retrieval. New York: Wiley, 1997.
7. Kittler,J., Hatef, M., Duin, R.P.W., Matas, J.: On Combining Classifiers. IEEE Transactions on Pattern Analysis and Machine Intelligence, Vol. 20, No. 3, March 1998.

Mismatch MB Retrieval for MPEG-2 to MPEG-4 Transcoding

Wang Xing Guo[1,2], Liu Ji Lin[1], Wei Guo Zheng[2], Ishfaq

[1]Zhejiang University, Hangzhou, P.R. China
[2]Multimedia Technology Research Center, Hong Kong University of Science and Technology
wangxg@ust.hk

Abstract. MPEG-4 is leading the compression of multimedia application into the fruitful future for it's affluent functions to support universal access and high performance compression[2]. But two excellent standard-compliant streams, MPEG-2 and MPEG-4 video, will be coexisting in different systems for a long time. This paper addresses the problems of transcoding MPEG-2 video to MPEG-4 compliant bitstream in compression domain to meet low complexity and low latency real-time application. The key issue about macroblock coding mode mismatch in transcoding processing will be discussed in detail. The reported simulation results authenticate the performance of the proposed transcoding algorithm in both objective and subjective quality.

1 Introduction

A number of international standards have been established based on different application, technology and era. Each of them is only optimized for a certain class of application. Generally, it is not economical and feasible to make any single media sever or terminal to support all kinds of encoding and decoding. Transcoding techniques that convert one format to another, preferably in the compressed domain, solve the problem of inter-standard operability.

MPEG-4, whose formal ISO/IEC designation is ISO/IEC14496 [2] was developed to fulfill the newer needs of emerging multimedia applications, such as object based coding, interaction and natural and synthetic data integration. To realize interoperation of MPEG-2 and MPEG-4 between different systems, an effective transcoder is desired for lots of multimedia applications.

An intuitionistic transcoding method is MPEG-2 decoding and MPEG-4 re-encoding, which achieves the conversion in the pixel domain. But the pixel approach has huge computation, memory, delay, and storage requirements. It has the greatest operation complexity because it includes the whole procedures of decoding and encoding. In addition, the quality of the target video will be deteriorated too, because the Motion Estimation has to base on the first generation distorted video [3].

An alternative solution is shown in Fig. 1, in which partially MPEG-2 decoding is used to get DCT coefficients and side information of the input macroblock. Then these data can be processed and organized based on the MPEG-4 syntax and algorithms to produce the MPEG-4 compliant video stream. This method has been studied deeply in MPEG-2 rate scaling and bitstream editing [4], but so far no such transcoder is available for MPEG-2 to MPEG-4 transcoding. Its major difficulties stem from that there are different coding modes between MPEG-2 and MPEG-4. What's more, many spatio-temporal dependencies in the highly compressed video data makes processing in MC-DCT domain even more complicated.

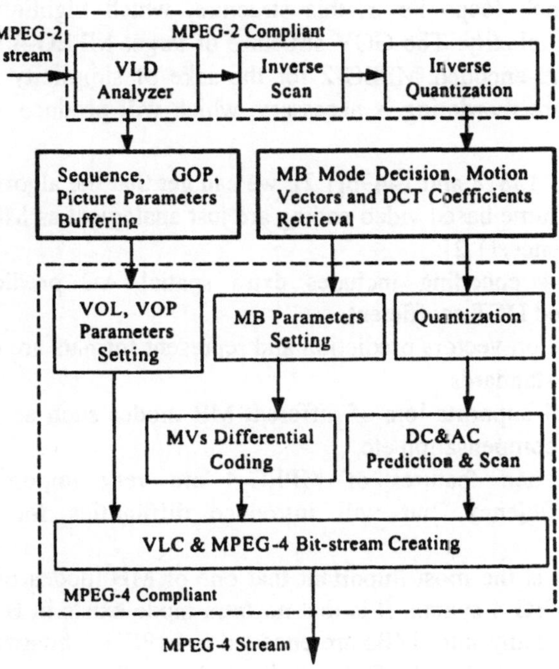

Fig. 1. MC-DCT domain transcoding

This paper is contributed to the design of MC-DCT domain transcoder and the mode mismatch MB processing. The paper is organized as follows. Section 2 gives a brief analysis on the conversion problems, e.g. MC-DCT transcoding structure and its characteristics. The different coding modes supported by MPEG-2 and MPEG-4 are listed here too. In Section 3 the limited motion estimation, mode decision and motion compensation in DCT are proposed to resolve the coding mode mismatch of Intra-coding MB in Bi-direction Picture. Experiment results are presented in Section 4. Section 5 is the conclusion remark.

2 MC-DCT Domain Transcoding

Fig.1 is the flow chart of the MC-DCT domain transcoding. The process for information extracting and setting is illustrated, from which it can be noticed that no motion estimation, motion compensation, DCT and IDCT are involved. So not only the operations are mostly reduced but also the buffer requirements are the lowest, which always results in low delay and simple hardware complexity. No coding or decoding feedback loops lie in this structure, which highlights the maximum reduction of complexity. The GOV structure of target MPEG-4 bit stream is kept unchanged as pre-encoded MPEG-2 for the sake of simplicity and low latency. Otherwise, picture reordering is necessary, which will produce a delay of several pictures.

From ISO/IEC 13818 and 14496[1,2], we can get that the algorithms of MPEG-4 for rectangular frame based video coding are just analogical as MPEG-2 except the following differences[1,2]:

- MPEG-4 encoding includes extra spatial AC prediction module of quantized DCT coefficient.
- The motion vectors prediction and represent formats are different between the two standards.
- MPEG-4 supports lots of different MB modes such as direct mode, 8x8 motion compensation etc.

The aforementioned features of MPEG-4 are very important to get high compression efficiency, but will introduce difficulties for MC-DCT based transcoding.

In addition, it is the most important that one of MB modes of MPEG-2 is not supported by MPEG-4 syntax. It is that no Intra mode exists in BVOP of MPRG-4 stream. Because many intra MBs are encoded in MPEG-2 bitstream, the MB data cannot be used directly in MPEG-4 encoding scheme. From simulation we can find without effective processing to retrieve these mismatch MB, the perceptual quality will be deteriorated seriously. As shown in Fig.4, the block artifact is very annoying though the objective PSNR is not degraded dramatically.

3 Mismatch MB Retrieval

In B-Picture of MPEG-2 there are four MB modes, Intra, Forward prediction, Backward prediction and Bidirectional interpolated prediction. During MPEG-2 encoding, in rich detail area of B-picture Inter coding mode will produce more bits than direct intra coding. So Intra mode will be selected without motion compensation. In BVOP of MPEG-4 there are four MB prediction modes, i.e., Direct, Forward prediction, Backward prediction, and Bidirectional interpolated prediction. MPEG-4 doesn't support Intra-coding mode in BVOP. When MPEG-2 B-pictures are transcoded to MPEG-4 B-VOP in MC-DCT domain, because no encoding loop are involved to form prediction, special processing should be performed to retrieve these Mismatch MBs. Generally there are three methods could be used:

- Force this kind MB as Direct mode;
- Force this kind MB as interpolation mode with zero motion vector and quantized DCT coefficients;
- Estimate the mismatch MB data from it's spatio-temporal neighbor MBs.

All these methods only approximate the data of the mismatch MB, and special block artifact is inevitable, which may result in obvious deterioration of the perceptual quality as Fig.4. From this point of view, these methods should be named as the mismatch MB concealment because no true MB data could be got. We proposed a

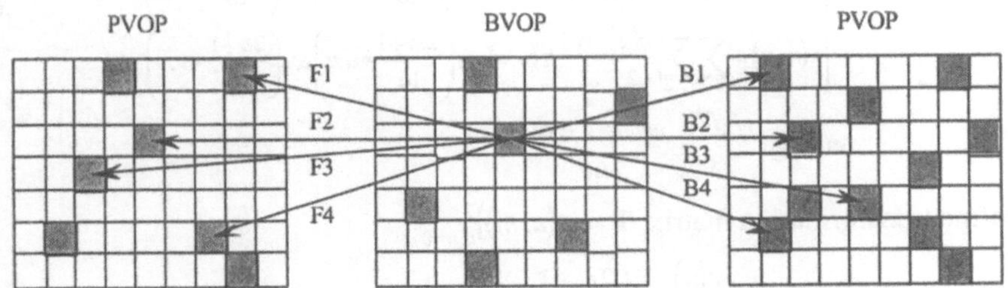

novel method to retrieve this mismatch MB based on special motion compensation in next section.

Fig. 2. Limited motion estimation and compensation in DCT domain, only Intra MB in bench VOP could be selected as motion match candidate.
■ Intra Coding MB, □ Inter Coding MB.

3.1 Restricted Motion Estimation

The special motion estimation/compensation for MB retrieval are illustrated as Fig.2. To transcode MPEG-2 B-picture to MPEG-4 BVOP in DCT domain, Intra MB could be compensated to one of MPEG-4 MB prediction modes based on restricted motion estimation. In Fig.1, no motion compensation loop is involved, so general motion estimation and compensation can't be adopted because reference picture in pixel domain are not available. Since both MPEG-2 and MPEG-4 syntax support Intra MB mode in I-picture (IVOP) and P-picture (PVOP), these Intra MBs in I and P pictures can be used as reference to predict the Intra MB of B-picture. Obviously the motion vectors only could be selected with MB alignment, it will affect the prediction precision and reduce the compression ratio. But all of the prediction operations can be completed fully in DCT domain; in addition there aren't many Intra MBs in B-picture so there is little impact on the global compression ratio.

The motion estimation in DCT-domain could be based on SAD (Sum of Absolute Difference). The search procedures and DCT domain mapping will be derived as follows.

$$SAD_N(x,y)=\sum_{i=1,j=1}^{N,16}\left|Ycurrent-Yreference\right| \quad (1)$$

$$x,y=\text{"up to [-64, 63]"},\ N=16 \text{ or } 8$$

Frame-base and Field-base prediction are corresponding to N=16 and 8 respectively. Equation 1 can be written as matrix form,

$$SAD_N(x,y)=\mathbf{Y}current-\mathbf{Y}reference \quad (2)$$

$$SAD_{inter}=\min(SAD_{frame}(x,y),\ (SAD_{top\_field}(x,y)+SAD_{bottom\_field}(x,y)) \quad (3)$$

DCT function

$$\begin{cases} X(u,v)=\dfrac{c(u)}{2}\dfrac{c(v)}{2}\sum_{m=0}^{7}\sum_{n=0}^{7}x(m,n)\cos\left(\dfrac{2m+1}{16}*u\pi\right)\cos\left(\dfrac{2n+1}{16}*v\pi\right) \\ x(m,n)=\sum_{u=0}^{7}\sum_{v=0}^{7}\dfrac{c(u)}{2}\dfrac{c(v)}{2}X(u,v)\cos\left(\dfrac{2m+1}{16}*u\pi\right)\cos\left(\dfrac{2n+1}{16}*v\pi\right) \end{cases} \quad (4)$$

$$c(k)=\begin{cases}1/\sqrt{2} & when\ \ k=0 \\ 1 & else\end{cases}$$

Define transformation matrix $\mathbf{T}=\{t(u,m)\}_{u,n=0}^{7}$

$$t(u,m)=\frac{c(u)}{2}\cos\left(\frac{2m+1}{16}*u\pi\right) \quad (5)$$

(4) can be written as matrix multiplication:

$$\begin{cases}\mathbf{X}=\mathbf{T}*\mathbf{x}*\mathbf{T}^T \\ \mathbf{x}=\mathbf{T}^{-1}*\mathbf{X}*\mathbf{T}^{-T}=\mathbf{T}^T*\mathbf{X}*\mathbf{T}\end{cases} \quad (6)$$

Obviously DCT/IDCT is a linear orthogonal operation, it is distributive to matrix addition and multiplication.

$$\begin{aligned} DCT(\mathbf{a}-\mathbf{b}) &= \mathbf{T}(\mathbf{a}-\mathbf{b})\mathbf{T}^T = \mathbf{T}\mathbf{a}\mathbf{T}^T-\mathbf{T}\mathbf{b}\mathbf{T}^T \\ &= DCT(\mathbf{a})-DCT(\mathbf{b}) \end{aligned} \quad (7)$$

So the SAD function may be realized in DCT domain just as in pixel domain, DCT/IDCT operations are not needed during the special motion estimation and compensation.

The search order is showed in Fig.3, here the priority of Euclidean distance is used. The mark "0" in reference VOP is the collocation of the current processing mismatch MB for BVOP.

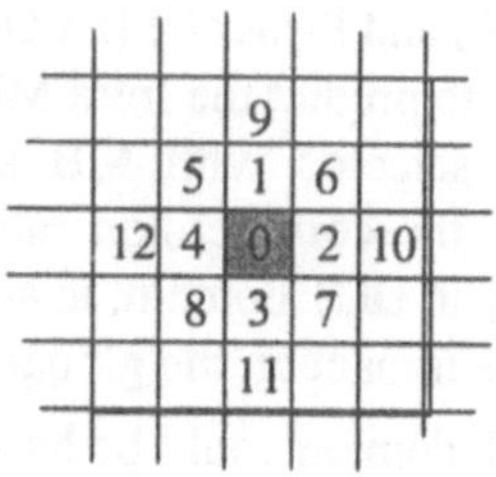

Fig. 3. Set search order based on short Euclidean distance priority

3.2 Motion Decision in DCT Domain

In order to reduce operation complexity and support low latency, only forward, backward and interpolate mode will be considered. The procedure can be described as

If ($SAD_{interpolate}$ <= min{$SAD_{interpolate}$, $SAD_{backward}$, $SAD_{forward}$})

interpolate mode

elseif ($SAD_{backward}$ <= min{$SAD_{interpolate}$, $SAD_{backward}$, $AD_{forward}$})

backward mode

else

forward mode

To deeply reduce operation, only forward prediction may be considered in limited motion estimation and mode decision. Here only frame-based prediction has been analyzed; it is convenient to extend to field-based prediction.

If I-picture is one of the references of B-picture, there always are enough Intra coding MBs for limited motion estimation. Otherwise, if all the references are P-picture, and no Intra coding MBs are involved in the MPEG-2 bitstream, there is no MB could be used in restricted motion estimation. Then the following approximation will be adopted to get the MB data.

The mismatch MB data in MPEG-4 bitstream, mode, motion vectors, and DCT coefficients, will be set the same as one of its neighbor MBs. How to select the reference MB from its neighbor candidates, the three criteria can be used: 1) Short distance priority criterion; 2) Consistent motion criterion; 3) Small DCT coefficient criterion. A small DCT coefficient guarantees that the corresponding prediction is more precise during the motion compensation. In general, the situation that no Intra MB exists in reference pictures appears so seldom that the approximation will not obviously affect the transcoding performance.

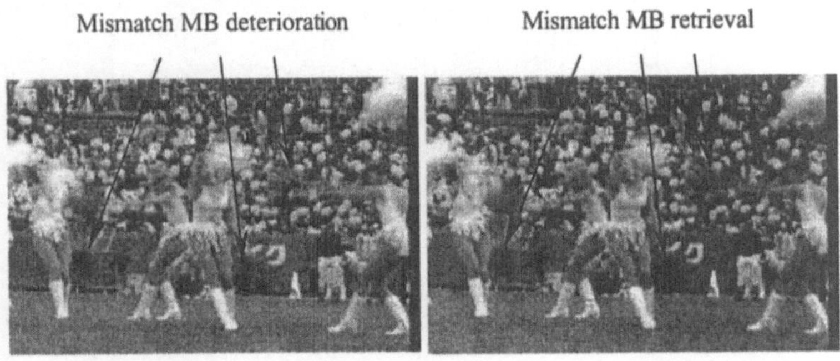

Fig. 4. Perceptual quality of target MPEG-4 video. Left: mismatch MBs were set as Direct mode; Right: mismatch MBs were processed with the proposed retrieval algorithm.

4 Simulation Result

Both progressive CIF sequences and interlaced CCIR-601 sequences had been simulated to verify the performance of the MC-DCT domain transcoding. Fig.4 shows the perceptual quality of CCIR-601 cheer sequences preencoded on 5Mbps with MPEG-2. It's noted that the annoying artifact has been removed effectively after the proposed algorithm processing.

Fig.5 is the test results of CIF Stefan sequences, which are encoded at 2Mbps with both MPEG-2 and MPEG-4. The GOP(GOV) structure is M=3, N=15 and TM5 rate-control was used in all encoder. Fig.5(b) is the average PSNR of 300 frames by different processing, while Fig.5(a) presents the PSNR of the first 30 frames.

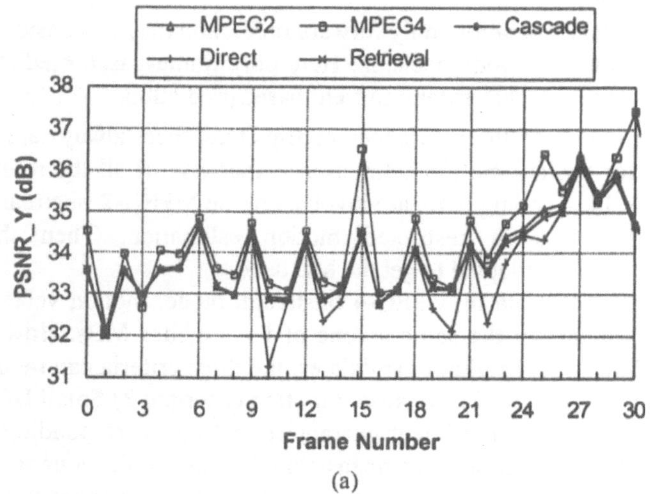

(a)

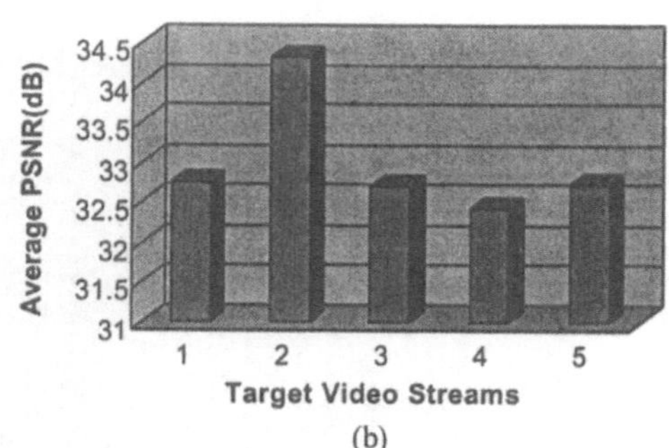

(b)

Fig. 5. PSNR of 300 Frame Stefan sequence at 2Mbps. In (b) 1. MPEG-2 encoding; 2. MPEG-4 encoding; 3. Cascade transcoding; 4. MC-DCT transcoding with Direct mode setting; 5. MC-DCT transcoding with the proposed processing.

From aforementioned curves, it is drawn that MPEG-4 can always get 2dB better quality than MPEG-2 at the same bitrate. Compared with decoding and re-encoding cascade method, MC-DCT transcoding didn't introduce the extra quality degradation. Even by the proposed algorithms processing, the average PSNR of target MPE-4 video is higher than cascade transcoding. The reason is that the Motion Estimation of the cascade method had to rely on the first generation distorted video, and the motion vectors of the compression domain transcoding are estimated from the original sequences. Although the proposed MB retrieval algorithm only got 0.3dB better average PSNR compared with Direct mode setting method, it can effectively overcome the annoying block artifact and picture flicker.

5 Conclusion

We have proposed a low complexity MC-DCT domain transcoder for converting MPEG-2 to MPEG-4, which features low latency and buffer requirements. The key issue, mode mismatch MB retrieval have be effectively solved by the novel restricted motion estimation & compensation. The simulation proved that the proposed transcoding could get better target visual and objective quality compared with the cascade architecture, and it is suitable for real time application because of its low operation complexity. The proposed transcoding architecture can be extended to the bitrate dynamic scaling application.

References

1. ISO/IEC 13818-2 Amendment 2?"Generic Coding of Moving Pictures and Associated Audio", *International Organization for Standardization*, Jan. 1996.
2. Information technology—Coding of audio-visual object: Visual," *ISO/IEC JTC1 CD 14496-2(MPEG-4)*, 1998.
3. P.A.A. Assuncao and M.Ghanbari, "A frequency-domain video transcoder for dynamic bit-rate reduction of MPEG-2 bit streams," *IEEE Trans. Circuits and Syst. video Technol.*, vol. 8, pp.953~967, Dec. 1998.
4. H. Sun, W. Kwok, and J. W. Zdepski, "Architectures for MPEG compressed bitstream scaling," *IEEE Trans. Circuits and Syst. video Technol.*, vol. 6, pp. 191-199, Apr. 1996.
5. S.Acharya and B.Smith, "Compressed domain transcoding of MPEG", *IEEE International Conference on Multimedia Computing and Systems*, pp.295~304, 1998.

On the Optimal Coding

Dongyang Long and Weijia Jia

Department of Computer Science, City University of Hong Kong
83 Tat Chee Avenue Kowloon, Hong Kong, PRC
{dylong, wjia}@cs.cityu.edu.hk

Abstract. Novel coding schemes are introduced and relationships between optimal codes and Huffman codes are discussed. It is shown that, for finite source alphabets, the Huffman coding is the optimal coding, and conversely the optimal coding needs not to be the Huffman coding. It is also proven that there always exists the optimal coding for infinite source alphabets. We show that for every random variable with a countable infinite set of outcomes and finite entropy there exists an optimal code constructed from optimal codes for truncated versions of the random variable. And the average code word lengths of any sequence of optimal codes for the truncated versions converge to that of the optimal code. Furthermore, a case study of data compression is given. Comparing with the Huffman coding, the optimal coding is a more flexible compression method used not only for statistical modeling but also for dictionary schemes.

1 Introduction

The Huffman coding [6] has been widely used in data, image, and video compression [2-3, 9-14]. For instance, the Huffman coding is used to compress the result of a quantitative stage in JPEG [9]. Huffman codes belongs into a family of codes with a variable length not a fixed length. That means that individual letter which makes a file encoded with bit sequences that have distinct length. This characteristic of the code words helps to decrease the amount of redundancy in message data i.e. it makes data compression possible. One of our motivations in conducting this research is to design a secure coding with high efficiency. In this paper a novel coding different from the Huffman coding is introduced.

Some of necessary concepts and notations are first introduced. An *alphabet* Σ is a finite set and Σ^* is the set of all finite length words formed from the letters of Σ (include *empty word* λ) and $\Sigma^+ = \Sigma^* - \{\lambda\}$. A subset $C \subseteq \Sigma^*$ is called a *code* [1, 7] (sometimes called an *uniquely decipherable code* [3, 10]) if, for all words $x_{i_1}, x_{i_2}, \ldots, x_{i_n}, x_{j_1}, x_{j_2}, \ldots, x_{j_m} \in C$, the equality $x_{i_1} x_{i_2} \ldots x_{i_n} = x_{j_1} x_{j_2} \ldots x_{j_m}$ implies m = n, $x_{i_1} = x_{j_1}$ and $x_{i_k} = x_{j_k}$, k = 2, ..., n. And any subset $C \subseteq \Sigma^*$ is called a *language* but not a code [1, 7]. A code $C \subseteq \Sigma^*$ is called a *maximal code*, if for any $x \in \Sigma^* - C$, $C \cup \{x\}$ is not a code. A code $C \subseteq \Sigma^*$ is called a *prefix* (or *instantaneous*) *code* [1, 6, 9] if $C \cap C\Sigma^+ = \emptyset$, that is, if no code word is a prefix of any other code word. A prefix code $C \subseteq \Sigma^*$ is a *maximal prefix code* if, for any $x \in \Sigma^* - C$, $C \cup \{x\}$ is not a prefix code.

An *information source* [3, 10] is an ordered pair $I=(\Sigma, P)$, where $\Sigma = \{s_1, s_2, ..., s_q\}$ is a *source alphabet* and P is a *probability* law that assigns to each element $s_i \in \Sigma$ a probability $P(s_i)$. For the measurement of the efficiency of a *coding*, we use the *average code word length* [3, 10]. Let $I = (\Sigma, P)$ be an information source, and (C, f) be a *coding* (or *encoding*), where $f: \Sigma \to C$ is a one-to-one mapping and C is a code, and $\Sigma = \{s_1, s_2, ..., s_q\}$ is a finite alphabet. The average code word length of (C, f) is $\sum_{i=1}^{q} l(f(s_i))P(s_i)$. A coding is said to be *maximal,* if the corresponding code of the coding is a maximal code. A coding is said to be *prefix* (or *instantaneous*), if the corresponding code of the coding is a prefix code. A *code* (*maximal code, prefix code, maximal prefix code*) is called *optimal* for a source alphabet Σ if no other code (maximal code, prefix code, maximal prefix code) has a smaller average code word length. Note that the *optimal code* here is different from one defined in [2-3], and [8]. All Huffman coding schemes for finite source alphabet Σ are prefix (or instantaneous) and have the shortest average code word length among all prefix coding schemes. And consequently all Huffman codes are optimal prefix codes for finite source alphabets [2-3, 8]. However, conversely optimal prefix codes need not be Huffman codes [5]. Therefore, the optimal code is not necessarily the Huffman code. For infinite source alphabets, several approaches have been taken to construct Huffman codes. Existence of Huffman codes for infinite source alphabets was shown in [8]. But, to the best of our knowledge there is no known discuss in the literature whether there exist optimal codes. From the viewpoint of data compression, study of existence of optimal codes is very significant.

2 Existence of Optimal Codes

First, we show that existence of the optimal coding for finite source alphabets and that all Huffman coding schemes are optimal coding schemes [4-5].

Theorem 1. *Let $I = (\Sigma, P)$ be an information source. Then all Huffman coding schemes for I are coding and have the shortest average code word length among all coding schemes for I. Conversely, the coding schemes are necessarily not to be the Huffman coding schemes.*

In order to show Theorem 1, we first give the following Lemmas [3, 10].

Lemma 1

(i) (McMillan's Theorem, [3, 10]) *Let $C = \{c_1, c_2, ..., c_q\}$ be a code over r letters alphabet and let n_i denote the length of code word c_i. Then the*

code word lengths n_1, n_2,..., n_q *must satisfy Kraft's inequality* $\sum_{i=1}^{q} r^{-n_i} \leq 1$.

(ii) (Kraft's Theorem, [3, 10]) *There exists a prefix code* $\sum_{i=1}^{\infty} p_i l(w_i)$. *over r letters alphabet, with code word lengths* n_1, n_2,..., n_q. *if and only if these lengths satisfy Kraft's inequality* $\sum_{i=1}^{q} r^{-n_i} \leq 1$.

(iii) *If there exists a code with code word lengths* n_1, n_2,..., n_q, *then prefix codes must also exist with these same code word lengths* n_1, n_2,..., n_q.

Lemma 2 *Any r-ary* (r ≥ 2) *Huffman code for a given finite information source alphabet is exactly corresponding to a complete r-ary tree.*

Proof: When r = 2, the conclusion is clearly. If r ≥ 3, we may not have a sufficient number of letters of the source alphabet so that we can combine them r at a time as we have done for r = 2. But in such a case, we can add dummy letters to the end of the information source alphabet and assign source probability zero to the added letters. The dummy letters are inserted to fill the tree. Since at each stage of the reduction, the number of letters is reduced by r – 1, we want the total number of letters to be 1 + k(r – 1), where k is the number of levels in the tree. Therefore, we add enough dummy letters so that the total number of information source alphabet is of r + k(r –1). The details of r-ary (r ≥ 3) Huffman codes can be referred to [3].

Proof of Theorem 1: Since the r-ary (r ≥ 2) Huffman code generated by the Huffman algorithm for any given finite information source alphabet is exactly corresponding to a complete r-ary tree (by Lemma 2). Also, it is known that a complete r-ary tree has to correspond to a maximal prefix code over the alphabet with *r* letters (see [1], p.85-88) Therefore, all Huffman codes are maximal prefix codes, and all Huffman coding schemes are coding schemes. Now, let $I = (\Sigma, P)$ be an information source, and let (C, f) be any coding scheme for Σ, where $C = \{c_1, c_2, \ldots, c_q\}$ is a code with code word lengths $n_1, n_2, \ldots, n_q$. By Lemma 1(iii), there must exist a prefix code $C_1 = \{d_1, d_2, \ldots, d_q\}$and a prefix coding scheme (C_1, g) for Σ such that $C_1 = \{d_1, d_2, \ldots, d_q\}$has the same code word lengths $n_1, n_2, \ldots, n_q$ as the code C. Again, let (C_h, h) be a Huffman coding scheme for Σ with code word lengths $m_1, m_2, \ldots, m_q$. By the Huffman algorithm [4, 7, 13], we know that

$$\sum_{i=1}^{q} l(h(s_i))P(s_i) = \sum_{i=1}^{q} m_i P(s_i) \leq \sum_{i=1}^{q} l(g(s_i))P(s_i) = \sum_{i=1}^{q} n_i P(s_i)$$

Since

$$\sum_{i=1}^{q} l(f(s_i))P(s_i) = \sum_{i=1}^{q} n_i P(s_i) = \sum_{i=1}^{q} l(g(s_i))P(s_i),$$

$$\sum_{i=1}^{q} l(h(s_i))P(s_i) = \sum_{i=1}^{q} m_i P(s_i) \leq \sum_{i=1}^{q} l(f(s_i))P(s_i) = \sum_{i=1}^{q} n_i P(s_i).$$

This shows that the average code word length of the coding scheme (C, f) is equal to or greater than the average code word length of a corresponding Huffman coding scheme (C_h, h). That is, all Huffman codes are optimal codes.

Conversely, all optimal codes need not to be Huffman codes. For example, for a given information source $I = (\Sigma, P)$ where $\Sigma = \{A, B, C, D, E\}$ and $P = \{0.50,0.25,0.14,0.09,0.02\}$. We easily deduce all the four Huffman codes $C_1 = \{1,01,001,0001,0000\}$, $C_2 = \{0,11,101,1001,1000\}$, $C_3 = \{1,00,011,0100,0101\}$, and $C_4 = \{0,10,111,1100,1101\}$. Clearly, the code $D = \{1,10,100,1000,0000\}$ is no Huffman code.

On existence of the optimal codes for infinite source alphabets, we have

Theorem 2 *Let X be a random variable with a countable infinite of possible outcomes and with finite entropy. Then for every D > 1, the following hold:*

(i) *There exists a sequence of D-ary truncated optimal codes for X, which converges to an optimal code for X.*

(ii) *The average code word lengths in any sequence of D-ary truncated optimal codes converge to the shortest average code word length for X.*

(iii) *Any optimal D-ary code for X must satisfy the Kraft inequality with equality.*

To facilitate proof, basic notations and definitions [1, 3, 8, 10] are first given. A *code* (*prefix code*) over a finite alphabet Σ (with D letters) is called a D-ary *code* (*prefix code*) over Σ. Let Z^+ denote the positive integers. A sequence of D-ary codes (prefix codes) C_1, C_2 *converges* to an infinite code (prefix code) C if for every $i \geq 1$, the ith code word of C_n is eventually constant (as n grows) and equals the ith code word of C. D-ary prefix codes are known to satisfy Kraft's inequality $\sum_{w \in C} D^{-l(w)} \leq 1$. Conversely, any collection of positive integers that satisfies Kraft's inequality corresponds to the code word lengths of a prefix code [3, 8, 10]. And D-ary codes satisfy Kraft's inequality $\sum_{w \in C} D^{-l(w)} \leq 1$. Conversely, any collection of positive integers that satisfies Kraft's inequality corresponds to the code word lengths of a code ([1], Proposition 4.4 in Chapter I, p.58-59).

Let X be a source random variable whose countable infinite range is (without loss of generality) Z^+, with respective probabilities $p_1 \geq p_2 \geq p_3 \geq \ldots$, where $p_i > 0$ for all i. The average code word length of a code $C = \{w_1, w_2, \ldots\}$ to encode X is $\sum_{i=1}^{\infty} p_i l(w_i)$. The *entropy* of the random variable X is defined as $H(X) = -\sum_{i=1}^{\infty} p_i \log p_i$. It is well known that the average code word length of an Huffman code is no smaller than $H(X)$ and is smaller than $H(X) + 1$ [3, 10]. According to Theorem 1, we easily obtain that:

Lemma 3 *The average code word length of an optimal code is no smaller than H(X) and is smaller than H(X) + 1.*

Lemma 3 plays a crucial role, which establishes existence of optimal codes for infinite source alphabets. By Theorem 1, we know that: *Huffman coding gives a method for constructing optimal codes for finite source ranges.*

Next, for each $n \geq 1$, let X_n be a random variable with a finite range, similar to truncated Huffman code [8], we define a *D-ary truncated optimal code* of size *n* for *X* as a D-ary optimal code for X_n.

Proof of Theorem 2: Using a minor modification of Theorem 1 in [8], only replacing a prefix code with a code in Theorem 1 of [8], we immediately get proof of Theorem 2.

3 A Case Study

In this section we will apply a coding to data compression. Different rations between the coding and the Huffman coding are also given.

For example, we encode the following file M: STATUS REPORT ON THE FIRST ROUND OF THE DEVELOPMENT OF THE ADVANCED ENCRYPTION STANDARD. According to Table 1, we easily calculate that the average code word length of the block code is 5 bits/symbol, and that the average code word length of the Huffman code C_2 is 342/87 bits/symbol. Therefore, the encoded file by the block encoding and the Huffman encoding C_2 will take up $87\times5=435$ bits and $87\times342/87 = 342$ bits respectively. By Theorem 1, we can give the optimal coding such as C_3 in Table 1. But the file encoded by C_3 will also need 342 bits. Next, in a non-statistical method, we will encode the file M by a coding different from the Huffman coding. First, a code is generated as follow: $C = \{010, 101, 110, 0000, 0001, 0110, 0111, 1001, 1111\}$. By Table 2, we will easily calculate that the encoded file will take up 92 bits. Clearly, the compression ratio is 435/92 = 4.73:1. However, the compression ratio of the Huffman coding scheme in Table 1 is 435/342 = 1.27:1. From the choice of the code *C* in Table 2, it easily follows that there exist many different coding schemes with the same compression ratio. Maybe it is one of the most difficult problems of the above coding how to give the code *C* in Table 2. Fortunately, an efficient algorithm generating a code is given. Denote the longest length of code words in the maximal prefix code *C* as max_length, the total number of code words in *C* as total_code, and the number of code checking as test_code.

Algorithm: Generating a code *C*

Input: An alphabet Σ

Output: A code *C*.

Step 1: Set *C* = empty, the number of code words in *C*, *m* = 0, and the code checking times, *t* =0.

Step 2: Repeat following steps 3 through 6 until *m* > total_code or *t* > test_code.

Step 3: Randomly generate an integer *n* as the length of word, $1 \leq n \leq$ max_length; *t* = *t* + 1.

Step 4: Randomly select a word *w* of length n from Σ^*.

Table 1. A Huffman coding for the file M

Letters of the file M	Probability	Huffman code C_2	No Huffman code C_1
(space)	13/87	010	101
T	10/87	101	010
E	9/87	110	001
N	7/87	0000	1111
O	7/87	0010	1101
D	6/87	0111	1000
R	6/87	0110	1001
A	4/87	1001	0110
S	4/87	1110	0001
C	3/87	00010	11101
F	3/87	00011	11100
H	3/87	00111	11000
P	3/87	00110	11001
I	2/87	10000	01111
U	2/87	10001	01110
V	2/87	11110	00001
L	1/87	111110	000001
M	1/87	1111110	0000001
Y	1/87	1111111	0000000

Table 2. A coding for the file M

Words of the file M	A code C
(space)	000
DEVELOPMENT	001
ENCRYPTION	100
THE	110
STANDARD	011
ADVANCED	0100
STATUS	0101
REPORT	1011
FIRST	1110
FOUND	1111
OF	10100
ON	10101

Step 5: Compare w with each word in C, if there exist prefix relations between w and a word in C, then go to step 3. Otherwise continue.

Step 6: $C = C + w$ (add the word w to C), $m = m + 1$, $t = t + 1$, go to step 3.

In fact, we are able to generate a prefix code efficiently. That is, the following Theorem 3 is shown. Proof of Theorem 3 is omitted here.

Theorem 3 *Let Σ be a finite alphabet and n be any positive integer. The above algorithm must generate a prefix code C containing n code words in polynomial time of n.*

In addition, to break a file [10] encoded by a code is a NP-complete problem.

Theorem 4 *Let M' be the file encoded by a code C and the length of M' be N. Then M' is encoded by at most 2^{N-1} variable length codes instead of block codes.*

Proof: Let $M' = a_1a_2a_3...a_N$, $a_i \in \Sigma$, $i=1, ..., N$. Suppose that $M' = c_1c_2... c_k$ such that $\{c_1, c_2, ..., c_k\}$ is a possible code. Since the length $l(c_j)$ of c_j satisfy $1 \le l(c_j) \le N$, c_j (j=1, ..., k) are able to choose all the sub-words of the word M' [1]. Let the number of the set $\{c_1, c_2, ..., c_k\}$ satisfying with $M' = c_1c_2... c_k$ be D_N. Then the number of the set $\{c_1, c_2, ..., c_k\}$ such that $a_2a_3...a_N = c_1c_2... c_k$ is D_{N-1}. Repeating the above discussion, we have that the number of the set $\{c_1, c_2, ..., c_k\}$ with $a_ia_{i+1}...a_N = c_1c_2... c_k$ is D_{N-i}. By the choice of c_j (j=1, ..., k), we easily obtain that $D_N = D_{N-1} + D_{N-2} + ... + D_{N-(N-1)} + 1$. Therefore, $D_N = D_{N-1} + D_{N-2} + ... + D_{N-(N-1)} + 1 = ... = 2^{N-2}(D_1 + 1) = 2^{N-1}$. Note that it is easy to verify that $D_1 = 1$ and $D_2 = 2$.

4 Conclusion

One disadvantage [14] of the Huffman coding is that it makes two passes over the data: one pass to collect frequency counts of the letters in the plaintext message, followed by the construction of a Huffman tree and transmission of the tree to the receiver; and a second pass to encode and transmit the letters themselves, based on the Huffman tree. This causes delay when used for network communication, and in file compression applications the extra disk accesses can slow down the scheme. Comparing with the Huffman coding, the coding may not collect frequency counts of the letters in the file. By the algorithm given in Section 3, we easily generate a code. This procedure is equivalent to constructing a Huffman code. Secondly, as seen in Section 3, the block coding is introduced, i.e., constructing suitable coding from the words of the file into the code words in a code. Usually, the Huffman coding only consider stream coding, that is, they are the functions from the letters of the file into the code words in a Huffman code. And the block coding has a better compression ratio than the stream coding. Thirdly, making use of abundant structure of codes and Theorem 1, to break a file encoded by an optimal code different from Huffman code [11] is much more difficult.

Acknowledgments: This work was partially sponsored by UGC Hong Kong under grant 9040511, the City University of Hong Kong under grants 7001060, 7100130, and 7100065, and by the National Natural Science of China (project No. 60073056) and the Guangdong Provincial Natural Science Foundation (project No. 001174).

References

1. Berstel, J., Perrin, D.: Theory of Codes. Academic Press, Orlando (1985)
2. Bell, T.C., Cleary, J.G., Witten, I.H.: Text Compression. Prentice Hall, Englewood Cliffs, NJ (1990)
3. Cover, T, Thomas, J.: Elements of Information Theory. New York, Wiley (1991)
4. Long, D., Jia, W.: The Optimal Encoding Schemes. Proc. of 16th World Computer Congress, 2000, Bejing, International Academic Publishers (2000) 25-28
5. Long, D., Jia, W.: Optimal Maximal Encoding Different From Huffman Encoding. Proc. of International Conference on Information Technology: Coding and Computing (ITCC 2001), Las Vegas, IEEE Computer Society (2001) 493-497
6. Huffman, D.A.: A Method for the Construction of Minimum-Redundancy Codes. Proc. IRE, Vol.40 (1952) 1098-1101
7. Jürgensen, H., Konstantinidis, S.: Codes. in: G. Rozenberg, A. Salomaa (editors), Handbook of Formal Languages, Vol.1, Springer-Verlag Berlin Heidelberg (1997) 511-607
8. Linder, T., Tarokh, V., Zeger, K.: Existence of Optimal Prefix Codes for Infinite Source Alphabets. IEEE Trans. Inform. Theory, 43(1997)6 2026-2028
9. Pennebaker, W.B., Mitchell, J.L.: JPEG: Still Image Data Compression Standard. New York (1993)
10. Roman, S., Introduction to Coding and Information Theory. Springer-Verlag New York (1996)
11. Gillman, David, W., Mohtashemi, M., Rivest, R.L.: On Breaking a Huffman Code. IEEE Trans. Inform. Theory, IT- 42(1996)3 972-976
12. Lakhani, G., Ayyagari, V.: Improved Huffman Code Tables for JPEG's Encoder. IEEE Trans. On Circuits and Systems for Video Technology, 5(1995)6, 562-564
13. Tzou, K.H.: High-order Entropy Coding for Images. IEEE Trans. Circuit Systems Video Technology, 2(1992) 87-89
14. Vitter, J.S.: Design and Analysis of Dynamic Huffman Codes. Journal of the Association for Computing Machinery, 34(1987)4 825-845

Dynamic Multi-reference Prediction in Video Coding for Improved Error Resilience over Internet

Yang Yu, Xuelong Zhu

Network and Speech Communication Group, Department of Electronic Engineering, Tsinghua University, Beijing 100084, P. R. China
yuyang97@mails.tsinghua.edu.cn
xlzhu@tsinghua.edu.cn

Abstract. When standard coded video is transmitted over Internet where packets may be lost, there exists the annoying problem of error propagation. In this paper we propose a new video coding scheme that dynamically chooses multiple references from multiple candidate frames in prediction, i.e., dynamic multi-reference prediction (DMRP). Based on the system model of the video codec with DMRP, we derive that the more candidate frames from which the references are chosen, the greater error resilience is achieved. Specifically we study the performance of video coding with two references selected from four candidate frames (2R4CF). The simulation results under the typical packet loss rates of Internet show that video coding with 2R4CF provides better error resilience than fixed two-reference video coding [4], single-reference four-frame video coding [3] and H.263 standard coding [5] with the coding efficiency nearly the same or a little higher than H.263 standard coding.

1 Introduction

With the increasing popularity of Internet and the ever growing network resources, video application over Internet is becoming an important part of today's Internet applications. However, today's Internet provides no or limited end-to-end QoS guarantees, so packets may be lost due to network congestion or buffer overflow. Furthermore, much of the efficiency of current video coding schemes comes from the inter-picture prediction mechanism, which makes the errors occurring in one frame propagate into the following frames until the intra-mode coding is applied.

To combat error propagation, it is proposed to utilize the feedback information [1]. However for real-time or multi-point applications, which are important applications in Internet, it is impractical to utilize the feedback information. So it is necessary to develop error resilience schemes without feedback information. Intra-mode refreshing can stop error propagation without feedback channel [2]. Yet intra-mode coding sacrifices too much coding efficiency, which makes it important to carefully select the regions to be intra refreshed. The ideal techniques should be those that achieve error resilience and at the same time sacrifice as small coding efficiency as possible. M. Budagavi [3] proposed multiframe video coding, which selects the best-matched block from the previous several frames as the prediction for the current block. It is shown that in multiframe video coding error propagates with smaller probability compared with traditional coding. Also as the search space of the matched block is enlarged, the coding efficiency for prediction error can be improved. However, in multiframe video coding, the error propagates with only smaller probability but with little change in values. Multi-reference motion compensated prediction (MCP) [4] obtains the prediction signal by averaging the best-matched blocks in the multiple previously reconstructed frames. It was shown [4] that with multi-reference MCP the propagation error can be attenuated, and at the same time, the coding efficiency for prediction error can be improved.

In this paper we propose video coding with dynamic multi-reference prediction (DMRP), i.e., choosing multiple references from multiple candidate frames, to achieve robustness to propagation error. From the system model of video codec, we observe that the use of DMRP can achieve greater propagation error resilience than fixed multi-reference scheme [4]. Simulation results of a specific scheme using two references from four candidate frames show that compared with fixed two-reference scheme [4], single-reference four-frame video coding [3], and H.263 standard coding [5], the proposed scheme is more resilient to packet loss.

The paper is organized as follows. In the next section, we will briefly describe the implementation of DMRP. Then we discuss the error robustness of the scheme in section 3. In section 4 simulation results are presented. Finally section 5 concludes.

2 Description of Dynamic Multi-reference Prediction

The main difference of video coding with DMRP from that of the baseline of H.263 standard coding [5] lies in the prediction signal. Similar to multi-reference MCP [4], the prediction signal in DMRP is the average of multiple motion compensated blocks. However, here the multiple motion compensated blocks are selected from multiple candidate frames. In order to avoid confusion from complex notations, in this and the next section we will take the special case of video coding using two references from K candidate frames (2RKCF) $(K > 2)$ without loss of generality. In this case the candidate frames are frame $n-1, n-2, \cdots, n-K$ with the current frame being n. Compared with the standard coding, the additional information needed to transmit in 2RKCF video coding is two motion vectors indicating the motions between the current block and the two best-matched blocks, and a sequence number (SN) designating the two best-matched blocks.

Denote the current block of size $B \times B$ in frame n to be coded is $s(x,y,n)$. To get the motion vectors, first we have to do K motion estimations, which is similar to that of the baseline of H.263 standard coding. Then C_K^2 prediction errors are obtained with the ith prediction error being:

$$pred\_err(i) = \sum_{\substack{x=k*B+1 \\ y=l*B+1}}^{\substack{x=(k+1)*B \\ y=(l+1)*B}} \left| s(x,y,n) - \frac{1}{2}\sum_{j=1}^{2} \hat{s}(x+dx_{n-\mu(i,j)}, y+dy_{n-\mu(i,j)}, n-\mu(i,j)) \right| \quad (1)$$

where $\hat{s}$ represents the reconstructed block at the encoder, $i(1 \le i \le C_K^2)$ is SN and $\mu(i,j)$ $(1 \le \mu(i,j) \le K, j=1,2)$ is the temporal distance between the selected reference frame and current frame n. The transmitted SN i_T is obtained as follows

$$i_T = \underset{1 \le i \le C_K^2}{Arg\ \min}\ pred\_err(i). \tag{2}$$

Then i_T, and the corresponding motion vectors $(dx_{n-\mu(i_T,j)}, dy_{n-\mu(i_T,j)})$ $(j=1,2)$ are coded and transmitted.

3 Error Robustness

3.1 Model of Video Codec

A hybrid video codec can be modeled as depicted in Fig. 1. In the model of the video encoder, as is shown in Fig. 1(a), the prediction signal $p(x,y,n)$ is obtained by passing the reconstructed signal $\hat{s}(x,y,n)$ through two filters $d(x,y,n)$ and $f(x,y)$. Here $f(x,y)$ represents the spatial filtering introduced in MCP, such as deblocking filtering and half-pixel interpolation. When only previous frame is utilized to obtain the prediction, as is done in most video coding standards,

$$d(x,y,n) = \delta(x+dx_{n-1}, y+dy_{n-1}, n-1) \tag{3}$$

where (dx_{n-1}, dy_{n-1}) is the estimated motion vector. In 2RKCF,

$$d(x,y,n) = \sum_{j=1}^{2} \frac{1}{2} \delta(x+dx_{n-\mu(i_T,j)}, y+dy_{n-\mu(i_T,j)}, n-\mu(i_T,j)). \tag{4}$$

The prediction error $e(x,y,n)$ acquired by subtracting $p(x,y,n)$ from the source signal $s(x,y,n)$ is intra-coded by an intra-encoder E. Then the encoded information $I(x,y,n)$ is transmitted, and the reconstructed prediction error $\hat{e}(x,y,n)$ from the local intra-decoder D is obtained to get the reconstructed signal $\hat{s}(x,y,n)$.

In the model of video decoder in Fig. 1(b), we omit the intra-decoder, as it has no effects on temporal propagation error concerned here. The decoded prediction error $e'(x,y,n)$ adds to the prediction signal $p'(x,y,n)$, which can be viewed as being obtained by passing the decoded signal $s'(x,y,n)$ through the filters $f(x,y)$ and $d'(x,y,n)$. Here $d'(x,y,n)$ is similar to $d(x,y,n)$ except that the spatial displacements are now the decoded motion vectors. Due to unreliable transmission, the decoded motion vectors and the signals at the decoder may be different from those coun-

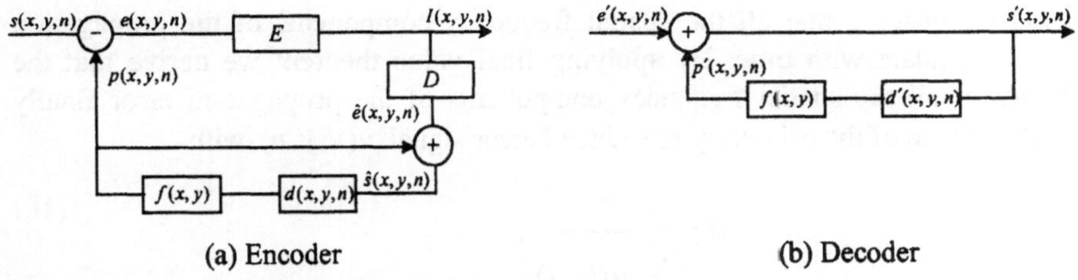

(a) Encoder (b) Decoder

Fig. 1. System model for hybrid video (a) encoder and (b) decoder

terparts at the encoder. Denote the introduced error signal due to packet loss is $u(x,y,n)$, i.e.,

$$u(x,y,n) = e'(x,y,n) - \hat{e}(x,y,n)\,. \tag{5}$$

From Fig. 1(b), we observe that we can take the video decoder as a linear system. Then the propagation error $v(x,y,n)$ is in fact the response of the linear system if the input signal is $u(x,y,n)$. So

$$v(x,y,n) = u(x,y,n) + v(x,y,n) * d'(x,y,n) * f(x,y)\,. \tag{6}$$

In the next subsection, we will discuss the propagation error in 2RKCF.

3.2 Propagation Error Resilience

As spatial translation of error signal has no influence on the amplitudes or energy of the error signal, here we don't take account of the influence of spatial displacement to propagation error. So in the analysis of propagation error, we assume that

$$d'(x,y,n) = \sum_{j=1}^{2} \frac{1}{2} \delta(x,y,n-i_T(j))\,. \tag{7}$$

Although the spatial filter $f(x,y)$ has the effects of filtering propagation error, it is too small to be error resilient and can be ignored. So we assume that

$$f(x,y) \doteq 1\,. \tag{8}$$

Then the propagation error $v(x,y,n)$ can be taken as the response of the linear system with transfer function

$$H(z_x,z_y,z_n) = \frac{1}{1 - \sum_{j=1}^{2} \frac{1}{2} z_n^{-\mu(i_T,j)}}\,. \tag{9}$$

From (9) we observe that all the spatial frequency components of the propagation error will attenuate with time. By applying final value theorem we derive that the amplitudes of all the spatial frequency components of the propagation error finally will be α of those of the originally introduced error signal $u(x,y,n)$ with

$$\alpha = \frac{2}{\sum_{j=1}^{2} \mu(i_T, j)} . \tag{10}$$

In the fixed two-reference coding scheme, frame $n-1$ and frame $n-2$ are used to get the prediction for current frame n with probability 1, i.e.,

$$E_{2R}[\alpha] = \frac{2}{3} . \tag{11}$$

In 2RKCF, the probability that the reference frames other than frame $n-1$ and $n-2$ are used in prediction is usually greater than zero, i.e.,

$$p(\mu(i_T,1) \neq 1, \mu(i_T,2) \neq 2) > 0 . \tag{12}$$

So

$$E_{2RKCF}[\alpha] = p\left(\mu(i_T,1) = 1, \mu(i_T,2) = 2\right) \cdot \frac{2}{3} + \sum_{\substack{\mu(i_T,1) \neq 1 \& \mu(i_T,2) \neq 2 \\ \mu \in \{1,2,\cdots C_K^2\}}} p(\mu(i_T,1), \mu(i_T,2)) \cdot \frac{2}{\mu(i_T,1) + \mu(i_T,2)} . \tag{13}$$

Comparing (11) and (13), we can see that the propagation error in 2RKCF is smaller than that of the video coding with fixed two-reference MCP. Also from (13) we derive that if we increase the number of candidate frames, i.e., the value of K, the error robustness can be improved.

It is not easy to analyze the error propagation property of DMRP and multiframe coding, as the probability of which reference frame is used as prediction is highly dependent on the video content. We will compare their performances through simulation in the next section.

4 Simulation Results

Although with the increase of K error robustness can be improved, the bit-rate for coding SN will increase, and the correlation between the current frame and the past frame decrease, so total coding efficiency gets lower and the speed of propagation error attenuation slows down. Further the complexity of coding is also increased with the increase of K. So it is not cost efficient if K is too large. Here we choose $K = 4$. We implement video coding with two references selected from four candidate frames (2R4CF) by revising the baseline of H.263 standard coding [5]. Then we compare the

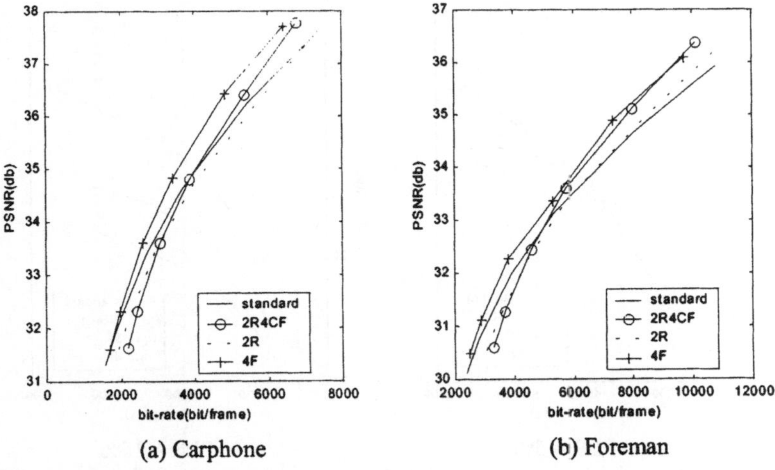

(a) Carphone (b) Foreman

Fig. 2. Comparison of R-D performance of (a) Carphone and (b) Foreman sequence coded by 2R4CF, H.263 standard, 2R video coding, and 4F video coding when PLR = 0%

performance of 2R4CF with that of the baseline of H.263 standard coding, video coding with fixed two-reference (2R) [4] MCP and four-frame (4F) video coding proposed in [3] under the simulation environment of packet loss in Internet.

The 2R4CF coder is implemented by modifying the baseline of H.263 standard coding. The syntax of H.263 bit-stream is extended as follows to include SN and additional motion vectors: 1. When a macroblock is not coded, which is indicated by the COD bits of H.263 and which is defined differently here as the associated motion vectors are both zeros and the DCT coefficients are all zeros, COD = 1 is output. After that SN which designates which of the two reference frames are used in prediction, is variable length coded. 2. For the macroblocks that are coded, COD = 0 is output. Then before coding the associated motion vectors, additional bits for SN are added. Finally in the field of motion vector data, i.e., MVD in H.263, two corresponding motion vectors are variable length coded.

The simulation environment is as follows. The test sequences are the standard 150-frame QCIF image sequences with a temporal resolution of 10 frames per second. The simulation is performed under the typical random packet loss rates (PLRs) of 5% and 15% in Internet [6]. The coded information for one frame is packetized in one RTP/UDP/IP packet. So the loss of one packet means the loss of the coding information for one whole frame. In case of packet loss, the concealment of direct temporal copying of the previous frame is performed. For each PLR 30 simulations are performed and the average luminance PSNR is computed.

First we will compare the rate and distortion (R-D) property of 2R4CF video coding, H.263 standard coding, 2R video coding and 4F video coding when PLR = 0%, which is shown in Fig. 2. From Fig. 2 we observe that 4F video coding achieves the best R-D performance when PLR = 0%. The PSNR of 4F video coding is about 0.2db

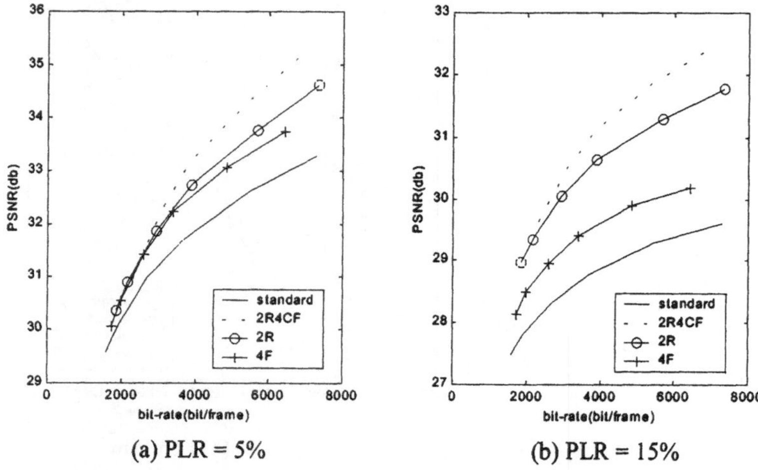

(a) PLR = 5%   (b) PLR = 15%

Fig. 3. The performance of Carphone sequence coded by 2R4CF, H.263 standard, 2R video coding, and 4F video coding when (a) PLR = 5% and (b) PLR = 15%

higher at low bit-rate and 0.7db higher at high bit-rate than that of the H.263 standard coder. The PSNR of 2R4CF video coding is a little smaller than that of 4F video coding. Comparing the PSNR of 2R4CF with that of H.263 standard coding at high coding bit-rate, we observe that the former is about 0.1-0.5db higher than the latter. At low coding bit-rate the PSNR of 2R4CF is about 0.1-0.5db lower than that of the standard coding. This is because at low bit-rate, the savings of the bit-rate for encoding the DCT coefficients can't totally counteract the almost constant bit-rate for SN and motion vectors. Finally it is observed that the PSNR of 2R video coding is very close to that of H.263 standard coding.

Fig. 3 and Fig. 4 show the performance of Carphone sequence and Foreman sequence coded by the above four schemes when PLR = 5% and PLR = 15%. As expected in section 2, 2R4CF outperforms the fixed 2R scheme. Fig. 3 and Fig. 4 also illustrate that 2R4CF video performs the best among all the schemes. Compared with H.263 standard coding, 2R4CF can achieve about 2db and 2.5db higher in PSNR when PLR = 5% and PLR = 15% respectively. We also observe that the performance of 4F video coding is worse than both 2R4CF video coding and 2R video coding. The reason is that although 4F video coding can reduce the probability of error propagation, it can't attenuate the propagation error, and the average performance is lower than that of 2R4CF video coding and 2R video coding.

5 Conclusion

We have shown that propagation error can be attenuated if we choose multiple references from multiple candidate frames. The more candidate frames the references are chosen from, the greater propagation error can be reduced. Considering the coding ef-

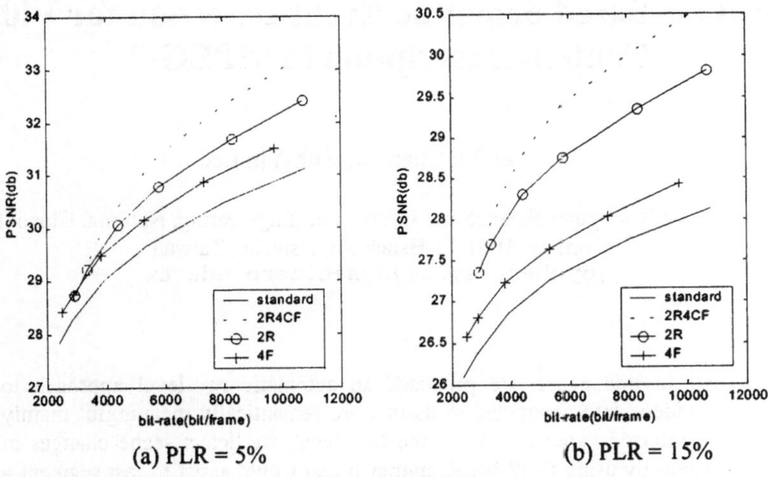

(a) PLR = 5% (b) PLR = 15%

Fig. 4. The performance of Foreman sequence coded by 2R4CF, H.263 standard, 2R video coding, and 4F video coding when (a) PLR = 5% and (b) PLR = 15%

ficiency and complexity issues, here we have specifically studied the video coding with 2R4CF. The simulation results show that 2R4CF video coding can provide significant performance improvement over H.263 standard coding with coding efficiency nearly the same or a little higher than H.263 standard coding.

Future work includes how to achieve optimal performance of coding efficiency and error resilience by selecting the reference frames. Additionally the proposed algorithm involves optimization and multiple motion estimations, which increase the algorithm complexity and may hinder its practical use. So properly utilizing the correlation in motion trajectory to reduce the complexity will also be the focus of future work.

References

1. Wada, M.: Selective Recovery of Video Packet Loss Using Error Concealment. IEEE J. Select. Areas Commun. Vol. 7 (1989) 807–814
2. Liao, Judy Y., Villasenor, J.: Adaptive Intra Block Update for Robust Transmission of H.263. IEEE Trans. Circuit and Syst. For Video Tech. Vol. 10 (2000) 30-35
3. Budagavi, M., Gibson, J.D.: Multiframe Video Coding for Improved Performance over Wireless Channels. IEEE Trans. Image Processing. Vol. 10 (2000) 252-265
4. Yu, Y., Zhu, X.: Multi-reference Motion Compensated Prediction for Error Resilience. International Symposium on Intelligent Multimedia, Video and Speech Processing. Hong Kong (2001) 217-220
5. ITU-T Recommendation H.263: Video Coding for Low Bit-Rate Communication (1996)
6. Boyce, J.M., Gaglianello, R.D.: Packet Loss Effects on MPEG Video Sent Over the Public Internet. ACM Multimedia. Bristol, UK (1998) 181-190

Motion-Based Semantic Event Detection for Video Content Description in MPEG-7

Duan-Yu Chen and Suh-Yin Lee

Department of Computer Science and Information Engineering, National Chiao-Tung University, 1001 Ta-Hsueh Rd, Hsinchu, Taiwan
{dychen, sylee}@csie.nctu.edu.tw

Abstract. In this paper, we proposed an automatic two-level approach to segment videos into abstracted shots that are semantically meaningful mainly based on inferred video events. In the first level, we detect scene changes in sports videos by using GOP-based approach that would assist to fast segment a video sequence into shots. In the second level, each of the shots generated from level-1 is analyzed by utilizing the information of camera operations and object motion that are computed directly from motion vectors of MPEG-2 video streams in compressed domain. Events in tennis videos are then inferred from both object trajectories and applied specific domain knowledge. Video shots are further segmented based on detected video events and hence semantically meaningful video clips can be generated and can assist to annotate video shots, summarize video content, and generate descriptions and description schemes in MPEG-7 standard. [1]

1 Introduction

More and more video information in digital form is available around the world. The number of users and the amount of information are progressing at a very rapid rate. Accordingly users need a content-based query method that is natural and friendly to search, filter and retrieve information. For more efficient and effective retrieval, it is necessary to extract high-level and semantic features for video content representation and indexing. The need of high-level and semantic features representation and indexing motivates the MPEG-7 standard, formally called multimedia content description interface.

High-level and semantic features can be inferred from the closed caption data [10], the variation of camera motions and also from spatial-temporal relationship of object locations in uncompressed [1][2][9] or compressed domain [3][6]. In order to save computation cost and storage space, recently more researches retrieve features or segment video data directly on compressed video data instead of uncompressed raw data. Some researches focus on classification of video content by identifying

[1] The research is partially supported by Lee & MTI Center, National Chiao-Tung University, Taiwan and National Science Council, Taiwan.

significant camera operations [7][8] by using motion vectors of MPEG video streams with specific domain knowledge.

In general, distinct camera operations would apply to different kinds of video events. For example, in a basketball game the slam dunk may correspond to the zoom-in operation and the fast break may be with panning camera motion. In addition, some researches separate video data into somewhat meaningful segments by analyzing macroblock coding types to detect scene change in consecutive frames [4][5]. However, previous researches either infer events from object locations in uncompressed domain or differentiate camera operations with domain knowledge to classify video events on compressed video data. Therefore, in this paper, we propose a two-level approach, that takes advantages of efficient scene change detection mechanism and the effectiveness of high-level features of objects' spatial-temporal relationships in MPEG compressed domain, to generate semantically meaningful video clips. Consequently, by utilizing the event information of associated video clips, video content descriptions and description schemes in MPEG-7 can be generated for high-level video content indexing and retrieval.

2 Overview of the Proposed Scheme

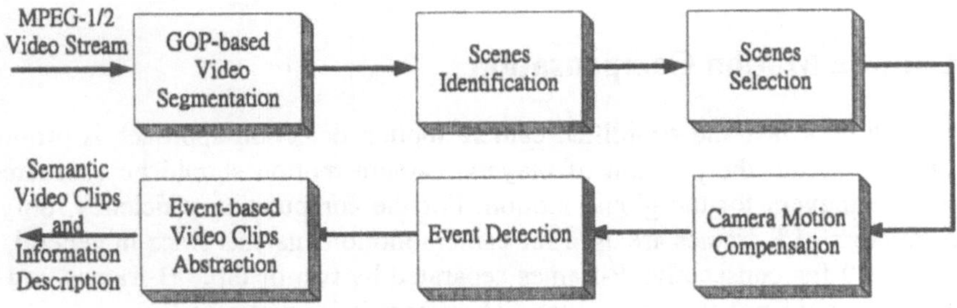

Fig. 1. Block Diagram of the Proposed Approach

Fig. 1 shows the block diagram of the proposed scheme. We use MPEG-2 compressed tennis video streams as the input. Video streams are first segmented into meaningful shots using the proposed GOP-based scene change detection approach. In this stage, advertisements and tennis court frames are identified and separated into individual clips. Video clips that contain tennis court frames are selected for analysis in the player detection stage. In the stage, only P-frames of the tennis court clips are used to obtain the motion information. Hence, camera motion in a frame can be computed directly from the motion vectors of P-frames and the positions of players can be correctly located after the process of camera motion compensation. Moreover, the trajectories of players in a video clip are used to infer high-level semantic events of tennis games with domain knowledge in the event detection stage, for example, serve and volley, baseline rally and passing shot. Video shots that are segmented in the GOP-based video segmentation module are further separated into semantically meaningful clips based on the inferred events in the previous stage. After the thorough procedure, semantic video clips are obtained and can be used to assist in video annotation, video descriptions generation and content-based query and retrieval. The details of each module are explained in the following sections.

3 Scene Change Detection

Video data is segmented into meaningful clips to serve as logical units called "shots" or "scenes". In our proposed GOP-based scene change detection approach [11], we first detect possible occurrences of scene change GOP by GOP (inter-GOP). The difference between each consecutive GOP-pair is computed by comparing first I-frames in each consecutive GOP-pair. If the difference of DC coefficients between these two I-frames is larger than the threshold, then there may have scene change between these two GOPs. Hence, the GOP that contains the scene change frames is located. In the second step – intra GOP scene change detection, we further use the ratio of forward and backward motion vectors to find out the actual frame of scene change within a GOP.

By this approach, we can differentiate between advertisement clips and tennis court clips, since the variation of DC values of I-frames in the advertisement clips are much larger than that in the tennis court clips. Hence, we can filter out advertisement clips and select only tennis court clips for further analysis.

4 Camera Motion Compensation

In this section, a fast and simplified camera motion detection approach is proposed. To correctly locate the position of players, camera motion should be estimated to compensate players for the global motion. For the computation efficiency, only the motion vectors of P-frames are used for camera motion analysis since in general, in a video with 30 fps consecutive P-frames separated by two or three B-frames, are still similar and would not vary too much. Therefore, it is sufficient to use the motion information of P-frames only to detect camera motions. However, the motion vectors of P-frames or B-frames in MPEG-2 compression standard may not actually represent correct motions in a frame. This problem in the tennis video streams is more serious since the consecutive frames in tennis court clips are very similar. This will lead to the situation that for a macroblock in tennis court, it may be to find a good match around its neighbor in the reference frame. However, this motion estimation does not mean that a macroblock does match the correct position in its reference frame.

Hence, in order to achieve more robust analysis, it is necessary to eliminate noisy motion vectors before the process of camera motion analysis. Motion vectors with the magnitude equaling or approximating zero are recognized as noise and hence not taken into consideration. On the contrary, motion vectors with larger magnitude are more reliable and are selected for camera motion estimation. After the noisy motion vectors are filtered out, the histograms of magnitude and direction of motion vectors are computed to acquire dominant motion direction and dominant motion magnitude to further identify whether camera motion, pan and tilt, happens or not. By the histogram-based approach, we can avoid matrix multiplications that are computationally inefficient when motion vectors are fitted to affine motion models. Furthermore, pan and tilt are two main camera motions in a tennis game and can be detected fast and correctly by the histogram-based approach. A threshold (150) can be defined from the experiments for magnitude and direction histograms of motion vectors and is used to identify the existence of camera motion in a frame. The magnitude and direction of camera motion are obtained by using Eq.(1) and Eq.(2).

$$SDMH_i = \#(Bin_{DMH-1,i}) + \#(Bin_{DMH,i}) + \#(Bin_{DMH+1,i}) \quad (1)$$

$$SDAH_i = \#(Bin_{DAH-1,i}) + \#(Bin_{DAH,i}) + \#(Bin_{DAH+1,i}) \quad (2)$$

DMH means the dominant magnitude of motion vector histogram, *DAH* the dominant direction of motion vector histogram, $SDMH_i$ the summation of the dominant and neighboring bins ($Bin_{DMH-1,i}$, $Bin_{DMH,i}$ and $Bin_{DMH+1,i}$) of magnitude histogram of the ith frame, $SDAH_i$ the summation of the three bins ($Bin_{DAH-1,i}$, $Bin_{DAH,i}$ and $Bin_{DAH+1,i}$) of direction histogram of the ith frame, and $\#(Bin_{j,i})$ represents the count of the jth bin in the ith frame. To tolerate the error of motion estimations, the values of $Bin_{DMH-1,i}$, $Bin_{DMH,i}$ and $Bin_{DMH+1,i}$ of magnitude histogram ($Bin_{DAH-1,i}$, $Bin_{DAH,i}$ and $Bin_{DAH+1,i}$ of direction histogram) are summed together to examine whether the summation $SDMH_i$ ($SDAH_i$) is larger than the threshold or not. If $SDMH_i$ and $SDAH_i$ are both larger than the predefined threshold, camera motion happened, and *DMH* and *DAH* are identified as magnitude and direction of camera motion in frame *i*. Moreover motion vectors, which are not recognized as noisy, are compensated with the magnitude and direction of camera motion for further player detections.

5 Tennis Events Analysis

To infer events of tennis games, we need to track the positions of two players in consecutive P-frames and generate a trajectory for each player. However, the intrinsic problem of motion estimation in MPEG-2 compression standard mentioned in the previous section makes players tracking more difficult. Moreover, the difficulty is also due to the varied shape or size of players in the consecutive frames. Therefore, in order to solve these problems, we propose a robust algorithm to track two players in consecutive P-frames and recognize the server further by utilizing the proposed server and receiver differentiation algorithm.

5.1 Players Tracking Algorithm

`Input:` P-frames in a video segment $\{P_1, \ldots, P_N\}$

`Output:` Macroblocks $\{MB_{1,i}, MB_{1,i}, \cdots, MB_{m,i}\}$ and center C_i ($C_{TP.i}$ or $C_{BP.i}$) of two players in frame *i*, $i \in$ *{1, ... , N}, where m is in the number of MBs in a frame*

$$C_i(x,y) = \frac{1}{m}\sum_{j=1}^{m} MB_{j,i}(x,y)$$

1. Analyze motion vector of inter-coded macroblocks in a P-frame to see if there is any camera motion.
2. If there is not any camera motion, go to step 3. If camera motion is detected, motion vectors that are not noisy are compensated with camera motion magnitude and direction.
3. Cluster motion vectors that are of similar magnitude and direction into the same group with region growing approach.
   3.1 Set search windows (*W*) size 3x3 macroblocks
   3.2 Search all macroblocks (*MB*) within *W*, and compute the difference ($diffMag_k$ and $diffAng_k$) of motion vector magnitude ($|MV|$) and direction ($\angle MV$) between center MV_{center} (*k=0*) within *W* and its neighboring eight motion vectors MV_k ($1 \leq k \leq 8$).
   $diffMag_k = abs(|MV_{center}| - |MV_k|)$, $diffAng_k = abs(\angle MV_{center} - \angle MV_k)$, *where*
   MV_{center} *is motion vector in the center position of W*
   $MV_k \in$ *motion vectors within W except* MV_{center}
   For all $1 \leq k \leq 8$, *flag* $F_k = \begin{cases} 1, & diffMag_k < T_{Mag} \text{ and } diffAng_k < T_{Ang} \\ 0, & \text{otherwise} \end{cases}$, *where*
   T_{Mag} *is the predefined threshold for motion vector magnitude and* T_{Ang} *is the threshold for motion vector direction*
   If $\sum_{k=1}^{8} F_k \geq 6$, Then *mark* F_{center} *of* MV_{center} *as 1, where* F_{center} *is the flag of the center motion vector within W.* Otherwise, *set all flags within W to 0.*
   3.3 Go to step 3.2 until all MBs are processed.
   3.4 Group MBs that are marked as 1 into the same cluster.
4. If there are more than two clusters, track forward and backward to eliminate noisy clusters.
5. Compute the center position of top and bottom players.
6. Update motion trajectories and go to step1 until all P-frames in a clip are processed.

5.2 Events Inference Model

Events inference model, as shown in Fig. 2, is used to infer events of tennis game from two trajectories of top and bottom players. In this paper, three events are identified: "serve and volley", "baseline rallies" and "passing shot". Notice that it is necessary to distinguish between server and receiver before event inferences. Server should be located for server related events, "serve and volley" and "passing shot". Therefore, we propose an algorithm to differentiate between server and receiver based on the fact that the shape of server varies more than receiver in consecutive P-frames from "two players ready" state to "one player serves" state.

- Server and Receiver Differentiation Algorithm

Input: Top player $\{ TP_1, TP_2, ..., TP_N \}$ and bottom player $\{ BP_1, BP_2, ..., BP_N \}$ in consecutive P-frames $\{ P_1, \dots, P_N \}$

Output: {Server, Receiver}

1. Set i =0, Stop = 0, $TP_{prob} = 0$ and $BP_{prob} = 0$
2. i = i + 1

   Compute the center position of Top Player TP_i and Bottom Player BP_i

   $C_{TP,i}(x,y) = \frac{1}{m}\sum_{j=1}^{m} MB_{i,j}(x,y)$, $C_{BP,i}(x,y) = \frac{1}{n}\sum_{j=1}^{n} MB_{i,j}(x,y)$, *where*

   $\{MB_{i,1}, MB_{i,2}, ..., MB_{i,m}\} \in TP_i$ *and* $\{MB_{i,1}, MB_{i,2}, ..., MB_{i,n}\} \in BP_i$
3. If $i = 1$, Then go to step2

   Else if $1 < i \leqq N$ Then

   If $Dist^{TP}_{i-1,i} = \| C_{TP,i-1}(x,y) - C_{TP,i}(x,y) \| < T$ and $Dist^{BP}_{i-1,i} = \| C_{BP,i-1}(x,y) - C_{BP,i}(x,y) \| < T$

   Then Compute $TP_{i-1} \otimes TP_i$ and $BP_{i-1} \otimes BP_i$

   If $\sum(TP_{i-1} \otimes TP_i) < \sum(BP_{i-1} \otimes BP_i)$ Then $BP_{prob} = BP_{prob} + 1$

   Else If $\sum(TP_{i-1} \otimes TP_i) > \sum(BP_{i-1} \otimes BP_i)$ Then $TP_{prob} = TP_{prob} + 1$

   Else Stop = Stop +1
4. If Stop < 3 and $i \leqq N$ Then go to step2
5. If $TP_{prob} > BP_{prob}$ Then $Server = TP$

   Else $Server = BP$

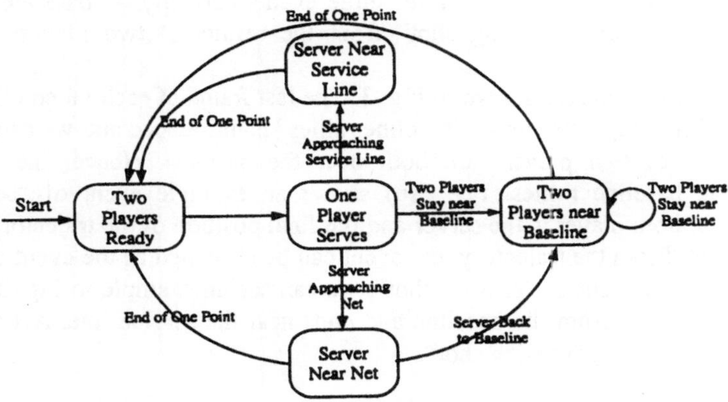

Fig. 2. Tennis Events Inference Model

In the server and receiver differentiation algorithm, we first compute the center of top and bottom player. The distance of top player (bottom player) between consecutive P-frames is computed in the third step. If both the distance $Dist^{TP}_{i-1,i}$ and $Dist^{BP}_{i-1,i}$ are smaller than T (T=16 pixels, width of macroblock), it means that players are still in "two players ready" state and do not actually move. In order to obtain the shape variations of two players, we utilize the exclusion Boolean operation $\otimes$ to compute the shape difference between consecutive P-frames. The center of TP_{i-1} and TP_i (BP_{i-1}

and BP_i) are overlapped and macroblocks in TP_{i-1} and TP_i (BP_{i-1} and BP_i) except center macroblock are excluded ($TP_{i-1} \otimes TP_i$ and $BP_{i-1} \otimes BP_i$). The exclusion results of each macroblock-pair are summed to be the shape difference between frame *i-1* and *i*. Bottom player is a potential server if its shape difference is larger than top player's and hence its possibility value BP_{prob} is accumulated. In contrast, if the shape difference of top player is larger than that of bottom player, the potential server is the top player and TP_{prob} is incrememted. Subsequently while the distance $Dist_{i-1,i}^{TP}$ or $Dist_{i-1,i}^{BP}$ is larger than threshold in successive three P-frames (*Stop* > *3*), two players are recognized as starting moving. The possibility values (TP_{prob} and BP_{prob}) of top and bottom player are examined to indicate which player is the server. Top player is the server if TP_{prob} is larger than BP_{prob} and bottom player is the server if BP_{prob} is larger than TP_{prob}.

6 Experimental Results

In the experiments, we take MPEG-2 compressed video streams as the input. The video streams are obtained from the channel of Star-Sports and at approximate 30 frames per second. The proposed two players tracking algorithm was tested over a video stream about 90 minutes segmented into 200 tennis court clips using the proposed GOP-based scene change detection approach. Moreover, the inference model for tennis events is used to infer three events correctly – "baseline rallies", "serve and volley" and "passing shot" from the results of two players tracking algorithm.

The experimental results are shown in Fig. 3. The last frame of each video clip is also displayed. In Fig. 3(a), an event of "baseline rallies" is introduced and we can see that the trajectories of two players are both near the baseline. Hence, the event is recognized as baseline rallies. Fig. 3(b) shows an example event of "serve and volley". The bottom player is the server and the final position of the trajectory is very close to the net. From the trajectory, the event can be classified as the event of "serve and volley". In the event of "passing shot", we can see an example in Fig. 3(c). The bottom player moves from the baseline and ends near the service line. Accordingly, the event is identified as "passing shot".

7 Conclusion and Future Work

In this paper, we utilize GOP-based scene change detection to fast segment video streams into advertisement and tennis court shots. Moreover, these two kinds of video shots can be correctly differentiated from the variation of I-frames. While the tennis court shots are identified, the proposed players tracking algorithm is utilized to locate the position of two players in consecutive P-frames and to generate trajectory of two players further. Furthermore, video events can be inferred from the generated trajectories based on the inference model with specific domain knowledge.

Experimental results show that the proposed approach can successfully detect events of tennis games. Therefore, two-level video segmentation approach are used to effectively segment tennis video streams into high-level semantic clips that can be used to assist in video annotation, video summarization, and description scheme (DS) and descriptor (D) generation in MPEG-7 standard. In the future, we will extend the approach of motion-based semantic event detection to more kinds of sports video to detect semantically meaningful video events. The description schemes and descriptors generations for effective content-based query are also the future research.

8 References

[1]. G. Sudhir, John C. M. Lee and Anil K. Jain, "Automatic Classification of Tennis Video for High-Level Content-based Retrieval," in Proc. IEEE International Workshop Content-Based Access of Image and Video Database, 1998, pp. 81-90.

[2]. H. Miyamori and S. I. Iisaku, "Video Annotation for Content-based Retrieval using Human Behavior Analysis and Domain Knowledge," in Proc. Fourth IEEE International Conference on Automatic Face and Gesture Recognition, 2000, pp. 320–325.

[3]. H. L. Eng, and K. K. Ma, "Bidirectional Motion Tracking for Video Indexing," in Proc. Third IEEE Workshop on Multimedia Signal Processing, 1999, pp. 153-158.

[4]. J. Nang, S. Hong, and Y. Ihm, "An Efficient Video Segmentation Scheme for MPEG Video Stream using Macroblock Information," ACM Multimedia 1999.

[5]. S. C. Pei, and Y. Z. Chou, "Efficient MPEG Compressed Video Analysis Using Macroblock Type Information," IEEE Transactions on Multimedia, Vol. 1, No. 4, December 1999.

[6]. L. Favalli, A. Mecocci, and F. Moschetti, "Object Tracking for Retrieval Applications in MPEG-2," IEEE Transactions on Circuits and Systems for Video Technology, Vol. 10, No. 3, April 2000.

[7]. R. Wang, and T. Huang, "Fast Camera Motion Analysis in MPEG domain," in Proc. ICIP 1999, Vol. 3, pp. 691-694.

[8]. Y. P. Tan, D. D. Saur, S. R. Kulkarni, and P. J. Ramadge, "Rapid Estimation of Camera Motion from Compressed Video with Application to Video Annotation," IEEE Transactions on Circuits and Systems for Video Technology, Vol. 10, No. 1, February 2000.

[9]. N. Haering, R. J. Qian, and M. I. Sezan, "A Semantic Event-Detection Approach and Its Application to Detecting Hunts in Wildlife Video," IEEE Transactions on Circuits and Systems for Video Technology, Vol. 10, No. 6, September 2000.

[10]. N. Babaguchi, S. Sasamori, T. Kitahashi, and R. Jain, "Detecting Events from Continuous Media by Intermodal Collaboration and Knowledge Use," in Proc. IEEE International Conference on Multimedia Computing and Systems, 1999, Vol. 1, pp. 782-786.

[11]. J. L. Lian, "Video Summary and Browsing Based on Story-Unit for Video-on-Demand Service," Master thesis, National Chiao Tung University, Dept. of CSIE, June 1999.

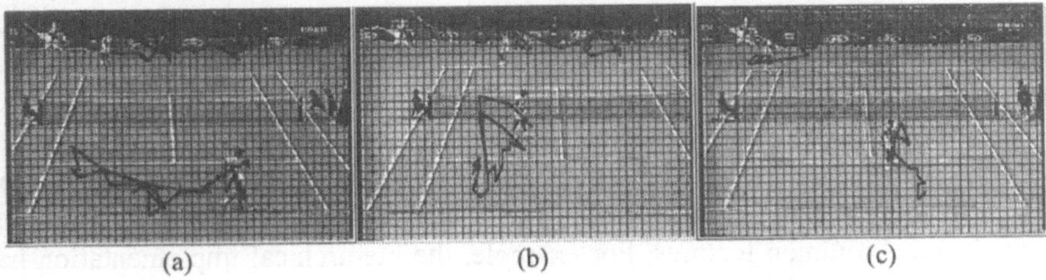

Fig. 3. Experimental Results of (a) baseline rallies, (b) serve and volley and (c) passing shot

Fast and Robust Sprite Generation for MPEG-4 Video Coding

Yan Lu[1], Wen Gao[1, 2], and Feng Wu[3]

[1] Department of Computer Science, Harbin Institute of Technology, Harbin, 150001, China
ylu@ieee.org

[2] Institute of Computing Technology, Chinese Academy of Sciences, Beijing, 100080,China
wgao@ict.ac.cn

[3] Microsoft Research China, Beijing, 100080, China
fengwu@microsoft.com

Abstract. This paper presents a fast and robust sprite generation algorithm for MPEG-4 video coding. Our contributions consist of two aspects. Firstly, a fast and robust Global Motion Estimation (GME) algorithm is proposed here. Spatial and temporal feature point selection schemes are incorporated into the hierarchical GME in order to speed up it. Experimental results demonstrate our method is up to seven times faster than the traditional one in MPEG-4 video verification model, and meanwhile the accuracy is slightly improved. Secondly, a sprite generation scheme with some novel techniques is developed. Rough image segmentation is also introduced for the purpose of image blending in sprite generation. The proposed algorithm can significantly improve the visual quality of the generated sprite image and the reconstructed background object in video coding. Furthermore, the proposed GME and sprite generation algorithms can be used for both frame-based and object-based video coding.
Keywords. video coding, global motion estimation, sprite generation, MPEG-4

1 Introduction

Sprite coding is one of the important components in MPEG-4 video coding, and the method for effectively compressing sprite image has been included in MPEG-4 video Verification Model (VM) [1]. However, how to generate sprite images still remains an open issue. A sprite, also referred to as mosaic [2], is an image composed of pixels belonging to a video object visible throughout a video sequence. Global Motion Estimation (GME) is the key part of sprite generation, and has attracted the attention of many researchers in the field of video processing and coding. Consequently, a number of GME methods have been developed in the past, which can be generally grouped into two categories: feature matching method [3][4] and gradient descent method [5][6]. Although each of these methods has its unique advantages and applications, they share some common features. For example, the hierarchical implementation has been adopted in most of these methods in order to speed up the GME process.

In this paper, a novel sprite generation technique is presented for video coding. Our GME algorithm for sprite generation is inspired by the earlier work in [6]. However, the difference is that the spatial and temporal feature point selection schemes are incorporated into the hierarchical GME in order to accelerate it. For video coding, the good visual quality and high coding efficiency are the fundamental goals, particularly for static sprite coding because the background object is normally reconstructed by directly warping the sprite according to MPEG-4 standard. However, few works have been done besides the global motion estimation in the earlier sprite generation methods. In this paper, a novel sprite generation scheme is proposed, which can generate sprite image with much better subjective visual quality. Furthermore, when no auxiliary mask information is available, the segmentation technique proposed in [7] is simplified and adopted in sprite generation, which can not only accelerate the motion estimation but also improve the visual quality of the generated sprite.

2 Global Motion Estimation

Global motion is normally relative to camera motion such as panning, tilting and zooming, and can be modeled on the basis of a parametric geometrical model. In this paper, the camera motion over the whole scene is parameterized by a perspective transformation as follows.

$$x' = \frac{m_0 x + m_1 y + m_2}{m_6 x + m_7 y + 1}, \quad y' = \frac{m_3 x + m_4 y + m_5}{m_6 x + m_7 y + 1} \tag{1}$$

Here $\{m_0, m_1, \ldots, m_7\}$ are the motion parameters. (x, y) and (x', y') are pair of coordinates whose positions are in correspondence between the two estimated images expressed in different coordinate systems.

A traditional hierarchical algorithm based on gradient descent method is adopted to estimate global motion parameters in this paper. Moreover, the spatial and temporal feature points selection schemes are developed and incorporated into the hierarchical algorithm in order to speed up the motion estimation. Fig. 1 shows the block diagram of the hierarchical implementation. The spatial and temporal feature point selection methods are described in the following paragraphs. The other part of implementation refers to [6].

Spatial Feature Points (SFPs) selection is performed on the image to be estimated prior to other operations in order to decrease the pixels involving in motion estimation. It is based on the fact that pixels with large gradient values dominantly contribute to prediction errors rather than those located in smooth areas. The key component of SFPs selection is to choose those pixels with the largest values in the Hessian image. The Hessian image $H(x, y)$ is calculated from the input image $I(x, y)$ using equation (2). Afterwards, the pixels with largest magnitudes in the Hessian image are selected, which normally correspond to peaks and pits in the image to be estimated.

$$H(x,y) = \left[\left(\frac{d^2 I(x,y)}{dx^2} \right) \left(\frac{d^2 I(x,y)}{dy^2} \right) - \left(\frac{d^2 I(x,y)}{dxdy} \right)^2 \right] \tag{2}$$

The Temporal Feature Points (TFPs) selection is done during the level transition in the hierarchical GME, which aims at further decreasing the pixels participating in the calculation of prediction errors. This operation is based on the fact that the pixels with larger temporal differences contribute more to the total prediction errors. The selection can be implemented as follows. Firstly, the temporal difference image between the current and the predicted image is calculated. The predicted image in term of current motion estimation has been calculated in the last step of previous GME level. Therefore the extra cost in time can be neglected. Secondly, the pixels with the largest absolute magnitudes in the temporal difference image are selected. This operation is the same as that in SFPs selection. Only those pixels involved in the previous GME level participate in the current TFPs selection.

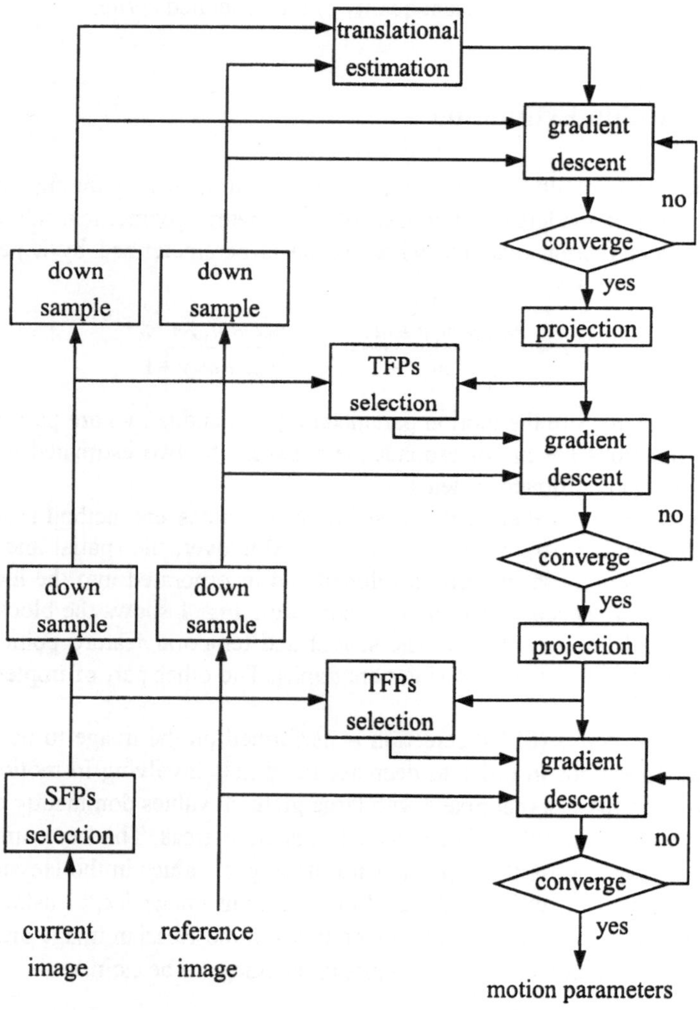

Fig. 1. Block diagram of the hierarchical GME implementation with spatial and temporal feature point selection

3 Sprite Generation

The described sprite generation structure bases on that in Appendix D of MPEG-4 Video VM [1]. However, in order to achieve fast and robust sprite generation, some novel techniques are introduced as shown in Fig. 2. Instead of estimating the global motion of the current image directly from the previous sprite, the described algorithm first warps the previous sprite and then calculates the global motion referencing the warped sprite image. This long-term motion estimation method can greatly decrease the error accumulations caused by the individual frame. The extra cost in memory is reasonable because the size of warped sprite is the same as that of current frame. Static sprite coding is normally used for object-based video coding, however sometimes auxiliary segmentation information is either unavailable or not accurate enough to mask out all moving objects from the scene. The rough segmentation technique developed in [7] is incorporated into the proposed sprite generation, which is usually used in this algorithm when no auxiliary segmentation masks are available.

The main goal of the described algorithm is to rapidly generate the background sprite with better visual quality. Assume that the video sequence comprises n frames, $\mathbf{I}_k$, $k = 0, 1, \ldots, n\text{-}1$. The sprite $\mathbf{S}_k$ is generated using $\mathbf{I}_i$, $i = 0, 1, \ldots, k\text{-}1$. $\mathbf{P}_k$ denotes the motion parameter estimated at the kth frame. The complete sprite generation algorithm at the kth frame is described as follows:

1) Divide $\mathbf{I}_k$ into reliable, unreliable, and undefined image regions.
2) Estimate global motion parameter $\mathbf{P}_k$ between $\mathbf{I}_k$ and $\mathbf{S}_{k-1}$.
3) If no auxiliary segmentation is available, then segment $\mathbf{I}_k$.
4) Warp image $\mathbf{I}_k$ towards sprite using $\mathbf{P}_k$.
5) Blending the warped image with $\mathbf{S}_{k-1}$ to obtain $\mathbf{S}_k$.

There are five modules used for processing each frame in the sprite generation, including Image Region Division, Fast and Robust Global Motion Estimation, Image Segmentation, Image Warping, and Image Blending. Bilinear interpolation is used for image warping, which is the same as that in MPEG-4 Video VM. Each module of the described algorithm is discussed in detail.

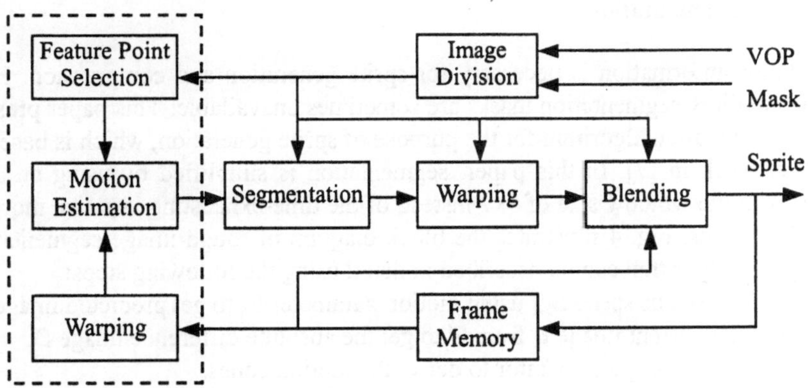

Fig. 2. Block diagram of fast and robust sprite generation

3.1. Image Region Division

According to the visual part of MPEG-4 standard, static sprite coding is normally used for object-based video coding. The described algorithm first derives the reliable masks from the segmentation masks by excluding some pixels along the borders of background object, as well as the frame borders. The excluded areas are defined as unreliable image region; the rest region in background object is defined as reliable image region. Moreover, the areas marked as foreground objects are defined as undefined image region. The core technique of image division is how to extract unreliable image region, which can be implemented by scanning the background object from four directions, i.e., left to right, top to bottom, right to left, and bottom to end. The sprite image is correspondingly divided into reliable, unreliable, and undefined regions. Reliable sprite region has been constructed from reliable image region. Unreliable sprite region was the visible part of unreliable image region. And undefined sprite region was not yet visible in previous images. An example of image division is shown in Fig. 3. The image division can contribute to sprite generation from two aspects. The first is only reliable region participates in motion estimation, which can not only speed up motion estimation but also eliminate the effect of foreground objects and frame borders. The second is that reliable, unreliable, and undefined regions are differently dealt with in image blending, which can improve the visual quality of generated sprite.

(a) Original segmentation

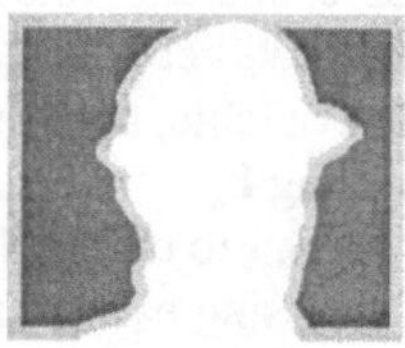

(b) reliability masks

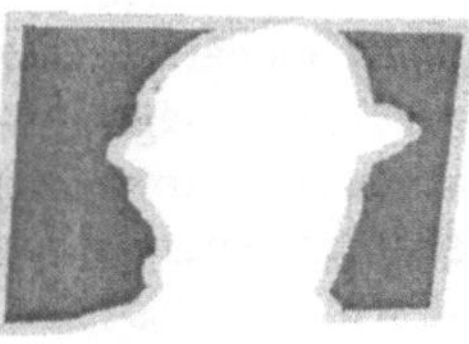

(c) warped sprite masks

Fig. 3. Illustration of image division. Light gray: unreliable region, dark gray: reliable region, and white: undefined region

3.2. Image Segmentation

Segmentation information is necessary for sprite generation and compression. However, the auxiliary segmentation masks are sometimes unavailable. This paper presents a rough segmentation algorithm for the purpose of sprite generation, which is based on our earlier work in [7]. In this paper, segmentation is simplified by using an *open* operator with the window size of 9x9 instead of the time-exhausting iterative morphological operations. Fig. 4 illustrates the block diagram of rough image segmentation. The proposed algorithm can be described in detail using the following steps:

1) Warp previous sprite $\mathbf{S}_{k-1}$ using motion parameter $\mathbf{P}_k$ to get predicted image $\mathbf{S}'$.
2) Subtract current image $\mathbf{I}_k$ from $\mathbf{S}'$ to get the absolute difference image $\mathbf{D}$.
3) Filter $\mathbf{D}$ using *open* operator to detect the motion zones.
4) Extract the final segmentation masks by thresholding the filtered image.

The detailed morphological operation can be found in [8]. Although the segmentation is not accurate, it is enough only for the purpose of eliminating the effect of foreground objects in background sprite generation. After the rough image segmentation, the background areas are marked as reliable image region, and the foreground areas are marked as unreliable image region. The image division results will contribute to the following image blending module.

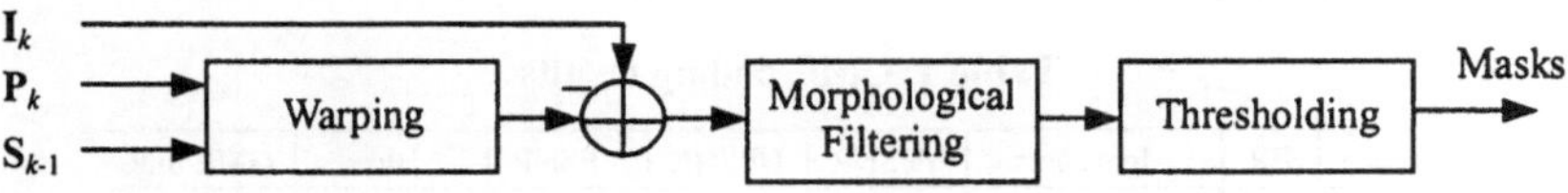

Fig. 4. Block diagram of image segmentation

3.3. Image Blending

In the described algorithm, reliable and unreliable image regions contribute differently to the sprite updating. The pixels located in reliable region are weighted to update the corresponding sprite pixels. However, for those pixels located in unreliable region, the corresponding sprite pixels are updated only when they have never been updated by reliable pixels. Undefined image region has no effect in this process. The proposed algorithm can produce sprite image with better visual quality due to two reasons. Firstly, the reliable region ensures that reliable image information contributes more to sprite updating because reliable region normally corresponds to the background object. Secondly, the unreliable region tackles the aperture problem when no reliable image information is available. The good trade-off between reliable and unreliable image division provides better visual quality of sprite than simply averaging images.

4 Experimental Results

According to MPEG-4 video coding standard, sprite coding can be classified into two categories: Global Motion Compensation (GMC) based video coding and static sprite coding. In order to be compared with MPEG-4 video VM, the proposed technique has been verified in both situations.

The comparison experiments were performed based on the platform of MPEG reference software for both frame-based and object-based video coding. Auxiliary segmentation masks came from [9]. No rate control mechanism was applied. Table 1 illustrates the experimental results on the *Stefan*, *coastguard*, and *foreman* sequences in CIF format (352 x 288), each of which has 10 seconds of video clips at frame rate of 30Hz. The results demonstrate that our proposed GME algorithm is up to 7 times faster than that in MPEG-4 VM, and meanwhile the PSNR is also slightly improved.

The same experimental conditions were also used for static sprite generation and coding. The static sprite was first generated using our proposed method and MPEG-4 VM, respectively. Afterwards, the generated sprite was encoded using MPEG-4 static sprite coding algorithm. The results shown in Table 2 further verify that our GME algorithm is faster and more robust. Moreover, the proposed algorithm can significantly improve the visual quality of the sprite image and the reconstructed background object. As an example, Fig. 5 shows the final sprite images generated from *Stefan* sequence using our proposed method. Undoubtedly, the sprite provides much better visual quality compared with that generated by averagely blending the contributing images, as shown in Fig. 6. Fig. 7(a) and Fig. 8(b) show the images reconstructed from the sprites generated from these two methods, respectively.

Table 1. GMC coding results

Sequence	BR	Algorithms	YPSNR	UPSNR	VPSNR	Bits	GME time
Stefan	500	MPEG-4 VM	28.62	33.79	33.51	5133465	1604
VO0		Proposed	28.62	33.81	33.51	5142881	233
Coast G	75	MPEG-4 VM	29.46	37.05	40.91	762133	676
VO3		Proposed	29.47	37.11	40.96	762701	136
Foreman	160	MPEG-4 VM	30.61	37.24	38.80	1635109	1660
VO0		Proposed	30.62	37.25	38.82	1644680	294
Stefan	540	MPEG-4 VM	28.54	33.71	33.42	5527824	1482
Rect		Proposed	28.54	33.74	33.42	5536516	224

Table 2. Static sprite coding results

Sequence	BR	Algorithms	YPSNR	UPSNR	VPSNR	Bits	GME time
Stefan	68	MPEG-4 VM	22.50	34.78	34.43	693729	1883
VO0		Proposed	22.69	34.93	34.60	709061	267
Coast G	10	MPEG-4 VM	26.29	36.98	41.88	93273	1035
VO3		Proposed	27.22	39.04	42.69	97708	161
Foreman	21	MPEG-4 VM	26.88	37.13	39.05	219833	1947
VO0		Proposed	26.93	37.46	40.27	218745	267
Stefan	70	MPEG-4 VM	21.97	34.04	33.62	680050	2038
Rect		Proposed	22.66	34.45	34.27	731022	297

Fig. 5. Background sprite of the *Stefan* sequence generated with our proposed method.

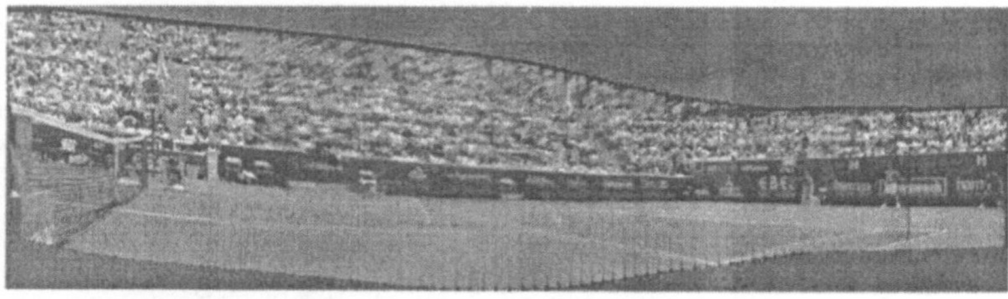

Fig. 6. Background sprite generated with averagely blending images in traditional methods.

(a)

(b)

Fig. 7. Sprite coding results for background object sequence *Stefan*, frame 190, 70kbit/s. (a) Proposed method, and (b) MPEG-4 Video VM

5 Conclusions

This paper presents a novel technique for background sprite generation. Our main contributions lie in two aspects. Firstly, the proposed GME algorithm incorporating spatial and temporal feature point selection schemes can significantly accelerate the sprite generation process. Secondly, the proposed sprite generation algorithm with some novel techniques can produce sprite image with much better subjective visual quality. In other words, the proposed GME and sprite generation technique can greatly optimize that in MPEG-4 Video VM.

References

1. MPEG-4 Video Group: MPEG-4 Video Verification Model Version 16.0. ISO/IEC JTC1/SC29/WG11, MPEG2000/N3312, Noordwijkerhout, Netherlands (2000)
2. Sikora, T.: The MPEG-4 Video Standard Verification Model. IEEE Trans. Circuits Syst. Video Technol., Vol. 5 (Feb. 1997), 19-31
3. Smolic, A., Sikora, T., Ohm, J-R.: Long-term Global Motion Estimation and Its Application for Sprite Coding, Content Description, and Segmentation. IEEE Trans. Circuits Syst. Video Technol., Vol. 9 (Dec. 1999), 1227-1242
4. Grammalidis, N., Beletsiotis, D., Strintzis, M.: Sprite Generation and Coding in Multiview Image Sequences. IEEE Trans. Circuits Syst. Video Technol., Vol. 10 (Mar. 2000), 302-311
5. Szeliski, R.: Image Mosaicing for Tele-reality. Digital Equipment Corp., Cambridge Research Lab., TR94/2. Cambridge, MA (May 1994)
6. Dufaux, F., Konrad, J.: Efficient, Robust, and Fast Global Motion Estimation for Video Coding. IEEE Trans. Image Processing, Vol. 9 (Mar. 2000), 497-501
7. Lu, Y., Gao, W., Wu, F., Lu, H., Chen, X.: A Robust Offline Sprite Generation Approach. ISO/IEC JTC1/SC29/WG11 MPEG01/M6778, Pisa (Jan. 2001)
8. Heijmans, H.: Morphological Image Operators. Academic Press, Boston (1994)
9. ftp://ftp.tnt.uni-hannover.de

Fast Motion Estimation Using N-Queen Pixel Decimation

*Shin-Wei Yang[1], Chung-Neng Wang[1], Chi-Min Liu[1], and Tihao Chiang[2]**

[1] Dept. and Institute of Computer Science and Information Engineering, National Chiao Tung University, Hsinchu, 30050, Taiwan
{swyang, cnwang, cmliu}@csie.nctu.edu.tw

[2] Dept. and Institute of Electronics Engineering, (NCTU), Hsinchu, 30050, Taiwan
tchiang@cc.nctu.edu.tw

Abstract. We present a technique to improve the speed of block motion estimation using only a subset of pixels from a block to evaluate the distortion with minimal loss of coding efficiency. To select such a subset we use a special sub-sampling structure, N-queen pattern. The N-queen pattern can characterize the spatial information in the vertical, horizontal and diagonal directions for both texture and edge features. In the 4-queen case, it has a special property that every skipped pixel has the minimal and equal distance of one to the selected pixel. Despite of the randomized pattern, our technique has compact data storage architecture. Our results show that the pixel decimation of N-queen patterns improves the speed by about N times with small loss in PSNR. The loss in PSNR is negligible for slow motion video sequence and has 0.45 dB loss in PSNR at worst for high motion video sequence.

1 Introduction

Several video coding standards including MPEG-1/2/4 contain block motion estimation as the most computational intensive module. Reducing the number of operations for block matching can speed up the motion estimation. There are three areas to improve the fast motion estimation including the number of search points [1], [2], the number of pixels from a block used for matching [3]-[6] and the distortion measure [1]. In the MPEG-4 reference software, it has provided two fast algorithms to reduce the search points [1], [2]. Both approaches have significantly improved the speed of the encoder. In this paper, we will focus on pixel decimation to achieve further improvement.

The pixel decimation can be achieved with either fixed pattern [3], [4] or adaptive pattern [5], [6]. As shown in Fig. 1(b), Bierling used a uniform 4:1 pixel decimation structure [3]. Liu and Zaccarin implemented the pixel decimation similar to the Bierling's approach with four sub-sampling patterns alternating among search steps so that all the pixels in the current block are visited [4]. The pixel decimation can be adaptive based on the spatial luminance variation within a frame [5], [6]. Adaptive technique can achieve better coding efficiency than that of the uniform subsampling schemes [3], [4] at the cost of overhead for deciding which pixel is more

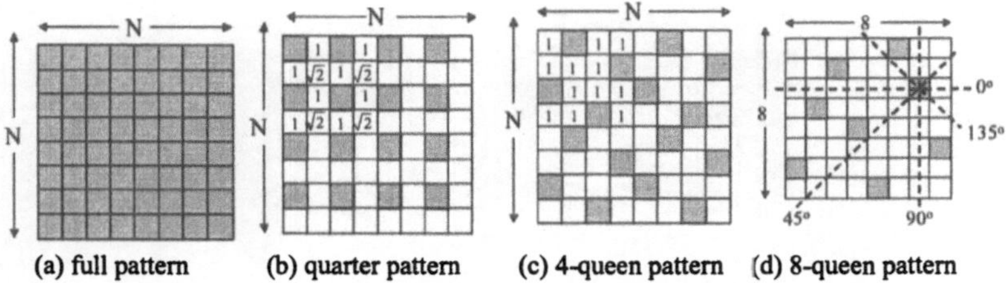

Fig. 1. The pixel patterns for decimation: (a) Full pattern with $N \times N$ pixels selected; (b) Quarter pattern uses 4:1 subsampling; (c) 4-Queen pattern is tiled with four idnetical patterns; (d) 8-Queen pattern. Figures (c) and (d) are derived from *N*-Queen approach with *N*=4 and *N*=8 respectively

representative. Furthermore, the irregular structure is challenging for hardware implementation.

In this paper, we present a regular and simple lattice for pixel decimation while the spatial luminance variation characteristics in all directions are captured. The goal is to find a sampling lattice that represents the spatial information in all directions and the pixels are distributed uniformly in the spatial domain. The major advantage of quarter pattern is its regular structure for pipelined processing and memory accessing. It has the disadvantage of having pixels with irregular distances of both 1 and $\sqrt{2}$. It also lacks half of the coverage in the vertical, horizontal and diagonal directions. To address the weakness of the quarter pattern, we discovered that the *N*-queen lattice improves the representation since it holds exactly one pixel for each row, column, and (not necessarily main) diagonal of a block as illustrated in Fig. 1. Thus, there are exactly *N* pixels for each $N \times N$ block. Our results will show that the quality is maintained about the same for *N* equals to 4 and 8.

2 The N-Queen Pixel Decimation

The idea is to select the most representative pixels based on the texture and edge information with the minimal number of pixels. As illustrated in Fig. 1(d), an edge can have 4 orientations in the horizontal, vertical and diagonal directions. Thus, it requires at least one pixel for each row, column, and diagonal of a $N \times N$ block. We realize that a solution to satisfy such a constraint is similar to the solution for the problem of placing N queens on a chessboard, which is often referred to as N-queen pattern. For a $N \times N$ block, as shown in the Fig. 1, every pixel of the N-queen pattern occupies a dominant position, which is located at the center. The surrounding pixels that intersect with the four lines with vertical, horizontal and diagonal orientations are removed from the list of the selected pixels. With such an elimination process, there is exactly one pixel selected for row, column, and (not necessarily main) diagonal of the block. Thus, the N-queen patterns present a N:1 subsampling lattice that can provide N times of speedup improvement.

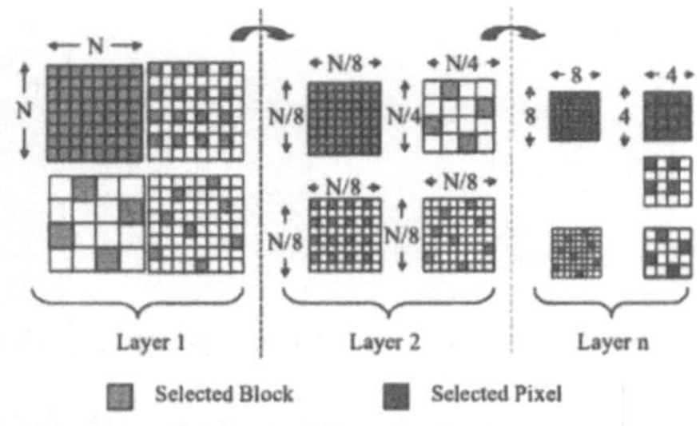

Fig. 2. Recursive structure of pixel decimation using various patterns at each layer.

The *N*-queen patterns in Fig. 1 (c) and (d) are not unique. For example, there are 92 8-queen patterns for a block of size 8×8. The issue is to identify which one provides a better representation. Fro each of the 92 patterns, we can compute the average spatial distance between the skipped pixels and the selected pixels. These 92 average distances are distributed between 1.29 and 1.37 pixels. Thus, the variation in average distances is only 0.08 pixel. We find that the 92 8-Queen patterns have almost identical performance with varying PSNR less than 0.1 dB.

The *N*-Queen lattice can also be used recursively to segment a frame into hierarchical layers. Each layer consists of *k* blocks of equal size $\frac{N}{k}\times\frac{N}{k}$. As shown in Fig. 2, we can select these *k* blocks using one of the sampling lattices at each layer except for Layer *n*. For each selected block, the same pixel decimation process can be applied recursively. A combination of various lattices offers great flexibility in performing motion estimation especially when global motion estimation at frame level is considered. The *N*-Queen lattice is applicable for non-square blocks used in H.26L.

3 Hardware Architecture

The architecture based on the N-queen lattice consists of three parts: the reshuffling, data accessing and pipelined matching modules. In the reshuffling module, we rearrange the pixels into smaller buffers for compact storage. Prior to the matching process, the starting addresses of the pixels are computed and the associated pointers are initialized for different buffers. With the starting addresses, we can overlap and pipeline the accessing and matching processes.

3.1 Compact Storage

For each $N\times N$ sub-block within a macroblock, the *N*-queen subsampling process transforms a 2-D $N\times N$ sub-block to a 1-D *N* pixel in a sequential manner, which is desirable for both the software and hardware implementation. To minimize the memory access bandwidth, we propose that separate frame memory buffers need to be allocated for each of the *N* locations. As illustrated in Fig. 3, the pixels located at non-overlapping checking points within a frame are put together to the four smaller buffers, for example, in which the pixels of the same column are moved into the rows of the buffer separately.

One of the special properties of this storage technique is that a macroblock resides in the continuous memory space which is easy to access. If we use a pipelined memory access strategy, a shift of one pixel in each frame buffer represents a spatial shift in *log(N)* pixels in the original frame. Thus, this data storage architecture can facilitate a *log(N)* search strategy easily. Another interesting observation is that each point can be easily accessible sequentially even though the search strategy is hierarchical. It basically provides an elegant solution to improve both search strategy and memory access.

Two approaches are used to store pixels: the row alignment and the column alignment. As illustrated in Fig. 3, the row alignment approach compresses pixels from the consecutive *N* columns together into a row and the column alignment approach compresses pixels from the consecutive *N* rows into a column. Obviously, for each row of the row-aligned buffers, the selected pixels from the same row of the original frame buffer are separated by an offset, which is 4 in Fig. 3. For each column of the row-aligned buffers, the selected pixels from the same column of the original frame are sequentially located. Within the column-aligned buffers, the pixels from the same row of the original frame buffer are sequentially placed in the corresponding rows while the pixels from the same column of the original frame buffer are separately stored in different columns.

3.2 Data Access

In each buffer, the selected pixels can be accessed in two steps: (1) compute the buffer indexes; (2) compute the starting addresses of the initial pixels. In the first step, the buffer index can be retrieved with a table lookup. The table is predetermined based on the specific *N*-queen patterns. For example, the 4×4 block on the left-top corner in Fig. 3 is used to construct such an index table which is defined as:

$$I[4][4] = \{\{4,1,2,3\}, \{2,3,4,1\}, \{1,2,3,4\}, \{3,4,1,2\}\}. \quad (1)$$

The table index is computed as

$$T(x, y)_k = I[(y+Q[k][1]) \bmod 4][(x+Q[k][0]) \bmod 4]. \quad (2)$$

where $k = 0,\ldots,3$.

The coordinates (x, y) represent the current locations of the blocks in the current frame and the function $Q[][]$ represents the offsets of the selected pixels in the *N*-queen pattern from the position (0,0) of the block with the coordinates (x, y). For example, the matrix of the offsets is defined as

$$Q[4][2] = \{\{1,0\}, \{0,2\}, \{2,3\}, \{3,1\}\}. \quad (3)$$

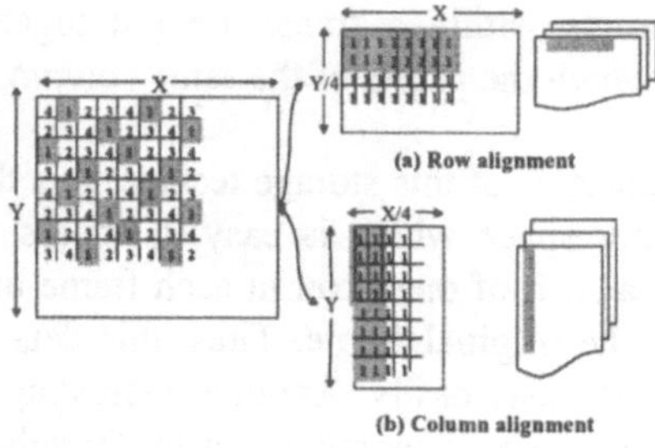

Fig. 3. The compact storages of the 4-queen pattern

In the second step, the starting addresses of the pixels within the indexed buffer $T(x, y)_k$ are computed as the following. For the row-alignment and column-alignment buffers, the addresses are computed as

$$col_k = (x + Q[k][0]),\ row_k = \lfloor (y + Q[k][1])/4 \rfloor, \quad (4)$$

and

$$col_k = \lfloor (x + Q[k][0])/4 \rfloor,\ row_k = (y + Q[k][1]), \quad (5)$$

respectively.

3.3 Parallel Block Matching

Based on our storage architecture, the continuous pixels in a row can be moved in a batch fashion from the buffer into a wide register of multiple bytes depending on the processor. For example, two registers of 64 bits can store 4 pixels from the current and reference blocks. Upon completion of the distortion computation, the reference register only needs to access next 64 bits that are located sequentially to implement a shift of four pixels in search points. Thus, our data storage structure can easily support pipelined memory access. The register with the 4 pixels can be processed in parallel. With the sequential nature of the storage, the data retrieval and the matching can be overlapped in a pipelined fashion.

A parallel matching algorithm is used for a group of the pixels within the search windows. Assume that the search range is 32×32 and the matching block has the size 16×16. Assume that several 64-bits or two 32 bits registers are available and each pixel is stored in 16 bits. For each operation, 4 pixels at the same row can be matched simultaneously. For the row-aligned buffers, the 16 pixels on the first column of the buffer can be placed into multiple registers. To process the next check point, the contents inside the overlapping 3 registers can be kept and the content of the first register is updated from the next 4 pixels in the same column. The same operations can be employed for each checking point at each row within the search window. Similarly, in the case of the column-aligned buffers, the 16 pixels at the first row of the buffer can be placed into multiple registers. When the matching process moves to the next checking points, the contents inside the overlapping 3 registers can be kept and the content of the first register is updated from the next 4 pixels at the same row. That is, the matching processes used for the column-aligned buffers are identical to the processes used for the transpose of the row-aligned buffers. The same operations are executed for the four buffers to find the motion vectors. Both the row-aligned buffer and the column-aligned buffers have high reusability and no overhead for collecting pixels in each step. Thus, either approach is useful to provide a pipelined memory access for parallel block matching.

4 Experimental Results

In our simulation, we use the MPEG-4 reference software and the distortion measure is Mean Absolute Difference (MAD), which is computed for a macroblock of size 16×16 and a search range of size 32×32.

The coding efficiency is analyzed based on the four parameters: sequences, sampling patterns, search strategies, and bit rates. We follow the recommended testing conditions as prescribed by the MPEG committee [1].

As for the sampling patterns, we use four patterns as described in Fig.1. The Full pattern ('F') selects all of the pixels in the current block. The Quarter pattern ('Q') is described in [3]. The 4-Queen ('4') pattern is constructed by tiling multiple small 4-Queen patterns for each 16×16 macroblock. The 8-Queen ('8') pattern is constructed by tiling similar to the 4-Queen pattern. Additionally, the two-layers recursive scheme ('4R') employs the same 4-Queen pattern at both the block layer and pixel layer.

For the search strategy, we used full search and two other techniques. The two approaches were adopted by the MPEG-4 committee which are often referred to as Motion Vector Field Adaptive Search Technique (MVFAST) [1] and Predictive Motion Vector Field Adaptive Search Technique (PMVFAST) [2].

In our table, MVFAST approach is denoted as 'MV' while the PMVFAST approach is 'PMV'. In Table 1, the first symbol denotes the search strategy and the remaining symbols denote the sampling pattern. For example, the notation 'PMV_8' represents the block motion vector estimation using PMVFAST approach and 8-queen pixel pattern. The bit rates (BR) are computed in kbps, the frame rates are represented in frames per second 'Fps', and the search range is denoted as 'SA'. The column 'PSNRY' denotes the average PSNR for the luminance. The 'ChkPt' indicates the actual number of checking points used. The 'Pixels' means the exact number of pixels for each checking point. The final column 'Ratio' is the improvement in speed as compared to the Full Search.

Table 1 demonstrates the performance for different testing conditions. Experimental results show that for various bit rates, frame rates, and picture sizes, the *N*-queen patterns has negligible degradation in video quality. For slow motion video such as 'Container' the loss in PSNR is less than 0.1 dB. For fast motion video, the loss in PSNR is less than 0.45 dB at worst. The 4-Queen pattern is always better than the Quarter pattern and the 8-Queen pattern is almost equivalent in PSNR. This is because the quarter pattern lacks half of the coverage in the vertical, horizontal and diagonal directions. When the search strategy is Full Search, the video quality is degraded more by *N*-queen patterns. The degradation may come from the fact that the no predictive vector is used as the other two approaches [1], [2].

It is more advantageous to use the recursive structure '4R' for larger picture size such as CCIR601 format. This is because the 16×16 block corresponds to 32×32 block at CCIR-601 resolution. Less spatial luminance variation occurs at larger picture size.

5 Conclusions

This paper has presented a fast and simple pixel decimation technique using *N*-queen patterns for the block based motion estimation. The advantages are multiple. The first obvious advantage is the reduction in computational complexity and memory bandwidth by a factor of *N*. The *N*-queen lattice is randomized and exhaustive in the vertical, horizontal and diagonal directions. Interestingly, such randomized lattice can be stored compactly with a sequential pipelined buffer access as demonstrated in this paper. Our architecture also facilitates parallel processing. The recursive nature of the *N*-queen sampling lattice has significant implications when the block is expanded to a picture for global motion estimation or sprite generation. With improvement in speed by a factor of *N*, our experimental results show no significant degradation in PSNR and have consistent performance for extensive tests as recommended by the MPEG committee.

References

1. Alexis M. Tourapis, Oscar C. Au, and Ming L. Liou, ore experiment on block based motion estimation, " *ISO/IEC JTC1/SC29/WG11 MPEG2000/M5867*, Mar. 2000.
2. Shan Zhu and K. -K. Ma, new diamond search algorithm for fast block-matching motion estimation," *IEEE Trans. Image Processing*, pp.287-290, vol.9, no.2, Feb. 2000.
3. M. Bierling, isplacement estimation by hierarchical block matching, " *Proc. SPIE Conf. Visual Commun. Processing'88*, vol. 1001, pp.942-951, 1988.
4. B. Liu and A. Zaccarin, ew fast algorithms for the estimation of block motion vector, " *IEEE Trans. Circuits and Systems for Video Technology*, pp.148-157, vol.3, no.2, Apr. 1993.
5. Y.-L. Chan and W.-C. Siu, ew adaptive pixel decimation for block motion vector estimation, " *IEEE Trans. Circuits and Systems for Video Technology*, pp.113-118, vol.6, no.1, Feb. 1996.
6. Y.K. Wang. Y.Q. Wang, and H. Kuroda, globally adaptive pixel-decimation algorithm for block-motion estimation, " *IEEE Tran. Circuits and Systems for Video Technology*, pp.1006-1011, vol.10, no. 6, Sept. 2000.

Table 1. The performance of the four pixel patterns and recursive structure, the three search strategies and the various video sequences on different testing conditions.

Sequence	Method	PSNRY	PSNRU	PSNRV	Δ PSN	ChkPt	Pixe	Ratio
Container QCIF BR=10 Fps=7.5 SA=16	Full Search	29.75	37.38	36.37		7501824	256	1
	Full_Q	29.60	37.22	36.36	-0.15	7501824	64	4
	Full_4	29.74	37.34	36.40	-0.01	7501824	64	4
	Full_8	29.31	37.19	36.08	-0.44	7501824	32	8
	MV_F	29.78	37.49	36.57	0.03	33436	256	224
	MV_Q	29.71	37.62	36.63	-0.04	35229	64	852
	MV_4	29.70	37.52	36.62	-0.05	33336	64	900
	MV_8	29.72	37.43	36.58	-0.03	34705	32	1729
	PMV_F	29.71	37.39	36.57	-0.04	24726	256	303
	PMV_Q	29.77	37.50	36.50	0.02	24682	64	1216
	PMV_4	29.77	37.63	36.52	0.02	23782	64	1262
	PMV_8	29.73	37.56	36.57	-0.02	23884	32	2522
Foreman CIF BR=112 Fps=10 SA=16	Full Search	30.05	36.73	37.49		40144896	256	1
	Full_Q	29.51	36.47	37.30	-0.54	40144896	64	4
	Full_4	29.79	36.70	37.49	-0.26	40144896	64	4
	Full_8	29.33	36.43	37.06	-0.72	40144896	32	8
	MV_F	29.89	36.88	37.66	-0.16	473299	256	85
	MV_Q	29.61	36.80	37.72	-0.44	446359	64	360
	MV_4	29.83	36.82	37.73	-0.22	453247	64	354
	MV_8	29.60	36.80	37.66	-0.45	444744	32	722
	MV_4R	29.06	36.56	37.41	-0.99	447622	16	1435
	PMV_F	29.97	36.94	37.76	-0.08	378736	256	106
	PMV_Q	29.66	36.83	37.71	-0.39	364766	64	440
	PMV_4	29.88	36.91	37.82	-0.17	366304	64	438
	PMV_8	29.65	36.71	37.65	-0.40	364337	32	881
	PMV_4R	29.10	36.54	37.35	-0.85	374118	16	1717
Stefan CCIR 601 BR=1M Fps=10 SA=16	Full Search	26.43	32.60	32.87		136857600	256	1
	MV_F	26.58	33.07	33.38	0.15	1584656	256	86
	MV_Q	26.38	32.87	33.18	-0.05	1376083	64	398
	MV_4	26.55	33.05	33.39	0.12	1397127	64	392
	MV_8	26.47	32.99	33.30	0.04	1365344	32	802
	MV_4R	26.24	32.76	33.02	-0.19	1385464	16	1581
	PMV_F	26.57	33.03	33.37	0.14	1414828	256	97
	PMV_Q	26.35	32.84	33.13	-0.08	1222771	64	448
	PMV_4	26.54	33.04	33.36	0.11	1251042	64	438
	PMV_8	26.46	32.98	33.28	0.03	1227809	32	892
	PMV_4	26.23	32.73	33.00	-0.20	1244059	16	1760

Improved MPEG-4 Visual Texture Coding Using Perceptual Dithering for Transparent Image Coding

Chung-Neng Wang[1], *Chi-Min Liu*[1], *and Tihao Chiang*[2]*

[1] Dept. and Institute of Computer Science and Information Engineering, National Chiao Tung University, Hsinchu, 30050, Taiwan
{cnwang, cmliu}@csie.nctu.edu.tw

[2] Dept. and Institute of Electronics Engineering, National Chiao Tung University (NCTU), Hsinchu, 30050, Taiwan
tchiang@cc.nctu.edu.tw

Abstract. MPEG-4 VTC provides coding efficiency using the zerotree entropy coding (ZTC) to remove the statistical redundancy among the coefficients within each wavelet tree. To improve the coding efficiency of ZTC, we propose an MPEG-4 compliant perceptual dithering coding (PDC) approach. In the ZTC technique, there is a parent-children relationship within each wavelet tree while the redundancy among the sibling nodes of different spatial orientations at the same frequency level is not exploited. The PDC approach perturbs the magnitudes of the sibling nodes for each wavelet tree according to the statistical distribution of AC coefficients within the subband at the same frequency level to achieve more energy compaction. The level of perturbation of each wavelet coefficient is constrained by the noise tolerance levels according to the perception model. For the same visual quality, we found that the PDC approach achieves bit savings over MPEG-4 VTC by 11~30%.

1 Introduction

MPEG-4 Visual Texture Coding (VTC) is a part of the MPEG-4 video specification [1]. MPEG-4 VTC contains three key elements including Discrete Wavelet Transform (DWT), zerotree entropy coding (ZTC) and adaptive arithmetic coding. The DWT decomposes an image into several logarithmically partitioned subbands as shown in Fig. 1. The subbands contain several levels of spatial frequency and various orientations for details such as texture and edge information. Since the wavelet coefficients are spatially localized, the coefficients at the same co-located subbands from lower frequency level to higher frequency level can be arranged as a wavelet tree. The ZTC is based on the strong correlation between the magnitudes of wavelet coefficients at different frequency levels while the scanning order can be adapted to further improve the correlation. Thus, the probability of the zero symbols is increased for each wavelet tree, which leads to higher compression. The ZTC exploits the correlations among levels of the wavelet tree but the correlation among the sibling nodes are not considered. In Fig. 1 we can observe that there is strong correlation among the wavelet coefficients at the sibling nodes. Thus, it is possible to improve the

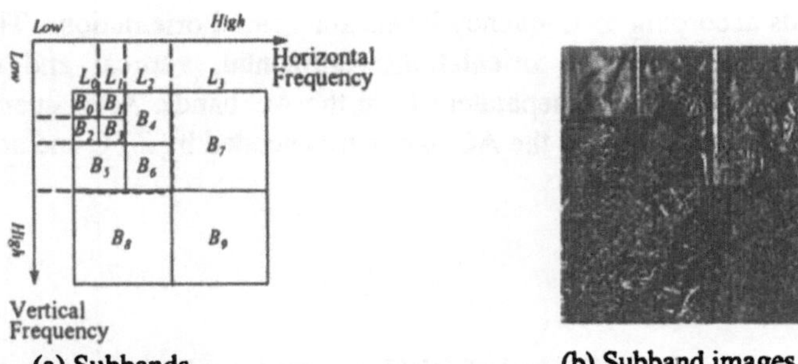

Fig. 1. The logarithmically partitioned subbands and wavelet trees of a 2-D image using the DWT. The symbol B_k denotes the k-th subband and the symbol L_k denotes the k-th level of the wavelet coefficients.

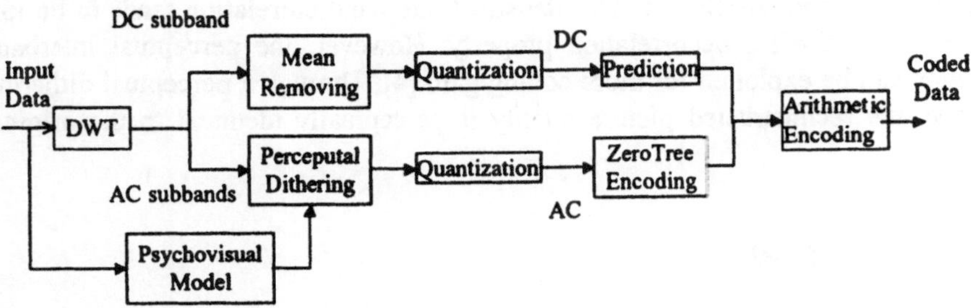

Fig. 2. Flow-chart of encoder and decoder for perceptual dithering coding

coding efficiency by removing the redundancy of each wavelet tree through preprocessing. For example, the edge-based vector quantization (EBVQ) [3] was proposed to provide better compression using vector quantization. The EBVQ technique requires edge-based codebooks and training session before the encoding process. It also requires decoder modification.

To remove the same redundancy while maintaining compatibility with MPEG-4 decoder, we proposed a perceptual dithering approach [4]. The key innovation is that we can use perceptual dithering to represent the original image with a visually equivalent image by exploiting the redundancy among sibling nodes and exploiting the fact that human visual system is less sensitive at the edge areas.

We develop a new technique to modify the statistical distribution of the AC coefficients such that the entropy is reduced while considering the psychovisual effects [5], [6]. Several images were tested to compare the proposed PDC and MPEG-4 VTC. Only the luminance component of color images and grayscale images were observed. To maintain the same visual quality, our results show that the PDC achieved bitrate reduction for about 11~30%.

2 Perceptual Dithering Coding

The encoder of the MPEG-4 VTC includes four basic modules: DWT, quantization process, ZTC and arithmetic coding. The DWT coefficients are grouped into DC band and AC bands according to frequency levels and spatial orientations. The DWT decomposes an image into three orientations: horizontal, vertical and diagonal directions. The DC band is coded separately from the AC bands. After quantization, the DC band is DPCM encoded and the AC bands are encoded by ZTC and arithmetic code.

2.1 Rationale

Fig. 1 (a) shows a logarithmically scaled DWT subbands and Fig. 1 (b) shows an instance of the wavelet decomposition that includes 7 subbands. There are similar patterns for the AC subbands which prompt the existence of the crossband correlation.

The correlations can be classified as the statistical interband correlation and the perceptual interband correlation. The statistical interband correlation tends to be low because of the DWT's decorrelation property. However, the perceptual interband correlation can be exploited for more coding gain [4]. Through a perceptual dithering technique, the reconstructed picture quality is perceptually identical to the original image.

2.2 Perceptual Model

The block diagram of the proposed PDC is shown in Fig. 2. In addition to the modules of the MPEG-4 VTC, the PDC adds the two more modules including the psychovisual model and the perceptual dithering.

For each wavelet coefficient, the perceptual model is constructed based on the visibility threshold, which is referred to as the pixel perceptual tolerable error (PPTE). The derivation of the PPTE, follows the approach as described in [5], which is based on both the background luminance perceptibility and the spatial masking effects.

Let the original image be the subband image at level *-1*. The full-band JND profile (JND_{fb}) is initially assigned as the PPTE for the subband image at level *-1*. For a gray-level still image with size $H \times W$,

$$PPTE_{0,-1}(m,n) = JND_{fb}(m,n), \; for \; 0 \le m \le H\text{-}1, \; 0 \le n \le W\text{-}1. \tag{1}$$

For the octave representation with L levels, the $PPTE_{q,l}(m,n)$ at position (m,n) of the q-th subband at level l is generated from the previous level in the following form:

$$PPTE^2_{q,l+1}(m,n) = \left[\sum_{i=0}^{1} \sum_{j=0}^{1} PPTE^2_{0,l}(i+m\cdot 2, j+m\cdot 2) \right] \cdot w_{q,l}, \tag{2}$$

for q=*0,..,3*, l=*0,..,L-1*, $0 \le m < \frac{H}{2(l+1)}$, and $0 \le m < \frac{W}{2(l+1)}$. $w_{q,l}$ is the perceptual weight of the q-th subband at level l. The perceptual weights [5] have been assigned as the inverse of the normalized spatial-frequency sensitivity of the human eyes to spatial frequencies in the q-th subband at frequency level l according to the MTF response curve [6].

Thus, the PPTE of each wavelet coefficient is adapted for the perceptually transparent coding of image. Assuming the transparent coding is not achievable for some applications requiring low bandwidth, some coding approach involving with minimally noticeable distortion (MND) would be required. For the low bit rate coding with minimally visible distortion, the visibility threshold of the minimally noticeable distortion is quantified as a multiple of the PPTE with the approaches in [5].

2.3 Perceptually Dithering

The dithering process moves the energy of the wavelet coefficients from the sibling subbands into a specific subband at the same frequency level. As shown in Fig. 3, the energy is concentrated by moving the wavelet coefficients toward the target vector V_{max}, which is the eigenvector with the maximum eigenvalue for the wavelet subbands at the particular frequency level. Obviously, most of the energy spread over the wavelet coefficients within the sibling subbands at the same frequency level will be concentrated at less wavelet coefficients. However, the energy movement process is controlled by the associated visibility threshold to keep the noise imperceptible. Thus, the perceptual dithering can compact the energy of the sibling subbands into the specified subband at the same frequency level without varying the perceptual fidelity.

As shown in [4], the dithering process consists of three phases. First, the autocorrelation matrix for the subband images is calculated. Second, the target vector V_{max} is evaluated. Third, each subband vector $S(m,n)$ is rotated to the vector nearest to the eigenvector $Vmax$ with a rotation quantity constrained by the rectangular box. The third phase involves the derivation of the desired vector, which depends upon the relative location between the box and the eigenvector. Trivially, as the eigenvector penetrates the box, the desired vector is identical to the eigenvector. As the eignevector does not penetrate the box, the desired vector is derived through the following steps.

1). Evaluate the first coordinate using the equations that describe the box surfaces.
2). Project the vectors $S(m,n)$ and V_{max} onto the surface from step 1 and reduce the problem to two-dimension.
3). In the projected plane, evaluate the remaining coordinates using the two projected vectors and the equations indicating the box boundaries.

Note that the energy of the vector $S(m,n)$ is conserved even though the vector was dithered. The energy is compacted with this dithering process so that the entropy is minimized. Assume that the vector S of the original coefficients is dithered and subsequently decorrelated into the vector S_Λ, for which the autocorrelation matrix is diagonalized. Under the same distortion that $D(\theta)=D(\theta_S)=D(\theta_{S_\Lambda})$, the bit saving per coefficient theoretically achievable can be computed as

$$G_{S\to S_\Lambda}=R_S(\theta_S)-R_{S_\Lambda}(\theta_{S_\Lambda})=\frac{1}{2}\log_2\left(\prod_{k=1}^{N}\sigma_k^2\right)^{\frac{1}{N}}-\frac{1}{2}\log_2\left(\prod_{k=1}^{N}\lambda_k\right)^{\frac{1}{N}} \tag{3}$$

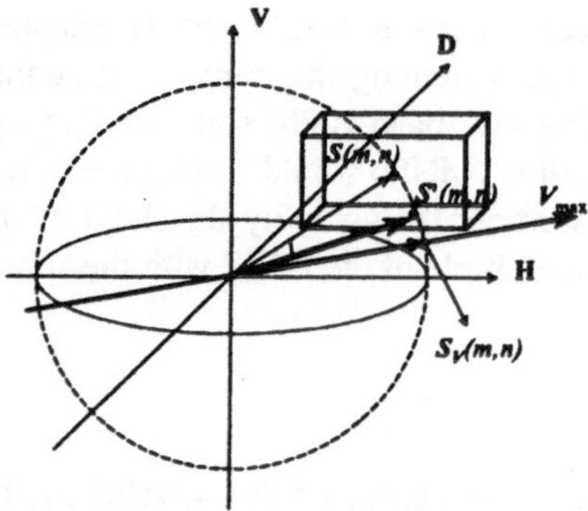

Fig. 3. Graphical illustration of the dithering along the eigenvector with maximum eigenvalue [4]. Where H, V, and D denote the spatial orientations respectively. *Vmax* is the target axis for energy compaction form the original vector *S(m,n)* to the dithered vector *S'(m,n)*. The box constrains the amnlitude the vector *S(m,n)* allowable to be changed without the nerreiving of

where σ_k^2 is the diagonal element of the autocorrelation matrix for S and λ_k is the diagonal element of the autocorrelation matrix for S_Λ.

Thus, for the same visual quality, the PDC reduced the bitrate with more energy compaction across the sibling nodes of every wavelet tree in the image.

2.4 Quantization Constraints

To prevent the coding distortion from being visible, the PDC should cope with the errors due to the quantization and the perceptual dithering processes. Let $S=[S_1,\ldots,S_k]^T$ be the vector of the wavelet coefficients and $\tilde{S}$ be a scalar quantization version of S. For each $n \in Z$, the quantized coefficients are either

$$\tilde{S}_i = \begin{cases} \left(n+\frac{1}{2}\right)\Delta_i, & S_i \in \left[n\Delta_i, (n+1)\Delta_i\right) \\ n\Delta_i, & S_i \in \left[\left(n-\frac{1}{2}\right)\Delta_i, \left(n+\frac{1}{2}\right)\Delta_i\right) \end{cases} \quad (4)$$

for any set of positive, finite quantization step sizes Δ_i , $i=1,\ldots,k$. The first quantization type in Eq. (1) is adopted by the MPEG-4 VTC. Thus, the quantized noise by the VTC is at most half of the quantization step size. Since the total noise comes from both the quantization and the dithering processes. Thus, the impact of the quantization noise on the reconstructed quality should be considered in computing the practical threshold. In order to maintain identical fidelity, the threshold for perceptual dithering is equivalent to the difference between the PPTE and the weighted value of the maximum quantization noise. The effect of the rounding errors should be included when integer representation is adopted for wavelet coefficients. Thus, the magnitude of each coefficient is only allowed to be modified within the following threshold

$$B_{q,l} = S_{q,l} - S'_{q,l} \le PPTE_{q,l} - \alpha\left(\frac{\Delta_l}{2}\right) - d_{rounding} \quad (5)$$

Table 1. The performance of PDC over MPEG-4 VTC with various quantization stepsize (Δ) and different weights (α) of quantization distortion for the images, Akiyo and Lena.

Akiyo	Δ	α	Bitrate			Bit saving (%)
			DC	AC	Total	
MPEG4	1	1	9023	322144	331167	
PDC	1	1	9023	213534	222557	32.80
	1	0.5	9023	211372	220395	33.45
	1	0	9023	209917	218940	33.89
MPEG4	2	1	9023	187760	196783	
PDC	2	1	9023	149873	158896	19.25
	2	0	9023	145500	154523	21.48
MPEG4	3	1	9023	129073	138096	
PDC	3	1	9023	112205	121228	12.21
	3	0.67	9023	110974	119997	13.11

Lena	Δ	α	Bitrate			Bit saving (%)
			DC	AC	Total	
MPEG4	1	1	30352	1142611	1172963	
PDC	1	1	30352	985576	1015928	13.39
	1	0.5	30352	969050	999402	14.80
	1	0	30352	962858	993210	15.32
MPEG4	2	1	30352	830837	861189	
PDC	2	1	30352	741244	771596	10.40
	2	0	30352	710948	741300	13.92
MPEG4	3	1	30352	638985	669337	
PDC	3	1	30352	570896	601248	10.17
	3	0.67	30352	594568	594568	11.17

where the $d_{rounding}$ equals to 1.0 here. The weighting value α indicates the percentage of the permissible quantization noise for modifying a coefficient to move energy around while keeping the degradation imperceptible.

3 Experimental Results

Both the PDC and the MPEG-4 VTC are tested. Table 1 shows the rate-distortion performance of the PDC and the MPEG-4 PDC techniques. To assess the visual quality of the reconstructed images and to evaluate the coding efficiency of the proposed PDC, a quality measure based on human visual system is used instead of the typical peak signal-to-nose ratio (PSNR). Thus, a fidelity measure is used to quantify the subjective quality of the reconstructed image. The subjective evaluation is processed in the wavelet domain, which can be converted to be the quality assessment in the spatial domain as in [5]. The new criterion, named as peak singal-to-perceptual-noise for subbands (PSPNRsub), is defined as

$$PSPNRsub = 10\log_{10}\left(255^2 / E[e^2]\right), \tag{6}$$

$$e_{q,l}(m,n) = \begin{cases} 0, & \text{if } |d_{q,l}(m,n)| \le PPTE_{q,l}(m,n) \\ e'_{q,l}(m,n), & \text{otherwise} \end{cases} \tag{7}$$

where $d_{q,l}(m,n) = S_{q,l}(m,n) - S'_{q,l}(m,n)$ is the coding error and the $e'_{q,l}(m,n) = |d_{q,l}(m,n| - PPTE_{q,l}(m,n)$ indicates the amount of the perceptible error. In our simulation using the MPEG-4 VTC with PDC, the reconstructed images are perceptually lossless, which was confirmed by evaluating the quality of each reconstructed image with the criterion in Eq. (6) and the subjective comparison on computer screen. Moreover, the DWT employed the default filter, as defined in the MPEG-4 VTC, with the filter length (9,3) and in integer type. The MPEG Single Quantization scheme [1] was used for all of the simulations.

The notation 'MPEG4' indicates the performance of the MPEG-4 VTC while the 'PDC' indicates the performance of PDC. The performance of the proposed PDC will be analyzed based on factors including the quantization step sizes, the weights of the quantization distortion. We used several grayscale images and color images in YUV format for testing. For the color images, only the luminance component (Y) was processed by the PDC. This paper illustrated only the results for the images in CIF (352x288) and YUV format, named as Akiyo. The result of the image with the size 512x512 and in grayscale format, named as Lena, was illustrated in Figure 4. For visually transparent coding of an image, a finer quantizer is used that the PDC achieved the bit savings about 11~30% on the average. For a coarse quantizer, the gain on the average are about 1~6% in bit reduction. As the quantization stepsize is increased, the coding gain is reduced since most of the AC coefficients, which have the energy smaller than the quantization scale, are zeroed out through quantization. In Table 1 we demonstrate the influences of the weighting values on the performance of the PDC. The difference of the coding gains with different weights indicates that an optimal weighting can be used to improve the coding efficiency of the proposed PDC.

4 Conclusions

This paper has presented a perceptual dithering coding (PDC) technique to improve the MPEG-4 VTC for images with transparent quality. The performance of the PDC is analyzed with two factors: the quantization step sizes and the weighting of the quantization distortion. The PDC achieves more coding efficiency due to the removal of the statistical redundancy and the perceptual redundancy that exists among wavelet coefficients. The coding gain is less at lower bitrates due to coarse quantization. We present an MPEG-4 compatible preprocessing approach that achieves significant improvements on coding efficiency by exploiting the perceptual correlation between the sibling subband nodes within the zero tree at the same frequency level for coding of images with transparent visual quality.

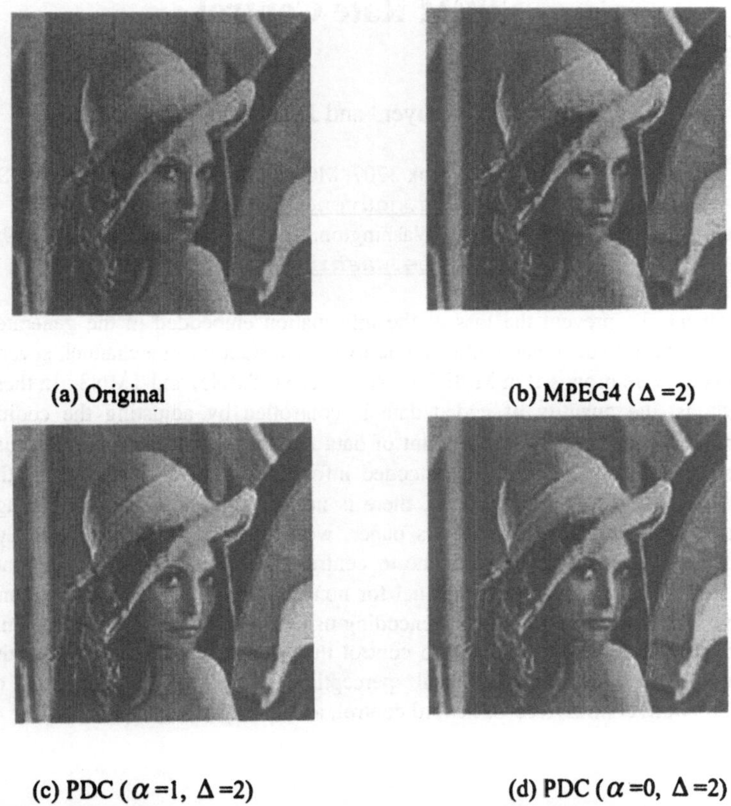

(a) Original (b) MPEG4 (Δ =2)

(c) PDC (α =1, Δ =2) (d) PDC (α =0, Δ =2)

Fig. 4. The reconstructions of the image with the size 512x512 and in grayscale format, named as Lena, through MPEG-4 VTC and the perceptual dithering coding. The quantization step size (Δ) used is 2 and the two weighting values (α) are used for perceptually dithering.

References

1. MPEG Video Group, "Information technology—Coding of audio-visual objects—Part 2: Visual & Amendment 1:Visual extension," *International Standard*, ISO/IEC JTC1/SC 29/WG 11 14496-2: 1999/Amd. 1:2000(E), Jan. 2000.
2. J. M. Shapiro, "Embedded image coding using zerotrees of wavelet coefficients," *IEEE Trans. Signal Processing*, vol. 41, no. 12, pp. 3445-3462, Dec., 1993.
3. N. Mohsenian and N. M. Nasrabadi, "Edge-based subband VQ techniques for images and video," *IEEE Trans. Circuits Systems for Video Techn.y*, vol. 4, no. 1, pp. 53-67, Feb. 1994.
4. C.-M. Liu and C.-N. Wang, "Perceptual interband correlation for octave subband coding of images," in *Proc. ISCAS* (Monterey, LA, USA), vol.4, May 1998, pp.166 –169.
5. C. H. Chou and Y. C. Li, "A perceptually tuned subband image coder based on the measure of just-noticeable-distortion profile," *IEEE Trans. Circuits Systems for Video Techn.*, vol. 5, no 6, pp. 467-476, Dec. 1995.
6. R. J. Safranek and J. D. Johnston, "A perceptually tuned subband image coder with image dependent quantization and post-quantization data compression," in *Proc. IEEE ICASSP*, vol. 3, 1989, pp. 1945-1948.

SPEM Rate Control

Anthony G. Nguyen[1] and Jenq-Neng Hwang[2]

[1]The Boeing Company P.O. Box 3707, MC 02-UT, Seattle, WA 98124 USA
Anthony.g.nguyen@boeing.com
[2]IP lab, Dept. of EE, University of Washington, Box 352500, Seattle, WA 98195 USA
hwang@ee.washington.edu

Abstract. To prevent the loss of the information embedded in the generated variable bit rate data that is transmitted over a constant bit rate channel, several methods were proposed in MPEG TMN5, H.263+ TMN5, and TMN8. In these methods, the quantity of coded data is controlled by adjusting the coding parameters according to the amount of data remaining in the buffer. Because this control is based on the past coded information and does not reflect the nature of the image being coded, there is no assurance that sufficient image quality will be obtained. In this paper, we present a Smooth Pursuit Eye Movement (SPEM) coding scheme to control the generated variable bit rate data over a constant bit rate channel for non real-time video applications and show the improvements over the encoding using the TMN H263+ codec. This can be considered as a method to control the bit rate in accordance with the characteristics of human visual perception using the combination of feedforward control, feed-backward control, and model-based approaches.

1 Introduction

Rate control is an essential part of most video encoders. Most video standards do not specify how to control the bit rate, the exact rate control of the encoder is generally left open to user specification. Ideally, the encoder should balance the quality of the decoded images with the channel capacity. This challenge is compounded by the fact that video sequences contain widely varying content and motion. The bit-rate control problem can be formulated as follows: given the desired bit-rate and the video sequences with a certain complexity, how do we efficiently encode the video sequences to achieve the highest quality (objective or subjective) of the encoded video. The problem of optimal bit allocation has been researched extensively in the literature. It remains a very active area of research in visual communication.

In this paper, we take into account the dependency of the frames in a video sequence and macroblocks within each frame together with video quality measures based on human visual perception. We also employ a rate-distortion framework and model-based approach to formalize the problem of optimizing the encoder operation on a macroblock by macroblock basis within each frame of a video sequence. In addition the combination of both feedforward [1] and feedbackward [4] bit rate control will be used to solve this optimization problem.

This paper is organized as follows. In section 2, we provide a Lagrangian-based solution for an arbitrary set of quantizers. We also present constraints imposed by the encoder and decoder buffers on both the encoded and transmitted bit rates in order to prevent the decoder buffer from overflowing or underflowing. In addition, we examine how channel constraints can further restrict the encoded and transmitted bit rates. In section 3, we propose our rate control for both frame and macroblock based on human visual perception. We apply rate distortion to the encoder operation using lagrange method and model-based approach on macroblock basis within each frame of a video sequence. The Simulation results are presented in section 4. Finally, section 5 provides a summary, and concludes the paper with our future works.

2 Optimization solution & buffer analysis

In section 2.1, we show how rate distortion formulation is applicable to our proposed rate control at macroblock layer, and give a solution based on Lagrange multipliers.

2.1 Lagrangian-based solution

The classical rate distortion optimal bit allocation problem consists of minimizing the average distortion D of a collection of signal elements subject to a total bit rate constraint R_c. Let's denote $r_k(q_k)$, $d_k(q_k)$, and q_k be the rate, distortion and quantizer of the kth macroblock in a picture. The quantization parameters for coding M macroblocks consist of a quantization state vector $\vec{Q} = (q_1, q_2, \ldots q_k)$. If the number of target bits R_T is given to a picture, then the optimal rate control is finding the state vector $\vec{Q}$, which minimizes the overall distortion.

$$D(\vec{Q}) = \sum_{k=1}^{M} d_k(q_k), \text{ Subject to } R(\vec{Q}) = \sum_{k=1}^{M} r_k(q_k) \le R_T$$

The constrained problem can be solved using Lagrange unconstraint problem:

$$J(\vec{Q}^*) = \sum_{k=1}^{M} \arg\min[d_k(q_k) + \lambda r_k(q_k)] = \sum_{k=1}^{M} J_k(q_k^*)$$ Where $J_k(q_k)$ is the Lagrange cost function for the kth macroblock and q_k^* is the optimal QP which minimizes $J_k(q_k)$ associated with the optimal Lagrange multiplier λ^*. Let Q be a set of allowed QPs. In the H263+ [3] video coding, the set Q consists of positive integer from 1 to 31 and $\vec{Q}^*$ is the set $q_k^* \in$ Q.

2.2 Buffer Analysis

In this section, we present the relationship between encoder and decoder buffers. Unless the instantaneous coding rate is constant, the encoder buffer is needed to smooth the variable output rate and provide a constant rate output.

We define $R_e(t)$, $R_c(t)$, and $R_d(t)$ to be the number of bits output by the encoder, channel bit rate, and decoder at time t respectively. $B_e(t)$, $B_d(t)$ are the instantaneous buffer fullness of the encoder and decoder. B_e^{max} , B_d^{max} are the maximum size of the encoder and decoder buffers. The delay from the encoder buffer input to the decoder buffer output, exclusive of channel delay, is L seconds. Next we present the conditions necessary to guarantee that the buffers at the video encoder and decoder do not underflow or overflow. Given B_e^{max} , the encoder buffer never overflows if:

$$0 \le B_e(t) \le B_e^{max} \tag{2.2.1}$$

If underflow or overflow never occurs then the encoder buffer fullness $B_e(t)$ is given:

$$B_e(t) = \int_0^t [R_e(\tau) - R_c(\tau)] d\tau \tag{2.2.2}$$

To ensure that the decoder buffer never underflows or overflows, the buffer fullness of the decoder must satisfy the following equation:

$$0 \le B_d(t) \le B_d^{max} \tag{2.2.3}$$

If underflow or overflow never occurs in either the encoder or decoder buffers, then the decoder buffer fullness $B_d(t)$ is given by:

$$B_d(t) = \begin{cases} \int_0^t R_c(\tau) d\tau & \tau \langle L \\ \int_0^t R_c(\tau) d\tau - \int_0^{t-L} R_d(\tau) d\tau & \tau \rangle L \end{cases} \tag{2.2.4}$$

Next we discretize all equations using uncoded frame period and we obtain the following expressions for the buffer constraint, the number of bits per coded frame for a given channel rate and the channel rate constraint:

$$0 \le B_d^i = B_d^0 - B_e^i \;\Rightarrow\; B_e^i \le B_d^0 = LR \tag{2.2.5}$$

$$R_c^i - B_e^{i-1} \le R_e^i \le R_c^i + B_e^{max} - B_e^{i-1} \tag{2.2.6}$$

$$B_e^{i-1} + R_e^i \ge R_c^i \ge B_e^{i-1} - B_e^{max} + R_e^i \tag{2.2.7}$$

Where R_e^i is the number of bits generated by the encoder and B_d^i is the decoder buffer fullness at frame i, B_e^i is the encoder buffer fullness after encoding frame i, B_d^0 is the initial fullness of the decoder buffer, R is the constant channel rate. The encoder buffer overflow and underflow can be prevented by constraining either the encoder bit rate per frame period as depicted by equation (2.2.6) or the transmitted bit rate per frame period as indicated by equation (2.2.7). From (2.2.5), if we choose

$B_e^{\max} = LR$ to ensure encoder buffer never overflows then the decoder buffer will never underflow. The decoder is much faster than the channel rate, therefore to prevent the decoder buffer overflow, the decoder buffer size can be chosen solely to ensure that it can handle the initial buffer fullness plus the number of bits for one frame (e.g.. $B_d^{\max} = LR$).

In summary, for CBR channel, to ensure the decoder buffer does not overflow or underflow, simply ensure the encoder buffer does not underflow or overflow.

Next we will discuss the choice of the delay L and show the relationship between the delay and the variable bit rate of the encoder. The encoder buffer fullness is given

$$B_e^i = \sum_{j=1}^{i} R_e^i - iR \leq B_e^{\max} = LR \tag{2.2.8}$$

Equation (2.2.8) indicates the trade-off between the necessary decoder delay and the variability in the number of encoded bits per frame. Because a variable number of bits per frame can provide better image quality, therefore equation (2.2.8) also indicates the trade-off between the allowable decoder delay and the image quality.

In the next section, we explain and present our proposed video encoding methods with the constraints derived in this section.

3 Proposed rate control method

One aspect of human visual perception we have considered in our rate control method is motion tracking ability without loss of spatial resolution, which is called Smooth Pursuit Eye Movement (SPEM) [2]. If the target is moving, our eyes can compensate this motion by SPEMs. The maximum velocity of SPEMs is about 18 to 27 pixels/frame under CCIR-500 [5] test conditions and image height of about 20 cm. Since a human observer is the end user of most video information, a video quality measure should be based on human visual perception for video quality prediction.

In the following sections, we propose non-real-time method to control the bit rate in accordance with human visual perception to improve the visual quality of an encoded video sequence over a constant bit rate channel using the combination of feed forward and backward control and model-based approach.

3.1 Rate control at frame-layer

Figures 3.1.1 shows the functional block diagram of the proposed bit rate control. In the proposed control bit rate, two blocks are added to the feedforward path and feedbackward path of the encoder. The motion analysis block is used to analyze the motion activities of the video sequence. The SPEM Q modifier block uses the motion information provided by Motion Analysis block together with human visual perception to modify the quantization step size of each frame in the video sequence. Thus, the base value of quantization step size for each frame will be calculated according to the line buffer occupancy. Then, based on the motion activity of each frame, the quantization step sizes of the frame will be modified.

Each frame in a video sequence can be categorized into one of 3 motion activity frame types (High, medium, low) depending on the total number moving vectors of the macroblocks in the frame. The ratio of moving blocks to coded blocks is also used to detect scenes where moving blocks dominate in coded blocks. After classifying motion activity frame type for a frame in the video sequence, quantization step sizes are modified for that frame. Let $\Delta Q = Q_{predict} - Q_{previous}$ be the feedback control value for the quantization step size from the previous frame to the present frame. To achieve a constant channel rate and satisfy the constraint of the buffer fullness, the quantization step size of the current frame has to be increased or decreased from the previous frame to adjust the number of bits that will be generated. Based on the human visual perception property SPEM, the current quantization should be calculated as $Q_{current} = Q_{previous} + \alpha * \Delta Q$,. the coefficient α is adjusted depending on the quantization step size in the previous frame. Table 3.1.1.1 summarized the detail how and when to modify the quantization step sizes based on the motion activity. In addition the proposed bit rate control will allocate more bits to those periods of high coding rate. This is because we consider the periods of high coding are the important periods that include the parts that the data wishes to convey, and so allocates more bits to those periods with high motion activity. Figure 3.1.2 shows the flow chart of the proposed rate control. $p_1 B \le R_e^{i} \le p_2 B$ expression is used to calculate the quantization for each frame, Where B is the buffer size and $p_1 = 1/p_2$ with $p_1 \ge 0$ and $p_2 \ge 0$. The $p_1 B$ and $p_2 B$ are established to guard against bit rate undershoot and overshoot, respectively, from the desired channel bit rate. The values of p_1 and p_2 vary from low coding rate to high coding rate periods. This allows more bits be allocated to the high coding rate period.

3.2 Rate control at macroblock layer

After each frame quantization is determined, then we apply rate distortion to the encoder operation on a macroblock basis within each frame of a video sequence. Next, we will use the Lagrange method and model-based approach with human visual perception to minimize the overall distortion incurred in coding one frame with a constraint that the overall bits do not exceed a given number of bits for that frame.

The bit count of macroblock for the low bit rate case can be approximated by:

$$B_i(\sigma^2, Q) = A[K \frac{\sigma^2}{Q^2} F(M_i, M) + C] \tag{3.2.1}$$

A is the number of pixels in a macroblock; K based on the statistics of the specific frame during encoding; σ_i is the variance of the ith macroblock; M_i is the motion activity of the ith macroblock; M is average motion activity of all macroblocks within a frame; $F(M_i, M)$ is a function of M_i and M; C is the average rate (in bits/pixel) to encode the motion vectors and the coder's header and syntax for the frame. The goal is to find an expression for the quantization parameters $Q_1^*, Q_2^*, \ldots, Q_N^*$ that minimize the distortion:

$$D = \frac{1}{N}\sum_{i=1}^{N} \alpha_i^2 \frac{Q_i^2}{12} \text{ and } \alpha_i = \begin{cases} 2\frac{B}{AN}(1-\sigma_i)+\sigma_i & \frac{B}{AN} < 0.5 \\ 1 & otherwise \end{cases} \quad (3.2.2)$$

where N is the number of macroblocks in a frame, α_i is the distortion weight of the ith macroblock, and B is total number of bits for a given frame. Using Lagrange theory, the unconstrained problem can be expressed as follows:

$$Q_1^*, Q_2^*, \ldots, Q_N^*, \lambda^* = \arg\min \frac{1}{N}\Sigma \alpha_i^2 \frac{Q_i^2}{12} + \lambda[\sum_{i=1}^{N} B_i - B] \quad (3.2.3)$$

Replace B_i in eq. 3.2.3 by eq. 3.2.1

$$Q_1^* .., Q_N^*, \lambda^* = \arg\min \frac{1}{N}\Sigma \alpha_i^2 \frac{Q_i^2}{12} + \lambda\left\{\sum_{i=1}^{N} A[K\frac{\sigma^2}{Q^2}F(M_i, M) + C] - B\right\} \quad (3.2.4)$$

By equating the partial derivatives of the right hand side to zero of equation 3.2.4, we obtain the following expression:

$$Q_i^* = \sqrt{\frac{AK}{B-ACN}\frac{\sigma_i}{F(M_i, M)\alpha_i}\Sigma \alpha_i \sigma_i F(M_i, M)} \quad (3.2.5)$$

Figure 3.2.1 is the flow chart for our proposed bit allocation algorithm in the macroblock level. First, we compute the variance and motion activity of the macroblock. Next the quantizer for the ith macroblock will be computed.. Finally compute the model parameters for the ith macroblock and these parameters will be used to encode the next frame.

4 Simulation results

In this section, simulations and subjective assessment are performed in order to confirm the effectiveness of our proposed scheme. Several QCIF sequences are used to test the proposed methods. Due to the space limitation, the only simulation results of the concatenated video sequence of the well-known Suzie and Miss America (Sm) video sequences will be presented in the paper. The other simulation results of the video sequences, which are captured from the movies, will not be included in this paper. We use Telnor's H263 codec (version 3.0) to test the proposed rate control methods. The subjective assessment is carried out under the following viewing conditions: The distance between a viewer and a display L = 20 in. and image size = QCIF. Ten Viewers (5 women and 5 men); Frame rate: 25 frames/sec; Bit rate: 64kbits/s and 32kbits/s.

The Simulation results indicate that our method achieves a bit rate closer to the target rate than H263 TMN (e.g. SPEM=64.17 and 32.10 Kbits/s, TMN=64.37 and

32.23 Kbits/s for 64 and 32 Kbit/s target rates). Also, the average PSNR of the encoded video sequence is higher than (or the virtually the same as) the average PSNR of the encoded sequence using H263 TMN (e.g. SPEM P+I frames PSNR=36.75, 35.94, TMN=36.25, 35.1; SPEM P frames PSNR=37.91, 35.49, TMN=37.93, 35.63). This indicates that re-allocating the bits within a video sequence by our proposed method improves the average PSNR of the video sequence. Fig. 4.1 includes the following items from top to bottom: PSNR luminance plot (64kbits/s); 2 encoded images (left with TMN right with SPEM); PSNR luminance plot (32kbits/s); 2 encoded images; Sum of motion vector.

For the subjective evaluations, more than 50% of the evaluators concluded that the video quality encoded by TMN is less than or equal to the video encoded by the SPEM. For Sm sequence 9 out of 10 said that the TMN encoded sequence quality is less than the encoded sequence using SPEM and one said that they are the same.

Overall, the simulation results indicate that the quality rating of a video sequence is strongly influenced by what the users see in the last several images of the sequence. If the last several images are of good quality, then the rating of the sequence tends to be high and vice versa. Also the quality rating of a video sequence is strongly influenced by what the users see in the high motion activity images.

5 Summary & Conclusion

The simulation results and subjective assessment indicate that our proposed rate control scheme encodes the video sequences with better PSNR and improves the subjective quality of the encoded video sequences.. The proposed method is effective when the variation in coding rate is large. Considering that video material usually consists of low-coding rate scenes in which the camera is fixed and subject movement is slight and high-coding rate scenes in which either the camera is moving or subject movement is large, the proposed method is expected to be effective in most cases.

Work to be done in the near future includes: 1) SPEM Online rate control. 2) The combination of SPEM for the frame level and Lagrange in the macroblock level without model-based. 3) Automatic setting of the thresholds for separating the video periods and automatic setting of thresholds for motion activity frame types.

6 References

1 A. Y. Lan, A. G. Nguyen, and J. N. Hwang, "Scene Context Dependent Reference-Frame Placement for MPEG Video Coding," IEEE Transactions on Circuits and Systems for Video Technology, Vol. 9, No. 3, April 1999.

2 D. A. Robinson, "The Mechanics of Human Smooth Pursuit Eye Movement," The Journal of Physiology, Vol 180, No. 3, October 1965.

3 ITU Recommendation H263, "Video coding for low bit rate communication".

4 U-T/SG-15, Video codec test model, TM5, Jan. 1995 and TM8, Jan. 1997.

5 "Method for the subjective quality assessment of TV pictures," CCIR Rec. 500-2, 1982

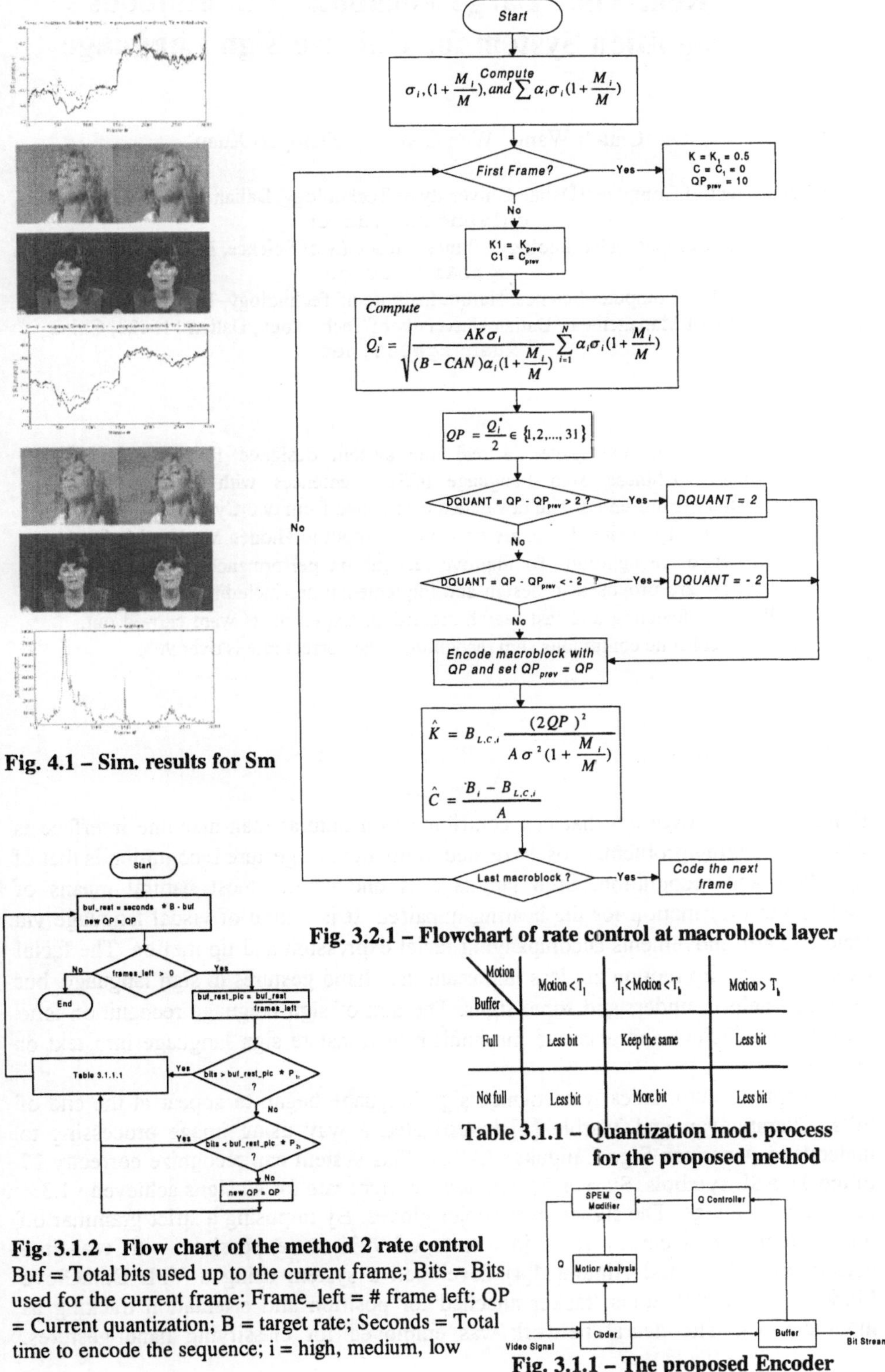

Fig. 4.1 – Sim. results for Sm

Fig. 3.2.1 – Flowchart of rate control at macroblock layer

Buffer \ Motion	Motion < T_l	T_l < Motion < T_h	Motion > T_h
Full	Less bit	Keep the same	Less bit
Not full	Less bit	More bit	Less bit

Table 3.1.1 – Quantization mod. process for the proposed method

Fig. 3.1.2 – Flow chart of the method 2 rate control
Buf = Total bits used up to the current frame; Bits = Bits used for the current frame; Frame_left = # frame left; QP = Current quantization; B = target rate; Seconds = Total time to encode the sequence; i = high, medium, low

Fig. 3.1.1 – The proposed Encoder

A Real-Time Large Vocabulary Continuous Recognition System for Chinese Sign Language

Chunli Wang [1] Wen GAO [2 3] Zhaoguo Xuan[4]

1 Department of Computer, Dalian University of Technology, Dalian 116023, China
chlwang@ict.ac.cn
2 Institute of Computing Technology, Chinese Academy of Science, Beijing 100080, China
wgao@ict.ac.cn
3 Department of Computer Science, Harbin Institute of Technology, 150001, China
4 Department of Management, Dalian University of Technology, Dalian 116023, China
xuan_zg@263.net

Abstract In this paper, a real-time system designed for recognizing continuous Chinese Sign Language (CSL) sentences with a 4800 sign vocabulary is presented. The raw data are collected from two CyberGlove and a 3-D tracker. The worked data are presented as input to Hidden Markov Models (HMMs) for recognition. To improve recognition performance, some useful new ideas are proposed in design and implementation, including states tying, still frame detecting and fast search algorithm. Experiments were carried out, and for real-time continuous sign recognition, the correct rate is over 90%.

1 Introduction

Hand gesture recognition that can contribute to a natural man-machine interface is still a challenging problem. Closely related to the field of gesture recognition is that of sign language recognition. Sign language is one of the most natural means of exchanging information for the hearing impaired. It is a kind of visual language via hand and arm movements accompanying facial expression and lip motion. The facial expression and lip motion are less important than hand gestures in sign language, but they may help to understand some signs. The aim of sign language recognition is to provide an efficient and accurate mechanism to translate sign language into text or speech.

Attempts to automatically recognize sign language began to appear at the end of 80's. Charaphayan and Marble [1] investigated a way using image processing to understand American Sign Language (ASL). This system can recognize correctly 27 of the 31 ASL symbols. Starner[2] reported a correct rate for 40 signs achieved 91.3% based on the image. The signers wear color gloves. By imposing a strict grammar on this system, the accuracy rates in excess of 99% were possible with real-time performance. Fels and Hinton[3][4] developed a system using a VPL DataGlove Mark II with a Polhemus tracker attached for position and orientation tracking as input devices. The neural network was employed for classifying hand gestures.

Takahashi and Kishino[5] investigated a system for understanding the Japanese kana manual alphabets corresponding to 46 signs using a VPL dataGlove. Their system could correctly recognize 30 of the 46 signs. Y. Nam and K.Y. Wohn[6] used three–dimensional data as input to HMMs for continuous recognition of a very small set of gestures. They introduced the concept of movement primes, which make up sequences of more complex movements. R.H.Liang and M.Ouhyoung[7] used HMM for continuous recognition of Tainwan Sign language with a vocabulary between 71 and 250 signs based Dataglove as input devices. Kisti Grobel and Marcell Assan [8] used HMMs to recognize isolated signs with 91.3% accuracy out of a 262-sign vocabulary. They extracted the features from video recordings of signers wearing colored gloves. C.Vogler and D.Metaxas[9] used HMMs for continuous ASL recognition with a vocabulary of 53 signs and a completely unconstrained sentence structure. C.Vogler and D.Metaxas[10][11] described an approach to continuous, whole-sentence ASL recognition that uses phonemes instead of whole signs as the basic units. They experimented with 22 words and achieved similar recognition rates with phoneme-based and word-based approaches. Wen Gao[12] proposed a Chinese Sign language recognition system with a vocabulary of 1064 signs. The recognition accuracy is about 93.2%. Chunli Wang[13] proposed a CSL recognition system with a vocabulary of 5100 signs. The best recognition accuracy of isolated signs is 95%.

By reviewing of foregoing research work we know that most researches on continuous sign language recognition were made on small test vocabulary. C. Vogler and D. Metaxas[14] pointed that the major challenge to sign language recognition is how to develop approaches that scale well with increasing vocabulary size. He used parallel HMMs (PaHMMs) to solve the problem. PaHMMs process multi streams independently. He ran several experiments with 22 sign vocabulary and demonstrated that PaHMMs could improve the robustness of HMM-based recognition even at a small scale. When streams are not frame synchronous, the complexity that the decoding algorithm requires may increase considerably. Results in speech recognition have indicated that allowing asynchrony among streams does not give any signification performance improvement.

Chinese Sign Language (CSL) consists of about 5500 elementary vocabularies including postures and gestures. Therefore the task of CSL continuous recognition becomes very challenging.

In this paper, a system is proposed to attempt to realize large vocabulary continuous CSL recognition. Two CyberGlove and a Pohelmus 3-D tracker with three receivers positioned on the wrist of CyberGlove and the waist are used as input device in this system. The raw gesture data include hand postures, positions and orientations. An algorithm based on geometrical analysis for purpose of extracting invariant feature to signer position and CHMMs with different number of states are used in this system. The description in detail can be found in [13].

In large vocabulary continuous speech recognition, phonemes are used as the basic units; the number of them is much smaller compared with those in CSL. There are 50~60 phonemes in speech and about 2500~3000 basic units in sign language. Therefore, the method to resolve large vocabulary continuous sign language recognition is different to that in speech recognition. Furthermore, it is impossible to build models for all the sign transitions between two signs (coarticulation or movement epenthesis). How to avoid the effect of coarticulation is very difficult. A modified Viterbi-beam algorithm is proposed here to tackle the problem movement epenthesis in sign language. The information of still frames at the end of a sign and the start of the next sign is used to set the punishing term during the decoding process at the sign transitions.

Another key factor for speeding up the recognition procedure and reducing the memory resources is how to pruning unlikely hypothesis as soon as possible. Selecting the candidate signs is used during the decoding process in this system. The experiments show that the sentences can be recognized in real-time.

The organization of this paper is as follows: Section 2 describes the outline of the designed system. Section 3 discusses approaches of sign language recognition. Section 4 demonstrates the performance evaluation of the proposed approaches. The summary and discussion are given in the last section.

2 System Architecture

The sign data collected by the gesture-input devices is fed into the feature extraction module, the output of feature vectors from the module is then input into the training module, in which one model is built for each sign. Because the system is signer dependent, there is only one mixture on each state. The parameters on the states are tied. The number of independent parameters in the models is reduced and the parameter estimation becomes simpler and more reliable. The language model that is used in our system is Bigram model. The search algorithm we used will be described in Sec.3. When the word sequence is output from the decoder, the sequence drives the speech synthesis module to produce the voice of speech.

3 Sign Language Recognition

The most popular framework for sign language recognition is the statistical formulation. Let $W = \{w_1, w_2, \ldots, w_N\}$ be a sequence of words. Suppose F is the feature extracted from input gestures. The recognizer must choose a word string W that maximizes the probability given that the feature evidence of F was observed. This problem can be significantly simplified by applying the Bayesian method to find $\hat{W}$:

$$\hat{W} = \arg_W \max P(F \mid W)P(W) \tag{1}$$

The probability, $P(F \mid W)$, that the feature F was observed if a word sequence W was gestured, is typically provided by the data model of hand gestures. A language model determines the likelihood $P(W)$ that denotes a priori chances of the word sequence W being gestured.

3.1. State Tying

Hidden Markov Models (HMMs)[15] have been used successfully in continuous speech recognition, handwriting recognition, etc. A HMM is a doubly stochastic state machine that has a Markov distribution associated with the transitions across various states, and a probability density function that models the output for every state. A key assumption in stochastic gesture processing is that the signal is stationary over a short time interval.

There are some gestures that appear in several signs, such as "Home", which is a part of "classroom", "school", "hospital" and "shop". Each state in HMMs are corresponding to a basic gesture, so there must be many parameters on the states are similar. The parameters can be tied. The aim of tying is to reduce computation load in decoding process. The tying can be carried out at different levels.

Sharing the same HMM among some different HMMs is named as "HMM tying in the whole sign space". This is the first level tying. Clustering different HMMs is very difficult because different HMMs may have different topologies, different transition probabilities and different state observation densities.

Clustering the Gaussians on the states of all of the models is named as "state tying in the whole sign space". This is the second level tying. Clustering the Gaussians means clustering the parameters.

From the temporal and spatial analysis, for each time instant, hand shape, hand position and hand orientation are three measurable factors forming a hand spatial unit in whole sign space. The basic spatial units include six data streams: the left hand shape, position, orientation, right hand shape, position and orientation. The number of possible combinations of these six parts can be approximately 10^8, so tying at state level for sign language recognition is not as effective as that for speech recognition.

Therefore, tying in each data stream or in sign subspace is proposed, where the data streams include hand shape, hand position and hand orientation. This is the third level tying. It is named as "stream state tying". The tied streams are called "codeword". This level tying is more efficient for calculating state observation probabilities for sign language recognition. Unlike state tying in speech recognition, the stream state tying is taken in each data stream of a hand gesture. The basic idea is as follows: first of all, a whole spatial vector is form by using all streams vectors. For each sign, its HMM is trained with training samples. After all HMMs have been trained, the observation probability densities in each data stream of all signs are tied with a few probability densities. The advantage of this approach is that the computation time is greatly reduced, because the state observation probability density in a whole gesture space is the product of the state observation probability densities of the six streams. And because the state probability in log domain can be computed by summing all stream state probabilities in log domain as follows:

$$\log b_i(x) = \sum_{l=1}^{6} \log b_{il}(x_j) \tag{2}$$

$b_i(x)$ is the i 'th state observation probability, $b_{il}(x_l)$ is the l 'th data stream observation probability in the i 'th state. For each data stream the stream state probabilities are clustered, the stream state probabilities belonging to the same class need to be computed only once. As the number of distinguishable patterns in each data stream is relatively small, for a given observation vector, after these six observation probabilities have been computed, the log likelihood of each signs can be easily gotten by a lookup table and by 5 times addition operations.

For the case of continuous sign recognition, even the network topology is linear, because the computation time for the state observation probabilities is relatively small, the probably active sign candidates can be quickly determined.

3. 2 Search Algorithms

Viterbi[15] search and its variant forms belong to a class of breadth-first search techniques. All hypotheses are pursued in parallel and gradually pruned away as the correct hypothesis emerges with the maximum score. In this case, the recognition system can be treated as a recursive transition network composed of the states of HMMs in which any state can be reached from any other state. The signal sequence cannot be segmented in advance. The recognition result cannot be gotten until the end of the sequence is reached. Viterbi algorithm has the function of segmentation. In order to conserve the computing and memory resources, it is imperative to prune the low-scoring partial paths. In Viterbi-beam search only the hypothesis whose likelihood falls within a beam are considered for further growth. The beam threshold with respect to the best path scoring at that level is computed. To speed up the decoding process and improve the recognition rate, the following techniques are proposed in time-synchronous search.

Word candidates

For each frame t, how to judge whether a sign is active is very important to speeding up the recognition process. Only the active signs need to be further searched, thus a large mount of computation load is reduced.

The approach to selecting the active signs at a frame is as follows: For each frame, compute the probabilities of all codewords of each stream. If the probability of a codeword is higher than a threshold, the codeword is active, otherwise inactive. After the active codewords of six streams are found. If the six codewords on a state are active, the state is active, and then the models including the state are active. The algorithm does not need compute all states probabilities of all signs.

Sometimes there are bad data gathered from the input devices. If this happens, the correct word may not be selected as the candidate at this frame. Because the errors cannot be corrected in Viterbi, the recognition result must be erroneous. To avoid the effect of the "noise", the word candidates should also include those previous word candidates, the scores of which are higher than a given threshold.

Still Frame Detecting

In the case of continuous sign language recognition, another difficult problem is the coarticulation, which means that both the sign in front and behind can affect a sign. If two signs are performed in succession, an extra movement from the end position of the first sign to the start position of the second sign appears sometimes. This phenomenon is called movement epenthesis. This problem is handled in speech recognition by adding extra context-dependent HMMs to describe the effect of coarticulation. But this idea is not efficient in large vocabulary sign language recognition. In speech recognition, phonemes are the basic units. There are about 50~60 phonemes. Plus context-dependent phonemes (TRIPHONE), there are about one thousand basic units. This number can be accepted. In CSL there are 2500~3000 "phonemes", so the number of possible "TRIPHONE" is too large to be accepted. In our system, the basic unit is the sign. In order to reduce the effect of the coarticulation, we use still frame detecting. The method is as follows. When a sign finishes, there maybe is a pause. So if a long standstill is detected, the probability of the current sign finishing is higher. In Viterbi search algorithm, when a step from one word to another one happens, a parameter is added to the current score. The parameter is set according to the number of the still frames. If there is no standstill or the standstill does not end, it is impossible that a sign ends, so the parameter is set to punish the transitions between signs. If the standstill finishes and the number of the still frames is big enough, it is probable that the current sign finishes, so the parameter is set to encourage the transitions. Besides, the next several frames maybe the movement epenthesis and their effect to the path should be reduced. With this method, the recognition rate can be improved greatly.

4 Experiment

The hardware environment is Pentium III 700MHz, with two CyberGloves and three receivers of 3D tracker; each Cyberglove is with 18 sensors. The baud rate for both CyberGlove and 3D tracker is set to 38400.

4800 signs in CSL are used as evaluation vocabulary. Each sign is performed five times. Four times are used for training and one for testing. The minimum number of states in HMMs is 3, and the maximum number is 5. The recognition rates of isolated signs with different numbers of the codewords are shown in Table 1. The test data are collected when the signs were recognized online.

According to Table 1, the numbers of codewords of right position, right orientation, left position, left orientation, left handshape and right handshape are set to 128, 128, 128, 128, 350, 350. The best recognition rate is 93.9%, and the recognition rate without state tying is 95%. The accuracy decreases little. It spends about 1 second to recognition a sign online. This result is encouraging. Real-time recognition has been realized.

Table.1. The recognition rates of signs for different numbers of codewords

The number of codewords						The Recognition Rates
Right Position	**Right Orientation**	**Left Position**	**Left Orientation**	**Left Hand Shape**	**Right Hand Shape**	
256	256	256	256	256	256	89.33%
128	128	128	128	256	256	92.73%
128	128	128	128	300	300	93.19%
128	128	128	128	350	350	93.74%
128	128	128	128	400	400	93.61%
128	128	128	128	512	512	93.91%

For continuous sentence recognition, 1000 sentences are test. These sentences are made randomly. Each sentence consists of 2 to 10 words. The result is shown in Table 2. The accuracy is over 90%.

Table 2. The results of sentences recognition

Without still frame detecting	H=6156,D=116, S=2401,I=467,N=8673
With still frame detecting	H=7819,D=42,S=812, I=243, N=8673

Note: H denotes the number of correct signs, D the number of delection errors, S the number of substitution errors, I the number of insertion errors, and N the total number of signs in the test set.

5 Conclusion

In this paper, a real-time continuous CSL recognition system based on large vocabulary is presented using HMM based technology. Our contributions within this system are three aspects: state tying, fast search technique and still frame detecting. Experimental results have shown that the proposed techniques are capable of improving both the recognition performance and speed. The idea for detecting the still frames is quite efficient for large vocabulary continuous sign language recognition. This system is for signer dependent recognition task. The system will be extended for the task of signer independent recognition in the future.

6 Acknowledgment

This research is sponsored partly by Natural Science Foundation of China (No.69789301), National Hi-Tech Program of China (No.863-306-ZD03-01-2), and 100 Talents Foundation of Chinese Academy of Sciences.

References

1. C. Charayaphan, A. Marble: Image processing system for interpreting motion in American Sign Language. Journal of Biomedical Engineering, 14(1992) 419--425.
2. T. Starner : Visual recognition of American Sign Language using hidden Markov models. Master's thesis, MIT Media Laboratory, July. 1995.
3. S. S. Fels, G. Hinton: GloveTalk:A neural network interface between a DataDlove and a speech synthesizer. IEEE Transactions on Neural Networks 4(1993) 2-8.
4. S. Sidney Fels: Glove –TalkII: Mapping hand gestures to speech using neural networks-An approach to building adaptive interfaces. PhD thesis, Computer Science Department, University of Torono, 1994.
5. Tomoichi Takahashi, Fumio Kishino: Gesture coding based in experiments with a hand gesture interface device. SIGCHI Bulletin (1991) 23(2) 67-73.
6. Yanghee Nam, K. Y. Wohn: Recognition of space-time hand-gestures using hidden Markov model. To appear in ACM Symposium on Virtual Reality Software and Technology (1996).
7. R. H. Liang, M. Ouhyoung: A real-time continuous gesture recognition system for sign language. In Proceeding of the Third International Conference on Automatic Face and Gesture Recognition, Nara, Japan (1998) 558-565.
8. Kirsti Grobel, Marcell Assan: Isolated sign language recognition using hidden Markov models. In Proceedings of the International Conference of System,Man and Cybernetics (1996) 162-167.
9. Christian Vogler, Dimitris Metaxas: Adapting hidden Markov models for ASL recognition by using three-dimensional computer vision methods. In Proceedings of the IEEE International Confference on Systems, Man and Cybernetics, Orlando, FL (1997) 156-161.
10. Christian Vogler, Dimitris Metaxas: ASL recognition based on a coupling between HMMs and 3D motion analysis. In Proceedings of the IEEE International Conference on Computer Vision, Mumbai, India (1998) 363-369.
11. Christian Vogler, Dimitris Metaxas: Toward scalability in ASL Recognition: Breaking Down Signs into Phonemes. In Proceedings of Gesture Workshop, Gif-sur-Yvette, France (1999) 400-404.
12. Wen Gao, Jiyong Ma, Jiangqin Wu, Chunli Wang: Large Vocabulary Sign Language Recognition Based on HMM/ANN/DP. International Journal of Pattern Recognition and Artificial Intelligence, Vol. 14, No. 5 (2000) 587-602.
13. Chunli Wang, Wen Gao, and Jiyong Ma. "A Real-Time Large Vocabulary Recognition System For Chinese Sign Language", The 4th International Gesture and Sign Language based Human-Computer Interaction, London, April 18th-20th, 2001.
14. Vogler C. Metaxas D. Parallel Hidden Markov Models for American Sign Language recognition. Proceedings of the Seventh IEEE International Conference on Computer Vision. IEEE Comput. Soc. Part vol.1,1999, pp.116-22, Los Alamitos, CA, USA
15. L Rabiner, B. Juang: Fundamentals of Speech Recognition. Publishing Company of TsingHua University.

Object Modeling, Coding, and Transmission for Multimedia Communications

Dongmei Wang[1] and Russell M. Mersereau[2]

[1] Agere Systems, StarCore Technology Center, Atlanta, GA 30328, USA,
[2] Georgia Institute of Technology, Center for Signal and Image Processing, Atlanta, GA 30332-0250, USA

Abstract. This paper discusses object modeling, coding, and transmission for multimedia communications in the desktop environment. To reduce video quality degradation caused by coding distortion and networking errors, we consider the compression and transmission of multimedia signals in a joint fashion. First, a three-level signal representation model is developed to connect 3-D graphics with video pixel information through 2-D object shapes. Second, nonrigid facial motion is modeled and is used to synthesize video images. Third, the video coding rates are adapted based on feedback of the network states and receivers.

1 Introduction

Data compression and data transmission are two key components in multimedia communications [1]. Data compression aims to achieve the best tradeoff between coding quality and bit rate, while data transmission concerns network protocols and their performance evaluation. Among the quality of service parameters, delay and packet loss are two major issues in real-world communications.

In this paper, we report object modeling, coding, and transmission for multimedia communications. The key strategy in this system is to model *a priori* knowledge of a video sequence so that the data needed for representing the object can be minimized. In particular, in video conferencing or video phone applications, the video frame usually contains a person. How should *a priori* information about the person be modeled? The first step is to build a 3-D human head-and-shoulder graphics model to describe the human object geometry. Among volume, surface, and polygonal representations, we choose a polygonal surface representation because of its rendering efficiency. This representation can be obtained by using a laser scanner type of data acquisition and processing system. To avoid cracks in the rendered images due to non-planar facets when the post-transformation model is projected back onto the display plane, we adopt a modified version of the 3-D model CANDIDE [2], which uses 160 vertices to form a triangular mesh. Because all facets are triangular, the three vertices always lie on a plane, even after transformation and numerical roundoff. Once the 3-D

* The work was performed at Georgia Institute of Technology with support from Intel Corporation.

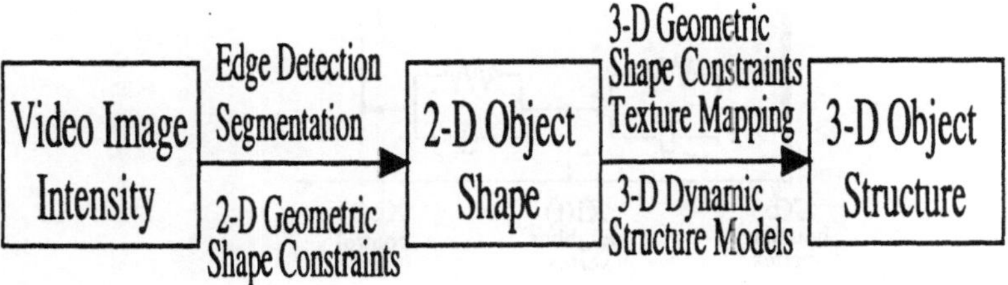

Fig. 1. Three-level signal representation

geometry is available, we manually adjust the generic 3-D head-and-shoulder model and map it to the neutral facial expression.

During the coding process, the encoder codes a texture frame with the neutral facial expression, extracts, and codes 3-D object structure and motion in contrast to encoding 2-D displacement vectors of image intensities. Our decoder extracts parameter set (texture, shape, and motion), synthesizes video using 3-D graphics models, and evaluates the synthesized video quality. The main challenge is to extract the motion from the video sequence. Global motion corresponds to head movement, while local nonrigid motion accounts for deformations of facial expressions. We focus on modeling and extracting facial nonrigid motion.

For video transmission, the TCP/IP protocol stack is used. TCP (Transmission Control Protocol) is slow and reliable. UDP (User Datagram Protocol) provides faster transmission, but its packets may get lost during routing, may arrive too late, or may be dropped due to buffer overflow. To reduce quality degradation when using UDP, we prototype an application content-level protocol that feeds the information of the network states and receiver capability back to the encoder to control coding rate.

2 Modeling

The only information directly available in the input video is the pixel intensities captured by a video camera. It is thus difficult to extract 3-D information from the pixel intensities. The object depth information is lost during video capture and the reverse process of extracting depth from intensity is ill-posed. Thus, we proceed by building higher-level models (structure level) for *a priori* information of the face. For this purpose, we develop a three-level signal representation that relates the input video to the output synthesized graphics (Figure 1). That is, in additional to the pixel-level intensity signal and the 3-D graphics model vertex values, we add a 2-D projection-plane shape description to capture the unique facial shape features (mouth, eyes, eyebrows, etc). The 2-D facial shape changes in the video sequence can be extracted using high-level computer vision techniques. These 2-D shape changes reflect the projected 3-D motion. Because the 3-D graphics model CANDIDE is based on a real person's face, the depth information about the human facial structure is available. Once the 2-D shape

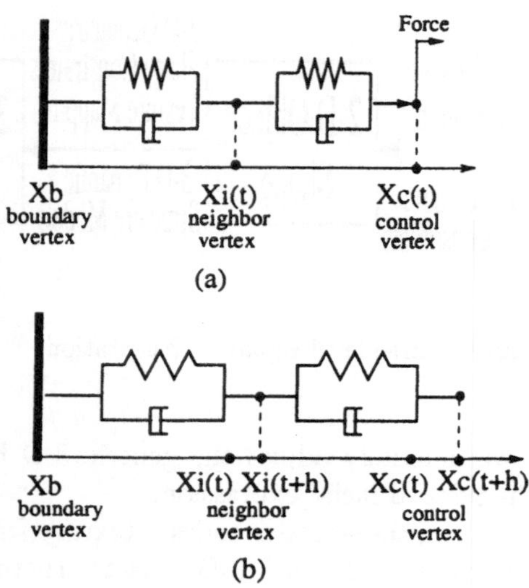

Fig. 2. The nodal displacement of a spring-mass-damper system shown in one dimension: (a) the initial equilibrium state at time t: x_b is the boundary vertex; x_c is the control vertex; and x_i is the neighboring vertex of the control vertex; (b) the final equilibrium state at time $t + h$.

movement is extracted from the encoder, the vertices on the 3-D model with respect to the 2-D shape can move accordingly. However, the real challenge is how other vertices (not shape feature vertices) would move! We proceed by building a facial motion simulation model based on the biophysical properties of human facial tissue. A physically-based simulation system models the 3-D face as a flexible structure. The continuous flexible structure is discretized spatially. It is then simulated temporarily by finite difference and iterative numerical techniques. Skin tissues posses elasticity and viscosity [3, 4]. The continuous material masses are redistributed to the discrete points as lumped masses. Because the CANDIDE model is already a one-layer discretization of 3-D facial structure shape in the spatial domain, it can be modeled by using the skin's biophysical properties. Thus, the subset of 3-D model vertices that correspond to the 2-D shape feature points is labeled as control vertices, and mass-spring-dampers units are used to interconnect these control vertices and their neighboring vertices to simulate the viscoelastic properties of facial tissue.

In mathematical terms, we assume that node i has point mass m_i, and define its spring position $\mathbf{x}_i(t)$, velocity $\mathbf{v}_i(t)$, and acceleration $\mathbf{a}_i(t)$ as

$$\mathbf{x}_i(t) = \begin{bmatrix} x(t) \\ y(t) \\ z(t) \end{bmatrix}, \qquad \mathbf{v}_i(t) = \frac{d\mathbf{x}_i(t)}{dt}, \qquad \mathbf{a}_i(t) = \frac{d\mathbf{x}_i^2(t)}{dt^2}.$$

Voight viscoelastic unit (spring and damper in parallel connection) is used to connect nodes i and j. $x_{ij}(t) = \|\mathbf{x}_j(t) - \mathbf{x}_i(t)\|$ denotes the actual spring length.

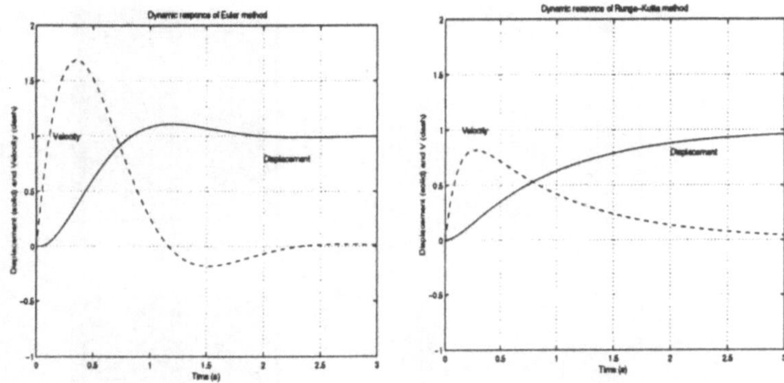

Fig. 3. Two numerical methods

The difference between $x_{ij}(t)$ and the rest spring length l_{ij} is the deformation $\Delta x_{ij}(t) = x_{ij}(t) - l_{ij}$. The skin tissue visco-elastic properties can be modeled by the stiffness coefficient k_{ij}, and velocity-dependent damping coefficient c_{ij}. Using Hooke's law, the spring's elastic force is $\mathbf{f}_{ij}^{s}(t) = k_{ij}\Delta x_{ij}(t)\frac{\mathbf{x_{ij}}(t)}{x_{ij}(t)}$, and the damper's viscous force is $\mathbf{f}_{ij}^{d}(t) = c_{ij}(\mathbf{v}_j(t) - \mathbf{v}_i(t))$. The total forces at node i are a combination of the net spring elastic forces $\mathbf{f}_i^S(t)$ and the net damping forces $\mathbf{f}_i^D(t)$. The external net force on node i includes driving image force $\mathbf{f}_i^E(t)$ and boundary constraints. By Newton's Second Law, the entire integrated dynamic node/spring system is

$$m_i \frac{d\mathbf{x}_i^2(t)}{dt^2} + \mathbf{f}_i^D(t) + \mathbf{f}_i^S(t) = \mathbf{f}_i^E(t).$$

In the state-space form,

$$\mathbf{y}_i = \begin{bmatrix} \mathbf{x}_i \\ \mathbf{v}_i \end{bmatrix}, \qquad and \qquad \mathbf{g} = \begin{bmatrix} \mathbf{v}_i \\ \dfrac{-\mathbf{f}_i^D - \mathbf{f}_i^S}{m_i} + \dfrac{\mathbf{f}_i^E}{m_i} \end{bmatrix}$$

or

$$\begin{cases} \dot{\mathbf{y}}_i &= \mathbf{g}(\mathbf{y}_i^{(t)}, t) \\ \mathbf{y}_i(0) = & \mathbf{y}_i^{(0)} \end{cases}$$

To solve the equations, we apply numerical methods [5] to iteratively displace the nodal points until the local contributions of all the adjacent elements are in equilibrium. An alternative approach, the second-order Runge-Kutta method, which has two evaluations of the system equations, is also used (Figure 3).

$$\begin{aligned} \mathbf{q}_i^1 &= \mathbf{g}(\mathbf{y}_i^{(t)}, t)\,\Delta\, t \\ \mathbf{q}_i^2 &= \mathbf{g}(\mathbf{y}_i^{(t)} + \mathbf{q}_i^1, t + \Delta t)\,\Delta\, t \\ \mathbf{y}_i^{(t+\Delta t)} &= \mathbf{y}_i^{(t)} + \frac{1}{2}(\mathbf{q}_i^1 + \mathbf{q}_i^2) + O(\Delta t^3). \end{aligned}$$

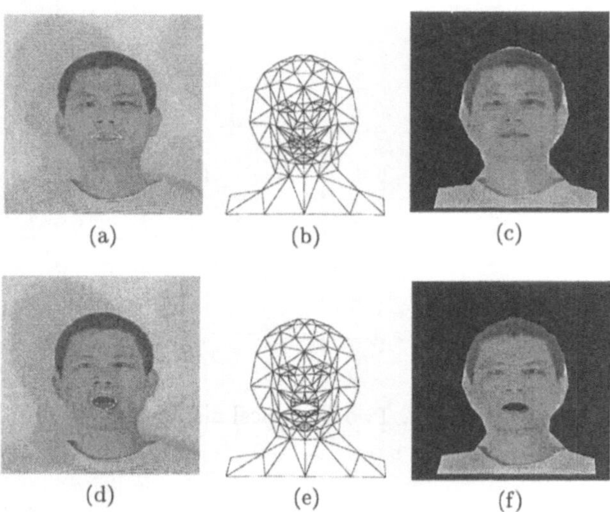

Fig. 4. Nonrigid facial motion tracking and synthesis using deformable template and 3-D biomechanical model: (a) placing mouth deformable template over frontal neutral face; (b) customizing CANDIDE model to fit to the person's neutral face; (c) texture mapping result; (d) tracking mouth movement using deformable template; (e) activating facial synthesis system to get 3-D geometry deformation; and (f) applying texture map to get the synthesis video image.

When the 2-D shape templates deform in the input video, the control vertices on the 3-D model move accordingly. Based on the above physical modeling and derivation, the neighboring vertices move also until the facial structure reaches a new equilibrium. The displacement is illustrated in a one-dimensional drawing of Figure 2 and the animation of 3-D graphics model is shown in Figure 4(e).

3 Coding

We use a finite sequence of typical human facial expression (Figure 5) as training set for the human facial structures, and obtain a codebook of 3-D facial structure parameters based on a facial action coding system [6] and a facial motion synthesis model presented above. In the training process, we collect human facial sequences representing several typical facial structures. To obtain facial structure deformation data that are as accurate as possible, we collect both front view and depth information of the person's facial structure. Then, we customize the 3-D model to the person by adjusting vertices in all three dimensions and obtain a texture map. We assume that only orthographic projection is employed in 3-D graphics rendering. To make the projected 3-D model animate in synchrony with the projected view of the face in the input video, we manually identify one-to-

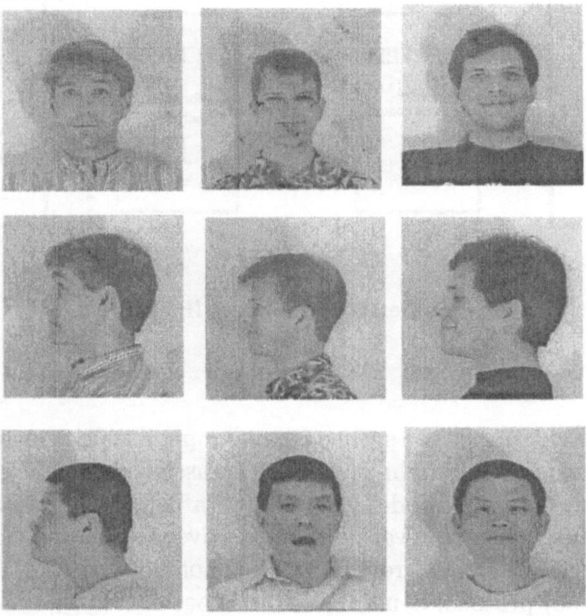

Fig. 5. Training sequences

one mapping between the feature points on the 2-D shape contour and a subset of 3-D vertices on the 3-D graphics model (Figure 4(a)). In subsequent video frames, we track the 2-D nonrigid shape changes using deformable templates (Figure 4(d)). Next, we deform the 3-D graphics model in synchrony with the input video using 2-D deformable templates. For different persons in different training sequences, the same 2-D shape changes in the 2-D image plane cause small variations in the 3-D facial structure deformation. This effect is controlled by adjusting the spring-damper parameters and comparing the input video to the synthesized video (3-D structure plus texture map). The 3-D structure deformation parameters are saved as a 3-D structure codebook for coding. When a new video sequence becomes available, we extract the 2-D shape moving scales as visual cues. We use these visual cues to help retrieve the 3-D structure deformation from the codebook. Then we apply the texture map to the 3-D structure to obtain synthesized images (Figure 4(f)). The 3-D structure codeset that produces the closest texture resemblance to the input video is transmitted.

4 Transmission

The types of data to be transmitted include the video texture, the 3-D graphics model parameters, structure motion, and other synthesis parameters (biome-

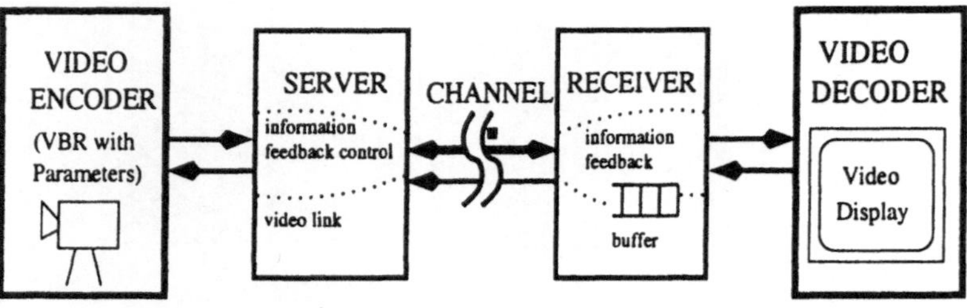

Fig. 6. Desktop video over IP system

chanical parameters such as the spring-mass-damper coefficients and time steps). The highest transmission reliability should be assigned to 3-D graphics model data (a list of the original model vertices and a list of the associated triangle topologies) because if the receiver does not receive the customized 3-D graphics model information, decoding (rendering) will not be possible. Thus, TCP (or an equally reliable) protocol is used. For other parameters, we use a UDP-type networking protocol to fulfill the real-time transmission requirement in videoconferencing. The UDP networking-related factors that could impact the decoded video quality include packet loss, packet delay, and buffer overflow. In a multicast session, receivers may have different rendering speeds. We categorize the network and receiver states as "loaded" if the client detects packet loss due to low receiving power and network congestion; "adequate" if the end user is able to decode and display the video properly; or "need-more-packets" if the client's decoder halts from time to time to wait for more packets to arrive. If too many receivers feed back network information at the same time, an implosion could occur. To avoid this, the server probabilistically selects a sample set of receivers for the state feedback information, and then for each client selected, the client delays a random time interval before sending the state information to the server. In our current system, once the server obtains the current network state information, it adjusts the encoded video stream with one appropriate bit rate that fits most of the clients as shown in (Figure 6). The future improvement would be to generate multiple video streams with different level of spatial resolution. This way, all users can pick a video rate that is the most appropriate to the network condition and its CPU. For video texture, because all of the subsequent frames are rendered on top of the texture with neutral facial expression, we implement a frame-based wavelet coder rather than a block-based coder to reduce blocking artifacts. For code generation, one approach is to entropy encode and packetize each subband independently [7], and the other is to encode symbols across different subbands using an interband tree-structured filterbank [8]. For the first one, if the most important low resolution subband in the wavelet decomposition is lost, we cannot reconstruct the basic image texture. Thus, we utilize an interband tree structure similar to the second one. We packetize the tree branches into different packets to avoid coding an entire band of signals in one.

5 Conclusion

In summary, we have developed both video coding and networking prototypes by using a three-level signal model, a nonrigid facial motion synthesis model, and network receiver feedback control strategy. The three-level signal model provides the foundation for 3-D object coding. Facial motion modeling simulates *a priori* knowledge of a real human face and is used for 3-D motion extraction from video sequences. Through interaction in the training phase, we have generated a codebook of 3-D structure parameters for coding. In the current model, we need approximately 13 kbps to code the structure motion parameters for video displayed at 10 frames per second. The wavelet coding of QCIF size color texture (with neutral facial expression) requires less than 19 kpbs.

For video transmission over IP, we feed back the network state and receiver rendering information to the server. This provides users at the receiving end with video at appropriate rates, avoids extensive frame hopping or stall. During initialization, we use TCP to transmit the model vertices. We use a frame-based tree-structured texture coding method that improves video quality at the same packet loss rate. Our demonstration shows that with a limited number of receivers in one communication session, the networking feedback criteria work well. In the Internet environment with potentially millions of users in one session, the performance of the feedback scheme needs to be further examined.

6 Acknowledgment

We are grateful to Dr. Tom Gardos, CSIP colleagues Sam Li, D. Anderson, J. Arrowood, M. Cobb, C. Lanciani, and J. Qin for their help.

References

1. F. F. Kuo, W. Effelsberg, and J. J. Garcia-Luna-Aceves, *Multimedia Communications: Protocols and Applications*, Prentice Hall PTR, Upper Saddle River, NJ, 1998.
2. M. Rydfalk, "Candide, a parameterized face," *Internal Report, Linkvping University*, Oct. 1987.
3. W. Larrabee, "A finite element model of skin deformation I. biomechanics of skin and soft tissue: A review," *Laryngoscope*, vol. 96, pp. 399–405, 1986.
4. W. Maurel, Y. Wu, N. M. Thalmann, and D. Thalmann, *Biomechanical Models for Soft Tissue Simulation*, Springer, Berlin, Heidelberg, New York, Barcelona, Budapest, Hong Kong, London, Milan, Paris, Santa Clara, Singapore, Tokyo, 1998.
5. W.H. Press, B.P. Flannery, S.A. Teukolsky, and W.T. Vetterling, *Numerical Recipes in C*, Cambridge University Press, New York, 1992.
6. P. Ekman and W.V. Friesen, *Facial Action Coding System (Investigator's Guide)*, Consulting Psychologists Press, Inc., Palo Alto, California, USA, 1978.
7. M. Vetterli, "Multidimentional subband coding: some theory and algorithms," *Signal Processing*, vol. 9, no. 2, pp. 97–112, Feb. 1984.
8. J. Shapiro, "Embedded image coding using zerotrees of wavelet coefficients," *IEEE Trans. on Signal Processing*, vol. 41, pp. 3445–3462, Dec. 1993.

Live Events Accessing for Multi-users with Free Viewpoints Using Stereo Omni-directional System

Hideki Tanahashi[1], Caihua Wang[1], Yoshinori Niwa[1], and Kazuhiko Yamamoto[2]

[1] Office of Regional Intensive Research Project, Softopia Japan (JST), 4-1-7 Kagano, Ogaki-City, Gifu, 503-8569 Japan
{tana,c-wang, niwa}@softopia.pref.gifu.jp
http://www.softopia.pref.gifu.jp/HOIP

[2] Department of Information Science, Faculty of Engineering, Gifu University 1-1 Yanagito, Gifu-City, Gifu, 503-1200 Japan
yamamoto@info.gifu-u.ac.jp

Abstract. In the Internet based live events accessing system, user interactions, such as changing a viewpoint or tracking an object, is an important aspect to be developed. This paper proposes a method to support live events accessing for multi-users with the ability to choose free viewpoints, using the stereo omni-directional system (SOS), which we have developed. This system can acquire all directional color images and stereo image pairs in real time. All cameras on this system operate simultaneously, and all images can be obtained synchronously. Using these images, we generate a VRML model of a 3D spherical representation of the live events. Users can manipulate the VRML model to view the events from a preferred viewpoint, and the images are updated at a rate which is nearly real-time.

1 Introduction

Live events broadcasting service via the Internet is considered to be an important application of multimedia and Internet technologies. With traditional services, all the users usually viewed the same scene that was produced by the server, and they didn't have much interaction with the server to meet individual demands while the event was playing. However, in recent years, due to developments in multimedia and Internet-based technologies, live events viewing that supports the individual demands of each user, such as changing viewpoints and tracking an object of interest, became a possible and useful application.

Generally, there are two ways to generate real-time images from arbitrary viewpoints for each user: one is to use multi-camera system[1-3] and another is to use the omni-camera system[4-8]. In the multi-camera system, a lot of cameras are set in the surrounding environment and take the real-time images of the event from many different viewpoints. Kanade[1] and Matsuyama[2] used those images to reconstruct a 3D model of the event in each frame and then generated videos with arbitrary moving viewpoints. The problem is that the reconstruction of 3D models of an event is time consuming and it usually can only be done off-line. On the other hand, Saito[3] generated the images of arbitrary viewpoints by using the images of the cameras which were located near the viewpoints. In this method, the objects in the event are approximated by planes, so it is effective when the event is viewed from far away.

In contrast to the former method, the omni-camera system only uses a few cameras, but each camera can take a 360° panoramic image of a scene. With such a panoramic image, it is very easy to respond to changes in viewing angles. The hyper omni-camera system, which has a hyperboloidal mirror mounted in the front of the lens, has been developed to obtain panoramic images[4-8]. As the image is taken from the scene reflected by a hyperboloidal mirror, the scene is somewhat distorted and needs to be transformed to a normal image of perspective projection. Yamazawa *et al.*[7] described a system which transforms the image taken by the hyper omni-camera into a cylindric image and displays the cylindric screen. Onoe *et al.*[8] presented a surveillance system which selects a region in the image taken by the hyper omni-camera according to the view direction of user, transforms and displays it to the user. Due to the nonlinear characteristics of the hyperboloidal mirror, the spatial resolution of the image obtained by the hyper omni-camera is not uniform. Moreover, a blind spot, such as the upper side of the sensor and center area, is caused due to the construction of the hyper omni-camera.

We have developed a system called Stereo Omni-directional System (SOS) [9]. This compact system can acquire all directional color and stereo images from the system, in real time, with uniform spatial resolution. In this paper, we propose a method of accessing live events for multi-users with free viewpoints, using the SOS we developed. Using real-time images obtained by SOS, we generate a VRML model of the 3D spherical representation of the live event. Users can manipulate the VRML model to view the event from their preferred viewpoint. The images are updated at a rate which is nearly real-time.

This paper is structured as follows. Section 2 describes the stereo omni-directional system (SOS), and section 3 describes the methods used to build a VRML model of a 3D spherical representation of the live event. Section 4 presents some examples of interactive viewing of live events using the constructed VRML model. Finally, section 5 summarizes the present work.

2 Stereo Omni-directional System (SOS)

Figure 1(a) shows a prototype of the Stereo Omni-directional System (SOS). The system is capable of obtaining color images and depth maps in all directions by using a component constructed of twenty stereo units. Each stereo unit is composed of three cameras, which are calibrated well and arranged to form two stereo pairs: top/bottom and left/right. Using both vertical and horizontal baselines, it is possible to obtain more precise and reliable stereo matchings. In addition, the three-camera system is more robust against occlusions. Table 1 shows the specifications of a stereo unit.

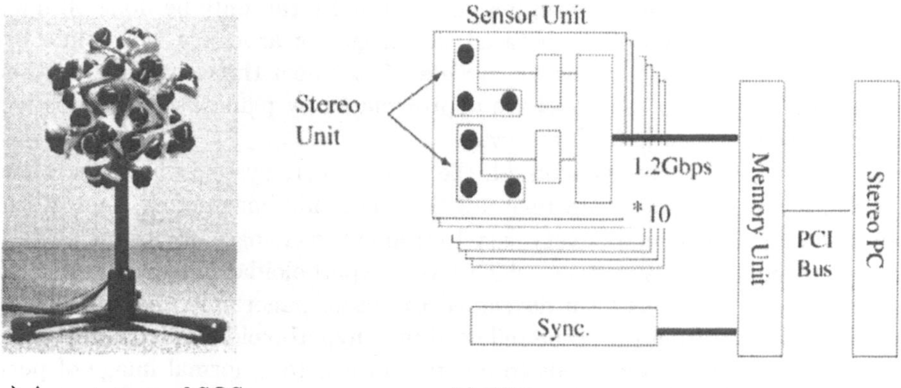

a) A prototype of SOS. b) SOS system construction

Fig. 1. A prototype of SOS and its system construction

In this system the stereo units are mounted at the center of each triangular plane of an icosahedron, and arranged so that they do not obstruct the view of each other. With this arrangement we can get a nearly uniform resolution of the whole space. All the cameras of this system operate concomitantly, and all images can be obtained simultaneously.

Table 1. Specifications of a stereo unit

Image Sensor	1/3' CMOS Color Image Sensor
Effective Resolution	640 (H) *480 (V)
Focal Length	2.9 (mm)
Field of View	96.6 deg (H)* 71.9 deg (V)
Baseline Length	90mm

As a result we succeeded in reducing the size of the entire system (diameter: 27cm; weight: 4.5 kg) securing the base line length (90 mm) to generate 3-D information with sufficient precision. Using this system, the depth resolution is 15cm at 2m given an image resolution of 640x480. The system view covers all the space outside of 40cm from the center of SOS. From each unit, a color image and two monochrome images are obtained. So, in total, twenty color images and forty monochrome images are obtained. These images are stored in a memory unit. After that, each pair of stereo images is sent to a PC, where stereo processing is carried out, as shown in Figure 1(b). The color image and the depth map of each direction are acquired at a speed of 15 frames per second.

In the following sections, we describe an application which uses SOS to provide real-time live events accessing for multi-users with free viewpoints.

3 Event Modeling Using SOS

As described in above section, an all-directional view of the event is obtained by SOS via its 20 stereo units. The 3D reconstruction of the event can be carried out using the stereo matching results on the images of the stereo units of SOS[9], but when considering computing costs, we decided to build a more simple model of a 3D spherical representation of the event. That is, we build a VRML model of a sphere and map the images of the 20 units of SOS to the sphere, getting a spherical movie of the event. All the users access the same spherical movie, but view it from their preferred viewpoint by manipulating the VRML model.

3.1 Integration of Images

Due to the geometries of SOS construction, we can cut out a triangular region from the image of the center camera of each stereo unit of SOS and integrate them into a image which corresponds to a polar expansion of an icosahedron. Because each camera is calibrated and the geometries of SOS are known, the center and the orientation of each triangular region in the image of each unit can be determined directly. The size of each triangular region depends on the depth of the scene, which can be computed as following.

$$S(d) = \frac{X_{size} tan(\Theta/2)d}{2tan(\Phi/2)(d-R)} \tag{1}$$

where d is the depth of scene, X_{size} is the horizontal size of the image of each camera, and Φ is the horizontal angle of the field of view, which is equal to 96.6 for the cameras used in SOS. Θ is the radial angle between the normals of two neighboring triangles on the icosahedron, and we know that $\Theta = 42.1$ from the geometry of an icosahedron. R is the distance between the center of SOS and the center of each triangle, where the central camera of the unit is mounted, and $R = 10.0$cm according to the design of SOS. Figure 2 shows the geometries for the computation of formula (1).

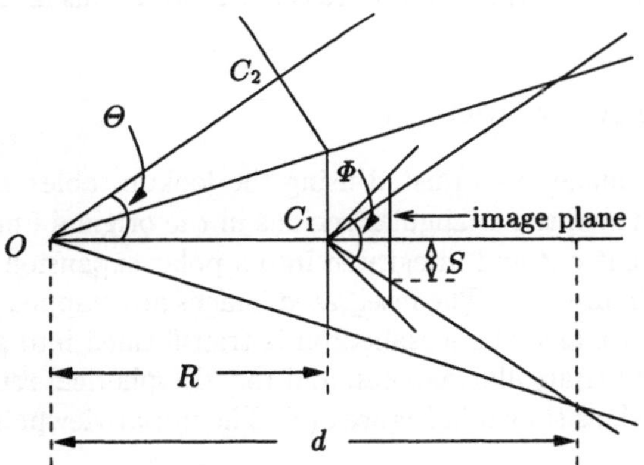

Fig. 2. FOV for a given depth

For a given range of depth (d_{min}, d_{max}), we can select the optimal size of the triangle region as $(S(d_{max}) + S(d_{min}))/2$, which minimizes the shift error in image integration caused by changes in depth. For example, given a range of depth of $(100cm, \infty)$, we can select $S = 73$ pixels in the case of resolution of 320×240, and the shift error will be within ± 2 pixels.

3.2 Color Fusion

Although the geometries of each camera are well calibrated, their white balances are only calibrated for a particular environment before SOS is shipped. So there may be no color consistency among the cameras in a new environment. In this research, we adopt a iterative color histogram normalizing approach which uses some sample images to build color lookup tables for each camera. Using this approach we can transform the colors of the image of each camera into globally consistent colors.

Using the geometries described above, we can determine the overlapping regions in the images of each pair of neighboring cameras. Let us consider the image I_i of the i-th camera and the image $I_{i_j}, j = 1,2,3$ of its three surrounding cameras. Let R_{i,i_j} and $R_{i_j,i}$ be the overlapped regions of I_i and I_{i_j}, respectively. We adjust the colors of I_i by iteratively normalizing the color histogram of $S_i = \bigcup_{j=1,2,3} R_{i,i_j}$ to that of $S_s = \bigcup_{j=1,2,3} R_{i_j,i}$, where $\bigcup$ stands for the union operator.

$$C_i^1(v) = (1-\alpha)C_i^0(v) + \alpha A_i^0(v) \tag{2}$$

$$A_i^0(v) = \max\{C_s^0(u) | F_i(C_i^0(v)) \leq F_s(C_s^0(u))\} \tag{3}$$

where $C_i^1(v)$ is the lookup table of color channels R, G or B for image I_i, and v is the index. $C_i^0(v) = v$ and $C_s^0(u) = u$ are the color channels of S_i and S_s. $F_*()$ is the accumulation of the normalized histogram. α is a factor to control the adjusting ratio, and it is set to 0.25 in the experiment.

After the lookup tables of all the images are computed, all the images are transformed using the lookup tables, and the same processing is iterated for the transformed images until the max iteration is reached.

Although the convergence of the above processing has not been proved theoretically, experiments show that a few iterations (10 iterations in the experiment) are sufficient.

3.3 Building VRML Model

The colors of each image are adjusted using the lookup tables which are computed in advance. Then, the triangular regions in the original images, as shown in Figure 3(a), are cut out and integrated into a polar expansion of an icosahedron, as shown in Figure 3(b). The integrated images are mapped to a 3D model of the icosahedron. Finally, the icosahedron is transformed into a sphere by iteratively splitting its triangular patches, and the 3D spherical representation of the scene is obtained, as shown in Figure 3(c). The initial viewpoint is set to the center of the sphere.

4 Events Accessing via Internet

Using the 3D VRML model of the 3D spherical representation of the event, users can access the same integrated image which is updated in real time, and manipulate the VRML model to view the event from their preferred viewpoint.

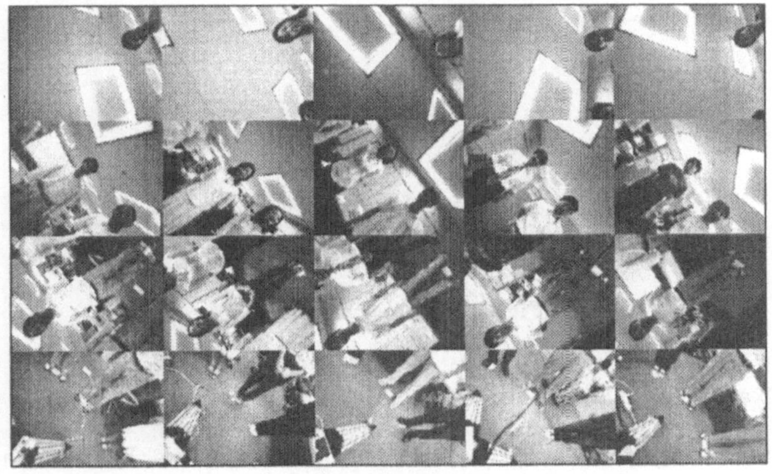

a) Original images

b) Integrated image c) Spherical model

Fig. 3. Integration of images

4.1 System Construction

The construction of the system, which supports access to live events by multi-users with individually selected viewpoints, is shown in Figure 4. The server captures images from SOS in real-time, adjust colors in each image using the lookup tables, which is described in above section, and integrates the images into a VRML model of 3D spherical representation. When accessing this system for the first time, each user receives a whole image and the VRML model from the server. The user may manipulate the VRML model to change a viewpoint, and the information of the new viewpoint is then sent to the server. The server selects adequate regions in the integrated image and sends it to the client of the user. Therefore the system can serve multi-users who can interact and adjust their viewpoint freely.

At present implementation, the server sends whole integrated images to each user, and the rate at which they are updated can reach 0.5 frames per second using one PC as the server.

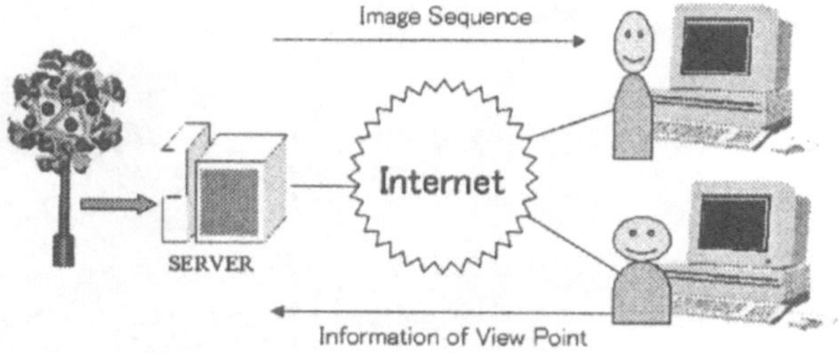

Fig. 4. System construction

4.2 Examples of Event Access

Figure 5 and Figure 6 show some examples of event access. Figure 5 shows a case in which two users access the same event simultaneously, but have different viewpoints. Figure 6 shows two frames of one user who is tracing his interested objects. In these figures, color inconsistency can be found occasionally. This is because we assumed that the overlapping regions of the neighboring cameras should contain strictly the same area, but this condition was not satisfied due to the depth change in the area. We are now considering a color calibration method using the know color patterns.

Fig. 5. Views of different users

5 Conclusion

In this paper, we proposed a method to support access to live events for multi-users with the ability to select viewpoints freely, using a stereo omni-directional system (SOS), which we have developed. This system acquired all directional color images and stereo image pairs in real time, and allows parallel accessing of multi-PC to the memory unit. Using these images, we generated a VRML model of a 3D spherical representation of the live event. Users can manipulate the VRML model to view the event from their preferred viewpoint. The images

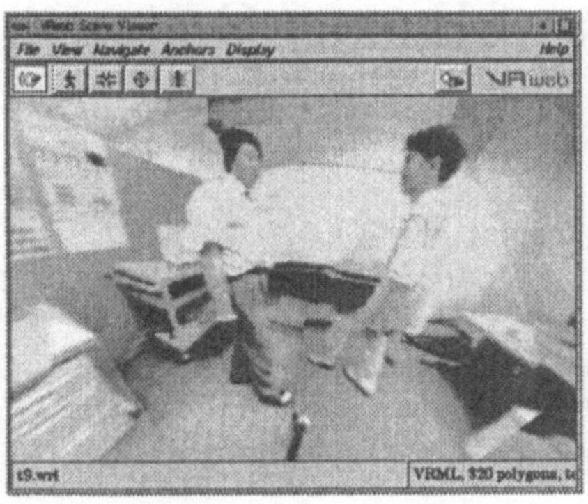
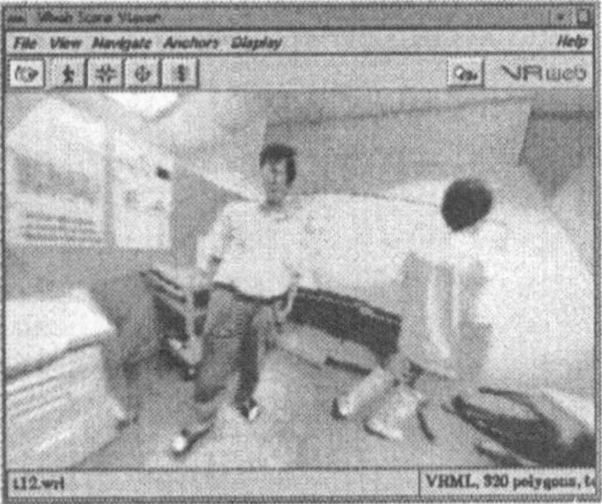

Fig. 6. Object tracking by user

are now updated at a rate of 0.5 frames per second and will achieve nearly a real-time rate by using PC cluster.

In the future, we will construct a PC cluster to support real-time application. We also plan to introduce recognition functions to support more complicated user interactions.

References

1. T.Kanede, P.Rander, and P.J.Narayanan. Virtualized reality: Constructing virtual worlds from real scenes. *IEEE MultiMedia*, 4(1):34–47, January 1997.
2. T.Matsuyama. Cooperative distribution vision – Dynamic integration of visual perception, action and communication. *Proc. of Image Understanding Workshop*, pp. 365-384, 1998.
3. H.Saito, S.Baba, M.Kimura, S.Vedula and T.Kanede. Appearance-based virtual view generation of temporally-varying events from multi-camera images in 3D room. *Computer Science Technical Report, CMU-CS-99-127*, 1999.
4. H.Ishigro and S.Tsuji. Omni-directional stereo. *IEEE Trans. Pattern Analysis and Machine Intelligence*, 14(2):257–262, February 1992.
5. Y.Nishizawa, Y.Yagi, and M.Yachida. Generation of environmental map and estimation of free space for a mobile robot using omnidirectional image sensor copis. *Journal of Robotics Society Japan*, 11(6):868–874, Jun 1993.
6. Y.Yagi. Omnidirectional sensing and its applications. *IEICE Trans. Information and Systems*, E82-D(3):568–579, March 1999.
7. K.Yamazaki, H.Takemura and N.Yokoya. Virtual tours into visualized dynamic real world using an omnidirectional video camera. *Proc. 4th ACCV*, Vol. 1, pp. 5-10, 2000.
8. Y.Onoe, N. Yokoya, K. Kazumasa and H.Takemura. Visual surveillance and monitoring system using an omnidirectional video camera. *Proc. ICPR*, pp. 588-592, 1998.
9. H.Tanahashi, K.Yamamoto, C.Wang, and Y.Niwa. Development of a stereo omnidirectional imaging system (sos). *Proc. IEEE IECON-2000*, pages 289–294, October 2000.

Unsupervised Analysis of Human Gestures

Tian-Shu Wang[1], Heung-Yeung Shum[2], Ying-Qing Xu[2], and Nan-Ning Zheng[1]

[1] Artificial Intelligence and Robotics Lab,
Xi'an Jiaotong University, Xi'an 710049, P.R.China
{tswang,nnzheng}@aiar.xjtu.edu.cn
[2] Microsoft Research, China,
No49, Zhichun Road, Haidian District, Beijing 100086, P.R.China
{yqxu,hshum}@microsoft.com

Abstract. Recognition of human gestures is important for analysis and indexing of video. To recognize human gestures on video, generally a large number of training examples for each individual gesture must be collected. This is a labor-intensive and error-prone process and is only feasible for a limited set of gestures. In this paper, we present an approach for automatically segmenting sequences of natural activities into atomic sections and clustering them. Our work is inspired by natural language processing where words are extracted from long sentences. We extract primitive gestures from sequences of human motion. Our approach contains two steps. First, the sequences of human motion are segmented into atomic components and clustered using a Hidden Markov Model. Thus we can represent the original sequences by discrete symbols. Then we extract lexicon from these discrete sequences by using an algorithm named COMPRESSIVE. Experimental results on music conducting gestures demonstrate the effectiveness of our approach

1 Introduction

Recognition of human gestures is important for human-computer interfaces, automated visual surveillance, and video library indexing[1]. This process, however, involves significant problems. Typically a large collection of training examples of gestures must be acquired in order to build models for the gestures. To obtain the training examples, a substantial number of gesture sequences must be segmented and aligned, typically by hand [2]. The common practice of manual segmentation and labeling is labor-intensive and error-prone. Worse, for many challenging applications, the set of gestures is not known in advance. In this paper, we present an approach for automatically segmenting and labeling a continuous sequence of human gestures.

Our approach makes no assumption about the presence of facilitative side information such as obvious segment points or the duration time of each gesture. Instead, we consider a sequence of human activities to consist of repetitive

* This work was performed while the first author was visiting Microsoft Research China.

gesture primitives with a high-level structure controlling the temporal ordering. This is analogous to the concept of words and grammar in natural language processing. The activities are exhibited by, for example, dance, Tai-chi, and sign language.

Human gestures are expressive human body motions, which generally contain spatial and temporal variation. To handle the variation, we need choose an appropriate representation. In one previous work, gestures are regarded as trajectory curves in a configuration space [3]. In our approach, we emphasize the dynamical part of gestures. We choose Hidden Markov Models (HMMs) to represent the dynamics. It has been demonstrated in [2] [4] that HMMs are effective for human gesture recognition.

The approach used in this paper is described as follows. The first step is to form a discrete representation of gestures. The observed continuous sequence is automatically segmented into atomic gestures. It is an over-segmentation process. And we use HMM models to separate atomics into several clusters. Thus by using cluster labels to replace atomics in the original sequence, we transform the continuous observation to a discrete symbol sequence. In the second step, we learn "words" from the discrete representation. Borrowing methods from natural language processing and data compression, we obtain structure from the symbol sequence and thus determine appropriate primitive gestures and labels of the original sequence. Although the computer is unaware of the meanings of the primitive gestures, the original sequences are effectively represented by them. For example, if we correspond word 16 to a waving hand gesture, we know that all other positions in the original sequence labeled by word 16 are waving hand.

In the reminder of this paper, we briefly overview related works in section 2, describe the details of our approach in section 3, present experiment results in section 4, and end with discussion and future work in section 5.

2 Related works

A vast amount of work in gesture recognition has been performed in the area of computer vision, and is reviewed in [4]. These works can be divided into two categories: trajectory-based and dynamics model-based. The trajectory-based approach matches curves in configuration space to recognize gestures [3]. The dynamics model-based approach learns a parametric model of gestures. HMM is a typical dynamics model and was proven to be robust in its recognition of gestures [2]. The HMM model has been extended to a more general model named Dynamic Bayesian Networks [5].

Several works involve unsupervised learning of video sequences and gestures. A HMM-based approach is used to cluster ambulatory audio and video content [6]. In it, the number of clusters must known a priori. An entropy training process of HMM is proposed in [7] and used to learn office activity. The whole sequence is used to train a single model, thus it is hardly suitable for handling large scale problems. An incremental learning framework of natural gestures is proposed in [8], but it does not involve learning the high level structure of gestures.

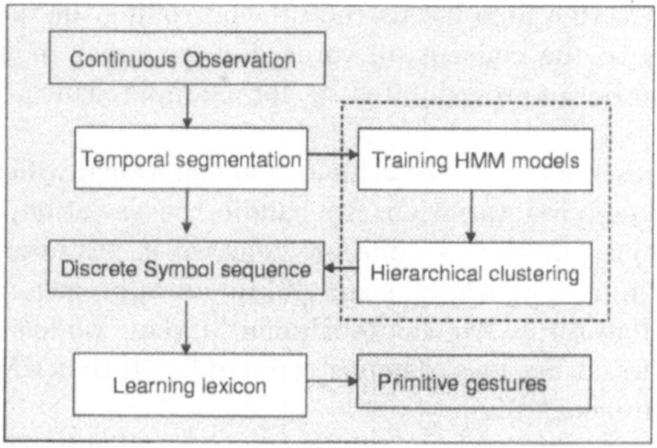

Fig. 1. Framework of the unsupervised learning approach

A relevant topic to this paper is learning the lexicon of a natural language. A classical MK10 algorithm is used to infer word boundaries from artificially generated natural language sentences in [10]. The sequitur algorithm is used to build hierarchical structure in an online process with linear calculation complexity in [9]. A dynamical programming-based approach for extraction of lexicon is proposed in [11]. The performance of different algorithms are not easily compared, but in terms of learning words, an offline algorithm is better than an online algorithm.

3 Approach

Human gestures can be represented as a sequence of hand positions in 3d-space. In a video sequence, the 3d space-curve is projected to a 2d image plane as a 2d trajectory. Thus the continuous observation of gestures is an ordered sequence of hand positions in a 2d image plane.

Figure 1 exhibits a framework of the learning approach. First, the continuous observation of human gestures is segmented into atomics movements. The segmentation involves identifying suitable break points at which to partition the gestures. The result of this process is an over-segmentation of gestures, in which every segment is only an atomic movement and without much meaning. Then we cluster those segments into several clusters by using Hidden Markov Models. This is done to learn a HMM for each segment using a hierarchical clustering method. The result of clustering gives a discrete representation of the original continuous observation, in which every segment is replaced by the cluster number that it belongs to. Finally, we infer the lexicon from the discrete symbol sequence. The details of each step are described in the following.

3.1 Temporal segmentation

The purpose of temporal segmentation is to split the continuous sequence into atomic segments. The atomic segments exhibit basic movements whose execution is consistent and easily characterized by a simple trajectory. As we need to extract meaningful gestures, the segmentation is overly fine and can be considered as finding the alphabet of motion.

The segmentation involves searching natural inconsistent points within the whole observation. A change in the type of human movement usually causes dips in velocity or abrupt variations in moving direction. We exploit this by finding the local minima of velocity and local maxima of change in direction. The minima (maxima) below (above) the certain threshold are selected as segment points. In practice, we found the calculation of change in direction to be prone to noise. So we apply a Gaussian smoothing filter to reduce noise.

3.2 Clustering by Hidden Markov Models

Humans perform gestures with variations in speed and position. To handle these variations, HMMs are used in this paper. An HMM is a probabilistic state machine and is widely used in recognition of dynamic processes. The Forward-Backward algorithm is an effective hill-climbing method for learning HMM parameters of observation sequences. And the Forward or Viterbi algorithm is used to evaluate the likelihood between observation and HMM[12].

HMMs provide a proper distance metric for sequence comparison. The distance between two sequences is computed as:

$$Dist(O_1,O_2)=\frac{1}{2}\left[\frac{1}{T_1}(P(O_1|\lambda_1)-P(O_1|\lambda_2))+\frac{1}{T_2}(P(O_2|\lambda_2)-p(O_2|\lambda_1))\right] \quad (1)$$

where λ_1,λ_2 denote two HMM models trained on sequences O_1, O_2; T_1,T_2 are the lengths of O_1, O_2, respectively.

The distance metric is used in [12] to compare HMM models. Considering the HMM as a generative model of sequences, the distance of models represent the distance of observations well.

Given a distance metric, many methods can be used to cluster the observation into several groups. In this paper, we choose hierarchical clustering to generate clusters from the observation[13]. The complete-link algorithm is used in this paper.

The operation of hierarchical clustering is a sequential process of merging the two most similar clusters to form a larger cluster. At the start, every sample is placed in its own cluster. The process is stopped when the distance between the two most similar clusters exceeds a threshold. In the complete-link algorithm, the distance between two clusters is maximum of all pairwise distances between samples in the two clusters. Compact clusters are produced by using the algorithm, and the result is fit for our purpose.

For N gesture segments, the whole clustering process requires training of N sequences, evaluation of N^2 distances, and a hierarchical clustering process on N samples. For large N, the process may be impractical. We can randomly select a set of segments to form the original clusters, use one HMM model to represent one cluster, and incrementally add the others.

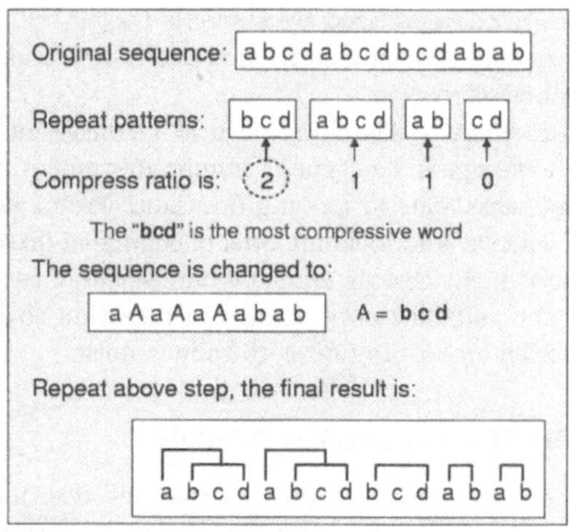

Fig. 2. An example of the COMPRESSIVE algorithm

3.3 Extracting Lexicon

Replacing each segment with its corresponding cluster number, we generate a discrete representation of the original continuous observation. Next we need to infer words from the sequence.

Extracting lexicon from a discrete sequence can be regarded as a language problem where we determine the basic vocabulary from a text. Considering the number of words, there may be a large number of possible solutions. We perhaps cannot find the true set of original base words, but such vocabulary has the property of providing a compact representation of the original data. So we can select an optimal solution by the MDL criteria, which is widely used in unsupervised learning and known to give interpretable results.

Directly finding the MDL solution is an NP-hard problem. Instead of finding the globally optimal solution, we adopt a heuristic approach called COMPRESSIVE [14]. It can be explained as selecting the word that provides the highest compression ratio of the input sequence. The compression ratio of a word is defined as:

$$\Delta DL = M \cdot N - (M + N + 1) \tag{2}$$

where M is the length of the word, and N is the number of repeated occurrences. This rule exhibits a tradeoff between pattern occurrence frequency and pattern length. In practice, the compressive first rule provides good performance for lexicon acquisition. An example is illustrated in Figure 2.

Our implementation uses a suffix-array [15]and has a complexity of $O(N^2)$. A suffix-array is a sorted list of all suffixes of a string, and can be constructed by initializing an array of pointers to every token in the string and sorting the array according to the lexicographic ordering of the suffixes denoted by the pointers.

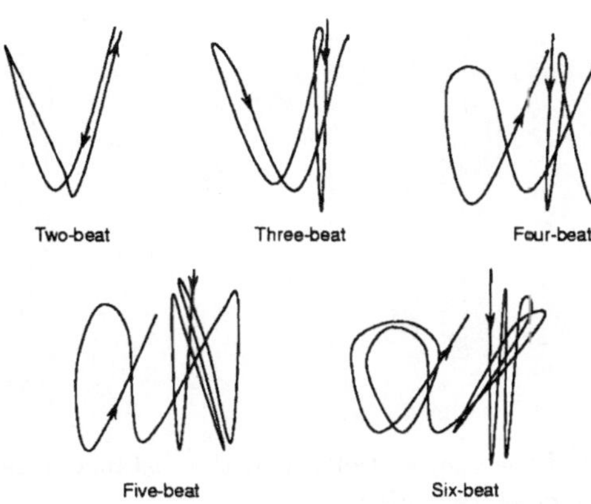

Fig. 3. Five basic conducting gestures.

To find the most compressed string, we need only scan the suffix array once and select one according to the Equation 2.

The lexicon obtained by our approach has a hierarchical structure. A word may contain other words. For example, in Figure 2, the string (*abcd*) has a sub-string (*abc*).

4 Experiment

To test our approach we carried out an experiment on musical conducting. It is natural to consider conducting as complex gestures consisting of a combination of simpler parts, for which we want to extract primitive patterns. We capture the data from a professional conductor who uses natural and precise conducting gestures.

We recorded about 8 minutes of conducting gestures. The whole sequence contains 5 basic beat-patterns, namely a two-beat pattern, three-beat pattern. Each basic pattern is performed many times. The prototype of each pattern is shown in Figure 3.

We use an optical motion capture system to obtain the 3d-position of the conductor's hand. The 3d-position is projected onto a virtual image plane, thus creating 2-d observation vector sequence contain the x, y position of conductor hand.

Totally 163 segments are obtained from temporal segmentation. We train a 5-state Gaussian HMM on each segment and calculate the distance matrix of sequences, which is shown in Figure 4. To choose the number of clusters, we draw a graph of the distance of the merged clusters. The cluster number can be estimated at a point, where increasing the number of clusters will merge very similar clusters. In our experiment the cluster number is selected as 15, as seen in Figure 4.

We obtain discrete representation of the original gesture sequence after the clustering process. The sequence is fed to the COMPRESSIVE algorithm to

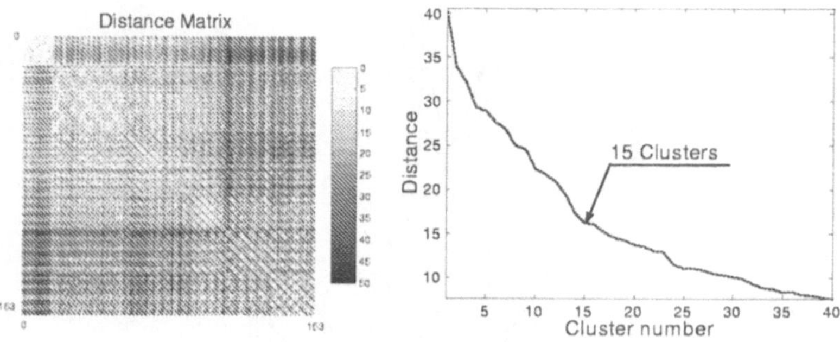

Fig. 4. Distance matrix of the samples(left), and the distance of merged clusters with respect to the number of clusters (right)

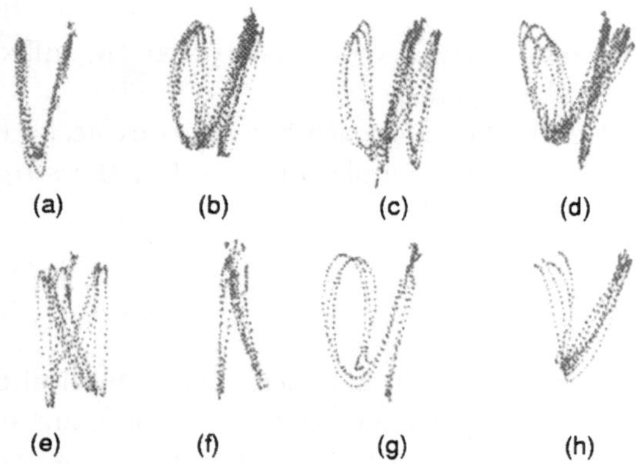

Fig. 5. The extracted patterns. (a) Two-beat. (b) Three-beat. (c) Four-beat. (d) Six-beat. Five-beat patterns are divided into (e) and part of (g). Within a hierarchical structure, (f) and (h) are part of (d) and (c),respectively.

determine words. Totally 8 words are extracted, including two-beat, three-beat, four-beat, and six-beat patterns. The five-beat pattern is not extracted because of few occurrences. The pattern is subdivided into two patterns as illustrated in Figure 5. The whole learning process takes approximate 4 minutes on a PIII 500MHZ CPU.

In the entire sequence, 104 of 163 segments are correctly labeled as prior known patterns. Although the rest are not recalled, they have been precisely assigned as new patterns.

It is shown that our algorithm can successfully segment and label continuous human gestures. Of course, this also reflects the limitation of the algorithm: it only extracts potential words instead of definite lexicon.

5 Conclusion

We have presented an approach for unsupervised clustering of human gestures. Our experiments show that our approach is feasible and useful. In addition, our approach can be easily adapted to incremental and online frameworks.

Our approach depends on the frequency of gestures. So it is suitable for structured human motion in which every gesture is repeated many times. Our future work will extend our approach to general human gestures. Another direction of interest is to apply our approach on partially labeled data.

References

1. D.M.Gavria. : The Visual Analysis of Human Movement: A Suvey. Computer vision and Image Understanding, Vol 73, 82-98,(1999).
2. T. Starner, A.Pentland.: Visual Recognition of American Language Using Hidden Markov Models. In Int workshop on Automatic Face and Gesture Recognition, 189-194, (1995).
3. Lee Campbell, Aaron.Bobick.: Recognition of Human Body Motion Using Phase Space Constraints, Fifth International Conference on Computer Vision, 624-630, Cambridge MA (1995)
4. Ying Wu, Thomas Huang.: Vision-Based Gesture Recognition: A Review. International Gesture Workshop, France, (1999)
5. Vladimir Pavlovic, James M.Rehg, John MacCormick.: Impact of Dynamic Model learning on Classification of Human Motion. International Conference on Computer Vision. (1999)
6. Brian.Clarkson, Alex.Pentland.: Unsupervised Clustering Of Ambulatory Audio and Video. AAAI99, (1999)
7. Matthew.Brand: Learning Concise Model of Human Activity from Ambient Video via a Structure-inducting M-step Estimator. MERL Technical report. (1997)
8. M. Walter, A.Psarrou, S. Gong.: An Incremental Learning Approach to Human Gesture Recognition Using Semi-CONditional DENSity PropagATION. International Conference on CARV, Singapore, (2000)
9. Nevil-Manning, and I. Witten.: Identifying Hierarchical Structure in Sequences: a Linear-time Algorithm. Artificial Intelligence Research, Vol 7, 66-82, (1997)
10. Wolff.J.G.: An Algorithm for the Segmentation of an Artificial Language analogue. British Journal of Psychology, vol 66, 79-90, (1975)
11. Kit. Chunyu.: A Goodness Measure for Phrase Learning via Compression with the MDL Principle. IESSLLI-98 Student Session, Chapter 13, 175-187, (1998).
12. L. Rabiner, B.Juang.: Fundamentals of Speech Recognition. Prentice Hall, New Jersey, USA (1993)
13. A.K.Jain, M.N.Murthy, P.J.Flynn.: Data Clustering: A Review. Technical report MSU-CSE-00-16, MSU, (2000).
14. Nevill-Manning, I. Witten.: Online and Offline Heuristics for Inferring Hierarchies of Repetitions in Sequence, Proceedings of the IEEE, in press.
15. K. Sadakane, H. Imai.: Constructing Suffix Arrays of Large Texts. Proc of DEWS98, (1998).

User Modeling for Efficient Use of Multimedia Files

Fan Lin[1] Liu Wenyin[2] Zheng Chen[2] Hongjiang Zhang[2] Tang Long[1]

[1]Dept. Computer Sci. and Tech., Tsinghua University, Beijing 100084,PR China
lfan98@mails.tsinghua.edu.cn
[2]Microsoft Research China, 49 Zhichun Road, Beijing 100080,PR China
{wyliu, zhengc, hjzhang}@microsoft.com

Abstract. It is very common that a user likes to collect many multimedia files of their interests from the web or other sources for his/her daily use, such as in emails, presentations, and technical documents. This paper presents algorithms to learn user models, in particular, user intention models and preference models from the usage of these files. Such usages include downloading, inserting, and sending multimedia files. A user intention model predicts when the user may want to involve some multimedia objects in his currently working environment (e.g., an email) and provides more convenient and accurate help to the user. A user preference model describes the types and classes of the user's favorite multimedia files and helps an offline crawler to autonomously collect more useful multimedia files for the user. The algorithms have been implemented in our media agents system and shown their effectiveness in user modeling.

1 Introduction

With the development of multimedia technologies and the Internet, the number of multimedia files available online increases rapidly and can be obtained more easily. The number of multimedia data that a single user may have accumulated is also continuously increasing. However, how to help the user efficiently manage and re-use his/her media collection, in particular, how to search for a particular media file or a set of media files from this collection, is a challenging problem.

Attempting to solve this problem, we have invented a media agents system [6] that autonomously collects and builds personalized semantic indices of multimedia data on behalf of the user and is able to provide intelligent suggestions to the user when appropriate. However, when and what to collect for the user and when and what to suggest to the user are among the most important decisions to make in the media agents system. These decisions are determined by the user models that represent the user's profile, in particular, the user's preferences and intentions. The media agents system needs to know user preference models that describes what are the user's favorite multimedia files such that the offline crawler can take the initiative to collect or index these files for the user. The user intention models can help the media agents system in predicting when is the proper time and what kind of multimedia files or which specific multimedia file the user may want to use.

In this paper, we present user modeling algorithms (e.g., how to build such user models) and their implementations in the media agents system. Since different users may have different models, a general user model cannot help accurate and proper decision-making. Hence, building specific user models for a particular user is necessary. We learn these from the user's previous experience of using these multimedia files, including downloading, inserting, and sending multimedia files.

In the media agents system, we record all activities the user has interacted with the system. A history of the user's actions is referred to as user log and is the data sources of learning the user models. For instances, frequently used media files usually show the user's strong preferences, and more accurate suggestions can be provided after learning from the records of whether or not the user has accepted those previously suggested items.

The rest of the paper is organized as follows. Section 2 presents algorithms of learning user models. Section 3 presents experiments and evaluations. We finally present concluding remarks in Section 4.

2 User Modeling Algorithms

2.1 Learn the User Intention Models

Many kinds of user activities, including mouse movement and typing can be used to learn and predict the user's intentions [3]. However, in order to make things simpler, we mainly consider learning the user's intentions from the text information he/she has typed. For instance, when the user is writing a new e-mail and has typed "Here is an interesting picture download from the web", the probability of the user's intention of inserting an image into the e-mail body as an attachment is very high. Therefore, the media agents can predict that user wants to insert an image in the e-mail. If the user's intention is to insert, we can further guess which image the user may want to insert based on other text information the user has typed or will type.

We refer to all the factors in the text that may imply the user's intentions as linguistic features. In order to use these features properly, we choose Bayesian Belief Network [4] to precisely represent the dependencies and probabilities among the linguistic features and the user's intentions. We have defined three levels of linguistic features in this paper: lexics, syntax, and partially instantiated sentence patterns. A lexical feature is a single word extracted from the text. A syntactical feature is the syntax structure of a sentence. An instantiated pattern feature is a frequently used sentence structure with some of its syntactical units instantiated with certain words, phrases, concept synonyms. The term "concept synonym" means a group of words that are different in meaning but imply the same user intention. For instance, if the word 'picture' or 'song' appears in the text that the user has just typed, the probability that he/she wants to insert an attachment is high. However, if the user has used word 'train' or 'building', such probability is low. Therefore, 'picture' and 'song' are of the same concept synonym here. "Here it is a...(concept synonym)" and "Attached please find...(concept synonym)" are examples of partially instantiated sentence pattern features. The Bayesian Belief Network we used to represent the user's intention model is illustrated in Figure 1.

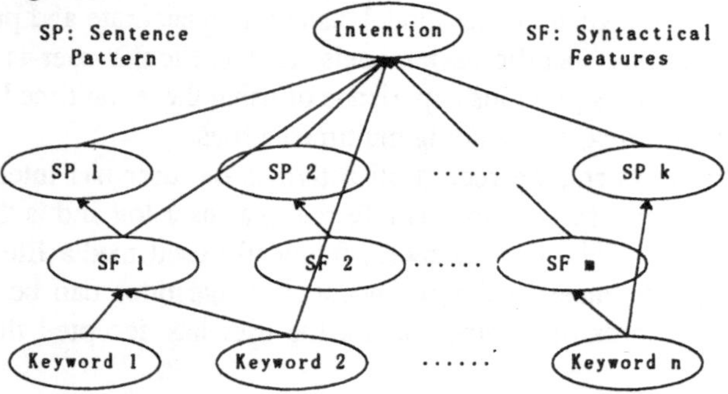

Figure 1. Intention modeling using a Bayesian Belief Network

Initially, such user intention model is empty but can be learned from the user log as the training data. We collect sufficient action records to train the intention model. Each user action record contains a text part and a tag of whether a media file is attached. The text part is then parsed such that all words (lexical features) are extracted from the sentences and are stemmed [5].

At the lexical level, direct association between keyword features and user intentions can be found through training. We use the fast algorithm proposed by Agrawal et al. [1] to generate association rules. The rules represent the causality relationship between keywords and intentions, e.g., given a keyword whether an insertion is intended. The causality rules are further constrained by two parameters: α (*Support of Item Sets*) and β (*Confidence of Association Rule*) [1]. The first one (α), which depicts the scope that the rules can be applied to, can be expressed by the percentage of those records that contain both the same keyword and an inserted attachment as evidence. The second one (β) depicts the probability that the rule stands, i.e., the probability of the intention given the appearance of the keyword. We evaluate the generated rules based on the values of these two parameters. The higher these two values, the better the rules. Those rules with parameters higher than certain thresholds are selected to build the Bayesian Belief Network.

Once training is completed, the intention model for the user is fully obtained and is used in the future to predict the user's intention based on what the user has just typed. The prediction process is as follows. First, a set of keyword features represented by (<a1, a2…an>) is extracted from the text typed by the user. The prediction module then calculates the probabilities of all predefined user intentions (V), and choose the one with the biggest probability (v_{map}) using the following equation [4].

$$\begin{aligned} v_{map} &= \arg\max_{vj\in V} P(v_j \mid a_1, a_2, \ldots, a_n) \\ &= \arg\max_{vj\in V} P(a_1, a_2, \ldots, a_n \mid v_j) P(v_j) \end{aligned} \tag{1}$$

where $P(a_1, a_2, \ldots, a_n \mid v_j) = \prod_{i=1}^{n} P(a_i \mid Parents\ (a_i), v_j)$.

However, lexical features do not work very well since they do not express much semantics (and intentions). More informative features are needed to precisely predict the user's intentions. Hence, we use natural language processing (NLP) technologies [2] to analyze sentence structures of the text. NLP can analyze a sentence and parse it into a tree structure. We use the highest-level sentence structures. For instance, we parse "Here are some photos" into the following sentence structure: AVP ("here"), VERB ("be"), NP ("some photos"). These syntactical features can dig out more useful information. We use the same method [1] to generate the association rules between these syntactical features and user intentions.

Using syntactical features, the prediction precision can be improved but is still limited. We find that some sentence patterns, such as, "here is something" in an e-mail, usually indicates that the user wants to insert an attachment. The sentence structure is AVP+VERB+NP. However, "how are you" has the same structure but indicates a different intention. Therefore, we further instantiate parts of the sentence structure and find several instantiated patterns that may strongly indicate user's intentions.

By instantiating parts of the syntactical features with certain frequently used words, phrases, or concept synonyms, we generate association rules at the instantiation pattern level, which is more general than the lexics level rules and more specific than the syntax level rules. Since each syntactical unit can be replaced by many words, we test all possible instantiations of syntactical units with corresponding words found in the training data and select those instantiated patterns with α and β parameters (of the association rules) larger than certain thresholds. In order to make the pattern features discriminative at a proper abstraction level, concept synonyms are used to instantiate some of the syntactical units. In order to do so, all NPs (noun phrases) are further parsed into sub-trees, each of which is searched in a breadth-first order. We refer to the noun found for the first time as the headword of the NP. We consider all headwords of those sentences that have been labeled with the same intention class (inserted or not) and have the same syntactical structure as the same concept synonym. As we can see from the experiments, user intention prediction based on this level rules is much better than using the rules at the other two levels.

2.2 Learn the User Preferences Models

The user's interests and preferences are learnt from the user's frequently used media files and described in user preference models. Once the user preferences models are known, it is possible for the media agents to provide better services, e.g., provide more appropriate suggestions or more preferred media files that have been collected automatically from all possible sources by an offline crawler. The media files on the local machine can also be automatically sought for better indexing, clustering, and/or classification at regular time as well. Other benefits includes media file sharing with other users having similar user preferences models.

We use two levels of semantic features in user preferences modeling: lexical features, which are exactly keywords, and modifier-headword features, which are headwords accompanied with some modifiers, as exemplified in Figure 2. A user may have several different preference models, each of which can be represented by a list of keywords, or more precisely, can be represented by a list of modifier-headwords features. For instance, a user may like classic music (headword) of Mozart (one modifier) and

Beethoven (another modifier). Keywords can be easily extracted from the environment context. However, a headword accompanied with some modifiers is more difficult to analyze. We obtain the headword of each sentence in the same way as discussed in the previous sub-section. In our algorithm, the nouns or adjectives that are headword's left brothers in the tree structure are considered the modifiers of the headword. This rule seems simple but is actually effective. Furthermore, we find those synonymous headwords with at least one-third modifiers in common and classify them into one synonym with the union of their modifiers.

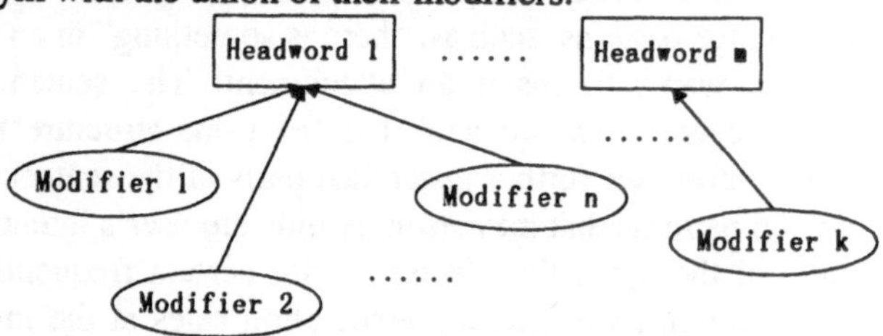

Figure 2. Illustration of Modifier-headword features

All user log records in the train data are clustered into several preferences clusters based on their semantic similarity, which can be measured using either levels of semantic features. Each cluster corresponds to a preference model for the user. At the lexical feature level, a user preference model is represented by a keyword frequency vector formed by the top 10 frequently used keywords (except for stop words) and their frequency in the user log cluster, e.g., $m=<k_1, k_2,...,k_{10}>$. Whether a multimedia file is of interest to the user depends on its semantic similarity to the user preferences models. We can also compare similarity between two user preference models by calculating the dot product of their keyword frequency vectors.

The above approach based on keyword frequency is simple for implementation but limited in performance. The Naïve Bayes approach has a good performance in classifying text documents and is therefore applied in the media agents to model the user's preferences based on the keyword probability.

In the Naïve Bayes approach, we use all words and their probabilities to form a keyword probability vector to model a preference. The probability of word w_k is estimated using the following equation described by [4].

$$P(w_k \mid m_j) = \frac{n_k + 1}{n + \mid Vocabulary \mid} \qquad (2)$$

where n is the total number of words existing within the training data, which are all user log records in the cluster corresponding to the user preference model m_j, n_k is the number of times that word w_k is found among these n words, and $|Vocabulary|$ is the total number of distinct words found in the training data. Actually, Eq. (2) is the term frequency combined with a smoothing function.

Given a multimedia file D represented by $<w_1, w_2,...,w_n>$, the most probable user preference model M_{NB} is calculated using the Naïve Bayes approach as follows.

$$m_{NB} = \arg\max_{mj \in M} P(m_j \mid w_1, w_2 ... w_n) \quad (3)$$
$$= \arg\max_{mj \in M} P(w_1, w_2 ... w_n \mid m_j) P(m_j)$$
$$= \arg\max_{mj \in M} P(m_j) \prod_k P(w_k \mid m_j)$$

$P(m_j)$ is the prior of m_j, which can be considered as of a uniform distribution initially. The approach assumes that the probability of a word is independent of others or its position within the text. Note that this assumption is not always true. However, in practice, the Naïve Bayesian learner performs remarkably well in many text classification problems despite the incorrectness of this independence assumption [4].

$P(m_j \mid w_1, w_2 ... w_n)$ is comparable among different m_j, and can therefore be used to find a better model. However, $P(m_j \mid w_1, w_2 ... w_n)$ is not comparable among different D, since it differs in magnitude for different lengths of keyword vectors. In order to judge whether D is of the user's interest, we need to find another metric that is comparable among different D such that a value larger than a threshold means that the document is of the user's preference. First al all, due to multiple multiplications in Eq (3), a geometrical mean is considered in normalizing $P(m_{NB} \mid w_1, w_2 ... w_n)$ as follows.

$$\log\left(\sqrt[n_w]{P(m_{NB}) \prod_i P(w_i \mid m_j)}\right) = \frac{\log(P(m_{NB} \mid w_1, w_2 ... w_n))}{n_w},$$

where n_w is the number of distinct keywords in document D matched with keywords in the model m_{NB}. Secondly, a factor of matched keyword percentage is considered such that the document containing a larger percentage of keywords in D matched in the model will get a higher metric value and is therefore more relevant to the user's preference model. Hence, $\frac{n_D}{n_w}$ is multiplied, where n_D is the total number of words in D.

Finally, we define the metric as follows, which is used to measure the relevancy of D to the user's preference model.

$$P_{norm}(D) = \frac{n_D * \log(P(m_{NB} \mid w_1, w_2 ... w_n)}{n_w^2} \quad (4)$$

Using the Bayesian method, the similarity between two user preference models can also be calculated. One of the metrics is as follows.

$$Sim(m_1, m_2) = \frac{P(m_1 \mid m_2) + P(m_2 \mid m_1)}{2}, \quad (5)$$

where, m_1 and m_2 are two user preference models represented by keyword vectors.

In addition, we use both modifier-headword features and keyword features in the Naïve Bayes approach to archive better performance.

3 Experiments and Evaluations

For user intention modeling, the training data are 200 records of user's e-mails, among which, 50 e-mails have attachments and the other 150 do not. Two-third of them were used for training and one-third for testing. In our experiments, the thresholds we used for α and β parameters discussed in Section 2.1 are 0.03 and 0.6.

First, we have used lexical features only. The precision of insertion prediction is about 80%. The result is fairly good, since most formal e-mails that contain attachments prefer to use "attach/attached/attachment", "see", and some other frequently used keywords, which can be easily judged at the lexics level. Nevertheless, a large number of informal emails do not use these obvious keywords. For example, some users like to type only a subject "an interesting song". These cases cannot be handled by the keyword feature extraction. Thus, we have added syntactic features to the model. The precision is about 5 percent higher. There are some sentence structures that always suggest insertion actions. For instance, only one noun phrase (NP), such as "an interesting song" in an e-mail usually implies that the user wants to insert an attachment. Adding partially instantiated sentence patterns, we successfully mined out several patterns such as "Here + be + concept synonym" and "Please see + concept synonym". Hence, the prediction precision can be as high as 97%. Figure 3 shows comparison of prediction precisions of using these three levels of features.

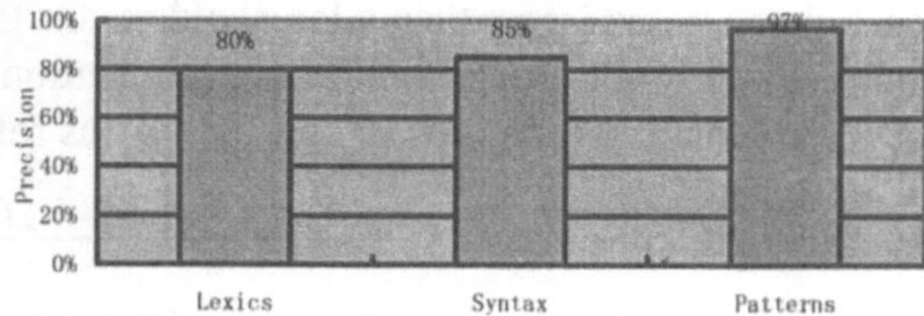

Figure 3. Performance of user intention modeling of using different level features

For user preferences modeling, we have let four users to search for their interested pictures on the web and download them. Their interests were: space photos, museum photos, football-game photos, and baseball-game photos. Each user downloaded 50 photos from web, 35 were use for training the user preference models and 15 were used for testing acceptance as relevant to the user preference model. Another 50 photos that were not in the four classes were downloaded for testing refusal.

Figure 4 shows performance of user preference modeling of the two approaches presented in Section 2.2. In the approach of top 10 keywords, the similarity threshold we used was 0.1. In the Naïve Bayesian approach, a threshold of –1.5 was used for the metric defined in Eq. (4).

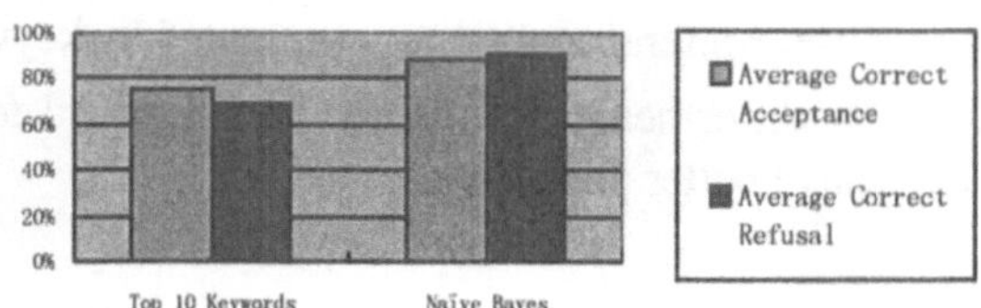

Figure 4. Performance of user preference modeling

Keyword features, headword features, and their combination were tested for comparison in preference modeling. The threshold of Naïve Bayes approach was kept unchanged. Performance comparison of these features in preference modeling is presented in Figure 5.

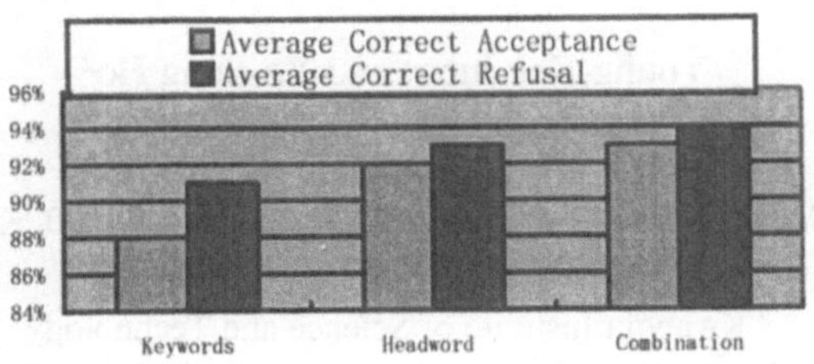

Figure 5. Comparison of different features in preference modeling

4 Concluding Remarks

In this paper, we have presented algorithms to learn user models, in particular, user intention models and user preference models in using accumulated multimedia files. The models can be learned more precisely after mining from a long time of action records of the user. The user preference models can help the media agents system to take the initiative to collect more media objects relevant to the user interests and provide the user with more satisfactory services. Even though the user has never seen these media files before, it is still possible for the media agents to find them for the user. The learned user intention model can help the media agents system to predict when it is the proper time to provide suggestions and what to suggest. Experiments have shown the usefulness and effectiveness of the developed algorithms.

References

[1] Agrawal R, et al. (1994) Fast Discovery of Association Rules. In: *Advances in Knowledge Discovery and Data Mining*, Fayyad UM, Piatetsky-Shapiro G, Smyth P, and Uthurusamy R (eds.), AAAI Press, California, pp. 307-328.

[2] Allen J (1994) *Natural Language Understanding*, University of Rochester, pp. 23-25.

[3] Horvitz E et al. (1998) The Lumiere Project: Bayesian User Modeling for Inferring the Goals and Needs of Software Users. In: *Proc. of the 14th Conference on Uncertainty in Artificial Intelligence*.

[4] Mitchell TM (1997) *Machine Learning*. McGraw-Hill.

[5] Porter MF (1980) An Algorithm for Suffix Stripping. *Program* 14(3):130-137

[6] Liu Wenyin, et al. (2001) A Media Agent for Automatically Building a Personalized Semantic Index of Web Media Objects. *To appear in Journal of the American Society for Information Science, 2001*.

A Feature-Based Vehicle Tracking System in Congested Traffic Video Sequences

Young-Kee Jung[1] and Yo-Sung Ho[2]

[1] Honam University
59-1 Seobong-Dong Kwangsan-Gu, Kwangju, 506-090, Korea
ykjung@mail.honam.ac.kr

[2] Kwangju Institute of Science and Technology
1 Oryong-Dong Puk-Gu, Kwangju, 500-712, Korea
hoyo@kjist.ac.kr

Abstract. This paper describes a new feature-based vehicle tracking system using trajectory matching, which extracts corner features of the vehicle and tracks the features using linear Kalman filtering, where features from the same vehicle are grouped together. We also propose a new grouping algorithm using trajectory matching to make our tracking system robust enough for segmenting different vehicles in the congested traffic situation. The proposed system has demonstrated good performance for crossway traffic video sequences.

1 Introduction

The red-light camera is popularly applied for traffic surveillance. It helps communities enforce traffic laws by automatically photographing vehicles whose drivers run red lights or do lane violation. A red-light camera system operates with a video-based vehicle tracking system to decide red-light or lane violation by its tracking trajectory.

In traffic surveillance applications, a video-based vehicle tracking system detects and tracks an individual vehicle that is moving through the camera scene. This system can provide traffic flows, such as normal traveling of vehicles, vehicle traveling in the wrong direction, and stopped vehicles.

Various tracking systems have been developed for detecting moving vehicles and tracing their locations based on the linear predictor model [1], [2], [3], [4]. One typical approach of video-based tracking is the feature-based tracking system where sub-features, such as distinguishable points or lines of the object, are traced [4]. The main advantage of this approach is that even in the presence of partial occlusion, some sub-features of the moving object remain visible. Therefore, this approach is appropriate for congested traffic in the crossway. Since a vehicle could have multiple sub-features, we have to group a set of features belongs to the same object.

Grouping of sub-features of the vehicles is based on common motion constraints. Previous grouping algorithms utilize only the spatial information that link sub-features together within a limited range [4]. In order to make the grouping robust enough for segmenting different moving vehicles, they keep track of relative distances of all feature pairs. If a feature pair has large variation of the relative distance, the grouping of the pair is broken. However, when the vehicle is turning left or right, the shape of the vehicle can be changed and tracking positions of the features become incorrect. Therefore, the conventional grouping rule does not guarantee stable vehicle tracking. In addition, the previous approaches are not appropriate for real-time object tracking due to their computational complexity for grouping.

In this paper, we propose a new feature-based tracking system where we design a robust grouping algorithm using trajectory matching., Fig. 1 shows key functional blocks of the proposed tracking system.

2 Feature-based Tracking System

As shown in Fig. 1, the proposed vehicle tracking system consists of three functional parts: feature detection, feature tracking and feature grouping.

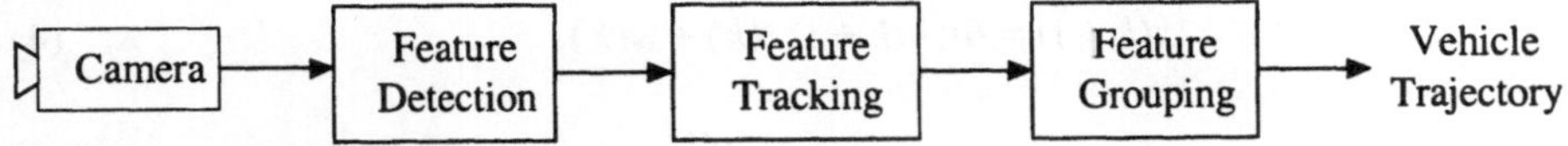

Fig. 1. Feature-based Tracking System

After we select features based on the measure of cornerness of the moving vehicle, we trace the detected features using linear Kalman filtering, which requires a modest amount of computation. In the grouping part, we group sub-features together that come from the same vehicle, which helps us to extract the vehicle trajectory.

2.1 Feature Detection

Corner points that can be traced reliably are chosen as sub-features of the vehicle. For corner point detection, we take gradient operations along the x and y directions over the 9x9 window, and compute the second moment matrix Z by taking average of the gradient values [5].

$$Z = \begin{bmatrix} g_x^2 & g_x g_y \\ g_x g_y & g_y^2 \end{bmatrix} \quad (1)$$

where g_x and g_y are the average gradient values along the x and y directions, respectively. If the matrix Z has two large eigenvalues, the original window contains a corner feature of high spatial frequency. Therefore, we can declare the corner point if $\min(\lambda_1,\lambda_2) > \lambda_c$, where λ_1 and λ_2 are two eigenvalues of the matrix Z and λ_c is a predefined threshold value.

2.2 Feature Tracking

Once a corner point is detected, we can track the feature efficiently by predicting the next coordinate from the observed coordinate of the feature point. We design a 2D token-based tracking scheme using Kalman filtering [1], [6]. The center position of the feature is used as the token $t(k)$. We assume the next token $t(k+1)$ is a sum of the current token $t(k)$ and the token change $\Delta t(k)$. We can define a simplified polynomial motion model as follows:

$$t(k+1) = t(k) + \Delta t(k) \tag{2}$$

Kalman filtering provides a sequential and recursive algorithm for optimal linear minimum variance (LMV) estimation of the system state $x(k)$. We define the state variable $x(k)$ as a two-dimensional vector, which represents the positional change of the token $\Delta t(k)$.

$$x(k) = \begin{bmatrix} \Delta x\_center(k) \\ \Delta y\_center(k) \end{bmatrix} \tag{3}$$

The Kalman filter algorithm tries to estimate system states based on a set of measurement errors. We assume that a state model is linear and it is defined by

$$x(k+1) = \Phi(k, k+1)x(k) + w(k) \tag{4}$$

$$\Phi(k, k+1) = \begin{bmatrix} 1 & 0 \\ 0 & 1 \end{bmatrix} \tag{5}$$

where $x(k)$ denotes the system state at time instant k, $\Phi(k,k+1)$ denotes a state transition matrix during the unit time interval, and $w(k)$ denotes an estimation error. Assuming that the trajectory of the target object varies with a constant acceleration, we can write the state transition matrix by Eq. (5).

We can also assume a linear relationship between the system state and a set of measurements as follows:

$$z(k) = H(k)x(k) + v(k) \tag{6}$$

$$H(k) = \begin{bmatrix} 1 & 0 \\ 0 & 1 \end{bmatrix} \tag{7}$$

where $x(k)$ denotes a set of measurements, $H(k)$ an observation matrix, and $v(k)$ measurement errors.

After we define a system model and a measurement model, we apply a recursive Kalman filtering algorithm to obtain LMV estimates of motion parameters. The recursive Kalman filtering algorithm consists of three steps of operations: initialization, state prediction, and measurement update.

In the initialization step, we determine the initial state estimate that are derived by discrete time derivatives of the feature center locations in the first two frames and determine the initial error covariance matrix which represents deviation of the initial state estimate from the actual initial state.

In the state prediction step, we determine a priori LMV estimate and its error covariance matrix for the current state based on the previous state estimate and error covariance. In the measurement update step, we combine the estimated information with new measurements to refine the LMV estimate and its error covariance matrix for the current state. We perform this correction process based on a set of measurement errors using normalized correlation. A small 9x9 gray-level template is extracted and used for calculating normalized correlation.

At each time frame, we use the Kalman filter to predict the search region for each corner point. The template that was extracted when the corner point was originally detected, is correlated in the search region. After we locate the correlation peak, we can update the system state and the error variance using Kalman filtering.

2.3 Feature Grouping using Trajectory Matching

The purpose of feature grouping is to cluster sub-features together that come from the same vehicle. Corner features that move together are linked into a single vehicle. Since there are many vehicles in traffic scenes, it is difficult to group sub-features. In order to resolve this segmentation problem, we develop trajectory approximation and trajectory matching algorithms.

For trajectory approximation, after we detect moving features in the traffic video sequence, we extract feature trajectories. A trajectory is aligned by the trail of the centroid of the feature in successive picture frames. Therefore, the feature trajectories that come from the same vehicle have similar shapes. We can approximate the *x* and *y* positions of the centroids over the frame time *t* by

$$\begin{aligned} x(t) &= a_{x0} + a_{x1}t + a_{x2}t^2 + \cdots + a_{xn}t^n \\ y(t) &= a_{y0} + a_{y1}t + a_{y2}t^2 + \cdots + a_{yn}t^n \end{aligned} \tag{8}$$

where $x(t)$ and $y(t)$ represent the *x* and *y* positions of the centroids, respectively, *n* is the approximation order, and a_{xk} (k=0,…,n) and a_{yk} (k=0,…,n) are approximated coefficients of $x(t)$ and $y(t)$, respectively.

If we approximate *m* known centroid points by a polynomial of order 3, the unknown coefficients, a_{x0}, a_{x1}, a_{x2}, and a_{x3}, can be found by least squares curve fitting, which minimizes the sum of the squares of the deviations of the data from the model. Clearly, this fitting does not make an accurate approximation of the data. However, the fitted curve represents a rough shape of the moving trajectory. This means that we can describe the moving trajectory only by a few polynomial coefficients.

Once all the feature points within a limited area are grouped into a single vehicle, we exclude some points that have different shapes of trajectories from the group. In this paper, we design the following trajectory matching rule to discriminate dissimilar trajectories from the group.

$$SM_x([P_x],[P'_x]) = w_0(a_{x0} - a'_{x0})^2 + w_1(a_{x1} - a'_{x1})^2 + w_2(a_{x2} - a'_{x2})^2 + w_3(a_{x3} - a'_{x3})^2 \quad (9)$$

$$SM_y([P_y],[P'_y]) = w_0(a_{y0} - a'_{y0})^2 + w_1(a_{y1} - a'_{y1})^2 + w_2(a_{y2} - a'_{y2})^2 + w_3(a_{y3} - a'_{y3})^2 \quad (10)$$

where SM_x and SM_y are defined as the x and y directional similarity measures (SM), respectively, $[P_x]$, $[P'_x]$, $[P_y]$ and $[P'_y]$ denote the coefficient value sets for the approximated trajectories to be compared, and w_k(k=0,1,2,3) are weight factors. If both SM_x and SM_y are lower than a predefined threshold value, we combine two feature points into the same group.

3 Simulation Results

We have performed computer simulations on several crossway traffic sequences and estimated the feature distance in the world coordinate system. We employ the least mean squares (LMS) method to find the translation vector and the projection matrix using 16 calibration points. In order to evaluate the performance of the proposed grouping algorithm, we compare tracking trajectories with other results.

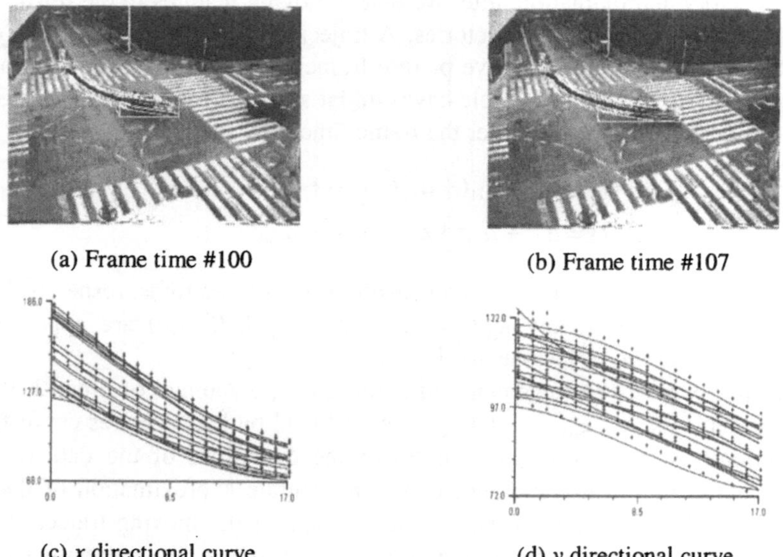

(a) Frame time #100 (b) Frame time #107

(c) x directional curve (d) y directional curve

Fig. 2. Tracking results of the grouping using only spatial information

As shown in Fig. 2(a), when we apply the grouping using only spatial information to the scene of a left-turning vehicle, one feature trajectory at the left lower region of the vehicle is deviated due to correlation mismatching between two adjacent frames. The feature point has been linked to other points within the vehicle until distances from this point to all the other features are larger than a given threshold value, which makes the grouping incorrect as shown in Fig. 2(b). Fig. 2(c) and Fig. 2(d) display approximated curves of the feature trajectories in the x and y directions, respectively, at frame time #100.

Fig. 3 demonstrates the tracking result by the grouping method using both the spatial information and trajectory matching for the same scene as in Fig. 2. As shown in Fig. 3(a), the feature point of a different shape of the trajectory is separated from the feature group of the left-turning vehicle since the similarity measure is smaller than a given threshold value. The result in Fig. 3(b) shows that the grouping is kept correctly. Fig 3(c) and Fig 3(d) display approximated curves of the feature trajectories in the x and y directions, respectively, at frame time #100.

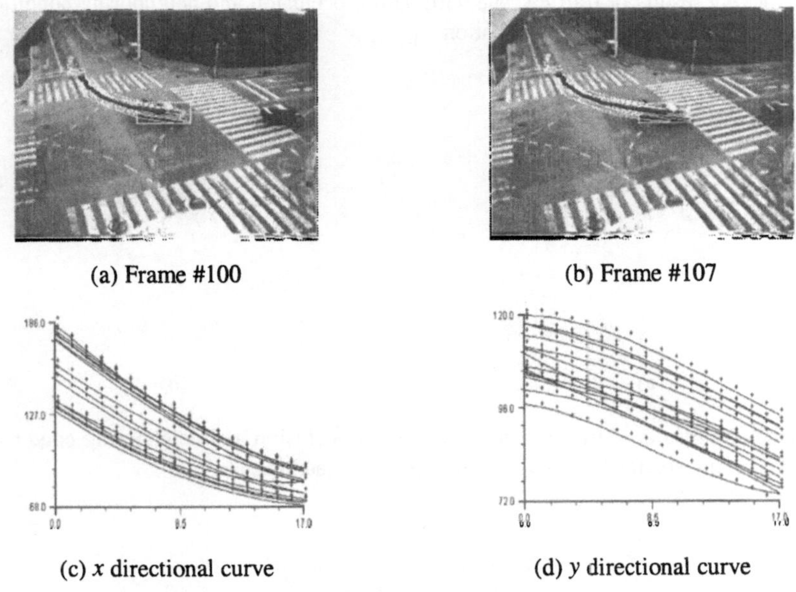

(a) Frame #100 (b) Frame #107

(c) x directional curve (d) y directional curve

Fig. 3. Tracking results of the grouping using spatial information and trajectory matching

In Fig. 4, we apply the grouping method using only spatial information to a traffic scene with partial occlusion and neighboring condition. There are two over-grouping errors in Fig. 4(a). Since two vehicles appear close to each other, it is difficult to separate two vehicles by the grouping method using only spatial information. If one vehicle passes by another vehicle, a visual occlusion can occur. Fig. 4(b) is the result including feature trajectory drawings.

Fig. 5 shows the tracking result by the grouping method using both the spatial information and trajectory matching for the same scene as in Fig. 4. When two vehicles appear close to each other, the trajectory matching algorithm can separate them easily at the initial time. For the partial occlusion, two vehicles are being merged during the initial period. However, as the two vehicles move down the road, they can be separated when they exhibit distinguishing motions.

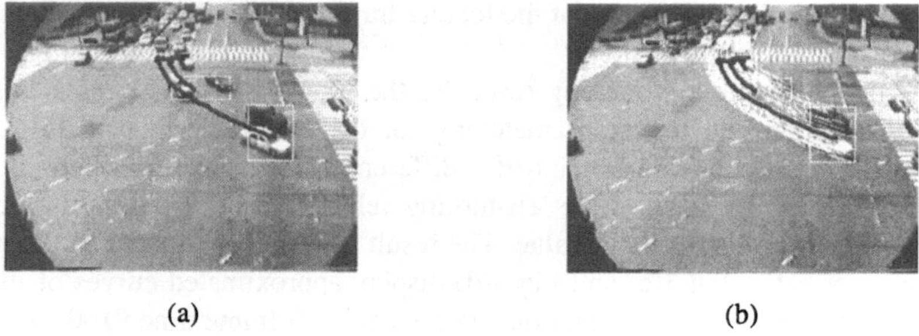

(a) (b)

Fig. 4. Tracking results of traffic scene with partial occlusion and neighboring condition by the grouping using only spatial information

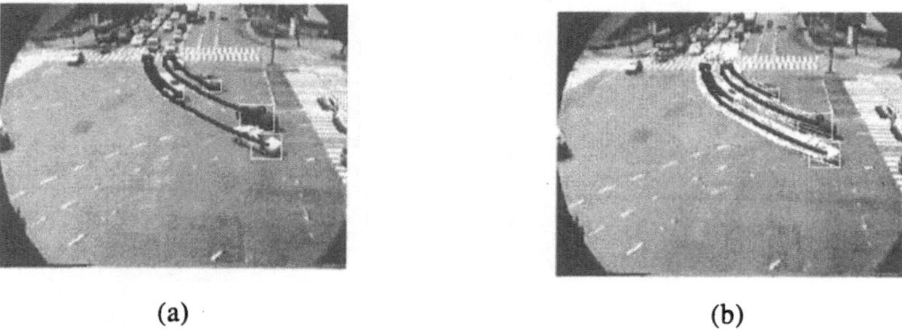

(a) (b)

Fig. 5. Tracking results of traffic scene with partial occlusion and neighboring condition by the grouping using spatial information and trajectory matching

Fig. 6. Tracking results of night traffic scene

Fig. 6 shows the tracking result of night traffic scene by using spatial information and trajectory matching. Especially, in case of night traffic, many noise trajectories are occurred by headlight. However, the noise trajectories are removed by trajectory matching, and our tracking algorithm tracks the vehicles successfully.

4 Conclusions

In this paper, we have proposed a feature-based vehicle tracking system with a new grouping scheme. We extract image feature points by a corner detection algorithm and trace the features using two-dimensional token-based Kalman filtering. The new grouping algorithm using trajectory matching makes the proposed tracking system robust even in the partial occlusion and neighboring conditions. We can extend the proposed system for more congested traffic scenes.

Acknowledgement

This work was supported in part by the Korea Science and Engineering Foundation (KOSEF) through the Ultra-Fast Fiber-Optic Networks (UFON) Research Center at Kwangju Institute of Science and Technology (K-JIST), and in part by Ministry of Education (MOE) through the Brain Korea 21 (BK21) project.

References

1. Jung, Y.K., Ho, Y.S.: Robust Vehicle Detection and Tracking for Traffic Surveillance. Picture Coding Symposium'99, (1999) 227-230
2. McFalane, N., Scholfield, C.: Segmentation and Tracking of Piglets in Images. Machine Vision and Application. Vol. 8 (1995) 187-193
3. Malik, J., Russell, S.: A Machine Vision Based Surveillance System for California Roads. PATH Project MOU- 83 Final Report, University of California, Berkeley (1994)
4. Beymer, D., McLauchlan, P., Malick, J.: A real-time computer vision system for measuring traffic parameters. Proc. IEEE Computer Society Conference on Computer Vision and Pattern Recognition, Vol. 12 (1997) 495-501
5. Forstner, W., Gulch, E.: A Fast Operator for Detection and Precise Location of Distinct Points, Corners, and Centers of Circular of Features. Proc. of the Intercommission Conf. On Fast Processing of Photogrammetric Data, (1987) 281-305
6. Rao, B.S.Y., Durrant-Whyte, H.F., Sheen, J.A.: A Fully Decentralized Multi-Sensor System For Tracking and Surveillance. The International Journal of Robotics Research, Vol. 12 (1993) 20-44

Movie Event Detection by Using Audio Visual Information

Ying Li and C.-C. Jay Kuo

Integrated Media Systems Center
Department of Electrical Engineering-Systems
University of Southern California, Los Angeles, CA 90089-2564
{yingli, cckuo}@sipi.usc.edu

Abstract. This work focuses on the detection of events including 2-speaker dialog scene, multiple-speaker dialog scene and hybrid scene from the daily movies. Specifically, we employ the visual information to detect all possible shot sinks by using a new method called a *window-based sweep algorithm*, then all detected shot sinks are categorized into 3 classes using the well-known K-means algorithm, which forms the basis of our proposed event-detection scheme. Furthermore, the accompanying audio cue will also be utilized for achieving more meaningful results. Our preliminary experimental results show that by integrating audiovisual information, meaningful events could be successfully detected and extracted.

1 Introduction

With the fast growing amount of multimedia information, content-based image/video indexing and retrieval have attracted more and more attentions these days. However, most existing solutions are based on low-level features, such as color, texture , shape and object spatial relations, keyframes, temporal variance, camera and object motions, etc. Although the extraction of above features is straightforward and relatively computationally simple, yet the corresponding query results are not always satisfactory due to the gap between low-level features and high-level semantics.

Recently, there have been some work on semantics extraction from multimedia data. Mahmood and Srinivasan [1] presented a query-driven approach to detect topical events by using image and text contents of query foils found in a lecture. While multiple media sources were integrated in their framework, the identification results were mainly evaluated in the domain of classroom lectures and talks due to the special features used. In Rui and Yeung's work [2] [3], video scenes were constructed from low-level shot sequence to serve as a video Table of Content (ToC). While scenes do capture more semantic meanings of the underlying video, not all constructed scenes contain meaningful themes due to their temporally adjoining nature. Sundaram and Chang [4] reported their work on determining computable scenes in films by combining audio and visual information as well as detecting dialog scenes by using a periodic analysis transform. However, since the arrangement of shot sequences in a dialog basically varies with the film genre and depends heavily on the directorial styles, periodic analysis appears too restrictive to take care of general scenarios. In addition, the problem becomes more complex when there are multiple speakers in a scene.

In this work, we propose to detect movie events by using a window-based sweep algorithm, where an event is typically a scene which contains a meaningful theme and is basically developing under a certain fixed environment. In particular, we first pool all similar shots into a shot sink, then each shot sink is classified into one of three predefined classes, from which the coarse-level events will be detected. Moreover, in order to better locate the dialog scenes, we further integrate the audio information into this framework.

The rest of paper is organized as follows. In Section 2, the proposed movie event detection algorithm is detailed. Section 3 gives the preliminary experimental results. Finally, concluding remarks and future work are given in Section 4.

2 Movie Event Extraction

Movie, known as a recording art, is practical, environmental, pictorial, dramatic, narrative and musical [5]. Since a film operates in limited time, all movie shots are efficiently organized by the film-maker in such a way that the audience will follow his/her own way of story-telling. Specifically, this goal is achieved by presenting the audience a sequence of cascaded events which gradually develop the movie plot. In this work, we consider the underlying event as the basic story unit of the movie. Detection of such events is very useful in a variety of applications including content-based video browsing, summarization and retrieval.

Basically, an event is a scene which contains a meaningful theme and is usually going on under a certain consistent environment. However, to some extent, an event is more than a scene since it does not have the restriction of consistent chromaticity, lighting conditions and ambient sound as imposed on scene definition [4]. In another word, as long as scenes share the same theme, they belong to the same event.

There are basically two ways to develop a thematic topic in an event: through actions where recorded movements tell the story or through dialogs where words carry the theme. Based on the film genre and film makers' directorial flavor, either of these two styles (or both) could be used frequently. However, no matter which filming style is used in an event, they share one common feature. That is, certain shots will present a repetitive visual structures. For instance, during a chase sequence, we frequently see shots of the pursued and the pursuer despite that the background is constantly changing. This repetitive pattern is even more distinct in a dialog scene. This is a very interesting observation, and the reason is perhaps due to the fact that since the drama of an event could only be developed within certain spatial and temporal localities, directors have to repeat some essential shots to convey the parallelism and continuity of activities due to the sequential nature of film making. In the rest of this section, we will elaborate on the proposed event detection algorithm which is partially developed based on this observation.

2.1 Computing Shot Sinks with Visual Information

Since an event is generally characterized by a repetitive visual structure, our first step is to extract all scenes which possess this feature. In particular, we introduce a new concept, shot sink, in this work. A shot sink contains a pool of shots which are visually similar to each other but largely different from those in other sinks.

Window-based Sweep Algorithm The window-based sweep algorithm is used to compute the shot sink for every shot from a given shot sequence. Since any event occurs within certain temporal locality, we naturally restrict our search range for visually similar shots within a window of length N as shown in Figure 1(a), where the current window contains $n - i + 1$ shots. Given shot i, we choose its keyframes to be its first and last frames and denote them b_i and e_i as shown in the same figure, then the similarity between shot i and j are defined as

$$\begin{aligned} Dist_{i,j} = \frac{1}{4}(W_1 * dist(b_i, b_j) + W_2 * dist(b_i, e_j) \\ + W_3 * dist(e_i, b_j) + W_4 * dist(e_i, e_j)) \end{aligned}$$

where $dist(b_i, b_j)$ is the standard Euclidean distance between the two keyframes b_i and b_j in terms of their color histograms and W_1, W_2, W_3 and W_4 are four weighting coefficients computed as

$$\begin{array}{ll} W_1 = 1 - \frac{L_i}{N}, & W_2 = 1 - \frac{L_i + L_j}{N}, \\ W_3 = 1, & W_4 = 1 - \frac{L_j}{N}. \end{array}$$

where L_i and L_j are lengths of shots i and j in terms of frames. Here, we do not consider the absolute time separation between shots i and j (i.e. the temporal distance between e_i and b_j) in computing $Dist_{i,j}$. The reason is that since we want to find all similar shots (thus, the name "sweep"), we shall not weaken shots similarity due to their physical separation as long as they are within the same timing window. However, we do have considered the relative distance between each keyframe by introducing the shot length parameters L_i and L_j into the weights. It is actually intuitive that, if shots i and j are similar shots, frames e_i should be more similar to b_j than b_i to b_j due to the motion continuity. Hence here we call $Dist_{i,j}$ a *time-adapted distance*.

Now, if $Dist_{i,j}$ is less than a predefined threshold T, we consider them to be similar, and throw shot j into shot i's sink. As shown in Figure 1(b), all shot i's similar shots are neatly linked together in their temporal order. One thing worth mentioning here is that if shot i's sink is not empty, we have to compute distances between the current shot, say, shot k, and all other shots in the sink (for example, shot i and shot j in this figure), and shot k is only qualified to be in the sink when the maximum of all distances is less than T.

We repeat this window-based sweep algorithm for every shot to compute their respective shot sink. However, if one shot has already been in other shot's sink, we skip the current shot and continue for the next one.

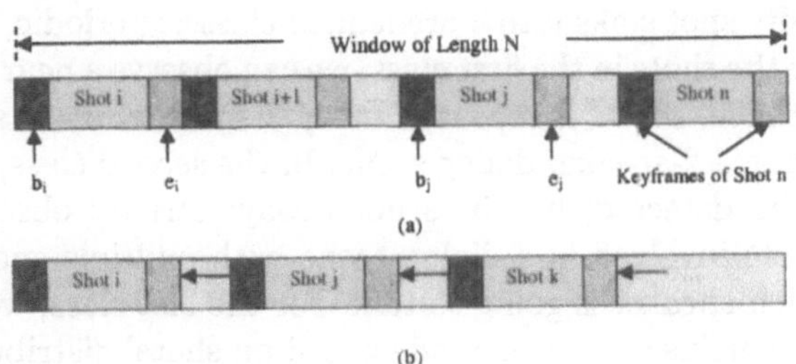

Fig. 1. (a) Shots contained in a window of length N, and (b) computed sink of shot i.

Determination of Parameters There are two parameters used in this algorithm, i.e. window length N and threshold T. For the algorithm to be of practical use, these parameters should be determined either automatically or easily by the user. We will discuss this issue below.

1). *Determining window length* N. We have tried two ways to choose parameter N in this work, i.e. a fixed value and an adaptive value that varies with every incoming movie. In the former case, we empirically set N to be a predefined value which covers the duration of a usual movie event. In the latter case, N is set to be proportional to the average video shot length, that is, $N = \alpha \times AvgShotLength$. Hence, the faster the movie rhythm, the shorter the window length. Based on our current experiments, a fixed value N produces better results, which is perhaps due to the reason that as a semantic unit, event is somehow independent of the underlying shot structure.

2). *Determining threshold* T. T is used to threshold the similarity measurement between two shots. Since our distance metric employs the color information and different movies will definitely have different primary hue, an empirically preset threshold will properly not work for all cases. In this work, we apply a Gaussian normalization procedure to resolve this problem. Specifically, for each shot in the current shot sequence, we compute its color distances to all other shots in the timing window. Then, we consider all computed distances as a sequence of Gaussian variables, and calculate its mean μ and standard deviation σ. Now, after we compute $Dist_{i,j}$ by using the previous equation, we normalize it by using μ and σ and then compare it with a predefined threshold T'. Since all distances have been normalized to the Gaussian distribution of zero mean and unit variance, it is easier to choose threshold T'. Moreover, once T' is adjusted, it will fit for all movies. Empirically, we find that $T' = -1.35$ produces a good similarity result. In this case, about 9% of the shots within the timing window are qualified for the corresponding shot sink as $P(X < x|x = T' = -1.35) = 0.089$.

2.2 Classifying Shot Sinks with K-means

Now, let us classify shot sinks into 3 predefined classes: periodic, partly-periodic, and random. For the shots in the first class, we can observe a near perfect periodic pattern. For instance, shot i is repeated every 2 shots which shall be frequently encountered during a 2-speaker dialog scene. In the second class, a certain rough periodicity will be detected, but it is not always strictly observed. Examples include those shots involved in a dialog scene with multiple speakers where we have no idea which speaker is going to talk. For the last class, we call it random since no specific conclusion can be made based on shots' distribution. Note also that if shot i's sink contains only one item (i.e. the shot itself), we exclude this shot for further consideration.

To detect the periodicity for each shot sink, we first calculate the relative temporal distance between shot i and its peers. Then, the mean μ and standard deviation σ of these distances are computed and considered to be the sink's features. Intuitively, a shot belonging to a periodic class will generally have smaller statistics than the one belonging to the random class.

After obtaining the two features for every shot sink, we choose to classify them by using the standard K-means algorithm. There are two reasons for using the K-means in this task. First, we can circumvent the trouble of determining a set of thresholds for our classification purpose. Second, K-means is a least-squares partitioning method which naturally divide a collection of objects into K groups. Hence, the K-means algorithm is more tolerant to "noisy" data as compared to others using rigid rules. For example, given a 2-speaker dialog scene, although typically we have a series of alternating close-up shots of two players, we can have characters in medium or long shots and shots with two present speakers . Moreover, different camera angles will definitely produce different shots even for the same speaker. Therefore, if we use an approach which strictly demands that every 2 shots should be similar while adjacent shots are different in a dialog scene [4], it will probably fail in some scenarios. However, if the K-means approach is applied, we may still get correct classification results. Figure 2 shows classification results for two movie clips. As one can see, all shot sinks have been well classified, where the leftmost group belongs to the periodic class and the rightmost one belongs to the random class.

2.3 Extracting and Classifying Events

Now, we are ready to organize all classified shot sinks into events. The first problem needs to be solved is the determination of the event boundary. The solution

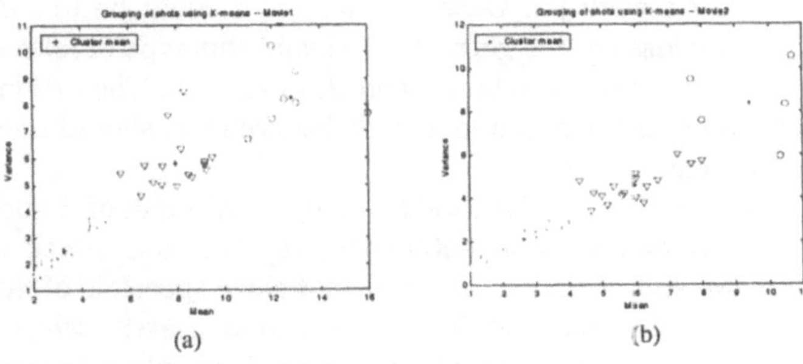

Fig. 2. Classifying shot sinks using K-means: (a) Movie 1 with 43 shot sinks, and (b) Movie 2 with 51 shot sinks.

actually resides in the definition of an event. Since each event has a certain thematic topic, thus basically events are not temporally sequential, which means that there will usually exist some progressive scenes between two consecutive events without any repetitive structure. Therefore in most of cases, a natural gap between unrelated shot sinks will be observed, which then serves as the event delimiter. Of course, it is still possible that two events are tightly developed one after another. However, it's very rare since the director will need time to establish the situation for the next event. The second problem is to assign appropriate types to each assembled event. Three event classes are considered in this work: the 2-speaker dialog scene, the multiple-speaker dialog scene and the hybrid scene. A set of simple rules are introduced here to accomplish this task.

1). If the event contains at least two periodic shot sinks, at most one partly-periodic, and no random shot sinks, it will be declared as a 2-speaker dialog scene. This is actually quite straightforward since during a typical movie conversation scene, the camera will track the speakers back and forth, producing a series of alternating close-up shots of the two players.

2). If the event contains several partly-periodic shot sinks, or if the periodic and random shot sinks coexist, we label it with a multiple-speaker dialog scene. Since we may have many speakers, and every speaker has an equal probability of talking, we may have random shot sinks in this case.

3). All left events are called the hybrid scene.

2.4 Integrating Audio Information

Since coarse-level events are detected based on pure visual information, false alarms will occur in some cases. For example, in one of our test movies, there is an event describing a hunter and his prey. The camera shuttles back and forth between them to generate a tense atmosphere. Naturally, this event is declared as a 2-speaker dialog scene since strong periodicity is detected. This type of events is actually not unusual in our daily movies and is called the "thematic dialog" in Sundaram's work [4]. Other similar cases could be found in events where two people are kissing, hugging, etc. To avoid this type of false alarms, we can integrate audio information into our detection scheme. The rationale here is quite intuitive: if an event is declared as a dialog scene, it should have a higher ratio of speech content.

For every shot in a dialog event, we'll classify it into one of 4 audio classes: speech, music, silence and environmental sound [6]. If it is a speech with music background shot, we still declare it a speech shot since speech is of more importance to us. An event can only be declared as a dialog event when its speech ratio is higher than a certain threshold. Otherwise, it is only a thematic scene.

3 Experimental Results

Three MPEG compressed movie clips are examined in our experiments, each of 1-hour long and belonging to one of following 3 genres: romance, adventure and action. Due to the subjectivity of the event definition, we will not lead discussions on the accuracy of extracted events since people's opinions may differ. Instead, we examine the correctness of the classified event classes since it's much easier to reach a common agreement. However, it's still our believe that all meaningful movie events have been correctly extracted using the proposed algorithm.

Experimental results are shown in Table 1 for all 3 movies. There are two parts in each sub-table: the results obtained by combing audio cue and the ones without audio. The precision and recall rates are computed to evaluate the performance where Precision = hits/(hits + false alarms) and Recall = hits/(hits + misses). In addition, because the hybrid event class contains the rest of events excluding the multi-speaker and the 2-speaker events, its extraction results are omitted from the table. Followings are some observations of the obtained results.

1. The event detection results are quite encouraging. All precision and recall ratios are higher than 83% when the audio information is integrated. Also, it is evident that by integrating the audio information into the proposed detection scheme, we have observed distinct improvements in the precision ratio for all cases.
2. The missed 2-speaker event in Movie 1 was misclassified as a hybrid one. In this scene, the two speakers are quite far apart at the beginning of the talk. Then, one of them walks towards the other which causes the change of the background and results in the irregularity of the periodicity. In Movie 2, a multiple-speaker scene is misclassified as a 2-speaker scene due to the fact that one of the speakers dominates the dialog. A similar case is also found in Movie 3.

4 Conclusion and Future Work

Event detection is essential to high-level semantic querying of video databases. It is also a very challenging problem to integrate evidences from multiple information modalities such as audio, video and language. A novel framework of

Table 1. Event detection results for Moviel, Movie2 and Movie3

Moviel – Tragic Romance										
	Combining Audio Information					Without Audio Information				
Event Class	Hit	Miss	False	Precision	Recall	Hit	Miss	False	Precision	Recall
Multi-speaker dialog	4	0	0	100%	100%	5	0	1	100%	83%
2-speaker dialog	6	1	0	86%	100%	9	1	3	90%	75%
Movie2 – Adventure										
	Combining Audio Information					Without Audio Information				
Event Class	Hit	Miss	False	Prec.	Recall	Hit	Miss	False	Prec.	Recall
Multi-speaker dialog	5	1	0	100%	83%	5	1	0	100%	83%
2-speaker dialog	14	0	1	93%	100%	16	0	3	84%	100%
Movie3 – Action										
	Combining Audio Information					Without Audio Information				
Event Class	Hit	Miss	False	Prec.	Recall	Hit	Miss	False	Prec.	Recall
Multi-speaker dialog	7	1	0	100%	88%	9	1	2	81%	90%
2-speaker	15	0	0	100%	100%	17	0	2	89%	100%

detecting movie events by integrating audio-visual cues was presented in this work. Specifically, coarse-level events were first extracted by using pure visual information. Then, the accompanying audio cue was utilized to refine the results. Encouraging preliminary experimental results have been obtained. In the future, we will apply some speaker identification technology to recognize speakers in the dialog scene, which should form an inseparable component in a practical content-based video indexing and retrieval system.

References

1. T. S. Mahmood and S. Srinivasan, "Detecting topical events in digital video," *Proc. of ACM Multimedia 2000*, pp. 85–94, Marina Del Rey, November 2000.
2. Yong Rui, Thomas S. Huang, and Sharad Mehrotra, "Constructing table-of-content for video," *ACM Journal of Multimedia Systems*, 1998.
3. Minerva Yeung, Boon-Lock Yeo, and Bede Liu, "Extracting story units from long programs for video browsing and navigation," *IEEE Proceedings of Multimedia*, pp. 296–305, 1996.
4. H. Sundaram and S. F. Chang, "Determining computable scenes in films and their structures using audio-visual memory models," *Proc. of ACM Multimedia 2000*, Marina Del Rey, November 2000.
5. James Monaco, *How to read a film: the art, technology, language, history and theory of film and media*, Oxford University Press, New York, 1982.
6. T. Zhang and C.-C. Jay Kuo, "Audio-guided audiovisual data segmentation, indexing and retrieval," *Proc. of SPIE*, vol. 3656, pp. 316–327, 1999.

Double Hierarchical Algorithm for Video Mosaics[1]

Peizhong Lu, Lide Wu

Department of Computer Sciences, Fudan University, Shanghai, 200433
Pzlu@fudan.edu.cn

Abstract. This paper presents a double hierarchical algorithm to construct large view mosaics of videos, taken with a camera that is free to pan, tilt, rotate, and zoom. Our method consists of two different hierarchical procedures. The first one deals with the estimation of global motion parameters between successive pairs of images. This is a modification of Mann s method based on a linear hierarchical technique combined with the associative law in group theory. The second one registers each three consequent images into an intermediate submosaic for the next hierarchical level. In order to improve the precision of the coordinate transformations between two frames we develop a local adjustment technique and a global feedback technique. The techniques significantly reduces the number of compositions of coordinate transformations from each frame to the reference frame, which results in significant decrease of accumulated registration errors mainly caused by rounding off in each matrix product. Plentiful experimental results show that our double hierarchical algorithm can efficiently control accumulated registration errors, thereby allowing the creation of high quality panoramic mosaics for perspective videos with great change of view.

1 Introduction

Automatic construction of video mosaic plays an important role in many fields, such as computer vision, image processing, and computer graphics[7]. For instance, the navigation of robots, ocean floor exploration [2], video compression [1], video indexing [3], super-resolution processing of digital camera [6], etc. The most difficult problem in procedures of video mosaic is how to control cumulative errors caused while registering many image frames to the same reference image. Mann and Picard [5] present a hierarchical algorithm that takes advantages of the associative law in group theory. Gracias[2] fulfils video mosaic by an algorithm based on feature point correspondences. The robustness of their algorithm relies on the correctness of the correspondences of feature points, which is also a difficult problem in computer vision.

In this paper, we present a double hierarchical and featureless algorithm to implement the automatic video mosaic. The videos we deal with in this paper are taken with a camera that is free to pan, tilt, rotate, and zoom. Our approach includes 4 main techniques: (1) local adjustment, (2) neighbor extension, (3) global adjustment, (4) global hierarchy. Key advantages of our techniques are: (i) significant decrease of accumulated registration errors, (ii) ability to register images even when the multiple

[1] Supported by National Funds of Nature Sciences of China (69935010), and Special Funds for Authors of Excellent Doctorate Dissertations of China.

images are of an extended scene with no overlap between the first, the middle, and the last frame in the sequence, (iii) high precision of the final mosaic image. Plentiful experimental results show that our new techniques can handle the problem of cumulative errors efficiently. They are also very robust and accurate. Even for the video taken from a camera with a long pan exceeding 90° degrees, our algorithm also produces compact mosaic image with high quality.

2 Motion Model

Let I_1, I_2 be two consequent frames. Due to the motion of camera, I_1 and I_2 have different coordinate system. To find out the coordinate transformation p from I_1 to I_2, we need to make an assumption that the transformation has a 8-parameter projective model.

$$p(x,y)=(x',y')=\left(\frac{a_{11}x+a_{12}x+a_{13}}{a_{31}x+a_{32}y+a_{33}},\frac{a_{21}x+a_{22}y+a_{23}}{a_{31}x+a_{32}y+a_{33}}\right) \tag{1}$$

If the consequent frames are taken with a camera undergoing a combination of pan, tilt, rotation, and zoom then we have proved in [4] that (1) satisfies. In this case, the matrix $(a_{ij})_{3\times3}$ is an invertible matrix, and is called a representation of p. We sometimes identify the matrix with the coordinate transformation if there is no confusions in context.

3 Mann s Featureless Algorithm

Let $I(x,y,t)$ be the frame at time t. Suppose most of pixels in $I(x,y,t+1)$ are induced by a very small movement of the camera. Then

$$I_x \cdot u + I_y \cdot v + I_t \approx 0, \tag{2}$$

where $(u,v) = (\frac{dx}{dt},\frac{dy}{dt})$ and $(I_x,I_y,I_t) = (\frac{\partial I}{\partial x},\frac{\partial I}{\partial y},\frac{\partial I}{\partial t})$ are respectively the velocity vector of the moving pixel and the vector of partial differentials in coordinate (x,y). I_x, I_y, and I_t can be approximated by average difference of the pixels near the point. By model (1), we have

$$((A\cdot X+b)-(c^T\cdot X+1)\cdot X)\cdot I_X+(c^T\cdot X+1)I_t \approx 0, \tag{3}$$

where $I_X = (I_x, I_y)^T$, and $A\in R^{2\times2}, b\in R^{2\times1}, c\in R^{2\times1}$.

Our task is to compute the unknown 8 parameters. By least square sums, the 8 parameters can be estimated by solving the solutions of the following equations:

$$\sum_{X \in S} (\Phi\Phi^T)[a_{11}, a_{12}, b_1, a_{21}, a_{22}, b_2, c_1, c_2]^T = \sum_{X \in S} (xI_x + yI_y - I_t)\Phi, \quad (4)$$

where $\Phi^T = [xI_x, yI_x, I_x, xI_y, yI_y, I_y, xI_t - x^2 I_x - xyI_y, yI_t - xyI_x - y^2 I_y]$.

But errors of partial differentials I_x, I_y, I_t will dramatically deteriorate the precision of the solutions. Moreover, according to calculus, approximations of I_x, I_y, and I_t are reasonable only if the ranges of motion between $I(x,y,t)$ and $I(x,y,t+1)$ are very small. Thus a hierarchical technique is a must if we want to find a better solution of equations (4).

Let the block in the first level have $m \times m$ pixels. For example, if the velocity of motions in the video is one frame per second, the moving distance of each pixel is $352/30 \approx 12$ pixels. To guarantee the condition that the range of moving is of less than 1 pixel, we must choose $m \geq 16$ in the first hierarchical level. The following algorithm is owed to Mann and Picard.

Algorithm 1. A revisited Mann's algorithm

1. Let $k = 4$, I the image to be transformated, J the reference image, p be the 3×3 identity matrix.

2. While $k \geq 0$

   Generate a virtue image $I' = p(I)$, which has same pixel at coordinate $p(x,y)$ as the pixel of I at (x,y).

   Construct the images I_k, J_k, which are the $2^k \times 2^k$ samples of I', J respectively.

   Solve equation (4) for transformation p_k from I_k to J_k.

   Let $p = p_k p$, $k = k-1$

3. Return p

Remark 1. The previous procedure of coarse to fine estimation uses compositions of intermediate transformations by group theory to enhance the accuracy and efficiency.

4 Double Hierarchical Mosaicing

It is the most difficult in video mosaic to handle the cumulative errors caused by registering hundreds of frames to the same one frame. Mann(1997) alleviates the cumulative errors by submosaic technique. Since the number of compositions of maps in Mann's method is linearly in proportion to the total number of frames in the video, the cumulative errors are still very great if the total number is large. In this section, we present a new featureless approach to control the cumulative errors for long video mosaicing. The number of compositions of maps in our method is logarithmic in proportion to the total number of frames. Our approach includes 4 main techniques: (1) local adjustment, (2) neighbor extension, (3) global adjustment, (4) global hierarchy.

4.1 Local Adjustor

While the global motion parameters are being estimated by hierarchical techniques, we delete in each intermediate step the pixels that do not overlap in the two images because these pixels will give negative effects on the precision of estimations.

Algorithm 2 (Local Adjustment)

Input: Two consequent images I_1, I_2.

Output: Finer transformation from I_1 to I_2

Initialization: k=1

1. Compute a coordinate transformation f_k from I_1 to I_2 in level k by Algorithm 1.

2. Generate the image $p_k(I_1)$ and find the overlap parts between $p_k(I_1)$ and I_2. The overlap parts are denoted as $p_k(I_1)'$ and I_2' respectively.

3. Use Algorithm 1 for $p_k(I_1)'$ and I_2' in levels k+1 to find the transformation Δ_{p_k}, and let $p_{k+1} = \Delta_{p_k} p_k$.

4. If $k+1$ level is the highest level then output p_{k+1} else $k = k+1$ and goto 1.

We call Δ_{p_k} the local adjustor of p_k. It eliminates negative effects of irrelative pixels, which results in improving the precision of motion estimation.

4.2 Neighbor Extension

If we can find a transformation p from I_1 to I_k such that $p(I_1)$ and I_k have larger than 60% coordinates overlapped, we call that I_k is a neighbor of I_1.

Neighbor extension means to find a neighbor as far as possible. Let p_i be the transformation computed by Algorithm 1 or Algorithm 2 from I_i to I_{i+1}, $i = 1,\dots,N-1$. We have the following Neighbor extension algorithm to find neighbors of I_1 in $I_1,\dots,I_N$.

Algorith 3: (Neighbor Extension Algorithm)

1. Initialize: $g = f_1$, $I_S = I_2, I_D = I_1$, i=1, $g_{K2D} = 1$.

2. While ($\text{Area}(g(I_S) \cap I_D) > \text{Area}(I_D) \times 60\%$)

   Use Algorithm 2 for images I_S and I_D to find the local adjustment: $g = \Delta_g g$. Let $g = p_{i+1} g g_{K2D}$, $I_S = I_{i+1}$, i=i+1.

3. $I_D = I_{i-1}, I_S = I_i$, $p_{K2D} = g_{i-1}$.

4. If i<N goto 2.

By previous algorithm, some key frames I_{ki} are chosen such that the consequent key frames are overlapped more than 60% coordinates, and such that the distance between two key frames is as far as possible.

4.3 Global Adjustor

By Algorithm 1, 2 and 3, we estimate the coordinate transformations p_i from I_i to I_{i+1}. We can construct a rough map $p_{ij} = p_j p_{j-1} \cdots p_i$ between images I_i and I_{j+1} with moderate long intervals $j+1-i$. The coarse map can be further adjusted by $\Delta_{p_{ij}}$ estimated from the overlap pixels of $p_{ij}(I_i)$ and I_{i+1}. Then $\Delta_{p_{ij}} p_{ij}$ is the adjusted fine transformation from I_i to I_{i+1}. We call $\Delta_{p_{ij}}$ the global adjustor.

4.4 Global Hierarchy

The principle of global hierarchical algorithm is showed in fig.1. The frames in level 1 are the key frames computed in Algorithm 3. An initial transformation from Submosaic 1 to Submosaic 2 is obtained by composing the transformations of the pairs (KeyFrame 2, KeyFrame 3), (KeyFrame 3, KeyFrame4) , and (KeyFrame4, KeyFrame5). When a video with *N* frames needs to be mapped into a panoramic image, the maximum number of coordinate transformations used to compose a map, from some frame to the mosaic, is less than $\log_8 N$.

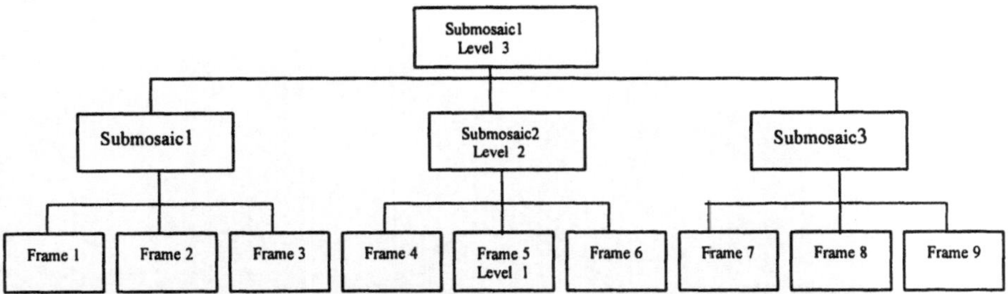

Fig. 1. Global Hierarchical Algorithm. The frames in level 1 are the key frames computed in Algorithm 3.

5. Experiment Results

The local adjustors can remarkably control the propagation of the cumulative errors. The results can be seen in Fig. 2. The following examples are the mosaic of videos taken with a series of pans and tilts. The total angle of pans is larger than 90°. The first frame has no pixels overlapped in the last frame. Our double hierarchical algorithms also fulfil the mosaic with high quality. Our Algorithm programmed in Borland C++ Builder 3.0 produces a panorama image for a 15-seconds-video in 2 minutes in a PC with a Pentium II 300.

The colors are not smoothed in our algorithm. Some color pre-filtering between pairs of frames may be helpful to enhance the quality of our algorithm. We also do not consider the case when the overlap of pairs of frames is less than 60% because we are dealing with video in the same shot instead of discrete images.

Fig. 2. The upper left mosaic image, size of 1001x1179, is made of 240 frames from a video size of 352x288. Since it is not controlled by local adjustors, the cumulative errors are very serious. The lower right mosaic size of 751x616 is made of the same frames. The cumulative errors are obviously alleviated by using local adjustments.

Fig. 3(a) The frames are selected from a segment video size of 352×288 in a VCD of The Chinese National Day Celebration. The video has a 15 seconds long pan segment (450 frames). The reference frame is the middle frame (the 250-th frame) which is not overlapped on any pixels with the first frame and the last frame. The luminosity of the first frame is obviously weaker than other frames in the video.

Fig. 3(b) The mosaic panorama made by our double hierarchical algorithm. The pan of the camera is larger than 90°. Its size is 1306×589.

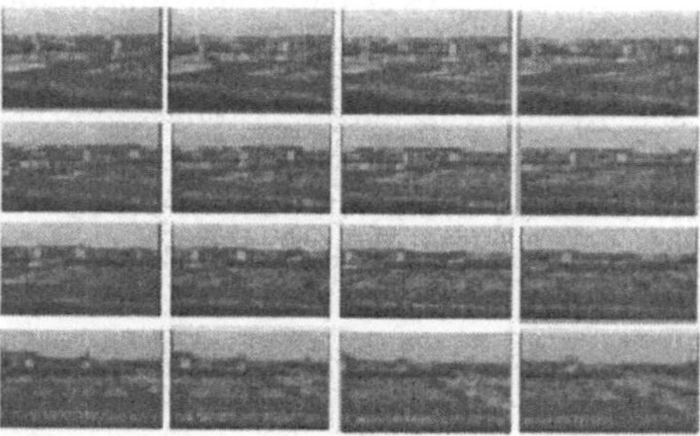

Fig. 4 (a) 16 frames from the video with 230 frames in The Chinese National Day elebration.

Fig. 4(b) The panorama mosaic of the 230 frames is made by Mann's classical methods. The size is 927x357.

Fig. 4(c) The panorama mosaic constructed by our algorithm.

6. Conclusions

In this paper, we present the double hierarchical algorithm to fulfil large scale mosaic for videos with large pan angle. The algorithm includes four main techniques. The local adjustment technique is used to eliminate the negative effects caused by irrelative pixels, which obviously improve the precision of the coordinate transformation between two consequent frames. The neighbor extension technique decreases the number of transformations used to compose a new transformation between frames with a long interval, and thus alleviates the cumulative errors. The global adjustment technique improves the precision of the coordinate transformation between two frames in long distance. The global hierarchical technique further controls the number of matrix multiplication. By combination of the four techniques, we obtain the new algorithm that produces mosaic images with higher quality. Experiment results show that our algorithm is quite successful.

References

[1] F.Dufaux and J.Konrad, Efficient, Robust, and Fast Global Motion for Video Coding, *IEEE Trans. On IP*, Val.9, NO.3, 2000, 497-501.

[2] N.Gracias and J.S.Victor, Underwater Video Mosaics as Visual Navigation Maps, *Computer Vision and Image Understanding* 79, 2000, 66-91.

[3] M. Irani and P.Anandan,Video Indexing Based on Mosaic Representations, *Proceedings of The IEEE*, Vol.86 No.5, 1998,905-921.

[4] P.Z. Lu, L.D. Wu, Algebraic Analyses of the Camera Motion Models in Videos, *Journal of Fudan University (Nature Sciences)*, Vol.38(4), 1999,350-357.

[5] S. Mann, R.W.Picard, Video Orbits of the Projective Group: A Simple Approach to Featureless Estimation of Parameters, *IEEE Trans. on IP,* Vol.6,No.9, 1997, 1281-1295.

[6] H.S.Sawhney and R. Kumar, True Multi-Image Alignment and Its Application to Mosaicing and Lens Distortion Correction, *IEEE Trans. On PAMI,* Vol.21, No.3, 1999, 235-243.

[7] H.Y. Shum and R.Szeliski, *Panoramic image mosaicing*. Technical Report MSR-TR-97-23, Microsoft Research, 1997.

Automatic Segmentation and Tracking of Moving Objects

Ming-Gang Liu, Chao-Huan Hou

Department of Integrated Digital System, Institute of Acoustics
Chinese Academy of Sciences, Beijing 100080, P. R. China

Abstract. A new automatic video sequence segmentation algorithm that extracts moving objects is presented in this paper. The algorithm exploits the local variation in the $L^*u^*v^*$ space, and combines it with motion information to separate foreground objects from the background. A new image segmentation algorithm based on graphic-theoretic approach is first employed to generate various regions according to local variation. Next, moving regions are identified by a new filter criterion, which measures the deviation of the estimated local motion from the synthesized global motion. In order to increase the temporal and spatial consistency of extracted objects, moving regions are tracked by a region-based affine motion model. Two-dimensional binary models are derived for the objects and tracked throughout the sequence by a Hausdorff object tracker. The proposed algorithm is evaluated for several typical MPEG-4 test sequences. Experimental results demonstrate the performance of the proposed algorithm.

1 Introduction

Traditional video standards such as MPEG-2, H.263 are low-level techniques in the sense that no segmentation or analysis of the scene is performed. They can just achieve high compression ratios. However, with the fast development of multimedia processing technique, new coding schemes with content-based interactivity is necessary. The new standard MPEG-4 [1] enables this kind of content-based functionalities by introducing the concept of video object planes (VOP's). VOP represents one object or "semantically meaningful objects" in a video. For each VOP, the motion, texture, and shape information is coded in separate bit streams. This allows separate modification and manipulation of every VOP.

Decomposing a video sequences into VOP's is very difficult. An intrinsic problem of VOP segmentation is that objects of interest are not homogeneous with respect to low-level features such as color, intensity, or optical flow. Most VOP segmentation algorithms [3-10] combine motion information of objects to separate objects from the background. Optical flow or motion fields could be used, but their accuracy is limited due to the noise and aperture problem. So extraction of objects contour only with motion information is difficult.

In this paper, a fast and robust video segmentation technique is proposed. First, a new image segmentation algorithm based on graphic-theoretic approach is first employed to generate various regions according to local variation. Next, moving regions are identified by the deviation of the estimated local motion from the synthesized global motion. In order to increase the temporal and spatial consistency of extracted objects, moving regions are tracked by a region-based affine motion model. The objects are tracked throughout the sequence by a Hausdorff object tracker.

The rest of this paper is organized as follows. Section II covers the segmentation of each frame into various regions base on graphic theory. Moving regions are identified in the next section. Moving objects are extracted and tracked in section IV. Final, the experimental results and the conclusion are presented.

2 Image segmentation using local variation

There are two kinds algorithms in moving objects segmentation techniques, one [3-6] is using image segmentation techniques to generate various regions, and then filtering regions segmented; the other is directly using filtering the image, such as CDM techniques, without initial segmentation. The first one generally can get better object contours than the second one.

Morphological segmentation techniques, such as Max-tree [3-4] can be used in the moving objects segmentation, but it usually generates too much regions. Guo [6] uses "mean shift" algorithm to segment image. Segmentation algorithms used in moving objects extraction should preserve the information of objects completely, because human eyes are sensitive to the contours of objects. Image segmentation based on local variation, or LV algorithm, can be used for this purpose.

LV algorithm is base on graphic theory. It first smoothes the image using a gaussian filter, and then transforms it to an undirected graph, $H=(V,E)$, where each pixel p_i has a corresponding vertex $v_i \in V$ and an edge $(v_i,v_j) \in E$ connects vertices v_i and v_j. The weight function $w((v_i,v_j))$ is based on the absolute intensity difference between the pixels. Then define S, a segmentation of V with a corresponding set of edges, thus every $C \in S$ corresponds to a component of the graph (V,E). Let C_i denote the component of S which contains vertex v_i. The internal variation of a component is defined as the maximum weight edge in any minimum spanning tree of that component

$$Int(C) = \max_{e \in MST(C,E)} w(e), \tag{1}$$

where $MST(C,E)$ is a minimum spanning tree of C with respect to E, and external variation between two components is defined as the lowest weight edge connecting them

$$Ext(C_1,C_2) = \min_{v_i \in C_1, v_j \in C_2} w((v_i,v_j)). \tag{2}$$

When two components are similar in the following sense, they should be merged into a single component

$$Ext(C_1,C_2) \le MInt(C_1,C_2), \tag{3}$$

where the minimum internal variation, *MInt* is

$$MInt(C_1,C_2) = \min(Int(C_1)+\tau(C_1), Int(C_2)+\tau(C_2)). \tag{4}$$

The function τ is relative to the size of the component, and adaptively controls the merging procedure, which is defined as

$$\tau(C) = k/\|C\|, \tag{5}$$

where $\|C\|$ denotes the size of C, and k is a constant.

LV algorithm can guarantee that under the frame defined, the segmentation result is neither over-segmented nor under-segmented. It runs in time nearly linear in the number of image pixels, and is fast in practice.

3 Motion filtering

The purpose of motion filtering is to detect independent moving regions. CDM [7] and HOS [10] techniques, which are based on DFD, can be a possible filtering method. But DFD technique may cause some problems. The DFD is low even for bad motion compensation as long as objects are warped to areas of similar intensity. On the other hand, highly textured regions usually have a high DFD even they are quite well compensated. Therefore, there is no grantee that the filtering results are correct.

We use an alternative approach to detect independently moving regions. For every frame, a dense optical flow filed is estimated by the techniques like Horn and Schunck [11], multiscale techniques [12-13], local relaxation [14] and block-matching [15] etc. Let $\mathbf{u}(\mathbf{x}) = (u,v)^T$ be the estimated flow vector at pixel (x,y) and let $\mathbf{x} = (x,y)^T$. The global motion is obtained using a six-parameter affine motion model

$$\hat{\mathbf{u}}(\mathbf{x}) = \mathbf{A}\mathbf{x} + \mathbf{b} \tag{6}$$

where, $\mathbf{A} = \begin{pmatrix} a_0 & a_1 \\ a_2 & a_3 \end{pmatrix}$, $\mathbf{b} = (b_0, b_1)^T$. We can use robust least median of square technique [5,8] to get $\mathbf{A}$ and $\mathbf{b}$. Thus for every pixel $\mathbf{x}$, we can get synthesized flow vector $\hat{\mathbf{u}}(\mathbf{x})$. The difference between the synthesized flow vector and the estimated flow vector is

$$M(\mathbf{x}) = \|\hat{\mathbf{u}}(\mathbf{x}) - \mathbf{u}(\mathbf{x})\|. \tag{7}$$

For the pixel $\mathbf{x}$ which conforms to the global motion, $M(\mathbf{x})$ is low, otherwise $M(\mathbf{x})$ is high. When $M(\mathbf{x})$ exceeds a threshold, we identify it as a moving pixel. If more than 60% of pixels in C_i are moving pixels, then the region is a moving region. The optical flow filed of frame Coastguard 240 is shown in **Fig.1.**(a) using the technique from Black [13], (b) is the square error after filtering, and (c) moving pixels.

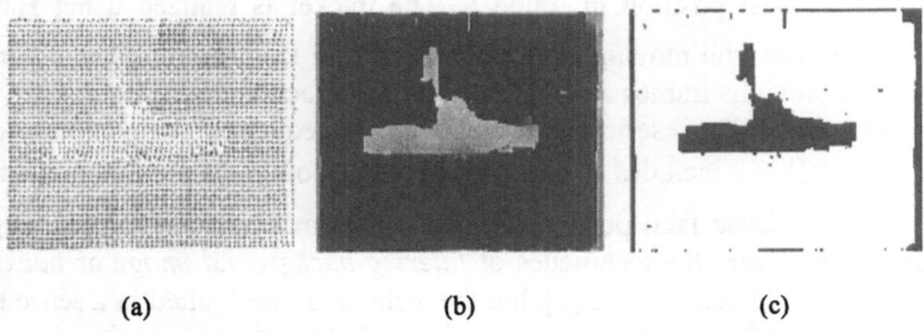

(a) (b) (c)

Fig. 1. Motion filtering, (a) optical flow field of Coastguard 240, (b) filter residue, (c) moving points (in black).

4 Moving objects extraction and tracking

4.1 Objects extraction

After motion filtering, we can get a series of moving regions. Independently Moving Component (IMC) is composed of connected moving regions. In order to avoid tracking noise regions, we only consider those IMC's with sizes exceeding a given threshold.

Meier and Ngan [5,7-8] uses the binary model of the object to get the complete object, or an VOP. The model is composed of rapid changing edge points $O_{t,i}^{rapid}$ and slowly changing edge points $O_{t,i}^{slow}$. Suppose, after motion filtering, we get N_t IMC's in frame t, and its edge set denotes E_t obtained by Canny [16] operator. Let $O_{t-1,i}$ be the object model in the frame $t-1$, $O_{t,i}$ be its model in the frame t, and $IMC_{t,i}$ be a part of $O_{t,i}$, then we have

$$O_{t,i}^{rapid} = \{e \in E_t \mid \min_{x \in IMC_{t,i}} \|e - x\| \le D_{rapid}\}. \tag{8}$$

$O_{t,i}^{rapid}$ includes the edge points with a value for the distance transform that is smaller than or equal to D_{rapid}. While, $O_{t,i}^{slow}$ is obtained by tracking the object from frame $t-1$,

$$O_{t,i}^{slow} = \{e \in E_t \mid \min_{x \in O_{t-1,i} \oplus p_i} \|e - x\| \le D_{slow}\} \tag{9}$$

where, p_i is the best position in frame t. The tracker is realized using Hausdorff distance. Therefore, the moving edge points detected from current frame and those detected from previous frames are combined to the object model .

However, there is a serious problem. In a sequence with more complex background, if $O_{t-1,i}$ includes a background edge point, then extrapolation using equation (9) will cause fatal positive feedback, thus may include many background edge points. Therefore, the techniques of *filtering background image* or *background edge points counting* can be used [7], but the techniques are limited in a sense that we do not know exactly whether a edge point is belonging to an object or to the background.

The model points obtained by the method mentioned above might not form a closed contour, which makes the extraction difficult. Meier and Ngan [5,8] uses Filling-in Technique plus Dijkstra's shortest path to get the closed object contour. For a simple background sequence, it works well. Guo [6] uses the gradient information in the color space, not luminance space, to guard extraction of object, but not all the sequences have a good gradient in color space, and also gradient in color space maybe too large or too small with respect to real object contour. So using the information gained through segmentation is important, we can track the regions once moved, and incorporated them in the object in case they stop moving for the moment.

For every region, we can use the affine motion model to get its motion, and then track it to the next frame. Thus, moving regions will be composed of moving regions currently being detected and those of previously being detected. We fill the holes in the moving regions, which are considered as parts of moving regions though they currently may not move.

4.2 Objects tracking

Hausdorff distance [17] is used to compare the similarity of two binary models. Let $O = \{o_1, \cdots, o_m\}$ denote the set of binary model points, where m is the number of model points, and $E = \{e_1, \cdots, e_n\}$ be the set of all edge pixels in the image. Then, the generalized Hausdorff distance is given by

$$h_K(O,E) = K_{o \in O}^{th} \min_{e \in E} \|o - e\|. \tag{10}$$

Instead of using the maximum value, the distances are sorted in an ascending order and the Kth value is chosen. Let $K = [fm]$, when $f = 1$, the distance will be the standard definition of Hausdorff distance. f can control the number of pixels that influences the Hausdorff distance. Similarly, we can define $h_R(E,O)$, and let $R=[rn]$. More details can be found in the reference [17].

Fig. 2 demonstrates that the binary model for the boat can be tracked successfully. The parameters used are $f=0.7, r=0.5, D_{match}=2$ ($D_{match}=2$ denotes that all the matching edge points are within the distance of 2 pixels).

Actually, we can also use the tracked models to extract the objects using the Filling-in Technique as Meier and Ngan [5,8] does.

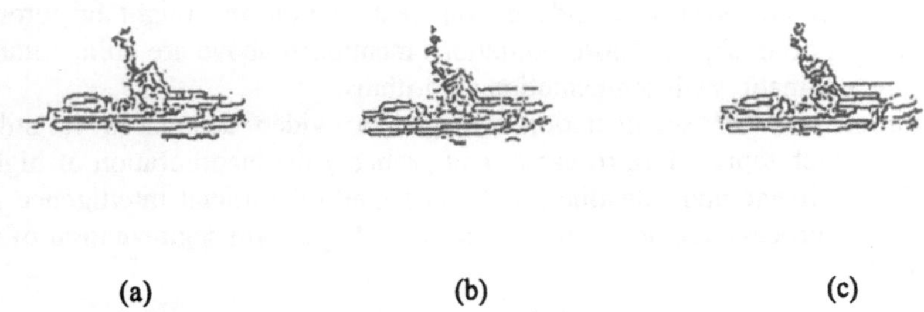

(a) (b) (c)

Fig. 2. Coastguard binary model tracking. (a) frame 230, (b) frame 240, (c) frame 250.

5 Experimental results

In this section, the results of the proposed algorithm are presented for three typical sequences, Claire, Mother&Daughter and Coastguard. When we use LV segmentation algorithm, more details should be preserved, because in coastguard sequence, the background is cluttered. The gaussian smooth parameter $\sigma=0.6$, and the constant parameter $k=100$. The parameters used in the Hausdorff tracker are $f=0.7, r=0.5, D_{match}=2$. We use the technique from Black [13] to estimate the optical flow field.

Claire is a typical "head-shoulder" sequence with stationary background, while Mother&Daughter with a litter more complex background. Fig.3 shows the original frame of Claire 30, segmented grayscale image, extracted object and its binary model. Fig. 4 shows the results for Mother&Daughter.

In the sequence Coastguard, the camera is following the boat so that the background appears to be moving. The boat, which is moving relative to the background, is proper extracted. However, because the cluttered background, the boundary is not as accuracy as "head-shoulder" sequence.

6 Conclusion

A new moving objects segmentation and tracking algorithm is proposed in this paper. After the initial segmentation, we can get a series regions, and then motion filtering technique is used to identify moving regions which compose the independently moving objects. The temporal correspondence is established by a Hausdorff tracker.

The experimental results show that the algorithm works well for automatic moving objects segmentation and tracking. However, there are also some limitations that should be mentioned. Since moving region is identified by the ratio of moving pixels in the region, sometimes due to the mal-segmentation or ill-motion estimation, the decision might be wrong, thus the boundaries of moving objects might not be very accurate. Furthermore, noise also induces apparent motion and might be wrongly picked up as part of an object. Those limitations mentioned above are quite common to the existing automatic VOP segmentation algorithms.

Fully automatic VOP segmentation for generic video sequences is still a challenging research topic. More research, and probably the incorporation of higher-level knowledge, image understanding, and some kind of artificial intelligence into the segmentation process, are necessary to successfully perform segmentation of real video sequences.

References

1 "MPEG-4 visual fixed draft international standard," ISO/IEC 14496-2, Oct.1998.

2 P.F. Felzenszwalb and D.P. Huttenlocher, "Image segmentation using local variation," Proc. IEEE Conf. Computer Vision Pattern Recognition, CVPR'98, pp.98-104, June 1998.

3 P. Salembier et al, "Antiextensive connected operations for image and sequence processing," IEEE Trans. Image Processing, Vol.7, No.4, pp.555-570, Apr. 1998.

4 L. Garrido, et al, "Motion analysis of image sequences using connected operators," SPIE, Vol.3024, pp.546-557.

5 T. Meier and K.N. Ngan, "Segmentation and tracking of moving objects for content-based video coding," IEE Proc. Visual Image Signal Processing, Vol.146, No.3, pp.144-150, June 1999.

6 J. Guo, et al, "Fast and accurate moving object extraction technique for MPEG-4 object-based video coding," in SPIE Visual Communication and Image Processing, VCIP'99, Vol.3653, pp.1210-1221, January 1999.

7 T. Merier and K.N. Ngan, "Automatic segmentation of moving objects for video object plane generation," IEEE Trans. Circuit and System For Video Technology, Vol.8, No.5, pp.525-537, Sept. 1998.

8 T. Meier and K.N. Ngan, "Extraction of moving objects for content-based video coding," in SPIE Visual Communication and Image Processing, VCIP'99, pp.1178-1189, January 1999.

9 R. Mech, M. Wollborn, "A noise robust method for 2D shape estimation of moving objects in video sequences considering a moving camera," Signal Processing, Vol.66, pp.203-217, 1998.

10 A. Neri, et al, "Automatic moving object and background separation," Signal Processing, Vol.66, pp.219-232, 1998.

11 B.K.P. Horn and B.G. Schunck, "Determining optical flow," Artificial Intell., Vol.17, pp.185-203, 1981.

12 M.R. Luettgen, et al, "Efficient multiscale regularization with application to the computation of optical flow," IEEE Trans. Image Processing, Vol.3, No.1, pp.41-63, January 1994.
13 Black, M. J. and Anandan, P., "A framework for the robust estimation of optical flow," Fourth International Conf. on Computer Vision, ICCV-93, Berlin, Germany, May 1993, pp. 231-236.
14 J.D. Kim and S.K. Mitra, "A local relaxation method for optical flow estimation," Signal Processing: Image Communication, Vol.11, pp.21-38, 1997.
15 M. Bierling, "Displacement estimation by hierarchical block-matching," in SPIE Visual Communication and Image Processing, VCIP'88, Vol.1001, pp.942-951, Nov. 1988.
16 J. Canny, "A computational approach to edge detection," IEEE Trans. Pattern Analy. Machine Intell., PAMI-8, pp.679-698, Nov. 1986.
17 Daniel P. Huttenlocher, et al, "Comparing images using the Hausdorff Distance," IEEE Trans. Pattern Analy. Machine Intell., PAMI-15, pp.850-863, Sept. 1993.

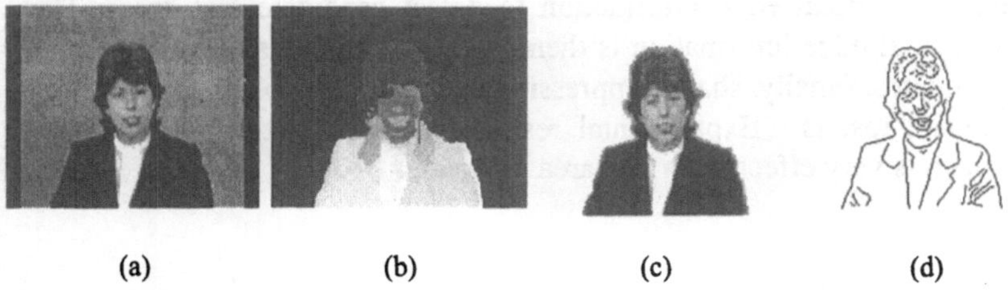

(a) (b) (c) (d)

Fig. 3. Sequence Claire, (a) frame 30, (b) segmented grayscale image, (c) extracted object, (d) object model.

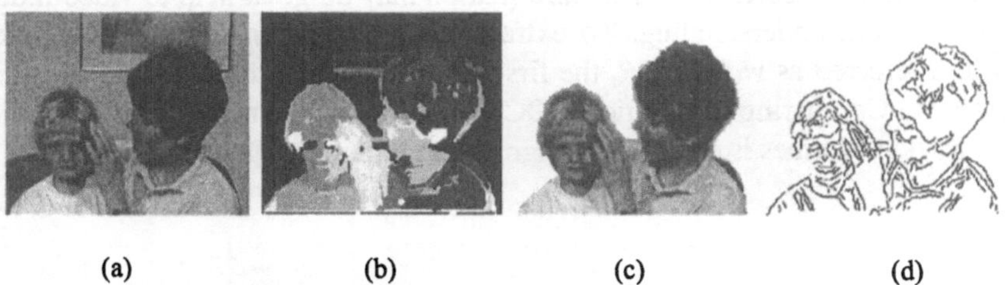

(a) (b) (c) (d)

Fig. 4. Sequence Mthr&Datr, (a) frame 30, (b) segmented grayscale image, (c) extracted object, (d) object model.

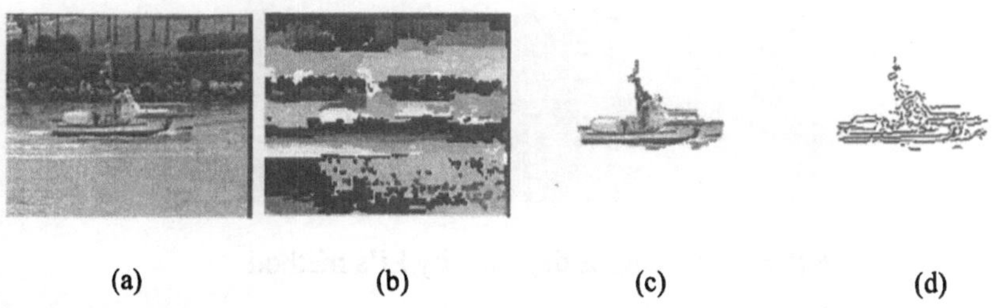

(a) (b) (c) (d)

Fig. 5. Sequence Coastguard, (a) frame 240, (b) segmented grayscale image, (c) extracted object, (d) object model.

Text Area Detection from Video Frames

Xiangrong Chen, Hongjiang Zhang

Microsoft Research China
hjzhang@microsoft.com

Abstract. Text area detection from video frame is an essential step for Video OCR. The key problem is the complex background of the video frames. This paper proposes a novel approach to this problem. First, we use the vertical edge information to detect candidate text areas. The horizontal edge information is then used to eliminate some of the false candidates. Finally, shape suppression technique is applied to further refine the results. Experimental results have shown the proposed approach is very effective in text area detection.

1 Introduction

Text embedded in video frames often carries the most important information, such as time, place, name or topics, etc. This information may do great help to video indexing and video content understanding. To extract text information from video sequence, which often referred as *video OCR*, the first essential step is to detect the text area in video frames. Comparing to traditional OCR application, the main difficulty to detect text area in video frames is complex backgrounds and low image resolution.

Fig. 1. Text regions detected by Li's method

There have been several published efforts in addressing the problem of text area detection in video. Li [1] used a hybrid wavelet/neural network segment approach based on 16×16 pixels blocks. Zhong, et al, [2] located caption in compressed domain using 8×8 DCT coefficients blocks. The main flaw of these two block-based methods is their inaccurate area boundary, as shown in **Figure 1**. Sato [3] applied a horizontal differential filter to the frame and detected text region that satisfies size, fill factor and horizontal-vertical aspect ratio constraints. However, this method also has no mechanism to constrain the boundary accurately. In addition, the above methods suffer when some non-text texture appears in the frame and thus increase the burden in the text recognition steps.

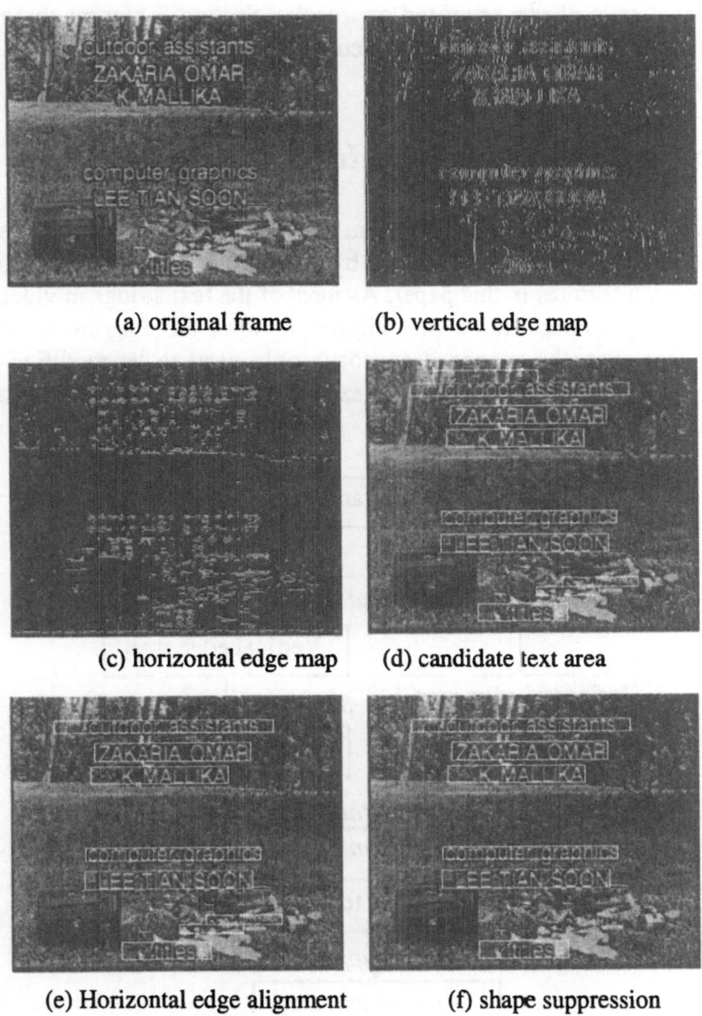

(a) original frame (b) vertical edge map

(c) horizontal edge map (d) candidate text area

(e) Horizontal edge alignment (f) shape suppression

Fig. 2. Examples of detection results by proposed method

In this paper, we propose a new approach to detecting text areas in video frames accurately and robustly in real time. As shown in **Figure 2**, we first apply a horizontal and vertical Sobel differential calculator, followed by an edge thinning process on the original image, (a), to obtain a vertical edge map, (b), and a horizontal edge map, (c). From the vertical edge map (b), we obtain candidate text areas, shown as the white rectangles in (d). Then, by using horizontal edge alignment, false candidates can be eliminated, as shown in (e). Finally, we use a shape suppression technique based on Bayesian decision theory to avoid false candidates resulting from non-text texture areas, as shown in (f). Experimental results have shown the proposed approach is very efficient and accurate in text area detection.

The remaining of this paper is organized as following. In section 2, we describe the diagram and details of our proposed approach. Section 3 present the experimental evaluation of the approach and Section 4 conclude the paper.

2 Detect Text Area Using Edge Information

Typically, text regions in video frames are strongly textured. There are several methods to describe such textures introduced by text strings. We use edge information to characterize such textures in this paper. As most of the text strings in video align horizontally, we only address this case. **Figure 3** shows the diagram of our proposed approach. However, the proposed approach only need to be modified slightly for detecting vertically aligned text string: to exchange the role of the horizontal edge map and the vertical edge map in Figure 3.

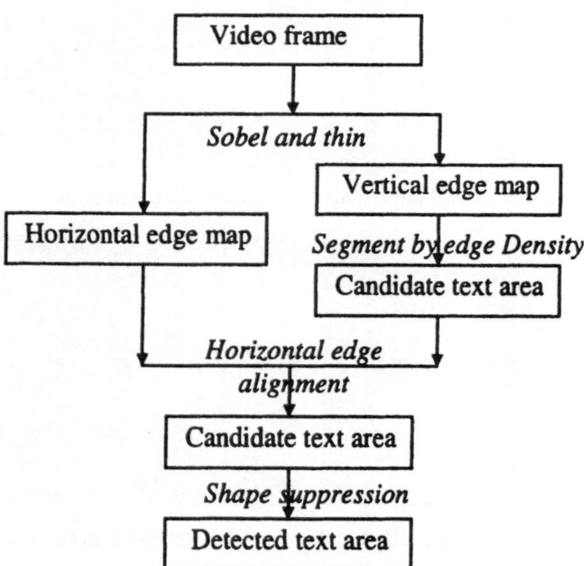

Fig. 3. Examples of detection results by proposed method

If you are unable to use LaTeX, you may use MS Word together with the template sv-lncs.dot (see Sect. 4) or any other text processing system. In the latter case, please follow these instructions closely in order to make the volume look as uniform as possible.

2.1 Edge Map Generation

We apply a 3×3 horizontal and vertical Sobel filter on a video frame to obtain two edge maps of the frame: vertical and horizontal, as shown in Figure 3. The Sobel operators are shown in **Figure 4.** A non-maxima suppression is then used to thin the edges. Isolated edge points in the edge maps are then filtered out by a de-noising processing.

-1	0	1
-2	0	2
-1	0	1

(a) Horizontal

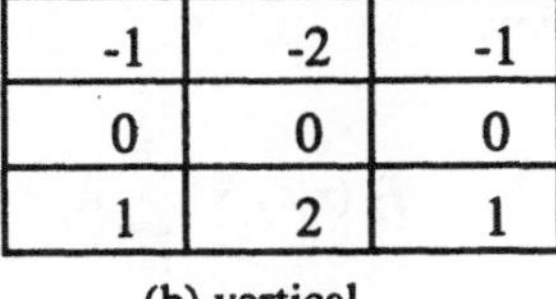

-1	-2	-1
0	0	0
1	2	1

(b) vertical

Fig. 4. Sobel operators

2.2 Finding Candidate Text Area

From the vertical edge map, we use edge density to find candidate text area. For a 352×288 PAL video frame, several heuristic rules are employed to embody the edge density: (1) Each scan line in the region should contain at least 6 edge points, (2) The edge density on each scan line in the region should be larger than 6 to 20, (3) The height of the region should be larger that 6 pixels. These heuristic rules can be adaptively modified for video frames of other systems and resolution.

2.3 Horizontal Edge Alignment Confirmation

For horizontal aligned text strings, there are many horizontal edges along the upper and bottom boundaries of the text area, as shown in Figure 2(c). This observation motivates us to eliminate some false candidates by using of the horizontal edge alignment confirmation. In Figure 2 (e), the candidates resulted from tree trunk is cleared up by applying this method.

2.4 Shape Suppression

After the above process, there still remain two kinds of problems: false candidates and inaccurate left and right text area boundaries, both rising from non-text textures.

These problems may increase the burden of the OCR procedures followed the text area detection. Therefore, it is desirable to do some preprocess to remove or at least reduce this problem. For this, we apply a shape suppression process based on Bayesian decision theory. The basic idea of shape suppression is to use shape information of character edge to reduce the effect of non-text texture. The probabilistic models required for the Bayesian approach are estimated with a Vector Quantization (VQ) framework [4].

VQ-based Bayesian Classifier

Considering ***n*** training samples from a class ***c,*** a vector quantizer is used to extract *m* (*m*<*n*) codebook vectors, v_i ($1 \le i \le m$), from the *n* training samples. Given class ***c,*** the class-conditional density of a feature vector ***x***, i.e., $f_X(x|c)$ can be approximated by a mixture of Gaussians with identity covariance matrices, each centered at a codebook vector, like below

$$f_X(x|c) \propto \sum_{i=1}^{m} w_i * \exp(-\|x - v_i\|^2 / 2) \tag{1}$$

where w_i is the proportion of training samples assigned to v_i. The Bayesian classifier is then defined using the maximum a posteriori criterion as follows

$$\hat{c} = \arg\max_{c \in \Omega}\{p(c \mid x)\} = \arg\max_{c \in \Omega}\{p(x \mid c)p(c)\} \tag{2}$$

where $\Omega=\{c_1,c_2\}$ is the set of shape class and $p(c)$ represents the priori class probability.

Feature Selection

A sample in training the codebook can be each consecutive thin edge within the candidate region in vertical edge map. Each feature vector consists of four elements:

$$v = (N/H,\ D/H,\ V_N/H,\ H_N/H)^T \tag{3}$$

where *H* is the pixel height of the candidate region; *N* the pixel number of the sample; V_N and H_N the pixel number of the sample's vertical projection and horizontal projection, respectively.

Training Phase

In our method, c_1 represents text shape class and c_2 non-text shape class. Training samples of class c_1 are from the vertical edge map of all the characters, both upper and lower cases, and digitals. Training samples of class c_2 consists of two parts. One is from the real data selected manually. The other is from a "bootstrap" process like in method presented in [5]. That is, to add samples incorrectly classified as text shapes to the training sample set of non-text shape class. The codebook size for each training set is empirically set to 4.

3 Experimental Results

We have tested our method on 2 hours CNN TV programs and a 21 seconds segment of MPEG-7 test data. The data contains many different sources, including TV business news, sport news, commercials, movies, weather reports, etc. With the proposed approach, over 95% of text regions have been detected correctly with a false detection rate lower than 5% in most cases except TV commercials. In TV commercials, characters in a same text region often vary to a large extent in both font and size, thus cannot pass the horizontal edge alignment confirmation. **Figure 5** shows results of example video frames.

We implemented our algorithm using a Media SDK 6.0 on a DELL PIII-500 PC. The system can detect text region from MPEG2 file in real time, i.e., 25fps with 352×288 frame size.

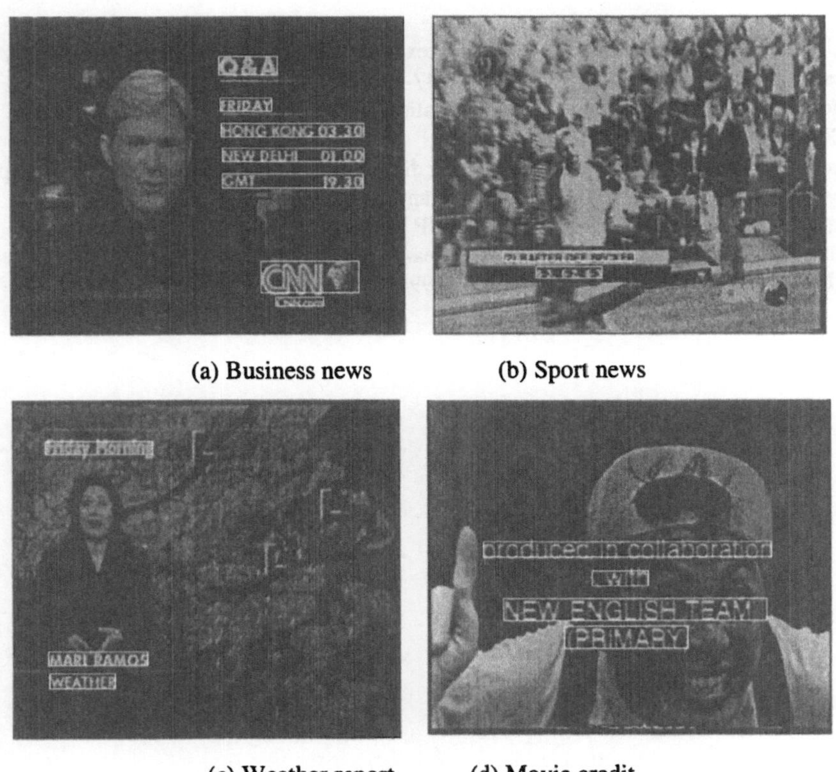

(a) Business news (b) Sport news

(c) Weather report (d) Movie credit

Fig. 5. Experiment results

4 Conclusions

In this paper, we have presented an approach to text area detection from video frames. The approach consists of four main processes, including edge map generation, candidate extraction, horizontal edge alignment confirmation and shape suppression. Experimental have shown the proposed approach is robust and accurate. In addition, the computational complexity of the proposed approach is very low such that it can satisfy real-time applications.

At the present, the proposed approach operates on single video frames, thus it can also applied directly text area extraction of still images. To improve the performance of the proposed approach, we are actively investigating methods for integrating temporal information available from video sequences, such as tracking text areas across multiple frames.

References

1. Li, H.; Doermann, D.; Kia, O.: Automatic text detection and tracking in digital video, IEEE Trans. on Image Processing, 9(1) (2000) 147-156
2. Zhong, Y., Zhang, H., Jain, A.K.: Automatic Caption Extraction of Digital Videos, Proc. ICIP'99, Kobe, (1999) 24-27
3. Sato, T., Kanade, T.: Video OCR: Indexing digital news libraries by recognition of superimposed caption. ICCV Workshop on Image and Video retrieval (1998)
4. Gray R.M.: Vector Quantization, IEEE ASSP Magazine, 1(2) (1984) 4-29
5. Sung, K., Poggio, T.: Example-based learning for view-based human face detection. A.I.Memo 1521, CBCL Paper 112, MIT (1994)

Interacting with 3D Graphic Objects in an Image-Based Environment

Yong Wang[1*], Jiang Li[2], Kun Zhou[3*] and Heung-Yeung Shum[2]

[1]Department of Electric Engineering, Tsinghua University, Beijing 100084, China
Joker_wang@hotmail.com
[2]Microsoft Research, China, 3F Sigma Building, 49 Zhichun Road, Beijing 100080, China
{jiangli, hshum}@microsoft.com
[3]State Key Laboratory of CAD&CG, Zhejiang University, Hangzhou, 310027, China
kzhou2k@hotmail.com

Abstract. This paper presents a novel hybrid rendering system, which allows users to interact with 3D graphic objects in an image-based environment. To represent a complex environment, we use a collection of images captured by a longitudinally aligned camera array, which rotates along a circle. The captured images are indexed and compressed for efficient rendering of the environment. Moreover, users can interactively deploy 3D graphic objects and move around in a constrained 3D cylindrical space in the image-based environment. Unlike traditional virtual reality systems that must take into account all the geometrical objects in the scene, the present 3D graphic rendering engine needs only to deal with a small number of foreground 3D graphic objects in the image-based environment, therefore significantly reducing the 3D graphic processing time. Experiments demonstrate that this system can be used as a new virtual and augmented reality platform for games, virtual tours, virtual real estate, and many other applications.

1 Introduction

Virtual reality is an attractive technology, which provides users an environment in which to navigate and play. Traditional virtual reality techniques are usually based on geometrical approaches, and the scenes may consist of millions or billions of polygons. The geometrical modeling and rendering approach has several main problems. First, it is very labor-intensive to construct a synthetic scene. Second, in order to achieve real-time performance, the complexity and rendering quality are usually limited by the rendering engine. Third, the requirement of certain acceleration hardware limits the wide application of the method.

Recently developed image-based modeling and rendering techniques [2, 8, 9, 12, 15] have made it possible to simulate photo-realistic environments. The advantages of image-based rendering methods are that the cost of rendering a scene is independent

---

* This work was done while these authors were interns at Microsoft Research, China.

of the scene complexity and that truly compelling photo-realism can be achieved since the images can be directly taken from the real world. One of the most popular image-based rendering software is Apple's QuickTime VR [3]. QuickTime VR has its roots in branching movies, e.g., the movie-map [11], the Digital Video Interactive (DVI) [14], and the "Virtual Museum" [13]. QuickTime VR uses cylindrical panoramic images to compose a virtual environment, therefore provides users an immersive experience.

An ideal virtual reality environment should basically provide users a 3D space to move and some virtual objects to interact with. In the image-based aspect, there have been some early efforts towards this goal. QuickTime VR uses a pop-up method to pop objects to the users. Specifically, a shooting game is demonstrated with the use of PanoVR SDK [5], a development kit for integrating photo-realistic panoramic images with 3D graphic objects in virtual worlds. Because a panorama only allows users to view the scene from a fixed location, users are not able to experience 3D motion.

Other approaches for image-based rendering [4, 6, 16, 17] that incorporate 3D graphic objects into scenes have also been studied. In these methods, the scenes again have to be reconstructed and represented by geometrical models. Efforts are made on recovering reflection properties of the captured objects and lighting conditions of the scene. These methods inevitably involve much more interaction and manipulation since structure from motion is regarded to be a difficult problem in computer vision.

Briefly, in the rendering aspect, the problem with a pure geometry-based virtual reality method is that the 3D rendering engine has to take into account all the geometrical objects in the scene, even if many of them simply act as part of the background. The situation is even worse when users only want to interact with a small number of foreground objects, because the selection engine has to process all geometrical objects in the scene, thereby increasing the response time significantly. According to current image-based virtual reality methods, either the user's motions are limited or the scenes have to be reconstructed manually.

An effective solution to the problem is to separate 3D graphic objects, which are used to interact with the users, from the background scene. The background scene is captured and then rendering by an image-based method. 3D graphic objects are introduced only if they are needed for interaction by the users. This kind of strategy leverages both the real property of the captured images and the interactive property of the 3D graphic objects.

In this paper, we will describe the architecture according to the above strategy. In Section 2, we introduce the processing of the user's actions, the rendering of the background and 3D graphic objects. A billiards game will be shown in Section 3. Finally, we conclude our work and discuss future directions in Section 4.

2 Architecture

As illustrated in Fig. 1, we capture scenes with a longitudinally aligned camera array [10]. The array is mounted on a horizontal arm supported by a tripod. The scene is captured while the array rotates along a circle, which is referred to as the "capture circle" (see Fig.2). Each pixel of the captured images is indexed by four parameters:

the rotation angle of the camera array, the longitudinal number of the camera, the image column number and the image row number. These images are compressed by the vector quantization method [7]. In addition, the radius R of the capture circle and the height H and the extension L of the camera array are recorded for references.

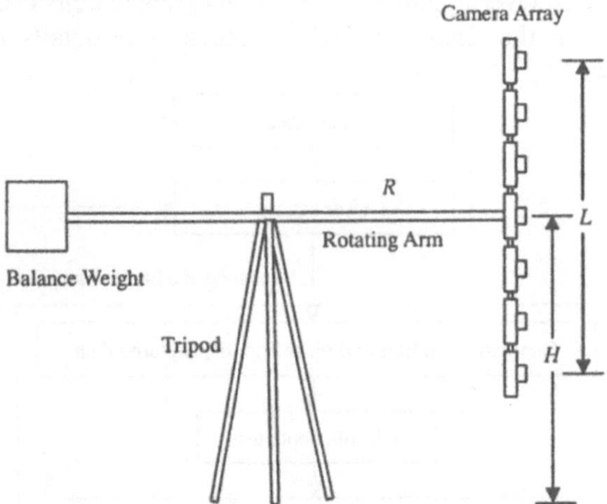

Figure 1: The setup of the capture system.

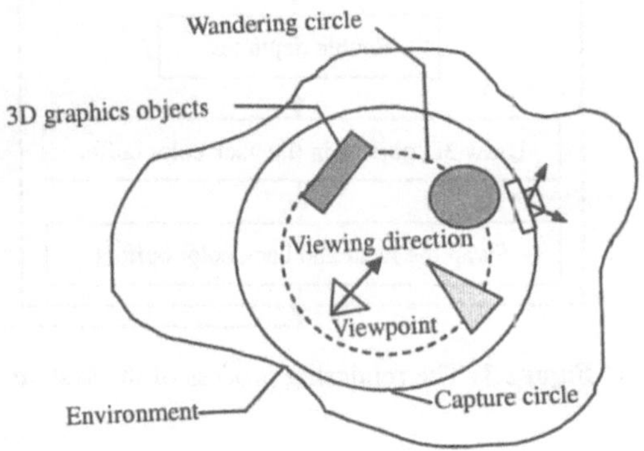

Figure 2: The top view of the environment and some 3D graphic objects.

In virtual reality applications, 3D graphic objects are deployed within the capture circle so that users can interact with them. Users are constrained to walk within a circle referred to as the "wandering circle". The magnitude of radius r of the wandering circle depends on both the lateral field of view φ_{fovc} of the capture camera and the radius R of the capture circle, and is equal to $R\sin(\varphi_{fovc}/2)$. It is obvious that any ray that is received at any viewing position within the circle can always be retrieved from the captured images.

Since 3D graphic objects are always located within the capture circle, no collision can occur between the 3D graphic objects and the surrounding environment. The rendering process is illustrated in Fig.3. First, the captured scene data are loaded into the main memory. The actions are processed, resulting with the viewing position and location of the user. These parameters are used in the generation of the background view of the environment. The same parameters are also employed in the rendering of the 3D graphic objects. Overlapping the view of 3D graphic objects on the view of the background results in the final view of the scene. The details of each step are described as follows.

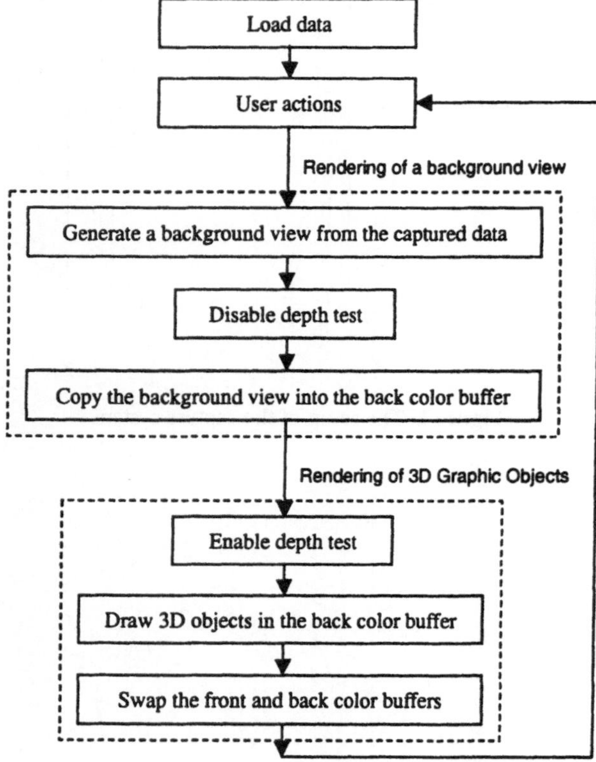

Figure 3: The rendering process of the system.

User Actions

Users can arrange the 3D graphic objects and interact with them. Mainly, users can translate, rotate, zoom in or out in the scene. The viewing position ***P***, the viewing direction ***T***, the longitudinal field of view $\Delta\theta_{fovo}$, and the lateral field of view $\Delta\varphi_{fovo}$ of the user are determined accordingly.

Rendering the Background

The detailed description of the background scene rendering can be found in [10]. Briefly, for each pixel in the view port to be rendered, a viewing ray is determined according to both the viewing position ***P*** and the viewing direction ***T*** of the user. The intersection point of the projection of the viewing ray on the capture plane and the capture circle is found. This intersection point indicates which image array is relevant to the viewing ray. Then, according to the horizontal angle between the viewing ray and the direction of the camera at the intersection point, a determination is made as to which image column in the image array has a corresponding viewing direction nearest to the direction of the viewing ray. Next, according to the elevation angle of the viewing ray, the intersection point of the viewing ray and the longitudinal camera array is calculated. This intersection point indicates which camera is relevant to the viewing ray. Finally, according to the elevation angle of the viewing ray, a determination is made as to which pixel contributes the color of the pixel in the rendered image.

Rendering 3D Graphic Objects

The rendering process of the 3D graphic objects is straightforward. We take the rendering in OpenGL as an example. As illustrated in Fig. 3, after the background view is generated, we disable the depth test and copy the resultant image to the back color buffer of an OpenGL driver. After that, we enable the depth test and draw the 3D graphic object in the back color buffer. Two key functions that define the view are

```
void gluLookAt(GLdouble eyex, GLdouble eyey, GLdouble eyez,
GLdouble centerx, GLdouble centery, GLdouble centerz,
GLdouble upx, GLdouble upy, GLdouble upz);
```

and

```
void gluPerspective(GLdouble fovy, GLdouble aspect, GLdouble
zNear, GLdouble zFar);
```

respectively, where the *eyex*, *eyey*, *eyez* arguments specify the desired viewpoint, which equals the view position ***P*** in the background rendering. The *centerx*, *centery*, *centerz* arguments specify the 3D coordinates of any point along the viewing direction, which can be chosen as ***P*** + ***T***. The *upx*, *upy*, *upz* arguments indicate the up direction of the view, which can be derived accordingly. The argument *fovy* equals the longitudinal field of view of the user θ_{fovo}. The argument *aspect* equals the ratio of the width of the view port to the height of the view port. The distances of near and far clipping plane *zNear* and *zFar* can be chosen by the user.

It should be noted that user operations such as selection and picking are implemented by the 3D rendering engine itself. Our programming interface is transparent to the 3D rendering engines.

3 Experimental Results

As an example, a billiard game is developed with the use of our application programming interface. Since it is hard to design an array with dozens of cameras at the present stage, we simulate the capture process in a synthetic scene. We adopt a scene "Brians Beach Bungalow" from 3DCAFE [1]. We set the radius of the capture circle to be 1.57 meters. Both of the longitudinal and lateral fields of view of the camera are 45°. Therefore, the radius of the wandering circle is 0.6 meters. We arrange 61 cameras in an array 2.7 meters high. The height of the rotating arm that supports the camera array is chosen to be 1.55 meters. Each camera captures 360 pictures in each rotation of the camera array. The resolution of the image is 256×256 pixels. It costs about 30 hours to generate a total of 21960 images on a Pentium III 500 PC. The amount of the resultant raw data is about 4GB. After vector quantization (12:1) and Lempel-Ziv coding (4:1), the size of the data file is reduced to 80MB. As for the 3D graphic objects, we deploy a billiard table into the scene. Users can navigate in the room or hit the billiard balls on the table. One important point in deploying the table is that one must put the table on the ground, i.e. the legs of the table must reach the ground. This can be guaranteed since the height of the camera array has been already recorded.

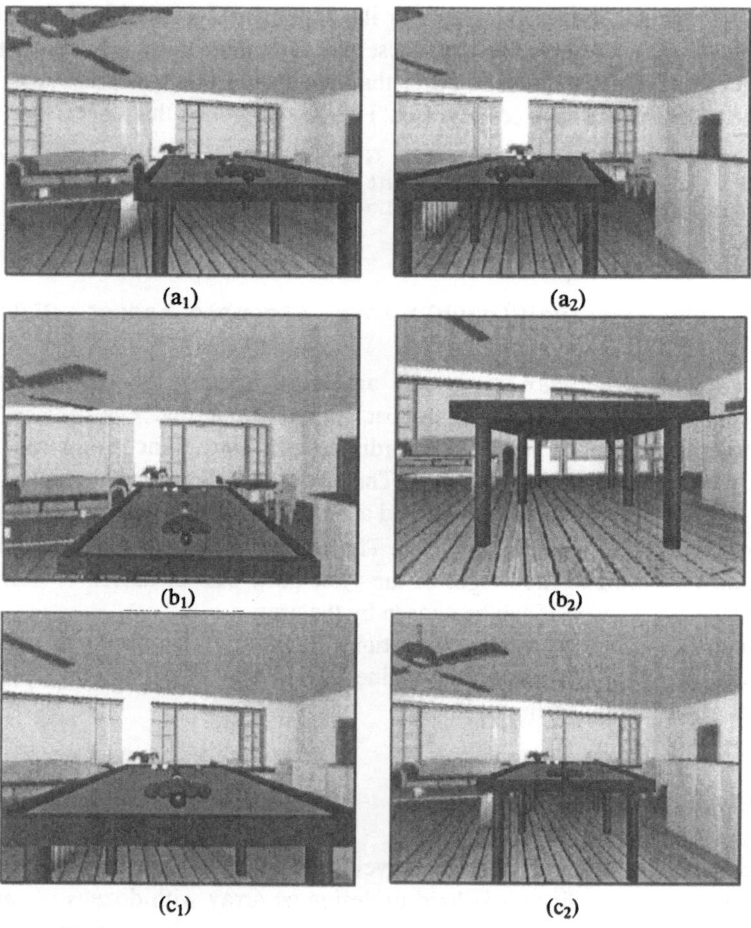

Figure 4: The views when the user moves left (a_1) and right (a_2), up (b_1) and down (b_2), and forward (c_1) and backward (c_2).

Fig. 4 shows views of the billiard table and the room when the user moves left (a_1) and right (a_2), up (b_1) and down (b_2), and forward (c_1) and backward (c_2). One can see that lateral and longitudinal parallaxes exist between the 3D graphic objects and the other objects in the room. In addition, the legs of the table are really fixed on the ground. The present system successfully keeps the geometrical consistency of 3D graphic objects and the surrounding scenes. Interested readers can visit http://research.microsoft.com/~jiangli/pcm2001demo.htm to view a video clip of billiard play. In that demo, the user first hit the balls and then viewed the billiard table and the surrounding scene at different locations and viewing directions while the balls are still rolling. Careful readers may find that the billiard table is so large that it may already exceed the range of the capture circle. This is true. Actually, users can deploy objects into any empty space so long as the objects do not intersect with the captured scene objects. In our system, this can be achieved by interactively moving the object and checking from different viewpoints just as what we do in the real world.

4 Conclusions

This paper presents a novel hybrid rendering system, which allows users to interact with 3D graphic objects in an image-based environment. With the use of this technique, users can move within a 3D cylindrical space and observe significant lateral and longitudinal parallaxes and lighting changes of the scene. The occlusions among the 3D graphic objects and the occlusions between 3D graphic objects and the background objects are obviously displayed. Moreover, users can interact with 3D graphic objects in the image-based scene.

The first feature of this technique is that the viewing rays that are needed for the rendering of surrounding scenes have already been captured in advance. The 3D graphic rendering engine need only take into account the relevant objects. Therefore, the 3D graphic processing time is significantly reduced. The second feature is that there is no need for any geometrical reconstruction in the rendering of image-based scenes. Since the scenes can be taken from any chosen place, it will be possible for us to vividly tour or play games in very complicated scenes such as forests that are uneasy to model. Furthermore, these beautiful scenes can also be stored in some web sites so that other people can download them and use them as backgrounds in their games or virtual tours.

The rendering of the background in our system represents a novel sampling pattern of a 4D plenoptic function. Compared to the light field, Lumigraph and other sampling methods of the 4D plenoptic function, our method provides an easier capture configuration, a uniform spatial sampling and an outward looking experience. Compared to concentric mosaics, our method eliminates vertical distortions and provides a 3D wandering experience without requiring depth correction.

In the present system, we only integrate 3D graphic objects into the image-based scene via an overlapping approach. Methods for incorporating lighting effects of the image-based scenes on the 3D graphic objects or including shadows of 3D graphic objects on the image-based scenes need to be developed in the future. Nevertheless, this technology has aided application developers in developing a wide range of virtual augmented reality applications, which need interaction with 3D objects in a complicated environment.

The authors would like to acknowledge Ka Yan Chan for proofreading the paper.

References

1. http://www.3dcafe.com/
2. S. E. Chen and L. Williams, View Interpolation for Image Synthesis, Computer Graphics Proceedings, Annual Conference Series, pages 279–288, Proc. SIGGRAPH 1993 (California), August 1993.
3. S. E. Chen, QuickTime VR – An Image-based Approach to Virtual Environment Navigation, Computer Graphics Proceedings, Annual Conference Series, pages 29-38, Proc. SIGGRAPH 1995 (Los Angeles), August 1995.
4. C.-S. Chen, Y.-P. Hung, S.-W. Shih, C.-C. Hsieh, C.-Y. Tang, C.-G. Yu and Y.-C. Cheng. Integrating 3D graphic objects into real images for augmented reality. In Proceedings of the ACM symposium on Virtual reality software and technology, 1998, pages 1-8.
5. Cheng-Chin Chiang, Alex Huang, Tsing-Shin Wang, Matthew Huang, Yunn-Yen Chen, Jun-Wei Hsieh, Ju-Wei Chen and Tse Cheng, PanoVR SDK -- a software development kit for integrating photo-realistic panoramic images and 3-D graphical objects into virtual worlds, Proceedings of the ACM symposium on Virtual reality software and technology, September 15-17, 1997, Lausanne Switzerland, pages 147-154.
6. Paul Debevec, Rendering Synthetic Objects Into Real Scenes: Bridging Traditional and Image-Based Graphics With Global Illumination and High Dynamic Range Photography, SIGGRAPH 1998.
7. A. Gersho, R. M. Gray, Vector Quantization and signal compression, Kluwer Academic Publishers, 1992.
8. S. J. Gortler, R. Grzeszczuk, R. Szeliski, and M. F. Cohen, The Lumigraph, Computer Graphics Proceedings, Annual Conference Series, pages 43-54, Proc. SIGGRAPH 1996 (New Orleans), August 1996.
9. M. Levoy and P. Hanrahan, Light Field Rendering, Computer Graphics Proceedings, Annual Conference Series, pages 31-42, Proc. SIGGRAPH 1996 (New Orleans), August 1996.
10. Jiang Li, Kun Zhou, Yong Wang and Heung-Yeung Shum, A Novel Image-Based Rendering System with A Longitudinally Aligned Camera Array, Eurographics 2000 Short Presentations, pp.107-114, Interlaken, Switzerland, 21-25 August, 2000.
11. A. Lippman, Movie Maps: An Application of the Optical Videodisc to Computer Graphics, Computer Graphics (Proc. SIGGRAPH 1980), pp. 32-43, 1980.
12. L. McMillan and G. Bishop. Plenoptic Modeling: An Image-based Rendering System, Computer Graphics Proceedings, Annual Conference Series, pages 39-46, Proc. SIGGRAPH 1995, August, 1995.
13. G. Miller, E. Hoffert, S. E. Chen, E. Patterson, D. Blackketter, S. Rubin, S. A. Applin, D. Yim, J. Hanan, The Virtual Museum: Interactive 3D Navigation of A Multimedia Database, The Journal of Visualization and Computer Animation (3): 183-197, 1992.
14. D. G. Riply, DVI- A Digital Multimedia Technology, Communications of the ACM, 32(7): 811-822, 1989.
15. H. Y. Shum and L. W. He, Rendering with Concentric Mosaics, Computer Graphics Proceedings, Annual Conference Series, pages 299-306, Proc. SIGGRAPH 1999 (Los Angeles), August 1999.
16. Y. Yu and J. Malik, Recovering Photometric Properties of Architectural Scenes from Photographs, ACM Computer Graphics, Proc. of SIGGRAPH 1996, pp.207–218, 1998.
17. Y. Yu, P. Debevec, J. Malik and T. Hawkins, Inverse Global Illumination: Recovering Reflectance Models of Real Scenes from Photographs, ACM Computer Graphics, Proc. of SIGGRAPH 1999, pp.215-224, 1999.

Robust Face Recognition with Light Compensation

Yea-Shuan Huang[1], Yao-Hong Tsai[1], Jun-Wei Shieh[2]

[1]Computer & Communications Research Laboratories
Industrial Technology and Research Institute, Taiwan
yeashuan@itri.org.tw
[2]Department of Electrical Engineering, YuanZe University

Abstract. This paper proposes a face recognition method which is based on a Generalized Probabilistic Descent (GPD) learning rule with a three-layer feed-forward network. This method aims to recognize faces in a loosely controlled surveillance environment, which allows (1) large face image rotation (on and out of image plane), (2) different backgrounds, and (3) different illumination. Besides, a novel light compensation approach is designed to compensate the gray-level differences resulted from different lighting conditions. Experiments for three kinds of classifiers (LVQ2, BP, and GPD) have been performed on a ITRI face database. GPD with the proposed light compensation approach displays the best recognition accuracy among all possible combination.

1 Introduction

Due to the rapid advance of computer hardware and the continuous progress of computer software, we are looking forward to developing more powerful and friendly computer use models so that computer can serve people in a more active and intelligent way. To this end, the computer naturally needs to have a surveillance ability, which enables it to detect, track, and recognize its surrounding people. This results in the situation that researches on face processing (including detection [1-2], tracking [3], and recognition [4-7]) are very prosperous in the last two decades. This paper mainly discusses our research effort on the face recognition (FR) issue.

The objective of our research is to develop a FR classifier which can recognize faces in a loosely controlled surveillance environment. This means the desired FR classifier can deal with the faces having different rotations, illumination, and backgrounds. Our approach is to train a three-layer feed-forward network by using a Generalized Probabilistic Descent (GPD) learning rule. GPD is originally proposed by Juang [8] to train a speech classifier, which is reported to have a much better recognition performance than the well-known Back-Propagation (BP) [9] training. However, to our best knowledge, GPD is rarely or even never used by the computer-vision community. Because GPD is based on minimizing a classification related error function, it theoretically can produce a better classification performance than the classifiers (such as BP) based on minimizing a least-mean-square error. Furthermore, to make FR insensitive to the illumination variation, a novel light compensation method is proposed to compensate the image variation resulted from the lighting factor.

This paper consists of five sections. Section 2 describes the used error function and the derived GPD weights updating rule. Section 3 describes the proposed light compensation method which can reduce the image difference occurred from the illumination variation. Section 4 specifies the ITRI (Industrial Technology and Research Institute) face database and its construction guidelines. Section 5 then performs several experiments and makes a performance comparison among LVQ2, BP, and GPD. Finally, Section 6 draws our conclusions and point out the future research directions.

2 A Generalized Probabilistic Descent Learning

The key idea in GPD formulation is the incorporation of a smooth classification-related error function into the gradient search optimization objective. In general, GPD can be applied to train various kinds of classifiers. Here, a three-layer feed-forward network is used to serve the classifier architecture.

Assume there are K persons in the concerned pattern domain, $C_1,\dots,C_K$, and the feature of an observed face is $x=(x_1,\dots,x_n)$, where n is the feature dimension. Let $g_i(x)$ be a discrimination function indicating the degree to which pattern x belongs to person i. In general, a pattern x is classified to be person M if $g_M(x)$ is the largest value among $\{g_i(x)\,|\,1\le i\le K\}$, that is $M=\arg\max_{1\le i\le K} g_i(x)$. In order to derive the optimized $\{g_i(x)\,|\,1\le i\le K\}$ which produce the best recognition accuracy, a training stage must be performed. Of course, a set of face training samples should be collected beforehand. During training, let T and M denote respectively the genuine person index and the person index having the largest discrimination function of pattern x. To simplify notation, g_i denotes $g_i(x)$. An error function $E(x)$ is defined to specify the possible classification error under the current classifier as

$$E(x)=\frac{1}{1+e^{\frac{g_T-g_M}{A(n)}}}$$

where $A(n)$ is a bandwidth parameter in iteration n governing the size of the active area of the sigmoid function, and $0\le A(n+1)\le A(n)$. When g_T is smaller than g_M, $E(x)$ becomes large, and when g_T is equal to g_M, $E(x)$ becomes 0.5 which is the smallest value among all possible $E(x)$. In fact, the more negative the value of

$g_T - g_M$ is, the larger $E(x)$ will be. This is a desired property because the small value of $g_T - g_M$ indicates the poor classification ability of the trained classifier. Therefore, the defined $E(x)$ is appropriate to serve as an error function. Consequently, to minimize $E(x)$ corresponds to derive a better classifier.

A three-layer network is used to classify an input face pattern, which consists of the input, hidden, and output layers. I_i denotes the i th node of the input layer which contains the value of the i th feature element of an input x, O_j is the output value of the j th node of the hidden layer, and O_k is the output value of the k th node of the output layer. In this network, g_k means O_k, and

$$O_j = \frac{1}{1+e^{-\sum_{1\le i\le n} W_{ij} * I_i}}, \quad O_k = \frac{1}{1+e^{-\sum_{1\le j\le m} W_{jk} * O_j}}, \text{ and}$$

$$E(x) = \frac{1}{1+e^{\frac{O_T - O_M}{A(n)}}}$$

where n and m are the node numbers of the input and hidden layers respectively, W_{ij} is the connection weight between the i th node of the input layer and the j th node of the hidden layer, and W_{jk} is the connection weight between the j th node of the hidden layer and the k th node of the output layer. Therefore, to minimize $E(x)$ corresponds to derive the optimized W_{ij} and W_{jk}. According to the generalized delta rule, W_{ij} and W_{jk} can be updated as follows:

$$\Delta W_{jk} = -\alpha(n)\frac{\partial E(x)}{\partial W_{jk}} \quad \text{and} \quad \Delta W_{ij} = -\alpha(n)\frac{\partial E(x)}{\partial W_{ij}}$$

where $\alpha(n)$ is a positive and monotonically-decreased learning rate. By using the chain rule with simple mathematical operations, it is easily to derive

$$\frac{\partial E}{\partial W_{jk}} = \begin{cases} \frac{E(1-E)}{A} O_l(1-O_k)O_j, & k = M; \\ -\frac{E(1-E)}{A} O_l(1-O_k)O_j, & k = T; \\ 0 & \text{, otherwise.} \end{cases} \quad \text{and}$$

$$\frac{\partial E}{\partial W_{ij}} = \frac{E(1-E)}{A}\left[O_M(1-O_M)W_{jM} - O_T(1-O_T)W_{jT}\right] * O_j(1-O_j)I_i.$$

3 Light compensation for Face Images

It is well known that the image colors (or gray levels) are very sensitive to the lighting variation. A same object with different illumination may produce considerably different color or gray-level images. The first row of Fig. 1 shows several face color images which are taken from different lighting conditions. In general, it is difficult to produce a good classification accuracy if face samples in the training and testing sets are taken from different lighting conditions. Therefore, a light compensation preprocessing is essential, which can reduce the image difference resulted from illumination variation to the minimum.

A novel light compensation method with a six-step processing procedure is proposed as follows:

Step 1: transform each face image pixel F(m,n) from the RGB space to the YC_bC_r space, where $1 \leq m \leq H$ and $1 \leq n \leq V$ (H is the pixel width of the face image and V is the pixel height of the face image) , and let P(m,n) be the gray level of F(m,n).

Step 2: mark each F(m,n) to be a skin-color pixel if it satisfies conditions defined in [10].

Step 3: approximate an equation Q(x,y) to all marked skin-color pixel's gray levels P(m,n). Here, Q(x,y) is designed to be a second-order equation. That is

$$\begin{aligned} P(x,y) &= Q(x,y) \\ &= ax^2 + bxy + cy^2 + dx + ey + f. \end{aligned}$$

Parameters a, b, c, d, e, and f can be derived from the least-mean square error between P(m,n) and Q(m,n) for all marked skin-color pixels. The derived Q(x,y) indeed approximates the background lighting distribution for the current face image.

Step 4: subtract Q(m,n) from P(m,n) to derive a subtracted image $P'(m,n)$, that is

$$P'(m,n) = P(m,n) - Q(m,n).$$

Step 5: compute the average gray level μ and the standard deviation d from the marked skin-color subtracted pixels. That is

$$\mu = \frac{1}{N} \sum_{F(m,n) \in \text{skin-color pixels}} P'(m,n), \quad \text{and}$$

$$d = \sqrt{\frac{1}{N} \sum_{F(m,n) \in \text{skin-color pixels}} (P'(m,n) - \mu)^2}$$

where N is the total number of pixels marked as skin color.

Step 6: normalize each pixel's gray level $P'(m,n)$ to generate a new value by the following equation

$$G(m,n) = 128 + \frac{(P'(m,n) - \mu)}{d} * \beta$$

where β is a scale factor which purpose is to make the range of the transformed gray levels between 0 and 255. It is worthwhile to mention that the transformed faces have an average gray level close to 128 and have similar gray-level standard deviations.

Before applying the proposed light compensation method, the face portion of image should be extracted from the whole image so that the skin-color-pixel detection can focus only on the face image. Fig. 1 shows respectively some face images (first row), skin-color-pixel images where white color denotes skin color and black color denotes non-skin color (second row), background lighting distributions (third row), subtracted images (fourth row), and normalized images (fifth row) by using the proposed light compensation method. From inspection, the final normalized images have more similar gray-level distributions so that a face classifier can learn the truly personal distinct characteristics..

4 Face Database Construction

Because we aim to recognize faces under a loosely controlled surveillance environment, it is important to consider many variation factors when collecting the face database, which includes

(1) Face rotation : Each person was asked to look at 14 marked points attached on walls, every two neighboring points approximately form a 10-degree viewing angle to this person.

(2) Background : Pictures are taken at two diagonal corners of an office room. The two corners look quite differently to each other; one is near windows which is a more homogenous background, and the other is near a door with a cluttered desk.

(3) Illumination : Since one background is close to window, it accepts sort of day light. Therefore, the taken images are brighter than those taken from the other background. Also, because the day light is not always normal to the people's faces, some face images present one side brighter than the other side.

There are 46 persons involved in our face database whose pictures are display on Fig 4. Each person was arranged to stand sequentially at two corners of one office room, and at each corner he/she was asked to rotate his/her head for about every 10 degrees by looking at 14 predefined wall marks. For each head rotation, a video camera (with-resolution 320*240) is used to take pictures. Therefore, there are 46*14 pictures in total. Fig. 2 shows the taken images of one particular person.

5 Experiment Results

Currently, the face images are extracted from the original whole images manually. In general, an extracted face image is the rectangular portion of image which contains eyebrows, eyes, nose, and mouth. Since the statistically-based classification approaches generally require a lot of training samples, it is important to increase the sample number of database images. However, it is expensive to collect the real face images. So, we increase the face images by two ways. The first one is to produce a mirror image for each photographed image, and the second one is to generate virtual images by rotating and shifting the original images

Each extracted face image is first processed by applying the proposed light compensation method and accordingly a compensated image G is generated. Then, G is normalized into a 25*25 image which is further mapped to a 40-LDA-eigen bases. Therefore, the total feature dimension is 40 and the three-layer network architecture is set to be 40 (input)-200(hidden)-46(output) here. The odd-numbered samples of the ITRI face data base are used to train the network, and the even-numbered ones of the same data base are used to test the trained network.

Three classification methods (LVQ2, BP, GPD) are implemented to make a performance comparison. LVQ2 [11] can construct the appropriate face prototypes of each person, and it classifies an input face pattern x to the person having the nearest prototype to x. Here, three prototypes for each person were constructed. Both BP and GPD use the same network architecture (40-200-46). For manifesting the effectiveness of the proposed light compensation method (LC), all the three classifiers are trained and tested both with and without CP. Table 1 displays the recognition results to the test database. From inspection, it obviously shows that (1) GPD performs better than the other two classifiers (BP and LVQ2) which confirms the efficiency of the proposed error function, and (2) the proposed light compensation method is effective because all the three classifiers with LC achieve higher recognition accuracy than their individual performance without LC.

6 Conclusions

Due to the huge amount of applications, face recognition technology has attracted a lot of research efforts. This paper proposes a GPD training approach based on a three-layer feed-forward network to recognize faces. GPD has been applied in speech processing, but it is rarely mentioned by the computer-vision community. From experiments. It shows GPD can produce a better performance than the well-known BP and LVQ2. A novel light compensation method is also described, which can compensate effectively the variation of the face images occurred from the illumination variation, and produce uniform-light gray-level face images with similar average gray level and standard deviation.

The experiment results, however, shows that even the GPD approach cannot have a secure enough recognition performance when dealing with face samples taken with several kinds of variations. It is necessary to design other efficient face features which are insensitive to camera variation. One feasible approach is to extract the individual face components, such as eyes, nose, and mouth, and classification is based on the total summation of individual component matching scores. Also, currently the face images are extracted manually. We are working on the face detection and extraction algorithms, which will further be integrated with the face recognition so that an automatic face detection and recognition system can be implemented in the near future.

Acknowledgements

This work is an outcome of the Network-Generation Human/Computer Interface Project (project code: 3XS1B11) supported by Ministry of Economic Administration (MOEA), Taiwan, R.O.C.

References

1. K.K. sung and T. Poggio, "*Example-Based Learning for view-Based Human Face Detection*," IEEE Trans. Patt. Anal. Machine Intell., Vol. 20, pp. 39-51, 1998.
2. H. A. Rowley, S. Baluja, and T. Kanade, "Neural network-based face detection," *IEEE transactions on PAMI.*, vol. 20, no. 1, pp. 22-38, Jan. 1998.
3. D. M. Gavrila , "The visual analysis of human movement: a survey," Computer Vision and Image Understanding, vol. 73, pp. 82-98, 1999.
4. M. Turk and A. Pentland, "*Eihenfaces for Recognition*", Journal of Cognitive Neuroscience, March, 1991.
5. R. Brunelli and T. Poggio, "*Face Recognition: Features Versus Templates*", IEEE Trans. Patt. Anal. Machine Intell. Vol. 15, No. 10, October, pp 1042-1052, 1993.
6. R. Chellappa, C. Wilson and S. Sirohey, "*Human and Machine Recognition of Faces: A Survey*", Proc. Of IEEE, Vol. 83, No. 5, May, pp 705-740, 1995.
7. A.K. Jain, R. Bolle and S. Pankanti, *Biometrics: Personal Identification in Networked Society*, Kluwer Academic Publishers, 1999.
8. B.H. Juang and S. Katagiri, "*Discriminative Learning for Minimum Error Classification*", IEEE Trans. On Signal Processing, Vol. 40, No. 12, December, pp 3043-3054, 1992.
9. B. Widrow and R. Winter, "*Neural Nets for Adaptive Filtering and Adaptive Pattern Recognition*", Computer, Vol. 21, No. 3, pp. 25-39, March, 1988.
10. C. Garcia and G. Tziritas, "*Face Detection Using Quantized Skin Color Regions Merging and wavelet Packet Analysis*", IEEE Trans. On Multimedia, Vol. 1 No. 3, pp 264-277, 1999.'
11. T. Kohonen, "*The Self-Organization Map*", Proc. Of IEEE, 78:1468-1680,1990.

Table 1. The test recognition rates of three face classifiers with and without light compensation

Approach	Recognition Rate
LVQ2	90.7%
BP	92.4%
GPD	94.6%
LVQ2 + LC	92.9%
BP + LC	94.6%
GPD + LC	96.1%

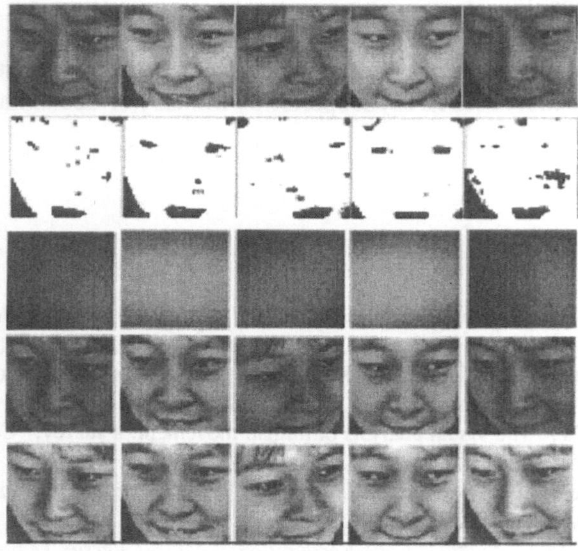

Figure 1. This figure shows respectively some face images (first row), skin-color-pixel images (second row), background lighting distributions (third row), subtracted images (fourth row), and normalized images (fifth row) by using the proposed light compensation method.

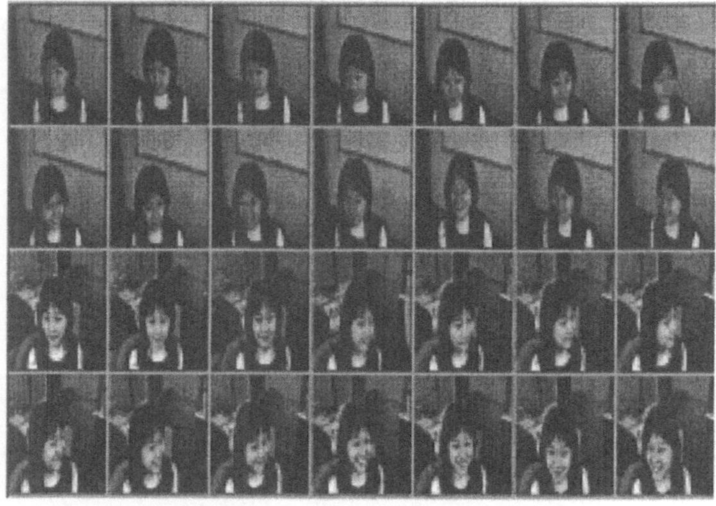

Figure 2 Pictures taken from different illumination and head rotation angles by a digit camera, the image size of each picture is 320*240.

Robust Head Pose Estimation Using Textured Polygonal Model with Local Correlation Measure

Yao-Jen Chang and Yung-Chang Chen

Department of Electrical Engineering, National Tsing Hua University
Hsinchu, Taiwan 30013
ycchen@ee.nthu.edu.tw

Abstract. In this paper, a robust head pose estimation algorithm is presented. In contrast with other approaches, the proposed algorithm adopts textured polygonal model generated from two orthogonal views for accurate head pose estimation. To achieve robust estimation under varying illumination, local correlation coefficient is taken as the similarity measure. The tracking is further improved by modeling head dynamics with Kalman filtering. Preliminary simulation results indicate that the proposed algorithm can reliably estimate the head pose under large rotation angles with varying illumination, and the average estimation error are all below 4 degrees.

1 Introduction

The information about where to the head faces and where at the eyes focus is an important factor for human communications. It also provides a natural means for human-computer interface. Head gesture recognition, facial expression analysis, and vision-based head animation need reliable 3-D head pose estimation as the pre-process, thereby making this topic receive wide attentions in the research field of computer vision. The head pose estimation can be decomposed into estimations of three orthogonal angles: the roll angle estimation, the yaw angle estimation, and the pitch angle estimation. Conventionally, the head pose estimation algorithms can be divided into four categories:

(1) Feature-points-based [1]: Some important and meaningful feature points such as eyes' centers and corners, nostrils, and lip corners are extracted and tracked from image sequences. The head pose is estimated from the distances between these facial feature points. The feature-points-based algorithm relies on the accurate extraction of feature points, which easily causes loss of tracking because some of these points may be occluded during rotations or may be deformed by rotations or facial expressions. And some angles like yaw and pitch cannot be estimated well if the distance changes between the user's head and the camera.

(2) Point-correspondences [2], [3]: The points selected from the face are salient points with high gradient. The 3-D location and movement of these points are estimated between successive frames using epipolar constraint [2] or solved in a structure from motion framework [3].

(3) Region-based: Qian Chen et al. [4] proposed an algorithm without any assistance from any facial features and any salient points. The algorithm relies on the extraction of skin and hair regions of the head. The roll angle estimation is calculated from the axis of the least inertia, and the yaw and pitch angles are estimated by approximation of the relationship between the head center and the skin area center. However, the hair color differs much from race to race, therefore, it is somewhat restrictive.

(4) Textured-model-based [5], [6], [7]: Recently, with the increasing rendering ability of graphics processor, several textured polygonal model assisted algorithms are presented. By using the analysis-by-synthesis approach, visually optimal solution can be found. La Cascia et al. [5] used a textured cylindrical model for head pose estimation. Schödl [6] and Eisert [7] used a full head model for more accurate head pose estimation. Since the matching measure is directly performed on the image intensity, this approach is sensitive to illumination. La Cascia et al. [5] handled illumination by combining illumination templates obtained by singular value decomposition (SVD) of a large set of textures corresponding to faces of different subjects under varying lighting conditions. Eisert [7] modeled the illumination as a point light reflected by a Lambertian surface. The illumination effects are estimated and compensated with the assistance of the accurate 3-D head model acquired by a 3-D laser scanner under controlled lighting conditions.

In this work, we extend the approach proposed by Schödl et al. [6] such that it can be used under varying illumination. The head model is obtained by adapting a generic facial model from two orthogonal views of user's face. Since the model is only an approximation and textures are generated without specific lighting condition, we adopt local correlation coefficient (LCC), which provides a good similarity measure under non-uniform illumination [8]. Furthermore, to accelerate the processing speed, the dynamics of head pose is modeled by Kalman filtering with a piecewise constant acceleration model. Thereby, the coarse head pose can be predicted which can greatly reduce the search time for fine pose estimation with the textured polygonal model. This paper is organized as follows. The facial model adaptation is introduced in Section 2. The head pose estimation algorithm together with the dynamic model of head movement is detailed in Section 3. The performance analysis is presented in Section 4. And finally, Section 5 concludes the paper.

2 Facial Model Adaptation

Before using a textured polygonal model to estimate head pose, the user's head model must be available. Since accurate model acquired from a 3D laser scanner is not affordable for ordinary users, we generate the facial model from two orthogonal views corresponding to user's frontal face and lateral face. Salient facial feature points are extracted to adjust a generic facial model, and then texture is mapped onto the facial model as an approximation to the real head.

2.1 Feature Point Extraction

To handle inter-personal variations of feature point distribution, a hierarchical approach is developed for reliable extraction of facial feature points [9]. It firstly detects face, then detects eyebrows, eye regions, mouth regions, and finally extracts feature points. The extracted facial feature points are eyebrows, eye centers, eye corners, and lip corners for the frontal face image. And feature points on the lateral face image and other important facial features such as ear outlines and face outline that cannot be reliably extracted are obtained with manual assistance.

2.2 Model Estimation

The extracted information in the above procedures provides estimation of 3-D locations for each feature point with correspondence in two views. These 3-D feature points are taken as control points for adjusting other vertices of the facial model, which forms a scattered data interpolation problem. Several interpolation methods including inverse distance weighted method [10], radial basis function [11], Dirichlet free-form deformations [12] can be utilized. For simplicity, we adopt the inverse distance weighted method. And to ensure the smoothness of the adjusted face, vertices on eyebrows, eyes, mouth, and chin outline are firstly interpolated by parabolas or third-order splines, and are taken as extra control points for adjusting the facial model.

2.3 Texture Mapping

Once the model is adapted, the texture is extracted for each triangular polygon, and a texture map is reconstructed on a virtual cylinder enclosing the 3-D face model [13]. The texture map is then blended from the extracted textures from two images; thereby the mismatch lighting conditions from the two orthogonal images can be compensated.

3 Head Tracking

3.1 Head Pose Estimation using Textured Polygonal Model

The proposed head pose estimation algorithm is a modification of the algorithm proposed by Schödl et al. [6]. In [6], the head movement is modeled as a set of points performing 3-D affine transform followed by projection to the image plane.

Therefore, the pose estimation is transformed to be an optimization problem for minimizing an error function:

$$e = \sum_p \rho(I(T(p, \{\alpha_i\})) - M(p)), \tag{1}$$

where p is one of 3-D model points, $M(p)$ is the associated intensity, $I(x)$ is the image intensity at location x, T is an affine transform followed by a perspective projection, the associated parameter set is $\{\alpha_i\}$ and ρ is the Geman & McClure robust error norm.

In our case, images are acquired by a monocular camera and depth value of the facial model is not reliable. Hence, we apply the approach with a weak-perspective projection [14]:

$$\begin{bmatrix} p'_x \\ p'_y \end{bmatrix} = s \underbrace{\begin{bmatrix} 1\,0\,0\,0 \\ 0\,1\,0\,0 \end{bmatrix}}_{\mathbf{P}_{\|}} \underbrace{\begin{bmatrix} 1 & -r_z & r_y & -t_x \\ r_z & 1 & -r_x & -t_y \\ -r_y & r_x & 1 & -t_z \\ 0 & 0 & 0 & 1 \end{bmatrix}}_{\mathbf{M}} \begin{bmatrix} p_x \\ p_y \\ p_z \\ 1 \end{bmatrix}, \tag{2}$$

where $(p_x, p_y, p_z)^{\mathrm{T}}$ is the 3-D coordinate in the world space, $\mathbf{M}$ is the applied affine transform matrix caused by small movement, $\mathbf{P}_{\|}$ is the orthographic projection matrix, s is the scaling factor whose physical meaning is camera focal length to average depth ratio, and $(p'_x, p'_y)^{\mathrm{T}}$ is the 2-D coordinate in the image plane.

Moreover, the intensity of face is subject to change under varying illumination and head movement. We therefore use local correlation coefficient as similarity measure [8]:

$$S = \sum_p LCC\left(I(T(\{q_p\}, \{\alpha_i\})), M(\{q_p\})\right), \tag{3}$$

where $\{q_p\}$ stands for the points in the neighborhood of point p and LCC stands for the local correlation coefficient function in $\{q_p\}$:

$$LCC\left(X_p, Y_p\right) = \frac{E\left[X_p Y_p\right] - E\left[X_p\right] E\left[Y_p\right]}{\sqrt{Var\left[X_p\right] \cdot Var\left[Y_p\right]}} \equiv \frac{f(X_p, Y_p)}{\sqrt{g(X_p, Y_p)}}. \tag{4}$$

To maximize the similarity function, the derivatives with respect to each parameter α_i is:

$$\frac{dS}{d\alpha_i} = \sum_p \frac{dLCC(X_p, Y_p)}{d\alpha_i} = \sum_p \left(\frac{f'(X_p, Y_p)}{\sqrt{g(X_p, Y_p)}} - \frac{1}{2} \frac{f(X_p, Y_p) g'(X_p, Y_p)}{\left(\sqrt{g(X_p, Y_p)}\right)^3} \right), \tag{5}$$

with

$$f'(X_p, Y_p) = \frac{1}{N} \left(\sum_{\{q_p\}} \left(Y_q - E\left[Y_q\right]\right) \frac{dX_q}{d\alpha_i} \right), \tag{6}$$

$$g'(X_p, Y_p) = \frac{2}{N} Var\left[Y_p\right] \left(\sum_{\{q_p\}} (X_q - E\left[X_q\right]) \frac{dX_q}{d\alpha_i} \right), \tag{7}$$

and

$$\begin{aligned} \frac{dX_q}{d\alpha_i} &= \frac{dI(T(q, \{\alpha_i\}))}{d\alpha_i} \\ &= I_x(T(q, \{\alpha_i\})) \cdot \frac{dT(q, \{\alpha_i\})_x}{d\alpha_i} + I_y(T(q, \{\alpha_i\})) \cdot \frac{dT(q, \{\alpha_i\})_y}{d\alpha_i}, \end{aligned} \tag{8}$$

where I_x and I_y are image intensity gradient at position $T(q, \{\alpha_i\})$ in x and y directions. And with weak perspective projection model in Eq. (2), the above derivatives with respect to each parameter can be derived as:

$$\begin{aligned} &\frac{dI}{dr_x} = -I_y q_z, && \frac{dI}{dr_y} = I_x q_z, && \frac{dI}{dr_z} = -I_x q_y + I_y q_x, \\ &\frac{dI}{dt_x} = -I_x, && \frac{dI}{dt_y} = -I_y, && \frac{dI}{ds} = I_x q_x + I_y q_y. \end{aligned} \tag{9}$$

With the above equations, we can adopt the gradient decent approach for finding the target affine transform and scale parameters. And Chan and Fallside's update strategy [15] is utilized for dynamic step size adjustment.

3.2 Head Pose Prediction using Kalman Filtering

The gradient search described in the above section requires iterative process, which is very time-consuming. Furthermore, the tracking can be easily trapped into local extremes due to the low-textureness of the face. Therefore, a prediction mechanism is necessary for finding the possible head pose in the next time stamp. This is achieved by modeling the head pose dynamics as a piecewise constant acceleration model with a Kalman filter [16]. The state equation is formed according to Newton's law:

$$\begin{bmatrix} x_{k+1} \\ \dot{x}_{k+1} \\ \ddot{x}_{k+1} \end{bmatrix} = \begin{bmatrix} 1 & T & T^2/2 \\ 0 & 1 & T \\ 0 & 0 & 1 \end{bmatrix} \begin{bmatrix} x_k \\ \dot{x}_k \\ \ddot{x}_k \end{bmatrix} + w_k, \tag{10}$$

where $x_k, \dot{x}_k, \ddot{x}_k$ stand for head pose position, velocity, and acceleration at time kT. $x_{k+1}, \dot{x}_{k+1}, \ddot{x}_{k+1}$ are predicted position, velocity, and acceleration at time $(k+1)T$. Therefore, the predicted measurement (the head pose) can be obtained by:

$$\hat{z}_{k+1} = \begin{bmatrix} 1 & 0 & 0 \end{bmatrix} \begin{bmatrix} x_{k+1} \\ \dot{x}_{k+1} \\ \ddot{x}_{k+1} \end{bmatrix}. \tag{11}$$

Start from the predicted head pose, the real head pose can be found with fewer iterations in the gradient search. And the difference between measured pose and the predicted pose forms the innovation process, which is utilized to adjust the state at time $(k+1)T$.

4 Simulation Result

Preliminary simulation is carried out on two test sequences consisting of 400 frames of image size 320×240 acquired from a Matrox Meteor-II image grabber at frame rate 30Hz. The first sequence is taken from normal lighting condition, while the second sequence is taken under a directional light from user's left side. Two similarity measures are compared: one is the sum of squared differences (SSD), which simulates the original approach in Eq. (1); and the other is the proposed approach using LCC with a uniform window of size 13×13 as similarity measure. Since the user only has small translations in these two test sequences, the performance comparison is focused on rotations. Tracking result is shown in Fig. 1, where truth values are depicted in thick solid lines while the estimated values are depicted in small circles connected with thin lines. The truth values are obtained by exhaustive search in the local area with LCC similarity measure and then refined with manual assistance. Table 1 lists the error mean and error standard deviation of two similarity measures. Obviously, the two similarity measures have competitive performance on the first test sequence. However, SSD fails to track the head pose for the second test sequence for it is sensitive to lighting condition such that it finds highest similarity on the wrong place, while LCC still performs well under the same condition. The tracking trajectory is shown in Fig. 2 and error measure of LCC is listed in Table 2.

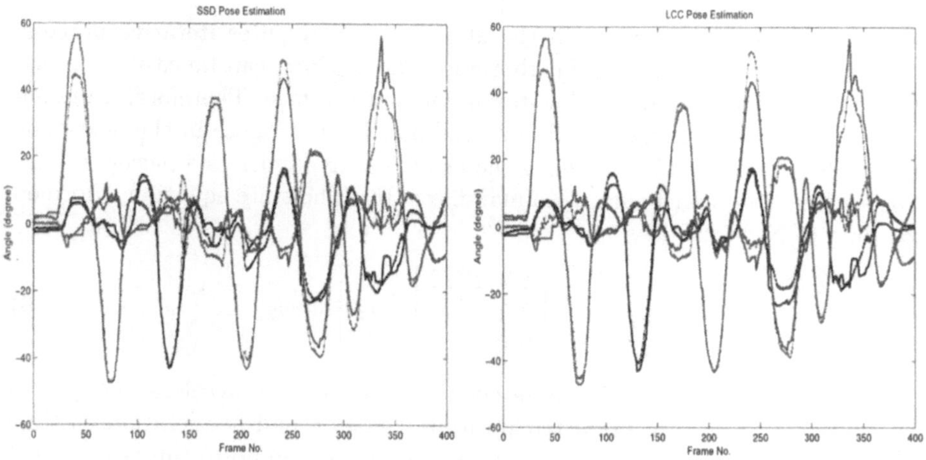

Fig. 1. Test sequence one: Tracking trajectory compared to ground truth data using SSD and LCC as similarity measure. (red: roll angle, green: yaw angle, blue: pitch angle)

Although accurate tracking results are obtained, the large computation is still a bottleneck. With an AMD Athlon 700 MHz CPU equipped with NVidia GeForce-2 graphics card running on the Windows 98 system, it requires 0.53

Table 1. Error Measure of Two Similarity Measures on Test Sequence One

	Mean			Std. Dev.		
	Pitch	Yaw	Roll	Pitch	Yaw	Roll
SSD	2.23°	3.65°	1.86°	2.03°	3.89°	2.43°
LCC	2.42°	2.59°	1.63°	2.06°	3.01°	2.15°

Table 2. Error Measure of LCC Similarity Measures on Test Sequence Two

	Mean			Std. Dev.		
	Pitch	Yaw	Roll	Pitch	Yaw	Roll
LCC	2.98°	3.98°	1.89°	2.99°	3.56°	2.32°

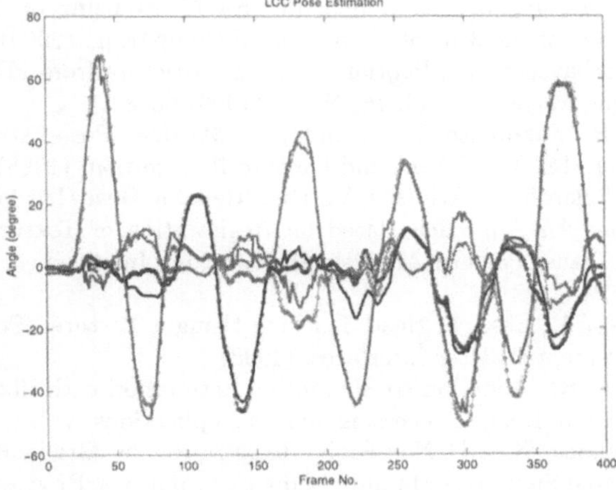

Fig. 2. Test sequence two: Tracking trajectory compared to ground truth data using LCC as similarity measure. (red: roll angle, green: yaw angle, blue: pitch angle)

to 4.88 seconds for the gradient search to reach convergence for each frame. The varying tracking time depends on the accuracy of head pose prediction using Kalman filtering described in Section 3.2. The average tracking speed per frame expressed in the form of (mean, std. dev.) is (2.06 sec, 1.01 sec) with the performed iterations statistics as (8.42 times, 4.55 times). Without Kalman filtering, the tracking speed degrades to (2.39 sec, 1.54 sec) with iterations as (10.58 times, 7.24 times). Therefore, the Kalman filtering does help speeding up the tracking speed and it also helps increasing the tracking accuracy from avoiding trapping into local extremes.

5 Conclusions

We have presented an algorithm of head pose estimation for image sequence acquired from a single uncalibrated camera. Using textured polygonal model with local correlation coefficient as similarity measure, accurate head pose estimation can be obtained under varying illumination condition. By modeling head pose dynamics as a piecewise constant acceleration model, the tracking speed is increased and the accuracy is also raised.

We are now improving the tracking speed for use in real-time applications. Better prediction mechanism such as the adaptive Kalman filter and performing gradient search in a hierarchical approach are under investigation.

References

1. Horprasert, T., Yacoob, Y., Davis, L.: Computing 3-D Head Orientation from Monocular Image Sequence. Int. Conf. Face and Gesture Recognition. (1996) 242–247
2. Liu, Z., Zhang, Z., Jacobs, C., Cohen, M.: Rapid Modeling of Animated Faces From Video. Proc. of the 3rd Int. Conf. Visual Computing. (2000) 58–67
3. Jebara, T., Azarbayejani, A., Pentland, A.: 3D Structure from 2D Motion. IEEE Signal Processing Magazine, Vol. 16, No. 3. (1999) 66–84
4. Chen, Q., Wu, H., Fukumoto, T., Yachida, M.: 3D Head Pose Estimation without Feature Tracking. Int. Conf. Face and Gesture Recognition. (1998) 88–93
5. La Cascia, M., Sclaroff, S., Athitsos, V.: Fast, Reliable Head Tracking under Varying Illumination: An Approach Based on Registration of Textured-Mapped 3D Models. IEEE Trans. Pattern Analysis and Machine Intelligence, Vol. 22, No. 4. (2000) 322–336
6. Schödl, A., Haro, A., Essa, I.: Head Tracking Using a Textured Polygonal Model. Workshop on Perceptual User Interfaces. (1998)
7. Eisert, P., Girod, B.: Model-based 3D Motion Estimation with Illumination Compensation. Int. Conf. Image Processing and its Applications, Vol. 1. (1997) 194–198
8. Cachier, P., Pennec, X.: 3D Non-Rigid Registration by Gradient Descent on a Gaussian Weighted Similarity Measure Using Convolutions. Proc. of MMBIA 2000. (2000) 182–189
9. Chang, Y. J., Chen, C. C., Chou, J. C., Chen, Y. C.: Virtual Talk: A Model-Based Virtual Phone Using a Layered Audio-Visual Integration. Proc. IEEE Int. Conf. Multimedia and Expo, Vol. 1. (2000) 415–418
10. Kampmann, M., Farhoud, R.: Precise face model adaptation for semantic coding of video sequences. Proc. Picture Coding Symposium'97. (1997)
11. Lavagetto, F., Pockaj, R.: The Facial Animation Engine: Toward a High-Level Interface for the design of MPEG-4 Compliant Animated Faces. IEEE Trans. Circuit, System, and Video Technology, Vol. 9, No. 2. (1999) 277–289
12. Lee, W. S., Thalmann, N. M.: Fast Head Modeling for Animation. Image and Vision Computing, Vol. 18. (2000) 355–364
13. Pighin, F., Hecker, J., Lischinski, D., Szeliski, R., Salesin, D. H.: Synthesizing Realistic Facial Expressions from Photographs. Proc. SIGGRAPH'98. (1998)
14. Shapiro, L. S., Zisserman, A., Brady, M.: 3D Motion Recovery via Affine Epipolar Geometry. Int. J. Computer Vision, Vol. 16. (1995) 147–182
15. Chan, L. W., Fallside, F.: An Adaptive Training Algorithm for Back Propagation Networks. Computer Speech and Language, Vol. 2. (1987) 205–218
16. Kiruluta, A., Eizenman, M., Pasupathy, S.: Predictive Head Movement Tracking using a Kalman Filter. IEEE Trans. System, Man, and Cybernetics-Part B: Cybernetics, Vol. 27, No. 2. (1997) 326–331

A Face Verification Algorithm Integrating Geometrical and Template Features

Feng Xie[1], Guangyou Xu[1], Eckart Hundt[2]

[1] Computer Science and Technology Department, Tsinghua University,
State Key Laboratory of Intelligent Technology and Systems,
Beijing 100084, PR China
xf@media.cs.tsinghua.edu.cn
[2] Corperate Technology, Siemens AG,D-81730, Munich,Germany

ABSTRACT. One of the key problems in a face recognition system is verification. This paper presented a verification algorithm using SVM classifier with integrated geometrical features and template features based on our multi-view face recognition system. By using only six feature points located during the process of template matching, improved system performance is achieved.

1 Introduction

High-security verification systems based on biometric modalities such as iris, retina and fingerprints have been commercially available for a long time. However, one of the most attractive sources of biometric information is the human face since it can be acquired without user interaction. Face recognition is a well established research field and a large number of algorithms have been proposed in literature. Popular approaches include those based on Eigenfaces[13], neural networks[16], and active appearance models [11]. These techniques vary in complexity and performance. Selection among these algorithms is typically dependent on the specific application.

On the other hand, the verification problem is much less explored. Previous work on this problem has primarily focused on integrating multiple biometric features to improve the performance of verification systems. Hong and Jain integrated faces and fingerprints for personal identification [1]. The key idea in their approach is based on PCA and the verification is achieved by comparing the computed measure with a pre-defined threshold. Brunelli and Falavigna have considered to integrate acoustic and visual features for identification [2]. They use a pre-trained linear classifier to achieve verification. Shingai and Takiyama unify profile curve identification and full face image identification to obtain better recognition rate [4]. They claim the combination of the two processes shows higher recognition rates than those obtained by two individual processes respectively.

Support Vector Machine(SVM) have been recently proposed by V. Vapnik and his co-workers as an effective and general purpose method of pattern recognition [12]. The applications of SVM for computer vision problems have been proposed recently. For example, Burel and Carel train a SVM for face detection [14]. An early study of

SVM in face verification has been reported by Phillips [15]. Compared with the standard PCA-based face authentication method, verification system based on SVM has shown to be significantly better.

In this paper we propose a fast verification algorithm, which integrates both template features and geometrical features. The output of SVM is used to verify an individual.

Our face identification system is based on the multi-view face recognition system described in [5,6]. The identification process consists of two steps. First, we use template matching approach to recognize the input image. Second, a trained SVM classifier is used to verify whether the image should be accepted as the recognition result or be rejected. The input vector of SVM integrates both geometrical features and template features. Based on a large database of 500 people face images (250 inside and 250 outside under ordinary illumination condition), we have achieved a very small average error rate (includes both recognition error and verification error).

The remainder of this paper is organized as follows. Section 2 outlines our identification system and the recognition algorithm. In Section 3, we describe the feature selection method and verification algorithm. Some experimental results will be demonstrated in Section 4. Finally, we conclude in Section 5 with discussions and future work.

2 Identification Algorithm

The verification process authenticates an individual's identity by comparing the individual only with his/her own template(s) (Am I whom I claim I am?). It conducts one-to-one comparison to determine whether the identity claimed by the individual is true or not. Generally, there are two classes of errors in a verification system: a genuine individual is rejected, and an impostor is accepted. More specifically, false acceptance rate (FAR) is defined as the probability of an impostor being accepted as a genuine individual. And false reject rate (FRR) is defined as the probability of a genuine individual being rejected as an impostor.

FAR and FRR are dual of each other. A small FRR usually leads to a larger FAR, while a smaller FAR usually implies a larger FRR. Generally, the system performance requirement is specified in terms of a fixed FAR or Equal Error Rate (the value when FRR equals to FAR). In this paper we use Equal Error Rate to evaluate the performance of verification.

The identification process in our face identification system consists of two steps. In the recognition process, we use template matching to get the highest score identity as the candidate. The second step is verification process in which we use a SVM classifier to verify whether the claimed candidate is true or not.

In our system, we use multi-view images to establish a face model which quantifies the continuous pose variations to multiple viewpoints. Then the system uses these normalized multi-view images to represent the different head poses. Because template matching is very effective under ordinary illumination condition, our method not only avoids the complexity of establishing 3D model, but also maintain the precision of recognition.

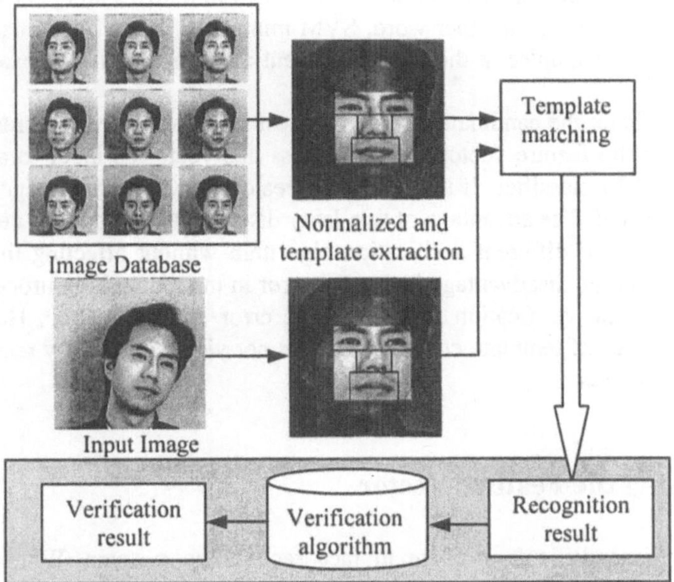

Fig. 1. Face verification system overview

Currently our system quantifies the horizontal axis and the vertical axis by 3 levels respectively, which results in a face model consisting of nine views. We extract four facial regions including face, eyes, nose and mouth as matching templates. In the recognition process, we extract these four templates from the input images and compare them with the templates in database [5].

For each person, we have captured nine images corresponding to different head poses to establish his face model (as shown in Fig. 1). First we detect the facial features, then normalize these image by affine transformation and extract the templates. The recognition method is based on template matching. The input image is normalized and templates are extracted as well. The average of template correlation for each person in database is calculated as the score of this person. Finally, the person with highest score is the output of the recognize system.

Although satisfactory results have been achieved by our previous approach, there remain many problems to be improved. One of the disadvantages lies in that we only use a threshold as the verification metric. Specifically, when the highest score is bigger than a specified constant, the input image is accepted, otherwise it is rejected. Because this approach only uses the information of one feature which makes it noise-sensitive, the average false rate is about 13%.

In order to solve this problem, we propose a novel method that integrates geometrical features and template features and uses the output of SVM classifier as the verification decision. SVM can be seen as a new way to train polynomial, neural network, or Radial Basis Functions classifiers. Most of the techniques used to train the above mentioned classifiers are based on the idea of minimizing the training error, which is usually called empirical risk. However, SVM operates on another induction principle, called structural risk minimization, which minimizes an upper bound on the generalization error. In the other word, SVM minimizes the error of misclassification not only for the examples in the training set but also for the unseen examples of the test set.

After we obtain the candidate with the highest score, we extract scores of template correlation as the feature vector. Then we pass this vector as input to a pre-defined two classes SVM classifier. If the output is greater then zero, the image is accepted, otherwise rejected. The advantage of two-layer discriminator is that we could compare the performance of different verification algorithm without affecting the process of recognition. But the disadvantage is that the error in the recognition process could not be rectified in the verification process so the error is accumulated. However, only using the features of template correlation could not yield satisfactory result. We have to find new features.

3 Choosing the Feature Vector

Verification is a difficult problem in face recognition systems. When the size of database is small, verification is relatively easy because the samples inside and outside the database could be easily distinguished in the feature space, and the distance between these two classes is distinct. When the size of database is small (i.e., 20 persons database), the FAR of this method could be less than 0.01% but the FRR is relatively much higher. So using multiple images of the same person could obtain satisfactory verification performance [9].

However, when the size of database is large, samples inside and outside the database will overlap in the feature space. Only using the feature of template correlation will result in more classification errors. One possible solution to this problem is to pursuit some other features such as geometrical features. However, face recognition systems based on geometrical features often need a lot of features. For example, Brunelli and Poggio extracted 35 dimensional geometrical features to describe the face [10]. Lanitis used a 83 parameters model to describe it [11].

We propose a verification method that integrates both geometrical features and template features. By using only six feature points located during the process of template matching, we have improved the system performance significantly.

Similar to the algorithm proposed by Poggio[7], we use the resident error of reconstruction as the geometrical feature. Consider a 2D view of a three-dimensional rigid object is defined in terms of pointwise features. It can be represented by the x, y-coordinates of its n feature points:

$$X = (x_1, x_2, \dots x_n)^T,\ Y = (y_1, y_2, \dots y_n)^T \tag{1}$$

Let us define the new view of the object as:

$$X_0 = (x_{0,1}, x_{0,2}, \dots x_{0,n})^T,\ \ Y_0 = (y_{0,1}, y_{0,2}, \dots y_{0,n})^T \tag{2}$$

and other two different views:

$$X_1 = (x_{1,1}, x_{1,2}, \ldots x_{1,n})^T, \quad Y_1 = (y_{1,1}, y_{1,2}, \ldots y_{1,n})^T \tag{3}$$

$$X_2 = (x_{2,1}, x_{2,2}, \ldots x_{2,n})^T, \quad Y_2 = (y_{2,1}, y_{2,2}, \ldots y_{2,n})^T \tag{4}$$

Then X_0 and Y_0 is a linear combination of X_1, Y_1 and X_2 (or Y_2):

$$X_0 = a_1X_1 + a_2X_2 + a_3X_3, \ Y_0 = b_1X_1 + b_2X_2 + b_3X_3 \tag{5}$$

Because each person has nine neutral expression images of different pose in our face database, we assume the face as a rigid object, thus make it applicable for this theorem. From the nine database images, two images are randomly selected and the coordinate vector is further calculated. Then we compute the coefficients of linear combination and the residual error use least-square method:

$$\text{Derr} = | a_1X_1 + a_2X_2 + a_3X_3 - X_0 | + | b_1X_1 + b_2X_2 + b_3X_3 - Y_0 | \tag{6}$$

According to 1.5 views theorem[7], if the input image and the image in database would be same person, the residual error Derr should be small, otherwise it should be large.

Since the verification problem only need to determine whether the identity claimed by the individual is true or not, it is a classification problem of two classes. SVM classifier is selected due to its significant performance. We integrated both template features and geometrical features as input vector of SVM classifier. The output of SVM classifier determines the verification decision. In the process of template matching, we extract four templates from each image and each person has nine images in database, so we could obtain 36 matching score. Plus the residual error Derr, we could get a 37D feature vector.

We select the Gaussian function as the kernel function of SVM:

$$K(x,y) = \exp(-(x-y)^2/2/\sigma^2) \tag{7}$$

So the optimal separating hyperplane in the feature space is given by,

$$f(x) = \text{sign}(\Sigma_i f_i y_i K(x,x_i) + b) \tag{8}$$

where (x_i,y_i) is the sample of training set, (f_i,b) is the output of training the SVM. Then the verification criteria is:

- if $f(x) >= 0$, accept as the recognition result,
- if $f(x) < 0$, reject.

4 Experimental Results

We randomly divide the 500 people database into two part, 250 people inside and 250 people outside. The training set contains 500 images, one image for each person. The test set contains the rest 980 images. We run this process four times. The performance of verification is list in Table 1. $\sigma = 1$ in kernel function.

Table 1. Performance of verification

	False Recognition	False Verification	Correct Identification Rate *
Group 1	14	57	92.76%
Group 2	16	50	93.27%
Group 3	10	45	94.39%
Group 4	19	57	92.24%

* Correct Identification Rate = 1- (False Recognition + False Verification) / Total Test Number

Comparison with other method such as Liu's generalized discriminant plane [8], Fisher Linear Discriminant Vector and nearest neighbor classifier is shown in Fig. 2. It can be seen that our approach has achieved much better performance over other method.

Another experiment shows the effectiveness of additional geometrical features. We train another SVM classifier only using the former 36 features that are the scores of template matching. The results are shown in Fig. 3. We could see that the additional geometrical features not only improved the performance of identification system significantly, but also improved the stability. The original correct rate of group No. 2 is relatively low, but after adding the geometrical features, a higher correct rate can be obtained.

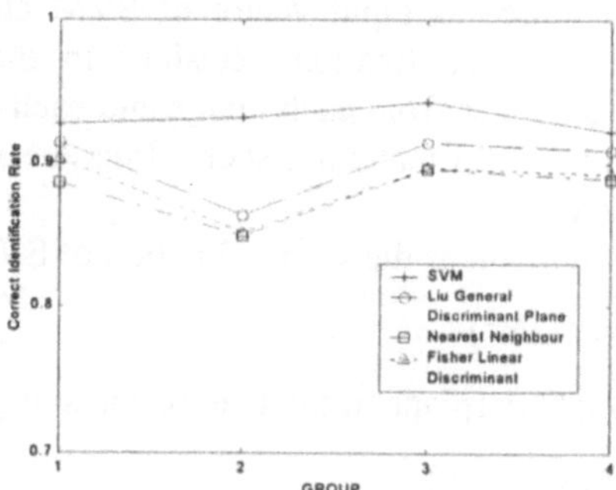

Fig. 2. Performance comparison between SVM, Liu General Discriminant Plane, Nearest Neighbour and Fisher Linear Discriminant

Experiments also show that the difference between different kernel functions is very small (as shown in Fig 4).

As shown in Fig. 3, after integrating geometrical features and template features, the performance and stability of identification have been improved significantly. Geometrical features show to be effective to improve the performance of face identification systems.

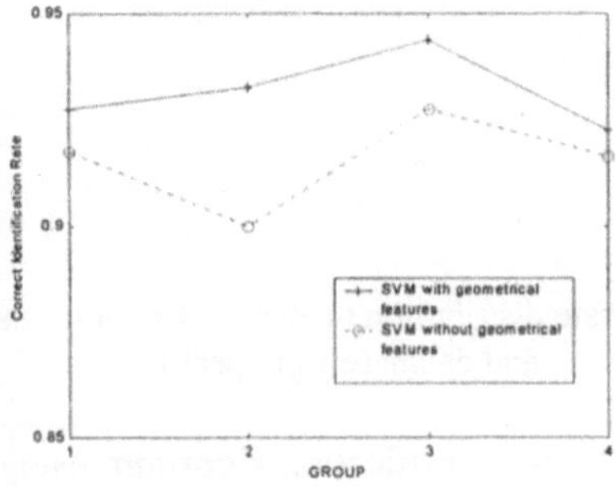

Fig. 3. Performance comparison between SVM with/without geometrical features

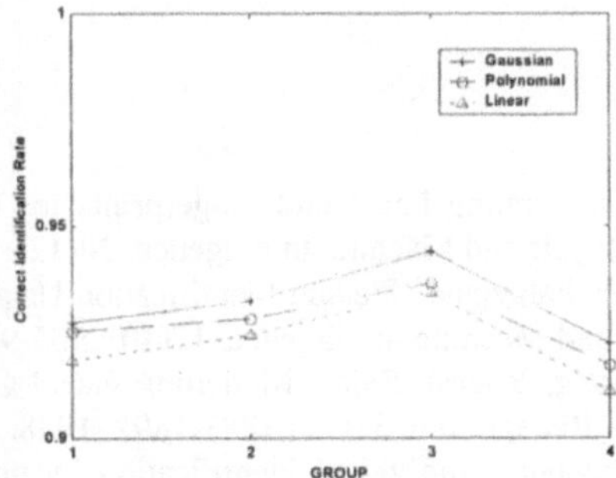

Fig. 4. Performance comparison between several kernel functions

5 Discussion and Conclusion

Considering the rapidity of verification process, we select the six feature points already located in the process of recognition. Though the distribution of residual error Derr of inside and outside partly overlapped, they are discriminable up to a scale (Fig. 5). So this feature could effectively improve the performance of verification. Certainly, if we extract more geometrical features or utilize the geometrical information more effectively, the performance could be better. This is one direction of future works.

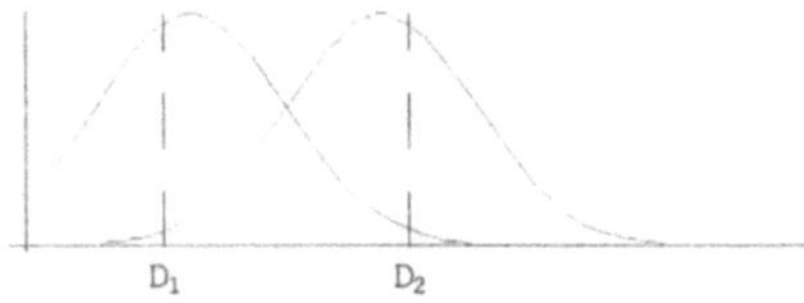

Fig. 5. The approximate distribution of Residual error of inside (left peak), and database(right peak)

This paper presented a effective verification algorithm using SVM classifier which integrating geometrical features and template features, based on the multi-view face recognition system described in [5,6]. Future work will focus on improving face model and extracting more geometrical features.

References

1. Lin Hong and Anil Jain, "Integrating Faces and Fingerprints for Personal Identification". IEEE Trans. On Pattern Analysis and Machine Intelligence, 20(12): 1295-1306, 1998.
2. Roberto Brunelli and Daniele Falavigna, "Person Identification Using Multiple Cues". IEEE Trans. On Pattern Analysis and Machine Intelligence, 17(10): 955-966, 1995.
3. S.J. Mckenna, Shaogang Gong, Yogesh Raja, "Modelling Facial Colour and Identity with Gaussian Mixtures". Pattern Recognition, 31(12):1883-1892, 1998.
4. Hiroto Shingai, Ryuzo Takiyama, "Individual identification by unifying profiles and full faces". IEICE Transactions on Information and Systems, E79-D(9):1274-1278, Sep 1996.
5. Peng Zhenyun, You Suya, Xu Guangyou, "Fast Face Feature Detection under Varying Pose". China Journal of Image and Graphic, 2(4): 225-229, Apr 1997.
6. Zhang Yongyue, Peng Zhenyun, You Suya, Xu Guangyou, "A Multi-View Face Recognition System". J. of Computer Sci, & Technol., 12(5):400-407, Sept 1997.
7. Tomaso Poggio and Thomas Vetter, "Recognition and Structure from one 2D Model View: Observations on Prototypes, Object Classes and Symmetries". A.I. Memo No. 1347, MIT Artificial Intelligence Laboratory, 1992.
8. K. Liu and J. Y. Yang, "A generalized optimal set of discriminant vectors". Pattern Recognition, 25(2): 817-829, 1992.
9. F. Xie, Zh. Peng, G. Xu, "Highly Reliable Face Identification System". The 4th China conference on Compute Intelligent Interface and Applications, pages 250-255, 1999.
10. Brunelli R. and Poggio T. "Face recognition: Features versus Templates". IEEE Trans. On Pattern Analysis and Machine Intelligence, 15(10):1042-1052, Oct. 1993.
11. Lanitis A., Taylor C.J., and Cootes T.F. "Automatic face identification system using flexible appearance models". Image and Vision Computing, 13(5): 393-401, Jun 1995.
12. Boser B.E., Guyon I.M., and Vapnik V.N. "A training algorithm for optimal margin classifier". Proc. 5th ACM Workshop on Computational Learning Theory, pages 144-152, Pittsburgh, PA, July 1992.
13. Turk M.A. and Pentland A.D. "Face recognition using eigenfaces". Proc. of Computer Vision and Pattern Recognition, 1991, pages 586-591.
14. Burel G. and Carel D. "Detection and localization of faces on digital images". Pattern Recognition Letters, 15: 963-967, 1994.
15. Phillips P.J. "Support vector machines applied to face recognition", NIPS'98, 1998.
16. Kohonen T. Self-Organization and Associative Memory. Springer, Berlin, 1988.

E-Partner: A Photo-Realistic Conversation Agent

Bo Zhang[1*] Changbo Hu[2*] Qingsheng Cai[1] Baining Guo[3] Harry Shum[3]

[1]Dept. of Computer Sci. & Tech.
Univ. of Sci. & Tech. of China
Hefei 230027, P.R.China

[2]Institute of Automation
Chinese Academy of Science
Beijing 100080, P.R.China

[3]Microsoft Research China
Microsoft Corporation
Beijing 100080, P.R.China

Abstract. An E-Partner is a photo-realistic conversation agent, which has a talking head that not only look photo-realistic but also can have a conversation with the user about a given topic. The conversation is multimedia-enriched in that the E-Partner presents relevant multimedia materials throughout the conversation. To address the challenges presented by the complex conversation domain and task, and to achieve adaptive behaviors, we have derived a novel dialogue manager design consisting of five parts: a domain model, a dialogue model, a discourse model, a task model, and a user model. We also extended existing facial animation techniques to create photo-realistic talking heads that facilitate conversational interactions. Some practical issues like how to handle the uncertainty from speech level are also discussed.

1 Introduction

Computer-animated characters, particularly talking heads, are becoming increasingly important in a variety of applications including video games and web-based customer services. A talking head attracts the user's attention and makes user interaction more engaging and entertaining. For a layperson, seeing a talking head makes interaction with a computer more comfortable. Subjective tests show that an E-commerce web site with a talking head gets higher ratings than the same web site without a talking head [7].

We describe a multimedia system for creating *photo-realistic conversation agents*, i.e. talking heads that not only look photo-realistic but also can have a conversation with the user. The conversation is *multimedia-enriched* in that the conversation agent presents relevant multimedia materials (audios, images, videos, etc.) throughout the conversation. We have built such a system, called *E-Partner*, which combines a number of component technologies including speech recognition, natural language processing, dialogue management, and facial animation. Integration of these technologies into an end-to-end system is by no means an easy task. In this paper, we describe the design of our system, with a focus on novel aspects of dialogue management and facial animation. We will also discuss practical issues, such as how to handle the uncertainty from speech level by using low-level information from an off-the-shelf speech API.

---

* This work was performed while the authors were visiting Microsoft Research China.

The dialogue manager in our system is designed so that the system can have an intelligent conversation with the user about a given topic. Specifically, our conversation agent is

Informative: the user can learn useful information through a multimedia-enriched conversation, and

Adaptive: the conversation agent can respond to the user's requests (e.g., skip part of the speech when being asked to) and adapt the conversation as the agent learns more about the user.

Later we will demonstrate these features through an example, in which the agent talks with the user about a tourist site.

Because it is informative, our conversation agent differs from chatter bots [10] and similar systems that use clever tricks to fake a conversation. More important, our system is different from simple-service dialogue systems [11], which allow the user to retrieve information or conduct transactions, and plan assistant dialogue systems [5], which can help the user execute a task. The conversation domain of our system is much more complex than that of the simple-service and plan assistant systems, and our conversation agent exhibits adaptive behaviors. The task of our conversation agent is also different from that of a plan assistant. To address the challenges presented by the complex conversation domain and task, and to achieve adaptive behaviors, we have derived a novel dialogue manager design consisting of five parts: a domain model, a dialogue model, a discourse model, a task model, and a user model.

Facial animation in our system is also crafted to facilitate conversational interactions. Existing techniques allow us to create a photo-realistic talking head for each individual sentence spoken by the conversation agent [2, 4]. In this work, we extend [2] so that the facial animations for individual sentences can be stitched together to provide a continuous presence of the talking head, which pauses between sentences and appears to listen (instead of just freeze) when the user speaks. The talking head can smoothly switch back and forth between the listening and talking states.

The remainder of this paper is organized as follows. In next section, we present the architecture of the E-Partner system. The dialogue manager is described in section 3. Section 4 is about the secret of the talking head. We conclude in section 5.

2 System Architecture

Fig.1 is a snapshot of a user interacting with Maggie the tour guide – our first application of the E-Partner system. The user converses with Maggie through a microphone. Maggie resides in the lower right corner of the screen. She talks with the user about different places of the Forbidden City, and presents multimedia materials (images, videos, etc.) in the *content window* in the upper left corner of the screen.

Fig. 1. A snapshot

1. M> Hi, I'm Maggie, your tour guide. Welcome to ...
2. U> Ok
3. M> [ShowPic 1] Below is an introduction to the Forbidden City.
4. M> Also known as the Imperial Palace Museum or Gugong, ...
5. U> I don't want to listen to this introduction part
6. M> Ok. Do you want to go to the Gate of Meridian?
7. U> Yes, go to that place
8. M> [ShowPic 2] Welcome to the Gate of Meridian.
9. M> The Meridian Gate is the southern entrance of the ...
10. U> Can you tell me the height of the meridian gate
11. M> The height of the Gate of Meridian is 35.6 meters. Do you want to know why it got its name Meridian Gate?
12. U> Yes
13. M> The Meridian Gate was so named because ...
14. M> We will leave the Gate of Meridian now. Do you want to go to the Gate of Supreme Harmony?
15. U> No, I want to go to that hall
16. M> Where do you want to go?
17. U> The hall of middle harmony
18. M> [ShowPic 3] Welcome to the Hall of Middle Harmony.
19. M> The Hall of Middle Harmony originally built in 1420 and ...
20. U> I want to leave this place
21. M> Ok. ...

Fig. 2. A dialogue example (M: Maggie, U: user)

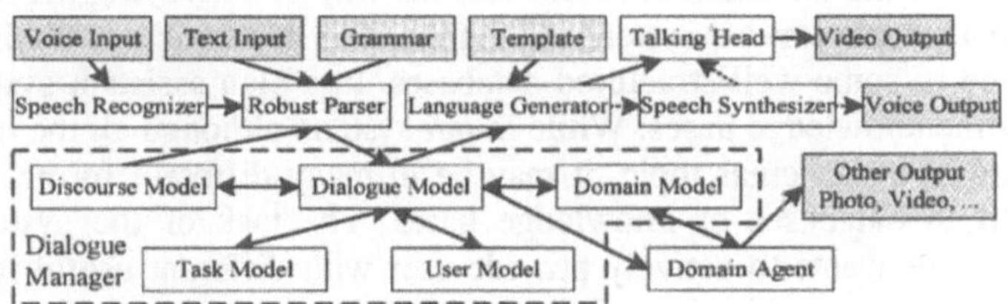

Fig. 3. Overall architecture of our system.

We illustrate some features of E-Partner through a dialogue example in Fig.2. If Maggie's sentence is too long for the user, he can barge in at any time (lines 1-2). The pictures are shown in the content window (line 3). Maggie has a tour plan for visiting different places within the Forbidden City. However, she can adapt to the user and skip sites when asked to (lines 5-6). She can answer the user's questions (lines 10-11). More important, she learns more about the user through these questions and takes high-level initiatives at appropriate situations (line 11). She also has the ability of limited story-telling (line 13). She takes the low-level initiative for form-filling (line 16), as well.

The main components of our E-Partner system (Fig.3) are:

- **Speech Recognizer:** get voice input and send the result to the parser. We use Microsoft speech recognition engine. In integration with other components, we gather rich low-level information (sound or phrase start event, recognition hypothesis, etc.) to aid the dialogue manager to handle the uncertainty. One example is to detect user barge-in before the recognition result. We also use the parser grammar to guide the selection of the candidate words.

- **Robust Parser:** get text input or recognition result; send the semantic interpretation to the dialogue manager. We use the robust parser [9] from the speech group of Microsoft Research. With LEAP grammar, it can handle many ill-formed sentences and is also capable of partial parsing.
- **Dialogue Manager:** select appropriate actions; send them to language generator or domain agent.
- **Domain Agent:** execute the non-verbal action, i.e., show pictures. It interacts with domain model intensively.
- **Language Generator:** execute the verbal action; send the result text to the talking head or speech synthesizer. A template-based approach is used to generate responses.
- **Speech Synthesizer:** generate voice from text; send it to the talking head. Now we use pre-recorded speech (Microsoft TTS engine if no talking head).
- **Talking Head:** synthesize video sequences from speech.

3 Dialogue Manager

Compared with simple-service systems and plan assistant systems, E-Partner differs in both the form of the information source and the way of conveying the information to the user. In a simple-service system, the information source is usually in a similar form and stored in some well-structured databases. In a plan assistant system, it can be stored in some knowledge bases. While in our system, although all the information remains related to a particular topic, it may be in many different forms, and is too complex to fit in databases or knowledge bases. The task of the system is also different. E-Partner wants to actively provide user with different useful information about a particular topic, while in a simple-service system, a correct answer for the user's current request is usually adequate, and a plan assistant system must help the user accomplish the task known to the system.

Our major problem here is how to represent and present the knowledge. E-Partner has many kinds of knowledge sources, which will play different roles in the dialogue system. The mixture of all these knowledge sources has a number of drawbacks [6]. In our system, we divide the knowledge sources into five parts: a domain model, a dialogue model, a discourse model, a task model, and a user model (Fig.3).

Besides the form of the domain model, the key difference from other systems is the complexity of the task model and the user model. The task model gives the E-Partner the ability to take the initiative in a high level, conveying the information to the user actively. The user model contains user preferences, which are built from the interaction between E-Partner and the user. User preferences can improve the quality of conversation, as well as user satisfaction.

Our dialogue manager receives the semantic representation from the parser, and then decides what to do by rule matching, which also takes the user model into consideration. If it does not get enough information, it prompts the user to give more information. If the user does not have a particular request, it takes the initiative according to the task scripts. By combining rule matching with form filling and task execution, we have a two-layer mixed-initiative dialogue system.

Dialogue Model

Our dialogue model is a combination of the dialogue grammar and frame-based approach [3]. We use rules to construct our dialogue model into hierarchical sub-dialogues. The dialogue manager chooses the appropriate sub-dialogue according to the discourse context and parser output. We can handle many kinds of conversation by providing carefully designed sub-dialogues.

Each rule specifies a list of actions to be executed sequentially when in a certain dialogue state (CONTEXT condition) and for a particular sentence input by the user (USER condition) (Fig.4). A USER condition is a form with many slots. If the dialogue manager finds any unfilled slot, it repeatedly asks for the missing slot, using a natural prompt specified by the designer, until all the missing slots are filled or the user gives up the current form. The parser focus is also set to reflect the form-filling status. Because the user can answer in any order they prefer, this can result in a low-level mixed-initiative behavior.

Discourse Model

The discourse model represents the current state of the dialogue. We use two kinds of data structures to represent the dialogue history: data objects constructed recently, in the form of a list of filled or unfilled slots, and a list of context variables, which can be read and written in a rule, indicating some special states.

Domain Model

The domain model holds knowledge of the world. It includes many kinds of information. The main structure is a tree, which provides a structured representation of many related concepts, i.e. a place tree contains different levels of places. Many other facts are directly or indirectly related to the different places in this place tree. LEAP grammar and the language template are also the implicit representation of part of the domain knowledge.

Task Model

The main task of the E-Partner is to actively provide the user with useful information related to a given topic. It is not a simple one-shot task. Usually, this task consists of many sub-tasks or primitive actions. The E-Partner should have the ability to fulfill these sub-tasks during the interactions with the user. Since the execution of a sub-task may be interrupted by the user when the user initiate a sub-dialogue, E-Partner should take the initiative again to continue its task after this sub-dialogue. So we have a high level mixed-initiative behavior when combining the task model with the original rule-based system.

A script language (Fig.4) is devoted to define the task structure using a hierarchical task tree. The leaf node represents the terminal task consisting of action sequence while the internal node represents the non-terminal task. Since there are many related concepts in the domain model, the tasks can be associated with different concepts.

When switching between different concepts, we also switch the current task to the associated task.

To prevent the task from disturbing the user, E-Partner executes the task only when it is not engaged in any sub-dialogue. The user can also ask E-Partner to skip the current task or parent task.

User Model

Our user model only includes the user preferences:

- If the user is in a hurry, skip some less important information. We assume that a hurried user likes to interrupt E-Partner.
- If the user does not like short stories, reduce the frequency of the story telling. We assume a user does not like stories if he often answers "no" when being asked whether he wants to hear a story, or interrupts a story.
- If the user likes to ask many questions, increase the frequency of question requests, which is a trick of saying something to lead the user to ask some particular questions that can be answered. This is very useful in increasing user satisfaction when many of their previous questions cannot be answered satisfactorily.

As long as the dialogue proceeds, the user's preferences will be changed dynamically and our dialogue manager can adapt to this kind of change by storing the parameters of the user preferences in the user model. Additional useful user preferences that may fit in the user model are currently being considered.

4 Facial Animation

For facial animation we use video rewrite [2], which is one of the most effective techniques for creating photo-realistic talking heads. However, video rewrite by itself cannot support conversational interactions as it is only a technique for creating a talking head for each individual sentence spoken by the conversation agent. We have extended [2] so that the facial animations of individual sentences can be stitched together to provide a continuous presence of the talking head, which pauses between sentences and appears to listen (instead of just freeze) when the user speaks. The talking head can smoothly switch back and forth between the listening and talking states.

The facial animation synthesized by video rewrite is a composite of two parts. The first part is a video sequence of the jaw and mouth, which is lip-synched according to the spoken sentence. The second part is a "background video" of the face. The mouth video sequence is generated from an annotated viseme database extracted from a short training video using a hidden Markov model (HMM). To support conversational interactions, we need a "background" video of the talking head that is alive and having a neutral expression. This ``background" video is taken from the training video. As mentioned, the training video is short. If the same background video is used repeatedly, the talking head appears artificial. Using video texture [8], we generate a "background" video that continues infinitely without apparent repetition. Similarly,

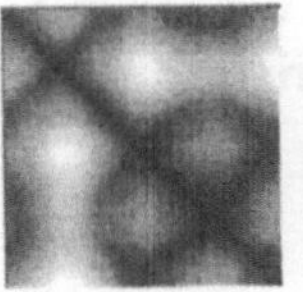

Distance matrix

Transmission loops

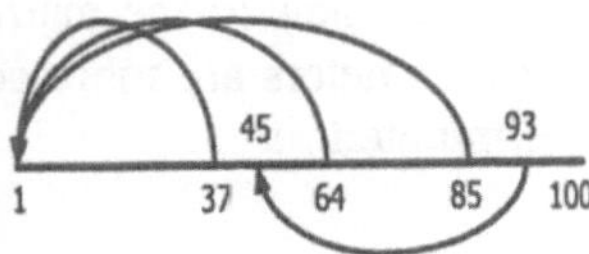

Possible transition graph

Fig. 5. Video texture of a background video with 100 frames

we use video texture to provide the talking head for the conversation agent when it is in the listening state.

Video texture generates infinitely long video from a short video sequence by jumping back to an earlier frame whenever there is a smooth transition from the current frame and an earlier frame. The smoothness of the transition is measured by the L2 distance between the frames. Fig.5 shows an analysis of a short video sequence. For this sequence, after dead-end avoidance and transitions pruning [8], the possible transmissions are (1, 37), (1, 64), (1, 85), (93, 45). In each transition point, we set a transition probability to decide the whether to jump back to an earlier frame.

A challenging issue in using video rewrite for conversational interactions is facial pose tracking. Accurate facial pose tracking is critical for the smooth transition between the talking and listening states, as well as for allowing natural head motion of the conversation agent when it is in the talking state. To allow a variety of head motions, the system warps each face image into a standard reference pose. The system tries to find the affine transform that minimizes the mean-squared error between face images and the template images [1]. The quality of facial animation largely depends on continuity of the facial pose. Even with a little error, the continuous mouth motion and the transition between talking and listening states become jerky.

We apply two strategies to improve the facial pose estimation. One is to apply second-order prediction to determine the initial pose. The other is to low-pass filter the pose parameters if abrupt motion exists. But in some cases there really exists large motions; we must eliminate the false alarm. We first interpolate the parameters of the pre frame and the post frame to obtain several different new parameters, and then compute the residue errors by each group of parameters. If the new error is greater than the original one, we believe that the abrupt motion is true. Otherwise, the parameters take the filter value. Linear interpolation directly on the affine parameters is not reasonable, because the parameters of the affine matrix do not correspond to the physical motion. So we decompose the affine matrix as the following:

$$\begin{bmatrix} a_1 & a_1 & a_2 \\ a_3 & a_4 & a_5 \\ 0 & 0 & 1 \end{bmatrix} = \begin{bmatrix} 1 & 0 & t_x \\ 0 & 1 & t_y \\ 0 & 0 & 1 \end{bmatrix} \begin{bmatrix} sx & k & 0 \\ k & sy & 0 \\ 0 & 0 & 1 \end{bmatrix} \begin{bmatrix} \cos\theta & -\sin\theta & 0 \\ \sin\theta & \cos\theta & 0 \\ 0 & 0 & 1 \end{bmatrix}$$

Note that the decomposition is not unique. If we maintain the order and assume some condition, the parameters can represent some physical meaning. For example, when k is small enough and $(sx\text{-}sy)$ is very small, the θ in fact is the rotation. We use k and θ to determine if abrupt motion occurs, and to predict and filter on the physical parameter. Then the new affine matrix can be computed. We conduct experiments to show that the parameters are more continuous than the original method, and that the jerkiness is eliminated.

5 Conclusion

In this paper, we present a photo-realistic conversation agent called E-Partner. The first application of the E-Partner project – Maggie the tour guide of the Forbidden City – has been demonstrated at Microsoft since last September. We have received positive feedback from many visitors. They think such a cyber companion will play a very important role in many similar applications. For example, in E-commerce applications to sell cars, an E-Partner can be a virtual expert on cars who can talk about cars with users. Other potential applications include some information-providing applications, interactive games, a lovely partner in a living room, etc.

References

1. Black, M.J., Yacoob, Y: Tracking and recognizing rigid and non-rigid facial motion using local parametric models of image motion. In *Proceedings of IEEE Intl. Conf. Computer Vision*, Cambridge, MA, 374-381, 1995.
2. Breglar, C., Covell, M., Slaney, M.: Video rewrite: Driving visual speech with audio. In *Proceedings of SIGGRAPH'97*, 353-360, July 1997.
3. Chu-Carroll, J.: Form-based reasoning for mixed-initiative dialogue management in information-query systems. In *Proceedings of Eurospeech'99*, 1519-1522, 1999.
4. Cossatto, E., Graf, H. P.: Photo-realistic talking-heads from image samples. *IEEE Trans. on Multimedia*, 2(3), September 2000.
5. Ferguson, G., Allen, J.: TRIPS: An Intelligent Integrated Problem-Solving Assistant. In *Proceedings of the Fifteenth National Conference on Artificial Intelligence*(AAAI-98), Madison, WI, 567-573, July 1998.
6. Flycht-Eriksson, A.: A survey of knowledge sources in dialogue systems. In *Proceedings of IJCAI-99 Workshop on Knowledge and Reasoning in Practical Dialogue Systems*, Stockholm, 1999.
7. Pandzic, I., Ostermann, J., Millen, D.: User evaluation: synthetic talking faces for interactive services. *The Visual Computer*, 15:330-340, 1999.
8. Schodl, A., Szeliski, R.: Video textures. In *Proceedings of SIGGRAPH'99*, 1999.
9. Wang, Y.: A robust parser for spoken language understanding. In *Proceedings of Eurospeech'99*, 1999.
10. Weizenbaum, J.: ELIZA - a computer program for the study of natural language communication between man and machine. *C. ACM*, 9:36-43, 1966.
11. Zue, V. et al.: JUPITER: A telephone-based conversational interface for weather information. *IEEE Transactions on Speech and Audio Processing*, 8(1), January 2000.

A Robust and Fast Face Modeling System

Zicheng Liu, Zhengyou Zhang, Dennis Adler, Erik Hanson, Michael Cohen

Microsoft Research, One Microsoft Way, Redmond, WA 98052-6399, USA
{zliu, zhang}@microsoft.com
http://research.microsoft.com/~zliu/

Abstract. In this paper, we describe our face modeling system which allows a user, with a PC and an ordinary video camera, to construct their own 3D face models with minimal manual work. Furthermore, the constructed face model can be animated right away. There are two technical innovations that make our system possible. The first is a robust head motion estimation algorithm that takes advantage of physical properties of the face feature points obtained from manual marking to reduce the number of unknowns. The second innovation is to fit a set of face metrics (3D deformation vectors) to the reconstructed 3D points and markers to generate a complete face geometry. We have done live demonstrations many times and constructed 3D faces for hundreds of people. The system has proven to be robust, fast, and easy to use.

1 Introduction

One of the most interesting and difficult problems in computer graphics is the effortless generation of realistic looking, animated human face models. Animated face models are essential to computer games, film making, online chat, virtual presence, video conferencing, etc. So far, the most popular commercially available tools have utilized laser scanners or structured lights. These systems produce more accurate data, but they are specialized equipment and expensive. In addition, in order to animate the model, the user still needs to register the model. Because inexpensive computers and cameras are widely available, there is great interest in producing face models directly from images. In spite of progress toward this goal, the available techniques are either manually intensive or computationally expensive.

The goal of our system is to allow an untrained user with a PC and an ordinary camera to create and instantly animate his/her face model in no more than a few minutes. The user interface for the process comprises three simple steps. First the user turns his/her head from one side to the other side in about 5 seconds. Second the user moves a slide to select a front view. Third, two images pop up and the user marks 5 feature points (eye corners, nose top, and mouth corners) on each of the two images. The Fourth step is optional: the user marks 3 points under the chin on the frontal view image. After these manual steps, the system then computes the 3D face geometry from the two images, and tracks the video sequences to create a complete facial texture map by blending frames of the sequence.

There are two technical innovations to make such a system robust and fast. The first is a robust head motion estimation algorithm that takes advantage of the physical properties of the face feature points obtained from manual marking to reduce the number of

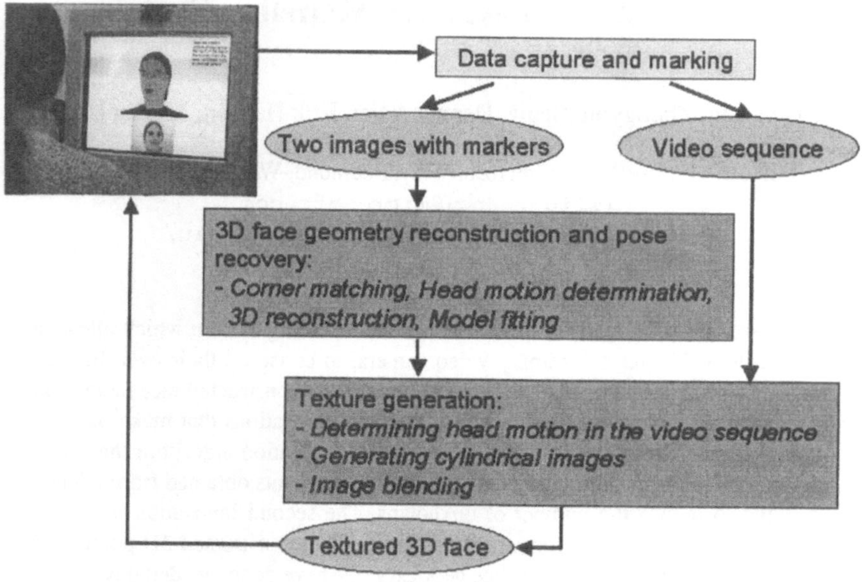

Fig. 1: *System overview*

unknowns. The second innovation is to fit a set of face metrics (3D deformation vectors) to the reconstructed 3D points and markers to generate a complete face geometry. Linear classes of face geometries and image prototypes have been used for constructing face models from images in a morphable model framework [2]. But we use linear classes of face metrics to interpolate a sparse set of 3D points. An earlier version of this face modeling system has been reported in an earlier paper [5]. This paper describes an improved system. This new system has incorporated the robust head motion estimation technique so that it is significantly more robust. In addition, the user interface is much simpler.

Facial modeling and animation has been a computer graphics research topic for over 25 years. The reader is referred to Parke and Waters' book [6, 5] for a complete overview.

2 System Overview

Figure 1 outlines the components of our system. The equipment include a computer and a video camera. We assume the intrinsic camera parameters have been calibrated, a reasonable assumption given the simplicity of calibration procedures [12].

The first stage is data capture. The user simply turns his/her head from one side all the way to the other side in about 5 seconds. Then the user moves a slide to select the frontal view. The system then displays the frontal view and its neighboring view, and have the user to mark 5 feature points (eye corners, nose top, and mouth corners) on each of the two images (see Figure 2 for an example). In the sequel, we call the two images the *base images*.

As an optional step, the user is instructed to put 3 markers below the chin on the frontal view (just one image).

The next processing stage computes the face mesh geometry and the head pose with respect to the camera frame using the two base images and markers as input.

The final stage determines the head motions in the video sequences, and blends the images to generate a facial texture map.

Fig. 2: *An example of two base images used for face modeling. Also shown are five manually picked markers indicated by yellow dots.*

3 Notation

We denote the homogeneous coordinates of a vector $\mathbf{x}$ by $\tilde{\mathbf{x}}$, i.e., the homogeneous coordinates of an image point $\mathbf{m} = (u, v)^T$ are $\tilde{\mathbf{m}} = (u, v, 1)^T$, and those of a 3D point $\mathbf{p} = (x, y, z)^T$ are $\tilde{\mathbf{p}} = (x, y, z, 1)^T$. A camera is described by a pinhole model, and a 3D point $\mathbf{p}$ and its image point $\mathbf{m}$ are related by

$$\lambda \tilde{\mathbf{m}} = \mathbf{A}\mathbf{P}\Omega\tilde{\mathbf{p}} \tag{1}$$

where λ is a scale, and $\mathbf{A}$, $\mathbf{P}$ and Ω are given by

$$\mathbf{A} = \begin{pmatrix} \alpha & \gamma & u_0 \\ 0 & \beta & v_0 \\ 0 & 0 & 1 \end{pmatrix} \quad \mathbf{P} = \begin{pmatrix} 1 & 0 & 0 & 0 \\ 0 & 1 & 0 & 0 \\ 0 & 0 & 1 & 0 \end{pmatrix} \quad \Omega = \begin{pmatrix} \mathbf{R} & \mathbf{t} \\ \mathbf{0}^T & 1 \end{pmatrix}$$

The elements of matrix $\mathbf{A}$ are the intrinsic parameters of the camera and matrix $\mathbf{A}$ maps the normalized image coordinates to the pixel image coordinates (see e.g. [3]). Matrix $\mathbf{P}$ is the perspective projection matrix. Matrix Ω is the 3D rigid transformation (rotation $\mathbf{R}$ and translation $\mathbf{t}$) from the object/world coordinate system to the camera coordinate system. When two images are concerned, a prime $'$ is added to denote the quantities related to the second image.

The fundamental geometric constraint between two images is known as the *epipolar constraint* [3, 11]. It states that in order for a point $\mathbf{m}$ in one image and a point $\mathbf{m}'$ in the other image to be the projections of a single physical point in space, or, in other words, in order for them to be matched, they must satisfy

$$\tilde{\mathbf{m}}'^T \mathbf{A}'^{-T} \mathbf{E} \mathbf{A}^{-1} \tilde{\mathbf{m}} = 0 \tag{2}$$

where $\mathbf{E} = [\mathbf{t}_r]_\times \mathbf{R}_r$ is known as the essential matrix, $(\mathbf{R}_r, \mathbf{t}_r)$ is the relative motion between the two images, and $[\mathbf{t}_r]_\times$ is a skew symmetric matrix such that $\mathbf{t}_r \times \mathbf{v} = [\mathbf{t}_r]_\times \mathbf{v}$ for any 3D vector $\mathbf{v}$.

4 Linear class of face geometries

Vetter and Poggio [10] represented an arbitrary face image as a linear combination of some number of prototypes and used this representation (called linear object class) for image recognition, coding, and image synthesis. Blanz and Vetter [2] used linear class of both images and 3D geometries for image matching and face modeling. The advantage of using linear class of objects is that it eliminates most of the non-natural faces and significantly reduces the search space.

Instead of representing a face as a linear combination of real faces, we represent it as a linear combination of a neutral face and some number of face *metrics* where a metric is vector that linearly deforms a face in certain way, such as to make the head wider, make the nose bigger, etc. To be more precise, let's denote the face geometry by a vector $\mathcal{S} = (\mathbf{v}_1^T, \ldots, \mathbf{v}_n^T)^T$ where $\mathbf{v}_i = (X_i, Y_i, Z_i)^T$ $(i = 1, \ldots, n)$ are the vertices, and a metric by a vector $\mathcal{M} = (\delta\mathbf{v}_1, \ldots, \delta\mathbf{v}_n)^T$, where $\delta\mathbf{v}_i = (\delta X_i, \delta Y_i, \delta Z_i)^T$. Given a neutral face $\mathcal{S}^0 = (\mathbf{v}_1^{0\,T}, \ldots, \mathbf{v}_n^{0\,T})^T$, and a set of m metrics $\mathcal{M}^j = (\delta\mathbf{v}_1^{j\,T}, \ldots, \delta\mathbf{v}_n^{j\,T})^T$, the linear space of face geometries spanned by these metrics is

$$\mathcal{S} = \mathcal{S}^0 + \sum_{j=1}^{m} c_j \mathcal{M}^j \quad \text{subject to } c_j \in [l_j, u_j] \quad (3)$$

where c_j's are the metric coefficients and l_j and u_j are the valid range of c_j. In our implementation, the neutral face and all the metrics are designed by an artist, and it is done once. The neutral face (see Figure 3) contains 194 vertices and 360 triangles. There are 65 metrics.

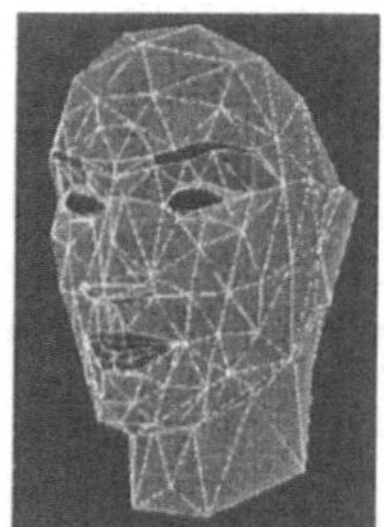

Fig. 3: *Neutral face.*

5 Face Geometry From Two Views

In this section, we describe our techniques to determine the face geometry from just two views. The two base images are taken in a normal room by a static camera while the head is moving in front. There is no control on the head motion, and the motion is unknown, of course. We have to determine first the motion of the head and match some pixels across the two views before we can fit an animated face model to the images.

5.1 Corner matching

One popular technique of image registration is optical flow [4, 1], which is based on the assumption that the intensity/color is conserved. This is not the case in our situation: the color of the same physical point appears to be different in images because the illumination changes when the head is moving. We therefore resort to a feature-based approach that is more robust to intensity/color variations. It consists of the following steps: (i) detecting corners in each image; (ii) matching corners between the two images; (iii) detecting false matches based on a robust estimation technique; (iv) determining the head motion; (v) reconstructing matched points in 3D space.

5.2 Robust head motion estimation

In this section, we describe a new algorithm to compute the head motion between two views from the correspondences of five feature points including eye corners, mouth corners and nose top, and zero or more other image point matches.

If the image locations of these feature points are precise, one could use five-point algorithm to compute camera motion. However, this is usually not the case in practice since a human in general cannot mark the feature points with high precision. When there are errors, a five-point algorithm is not robust even when refined with a bundle adjustment technique. The key idea of our algorithm is to use the physical properties of the feature points to improve robustness. We use the property of symmetry to reduce the number of unknowns. We put reasonable lower and upper bounds on the nose height and represent the bounds as inequality constrains. As a result, the algorithm becomes significantly more robust.

5.3 3D reconstruction

Once the motion is estimated, matched points can be reconstructed in 3D space with respect to the camera frame at the time when the first base image was taken. Let $(\mathbf{m}, \mathbf{m}')$ be a couple of matched points, and $\mathbf{p}$ be their corresponding point in space. 3D point $\mathbf{p}$ is estimated such that $\|\mathbf{m} - \hat{\mathbf{m}}\|^2 + \|\mathbf{m}' - \hat{\mathbf{m}}'\|^2$ is minimized, where $\hat{\mathbf{m}}$ and $\hat{\mathbf{m}}'$ are projections of $\mathbf{p}$ in both images according to (1).

5.4 Fitting a face model

The face model fitting process consists of two steps: fitting to 3D reconstructed points and fine adjustment using image information.

3D fitting. Given a set of reconstructed 3D points from matched corners and markers, the fitting process searches for both the *pose* of the face and the metric coefficients to minimize the distances from the reconstructed 3D points to the face mesh. The pose of the face is the transformation $\mathbf{T} = \begin{pmatrix} s\mathbf{R} & \mathbf{t} \\ \mathbf{0}^T & 1 \end{pmatrix}$ from the coordinate frame of the neutral face mesh to the camera frame, where $\mathbf{R}$ is a 3×3 rotation matrix, $\mathbf{t}$ is a translation, and s is a global scale. For any 3D vector $\mathbf{p}$, we use notation $\mathbf{T}(\mathbf{p}) = s\mathbf{R}\mathbf{p} + \mathbf{t}$.

The vertex coordinates of the face mesh in the camera frame is a function of both the metric coefficients and the pose of the face. Given metric coefficients $(c_1, \ldots, c_m)$ and pose $\mathbf{T}$, the face geometry in the camera frame is given by

$$\mathcal{S} = \mathbf{T}(\mathcal{S}^0 + \sum_{i=1}^{n} c_i \mathcal{M}^i). \qquad (4)$$

Since the face mesh is a triangular mesh, any point on a triangle is a linear combination of the three triangle vertexes in terms of barycentric coordinates. So any point on a triangle is also a function of $\mathbf{T}$ and metric coefficients. Furthermore, when $\mathbf{T}$ is fixed, it is simply a linear function of the metric coefficients.

Let $(\mathbf{p}_1, \mathbf{p}_2, \ldots, \mathbf{p}_k)$ be the reconstructed corner points, and $(\mathbf{q}_1, \mathbf{q}_2, \ldots, \mathbf{q}_5)$ be the reconstructed markers. Denote the distance from $\mathbf{p}_i$ to the face mesh $\mathcal{S}$ by $d(\mathbf{p}_i, \mathcal{S})$. Assume marker $\mathbf{q}_j$ corresponds to vertex $\mathbf{v}_{m_j}$ of the face mesh, and denote the distance between $\mathbf{q}_j$ and $\mathbf{v}_{m_j}$ by $d(\mathbf{q}_j, \mathbf{v}_{m_j})$. The fitting process consists in finding pose $\mathbf{T}$ and metric coefficients $\{c_1, \ldots, c_n\}$ by minimizing

$$\sum_{i=1}^{n} w_i d^2(\mathbf{p}_i, \mathcal{S}) + \sum_{j=1}^{5} d^2(\mathbf{q}_j, \mathbf{v}_{m_j}) \tag{5}$$

where w_i is a weighting factor.

To solve this problem, we use an iterative closest point approach.

Fine adjustment using image information. After the geometric fitting process, we have now a face mesh that is a close approximation to the real face. To further improve the result, we search for silhouettes and other face features in the images and use them to refine the face geometry. The general problem of locating silhouettes and face features in images is difficult, and is still a very active research area in computer vision. However, the face mesh that we have obtained provides a good estimate of the locations of the face features, so we only need to perform search in a small region.

6 Face Texture From Video Sequence

Now we have the geometry of the face from only two views that are close to the frontal position. For the sides of the face, the texture from the two images is therefore quite poor or even not available at all. Since each image only covers a portion of the face, we need to combine all the images in the video sequence to obtain a complete texture map. This is done by first determining the head pose for the images in the video sequence and then blending them to create a complete texture map.

Successive images are first matched using the same technique as described in Section 5.1. We could combine the resulting motions incrementally to determine the head pose. However, this estimation is quite noisy because it is computed only from 2D points. As we already have the 3D face geometry, a more reliable pose estimation can be obtained by combining both 3D and 2D information.

After the head pose of an image is computed, we use an approach similar to Pighin et al.'s method [7] to generate a view independent texture map. We also construct the texture map on a virtual cylinder enclosing the face model. But instead of casting a ray from each pixel to the face mesh and computing the texture blending weights on a pixel by pixel basis, we use a more efficient approach by using graphics hardware.

7 Animation

Having obtained the 3D textured face model, the user can immediately animate the model with the application of facial expressions including smiles, sad, thinking, etc. The model can also perform text to speech.

To accomplish this we have defined a set of vectors, which we call *posemes*. Like the metric vectors described previously, posemes are a collection of artist-designed displacements. We can apply these displacements to any face as long as it has the same topology as the neutral face. Posemes are collected in a library of actions, expressions, and visems.

8 Results

We have constructed 3D face models for well over a hundred of people. We have done live demonstrations at ACM Multimedia2000, ACM1, and CHI2001, where we set up a booth a construct face models for visitors. At each of these events, the success rate is 90% or higher. In ACM1, most of the visitors are kids or teenagers. Kids are usually more difficult to model since they have smooth skins, but our system worked very well. We observe that the main factor for the occasional failure is the head turning too fast.

Figure 4 shows side-by-side comparisons of eight reconstructed models with the real images. In these examples, the video sequences were taken using ordinary video camera in people's offices. No special lighting equipment or background was used. After data-capture and marking, the computations take about 1 minute to generate the synthetic textured head. Most of this time is spent tracking the video sequences.

Fig. 4: *Side by side comparison of the original images with the reconstructed models of various people.*

9 Conclusions

We have developed a system to construct textured 3D face models from video sequences with minimal user intervention. With a few simple clicks by the user, our system quickly generates a person's face model which is animated right away. Our experiments show that our system is able to generate face models for people of different races, of different ages, and with different skin colors. Such a system can be potentially used by an ordinary user at home to make their own face models. These face models can be used, for example, as avatars in computer games, online chatting, virtual conferencing, etc.

10 Future work

In our current system, the face geometry is determined from only two views, and video sequences are used merely for creating a complete face texture. We are working on using all the images in the video sequence to improve the geometry, and some of the initial results are reported in [9]. We are planning on incorporating this work into our system.

The current face mesh is very sparse. We are investigating techniques to increase the mesh resolution by using higher resolution face metrics or prototypes. Another possibility is to compute a displacement map for each triangle using color information.

Several researchers in computer vision are working at automatically locating facial features in images [8]. With the advancement of those techniques, a completely automatic face modeling system can be expected, even though it is not a burden to click just five points with our current system.

Additional challenges include automatic generation of eyeballs and eye texture maps, as well as accurate incorporation of hair, teeth, and tongues.

References

1. J. Barron, D. Fleet, and S. Beauchemin. Performance of optical flow techniques. *The International Journal of Computer Vision*, 12(1):43–77, 1994.
2. V. Blanz and T. Vetter. A morphable model for the synthesis of 3d faces. In *Computer Graphics, Annual Conference Series*, pages 187–194. Siggraph, August 1999.
3. O. Faugeras. *Three-Dimensional Computer Vision: a Geometric Viewpoint*. MIT Press, 1993.
4. B. K. P. Horn and B. G. Schunk. Determining Optical Flow. *Artificial Intelligence*, 17:185–203, 1981.
5. Z. Liu, Z. Zhang, C. Jacobs, and M. Cohen. Rapid modeling of animated faces from video. In *Proceedings of Visual 2000*, pages 58–67, 2000.
6. F. I. Parke and K. Waters. *Computer Facial Animation*. AKPeters, Wellesley, Massachusetts, 1996.
7. F. Pighin, J. Hecker, D. Lischinski, R. Szeliski, and D. H. Salesin. Synthesizing realistic facial expressions from photographs. In *Computer Graphics, Annual Conference Series*, pages 75–84. Siggraph, July 1998.
8. T. Shakunaga, K. Ogawa, and S. Oki. Integration of eigentemplate and structure matching for automatic facial feature detection. In *Proc. of the 3rd International Conference on Automatic Face and Gesture Recognition*, pages 94–99, April 1998.
9. Y. Shan, Z. Liu, and Z. Zhang. Model-based bundle adjustment with application to face modeling. In *International Conference on Computer Vision (ICCV'2001)*, 2001.
10. T. Vetter and T. Poggio. Linear object classes and image synthesis from a single example image. *IEEE Transations on Pattern Analysis and Machine Intelligence*, 19(7):733–742, 1997.
11. Z. Zhang. Determining the epipolar geometry and its uncertainty: A review. *The International Journal of Computer Vision*, 27(2):161–195, 1998.
12. Z. Zhang. Flexible camera calibration by viewing a plane from unknown orientations. In *International Conference on Computer Vision (ICCV'99)*, pages 666–673, 1999.

Automatic Human Face Recognition System Using Fractal Dimension and Modified Hausdorff Distance[1]

Kwan-Ho Lin, Baofeng Guo, Kin-Man Lam and Wan-Chi Siu

Centre for Multimedia Signal Processing
Department of Electronic and Information Engineering
The Hong Kong Polytechnic University, Hong Kong
enkmlam@polyu.edu.hk

Abstract. In this paper, an efficient automatic human face recognition system is proposed. Fractal dimension is an efficient representation of texture which is used to locate the eyes in a human face. We propose a modified approach to estimate the fractal dimensions which is less sensitive to lighting conditions and provides information about the orientation of an image under consideration. Based on the position of the eyes, two face images are normalized, aligned and then compared by a new modified Hausdorff distance measure. As different facial regions have different degrees of importance for face recognition, the modified Hausdorff distance is weighted according to a weighted function derived from the spatial information of the human face. Experimental results show that our approach can achieve recognition rates of 76%, 84%, and 92% for the first one, the first five, first ten likely matched faces, respectively. If the position of the eyes is selected manually, the corresponding recognition rates are 82%, 95% and 98%, respectively. The average processing time for detecting the eyes and recognize a human face is less than two seconds.

1. Introduction

Facial feature detection is an important step for an automatic human face recognition system [1][2][3]. The system has a wide range of applications such as security systems, credit card verification, etc. Although the subject of automatic human face recognition has been studied for more than 20 years, it still presents a challenge because the human face may change its appearance.

The success of an automatic human face recognition system relies not only on an efficient face recognition method, but also on the accuracy of the location of the facial features. There are several approaches for locating the facial features [4][5] and recognizing the human face [6][7]. However, they are computationally intensive approaches.

In this paper, an efficient method for locating the two eyes and recognizing the human face is proposed. In our method, the position of the two eyes are located based on the valley field detection and measurement of fractal dimensions. Fractal

[1] This work is supported by HKPolyU research grant G-V498

dimension is an efficient representation of the texture of facial features. The detection procedure of the two eyes is divided into three levels. The first level locates the possible eye candidates which exhibit themselves as a valley in the image space. Two possible eye candidates with similar fractal dimensions are grouped to form a possible eye pair in level 2. The possible eye pairs are then further verified based on the fractal dimensions of the eye-pair windows and face regions in level 3.

After the eyes are located, a modified Hausdorff distance proposed in this paper will be used to compare two human faces. Humans have the ability to categorize faces at a glance and recognize the line drawings of objects as accurately as photographs [6]. It is suggested that the edge-like retinal images of faces are useful and efficient in face identification. Takács [6] introduced a method of comparing face images using the "doubly" modified Hausdorff distance, which is a similarity measure derived as a variant of the Hausdorff distance. This modified Hausdorff distance introduces the notion of neighborhood function N_B^a and assoicated penalty (P), which is called 'doubly' modified Hausdorff distance (M2HD). This modified Hausdorff distance is defined as follows:
Given two finite point sets

$$A=\{a_1,\dots,a_p\} \text{ and } B=\{b_1,\dots,b_q\},$$

$$H(A,B)=max\{h(A,B),\ h(B,A)\} \tag{1}$$

where $$d(a,B)=\max(I\cdot \min_{b\in N_b^a}\|a-b\|,(1-I)\cdot P) \text{ and } \mathrm{h(A,B)}=\frac{1}{N_a}\sum_{a\in A} d(a,B)$$

In this modified definition, N_B^a is the neighborhood of point a in set B. I is an indicator, which is equal to 1 if there exists a point $b\in N_B^a$, and 0 if otherwise. This formulation may have two different values for $h(A,B)$: when all matching pairs fall within a given neighborhood, its value will be the same as the original Hausdorff distance; however, if no matching pair is found, then the penalty value P is considered. This modified Hausdorff distance therefore accounts for small and non-rigid local distortions. However, this distance measure does not consider the spatial information of the human face such as the eyes and mouth. Hence, in this paper, a new method for human face recognition is devised that utilizes a modified type of Hausdorff distance by incorporating the spatial information of a human face. In order to evaluate this combined new method, the ORL database is used in the experiment. The experimental results show that the proposed method is efficient and can achieve a reasonable recognition rate.

This paper is organized as follows. Section 2 presents a new approach to locating the eyes. A new modified Hausdorff distance, namely spatial weighted Hausdorff distance, is defined in Section 3. Section 4 presents the experimental results. Finally, conclusions are given in Section 5.

2. Detecting the Eye Pairs

In this section, we propose a new approach for locating the eye pairs in an image. Our new approach is based on the surface roughness of facial features by means of fractal dimension. Box-counting [8] is one of the methods which estimates the fractal dimension. This method is an efficient technique for estimating fractal dimensions, and can be applied to gray-level images and binary images [9]. Our detection scheme can be divided into three stages. First, all the valley regions in an image are detected and tested for possible eye candidates. Valley positions that have features similar to the eyes are considered as possible eye candidates, and will be passed to the second stage to form possible eye pairs. At the second stage, possible eye pairs are formed from the eye candidates based on the eye features and our proposed oriented fractal dimension. In the third stage, the possible eye pairs are then further verified based on the fractal dimensions of the eye-pair windows and face regions. The detailed procedures for locating the eye pairs and the face regions are described below.

2.1 Valley Detection of the Eyes

As the iris has a relatively low gray-level intensity in a human face, a valley exists at an eye region. The valley field, Φ_v, is extracted by means of morphological operators. A possible eye candidate is identified at position (x,y) if the following two criteria are satisfied:

$$f(x,y) < t_i \text{ and } \Phi_v(x,y) > t_v \tag{2}$$

where $f(x,y)$ is a facial image, and t_i and t_v are thresholds. A number of regions of possible eye candidates are detected, and are then reduced to a point by choosing the best candidate in each of the regions. Two functions, $v_1(x,y)$ and $v_2(x,y)$, are used to locate the best eye candidate in each region. The two functions are defined as follows:

$$v_1(x,y) = C_{1,1}\Phi_{1,1}(x,y) + C_{1,2}\left(\frac{f(x-2,y)+f(x+2,y)}{2} - S_{1,1}(x,y)\right)$$
$$v_2(x,y) = C_{2,1}\Phi_{2,1}(x,y) + C_{2,2}\left(\frac{f(x-3,y)+f(x+3,y)}{2} - S_{2,1}(x,y)\right) \tag{3}$$

where C's are weighting factors, $\Phi_{1,1}(x,y)$ and $S_{1,1}(x,y)$ are the average valley intensity and the average gray-level intensity inside a 3×3 window, respectively, while $\Phi_{2,1}(x,y)$ and $S_{2,1}(x,y)$ are the corresponding values inside a 5×5 window.

2.2 Grouping the best eye candidates to form possible eye pairs

Two eye candidates are paired to form a possible eye pair. We assume that the rotation of the human face is less than 45°. The two eyes of a face should have similar orientations and be of similar size. Moreover, the roughness of the two eye regions should be close to each other.

Based on the inter-distance between the two eye candidates, we can set up the corresponding windows to cover each of the two eye regions. The height, h, and width, w, of the windows are equal to a quarter of the inter-distance, L. As fractal dimension is sensitive to lighting conditions, the average gray-level intensities of the two eye windows are therefore adjusted to 180. This arrangement alleviates the effect of uneven lighting conditions on each half of the face. When two eye candidates are paired, they should have similar fractal dimensions, as well as orientation. However, owing to the use of square boxes in counting, fractal dimension lacks this information about orientation. In our approach, we use two rectangular boxes, as shown in Fig 1, namely a vertical rectangular box and a horizontal rectangular box of different orientations instead of a square box in box-counting. The two measured fractal dimensions are called horizontal fractal dimension, FD_h, and vertical fractal dimension, FD_v, respectively. The two fractal dimensions, FD_h and FD_v, for a human face are different from each other, and change according to the orientation of the eyes. For any given image region, the texture inside will remain more or less the same under different rotations, but both the FD_h and FD_v will change. Nevertheless, when the FD_h decreases, the FD_v will increase, and vice versa. This is due to the fact that the total number of boxes required to cover the image area or space should change only slightly even when the image is rotated. The sums of FD_h and FD_v for the eye samples under different rotations remain fairly constant. Thus, a valid eye pair can be selected if the following criteria are satisfied.

$$\begin{aligned} &|FD_h(x_0, y_0) - FD_h(x_1, y_1)| < t_1 \text{ and } |FD_v(x_0, y_0) - FD_v(x_1, y_1)| < t_2 \text{ and} \\ &|(FD_h(x_0, y_0) + FD_v(x_0, y_0)) - M_{eye}| < t_3 \text{ and} |(FD_h(x_1, y_1) + FD_v(x_1, y_1)) - M_{eye}| < t_4 \end{aligned} \quad (4)$$

where (x_0, y_0) and (x_1, y_1) are the locations of the left- and right-eye candidates, M_{eye} is the average fractal dimension of the eye windows, and t_1, t_2, t_3, and t_4 are thresholds. For a valid pair, the respective differences should be less than certain thresholds. The possible eye candidates are then validated by the oriented fractal dimension to form possible valid eye pairs. Our experiments show that by using the oriented fractal dimension we can form eye pairs more reliably than cases where the conventional fractal dimension is used. As the oriented fractal dimension matches eye pairs more accurately, the total amount of computation required in stage three can be reduced.

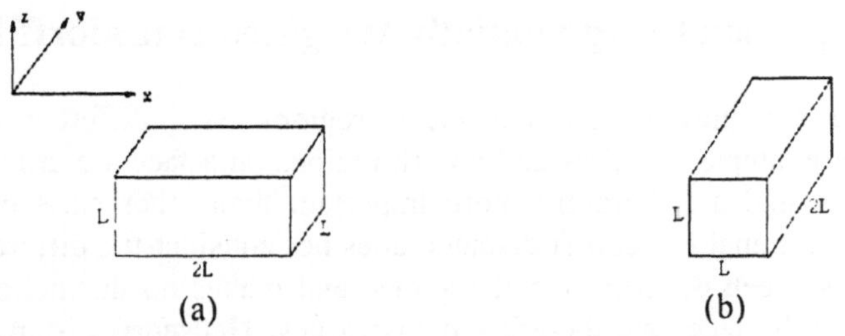

Fig. 1. Rectangular boxes used for measuring (a) FD_h, and (b) FD_v.

2.3 Verification of eye pairs

The eye pairs selected in stage two are passed to the next stage for further verification. At stage three, the measurement of each possible eye-pair region and its corresponding face region will be computed by means of fractal dimension. In order to reduce the effect of lighting conditions, the edge images are used in the computation of the fractal dimensions.

Based on the inter-distance L between two eye candidates, the eye-pair region and its corresponding face region can be extracted. In order to verify whether a selected eye-pair candidate is valid, the average fractal dimensions of the eye-pair regions, M'_{eye}, and the face regions, M'_{face}, are computed. In our study, we computed the fractal dimensions of a number of eye-pair windows and face windows. The corresponding means and variances of the fractal dimensions are 1.7298 and 0.0015, respectively, for the eye-pair region and 1.9469 and 0.0027, respectively, for the face region. The computed fractal dimensions of the eye-pair regions and face regions show a small variance under different scales. A large difference is found between the fractal dimensions for facial images and those for non-facial images. Thus, a valid eye pair can be selected if the following criteria are satisfied.

$$| F_{face}(x,y) - M'_{face}(x,y) | < t_5 \text{ and}$$
$$| F_{eye}(x,y) - M'_{eye}(x,y) | < t_6 \tag{5}$$

where (x,y) represents the position of the eye-pair window and the face windows, F_{eye} and F_{face} are the fractal dimensions of the eye-pair and face regions, M'_{eye} and M'_{face} are the average fractal dimensions of the two windows, and t_5 and t_6 are the thresholds. However, it is possible to detect more than one valid eye pair, which cluster around the valid eye-pair region. In making a selection among the overlapping valid eye pairs, the one with the lowest value of $| F_{eye}(x,y) - M'_{eye}(x,y)| + | F_{face}(x,y) - M'_{face}(x,y)|$ should be selected as the best eye pair in the overlapping region.

3. Face Recognition Using Spatially Weighted Hausdorff Distance

In human face recognition, different facial regions have different degrees of importance. For example, the eyes and mouth regions on a face are crucial features for identification and are therefore more important than other parts of the face. However, the traditional Hausdorff distance does not consider the different degrees of importance between different facial regions, and makes no distinction between different parts of the face. We therefore devise a new Hausdorff distance measure that is specific to face recognition and put more emphasis on the crucial facial features, including the eyes and mouth regions.

The modified Hausdorff distance measure incorporates a weighted function which is defined according to the spatial position of the respective regions of the facial features; hence it is called Spatially Weighted Hausdorff Distance (*SWHD*). The following is the definition of the new Hausdorff distance:

Given two finite point sets $A=\{a_1,\ldots, a_p\}$ and $B=\{b_1, \ldots , b_q\}$, the spatially weighted Hausdorff distance is defined as follows:

$$H(A,B) = \max(h_{sw}(A,B), h_{sw}(B,A)) \tag{6}$$

$$h_{sw}(A,B) = \frac{1}{N_a} \cdot \sum_{N_a} w(b) \min_{b \in B} \|a - b\| \tag{7}$$

N_a is the number of points in set A; $w(x)$ is a weighted function, whose definition is:

$$w(x) = \begin{cases} 1 & x \in R_i \\ w_v & x \in R_u \\ 0 & x \in R_b \end{cases} \tag{8}$$

where R_i represents the important facial regions, such as the eyes and mouth, which should be emphasized; R_u is the unimportant facial regions, which are the facial regions other than the important facial regions; and R_b is the background region that contains no facial parts. With this weighted function, an edge point that occurs in the background will be ignored. All points in the unimportant facial regions, R_u, will be suppressed by a weighted value, w_v, which is less than one. All points in the important facial regions, R_i, are fully counted.

In our new approach, the two eyes in a facial image are located using fractal dimensions, as described in Section 2. After detecting the two eyes, a rectangular face window, the two eye windows and the mouth window can be set by means of anthropometric measure. In order to avoid interference from the background and noise, the four corners of the face picture are considered as non-facial regions and are discarded. In normal situations, these regions do not contain any useful facial edge.

In this weighted function, the weight of the eyes and mouth regions (important region R_i) has a value of 1; the weight of the background region, R_b, is 0; and the weight of the remaining face region, R_u, is 0.5. Due to the weighted function, only those edge points in the face region are considered when computing the Haudorff distance. These important regions for recognition have a higher weight (i.e., 1); therefore, this modified Hausdorff distance is more effective in capturing the salient features of human faces. Because the weight of the background is 0, the noise points and non-facial points in these areas will be ignored, resulting in a better noise immunity.

4. Experimental Results

The input to our automatic human face recognition system is a facial image. The system locates the position of the two eyes automatically. The face region is then normalized according to the inter-distance of the two eyes, and the weighted function for the input face can then be generated. Based on the position of the two eyes, we can also estimate the face region. The corresponding edge map of the face region is then produced and two human faces, one from the input and the other from the face gallery, are compared using the spatially weighted Hausdorff distance.

We used the ORL face database in the experiment. An upright frontal view of each of the 40 subjects with a normal facial expression was chosen in our experiment. Among the rest of the faces, 6 images for each of the 40 subjects were selected to form a pool of 240 faces as a testing set.

Figure 2 shows the cumulative recognition rates from our experiment based on automatic and manual selections of the eyes, as well as the results based on the doubly modified Hausdorff distance with manual selection. The automatic face recognition system can achieve recognition rates of 76%, 84% and 92% for the first one, the first five, and the first ten likely matched faces, respectively. The corresponding recognition rates using spatial weighted Hausdorff distance (SWHD) and "doubly" modified Hausdorff distance (W2HD) with manual selection are 82%, 95% and 98% and first one, first five and first ten likely matched faces, respectively. The experiments were conducted on a Pentium III 733MHz computer. The average runtime for detecting the eyes and recognizing a human face input from a database of 240 faces is less than two seconds: slightly less than one second for eye detection, and slightly more than one second for face recognition

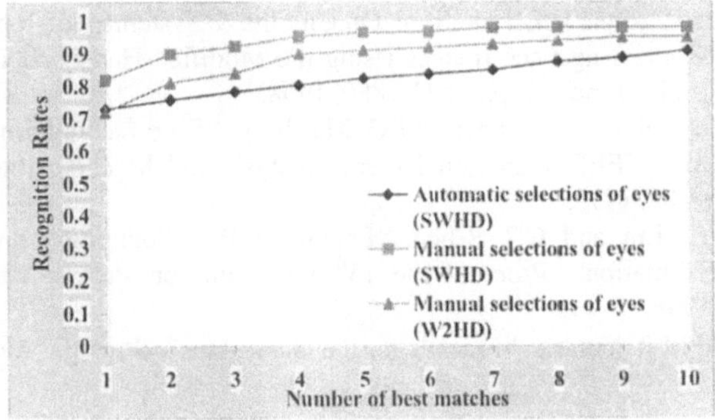

Fig. 2. Overall recognition rates using 240 testing face images.

5. Conclusion

An automatic human face recognition is proposed which combines the detection of the two eyes by fractal dimension, and face recognition by a modified Hausdorff distance. We have proposed an oriented fractal dimension to accurately extract the eye pairs. The effect of uneven lighting conditions on the left-eye and the right-eye can be reduced by normalization to a specific gray-level intensity. Moreover, when grouping a left eye candidate with a right eye candidate to form an eye pair, the oriented fractal dimension provides a higher level of matching accuracy. A spatially weighted Hausdorff distance is also proposed in this paper for human face recognition. Since different facial regions have different degrees of importance for face recognition, this new distance measure incorporates the *a priori* structure of a human face by emphasizing the important facial regions. This can reduce the effect of outliers on the image. Experimental results based on the ORL database show that our automatic human face recognition can achieve recognition rates of 76%, 84%, and 92% for the first one, the first five, the first ten likely matched faces, respectively. The corresponding recognition rates manual selection of the two eyes are 82%, 95% and 98%, and the first one, the first five and the first ten likely matched faces respectively.

References

1. K.M. Lam and H. Yan, "An analytic-to-holistic approach for face recognition based on a single front view", IEEE Trans. on Pattern Analysis and Machine Intelligence, vol. 20, no.7, pp.673-686, 1998.
2. T. Kondo and H. Yan, "Automatic human face detection and recognition under non-uniform illumination", Pattern Recognition, vol 32, no 10, pp. 1707-1718, 1999.
3. H. Liu, M. Wu, G. Jin, G. Cheng and Q. He, "An automatic human face recognition system", Optics and Lasers in Engineering, vol 30, no. 34, pp.305-314, 1998.
4. A.L. Yuille, "Deformable templates for face recognition", J. Cognitive Neuroscience, vol 3, no.1, pp. 59-70, 1991.
5. K.M. Lam, "A fast approach for detecting human faces in a complex background", ISCAS'98, Proc. of the IEEE Int. Sym. On Circuits & Systems, vol 4, pp. 85-88, 1998.
6. B. Takács, "Comparing Face Images Using the Modified Hausdorff Distance", Pattern Recognition, vol. 31, no. 12, pp.1873-1880, 1998.
7. L. Wiskott, J. Fellous, N. Kruger and C. Malsburg, "Face recognition by elastic bunch graph matching", IEEE Trans. on Pattern Analysis and Machine Intelligence, vol.19, no.7, pp. 775-779, 1997.
8. J. Feng, W.C. Lin and C.T. Chen, "Fractional Box-Counting Approach to Fractal Dimension Estimation", Proc. of the 13th Int. Conf. on Pattern Recognition, vol.2, pp.854-858, 1996.
9. P.J Saupe and M.P. Yunker, "Fractals for the classrooms", Strategic Activities Vol. One, Springer-Verlag.

Similarity Retrieval in Image Databases by Boosted Common Shape Features Among Query Images

Jiann-Jone Chen[1], Cheng-Yi Liu[1], Yea-Shuan Huang[1], and Jun-Wei Hsieh[2]

[1] E000/CCL, Industrial Technology Research Institute,
Bldg. 51, 195-11 Sec. 4, ChungHsing Rd. ChuTung, HsinChu, 310 Taiwan
{chenjj, bruceliu, yeashuan}@itri.org.tw
[2] Depart. of Electrical Engineering, Yuen-Ze Univ.,
No. 135 Yuan-Tung Rd. ChungLi, TaoYuen, Taiwan
shieh@saturn.yzu.edu.tw

Abstract. We present an on-line query mechanism for shape-based similarity retrieval of image databases. It successively boosts salient common features among query samples, in which weak classifiers are tuned and selected to contribute to a final strong classifier. The similarity between two shape samples was measured in statistic space of features, through which relative instead of absolute similarity was targeted for visual information retrieval. Experiments of query by the boosted features on thirty thousand trademark images showed that the retrieved results meet visual similarity of shape very well. Only 5 - 7 boosted features out of 100 or more were enough to represent subjective recognition on shape similarity.

1 Introduction

Content-based similarity retrieval for multimedia data becomes important after international coding standard, such as JPEG, MPEG-1, -2, had been widely used and distributed over Internet. The multimedia content description interface, MPEG-7 [1], had been proposed to provide normal descriptors for database search engine. For 2D shapes, contour-based and region-based descriptors, shown in Fig. 1, have been proposed in MPEG-7. Describing shapes of image content by contours with Fourier descriptors (FDs) [2] yields size, rotation and transition invariant descriptors for indexing. However, FDs are sensitive to noises. A multiscale, curvature scale space descriptors had been proposed to improve the stability in contour description and matching [3]. For region-based descriptors, Zernike and psuedo-Zernike moments (ZMs and PZMs) also provide size, transition and rotational invariant descriptors for similarity retrieval [4]. In general, there's no one set of universal shape descriptors could meet all specific requirements in similarity retrieval. The indexing system, though feature sets accommodated are plural, is with single similarity retrieval target. In [5], visually salient feature is determined using probabilistic distribution model of features from trademark databases, however, feedback control had not been investigated.

For similarity retrieval, each user has his definition on shape similarity that the query system usually provides relevance feedback or multi-instances to learn. In [6], the visual concept is selected according to the importance of each instance feature from user's feedback. Other learning approach could be found in [7]. We proposed to boost salient common features among query samples such that user's recognition on similarity is targeted. The boosting algorithm consistently selects weak hypotheses that are slightly better than random guessing, and the error of the final hypothesis would drops exponentially fast [8]. In general, only global shape contents are subjectively recognized for similarity measure [5]. We thus proposed to successively boost one salient common feature under the boosting framework. Similar concept can be found in [9]. In addition, when both positive and negative query images are provided, it's proper to actively choose converging positive features while excluding negative ones, which are usually sparse and diverse, passively. This paper is organized as follows. In section 2, descriptors for shape content in images are presented. Pre-processing for each image is introduced in section 3. The query mechanism by boosting salient common features is described in section 4. Simulation study is provided in section 5. Section 6 concludes the paper.

(a) (b)

Fig. 1. Shape description by (a) shape-contour and (b) shape-region.

2 Shape Descriptors

Shape descriptors are extracted from image contents according to applications of indexing. For shapes in images, we use region-based shape descriptors, Zernike and pseudo-Zernike moments [10], as the basic feature sets.

2.1 Zernike Moments

Zernike moments are defined inside the unit circle, and the radial polynomials $R_m(\rho)$ are defined as:

$$R_{mn}(\rho) = \sum_{s=0}^{\frac{(n-|m|)}{2}} (-1)^s \frac{(n-s)!}{s!(\frac{(n+|m|)}{2}-s)!(\frac{n-|m|}{2}-s)!}\rho^{n-2s}, \tag{1}$$

where $n = 0, 1, 2, \cdots, \infty, |m| \leq n$ and $n - |m|$ is even. The two-dimensional zernike moment with order n and repetition m of an image, $I(\rho, \theta)$ in polar coordinate is defined as:

$$A_{nm} = \frac{n+1}{\pi} \sum_{\rho} \sum_{\theta} [V_{nm}(\rho, \theta)]^* \cdot I(\rho, \theta), \ s.t. \ \rho \leq 1. \tag{2}$$

The Zernike basis polynomials, $V_{nm}(\rho, \theta)$, are defined as

$$V_{nm}(\rho, \theta) = R_{nm}(\rho) \cdot \exp(-jm\theta). \tag{3}$$

2.2 Pseudo-Zernike Moments

Pseudo-Zernike moments are another set of orthogonal polynomials with similar properties to Zernike polynomials. The psuedo-Zernike radial polynomials are defined as

$$R_{nm}(\rho) = \sum_{s=0}^{n-|m|} (-1)^s \frac{(2n+1-s)!}{s!(n-|m|-s)!(n+|m|+1-s)!} \rho^{n-s}. \tag{4}$$

The two-dimensional pseudo-Zernike moment can be defined similarly to (2). Normalized projections vector, $\hat{f} = \{A_{nm}\}/|A_{00}|$, of both ZMs and PZMs are the desired shape descriptors. In general, PZMs are less sensitive to noises than are ZMs.

3 Pre-processing

Both ZMs and PZMs provide orientation invariant feature for shapes. Both ZMs and PZMs are projections of signals representing shape content on a complete set of complex-values functions orthogonal on the unit disk, $x^2 + y^2 \leq 1$. To achieve transition invariance, the coordinate zero are moved to shape centroid, i.e., $(E[x_i], E[y_i])$, where $(x_i, y_i)s$ belong to points of object shape. The scale invariance is accomplished by enlarging or reducing each shape such that its zero-th order moment equals to a predetermined value. Both pre-processing steps are designed for discrimination of different shapes or identification of the same shapes, which are not quite the same when dealing with retrieval of similar shapes from image databases. For this, we intend to accommodate shape content in image with minimum bounding circle (MBC). We have devised a fast algorithm for locating the MBC of shape content, i.e., center and radius, which excludes erroneous noises, when computing ZMs and PZMs, outside the circle. Experiments show that shape features computed with the MBC center do perform better in similarity retrieval of shapes than do with shape centroid. Note that with the MBC, the projections of shape content on Zernike bases could be computed efficiently, i.e., less computation time and less erroneous noises.

4 Boosting

Shape feature sets are defined according to specific database and user's requirements. They are efficient in similarity retrieval for their applications. Nonetheless, it's clear there's no one set of universal descriptors could satisfy all requirements. In addition, users may need specific combination of features for their retrieval target, either query by multi-instance or relevance feedback. The query mechanism thus must accommodate plural features sets while being flexible in selecting proper features to figure out user's definition on shape similarity. Note that the target, by nature, of visual information retrieval is *relative* instead of *absolute* similarity. We intend to measure similarity between samples in the supervised approach, such as those in statistical space [5]. To reflect visual similarity, the on-line learning mechanism should bring up subjectively similar features among query samples for refined query. For this, we propose to choose features by boosting salient common ones to meet visual similarity.

4.1 Similarity Measurement

To measure relative similarity between shape samples in statistic space, the probability distribution of each shape feature was modelled by gamma distribution function with parameters α and β:

$$\begin{aligned} p(f_i;\alpha,\beta) &= \tfrac{1}{\beta^\alpha \Gamma(\alpha)} {f_i}^{\alpha-1} \exp(-f_i) U(f_i) \\ \Gamma(\alpha) &= \textstyle\int_a^b x^{\alpha-1} e^{-x}\, dx. \end{aligned} \tag{5}$$

The parameters,α and β could be computed from $\alpha = \frac{m_i^2}{\sigma_i^2}$ and $\beta = \frac{\sigma_i^2}{m_i}$, where m_i and σ_i are the mean and standard deviation of feature f_is of all images in database. Dissimilarity between feature value a and b thus could be measured by the following probability distance:

$$P(a,b) = \int_{\min(a,b)}^{\max(a,b)} p(f_i)\, df_i \tag{6}$$

4.2 Boosting Algorithm

The basic idea of boosting algorithm is to collect weak hypotheses to form a single highly accurate prediction rule. If weak hypotheses are slightly better than random guessing, the error of the final hypothesis would drops exponentially fast [8]. For shape-based similarity retrieval, visual perception would appreciate global instead of detailed shape contents in images [5]. This boosting algorithm is thus designed to successively select one highly deterministic feature among query shape images to output robust global classifier. We describe the boosting procedure with the following control steps:

- Input: query images $(x_1, y_1), \cdots, (x_N, y_N)$, weak learning algorithm **WeakLearn**, integer T specifying the number of iterations
- Do for $t = 1, 2, \cdots, T$:
  1. Get the distribution by: $\boldsymbol{p}^t = \frac{\boldsymbol{w}^t}{\sum_{i=1}^N w_i^t}$
  2. Call function **WeakLearn**($\boldsymbol{p}^t$) and return *one* hypothesis h_j for each feature j and compute its error

$$\varepsilon_j = \sum_{i=1}^{N} p_i^t \cdot |h_j(x_i) - y_i|. \tag{7}$$

  3. Set $h_t(\cdot) = h_k(\cdot)$, where k is feature index such that

$$\varepsilon_k = \min\{\varepsilon_j\}_{j=1,\cdots,F}. \tag{8}$$

  4. Let $\beta_t = \frac{\varepsilon_t}{1-\varepsilon_t}$ and set the new weight vector to be:

$$w_i^{t+1} = w_i^t \cdot \beta_t^{1-|h_t(x_i)-y_i|}. \tag{9}$$

- Output the hypothesis

$$h(x) = \sum_{t=1}^{T} (\log \frac{1}{\beta_t}) \cdot h_t(x) \geq \frac{1}{2} \sum_{t=1}^{T} (\log \frac{1}{\beta_t}). \tag{10}$$

The **WeakLearn** function is designed to locate the decision boundaries for each hypothesis by finding the minimum error with function $\varepsilon_j(m_i)$ in eq. 7, in which $m_j = \frac{1}{N} \sum_{i=1}^N f_j(x_i)$ and

$$h_j(\cdot) = \begin{cases} 0 & \text{if } P(f_j(x_i), m_j) \leq P_T \\ 1 & \text{otherwise,} \end{cases} \tag{11}$$

where P_T could be the constant threshold to determine whether features j of two samples are relatively similar or not. The boosting mechanism could be easily understood with the aids of Fig. 2. With P_T specifying the shaded region, the weaklearn hypotheses are designed to accommodate salient common (converging) features among query samples, such as feature of samples 1 and 2 with the hypothesis $h_l(\cdot)$ in Fig. 2 (a). Excluded samples, such as samples 3, 4 and 5 in Fig. 2 (a)(b), are weighted heavily to make them easily boosted thereafter. As seen in Fig. 2 (b), feature m of samples 4 and 5 are boosted and heavily weighted sample 3 is then targeted. Possible hypothesis could be as that shown in Fig. 4 (c). The final strong hypothesis is thus a greedy collection of deterministic weak hypotheses. Note that only positive features are plotted in Fig. 2. The weak hypothesis could accommodate negative samples as well.

5 Experiment Study

Thirty thousand registered Taiwan trademarks were collected. They contain text pattern, animal, regular geometrical shape and shapes with text et al. Each image is pre-processed by locating MBC of the trademark shape region for both normalization and feature extraction. Magnitudes of ZMs and PZMs for each sample image are computed by lookup-tables to speed up processing of database images. With order n=10, the number of ZMs and PZMs are 36 and 66, respectively. Fig. 3 shows the retrieval results of one query image in the upper-left corner. The similarity ranking is from left to right and up to down. In Fig. 3 (a), the retrieved shape images are not coherent in subjective similarity since only one query image was given. When one positive sampled were added for refined query, more visually similar shape were retrieved as shown in Fig. 3 (b). Giving more positive samples, the salient and common features were boosted and the retrieved results demonstrate convergence toward subjective similarity very well, as images shown in Fig. 3 (c) circled with dotted line.

6 Summary

We presented a query mechanism for shape-based similarity retrieval in image databases, by which salient common features among query samples are boosted successively. The rule for determining the weak hypothesis is actively choosing converging features of positive samples while excluding passively negative ones. The most distinguished functionality of the proposed method is that visual similarities could be targeted well from multiple sets of features. Experiments showed that the retrieved results by the proposed boosting algorithm meet subjective similarity very well.

7 Acknowledgements

This work was supported by Ministry of Economic Affairs of Taiwan under grant 903XS1B11 conducted by ATC/CCL/ITRI.

References

1. Overview of the MPEG-7 Standard (version 4.0), ISO/IEC JTC1/SC29/WG11 N3753, Oct. 2000.
2. C. T. Zhan, et al., "Fourier descriptors for plane closed curves," *IEEE Trans. Computer,* vol. 21, pp. 269-281, 1972.
3. F. Mokhtarian, et al., "A theory of multi-scale, curvature-based shape representation for planar curves," *IEEE Trans. Pattern Aanalysis & Machine Intelligence,* vol. 14, no. 8, pp. 789-805, 1992.
4. A. Khotanzad and Y. H. Hong, "Rotational invariant image recognition using features selected via a systematic method," *Pattern Recognition,* vol. 23, no. 10, pp. 1089-1101, 1990.

5. Y. S. Kim et al., "Content-based trademark retrieval using visually salient feature," *IEEE Proc. Comput. Vision & Pattern Recog.*, pp. 307-312, 1997.
6. J. W. Hsieh, et al., "Using relevance feedback to learn visual concepts from image instances," *IEEE Int. Conf. Image Analysis and Processing,* pp. 692-698, 1999.
7. I. El-Naqa, et al, "Image retrieval based similarity learning," *IEEE Conf. Image Processing,* vol. III, pp. 722-725, 2000.
8. Y. Freund and R. E. Schapire, "A decision-theoretic generalization of online learning and an application to boosting," *Journal of Comp. & Sys. Sci.*, 55(1): 119-139, 1997.
9. K. Tieu and P. Viola, "Boosting image retrieval," *IEEE Conf. Comput. Vision and Pattern Recog.*, vol. 1, pp. 228-235, 2000.
10. C.H. Teh, R. T. Chin, "On image analysis by the methods of moments," *IEEE Trans. Pattern Analysis & Machine Intelligence,* Vol. 10. No. 4. pp. 496-513, July 1988.

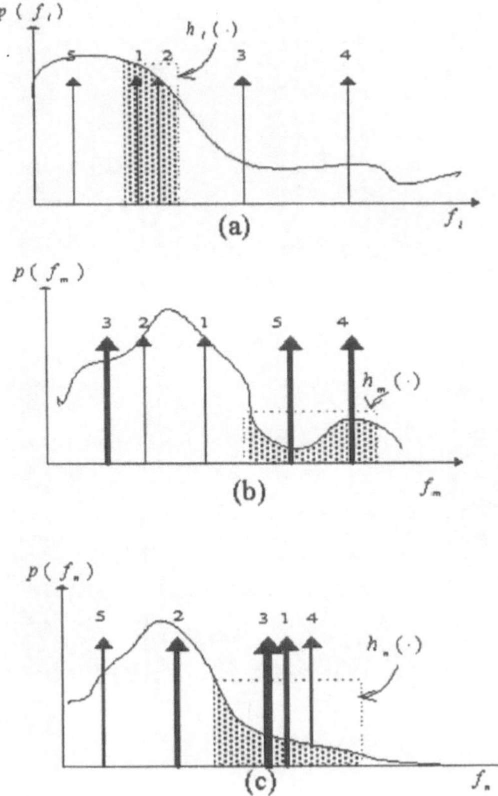

Fig. 2. Locate weak classifiers by greedily covering, while excluding negative ones, possible salient common features. The width of line denotes the weighting of the corresponding sample.

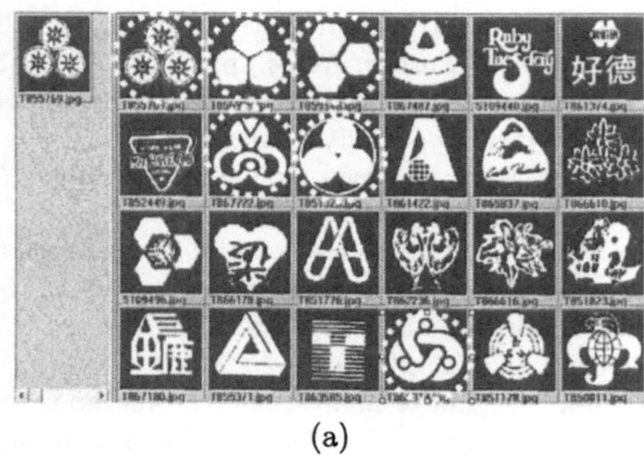

(a)

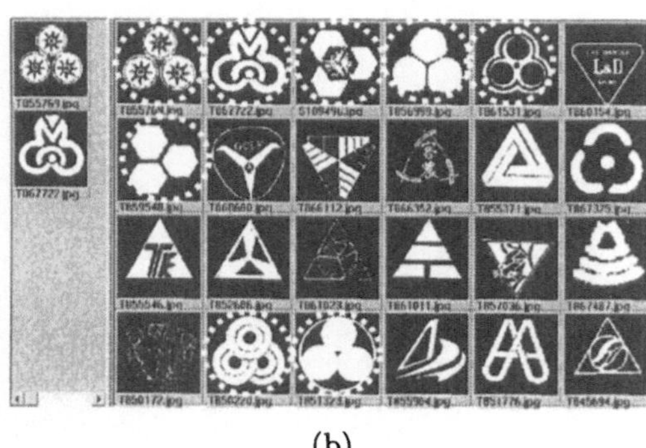

(b)

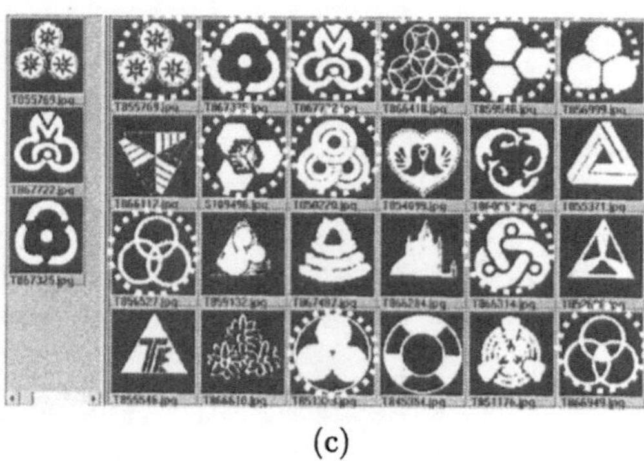

(c)

Fig. 3. Retrieved results by the boosting algorithm with (a) one, (b) two and (c) three query images. As shown, when more shape images were given, more subjectively similar shapes were retrieved by the proposed algorithm

Combining Configurational and Statistical Approaches in Image Retrieval

Huizhen Yu and W. Eric L. Grimson

Artificial Intelligence Laboratory,
Massachusetts Institute of Technology,
Cambridge, MA 02139, USA
{janey, welg}@ai.mit.edu

Abstract. We develop a framework for combining configurational and statistical approaches in image retrieval. While configurations have semantic description power, the explicit representation of an image by a set of configurations lacks the vector space structure from which the statistical feature-based representations have benefitted. That makes concept learning and prediction harder. Our framework treats configurations analogously to words occurring in a document. It combines a configuration-based approach with statistical approaches to take advantage of both the semantic description power of the former, and the simple vector-space structure of the latter.

1 Background

A key goal in image indexing is to create methods that efficiently retrieve images from large collections. Critical issues for efficient indexing are designing good image representations, and learning query concepts from user interactions.

Two alternative representation schemes are vectors and sets. When each image is mapped to a feature vector (especially with pixel-level features), learning a visual concept is transformed into a supervised learning problem (e.g., [8, 10]). Unfortunately, a vector representation poorly preserves relevant information about spatial layout, making the design of a proper metric for the vector space difficult.

In case of the set representation, images are described by the generic elements they contain. An example is the attributed graph [3], a structure composed of attributed parts (e.g. color, shape), and attributed relations such as relative brightness, relative texture change, and relative positions. We call subgraphs of these attributed graphs "configurations". This structured composition is convenient for representing contextual information in an image. It is a natural way for a user to directly specify a query concept (e.g., [6]), and has also been shown to be successful for retrieval when the configuration is representative of the scene or the appearance of the object (e.g.,[5, 2]).

* This work is supported by ITRI.

However, when the input to the system contains only labeled images (positive or negative examples), learning the common structure becomes difficult. There is some work on learning a concept under a set representation (e.g., [4, 7]). In [4], an implicit set representation was used, but the method was computationally costly, and negative examples were not used in concept learning. In [7] an explicit set representation was used by fixing the structure of the configurations and representing images by a few of the major configurations they contain. This transforms concept learning into maximum likelihood parameter estimation. However, the structure of the configuration is not as flexible as in the implicit set representation.

Inspired by the analogy of words to documents, we extend [4] using the attributed graph representation. The key idea is to derive a secondary vector representation after extracting candidate configurations. The framework can incorporate expert object detectors as well as statistical feature-based classifiers, and accounts for uncertainty in these modules.

2 An Overview

The key idea for merging configurational and statistical methods is to use a vector representation of images, based not on pixel qualities, but rather on the occurrence of configurations. We obtain a "secondary" feature vector for each image, where feature i corresponds to "whether configuration i has occurred in it." The value of features can be binary, or continuous (e.g., a probability, or similarity measure.)

Given this approach, we preprocess the database by computing an attributed graph for every image, based on a color segmentation of the image. The component attributes we use are HSV color and shape moments of regions. The attributed relation is the direction between two neighboring regions, and the assumption we make is that vertical order is important while horizontal order is not. Upon query, the system extracts candidate configurations from example images and trains an inference module to softly select among these configurations. Then it predicts over the dataset to retrieve relevant images.

The main challenge is speed, because these "secondary" features can only be constructed at the query step, and the comparison between them involves graph checking steps performed on each image. Since graph matching is NP complete, finding relevant configurations requires a fast greedy algorithm. We pairwise sample example images to feed to this matching algorithm. We describe finding configurations and the structure of the inference module below.

3 Extract Informative Configurations

Finding common patterns between images can be formulated as a subgraph isomorphism problem when only binary relations between regions are considered, and more generally a relational homomorphism where relations can be N-ary. (See [3] for a comprehensive analysis of such approaches.)

Two major differences between the traditional problem setting and our case make old algorithms not suitable here. First, one graph is usually a model that needs to be found in the second graph. But in our case the common subgraph may be partial to both graphs. The second difference is that fixing the matching range of the component attributes is not suitable here, for objects/scenes can have large variability in appearance, due to lighting changes, for example. This range should be determined adaptively from the common subgraph, thus creating a self loop. Because of these difficulties, as well as the high computational demand of on-line response, we use an extension of the maximal clique method for extracting common subgraphs, whose attributes are then naturally determined by the matching.

The maximum clique method has previously been used in model based registration [1], and a key conclusion is to form a set of good hypotheses based on consistent matching. Our method first constructs a decision graph $G = (V, E, h)$. Each vertex $v \in V$ assigns a pair of neighboring regions in one image to a pair in another image. To relax the constraint of hard assignments, we introduce a height label $h(v) \in [0, 1]$ for each vertex. It indicates the quality of the assignments, and is constructed to be a continuous function of the similarity (measured by the color and shape attributes) between corresponding regions and the angle between the vertical directions of the two pairs. Two vertices are considered compatible if their assignments satisfy the one-to-one matching constraint. Two compatible vertices share an edge, i.e., $E = \{(v_1, v_2) \mid v_1,\ v_2 \text{ are compatible.}\}$. Beginning from a height level, the maximal cliques are found on the induced decision graph. They form a set of hypotheses regarding possible matches. The details of the algorithm are listed in Fig. 1. Between the clique growing stages, several criteria (e.g., large contrast or scale) are used to further select informative configurations. In the image plane, we can think of it as growing configurations from the best matching spots. The stopping criterion can be the size of the cliques or the height of the induced graph. Figure 2 shows an example of snowy mountain configuration selected by the largest contrast criterion. Note the two subgraphs are almost horizontal reflections of each other.

Given: clique-selecting agents; a stopping criterion;
a decision graph $G = (V, E, h)$;
Initialize: $h = h_0$; step δh; $\{C_i\} = \emptyset$;
Repeat until satisfying the stopping criterion:

1. G_h = subgraph of G induced by $\{v \in V \mid h(v) > h_0\}$;
2. $\{C_j\}$ = maximal cliques grown from C_i in G_h;
3. $\{C_j\}$ = selected cliques from $\{C_i\}$ by the clique-selecting agents;
4. $h = h - \delta h$; go to 1.

Fig. 1. Extended maximal clique algorithm.

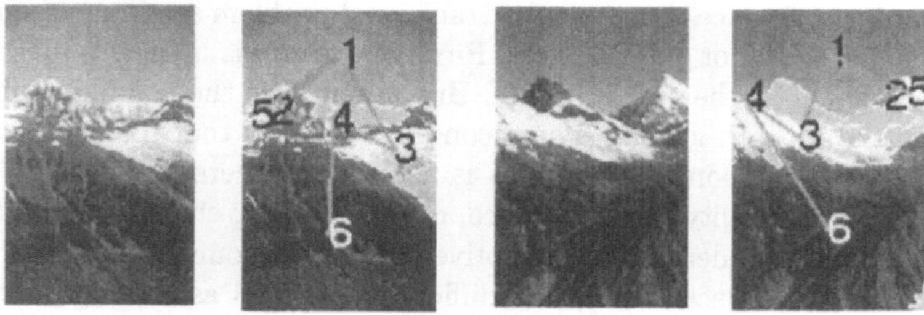

Fig. 2. An extracted common subgraph superimposed on the original images with non-matched regions blanked out.

Ideally, we should take the extracted configuration in whole and find its best match in each image from the database. But for large databases, doing even greedy graph matching is too expensive. We therefore break the configurations into smaller parts, each a superclique induced by one component and its edges, so that the checking algorithm only needs to find the "dominant" region and then check the compatibility of its neighbors.[1] It is worth to note that this flexibility is also due to the following learning module that selects reliable detectors.

4 Concept Learning and Predicting

Once we have a set of candidate configurations, the simplest vector representation would be binary bits, each indicating the occurrence of the corresponding configuration in an image. Unlike words occurring in documents, this is not suitable for visual tasks because of the uncertainty in the measurements. A direct extension is mapping an image into a real valued feature vector, where each feature indicates the probability of the occurrence of the corresponding configuration. We now describe formally the procedure of concept learning and making predictions, beginning from the simplest setting.

4.1 A Naive Setting

Let S^+, S^- be the set of positive and negative images respectively, and $S = S^+ \cup S^-$. Let Y be the class label (1/0 for positive/negative), and $\{C_i\}_1^n$ the configurations extracted from the previous stage. We define X_i to be 1 if C_i occurred, 0 otherwise. If x_i is obtainable from the graph matching algorithm, the observations $(\hat{x}_1^j, \ldots, \hat{x}_n^j, \hat{y}^j)$ for each example image $j \in S$ form a training set for the inference network. After training, the network can predict Y for an unlabeled observation $(x_1, \ldots, x_n)$ in the database, thus classifying or ranking images according to the posterior probabilities.

[1] Alternatively, we could maintain them as one configuration, but allow the checking algorithm approximately "find" that configuration.

4.2 Allow Uncertain Measurements

In practice, the matching algorithm cannot make binary decisions with complete certainty. Assigning real values can indicate quality of match. To allow this uncertainty and at the same time not increase the complexity of training the inference network, we use the network shown in Fig. 3. A difference to the previous model is that the values of X_is are now unobservable.

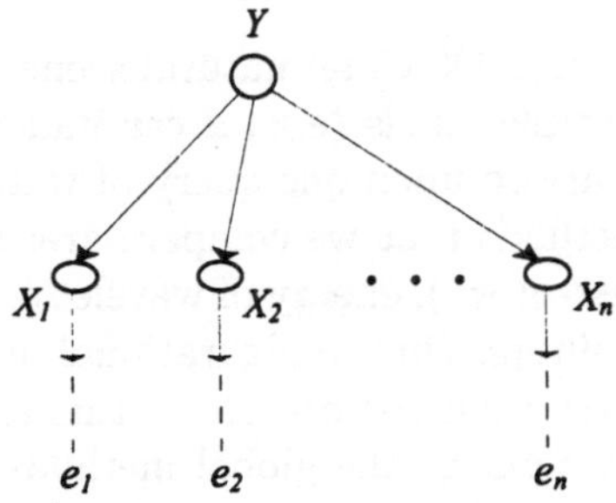

Fig. 3. Naive Bayesian network with latent variables.

For each configuration C_i, we model the associated graph checking algorithm as an autonomous agent [9] from whom we receive information, but have no clear knowledge of how this information is gathered. The *dummy node* e_i represents the virtual evidence "observed" from an image by the checking algorithm, who then reports us the likelihood ratio $P(e_i \mid X_i = 1) : P(e_i \mid X_i = 0)$.

Denoting all evidence by e, and assuming uniform prior on class labels,

$$P(Y \mid e) \propto \prod_i \sum_{x_i} P(e_i \mid x_i)\, P(x_i \mid Y) . \tag{1}$$

Therefore, the likelihood ratio $\frac{P(e_i|X_i=1)}{P(e_i|X_i=0)}$ suffices for calculating the posterior probabilities $P(Y \mid e)$.

The parameters, $P(X_i \mid Y)$, are estimated in training by (Expectation-Maximization (EM). Let $\theta_{i1} = P(X_i = 1 \mid Y = 1)$, $\theta_{i0} = P(X_i = 1 \mid Y = 0)$. The updating rules are:

$$\theta_{i1}^{(t+1)} = \frac{1}{|S^+|} \sum_{j \in S^+} P(X_i = 1 \mid Y{=}1, e_i^j, \theta_i^{(t)}) , \tag{2}$$

$$\theta_{i0}^{(t+1)} = \frac{1}{|S^-|} \sum_{j \in S^-} P(X_i = 1 \mid Y{=}0, e_i^j, \theta_i^{(t)}) , \tag{3}$$

where

$$P(x_i \mid y, e_i, \theta_i) = \frac{P(x_i \mid y)\, P(e_i \mid x_i)}{\sum_{x_i'} P(x_i' \mid y)\, P(e_i \mid x_i')} . \tag{4}$$

Again, only the likelihood ratios between $P(e_i \mid x_i)$ are needed to calculate (4).

After training, we can eliminate less informative features, for example, features s.t. $P(x_i \mid Y = 1) = P(x_i \mid Y = 0)$. With k configurations being deactivated from the configuration set, we save k graph checking steps per image in the database, thus speeding up the predicting process.

5 Experiments

We have tested the system on 1000 Corel natural scene images. They are manually labeled and have multiple labels (e.g., a car under the sunset). Figure 4 shows a performance comparison upon one query of waterfall scene. The global statistical feature-based methods that we compare are: histogram on opponent color space (denoted as "hist-rgby"), energy of wavelet coefficients and energy of the responses from Gabor filters. Our configurational approach (labeled "Config") does significantly better than the others. In this experiment, no methods get negative examples (the input to the global methods is one image from the two images given to our system.) Without negative images, our system forges negative points complementary to the positive vectors at its training stage, which is equivalent to weighting candidate configurations equally when no evidence so far indicates bias.

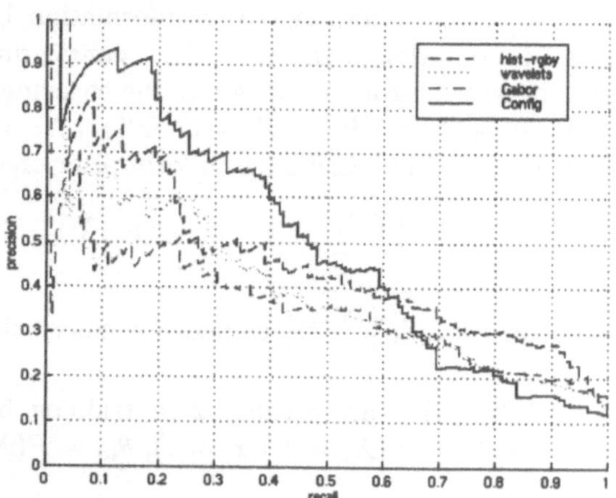

Fig. 4. Comparison on a waterfall example.

Figure 5 and 6 demonstrates how negative examples help selecting discriminative configurations. In Fig. 5, an extracted common subgraph is superimposed on one of the two example images.[2] Seeing only two examples, the system believes

[2] Note the two connected components in this subgraph correspond to only one optimal clique in the decision graph.

all the supercliques, configuration C_1 to C_6, are equally important. Figure 6(a) shows the retrieved images. The decimal numbers above each image are the log posterior probabilities. Given additional 5 examples (among which 3 negatives are 841, 582 and 435), the system deactivates C_5 and C_6 as less informative, and penalizes for containing C_4. Non-waterfall images having this white-white pattern will thus be penalized much more than waterfall images that also have pattern C_1 to C_3, which, translated to our language, are describing the concept as a vertical white region with dark and green surround. The improved retrieval result is shown in Fig. 6(b).

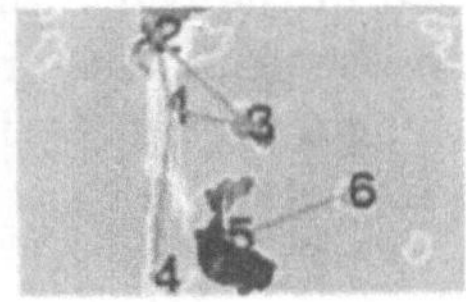

Fig. 5. A waterfall configuration.

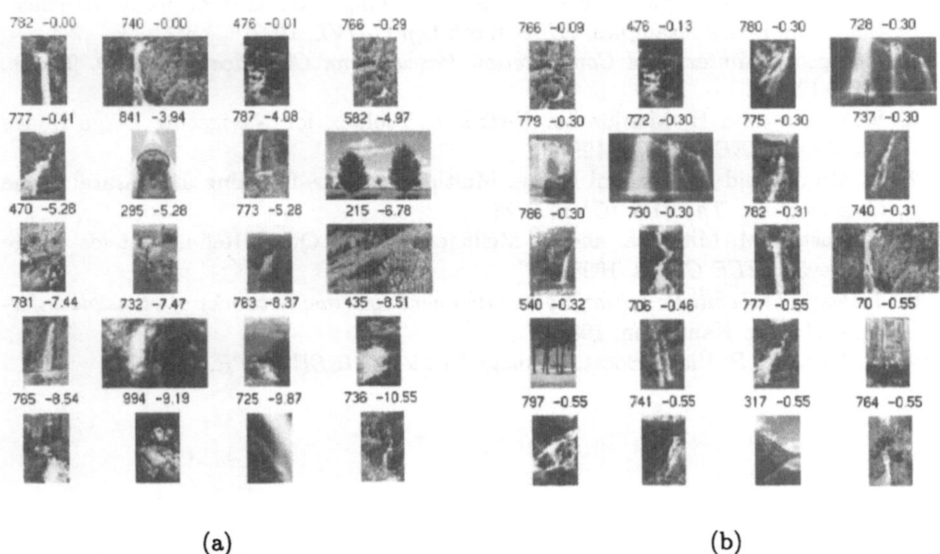

Fig. 6. Retrieval results without(left) and with(right) negative examples.

6 Discussion

The work presented here exploits the richness in the structured description of visual contents as well as the simplicity of a vector representation. An advantage of the framework is that it separates decision from the inexactness in modeling and the uncertainty in measurements. It uses an inference process to judge from the training data which subgraphs, together with their detectors, are reliable indicators for prediction. This is beneficial when perfect detectors are not obtainable (e.g., due to inaccurate image segmentation), or not affordable due to efficiency reasons.

We consider the limitation of the current work to be the conditional independence assumption in the Naive Bayesian network. We are working towards handling correlation between detectors, as well as improving both the representation and the learning algorithm by incorporating statistical features and prior information in a systematic way.

References

1. R.C. Bolles and R.A. Cain. Recognizing and Locating Partially Visible Objects. *The International Journal of Robotics Research*, Vol. 1, Num. 3, 1982.
2. M. Das, E. Riseman, and B. Draper. FOCUS: Searching for Multi-colored Objects in a Diverse Image Database, *IEEE CVPR*, 1997.
3. R. Haralick, and L. Shapiro. *Computer and Robot Vision*, Addison-Wesley, 1992.
4. A. Lakshmi Ratan, and W.E.L. Grimson. Training Templates for Scene Classification using a Few Examples, *IEEE Workshop CAIVL*, 1997.
5. P. Lipson. *Context and Configuration Based Scene Classification*, Ph.D. Thesis, MIT, 1996.
6. W.Y. Ma, and B. Manjunath. NeTra: A Toolbox for Navigating Large Image Databases. *IEEE CVPR*, 1997.
7. O. Maron, and A. Lakshmi Ratan. Multiple Instance Learning for Natural Scene Classification. *The 11th ICML*, 1998.
8. C. Nastar, M. Mitschke, and C. Meilhac. Efficient Query Refinement for Image Retrieval, *IEEE CVPR*, 1998.
9. J. Pearl. *Probabilistic reasoning in intelligent systems: networks of plausible inference*, Morgan Kaufmann, 1988.
10. K. Tieu and P. Viola. Boosting Image Retrieval, *IEEE CVPR*, 2000.

Digital Image Coding with Hybrid Wavelet Packet Transform

Pei-Yuan Huang and Long-Wen Chan

Department of Computer Science
National Tsing Hua University
Hsinchu, Taiwan, Republic of China
lchang@cs.nthu.edu.tw

Abstract. The hybrid wavelet packet improves the performance of wavelet packet transform by choosing appropriate quadrature mirror filters. Therefore, it is proposed for digital image compression in this paper. We use a top-down scheme to optimize the hybrid wavelet packet and the wavelet coefficients are quantized with a successive approximation algorithm and then coded with context-based arithmetic coding. Experimental result shows that the proposed algorithm has better performance than SPIHT and EZW for images with complex texture.

1 Introduction

Wavelet transform based image coding has a better performance than the DCT-based method. Several wavelet-transform based methods, such asembedded zerotree wavele EZW [1], set partitioning in hierarchical trees SPIHT [2], and morphological representation wavelet data MRWD [3] have been proposed to exploit the spatial oriented tree structure proposed by Shapiro[1]. It performs very well for compressing the common image, however, it is not suitable for the image containing much texture. In contrast to the wavelet transform, wavelet packets[4] can do further decomposition on any subband rather than only on the low frequency band. For this reason, wavelet packets can provide rich library of wavelet packet bases and are suitable for the analysis of non-stationary signals.

The hybrid wavelet packet transform improves the performance of wavelet packet transform by choosing appropriate QMFs [5-6]. The choice of appropriate QMF is not only signal dependent, but also scale dependent. It can provide a richer library of wavelet packet bases. To select the best basis over all possible wavelet packet bases of the given image we use the top-down method to prune the wavelet packet tree with the cost function of entropy. In order to generate the embedded bit stream for progressive transmission we reorder the transformed coefficients with successive approximation quantization to construct a prioritized quantization scheme. This leads to simple implementation and high coding efficiency for progressive transmission.

2. The Proposed Image Coding with Hybrid Wavelet Packet

The coding algorithm with the hybrid wavelet packet transform can produce an embedded bit stream for progressive transmission. The basic concept is the order-by-magnitude transmission which is used by Huang's partition priority coding for progressive DCT image compression [8] and by Shapiro's embedded coding property of bit-plane [1]. The bits conveying more significant information are in front of the bit stream. In the hybrid wavelet packet analysis, given m filter banks, the number of bases contained in an the L+1 level is given recursively by $B_{L+1} = m(B_L{}^2 + 1)$, where B_L is the number of bases at the level L. Thus, we must do some modification of the algorithm in [9] for best basis selection. Note that the information cost in is the first-order entropy of wavelet coefficients H(S). The top-down algorithm for best basis selection [7] is given as below:

1. We apply the hybrid wavelet packet transform on the original image. Each time we adopt m QMF pairs to the hybrid wavelet packet tree analysis. For each node, there are m children branches corresponding to the wavelet coefficients that result from the application of the m QMF pairs. Every branch is composed of four nodes. The procedure begins at the root node as the first parent node, which corresponds to the image.

2. The entropy of each children branch of a parent node is computed. If any branch has not the entropy less than the parent's, all m branches are pruned; otherwise the four nodes of the branch with the lowest entropy are chosen as new nodes in the next level and all other m-1 branches are pruned. We also have to record the associated quadrature mirror filters(QMFs).

This method is then only applied to those new nodes in the next level from left to right recursively until the expected level is reached and all nodes are traversed.

2.1 Scanning Order of Wavelet Coefficients

In the progressive transmission, the large significant coefficients should be transmitted first then the small significant coefficients are refined later. The coefficients in the coarser scale represent the kernel of the image. As long as these coefficients are lost, the image has serious distortion. Therefore, the scan order is from coarse to fine. It means that the LL band must first be scanned then the HL, LH, and HH band according to the optimal hybrid wavelet packet tree. However, in the same frequency band, the scan order is in raster scan. The scan orde of the wavelet coefficient is denoted as $S_{i,j}$, $0 \le i, j \le N-1$, where NxN is the size of the image.

In priority progressive transmission [8], the transformed coefficients are ordered by their magnitude in the order that the largest coefficient is encoded first. The wavelet-transform based coding algorithm such as EZW and SPIHT also follow this spirit but use some different way to deal with these coefficients. The prioritized coding schemes are suitable for embedded image coding. A coefficient $S_{i,j}$ is called significant if it is greater than or equals to the threshold Q, otherwise it is called insignificant. The insignificant coefficient is implicitly quantized to zero by the threshold Q. We can generate the embedded sequence by allowing non-uniform quantization. In the successive partition coder, the magnitude range R of the wavelet coefficients is divided into several variable-sized partitions $\{L_i\}$, where $L_i = \{m \mid 2^{n-i-1} \le m < 2^{n-i}\}$.Let $\{L_0, L_1, L_2 .... L_n\}$ be the partitions on the magnitude range M of the wavelet coefficient $S_{i,j}$ where $0 \le |S_{i,j}| \le M$ such that L_i are disjoint nonempty and bound by 2^{n-i-1} to 2^{n-i} where $n = ceiling[\log_2(\max(|S_{i,j}|))], 1 \le i, j \le N-1$. For each partition step, we use the different step sized quantizer $\{Q_0, Q_1, Q_2 ...... Q_n\}$, where $Q_i = Q_{i-1}/2$. The initial threshold Q_0 is chosen as the power of two and has to satisfy $|S_{i,j}| < 2Q_0, 1 \le i, j \le N-1$.

Each L_i can be viewed as a quantization pass. In each pass, the coefficients compare with the current threshold to determine their significance. If $|S_{i,j}| \in L_i$, $S_{i,j}$ is significant and 1 is encoded followed by the sign bit to indicate its significance. Then, the residue $R_{i,j} = |S_{i,j}| - LB(L_i)$ is put to the list to be refined in the next quantization pass, where $LB(L_i)$ stands for the lower bound of L_i. The bit stream is generated by encoding the bit plane which consist of the bits contributed from each coefficient with arithmetic coding. In the encoding pass, we encode one bit of each coefficient from the most significant bit to the less significant bit. The magnitude bit and sign bit are encoded with different context models applied in arithmetic coding. The encoding process stops until all bits of coefficient are encoded.

In our coding procedure, we also use the context-based arithmetic coding scheme [10-12], which is used for the bi-level image compression to encode them.

3. Experimental Results

In our simulation, we use are biorthogonal 7-tap filter, 12-tap Coiflet filter, and 6-tap Daubechies filter. Figures 1 (a) and (b) show the magnified view of an area of the boat imag at 0.25 bit/pixel for EZW and the proposed coder, respectively. Figure 2 (a), (b) shows the magnified view of thr Babara's right leg of the reconstructed Babara image at 0.25 bit/pixel with SPIHT and thr proposed algorithm, respectively. From above observations, we find our coder with hybrid wavelet packet transform could preserve the texture of the image much better than SPIHT. It is because the hybrid wavelet packet can better match the texture than wavelet transform.

4. Conclusion

Our coding algorithm based on the hybrid wavelet packet which allows multiple quadrature mirror filters to be used is adapted for any images. The top-down best basis selection scheme is used to save the time and memory for the exhaustive search process.. From the experimental results we can see that our coder always has better performance than SPIHT for the image with much texture. Besides, our coder also has better performance than the coder which uses the wavelet packet transform.

References

[1] J. M. Shapiro, "Embedded Image Coding Using Zerotrees of Wavelet Coefficients", IEEE Transaction on Signal Processing, vol. 41, no. 12 pp. 3445-3462, December 1993.

[2] A. Said and W. A. Perlman, " A New, Fast, and Efficient Image Codec Based on Set Partitioning in Hierarchical Trees", IEEE Transaction on Circuits and System for Video Technology, vol. 6, no. 3 pp.243-250, June 1996.

[3]Servetto, S.; Ramchandran, K.; Orchard, M. ,"Morphological Representation of Wavelet Data for image coding", Acoustics, Speech, and Signal Processing, 1995. ICASSP-95., 1995 International Conference on vol. 4 , PP. 2229 –2232, 1995.

[4]R. Coifman, Y. Meyer, S. Quake and V. Wickerhauser, "Signal processing and compression with wavelet packet", Numerical Algorithm Research Group, Yale University, April 1990

[5]R. A. Hedges and D. Cochran, "Hybrid wavelet packets: a top down approach", 1998. Conference Record of the Thirty-Second Asilomar Conference on Signals, Systems & Computers , Vol. 2 , 1998 , pp. 1381 –1385.

[6] R. A. Hedgess, "Hybrid wavelet packet analysis", in Proceedings of the IEEE-SP International Symposium on Time-Frequency and Time-Scale Analysis, 1998.

[7]A.S. Lewis and G. Knowles, "Image Compression Using the 2-D Wavelet Transform", IEEE Transaction on Image Processing, vol. 1, no. 2, pp. 224-250, April 1992.

[8]Y. Huang, H. M. Drizen, and N. P. Galatsanos, "Prioritized DCT for Compression and Progressive Transmission of Images", IEEE Transaction on Image Processing, vol. 1, no. 4, October 1992

[9]R. Coifman and V. Wickerhauser, "Entropy-Based Algorithms for Best Basis Selection", IEEE Transaction on Information Theory, vol. 38, no. 2, pp. 713-718, March 1992.

[10]H. Witten, R. M. Neal and J. G. Cleary, "Arithmetic Coding for Data Compression", Comm. ACM, vol. 30, pp. 520-540, June 1987.

[11]Xiaolin Wu, and Nasir Memon, "Context-Based, Adaptive, Lossless Image Coding", IEEE Transaction on Communications, vol 45, no. 4, pp. 437-444, April 1997.

[12]S.Y. Wang, K.W. Cheung, C. H. Cheung, L. M. Po, "Embedded Lossless Wavelet-Based Image Coding algorithm with Successive Partitioning and Hybrid bit scanning", IEEE Signal Processing Society 1999 Workshop on Multimedia Signal Processing September 1999, Copenhagen, Denmark

(a)

(b)

Fig. 1 (a) The EZW coder. (b) Our proposed coder.

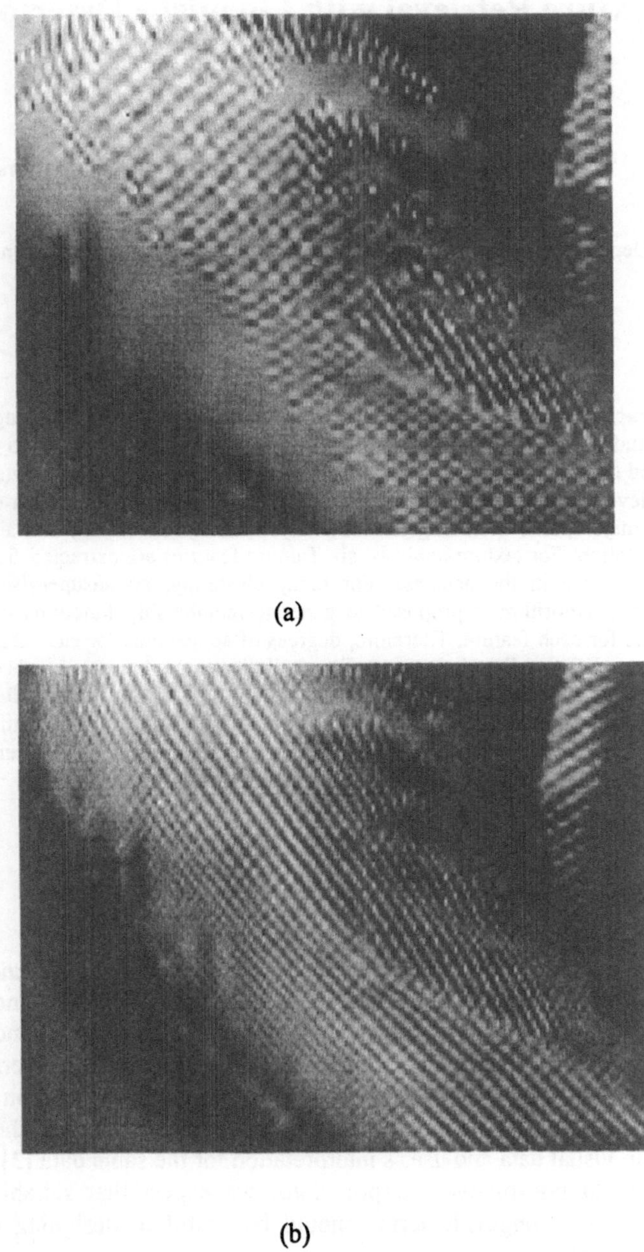

(a)

(b)

Fig. 2 (a) The SPIHT coder. (b) Our proposed coder.

Texture Retrieval with Linguistic Descriptions[1]

Chih-Yi Chiu[1], Hsin-Chih Lin[2], Shi-Nine Yang[1]

[1] Department of Computer Science, National Tsing Hua University, Hsinchu, Taiwan 300, ROC
{cychiu, snyang}@cs.nthu.edu.tw
[2] Department of Information Management, Chang Jung Christian University, Tainan, Taiwan 711, ROC
hclin@mail.cju.edu.tw

Abstract. A texture retrieval system with linguistic descriptions is proposed in this study. Users can pose textural descriptions or visual examples to find the desired texture. A mapping mechanism between low-level statistic features and high-level semantic information is formulated. The proposed system contains three major parts, including texture analysis, fuzzy clustering, and similarity computation. For texture-analysis, six Tamura features are extracted from each texture image in the database. For fuzzy clustering, an unsupervised fuzzy clustering algorithm is proposed to generate membership functions with five degrees for each feature. Therefore, degrees of appearance for each feature are interpreted as five linguistic terms. For similarity computation, a user's query is first translated into a query matrix through the generated membership functions. A similarity metric is proposed to compute the similarity between the query matrix and feature matrix of corresponding texture images. Several empirical tests are given to demonstrate the performance of the proposed system.

1 Introduction

In content-based image retrieval, perceptual features of images are known as color, texture, shape, spatial layout, and so on [1]. According to MPEG-7 standard [2], these perceptual features are the lowest abstraction level called descriptors and the semantic information of the media object belongs to the highest level. However, the mapping between low-level image features and high-level semantic information is not trivial. The semantic gap comes from the lack of consistence between the information extracted from visual data and user's interpretation for the same data [3]. As linguistic descriptions yield informative interpretations, we expect that suitable methods to transfer images into linguistic terms should be useful in designing content-based image retrieval systems.

The Picasso system [4] used Itten's color language to expresses the semantics associated with the combination of chromatic properties of color images. Comparing with color, texture is more difficult to express in words. Many research efforts have

[1] This study was supported partially by National Science Council, R.O.C. under Grant NSC89-2218-E-309-001 and Ministry of Education, R.O.C. under Grant 89-E-FA04-1-4

been made to characterize textures through a set of features in either the spatial or frequency domain. However, little semantic referent is offered in visual perception. Tamura *et al.* [5] proposed six basic visual features for a texture, including coarseness, contrast, directionality, line-likeness, regularity, and roughness. The Photobook system [6] proposed following three Wold features for a texture: periodicity, directionality, and randomness. Both Tamura and Wold features are related to human visual perception. Mojsilovic *et al.* [7] proposed five perceptual criteria (vocabularies) used in the comparison among color patterns, as well as a set of rules (grammars) governing the use of these criteria in similarity judgment. The vocabulary and grammar can provide a simple linguistic description for visual qualities of textures.

In this study we propose a novel system for texture retrieval. The six Tamura features are extracted for each image in the database. For each statistic feature, an unsupervised fuzzy clustering algorithm is proposed to generate membership functions. Then the system will automatically produce linguistic descriptions for textures according to membership functions. For query, users can describe the desired textures with linguistic terms, such as "fine and very regular," to find textures with similar degree of descriptions. Accordingly, it provides not only the low-level texture features but also the high-level semantic information. The proposed system is composed of construction phase and query phase. The construction phase contains texture analysis and fuzzy clustering. The query phase allows users to pose linguistic descriptions or visual examples to find the target texture images in the database. Fig. 1 shows the proposed system architecture.

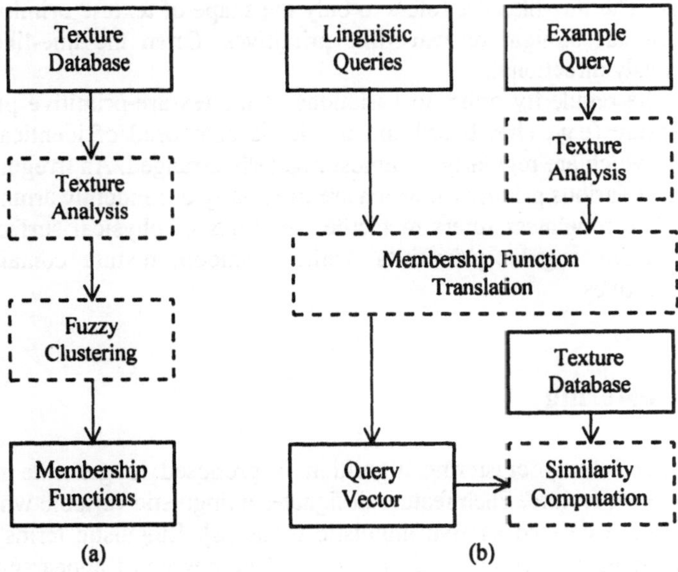

Fig. 1. (a) Construction phase (off-line). (b) Query phase (on-line)

The rest of this paper is organized as follows. Section 2, 3, and 4 present three major parts of the system, including texture analysis, fuzzy clustering, and similarity computation, respectively. Section 5 reports on experimental results and performances. Conclusions and future work are given in the last section.

2 Texture Analysis

The six Tamura features, including coarseness, contrast, directionality, line-likeness, regularity, and roughness, are extracted from each texture image in the database. Definitions and computational procedures of the six features can be found in [5]. We summarize visual properties of the six features as follows:

Coarseness: The coarseness is the most fundamental feature in analyzing a texture. This feature refers to the size and number of texture primitives. A coarse texture contains a small number of large primitives, while a fine texture contains a large number of small primitives.

Contrast: The contrast stands for image quality in the narrow sense. This feature refers to the difference in intensity between neighboring pixels. A texture of high contrast has large difference in intensity between neighboring pixels, while a texture of low contrast has small difference.

Directionality: The directionality is a global property over the given region. This feature refers to the shape of texture primitives and their placement rule. A directional texture has one or more recognizable orientation of primitives.

Line-likeness: The line-likeness refers to only the shape of texture primitives. A line-like texture has straight or wave-like primitives. Often the line-like texture is simultaneously directional.

Regularity: The regularity refers to variations of the texture-primitive placement. A regular texture (e.g., chessboard and textile) is composed of identical or similar primitives, which are regularly or almost regularly arranged. An irregular texture is composed of various primitives, which are irregularly or randomly arranged.

Roughness: The roughness refers to tactile variations of physical surface. A rough texture contains angular primitives, while a smooth texture contains rounded blurred primitives.

3 Fuzzy Clustering

An unsupervised fuzzy clustering algorithm is proposed to generate membership functions for each feature. Each feature designates a linguistic variable whose degrees of appearance are defined as five linguistic terms [8]. Linguistic terms for the six linguistic variables are summarized in Table 1. The degree of appearance increases from left to right in this table. The linguistic term is considered as a fuzzy set, which is represented as a triangular membership function. The proposed fuzzy clustering algorithm is given as follows.

Linguistic Variables	Linguistic Terms				
Coarseness	very fine	fine	medium on coarse	coarse	very coarse
Contrast	very low on contrast	low on contrast	medium on contrast	high on contrast	very high on contrast
Directionality	very non-directional	non-directional	medium on directional	directional	very directional
Line-likeness	very blob-like	blob-like	medium on line-like	line-like	very line-like
Regularity	very irregular	irregular	medium on regular	regular	very regular
Roughness	very smooth	smooth	medium on rough	rough	very rough

Table 1. Linguistic terms for the six linguistic variables

Fuzzy Clustering Algorithm
Input: Feature values $x_1, x_2, \ldots, x_n$ of a linguistic variable in given database containing n texture images.
Output: Membership functions with five linguistic terms for the linguistic variable.

1. Initialize five evenly distributed triangular membership functions (see Fig. 2).

$$c_j = c_{\min} + \frac{j}{6} \times (c_{\max} - c_{\min}). \tag{1}$$

   where $c_1, c_2, \ldots, c_5$ denote class centers of the initial fuzzy partition, c_{min}= min(x_1, $x_2, \ldots, x_n$), c_{max} = max($x_1, x_2, \ldots, x_n$), j = 1, 2, 3, 4, 5.

2. Set membership matrix $U = 0$. For each pattern x_i, update the membership value u_{ij} using one of the following rules, where u_{ij}, $1 \le i \le n$, $1 \le j \le 5$, denotes the i-th pattern belongs to the j-th linguistic term.
   Rule 1. If $x_i \le c_1$, $u_{i,1} = 1$ and $u_{i,k\neq 1} = 0$.
   Rule 2. If $c_j < x_i \le c_{j+1}$, compute

$$u_{ij} = \frac{c_{j+1} - x_i}{c_{j+1} - c_j}, \; u_{i,j+1} = 1 - u_{ij}, \text{ and } u_{i,k\neq j,j+1} = 0. \tag{2}$$

   Rule 3. If $x_i > c_5$, $u_{i,k\neq 5} = 0$ and $u_{i,5} = 1$

3. Compute $c_1, c_2, \cdots, c_5$ using the following equation:

$$c_i = \frac{\sum_{j=1}^{n} u_{ij} x_j}{\sum_{j=1}^{n} u_{ij}}. \tag{3}$$

   If $c_1, c_2, \cdots, c_5$ are unchanged, the algorithm stops; otherwise go to Step 2.

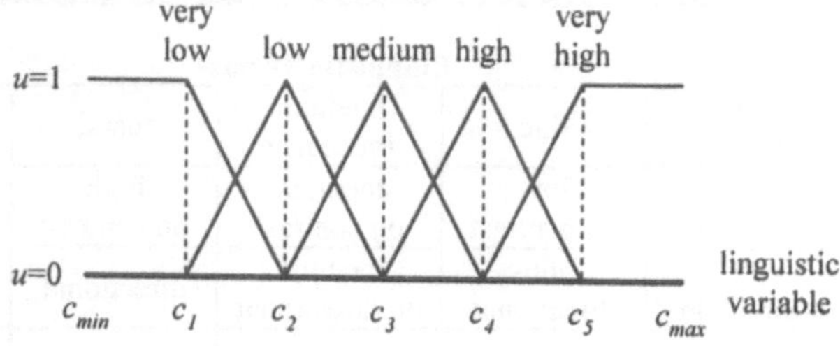

Fig. 2. Initial membership functions with five linguistic terms for a linguistic variable

The proposed algorithm obtains all membership functions for the six Tamura features. The membership vectors of each texture images in the database are then computed through the generated membership functions. The description of the texture depends on its membership vectors. For example, the contrast membership vector of the image D3 in Fig. 4 is (0, 0, 0, 0.92, 0.08), which is classified in linguistic term as "high on contrast". Fig. 3 shows the two-dimensional spatial distribution of some texture images after fuzzy clustering. In this figure, the horizontal axis represents the coarseness dimension, whereas the vertical axis represents the contrast dimension. Each texture image, together with its Tamura features and linguistic terms, is organized and stored in an image database for further applications.

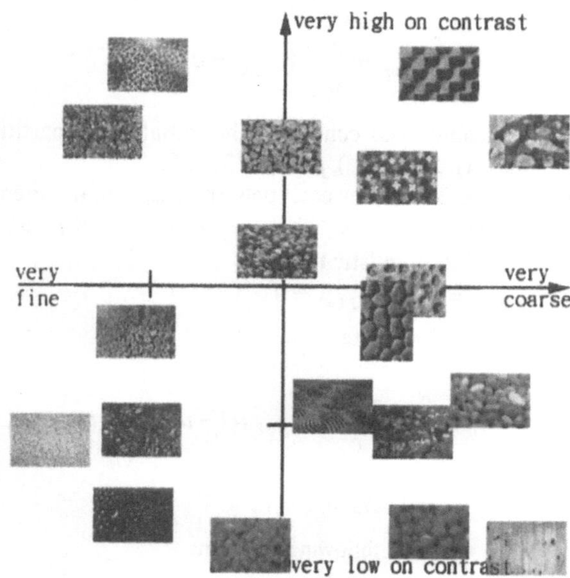

Fig. 3. Two-dimensional spatial distribution of some textures

4 Similarity Computation

The proposed system offers two query methods to retrieve textures: one is based on linguistic descriptions and the other is based on visual examples.

First, we associate each image in the database a feature matrix *FM* by collecting all its membership vectors. In other words, the membership vector of the *i*-th feature of the image is assigned to the *i*-th row of the matrix *FM*. When posing a linguistic description, a user can select some target features and their respective linguistic terms for query condition. Then each linguistic term is translated into a membership vector. Finally these membership vectors are formed a query matrix *QM*. For example, users may specify a linguistic query such as "very fine and medium on contrast." Then the corresponding query matrix is shown as follows:

$$\begin{bmatrix} 1 & 0 & 0 & 0 & 0 \\ 0 & 0 & 1 & 0 & 0 \\ * & * & * & * & * \\ * & * & * & * & * \\ * & * & * & * & * \\ * & * & * & * & * \end{bmatrix}$$

Note that the membership vector of unspecified features are recorded as (* * * * *).

When issuing a visual example, users can select a sample image together with some features as the query condition. Then system computes the query matrix to perform the query. According to the query condition, each feature value is converted into membership vector and the query matrix.

To measure the degree of similarity, we define the similarity function as follows:

$$Similarity(i) = \frac{1}{1 + \|QM - FM(i)\|} \tag{4}$$

where $\| \cdot \|$ is the Euclidean distance and *i* is the *i*-th texture image in the database.

5 Experimental Results

The proposed system is implemented in Matlab script on a PC with an AMD K7 Athlon 650 CPU, 128MB RAM, and Microsoft Windows 98SE. The database contains 1500 192x128 Corel true-color texture images. These images are transformed to gray-level images before extracting the six Tamura features. The average time required for feature extraction of a texture image is about 1.86 seconds.

To demonstrate the performance of the proposed system, a subset of Brodatz textures [9] and Corel images are tested in our experiments. Fig. 4 shows resulting descriptions of some texture images. The average time required for each texture description is less than 2 seconds.

Fig. 5 and Fig. 6 show retrieval results for linguistic descriptions. The retrieved images are displayed in descending similarity order in from left to right. Fig. 7, 8 and 9 show retrieval results of visual examples. The left-most image is the query image and the retrieved images are displayed in descending similarities order. According to these empirical tests, the retrieval results are perceptually satisfactory. The average retrieval time is about 3 seconds. A speedup can be expected by a better indexing scheme in the database.

6 Conclusions and Future Work

A texture retrieval system with linguistic descriptions is proposed in this paper. Users can pose textural descriptions or visual examples to find the desired texture. A mapping mechanism between low-level texture features and high-level semantic information is formulated through the proposed fuzzy clustering algorithm. According to the experimental results, the fuzzy clustering algorithm generates satisfactory membership functions for each linguistic variable. The texture image can be described in feasible linguistic terms; and the retrieved images are indeed perceptually similar according to the linguistic terms.

For future work, we try to extend the linguistic descriptions to more perceptual features, such as color, shape, and spatial layout. Besides, the weighted feature descriptors may be combined according to description schemes to obtain high-level descriptions for special applications. Furthermore, we will explore some alternative approaches to find more effective similarity functions. For example, fuzzy inference and Bayesian probabilistic are two possible candidates.

References

1. A. Del Bimbo, *Visual Information Retrieval*, Morgan Kaufmann Publishers, 1999.
2. MPEG Requirement Group, "MPEG-7 Requirements Document V.13," *Doc. ISO/MPEG N3933*, MPEG Pisa Meeting, January 2001.
3. W. M. Smeulders, M. Worring, S. Santini, A. Gupta, R. Jain, "Content-based image retrieval at the end of the early years," *IEEE Transactions on Pattern Analysis and Machine Intelligence*, Vol. 22, No.12, pp. 1349-1380, 2000.
4. Corridoni, J.M., A. Del Bimbo, P. Pala, "Image retrieval by color semantics", *ACM Multimedia Systems Journal*, Vol. 7, Issue 3, pp. 175-183, 1998.
5. H. Tamura *et al.* "Textural features corresponding to visual perception," *IEEE Transactions on Systems, Man, and Cybernetics*, Vol. 8, No. 6, pp. 460-473, 1978.
6. F. Liu and R. W. Picard, " Periodicity, directionality and randomness: Wold features for image modeling and retrieval," *IEEE Transactions on Pattern Analysis and Machine Intelligence*, Vol. 18, No. 7, pp. 722-733, 1996.
7. Mojsilovic, J. Kovacevic, J. Hu, R. J. Safranek, and S. K. Ganapathy, "Matching and retrieval based on the vocabulary and grammar of color patterns," *IEEE Transactions on Image Processing*, Vol.9, No.1, pp. 38-54, 2000.
8. J. S. R. Jang *et al.* Neuro-Fuzzy and Soft Computing, Prentice Hall, 1997.
9. P. Brodatz, Textures: A Photographic Album for Artists and Designers, Dover, New York, 1966.

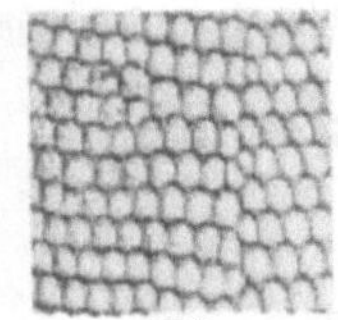
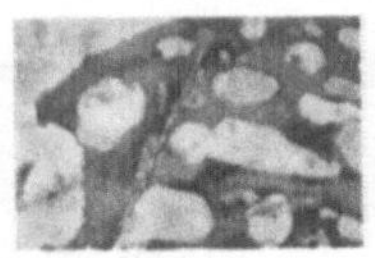

D15	D3		
fine (0.88)	very fine (1.00)	very coarse (0.78)	fine (0.75)
high on contrast (0.92)	high on contrast (0.92)	high on contrast (0.75)	very low on contrast (0.76)
very directional (0.89)	non-directional (0.88)	very non-directional (0.69)	directional (0.62)
line-like (0.74)	very blob-like (0.54)	blob-like (0.82)	very blob-like (1)
medium on regular (0.70)	very regular (1.00)	irregular (0.99)	regular (0.89)
medium on rough (0.78)	smooth (0.8)	very rough (1)	very smooth (0.88)

Fig. 4. Texture description: linguistic terms with membership value.

Fig. 5. Retrieval results of linguistic queries "very directional, very line-like, and very regular."

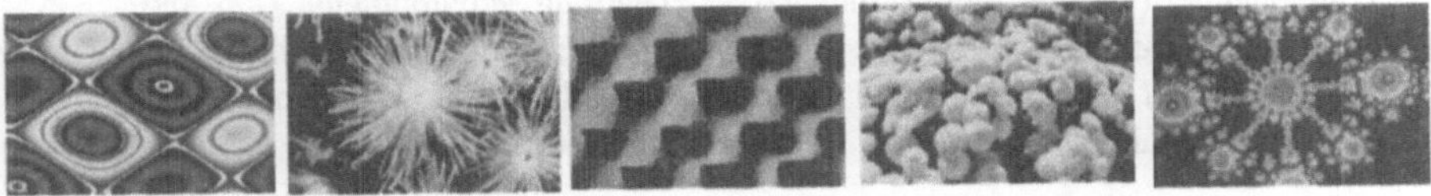

Fig. 6. Retrieval results of linguistic queries "very coarse and very high on contrast."

Fig. 7. Retrieval results of visual example for the condition "similar on coarseness, contrast, and line-likeness."

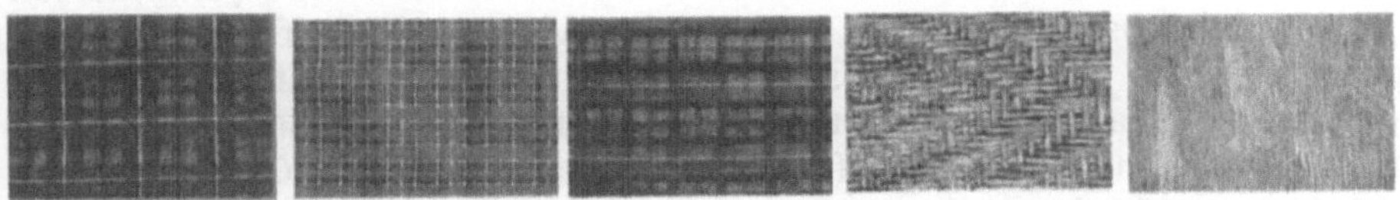

Fig. 8. Retrieval results of visual example for the condition "similar on contrast, directionality, line-likeness, and roughness."

Fig. 9. Retrieval results for an visual example with the given condition "similar on directionality and line-likeness"

Implementation of the Virtual School : Best Cyber Academy

Chi-Syan Lin

Associate Professor
Institute of Computers and Information Education
National Tainan Teachers College
GSM: +886-0932-830-451
linc@ipx.ntntc.edu.tw

Abstract. The article discusses the architecture and implementation issues of a virtual school --- Best Cyber Academy. Best Cyber Academy is being implemented following the principles of distributed learning in order to create a web-based learning environment for elementary and junior high students to enjoy learning constructively in an authentic collaborative manner. It is suggested that the architecture of a virtual school should consist of three components: (1) the highly interactive eLearning environments, (2) the profound eLearning content and (3) the concrete eLearning community. To implement and maintain a virtual school successfully, three components above are all essential.

1 Introduction

Taiwan government has been advocating the education reform that focuses on the change of learning paradigm. It is widely accepted in the field of school education that constructivism should be the guideline for instructional design. Hence, we need to provide students an active learning environment that is full of collaborative and adaptive learning opportunities with the claims of constructivism. It has been discussing that Internet is a feasible tool for creating such environment. There are huge efforts around the world have been devoted to the creation and experimentation of educational websites. However, there are few evidences that fulfill the claims of Internet advocates in the field of school education. It seems that Internet is far beyond what we have realized about in terms of education application. This paper aims to propose the architecture of a Taiwan virtual school, Best Cyber Academy which has over 80 thousands members and is one of the most popular education websites in Taiwan (http://linc.hinet.net/), and the implementation of it for helping primary and secondary schools to meet the challenge of the 21st century.

2 The Rationales of Best Cyber Academy

Constructive Learning Theory is the primary principle for designing Best Cyber Academy. By means of the Internet, Best Cyber Academy is intended to construct an authentic collaborative learning environment that could serve as a virtual school and provide eLearning services to the pupils around the world. In such an environment, pupils are able to pursue individual and adaptive learning needs without the constraints of time and pace. Moreover, pupils can learn collaboratively at anytime and anywhere with their distant peers or even the citizens around the world. This is to say, Best Cyber Academy provides a new teaching method and learning media with the features of anytime, anyplace, anyway and anyone. Best Cyber Academy represents a new paradigm of education.

3 The Collaborative Learning Environments of Best Cyber Academy

It is suggested that the primary concern of an eLearning environment is to stress the function of interpersonal interaction in order to meet the needs of active and collaborative learning. Based on the rationales mentioned in the previous section and the concern of an eLearning environment, Best Cyber Academy has researched and developed an eLearning environment equipped with six infrastructures: (1) identification system, (2) communication tools, (3) collaborative learning tools, (4) instructional management system, (5) repository, retrieval, and representation of learning resources, and (6) the application of intelligent agents.

3.1 Identification System

To assure the authenticity of the users' information and manage pupils' learning processes, it is essential to build an identification system in an eLearning environment. As a matter of facts, identification system is the key for an eLearning environment in terms of providing high-end learning services such as adaptive learning and supports. After spending several years on trial and error, Best Cyber Academy has developed a feasible identification system. By means of manual and system automatic identification, upon registering on line pupils can immediately login to the Best with their identification and enjoy the personal learning services.

3.2 Communication Tools

All pupils participating in eLearning activities should be able to employ interpersonal communication tools. By means of them, pupils can discuss, share and cooperate with their peers. The tools could be divided into two categories in terms of time phase: asynchronous and synchronous.

3.3 Collaborative Learning Tools

Collaborative learning tools provide users with the function needed for Web-based collaborative learning. These tools help users proceed to collaborative learning activities freely and easily.

3.3.1 Auto-Grouping Mechanism

Best Cyber Academy is equipped with a users learning activities tracking system that is able to record learners' learning behaviors and web pages navigated. According to theses data provided from the tracking system, a grouping mechanism can divide learners into groups with desired design and help them achieve their learning goals of collaborative learning and reach higher learning performance.

3.3.2 Artifact Center

Artifact Center, helping users have the sense of learning community, is an important eLearning tool in terms of constructing knowledge and collaborative learning. By means of it, users can show their works publicly and receive feedback from others such as peers, domain experts, and even parents. Therefore, to enhance the result of eLearning, Artifact Center is contained in all learning sessions of Best Cyber Academy such as "Internet eFamily Book", "WebTheme Curriculum", "Collaborative Learning Projects" and "eLearning Materials".

3.3.3 Collaborative Notebook

Collaborative Notebook, a tool for team members to record the processing information or idea during collaborative learning events, is one of the most significant collaborative tools in Best. It can help learners deduce constantly and think logically in collaborative learning. Its design is corresponding with the Auto-Grouping mechanism and it is embedded in all the collaborative learning projects or activities.

3.4. Instructional Management System

The purpose of Instructional Management System is to manage learners' personal information and their learning records.

3.5. Repository, Retrieval, and Representation of Learning Resources

In an eLearning environment, searching and organizing learning resources are very important learning activities. However, the present search engines provide little requested information for the learners; they are not designed for assisting pupils' learning; their interface and function also concern little about the needs of pupils in primary and secondary schools. For better utilization of learning resources on the Internet, Best Cyber Academy has designed two systems: (1) digital library and (2) learning performance indicators search engine.

3.5.1 Digital Library

Digital Library is designed in light of pupils eLeaning needs with special information repository, retrieval, and representation considerations. By means of it, teachers or experts can login to utilize the learning resources; teachers and pupils can engage in inquiry learning.

The content of digital library system is divided into eight learning domains and based on a subject classification model that is created following the Governmental Curriculum Scheme. The subject classification model helps the Best manages Internet learning resources efficiently. Pupils or teachers can retrieve appropriate and useful learning resources with learning domain, grade level and performance pointer search engines. With the help from digital library, learning in cyber space will become more efficient and enjoyable for students.

3.5.2 Learning Performance Indicators Search Engine

This search engine covers eight domains and six learning issues that are regulated by MOE of Taiwan. The user could either uses keywords to search the detailed learning performance indicators of each learning activity or apply alternatively the indicators to search required supporting learning resources. To use this tool, the user should follow three steps: (1) click "Performance Indicators Search Engine", (2) enter keywords to search relative performance indicators and (3) select the preferred performance indicators and retrieve the relevant learning resources from Digital Library.

3.6 IA : Intelligent Agents

Intelligent Agent is the newest technology and concept in the field of Internet. In an eLearning environment, intelligent agents could provide all kinds of learning supports and make adaptive learning possible. Furthermore, intelligent agents are one of the most significant tools for achieving the sense of community and its identification. Intelligent agents could play the role of a teacher and monitor pupils' learning behaviors, to record learning processes, to understand pupils' level of learning and to assist pupils at any time. Thus, IA will affect the result of eLearning dramatically.

At present, Best Cyber Academy is researching and developing six IAs for eLearning environments: (1) Avatars, (2) Learning Companion, (3) Moderator, (4) Genie, (5) Digital Librarian and (6) Evaluator.

3.6.1 Avatars

They are the representatives of individual learners on the cyber space. They can record and track learning process for learners individually. Avatars are the central pieces of intelligent agents in Best Cyber Academy. They are the databases and information providers for other agents.

3.6.2 Learning Companion

It is the friend to users. Usually, its roles are to learn together with pupils, give support to pupils, interact with pupils and reduce pupils' learning pressure. For now, Best Cyber Academy has developed a learning companion–WuKong. With WuKong's help, pupils can improve learning motivation and performance, and increase interpersonal interaction.

3.6.3 Moderator

It can track learning schedule and monitor learning outcome in a collaborative eLearning event. An experienced Moderator will guide pupils to interact with others and increase the frequency of interaction.

3.6.4 Genie

It represents the expert in eLearning environment. It can examine and search the database of pupils' model, understand an individual pupil's learning situation and difficulties, answer learners' inquiries and give pupils appropriate assistant.

3.6.5 Digital Librarian

It can search, filter and organize information to suit individual needs and cope with chores automatically. Through the help from digital librarian, pupils can receive the information they really need; this helps their learning considerably.

3.6.6 Evaluator

It can give assessment to an individual pupil based on pupils' student model database. After evaluation, evaluator will provide immediate, individualized feedback and synchronous online guidance to pupils.

4 eLearning Content

The eLearning content in Best Cyber Academy is divided into six categories: (1) eLearning materials, (2) WebTheme, (3) collaborative learning projects, (4) online forestall quiz, (5) witty playground, and (6) Go Go Mall.

4.1 eLearning Materials

Following the standard of Governmental Curriculum Scheme, eLearning materials consist of eight subjects: (1) Language, (2) Mathematics, (3) Social Study, (4) Life Study, (5) Science and Life Technology, (6) Arts and Humanities, (7) Health and PE, and (8) General Activities. Each subject covers four levels: grade 1-2, grade 3-4, grade 5-6 in primary schools and all grades in the middle schools. eLearning materials are targeted at providing individual learning materials and are much like a conventional CD title except the networked features. For now, over eighty eLearning materials are presented in Best Cyber Academy.

Based on constructivism and the features of eLearning technology, eLearning materials of Best Cyber Academy usually require three learning activities: navigation, ongoing assessment and communication.

4.1.1 Navigation

Navigation means pupils utilize the browser to navigate different learning resources suitable for them. This is to say that learners use their sense of "look" and "hearing" to obtain semantic knowledge. Therefore, navigation is a perceptive learning activity.

4.1.2 Ongoing Assessment

As far as learning hierarchy is concerned, ongoing assessment is a higher learning activity than navigation. Ongoing assessment implies that learners utilize online test, search engine, assignments or artifacts to assess or examine their own present learning status for receiving procedural and strategic knowledge. Therefore, ongoing assessment usually incorporates learning activities such as presentation, evaluation and reflection.

The main purpose of ongoing assessment is to help the learners rethink the information they have just navigated and plan further learning path and objectives.

4.1.3 Communication

Communication means discussion, emulation and collaboration among people. According to the learning theory, interpersonal communication is the highest cognitive activity. Learners can construct constructive knowledge (meta-cognitive knowledge) by means of interpersonal communication.

4.2 WebTheme

WebTheme combines the theories of inquiry learning, project-based learning, engaged learning, collaborative learning and web-based inquiry learning for offering pupils, guardians and teachers an alternative eLearning approach. The unique features of WebTheme are (1) pupils study in a team, (2) the team members work together with collaborative tools to find the solutions of driving questions in an interdisciplinary manner, and (3) finish the tasks and present them in public by using multimedia tools.

4.3 Collaborative Learning Projects

To go beyond the traditional teaching methods and institutional settings, schools around the world could incorporate information technologies and work on collaborative projects together and develop the essence of open education. Best Cyber Academy designs and operates three kinds of collaborative learning projects: interschool, international and WebQuest.

4.4 Online Forestall Quiz

On the basis of online test database and game style, Online Forestall Quiz, enabling multiple users to play simultaneously, pops up the question randomly. All users can use "Question-Giver" to provide questions. "Online Forestall Quiz" will make "Ongoing Assessment" more interesting and meaningful. The immediate feedback and competition feature of the Quiz will enhance pupils' learning interests and engagement during their learning process.

4.5 Witty Playground

Witty Playground is a special zone designed to relieve pupils' pressure and provide recreation. This zone consists of intelligent computer or online games and is full of entertainment and pupils can train their thinking and reaction abilities. Furthermore, all games are designed and created by teachers of primary and secondary schools those who put more focus on learning than entertainment.

4.6 Go Go Mall

Go Go Mall is a place where pupils can enjoy online shopping, participate in all sorts of community parties, and receive educational eCommerce service. Pupils can search and sell goods relating to education. This Mall will also build a platform providing pupils to have deal with others and an eCommerce area for exhibition and arts fairs. The teachers can help pupils learn correct Internet transaction knowledge and proper Internet behavior; the pupils can exchange knowledge with others in this Mall.

5 eLearning Community:

The sense of learning community in a virtual school could glue members together and create the ownership among members. Therefore, learning community is the key for maintaining the momentum of a virtual school. The learning community is resulted from the interaction between virtual learning community in networked learning environments and real associations that are associated with the virtual school.

The best way to create a virtual learning community in virtual schools is to provide a learning environment that members are able to both take part in the learning activities actively and also control their own learning pace and incorporate their own learning styles. As to the real associations, three communities are formed in Best Cyber Academy currently: (1) eLearning teachers, (2) eLearning tutors and (3) news community.

5.1 eLearning Teachers

One important mission of Best Cyber Academy is to develop eLearning materials. To help pupils learn actively, the content should be attractive to them. Teachers of primary and secondary schools stand on the frontline of teaching; they understand best the pupils' needs and their learning behaviors. Thus, they are the best candidates to develop and design the draft of eLearning materials.

eLearning materials should be developed and designed under the consideration of meeting different pupils' needs. eLearning materials designers should have a place to offer opinions and receive support in the process of designing eLearning material, so it is a must for Best Cyber Academy to form a learning-oriented teacher community. The initial plan for this community is to form a group of key members and then these members will be the leaders to help others develop local and regional learning community physically and virtually.

5.2 eLearning Tutors

Best Cyber Academy employs the Internet features to develop learning mechanisms that are manual, automatic, synchronous and asynchronous to help pupils obtain individual and adaptive learning content and counseling.

Best Cyber Academy has been recruiting and training teachers and pre-service teachers as the online tutors to provide online learning supports. Tutors will answer pupils' questions with all kind of communication tools mentioned above such as Forums and Best GSM. The eLearning tutors community has formed Best Cyber Academy an educational website with harmless, excellent and perfect learning environments.

5.3 News Community

News Community is intended for members to report and share latest information regarding to education and campus activities. The information providers are pupils and teachers of primary and secondary schools. Periodically, exclusive about people or particular news will be reported. At the same time, Best Cyber Academy also recruits Campus Journalists, Reporters, Correspondents to contribute their works and interact with the members of News Community.

6 Conclusion

In this paper, a proposal about a virtual school is suggested. To build a sound virtual school, three components should be equipped: eLearning environment, eLearning content and eLearning community. As far as eLearning environment is concerned, the infrastructure should contain: (1) identification system, (2) communication tools, (3) collaborative learning tools, (4) instructional management system, (5) repository, retrieval, and representation of learning sources and (6) the application of IA. To help pupils learn actively and collaboratively, six categories of eLearning content are suggested: (1) eLearning materials, (2) WebTheme curriculum, (3) collaborative learning project, (4) online forestall quiz, (5) witty playground and (6) Go Go Mall. Apart from eLearning environment and eLearning content, a virtual school needs "users" to build up a brand community. Both virtual learning community and real associations that are associated with the virtual school constitute the community.

References

1. Brenner, W., Zarnekow, R., & Wittig, H. (1998). Intelligent Software Agents: Foundations and Applications. Berlin, Germany: Springer-Verlag.
2. Cockayne, W. R., & Zyda, M. (1998). Mobile Agents. Greenwich, CT: Manning Publications Co.
3. Davidson, K. (1998). Education in the Internet – Linking Theory to Reality. http://www.oise.on.ca/~kdavidson/cons.html.
4. Lin, Chi-Syan, & Wu, Tieh-Hsiung, (1998). The Design and Application of Tracking Systems for the Web Learning Environments. Proceedings of ED-MEDIA and ED-TELECOM 98: 10th World Conference on Educational Multimedia and Hypermedia & World Conference on Educational Telecommunications, June 20-25, 1998, (1) (pp. 825-830). Freiburg, Germany: AACE.
5. Lin, Chi-Syan, (1998). Pathfinder: A Web Learning Environment for Elementary School Students at Taiwan. (CD ROM of WebNet 98 Proceeding, Nov.).
6. Lin, Chi-Syan, (1999). Pathfinder: The Design and Application of a Web Learning Environment for Elementary Schools in Taiwan. (CD ROM of EdTech 99 Procedding, Ministry of Education, Singapore).
7. Wallace, R., Krajcik, J., & Soloway, E. (1996). Digital Libraries in the Science Classroom: An Opportunity for Inquiry. http://www.dlib.org/dlib/september96/09wallace.html

Applying Process Improvement Approach to the Design and Development of a Multimedia-Based Training Management System

Jihn-Chang J. Jehng

Inst. of Human Resource Management
National Central University
Chung-Li, Taiwan 32054
jehng@src.ncu.edu.tw

Jia-Sheng Heh

Dept. of Info and Computer Eng.
Chung-Yuan Christian University
Chung-Li, Taiwan 32054
jsheh@ice.cycu.edu.tw

ABSTRACT. Multimedia-based training management has been challenged for its administrative efficiency in managing the training process. The problem could arise from the system design and development that often focuses on the functional deployment instead of the process redesign. This article proposes a process improvement approach by applying process flowcharting and value analysis techniques. This approach first analyzes and diagnoses specific tasks occurring in the entire training management process. Unnecessary tasks were then integrated, redesigned or eliminated so that the restructured process can be more simple, flexible and at a low cost. The design of the MTI multimedia-based training management system is described for illustration. Results of the system performance evaluation showed that the amount of in-house training management works have been reduced and the entire process has been condensed into one fourth of the original cycle time.

1. Introduction

One of the central principle of applying advanced computer and telecommunication technology to human resource management is to change the way people work [6]. This is particularly critical in training management, which has shown laggard to arrive at information management systems and continues to face obstacles to full automation, starting with the indisputable fact that the basic subject matter of training - people - are definitely variable and constantly changing. A multimedia-based training management system is more than a database of information about people who receive training. It is, or should be, a technology that automates an expanding range of administrative processes and procedures needed to manage training affairs effectively. However, merely throwing computers into an existing management process and automating it does not guarantee the process to be improved into a more effective and efficient way. In fact, the misuse of technology can block process improvement altogether by reinforcing old ways of thinking and old behavior patterns [3].

The initial step to fully exploit multimedia-based training management technology has already been taken in many organizations. The traditional approach, however, has not worked well in the human resource department. The traditional approach is to look at existing tasks, procedures, activities, and data requirements as given, needs that are accepted as requirement, and simply to automate these functions. Thus, the traditional approach to systems development, which has worked well for many non-HR systems, such as accounting and material resource management, goes to work on a function as it exists. It breaks the function down into inputs, processes, and outputs; traces the information flow; identifies needed data elements; and then automates at the end, depending on the need for human intervention and the technological environment. Very often, system designers have avoided the most difficult parts of the function, or made a case for a trade-off between 90 percent mechanization and a more costly system. Usually, the basic approach to training management system development has usually been the same: Automate the function and its surrounding administrative processes and procedures; don't question the validity or effectiveness of the function itself. However, automation sometimes simply provides more efficient ways of doing the wrong types of things.

Such systems development could go on and on, given the complexity and diversity of training management in an organization, and the processes and procedures that support it. Underlying this diversity is the plain fact that employee training is not the same as accounting or material resource control - both relative rigid disciplines with universally applicable standards and optimal procedures. The processes and procedures of training are usually company-specific depending on a company's HR policies and strategies. Quite often the right way of handling a training function at A company would not apply in B company - due to differences in workforce characteristics, internal customer service goals, skills requirements, or many other variables that influence optimal training processes in different organizations.

In this article we propose a process improvement approach that could be applied to the design and development of multimedia-based training management systems. This approach employs a wide range of ideas from industrial engineering, job restructuring, organizational effectiveness, and chronological flow techniques [4][5]. The goal is not only to make training management systems be more efficient but to make sure the right systems are being done in a more effective manner.

2. Process Improvement/Workflow Analysis

When designing multimedia-based training management systems, the critical questions have usually been ignored. Is this administrative process or procedure necessary? How can the process be improved, not just automated? In short, how can and should the administrative work itself be improved by technology? The goal should be to raise the quality and improve training management, not merely provide data faster, more uniformly, less expensively, or more efficiently. This is the central issue of training management if the final system is to be genuinely effective in serving business and HR objectives.

The process improvement approach aims at making an administrative process be simpler, more flexible and at a low cost. It applies two techniques, process flowcharting and value analysis, to analyze the specific activities occurring within an existing process of a training function. This approach is also known as workflow analysis, which is generally defined as the analysis of work over time on a sequential basis, as it passes from person to person or place to place, at the greatest possible level of detail [1] [2]. As this concept is applied to training management, it involves the reexamination of all management tasks, procedures, and processes for a system. Thus, workflow analysis in this context will identify opportunities to eliminate some tasks and procedures, simplify others, and so on. The overriding objective is to create an optimal state for all management tasks, before they are automated or presented to system developers for mechanization.

2.1 Flowcharting the process

While implementing the process improvement approach, the process flowcharting technique is first used by interviewing and observing people who perform the tasks. A workflow chart contains a sequential series of tasks from a trigger event that starts the process to the completion of the process. In this step, everything that is being done - whether or not it makes sense - is identified and described.

The project team responsible for identifying and mapping the current process should avoid giving the impression that they are judging the tasks in any way. The objective of this stage is to learn what is happening now, not whether what's happening is a good idea. On the other hand, if an interviewee provides comments or ideas on how to improve a task or a series of tasks, these should be noted for possible use in the next step, when tasks will be analyzed for improvement.

2.2 Analyzing process for improvement

Once current processes have been charted, project team, then, works with people in the human resource department to evaluate and determine which tasks can be eliminated, which can be integrated, which should be improved, and how the overall process can be made both more efficient and more effective. Using the workflow documents as walk-through documents, the project team could diagnose every task within the overall context of the purpose of the process. Although a process and its associated tasks represent unique opportunities for improvement, the following questions are usually applicable in most cases:

- Is this process necessary? Why is it so necessary?
- Can it be done by someone else in a more effective manner?
- Are all tasks in the process essential?
- Which task or tasks can be eliminated or combined?
- What can be automated?
- What's the optimal or "should be" solution in the long run?
- What can be done now as an interim solution?

Answers to these questions are confined in terms of organizational priorities, business needs, and the objectives of the process being analyzed. Sometimes, processes or tasks that need to be improved are practically evident. For example, a process that includes the need for three or four approvals when an employee changes her name or address is obviously bureaucratic and unnecessary. At other times, workflow analysis will show that changes are being forwarded to people or functions that neither approve nor need to know the changes, just because that is the way they have always done and take for granted.

While the outright elimination of tasks or procedures is not always a first consideration, most work analyzed in this phase is more susceptible to restructuring or redesigning than total elimination. In this context, restructuring means job redesign, such as the combining of work done in two places and reassignment of tasks that can be done more effectively at another level.

Throughout this stage of workflow analysis, automation should remain in the forefront of the team's thinking. As a general rule, work that cannot be eliminated should be automated now or in the long-range visionary process.

2.3 Value analysis

The next step for the project team is to take the information they learned from the process flowcharting and conduct a value analysis. Using the process flowchart as its blueprint, the project team estimates the percentage of value a given process provides to the customers. First, the team evaluates each activity on the process flowchart individually and places it into appropriate category which will be evaluated and classified as either value-added or nonvalue-added steps based on the following questions:

- Is it linked directly to a customer need?
- Does it bring you one step closer to a finished work?
- Is it linked directly to the functional mission?

If any of these questions can be answered "yes," the activity adds value. If the answer to preceding questions is collectively "no," most likely the activity is nonvalue-added and should be placed in the appropriate nonvalue-added category. If project team still isn't sure, they need to answer the following questions:

- Does it relate to fixing a problem?
- Is it compensating for poor performance somewhere else?

If the answer is "yes" to either of these questions, the activity does not add value and should be categorized as nonvalue-added. The project team, then, evaluates the categorized steps for individual process time and the percentage of workflow through each step.

With value analysis, the project team can also compare its total process time yield to actual cycle time estimates. Though this type of data comparison is nothing new, through it a team can quickly arrive at a fairly accurate delay time estimate to use as a basis for process improvement.

2.4 Model testing and implementation

The selection of an optimal process for test is based on standards of both effectiveness and efficiency, and involves consideration of a broad range of technical, operational, economic, human, and policy issues. Testing a new process has two important objectives. First, and most important, it gives the project team a chance to correct mistakes or make necessary adjustments. The trial provides designers with the opportunity to see a "drawing board" optimal model come to life, so that it can be fine-tuned at least, and totally restructured if necessary. The second benefit of testing is that it provides users with early exposure to the new ways of handling work. Getting people to change the way they perform work is always difficult. But when they are asked to participate in a test of a new process, rather than being presented with the final, unchangeable version, the implementation of change is usually more manageable.

With the results of testing in hand and any alterations decided upon, the new process is subject to automation. Usually, the process improvement approach should have developed a set of benchmarks of organizational effectiveness that can be applied after implementation. The measurements and standards used in cost/benefit analysis should be applied to see if they actually occurred in operation. The application of cost/benefit analysis to the results of implementation, however, is beyond the scope of discussion in this article.

3. A Case Illustration

In order to describe in detail how a process improvement approach is applied to the design and development of multimedia-based training management systems, an actual case is selected for illustration. The training management system is developed in a joint effort between the Institute of Human Resource Management at the National Central University, Taiwan, and the HR department in Microelectronics Technology Inc., a high-tech firm located in the Hsin-Chu Science-based Industrial Park, Taiwan.

3.1 The company' training system

Microelectronics Technology Inc. (MTI), which is first microwave technology firm in Taiwan, was founded in 1983. Currently, there are more than eight hundred full-time employees in MTI. Most of them have received education at the college level. The board of trustees has addressed that the corporate business goal of continual pursuit of business growth and a high level of customer satisfaction should be ensured. The top management emphasizes the quality human resources and recognizes each individual employee's work value and achievement.

In order to attain its corporate goal and fulfill business strategies, the primary mission of MTI's HRD program is to maintain and develop its quality human resource so that its business competitive advantages can be assured. The MTI's employee training program is designed based on its overall business strategies, job analysis, performance appraisal, and the demand of each individual employee's self-development. The HR department is mainly responsible for arranging strategy management courses for different levels of managers and developing general courses based on the job analysis. Functional departments are responsible for designing various types of professional training. Specific training assigned to each individual employee is based on the annual performance appraisal. HR also arranged courses for developing licensed in-house trainers. The MTI's training program mainly contains seven tracks of courses: business strategies, in-house trainer development, quality control, function-specific, new-comer, general education, and self-development. Basically, the HR is responsible for arranging courses in business strategies, new-comer, general education, and self development four tracks. Training specialists in each functional department take charge of in-house trainer development, quality control, and function-specific training three tracks. The training program is customized so that employees can develop appropriate skills for their individual needs. Due to the complexity of training process management, the HR department desperately needs to apply information technology to manage its training program.

3.2 Implementing the process improvement

Before developing the system, the project team first applied the flowcharting technique to evaluate current training management process. Forty-six tasks were identified in the process of in-house training. At the beginning of each fiscal year, the HR conducts a training need survey by requesting functional managers and department training specialists to specify their individual department's training needs. The HR also requests information from functional managers about each individual employee's performance evaluation in the previous year. Based on information from the survey and employees' performance evaluation, the HR determines the number of employees who need to receive training and the number of courses that needs to be developed within the constraint of training budget. In the next step, the HR will seek, interview, and select appropriate trainers for different courses. After all trainers are identified, the HR selects classrooms, decides class schedules and prepares the syllabus for each individual course.

At the same time, each individual employee sends course application forms to his/her functional manager for approval. The functional managers evaluate each individual worker's prior work performance and, then, either approve or reject his/her application. After approval, employees start to register courses.

The HR processes registration and determines the number of persons for each course. They, then, prepare course materials, arrange classrooms, and inform participants to attend classes. After all workers have taken courses, the HR figures out each course's participation rate, work out each individual worker's training cost and request functional managers to evaluate training courses. At the same time, the HR establishes each individual worker's training record. Finally, the HR furnishes both execution and evaluation reports for the entire training program. Figure 1 shows the workflow.

Figure 1. The original in-house training management workflow containing 46 tasks

After interviewing the MTI HR manager who takes charge of the training program, the project team decides to restructure the entire process by asking questions addressed above. The new process contains 23 tasks, which are a half of total tasks occurred in the current process. The major improvement of current training management process appears as follows:

- All paper works are converted into electronic ones. Therefore, training needs survey, performance evaluation request form, course application, training effectiveness evaluation, and individual employee's training records are all done electronically.
- All numerical calculations are executed automatically by computers, such as head count of participants in each course, each individual employee's training cost and participation rate of each course.
- All communications are done electronically, such as course announcement, course schedule notification, and learning materials distribution.

In the restructured process, nearly 80% works are completed on-line. At the initial training preparation stage, the HR executes an on-line training needs survey and identifies needed courses immediately once all functional managers responds and returns the survey. He/She then searches, interviews, selects appropriate instructors for each courses and makes an on-line announcement of those courses.

At the training implementation stage, the HR processes applicants' registration and prepares student name lists for each course after functional managers approve and send individual workers' registration form to the HR on-line. Each individual worker is then notified by the e-mails about the course schedules.

At the end of training, each course's participation rate and each individual worker's training cost and training performance records are processed on-line by the HR. Finally, the HR prepares both execution and evaluation reports for the entire training. Figure 2 shows the workflow after reengineering.

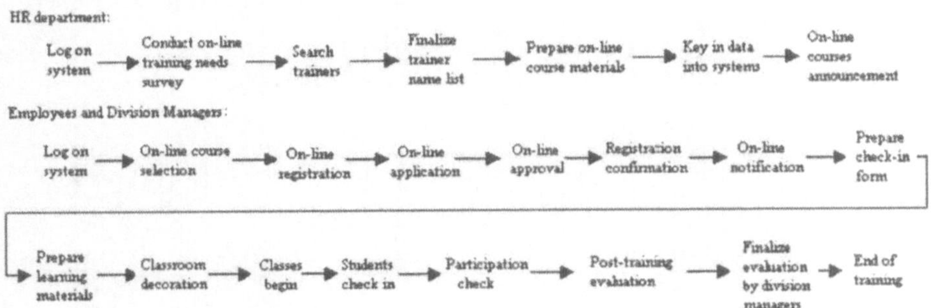

Figure 2. The in-house training management workflow after reengineering

The same reengineering effort was also applied to the external training management. Twenty-three percent of tasks were reduced in the external training management after reengineering and almost 67% of the work is selected for automation.

3.3 System functional architecture

The system, which runs in the UNIX environment, was written with the Lotus NOTES software application. The architecture of the system is shown in Figure 3.

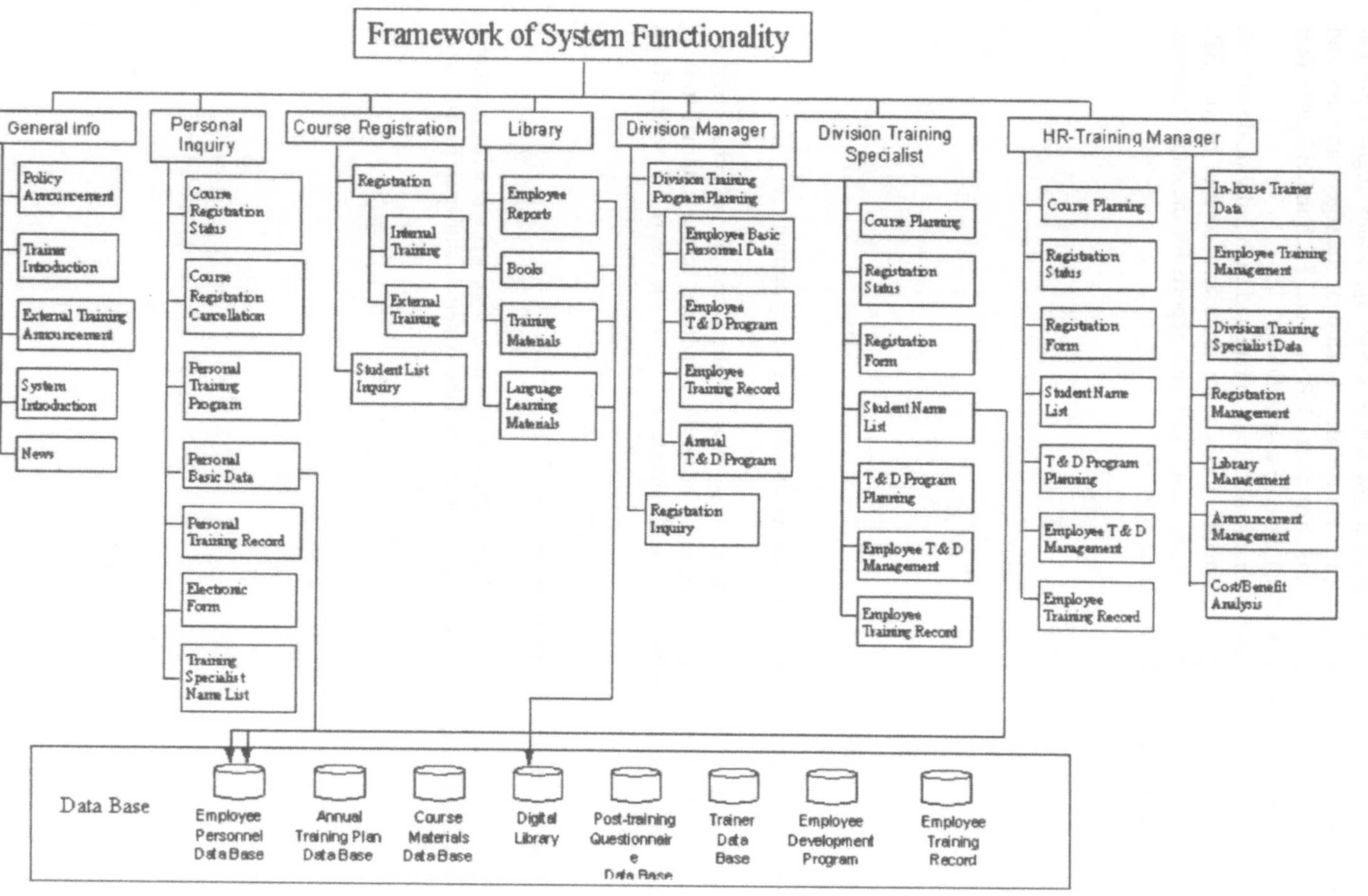

Figure 3. System architecture

The system includes seven functions. The "General Info" function allows users to get access to information about the company's training policy, the system, in-house trainers and recent news about the training program. The "Personal Inquiry" function allows users to get access to information about their course registration status, each individual employee's training program, each individual employee's training record, and their divisional training specialist. Under the "Course Registration" function, users can register in-house/external training courses and check student directory in each course. Users can use the "Library" function to get access to reading other employees' reports, checking out books, downloading course materials and borrowing language learning materials. Division managers are authorized to use the "Division Manager" function to plan divisional training program, evaluate their subordinates' training records, review/plan each year's training program, and check their subordinates' course registration status. Division training specialists are authorized to use the "Division Training Specialist" function to design professional training courses, design/distribute registration forms, manage their divisional employees' training record. The HR training manager is the entire system function manager who is allowed to oversee the entire function of the system. He/she is allowed to use the "HR-Training Manager" to manage all training works, including corporate training program, course registration, in-house trainers, students' training records, the digital library, training cost/benefit analysis, etc.. In a short, almost all training management works can be completed by means of these seven functions.

3.4 Value Analysis - Quantitative valuation of system contribution

Results of value analysis of the system performance are described in the table 1. The total number of tasks in the original process of in-house training management has been reduced into a half, from 46 to 23. The process time has been decreased from four into one week. The improvement rate is 75%. The total number of tasks in the original process of external training management has been reduced from 37 to 29, and the process time has been decreased from five weeks into two weeks. The improvement rate is 67%. The process time saved by the system has shown that the system has dramatically improved the effectiveness and efficiency of training management.

Table 1. Value analysis of workflow improvement

	No. of tasks in the original process	No. of tasks in the reengineered process	Improvement rate	Time spend in the original process	Time spend in the reengineered process	Improvement rate
In-house training	46	23	50%	4 weeks	1 week	75%
External training	37	29	23%	3 weeks	1 week	67%

4. Summary

This article indicates that the application of the process improvement approach to the design and development of a multimedia-based training management system has dramatically improved the system performance. Through the process improvement approach, not only the entire work processes of training management were simplified, effects of work automation has also been enhanced. Results of value analysis reveals that the process reengineering plus automation will have greater impact on effects of information system performance than simply automating the process.

5. References

[1] Gruhn, V. "Business process modeling and workflow management". International Journal of Cooperative Information Systems, 4(2 &3): 145-164.

[2] Hammer, M. and Stanton, S. A. The reengineering revolution: A handbook. HarperCollins Publishers, Inc., New York, 1995.

[3] Hammer, M. and Champy, J. Reengineering the corporation: A manifesto for business revolution. HarperCollins Publishers, Inc., New York, 1993.

[4] Leymann, F. and Roller, D. "Workflow-based application". IBM System Journal, 36(1): 102-123.

[5] Selander, J. P. and Cross, K. F. "Process redesign: Is it worth it?" Management Accounting, 80(7): 40-44.

[6] Walker, A. J. Handbook of human resource information systems: Reshaping the human resource function with technology. McGraw-Hill, Inc., New York, 1993.

IP Traffic Monitoring: An Overview and Future Considerations [†]

Dong Wei and Nirwan Ansari

Advanced Networking Lab
Department of Electrical & Computer Engineering
New Jersey Institute of Technology, University Heights
Newark, New Jersey 07102
{dxw3077, nirwan.ansari}@njit.edu

Abstract. An overview on emerging IP traffic monitoring is presented. Important parameters to characterize the traffic, network and QoS, are discussed. The infrastructure and methodology to measure those parameters directly or to compute them based on other measurements are described. We also present a discourse on coping with the challenge of new transport architectures and technologies. In summary, a framework of IP traffic monitoring is presented.

1. Introduction

Rapid growth of the Internet is evidenced by unceasing increased traffic volumes due to new applications and users. Main reasons for the necessity to understand and measure traffic patterns and characteristics are: 1) network optimization and planning, i.e., more efficient usage of the network resources, 2) appropriate provisioning of QoS for all applications, and 3) detection of network security violations. However, Internet traffic is heterogeneous and highly dynamic, and, as a consequence, is difficult to predict. Furthermore, it is also difficult to observe Internet traffic owing to large network size, huge traffic volume, relatively distributed administration, and heterogeneous media. Current understanding of the traffic pattern and measuring methods are rather rudimentary, and further study on IP monitoring becomes increasingly important and urgent as traffic grows exponentially.

This paper presents current state of the art on IP traffic measurement and characterization, and attempts to answer the following questions:

- Why is IP traffic monitoring necessary?
- What parameters can characterize the traffic, the network, and QoS?
- How can these parameters be collected? By measuring directly or computing based on other measurements?
- What kinds of network infrastructures or protocols are needed for these methods?

[†] This work was supported in part by OpenCon Communication Systems Inc., the New Jersey Commission on Science and Technology via the NJ Wireless Telecommunication Center, and the New Jersey Commission on Higher Education via the NJI-TOEWR project.

- How can these measurements be used to improve the efficient usage of the network resources?
- How can these measurements be employed to provision appropriate QoS for all applications?
- What should be considered to meet the rapid growth of traffic and new technologies, especially with the emergence of traffic engineering technology?

The rest of the paper is organized as follows. Section II presents the background and motivations of IP traffic monitoring. Section III discusses IP traffic pattern, modeling and characteristics. The infrastructures and methods to collect measurements and compute parameters are presented in Section IV. Further discussion on efficient IP traffic measurement is presented in Section V. This paper ends with some concluding remarks in Section VI.

2. Motivations Behind IP Traffic Monitoring

Network traffic measurements and characterizations are needed by ISPs for the following reasons [1]-[5]:

1) To understand macroscopic, infrastructure-wide traffic behavior (from the perspective of the entire network) for network optimization and planning:

- Network design, operation and flow management, i.e., traffic load balance, and efficient resource usage by adapting network configuration to tackle problems such as congestion and so forth.
- Identify and eliminate unnecessary protocols, hence increasing the efficiency of IP networks
- Identify sub-optimal routing
- Billing and pricing

Long-term measurement and optimization as a whole are needed to meet the above requirements.

2) To provision appropriate QoS for each application (from the microscopic perspective, per flow, session, or connection):

Network configuration should be dynamically and autonomously adapted, and resources should be re-allocated to provision appropriate QoS in terms of 1) transmission rate; 2) delay; 3) delay jitter; 4) packet loss rate, and so forth. Real time measurement and control are needed to meet the QoS requirement.

3) Detection of network security violation and abnormalities

This task includes detecting potentially dangerous traffic conditions, pinpointing where and understanding how they are originated, performing designated actions to block the abnormalities, and hence limiting their extension to the entire network.

For different motivations, measurements can be classified as 1) long-term, and 2) real time. They span on different time scales, from months, weeks down to seconds and even milliseconds.

3. IP Traffic Pattern, Modeling and Characteristics

<table>
<tr><td>HTTP</td><td>FTP</td><td>Telnet</td><td>SMTP</td><td>Others</td><td>RIP</td><td>SNMP</td><td>DNS</td><td>Other</td></tr>
<tr><td colspan="5">TCP</td><td colspan="4">UDP</td></tr>
<tr><td colspan="4"></td><td>ICMP</td><td>ARP</td><td colspan="3"></td></tr>
<tr><td colspan="9">IP</td></tr>
</table>

Fig. 1. The Composition of IP Traffic

Fig. 1 shows various protocols in the IP protocol suite [7]. Roberts [8] showed that about 90 to 95% of Internet packets use TCP and correspond to the transfer of digital documents of one form or another (Web pages, data transfer, MP3 tracks, etc.). Thompson, *et al*, showed [9] that:

- Of IP traffic, TCP accounts for 95% or more of bytes, 85-95% packets, and 75-85% of the flows. ICMP packets account for less than 1% of all packets. UDP makes up the remaining IP traffic.
- About 40% of all packets are 40 bytes (TCP ACK, RST and FIN, SYN), 5% of 44 bytes, 5% of 552 bytes, 6% of 576 bytes, 10% of 1500 bytes. 90% of packets are 576 bytes or smaller.

The above data show that TCP packets dominate the IP traffic, and short packets (40 or 44 bytes long) occupy more than half of the IP packets. Thus, the statistical characteristics of TCP packets dominate the statistical characteristics of IP.

According to different QoS requirement, Roberts [8] classified the IP traffic into two categories: 1) elastic flow, where the packets of a document are transferred, requiring zero packet loss rate; and 2) streaming flow, where the packets represent an audio or video signal being transferred, requiring end-to-end delay and delay jitter guarantees.

The development of new Internet applications could change the composition of IP traffic through new protocols or QoS requirement, and thus could change the statistical characteristics of IP traffic. Nevertheless, the study of current IP pattern is still necessary and urgent for both the academic and industry.

Traditionally, analysis of IP traffic is based on two assumptions: 1) the arrival of traffic is independently Poisson distributed; 2) the service time is exponentially distributed. Thus, Markov process can be employed to predict the average performance in terms of queuing delay, packet queue size, and so forth. However, in the past few years, many studies [10]-[15] showed that IP traffics do not follow those two assumptions and show self-similarity in different time scales. There are two important characteristics with IP traffic: burstiness and long-dependency, i.e., packets come in burst and the autocorrelation of traffic can span a large time scale. It is tempting to think that the aggregation of IP traffics should be Gaussian distributed, and the burstiness could be smoothed by aggregation, but on the contrary, reference [10] and [12] demonstrated by experiments that the aggregation of IP traffic can intensify burstiness.

Paxson and Floyd [11] showed that, in conventional Markov process, self-similarity in a network is ignored, the burstiness of traffic is underestimated, and the performance is overestimated. As a consequence, resource allocation based on

Markov assumption is inadequate, resulting in the unexpected bigger delay, bigger queue size, and higher packet loss rate.

Many studies showed the existence of self-similarity in IP traffic. However, no model can provide both qualitative insights and quantitative predictions on the performance of IP networks so far.

In order to simulate IP traffic, three most widely used methods to generate self-similar traffic are:

- Pareto distribution [11]
- Fractional Brownian motion [16][17]
- ON-OFF sources [10][18]

Hurst parameter ***H*** is the parameter to characterize a self-similar random process. Gomez and Santonja [19] enumerated three methods to estimate ***H***:

- R/S analysis
- Variance-time plot
- Periodogram-based analysis (wavelet, energy-scale index relation)

In order to provide qualitative insights of traffic and network, the following parameters need to be collected and analyzed:

1) Parameters to characterize IP traffic patterns:

- Primary data that can be collected
  - Packet arrival rate
  - Packet inter-arrival time
  - Packet length distribution
  - Link lifetime
- Statistical data
  - Mean
  - Peak
  - Burstiness (standard deviation)
  - Self-similarity (Hurst parameter ***H***)

2) Parameters to characterize networks (not only in Internet):

- Utilization and throughput
- Quiescence (indicates the occupancy of a link) [6]
- Unpredictability (indicates the stability and consistency of a link) [6]
- Responsiveness to the change of IP traffic
- Routing stability
- Reliability (ability to pinpoint some anomalous traffic conditions and block them)
- Granularity

3) Parameters to characterize the QoS of a link:

- End-to-end delay
- Delay jitter
- Packet loss rate
- Round trip time (RTT)

IPPM (IP Performance Metrics) working group of IETF has developed some metrics of quantities to characterize the performance and reliability of the Internet [22].

4. The Infrastructure and Methodology of IP Traffic Measurement

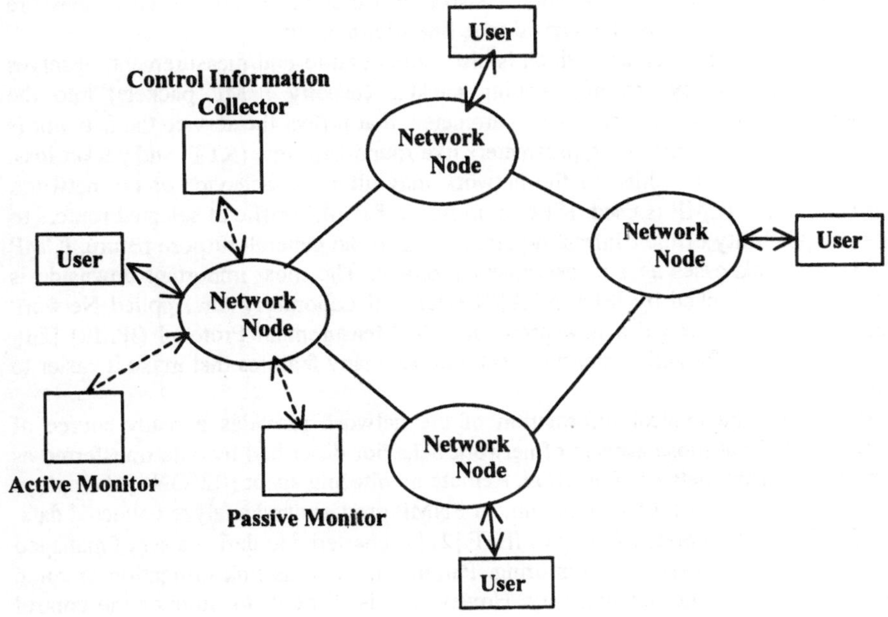

Fig. 2. Infrastructure of IP Traffic Measurement

Some parameters, such as delay jitter and H, are not observable directly. These parameters could be calculated from other measurements.

There are three methods of collecting data of network behavior [1][5]:

- Passive measurement: a probe, which resides at the import of a network node, and records network activities, is inserted into this node. Most commonly, the probe is attached to a link between network nodes, and summarizes and records information about the traffic flowing on that link.
- Active measurement: the behavior of the network is studied by sending data (usually a probing packet, from end to end) through the network and observing the results, including the time taken to send the data. Internet Control Message Protocol (ICMP) and IP Measurement Protocol can be used here.
- Control information monitoring: network control information such as routing or network management information (SNMP derived data and BGP router-based data) is captured and analyzed.

These three approaches focus on different perspectives of network behavior, and each method has its advantages and disadvantages. All of them are often employed together to develop an understanding of the entire network's behavior.

Passive measurement, which is also called per-hop measurement, observes the behavior of a network at a specific point; it does not add to or modify the data carried by the network. Consequently, it has no impact on the behavior of the network. A very detailed understanding of the behavior at the point of measurement can be developed, but it is difficult to gain an understanding of the network as a whole, or the end-to-end behavior of the network. Passive measurement is often used to measure traffic patterns, such as packet arrival rate, link lifetime, etc.

Since active measurement, which is also called end-to-end measurement, observes network behavior by sending probing packets (usually ICMP packets) into the network, it lends itself to measuring parameters that reflect the service the network is offering to its users, including parameters like round-trip time (RTT) and packet loss. However, the traffic added to the network may alter the behavior of the network. Furthermore, if ICMP is used, ISPs could turn off ICMP traffic at selected routers to limit the visibility of their infrastructure. Owing to the general-purpose nature, ICMP has some weaknesses as a measurement protocol. The most important downside is that it can be blocked by ISPs. NLANR (National Laboratory for Applied Network Research) has developed a new protocol – IP Measurement Protocol (IPMP) [20], which is tailored for active measurement and has many features that make it easier to process.

Monitoring the control information of the network provides a ready source of information about those aspects of network behavior described by data transferred as part of the normal network operation. Remote monitoring agent (RMON) [4] employs this approach to configure and instrument SNMP properly and analyze collected data. The RMON MIB Working Group of IETF [21] is chartered to define a set of managed objects for remote network monitoring. Parameters such as link utilization or route stability may be collected this way. However, it is difficult to monitor the control information when the network size is large.

To provision appropriate QoS, traffic pattern should be measured, bandwidth and buffer are reserved accordingly; network status should be monitored to avoid congestion and to balance traffic load to improve the throughput of the entire network.

5. Further Considerations On IP Traffic Monitoring

Owing to the increased need for Internet usage and demand for provisioning quality of service, IP traffic engineering technologies become monumentally important, and thus traffic-engineering-oriented measurement is required. In order to develop general and operational measurement infrastructure and methodology, the following issues should be considered [23]-[26]:

1) Protocol-independent and traffic engineering aware measurements - an IP link can be arbitrarily specific, e.g., via MPLS or DiffServ, and thus IP links have many varieties, supported by different protocols. An efficient measurement should be designed for generic IP traffic, which is independent of protocols and portable across different platforms. Furthermore, the measurement should be traffic engineering aware too. For example, in DiffServ, many packets may pass the same path (from end to end), but they may have different classes of service (CoS), different priority queues, and thus different delay, etc. The measurement methodology should be aware of these classes of service, and collect and analyze data accordingly.

2) Scalability – a measurement infrastructure must be able to scale with the size and speed of a network as it evolves.
3) Timing optimization and orthogonality of collected data – minimize the amount of data to be collected without compromising the necessary accuracy, thus preventing network performance from being adversely affected by unnecessarily loading of processors, memories, transmission facilities and the administrative support systems.
4) Feedback mechanism for topology state – in order to provision appropriate QoS, constraint-based routing measurement is employed, in which all network nodes require topology state information, such as link availability and maximum resource, etc. However, the information could fluctuate immediately while it is distributed in the network. To acquire accurate topology state information, a feedback mechanism can be employed by traversing the IP link.
5) Security – ensure correctness and reliability of the measurements.
6) Active measurements that are less invasive and do not provoke ISPs to block them.
7) Aggregating, mining, and visualizing the massive data sets in ways that are useful to multiple users
8) Traffic prediction based on measurements and modeling – by capturing the statistical nature of traffic from previous measurements, resources can be re-allocated and network can be re-configured accordingly by predicting the subsequent traffic, such that the performance in terms of efficiency and QoS can be improved.
9) Optical consideration – optical network is going to play a major role in the Internet. It is imminent to develop IP traffic monitoring over optical channels and labels. This is an emerging research.

6. Conclusions

With the development of traffic engineering technologies, IP traffic monitoring can have a wide range of influence on network performance. The current infrastructure and methodology of IP traffic monitoring cannot meet the demand for provisioning appropriate QoS for IP applications. Some issues, which need to be considered when the new infrastructure and methodology of IP traffic monitoring are developed, have been discussed in this paper.

References

1. K.C. Claffy, "Measuring the Internet," *IEEE Internet Computing*, vol.4, no.1, Jan.-Feb. 2000, pp. 73 – 75.
2. A. Adams, *et al*, "The Use of End-to-End Multicast Measurements for Characterizing Internal Network Behavior," *IEEE Communications Magazine*, vol.38, no.5, May 2000, pp.152-158.
3. R. Caceres, *et al*, "Measurement and Analysis of IP Network Usage and Behavior," *IEEE Communications Magazine*, vol.38, no.5, May 2000, pp.144-151.

4. Luca Deri, Stefano Suin, "Effective Traffic Measurement Using ntop," *IEEE Communications Magazine*, vol.38, no.5, May 2000, pp.138-143.
5. T. McGregor, H. Braun, J. Brown, "The NLANR Network Analysis Infrastructure," *IEEE Communications Magazine*, vol.38, no.5, May 2000, pp.122-128.
6. W. Matthews, Les Cottrell, "The PingER Project: Active Internet Performance Monitoring for the HENP Community," *IEEE Communications Magazine*, vol.38, no.5, May 2000, pp.130-136.
7. Gil Held, *Voice & Data Internetworking*, McGraw-Hill, 1998, pp.35.
8. Jim W. Roberts, "Traffic Theory and The Internet," *IEEE Communications Magazine*, vol.39, no.1, Jan. 2001, pp.94-99.
9. Thompson, K.; Miller, G.J.; Wilder, R., "Wide-area Internet traffic patterns and characteristics," *IEEE Network*, vol.11, no.6, Nov.-Dec.1997, pp. 10 –23.
10. W.E. Leland, W. Willinger, *et al*, "On the self-similar nature of Ethernet traffic (Extended Version)," *IEEE/ACM Transaction on Networking*, vol.2, no.1, Feb.1994, pp. 1-15.
11. V. Paxson and Sally Floyd, "Wide Area Traffic: The Failure of Poisson Modeling," *IEEE/ACM Transaction on Networking*, vol.3, no.3, June 1995, pp.226-244.
12. W. Willinger et al, "Self-Similarity Through High-Variability: Statistical Analysis of Ethernet LAN Traffic at the Source Level," *IEEE/ACM Transaction on Networking*, vol.5, no.1, Feb.1997, pp.71-86.
13. J. Beran, R. Sherman, M.S. Taqqu, W. Willinger, "Long-Range Dependence in Variable-Bit-Rate Video Traffic," *IEEE/ACM Transaction on Communications*, vol.43, no.2, Feb.-March-April 1995, pp. 1566-1579.
14. M. Crovella and A.Bestavros, "Self-Similarity in World Wide Web Traffic: Evidence and Possible Causes," *IEEE/ACM Transaction on Networking*, vol.5, no.6, June 1997, pp. 835-846.
15. B. Tsybakov and N. Georganas, "Self-Similar Processes in Communications Network," *IEEE Transaction on Information Theory*, vol.44, no.5, Sep.1998, pp.1713-1725.
16. W. Willinger *et al*, "Self-Similar Traffic Generation: The Random Midpoint Displacement Algorithm and Its Properties," *1995 IEEE International Conference on Communications*, vol. 1, pp. 466-472.
17. F. Chen, *et al*, "A Hybrid Approach for Generating Fractional Brownian Motion," GLOBECOM '96, Communications, vol.1, pp. 591–595.
18. P. Pruthi and A. Erramilli, "Heavy-Tailed ON/OFF Source Behavior and Self-Similar Traffic," *ICC '95 Seattle*, vol. 1, pp.445–450.
19. M.E. Gomez and V. Santonja, "Self-Similarity in I/O Workload: Analysis and Modeling," *Workload Characterization: Methodology and Case Studies*, 1999, pp. 97-104.
20. http://www.nlanr.net/ActMon/IPMP/
21. http://www.ietf.org/html.charters/rmonmib-charter.html
22. Paxson V., Almes G., Mahdavi J., Mathis M., "Framework for IP Performance Metrics," http://www.ietf.org/rfc/rfc2330.txt
23. Christian B., Davies B., Tse, H., "Operational measurements for Traffic Engineering," http://search.ietf.org/internet-drafts/draft-christian-tewg-measurement-00.txt
24. Lai W.S., "A Framework for Internet Traffic Measurement," http://www.ietf.org/internet-drafts/draft-wlai-tewg-measure-00.txt
25. Awduche, Elwalid, Widjaja, Xiao, "A Framework for Internet Traffic Engineering," http://search.ietf.org/internet-drafts/draft-ietf-tewg-framework-02.txt
26. Van den Berghe S., Vanheuven P., Demeester P., Asgari H., "Some Issues for Designing a Measurement Architecture for Traffic Engineered IP Networks," http://search.ietf.org/internet-drafts/draft-svdberg-temon-00.txt

Efficient Dynamic Image Retrieval Using the Á Trous Wavelet Transformation

G.R. Joubert and O. Kao

Department of Computer Science, Technical University of Clausthal
38678 Clausthal-Zellerfeld, Germany
e-mail: {joubert,okao}@informatik.tu-clausthal.de

Abstract. The increasing use of digital images in applications ranging from remote sensing to medical applications and industrial control systems results in a demand for well-suited and efficient techniques for their storage, management and retrieval. The state-of-the-art approach for image retrieval considers a priori extracted features, which are compared to query information supplied by a user in the form of, for example, a list of keywords or the corresponding features of a sample image or sketch. In this paper an alternative, object-based approach for image retrieval is presented. This allows the user to specify and to search for certain regions of interest in images. The marked regions are represented by wavelet coefficients and searched in all image sections during query runtime. All other image elements are ignored, thus a detailed search can be realised. The resulting computational effort can be overcome by utilisation of parallel architectures. An example for a cluster-based image database is discussed in the last part of this paper.

1 Introduction

Image databases are used to organise, manage and retrieve different classes of images. They allow searches for a *number of images* that are similar to a given sample image or sketch.

The importance of image databases increased dramatically in recent years. One of the reasons is the spreading of digital image technologies and multimedia applications producing petabytes of pictorial material per year. The application areas are numerous. Document libraries offer e.g. their multimedia stock all over the world. This is also true for art galleries, museums, research institutions, photo agencies for publishing houses, press agencies, civil services, etc. managing many current and archived images. Some well-known research systems are QBIC [1], SURFIMAGE [2] and VISUALSEEK [3].

An image is a complex data structure containing syntax and semantic information. In addition to the raw image data, technical and world-oriented information, a number of extracted features is used for image representation in a database system. These are usually related to colour, shape and texture. Additional knowledge-based information describes the relationship between the image elements and the real world entities. The raw image data, the technical and the world-oriented information are modelled by standard data structures and stored in existing databases. The user can either browse the database or search it by entering keywords. Examples for such *databases with images* [4] are widely available on the Internet, e.g. web presentations of museums, art galleries, etc.

These methods require laborious manual annotation of individual images stored as well as time intensive construction of appropriate keyword combinations to facilitate the retrieval process. An image database should support improved querying, retrieval and annotation methods, which enable a content based – syntax and semantic – similarity search in a general set of images.

The state-of-the-art approach for the creation and retrieval of image databases is based on the extraction and comparison of a priori defined features. At query time the user creates a sample sketch or loads a sample image, which is then processed in the same manner as the images in the database. Subsequently, the distances between the vector of the query image and the vectors of all images in the database are calculated. Each of these results gives an indication about the similarity of the compared images. The images with the smallest difference are the most similar and the corresponding raw data is sent to the user interface for visualisation. The user must then decide whether one or more of the displayed images meet his requirements.

Acceptable system response times are achieved, because no further processing of the image raw data is necessary during query runtime. This results in a considerable reduction of compute times. The straightforward integration into existing database systems is a further advantage of this approach.

However, extraction of simple features often results in a disadvantageous reduction of the image content. The individual objects are not satisfactorily considered in the retrieval process. Furthermore, it is not clear whether a suitable combination of the known relatively simple features can be formulated for the retrieval of all kinds of images.

2 Feature Extraction using the Á Trous Wavelet Transformation

An alternative approach for image retrieval is based on the analysis and description of manually chosen regions of interest, which are subsequently compared to all image sections in the database. A selected region forms the starting point of the search. The whole target image is searched for a region(s), which closely resemble the characteristics of the selected region.

A well-known method for dynamic retrieval is template matching, where the region is represented by a minimal bounding rectangle and correlated with all images in the database, e.g. by subtraction of the corresponding colour values. These are added to a sum describing the similarity of the examined sections. Disadvantages are given by the poor rotation and size invariance, which requires a repeated analysis of the region for every possible slope and size. Moreover, small colour deviations lead to large differences in the computed similarity.

This paper presents an approach called wavelet-based template matching, where the similarity of corresponding wavelet coefficients in the sample and target image is examined. All images in the database are transformed using the so-called á trous wavelet algorithm. This discrete approach to the classical continuous wavelet transform offers a denser time-scale plane as obtained with the fast wavelet transform (e.g. [5, 7, 8]). The foundation of the algorithm is a low pass filter h defined as $h = (1/2, 1/4, 1/2)$ (*linear Lagrange filter*) [6]. For the transformation of two-dimensional image data expanded to the next $2^n \times 2^n$ dimension the convolution matrix $FM(f_x, f_y) = h * h^T$ is used.

In contrast to the common wavelet transform no classification into horizontal, vertical and diagonal coefficients is performed. The detail coefficients are created by subtraction of corresponding approximation coefficients on two consecutive decomposition levels. An important property of the á trous transformation is given by the fact that downsampling is not applied and thus the number of approximation coefficients equals the number of image points.

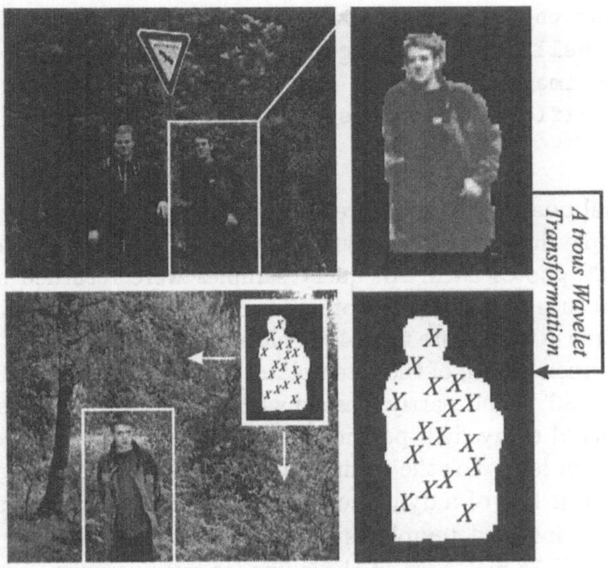

Fig. 1. Image retrieval with dynamically extracted features: the user-defined object is transformed and represented by a number of wavelet coefficients (X)

An increased computational effort compared to the standard wavelet transform is required. However, this is not a decisive disadvantage, as all images are transformed only once when they are inserted in the database. The result is stored as an a priori extracted feature and only the selected coefficients are compared during retrieval runtime.

A query starts with the selection of a region of interest. The background is set with a neutral colour and the object is represented by a minimal bounding rectangle. Thereafter, the region is transformed using the á trous wavelet algorithm and represented by the n absolute largest wavelet coefficients as shown in Figure 1. Subsequently, all image sections are searched for the occurrence of a similar feature vector. Retrieval tests with standard objects such as symbols and traffic signs showed that a direct comparison of the extracted coefficients leads to poor differentiation between hits and misses. Therefore, characteristic properties such as maximal and minimal coefficients, standard deviation and average value are evaluated and combined into a similarity index. The similarity check between the object and the section to be examined is realised according to the following algorithm:

```
Total similarity = 0
FOR all decomposition levels BEGIN
     Extract the absolute largest coefficients at the same
          positions as in the object
     Calculate the difference between the minimum and maximum
          as well as the average and standard deviation of
          the image and object coefficients
     Add all differences to the similarity value
END
```

The retrieval quality was measured experimentally in three steps using collections of sample images. Firstly, symbols and traffic signs were searched in a collection of 100 photos each. All query samples were returned as a best hit, thus a retrieval rate of 100% was obtained. Subsequently, a number of images (14) in the database with more than 4000 pictures was modified by insertion of a template of a person. Seven of these templates were rotated (15°, 90°), mirrored, downsized (50%, 80%) and partly masked with another object. The retrieval operations considered every fifth position in a row and used 448 coefficients and two decomposition levels for the computation of the similarity degree. Figure 2 shows the best four hits of a dynamic image retrieval using á trous coefficients.

Eleven of the inserted templates were recognised as similar, which corresponds to a rate of 78,6%. Nine of these images were returned within the best 32 hits (64,3%) and three within the best four hits. Not recognised were the 90° rotated, 50% reduced and the horizontally mirrored template.

The third experiment considered "real" images showing the same person in forest scenes. Different lightning conditions, varying distances to the camera as well as gestures and facial play increase the complexity significantly. Figure 3 depicts four hits retrieved from the forest series. The query object is the person marked in Figure 1. In contrast to the high retrieval rate achieved with the inserted templates only five of the 14 possible images were found in the first 32 retrieval hits. The poor result of 21,7% shows that this method is only partly suitable for retrieval of "real" images. This rate is significantly improved, when a multi-scale and multi-rotation search is performed.

Fig. 2. Retrieved pictures on the first four positions using wavelet-based template matching

An alternative approach is given by transforming the query and the target section using the standard wavelet algorithm and comparing the largest coefficients directly. This is an adaptation of the wavelet-based method for image comparison proposed by JACOBS ET AL. [9]. However, the retrieval rate in real images remains nearly unchanged and amounts to less than 20%. A disadvantage of this standard method compared to the introduced á trous approach is that online computation of the wavelet decomposition for the target sections is required. This necessitates the availability of huge computing resources.

3 Cluster Architecture for Efficient Retrieval

Dynamic image retrieval requires the analysis of all *image sections* in the database and produces a big processing load in addition to the large storage demands. Image storage and retrieval applications are thus both time and space complex. It is well-known that parallel processing potentially offers effective and efficient solutions to such problems. Cluster architectures are cost-effective MIMD-platforms due to the fact that standard hardware and software components can be used.

Fig. 3. Retrieved pictures from a "real" photo series showing a person in different forest scenarios

A disadvantage of clusters is the relatively narrow intra-node communication bandwidth.

PFISTER [10] defines a cluster as a parallel or distributed system consisting of a collection of interconnected stand-alone computers and used as a single, unified computing resource. The best-known cluster platform is *Beowulf*, a trivially reproducible multi-computer architecture [11]. Clusters have the advantage that each node has its own primary and secondary memories. This avoids the communication bottleneck common to shared memory architectures. Moreover, the reasonable price per node enables the creation of systems with a large number of processing elements (PE's). This section gives a short overview over a special cluster-based architecture for image retrieval with dynamically extracted features called Cairo.

Cairo is based on a Beowulf cluster with 16 SMP (Symmetrical Multiprocessing) nodes, each of them with two PE's. Thus parallelism on a global and a local level can be combined within an individual query. Based on the functionality the nodes are subdivided into:

- Query stations, which host the graphical user interface and provide a web-based access to the image database.

- Master node, which controls the cluster, receives the query requests, and broadcasts the algorithms, search parameters, the sample image and the features to the computing nodes. Furthermore, it unifies the sub-results and produces the final ranking.
- Computing nodes, which perform the image processing and comparisons. Each of these nodes contains a disjunctive subset of the existing images and executes all operations with the data stored on the local devices. The sub-results are sent to the master node.

The partitioning and the distribution of the image set across the individual cluster nodes are decisive for the retrieval efficiency. A reliable, content-based partitioning of the images into independent subsets is, however, currently not realisable. This is especially the case when a general image stock is used. An unsuitable assignment can lead to some images being unfindable, since they are not even considered during the corresponding queries.

This is the reason why the initial partitioning of the Cairo image set B uses a content-independent, size-based strategy, that leads to a set of partitions $P = P_1, P_2, \ldots, P_n$ with the following characteristics:

$$\forall P_i, P_j \subset B : P_i \cap P_j = \emptyset, \quad size(P_i) \approx size(P_j) \quad i,j = 1, \ldots, n,\ i \neq j. \quad (1)$$

The processing of a partition $P_i = \{b_{i1}, b_{i2}, \ldots, b_{in_i}\}$ is executed per image, i.e. the individual operations are independent of one another. This initial partitioning makes it possible for all nodes to have uniform processing times, assuming a homogenous, dedicated execution platform, if a query needs to analyse all images in the database.

The distribution of the data across a number of nodes enables a parallelisation of the retrieval by executing the same operations on all nodes and only considering the local image subset. Components called *Transaction*, *Distribution*, *Computation* and *Result manager* based on the parallel libraries PVM and MPI are necessary to implement this approach. The transaction manager determines the order of the operations to be executed and controls the module for workload balancing by dynamic re-distribution of images between the nodes. The distribution manager generates the program calls for the image analysis according to the PVM and MPI syntax and sends these to all computing managers on the cluster nodes, which control the execution of the extraction algorithms with the local data. The result manager unifies all sub-results and submits the final ranking to the user interface for visualisation.

The evaluation of a priori extracted features in the first stage reduces the set of images to be analysed dynamically. Thus, the even distribution of the images over the cluster nodes is distorted and the gain through parallel processing is limited. The workload across the cluster is balanced by moving images permanently or temporarily to idle nodes. It can be proven that this problem is NP-complete [12] and no exact polynomial algorithm exists (unless P = NP). Therefore, heuristic strategies for workload balancing such as LTF (*Largest Task First*) are developed, which enable a significant reduction of the system response time [13].

4 Conclusions

This paper introduces a wavelet-based approach for image retrieval using dynamically extracted features. All images are transformed with the á trous algorithm, thus the number of created approximation coefficients equals the number of pixels. This is important for the a priori computation of the wavelet images. A user-defined region of interest is represented by a number of coefficients and compared to all sections in the database. All other image elements are ignored, so a detail search can be realised. The related computational requirements are satisfied by using a high performance cluster architecture for image retrieval.

Future work includes the examination of further methods for dynamic retrieval, e.g. Gabor-Wavelets [14] are a promising approach. Other similarity criterions in combination with the fast wavelet transform have to be examined in more detail.

References

1. J. Ashley et al. Automatic and semi-automatic methods for image annotation and retrieval in QBIC. In *Proceedings of Storage and Retrieval for Image and Video Databases III*, volume 2420, pages 24–35, SPIE, 1995.
2. C. Nastar et al. Surfimage: A flexible content-based image retrieval system. In *Proceedings of ACM Multimedia*, pages 339–344, 1998.
3. J.R. Smith, S.-F. Chang. Visualseek: a fully automated content-based image query system. In *Proceedings of ACM Multimedia*, pages 87–98, 1996.
4. S. Santini, R. Jain. Image databases and not databases with images. In *Proceedings of Conference on Image Analysis and Processing*, pages 38–48, 1997.
5. S. Mallat. *A Wavelet tour of signal processing.* Academic Press, 1998.
6. M. Feil, A. Uhl. Real-time image analysis using wavelets: the a trous algorithm on MIMD architectures. *IS&T/SPIE's Imaging Newsletter*, 9(2):4–5, 1999.
7. M. Shensa. Wedding the á trous and the mallat algorithms. *IEEE Transactions on Signal Processing*, 40(10):2464 - 2482, 1992.
8. P. Dutilleux. An implementation of the algorithm á trous to compute the wavelet transform. In *J. Combes, A. Grossmann, P. Tchamitchian (Edts.): Wavelets: Time-Frequency Methods and Phase-Space*, pages 298 - 304. Springer, 1989.
9. C. E. Jacobs, A. Finkelstein, D. H. Salesin. Fast multiresolution image querying. In *Proceedings of ACM Siggraph 95*, pages 277 - 286. Springer, 1995.
10. G. F. Pfister. *In Search of Clusters.* Prentice Hall, 2. edition, 1998.
11. D.F. Savarese, T. Sterling. Beowulf. In *R. Buyya (Edt.): High Performance Cluster Computing - Architectures and Systems*, pages 625–645, Prentice Hall, 1999.
12. R. Karp. Reducibility among combinatorial problems. In *Complexity of Computer Computations*, pages 85–104. Plenum Press, 1972.
13. O. Kao, G. Steinert, F. Drews. Scheduling aspects for image retrieval in cluster-based image databases. In *Proceedings of the IEEE/ACM International Symposium on Cluster Computing and the Grid (CCGrid 2001)*, pages 329–336, 2001.
14. V. Krüger, G. Sommer. Gabor wavelet networks for object representation. Technical Report 2002, University of Kiel, February 2000.

Image Retrieval in Multimedia with Emergence Index

Sagarmay Deb, Yanchun Zhang
Dept. of Maths & Computing
Univ. of Southern Queensland
Toowoomba,QLD 4350 Australia
debsc@idx.com.au

Abstract. Emergence is a phenomenon where we study the implicit or hidden meaning of an image. We introduce this concept in image database access and retrieval of images using this as an index for retrieval. This would give an entirely different search outcome than ordinary search where emergence is not considered, as consideration of hidden meanings could change the index of search. We discuss emergence, emergence index and accessing multimedia databases using emergence index in this paper.
Key words: Content-based image retrieval, Emergence index, Multimedia Databases

1 Introduction

Content-based image retrieval (CBIR) is a bottleneck of multimedia database access. Although extensive research has been done during the last decade, it has yet to attain maturity. Original text-based approach in image retrieval was time consuming and expensive as it involved manual processing of image data which could sometime be very voluminous. Attempts have been made to combine text-based and content-based retrieval [5] and quite a few models like QBIC, Virage, Excalibur, Attrasoft, Pichunter, VisualSEEK, Chabot, Photobook and so on have been developed. Fully automated CBIR has come into being very recently using low-level features like color, texture, shape and spatial locations. Few models are now commercially available like QBIC, Virage, Excalibur, Attrasoft and others. Also non-commercial models developed by universities and research institutions are also available. But they do an approximate match between input and objects of image database. Thorough image segmentation, which is important for very accurate retrieval is still a problem.

CBIR has been defined in three levels. Level 1 is about finding symmetry between input image and images of database. As we mentioned, success to some extent has been achieved in this level. Level 2 is about extracting semantic meaning out of the image like 'Find a double-decker bus in an image'. Only very limited success has been achieved in this field. One of the best known works in this field is of Forsyth and others [2] by successfully identifying human being within image and this technique has been applied for other objects. Level 3 is about finding inner meanings of an image like 'Find pain in an image'. This requires very sophisticated and complex logic and segmentation. Very little has been achieved so far in this level with current technology [1].

Multimedia databases. The ultimate goal of multimedia database is to have all information types digitized and computerized. But this has not yet been achieved. The multimedia database could contain, as we know, text, audio, still images, digital video and graphic objects.

Multimedia database is highly efficient database that supports multimedia data types, alphanumeric types and handle very large volumes of information. The multimedia database management system consists of three capabilities, conventional database system and hierarchical storage system support and information retrieval capacity.

In multimedia databases queries are more often based on content of the objects. As we discussed, images can be accessed based on their contents and spatial relationships among various objects within the image. For voice data, the index could be based upon speaker of the voice information. For color image, color histograms could be used as index for search and access. For video images, it could be scenes. For text data, the search attributes could be nonstop words. Once we define the attributes and features of multimedia data, they could be used as index in searching multimedia database. Images take lot of space on our hard disks. A multimedia database can help us wrangle these files. They allow us to view an image, play a movie or hear a sound even if we do not have the program that created it. This could be time saver. We do not need to launch several applications to look through a variety of files. We can drill down in search through the results of a previous search to find an image, then drag it into a page layout program [6]. From commercial point of view, the multimedia database is nothing but glorified file management system. In terms of research it means to do more in terms of finding semantic meanings of image [7].

The paper provides definition and application of emergence index using pictures and application of emergence index in image query processing. Section 2 gives the definition and section 3 the access of multimedia database. We make our conclusion on section 4.

2 Emergence Index

Feature of an image, which is not explicit, is emergent feature if it can be made explicit.

Examples of emergence. Shape emergence is associated with emergence of individual or multiple shapes. Figure 1 contains examples of shape emergence.

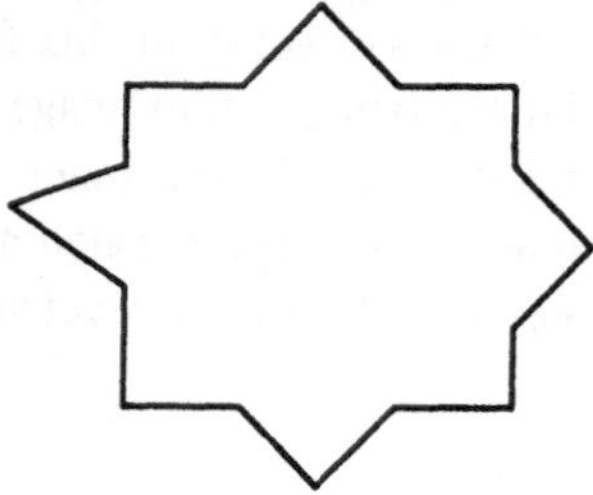

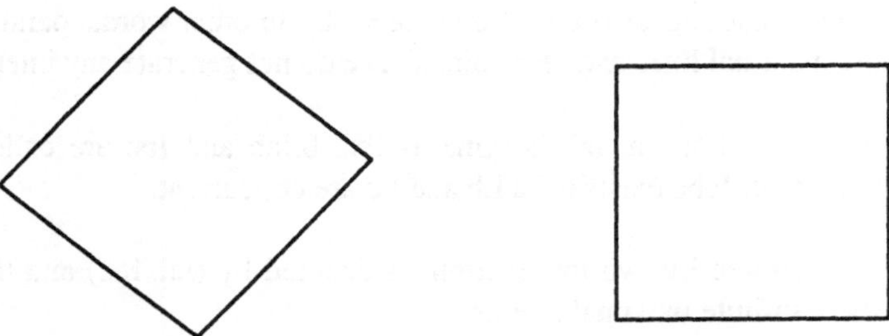

Figure 1 Two Emergent shapes derived from the existing one. The first one is the existing shape
whereas the other two are emergent shapes from the first [4]

2.1 Definition of Emergence Index

Image retrieval where the hidden or emergence meanings of the images are studied and based on those hidden meanings as well as explicit meanings, where there is no hidden meaning at all, an index of search is defined to retrieve images is called emergence index.

2.2 Semantic Representation of images

Symbolic Representation of images. The symbolic representation of shapes can be defined using infinite maximal lines as

$$I = \{N; constraints\} \quad (1)$$

Where N is the number of infinite maximal lines which effectively constitutes image I and constraints are restrictions which define behaviors or properties that come out from the infinite maximal lines [3].

2.3 Various mathematical tools that would be used in the definition of the image

Geometric property. There are four geometric properties involved in infinite maximal lines: a. Two lines La and Lb are perpendicular, $La \perp Lb$. b. Two lines La and Lb are parallel, La // Lb. c. Two lines La and Lb are skewed, $La \times Lb$. d. Two lines La and Lb are coincident, La = Lb

Topological property. Intersection and segment are two properties of a set of infinite maximal lines. If La and Lb are two infinite maximal lines then intersection Iab would be denoted by a. $La \times Lb \Rightarrow Iab$, b. $La \perp Lb \Rightarrow Iab$ where => means 'implies'. The first case of the above is the skewness whereas the second case is perpendicularity of the geometric property.

The intersection cannot occur if La // Lb or La = Lb. In other words, parallel behavior of two infinite maximal lines and also coincidence do not generate any intersection.

Properties of intersection a. Iab is same as Iba. b.Iab and Ibc are called collinear intersection in Lb. c. Iabc exists if La,Lb and Lc are concurrent.

The segment generated by two intersections is denoted by (Iab,Ibc) and this segment lies obviously in infinite maximal line Lb.

There are three types of intersection groups: ordinary groups, adjacent groups and enclosed groups. These three groups indicate three kinds of topological structures, which define intersections and line segments in different ways. Ordinary group could be expressed by a pair of '(' and ')' parentheses. In this case a line segment could be defined by two intersections. If La,Lb and Lc are three lines, then segment of line would be (Iab,Icb). The adjacent group is defined by a pair of angle '<' and '>' brackets. Here only two adjacent intersections can represent line segment of the order <Iab,Iac>. An enclosed group, defined by a pair of square '[' and ']' brackets represent a circuit of line segments. For a triangle it would be [Iab,Iac,Ibc].

Dimensional property. The length of the segment of two intersections is the dimensional property and is denoted by d(Iab,Ibc).

3 Accessing Multimedia Databases

In this section we discuss the methodology we follow in accessing multimedia databases. We have pointed out that CBIR is a bottleneck in accessing multimedia databases. We attempt to establish symmetry between input and images of multimedia database on contents using emergence index.

3.1 Symmetry between input and images of database

Calculation of index of input. Let us suppose our input image is of the kind shown below.

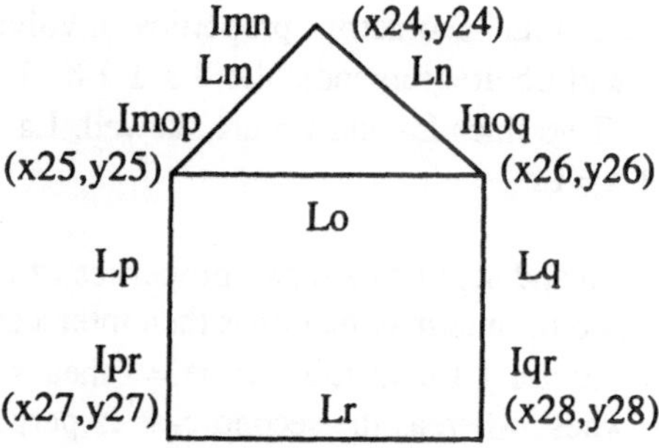

Figure 2 input

This is the image of a house. In the input image, coordinates are obviously (x24,y24),(x25,y25),……,(x28,y28). We notice if Lm,Ln,Lo,Lp,Lq and Lr are the six lines constituting the house, then Lp//Lq,Lo//Lr. Also the number of sides is 6.

The distance between (x25,y25) and (x27,y27) is same as the distance between (x26,y26) and (x28,y28). This can be defined as d{(x25,y25), (x27,y27)} = d{(x26,y26), (x28,y28)} which is d(Imop,Ipr) = d(Inoq,Iqr).

Again the distance between (x24,y24) and (x25,y25) is same as the distance between (x24,y24) and (x26,y26). This can be defined as d{(x24,y24), (x25,y25)} = d{(x24,y24), (x26,y26)} which is d(Imn,Imop) = d(Imn,Inoq).

Also the distance between (x25,y25) and (x26,y26) is same as the distance between (x27,y27) and (x28,y28) and this can be defined as d{(x25,y25), (x26,y26)} = d{(x27,y27), (x28,y28)} which is d(Imop,Inoq) = d(Ipr,Iqr).

Calculation of index of image. In the example image, we have three objects O1,O2,O3. O1 is the lake, O2 a house and O3 is also a house. Coordinates for O1 are C1=(x1,y1), C2=(x2,y2),…….. C13=(x13,y13). Coordinates for O2 are C14=(x14,y14), C15=(x15,y15), …. , C18=(x18,y18). The six sides are La,Lb,Lc,Ld,Le and Lf. Coordinates for O3 are C19=(x19,y19), C20=(x20,y20), …., C23=(x23,y23). The six sides are Lg,Lh,Li,Lj,Lk and Ll.

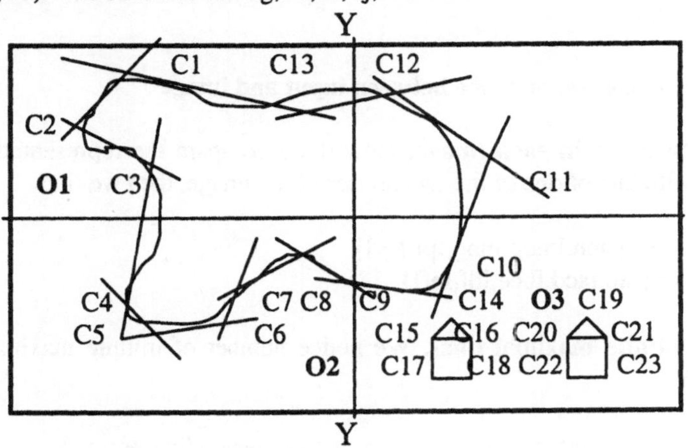

Figure 3 Image of multimedia database

Constraints. According to equation (1) in Section 2.2, constraints for O1,O2 and O3 are as follows:

For O1, I = {13;C1,C2,C3,….,C13}.
For O2, the number of sides is 6 and the distance between (x15,y15) and (x17,y17) is same as the distance between (x16,y16) and (x18,y18). In other words, d{(x15,y15),(x17,y17)} = d{(x16,y16),(x18,y18)} which is d(Iacd,Idf) = d(Ibce,Ief).

Also distance between (x14,y14) and (x15,y15) is same as the distance between (x14,y14) and (x16,y16). In other words,
d{(x14,y14),(x15,y15)} = d{(x14,y14),(x16,y16)} which is d(Iab,Iacd) = d(Iab,Ibce).

And distance between (x15,y15) and (x16,y16) is same as the distance between (x17,y17) and (x18,y18). In other words,
d{(x15,y15),(x16,y16)} = d{(x17,y17),(x18,y18)} which is d(Iacd,Ibce) = d(Idf,Ief).

Then Ld//Le, Lc//Lf.

For O3, the number of sides is 6 and the distance between (x20,y20) and (x22,y22) is same as the distance between (x21,y21) and (x23,y23). In other words, d{(x20,y20),(x22,y22)} = d{(x21,y21),(x23,y23)} which is d(Igij,Ijl) = d(Ihik,Ikl).

Also distance between (x19,y19) and (x20,y20) is same as the distance between (x19,y19) and (x21,y21). In other words,
d{(x19,y19),(x20,y20)} = d{(x19,y19),(x21,y21)} which is d(Igh,Igij) = d(Igh,Ihik).

And distance between (x20,y20) and (x21,y21) is same as the distance between (x22,y22) and (x23,y23). In other words,
d{(x20,y20),(x21,y21)} = d{(x22,y22),(x23,y23)} which is d(Igij,Ihik) = d(Ijl,Ikl).

Then Lj//Lk, Li//Ll.

3.2 To establish correspondence between input and image

Group intersections in each image. Now if we compare the representation of this input image with that of one of the two houses of the image, then we find

Input = {6;[Imn,Imop,Inoq,Ipr,Iqr]}
O2 = {6;[Iab,Iacd,Ibce,Idf,Ief]}

Number of infinite maximal lines. We notice number of infinite maximal lines in each case is 6.

Corresponding equivalence. Considering the corresponding equivalence of various segments, we get

La ⇔ Lm ^ Lb ⇔ Ln ^ Lc ⇔ Lo ^ Ld ⇔ Lp ^ Le ⇔ Lq ^ Lf ⇔ Lr

And the corresponding equivalence of various intersections are

Iab ⇔ Imn ^ Iacd ⇔ Lmop ^ Ibce ⇔ Inoq ^ Idf ⇔ Ipr ^ Ief ⇔ Iqr

Number of intersections. The number of intersections in each case is 5.

Geometric constraints of infinite maximal lines. Input has

Imn ⇔ Lm × Ln
Imo ⇔ Lm × Lo
Ino ⇔ Ln × Lo

So Lm × Ln × Lo is established since they intersect each other.

O2 has Iab ⇔ La × Lb
Iac ⇔ La × Lc
Ibc ⇔ Lb × Lc

So La × Lb × Lc is established since they intersect each other.

Dimensional constraints of segments. Since the number of intersections in input and O2 is same, we deduct

In input Lm × Lo ^ Lm × Ln ⇔ (Imo, Imn)
Ln × Lo ^ Ln × Lm ⇔ (Ino, Imn)
Lo × Lm ^ Lo × Ln ⇔ (Iom, Ion)
Lp × Lo ^ Lp × Lr ⇔ (Ipo, Ipr)
Lq × Lo ^ Lq × Lr ⇔ (Iqo, Iqr)
Lp × Lr ^ Lq × Lr ⇔ (Ipr, Iqr)

So dimensional constraints in input is
d(Imo, Imn),d(Ino, Imn),d(Iom, Ion),d(Ipo, Ipr),d(Iqo, Iqr),d(Ipr, Iqr)

In O2 La × Lc ^ La × Lb ⇔ (Iac, Iab)
Lb × Lc ^ Lb × La ⇔ (Ibc, Iab)
Lc × La ^ Lc × Lb ⇔ (Ica, Icb)
Ld × Lc ^ Ld × Lf ⇔ (Idc, Idf)
Le × Lc ^ Le × Lf ⇔ (Iec, Ief)
Ld × Lf ^ Le × Lf ⇔ (Idf, Ief)

So dimensional constraints in input is
d(Iac, Iab),d(Ibc, Iab),d(Ica, Icb),d(Idc, Idf),d(Iec, Ief),d(Idf, Ief)

Corresponding intersections

Lm ↔ La ^ Ln ↔ Lb ^ Lm × Ln ^ La × Lb => Imn ↔ Iab
Lm ↔ La ^ Lp ↔ Ld ^ Lm × Lp ^ La × Ld => Imp ↔ Iad
Ln ↔ Lb ^ Lq ↔ Le ^ Ln × Lq ^ Lb × Le => Inq ↔ Ibe
Lp ↔ Ld ^ Lr ↔ Lf ^ Lp × Lr ^ Ld × Lf => Ipr ↔ Idf
Lq ↔ Le ^ Lr ↔ Lf ^ Lq × Lr ^ Le × Lf => Iqr ↔ Ief

So we see the symmetry between the input and image O2 although they are not of the same size. Also, the image in the database is that of a locality. But our input, which comes as the image of a house, selects this image although they are not same image. This is the emergence index search.

4 Conclusion

We have discussed accessing multimedia databases using emergence index. We have shown how emergence can give rise to altogether different meaning of an image. This could help us explain and interpret images in a more accurate way. More research works need to be done to apply this concept in practical problems of finger-print analysis, understanding cloud behavior in weather forecasting or selecting geographic location in the image database. That way we should be able to find more meanings and hidden patterns of those images which not only would enable us to define them more accurately but also should establish more appropriate symmetry with other images when needed.

To implement this concept, we require thorough image segmentation and also to extract semantic meanings out of an image. As we mentioned in section 1, the current technology still lacks these facilities. However, given the pace of technological advancements in this field, it should not be too long before technology should be able to support us to implement these concepts in practice.

References

1. Eakins, J.P. and Graham, M.E.: Content-based image Retrieval: A report to the JISC Technology Application Program. Institute for Image Data Research, University of Northumbria at Newcastle,U.K.(1999)
2. Forsyth.D.A and others. :Finding pictures of objects in large collections of images. Digital Image Access and Retrieval: 1996 Clinic on Library Applications of Data Processing (Heidon,P.B and Sandore,B,eds), Graduate School of Library and Information Science, University of Illinois at Urbana-Champaign,118-139
3. Gero, J.S. : Shape emergence and symbolic reasoning using maximal lines.Unpublished Notes, Design Computing Unit, Department of Architectural and Design Science, University of Sydney, Sydney(1992)
4. Gero,J.S.: Visual emergence in design collaboration, Key Center of Design Computing, University of Sydney (Year Unknown)
5. Gudivada,V.N. and Raghavan,V.V.: IEEE.Content-Based Image Retrieval Systems (1995)
6. Sandsmark, F.: Multimedia Databases bring Order to Images(1997)
7. Swiderski, Z. :Multimedia Information Systems: Multimedia Databases(1998)

Efficient Multimedia Database Indexing Using Structural Join Index Hierarchy*

Chi-wai Fung [1] and Qing Li [2]

[1] Department of Computing, Institute of Vocational Education, VTC, Tsing Wun Road, NT, Hong Kong, CHINA
cwfung@vtc.edu.hk

[2] Department of Computer Science, City University of Hong Kong, Tat Chee Ave., KLN, Hong Kong, CHINA
csqli@cityu.edu.hk

Abstract. In this paper, we introduce structural join index hierarchy (SJIH) indexing mechanisms that mimic the class composition hierarchy of the complex objects to provide direct access to multimedia objects and/or their component objects. A cost model for processing the queries and maintaining the indices is developed. A heuristic algorithm is designed to select appropriate indices to efficiently process a given set of multimedia queries. Through the use of a News-on-Demand example, we show that SJIH indexing mechanisms facilitate efficient query processing in multimedia applications.

1 Introduction

Performance is a key factor for the success of multimedia database systems, especially when supporting semantically rich applications such as Video Database Management Systems [2,3,10]. For these applications, multimedia object query processing has a major impact on the cost of query processing. One of the ways to improve the performance of query processing is to make use of index. This is because without any particular access structure, query processings are processed by pointer traversal and sequential scanning of the multimedia database. But the cost of multimedia object query processing using pointer traversal and sequential scanning is very high, especially when: (a) the multimedia objects are large, which is the usual case; (b) component multimedia objects to be retrieved are deep inside the class composition hierarchy (*CCH*); (c) the user may be interested more in the relationship among the complex multimedia object/component objects than in their actual contents in some cases.

For these reasons, we have been developing a uniform framework of structural join index hierarchy (*SJIH*) [6,7,8]. Our main contributions along this research direction include the following: (a) a unified framework of SJIH which subsumes previous work in OODB indexing methods and yet provides efficient support for complex object

* This work was mainly supported by a grant from City University of Hong Kong Strategic Research Grants [Project No. CityU 7001073].

retrieval; (b) a detailed cost model for the retrieval cost, the storage cost and the index maintenance cost for SJIH; and (c) analytical experiments have been conducted to show that there is a wide range of parameters for which SJIH is beneficial. In this paper, we further present experiments on a heuristic SJIH selection algorithm being developed for optimal or near-optimal index selection, and show that the algorithm is both efficient and effective in reducing multimedia object query processing cost.

Our subsequent discussion is based on the running example schema as illustrated in Figure 1. The figure shows a schema of an News-on-Demand video database application. A news video (*News*) has a number of headlines (*Headline*) and a number of stories (*Story*). A headline in turn can have a number of headline video segments (*HSegment*) and a number of keywords (*Keyword*). On the other hand, a story has a number of story video segments (*SSegment*) and a number of bib information (*Bib*). Furthermore, each bib information consists of a number of bib terms (*BibTerm*).

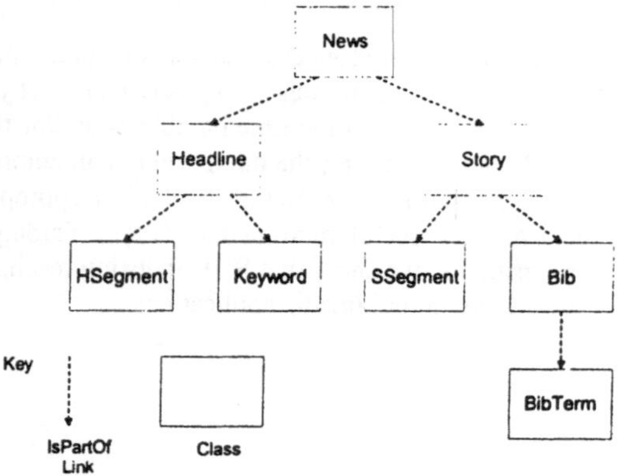

Fig. 1. News-on-Demand database schema

The rest of the paper is organized as follows: Section 2 reviews background work on indexing schemes and index selection algorithms, Section 3 formulates our SJIH indexing framework and Section 4 discusses cost model and index selection algorithm. Conclusions are given in Section 5.

2 Background Work

There has been some work done on indexing techniques for efficient query processing along a CCH. These techniques include: Multi-index (MI) [11], Join index (JI) [12], Nested index (NI) [1], Path index (PI) [1], Access Support Relation (ASR) [9] and Join index hierarchy (JIH) [13]. By comparing the previous work on indexing methods, we note the following points: (a) In terms of the number of index lookups required for query processing, NI, PI, ASR and JIH are better than MI and JI. (b) MI, NI and PI only support reverse traversal, but JI, ASR and JIH support traversals in multiple directions. (c) All of the above indexing methods index on classes along a *single path*, hence for complex object retrieval that requires results from classes on multiple paths, extra processing is required. In contrast, our SJIH framework supports *multiple path* queries, facilitates traversal in both forward and reverse direction, and at the same time is extensible for accommodating new user requirements [8].

Upon input of the database characteristics and query processing characteristics, an index selection algorithm can be devised to determine the optimal or near-optimal indexing method to process a set of queries. As shown in [8], the number of different index configurations grows quickly as the number of classes in an OODB schema increases. Hence the search space for index selection also grows quickly, implying brute force method does not work for index selection problem. Previous work on index selection includes [4], in which an optimal index configuration for a path is achieved by splitting the path into subpaths and optimally indexing each subpath. But they only considered multi-index and nested index along a single path in a CCH. In [5], the index selection problem is addressed based on nested index, with the following index selection algorithms analyzed: a naive scheme, an algorithm based on profit ordering, a greedy algorithm, and a sophisticated look-ahead algorithm.

3 SJIH Mechanisms

3.1 Basic Definitions

We use the join index approach to store OIDs in the form of tuples for efficient complex object retrieval. In the SJIH framework, we present the following index categories: (1) base join index (BJI) ([13]), (2) derived join index (DJI) ([13]), (3) hyper join index (HJI) (our contribution), and (4) structural join index (SJI) (our contribution). Furthermore, BJI and DJI are defined over a single path, whereas HJI and SJI are defined over multiple paths.

The most primitive index under SJIH is the BJI: a BJI is used to support navigation between two adjacent classes. A BJI is a binary relation with the two attributes being the OIDs of two neighbouring classes. Furthermore, BJIs are also useful in building up more complex higher level indices.

A DJI is a ternary relation with the first two attributes being the OIDs of two classes along the same path, and the third attribute (*dup*) is a duplicating factor which records the number of duplicates. As in [13], a *dup* value greater than 1 means that there is more than one connection relating the OIDs of two classes in the OODB. These duplicate factors facilitate the management of the impact of object deletions on the DJI. DJIs are "derived" from the BJIs. While a BJI relates two adjacent classes in the OODB schema, a DJI relates classes that are one or more classes apart and on the same path. In a more complex OODB schema, a DJI can also be derived from other DJIs and/or BJIs.

A HJI is also a ternary relation, where the first two attributes are the OIDs of two classes (over two paths). The third attribute is still the duplicating factor. HJIs also relate objects of two classes in an OODB schema and consists of two OIDs. But HJI can involve classes from two different paths. Note that a DJI is a special case of a HJI when the two classes are from the same path.

For a SJI which indexes on n classes and hence containing a total of n OIDs, the SJI is an $n+1$-ary relation, where the first n attributes are the OIDs of the classes. The last attribute is still the duplicating factor. An SJI is a sophisticated structure as it may contain more than two OIDs from classes in an OODB schema. In fact, an SJI may even cover the whole schema structure (complete SJI), though more often it covers part of the schema structure (partial SJI). From the design point of view, an SJI is a high level abstraction of the original OODB schema that contains the OID information about the classes that are indexed by the SJI.

3.2 Types of SJIH

In a query processing environment with multiple queries, one single indexing method is often not enough to expedite all queries. Furthermore, the user requirements and query patterns may change, requiring accesses to different classes during query processing. Our framework solves this problem by having a SJIH. An SJIH can consist of a set of partial SJIs (or even a complete SJI) coupled with some simpler BJIs, DJIs and HJIs. An ideal SJIH should expedite most of the queries in the query processing environment. When the query pattern changes, we can use the existing indices in the SJIH to form new indices. The following classifications of SJIHs are introduced for a given OODB schema:

Complete-SJIH (CSJIH): It is a single large SJI that covers every class in the schema. CSJIH is the most powerful as all the OID information and hence all the relationships between objects in all the classes are captured. The more the number of classes an SJIH has, the more complex it is. The major problem with CSJIH is its large storage and maintenance cost, especially for a high degree of sharing between composite objects and their component objects.

Partial-SJIH (PSJIH): A PSJIH may contain a number of partial SJIs and some other simpler BJIs, DJIs and HJIs. Since not all the OID information is stored but is spread over a number of indices, we may need to combine these indices to obtain the results for query processing. PSJIH has the advantage of lower maintenance cost, but it may imply higher query processing cost. For cases with a high degree of sharing, the storage overhead will be much lower than that of the CSJIH.

Base-SJIH (BSJIH): It is the collection of all the BJIs between every two neighbouring classes in the OODB schema. Query processing requires combining the relevant BJIs to obtain the result. The main advantage of the BSJIH is its low storage cost even in the case of a high degree of sharing. Another advantage is that it is efficient to maintain a BJI. The main problem with the BSJIH is that the performance of query processing may not be as good as that of the CSJIH or a PSJIH, due to the large number of BJIs involved.

3.3 Examples of SJIH

Figure 2 shows an example occurrence of the *News* object with OID N[1]. Note that we use notations similar to [1], the N[], H[], HS[], S[], SS[], B[] and T[] are OIDs for classes *News*, *Headline*, *HSegment*, *Story*, *SSegment*, *Bib* and *BibTerm*, respectively. From the News-on-Demand application semantics, there is a constrained pair-up [8] between object instances of classes *Headline* and *Story* from the two branches in the schema, that means, headline H[1] is paired-up with story S[1] but not S[2]. Similarly H[2] is only paired-up with S[2].

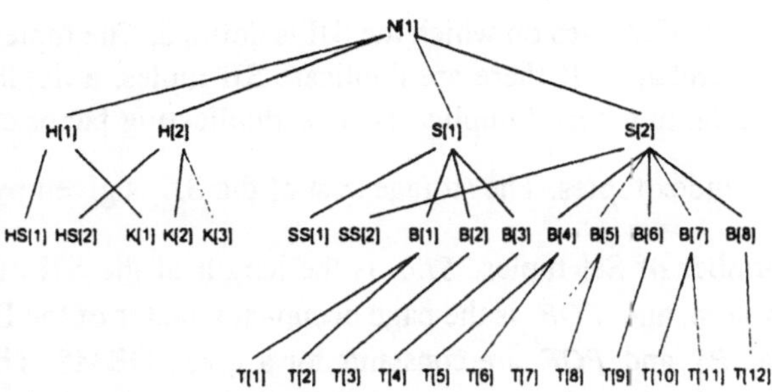

Fig. 2. An example News object

An CSJIH consists of a single complete SJI that stores OIDs of all the classes in the schema. Due to the page limit, only some of the CSJIH index tuples are shown below:

<N[1],H[1],HS[1],K[1],S[1],SS[1],B[1],T[1],1>
<N[1],H[1],HS[1],K[1],S[1],SS[1],B[1],T[2],1>
<N[1],H[1],HS[1],K[1],S[1],SS[1],B[2],T[3],1>
<N[1],H[1],HS[1],K[1],S[1],SS[1],B[3],T[4],1>
<N[1],H[2],HS[2],K[2],S[2],SS[2],B[4],T[5],1>
... (a total of 20 index tuples)

On the other hand, an BSJIH consists of 7 BJIs that index on every pair of neighbouring classes. They are <N[],H[]>, <N[],S[]>, <H[],HS[]>, <H[],K[]>, <S[],SS[]>, <S[],B[]> and <B[].T[]>. Example BJI index tuples that index on classes *News* and *Headline* are:

<N[1],H[1] >
<N[1],H[2] >
(a total of 2 index tuples)

Finally, an example PSJIH that consists of 3 SJIs: an SJI <N[],H[],HS[],K[],S[],SS[],*dup*>, an SJI/BJI <S[],B[]> and an SJI/BJI <B[],T[]>. Example SJI index tuples for <N[],H[],HS[],K[],S[],SS[],*dup*> are:

<N[1],H[1],HS[1],K[1],S[1],SS[1],1>
<N[1],H[2],HS[2],K[2],S[2],SS[2],1>
<N[1],H[2],HS[2],K[3],S[2],SS[3],1>
(a total of 3 index tuples)

4 Cost Model and Index Selection Algorithm

In this section, we summarize the characteristics of the SJIH cost model that includes storage cost, index maintenance cost and query processing cost. We then use the News-on-Demand example for illustration. Furthermore, we report on the effectiveness and efficiency of our heuristic index selection algorithm which finds the optimal or near optimal SJIH.

4.1 Cost Model

We store OIDs of an SJI in the form of tuples in the leaf level of a clustered B^+ tree index. We can also build non-clustered indices on the SJI tuples if required. The index tuple consists of OIDs of classes on which the SJI is defined. The tuples are stored as a relation with no redundancy. If there are duplicate SJI tuples, a duplicating factor is used to record the total number of duplicates. This duplicating factor can facilitate the management of the index tuples. The storage cost of the SJI is given by: $\left\lceil \frac{n \times STJI}{PS \times POF} \right\rceil$, where n is the number of SJI tuples, $STJI$ is the length of the SJI tuples, PS is the page size of the system, and POF is the page occupancy factor of the B^+ tree index. In the above formula, PS and POF are constants for a given DBMS. The length of the SJI tuples is proportional to the number of OIDs being indexed. We find that the constrained pair-up between the classes in the different branches of the CCH influences on the number of SJI tuples. Constrained pair-up (between two classes A and B), means that there are constraints on the pairing up of actual objects (between classes A and B). If the two classes A and B are unconstrained pair-up, the objects in the two classes can be paired up freely without any constraint.

Due to the space limit, interested readers are referred to [7] for the detailed index maintenance and query processing cost model for SJIH. The general features are summarized as follows: (a) Similar to the storage cost, the constrained/unconstrained pair-ups between the different branches of the CCH have a great impact on the index maintenance and query processing cost. The index maintenance and query processing cost of SJIH on CCH with constrained pair-up branches is much less than that with unconstrained pair-up. (b) Within a branch of the CCH, high forward/reverse fan-outs values lead to high index maintenance and query processing cost.

We note from [7] that both the index maintenance cost and query processing cost are highly dependent on the storage cost. The storage cost in turn is dependent on the number of classes, hence number of OIDs being indexed. Furthermore, the storage cost is also dependent on the number of index tuples in the SJIH, in turn dependent on the constrained/unconstrained pair-up between the classes. From the above, we define the term $overhead = \sum_i (numOID_i \times n_i)$, where the summation is over all SJIs in the SJIH, with $numOID_i$ is the number of OIDs and n_i is the number of SJI tuples in the i th SJI.

To illustrate the cost model characteristics by our News-on-Demand schema and example occurrence, we show in Table 1 the overhead and the number of SJIs for each of the following indexing schemes: PSJIH, BSJIH and CSJIH (as illustrated in Section 3.3). From Table 1, we see that in terms of the storage cost/overhead, the use of PSJIH will be the best (with minimum overhead); BSJIH is close to PSJIH; and CSJIH will be the worst. In addition to the storage overhead, the query processing cost is also dependent on the number of SJIs in the SJIH. If the number of SJIs is high, extra processing is required to join back the results. Still from Table 1, we observe that for our running example, PSJIH is still the best in terms of query processing, as it has the minimum overhead and a low number of SJIs. BSJIH is efficient in terms of index maintenance (it has an overhead quite close to that of PSJIH), but for query processing, it is not as efficient as PSJIH due to its larger number (viz., 7) of SJIs involved. Finally, CSJIH is inefficient in terms of index maintenance, as its storage overhead is nearly triple that of PSJIH. So in terms of query processing, although CSJIH has some advantages over BSJIH with its smallest number of SJI involved, it still cannot compete with PSJIH due to its overly large storage overhead [8].

Table 1. Summary of overhead and number of SJIs

Index	*Overhead*	*Number of SJIs*
PSJIH	58	3
BSJIH	62	7
CSJIH	160	1

4.2 Index Selection Algorithm

Index selection algorithm that minimizes query processing cost has been regarded as a tough problem. In particular, for an OODB schema with *n* classes, the number of possible SJIHs grows very quickly [8]. For large *n*, the total number of possible SJIHs approaches 2^{n^2} . In [7], we have described a hill-climbing heuristic SJIH selection algorithm (*HCHSSA*) for finding optimal or near-optimal SJIH based on the input of database characteristics and query characteristics. The design of the HCHSSA is based on the following rationale: (a) As the set of queries in the query processing environment usually does not involve all the classes in the OODB schema, the query graph (*QG*) has fewer or the same number of nodes as the schema graph (*SG*). Dealing with a QG instead of the SG can thus potentially reduce the search space of the HCHSSA. (b) Forming an SJI that covers unconstrained pair-up branches in the QG is expensive both in terms of storage space and retrieval/maintenance cost. We avoid this by separating unconstrained branches from the QG. We break the QG into a number of simpler QGs: one QG contains the constrained pair-up branches, and the other QGs contain one unconstrained pair-up branch in each QG. By doing this, the search space is significantly trimmed down by breaking the QG into a set of simpler QGs (SQG).

For an example CAD schema (which has 11 classes and is similar to the News-On-Demand schema) and query processing environment [7], we have performed analytical evaluation on our HCHSSA. In the first part of the evaluation, we used Exhaustive Enumeration Algorithm (*EEA*) to exhaustively enumerate all possible SJIHs to find the minimum cost SJIH. This absolute minimum cost SJIH serves as a measure to the quality of the output of the HCHSSA. In the second part of the experiment, we used our HCHSSA. The HCHSSA produces the same final SJIH as the EEA, which means that the HCHSSA finds the optimal solution in its hill-climbing process. In terms of effectiveness, HCHSSA finds the optimal solution in all three sets of queries, which means HCHSSA is quite effective when compared with the EEA. In terms of efficiency, the efficiency of the algorithm to find the optimal SJIH is dictated by the number of SJIHs probed during the search. HCHSSA is also highly efficient when compared with the EEA. We further note that the process of branch separation greatly reduces the number of SJIHs to be probed in the later stages of the algorithm. For a query graph (without branch separation) with 11 classes, for example, the number of SJIHs probed in the EEA will be approximately 3×10^{26} as compared with 17,901 in HCHSSA. Finally, in the case where there is only limited storage space available for storing the indices, from the lower envelop of the scatter plot of storage space vs. total cost, HCHSSA facilitates selection of a near-optimal set of indices for efficiently executing the set of queries.

5 Conclusions

Queries in multimedia database systems typically access complex objects and/or their component objects. In order to support their efficient processing, it is important to provide suitable access methods for retrieving complex multimedia database objects. Earlier work on OODB indexing has addressed efficient navigation through path expressions. We have extended existing work by advocating the Structural Join Index Hierarchy (SJIH) mechanism for retrieving complex multimedia database objects. A cost model for processing the queries and maintaining the indices is developed. Our performance results demonstrated the utility of the SJIH, and showed the superiority of a selected SJIH over other indexing schemes, such as nested index, multi-index and access support relation. A heuristic algorithm HCHSSA is developed to select appropriate indices to efficiently process a given set of queries over an example database schema. Our results show that, given a set of queries, the heuristic algorithm facilitates fast selection of the optimal or near-optimal set of indices for efficiently executing the queries.

References

1. E. Bertino and W. Kim, "Indexing Technique for Queries on Nested Objects", in *IEEE Trans. on Knowledge and Data Engineering*, 1(2): 196-214, 1989.
2. S. Chan and Q. Li, "Developing an Object-Oriented Video Database System with Spatio-Temporal Reasoning Capabilities", in *Proc. of Intl. Conf. on Conceptual Modeling (ER'99)*, LNCS 1728, 47-61, 1999.
3. S. Chan and Q. Li, "Architecture and Mechanisms of a Web-based Video Data Management System", in *Proc. of IEEE Intl. Conf. on Multimedia and Expo (ICME'2000)*, 2000.
4. S. Choenni, E. Bertino, H. M. Blanken and T. Chang, "On the Selection of Optimal Index Configuration in OO Databases", in *Proc. Intl. Conf. of Data Engineering*, p526-537, 1994.
5. Sudarshan S. Chawathe, Ming-Syan Chen, Philip S. Yu, "On Index Selection Schemes for Nested Object Hierarchies", in *Proc. Intl. Conf. on Very Large Data Bases*, p331-341, 1994.
6. C. W. Fung, K. Karlapalem and Q. Li, "Structural Join Index Hierarchy: A Mechanism for Efficient Complex Object Retrieval", in *Proc. of 5th Intl. Conf. on Foundations of Data Organization (FODO'98)*, Kobe, Japan, p127-136, 1998.
7. C. W. Fung, K. Karlapalem and Q. Li, "Complex Object Retrieval via Structural Join Index Hierarchy Mechanisms: Evaluation and Selection Approaches", in *Proc. of 9th ACM Intl. Conf. on Information and Knowledge Management*, p150-157, 2000.
8. C. W. Fung, "Vertical Class Partitioning and Complex Object Retrieval in Object Oriented Databases", PhD Thesis, Department of Computer Science, Hong Kong University of Science & Technology, December, 1998.
9. A. Kemper and G. Moerkotte, "Access Support in Object Bases", in *ACM-SIGMOD Intl. Conf. on Management of Data*, Atlantic City, N.J., p364-374, 1990.
10. Q. Li, S. Chan, Y. Wu and Y. Zhuang, "Web-based Video Database Management: Issues, Mechanisms, and Experimental Development", *Proc. 7th Int'l Conference on Distributed Multimedia Systems (DMS'2001)*, Taipei, Taiwan, Sept.26-28, 2001.
11. D. Maier and J. Stein, "Indexing in an object-oriented DBMS", in *Proc. IEEE Intl. Workshop on Object-oriented Database System*, p171-182, Asilomar, Pacific Grove, CA, September 1986.
12. P. Valduriez, "Join indices", in *ACM Trans. on Database Systems*, 12(2):218-246, 1987.
13. Z. Xie and J. Han, "Join Index Hierarchies for Supporting Efficient Navigations in Object-Oriented Databases", in *Proc. Intl. Conf. on Very Large Data Bases*, p522-533, 1994.

Modeling of the HLA-based Simulation System

Jiung-Yao Huang[1] and Lawrence Y. Deng

Department of Computer Science and Information Engineering,
Tamkang University, Tamsui, Taipei, Taiwan 251
[1]jhuang@mail.tku.edu.tw

Abstract. High Level Architecture is the IEEE standard 1516 to build a large scale distributed virtual environment over the Internet. This paper proposes a Colored-Timed Petri Net(CTPN) model to analyze and design an HLA-based simulation, called federation. The proposed model aims to assist the Federation Development and Execution Process(FEDEP) to facilitate the process of creating a federation. The paper strictly follows the HLA specification to analyze and develop the proposed model so that it can later become a template for the designer to develop a federation. With the developed CTPN model, a system developer can modularly design a federation by cost effective method. At the end of this paper, a demo game is developed to verify the effectiveness of the proposed model.

1 Introduction

The distributive virtual environment is a computer-generated synthetic world on the network in which users can navigate and interact with each other. Previous work on this effort includes: VERN, DIVE, RING, BRICKNET[1] and SharedWeb[2]. Unfortunately, most of the previous researches defined their own proprietary protocols that are not compatible with each other, let alone interoperation together. To solve this problem, the Defense Advanced Research Project Agency (DARPA) of America with the Army initiated a project called Simulation Network (SIMNET) in 1983 to study the protocol of interconnecting existing simulators to perform the military drill. With the experience from SIMNET, the Distributed Interactive Simulation (DIS) technology followed in 1989. DIS later became the international standard, IEEE 1218, of the communication protocol for the 3D interactive multiple participants virtual environment.

In 1995, Department of Defense, US, proposed a new communication architecture called High Level Architecture(HLA) which has become the international standard, IEEE 1516, in year 2000.[3] The goal of the HLA is to provide a structure that supports reusability and interoperability among different types of simulation. According to the HLA terminology, the simulating system is called the federate and the simulation environment that is composed of multiple federates is called the federation. The HLA specification itself does not furnish enough information for the developer to design a complete HLA-based simulation environment. To alleviate this situation, DMSO proposes a standardized procedure to develop and execute a federation, called

Federation Development and Execution Process(FEDEP)[4].

FEDEP, however, is not a method to build a federation. Instead, it is a guideline document for the developer to comply when he designs a federation. The goal of this paper is to propose a Colored-Timed Petri Net(CTPN) model for the federate developing process to facilitate the process of creating a federation. This paper strictly follows the HLA specification to analyze and develop the proposed model so that it can later become a template for developing a federation. In the following sections, the concept of HLA and the modeling tool is introduced first. The process of developing the proposed model then follows. Finally, in order to verify the effectiveness of the proposed model, a demo game is implemented and briefly discussed at the end.

2 Related Works

2.1 High Level Architecture(HLA)

The objective of HLA is to provide a common simulation framework to facilitate the interoperability of all types of simulations, analysis tools, and live players. In addition, the HLA standard aims to promote the reuse of these modular Modeling and Simulation components. The HLA is defined by three concepts: [3]

Object Model Templates(OMT);
Interface Specification;
HLA compliance rules.

The Interface Specification defines programming interfaces with six types of services, which are Federation Management, Declaration Management, Object Management, Ownership Management, Time Management, and Data Distribution Management. The software that realizes these six service groups is called Run Time Infrastructure(RTI).

The OMT is a template for documenting HLA-relevant information about classes of simulation or federation objects and their attributes and interactions. This common template facilitates understanding and comparisons of different simulations/ federations, and provides the format for a contract between members of a federation on the types of objects and interactions that will be supported across its multiple interoperating simulations. When this template is used to describe an individual federation member (federate), it is called a Simulation Object Model (SOM). On the other hand, when this template documents a named set of multiple interacting federates (federation), it is called a Federation Object Model (FOM).

The HLA Rules is a set of ten rules that define the relationship and rationale among federate, federation, FOM, SOM and RTI. Among these ten rules, five rules are applied to federation and other five are to regulate federate. In brief, these rules describe that each federate should have a SOM whereas each federation should have a single FOM. Moreover, the rules say that the operation of a federation is confined by the FOM and the SOM regulates the operation of a federate.

2.2 FEDEP

The FEDEP (**FE**deration **D**evelopment and **E**xecution **P**rocess) is aimed as the completed guiding documents for the federation development and it starts from the objective definition, followed by the designing steps of the federation and execution, and concludes with the assessment of the execution result.[4] The FEDEP is identified by a sequence of six abstract steps: *Define Federation Objectives*, *Develop Federation Conceptual Model*, *Design Federation*, *Develop Federation*, *Integrate and Test Federation*, and *Execute Federation and Prepare Results*.

Even though FEDEP clearly defines the procedures to develop the federation, it is simply a guiding document for the federation developer. It is not a formal methodology for the user to follow or use. This paper proposes a model and a methodology based on Colored-Timed Petri Net for the developer to easily design an HLA-based simulation system.

2.3 The Colored-Timed Petri Net

The Petri Net was originally proposed by C. A. Petri which attempts to develop a formal methodology to describe and analyze a system behavior. The Petri Net model is a graphical and mathematical modeling tool that is especially useful to capture the synchronization characteristic among modules of a system. However, a developer often found out that the Petri Net model could easily grow enormously even when modeling a simple system. This situation is due to the existence of several subnets that possess the same functionality in this large net. To effectively reduce the size of a large net as well as solve the problem of redundant subnets in a net, the Colored Petri Net(CPN) was proposed[5].

The Colored-Timed Petri Net(CTPN)[6] is an enhancement of CPN which takes the timing delay into consideration. The CTPN follows the same disciplines sketched by CPN, except adding the time transition mechanism into the model. In addition, in order to model the distributed system, the CTPN was further extended[7] by adding five communication objects. These five extended objects enable two CTPNs to pass token(s) among them to model the process of distributive computation.

3 Modeling of the Federation

The goal of the HLA is to define a distributive common infrastructure that not only can interoperate different types of simulation systems but also put the evolvement of the future technology into consideration. Due to the vision of this goal, no implementation methodology is limited in constructing an HLA-based simulation environment. Hence, a formal model is required for the developer to design a federation. This model must obey the rules set by the HLA specification and fit tightly to the essence of the HLA standard.

3.1 The Mapping of the CTPN Components

Based upon the HLA specification and the FEDEP, this paper purposes a CTPN model to fully explore the functionalities of a federation execution. Since the HLA environment is a fully distributive simulation environment, the proposed model must fully conform to the designated features of the HLA standard. There are three distinct essences of the HLA specification, which are *distributive*, *modular and reusable*, and *interactive*. Accordingly, the bases of employing CTPN to model the HLA-based simulations must conform to these three essences. Hence, the mapping of components of the CTPN model to a simulation system(federation) is as follows.

CTPN: Since a federation execution represents a distributive computing of a simulation, the entire federation execution is modeled as a complete CTPN. The simulated entities that constitute a federation are modeled as sub-CTPNs. Furthermore, each sub-CTPN models the operation of an object instance and adheres to the information defined in the Federation Object Model (FOM).

Sub-CTPN: Each sub-CTPN is analyzed and designed based upon the information recorded in SOM and each sub-CTPN may be further subdivided into several sub-CTPNs.

Colored Token: The color token is employed to model an object instance with each color representing a category of object. Since each federate must have a unique ID inside a federation execution, each color is also unique inside the CTPN to uniquely model a category of an object.

Immediately Transition: The HLA standard defines a message-based distributive simulation infrastructure. Two categories of messages are identified which are time-based and event-based messages. The event-based message is the message without time stamp and is handled by the RTI immediately after the event is triggered. To exhibit this phenomenon, the Immediate transition is used to model the mechanism of event-based message passing.

Timed Transition: Contrary to the Immediate transition, the time-based message is modeled by the Timed transition of CTPN model.

Macro Transition: As discussed in the previous section, the macro transition is employed to model the transition among sub-CTPNs. Since the entire FOM is modeled as a complete CTPN and each SOM is modeled by a sub-CTPN, the Macro transition models the connection between FOM and SOM.

Place: The place is modeled as a snapshot of the status of a federate. A place represents the current status of a federate during the federation execution.

3.2 Analysis and Design A Federation Execution Model

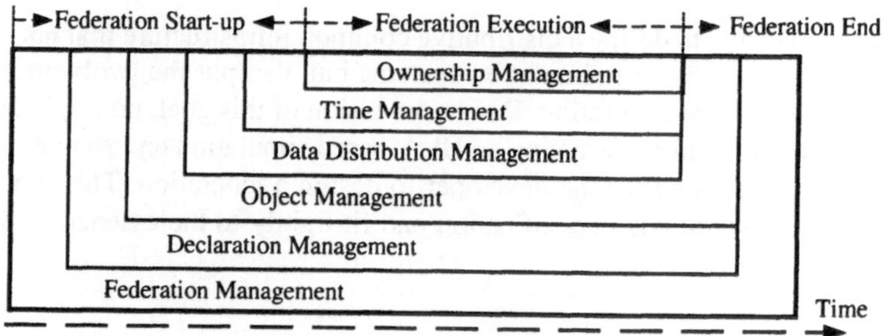

Fig. 1. The federate execution cycle

From the HLA Rule 4, in order to achieve the consistency and validity among messages passed by RTI, each federate must follow the definition of HLA interface specification to request services from RTI. As shown in Fig. 1, a federation execution cycle is composed of three phases, which are Federation Start, Federation Execution and Federation End phases.

These three phases are conjuncted with FOM and SOM to form a complete HLA-based simulation. Furthermore, as shown in Fig. 1, services from the six service groups of the HLA Interface specification must be invoked in the designated order.

The Main CTPN Model. As discussed previously, a federation execution is modeled as a complete CTPN model as depicted in Fig. 2, and it is called the main CTPN model. Following the execution cycle sketched in Fig. 1, the CTPN model in Fig. 2 is mainly composed of a sequence of Pitch down places and Catch up places to modular model the Federation Start-up phase(Fig. 3), the Federation Execution phase(Fig. 5), and Federation End phase(Fig. 6).

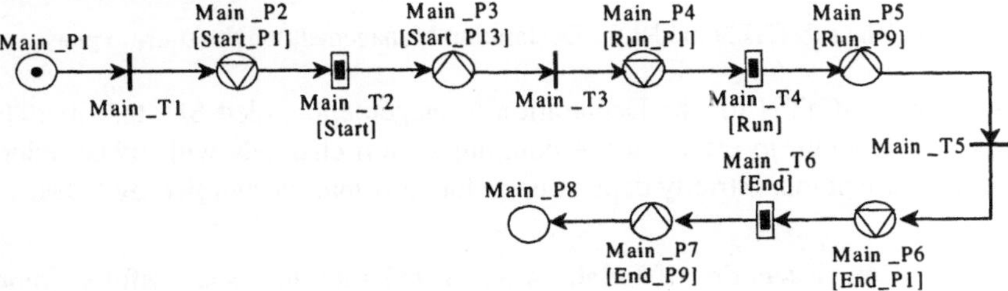

Fig. 2. The main CTPN model

The Federation Start-up Model. Fig. 3 depicts the sub-CTPN model of the HLA-base simulation at the start-up phase.

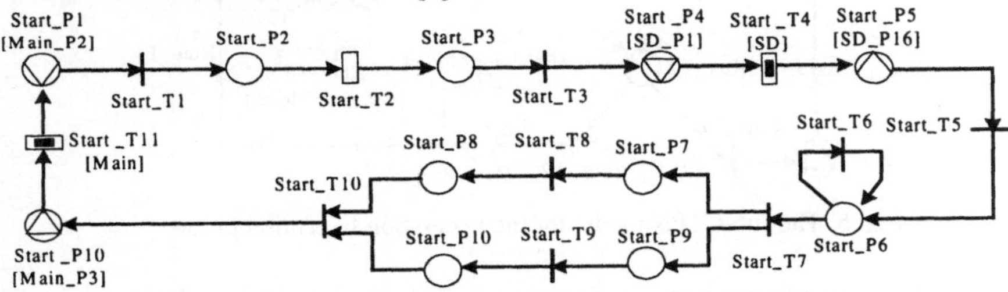

.**Fig. 3.** The sub-CTPN model for the Federation Start-up phase

The Federation start-up phase begins with the transition Start_T1 that models createFederationExecution service call from Federation Management to create a new federation execution if it does not exist. The transition Start_T2 then follows to model joinFederationExecution service call. When a colored token appearing on place Start_p3 indicates that a federate has already successfully joined a federation. The start-up phase then enters another sub-CTPN, called SD, through transition Start_T3. The sub-CTPN, as shown in Fig. 4, is to model the Declaration Management service. After returning from the sub-CTPN SD, a federate then begins to instance and register the simulated objects inside the virtual world by looping the place Start_p6 and the transition Start_T6 to model the Object Management service. Finally, the transition Start_T7 conveys the start-up phase to the Time Management service to activate the time-based messages delivering service. The transition Start_T8 is to model the action of a federate to set itself as a time regulating federate, whereas the transition Start_T9 is to set a time constrained federate.

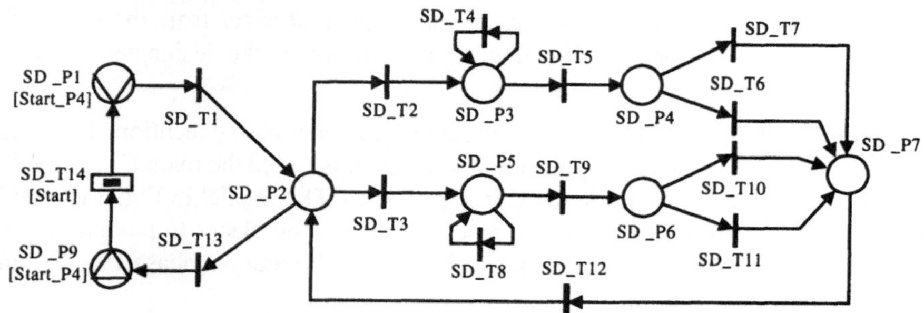

Fig. 4. The sub-CTPN model for Declaration Management on the start-up phase

Fig. 4 is the sub-CTPN for the Declaration Management, called SD, that models the process of a federate to establish the communication channels with other federates. This establishment must strictly depend upon the information supplied by FOM.

The Federation Execution Model. After a federate has successfully joined a federation execution and declared all of the required object classes and interaction types, it then begins to interact with other federates by sending and receiving messages as shown in Fig. 5.

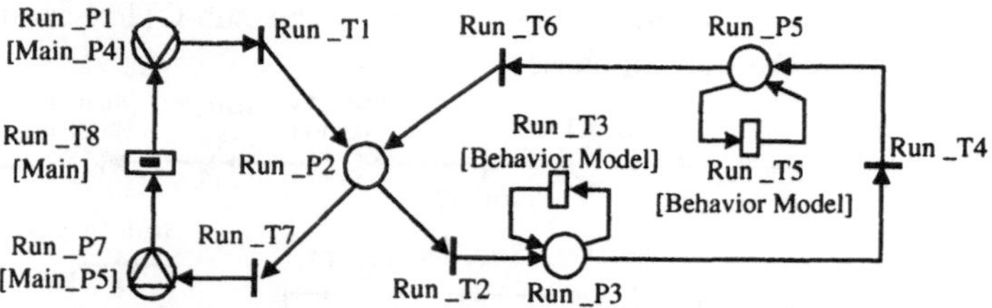

Fig. 5. The sub-CTPN model for the Federation Execution phase

During the federation execution, as depicted in Fig. 5, the simulated federate will repeatedly send the messages of its simulated object(s) and receive events from other federates until condition(s) defined in the place Run_P2 is satisfied. On each bout of the simulation loop, the transition Run_T2 models the beginning of the loop and the transition Run_T6 marks the end. The transition Run_T3 is triggered by every generated object attribute and interaction recorded in SOM. Furthermore, the transition Run_T3 is depended upon the modeled simulated object and need to be further modeled for each specific application. Similar to the event-receiving phase, the transition Run_T5, which models reflectAttributeValues and receiveInteraction service calls defined in Object Management, represents the reaction of federate when receiving events.

The Federation End model. According to Fig. 1, when a federate wants to leave a federation execution, it must first invoke services from Declaration Management and Object Management to relinquish its published and subscribed data before it can use Federation Management to resign from the participated federation. Furthermore, since this relinquishing process must be executed according to the information recorded in FOM and SOM, a sub-CTPN to model Declaration Management is designed as shown in Fig. 7 to fully explore its connection with FOM and SOM.

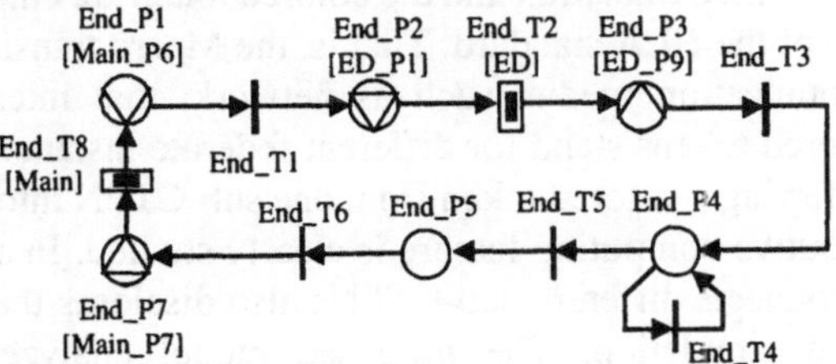

Fig. 6. The sub-CTPN for the Federation End phase

After returning from sub-CTPN ED, the simulated federate then triggers the transition End_T3 to begin to remove its object classes from the federation execution. Finally, the transition End_T5 that models resignFederationExecution service call and the transition End_T6 that models destroyFederationExecution service calls from Federation Management are invoked in order to formally leave the federation.

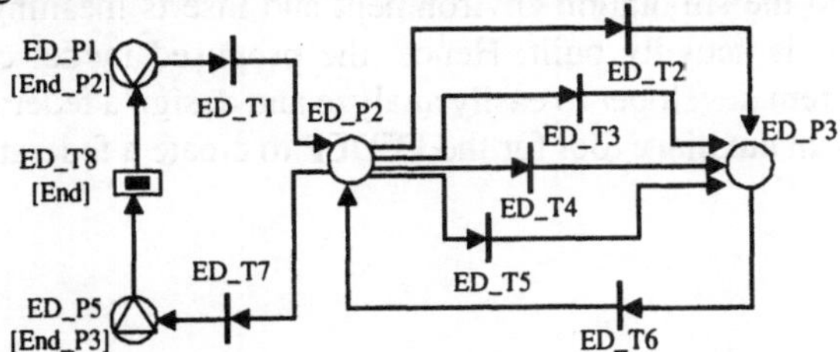

Fig. 7. The sub-CTPN for Declaration Management on the ending phase

4. An Example

To verify the correctness of the proposed CTPN model, an HLA-based gaming demo was designed and experimented. This simplified demo game contains only two types of objects. One is a tank and the other is a helicopter. Furthermore, since the designed federate is used to demo the feasibility of the proposed CTPN model, the interactions among objects for this federation are sending object's status information and firing weapon at each other only. As far as the SOM for the federation, since the designed game is simply a proof-of-concept demo, SOM is exactly the same as FOM. The demo game was implemented under Microsoft Windows 2000 using OpenGL library and GForce II MX 3D acceleration card to display the 3D scene. The machine that runs the demo game is a desktop computer with Pentium III 600 CPU.

5. Conclusion

This paper proposed a CTPN model for the HLA-based simulation system. The proposed model provides an infrastructure for the developer to study and analyze the status of the federation execution. Reusable processes are also explored by the proposed model when we develop an HLA application and efficiently reduce the developing time. The Macro transition and the colored token are employed to model the distributive property of the HLA standard. That is, the Macro transition may implicitly represent the communication media, such as network, that interconnects different sub-CTPNs and colored tokens stand for different federate instances that interact with each other. By transferring a colored token from one sub-CTPN into another via Macro transition, the distributive computing feature is clearly studied. In addition, the Macro transition that interconnects different sub-CTPNs also discloses the modularity of the modeled HLA-based simulation. The proposed model analyzes the HLA-based simulation into a hierarchy of sub-CTPNs. This hierarchy further explores the reusability of the modeled federation execution.

Under the HLA Rules, the federation execution is inseparable from FOM and SOM. But, the HLA specification does not explicitly explain how a federate is collaborated with FOM and SOM. The model proposed in this paper fully investigates this issue by CTPN while adhering to the HLA standard. By naming each color token as a simulation instance and assigning attributes to that token, the proposed model tightly integrates the FOM and SOM into the simulation environment and inserts meaning to the modeled simulation before it is actually built. Hence, the proposed model can be used as a template for the system developer to easily analyze and design a federation. This model can also be used as an auxiliary tool for the FEDEP to create a federation execution.

Reference

1 Singhal, S., Zyda, M.: Networked Virtual Environment: Design and Implementation. ACM Press, January (2000)

2 Huang, J. Y., Fang-Tson, C. T., Chang, J. L.: A Multiple User 3D Web Browsing System. IEEE Internet Computing, Vol. 2, No. 5, Sept/Oct (1998) 70-80

3 Calvin, J. O., Weatherly, R.: An Introduction to the High Level Architecture (HLA) Run-Time Infrastructure(RTI). 14th DIS Workshop, Orlando, FL, March (1996) 705-716

4 Federation Development and Execution Process (FEDEP). [http://www.dmso.mil/briefs/msdocs/guide/fedepv15.pdf]

5 Jensen, K.: Colored Petri Nets and The Invariant Method. Theoretical Computer Science, Vol. 14 (1981) 317-336

6 Christensen, S., Petrucci, L.: Towards a Modular Analysis of Coloured Petri Nets. Lecture Notes in Computer Science, Vol 616, ISBN 3-540-55676-1 (1992) 113-133

7 Kuo, C.H., Huang, H.P., Yeh, M.C.: Object-Oriented Approach of MCTPN for modeling Flexible Manufacturing System. Advanced Manufacturing Technology, Vol. 14, (1998) 737-749

An End-to-End Delivery Scheme for Robust Video Streaming

Jen-Wen Ding[1], Yueh-Min Huang[1], and Cheng-Chung Chu[2]

[1] Department of Engineering Science, National Cheng Kung University,
Tainan, Taiwan, R.O.C.
jwding@mail2000.com.tw; raymond@mail.ncku.edu.tw

[2] Department of Computer Science and Information Engineering, Tunghai University,
Taichung, Taiwan, R.O.C.
chu@csie.thu.edu.tw

Abstract. In this paper, we propose a novel robust end-to-end approach, referred to as packet permutation (PP), to deliver pre-compressed video streams over the Internet. We focus on reducing the impact caused by the bursty loss behavior of the Internet. PP is designed to be both orthogonal and complementary to traditional error control schemes, such as forward error correction (FEC) and feedback/retransmission-based schemes. With the use of PP, the probability of losing a large number of packets within each video frame can be significantly reduced. Our simulation results show that PP greatly reduces the overhead required by FEC (or feedback/retransmission-based schemes) to recover the damaged or lost data in order to achieve a predefined quality of service (QoS).

1 Introduction

1.1 Motivation

With the rising popularity of the Internet and the dramatic evolution in multimedia and communications technologies, there is a growing demand to support video streaming over the Internet. However, the current Internet is unsuitable for supporting video streaming since it offers only a single class best effort service. One of the main drawbacks of this simple service model is that packets may be damaged or lost during transmission. In particular, successive packets are often dropped by routers when the network becomes congested, resulting in bursty packet losses [1], [6], [8]. Previous studies on packet loss on the Internet have indicated that this behavior is primarily caused by the drop-tail queuing discipline employed by many Internet routers [5].

Previous studies on video viewing have shown that packet losses as well as other problems, such as varying transmission delay and bandwidth, have annoying effect on the perceptual quality of video data. In particular, since numerous video compression algorithms apply inter-frame compression techniques [3], the effect caused by packet losses may be significant. With inter-frame dependancy, losing any packet of an intra-frame (also known as a reference frame) is equivalent to losing all interframes related to that intraframe. In this paper, we focus on reducing the annoying effect caused by bursty packet losses. We propose a novel robust end-to-end delivery scheme, termed packet permutation (PP), for pre-compressed video streams over a wide-area network with bursty packet loss behavior, such as the Internet. At the server side, PP permutes the normal packet delivery sequence of video files prior to transmission. At the client side, PP re-permutes the received packets back to the original delivery sequence before they are presented to the application. Therefore, as will be explained in Section 2, when a bursty loss occurs, the probability that a video frame loses consecutive packets can be greatly reduced. More importantly, the probability that a frame loses a large number of packets is also reduced. This effect is significant since it implies that the overhead required to recover the lost packets of all reference frames of a video stream to achieve a predefined QoS can be greatly reduced by PP. The effectiveness of PP is validated via a series of trace-driven simulation experiments presented in Section 3.

1.2 Previous Work and Research Contributions

To handle the bursty loss behavior on the Internet, Varadarajan et al. have recently proposed several error spreading algorithms for video streaming [4], [7]. Their work permutes the data of video streams at the video frame level, while PP performs error spreading at the packet level (certainly, the permutation algorithms of PP and previous work are quite different). Their intention is to reduce the maximum number of consecutive lost frames, referred to as consecutive loss factor (CLF), caused by bursty packet losses. However, the unit of bursty packet losses is a packet, rather than a video frame. The size of a video frame is typically much larger than that of a packet, and different types of frames have very different sizes. For example, for MPEG video, an *I* frame can be divided into approximately 37 packets of 576 bytes, the Internet standard MTU. On the other hand, the length of a bursty loss observed by an end-to-end connection generally ranges from two to six packets in the current Internet [1], [8]. Thus, the probability that many consecutive video frames are damaged by a bursty loss is very low. As a result, although "frame permutation" alleviates the worst case (i.e., reducing the maximum number of consecutive lost frames), the probability distribution functions of packet losses within each video frame remain essentially unchanged. As will be shown in Section 3, while PP significantly reduces the overhead required by error recovery to achieve a predefined QoS, frame permutation fails to reduce this overhead.

PP has three salient features. First, it is orthogonal and complementary to conventional error control schemes such as FEC and feedback/retransmission-based schemes. Note that since it can work synergistically with FEC, it is very suitable for video applications using multicast. Second, PP can be applied to many types of video formats with interframe dependency. To illustrate PP, we primarily apply it to MPEG video, a prevalent video compression format, in this paper. Nevertheless, the algorithm presented in this paper can be extended to other video formats with similar structure. Third, PP has very low computational complexity, which makes the implementation practical.

The rest of this paper is organized as follows. Section 2 details PP and Section 3 presents the results of the trace-driven simulations. Finally, Section 4 concludes this paper.

2 Packet Permutation

2.1 Impact of Bursty Packet Losses

Consider transmitting an MPEG video stream over the Internet. Whenever a bursty loss occurs in the stream (i.e., successive packets of the stream are dropped), three types of situations may occur for the *I* frames of the stream as shown in Figs. 1(a)-(c), where NDS refers to normal delivery sequence. For MPEG video, it is known that losing any of the *I* frame packets will result in a significant impact on the visual quality of the stream since the loss of an *I* frame will render the whole GOP (group of pictures) related to that *I* frame useless. A GOP may contain 12 or 15 frames or hundreds of packets. Hence, it is vital to recover all lost packets for *I* frames. However, this is not an easy task. If FEC is employed, because of the unpredictable behavior of bursty losses, in order to receive all *I* frames correctly, each *I* frame must use a large enough redundancy (i.e., repair packets) in order to recover from the worst case created by bursty losses (e.g., see Fig. 1(c)). If feedback/retransmission-based schemes are employed, there may exist some situations where so many packets of an *I* frame are lost such that it is difficult to retransmit them on time (e.g., see Fig. 1(c)).

Observe from Figs. 1(b) and 1(c) that if the distance between any two consecutive *I* packets can be increased, then the number of *I* packets dropped in a bursty loss will be reduced. The longer the distance, the less the loss. A direct method to achieve this goal is to spread all *I* packets across the entire delivery sequence, as shown in Fig. 1(d). In this way, we can eliminate many ill conditions incurred by bursty losses. In other words, the number of *I* packets dropped in a bursty loss can then be reduced to a small number. Although this method reduces the probability of losing larger numbers of *I* packets, it also increases the probability of losing smaller numbers of *I* packets. This is because when all *I* packets are spread out, an *I* packet is more likely to encounter a bursty loss. Therefore, spreading all *I* packets out reshapes the probability function of the number of lost packets within each *I* frame as depicted in Fig. 2. Obviously, the reshaped function is better. For FEC it substantially reduces the redundant information required to protect all *I* frames. For feedback/retransmission-based schemes, it virtually eliminates events in which so many *I* frame packets are lost that they cannot be retransmitted on time.

Similarly, it is desirable to reduce the probability of losing larger numbers of packets for P_1 frames since the loss of a P_1 frame will render the subsequent *P* frames and all *B* frames within the same GOP useless. Therefore, it is also desirable to spread all packets of P_1 frames across the entire delivery sequence. A similar argument applies to the remaining reference frames. Actually, increasing the distance between any two consecutive packets belonging to the same reference frame is the main idea behind PP.

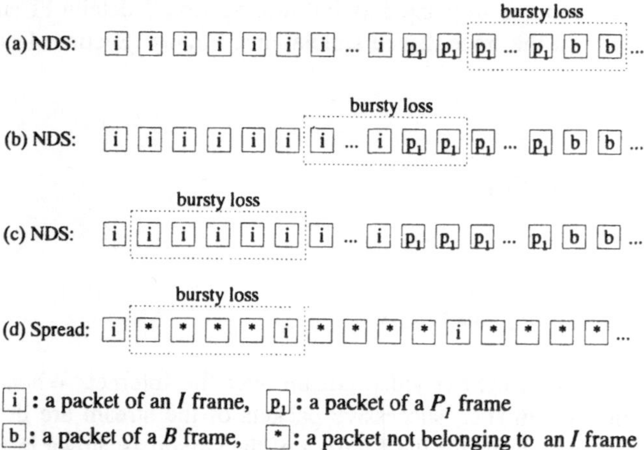

Fig. 1. Impact of a bursty loss on *I* frames.

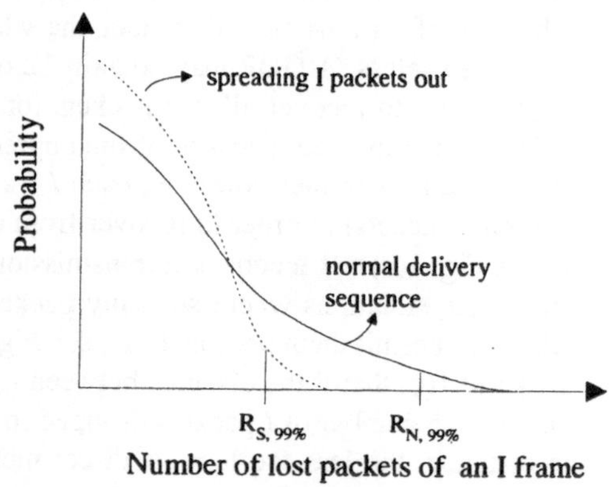

Fig. 2. The probability distribution function of the number of lost packets of an *I* frame.

2.2 Packet Permutation Algorithm

To spread the packets of each frame type across the entire delivery sequence, PP interleaves the packets from distinct frames. The size of a packet is set to the Internet standard MTU, 576 bytes. The unit of packet permutation may be one or several GOPs, and is an adjustable parameter. PP permutes the normal packet delivery sequence of one or several GOPs before transmitting them to the client. At the client side the permuted packets are re-permuted back to the original delivery sequence before they are presented to the application. For simplicity of presentation, we first consider the case with one GOP as the unit of permutation. In this case, PP alters the packet delivery sequence within each GOP, but preserves the order in which distinct GOPs are sent. The delivery sequence generated by PP is referred to as the packet permutation sequence (PPS). Let i_k^g denote the kth packet of the I frame in the gth GOP, $p_{j,k}^g$ denote the kth packet of the P_j frame in the gth GOP, and b_k^g denote the kth packet of the B frames in the gth GOP. Fig. 3 illustrates how the PPS of a GOP is generated (with the abbreviation of the corresponding superscripts). Initially, PP adds the most significant frame packets (i.e., I frame packets) to PPS. Then, it inserts each of the second most significant frame packets (i.e., P_1 frame packets) between every two consecutive I packets. Next, it similarly inserts the third most significant frame packets (i.e., P_2 frame packets) into the other consecutively arranged I packets. Other frames are similarly inserted based on their significance. After there is a packet inserted between every two consecutive I packets, the insertion operation returns to the beginning of the PPS and then continues. A similar process is repeated until all packets have been added to the PPS. Note that since PP inserts packets in the order of their importance, first, the largest distance is between consecutive I packets, and the next largest distance is between consecutive P_1 packets, and so on. Consequently, the impact caused by bursty losses on I frames is the smallest, that upon P_1 frames is the next smallest, and so on.

PP can also use two or more GOPs as the unit of permutation. The advantage of permuting several GOPs at a time is that the distance between consecutive packets belonging to the same reference frame can be extended even more. The drawback is that this may incur a slightly longer initial delay and a larger buffer requirement. The additional delay introduced by permuting an additional GOP is approximately 0.5 seconds (if a GOP contains 15 frames and the playback rate is 30 frames/second); and the additional buffer space needed is approximately 76KB (if the average bit rate is 1.2Mbps). Fortunately, such extra delays and buffer space are acceptable for most applications [2], [3]. The way multiple GOPs are permuted is similar to that discussed above. The main difference is that the frames of the same type in distinct GOPs are merged and treated as a single frame with their packets interleaved with each other. To better explain this idea, assume that two GOPs are permuted. Then, in the generated PPS, the next I packet after i_1^1 is i_1^2; the next P_1 packet after $p_{1,1}^1$ is $p_{1,1}^2$; and so on. As a result, the distance between any two consecutive packets belonging to the same reference frame is even larger, which increases the robustness of the delivery sequence. Due to limited page space, the formal algorithm of PP is abbreviated here. However, it can be seen from Fig. 3 that the computational complexity of PP is $O(T \cdot G \cdot m)$, where T is the number of frame types in a GOP, G is the number of GOPs permuted at a time, and m is the maximum number of packets in a frame. This low computational complexity makes the implementation practical. It is worth mentioning that PP can be used in conjunction with FEC easily: it simply handles the repair packets generated for each reference frame as part of each reference frame.

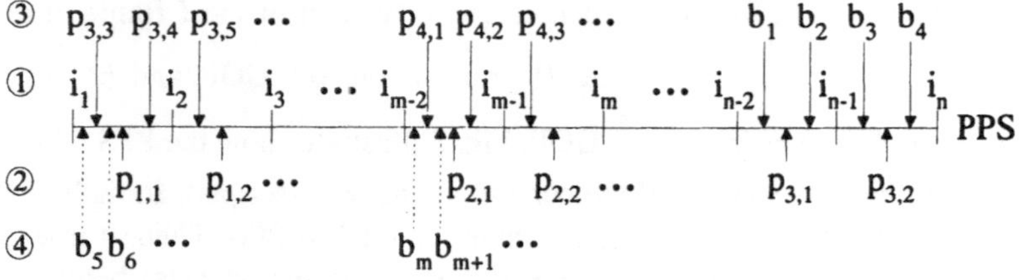

Fig. 3. Generating packet permutation sequence for a GOP.

3 Performance Evaluation

3.1 Simulation Model

Recent work has shown that the end-to-end packet loss behavior on the Internet can be modeled by a two-state Markov chain, know as the Gilbert model, in which state "1" represents a lost packet and state "0" represents a packet successfully reaching its destination [1], [4], [7], [8]. In our simulation, the Gilbert model was employed to simulate the packet loss behavior on the Internet. The video stream tested is a variable-bit-rate (VBR) MPEG-1 file named "cnn.t", whose bit rate trace can be obtained from [9]. The stream has an average bit rate of 1.2Mbps with a frame rate of 30 fps, and a GOP pattern of "IBBPBBPBBPBBPBB." In each simulation, 2000 GOPs were transmitted with the packet size set to 576bytes, the Internet standard MTU; that is, about 300,000 packets were transmitted in each simulation. With the simulation model described above, a series of experiments were conducted to compare the performance of the delivery schemes using NDS (normal delivery sequence) and PPS (packet permutation sequence).

3.2 Simulation Results

In the first experiment the average packet loss rate was set to 5%, the average number of packets dropped in a bursty loss was set to three packets, and the buffer size employed by PP was set to one GOP. No FEC repair packets were encoded for both the delivery schemes using NDS and PPS. Fig. 4 shows the probability that a GOP loses *l* packets. Since the probability distribution functions of P_1, P_2, P_3, and P_4 frames are similar to that of P_1, they are not shown here. It is clear from the plots in Fig. 4 that PP reshapes the probability functions so that for each frame the probability of losing larger numbers of packets is significantly reduced, which validates our claim.

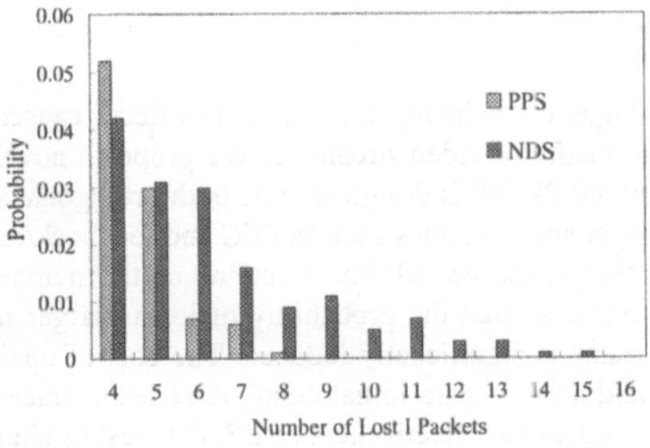

Fig. 4. The probability that a GOP loses *I* packets.

In the second experiment, we encoded FEC repair packets for all reference frames in each GOP, and compared the number of repair packets required by NDS and PPS to achieve a particular QoS. Fig. 5 shows the number of repair packets required by NDS and PPS for guaranteeing that 95% and 99% of the GOPs transmitted will not lose any of the reference frame packets (i.e., *I*, P_1, P_2, P_3, and P_4 packets). As expected, PP substantially reduces the number of repair packets required for protecting all reference frames. To examine the effect of permuting data at video frame level, we repeated this experiment for numerous frame permutation sequences. We found that permuting only frames cannot reshape the probability function of the number of lost packets within each video frame as PP does, and therefore the results of other sequences tested are similar to that shown in Fig. 5. In this experiment, the extra cost incurred by PP is the initial delay of 1.5 seconds and the memory space of about 230KB required by both the sender and receiver. In practice, this extra cost is acceptable for most video applications [2], [3].

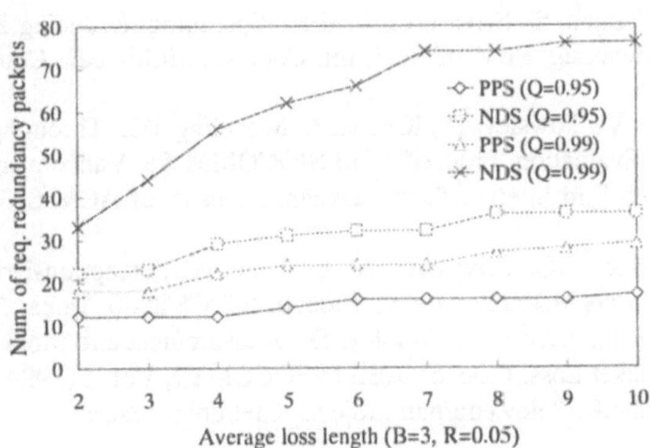

Fig.5. The number of FEC repair packets required by each GOP for guaranteeing that Q percent of GOPs will not lose any reference frame (buffer size = 3 GOPs, average loss rate = 5%).

4 Conclusions

In this paper, we focus on reducing the annoying effects caused by bursty packet losses on the visual quality of video streaming. We propos a novel robust end-to-end delivery scheme, termed PP. PP is designed to be both orthogonal and complementary to conventional error control schemes such as FEC and feedback/retransmission-based schemes. PP can reshape the probability functions of the number of packet losses within each video frame so that the probability of losing larger numbers of packets within each video frame is significantly reduced. The cost of applying PP is a small extra buffer space and a short extra initial delay. A series of trace-driven simulations were conducted to validate the effectiveness of PP. Our results showed that in various network conditions, PP effectively reduces the probability of losing larger numbers of packets for each video frame. If combined with FEC, PP will greatly reduce the number of repair packets required to protect reference frames. If combined with feedback/retransmission-based schemes, it will substantially reduce the events in which so many reference frame packets are lost that they cannot be retransmitted on time. From these results, we conclude that PP is a robust transmission technique for video streaming over a wide-area network with bursty packet loss behavior.

References

1. Bolot, J.C., Garcia, A.V.: The Case For FEC-Based Error Control for Packet Audio. Proc. of ACM Int. Conf. on Multimedia (1996)
2. Ding, J.W., Huang, Y.M.: Resource-Based Striping: An Efficient Striping Strategy for Video Servers using Heterogeneous Disk-Subsystems. Multimedia Tools and Applications, Vol. 18, No. 2 (2002)
3. Kuo, F., Effelsberg, W., Garcia-Luna-Aceves, J.J.: Multimedia Communications. Prentice Hall PTR (1998)
4. Ngo, H.Q., Varadarajan, S., Srivastava, J.: Error Spreading: Reducing Bursty Errors in Continuous Media Streaming. Proc. of IEEE Int. Conf. on Multimedia Computing and Systems. (1999) 314-319.
5. Padhye, J., Firoiu, V., Towsley, D., Kurose, J.: Modeling TCP Throughput: A Simple Model and its Empirical Evaluation. Proc. of ACM SIGCOMM '98, Vancouver, CA (1998)
6. Paxson, V.: End-to-End Internet Packet Dynamics. Proc. of ACM SIGCOMM'97, Cannes, France (1997)
7. Varadarajan, S., Ngo, H.Q., Srivastava, J.: An Adaptive, Perception-Driven Error Spreading Scheme in Continuous Media Streaming. Proc. of ICDCS'2000, Taipai, Taiwan (2000)
8. Yajnik, M., Moon, S., Kurose, J., Towsley, D.: Measurement and Modeling of the Temporal Dependence in Packet Loss. Proc. of IEEE INFOCOM'99, Vol. 1 (1999) 345-352
9. Available: ftp://tenet.berkeley.edu/pub/projects/tenet/dbind/traces/

Customer Identification for MPEG Video Based on Digital Fingerprinting

Jana Dittmann[a], Enrico Hauer[a,b], Claus Vielhauer[b], Jörg Schwenk[c], Eva Saar[c]

[a]GMD Research Center of Information technology, Darmstadt, Germany
[b]Platanista GmbH, Darmstadt, Germany
[c]T-Nova GmbH, Technology Center, Germany

ABSTRACT. In our publication we present a fingerprint watermark for the compressed video formats MPEG1/2 to ensure customer identification. The basic customer information is a watermark, which was developed for still images. We transfer it into the video area and adjust it to the special facts of MPEG video to be resistant against coalition attacks.

Keywords
Fingerprint watermark, coalition security, MPEG-video, data hiding, customer vector

1. Motivation

Digital Watermarking offers various security mechanisms, like protection of integrity or copyright, among others. The field of application is important for the design. A watermark can, for instance, embed customer identification into a carrier signal, like image, video, audio or 3D and each customer gets a special copy with his identification. But with customer copies it is possible to commit a coalition attack: Two or more customers work together and compare their copies pixel by pixel. They can detect differences between the copies and identify them as the watermark. After changing the values at these positions, where the differences are, it is usually impossible to retrieve the correct watermark information.

Currently we find a lot of digital watermarking techniques some examples can be found in [7,8,9], but only few are focused on the coalition attack, especially in the area of video watermarking we could not find any evaluation. Therefore on the basis of a digital watermark [1][2] we develop a robust fingerprint watermark algorithm for MPEG1/2 video. The basis derives from the image area and is adjusted to MPEG standards for compressed videos. The watermark information is a customer identification number (chapter 2). The two fingerprint algorithms, which we test, are the Boneh-Shaw Scheme [3] and the Schwenk Scheme [2]. We represent the watermarking algorithm in chapter 3. Finally we test the two fingerprint algorithms which should offer security against the coalition attack. The watermark will be optimized by the parameter complexity, capacity, transparency and robustness.

2. Digital Fingerprint Algorithm

To solve the problem of the coalition attack, we use the Boneh-Shaw fingerprint and the Schwenk fingerprint algorithm [3][2]. With the algorithms we can find the customers, which have committed the coalition attack. To mark images, we generate positions within the image to embed the watermark information (in the video the positions stand for scenes). Each customer has his own fingerprint, which contains a number of "1" and "0". Each fingerprint vector is assigned to marking positions in the document to prevent the coalition attack. The only marking positions the pirates cannot detect are those positions which contain the same letter in all the compared documents. We call the set of these marking positions the intersection of the different fingerprints. To this purpose we use two schemes:

2.1. Schwenk Fingerprint Scheme

This first approach puts the information to trace the pirates into the intersection of up to d fingerprints. In the best case (e.g. automated attacks like computing the average of fingerprinted images) this allows us to detect all pirates, in the worst case (removal of individually selected marks) we can detect the pirates with a negligibly small one-sided error probability, i.e. we will never accuse innocent customers.

The fingerprint vector is spread over the marking positions. The marking positions for each customer are the same in every customer copy and the intersection of different fingerprints can therefore not be detected. With the remaining marked points, the intersection of all used copies, it is possible to follow up all customers, which have worked together.

2.2. Boneh-Shaw Fingerprint Scheme

The scheme of Boneh and Shaw [3] is also used to recognize the coalition attack, but it is an other scheme. Here it is noticeable, that you do not necessarily find all pirates, with a (any arbitrary small) probability ε to get the wrong customer and every fingerprint has a different number of zeros.

The number of customers is q and with q and ε you can get the repeats d. The fingerprint vector consists of (q-1) blocks of the length d ("d-blocks"), the whole length is $d*(q-1)$. The first customer has the value 1 in all marked points, in the second customer all marked points without the fist "d-block", in the third all marked points without the first two "d-blocks". The last customer has the value 0 in all marked points.

With a permutation of the fingerprint vector we get a higher security, because the pirates can find differences between the copies, but they can't assign it to a special d-block.

3. Digital Watermark for MPEG1/2 Videos

In this chapter we introduce a digital watermark for MPEG video. First we analyze the general demands for watermarks for MPEG videos. The second part is the design of our watermark including embedding and retrieval process.

3.1. Demands of MPEG watermarks

With [4] the demands of MPEG fingerprint watermarking can be divided into the following characteristics:

- Robustness, Capacity, Transparence, Security, Complexity, Verification, Invertibility

For the fingerprint watermarking in MPEG videos, the following parameters are important:

- Robustness: Resistance to
  - Frame cutting and frame changing, Digital-Analog-Digital Transformation, Decoding-encoding processes with changing of the data rate, Format conversion
- Capacity
  - quantity of information, which can be embedded without significant increase of the data volume
- Transparence: - prevent visual artifacts in a frame and in a sequence of frames
- Security: - Resistance against coalition attacks
- Complexity: - blind or non-blind algorithm and run time performance
- Verification: - public or private algorithm
- Invertion: - restoration of the original

In our current version we focus on the resistance of frame cutting, frame changing and decoding and encoding processes.

The capacity describes the amount of information that can be embedded into the video. If the embedding information increases the data rate, the video has to be resynchronized.

For the embedding of the fingerprint information the watermark must be transparent. The luminance blocks in the MPEG video are a good carrier signal, because changes in the luminance values are only fairly visible for the human eyes. It is also important to consider the relations to the frame types, to prevent visual artifacts [6].

The important security aspect for fingerprint watermarks is the security against the coalition attack. Therefore the fingerprint bits will be embedded at the same positions in the I-Frame. The idea is to mark for each customer the scenes differently, but several customers have enough identical marked scenes so that the rest amount remains after a coalition attack, to trace the pirates.

The complexity of the watermarking algorithm depends on the runtime performance and the use of the original. The watermarking algorithm is a non-blind algorithm and depends on the original. This dependence is disadvantageous. To improve the runtime performance we embed the watermark information into the temporary frame information during the decoding of the video. We decode the video only partially and use only I-Frames. Our carrier signal consists of four luminance blocks in a macroblock.

3.2. Watermarking design

Three general problems emerge during the development of the watermark:

(a) Robustness

To improve the robustness against the coalition attack, we embed one fingerprint vector bit in a whole scene. So we reach a resistance against statistical attacks, like average calculation of look like frames. With this method we can make the frame cutting and frame changing ineffective. We have not contemplated the cutting of a whole scene yet. In the current prototype we mark a group of pictures GOP for one fingerprint bit. We add a pseudo random sequence to the first AC values of the luminance DCT blocks of an intracoded macroblock in all I-Frames of the video.

(b) Capacity

The basis of the video watermark is an algorithm, which was developed for still images [1][2]. In still images the whole fingerprint is embedded into the image and the capacity is restricted. With the I-Frame in a video, the capacity is much better. To achieve high robustness, we embed one watermark information bit into a scene. Thus the video must have a minimal length. Additional to the embedding of the watermark, the data rate can increase. The problem of synchronization between the audio and video stream can arise or data rate is raised. Basically, with the embedding of the watermark we must synchronize the audio and video stream.

(c) Transparence

To improve the transparency we use a visual model [4]. With the visual model the watermark strength is calculated for every marking position individually. Additionally, we use the same marking position for each frame.

3.3. Embedding process of the watermark algorithm

The fingerprint algorithms [2] and [3] produce the watermark information, the fingerprint bit vector, which we want to embed into the video. The starting parameters are:

- Original video V and User key UK
- Fingerprint vector FPV with the Length l
- Range, the values of the watermark sequence are between [-Range, +Range]
- Watermark strength ws
- number of marked DCT blocks per frame r_1 in % and of marked AC values r_2
- minimal number of marked GOP per bit of the watermark information r_3

The watermark algorithm supports MPEG1 system stream and MPEG2 program stream. First we split the system stream into the audio and video stream. The next step is a check, that the video has enough GOPs n to embed the information.

$$n >= \text{Length } l * r_3 (1)$$

If the video has not enough GOPs the embedding process is stopped with an error message.

After the splitting of the fingerprint vector FPV into its bits we embed one bit of the fingerprint vector FPV, the watermark information, in every GOP. If the number of GOP n is more than Length l * r3 we repeat the embed of the information in the next GOPs of the video.

The next steps are repeated for every GOP in the video:

a) If the watermark bit is a 1 the GOP will decode, if it's a 0 we go to the next GOP of the video. Calculate the number of DCT blocks in the intra-coded frame

$$m = height_{frame}/8 * wide_{frame}/8 \qquad (2)$$

b) Calculate number of DCT blocks, which will be marked

$$p = m * r1 \qquad (3)$$

c) For the first frame we build a pseudo random sequence $B=(B_0, B_1, B_2, \ldots, B_{p-1})$ for the marking position in the frame, the sequence B will be used for every marked frame

d) Building of a pseudo-random sequence $R(R_0,R_1,R_2, \ldots, R_{p-1})$, every R_i consists of r_2 elements with values between –Range and +Range

e) For each selected luminance DCT block for i= 0 to p-1
   1. Extract the luminance DCT block B_i of the Frame I
   2. Multiplication of watermark strength ws with the R-Sequence R_i

      $$R_i' = R_i * ws \qquad (4)$$

   3. Inverse quantization of luminance DCT block B_i
   4. Add the R-Sequence R_i of the first r_2 AC values in zig-zack-scan

      $$B_i' = \sum R_{ij} + B_{ij} \text{ for } j = 1 \text{ to } r_2 \text{ in zig-zag-scan} \qquad (5)$$

   5. Quantization of luminance DCT block B_i'

f) To get the marked video frame I' write all marked luminance DCT Block back into the original frame

g) Write the marked frame I' in the Video V to produce the marked Video V'

A schematic illustration of the embed process is at http://www.darmstadt.gmd.de/~hauer/pcm2001.

3.4. Retrieval process of the watermark algorithm

In the retrieval process we need the original video. The watermark algorithm retrieves the fingerprint vector and the fingerprint algorithm analyzes the vector to get the customer. The starting parameters are:

- Original video Vand marked video V'
- Userkey UK
- Range, the values of the watermark sequence are between [-Range, +Range]
- number of marked DCT blocks per frame r_1 in %
- number of marked AC values r_2
- minimal number of marked GOP per bit of the watermark information r_3
- tolerance value t

The first steps of splitting the video stream and the check for enough GOPs are the same as in the embedding process.

As we embed the bits of the fingerprint vector FPV in the I-Frame of the GOP, we analyze the I-Frames in the video only.

The next steps are:

a) Calculate the number of DCT blocks in the intracoded frame
   $m= height_{frame}/8 * wide_{frame}/8$ (6)
b) Calculate number of DCT blocks, which will be marked $p= m * r1$ (7)
c) For the first frame we build a pseudo random sequence $B=(B_0, B_1, B_2..., B_{p-1})$ for the marking position in the frame, the sequence B will be used for every marked frame
d) Building of a pseudo-random sequence $R(R_0,R_1,R_2, ..., R_{p-1})$, every R_i consists of r_2 elements with values between –Range and +Range
e) For each selected luminance DCT block for i= 0 to p-1
   1. Extract the luminance DCT block B_i of the frame I in video V
   2. Extract the luminance DCT block B_i' of the frame I' in video V'
   3. Calculate the difference block Bi'' $B_i'' = B_i' - B_i$ (8)
   4. Read the watermark sequence WM_i (the first r_2 AC values in B_i'' in zig-zag-scan)
   5. Compare watermark sequence WM_i with R_Sequence R_i
      a. If $WM_i = R_i$, the bit has the value 1, other bit has the value 0
   6. If the fingerprint vector is more than once in the video, we build a sum for every bit at each position. We compare the redundancy at the end of video.
      a. Analyze the information and evaluate the customer ID

A schematic illustration of the retrieval process is at http://www.darmstadt.gmd.de/~hauer/pcm2001.

4. Test results

The test of the prototype concentrates on: the transparency, the MPEG re-encoding and the coalition security. We use four different test videos: a news program (video 1), cartoon (video 2), movie trailer (video 3) and commercial (video 4).

(a) Transparency

The tools, which we used, can estimate the quality differences between the original and marked video. The base of the tool is the JND algorithm [5]. The assess lies between 1 and 6. At 1 there are no differences between the original and the copy. At 4 it is possible to see the watermark. At 6 you can see the watermark. The to compared objects are the intracoded frames between frame number 1 and 36. These frames are marked with the watermark. The parameters, with which we measure the transparency, are the Range R of the pseudo random Sequence R and the watermark strength ws. Details of table are at http://www.darmstadt.gmd.de/~hauer/pcm2001.

In all test results it is possible to retrieve the fingerprint vector correctly. The tests are based on the Boneh-Shaw Scheme [3]. The parameters of the fingerprint vector are q=4, d=3 and the customer ID=3.

With the quality assess of Q=3 it is possible to see the watermark. We observed that Range and watermark strength ws together influence the quality. If the product of Range * ws is smaller than 6 there is a good to very good visual quality. With a forward increase of the parameter the watermark will be more visible. If the product of Range * ws is smaller 4 the watermark is invisible but it is impossible to readout the watermark.

Differences between the videos are only in the movie trailer. The video needs higher values of Range and ws nowever the watermark is visible.

(b) MPEG robustness

We measure the robustness with a re-encoding process. We work with different data rates. The data rates are 600 kB/s, 800 kB/s, 1MB/s, 1,5 MB/s. With the increase of the Range to 20 it is impossible to detect the right watermark after the re-encoding. The retrieved information is complete different from the embedded information or sometime there are some segments of the customer vector, but this is insufficient for the exact determination of the customer.

(c) Coalition security

There are more possibilities, to carry out a coalition attack:

1. Attacks to separate frame areas
2. Attacks to whole frame
3. Attacks to whole scenes

The time and practical effort grows from (1) to (3). The video must be split in the important areas. Additionally there must be knowledge about the MPEG video format.

With weak spots in the transparency it is possible to detect parts of watermark in separate frame areas. But for the coalition attack this attack is relative irrelevant, because we embed the fingerprint bit over the whole frame and several times over the whole video. The attack over whole frames, like the exchange of frames, is only possible with visual similar frames, because with different frames the semantic of the frames can be destroyed. Only for attacks over whole scenes the watermark has no robustness, because one bit of the fingerprint vector will be cut out. But with the cut off of whole scenes the semantic of the video will be decreased. We have not note this attack for this prototype.

5. Conclusion

In this contribution we have described a watermark algorithm for MPEG video with special marking positions, based on the mathematical model of [2] and [3]. With the watermark algorithm we embed generated fingerprint vectors, which embed customer identification.

The algorithms work on intracoded frames and embed the customer information to the DCT values. The tests examine the transparency, robustness and coalition security. The transparency has shown, that with the parameter Range it is possible, to adapt the visual quality. With high transparency the robustness cannot meet, especially during a re-encoding process. The results are very good to the coalition attack. Generally for a high number of customers the length of the fingerprint vectors is very high. The optimization of the fingerprint algorithms is an important point for the future research. The problem is to embed the customer vector in material with restricted size.

6. References

[1] Dittmann, Jana; Stabenau, Mark; Schmitt, Peter; Schwenk, Joerg; Saar, Eva; Ueberberg, Johannes (1999), *Digitale Fingerabdrücke als digitale Wasserzeichen zur Kennzeichnung von Bildmaterial mit kundenspezifischen Informationen*. In: Baumgart, Rannenberg, Wähner, Weck: Verläßliche IT-Systeme, DuD Fachbeiträge. Braunschweig/ Wiesbaden: Vieweg, 1999, S. 243 - 262, ISBN 3-528-05728-9.

[2] Dittmann, Jana; Behr, Alexander; Stabenau, Mark; Schmitt, Peter; Schwenk, Joerg; Ueberberg, Johannes (1999), *Combining digital Watermarks and collusion secure Fingerprints for digital Images*, Proceedings of SPIE Vol. 3657, [3657-51], Electronic Imaging '99, San Jose USA, 24-29 January 1999

[3] D. Boneh and J. Shaw, *Collusion-Secure Fingerprinting for Digital Data.* Proc. CRYPTO'95, Springer LNCS 963, S. 452-465, 1995.

[4] Dittmann, Jana, *Digitale Wasserzeichen*, Springer Verlag 2000, S. 62-53, ISBN 3-540-66661-3

[5] Steinebach, Martin; Dittmann, Jana; Mukherjee, Anirban: *Computer-aided visual model for ensuring video watermarking transparency*, to appear in Proceedings of SPIE: Security and Watermarking of Multimedia Contents III, 21-26 January 2001, San Jose, California, USA, Vol. 4314, 2001

[6] Hartung, Frank, Digital Watermarking and Fingerprinting of Uncompressed and Compressed Video, Shaker Verlag 2000, S. 79-82, ISBN 3-8265-7052-9

[7] Cox, Ingemar J, and Linnartz, Jean-Paul M.G.: Public watermarks and resitence to tampering, Proceedings of IEEE Int. Conf. O Image Processing, 1997, av. only on CD-ROM

[8] B Pfitzmann, *Trials of Traced Traitors*, In Proc. of First International Workshop on Information Hiding '96, 30 May - 1 June 1996, Isaac Newton Institute, Cambridge UK; proceedings published by Springer as Lecture Notes in Computer Science v 1174, pp. 49-64, 1996.

[9] S. Pereira, J.J.K. Ó Ruanaidh, T. Pun: *Secure robust digital watermarking using the lapped othogonal transform*, In Proc. of the SPIE Conference on Electronic Imaging '99, Security and Watermarking of Multimedia Contents, 24-29 January 1999, San Jose USA, Proceedings of SPIE Vol. 3657, [3657-51], pp. 21-30, 1999

Performance Analysis of Data Hiding

Shuichi Shimizu

IBM Japan, Tokyo Research Laboratory
1623-14 Shimotsuruma, Yamato-shi, Kanagawa 242-8502, Japan
shue@jp.ibm.com

Abstract. This paper presents a theoretical performance analysis of data hiding, which inserts invisible/inaudible digital watermarks in media data. The analysis relates payload limit, minimum watermark-signal-to-noise ratio, probability of watermark detection error, and bandwidth of the watermarking channel. The usage of such a channel for large payload, direct sequence spread spectrum (DSSS) with and without coding for error recovery is discussed. The paper finally illustrates how the analytical results can be applied in practice, in terms of selecting parameters of watermarking under quantization, by introducing analytical prediction of the decreasing SNR against quantization step size.

1 Introduction

Data hiding, the insertion of imperceptible digital watermarking (invisible for video and image and inaudible for audio applications) into a host media data, offers a way to carry secondary information such as annotation which is tightly coupled with primary host data. The maximum amount of information bits which the watermark is able to carry is called payload and is an important issue for digital watermarking. Payload limit in terms of channel capacity was discussed in [1, 2]. This paper presents an analysis on watermarking performance in terms of the payload limit, minimum watermark-signal-to-noise ratio, probability of watermark detection error, and bandwidth of watermarking channel. Also presented are results on the effect of quantization such as from lossy compression against watermarks with minimum SNR. In Section 2, we review the watermarking processes, in Section 3, we analyze the performance of watermarking in terms of payload and the robustness margin to be introduced for realizing the reliable detection, and in Section 4, we give the practical performance analysis and experimental results on the effect of quantization.

2 Watermark Creation and Detection

Digital watermarking may be classified as robust or fragile. In this paper, we shall be concerned only with robust watermarking which refers to those methods for which the inserted watermark are still detectable after certain signal processing or deliberate attack. Most of robust watermarking schemes [3, 4] are based on some form of spread spectrum techniques, in which watermark creation and detection may be regarded as an application of digital communications. For these schemes, because a large amount of redundancy is required to overcome the effect of processing or attack on the watermark signal, the bandwidth W of the inserted watermark is much greater than the information rate R.

Watermark creation is mainly composed of the following three steps: (1) Channel coding generates a code word from the information bits. This code word can be viewed as a binary baseband signal. We denote by c_{ij} the j-th bit in the i-th code word, where $1 \leq i \leq 2^R$ and $1 \leq j \leq W$. We refer to the simple repetition of the bits to expand R to W as the uncoded case. (2) Spectrum spreading, or more specifically direct sequence spread spectrum (DSSS), multiplies a pseudo random number (PN) sequence $\{b_j\}$ by the baseband signal to generate another sequence, $g_j = (2c_{ij} - 1)(2b_j - 1)$ for the i-th code word. The symbol unit of spreading is called a chip. (3) Modulation segments the host data into a number of blocks, applies discrete Fourier transform (DFT) or other transforms to each of the blocks, and selects a frequency component to carry g_j. The j-th transmitted signal for the i-th code word is represented by

$$w_{ij} = (2c_{ij} - 1)(2b_j - 1)\mu_j, \tag{1}$$

where the positive number μ_j is the strength of the watermark. The case when no transform is applied, or when transform is applied to the host data without segmenting into blocks is also treated as modulation in this paper.

Watermark detection is also composed of three steps, which are the inverses of those in the creation process. (1) Demodulating converts the observed waveform signal to baseband based on carrier frequencies for the case of modulation with carrier, or extracts appropriate pixels or coefficients to make the baseband signal for the case of modulation without any carrier. For simplicity, we assume synchronization prior to the modulation step. Then, the j-th received signal is $r_j = w_j + n_j$, where the code word is unknown and n_j indicates the additive noise that has been introduced in the channel. (2) Despreading multiplies the baseband signal with the same PN sequence used in the creation stage. (3) Decoding determines the most likely embedded information bits by using soft-decision on the continuous baseband signal obtained through the above two steps. In this step, the correlation metric is calculated for the k-th code word as follows:

$$M_k = \sum_{j=1}^{W} (2c_{kj} - 1)(2b_j - 1)r_j, \tag{2}$$

and the one with the maximum value is selected.

3 Basic Performance Analysis

In general, there is a trade-off between the payload and robustness. Namely, the higher the payload, the less robust the watermark. In the following, we analyze watermarking performance in terms of the payload and robustness under the detection error rate.

3.1 Detection Error Rate

For linear codes, the difference between correlation metrics of any code words can be mapped into metrics of all-zero code word (M_1) and the corresponding one (M_m), and so the distance between any two of them can be represented by

$$D_m = M_1 - M_m = 2\sum_{j=1}^{W} c_{mj}\mu_j - 2\sum_{j=1}^{W} c_{mj}(2b_j - 1)n_j. \tag{3}$$

In the case that the watermark strength is constant in each chip ($\mu_j = \overline{\mu} = \mu_{\rm S}$), it is known [5] that the distance converges to a normal distribution with mean $2w_m\mu_{\rm S}$ and variance $4w_m\sigma_{\rm N}^2$, when the number of non-zero c_{mj} is large enough. Thus, the probability of code word error between the two is

$$P_2(w_m) = \text{Prob}[D_m < 0] = Q\left(\sqrt{\frac{\mu_{\rm S}^2}{\sigma_{\rm N}^2} w_m}\right), \tag{4}$$

where $Q(x)$ is the tail of Gaussian density:

$$Q(x) = \int_x^\infty \frac{1}{\sqrt{2\pi}} e^{-t^2/2} dt. \tag{5}$$

Denote by $E_{\rm c}$ the energy per chip, N_0 the single-sided noise power spectral density, $E_{\rm b}$ the energy per bit, and $R_{\rm c}$ the code rate. Thus $E_{\rm c} = R_{\rm c}E_{\rm b}$ and $E_{\rm c}/N_0 = \mu_{\rm S}^2/(2\sigma_{\rm N}^2)$. By noting $S = E_{\rm b}R$ and $N = N_0W$, (4) can be rewritten as[1]

$$P_2(w_m) = Q\left(\sqrt{2\frac{S}{N}\frac{W}{R}R_{\rm c}w_m}\right). \tag{6}$$

Note that it is not necessary that the additive noise follows a normal distribution in this analysis. However, when the noise follows a Gaussian distribution, then it is know that the correlator produces the maximum SNR, and thus it is optimum. It is also not necessary that they are individually distributed, however, it is required that they are identically distributed or wide-sense stationary.

If the strength u_j is not constant, (6) still holds. In this case, the distance D_m is the sum of two uncorrelated random variables, and its mean is $2w_m\mu_{\rm S}$. When the μ_j's are uncorrelated, its variance is $4w_m(\sigma_{\rm N}^2 + \sigma_{\rm S}^2)$, where $\sigma_{\rm S}^2$ is the variance of μ_j.

3.2 Payload and Minimum SNR for Uncoded and Coded DSSS

Now, we discuss the uncoded and coded DSSS watermarking channel as practical schemes. The uncoded DSSS does not employ any code word and its robustness

[1] When the code is concatenated as an outer code with a binary repetition code, then the coding gain of the combined code is $R_{\rm c}w_m = R_{\rm c}^{\rm o}w_m^{\rm o}$, where $R_{\rm c}^{\rm o}$ and $w_m^{\rm o}$ are the code rate and weight of the outer code.

is supported by the DSSS only. In the simple repetition code (i.e., no code word), the minimum of w_m is W/R, the code rate is $R_c = R/W$. The probability of decoding error on $M = 2^R$ code words is upper-bounded by

$$P_M \leq \sum_{m=2}^{M} P_2(w_m) \simeq RQ\left(\sqrt{2\frac{S}{N}\frac{W}{R}}\right). \tag{7}$$

In the case that the (n, k) convolutional code is introduced to the watermark creation stage, and soft-decision such as Viterbi algorithm is applied to extract the information bits, the upper bound of the equivalent bit error rate is [5],

$$P_b \leq \frac{1}{k} \sum_{d=d_{free}}^{\infty} \beta_d P_2(d), \tag{8}$$

where k is the number of input bits for the convolutional encoder, d_{free} is the minimum free distance of the convolutional code, and the coefficients $\{\beta_d\}$ are obtained from the transfer function of the code. Thus, the probability of code word error can be bounded by

$$P_M = 1 - (1 - P_b)^R < \frac{R}{k} \sum_{d=d_{free}}^{\infty} \beta_d Q\left(\sqrt{2\frac{S}{N}\frac{W}{R}R_c^\circ d}\right), \tag{9}$$

if the information bits are assumed to be independent.

When the maximum error rate P_M, bandwidth W, and channel coding parameters k, β_d, R_c° are given, then the maximum payload R and minimum SNR S/N are determined from Equation (7) or (9), which are plotted in Fig. 1 with the inequality sign replaced by equal sign.[2] Also included in Fig. 1 is the Shannon's channel capacity as a reference of payload upper limits. For example, when the coded DSSS is employed, then a 256-bit payload is obtained with −18.5 dB minimum SNR. When the error rate and/or the bandwidth are allowed to be greater, then the maximum payload can be greater and/or the minimum SNR can be smaller.

Note that the well-known watermarking scheme of [3] employs M-ary orthogonal signals with $M = 1000$ (about 10-bit payload) and bandwidth $W = 1000$. Assuming an additive white Gaussian noise (AWGN), then the minimum SNR is about −15.1 dB for the 10^{-5} error rate.[3] By shifting Fig. 1 by about 18.2 dB (i.e., 65536/1000), it is found that the minimum SNR for the uncoded DSSS is −9.5 dB under a 10^{-5} error rate. Thus, the M-ary orthogonal channel coding contributes about 5.6 dB gain.[4]

---

[2] In (9), R is the payload plus the constraint length K, and the summation is calculated until $d = 64$ because the terms for $d > 64$ are small enough with comparison to the given error rate for drawing Fig. 1.

[3] From [5], $P_M = \frac{1}{\sqrt{2\pi}} \int_{-\infty}^{\infty} \{1 - (1 - Q(y))^{M-1}\} \exp\left\{-\frac{1}{2}\left(y - \sqrt{2(S/N)W}\right)^2\right\} dy$

[4] However, the use of larger M is not practical in terms of computational costs.

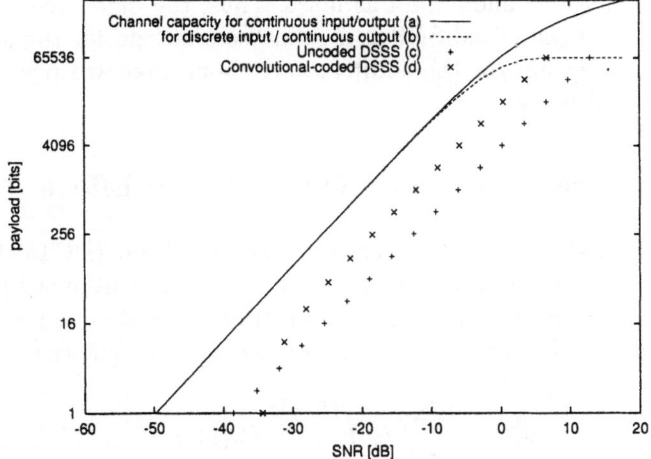

Fig. 1. Trade-offs between the payload and minimum SNR for (a) Shannon's channel capacity with continuous input and output, (b) channel capacity with discrete input, (c) the uncoded DSSS, and (d) the convolutional-coded DSSS with rate $R_c^\circ = k/n = 1/2$, constraint length $K = 7$, minimum free distance $d_{free} = 10$, coefficients $\beta_{10} = 36$, $\beta_{11} = 0$, $\beta_{12} = 211 \cdots$, bandwidth $W = 65536$, and error rate $P_M = 10^{-5}$.

3.3 Decision Rule

In practice, the SNR is unknown to the detector, and so it is necessary to estimate the SNR from the received signals, $z_{lj} = (2c_{lj} - 1)(2b_j - 1)r_j$, where $l = \arg\max_k M_k$. As the sample mean $\hat{\mu}_{z_l}$ and variance $\hat{\sigma}^2_{z_l}$ are the minimum-variance unbiased estimators, thus the SNR can be estimated by $\hat{\mu}^2_{z_l}/(2\hat{\sigma}^2_{z_l})$. The decision rule to employ the output from the decoder is then as follows:

$$\delta = \begin{cases} 1 & \text{if } \hat{\gamma}_l \stackrel{\triangle}{=} \hat{\mu}^2_{z_l}/(2\hat{\sigma}^2_{z_l}) \geq T, \\ 0 & \text{otherwise} , \end{cases} \tag{10}$$

where the threshold T corresponds to the minimum SNR.

Note that Equation (10) is designed to be optimum for the binary hypothesis testing of acceptance of code word, but it should not be applied as a decision rule for another binary hypothesis testing that tests existence or absence of watermark, because it is not optimum for that purpose. The false alarm rate might be much higher than the code word error rate when the above decision rule is applied.[5]

3.4 Robustness Margin

The SNR is closely related to the robustness of watermarks. Just after watermark is embedded, the initial SNR is the ratio of the watermark signal to the power

[5] In the uncoded DSSS, $P_M \simeq RQ(\sqrt{2TW/R})$ and $P_{FA} \simeq Q(\sqrt{R/\sqrt{2}}(\sqrt{2T} - 1))$.

of the original image or audio data as noise. Thus, the difference between the minimum SNR and the initial SNR is a robustness margin for the attenuation of watermark signals and/or the additive noise from unknown post processing such as lossy compression.

4 Performance Analysis on Quantization Effect

Quantization is performed on a discrete cosine transform (DCT) domain for JPEG and MPEG [6]. Given a random variable Y with continuous probability density function (PDF) $P_Y(y)$, a uniform quantizer with step size q produces a discrete PDF $P_Z(z)$. The first and second moments of the quantizer output are

$$\mathrm{E}[Z] = \sum_{i=-\infty}^{\infty} iq \int_{(i-\frac{1}{2})q}^{(i-\frac{1}{2})q} P_Y(y)dy, \tag{11}$$

$$\mathrm{E}[Z^2] = \sum_{i=-\infty}^{\infty} (iq)^2 \int_{(i-\frac{1}{2})q}^{(i-\frac{1}{2})q} P_Y(y)dy, \tag{12}$$

and the variance is $\sigma_z^2 = \mathrm{E}[Z^2] - \mathrm{E}^2[Z]$. We shall assume that the original host signal follows the generalized Gaussian PDF:

$$P_X(x) = \frac{c_1(\beta)}{\sigma} \exp\left(-c_2(\beta)\left|\frac{x}{\sigma}\right|^{\frac{1}{\beta}}\right), \tag{13}$$

where

$$c_1(\beta) = \frac{\Gamma^{\frac{1}{2}}(3\beta)}{2\beta\Gamma^{\frac{3}{2}}(\beta)}, \quad c_2(\beta) = \left[\frac{\Gamma(3\beta)}{\Gamma(\beta)}\right]^{\frac{1}{2\beta}} \tag{14}$$

and $\Gamma(x)$ is the Gamma function. Note that $\beta = 1/2$ represents the Gaussian PDF and $\beta = 1$ represents the Laplacian PDF.

These equations allow us to compute the watermarking SNR vs. the normalized quantization step size. The solid line (a) in Fig. 2 is from analysis, showing SNR decreasing with increasing quantization step size for "Lena" image with the constant-strength watermarking scheme or

$$Y = X + a\sigma. \tag{15}$$

That is, by substituting $P_Y(y) = P_X(y - a\sigma)$ in Equation (11) and (12). In the figure, the scaling factor[6] is set to $a = 0.5$, and the horizontal axis is normalized to q/σ. It is found that the SNR rapidly decreases when the quantization step size exceeds twice the watermark strength or $q/\sigma > 2a$. The points marked with "+" are from measurement. For the experimental measurement, the watermark is created on 16 coefficients in the middle range of each 8×8-DCT block. In general,

[6] The scaling factor $a = 0.5$ makes PSNR 42 [dB] with 4 [dB] standard deviation for the 100 sample natural images used in the experimental measurements. In the PSNR, the signal is (peak) power of image, and the noise is power of watermark.

the variance is greater on a lower frequency than on a higher frequency in natural images, and so the 16 coefficients are separately manipulated to represent the watermark so that the amount of manipulation would be proportional to the standard deviation σ_i of the i-th coefficient or $Y_i = X_i + a\sigma_i$. In the detection stage, the Quantizer outputs $\{Z_i\}$ are normalized prior to summing up them so that the watermark signal could be maximized, by dividing them with the sample standard deviation $(\hat{\sigma}_z)_i$. Thus, the SNR is estimated by

$$\hat{\gamma} = \frac{1}{2}\left[\frac{1}{n}\sum_{i=1}^{n}\left(\frac{\hat{\mu}_z}{\hat{\sigma}_z}\right)_i\right]^2, \tag{16}$$

where n is the number of the coefficients manipulated in each DCT block, and $(x)_i$ indicates the statistics in the i-th coefficient.

The dotted line (c) shows the analysis on another watermarking scheme, namely, adaptive-strength scheme or

$$Y = X + a|X|, \tag{17}$$

in which the strength of watermark signals is proportional to the strength of host signals. The PSNR is the same as in the constant-strength scheme, because the mean of watermark power is the same, i.e., $\mathrm{E}[(a|X|)^2] = a^2\sigma^2$. The points marked with "x" are from measurement. The deviation caused by various assignments of PN sequence and code word may be negligible because of the high bandwidth.

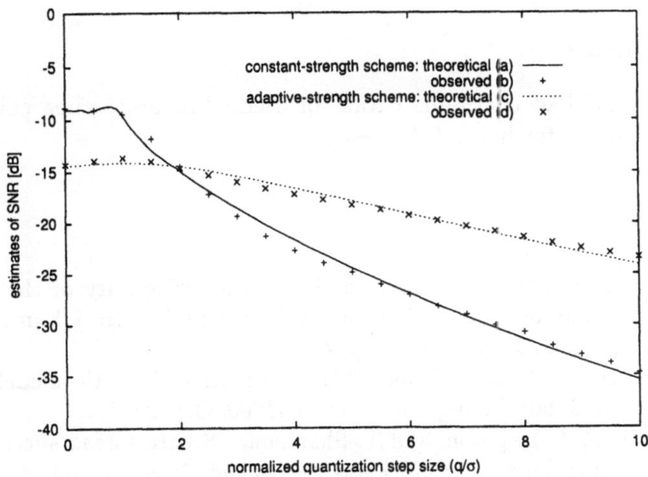

Fig. 2. Theoretical and observed estimates of SNR on a "Lena" image for the constant-strength and adaptive-strength schemes, in which a generalized Gaussian PDF is assumed, and $\beta = 1.77$ is fitted to the image.

It is found from Fig. 1 and Fig. 2, that the 256-bit payload in the bandwidth $W = 65536$ can be achieved as long as the quantization step size is less than about 6 times of the standard deviation of the host signal for the adaptive-strength watermarking scheme with the watermark strength $a = 0.5$, because the SNR is able to decrease down to about -18.5 dB, which was found from Fig. 1. Note that in our 100 sample natural images, the difference between analysis and measurement shows -0.03 [dB] mean with 1.60 [dB] standard deviation, which indicates that the theoretical estimates fit the observed estimates on average.

Consequently, when the generalized Gaussian PDF parameters, $\{\sigma_i\}$ and β, are known for the given host image, then the SNR can be predicted from the quantization weights, and thus the upper limit of compression rate is found or the minimum watermarking strength can be determined under the given compression rate. For the case of "cjpeg" [7], the SNR can be predicted based on a "quality" parameter and the predefined quantization table which describes the weights of quantization for DCT coefficients, and thus the minimum watermarking strength can be determined under the quality parameter given as compression rate.

5 Conclusion

We have analyzed the performance of data hiding in terms of the payload limit, the minimum SNR, the probability of detection error, and the bandwidth of the watermarking channel. We have illustrated how the analytical results can be applied in practice in terms of selecting parameters of watermarking under quantization.

Acknowledgments

The author would like to thank Professor Bede Liu and other colleagues at Princeton University for helpful discussions.

References

[1] M. Barni, F. Bartolini, A. de Rosa, and A. Piva, "Capacity of the watermark channel: How many bits can be hidden within a digital image ?," in *Proc. SPIE*, San Jose, CA, Jan. 1999, vol. 3657, pp. 437–448.
[2] G-I. Lin P. Moulin, M.K. Mihcak, "An information-theoretic model for image watermarking and data hiding," in *Proc. ICIP'00*, Oct. 2000.
[3] I. Cox, J. Kilian, T. Leighton, and T. Shamoon, "Secure spread spectrum watermarking for multimedia," *IEEE Trans. on Image Procesing*, vol. 6, no. 12, pp. 1673–1687, Dec. 1997.
[4] M. Barni, F. Bartolini, and A. Piva, "A dct-domain system for robust image watermarking," *Signal Procesing*, vol. 66, no. 3, pp. 357–372, May 1998.
[5] J. Proakis, *Digital Communications, 3rd ed.*, New York: McGrawHill, 1995.
[6] G. K. Wallace, "The jpeg still picture compression standard," *Communications of the ACM, CACM*, vol. 34, no. 4, pp. 30–44, 1991.
[7] Independent JPEG Group, "jpegsr6b.zip," http://www.ijg.org.

Data Encryption Using MRF with an RSA Key

Chaur-Chin Chen

Department of Computer Science
National Tsing Hua University
Hsinchu, Taiwan 300
Tel: +886 3 573 1078
Fax: +886 3 572 3694
E-mail: cchen@cs.nthu.edu.tw

June 21, 2001

Abstract In a digital multimedia era, the security of multimedia over network transmission becomes a challenging issue. A strategy, combining cryptography with steganography, is investigated to overcome the problems in hand. This paper proposes hiding secret messages,represented as a binary image, by covering a binary random texture synthesized from a 2D Ising Markov random field with an authorized RSA key as the seed. Experiments show that an unauthorized key may never recover the message even it is close to the authorized one.

1. Introduction

The security of multimedia over network transmission and information concealment raises an increasing interest in a digital multimedia era. The issues are discussed in E-commerce and Web-commerce sporadically. Petitcolas et al. [5] reported a survey of information hiding methods. Cox et al. [1] and Wolfgang et al. [8] reviewed the watermarking techniques. As the technology moves, a new scheme, based on combining the concept of cryptography [4] and steganography [3] using a probabilistic texture image model, is investigated for hiding secret messages.

Steganography [3] is a Greek ancient art of hiding information and is currently exploited to either put a digital image on the secret messages to hide the information or insert watermarks [1,6,9] into a digital image, audio, and/or video, to preserve an intellectual property or to claim the copyright. The research of using steganography is to invent an intelligent use of camou
flage such that no one except the authorized person can read the secret message after decryption.

Cryptography [4], on the other hand, is concerned with strategies based on a secret key for enciphering or concealing data such as text, image, audio, and video data. A commonly used cryptographic system, RSA system [7], based on Euler and Euclidean theorems from Number Theory, may encrypt a plaintext with a binary representation into a ciphertext with a public key (a, n), where $n = pq$ is a large number, $3 < a < m = (p - 1)(q - 1)$, and $\gcd(a, m)=1$. Presumably, an RSA system realizes that only an authorized person knows how to factor n into the product of two primes, p and q, and so does the private key b (that requires solving ax ≡ 1 mod m) to decrypt the ciphertext, The usage of RSA system is based on issuing a very large number n = pq such that for intruders using trial and error approaches can never find the secret key b in their lifetime.

This paper assumes that the secret message is represented as a binary image. To hide the secrets, a synthesized texture, like a rain pattern, from a second order Ising Markov random field with parameters (1, 1, 1,-1) [2] with an authorized RSA key [4] as the seed covers on the message by means of a simple image processing operation like "pixel exclusive-or" to encrypt and hide the secret message. Only the one who knows the authorized key may recover the information

2. The Algorithm

Suppose that a secret message to be hidden is represented as an $N \times N$ binary image, X. We will implement the following steps.

1. Issue an RSA key (a,n), where n=pq, p and q are large prime numbers, m=(p-1)(q-1). gcd(a,m)=1 and ab≡1 mod m must 3 be satisfied [4].
2. Use an Ising Mrf model to generate a binary texture image W by the use of the authorized key b obtained in (1) as the initial seed for the Mrf synthesizer [2].
3. Cover the image X with W by $Y=X \oplus W$, where each pixel of Y is obtained by $x \oplus w$, where $x \in X$ and $w \in W$ are the corresponding pixels (bits).
4. Get a word, y, an integer of k^2 bits long by rearranging a block of $k \times k$ pixels from the image, Y , the secret message covered by a binary texture.
5. Encrypt each word obtained in (4) by the strategy of an RSA system to get the enciphered image Z.
6. To decrypt and recover the message, an authorized person must know b, the factors p and q of n, and the parameters of Mrf synthesizer which is extremely diÆcult although not unsolvable.

3. Experiments

To demonstrate how our algorithm works. Suppose Figure 1(a) contains the original message which is a 64×64 0-1 binary image. We follow the algorithm.

For step 1, we select two prime numbers p = 127 and q = 193 such that n = pq = 24511 and m = (p-1)(q-1) = 24192. We further elect a = 2731 which is relatively prime to m. Thus, b = 18691 is the unique solution of ax ≡ 1 mod m.

For step 2, we synthesize a binary texture, W, from an Ising Markov random field [2] with the authorized key b = 18691 as the initial seed.

For step 3, the message shown in X is now hidden as $Y=X \oplus W$ as shown in Figure 1(b).

For step 4, we first partition the image into $32 \times 32=1024$ 2×2 blocks, then pack each 2×2 block with bits y0, y1, y2, and y3 into a 16-bit integer by y = 2048 * y3 + 256* y2 + 16 * y1 + y0.

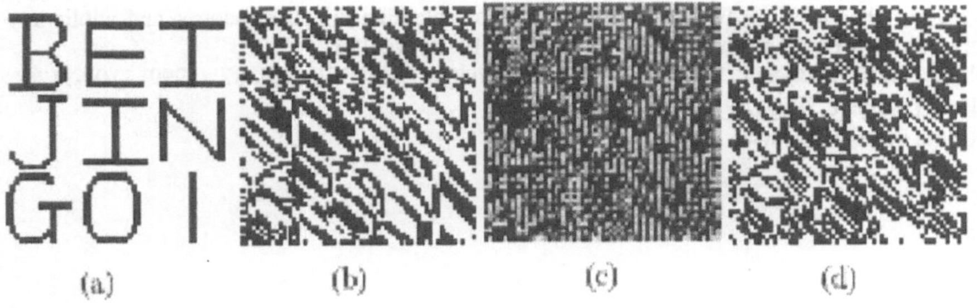

Figure 1: (a) Original, (b) Concealment, (c) Encipherment, (d) Intrusion

For step 5, we encipher each y obtained in (4) as $z \equiv y^a \bmod n$ and then unpack the word z as four 8-bit integers to get the enciphered message Z as shown in Figure 1(c).

Figure 1(d) shows the decrypted message by randomly guessing the key $\bar{b} = 18693$ instead of using the correct key b = 18691. Note that the original message will be completely recovered if the correct key is chosen.

4. Discussion and Conclusion

This paper proposes a framework of using a cryptographic algorithm associated with an Ising Mrf to cover a secret message to achieve information concealment. The issue is that the synthesized texture by an Mrf using the authorized key of an RSA system is presumably diÆcult to be revealed. Furthermore, the Mrf parameters are floating-point numbers which increases the complexity of intrusion. For the future work, some other texture models such as Gaussian Mrf models, fractal models, Gabor _lters, and time series models [2] can also be used instead of Ising Mrf for information concealment under our proposed paradigm. Other cryptographic algorithms such as the one based on an elliptic curve [4] might also be considered.

References

[1] Cox, I.J., Kilian, J., Leighton, T., Shamoon, T.: Secure, spread spectrum watermarking for multimedia, IEEE Trans. Image Processing, Vol. 6, No. 12, (1997) 1673-1687

[2] Dubes, R.C., Jain, A.K.: Random field models in image analysis, Journal of Applied Statistics, Vol. 16, (1989) 131-164.

[3] Johnson N.F., Jajodia, S.: Exploring steganography: Seeing the unseen, IEEE Computer Magazine, Vol. 32, (1998) 26-34.

[4] Van Der Lubbe, J.C.A.: Basic methods of cryptography, Cambridge University Press, (1999)

[5] Petitcolas, F.A.P., Anderson, R.J., Kuhn, K.G.: Information hiding - A survey, Proceedings of the IEEE, Vol. 87, (1999) 1062-1078

[6] Pitas, I.: A method for watermark casting on digital images, IEEE Trans. Image Processing, Vol. 8, (1998) 775-780

[7] Rivest, R., Shamir, A., Adleman, L.: A method for obtaining digital signatures and public-key cryptosystems, Communications of ACM, Vol. 21, (1978) 120-126
[8] Wolfgang, R.B., Podilchuk, C.I., Delp, E.J.: Proceedings of the IEEE, Vol. 87, (1999) 1108-1126
[9] Website Digimarc, http://www.digimarc.com
[10] Website Stego, http://www.stego.com

Digital Watermarking for Forgery Detection in Printed Materials*

Y.J.Song, R.Z.Liu, T.N.Tan

National Lab of Pattern Recognition
Institute of Automation, Chinese Academy of Sciences
P.O.Box 2728 Beijing, 100080, P.R.China
{yjsong,liurz,tnt}@nlpr.ia.ac.cn

Abstract. Forgery prevention and detection are of great social importance.This paper attempts to apply digital watermarking into forgery prevention.To embed a watermark,the wavelet transformation is first applied to the original image and the corresponding approximation image and detail images are obtained.The digital watermark is embedded into the most important DCT coefficients of the approximation image except the DC coefficient of the detail image through linearly additive operation.The corresponding watermark is extracted throught threshold judgement and the threshold is determined through the difference of two cycle print&scan and one cyle print&scan of the images.To improve the robustness of the orgorithm, the simple and effective repetition is applied to watermark configuration.And the CIE Lab color space is chosen to guarantee the repetition of the results and minimize the error brought by the transference of images between differnt equipments.Experimental results show that the proposed algorithm can satisfy the requirements of forgery prevention for ordinary images, that is to say the digital watermark is robust to one cycle print&scan and fragile to two cycle print&scan. Compared with other forgery prevention and detection techniques, the algorithm described in this paper reduced the computation cost considerably as no other special material or equipment is required and ordinary user can verify the authentication of printing materials. This algorithm can also be used in printing materials copyright protection,such as the owner verification in certificates,passports,ect.

1 Introduction

The increasingly networked society calls for effective measures for copyright protection, image authentication, etc. Digital watermarking thus comes into being and promotes the progress of the field. But we should not neglect those images largely in the form of presswork (trademarks, pictures, certification, ID cards, paper currency, passports, etc). For recent years, many people have been engaged in forgery of printed materials for illegal economic profit. The identical printing process brings the fact that

* This work is supported by the Chinese NSF (Grant No. 59825105) and the Chinese Academy of Sciences.

it is easy for a forger to make illegal copies of the original. Just take the passports as an example, from the China Police Department statistics, there are about 3 million false passports all over the world. And a comparative portion is absolutely counterfeited. The strike on counterfeit has never been stopped. People have thought of many different forgery prevention methods on color printing, such as laser forgery preventing, telephone code forgery preventing, computer network counterfeit preventing, etc. All these forgery-prevention techniques have worked on a certain degree, but the cost has increased greatly. People are looking forward to more cost-effective schemes.
In this paper, we attempt to apply digital watermarking into the forgery prevention field. The paper is organized as follows. Section 2 introduces the recent progresses of watermarking in printing systems. Section 3 puts forward the implementation scheme. Section 4 outlines the experimental results. And Section 5 makes the conclusions and presents the work to be continued.

2 Recent Progresses of Watermarking in Printing

Recent public literatures show that some researchers have tried to apply watermarking into printing system. The watermarking scheme invented in Digimarc Company has been integrated in the most popular image processing tool-PhotoShop. The embedded watermark can survive printing and scanning on some degree. But the amount of watermark is very limited and the content of watermark is restricted in Digimarc ID, Distributor ID, Copyright Year, etc. Also it is sensitive to geometric transform. Pun [1] has devised a watermarking algorithm robust to printing and scanning. The PhotoCheck software developed in AlpVision Company by Kutter [2] is mainly focused on authentication detection of passports. As a passport belongs to the owner with his photo, this belongs to a content-based watermarking technique. When the photo is changed, the image with the watermark is of course lost and this just requires that the watermark hidden in the owner's passport is robust to one cycle of print and scan. Considering the special characteristic of FFT on rotation, scaling and cropping, Lin [3][4] has carried out the research on fragile watermarking rather early and obtained many useful conclusions on the distortion brought by print and scan. Researchers in China [5] began to hide some information in printing materials, using the function offered by PhotoShop. All these are focused on the watermark robust to one cycle of print and scan. For real forgery prevention, there are some other requirements as discussed in the following.

Figure 1 and 2 illustrate watermark embedding and extraction processes both for a copyrighted product and a forged one. From the figures, we can see that the difference between the copyrighted and the forged is the process before watermark extraction. The copyrighted only needs one scan, while the forged requires more than one cycle of print and scan. It will be ideal if the watermark is robust only to the first cycle of print&scan, but fragile to the second cycle of print&scan.

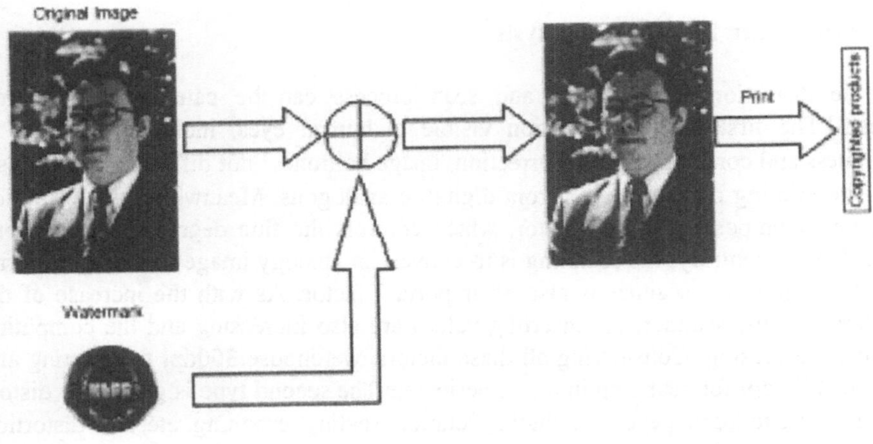

Fig. 1. Embedding Process

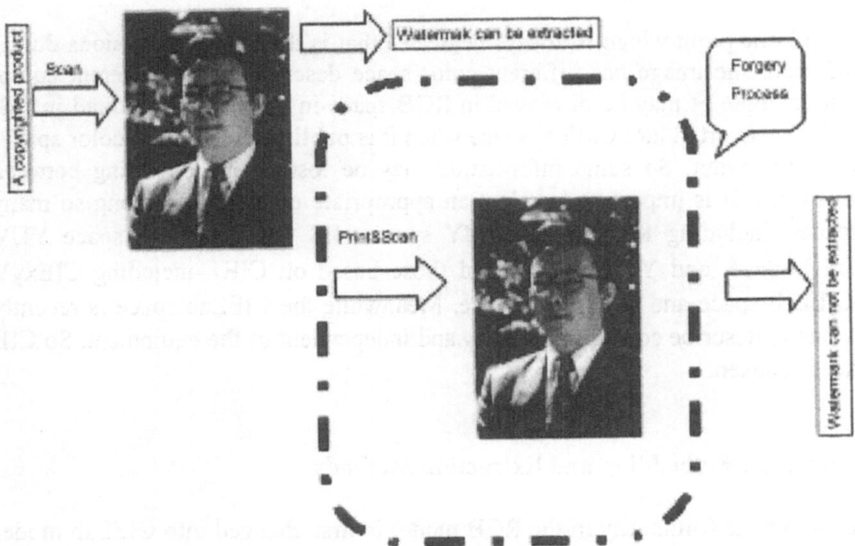

Fig. 2. Extracting Process

3 Implementation Method

3.1 Print&scan Distortion Analysis

All the distortion in the print and scan process can be categorized into two types[3].The first type is distortion visible to human eyes, including changes of brightness and contrast, gamma correction, image halftone, dot diffusion, edge noise, etc. The printing of an image is from digital to analogous. Meanwhile, the resolution of a photocomposer is a key factor, which controls the fine degree of the halftone grids. On the contrary, the scanning is to convert an analogy image to its digital form. The resolution of a scanner is also an important factor. As with the increase of the resolution of the scanner, the inserting values are also increasing and the computing speed is decreasing. Considering all these factors, we choose 300dpi for printing and 600dpi~1200dpi for scanning in our experiments.The second type is geometric distortion invisible to human eyes, including rotation, scaling, cropping, etc.This distortion always occurs when locating the corresponding portion in the printing sheet with the original digital images. Some rotation is needed, as a sheet may not be very horizontal when it is put on the surface of a scanner. Numerous experiments show the rotation angle is at about $-0.5°\sim 0.5°$. A certain cropping is necessary to cut the margins. And scaling is always indispensable, as the printing resolution and the scanning resolution are always inconsistent.

There is still one point which is always neglected,that is the color conversions during print and scan.One image has different color space descriptions on different equipment. For example, it may be displayed in RGB space in computer, be edited in HSI space and be converted into CMYK space when it is published. Different color spaces have different gamut. So some information may be lost when converting between different spaces. It is important to select an appropriate color space among so many color spaces, including RGB space, CMY space, HIS (HLS, HSB) space YUV space, YIQ space, and YCrCb space and those based on CIE, including CIExyY space, CIELab space and CIELu*v* space. Meanwhile the CIELab space is recently the only one to describe color most exactly and independent of the equipment. So CIE Lab space is chosen.

3.2 Watermark Embedding and Extraction Methods

The original image (ordinarily in the RGB mode) is first changed into CIELab mode, and the L portion is chosen to carry the watermark. The watermark '*This belongs to NLPR*' is taken as an example (the length of the watermark is defined as l).
Firstly, each bit of the watermark is extracted and a sequence composed of 0 and 1 is obtained. 0 is changed to –1, 1 remains unchanged. The above sequence is repeated m times and the size of the total sequence is $8l*m$. Secondly, a two-level multi-resolution representation of the original image is obtained using a Haar wavelet transform.The

DCT transform is applied to the approximation image, the $8l*m$ largest coefficients are selected and the watermark is added with a linear additive function, just as Cox's method [6]. The strength of the watermark is controlled by a. Lastly, the inverse DCT of the above sequence is made,the corresponding inverse wavelet tranform is done to get the watermarked image which can be printed later.

It is time to distinguish the copyrighted products and the forged ones. Firstly, one of the presswork is scanned and a scanned image with some margin is obtained (The sheet should better be put as horizontal as possible.). Secondly, the corresponding area with the original digital image is located. Thirdly a sequence W_j (i) is computed using the minus operation with the embedding process. M is chosen as a threshold, if the current value of W_j (i) is greater than M, then W_jj (i) is set to 1,otherwise is set to 0. If the number of 1s is greater than that of 0s in a bit of a character, then the bit is considered as 1s,otherwise 0.By repeating the above operation for all other bits, the watermark is extracted.

At the same time, the bit-error rate curve can be obtained. If the whole eight bits of a character can be extracted (or the bit error rate of each bit of a character is less than 50%), then the extracted character is considered as correct. If all the characters can be extracted from the first cycle of the print&scan image, the watermark is considered robust to the first cycle of print&scan. If all the characters can not be extracted from the second cycle of the print&scan image, the watermark is defined fragile to second cycle of print&scan. Thus the watermark can claim the owner of the copyright and detect the forgery images.

Now the pirating technique is becoming more sophisticated. That is to say the difference between the first cycle of print&scan image and the second cycle of print&scan image is small. If the above scheme works, the difference between the sequences extracted after the copyrighted image and the forgery must be found. Many repeated experiments (100 times) with the approximately same conditions demonstrate that the mean of the sequence extracted from copyrighted image stabilizes at a certain value M_1 (the variance is between -0.1 and 0.1). Many repeated experiments (100 times) with other conditions different from the copyrighted print and scan show the mean of the sequence extracted from forgery image stabilizes at another certain value M_2 and M_2 is ten times greater than M_1.So M_1 is chosen as the decision threshold.

4 Experimental Results

4.1 Parameter Optimization

Channel capacity is a key factor in the watermark insertion and detection. It is well connected with the robustness and the invisibility of the watermark. Robustness need more watermark capacity and invisibility requires capacity should not exceed a certain value. From the point of information theory, MIT lab's Smith and Comiskey [7] ever

made some capacity estimation on the data hiding system. They obtained the conclusion that the channel capacity is proportional to the ratio of signal-noise of the system on the condition that Gaussian noise channel is the basic model of the system and the ratio of signal-noise is low.Ramkumar [8] made some improvement on the above model and also made some quantitative analysis. Although this model still have many presumptive conditions, but it offered a useful reflection. In this paper, we used the formula proposed [8] and estimate that we can embed 1000 bits at best robust to first cycle of print&scan in a 256*256 pixel if we just use luminance of the image. For more details [8] can be referred to.
The invisibility of a watermark is weighted by the image quality evaluation. PSNR is chosen for simplicity. Generally, the PSNR should be chosen to be 38dB for watermark invisibility and more powerful watermark.The robustness is connected with the following factors:Watermark strengthen factor *a,* watermark sequence repeat times *m*, watermark sequence length *l*, etc. PSNR is defined no less than 38dB, the whole length of the adding sequence ($8*m*l$) is *computed* to be 1000 at most.The optimized value of *a* is 0.2 on the condition that watermark sequence is consist of 1, -1, PSNR is 38dB and $8m*l$ is1000. Of course, the robustness is connected with printing quality and the resolution of the original image.

4.2 Parameter Optimization

The most popular attack tool-Stirmark3.1 is first selected to test the robustness of the algorithm. The following Table1 is statistical results.
The watermark shows good robustness to JPEG compression, scaling, changes in the x-y axis display, removal of the rows and columns symmetrical or not; it shows some robustness on central cropping, rotation with scaling and cropping, x-y direction cropping to some extent; and it is fragile to Linear geometry conversion.The above robustness can satisfy the process of the printing and scanning which includes some rotation (-0.5 degree to 0.5 degree), some cropping (about 1%), scaling, JPEG compression for fast transmission, random error, etc.

Test type	Test numbers	Right Tests numbers
Remove the rows and columns symmetrical or not	5	5
Filtering (median、Gaussian、FMLR、sharping)	6	5
JPEG compression	12	12
Cropping	9	2
Linear geometry conversion	3	0
Change the x-y axis display	8	8
Rotation with cropping ,without scaling	16	6
Rotation with cropping and scaling	16	6

Scaling	6	6
x – y direction cropping	6	3
Stirmark random bend	1	0
sum	88	53

Table 1. Stirmark3.1 test results

4.3 Print&scan Results

Figure 4 is a typical result chosen from 100 experiments. It shows bit error rate comparison between the copyrighted and forgery images. As when the bit error rate is lower than 35%, the extracted bit is considered correct. The bit error rate of each bit from the copyrighted image is all below 50%, thus the watermark can be fully extracted.

While the bit error rate from the forgery image is above 35%,only about half of the bits can be extracted correctly and now the embedded watemark has become meaningless. So we can make a decision that when the watermark can be 85% or above extracted, the image is considered copyrighted product; otherwise the image will be considered forgery product.

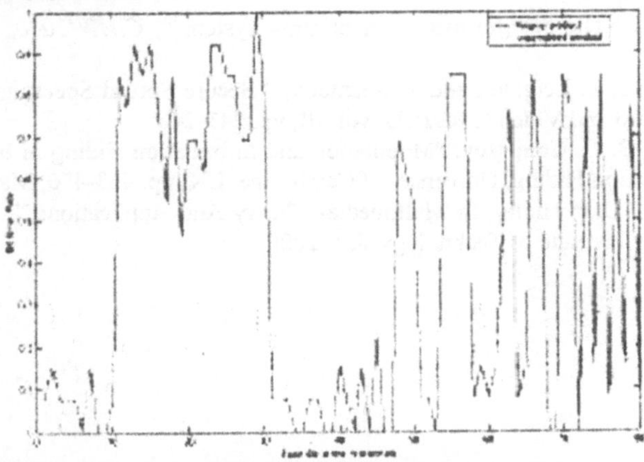

Fig. 3. Bit Error Rate Comparison (Copyrighted and Forgery Images)

5 Conclusions

The above experiments show that the proposed scheme can satisfy the requirement of forgery preventing for ordinary images. Also it can be used in situations where only the robustness to one cycle of print&scan is needed, such as the ID card, passports, etc. The most excellent point is that the cost of this scheme is largely reduced compared with other forgery techniques and ordinary people can authenticate their products. The combined wavelet and DCT transform is applied to the original image and the watermark is linearly added to the most energy-concentrated oefficients.The CIE lab color space makes it possible that the watermark technique can be used in forgery prevention field. The repeated experiments for the same watermark and same image under the same parameters are considered on the same environment equipment (including the scanner, printer, etc.). The optimization may vary with different equipment.

There is still much work to do from the point of research. If we take the color difference (a* and b*) into account, more watermarks can be added and PSNR will not work. Future work will focus on these.

References

1. Joe J. K. Ó Ruanaidh, Thierry Pun, " Rotation, scale and translation invariant spread spectrum digital image watermarking", *Signal Processing* vol. 66(III), pp.303-317, May 1998.
2. M. Kutter, F. Jordan, F. Bossen, "Digital signature of color images using amplitude modulation", Journal of Electronic Imaging, vol. 7, no. 2, pp. 326-332, April, 1998.
3. C.Y.Lin and S.F.Chang, " Distortion Modeling and Invariant Extraction for Digital Image Print-and-Scan Process ", *ISMIP 99*, Taipei, Taiwan, Dec. 1999.
4. C.Y.Lin, " Public Watermarking Surviving General Scaling and Cropping: An Application for Print-and-Scan Process ", *Multimedia and Security Workshop at ACM Multimedia 99*, Orlando, FL, Oct. 1999.
5. Z.Y.Li, Z.Z.Fu, " Hiding information in printing system ", *CIHW'2000*, Beijing, China, Jun.2000.
6. I.J. Cox, J. Kilian, T. Leighton and T. Shamoon, " Secure Spread Spectrum Watermarking for Images, Audio and Video ", *ICIP'96*, vol. III, pp. 243-246.
7. J. R. Smith and B. O. Comiskey, "Modulation and Information Hiding in Images ", Workshop on Information Hiding, University of Cambridge, UK, pp. 463-470, May 1996.
8. M. Ramkumar, " Data Hiding In Multimedia- Theory And Applications ", Ph.D. Dissertation, New Jersey Institute of Technology, Jan. 2000

Improvement and Comments on Image Watermarking Using Complementary Modulation

I. Wiseto Agung and Peter Sweeney

Centre for Communication Systems Research (CCSR), University of Surrey, Guildford GU2 7XH, United Kingdom
w.agung@surrey.ac.uk

Abstract. An improved method for watermarking images in the discrete wavelet transform domain is introduced based on complementary modulation proposed by Lu *et al.* The enhancement is performed by utilizing Reed Solomon error control coding, and modulate the data and parity separately. In addition, we raise comments on the method for combating StirMark random geometric attack which was suggested by those authors, and we offer an alternative method to do so.

1. Introduction

The production and distribution of multimedia data in digital format, raises the problem of protecting intellectual property rights (IPR), since the digital data can be easily copied without degradation in quality. With digital watermarking, information including origin, status, and/or destination of the data, can be imperceptibly and robustly embedded in the host data, either in the spatial domain or in a transform domain.

Robustness of watermarking systems can be improved by applying diversity. In [3], Kundur presented analysis of improving the robustness by repeatedly embedding the watermark and characterizing the attacks. Lu *et al.*[5] embedded the watermark data by using complementary modulation, which consists of positive and negative modulations.

In this paper we suggest an enhancement of the method in [5] if binary data is applied as a watermark. The proposed method uses a Reed Solomon code on the watermark, then embeds data and parity separately in negative and positive modulation respectively to the discrete wavelet transform coefficients.

To cope with the StirMark random geometric attack [6], the authors in [5] suggested a relocating method based on the watermarked image prior to the detection. However, from our simulation it was found that this method can produce a false positive result. Then, we propose another method to deal with this attack which is valid.

The reminder of this paper is organized as follows. In Section 2, the complementary modulation concept is reviewed. Then, in Section 3 an overview of Reed Solomon error correcting code and its properties is given. Section 4 and Section 5 describe our proposed watermarking scheme and its experimental results respectively. The issue of combating the random geometric attack is discussed in Section 6. Finally, the conclusion will be given in Section 7.

2. Complementary Modulation

In order to be robust against attacks, many watermarking schemes such as [2] or [8] embed the watermark by slightly changing or modulating the magnitude of the significant transform coefficients. If the watermark has positive value, the coefficient magnitude is increased. Conversely, if the watermark has negative value (or 0 or –1 for binary type) the magnitude is decreased.

The authors in [5] observed that an arbitrary attack usually tends to increase or decrease the magnitudes of the majority of the transformed coefficients. Or, in other words, the chance that an attack will make the number of increased and of decreased coefficients equal is very low. So, they proposed a scheme which aims to detect the watermark from the less distorted coefficients. They use two different modulation rules: positive modulation and negative modulation. If a modulation operates by adding a positive quantity to a positive coefficient or by adding a negative quantity to a negative coefficient, then it is called positive modulation. Otherwise, it is called negative modulation. Then, in the detection, the best result that survives against attacks is chosen.

3. Reed Solomon Codes

Digital watermarking embedding and detection can be observed as a communication system where the information (i.e. the watermark) is transmitted through a channel to the receiver. To overcome the error which may occur in the channel (i.e. the attacks), an error control coding can be utilized, where in our proposed scheme, the Reed Solomon code is used. A brief summary of RS code and its terminology will be given as follows.

A Reed Solomon code [4,7] is usually specified as RS(n,k), where k data symbols of s bits each are added by (n-k) parity symbols to make n symbols codeword. The code rate is equal to k/n. The RS decoder can correct *errors* and *erasures*. If the position of the incorrect symbol is known, it can be categorized as an erasure. A decoder can correct up to $(n\text{-}k)/2$ symbol errors or up to n-k symbol erasures. To fit the specific implementation, RS codes can be *shortened* by making several data symbols zero at the encoder, not transmitting them, and inserting them in the detection prior to the decoding.

4. Proposed Scheme

A block diagram of improved complementary modulation watermarking is shown in Figure 1. Firstly, the original image is decomposed into three levels using the discrete wavelet transform. Like the method of Xia *et al.*[8], the watermark will be embedded only in the largest coefficients at the high and middle frequency bands. The DWT coefficients at the lowest resolution are not changed.

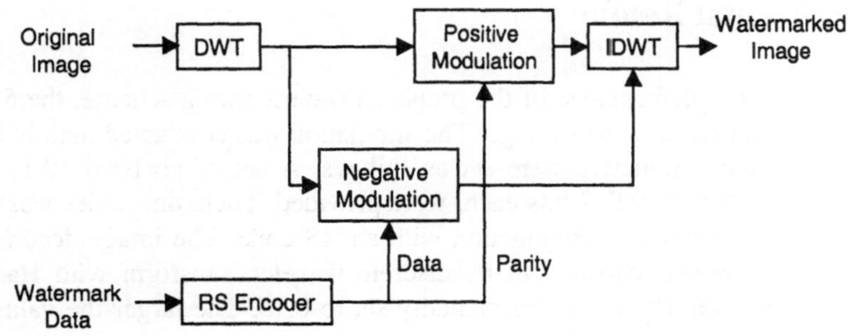

Fig. 1. Proposed embedding scheme

For the watermark, *d* bits of random {0,1} binary data are used, and they are encoded by a Reed Solomon error correcting code into *(d+p)* bits, before being embedded into the required DWT coefficients.

Next, the high and mid band coefficients of the host image (*V*) are sorted in increasing order. Then, the positive and negative modulations are applied to the parity and data (*W*) respectively, constructing watermarked coefficients (*V'*), using the following rules:

Parity / Positive Modulation:

$$v_i^{'} = \begin{cases} v_i(1-\alpha), & w=0, \quad i: odd \\ v_{\max-i}(1+\alpha), & w=1, \quad i: odd \end{cases} \tag{1}$$

Data / Negative Modulation:

$$v_i^{'} = \begin{cases} v_i(1+\alpha), & w=0, \quad i = even \\ v_{\max-i}(1-\alpha), & w=1, \quad i = even \end{cases} \tag{2}$$

Finally, after the coefficients are set to their original order, they are reconstructed by inverse discrete wavelet transform to form the watermarked image. The scaling factor α. is used to adjust the watermark level, so that it is imperceptible.

In the detection, by using the original image, the data and parity extraction from the suspected image are performed by the inverse of the process in Figure 1 and the above rules in equation (1) and (2). Then, by applying the RS decoder the watermark can be reconstructed.

Finally, the extracted watermarked W^* is assessed by comparing it to the original watermark data *W* using a similarity correlation suggested by Cox *et al.*[2]:

$$SIM(W,W^*) = \frac{W^*.W}{\sqrt{W^*.W^*}} \tag{3}$$

A set of m randomly generated watermarks with d bits each is used to check that the detection best matches the original watermark.

5. Experimental Results

To evaluate the performance of the proposed watermarking scheme, the 512×512 Lena image was used as a host image. The simulation was conducted mainly by using Matlab where the parameters were set as follows. A set of m=1000 {0,1} random binary data with length d=992 bits each, were provided. Then, one series was selected and used as a watermark in conjunction with an RS code. The image decomposition and reconstruction was carried out by discrete wavelet transform with Haar filter. The watermark level α was experimentally set to 0.15. The larger the value of α, the more the watermarked image degraded.

The performance of the proposed scheme is compared to complementary modulation (Lu *et al.*) methods. In order to make a fair comparison, where each method carries the same amount of data, the (248,124) and (248,62) RS codes were used for the Lu *et al.* method and the proposed method respectively. In the detection of the proposed method, the decoder used both (248,62) and (124,62), using erasures, for each of the two modulations subsequently taking the best result.

Then, several attacks were applied by using Matlab functions and StirMark 3.1 [6] to test the robustness of those algorithms before detection. Table 1 shows the maximum attack level, which the watermark still can survive. The embedded watermark is categorized as successfully detected if its SIM is maximized and can be distinguished clearly from the SIMs of other 999 data.

As can be seen from Table 1, the proposed scheme is more robust for these attacks: Gaussian noise, low JPEG compression, rotation, and scaling. Like the other scheme, the proposed method is not robust against the StirMark random geometric attack. However, this issue will be discussed in Section 6.

Table 1. Robustness against various attacks

Attacks	Lu *et al.* method	Proposed method
Gaussian noise, mean=0	var < 0.01	var < 0.03
Low JPEG	QF > 13	QF > 1
Rotation: 1. detect directly	offset < 0.5°	offset < 0.9°
2. re-rotate	any angle	any angle
Scaling	SF > 0.45	SF > 0.35
Cropping	cropped < 85%	cropped < 85%
StirMark Random Geometric	fail	fail

Figure 2 shows the SIM of the two methods against other attacks, i.e. FMLR, median filter, sharpening, linear geometric transforms, aspect ratio changing, and row & column removing, where for these attacks the proposed scheme is better and the watermarks can be detected successfully.

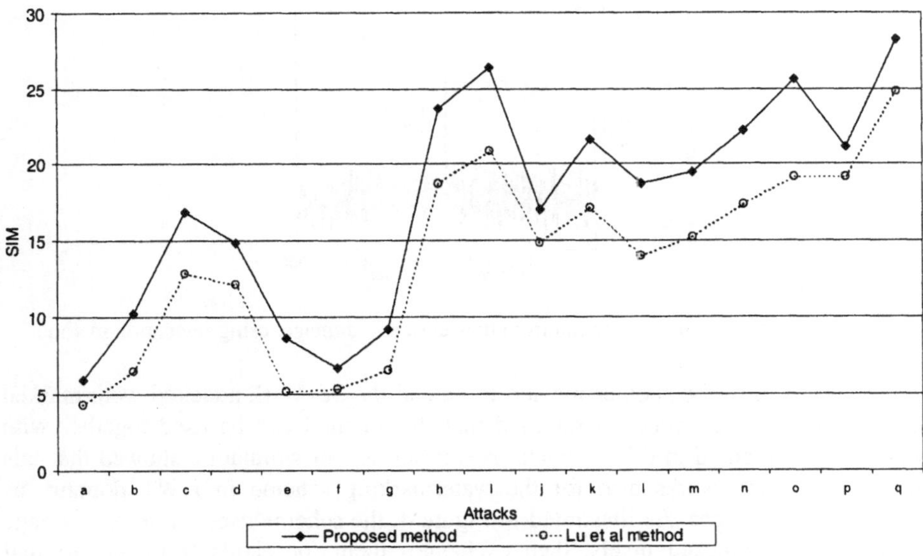

Fig. 2. Robustness Against Various Attacks : *(a)FMLR (b)2x2 Median Filter (c)3x3 Median Filter (d)Sharpening 3x3 (e)Linear Geometric Transform 1.007,0.010, 0.010,1.012 (f)Linear Geometric Transform 1.010, 0.013, 0.009, 1.011 (g)Linear Geometric Transform 1.013, 0.008, 0.011, 1.008 (h)Aspect Ratio x:0.8 y:1.0 (i)Aspect Ratio x:0.9 y:1.0 (j)Aspect Ratio x:1.0 y:0.8 (k)Aspect Ratio x:1.0 y:0.9 (l)Aspect Ratio x:1.0 y:1.1 (m)Aspect Ratio x:1.0 y:1.2 (n)Aspect Ratio x:1.1 y:1.0 (o)Aspect Ratio x:1.2 y:1.0 (p)17 Row 5 Col Removed (q)1 Row 5 Col Removed*

6. Combating Random Geometric Attack

To cope with the StirMark random geometric attack [6], the authors in [5] suggested a relocating method based on the watermarked image prior to the detection. In this method, the wavelet coefficients of the attacked watermarked image A and the watermarked image V' are both sorted. Then, the ith coefficient of A, $A(i)$, is put into the position of the ith coefficient of V', $V'(i)$, for all i.

A simulation to test the validity of this method against false positive was carried out by applying an image with no watermark as an 'attacked watermarked image'. Surprisingly, as can be seen from Figure 3, the 'watermark' can be detected. Then, for further validation, this relocating method was also applied to watermarking scheme with single modulation [8] for both binary and real watermark data, where similar false positives were also shown. It is therefore believed that the amending method described in [5] is invalid. However the authors claim that, since we have original image for the detection, the above problem can be avoided if an image recognition, which requires user assistance, is performed prior to the detection.

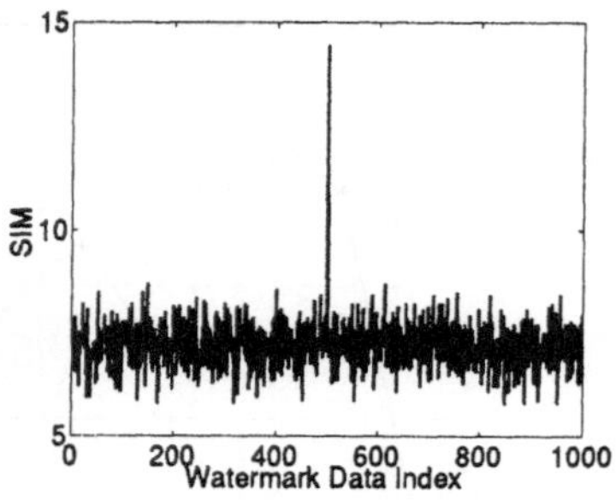

Fig. 3. False positive detection from unwatermarked image, using relocation method

Instead, we propose another method to amend the StirMark attacked watermarked image. Our previous work [1] reported that this method can be used together with watermarking method in DCT domain. Nevertheless, our simulation showed that this amending method works also for the watermarking scheme in DWT domain, as proposed in this paper. As illustrated in Figure 4, the scheme uses a reference image to identify the attacked pixels, then exchanges them for pixels from the original unwatermarked image.

The attacked pixels can be approximated by taking a difference between the attacked watermarked image (suspect image) and a reference image. Ideally, the watermarked image containing the same watermark as the suspect image should be used as the reference image. Nevertheless, in a fingerprinting application where each recipient has a unique watermark, it is not possible to identify which watermark was being embedded into the suspect image. Hence, alternatively, we can use the original image as a reference.

By using this difference, we can determine how many pixels should be changed. Then, after replacing the attacked pixels by pixels from the original image, the detection can be completed. It should be noted that there is a trade off in determining the number of attacked pixels that should be changed. Changing only few pixels may not reduce the effect of the attack. On the other hand, replacing too many pixels, which is similar to applying severe cropping, may reduce the robustness of the scheme.

From the simulation it was shown that by replacing around 35% - 45% of the pixels, a valid detection result can be obtained. Furthermore, the false positive detection does not occur.

7. Conclusions

A robust image watermarking method in DWT domain by using error control coding with separate data and parity embedding is presented. The watermarks embedded using the proposed schemes can be successfully detected from images degraded by various attacks. Moreover, the proposed scheme is more robust than the other method which uses complementary modulation. Furthermore, we suggest a valid method to combat the Stirmark random geometric attack which can be used in association with watermarking scheme in DCT or DWT domain, including our proposed watermarking method.

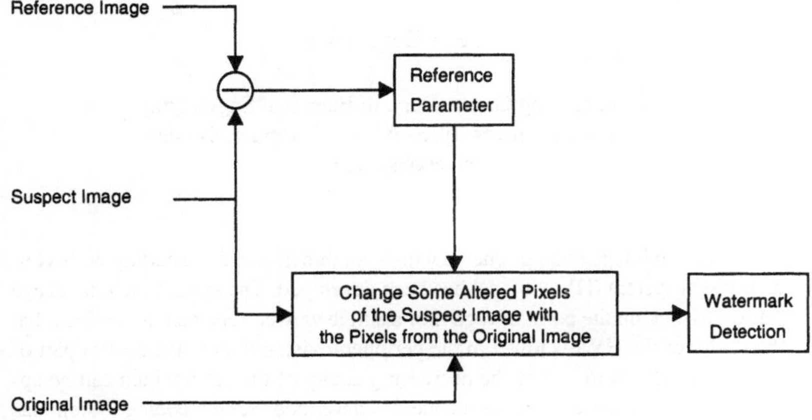

Fig. 4. Proposed scheme to combat random geometric attack

References

1. Agung, I.W., Sweeney, P.: Method for Combating Random Geometric Attack on Image Watermarking, IEE Electronics Letters, Vol.37, No.7, pp.420-421, 29 March 2001
2. Cox, I.J., Killian, J., Leighton, F.T., Shamoon, T.: Secure Spread Spectrum Watermarking for Multimedia, IEEE Transactions on Image Processing, vol.6, no.12, pp.1673-1687, December 1997
3. Kundur, D.: Improved Digital Watermarking through Diversity and Attack Characterization, Proc. Workshop on Multimedia Security at ACM Multimedia '99, Orlando, Florida, pp. 53-58, October 1999.
4. Lin, S., Costello, D.J.: Error Control Coding Fundamentals and Applications, Prentice Hall, Englewood Cliffs, NJ, 1983
5. Lu, C.S., Huang, S.K., Mark Liao, H.Y., Sze, C.J.: Cocktail Watermarking For Digital Image Protection', IEEE Trans. On Multimedia, Vol.2, No.4, pp. 209-224, 4 December 2000
6. Petitcolas, F.A.P., Anderson, R.J., Kuhn, M.G.: Attacks on Copyright Marking Systems, David Aucsmith (Ed) Second Workshop on Information Hiding, vol. 1525 of Lecture Notes in Computer Science, Portland, Oregon, USA, pp.218-23814-17, April 1998
7. Sweeney, P.: Error Control Coding An Introduction, Prentice Hall International (UK), 1991
8. Xia, X., Boncelet, C.G., Arce, G.R.: Wavelet Transform Based Watermark for Digital Images, Optics Express vol.3, no.12, pp.497-511, 7 December 1998

An Eye-Movement Controlled Wavelet Based Image Coder

Peter Bergström

Image Coding Group, Dept. of Electrical Engineering
Linköping University, S-581 83 Linköping, Sweden
peter@isy.liu.se

Abstract. An image coding scheme which combines transform coding with a human visual system (HVS) model has been developed. The system include an eye tracker to pick up the point of regard of a single viewer. One can then utilize that the acuity of the HVS is lower in the peripheral vision than in the central part of the visual field. A model of the decreasing acuity of the HVS which can be applied to a wide class of transform coders is described. Such a coding system has a large potential for data compression.

In this paper we have incorporated the model into an image coder based on the discrete wavelet transform (DWT) scheme.

1 Introduction

The field of image coding deals with efficient ways of representing images for transmission and storage. Most image coding methods have been developed for TV-distribution, tele-conferencing and video-phones. Few efforts have been devoted towards coding methods for interactive systems. One example where interactive systems exists is in tele-robotics, where a human operator controls a robot at a distance. Interactive systems usually have only one observer of the transmitted image. In such a system one can include an eye tracker to pick up the point of regard of the viewer.

The human visual system (HVS) works as a space variant sensor system providing detailed information only in the gaze direction. The sensitivity decreases with increasing eccentricity and is much lower in the peripheral visual field. Thus, in a system with a single observer whose point of gaze is known, one can allow the image to be coded with decreasing quality towards the peripheral visual field.

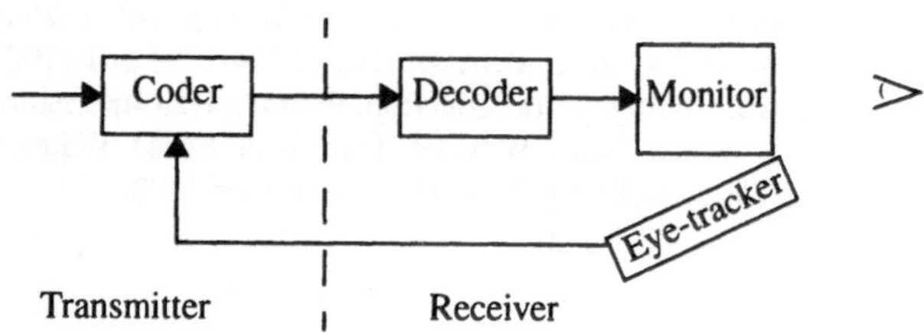

Figure 1. An eye-movement controlled coding system.

In a previous work we have incorporated the model of the HVSs acuity described in section 2 into the JPEG coder with good results [1]. The JPEG coder applies a block based decomposition scheme in combination with the discrete cosine transform (DCT). In this work we will apply the HVS model to a coder based on the DWT decomposition scheme.

To be as similar as possible to the JPEG coder except for the decomposition step the DWT coder in this work is made up of four modules. The image is first decomposed into an octave-band representation. Secondly the transform coefficients are quantized, zero-tree scanned and finally entropy coded [4]. In the decomposition step we have used the Daubechies 9/7 biorthogonal filter bank [2], an excellent filter bank for image compression [3]. The quantizer consists of one uniform scalar quantizer for each subband. A quantization matrix contains the quantization steps. For each image the best quantization matrix is estimated in a rate-distortion sense [4].

The outline of this paper is as follows. Next, the model of the visual acuity will be described. The proposed scheme is presented in section 3 followed by simulation results in section 4. Finally, section 5 draws up the final conclusions.

2 A Visual Acuity Model

Due to the uneven distribution of cones and ganglion cells in the human retina, we have truly sharp vision only in the central fovea. This, covers a visual angle of less than 2 degrees. The ability to distinguishing details is essentially related to the power to resolve two stimuli separated in space. This is measured by the *minimum angle of resolution* (MAR) [6, 7, 8]. The MAR depends on the *eccentricity*, which is the angle to the gaze direction. In this work we will use the MAR measured by Thibos [6].

The related size in the image to a MAR value is called the *minimum size of resolution* (MSR). This size depends on the current viewing conditions. We will assume that the display is flat. Figure 2 shows the viewing situation.

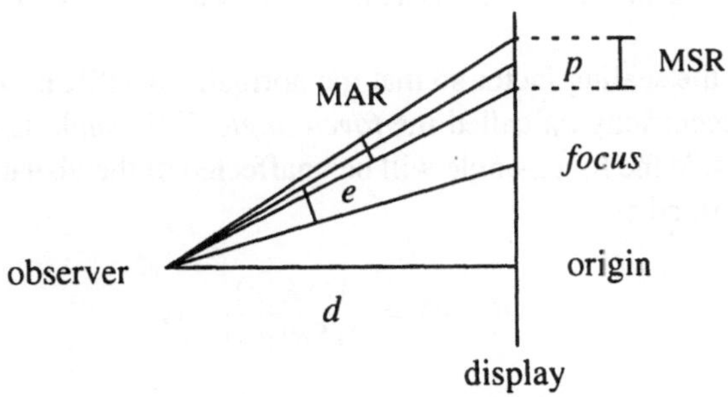

Figure 2. Viewing situation.

With a position tracker and an eye tracker we will get the distance between the observer and the display, denoted *d*, and the point of regard in the image which will be called the *focus*. From these values, one can calculate the *eccentricity*, *e*, for any point, *p*, in the image plane. Furthermore, the minimum size of resolution for the point p is equal to,

$$MSR_{\perp r}(e) = 2\sqrt{d^2 + r_p^2}\tan\left(\frac{MAR(e)}{2}\right) \quad (1)$$

where r_p is the distance between the current point and origin. The MSR in Equation 1 is calculated perpendicular to the r_p-direction. For a computer display the MSR is almost equal for all directions. For larger eccentricities the region which is covered by the MAR will have the form of an oval. However, the $MSR_{\perp r}$ is used since it is the minimum MSR for all directions. This will guarantee that we will not erase visible details.

The MSR-bound can be expressed as a visual frequency constraint. Thus, an image frequency must be less than,

$$f_{vc}(e) = \frac{1}{2 \cdot MSR(e)} \quad (2)$$

if an observer shall be able to perceive it.

2.1 Normalized MSR

The model above is a *just-noticeable distortion* (JND) bound. The possibility to utilize this for compression will occur if we use a large or a high resolution display. However, for many computer displays with normal pixel-resolution the MSR-value will be less than the size of a pixel in large parts of the image. If we, in these cases want to increase the compression we have to go from a JND-bound to a MND-bound (*minimum noticeable distortion*). A MND-bound can not be measured it has to be estimated. This is achieved by normalization of the JND-bound [6].

The normalization will be done such that the relative difficulty to catch details at different eccentricities is kept. This is equal to scaling the stimulated area on the retina equally at different eccentricities. This is achieved by scaling the MSR equally at all eccentricities.

We will define the scaling factor so that the normalized MSR is equal to the width of a pixel at the eccentricity e_f, called the *fovea-angle*. This angle is set to 2 degrees. Thus, the region inside the fovea-angle will be unaffected of the visual model. The normalized MSR is defined as,

$$MSR_N(e) = \frac{MSR(e)}{MSR(e_f)} \cdot ps_w \quad (3)$$

where ps_w is the width of a pixel. The parameter ps_w is equal to $ps_w = is/ir$ where *is* and *ir* are the size and pixel resolution of the image.

3 Modified DWT Coder

The discrete wavelet transform divide the frequency domain into an octave-band representation. To preserve the space frequency resolution and thereby a constant number of coefficients, the scheme consists of down sampling after each filtering. The result is that the coefficients for each decomposition level will represent a larger spatial region. To estimate the spatial and frequency region related to a coefficient we will not take the current filters into consideration. Instead, we will use the decomposition dependent regions pointed out by the *Heisenberg boxes* [9, 10]. Figure 3 (*left*) illustrates the space frequency decomposition for a DWT scheme. Each coefficient is associated with a Heisenberg box. These indicates the time and frequency intervals where the energy of the coefficients are mostly concentrated.

The Heisenberg boxes will for each level, l, divide the space into squares. Each square has the size,

$$\begin{matrix} 2^l \times 2^l \\ 2^L \times 2^L \end{matrix} \quad \text{if} \quad \begin{matrix} 0 \le l \le L \\ l = L+1 \end{matrix} \tag{4}$$

where L is the number of decompositions (L+1 levels).

In the frequency domain, the one-dimensional lower frequency border of subband number l, starting with one at the high pass band, is calculated according to (f_y is calculated in the same way),

$$f_x(l) = \begin{cases} 0.5 \cdot 0.5^l & \text{if} \quad 0 \le l \le L \\ 0 & \phantom{\text{if}} \quad l = L+1 \end{cases} \tag{5}$$

where L is the number of decompositions (L+1 levels). In the two dimensional case each level (except the dc-level) consists of three subbands, representing horizontal, vertical and diagonal frequencies. For the diagonal subbands both f_x and f_y are calculated according to Equation 5. For the vertical and horizontal subbands either f_x or f_y are calculated according to Equation 5 while the other is equal to 0.

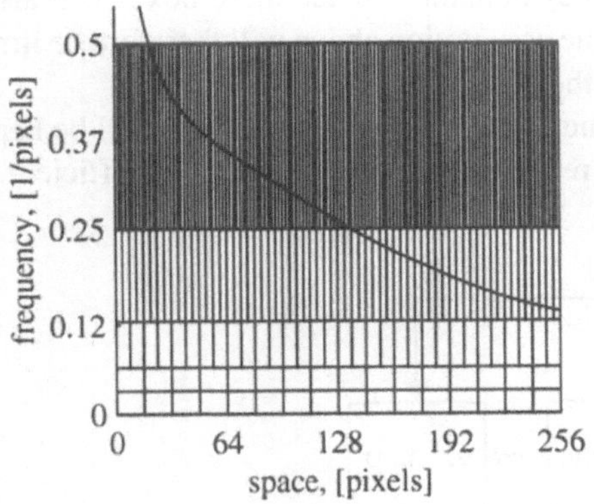

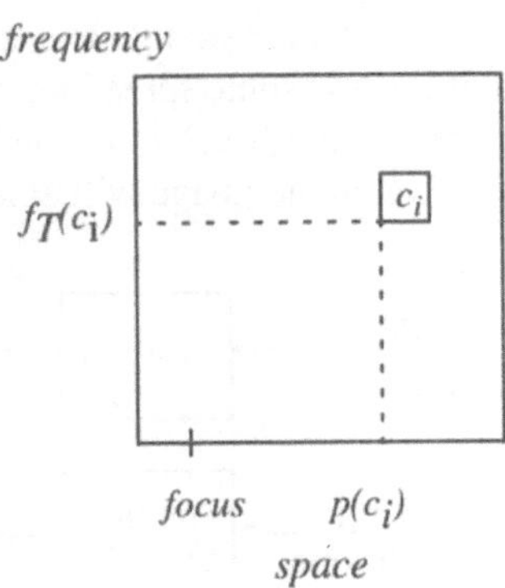

Figure 3. Space frequency decomposition for the DWT scheme (left). Visual description of the position $p(c_i)$ and lower frequency range $f_T(c_i)$ corresponding to coefficient c_i (*right*).

Assume that the viewing conditions are equal to, d=0.5m, is=0.3m, ir=512 pixels, e_f=2 degrees and focus in the centre of the image. Consider the space frequency decomposition along the positive x-axis. Figure 3 (left) shows this space frequency decomposition and the current visual frequency constraint.

A transform coefficient will respond above all to signals whose location and frequency are covered by the corresponding Heisenberg box. The response to other signals will decrease with the distance to the box. We will assume that the coefficients response to signals which are not covered by the corresponding box can be neglected. Thus, a coefficient whose Heisenberg box entirely is above the visual constraint can and will be set to zero.

Let $f_T(c_i)$ denote the lower range of the frequency interval of the Heisenberg box corresponding to coefficient c_i and let $p(c_i)$ denote the point in the space interval which is closest to *focus*. Figure 3 (*right*) shows an example. Thus, the strategy above can be expressed as,

$$f_{vc}(d, focus, p(c_i)) < f_T(c_i) \quad \Rightarrow \quad c_i = 0 \tag{6}$$

where d is the distance to the observer and *focus* the point on the display which is pointed out by the gaze direction. With the three parameters d, *focus* and $p(c_i)$ we can calculate the current eccentricity and then apply Equation 2 to get the visual frequency constraint, f_{vc}. The frequency f_T is equal to,

$$f_T = \sqrt{f_x^2 + f_y^2} \tag{7}$$

where the frequencies f_x and f_y are the lower borders of the one dimensional horizontal and vertical subbands.

Note that, since the visual constraint is a decreasing function, a Heisenberg box which is above the visual constraint can only have one corner near the visual constraint. Thus, the most part of the space and frequency domains outside these boxes will also be above the visual constraint. The error in the assumption above will therefore be limited even if there is some spreading outside the Heisenberg boxes.

Furthermore, the f_T value for the baseband is zero. Thus, the baseband will be kept and every pixel in the image will at least be represented by one transform coefficient.

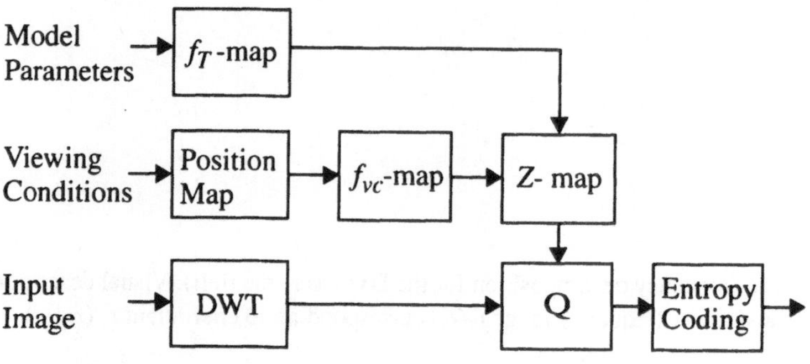

Figure 4. The modified DWT-encoder.

Figure 4 shows a block diagram of the modified DWT-coder. In an initial stage a f_T value is estimated for each subband. Then, whenever the focus is moved a position map is estimated. It contains the position for each coefficient which has the minimum distance to the current focus. Note that three coefficients at each level will have the same position. This position is used to calculate the eccentricity which is put into Equation 2 to calculate the visual frequency constraint for each coefficient. Those coefficients whose f_T value is larger than its visual frequency constraint, f_{vc}, are marked with a zero in the Z-map and the rest with a one. Transform coefficients which are marked with a zero are finally set to zero. This can be done before or after the quantization or by adapting the quantization matrix.

3.1 An Alternative Implementation

Instead of calculating a visual frequency constraint for each coefficient we can utilize Equation 2 and transform the f_T values to MSR related values. The distance to focus which corresponds to each of these MSR related values are then estimated. These values, one for each subband, are called visual distance constraint, denoted d_{vc}. A coefficient will be kept if the minimum distance between the coefficient and the focus is smaller than the current d_{vc} border.

Thus, instead of calculating one f_{vc} value for each coefficient, we only have to calculate one d_{vc} value for each subband. The other steps in the two implementations are equal or comparable considering the requirement of computations.

A factor which will affect the computation gain is the pixel resolution, a higher pixel resolution will increase the number of coefficients but not the number of subbands.

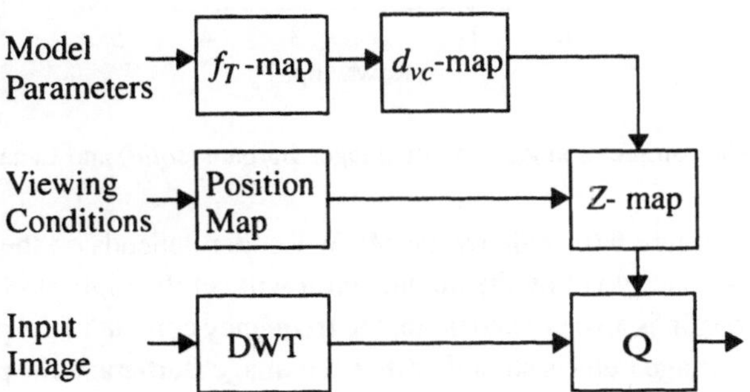

Figure 5. An alternative implementation.

4 Simulation Results

The modified coder described in this paper will be called the MDWT coder. The same coder but without applying the visual constraint will be called the DWT coder.

It is well known that there does not exist any objective distortion measure which completely mirrors the perceived image quality [8]. Furthermore, there are no distortion measurement which consider the acuity of the HVS.

We will instead compare the bit rate for the MDWT coder and the DWT coder when they use the same quantization matrix. That way all maintained coefficients will be quantized in the same way and the quality in the fovea region will be equal.

Thus, the procedure has been the following. For a given image we estimate the best quantization matrix in a rate-distortion sense which results in a certain bit rate for the DWT coder [5]. The image is then coded in the two coders using this quantization matrix. Denote the resulting bit rates with R_{DWT} and R_{MDWT}. We define the compression gain for the modified coder as,

$$Gain = R_{DWT}/R_{MDWT} \tag{8}$$

Figure 6 shows the results when the images Barbara and Lena are coded. The viewing conditions are set to, *d*=0.5m, *is*=0.3m, *ir*=512, e_f=2 degrees and focus in the centre.

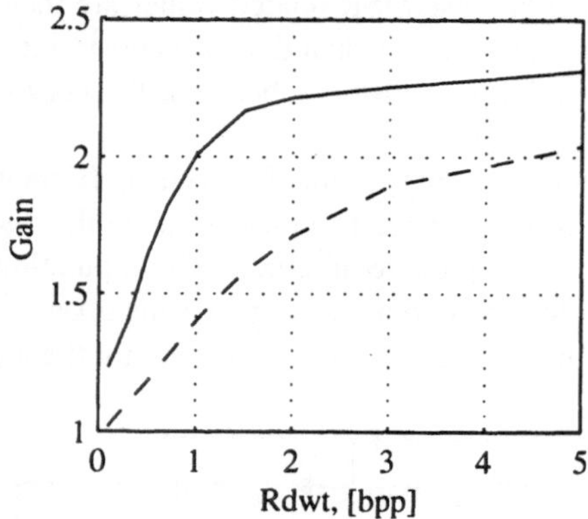

Figure 6. The compression gain for the images Barbara (*solid*) and Lena (*dashed*).

As can be seen in Figure 6 the gain by the MDWT coder depends on the required quality. If the required quality is low the quantization will set the high-pass coefficients to zero anyway. The gain is also dependent on the frequency content in the peripheral parts of the image. The image Lena is smoother than the image Barbara in the peripheral parts and the gain is therefore less for this image.

5 Conclusion

The coder described in this paper shows that there is a considerable additional potential for data compression if one takes into account the point of regard of the observer. The gain is dependent on the high frequency content in the peripheral regions of the image and on the quality that is required. The benefit of the proposed coder is therefore most prominent in a situation where the required quality is high.

In a previous work [1] we applied the visual acuity model described in section 2 to a DCT based coder. The result was higher compression gain than for the MDWT coder described in this work. A research direction is therefore to investigate why. Probably is the reason a better correspondence between the space frequency decomposition and the visual constraint in section 2. A more adaptive decomposition of the space and frequency domain will probably result in an even better correspondence with the visual constraint. It would therefore be of interests to incorporate the visual constraint into a wavelet packet coder.

Our future work will also be directed towards investigating the filter spreading outside the Heisenberg boxes. The result could be a better method to predict the effective size of the filters in the space and frequency domain.

Another direction will be to investigate the real-time performance. Simple visual tests with static images under fixation of the focus have been done. The observers have then only reported minor artifacts. However, a real-time system is necessary too investigate the visual aspects better.

A necessary requirement for a system which uses an eye-movement controlled coder is that it can handle the delay introduced by the encoder and the transmission. This is an issue which is not covered in this paper but which will require special attention [11].

References

[1] P.Bergström, R.Forchheimer, "An eye-movement controlled DCT-coder.", In Proc. of the SSAB Symposium in Image Analysis, 2000.

[2] M.Antonini, M.Barlaud, P.Mathieu, I.Daubechies, "Image coding using wavelet transform.", IEEE Trans. in Image Proc., vol. 1, pp. 205-220, 1992.

[3] J.D.Villasenor, B.Belzer, J.Liao, "Wavelet filter evaluation for image compression.", IEEE Trans. in Image Proc., vol. 2, pp. 1053-1060, 1995.

[4] G.Strang, T.Nguyen, "Wavelets and filter banks.", Wellesley-Cambridge Press, ISBN 0-9614088-7-1, 1996.

[5] L.N.Thibos, "Retinal limits to the detection and resolution of gratings.", J. Opt. Soc. Am., vol. 4, no. 8, pp. 1524-1529, 1987.

[6] F.W.Weymouth, "Visual sensory units and the minimum angle of resolution.", Am. J. Ophthalm., vol. 46, pp. 102-113, 1958.

[7] G.Westheimer, "The spatial grain of the perifoveal visual field.", Vision Res., vol. 22, pp. 157-162, 1982.

[8] N.Jayant, J.Johnston, R.Safranek, "Signal compression based on models of human perception", Proc. IEEE vol. 81, pp. 1383-1422, 1993.

[9] M.V.Wickerhauser, "Adapted wavelet analysis from theory to software.", AK Peters, Wellesey, ISBN 1-56881-041-5, 1994.

[10] S.Mallet, "A wavelet tour of signal processing.", Academic press, ISBN 0-12-466605-1, 1998.

[11] B.Girod, "Eye movements and coding of video sequences.", Visual Com. and Image Proc., SPIE, vol. 1001, 1988.

Variable Frame-Rate Video Coding Based on Global Motion Analysis

Yuwen He, Xuejun Zhao, Shiqiang Yang, Yuzhuo Zhong

Computer Science and Technology Department, Tsinghua University
Beijing 100084, P.R.China

Abstract. This paper proposes a variable frame-rate video coding method based on global motion analysis for low bit rate video coding. Variable frame-rate video coding outperforms fixed frame-rate coding taking full adavantage of adjusting coding frame-rate according to the motion activity of video segments in the video sequence to be coded. Bit-rate can be reduced greatly in those video segments with low motion activity because lower coding frame-rate is used. Global motion analysis is utilized to evaluate the motion activity. The video sequence is classified into segments with low, medium and high motion activity according to global motion intensity. The results of variable frame-rate coding and fixed frame-rate coding methods are compared with test model of H.263 in order to evaluate the performance of proposed variable frame-rate coding method. Bit rate is reduced compared with fixed frame rate coding with the same image quality.

1 Introduction

Traditional video coding scheme, such as MPEG-1/MPEG-2, is fixed frame-rate (FFR) and based on statistical principle. It is independent on video contents, so the optimal compression performance usually can not be gotten with it. FFR coding will waste valuable resources in many situations because there are quite a few shots consisting of still images or low motion activity. There is no need to transmit still images at 25 frames/s or 30 frames/s. Nowadays more and more researchers focus on video content analysis. Much research achievements have been made in content-based video analysis [1]. So content-based video coding is becoming possible. MPEG-4 is the object-based coding standard, which supports object-oriented interactivity, and it has better compression performance compared with conventional frame-based coding because different coding scheme is selected to use for different video object according to its specific attributions. MPEG-7 is a new developing standard, which will provide a multimedia content description interface standardizing the content description. When a video is decomposed into more meaningful segments with some homogeneous attributes, compression could be optimized in source coding. Tian and Zhang [1] introduce the concept of content-based variable frame-rate (VFR) compression, which belongs to content-based video compression. In that concept there are three kinds of frame-rate, one is the source frame-rate, the second is transmission frame-rate and the third is playback frame-rate. They can be different in content-based video coding. The transmission frame-rate maybe is much lower than playback frame-rate or source frame-rate, and it is determined based on various factors such as activity levels of shots and communication channel capacity. Taking the low frame-rate as transmission frame-rate can save transmission bandwidth, storage space. Saw [3] investigates the video coding system with content analysis. The system performance is improved because of utilizing the analysis results in coding. Content-based video coding is a good solution of low bit-rate video coding. Variable frame-rate coding method proposed by Guaragnella [6] uses frame difference to evaluate the motion activity, but it can only be available for the videos with still background and frame difference usually can not reflect the motion activity correctly when motion change is large. Kim [7] selects coding frame-rate according to the current available transmission bandwidth of network. The system emphasizes the transmission quality not on the compression performance. Chen [8] proposes a source model in coding, which can estimate the number of coded bits when a given quantization step is used. Then they can select the frame-rate in order to get the constant image quality. Their method is still based on statistics without content analysis. The availability of the prediction model is very important in their system, but there is no general model in existence.

Motion information is a very important factor in the compression. The effect of motion compensation will determine the compression performance directly. There are two kinds of motion in the video: the one is global motion of background, and the other is the local motion of foreground. The area of background is usually larger than that of foreground. So the motion of background is more important than the local motion with regard to compression performance. In this paper we will use the global motion as the main cue in the video content analysis, which can reflect the motion activity of background. Robust and fast global motion estimation (GME) is our former research work in global motion compensation coding in MPEG-4 [4][5]. We classify video sequence into coding segments with low, medium and high motion activity. The motion activity is measured with global motion parameters. In this paper we only use two translational motion parameters mainly. The different coding frame-rate is applied in different segments according to its motion activity.

The paper is organized as follows. The methodology of variable frame-rate coding is explained, and the method of motion activity analysis is introduced in detail in section 2. Experimental evaluation is given in section 3. The comparison is made between VFR and FFR coding with test model (TM) of H.263. A short discussion and conclusion are presented in section 4.

2 Variable Frame-Rate Video Coding

There are two main modules in the VFR video coding system with different functions. The first is video content analysis module, which will decompose the video into segments with different motion activity and determine the motion activity level of every segment. The second is the variable frame-rate coding module, which will encode the given segments with different frame-rate according to its motion activity level. They

will be discussed in detail in the following parts. There are three main steps in VFR coding system.
(1) Calculate translation motion parameters of two consecutive frames with global motion estimation;
(2) Decompose the video sequence into coding segments with different motion activity according to the intensity of translation motion;
(3) Encode the coding segments with different frame-rate according to motion activity.

2.1 Motion Activity Analysis

MPEG-7 defines motion activity of video shot [2]. But their aim is for content-based retrieval. In VFR coding, motion activity analysis is to analysis the motion intensity in order to determine the coding frame-rate. The coding frame-rate of high motion activity will be higher than that of low motion activity. Global motion is the motion of background, which is induced by camera motion, and it is dominant motion because the area of background is usually larger than that of foreground. Thus global motion will determine the coding performance. So global motion will be used to determine the motion activity of the given segment. There are three levels of motion activity according to the intensity of global motion: low, medium and high.

In global motion estimation six-parameter affine motion model is used, which is represented in equation (1). $[x, y]^T$ is a pixel's position in the current image, and $[x', y']^T$ is the corresponding pixel's position in the reference image. The relation between them is:

$$\begin{cases} x' = ax + by + c \\ y' = dx + ey + f \end{cases} \quad (1)$$

Detailed algorithm of robust GME can be referred in [4][5]. In affine models of equation 1, parameter c and f is the translation motion parameters in horizontal and vertical directions. We will identify the motion activity of segment according to these two translation motion parameters.

Figure 1 (page 4) shows the motion activity segment result of stefan sequence according to two global motion parameters. There are three levels of motion intensity: low motion activity (LMA), medium motion activity (MMA), and high motion activity (HMA). We first set two predefined thresholds: Threshod_L and Threshold_M.

$$\text{Threshod}_L = SR/4\ ,\ \text{Threshold}_M = SR/2\ ; \quad (2)$$

In equation (2) SR is the searching range of motion estimation in video coding. SR is 16 in the experiment. The motion activity determination rule of frame is presented as follows (TM_x and TM_y represent translation motion parameter in X and Y direction respectively):

If (($|TM_x| < \text{Threshold}_L$) and ($|TM_y| < \text{Threshold}_L$))
  Then current frame belongs to LMA;
Else If ((($\text{Threshold}_L<|TM_x|<\text{Threshold}_M$)and($|TM_y|<\text{Threshold}_M$))
    or (($\text{Threshold}_L<|TM_y|<\text{Threshold}_M$) and ($|TM_x|<\text{Threshold}_M$)))
  Then current frame belongs to MMA;

Else If (($|TM_x|$>$Threshold_M$) or ($|TM_y|$>$Threshold_M$))
  Then current frame belongs to HMA;
End If

After determining the motion activity of every frame then we can group the continuous frames with same motion activity into segments, which will be regarded as coding units with fixed frame-rate. But there will be some segments with only a few frames. In order to deduce the number of segments, we add a constraint in grouping. The segment will be incorporated into adjacent segment with higher motion activity between its two adjacent segments if the total frame number of this segment is less than 10.

There are ten segments in according to the two thresholds and the segmenting constraint in figure 1. The frames of every segment are no less than 10.

2.2 Variable Frame Rate Coding

Variable frame-rate video coding module will encode the decomposed segments with different coding frame-rate according to the motion activity. There are three kinds of coding frame-rate corresponding to three kinds of motion activity level. We define these coding frame-rate as follows:

$$FR_L = a{*}FR_s,\ \ FR_M = b{*}FR_s,\ \ FR_H = FR_s; \qquad (3)$$

FR_L, FR_M and FR_H represent the coding frame-rate for low motion activity, medium motion activity and high motion activity respectively. FR_s is the source frame-rate of video sequence. We set a and b parameters in the experiment as: a=1/3, b=1/2. The motion intensity increases because lower frame-rate is used in the low motion activity segment. But there usually exists a constraint in order to guarantee that the motion vector does not exceed the searching range of motion estimation in coding.

$$Threshold_x{*}\ (FR_s / FR_x) \leq SR, \text{ where x is L or M} \qquad (4)$$

The first frame of coding segment will be encoded as I-Frame in the VFR coding module, so that the quality of successive frames encoded as P-Frame can be improved and the image quality will not change too much between continuous segments. And then the coding module will use the predefined I-Frame gap to encode the segment. Figure 2 (page 4) shows the whole procedure of VFR coding.

3 Experimental Evaluation

In order to evaluate the VFR coding method proposed in this paper. VFR and FFR coding schemes are compared with the test model (TM) of H.263. Some video testing sequences in MPEG-4 testing data are selected. They are listed in table 1. All these sequences have strong global motion, and they are used to evaluate global motion estimation and global motion compensation coding by MPEG-4 video group. Coding segments in table 1 is the number of segments decomposed from the video according to the global motion parameters. The coding results are shown in the graph of PSNR and Bit-Rate. PSNR of luminance (Y) and two color components (Cb,Cr) with two coding schemes are drawn in the graph. In experiment fix quantization parameter is used and no rate control is applied.

Table 1. Testing sequences

Sequence	Format/Frames	Source FR (fps)	Coding Segments
Stefan	SIF/300	30	10
Bus	SIF/298	30	6
Coastguard	CIF/300	30	3

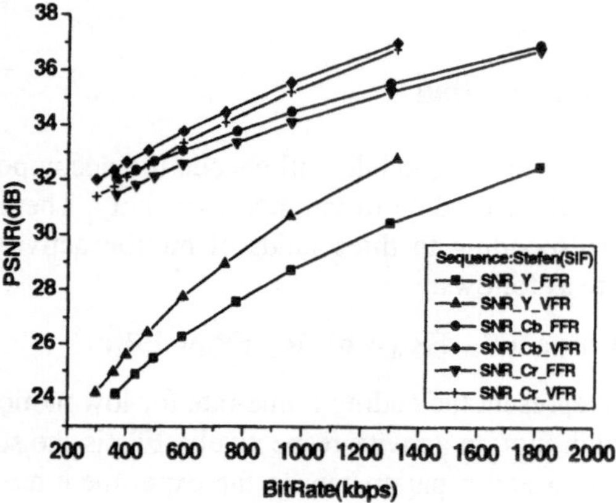

Figure 3. Coding results of stefan sequence

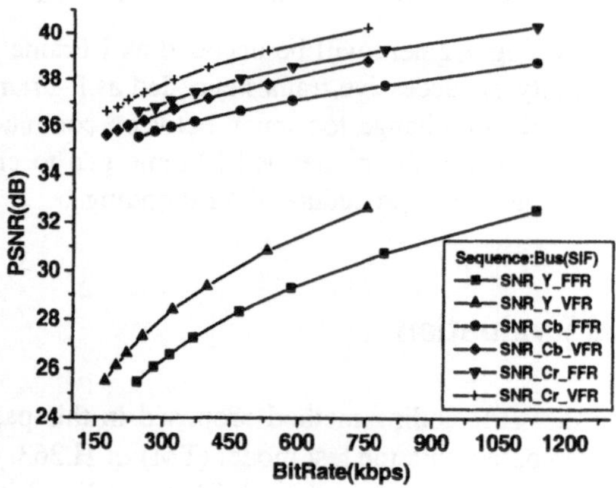

Figure 4. Coding results of bus sequence

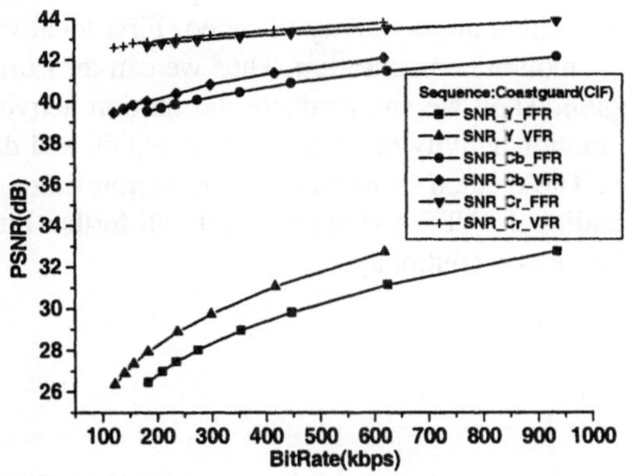

Figure 5. Coding results of coastguard sequence

VFR coding scheme outperforms FFR coding scheme from the comparisons of the figure 3, figure 4 and figure 5. There is 1.0dB-2.0dB objective quality increment for PSRN-Y (luminance) on condition of the same bit-rate for all these three sequences compared to FFR coding, and PSNR of Cb and Cr of VFR is also higher than that of FFR considering the same bit-rate. On the other hand there is about 40% bits saving with VFR coding scheme under the condition of the same PSNR-Y. We also evaluate the subjective decoded image quality. The image quality of VFR is better than that of FFR under the condition of the approximate same bit-rate. The improvement is visible.

4 Summary

Variable frame-rate video coding is a potential coding scheme because it is based on video content analysis, which has a high compression performance. From the comparisons of FFR coding, the method of evaluating motion activity is effective and VFR coding method proposed in this paper is available, and the gain of coding performance is substantial. There are two main modules in VFR coding system proposed in the paper. The first is motion analysis module and it classifies the video into coding segments. The second is coding module, and it encodes coding segments with variable frame-rate according to motion activity level. The key problem in VFR coding is how to analysis the motion activity from video content. This paper investigates the motion analysis with global motion information. The proposed system is more complex than that of conventional coding system such as H.263 because content analysis is added. But the performance of our VRF coding system will be improved with robust and fast global motion estimation. The global motion information can also be referred in local motion estimation in the latter coding module, so that the speed of coding module can be accelerated greatly. Thus global motion estimation is very valuable in our VFR coding system.

The compression performance will be better if global motion and local motion are considered to evaluate the motion activity of video. First local motion region can be extracted with global motion compensation. Thus we can measure the motion activity of local motion region. Then we can evaluate the motion activity of video with the combination of the motion activity of global motion region and the motion activity of local motion region. The method of motion compensation frame interpolation is also important when decoding the VFR coded stream. It will further improve the subjective quality especially the motion continuity.

References

1. Chang Wen Chen, Ya-Qin Zhang, Visual Information Representation Communication, and Image Processing, NewYork Basel, 1999, pp250.
2. Akio Yamada, Mark Pickering, Sylvie Jeannin, Leszek Cieplinski, Jens Rainer Ohm, Munchurl Kim, "MPEG-7 Visual part of eXperimentation Model Version 9.0", ISO/IEC JTC1/SC29/WG11/N3914, Pisa Jan.2001.
3. Yoo-Sok Saw, Rate-Quality Optimized Video Coding, Boston: Kluwer Academic Publishers, c1999.
4. Yuwen He, Wei Qi, Shiqiang Yang, Yuzhuo Zhong, "Feature-based Fast and Robust Global Motion Estimation Technique for Sprite Coding", ISO/IEC JTC1/SC29/WG11, MPEG00/M6226, July 2000.
5. Yuwen He, Bo Feng, Shiqiang Yang, Yuzhuo Zhong, "Fast Global Motion Estimation for Global Motion Compensation Coding", International Symposium on Circuits and Systems (ISCAS2001), May 2001.
6. Cataldo Guaragnella, Eugenio Di Sciascio, "Variable Frame Rate for Very Low Bit-Rate Video Coding", 10th Mediterranean Electrotechnical Conference, MeleCon 2000, Vol.2, pp503-506.
7. JongWon Kim, Yung-Gook Kim, HwangJun Song, Tien-Ying Kuo, Yon Jun Chung, C.-C. Jay Kuo, "TCP-Friendly Internet Video Streaming Employing Variable Frame-Rate Encoding and Interpolation", IEEE Trans. on Circuits and System for Video Technology, Vol. 10, No.7, Octobler 2000, pp1164-1174.
8. Jiann-Jone Chen, Hsueh-Ming Hang, "Source Model for Transform Video Coder and Its Application-Part II: Variable Frame Rate Coding", IEEE Trans. on Circuits and Systems for Video Technology, Vol.7, No.2, April 1997, pp299-311.

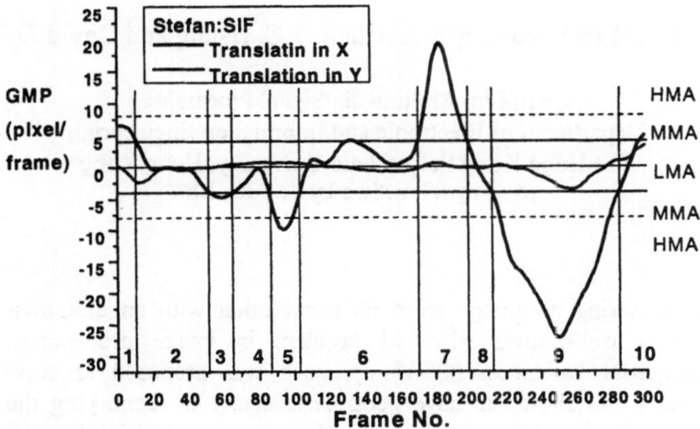

Figure 1. Motion activity segment result of stefan sequence according to global motion parameters (LMA: Low Motion Activity, MMA: Medium Motion Activity, HMA: High Motion Activity)

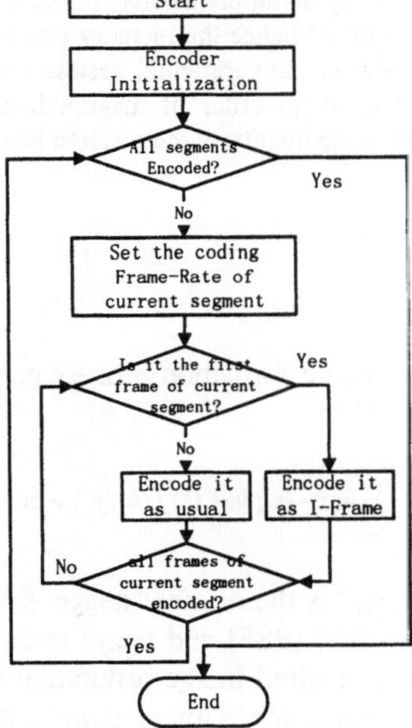

Figure 2. The flowchart of VFR coding module

Efficient Blind Image Restoration Based on 1-D Generalized Cross Validation

Daniel P.K. Lun*, Tommy C.L. Chan, T.C. Hsung and David D. Feng

Centre for Multimedia Signal Processing
Department of Electronic and Information Engineering
The Hong Kong Polytechnic University, Hong Kong
* enpklun@polyu.edu.hk

Abstract. Restoring an image from its convolution with an unknown blur function is a well-known ill-posed problem in image processing. The generalized cross validation (GCV) approach was proposed to solve the problem and it has shown to have good performance in identifying the blur function and restoring the original image. However, in actual implementation, various problems incurred due to the large data size and long computational time of the approach are undesirable even with the current computing machines. In this paper, an efficient algorithm is proposed for blind image restoration. For this approach, the original 2-D blind image restoration problem is converted into 1-D ones by using the discrete periodic Radon transform. 1-D GCV algorithm is then applied hence the memory size and computational time required are greatly reduced. Experimental results show that the resulting approach is faster in almost an order of magnitude as compared with the traditional approach, while the quality of the restored image is similar.

1 Introduction

In many practical situations, image formation process can be adequately formulated by the following linear model [1]:

$$g(x,y)=\sum_{x'=0}^{N-1}\sum_{y'=0}^{N-1}h(x-x',y-y')f(x',y')+n(x,y) \tag{1}$$

where N is the image size, $f(x,y)$ is the original image, $g(x,y)$ is the observed image, $h(x,y)$ is the point spread function (PSF) and $n(x,y)$ is the additive noise due to the imaging system. The problem of blind image restoration is to recover the unknown original image $f(x,y)$ from a given blurred image $g(x,y)$ without the knowledge of the PSF $h(x,y)$. One of the important classes of approach for solving the blind restoration problem is by modeling the true image as a 2-D autoregressive (AR) process and the PSF as a 2-D moving average (MA) process. Based on these models, the resulting blurred image is represented as an autoregressive moving average (ARMA) process. Identifying the ARMA parameters allows us to identify the true image and PSF.

One of the most popular methods in this class is the generalized cross-validation (GCV) approach [2]. The GCV approach determines the parameters by minimizing a weighted sum of prediction errors. This criterion has been shown to possess certain properties that are superior to other approaches in the context of regularization parameter estimation [3]. Nevertheless, the GCV approach is often criticized due to the extensive numerical searches for minimizing the GCV score. Efficient approach [4] was proposed to first estimate the unknown PSF parameter set and regularization parameter from raw data, and then make use of a computationally inexpensive preconditioned conjugate gradient algorithm to solve the non-blind problem. Efficient estimation of the PSF becomes the major concern. In this paper, we consider adopting the discrete periodic Radon transform (DPRT) [5] for the estimation of the PSF. By using the DPRT, a 2-D signal can be processed by some 1-D approaches to reduce the complexity. Experimental results show that the new approach is much faster than the traditional one, while the quality of the restored image is similar.

1.1 Discrete Periodic Radon Transform

The DPRT on Z_P^2 and $Z_{2^n}^2$, and their inversions are proposed in [5], where P is a prime integer and n is any positive integer. Due to page length limit, we describe only the prime length case. Let $f(x,y)$ be a 2-D function, where $x,y \in \{0, 1, ..., P\text{-}1\}$; P is prime. The DPRTs of $f(x,y)$ on Z_P^2 is given as follows [5]:

$$f_m^c(d) = \sum_{x=0}^{P-1} f(x, <d+mx>_P)\ ; \quad f_0^b(d) = \sum_{y=0}^{P-1} f(d,y) \tag{2}$$

where $<A>_D$ means the residue of A modulo D; $d,m \in \{0,..,P\text{-}1\}$. The DPRT has a few useful properties. Among them, the circular convolution property is particularly relevant to the current problem. It is shown in [5] that the circular convolution of two functions with size PxP (where P is prime) can be converted into $P+1$ 1-D length-P circular convolutions in the transform domain. That is, if $g(x,y)$ is the result of the 2-D circular convolution between two 2-D functions $f(x,y)$ and $h(x,y)$, then

$$g_m^c(d) = h_m^c(d) \otimes f_m^c(d)\ ; \quad g_0^b(d) = h_0^b(d) \otimes f_0^b(d) \tag{3}$$

where m $\in \{0,...,P\text{-}1\}$ and $\otimes$ stands for 1-D circular convolution. The functions $\{g_m^c(d), g_0^b(d)\}$, $\{h_m^c(d), h_0^b(d)\}$, and $\{f_m^c(d), f_0^b(d)\}$ are the DPRT of $g(x,y)$, $h(x,y)$, and $f(x,y)$, respectively. By performing the inverse DPRT on $g_m^c(d)$ and $g_0^b(d)$, $g(x,y)$ can be obtained. The inverse DPRT on Z_P^2 is given in [5]:

$$f(x,y) = \frac{1}{P}\left[\sum_{m=0}^{P-1} f_m^c(<y-mx>_P) - \sum_{d=0}^{P-1} f_0^b(d) + f_0^b(x)\right] \tag{4}$$

1.2 GCV For Image Restoration

The image formation process can be modeled as a 2-D AR process:

$$f(p,q) = \sum_{(k,l)\in R_a} a_{kl} f(p-k, q-l) + u(p,q) \tag{5}$$

where f is the original image; u is an independent zero-mean white noise process with variance σ_u^2. R_a is the nonsymmetric half-plane support of the AR process. Eqns.1 and 5 can be rewritten in matrix form as follows:

$$f = af + u \; ; \; g = hf + n \tag{6}$$

where the 2-D signals have been lexicographically ordered and expressed in matrix-vector notation. Eqn.6 can be combined to form a single equation:

$$g = h(I-a)^{-1}u + n \tag{7}$$

The blur identification problem becomes a matter of determining the parameters of an ARMA model. It can be achieved using the GCV algorithm.

The concept of applying cross-validation to image restoration is quite simple. For a fixed value of the model parameters, a restored image is determined using all but one values from the observed image. The restored mage is then reblurred to predict the observation that was left out of the restoration. The parameter set which minimizes the mean-square prediction error over all the observations is chosen as the optimal estimate. Due to the difficulty in implementation, the cross-validation approach is modified [2] to become the generalized cross-validation approach. The parameter set which minimizes the GCV score as follows is taken to be the final solution:

$$V(\theta) = \frac{\dfrac{1}{N^2}\sum_{p=1}^{N}\sum_{q=1}^{N}\left(1-\dfrac{(H^*.H)_{p,q}}{(H^*.H)_{p,q}+\alpha(B^*.B)_{p,q}}\right)^2 \left|G_{p,q}\right|^2}{\left[1-\dfrac{1}{N^2}\sum_{p=1}^{N}\sum_{q=1}^{N}\dfrac{(H^*.H)_{p,q}}{(H^*.H)_{p,q}+\alpha(B^*.B)_{p,q}}\right]^2} \tag{8}$$

where H, A and G are the DFT of h, a and g, respectively; H^* and B^* are the complex conjugate of H and B, respectively; and $B = 1 - A$. Here we assume that the matrices a and h are circulant, i.e. the image is blurred by a circular convolution operation. Besides, the following assumptions are often made to further reduce the complexity [2,6]: (i) the AR model can be adequately described by only two parameters: $a_{10} = \rho_v$, $a_{01} = \rho_h$, and $a_{11} = -\rho_v\rho_h$; (ii) the blurring process is energy conservative.

2 Converting 2-D GCV To 1-D GCV

The idea of using the DPRT for blind image restoration is very simple. Recall eqn.6 and rewrite it using the 2-D circular convolution operator $\otimes_2$:

$$f = \tilde{a} \otimes_2 f + u; \quad g = \tilde{h} \otimes_2 f + n \tag{9}$$

Since the supports of the PSF and AR model are often much smaller than the image, the functions $\tilde{h}$ and $\tilde{a}$ as shown in eqn.9 refer to the original h and a padded with appropriate number of zeros to enable them to have the same size as the image support. Assume that the DPRT of g, f, $\tilde{h}$, $\tilde{a}$, u and n are $\left(g_m^c, g_s^b\right)$, $\left(f_m^c, f_s^b\right)$, $\left(\tilde{h}_m^c, \tilde{h}_s^b\right)$, $\left(\tilde{a}_m^c, \tilde{a}_s^b\right)$, $\left(u_m^c, u_s^b\right)$, and $\left(n_m^c, n_s^b\right)$, respectively, where $m = 0, \ldots, 2^n-1$; $s = 0, \ldots, 2^{n-1}-1$ and the size of all functions are NxN, where $N = 2^n$; $n \in Z$. Then from the circular convolution property of the DPRT, we have

$$\begin{aligned} f_m^c &= f_m^c \otimes \tilde{a}_m^c + u_m^c & \qquad g_m^c &= f_m^c \otimes \tilde{h}_m^c + n_m^c \\ f_s^b &= f_s^b \otimes \tilde{a}_s^b + u_s^b & \qquad g_s^b &= f_s^b \otimes \tilde{h}_s^b + n_s^b \end{aligned} \tag{10}$$

Eqn.10 shows that the original 2-D problem is converted into $3N/2$ 1-D blind image restoration problems. 1-D GCV algorithm can be applied to estimate $\left(\tilde{h}_m^c, \tilde{h}_s^b\right)$, $\left(\tilde{a}_m^c, \tilde{a}_s^b\right)$ from $\left(g_m^c, g_s^b\right)$. The 1-D GCV score for the m projections become:

$$V(\theta_m) = \frac{\frac{1}{N}\sum_{p=1}^{N}\left(1 - \frac{((\tilde{H}_m^c)^* . \tilde{H}_m^c)_p}{((\tilde{H}_m^c)^* . \tilde{H}_m^c)_p + \alpha_m((\tilde{B}_m^c)^* . \tilde{B}_m^c)_p}\right)^2 \left|G_m^c(p)\right|^2}{\left[1 - \frac{1}{N}\sum_{p=1}^{N}\frac{((\tilde{H}_m^c)^* . \tilde{H}_m^c)_p}{((\tilde{H}_m^c)^* . \tilde{H}_m^c)_p + \alpha_m((\tilde{B}_m^c)^* . \tilde{B}_m^c)_p}\right]^2} \tag{11}$$

where $\tilde{H}_m^c$ is the DFT of $\tilde{h}_m^c$ and $(\tilde{H}_m^c)^*$, $(\tilde{B}_m^c)^*$ are the complex conjugate of $\tilde{H}_m^c$, $\tilde{B}_m^c$. The parameter set θ_m becomes $\left\{\alpha_m, \tilde{h}_m^c, \tilde{a}_m^c\right\}$. The 1-D GCV scores for the s projections are similar to eqn.11 with all m replaced by s. Based on the result obtained from the 1-D GCV estimation, we can reconstruct $\tilde{h}$ and $\tilde{a}$ based on $\left(\tilde{h}_m^c, \tilde{h}_s^b\right)$, $\left(\tilde{a}_m^c, \tilde{a}_s^b\right)$ using the inverse DPRT [5]. The restored image can be obtained by any computationally inexpensive restoration algorithm based on $\tilde{h}$ and $\tilde{a}$.

Unfortunately, this intuitive idea in general does not work properly. As the DPRT is non-orthogonal, the 3N/2 1-D GCV restorations have the total computational complexity not so much lower than the original 2-D problem. Furthermore, the DPRT of a compact-supported function may not be compact-supported. It implies that more parameters will be required to estimate than the original 2-D approach. Let us use an example to illustrate the problem. Assume that both g and f have the size of $256x256$. Assume also that h and a have the size of $5x5$ and $2x2$, respectively. Hence originally the parameter set contains only 30 parameters required to be estimated. In eqn.10, the support for $\left(\tilde{h}_m^c, \tilde{h}_s^b\right)$, $\left(\tilde{a}_m^c, \tilde{a}_s^b\right)$ can be up to 256, i.e. the size of the image support. Hence for each m and s, up to 256 parameters are to be estimated.

3 Proposed Approach

An alternative approach is proposed. First, it is interesting to note that, depending on the size of h and $\tilde{h}$, some of the projections of $\tilde{h}$ are compact-supported.

Lemma 1: Given that a function $\tilde{h}$ with size *NxN* is formed by padding appropriate number of zeros to another function h with size *PxP*, where $N = 2^n$; $n \in Z$ and P is a prime integer. If the DPRT of $\tilde{h}$ is $\left(\tilde{h}_m^c(d), \tilde{h}_s^b(d)\right)$, where m, $d = 0,\ldots,N-1$; $s=0,\ldots,N/2-1$, then

$$\begin{aligned} \tilde{h}_m^c(d) = 0 \quad & \text{if } \{P \le d \le N-1-m(P-1) \;\; and \;\; m < R\} \\ & and \text{ if } \{P+(N-m)(P-1) \le d \le N-1 \;\; and \;\; m > N-R\} \\ \tilde{h}_s^b(d) = 0 \quad & \text{if } \{P \le d \le N-1-2s(P-1) \;\; and \;\; s < R/2\} \\ & and \text{ if } \{P+(N-2s)(P-1) \le d \le N-1 \;\; and \;\; s > N-R/2\} \end{aligned} \tag{12}$$

where $R = (N - P) / (P - 1)$. The proof of Lemma 1 can be found in [7]. Lemma 1 shows that when m and s are very small or big numbers, there will be a consecutive sequence of zeros exists in the corresponding projections. This implies that the first and the last few projections of the total $3N/2$ projections are essentially compact-supported. When applying the 1-D GCV algorithm to these projections, the number of parameters to be estimated is much less than the others. Besides, we now further show that only some of these essentially compact-supported projections are useful for reconstructing the original compact-supported PSF h.

Lemma 2: Given that a function $\tilde{h}$ with size *NxN* is formed by padding appropriate number of zeros to another function h with size *PxP*, where $N = 2^n$; $n \in Z$ and P is a prime integer. Assume that the DPRT of $\tilde{h}$ is $\left(\tilde{h}_m^c(d), \tilde{h}_s^b(d)\right)$, where m, $d = 0,\ldots,N-1$; $s = 0,\ldots,N/2-1$, and the DPRT of h is $\left(h_m^c, h_0^b\right)$, where m, $d = 0,\ldots,P-1$. Assume also that $N > (P^2+1)$, then

$$\text{(i)} \quad h_0^b(d) = \tilde{h}_0^b(d) \tag{13}$$

$$\text{(ii)} \quad h_m^c(d) = \sum_{n=0}^{m-\lfloor m/P \rfloor} \tilde{h}_m^c(<d+P(N-n)>_N)$$

$$\text{(iii)} \quad h_{P-1-m}^c(d) = \sum_{n=0}^{m-\lfloor m/P \rfloor} \tilde{h}_{N-1-m}^c(<d+Pn>_N)$$

for $0 \le m < P/2$ and $d = 0,\ldots,P-1$. The proof of Lemma 2 can be found in [7]. Lemma 2 shows that by appropriately adding the data of the essentially compact-supported projections obtained from $\left(\tilde{h}_m^c(d), \tilde{h}_s^b(d)\right)$, we can reconstruct $\left(h_m^c, h_0^b\right)$. More importantly, only $P+1$ projections are required for the reconstruction of $\left(h_m^c, h_0^b\right)$ as compared to the original $3N/2$ projections. The complexity is greatly reduced.

Besides estimating the PSF h, the estimation of the image model parameter a is also important. Recall that images are assumed to be represented by an AR model a_{ij} with only two unknowns: $a_{10} = \rho_v$, $a_{01} = \rho_h$, and $a_{11} = -\rho_v\rho_h$. With this simple structure, all parameters can be obtained from the DPRT projections of a as follows:

$$\tilde{a}_0^c(0) = \rho_v, \tilde{a}_0^b(0) = \rho_h \tag{14}$$

Hence once $\tilde{a}_0^c$ and $\tilde{a}_0^b$ are obtained from the 1-D GCV algorithm, ρ_v and ρ_h can also be obtained. The proposed DPRT blind restoration algorithm is summarized below:

1. Perform the DPRT on g to obtain $\left(g_m^c, g_s^b\right)$.
2. Select g_0^b and P other projections from g_m^c of which the corresponding projections of $\tilde{h}_m^c$ are compact-supported. More specifically, we select the first $\lceil P/2 \rceil$ and the last $\lfloor P/2 \rfloor$ projections of g_m^c and projection g_0^b.
3. 1-D GCV algorithm is then applied to identify $\left(\tilde{h}_m^c, \tilde{h}_0^b\right)$ and $\left(\tilde{a}_m^c, \tilde{a}_0^b\right)$ for the selected projections.
4. Reconstruct $\left(h_m^c, h_0^b\right)$ from $\left(\tilde{h}_m^c, \tilde{h}_0^b\right)$ using eqn.13.
5. Obtain a from $\left(\tilde{a}_0^c, \tilde{a}_0^b\right)$ using eqn.14.
6. Obtain h from $\left(h_m^c, h_0^b\right)$ using the inverse DPRT algorithm.
7. Based on the estimated h and a, obtain α by direct searching and using the 2-D GCV score as the stopping criterion.
8. Restore the image using the estimated h, a, and α.

4 Experimental Results

Both the traditional 2-D GCV blind image restoration algorithm and the proposed DPRT based algorithm were implemented using Matlab. Standard testing images, such as, Lenna and Pepper, etc. were used and blurred by a symmetric 5x5 PSF. Additive white Guassian noise was then added to the blurred images in two different noise levels: BSNR = 30dB and 40dB. The numerical search of the GCV algorithm was implemented using the Matlab routine *fmincon*. The initial conditions for the 2-D GCV approach were:

$$\{\alpha = 0.0001;\ \rho_v = 0.8;\ \rho_h = 0.8; h_{00} = 1;\ h_{ij} = 0 \ \ if \ \ i, j \neq 0\}$$

The initial conditions for the DPRT based algorithm were:

$$\{\alpha_m = 0.0001; \rho_v = 0.8; \rho_h = 0.8; \tilde{h}_m^c(0) = 1;\ \tilde{h}_m^c(d) = 0 \ \ if \ \ d \neq 0\}$$

The results in terms of accuracy and complexity in all experiments were recorded and averaged. Table 1 shows the comparison result. It is noted that, in both noise levels, the total number of operations required for the proposed approach is only about 4% of the 2-D GCV algorithm. This result is foreseeable because the major operation done in each iteration of the GCV algorithm is an FFT. By converting the 2-D GCV algorithm to become *P+1* 1-D ones, the 2-D FFT required in each iteration is also converted into *P+1* 1-D FFTs. Hence the complexity is greatly reduced from $O(N^2 \log_2 N^2)$ to $O((P+1)N\log_2 N)$, where $N >> P$.

Table 1. Comparison in terms of arithmetic operations

	2-D GCV			**Proposed DPRT approach**		
BNSR	Iteration number (I)	Flops per iter. (F)	I*F	Iteration number (I)	Flops per iter. (F)	I*F + DPRT
40dB	361	5.6×10^6	2.0×10^9	1,515	40,759	6.3x10 7
30dB	318	5.6×10^6	1.8×10^9	1,648	40,759	6.8x10 7

Table 2. Comparison in terms of accuracy achieved

	2-D GCV		**Proposed DPRT approach**	
BNSR	Restored image (SER)	Estimated PSF accuracy (SER)	Restored image (SER)	Estimated PSF accuracy (SER)
40dB	25.82 dB	14.16 dB	26.78 dB	14.12 dB
30dB	23.10 dB	12.68 dB	23.42 dB	13.84 dB

Table 2 illustrates the accuracy of both approaches. The results in Table 2 show that the accuracy of the proposed DPRT approach is not inferior to the traditional 2-D approach, particularly in high noise level. Fig.1 to 4 show the actual restored images given by both approaches. It is seen that no observable difference can be found from the restored images obtained by the two approaches.

5 Conclusion

In this paper, efficient algorithms are proposed for blind image restoration. By using DPRT, the original 2-d blind image restoration problem is converted to some 1-d ones hence greatly reduces the memory size and computation time. Experimental results show that the proposed DPRT based approach consistently uses less arithmetic operations than the 2-D GCV approach. The overall saving can be as much as 96%. Apart from the saving in computation time, the accuracy of the proposed approach is not inferior to the traditional one in both objective and subjective measures.

References

1. Andrews, H.C. and Hunt, B.R., *Digital image Restoration*, Englewood Cliffs, NJ: Prentice-Hall, (1977).

2. Reeves, S.J. and Mersereau, R.M.: Blur Identification by the Method of Generalized Cross-Validation. IEEE Trans. on Image Processing, Vol.1(3). (1992) 301-311.
3. Wahba, G.: A Comparison of GCV and GML for Choosing the Smoothing Parameter in the Generalized Spline Smoothing Problem. Annals Statistics, Vol.13(4). (1985) 1378-1402.
4. Nguyen, N., Golub, G. and Milanfar, P.: Blind Restoration / Superresolution with Generalized Cross-Validation Using Gauss-Type Quadrature Rules. Proceedings, Thirty-Third Asilomar Conf. on Signals, Systems, and Computers, Vol.2. (1999) 1257 –1261.
5. Hsung, T.C., Lun, D.P.K. and Siu, W.C.: The Discrete Periodic Radon Transform. IEEE Trans. on Signal Processing, Vol.44(10). (1996) 2651-2657.
6. Lagendijk, R.L., Biemond, J. and Boekee, D.E.: Identification and Restoration of Noisy Blurred Images Using the Expectation-Maximization Algorithm. IEEE Trans. on ASSP, Vol.38(7). (1990) 1180-1191.
7. Lun, D.P.K., Chan, Tommy C.L., Hsung, T.C., Feng, D. and Chan, Y.H.: Efficient Blind Image Restoration Based on Discrete Periodic Radon Transform, Submitted to IEEE Trans. on Image Processing.

Fig. 1. Original Image

Fig. 2. Blurred and noisy image (BSNR = 30dB)

Fig. 3. Restored image using 2-D GCV (SER = 22.01dB)

Fig. 4. Restored image using the proposed approach (SER = 22.66dB)

Acknowledgement. This work is supported by the Hong Kong Polytechnic University under research project A418.

Block Reordering Wavelet Packet SPIHT Image Coding

Ta-Te Lu, Kuo-Wei Wen, and Pao-Chi Chang

Department of Electrical Engineering, National Central University, Chung-Li, Taiwan 320
E-mail : pcchang@ee.ncu.edu.tw

Abstract. The set partitioning in hierarchical trees (SPIHT) coding algorithm, proposed by Said and Pearlman, provides effective progressive and embedding property. However, for images with high energy that is randomly dispersed throughout high frequency subbands in the wavelet domain, the SPIHT does not fully exploit energy compaction of the wavelet transform and thus becomes less efficient to represent these images. This paper presents an energy compaction method, block reordering wavelet packet SPIHT (BRWP-SPIHT) coding, to enhance the image visual quality. The block reordering technique divides the wavelet coefficients into blocks and reorders these blocks depending on the significance of each block. The simulation results show that BRWP-SPIHT is superior, on average, to SPIHT by 0.6 dB for texture rich images. Subjectively, it also shows significant enhancement to the quality of the reconstructed image, particularly for images with fractal and oscillatory patterns.

Index Terms – Block reordering, Energy compaction, Wavelet packet, SPIHT, image coding....

1 Introduction

Many wavelet-based embedded image coders, such as Shapiro's embedded zerotree wavelet coding (EZW) [1], Said and Pearlman's set partitioning into hierarchical tree (SPIHT) [2], Chai's significance-linked connected component analysis (SLCCA) [3], and Taubman's embedded block coding with optimized truncation (EBCOT) [4], provide progressive coding properties.

Said and Perlman's SPIHT with a set partitioning sorting algorithm with ordered bit plane transmission generally performs better than EZW for still images. However, SPIHT coding is less efficient to represent an image that has randomly dispersed horizontal or vertical energy distributions in the high frequency subbands of wavelet transform, such as the test image "Barbara". Some of the images, such as "Goldhill" and "Fingerprints", have fractal patterns that are important to human visual quality. Unfortunately, those fractal patterns have small corresponding wavelet coefficients and are often quantized to zero by SPIHT at a low to medium bit rate.

Most zerotree coding algorithms, such as EZW, SPIHT and SLCCA [1]-[3], are based on the wavelet decomposition tree structure of Mallat. Taubman used the wavelet packet decomposition for EBCOT [4]; Meyer proposed the fast adaptive wavelet packet for oscillatory textured images [5]. All these authors support the claim that the wavelet packet performs preferably visual quality for those images with fractal patterns than the conventional wavelet decomposition structure [4]-[6]. In this paper, we apply SPIHT to wavelet packet decomposition and propose a block reordering technique for increasing coding efficiency. In LH, HL, and HH high frequency subbands of the first layer of DWT, a subband is divided into a number of blocks and SPIHT is operated on each subband independently. The energy compaction is achieved by the reordering technique which reorders the wavelet blocks according to the energy of each block. Hence, SPIHT can be applied in a more effective way and results in more efficient compression. Section II describes the block reordering wavelet packet SPIHT (BRWP-SPIHT) algorithm. Section III presents the variable block size BRWP-SPIHT method (VBRWP-SPIHT) that is a recursive version of BRWP-SPIHT. The results of the simulation comparison of SPIHT, MRDW, SLCCA, BRWP-SPIHT, and VBRWP-SPIHT are shown in Section IV. Conclusions are given in the final section.

2 Block Reordering Wavelet Packet SPIHT

In SPIHT algorithm, the wavelet coefficients are first organized into spatial orientation trees. The SPIHT algorithm consists of two passes, namely the sorting pass and the refinement pass. The sorting pass is used to find these significant pixels that were defined as insignificant before the current threshold scan. Those pixels transmitted in a previous sorting pass, are set as the refinement pass. The list of insignificant pixels (LIP), the list of significant pixels (LSP), and the list of insignificant sets (LIS) are used to indicate whether these pixels are significant or not.

2.1 Energy Compaction

The SPIHT coding is based on the pyramid structure to exploit the correlation among subbands. Some of images have large energy which is randomly dispersed in high frequency subbands. Unfortunately, the original SPIHT requires a significant amount of bits to exploit the correlation between the lowest band and the high frequency subbands for this kind of images. The block diagram of the BRWP-SPIHT method proposed in this paper is shown in Fig. 1. Images are first decomposed into four subbands by discrete wavelet transform (DWT). All subbbands in the first layer are again decomposed by a five-level pyramid DWT. Since the high frequency subbands are further decomposed, the overall decomposition process is in the category of wavelet packet transform. The original SPIHT is applied to the LL band as the convential approach does. For increasing the SPIHT coding efficiency, high frequency subbands are rearranged before SPIHT is applied. Each high frequency subband in the first layer with five-level pyramid structure, i.e., LH, HL, and HH, is divided into a number of blocks B_n , where n=1, 2, 3, representing three high frequency bands. If any wavelet coefficient in block b exceeds the scan threshold T_i (the initial threshold T_0 is half of the maximum magnitude of wavelet coefficients) of SPIHT then the wavelet block b is considered as significant and the block counter N_b increases by one. These wavelet blocks are reordered according to the number of significant wavelet coefficients in N_b, with the maximum N_b in the top left corner, to obtain the energy compaction of these high frequency subbands.

We search over all coefficients and find all of the significant wavelet blocks at T_i, then these blocks are zig-zag scanned for SPIHT, shown as in Fig. 2. In the next threshold T_{i+1} search, wavelet blocks which are insignificant at T_i can be identified as new significant wavelet blocks based on the block counter. A reordering example for the HL subband of Barbara is shown in Fig. 3. Fig. 3(a) shows the three-level DWT of Barbara in the HL band. The reordered result of 64 wavelet blocks in the HL band is shown in Fig. 3(b). It is easily observed that energy is more concentrated at the upper left corner after reordering. By experiments, the 256-wavelet block for 512 x 512 images is the best choice when both the bitrate overhead and the performance are taken into account.

2.2 Bit Allocation

Bit allocation aims to adjust the bit rate r_n of each subband in the first layer, where n=0, 1, 2, 3, representing LL, LH, HL, and HH subbands, to minimize the reconstruction error for a fixed total rate R_c. Because each significant coefficient will be quantized by SPIHT explicitly, the bit allocation is determined by the number of blocks in each subband.

$$r_n = \frac{S_n \times w_n}{\sum_{n=0}^{3} S_n} \times R_c \qquad (1)$$

Where w_n is the weighting factor for each subband, and S_n is the sum of significant blocks in the n-th band. From the simulation results, $w_0 = 1$, and $w_n = 1.1$, n=1, 2, 3, yields the best input quality for texture images.

3 Variable Block Size with Block Reordering Wavelet Packet SPIHT

In this section, a multiple-layer variable block size BRWP-SPIHT (VBRWP-SPIHT) is proposed. It has two differences from the previous BRWP-SPIHT. Namely, the reordering is restricted in the upper left quadrature and the upper left quadrature blocks can be divided recursively, shown as in Fig. 4. To further achieve energy compaction, the first block in the zigzag scan, i.e, the most upper left block, is divided into four sub-blocks. The block division in the left quadrature blocks can be performed in multiple layers to achieve maximum energy compaction.

In the sorting process of BRWP-SPIHT the block position must be recorded, and transmitted to the decoder as side information. The upper-left quadrature is usually the most energy concentrated area, where block reordering has significant effect in energy compaction, while the others have less reordering effect. In VBRWP-SPIHT, the amount of recorded information can be reduced significantly.

4 Experimental Results

4.1 PSNR Comparisons

We perform simulations with various DWT based coding algorithms, including SLCCA [3], MRWD [7], SPIHT [2], as well as the proposed BRWP-SPIHT and VBWP-SPIHT methods, at the same bit rate to compare peak signal-to-noise ratios (PSNR). The 9-7 biorthogonal wavelet filters of Daubechies [8] and 512 x 512 Barbara, Goldhill images are used. In BRWP-SPIHT, 256 wavelet blocks are used for each high band. In VBRWP-SPIHT, 64 wavelet blocks are used for each high band in each layer of a three-layer structure. Table 1 compares the performance at various bit rates of SLCCA, MRWD, SPIHT, BRWP-SPIHT, and VBRWP-SPIHT for Barbara and Goldhill. For Barbara, on average, VBRWP-SPIHT outperforms SPIHT by about 0.6 dB, SLCCA by about 0.12 dB, and MRWD by about 0.45 dB. The BRWP-SPIHT outperforms SPIHT by about 0.58 dB, SLCCA by about 0.11 dB and MRWD by about 0.44 dB. For Goldhill, on average, VBRWP-SPIHT and BRWP-SPIHT perform about equally as SPIHT based on PSNR. These results show that the block reordering technique of our proposed algorithms provide more efficient way to encode the significant wavelet coefficients than others methods.

4.2 Perceptual Quality

Fig. 5(b)-(d) shows the results for the pants of Barbara using SPIHT, BRWP-SPIHT and VBRWP-SPIHT at 0.25 bpp. Fig 5(a) shows the original source of Barbara. It is observed that the oscillating patterns are blurred by SPIHT coding, as shown in Fig. 5(b). However, the proposed methods still maintain good perceptual quality at low bit rates. Fig. 6(b)-(d) shows the reconstructed results for Goldhill using SPIHT, BRWP-SPIHT and VBRWP-SPIHT at 0.444 bpp. Fig 6(a) shows the original source of Goldhill. Most details on the roof of the house are erased by SPIHT as shown in Fig. 6(b). However, BRWP-SPIHT and VBRWP-SPIHT can maintain those details as shown in Fig. 6(c)-(d). It is observed that those oscillating patterns can be truly preserved by VBRWP-SPIHT and BRWP-SPIHT.

5 Conclusion

We have presented the block reordering technique for wavelet packet SPIHT. It is particularly suitable for images with fractal patterns or oscillating patterns. The block reordering algorithm with wavelet packet has three advantages: 1) the energy compaction in the upper left of high frequency subbands can improve the SPIHT coding efficiently. 2) the wavelet packet decomposition provides flexible structure for high frequency subbands, and thus yields better performance with SPIHT coding. 3) the multiple layer with partial reordering can make the block reordering fast. According to the experimental results, the proposed methods improve not only the PSNR values but also perceptual image quality.

References

1. J. M. Shapiro, "Embedded image coding using zerotrees of wavelet coefficients," IEEE Trans. Signal Processing, Spec. Issue Wavelets Signal Processing, vol. 41, pp. 3445-3462, Dec. 1993.
2. A. Said and W. A. Pearlman, "A new fast and efficient image codec based on set partitioning into hierarchical trees," IEEE Trans. on Circuits and Systems for Video Technology, vol.6 pp.243-250, June 1996.
3. B. B. Chai, J. Vass and X. Zhuang, "Significance-linked connected component analysis for wavelet image coding," IEEE Transactions on Image Processing, Vol. 8, pp. 774-784, June 1999.
4. D. Taubman, "High performance scalable image compression with EBCOT, " IEEE Transactions on Image Processing, Vol. 9, pp. 1158-1170, July. 2000.
5. F. G. Meyer, A. Z. Averbuch, "Fast adaptive wavelet packet image compression," IEEE Transactions on Image Processing, Vol. 9, pp. 792-800, May 2000.
6. N. M. Rajpoot, F. G. Meyer, R. G. Wilson and R. R. Coifman, "On zerotree quantization for embedded wavelet packet image coding," in Proc. Int. Conf. Image Processing, 1999.
7. S. D. Servetto, K. Ramchandran and M. T. Orchard, "Image coding based on a morphological representation of wavelet data," IEEE Transactions on Image Processing, Vol. 8, pp. 1161-1174, Sept. 1999.
8. M. Antonini, M. Barlaud, P. Mathieu and I. Daubechies, "Image Coding Using Wavelet Transform", IEEE Trans. on Image Processing, vol. 1, no 2, April 1992.

TABLE 1. Comparisons of reconstructed images with various compression methods for "Barbara" and "Goldhill".

Barbara

	BRWP-SPIHT	VBRWP-SPIHT	SPIHT	SLCCA	MRWD
0.12bpp	25.33	25.36	24.86	25.36	25.27
0.25bpp	28.10	28.12	27.58	28.18	27.86
0.50bpp	32.12	32.15	31.40	31.89	31.44
0.75bpp	34.85	34.86	34.26	---	---
1.00bpp	37.00	37.02	36.41	36.69	36.24

Goldhill

	BRWP-SPIHT	VBRWP-SPIHT	SPIHT	SLCCA	MRWD
0.12bpp	28.50	28.52	28.48	---	---
0.25bpp	30.58	30.60	30.56	30.60	30.53
0.50bpp	33.13	33.15	33.13	33.26	33.15
0.75bpp	34.90	34.91	34.95	---	---
1.00bpp	36.40	36.41	36.55	36.66	36.56

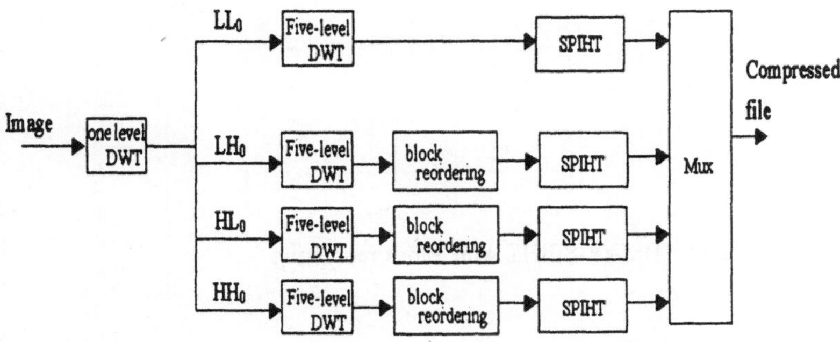

Fig. 1. BRWP-SPIHT encoder block diagram

Fig. 2. Zig-zag scan for block reordering in BRWP-SPIHT.

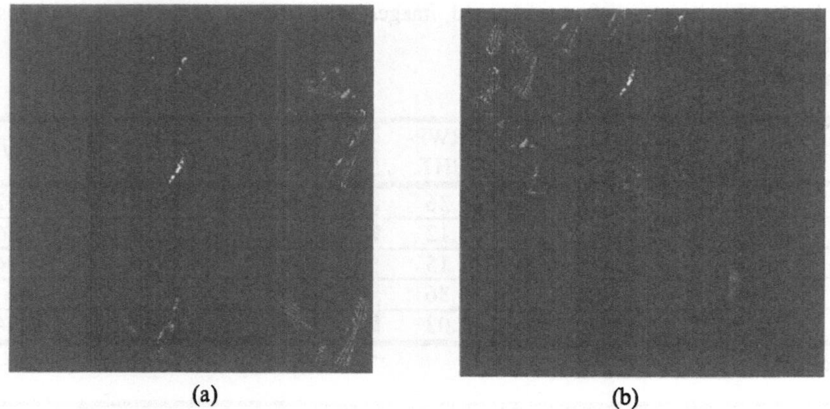

(a) (b)

Fig. 3. Block reordering example (a) DWT with three layer in HL band of Barbara (b) Energy compaction after reordering for HL band with three layer decomposition

Fig. 4. Zig-zag scan for VBRWP-SPIHT with block reordering

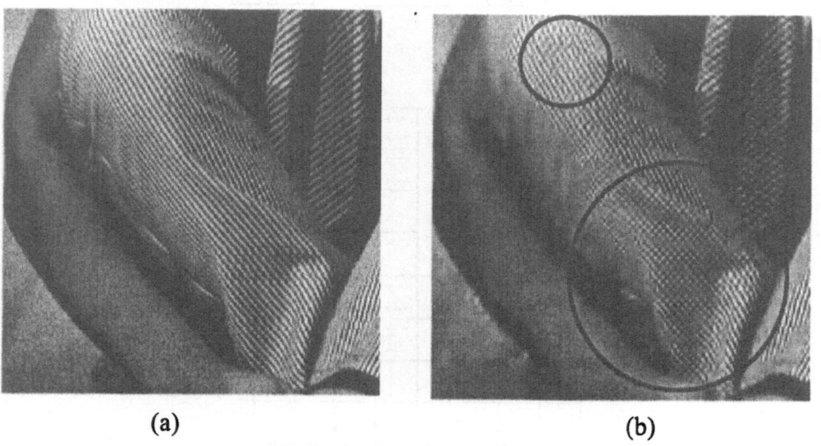

(a) (b)

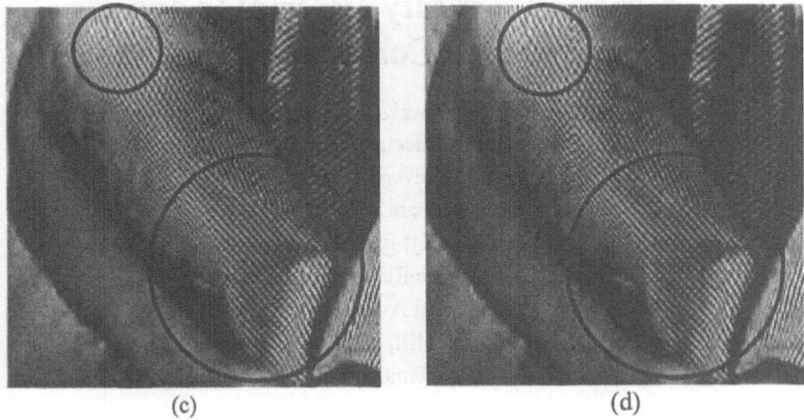

(c) (d)

Fig. 5. Magnified detail at 0.25 bpp for Barbara image. (a) Original (b) SPIHT, PSNR=27.46dB (c) BRWP-SPIHT, PSNR=28.10dB (d) VBRWP-SPIHT, PSNR = 28.11dB.

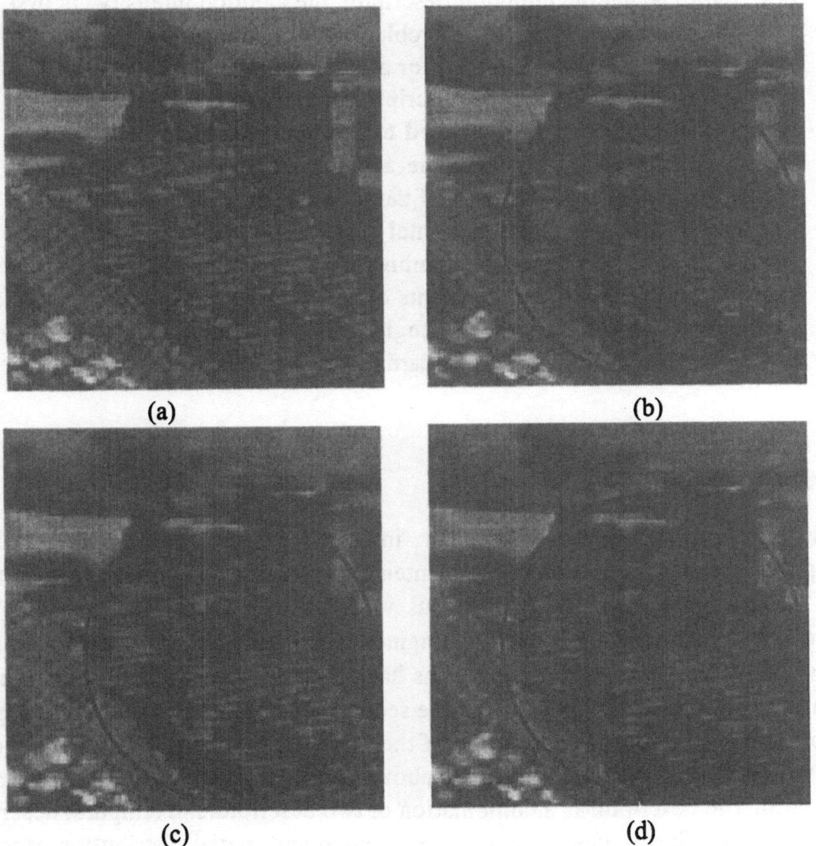

(a) (b) (c) (d)

Fig. 6. Coding results at 0.444 bpp for Goldhill image. (a) Original image. (b) SPIHT, PSNR = 32.62dB.(c) BRWP-SPIHT , PSNR = 32.60dB. (d) VBRWP-SPIHT,PSNR = 32.62dB.

A Motion Activity Descriptor and Its Extraction in Compressed Domain

Xinding Sun, Ajay Divakaran⁺, B. S. Manjunath**
*Department of Electrical and Computer Engineering, University of California, Santa Barbara, CA 93106
{xdsun, manj}@ece.ucsb.edu
⁺Mitsubishi Electric Research Laboratories, 571 Central Avenue, #115
Murray Hill, NJ 07974
ajayd@merl.com

Abstract. A novel motion activity descriptor and its extraction from a compressed MPEG (MPEG-1/2) video stream are presented. The descriptor consists of two parts, a temporal descriptor and a spatial descriptor. To get the temporal descriptor, the "motion intensity" is first computed based on P frame macroblock information. Then the motion intensity histogram is generated for a given video unit as the temporal descriptor. To get the spatial descriptor, the average magnitude of the motion vector in a P frame is used to threshold the macro-blocks into "zero" and "non-zero" types. The average magnitude of the motion vectors and three types of runs of zeros in the frame are then taken as the spatial descriptor. Experimental results show that the proposed descriptor is fast, and that the combination of the temporal and spatial attributes is effective. Key elements of the intensity parameter, spatial parameters and the temporal histogram of the descriptor have been adopted by the draft MPEG-7 standard [10].

1. Introduction

How to characterize the degree or intensity of a scene change and the corresponding temporal pattern of that intensity is of great significance in content-based system applications. Most previous work such as UCSB Netra V [2], IBM CueVideo [9], Columbia Video Search Engine[1], etc. has applied motion feature for content analysis, but none of the systems have addressed the above issue. It is the first question addressed in this paper. The second question addressed in this paper is how to describe the spatial distribution of the motion in a scene, i.e. how the motion varies within a given frame. To solve the above problems, a motion activity descriptor is proposed. The descriptor is a combination of two descriptors: a temporal descriptor and a spatial descriptor, which address the temporal and spatial distribution of motion respectively.

In obtaining the temporal descriptor for motion activity, we first characterize a scene change into different intensity levels, called ***motion intensity***. This is based on the following observation. When describing video scene motion intensities, a person usually uses several levels of description, for example, high, low, medium, etc. In sports videos, a play can be characterized in terms of these intensity levels very clearly. At the beginning of the play, the intensity of motion is small, and it goes up and down with the progression of the play. This pattern is very similar to that of audio, which can be characterized by rhythm. After we get the intensity level of a scene, we can further characterize the temporal change of the scene. Suppose that the video sequence has been segmented into small units based on different measures [7], we can then use the histogram of the intensity, here we call it ***motion intensity histogram*** (MIH), to characterize the change of it. The MIH is taken as our temporal descriptor.

In obtaining the spatial descriptor for motion activity, we use motion vectors to characterize the video frames into spatial regions. Motion segmentation of image into regions tends not to be robust in practical applications. Therefore, instead of working on the segmentation, we pursue a statistical approach. The general idea is to threshold the macroblocks into zero and non-zero types based on whether it is above or below the average motion magnitude. The average magnitude and the runs of zero types can then be used to describe the spatial distribution of the motion and taken as our spatial descriptor.

The primary reason for compressed domain video processing is that it can achieve high speeds (see for example [8]). Therefore, in this paper we extract features from compressed domain information directly. Since the P frames of a video are good sub-samples of the original video, we confine our extraction to them.

2. Extraction of Temporal Descriptor for Motion Activity

2.1 Motion Intensity

To exploit temporal redundancy, MPEG adopts macroblock level motion estimation. In order to reduce the bit rate, some macroblocks in the P or B frames are coded using their differences with corresponding reference macroblocks. Since only P frames are used for later discussion of camera control, the following discussion applies to P frames only. During motion estimation, the encoder first searches for the best match of a macroblock in its neighborhood in the reference frame. If the prediction macroblock and the reference macroblock are not in the same positions of the frames, motion compensation is applied before coding. No_MC means no motion compensation. When a macroblock has no motion compensation, it is referred to as a No_MC macroblock. Generally, there are two kinds of No_MCs: one is the No_MC intra-coded and the other is the No_MC inter-coded. In typical MPEG encoder architecture, there exists an inter/intra classifier. The inter/intra classifier compares the prediction error with the input picture elements (pels). If the mean squared error of the prediction exceeds the mean squared pel value then the macroblock is intra-coded, otherwise it is inter-coded. The No_MC intra-coded and inter-coded scheme can be obtained correspondingly.

Only P frames of MPEG macroblocks have No_MC inter-coded macroblocks. In fact, in a special case, when the macroblock perfectly matches its reference, it is skipped and not coded at all. To simplify the illustration, the skipped frames are categorized the same as No_MC inter-coded frames as shown in figure 1.

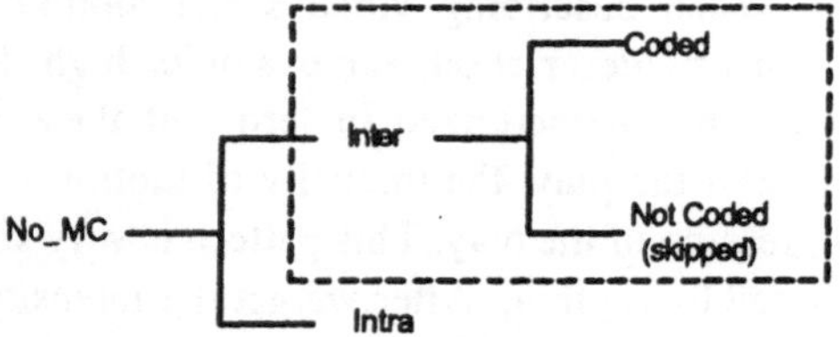

Figure 1. No_MC in MPEG video macroblocks.

According to the definition of inter No_MC, we can see that when the content of video changes are not too significant, and thus many macroblocks can be matched by their reference frames, the number of inter No_MC macroblock in a P frame would be high. For example, pauses in sports games often coincide with small object motion and fixed cameras in videos, so the corresponding number of inter No_MC macroblocks would be very high. On the other hand, when the content of the video changes rapidly, and thus many macroblocks cannot be matched by their reference frames, the number of inter No_MC macroblock in a P frame would be small. Here, we define the α-ratio of a P frame as:

$$\alpha = \frac{Numberof\ \text{inter}\ No\_MC\ Macroblocks}{TotalNumberof\ FrameMacroblocks}\ . \qquad (1)$$

From our experiments, we found that this ratio is a good measure of scene motion intensity change and it conforms with human perception very well. The higher the ratio is, the lower the scene motion intensity change is. Figure 2 shows two frames from a football video, the first one extracted from the start of a play, which has a high α = 86%, and the second one corresponding to the play in progress, which has a low α = 5%.

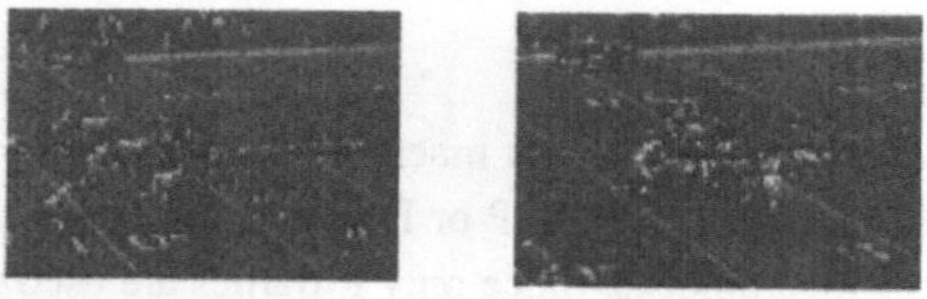

Frame 1. α=0.86 Frame 2. α=0.05

Figure 2. Two video frames with different inter No_MC ratios

As our objective is to find motion intensity levels, it is not necessary to use α-ratios directly for video motion description. So, we further quantize the ratio into several levels. Here we use the logarithmic compandor [4] that has been widely applied to speech telephony for quantization. First we compress the ratio into $G_u(\alpha)$ using the μ_law characteristic. By using this method, we can keep quantization steps higher for high ratio values. Next, we use vector quantization methods to transform $G_u(\alpha)$ into N_l quantized change levels. A codebook of N_l entries is extracted from the $G_u(\alpha)$ data set first, then $G_u(\alpha)$ values are indexed using this code book. In our experiments, we set N_l =5. We use the index of $G_u(\alpha)$ as the quantized level, therefore the motion intensity of a scene can be characterized by a level L =i, where i=1,2,3,4, 5.

Figure 3 shows such quantization results on P frames 1500 to 2000 of a soccer video (from MPEG 7 test data V18). The I and B frames in this interval are not used. The original α-ratios are shown in figure 3.a. The quantized change levels are shown in figure 5.b. Within the time range betweenframes 1880 to 1970, there is a pause of the play. During the pause, the scene change has a very lowvalue and the P frames within the pause have high quantized levels.

a. Original α-Ratio

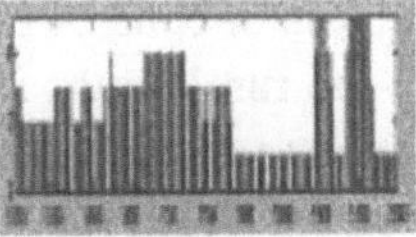

b. Quantized α Level

Figure 3. The α-ratios and their quantized levels from part of the MPEG-7 data set.

2.2 Motion Intensity Histogram

Assume a video has been segmented into temporal segments (called *video units*), where these video units can be a video sequence, a shot, or small temporal segments. Then the histogram of the above levels can be used to characterize the segments' temporal intensity distributions. Note that the histogram is not dependent on the video segment size, therefore it can be easily scaled to multiple video levels. Therefore, it supports hierarchical video content description. While much research effort has been expended on frame level motion feature description, we believe that we discuss the temporal intensity distribution for the first time. The temporal intensity distribution is similar to the histogram analysis that has been used for region based image processing [6].

Given a video unit, we define our temporal descriptor as the corresponding motion intensity histogram of the unit: MIH=$[p_0, p_1, p_2, p_3, \cdots p_{N_l}]$. Where p_i is the percentage of the quantized motion corresponding to the *i*-th quantization level, and $\sum_{i=1}^{N_l} p_i = 1$. Here we set N_l =5. The intensity level within a small video temporal region usually keeps stable. Therefore this vector also conforms to human perception very well.

3. Extraction of Spatial Descriptor for Motion Activity

We use the magnitude of motion vectors with a run-length framework to form a descriptor [2]. The extraction is as follows:

For a given P frame, the "spatial activity matrix" C_{mv} is defined as: $C_{mv} = \{R(i,j)\}$, where $R(i,j) = \sqrt{x_{i,j}^2 + y_{i,j}^2}$ and $(x_{i,j}, y_{i,j})$ is the motion vector associated with the $(i,j)th$ block. For Intra-coded blocks, $R(i,j) = 0$.

The average motion vector magnitude per macro-block of the frame/object C_{mv}^{avg} is given by: $C_{mv}^{avg} = \frac{1}{MN}\sum_{i=0}^{M}\sum_{j=0}^{N} C_{mv}(i,j)$ where M and N are the width and height of the macroblocks in the frame.

We use C_{mv}^{avg} as a threshold on C_{mv} to get a new matrix as:

$$C_{mv}^{thresh}(i,j) = \begin{cases} C_{mv}(i,j), \text{ if } C_{mv}(i,j) \geq C_{mv}^{avg} \\ 0, \text{ otherwise} \end{cases}$$

Then we compute lengths of runs of zeroes in the above matrix, using a raster-scan order. Next we classify the run-lengths into three categories, short, medium and long, which are normalized with respect to the object/frame width. In this case we have defined the short runs to be 1/3 of the frame width or lower, the medium runs to be greater than 1/3 but less than 2/3 of the frame width, and the long runs to be all runs that are greater than or equal to the width. N_{sr} is the number of short runs, with N_{mr}, N_{lr} similarly defined. We use such "quantization" of runs to get some invariance with respect to rotation, translation, reflection etc.

The spatial descriptor can then be constructed as $SD = (C_{mv}^{avg}, N_{sr}, N_{mr}, N_{lr})$. Note that the descriptor indirectly expresses the number, size, and shape of distinct moving objects in the frame, and their distribution across the frame. For a frame with a single large object such as a talking head, the number of short run-lengths is high, whereas for a frame with several small objects, such as an aerial shot of a soccer game, the number of short run-lengths is lower.

4. Similarity Measure

After we obtain the motion activity descriptors for different video data sets, the MPEG-7 enabled applications can be performed based on them. However, in order to compare feature vectors, we need to provide a similarity measure. Generally, the feature vector components propose above are correlated. Therefore, when computing the similarity between two feature vectors, we use the Mahalanobis distance. The Mahalanobis distance between two feature vectors: Q_1 and Q_2 is given by:

$$D_M(Q_1,Q_2) = [Q_1\text{-}Q_2]M^{-1}[Q_1\text{-}Q_2] \ . \tag{2}$$

Where M is the covariance matrix of the feature vector. Since M^{-1} is symmetric, it is a semi or positive matrix. So we can diagonalize it as $M^{-1} = P^T \Lambda P$, where Λ is a diagonal matrix, and P is an orthogonal matrix. Then computation of (2) can be simplified in terms of Euclidean distance as follows:

$$D_M(Q_1,Q_2) = D_E\left(\sqrt{\Lambda}PQ_1, \sqrt{\Lambda}PQ_2\right) \ . \tag{3}$$

Since Λ and P can be computed directly from M^{-1}, the complexity of the computation of the vector distance can be reduced from O(n^2) to O(n).

5. Experimental Results

We have implemented the descriptor for MPEG-7 data sets for the applications of video classification, retrieval, browsing, etc. Since the temporal and spatial descriptors cover two different aspects of motion activity, we first show experimental results of the two separately, then we show how to combine the two together for more powerful applications. To test the descriptors, a video is first segmented into small video units (clips) using the method proposed in [7]. The number of clips is 5% of the total video length. Therefore, a video with 100,000 frames will be segmented into 5000 small clips.

To get the temporal descriptor, the MIH is computed for each video clip. An example

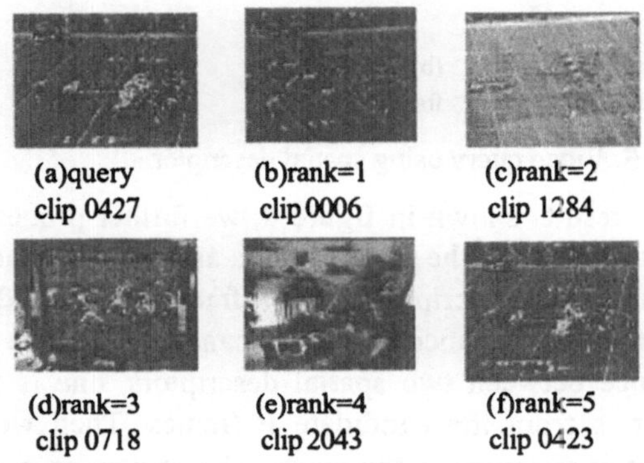

Figure 4. Video query using temporal descriptor

of searching for similar video clips using the MIH descriptor and the similarity measure is shown in figure 4. The first P frame from each clip is used to represent the whole clip. The query frame shows a scene where a football game starts and there is very little motion in the scene. The 5 retrieved clips, ranked in order from 1 to 5, are displayed in the figure. As we expect, similar scenes are retrieved from the video.

Figure 5 shows the experimental results on a retrieval of a similar scene, based on the spatial descriptor SD. The first P frame from each video clip is shown in the figure. The query is an anchorperson in the news. We observe that the scenes with the anchorperson showing similar gestures are retrieved from the video stream.

A general motion activity descriptor can be constructed from its temporal and spatial parts as $Q = (\text{MIH}, SD)$. Now we explain how to use the general descriptor. First, note that the temporal attributes can apply to an entire video sequence, not necessarily to just a shot, and still be meaningful. For example, a high action movie like "The Terminator" could get a quantized intensity value that indicates high action. Moreover, the proposed temporal histogram would be even more meaningful in describing an entire movie or any other long video sequence. It immediately follows that the intensity histogram can serve to filter at the video program or sequence level. However, once we have located the program of intere st, the spatial attribute becomes meaningful, since it effectively locates similar activities within a program, and thus facilitates intra-program browsing. This is a capability unique to the motion activity descriptor among all other MPEG-7 visual descriptors.

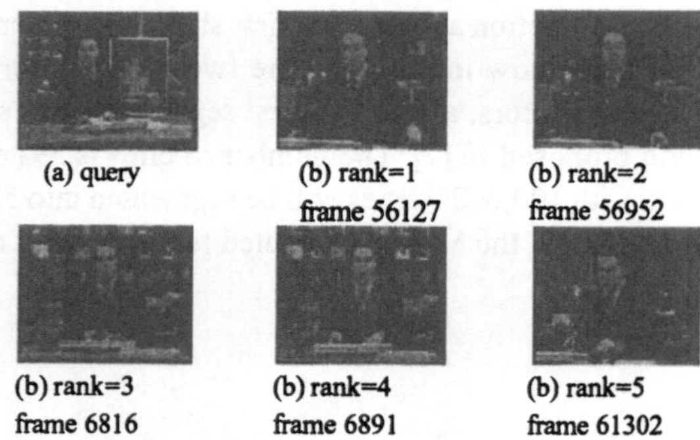

Figure 5. Video query using spatial descriptor..

Based on the query results shown in figure 4, we further process the query video using the general descriptor. All the query results are used as candidates for further spatial processing. The spatial descriptor for all P frames in all candidate clips and the query clip are computed. The distance between a candidate and the query is computed as the smallest distance between two spatial descriptors, one is from the query P frames and the other is from the candidate P frames. Then we can reorder the candidates based on their distances to the query. The new order is shown in Figure 6. Clip0423 is our target, but it is the last one among the temporal query result candidates. After further spatial processing, it moves to rank 1 as expected.

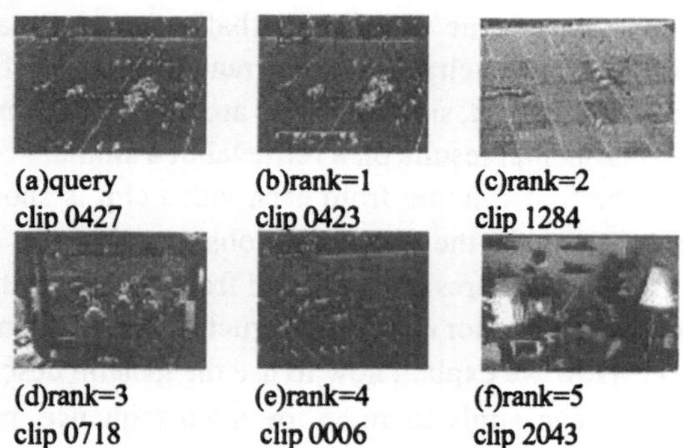

Figure 6. Results from figure 4 re-sorted with the spatial

6. Conclusions

In this paper we present a novel motion activity descriptor, which includes both temporal and spatial features of motion. The proposed descriptor can be extracted using compressed domain information. It supports both similarity-based classification and retrieval, as well as other applications such as surveillance, video abstraction, content re-purposing etc. The core of our descriptor, viz. the intensity, spatial and temporal attributes, has been accepted into the draft MPEG-7 standard motion activity descriptor.

The descriptor can be efficiently computed since only P frames of a video are processed and the descriptor can be processed directly in the compressed domain. While the temporal feature of the descriptor can be scaled to support multi-level representation and provides a basis for hierarchical video content analysis, the spatial feature can be easily scaled for different frame sizes as well.

Since the descriptor is a low level and simple descriptor, it does not carry out semantic matches. Therefore, as a standalone feature descriptor it only targets MPEG-7 enabled applications like media filtering, multimedia presentation etc. However, we can combine it with other visual features to make it more powerful in content-based multimedia applications. Future research also includes how to process the descriptor in both compressed domain and spatial domain more effectively.

Acknowledgement. This research is in part supported by the following grants/awards: NSF #EIA-9986057, NSF#EIA-0080134, Samsung Electronics, and ONR#N00014-01-1-0391. The first author would like to thank Dr. Yanglim Choi, Samsung electronics, for many fruitful discussions.

7. Reference

[1] Shih-Fu Chang, William Chen, Horace J.Meng, Hari Sundaram and Di Zhong, "A Fully Automated Content-Based Video Search Engine Supporting Spatiotemoral Queries", *IEEE Trans. on Circuits and Systems for Video Technology*, 8(5), pp.602-615, 1998.

[2] A. Divakaran and H. Sun, "A Descriptor for spatial distribution of motion activity", *Proc. SPIE Conf. on Storage and Retrievalfrom Image and Video Databases*, San Jose, CA 24-28 Jan. 2000.

[3] Y.Deng and B.S.Manjunath, "NeTra-V: toward an object-based video representation", *IEEE Transactions on Circuits and Systems for Video Technology*, vol.8, (no.5), p.616-27, Sep 1998.

[4] A. Gersho and R.M. Gray , "Vector Quantization and Signal Compression, " *Kluwer Academis,* 1991

[5] B. G. Haskell, A. Puri and A. N. Netravali, "Digital Video: An Introduction to MPEG 2," *Chapman and Hall*, 1997.

[6] W. Y. Ma and B. S. Manjunath, "NETRA: A toolbox for navigat ing large image databases," *IEEE International Conference on Image Processing*, pp. 568-571,1997

[7] X. Sun, M. Kankanhalli, Y. Zhu and J. Wu, "Content-Based Representative Frame Extraction for Digital Video," *International Conference on Multimedia Computin g and Systems,* pp. 190-194, 1998

[8] Hongjiang Zhang, Chien~Yong Low, and Stephen W. Smoliar, "Video parsing and browsing using compressed data," *Multimedia Tools and Applications*, 1(1): pp.89-111, 1995.

[9] URL: http://www.almaden.ibm.com/cs/cuevideo

[10] URL: http://www.cselt.it/mpeg/, official MPEG site.

A Fast and Effective Block-Matching Error Concealment Scheme

Jian Wang[1] and Chang Wen Chen[2]

[1] Dept. of Electrical Engineering, University of Missouri, Columbia, MO 65211
jwang@ee.missouri.edu

[2] Interactive Media Group, Sarnoff Corporation, Princeton, NJ 08543
cchen@sarnoff.com

Abstract. In the transport of compressed video over error prone channels, motion vectors and displaced frame differences may be lost or received with errors. The effect of such information loss can be devastating because any damage to the motion vector may lead to severe error propagation and significant visual distortion over several video frames at the decoder. To resolve such problem, several block-matching based techniques have been proposed to conceal the transport error. However, the corresponding computational expense required by these schemes has been too intensive for a practical video decoder. In this paper, we introduce a technique that makes use of correctly received motion vectors of neighboring macroblocks around the lost macroblock to achieve an effective block-matching. This technique enables us to reduce the computational expense to a great extent. Experimental results show that the proposed error concealment method can produce a high quality video while consuming reasonable computational power.

1 Introduction

Video compression is usually achieved by reducing two kinds of redundancy, i.e. spatial redundancy and temporal redundancy. For example, in the MPEG-2 video compression standard [1], three types of frames, namely intra frame(I), predictive frame(P) and bi-directional predictive frame(B), are defined and most macroblocks are inter coded macroblocks. For inter coded macroblock, motion vector (MV) and displaced frame difference (DFD) are encoded and transported to the decoder. For practical channels, the transport of compressed video is subject to error corruption. The transport errors may result in the lost of decoding synchronization and eventually the loss of MV and DFD as they are coded with the variable-length codes. The effect of such information loss can be devastating for the transport of compressed video over error prone channels because the errors in the compressed bit stream may lead to significant visual distortion over several consecutive frames [2].

The error concealment techniques are essentially post-processing techniques, aiming at alleviating the visual distortion caused by the loss of bitstream segments using information of correctly received neighboring macroblocks or frames at the decoder. In the past 10-15 years, many error concealment methods have been proposed. Generally, all these techniques make use of the correlation between a lost macroblock and its adjacent macroblocks in the same frame and/or the previous frame in order to accomplish error concealment. Recently, some researchers [3, 4] borrowed the idea of block-matching motion estimation and compensation in the video encoding and introduced block-matching based error concealment methods. Because it is usually true that there is strong temporal correlation between the neighboring frames, such block-matching based methods can achieve very good results. However, the existing block-matching based methods employ full search to find the best candidate. As a result, the corresponding computational expense is very high which prevents these techniques from being used in the real-time decoder. In this paper, we propose a technique that takes advantage of existing motion vectors (MV) of neighboring inter macroblocks around the lost macroblock to achieve an effective block-matching. This technique enables us to virtually avoid the time-consuming full search and therefore reduces the computational expense to a great extent.

This paper is organized as follows. In section 2, we first review some existing block-matching based error concealment methods. We then propose a fast and effective block-matching error concealment method to recover the lost information. Experimental results that demonstrate the effectiveness of the proposed error concealment scheme are shown in Section 3. Finally, we conclude this paper in Section 4 with some discussions.

2 Fast and Effective Block-Macthing Error Concealment Method

2.1 Review of Existing Block-Matching Based Methods

It is well known that the pixels among consecutive video frames have strong correlation known as temporal redundancy. In several current video compression standards, for example MPEG-2, block-matching based motion estimation and compensation is employed to reduce such redundancy. After motion estimation, MV and DFD are encoded at the encoder and transported to the decoder. It is well known that transport of compressed video is subject to error corruption. Such transport errors may result in the lost of decoding synchronization and eventually the loss of MV and DFD. Most existing error concealment techniques have been exploring the correlation of MV between neighboring macroblocks as well as neighboring frames in order to recover the lost MV and DFD. Recently, Zhang [3] borrowed the idea of block-matching and developed an error concealment method based on decoder motion-vector estimation (DMVE). Suppose both MV and corresponding DFD of an inter macroblock are lost due to the errors in the transport process. They examined the relationship between the error corrupted macroblock and its neighbors. In particular, they consider several lines, e.g. two to eight, of pixels around the lost macroblock. Based on the gray scale value of these pixels, they search for a best candidate in both past and subsequent reference frames using a pre-defined error criterion. Once the block with the least matching error is found, the macroblock surrounded by these pixel lines is assumed to be the best candidate to replace the lost macroblock.

Tsekeridou [4] also proposed a block-matching based error concealment method. The difference between Tsekeridou's and Zhang's method is that Tsekeridou employed different shape and size of blocks to perform block-matching. From these candidates, the one with least matching error is selected and the corresponding macroblock is used to conceal the lost one.

In order to obtain a good effect of estimation, the existing schemes all employed full search within a range for block-matching based error concealment. Consequently, these schemes result in heavy computational burden and make them difficult to be employed in practical applications. Although several attempts [4] have been made to address this issue, the intrinsic nature of the full search has not been changed. A modified full search strategy is often inadequate to reduce the computational expense significantly enough for practical applications. It is therefore desired to develop a fast and effective block-matching error concealment method so that it can be employed in real time applications.

2.2 The Proposed Error Concealment Scheme

Intuitively, the full search block matching and simple copy of loss block are two extremes of error concealment strategies. The full search-based scheme can be considered optimal in terms of concealment performance. However, the computational requirement is the most demanding one though. On the other hand, the simple copy of loss block requires minimum computational burden. However, its concealment performance is expected to be the most inferior.

To reduce the computational requirement for the block matching based error concealment, we would need to avoid the extensive computations of the matching errors. Notice that, if a neighboring macroblock of the lost macroblock are decoded without error, we shall try to recover the lost macroblock using the information derived directly from its neighboring macroblock. In particular, we should make full use of the motion vector and the displaced frame difference since these two important quantities can be used directly without additional computation. Consequently, the scheme of error concealment will need to be based on neighboring macroblocks, instead of arbitrary lines of neighboring pixels as reported in [3].

There are several assumptions that have been considered in the design of a fast and effective error concealment algorithm design. First, we assume that the error concealment can be designed based on neighboring macroblocks, instead of neighboring pixels. This allows us to make full use of motion vectors and displaced frame differences from correctly decoded neighboring macroblocks. Second, we assume that the motion of at least one neighboring macroblocks would be approximately the same as that of the lost macroblock. Therefore, we assume that we can always find a candidate macroblock in the reference frame to replace the lost macroblock with high visual fidelity. Third, we assume that the displaced frame differences of neighboring macroblocks can be used to measure the goodness of the block-matching in the search for a candidate macroblock to replace the missing macroblock. Essentially, we will link the missing macroblock to one of neighboring macroblock to form an extended block to compute the goodness of the block matching. Three different combination of the missing macroblock and its neighboring macroblock are shown in Figure 1.

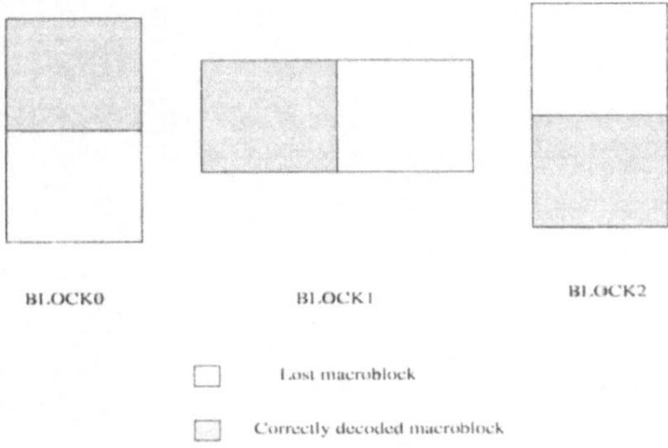

Fig. 1. Three types of BLOCK in the proposed method.

As we move from the pixel-based approach to the macroblock-based approach, we are able to save significantly the computational requirement because we can directly make use of the motion vectors and displaced frame differences of its neighboring macroblocks. Although the scheme proposed in [4] is also based on macroblocks, direct use of the information from neighboring macroblocks was not exploited. It is this direct use of the available information from neighboring macroblocks that enables us to significantly reduce the computational requirement in the block-matching-based error concealment.

In this research, we consider the case that both MV and DFD of an inter-coded macroblock are lost or cannot be recovered. This is the worst case for inter macroblock decoding because no information about this macroblock is available for error concealment. Because video signals are highly correlated in both spatial and temporal domains, if we assume that its neighboring macroblocks are decoded without error in the current frame, we shall be able to make full use of the correctly decoded information to conceal the error macroblock based on a block-matching scheme.

Figure 2 illustrates the basic idea of the proposed scheme. We first construct an extended block consisting of the missing macroblock and one of its neighboring macroblocks. Suppose that MB3 is the erroneous macroblock, MB0, MB1, and MB2 are three neighboring macroblocks around the erroneous macroblock. Then, the extended block BLOCK 0 will consist of the missing macroblock and its top neighbor. Similarly we can define two other extended blocks, BLOCK 1 and BLOCK 2, as shown in Figure 2.

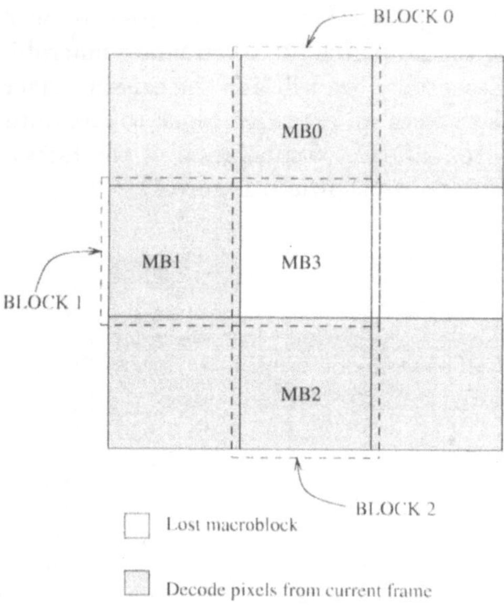

Fig. 2. Matching areas employed in the proposed method.

In the ideal case when all four macroblocks, MB0, MB1, MB2, and MB3, are from the same object, the motion vectors for MB0, MB1 and MB2 should be nearly identical. In this case, the error concealment become simple and can be accomplished by directly copying the corresponding macroblock in the reference frame to conceal this erroneous macroblock.

In real compressed video, these four macroblocks rarely have completely identical motion vectors. A more reasonable hypothesis is to assume that two neighboring macroblocks having the same motion characteristics. This assumption is the base for constructing the extended blocks as shown in Figure 1. The size of three BLOCKs, BLOCK 0, 1, and 2, are 16×32, 32×16, and 16×32, respectively. As an extended block includes a completely decoded macroblock, it facilitates the full use of the information of the correctly decoded macroblock for motion estimation of the extended blocks. Notice that, if these macroblocks are inter coded, the motion vectors are readily available for MB0, MB1, and MB2. Moreover, the displaced frame differences are also available. As a result, we can use these prediction errors to represent the goodness-of-matching for the extended blocks. Therefore, the prediction error of BLOCK 0 can be represented by the absolute sum of prediction errors computed from MB0, and similar representations of prediction errors for BLOCK 1 and BLOCK 2 can also be defined. With all these prediction errors, we can therefore determine the motion vector for the missing macroblock by selecting the motion vector that is associated with the least absolute sum of prediction errors among these extended blocks.

In practical MPEG-2 video, the decoder may not re-gain synchronization until the end of a slice. Therefore, we often encounter the cases when consecutive loss of macroblocks occurs within a slice. In this case, the current missing macroblock MB3 will become MB1 in the next step of error concealment. Hence, we actually use MB0 and MB1 in this research to decide the final MV for each missing macroblock. The proposed fast motion estimation error concealment method can be summarized as follows:

1. If both MB0 and MB2 are intra type, a copy of the corresponding macroblock in the previous frame will replace the erroneous macroblock MB3;
2. If one of MB0 and MB2 is intra type and another one is inter type, we will copy the corresponding macroblock according to the motion vector information of their inter type macroblock;
3. If both MB0 and MB2 are inter type, the motion vector with smaller sum of prediction error will be selected as the MV of MB3 and the corresponding macroblock in the reference frame will replace the erroneous macroblock.

3 Experimental Results

Several well-known HDTV video test sequences, including flower garden, table tennis, and Susie, are used to test the proposed error concealment scheme. In addition, some scene change frames are constructed with above sequences. The format for these video sequence is 720×576 in size and 4:2:0 in format. The compressed bitstream is generated by a MPEG-2 encoder with TM5 [5] encoder and corresponding parameters for this CBR encoder is shown in Table 1.

Table 1. Parameters of CBR Encoder.

Bit rate (Mbps)	Length of GOP	Distance between two P frames	Buffer Size (Kbytes)
4.0	12	3	224

Since the error concealment for inter macroblocks is the most challenging task, we limit the errors to occur in the inter-coded macroblocks within an inter-coded frame. Therefore, we did not employ any channel model to stimulate the random or bursty error in the process of transport. Furthermore, we assume there is only one slice for each macroblock row, that is, 45 macroblocks per slice.

We compare the proposed scheme to two error concealment schemes. One is the simple replacement which conceals the lost macroblock by simply copying the block located in the corresponding position in the previous frame. Another one is the DMVE scheme [3]. Eight additional lines are used in DMVE, so the size of the extended block is 24×32. The search range is from -16 to 16.

Table 2 shows the numerical results by all these error concealment schemes. From this table, we can see that DMVE is capable of achieving good result for many sequences. This is expected as the DMVE scheme employs full search which enables the algorithm to obtain the optimal match. However, the computational expense for the DMVE scheme is prohibitive for many practical applications. In contrast, the proposed method presents a good trade-off between the performance and computational expense. The proposed scheme consistently outperforms the simply replacement scheme with significant margins and the PSNRs are very close to, or even higher than, the results by DMVE.

Table 2. The performance comparison of three error concealment methods (PSNR:dB).

	Proposed method	DMVE	Replacement
Flower and Garden	29.067	29.46	28.12
Susie	34.98	36.47	34.59
Leaves and Wind	32.67	32.57	32.22
Table Tennis	30.36	31.4	29.18
Calendar	28.212	28.07	26.53
Scene Changel	29.24	29.884	22.191
Scene Change2	32.255	33.158	28.677
Scene Change3	31.884	31.968	26.156
Scene Change4	26.57	26.328	24.072

The greatest advantage of the proposed scheme is the significant reduction of the the computational expense. In the case of DMVE, if the search range is from $-N$ to N and the pixel lines selected for the search is n, the computational expense can be represented by $4N^2 \times (48n + 2n^2)$ addition (subtraction) operations, $4N^2 \times (48n + 2n^2)$ absolute value operations, $4N^2 \times ((48n + 2n^2) - 1)$ addition operations, and $4N^2 - 1$ comparison operations. For the typical parameters of $N = 16$ and $n = 8$, the corresponding operations for DMVE will be 524288 additions (subtractions), 524288 absolute value calculations, 523264 additions, and 1023 comparisons, respectively. In the case of the proposed scheme, however, we only need 512 absolute value operations, 510 addition operations, and one comparison operation. The saving of computational expense is more than 1000:1.

4 Conclusion

In this paper, a fast and effective block-matching-based error concealment scheme has been proposed. We make full use of existing MV information of neighboring macroblocks around the erroneous macroblock. Such a scheme enables significant reduction of the computational expenses of the full search in the existing schemes. We provided an analysis of the computational requirements for both the DMVE scheme and the proposed scheme and showed that more than

1000:1 of speed-up can be achieved. The experimental results on several HDTV test sequences demonstrated that the proposed scheme can also achieve excellent error concealment performance compared with the DMVE scheme. We believe the proposed scheme can be readily adopted in various practical video communication applications.

References

1. ISO/IECJTC1/SC29/WG11, "Generic coding of moving pictures and associated audio," ISO/IEC 13818-2 1995.
2. Y. Wang and Q. F. Zhu, "Error control and concealment for video communication: a review," *Proc. of the IEEE*, vol. 86, No. 5, pp. 974–997, May 1998.
3. J. Zhan, J. F. Arnold, and M. R. Frater, "A cell-loss concealment technique for MPEG-2 coded video," *IEEE Trans. on Circuits and Systems for Video Technology*, vol. 10, No. 4, pp. 659–665, June 2000.
4. S. Tsekeridou and I. Pitas, "MPEG-2 error concealment based on block-matching principles," *IEEE Trans. on Circuits and Systems for Video Technology*, vol. 10, No. 4, pp. 646–658, June 2000.
5. ISO/IEC/JTC1/SC29/WG11, "Test model 5," Draft, Apr. 1993.

Bit Allocation for Video Coding with Temporal-Spatial Tradeoff

Shan Liu, JongWon Kim, and C.-C. Jay Kuo

Integrated Media Systems Center
Department of Electrical Engineering-Systems
University of Southern California, Los Angeles, CA 90089-2564
{shanl, jongwon, cckuo}@sipi.usc.edu

Abstract. Bit allocation with joint temporal-spatial consideration for video coding and motion-compensated frame interpolation at low bit rates is investigated. In contrast with traditional approaches where the frame-rate control and the quantization parameter selection are treated separately, they are jointly optimized in this work. In our framework, an affine warping based on triangular patch is adopted to interpolate skipped frames. Both skipped and coded frames contribute to the operational rate-distortion (R-D) function, and bit allocation is formulated as an optimization problem. A heuristic approach using iterative greedy pruning is proposed to solve this problem. It provides a suboptimal solution at a reasonable complexity. Experimental results show that, with various temporal (frame skipping) and spatial (quantizer) combinations, the proposed algorithm can achieve an average PSNR that is $0.3 \sim 1.0$ dB better than that of ITU-T H.263+/TMN8. Moreover, consistency of visual quality has significantly improved as evidenced by the reduced PSNR variance among frames.

1 Introduction

Video compression is often processed in both temporal and spatial domains. Temporal compression techniques such as motion compensated prediction (MCP) and frame skipping (temporal sub-sampling) are widely used in state-of-the-art standards to reduce temporal redundancy, while still image compression methods such as DCT and quantization are adopted to reduce spatial redundancy within each frame. Under a certain budget, more skipped frames result in worse temporal quality, whereas each coded frame can achieve higher spatial quality. Thus, temporal and spatial resolutions are to be adaptively compromised for the optimal joint quality. Moreover, temporal quality can be enhanced by applying motion compensated interpolation (MCI) to reconstruct skipped frames [1]. However, due to its complicated dependency relationship, temporal-spatial quality tradeoff for adaptive frame skipping has to be studied carefully for the purpose of achieving the best visual quality for the entire sequence.

There has been relevant research work on temporal and spatial bit allocation. First, given a frame-type combination and frame-rate, Ortega and Ramchandran [2, 3] investigated the optimal bit allocation problem for dependent quantization. Quantization parameters (QPs) were adaptively selected under a buffer constraint, resulting in spatially oriented allocation regardless of the temporal frame activity. Song *et al.* [4] proposed a frame-rate control scheme that adjusted the encoding frame-rate based on the inherent motion activity. The proposed Lagrangian solution adjusted the frame rate in a smoothly changing fashion, relying on the proposed frame-layer R-D (rate-distortion) model. Then, the MB-layer R-D model of ITU-T H.263+/TMN8 was used for rate allocation (i.e. QP adjustment) within a frame. However, due to R-D modeling, its performance is subject to modeling errors and the resulting quality degrades at initialization and sudden variations. Thus, though being confined to the INTRA-frame type, a more computationally aggressive approach based on dynamic programming was recently proposed by Reed and Lim [5]. Temporal-spatial quality was jointly optimized by adapting both FS (frame skipping) and QP based on measured (or estimated) operational R-D functions. Unfortunately, the I-frame limitation, which has been adopted to avoid computational difficulty of prediction dependency, imposes some restriction on its applicability to motion-compensated video coders such as ISO/IEC MPEG-4 and ITU-T H.263+. Also, simple frame repetition (FR) was used in [5] to reconstruct skipped frames so that even interpolation dependency is greatly simplified.

A joint temporal-spatial bit allocation scheme considering both frame coding and interpolation dependency is examined in this paper. Both INTRA and INTER frame types are treated, and skipped frames with MCI are adopted. Affine warping with triangular patches is used in motion-compensated interpolation of skipped frames, and both skipped and coded frames contribute to the operational R-D function. Dynamic programming has been widely used to solve the independent R-D optimization problem. However, it does not provide an optimal solution to dependent problems effectively [2]. Exhaustive search is often required to guarantee the solution optimality, but it is not practical due to its high computational complexity. In this work, a heuristic iterative algorithm based on greedy pruning is proposed to achieve a near optimal solution at a reasonable cost. Experiments show that the proposed algorithm can improve overall video quality by around 0.3 $\sim$ 1.0dB in average PSNR on various test cases. Moreover, the PSNR variance is much smaller. That is, the output visual quality is more consistent for the entire sequence, which is preferred by human beings.

The rest of the paper is organized as follows. The joint temporal-spatial rate allocation problem is formulated in Section 2, which covers independent and dependent frame coding scenarios as well as frame skipping. The proposed solution is detailed in Section 3 and experimental results are provided in Section 4. Finally, concluding remarks are given in Section 5.

2 Temporal-Spatial Dependent Rate Allocation: Problem Formulation

The classical rate allocation problem has been studied with and without temporal dependency [2], [3]. Given N dependent coded frames, the frame rate is usually fixed prior to allocation. In [2] and [3], the focus was on adapting QPs for all frames, $\{Q_i, i = 1, \ldots, N\}$, to achieve the best spatial quality . Mathematically, the problem can be written as

$$\min_{Q_1,\ldots,Q_N} \sum_{i=1}^{N} D_i(Q_1, \ldots, Q_i), \quad \text{s.t.} \quad \sum_{i=1}^{N} R_i(Q_1, \ldots, Q_i) < B_{budget}, \tag{1}$$

where $D_i(\cdot)$ and $R_i(\cdot)$ are the distortion measure and the rate of the ith frame under the given QP selection, respectively. Also, B_{budget} stands for the total bit budget.

In contrast, typical frame-rate control algorithms adopt frame skipping (FS) according to the underlying motion to achieve better temporal quality, while selecting QPs independently. If the temporal-spatial trade-off can be exploited simultaneously, it is natural that rates can be more efficiently allocated.

No matter how a video input is compressed and transmitted, the visual quality at the receiver can be best evaluated with respect to its quality in a full frame-rate playback. That is, in measuring the quality of video, not only coded frames but also skipped frames should be included. Here, we use the convention for frame set $\mathbf{S}$ to indicate FS, i.e.

$$\mathbf{S} = [S_1, S_2, \ldots, S_N], \quad S_i \in [0, 1], \quad i = 1, \ldots, N. \tag{2}$$

where $S_i = 1/0$ indicates a coded/skipped frame among total N frames. Similarly, the QP set $\mathbf{Q}$ can be written as

$$\mathbf{Q} = [Q_1, Q_2, \ldots, Q_N], \quad Q_i \in [Q_{min}, Q_{max}], \quad i = 1, \ldots, N. \tag{3}$$

When frames are skipped, a frame-rate up-conversion scheme should be used to reconstruct skipped frames with neighboring coded (reference) frames. Although any method can be applied, including frame repetition (FR), frame averaging (FA), and MCI [1], the 6-parameter affine warping model [6] is adopted here to achieve better interpolation. The 6-parameter affine model is defined as

$$x_i' = a_0 + a_1 \times x_i + a_2 \times y_i,$$
$$y_i' = b_0 + b_1 \times x_i + b_2 \times y_i,$$

where (x_i', y_i') is the coordinate of the interpolated pixel in the reconstructed frame and (x_i, y_i) is that of the corresponding pixel in the reference frame. Different interpolation schemes result in different values of D_i.

Temporal dependency is generally unavoidable in video coding, especially at bit rate goes lower. Most video coding techniques use INTER frames for compression efficiency, which introduces temporal dependency among frames. Also, frame interpolation introduces dependency as discussed above. The total distortion can be expressed by

$$\sum_{i=1}^{N} D_i(\mathbf{Q},\mathbf{S}) = \sum_{i=1}^{N} \left\{ D_i(Q_i, Q_{i_r}) | (S_i = 1) + D_i(Q_{i_p}, Q_{i_n}) | (S_i = 0) \right\}, \quad (4)$$

where the current P frame is predicted from the i_r^{th} I or P frame or interpolated from both i_p^{th} and i_n^{th} I or P frames. Since skipped frames do not cost any bit, the total rate is

$$\sum_{i=1}^{N} R_i(\mathbf{Q},\mathbf{S}) = \sum_{i=1}^{N} R_i(Q_i, Q_{i_r}) | (S_i = 1). \quad (5)$$

The resulting rate allocation problem is to find $\mathbf{Q}^*$ and $\mathbf{S}^*$ such that

$$[\mathbf{Q}^*, \mathbf{S}^*] = \arg\min_{\mathbf{Q},\mathbf{S}} \sum_{i=1}^{N} D_i(\mathbf{Q},\mathbf{S}), \quad (6)$$

$$\text{subject to} \quad \sum_{i=1}^{N} R_i(\mathbf{Q},\mathbf{S}) < B_{budget},$$

where $D_i(\mathbf{Q},\mathbf{S})$ and $R_i(\mathbf{Q},\mathbf{S})$ are the distortion and the bit budget of the ith frame under the given frame and QP sets, respectively. Usually, D is represented in terms of the mean square error (MSE).

This problem can be greatly simplified by removing temporal dependency as done in [5]. That is, all coded frames must be INTRA-frames to avoid coding dependency, and FR is used (instead of bidirectional interpolation methods such as FA and MCI) to avoid interpolation dependency. Dynamic programming is utilized to solve this independent R-D optimization. Note, however, this approach is not adequate in solving the dependent problem as given by (6), since frame coding and MCI dependency are interconnected.

3 Proposed Algorithm for Rate Allocation

To find the optimal solution to the dependent problem, exhaustive search is typically required. By checking all possible combinations, exhaustive search can guarantee the optimal solution. However, the extremely high computational cost prevents it from being a practical approach. If there are N frames in the sequence and the total number of possible QP in a frame is M, there are totally $\sum_{i=0}^{N-2} M^{N-i} C_i^{N-2}$ possible paths, among which the best one should be selected, given that any frame except for the first and the last can be skipped. Hence, the complexity of exhaustive search is $O(M^N \sum_{i=0}^{N-2} C_i^{N-2}/M^i)$.

To reduce the complexity and make the problem computationally feasible, a heuristic iterative algorithm based on greedy pruning is proposed. To simplify further, we assume the IPPP... structure, where the first frame is coded in the INTRA mode and all subsequent frames are coded as P-frames. This is nevertheless a very typical coding structure. Furthermore, all derivations given in this section can be easily extended to multiple I-frames with additional B-frames.

3.1 Cost Function and Frame Skipping

First, a cost function J is defined to model the R-D performance of a selected path with the Lagrangian multiplier λ:

$$J(q,j) = D(q,j) + \lambda R(q,j), \tag{7}$$

where D and R are the total distortion and rate for q^{th} path up to the jth frame. Note that λ controls the cost J by starting from high and low boundary values and these values converge during iteration.

Without MCI dependency, each coded frame is represented by a 'node' in the trellis, which represents coded frames with different QPs. If there is frame skipping, an extra node, denoted as the 'skip node', is introduced. Unlike regular nodes which correspond to coded frames and thus have calculated rate and distortion values, the frame on the skipped node cannot be reconstructed at the current stage. Instead, the cost of the skip node can only be computed when the next coded frame is available. Therefore, the skip node at the current stage will not be pruned.

The maximal number of skipped frames is $N-2$ in a sequence consisting of N frames. However, the temporal quality is unacceptable when the number of skipped frames exceeds a certain value. Besides, a high number of skipped frames may result in higher complexity, since all paths passing skipped frames should be reserved until the next coded frame is reached. Hence, to ensure reasonable temporal quality as well as to control the complexity, we set an upper bound by S_{max} on the number of successively skipped frames.

3.2 Search Reduction with Monotonic Property

Ramchandran *et al.* [3] explored the monotonic property of the R-D curve to reduce the complexity. Under this property, for any $\lambda \geq 0$, we have

$$J(q,j) \leq J(q',j), \quad if \quad q \leq q', \tag{8}$$

where q represents the QP level from low (fine) to high (coarse) levels. This monotonic property implies that a better (finer QP with higher PSNR) predictor will lead to more efficient coding.

With the addition of MCI dependency, we can further claim that a better reference will result in more accurate reconstruction of a skipped frame. Since better references (I or P frames) come from better predictors, the monotonic property can be extended to the current case. The resulting pruning scheme is called "monotonic pruning". Note that this property was only verified by experiments but not proved in [3]. Thus, the solution obtained by selective iteration, which exploits this monotonic property, should not be claimed as the strict optimum.

3.3 Search Reduction via Greedy Pruning

Even with monotonic pruning, the complexity is still quite high. To further reduce the complexity, another simplification, called greedy pruning, is proposed. Instead of pruning nodes that violate the monotonic property, only the 'best' and 'pending' nodes are kept, while all others are eliminated. The best node corresponds a coded frame at a certain QP, passed by the path with the minimum cost J. The pending node is a node corresponding to a skipped frame, through which more than one path may be reserved. Note that pending nodes are constrained by the maximum allowed number S for successively skipped frames.

3.4 Proposed Algorithm

The final search algorithm is described below with an example shown in Fig. 1.

Step1: Initialize the value of λ.
Step2: Calculate $J(q, 1)$ for the first frame, which is the I-frame, for each QP within $q \in [Q_{min}, Q_{max}]$ as shown in Fig. 1(a).
Step3: Select the I-frame with the lowest cost J. Refer to Fig. 1(b).
Step4: Grow the trellis to stage 2 by coding the first P-frame with all QP values. The skip node is reserved. Refer to Fig. 1(c).
Step5: Keep the node with the lowest cost J and prune all others except for the skip node as shown in Fig. 1(d).
Step6: Grow the trellis to one more stage, and the skipped frames in previous stages are reconstructed as shown in Fig. 1(e).
Step7: Prune all nodes except the best and skip nodes. Refer Fig. 1(f).
Step8: Grow trellis to stage 4 as shown in Fig. 1(g).
Step9: Prune paths which have more successive skipped frames than S ($S = 2$ in this example) as shown in Fig. 1(h).
Step10: Prune nodes as done in *Step*7. See Fig. 1(i).
Step11: Continue the above process until the last frame is reached. Update λ and return to *Step*2.
Step12: Stop when λ converges.

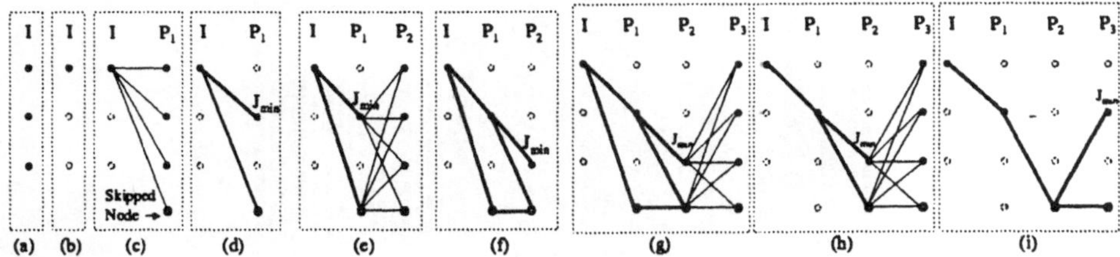

Fig. 1. A search example with greedy pruning.

Since the I-frame will normally affect the quality of the following P-frames, and thus the overall quality of the whole sequence, we can slightly modify the above algorithm to keep all possibilities (QPs) of the first I-frame, and apply only monotonic pruning to the first I-P stage. Experiments show that this modification slightly enhance the optimization and speed up the convergence of λ.

The complexity of the proposed search algorithm greedy pruning is tremendously reduced compared to exhaustive search. Since the number of reserved paths at each stage is fixed $(S + 1)$, the complexity in one iteration is $O(S \cdot N)$.

4 Experimental Results

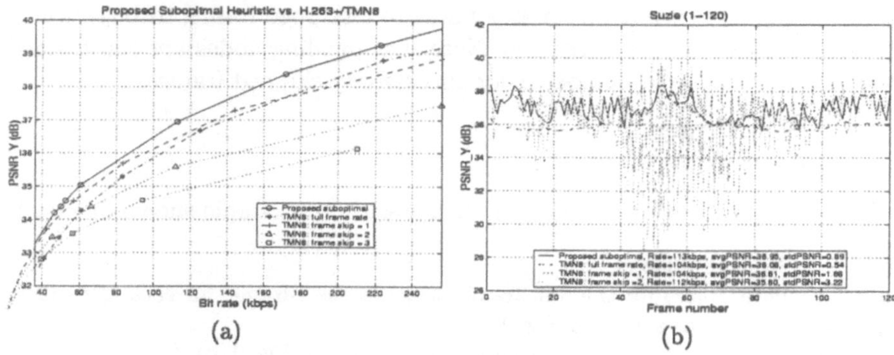

Fig. 2. (a) The R-D performance comparison for the 'Suzie' sequence, (b) PSNR_Y comparison for each frame of the 'Suzie' sequence at 113kbps.

Simulations on various test sequences are performed by utilizing the H.263+/TMN8 codec. However, due to the space limit, only results from the 'Suzie' and 'Coastguard' sequences are presented. Fig. 2(a) compares the R-D performance of the proposed solution and that with fixed QP/FS on 'Suzie'. Fig. 2(b) shows the empirical PSNR curves at a budget rate of 113kbps. These figures show that the proposed method achieves a better R-D performance and outperforms all fixed QP/FS cases. The average PSNR is enhanced by 0.3 to 1.0 dB, and the PSNR is more consistent. The adaptive QP and FS selection by the proposed method is depicted in Fig. 3, where $QP = 0$ stands for skipped frames.

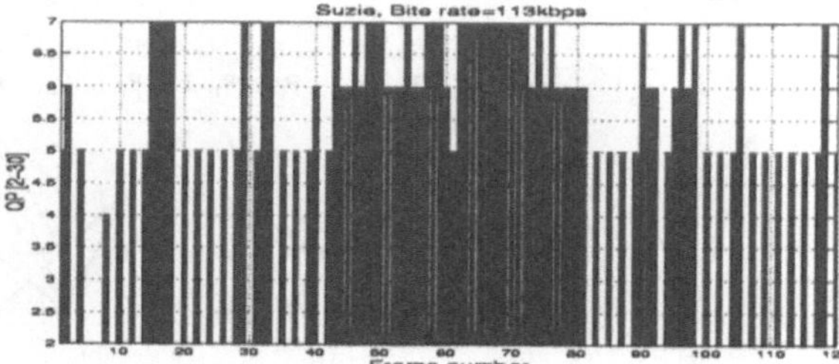

Fig. 3. Illustration of adaptive QP and FS selection for the 'Suzie' sequence at 113kbps.

Table 1 presents the performance comparison in terms of the average PSNR and PSNR variances for the proposed algorithm under various budgets on sequences 'Suzie' and 'Coastguard', respectively. We can conclude that the proposed greedy iteration always achieves higher overall quality (higher average PSNR) while maintaining consistence quality (lower PSNR variance).

Table 1. Performance comparison in terms of actual bit rates, average PSNR, and PSNR variance for 'Suzie' and 'Coastguard' sequence.

'Suzie'				'Coastguard'			
Budget = 40kbps	Rate (kbps)	Average PSNR (dB)	PSNR Variance	**Budget = 40kbps**	Rate (kbps)	Average PSNR (dB)	PSNR Variance
Greedy Iteration	39.27	33.68	0.38	Greedy Iteration	40.80	26.78	0.42
FS=0, QP=15	38.39	32.61	0.22	FS=0, QP=29	40.80	25.60	0.28
FS=1, QP=11	38.69	33.41	0.85	FS=1, QP=22	40.10	26.41	0.62
FS=2, QP=9	40.10	33.18	3.72	FS=2, QP=19	40.01	26.61	1.90
FS=3, QP=8	39.37	32.80	7.90	FS=3, QP=17	39.92	26.48	3.85
Budget = 60kbps	Rate (kbps)	Average PSNR (dB)	PSNR Variance	**Budget = 61kbps**	Rate (kbps)	Average PSNR (dB)	PSNR Variance
Greedy Iteration	60.66	35.05	0.38	Greedy Iteration	61.40	27.90	0.45
FS=0, QP=10	61.01	34.23	0.25	FS=0, QP=21	62.50	26.94	0.25
FS=1, QP=8	57.07	34.57	1.39	FS=1, QP=17	58.84	27.53	0.94
FS=2, QP=6	66.34	34.39	6.14	FS=2, QP=14	60.60	27.72	2.92
FS=3, QP=6	56.37	33.58	10.78	FS=3, QP=12	63.70	27.56	5.82
Budget = 113kbps	Rate (kbps)	Average PSNR (dB)	PSNR Variance	**Budget = 84kbps**	Rate (kbps)	Average PSNR (dB)	PSNR Variance
Greedy Iteration	113.04	36.95	0.48	Greedy Iteration	84.20	28.85	0.39
FS=0, QP=7	103.34	36.08	0.27	FS=0, QP=17	85.30	27.90	0.22
FS=1, QP=5	111.00	36.61	3.43	FS=1, QP=13	86.84	28.75	1.50
FS=2, QP=4	112.12	35.60	10.39	FS=2, QP=11	87.62	28.66	4.12
FS=3, QP=3	140.42	35.52	22.74	FS=3, QP=10	81.80	28.13	7.14

5 Conclusion

A heuristic greedy pruning was proposed to solve the joint temporal-spatial dependent R-D problem with both frame encoding and frame skipping dependency. Both frame skipping and quantization parameters are jointly determined so that the trade-off between temporal and spatial quality can be addressed simultaneously. Experimental results show that the proposed method does enhance the overall video quality with respect to the full frame-rate playback quality.

References

1. A. M. Tekalp, *Digital Video Processing*, Prentice hall, NJ, 1995.
2. A. Ortega, *Optimization techniques for adaptive quantization of image and video under delay constraints*, Ph.D. thesis, Dept. of Electrical Engineering, Columbia University, Jun 1994.
3. K. Ramchandran, A. Ortega, and M. Vetterli, "Bit allocation for dependent quantization with application to multiresolution and mpeg video coders," in *IEEE Trans. on Image Processing*, September 1994, vol. 3, pp. 533–545.
4. H. Song, J. Kim, and J. Kuo, "Real-time h.263+ frame rate control for low bit rate VBR video," in *Proc. IEEE International Symposium on Circuits and Systems*, 1999, vol. 4, pp. 307-310.
5. E. C. Reed and J. S. Lim, "Multidimensional bit rate control for video communication," in *Proc. SPIE*, San Diego, CA, July 2000, vol. XXIII, pp. 277–288.
6. T. Kuo and C.-C. Jay Kuo, "Motion-compensated interpolation for low-bit-rate video quality enhancement," in *Proc. SPIE, Applications of Digital Image Processing*, 1998, vol. 3460, pp. 277–288.

An Evaluation of the Robustness of Image Retrieval Based on Vector Quantization

Shyhwei Teng and Guojun Lu

GSCIT, Monash University, Gippsland Campus
Churchill, Vic 3842
AUSTRALIA
E-mail: shyh.wei.teng@infotech.monash.edu.au

Abstract. Image retrieval based on vector quantization (VQ) is a content-based image retrieval that we have proposed recently. However, it is noted that a potential problem of the proposed method is that it may be not robust in the sense that its performance may be sensitive to small changes in images. This paper investigates if this is a problem in practical image retrieval systems. Our experimental results and analysis show that image retrieval based on VQ is robust.

1 Introduction

With growing utilization of digital image libraries in recently years, content-based image retrieval techniques are developed to allow information to be managed efficiently and effectively. Such techniques use image features such as colour, shape and texture for indexing and retrieval [1, 2, 3, 4, 5]. To date, colour-based image retrieval techniques are the most popular and are commonly implemented in many content-based image retrieval applications [6]. Its popularity is mainly due to two reasons. Firstly, compared to shape and texture, it is normally much easier to remember the colour elements in the images. Secondly, not only are image retrieval techniques relatively easier to implement, but also effective.

In colour-based retrieval techniques, each image in the database is represented by a colour histogram [1, 3, 5]. Traditionally, the histogram H(M) is a vector (h_1, h_2,..., h_n), where each element h_j represents the number of pixels falling in bin j in image M. Each bin denotes an interval of a quantized colour space. During image retrieval, a histogram is found for the query image or estimated from the user's query. A metric is used to measure the distance between the histograms of the query image and images in the database. (If images are of different size, their histograms are normalized.) Images with a distance smaller than a pre-defined threshold are retrieved from the database and presented to the user. Alternatively, the first k images with smallest distances are retrieved.

Recently, we have proposed a retrieval technique that is based on vector quantization (VQ) compressed image data. In concept, it is similar to the method based on colour histograms. The difference is that in VQ-based method, the histogram represents the number of blocks using a particular codeword in the codebook, instead of a particular colour. With such histogram, spatial relationships among the image pixels are captured. Initial studies show that the proposed scheme is more effective than traditional colour-based methods [7, 8].

However, it is noted that the VQ-based method may have a potential robustness problem. The problem can be explained as follows. The image encoding in VQ consists of two stages. First, the image is segmented into equal blocks of MxN pixels. The block size must be equivalent to the codeword size. Then, each image block is compared with the codewords to find the best match. The index of the best matching codeword is now used to represent the image block. Due to the manner images are encoded, it is possible that two similar images, where one is a slight translated image of another, have two very different sets of codewords representing their image blocks. Even though majority of the pixels in the two images are the same, the positions of the pixels in their respective images are different. The pixel position difference might cause the pixels to be grouped differently and coded with different codewords. Since the retrieval of the proposed VQ scheme is based on the codewords, the distance of the two images can be large, though perceptually, they are almost the same.

In this paper, we investigate the retrieval robustness of the VQ-based method in practice. The following sections are organized as follows. Next section describes the main concepts of image indexing and retrieval based on VQ compressed image data. Section 3 presents some robustness studies on the retrieval performances of VQ-based method. Finally, Section 4 concludes the paper.

2 Image Indexing and Retrieval Based on VQ Compressed Data

VQ is an established compression technique that has been used for image compression in many areas [7-11]. A vector quantizer can be defined as a mapping Q of K-dimensional Euclidean space R^K into a finite subset Y of R^K, that is
$Q: R^K \text{-->>} Y$,

where $Y = (x'_i;\ i = 1, 2, \ldots.\ N)$, and x'_i is the ith vector in Y.

Y is the set of reproduction vectors and is called a VQ codebook or VQ table. N is the number of vectors in Y. At the encoder, each data vector x belonging to R^K is matched or approximated with a codeword in the codebook and the address or index of that codeword is transmitted/stored instead of the data vector itself. At the decoder, the index is mapped back to the codeword and the codeword is used to represent the original data vector. In the encoder and decoder, an identical codebook exists whose entries contain combinations of pixels in a block. Assuming the image block size is (n x n) pixels and each pixel is represented by m bits, theoretically, $(2^m)^{n \times n}$ types of blocks are possible. In practice, however, there are only a limited number of combinations that occur most often, which reduces the size of the codebook considerably. This is the basis of vector quantization. If properties of the human visual system are used, the size of the codebook can be reduced further and fewer bits can be used to represent the index of codebook entries.

To index an image, the number of occurrences of each index is calculated to obtain an index histogram $H(v_1, v_2, \ldots, v_i, \ldots, v_n)$, where v_i is the number of times codeword i is used by the image, and n is the total number of codewords in the codebook. Since each index is unique for each codeword in the codebook and each block of pixels is represented by an index number, this histogram will be able to characterise the major features of the image.

During image retrieval, an index histogram $H(q_1, q_2, \ldots, q_i, \ldots, q_n)$ is calculated for the query image. Then the distance between the query image Q and the target image V is calculated as follows :

$$d(Q,V) = \sum_{i=1}^{n} |q_i - v_i|$$

Images can be ranked in an ascending order of calculated distances.

After describing the main concepts of image indexing and retrieval based on VQ compressed image data, we will now illustrate the potential problem of this method with an example.

Fig. 1 shows four images (dimension of 8x4 pixels) where, image B, C and D are image A translated right by 1, 2 and 3 pixels respectively. After translation, perceptually, the four images are still very similar. However, in VQ process, we have 8 distinct blocks if the block size is 4x4 pixels. Each distinct block may be coded into different codewords, thus these images may have totally different VQ histograms. This is a possibility. We want to determine what is the effect of this potential problem on image retrieval performance.

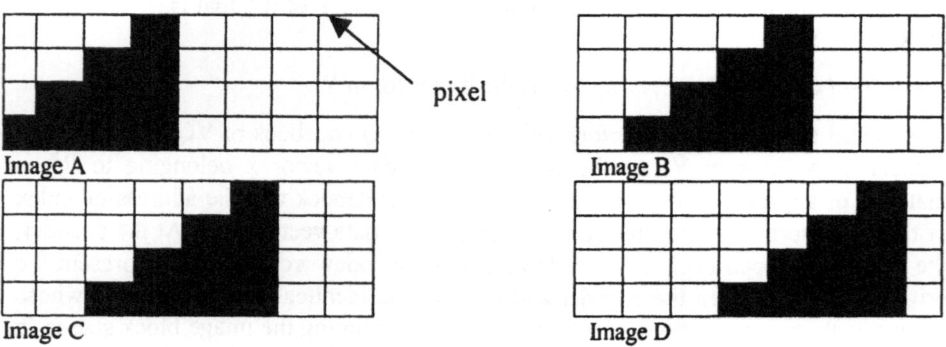

Fig. 1. Perceptually similar images that differ by a slight pixel shift

3 Robustness Studies on Image Retrieval of the VQ Scheme

To investigate the effects the image translation problem has on retrieval performance of the VQ scheme, two sets of experiments are conducted. The first experiment studies the VQ histograms of the images and their translated images. We investigate if the slight translations in the images cause great change in the histogram. The purpose of the second experiment is to compare the retrieval performance based on the recall and precision curves [11,12] of the VQ scheme on databases before and after translated images are added. For both experiments, the codebook size is 1024 and the dimension of the codeword is 4x4 pixels. The dimension of the images used is 256x256 pixels.

3.1 Histogram Studies

To conduct the first experiment, 200 images are randomly chosen. For each image, eight translated images (four translated to the right by 1, 2, 3, 4 pixels; four translated diagonally down by 1, 2, 3, 4 pixels) are produced from it. With the original image as the query, the distances between the query and each of its reproduced images are calculated. The largest distance between each query and their translated images are added and the average difference is 10.76% of the maximum possible distances between two images (twice of the number of blocks). This means that between the queries and their images that are most affected by the translation, only an average of 10.76% of the blocks are represented by different codewords. Thus, these results show that in practice, the number of image blocks affected by the translation is a lot smaller compared to what is suggested in theory.

To investigate the results above, we take a closer look into one of the 200 images above. Fig. 2 shows 2 images, where MT5D3 is one of the translated (diagonally down by 3 pixels) image of the query image MT5Q. Among the translated images and the query, MT5D3 has the largest distance to MT5Q. However, their histograms are similar and the percentage of difference is 14%. With such percentage of difference, the translated images of MT5Q are ranked among the closest when retrieved from database. Actually, this distance is much smaller than that (53%) between MT5Q and VC14 (Fig. 4) which is a similar face to MT5Q.

MT5Q.JPG

MT5D3.JPG

Fig. 2. MT5Q and its translated image, MT5D3

The reasons for the difference between what is suggested in theory and the results obtained in practice are as follows:

- Generally, for an image to be meaningful, majority of the pixels and their neighbours are correlated. For example, in Fig. 2, large patches of pixels in the areas like hair, face and background have similar colour. When the image is translated by a few pixels, pixels that are shifted out of the VQ segmented blocks and the pixels shifted into them actually have the similar colour. Since there is little pixel colour change in the blocks, the codeword that is closest will likely to stay unchanged. The image blocks that are affected are the ones which contain edges of the picture. The percentage of such blocks in a image is normally small.

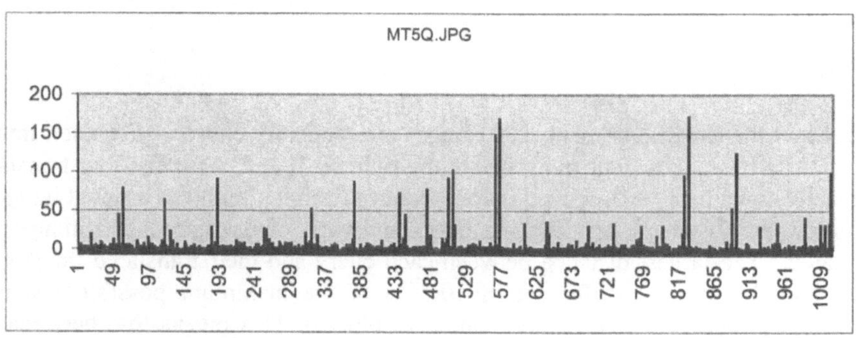

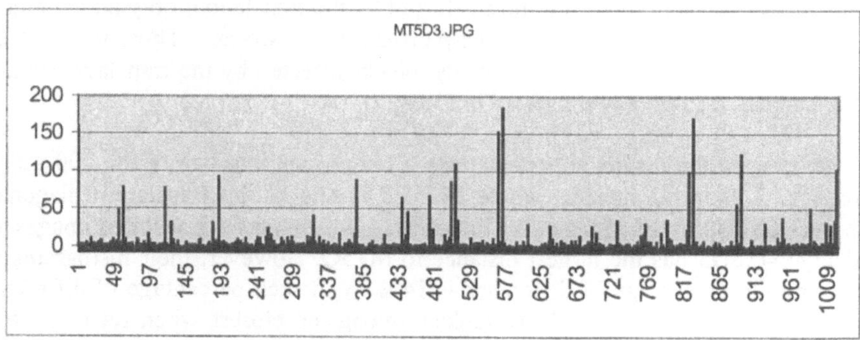

Fig. 3. VQ based histograms of "MT5Q.JPG" & "MT5D3.JPG"

- From Section 2, we see that VQ uses the properties of human visual system to achieve better compression. Image blocks which are perceptual similar are therefore represented by the same codeword. Thus, the codebook does not contain all the possible distinct blocks in the database images. Thus, majority of the codewords used to represent the query blocks are still the closest to the translated blocks.

3.2 Recall and Precision Studies

In the second experiment, two image databases are used. The first database consists of 2165 randomly chosen general images. The second database consists of the images in the first database and 48 added translated images. The 48 translated images are produced from six query images randomly chosen from the first database (8 from each query). The retrieval performances of the VQ scheme in both databases is evaluated by comparing to the retrieval results based on the colour histogram method used in the commercial product *QBIC*[1] from IBM [8, 9, 10]. The colour histogram method used in the QBIC system is an improved version of the traditional colour histogram method as it takes into account the contributions of perceptually similar colours in the distance calculation [5, 10].

Fig. 5 shows the retrieval performances of both systems on the two databases. From the retrieval results of the first database (before the translated images are added), we see that the recall and precision curve of the VQ method is further away from the origin compared to the curve of QBIC's colour histogram method starting from recall value of about 20%. Thus, VQ method performs better than the QBIC's colour histogram method before the translated images are added. According to the recall and precision curves plotted from the retrieval results of the two systems on the second database, we see that the retrieval performances of both systems have improved. Until the recall value of about 70%, both systems' curves have precision of 1. The reason for the QBIC's colour histogram curve having the precision of 1 is because this method is invariant to translation [13]. Thus all the added translated images are retrieved in the QBIC system. As for the VQ-based system, all the added translated images are also retrieved (Fig. 4) due to the reasons we have discussed in Section 3.1. Above the recall value of 70%, the recall and precision curves show that the VQ-based method performs better than the colour histogram method. VQ-based method performs better because besides retrieving the added translated images, it is also able to retrieve more database images that are considered as relevant to the queries compared to the colour histogram method.

3.3 Further Analysis on Experimental Results

The results in Sections 3.1 and 3.2 demonstrated that the VQ-based method is robust. This can be further explained as follows.

- The first database used above consists of general images that are randomly chosen without any bias. If the retrieval results of VQ-based method are better than QBIC on the first database, the same should be true for the second database which is just another database with more similar images to queries.
- In content-based image retrieval technique, the retrieval is not based on exact match and the retrieved database images are normally ranked based on their similarity to the query. Since the difference between the query and its translated images are relatively small, the translated images should still be ranked higher among the retrieved image.

In our current experiments, similarities between codewords/bins are ignored. We believe that the effect of small changes in images on image retrieval performance and VQ histogram will be even smaller when similarities between codewords are considered. We will investigate this further.

---

[1] QBIC is a trade mark of IBM.

4 Conclusion

Our work shows that in practice, the VQ scheme is capable of retrieving images that only differ from their query by a slight translation. It also shows that its retrieval performance is also better compared to the colour histogram method used in QBIC, before and after adding shifted images into the database. Thus, the proposed VQ based method is a robust image indexing and retrieval scheme.

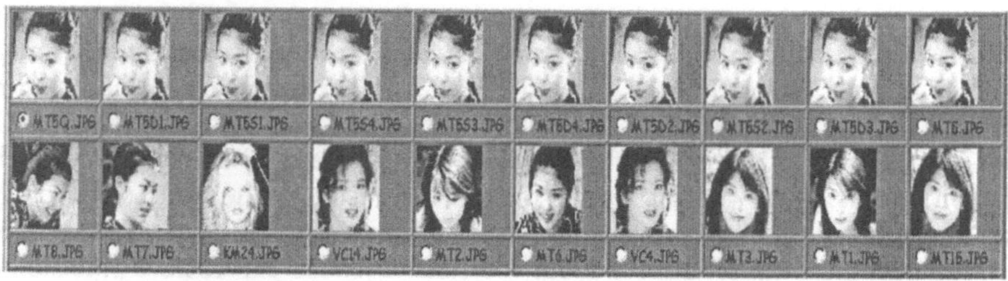

Fig. 4. An example of VQ based retrieval result of query image "MT5Q.JPG"

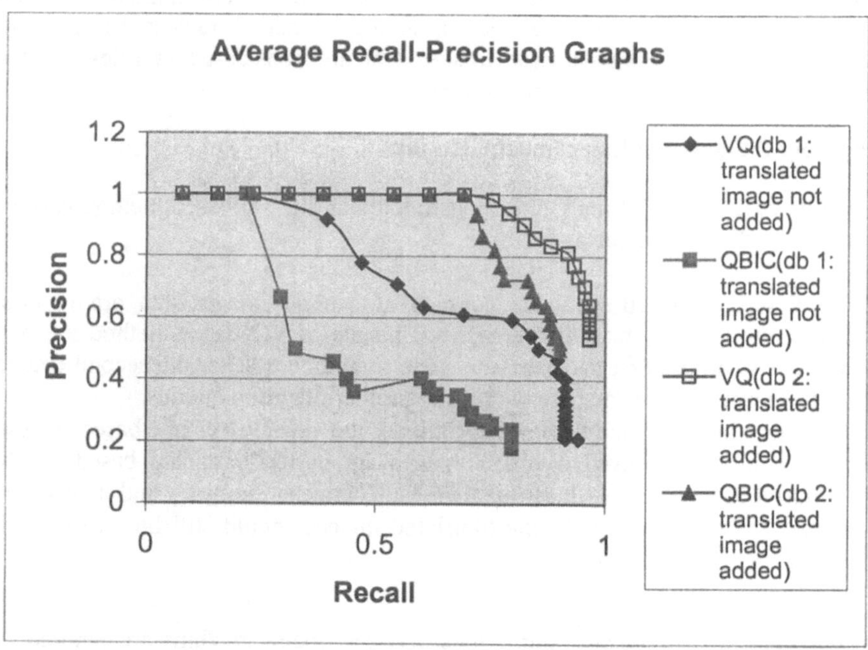

Fig. 5. Performance comparison among VQ-based and QBIC

References

[1] Y. Gong, H. Zhang and C. Chuan, "An image database system with fast image indexing capability based on colour histograms", Proceedings of IEEE 10's Ninth Annual International Conference, Singapore, 22-26 August 1994, pp.407-411.

[2] S. K. Chan, Content-based Image Retrieval, MSc thesis, National University of Singapore, 1994.

[3] M. J. Swain and D. H. Ballard, "Color indexing", Int. J. Comput. Vision, 7:11-32. 1991.

[4] G. D. Finlayson, Colour Object Recognition, MSc Thesis, Simon Fraser University, 1992.

[5] W. Niblack et al, "QBIC Project: querying images by content, using colour, texture, and shape" Proceedings of Conference on Storage and Retrieval for Image and Video Databases, 1-3 Feb. 1993, San Jose, California, US, SPIE Vol. 1908, pp.1908-1920.

[6] V.D. Lecce and A. Guerriero, "An elvalution of the effectiveness of image features for image retrieval", Journal of Visual Communication and Image Representation 10, 1999, pp. 351-362.

[7] G. Lu and S. Teng, "A Novel Image Retrieval Technique based on Vector Quantization", Computational S. Intelligence for Modeling Control and Automation, February 1999, Australia, pp.36-41.

[8] S. Teng and G. Lu, "Performance study of image retrieval based on vector quantization", ICCIMADE'01: International Conference on Intelligent Multimedia and Distance Education Conference, 1-3 June 2001, Fargo, ND, USA.

[9] W. Niblack et al, "QBIC Project: querying images by content, using colour, texture, and shape" Proceedings of Conference on Storage and Retrieval for Image and Video Databases, 1-3 Feb. 1993, San Jose, California, US, SPIE Vol. 1908, pp.1908-1920.

[10] QBIC Home Page, http://wwwqbic.almaden.ibm.com/

[11] G. Salton, Introduction to Mordern Information Retrieval, McGraw-Hill Book Company, 1983.

[12] G. Lu and A. Sajjanhar, "On performance measurement of multimedia information retrieval systems", International Conference on Computational Intelligence and Multimedia Applications, 9-11 Feb. 1998, Monash University, pp.781-787.

[13] M.J.Swain, "Interactive indexing into image database", Proceedings of Conference on Storage Retrieval Image Video Databases, W, 1-3 Feb. 1993, San Jose, California, US, SPIE Vol. 1908.

Search for Multi-modality Data in Digital Libraries

Jun Yang [1] Yueting Zhuang [1] Qing Li [2]

[1] Microsoft Visual Perception Laboratory of Zhejiang University
Hangzhou, 310027, China
i_jyang@yahoo.com yzhuang@cs.zju.edu.cn
[2] Department of Computer Science, City University of Hong Kong
Kowloon, HKSAR, China
csqli@cs.cityu.edu.hk

ABSTRACT. Developing effective and efficient retrieval techniques for multimedia data is a challenging issue in building a digital library. Unlike most previously proposed retrieval approaches that focus on a specific media type, this paper presents *2M2Net* as a generic framework for retrieval of multi-modality data in digital libraries. As its specific approaches, a learning-from-elements strategy is devised for propagation of semantic descriptions, and a cross media search mechanism with relevance feedback is proposed for evaluation and refinement of user queries. Experiments conducted on a digital encyclopedia manifest the effectiveness and flexibility of our approaches.

1. Introduction

Digital libraries are becoming the most complex and advanced form of information systems that are used to store, access, share and disseminate multimedia data of various types including text, image, audio and video. A challenging issue in building a digital library is to support effective and efficient retrieval of such multi-modality data in the whole library.

Currently, many digital library systems rely on text-based retrieval [5] technologies for retrieving information from the library. While such technologies could be tolerable for textual documents, they have limited applicability to digital libraries due to lack of effective means to specify queries for multimedia data. The problem is even amplified when the multimedia data are not well annotated. In contrast, content-based retrieval has been proposed to index and search multimedia data by their low-level features. This approach has been respectively adopted to image, video and audio retrieval [1][2]. Formulating a query in this approach is to create or select a representative media object as query example and search for other objects that resemble to it in terms of low-level features, denoted as query-by-example. However, the performance of this approach is very low when the low-level features of the multimedia data cannot be readily mapped to their semantics.

Not surprisingly, most approaches currently available for multimedia retrieval are dedicated to a certain media type and thus inapplicable to a digital library that contains multi-modality data. Moreover, there are great constraints on the means by which a user can formulate his/her query. A user must know clearly which media type to search for, and has an appropriate retrieval example to express the query. However, this is very inconvenient and inflexible in the context of a digital library. Quite often, a user may have only a vague idea of his/her information need, or has no appropriate query example at hand that can be used to express the information need.

To address the limitations of the current retrieval technologies, we propose a seamless integration framework, *2M2Net*, for retrieval of multi-modality data in digital libraries. It features a learning-from-elements strategy for propagation of the semantic descriptions, as well as a cross media search mechanism with relevance feedback that is tailored to multi-modality data. High-level semantics and low-level features are integrated during the retrieval process towards high retrieval performance. Within this framework, user queries can be (re-) formulated in a flexible and convenient way. Finally, a retrieval system using the proposed framework has been built on a digital encyclopedia. This framework distinguishes from the previous retrieval systems, such as QBIC[2] for image retrieval and VideoQ[1] for video retrieval, in that it support retrieval of multi-modality data, as well as employ an integration approach to enhance the retrieval performance.

This paper is organized as follows. In Section 2, we present the architectural framework of *2M2Net.* Two specific approaches of the framework are described in Section 3. In Section 4 we present the implementation issues and the experimental evaluations of the system. Conclusion and future works are given in Section 5.

2. The Architectural Framework

Our proposed framework does not simply put together the existing retrieval methods specific to each media type in order to handle multi-modality data. Instead, it fully explores the semantic correlation existed among various media objects in a digital library to enhance the retrieval performance. It is named as *2M2Net* due to our intension to model the multi-modality (the first "2M"), multimedia data (the second "2M") in a digital library as a *Net*work at the semantic layer.

A digital library can be viewed as a collection of *multimedia documents*[1], which is recursively defined as a logical document consisting of several elements that are multimedia documents by themselves or individual media objects such as text, image, video and audio. Each document has a semantic subject that is applicable to all of its elements. The concrete forms of multimedia document include web page(s), a portion of encyclopedia and other forms of multimedia data collection.

The framework of *2M2Net* is illustrated in Figure 1. Multimedia documents are firstly pre-processed so that their various elements are extracted out and stored into the corresponding databases in the *Storage Subsystem.* In *2M2Net,* a multimedia document *D* is represented by means of its semantic skeleton, S^D= *(ID, Title, URL, Keyword-list, Element-set)*, where *Keyword-list* is a list of weighted keywords describing the document semantics, and *Element-set = (Texts, Images, Videos, Audios, ...)* is a set of component media objects. Each media object is represented by its low-level features and semantics as descriptive keywords, e.g., *Image* =

---

[1] If not indicated explicitly, document is referred to multimedia document in this paper.

(Keyword-list, Image-features). In the pre-processing phase, the semantics and low-level features of each media object are extracted. The semantics of text object is directly extracted from itself using the traditional IR techniques. For non-textual objects such as image and video, the semantics can be obtained from the accompanying textual descriptions (e.g. surrounding text, captions, HTML tags), depending on the specific form of the document. The extracted features and semantics are stored into semantic skeleton base to construct the initial semantics skeleton.

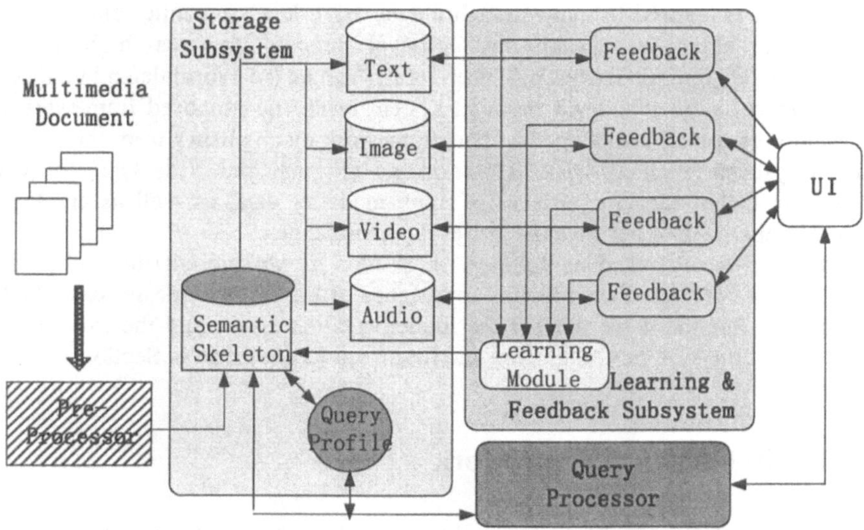

Fig. 1. The *2M2Net* Framework

User query is processed based on semantic skeleton by the *Query Processor*, which conducts a cross-media search to retrieve relevant documents or media objects. This mechanism allows a simple keyword-based search to induce a suite of more sophisticated content-based retrievals to be conducted. User feedback is accepted and handled by the *Feedback & Learning Subsystem*. It conducts a parallel session of relevance feedback on each media type to improve the retrieval results immediately. Meanwhile, a learning-from-element process is performed to propagate descriptive keywords among semantically related documents and media objects, which is likely to enhance the retrieval performance in a long term. The *Query Profile* is designed (but not implemented) to expedite and optimize the retrieval process by memorizing the history of complex queries previously processed and their resolutions.

3. The Specific Approaches

In this section, we describe two key approaches employed by the proposed framework, which are learning-from-elements strategy and cross-media search mechanism with relevance feedback.

3.1 Learning-from-Elements

In practice, the initial semantics acquired for documents and their elements in the pre-processing phase are imprecise, insufficient or even non-existing. In view of this, we devise a machine learning strategy, learning-from-element, to supplement their semantics by propagating descriptive keywords among them. It is triggered whenever a user marks a set of the documents and media objects as feedback examples for a given set of query keywords. As illustrated in Figure 2, there are four directions in which keyword propagation can take place: from user query to feedback examples as documents or media objects (type A), from a document to its elements (type B), from a media object to its parent document (type C) and from a media object to visually similar ones of the same media type (type D).

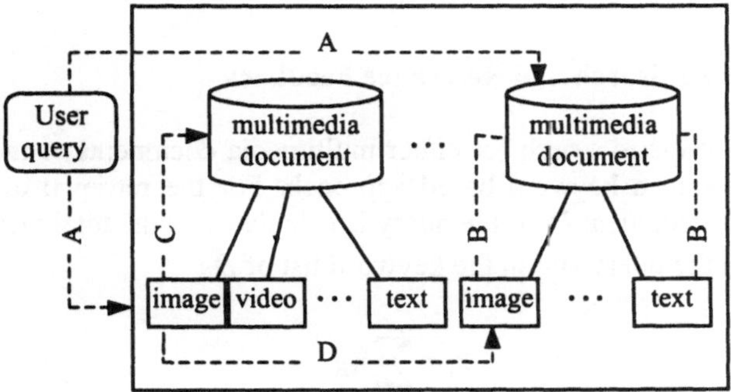

Fig. 2. Keyword Propagation Scheme

Propagation from the query to the feedback examples (type A) serves as the starting point of the whole learning process. Its mechanism is described as follows. For a positive example, we add each query keyword into its keyword list. If the query keyword is already in the list, its weight is increased by a certain step. For a negative example, if there is any query keyword is in its keyword list, we remove it from there. By conducting this propagation for each feedback example, the semantics of these documents and media objects are implicitly learnt from users. Also, the representative keywords with a majority of user consensus are likely to receive a large weight.

Propagation types B and C are more ambitious schemes that utilize the semantic correlation among the elements of a document. If the positive example is a media object, the keywords inserted or updated (in term of weights) by type A are further propagated to its parent document (type B); otherwise if the positive example is a document, some of its keywords are pass to its elements (type C). Both propagations are carried out with great care to avoid spreading erroneous keywords. Currently, we apply a simple verification process by examining if each keyword to be propagated is the one with largest weight in the keyword list. The top keyword is likely to represent the actual semantics of the document/object and therefore qualified for further propagation. The negative examples are not considered for such propagations, lest correct keywords to be removed from other documents/objects by erroneous propagation. Both schemes are particularly advantageous when users are reluctant to give many feedbacks, since they can spread the query keywords to more documents or media objects including those that are not designated as feedback examples. A likely concern of using these two schemes is the tradeoff between a wide coverage of keywords and the possible erroneous keywords. We argue that a rich set of keywords (perhaps imperfect) is more desirable than a small set of precise keywords for retrieval purpose, and erroneous keywords are easy to identify and correct.

Type D is applied each time a new image or video is registered into the system. Considering the difficulty of extracting semantics for such non-textual object, this scheme attempts to make some guesses of its semantics based on low-level features. That is, for each new image or video, a content-based search is performed to find other images or videos that visually resemble it. The keywords collected from the top *N* matches are inserted into the keyword list of the new object. Evidently, due to the inherent limitation of low-level features, this scheme is very unreliable.

3.2 Cross Media Search and Relevance Feedback

2M2Net allow users to search for either multimedia documents or media objects of a certain type, using a keyword-based approach. For the retrieval of documents, the similarity R_i of document D_i to the query is calculated as the total weight of keywords coexist both in the query and in the keyword list of D_i:

$$R_i = \sum_{k=1}^{M} w_{ik} \tag{1}$$

where M is the number of common keywords between D_i and the query, w_{ik} is the weight of the *k*th such keyword of D_i. All the candidate documents are compared with the query and ranked in the descending order of their similarity. The retrieval of media objects can be processed in a similar way.

Since the keyword descriptions are insufficient initially, the matches returned by the keyword-based search can be quite limited. In this case, a suite of more sophisticated keyword- or content-based search is triggered intending to find more promising candidates. If the query is for documents, an exhaustive keyword search is conducted. That is, for each unmatched document, we merge the keywords of all its elements and re-evaluate the similarity by comparing the query against this combined keyword list. Otherwise if the query is for a specific media, we conduct a content-based search to find more media objects that are visually similar to top match retrieved in the keyword-based search. The documents or media objects obtained in this second-pass search are ranked behind the matches of the keyword-based search.

The system proceeds to the feedback phase when the user marks a set of documents or media objects as feedback examples. The feedback process is carried out based on the high-level semantics as well as on the low-level features. At the semantic level, the learning-from-elements strategy described in Section 3.1 is applied to propagate the keywords among the involved documents or media objects. At the feature level, certain content-based relevance feedback technique is used according to the media type of the feedback examples. Currently, we use the feedback technique proposed by Rui [4] for images, and that proposed by Wu [6] for videos. However, any other feedback techniques can be easily incorporated into this framework.

We then reevaluate the retrieval results based on the improved semantics and feature representation (weights). A hybrid approach of semantics- and feature-based relevance feedback is proposed by Lu et al. [3] for image retrieval. We generalize this method to accommodate all kinds of media. It is formulated as a uniform distance metric function that measures the similarity between a media object and the query:

$$S_i = \alpha R_i + \beta\left\{\frac{1}{N_R}\sum_{k\in O_R}[(1+R_{ik})S_{ik}]\right\} - \gamma\left\{\frac{1}{N_N}\sum_{k\in O_N}[(1+R_{ik})S_{ik}]\right\} \quad (2)$$

where α, β and γ are suitable constants, O_R and O_N are set of relevant and irrelevant media objects of a certain type, N_R and N_N are the number of objects in O_R and O_N. R_i is the semantic similarity between the *i*th candidate object and the initial query defined in (1). R_{ik} is the similarity between the *i*th object and the *k*th positive/negative feedback example, which is also calculated using (1). S_{ik} is the their similarity on the low-level features. For textual object that has no low-level features, S_{ik} is set to 1. This function can be adapted to multimedia document, by regarding O_R and O_N as the relevant and irrelevant document collections and setting each S_{ik} to 1. Therefore, we can adopt (2) to calculate the improved retrieval results as either media objects of a specific type or the whole documents.

4 Implementation and Experiments

To show the effectiveness of the proposed framework, a prototype system using this framework has been established for multimedia retrieval in a digital encyclopedia.

Fig. 3. The query results of multimedia documents

The system consists of a back-end and a front-end. The back-end is responsible for the processing, storage, authoring and retrieval of multimedia data. The front-end is a web-accessible interface that handles all user-system interactions. The main user interface is as shown in Figure 3, which displays the relevant documents retrieved for the query of “water”. A multimedia document is visualized as its sketch, i.e. abstracts for text, thumbnails for images and key-frame lists for videos. The keyword search can be aimed at a certain media type as well. In addition to the keyword-based search paradigm, the user can perform a content-based search using a specific media object as the query example by clicking on the “Similar” link below it. Each document or media object has a “ ” and a “×” icon attached to it, denoting positive and negative example respectively. The user can indicate feedback examples by clicking on them and then press the “Feedback” button to activate the feedback process.

Some simple experiments are conducted to show the effectiveness of the system. The test data are collected from Microsoft Encarta Interactive World Atlas 2000, as a part of the Encarta Encyclopedia. The “World Tour” part of the atlas has 19 categories, with each category being further divided into several topics (totally 160 topics). Each topic usually has several images, text paragraphs and sometimes a video clip in it. We regard each topic as a multimedia document and manually feed its media objects into the system. The initial semantics are obtained from the title of category and topic (for document), and from the caption (for image and video).

In the experiments, we input some keywords to search for multimedia documents and perform feedbacks by marking relevant documents as positive examples. It is noticed that after an average of 4 iterations, the query keywords are spread from the involved documents to 90% of their elements, along with a remarkable rise of retrieval performance. A similar experiment is conducted on a specific media such as image, which shows that the keywords can be also efficiently propagated from media objects to their parent document.

A performance evaluation in terms of precision and recall is not conducted for two reasons. First, a ground-truth database indispensable to performance evaluation is very hard to construct, since most digital libraries are not well annotated, indexed or classified. In addition, considering the variety of search and feedback options supported by the system, a survey has to be made to study the user behaviors of posting queries and giving feedbacks. However, such a survey requires the help from a large number of human subjects, which is not currently available to us.

5 Conclusion and Future Work

In this paper, we have presented a novel framework of *2M2Net* for retrieval of multi-modality data in digital libraries. As its specific approaches, the learning-from-elements strategy is devised for interactive propagation of keyword descriptions, and the cross media search mechanism with relevance feedback is proposed for evaluation and refinement of user queries. The major contribution of our work is providing a generic framework for retrieval of multi-modality data, instead of any specific retrieval technique dedicated to a certain media. This framework is general and open enough to accommodate other media types (such as audio), or incorporate any retrieval or feedback algorithm specific to each media type.

However, the current design of *2M2Net* still has its weaknesses and limitations, some of which are identified as follows:

- *The system does not support browsing or navigation of multimedia data.* As popular user behaviors, the user should be able to browse multimedia documents by subject categories, or navigate from one document to related ones. However, the current design does not include the concept of subject category, nor does it track the links between documents or objects through which user can navigate.
- *The feature-level relevance feedback has no memory.* While the semantic-level feedback remembers the history by progressive propagation of keywords, the feature-level feedback technique discards the optimized feature weights in the previous query sessions and starts from scratch in the future queries. It thus makes no contribution to the long-term retrieval performance, which can be otherwise improved progressively by remembering the optimized feature weights.

We also propose the following foreseeable future works:

- *Using lexical thesaurus to define semantic similarity metric.* The semantic similarity metric based on exact keyword match cannot address the relevancy between different keywords. A thesaurus-based semantic similarity metric can overcome this problem and therefore improve the retrieval accuracy.
- *Constructing query profile.* The query file intends to memorize the history of some complex queries as a sequence of user-system interaction, as well as the resolutions to them. The next time a similar query is encountered, the results can be directly deduced from the query profile without exhaustively searching the whole library, thereby optimize and expedite the retrieval process.
- *Exploiting link analysis.* Structural and semantic links between multimedia documents widely exist in a digital library, indicated by either structural neighborhood or hyperlinks. These link structures can be analyzed off-line to deduce the semantics of non-textual media objects, or explored on-line during the retrieval process as a cue of relevancy between media objects

References

1 Chang, S. F., Chen, W., Meng, H. J., Sundaram, H., Zhong, D., "VideoQ: An Automated Content Based Video Search System Using Visual Cues", ACM Multimedia, 1997.

2 Flickner, M., Sawhney, H., Niblack, W., Ashley, J., "Query by image and video content: The QBIC system." *IEEE Computer*, 1995.

3 Lu, Y. et al, "A Unified Framework for Semantics and Feature Based Relevance Feedback in Image Retrieval Systems", ACM Multimedia, 2000.

4 Rui, Y., et al, "Relevance Feedback: A Power Tool for Interactive Content-based Image Retrieval", *IEEE Trans. on Circuits and Video Technology,* 1998.

5 Salton, G., Buckley, C. "Introduction to Modern Information Retrieval", McGraw-Hill Book Company, New York, 1982.

6 Wu, Y., Zhuang, Y. T., Pan, Y. H., "Relevance Feedback of Video Retrieval", in Proc. of the first IEEE Pacific Rim Conference on Multimedia, pp 206-209, December, 2000.

Compressed Domain Summarization of Digital Video

C.M. Chew[1] and M.S. Kankanhalli[1]

[1] School of Computing, National University of Singapore
{chewchor, mohan}@comp.nus.edu.sg

Abstract. Video data is usually voluminous and it is desirable that one be able to get a quick idea of the content before actually watching a video or downloading it from the web. In this paper, we present a video summarization algorithm that works in the compressed domain, in particular MPEG videos. The algorithm is based on an existing one used in the uncompressed domain. To adapt it for MPEG videos, we make use of a feature known as DC histogram that can be extracted from MPEG videos without full decompression. A video summarizer based on our algorithm is implemented and experiments are conducted to examine its effectiveness. Results show that the summarizer performs quite well to user expectations.

1 Introduction

With the recent and rapid advances in multimedia technology and computing power, digital video is increasingly becoming a popular and valuable information resource. However, the sheer amount of data in a video when compared with other forms of media such as text and audio makes management and manipulation very difficult. To reduce the amount of storage needed, most video clips are compressed into a smaller size using a compression standard such as MPEG [1, 2].

However, even after going through compression, compressed videos are still too big to transfer over general-purpose networks such as the Internet. Even if a user has a complete video clip, he or she may just want to view a summary of the video instead of watching it from the beginning till the end. Thus browsing and summarization tools that would allow the user to quickly get an idea of the overall content of the video footage are very useful. This functionality will become very important in the coming years when TV broadcasts worldwide will be done in a fully digital format.

Much of the research work done on video summarization methods has only focused on the uncompressed domain [3]-[7]. They cannot be used directly on compressed videos such as MPEG files. An MPEG video will have to be decompressed back to its original uncompressed form before the summarization can be performed. This is very time consuming and requires a huge amount of space, which defeats the original purpose of compressing videos. Moreover recompression back to compressed form after summarization may result in loss of picture quality due to re-quantization.

In this paper, we propose a video summarization algorithm that operates directly in the compressed domain. The algorithm uses an adaptive clustering method that has been employed in the uncompressed domain. This clustering method does not rely on shot detection techniques which most of the previous work, e.g. [8]-[10], have been based on. We also show how to extract a feature from MPEG videos without full frame decompression such that the feature still captures the essential information of the video frames.

2 Summarization Algorithm

2.1 Clustering Method

The main aim of our summarizer is to analyze a given video clip and extract the important frames that reflect the content changes of the video. We call these important frames *representative frames (R-frames)*. Since it is still not possible today for computers to understand the semantics of video images, we will base our summarizer on low-level features such as color, motion, etc. However, we do not assume that all low-level features change somewhat abruptly at shot boundaries. Instead we will use a clustering method to remove redundant frames and retain the important frames. In particular, we will extend an earlier work [7] and apply the technique described in that paper to compressed domain videos.

The nature of the spatial distribution of the points corresponding to video frames can be described as clusters connected by abrupt or gradual changes. So it is possible to divide a video V into N' clusters. We call these clusters *units*. If we represent frame 1 of all the units' representative frames using R_{p1} to $R_{pN'}$, V can then be described as:

$$V = U_1 \circ U_2 \circ \ldots \circ U_{N'}$$

where

- $U_i = \{ R_{pi}, R_{pi1}, \ldots, R_{p(i+1)} \}, \ i \in [1, N']$
- $\circ$ is the temporal concatenation operation

Since the units are in temporal order, we can define the unit change as the difference between two consecutive representative frames, i.e.

$$Change(U_i) = D(R_{pi}, R_{p(i+1)})$$

In order to extract good representative frames, we should aim to divide the video into units that have very similar unit changes. This can be described as to minimize:

$$\sum_{i=1}^{N'-1} \sum_{j=i+1}^{N'-1} \left| Change(U_i) - Change(U_j) \right|$$

By having units that have very similar unit changes, we are actually dividing the videos into individual sections whose length corresponds to the amount of content changes within the particular section. For example, a high action scene is usually divided into more units than a relatively static scene since the content of the high action scene changes much quicker. This concept is what we will base our clustering algorithm on.

Our clustering algorithm works in an iterative fashion. We start initially with all the frames of the video and iteratively drop frames until the desired result is obtained. For a given video V with length N, suppose we want to extract N' representative frames. The feature of each frame in V is computed first. Then the video is partitioned in small units whose lengths are all L. All the units are temporally contiguous. For example, Figure 1 shows the partitioning with L=2 and L=3. So the units for L=3 are {(0,1,2), (2,3,4), (4,5,6), (6,7,8)}. In each unit, the unit change is computed, which is the distance between the first frame and the last frame of the unit.

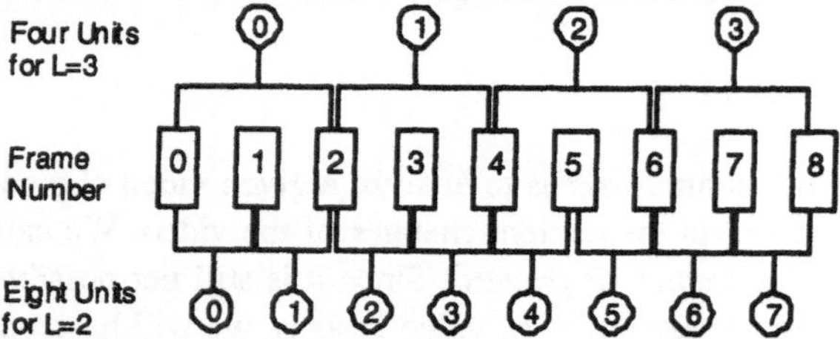

Figure 1: Partitioning a Video into Units

After all the unit changes are computed, these values will form an array of length $K=\lceil N/(L-1)\rceil$. Because our objective is to extract representative frames according to frame content changes, the values in the array do reflect the actual degree of content change in all the units. The values are then sorted in ascending order. After sorting, the elements that are located at the beginning represent the frames where there are small changes, while the units in the later part consist of frames having large changes.

By selecting a ratio $0<r<1$, we cluster the array into two clusters according to the value of unit change. The first cluster comprises of the smallest elements of the array and its length is K^*r. We call this cluster the *small-change cluster*. The rest of the elements comprise the *large-change cluster*.

If the change of a unit belongs to the large-change cluster, we take all of its frames as part of the current extracted representative frames. If the change of a unit belongs to the small-change cluster, then we delete all the frames except the first and the last from the unit. The first and the last frames are retained as part of the current extracted representative frames. After the deletion process, $K^*r^*(L-2)$ frames will be deleted.

Suppose the number of frames left is N". If N' is greater than or equal to N" then we have achieved the desired result and we can stop the algorithm. If not, we regroup all the retained frames as a new video and repeat the last procedure. With the decrease in the number of frames after each iteration, small units are consequently clustered together. A unit will physically span across more frames in the original video. So it will represent a larger range of frame changes. Frames are deleted from the sequence after each iterative process, so the overall number of frames left will decrease each time. Therefore, no matter how small a number may be required, the algorithm will converge to the desired requirement.

Another characteristic of the clustering method is that it is general, i.e. it can use any low-level content as a feature to calculate the difference between two frames in a video. For example, the feature could be color, motion, shape or texture. The feature used in our summarizer is discussed in the next section.

After extraction of representative frames from a video, users can make use of a browsing tool that provides interactive functions for traversal between these frames. However this process requires a lot of feedback between the user and the computer, since thousands of representative frames can be generated for an hour of video. This may be too time consuming for some users and therefore, a grazing view is preferred in this case, i.e. a video summary is generated from the representative frames which the user will view in order to get a general idea about the original video.

One way of generating the summary is to output the representative frames sequentially to a new video. However, this approach is not really useful because when the summary is played at the normal frame rate, users will find it very difficult to grasp information from it. This is because the pace of the summary will be too fast and jerky. To solve this problem, *representative sequences (R-sequences)* are used. An R-sequence consists of a representative frame plus its several successive frames. The length of the following frames is called the *smoothing factor S*. From experiments, it has been found that the smoothing factor has to be greater than or equal to 5 in order to obtain a visually pleasing result.

2.2 Feature Extraction

In order to work directly on an MPEG video, we need to find a feature with these properties: 1) it can be extracted efficiently from the video; and 2) it can capture the essence of each video frame such that analysis can still be carried out without much error. In this paper, we will utilize a feature known as DC histogram that is based on the DC image proposed by B.L. Yeo and Bede Liu [11].

The compression of MPEG video is carried out by dividing each frame of the video into 8x8 pixel blocks. The pixels in the blocks are transformed into 64 coefficients using Discrete Cosine Transform. The DC term $c(0,0)$ is related to the pixel values $f(i,j)$ via the following equation:

$$c(0,0) = \frac{1}{8} \sum_{x=0}^{7} \sum_{y=0}^{7} f(x,y)$$

In other words, the value of the DC term is 8 times the average intensity of the pixel block. If we extract the DC term and subsequently the average intensity of all the blocks in an image, we can use the average values to form a reduced version of the original image. This smaller image is known as the DC image.

Although the size of the DC image is only 1/64 of that of the original image, it still retains significant amount of information. This suggests that scene operations of a global nature originally performed on the original image can also be applied on the DC image.

For the sake of efficiency, we will only consider luminance blocks when forming the DC image. This is because the eye is sensitive to small changes in luminance, but not in chrominance. Thus we can discard the chrominance information without affecting the quality of the extracted DC image much.

It is trivial to extract a DC image from an I-frame in MPEG since all blocks are intra-coded. The average intensity of each block is 1/8 the DC-coefficient of that block. However, extracting DC images from P and B frames involves more effort as motion compensation and differential coding are used in these frames.

To obtain the DC coefficients of a P frame, we need to use the coefficients in the reference I or P frame. This is illustrated in Figure 2. Consider the current block in a new P frame. This block can be reconstructed from the information in the reference block in a previous I or P frame referred to by the motion vector. Thus, by using the DC coefficients of P1, P2, P3, and P4, the DC coefficient of the current block, D_c, can be reconstructed by

$$D_c = \frac{1}{64}\sum_{i=1}^{4}[DC(P_i)]_{00} w_i h_i + e$$

where $[DC(P_i)]_{00}$ refers to the DC coefficient of the block Pi and e is an error term. In practice, e is found to be small and thus the first term is a good enough approximation of the desired DC coefficient.

Figure 2: Determining DC coefficient of a P frame

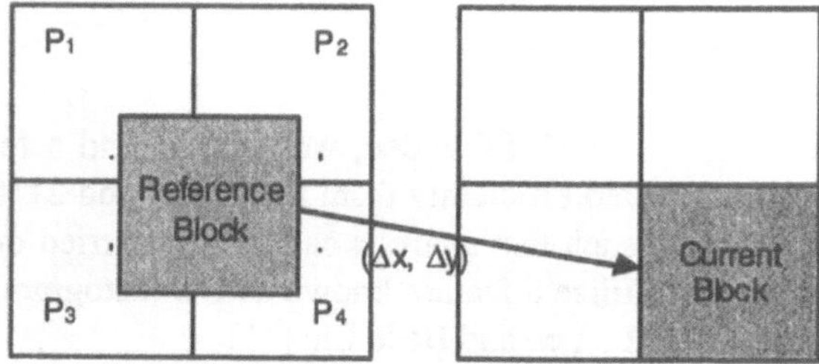

The same technique can also be applied to B frames which are forward-only or backward-only predicted. For bi-directional frames, two DC coefficients are first obtained in each prediction direction and the final coefficient value is the average of the two.

Although DC images are 1/64 the size of the original video frame size, they are uncompressed and thus takes up a substantial amount of space. For example, a DC image for a 320 x 240 video frame will occupy 40 x 30 = 1200 bytes. Assuming a frame rate of 30 fps, the total amount of space required for a 2 hour video is 1200 x 30 x 60 x 60 x 2 = 247.2 MB. This number will be even larger for higher resolution videos such as DVD and Digital TV.

To reduce the amount of data to be processed, we will use a DC histogram as the feature for each frame instead of the DC image. The histogram will be divided into 64 bins, i.e. each bin will account for 4 luminance values. Since luminance values ranges from 0 (black) to 255 (white), we can assume that this range is linear and thus values close together are similar. The cost of computing the histogram is very low and each frame now only takes up 64 x 2 = 128 bytes (assuming a 16-bit integer is used for the value of each histogram bin) regardless of the frame size. So a 2 hour video will only occupy 128 x 30 x 60 x 60 x 2 = 26.4 MB, a figure that average computers nowadays can handle quite easily. To calculate the difference between two histograms, the sum of the absolute bin-to-bin difference is taken.

3 Experimental Results

Evaluating the quality of a video summary is difficult as the factors to consider are highly complex and difficult to quantify computationally. Some methods based on shot detection have used the number of shots detected as their metric. However, as our algorithm is not based on shot detection, this metric cannot be used for our summarizer. Since there is no absolute measure of summarization quality available today, we decide to measure the quality of our summaries by user questioning.

For the experiment, we used 10 persons as our test subjects. Three video summaries generated using our summarizer were used as the test videos. Information about the summaries is shown in Table 1. P refers to the summarization percentage, L the unit length, r the clustering ratio and S the smoothing factor applied.

Video	Genre	Original Length	Summarization Parameters	Summary Length
A	Movie	1h 59m 34s	P=1.5%, L=5, r=0.3, S=5	5m 10s
B	News	21m 20s	P=2%, L=12, r=0.3, S=20	2m 17s
C	Movie	2h 28m 32s	P=0.2%, L=11, r=0.3, S=20	1m 51s

Table 1: Details of Video Clips used for User Evaluation

Before viewing the video summaries, the test subjects were given some information about each summary such as the genre and the aim of the summary. After viewing each summary, each person was then asked to rate the summary in four categories (Clarity, Conciseness, Coherence and Overall Quality) on a scale of 1 to 7, corresponding to worst and best respectively. At the end of the questionnaire, the person is then requested to rate the automatically generated summaries against their opinions of human-generated ones. Table 2 shows the average scores of the evaluation exercise.

Video	Clarity	Conciseness	Coherence	Overall Quality
A	5.2	5.7	4.8	5.3
B	6.0	6.2	5.8	6.0
C	5.2	5.2	5.2	5.2
Average	5.5	5.7	5.3	5.5

Table 2: Results of User Evaluation

From the table, we can see that on the whole, the summaries performed quite well with scores of over 5 in all but one category. Looking at the performance of each individual summary, Video A scored highly in conciseness but got the lowest coherence score among the three videos. This is expected since the aim of the summary is to portray the complete story of the original video as much as possible to the viewer within the 5 minutes. The smoothing factor has to be set to a relatively low value of 5 in order to keep the length of the summary within the desired length. This results in a certain degree of choppiness when viewing the video, thus affecting the coherence score.

Video B scored the highest in all categories. A news programme usually cycles between the news presenter and the video footage of the story currently presented. The luminance difference between these two kinds of scenes is usually quite large, so our video summarizer was able to extract all the segments in the programme. Coupled with the fact that a large smoothing factor of 20 was used, the resultant summary was very clear and smooth flowing.

Video C's score was the same for all the categories. Since the aim of this summary is to give a general idea of the movie's content rather than portraying the whole plot (which is the case for the summary of Video A), the parameters used for summarization (smaller percentage, larger unit size and smoothing factor) were different from those used for Video A. Therefore, the amount of content covered is less (accounting for the lower conciseness score) but the summary is more fluid (accounting for the higher coherence score).

The last question of the survey asked the viewer to rate the automatically generated summaries against their opinions of human-generated ones. The average score for this question is 5.00 (out of a maximum of 7), which means that the users agree to a limited extent that the quality of the summaries is comparable to that of human-generated ones. This is quite a good score for an automated summarizer. Since our summarizer is still based on a low-level feature, it is expected that the automatically generated summaries are still inferior to human-generated summaries that are based on semantics.

4 Summary

We have presented a video summarization algorithm that operates directly in the compressed domain (MPEG videos) without employing shot detection techniques. We extract the DC histogram feature from each frame of the MPEG video and use it together with an adaptive clustering method to extract representative frames to form the summary. User surveys conducted have shown encouraging results.

An area for further investigation is the use of other features such as motion vectors. We have explained that our clustering method is general, i.e. it can use any low-level content of a video as the feature for summarization. Therefore it would be interesting to study how different features affect the quality of summarization and the effectiveness of these features in the various genres of video.

References

[1] ISO/IEC 11172-2, Coding of Moving Pictures and Associated Audio for Digital Storage Media at up to about 1.5 Mbit/s, Part 2: Video.

[2] ISO/IEC 13818-2, Generic Coding of Moving Pictures and Associated Audio Information, Part 2: Video.

[3] JungHwan Oh, Kien A. Hua, "An Efficient Technique for Summarizing Videos Using Visual Contents", *Multimedia and Expo, 2000. ICME 2000. IEEE International Conference, Vol. 2, pg 1167 – 1170, Jul 2000.*

[4] Yihong Gong, Xin Liu, "Generating Optimal Video Summaries", *Multimedia and Expo, 2000. ICME 2000. IEEE International Conference, Vol. 3, pg 1559 – 1562, Jul 2000.*

[5] D. DeMenthon, V. Kobla, D.Doermann, "Video Summarization by Curve Simplification", *Technical Report LAMP-TR-018, CS-TR-3916, University of Maryland, College Park, 1998.*

[6] Rainer Leinhart, Silvia Pfeiffer, Wolfgang Effelsberg, "Video Abstracting," *Communications of the ACM, Vol. 40, No. 12, Dec 1997.*

[7] X. Sun, M. Kankanhalli, "Video Summarization Using R-Sequences", *Journal of Real-Time Imaging, Vol. 6, No. 6, pp. 449-459, Dec 2000.*

[8] N. Gamaz, X. Huang, S. Panchanathan, "Scene Change Detection in MPEG Domain", *Image Analysis and Interpretation, IEEE Southwest Symposium, pg 12 – 17, Apr 1998.*

[9] Ali M Dawood, Mohammed Ghanbari, "Clear Scene Cut Detection Directly from MPEG Bit Streams", *IEEE Image Processing and its Applications, No. 465, Vol. 1, pg 285 – 289, Jul 1999.*

[10] Jongho Nang, Seungwook Hong, Youngin Ihm, "An Efficient Video Segmentation Scheme for MPEG Video Stream using Macroblock Information", *7th ACM international conference on Multimedia, pg 23 – 26, Oct 1999.*

[11] B. L. Yeo and B. Liu, "Rapid Scene Analysis on Compressed Video," *IEEE Transactions on Circuits and Systems for Video Technology, Vol. 5, No. 6, Dec 1995.*

[12] H.S. Chang, S. Sull, and S.U. Lee, "Efficient Video Indexing Scheme for Content-based Retrieval", *IEEE Transactions on Circuits and Systems for Video Technology, Vol. 9, No. 8, pp. 1269-1279, Dec 1999.*

[13] A. Hanjalic and H.J. Zhang, "An Integrated Scheme for Automatic Video Abstraction Scheme Based on Unsupervised Cluster-validity Analysis", *IEEE Transactions on Circuits and Systems for Video Technology, Vol. 9, No. 8, pp. 1280-1289, Dec 1999.*

Automatic Segmentation of News Items Based on Video and Audio Features

Weiqiang Wang   Wen Gao

Institute of Computing Technology, Chinese Academy of Sciences, Beijing , China, 100080
Email: {wqwang, wgao}@ict.ac.cn

Abstract. In the paper, we present an approach that exploits audio and video features to automatically segment news items. Integration of audio and visual analysis can overcome the weakness of the approach only using the image analysis techniques. It brings our approach with more adaptation to variable existence situations of news items. The proposed approach identifies silence segments in accompanying audio, and integrates with shot segmentation results, as well as anchor shot detection results, to determine boundaries between news items. Experiments show that the integration of audio and video features is effective to solve the problem of automatic segmentation of news items.

1. Introduction

Most early studies in video structure analysis are based on visual information. To effectively index and retrieve video documents, they are segmented into scenes[1,2]. Furthermore, Shot boundaries are determined to characterize content details[3,4], and key frames are extracted to construct index[5,6].

Audio, as another time-dependent media in video documents, can supplement visual information, and supply a unique cue for video content analysis. For instance, in anchor shots of CCTV news, visual content is almost unchanged, but it is possible multiple news items are reported by anchorpersons synchronously. In a movie, a group of consecutive shots maybe differ drastically in visual content, but the accompanying music indicates they belong to the same semantic clip. Recently, more literatures proposed to apply audio analysis techniques in characterizing video content. [7] exploited multiple audio features and a neural net classifier to differentiate five classes of TV programs, including advertisement, basketball, football, news, weather. [8] proposed a heuristic rule-based approach for the segmentation and annotation of generic audio data. Audio recordings are segmented and classified into basic audio types such as silence, speech, music, environmental sound, etc. [9,10] combined audio and visual features to detect shot boundaries. Based on audio and visual features, [11] applied the HMM classifier to segmentation and classification of video scenes.

Automatic segmentation of news items is a significant research topic for implementing an automatic cataloging system of news video. That makes users browse video content quickly on the story level. Based on domain knowledge, [12] exploited image analysis techniques to automatically parse news video. The kernel of their system is the algorithm that locates and identifies anchorperson shots. Since they assume each news item starts with an anchor shot followed by a sequence of news shots, their system cannot identify the news items only read by anchorperson without news shots, and those starting without an anchorperson shot. The limitation cannot be overcome by only analyzing visual signals.

The paper presents an approach, which integrates audio and visual information to segment news items. It overcomes the limitation of the system aforementioned. First, silence segments in the audio channel are located. Then they are integrated with shot segmentation and anchor shot detection results from the visual channel, to determine the boundaries between news items.

The rest of the paper is organized as follows. Section 2 first overviews the whole system. Then follows a detailed description of the audio analysis algorithm, as well as the discussion of visual cues used. At the end of the section, an approach of news item extraction through multi-model information fusion is presented. In section 3, experiment results and analysis are given. Section 4 concludes the paper.

2. Segmentation of TV News Items

TV news usually has a very straightforward temporal syntax. Experience implies usually there is a relatively long silence between consecutive news items, and the synchronized video clip involves shot transitions. An exception is that in anchor shots the silence segment does not go with shot transitions. Based on the above observations, audio and visual analysis can be integrated to extract news items in TV news programs. Though commercials exist in some TV news, we assume some preprocessor has filtered them out here. The framework of the system is summarized in Fig. 1. The following sections will describe the modules further.

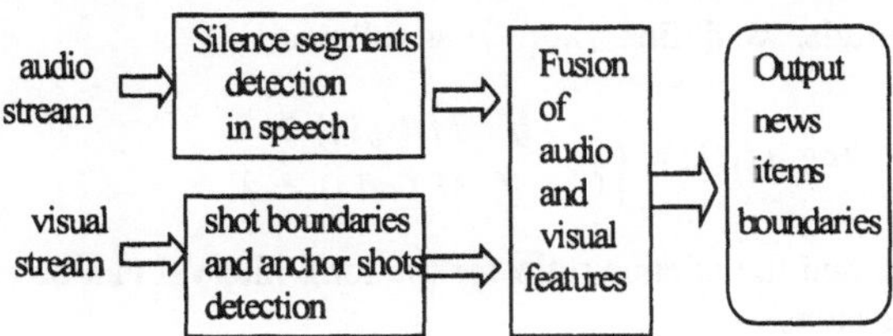

Fig. 1. The framework of our system

2.1 Detecting silence segments

International standard MPEG-1,2 exploit the perception-based high performance encoding schemes to compress audio. The standards specify three layers of encoding schemes for audio. Higher the layer is, more complex the encode/decode computation is, and higher compression ratio is obtained. Since audio in digital TV programs is commonly encoded with layer II, we assume the audio involved in the paper is also the case. The audio elementary stream consists of a sequence of audio frames. Each frame contains a fixed number of samples, such as 1152 samples for layer II. The short time average magnitude of each frame can be calculated using the following expression,

$$M_m = \frac{1}{N}\sum_{n=0}^{N-1}|x(n)| \tag{1}$$

where $x(n)$ is the nth sample value in the frame m, N is the number of samples in each frame. Since the synthesis of sub-band filtered data in decoding process of MPEG audio is a linear computation, the average magnitude can be approximated as the following expression,

$$M_m = \frac{1}{32*K}\sum_{i=0}^{32}\sum_{n=0}^{K-1}|s_i(n)| \tag{2}$$

where $s_i(n)$ is the nth sample of sub-band i, K gives the number of samples in each sub-band. If $M_m < \lambda$, then we consider the frame m is in the state of silence, where λ is a threshold. For an audio stream with the sample rate of 48 KHz/s, each audio frame lasts about 24ms. To identify various types of clips, we select a relatively long interval and consider its features. Let T represent the length of the interval, and each audio frame lasts τ, thus the interval contains about $L = \lceil T/\tau \rceil$ audio frames. In our system, T is chosen about one second.

When an anchorperson reports news, pauses with different lengths exist between words, sentences, as well as news items. Some music clips or some clips with music background also exist in the TV news program. Accurate identification of them is very helpful to parse TV news. For the purpose, the pause rate and the silence ratio are calculated for those relatively long intervals. Assume $AC_i\ (i = 0,1,\ldots)$ is a long interval, $af_{ij}\ (j = 0,1,\ldots,L-1)$ represents the jth audio frame and $M(af_{ij})$ is its short time average magnitude, we define $Tag(i,j)$ as follows:

$$Tag(i,j) = \begin{cases} 1 & if\ \ M(af_{ij}) \geq \lambda \\ 0 & if\ \ M(af_{ij}) < \lambda \end{cases} \tag{3}$$

Then the pause rate and the silence ratio for the long interval can be calculated using the following expressions.

$$C(i,j) = \begin{cases} 1 & if\ Tag(i,j) = 0\ and\ Tag(i,j-1) = 1, j \geq 1 \\ 0 & else \end{cases} \tag{4}$$

$$PauseRate(i) = \sum_{j=0}^{L-1} C(i,j) \tag{5}$$

$$SilenceRatio(i) = 1 - (\sum_{j=0}^{L-1} tag(i,j))/L \tag{6}$$

Using the two features, the music clips or the clips with background music in TV news can be identified. For an audio clip, if each $AC_i\ (i = s, s+1,\ldots,t-1,t)$ satisfies

$PauseRate(i)$=0, $SilenceRatio(i)$=0, then we label the clip as music. After that, we apply the following algorithm to identify the pauses in speech, which are considered as potential silence intervals between news items.

Algorithm 1: Select Candidates of the Silence Intervals between News Items

IF ($PauseRate(i) \neq 0$)

    IF ($SilenceRatio(i) / PauseRate(i) > \alpha$)

        AC_i will be chosen as a candidate silence clip

    ELSE

        AC_i is not a candidate silence clip

ELSE

    IF ($SilenceRatio(i) > \beta$)

        AC_i will be chosen as a candidate silence clip

    ELSE

        AC_i is not a candidate silence clip

Where α , β are thresholds and $\beta > \alpha$. They are related with $L*\tau$. The larger $L*\tau$ is, the less α , β should be chosen. Since we choose $L*\tau$ =1 second, α=0.27, β =0.85 are correspondingly chosen experientially.

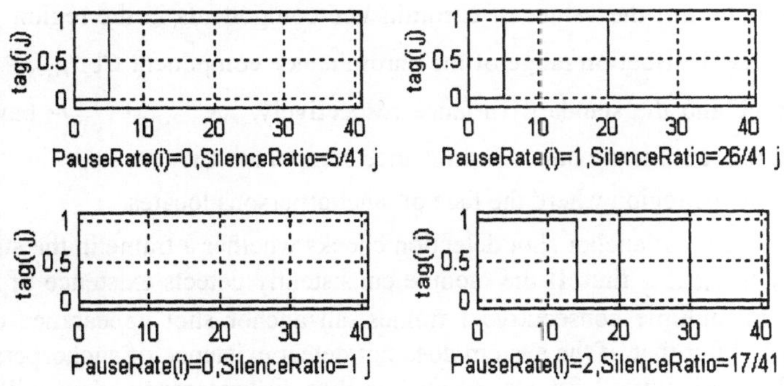

Fig. 2. Typical wave images of $Tag(i, j)$

For a long interval, Fig. 2 gives several typical wave images of $Tag(i,j)$, and the corresponding $PauseRate(i)$ and $SilenceRatio(i)$. After the candidates of the silence intervals are identified, the silence segment $SG\ (n)$ can be further determined through clustering the intervals, i.e., $SG(n) =< s_n, e_n >$, $n, s_n, e_n = 1,2,....$, and $s_n \leq e_n$, which means in the audio clip AC_{S_n-1} AC_{S_n} ... AC_{e_n} AC_{e_n+1} , only AC_{S_n-1} , AC_{e_n+1} are not the candidates. We consider the clip $SG(n)$ is where news item changes with the most probability.

2.2 shot segmentation and anchor shot detection

Generally, TV news involves two classes of shots, i.e., anchor shots and news shots. The former only uses audio to present the content while the latter uses the visual and audio stream synchronized to do that. Therefore, if an anchor shot involves multiple news items, vision-based analysis is not able to provide any cues for news item segmentation. For a clip made up of multiple news shots, if a news item is changing to another news item among it, the boundary between them must also be a shot boundary. In this case, shot segmentation is significant, since it will provide potential candidates of news item boundaries.

Anchor shot detection is another significant aspect of the system. The detection results are used to determine which channels are used to extract news items. In news programs produced by different broadcast corporations, a frame in an anchor shot usually involves two common objects, an anchorperson and a background. Anchorpersons may differ, or the same person is in different dresses on different days, but the whole background or some local region in the background usually keeps unchanged for a long period. Therefore, a model of anchor shots can be constructed to characterize the content of the unchanged region and the system uses the model to detect the anchor shots. In our system, the model is represented as:

$$AnchorShot = < R, C, F > \tag{7}$$

- R is a region in the background object, the content of which keeps almost the same on different days and has consistent color texture.
- C is a feature vector $< rv^{cb}$, $ravg^{cb}$, rsd^{cb}, rv^{cr}, $ravg^{cr}$, $rsd^{cr} >$, which models the distribution of the values of chrominance components in the region R. rv^{cb} is the dynamic distribution range of the chrominance component Cb. $ravg^{cb}$, rsd^{cb} are the average and the standard variance respectively. rv^{cr}, $ravg^{cr}$, rsd^{cr} have the similar meaning, but for the other chrominance component Cr.
- F is the region where the face of anchorpersons locates.

The module of anchor shot detection checks whether a frame in the stream satisfies the model $< R, C >$ first. If the module consistently detects existence of anchorperson frames in multiple consecutive I frames, an anchor shot appearance event will be declared. After that, if the system does not detect existence of anchorperson frames in multiple consecutive I frames, an anchor shot disappearance event will be declared. The step has the power to identify most of anchor shots accurately. If the system pursues higher accuracy, face detection in the region F is imposed to refine the results further. The algorithm does not involve shot segmentation, and operates in compression domain, involving only simple computation, which makes the detection very fast. In evaluation experiments on a big test set, more than 98% accuracy and 100% recall are gained. Due to the primary purpose of the paper, more details of the algorithm will be presented in another paper.

2.3 Automatic segmentation of news items

For each silence segment $SG(n) = < s_n, e_n >$, there is a synchronized video segment $< Vs_n, Ve_n >$, where Vs_n, Ve_n are its start frame and end frame. We specify that if a news item consists of an introductory anchor shot and some news shots, it will be considered as two items. One is the anchor shot, and the other consists of all news shots. The processes described in the sections 2.1, 2.2, provide useful visual and audio cues to segment news items. The whole segmentation process involves two steps. First, the anchor shot detection module segments the stream into two classes of clips interleaved, i.e. anchor shot clips and news shot clips. Fig.3 illustrates the result after that. Then we use the following rules to refine the results, to check if there are still news items boundaries in each clip.

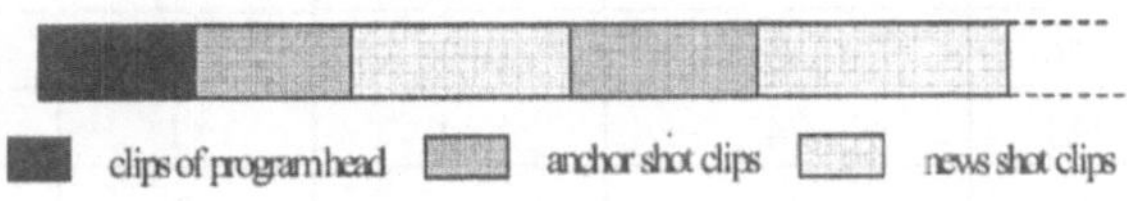

Fig. 3. The result generated after the anchor shot detection

Rule 1 if the segment $< Vs_n, Ve_n >$ belongs to an anchor shot, and the corresponding silence segment $SG(n)$'s total silence ratio $\eta = \sum_{i=Sn}^{en} SilenceRatio(i)$ satisfies $\eta > \zeta$, ζ is a threshold, then the frame at the position $\lfloor (Vs_n + Ve_n)/2 \rfloor$ is chosen as a boundary of news items.

Rule 2 if the segment $< Vs_n, Ve_n >$ covers two different shots, represented by s_k and s_{k+1}, $k = 0,1,\ldots$, and the corresponding silence segment $SG(n)$'s total silence ratio $\eta = \sum_{i=Sn}^{en} SilenceRatio(i)$ satisfies $\eta > \sigma$, σ is a threshold, then $shot(k)$ is considered as the last shot of the foregoing news items, and $sho(k+1)$ as the first one of the following news item.

If the rules cannot be applied to a clip generated by step 1, then the clip itself is considered a news item. For instance, if no silence segment in an anchor shot satisfies the rule 1, the anchor shot forms an item itself. For news shot clips, the silence segment in the middle of a shot only means a common pause during reporting a news item. Usually the contents of TV news are compact. The silence segment $SG(n)$ in the audio channel is very short, generally less than 3.5 seconds. On the other hand, to impress the viewer and make them comfortable visually, two shot transitions within the 3.5 seconds do not occurs generally. Therefore we can assume the segment $< Vs_n, Ve_n >$ covers two shots at most. Our observation of CCTV news has also verified the characteristics.

3. Experiments and Evaluation

We implement the system described in section 2, and random choose 4 days' MPEG CCTV news from video program database as test data to validate the algorithm. The whole experiments are conducted on the PC with PIII-450 CPU and 64M memories. The frame rate of test data is 24f/s with frame size 720*576 pixels. The test data set contains 184100 frames, and lasts two hours or so in total. Before testing, we label manually all the news items in the four days of news, as a standard reference to evaluate the performance of the algorithm. When labeling, introductory anchor shots and following news shots involving the same topic are considered as different items.

Table 1. Experiment results of news item segmentation

Programs	Shots	News Items(S)	Output(D)	Error (E)	Missed (U)
News0	276	33	40	8	1
News1	243	24	34	11	1
News2	305	28	33	7	2
News3	274	18	24	7	1
Total	1098	103	131	33	5

Table 2. Experiment results to the two complex cases

Pro-grams	Actual Boundaries		Ones Detected Accurately	
	A	B	A	B
News	3	3	3	2
News	2	5	2	4
News	2	3	1	2
News	0	6	0	5
Total	7	17	6	13

Note: A—multiple items in an anchor shot; B— news items with no introductory anchor shots

Compared to accuracy, we pay more attention to recall, since the latter means less manual effort of a user to correct the results automatically generated by the system. Therefore, the following parameters values are chosen, α =0.27, β =0.85, ζ =1.6, σ =1.31, and the experiment results are tabulated in table 1. According to the statistics in table 1, the accuracy of news item segmentation $P = 1-\frac{E}{D}=1-\frac{33}{131}=74.8\%$ and the recall $R=1-\frac{U}{S}=1-\frac{5}{103}=95.1\%$ are calculated out. During the experiments, the less ζ , σ are chosen, the higher recall can be obtained. But the accuracy becomes less, since the higher recall also brings more false boundaries. Our analysis found the missed boundaries are mainly caused by disturbs of background sound occurring on the boundaries, which confuse the detection of silence segments. For false segmentations, they also result from scene sound. For instance, during an interview, the speaker altercations between a reporter and an interviewee bring some silence segments in audio channels. If a shot transition accompanies, then false claims may occur. The two cases, which cannot be handled by [12], are ubiquitous in CCTV news. The experiment results related to them are summarized and tabulated in table 2. The statistics in it shows our algorithm is valid and it can accurately identify most of the boundaries in the two cases. It should be pointed out, almost all false claims in table 1 result from the effort to identify them.

4. Conclusions

The paper explores integration of audio-visual cues to automatic segmentation of news items. A novel approach has been proposed. It overcomes the limitation of the approach in [12], and brings more adaptation. The experiment results show the algorithm is valid and robust. The recall 95.1% and the accuracy 74.8% have been achieved when the system identifies boundaries between news items. The experiments also imply integration of audio-visual cues is effective to parse high-level structures of video. Though the method is designed specifically for parsing TV news, its analysis of audio signals, as well as integration strategy of audio-visual cues can also be applied to the scene analysis of other video classes.

5. References

[1] M. M. Yeung and B. L. Yeo, " Time-constrained clustering for segmentation of video into story units," in int. Conf. Pattern Recognition(ICPR '96), pp375-380, Aug, 1996.

[2] Yong Rui, Thomas S. Huang and Sharad Mehrotra, "Exploring Video Structure Beyond The Shots," Proc. of IEEE International Conference on Multimedia Computing and Systems (ICMCS), Austin, Texas USA, pp237-240,1998.

[3] B.L. Yeo and B. Liu, "Rapid Scene Analysis on Compressed Videos", in IEEE Transactions on Circuits and Systems for Video Technology, Vol. 5, No. 6, pp. 533-544, December 1995

[4]J.S. Boreczky and L.A. Rowe, "Comparison of Video Shot Boundary Detection Techniques.", Proc. SPIE Conf. Storage and Retrieval for Video Databases IV, San Jose, CA, February 1995.

[5]Yueting Zhuang, Yong Rui, Thomas S. Huang, and Sharad Mehrotra, "Adaptive Key Frame Extraction Using Unsupervised Clustering," in Proc. of IEEE Int Conf on Image Processing , Oct, 1998, Chicago, IL. pp866-870.

[6]A. Girgensohn and J. Boreczky, "Time-Constrained Keyframe Selection Technique.", In IEEE Multimedia Systems '99, IEEE Computer Society, vol. 1, pp. 756-761, 1999.

[7] Z. Liu, J. Huang, Y. Wang and T. Chen, "Audio Feature Extraction & Analysis for Scene Classification," IEEE Signal Processing Society 1997 Workshop on Multimedia Signal Processing, June 23 - 25, 1997, Princeton, New Jersey, USA.

[8] Tong Zhang and C.-C. Jay Kuo, "Heuristic approach for generic audio data segmentation and annotation," ACM Multimedia Conference, pp. 67-76, Orlando, Nov. 1999.

[9] J.S. Boreczky,L.D. Wilcox,"A Hidden Markov Model Framework for Video Segmentation Using Audio and Image Features," in ICASSP'98, pp.3741-3744, Seattle, May 1998.

[10]J. Nam and A.H. Tewfic, "Combined Audio and Visual Streams Analysis for Video Sequence Segmentation", Proc. ICASSP'97, Vol.4, Munich, Germany, pp2665-2668,1997.

[11] J. Huang, Z. Liu, and Y. Wang, "Joint Video Scene Segmentation and Classification Based on Hidden Markov Model," ICME-2000, New York, NY, July 30 - Aug. 2, 2000.

[12]H. J. Zhang, S.Y. Tan, S. W. Smoliar and Y. Gong, "Automatic Parsing and Indexing of News Video", Multimedia Systems, 2: 256-266, 1995.

Association Feedback: A Novel Tool for Feature Elements Based Image Retrieval

Yin Xu[1], Yujin Zhang [2]

Department of Electronic Engineering, Tsinghua University, P.R.China
[1]xuyin97@mails.tsinghua.edu.cn
[2]zhangyj@ee.tsinghua.edu.cn

Abstract. Different from the traditional image retrieval systems, our retrieval framework bases on feature elements but not feature vectors. The retrieval task is to judge whether the image holds the feature elements of the demand set. As the opposite interactive tool to the relevance feedback for the current feature vector based retrieval, this paper proposes a new approach: association feedback. It analyzes synthetically the feedback data, retrieval history and existing result to find out the associated elements that potentially hit the retrieval target. And it can easily implement interest switch, by using associated part as the bridge. Experimental result shows inspiring future for the new approach.

1 Introduction

Nowadays the mainstream of image retrieval is content-based retrieval (CBIR). Some of the systems even declaim to be able to achieve semantic retrieval.

While most CBIR systems extract features from the images, and use the features as the image "labels" to identify the image similarity. The popular way to deal with the features is to combine them as vectors. Thus retrieval task becomes searching in the multi-features vector space.

Feature vectorization makes it easy to implement similarity match, multi-feature combination, and image feature database organization. Besides, a powerful tool for retrieval interaction, relevance feedback [1,2], attempts to meet the user requirement by adjusting the term weightings of the feature vectors.

While we break the features into separate units with clear visual meaning, and call them feature elements (FEs). It is the feature element but not the feature vector that plays the key role in the human mind-retrieval. Thus the retrieval task is transformed into judging whether the images hold the demand feature elements [3].

At the interactive stage, as an equivalent tool, association feedback is proposed in this paper. Different from relevance feedback, it tries to detect the associated parts between the retrieval result and user feedback, then estimates the user intent on the selection of the feature elements or FEs characteristic adjustment.

In section 2, feature element theory is briefly reviewed, and the retrieval process is described in short. The mechanism of association feedback will be particularly described in section 3. Experiments result and conclusions will be given in section 4 and 5 respectively.

2 Feature Element Based Retrieval

In the proposed framework, feature extraction stage generates feature elements directly. Then some evaluations are done to pick out the potential important ones. Grid index is used to organize up the feature element database.

2.1 Feature Element Generation and Evaluation

The feature vector presents a statistical view of the image. While feature element tries to catch the concept factor in visual sense, which makes them more intuitive.
For each FE, we define one primary value and several secondary values. Primary value is taken as its identifying label, while secondary values represent some other accessory visual characteristics.

In our system, color distribution feature element (cdFE) is developed. For this FE, color cardinalities obtained by dynamic clustering in the HSV space [4] are taken as the feature elements. Its primary value is the Hue (Hbin). There are three secondary values added to the cdFE: Saturation (Sbin), Color Coherence Value (CCVbin) [5] and Color AutoCorrelogram Value (CACbin) [6]. The latter two contain spatial information of the color cardinality.

Feature element evaluation is done next to estimate the potential importance of the FEs. From some literature investigating on the visual perception psychology, several principles for evaluation are drawn to help us to establish a priority level system that also meets some requirement of fuzzy effect [7,8,9]. The evaluation process partitions the FEs into three sets: important FEs (iFEs), extend FEs (eFEs), and trivial FEs (tFEs). Among them, iFEs usually are the retrieval targets, eFEs will be used to extend the potential interest, while tFEs are often discarded.

2.2 Grid-Index And Retrieval Session

Different from the popular clustering organization method [10,11] in the stage of image data popularization, we put forward one relative simple and stable approach, grid-index. Feature elements are put into grids according to their values. For example, the primary value of cdFE: Hbin, is divided into 360 grids evenly. The image that contains one FE whose Hbin is 60°, is registered into the $Hbin = 60°$ grid. Thus, the grid-index system with all the images registered in is built up.

Here retrieval session is used to define the process, which starts with the retrieval request submitted and ends with the satisfied result accepted by the user. At the beginning, user's retrieval demand, QBE or natural language instruction, is translated into a set of target FEs. Then from the grids that match the values of the target FEs, all the images registered in are picked out to form the result list. The preliminary retrieval outcome is available now.

More details about the feature element theory and grid-index can be found in [3].

3 Association Feedback

At the interactive stage, users often show their favor by feedback action. They may not feel satisfied with the result provided: low recall or low precision. And as an even greater challenge, users may have some association on the current circumstance. Association feedback tries to find out the associated part, which is the bridge between the user intent and current result.

3.1 Feedback Data Collection

In the retrieval framework, user may say "yes" or "no" to the preferred or not-preferred image to show his inclination as the traditional way. The yes-no feedback data are collected to analyze the genuine intent of the user. We believe that in fact user like some elements or dislike some others in subconscious.

3.2 Hit Ratio Analysis

Image marked with "yes" and those with "no" are gathered into the yes-group and no-group separately. For each group, the "yes" or "no" hit ratio for the elements is calculated. The yes-hit-ratio is the ratio of the images in the yes-group, which contain the FE that hit at least one in the demand FE set, to all the yes-group images, the no-hit-ratio can be computed in the similar way, $F(I)$ means the feature element set contained by image I :

$$H_k^Y = \frac{\left\| \{ I_{Y_j}, j = 1, \cdots, M \mid \exists FE_{Y_j} \in F(I_{Y_j}), P(FE_{Y_j}) \overline{M} P(FE_k) \} \right\|}{\left\| \{ I_{Y_j}, j = 1, \cdots, M \} \right\|} \tag{1}$$

$$H_k^N = \frac{\left\| \{ I_{N_j}, j = 1, \cdots, N \mid \exists FE_{N_j} \in F(I_{N_j}), P(FE_{N_j}) \overline{M} P(FE_k) \} \right\|}{\left\| \{ I_{N_j}, j = 1, \cdots, N \} \right\|} \tag{2}$$

H_k^Y and H_k^N mean the yes and no hit ratio of the kth demand feature element respectively. I_{Y_j} and I_{N_j} mean the jth yes or no image respectively. While $\overline{M}$ means successful match of FE primary value. $P(FE)$ presents the primary value. And $\| A \|$ calculates the cardinality of the set A.

Obviously the FEs get much more "no" than "yes" usually hit the user's distaste, otherwise, FEs hit more "yes" than "no" implies their importance. And the common elements the yes images hold, though not in the demand set, still have the opportunities to be promoted to the iFE set. Thus new set of demand FEs generates by hit ratio analysis.

3.3 Hit Density Calculation

The next step is to adjust the values of these FEs, because the user may not accept the original values of them. The goal of the value adjustment is to determine the new domain match boundary of the FE values. Hit density set is introduced to calculate the new value distribution. The value of FEs in yes-group is denoted as v^+, while v^- represents the values in the no-group. Thus, the yes and no sets are combined to form the original hit density set, then all the bins are rearranged as sort ascending:

$$HD_o = \{v_1^+, \cdots, v_N^+\} \bigcup \{v_1^-, \cdots, v_M^-\} = \{v_1 \le \cdots \le v_{N+M}\} \tag{3}$$

As the HD_o data is discrete, interpolation is needed to get the continuous distribution. Firstly the density of each bin is calculated as follow:

$$d_i = \sum_j^{N+M} (1 - \frac{\min(|v_j - v_{d_i}|, T)}{T}) \tag{4}$$

Here, T is set to limit the neighborhood range. Then between two discontinuous and homo-sign bins, linear interpolation of the bin density is done to obtain the continuous density distribution. Naturally normalization is a must. Due to the incompleteness and insufficiency of the user feedback data, there are still some bins that are uncertain of their signs, one classical continuous hit density set is presented as follow:

$$HD_c = \{0, \cdots, d_i^-, \cdots, d_{i+p}^-, 0, \cdots, d_j^+, \cdots, d_{j+q}^+, 0, \cdots, d_k^-, \cdots, d_{k+r}^-, 0, \cdots\} \tag{5}$$

Usually the bins from ith to $i+p$th and from kth to k+rth are all below zero (refused), whereas, the bins from jth and $j+q$th are positive (accepted).

3.4 Accepted Domain Match Boundary Decision

The consequent task is to ascertain the accepted domain boundary of FE values. Applying rough set theory [12], we can define lower approximation boundary set $S_l = \lfloor d_j, d_{j+q} \rfloor$ and upper approximation boundary set $S_u = \lfloor d_{i+p+1}, d_{k-1} \rfloor$. Obviously, the genuine boundary set, $S_g = \lfloor d_s, d_t \rfloor$, obeys: $S_l \subseteq S_g \subseteq S_u$.

Because of the feedback data incompleteness, the history data and some hypothesis must be adopted. The history data include original values of FEs and all previous user feedback data. It is supposed that during one retrieving session, the feedback data always stick to one retrieval goal. Thus all these data can be integrated to reduce the roughness of S_g. To be simple, S_g is set as $\lfloor d_{(i+p+1+j)/2}, d_{(j+q+k-1)/2} \rfloor$.

Now, the new demand set of FEs and their adjusted values are available for the next round retrieval.

3.5 Interest Switch Realization

During one retrieving session, the user would submit one retrieval request, but he may partially take the request as the ultimate goal or even change his mind during the session. We name it *interest switch*. Applying association feedback, it is easy to get the associated part, which is usually a subset of the demand FEs set, i.e., the bridge to the new retrieval. While new FEs will be added to the demand set. Thus some potential FEs will be promoted into the demand set.

4 Experimental Results and Discussions

Our image database consists of 1848 color images. Three groups of experimental result data on the archive of images are given as Table 1.

All the retrieval sessions start with the image of a sunflower under blue sky. Feature element generation and evaluation produce two important cdFEs with hue yellow and blue as their primary value respectively. The task of session A is to find out many small yellow flowers, task B tries to retrieval big yellow flowers, while the destination of C is to obtain small red flowers. All sessions involve interest switch. *Ft* represents the feedback rounds to reach the satisfied result. *N* is the amount of the final images in the result list, which belongs to the respective groundtruth set. R_p and R_t are retrieval recalls:

$$R_p = \frac{\textit{relevant images in final result}}{\textit{groudtruth images after FE evaluation}} \times 100\% \tag{6}$$

$$R_t = \frac{\textit{groudtruth images after FE evaluation}}{\textit{all groudtruth images}} \times 100\% \tag{7}$$

Pr represents the precision defined in [2]. Due to the complexity and diversity of the images in the database, and most important, lack of sufficient semantic identification, the low precision now is somehow understandable. Besides, some new kinds of feature elements are needed.

The retrieval session of each task is illustrated in Fig. 1-3. In session A, user selects images with small yellow flowers, while say no to the "big" ones. In the second round, the requirement is confirmed and images only with blue are refused. Thus leads to the fine result. Task B is similar to A. While task C is a little more complicated, as red is not the important FE. By emphasizing on red information, red cdFE is promoted gradually from eFE to iFE, and in the same way to A and B, yellow is refused.

Table 1. Experimental result of the 3 retrieval sessions

	Ft	N	R_p	R_t	Pr
A	2	42	91.30%	88.46%	51.85%
B	1	41	83.67%	87.50%	51.90%
C	2	108	74.03%	90.80%	57.47%

1 2 3

Fig. 1. Three retrieval sessions - Session A. Note: the ranking of images is rearranged to show more relevant images in one page.

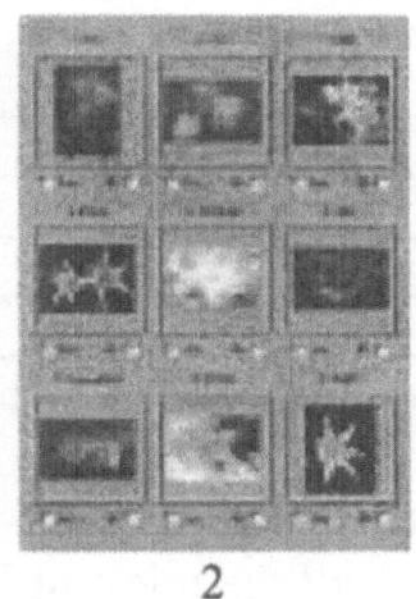

1 2

Fig. 2. Three retrieval sessions - Session B. The same note as A.

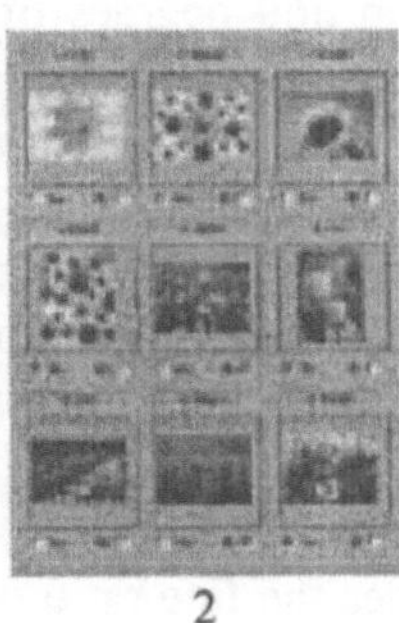

1 2 3

Fig. 3. Three retrieval sessions - Session C. The same note as A.

Table 2. FE data change during each retrieval session

	Hbound	CCVbound	Importance
A, B, C	[198, 237]	[0, 14]	iFE
	[36, 75]	[0, 14]	iFE

(a) Original FE data after direct retrieval, 3 tasks start at the same scratch line.

		Hbound	CCVbound	Importance
A	1	[29, 58]	[6, 14]	iFE
	2	[196, 235]	[0, 3]	eFE
B	1	[38, 67]	[0, 6]	iFE
C	1	[36, 65]	[6, 14]	iFE
	2	[342, 19]	[0, 8]	eFE

(b) After first round retrieval, task B reaches its end point. For A, blue element is degraded as eFE, while for C, red is promoted into eFE.

	Hbound	CCVbound	Importance
A	[35, 64]	[6, 14]	iFE
C	[351, 35]	[0, 6]	iFE

(c) Now all the tasks reach their goals, session A only contain small yellow FE, session C kicks yellow out at last.

	Hbound	CCVbound
A	[25, 75]	[6, 14]
B	[25, 75]	[0, 5]
C	[335, 25]	[0, 5]

(d) These are the authentic FE values that required by evaluated groudtruth.

Table 2 illustrates the change of the FE data in the retrieval session. For each task, in one retrieval round, all the relevant FEs are listed out. Of each FE, two of the most relevant values, Hbin and CCVbin, are chosen to be presented. Hbound and CCVbound mean the domain match boundary of respective value. Domain of Hbin is [0, 360] which is corresponding to 360 degrees of Hue. While the value span for CCVbin is from 0 to 14, the higher, the more scattering the color cardinality is, and low value present compactness and largeness. Importance points out which set, iFE or eFE, the FEs belong to.

The border between iFE and eFE decides the amount of probable evolved results during retrieval. If more eFEs are taken as iFEs, more result images are at hand for choice, otherwise, maybe more accurate outcomes are available. To cope with the dilemma is a crucial task for future work.

What is remarkable is that besides the fine ratio of recall, the amount of feedback rounds for the user to achieve his goal (even include interest switch) is quite few. While the low precision problem involve the image recognition problem in general circumstances. To our opinion, the task of retrieval is to find as many similar one as possible, but no to recognize and understand accurately. Besides, an integrated semantic recognition framework based on the feature element theory is under developing. We hope the intuitive and flexible nature will help this framework achieve more general and finer semantic result.

5 Conclusion

Unlike the traditional image retrieval systems, where features are taken as vectors, the proposal brand new approach is based on the feature element theory. And the association feedback mechanism is developed to help user handle the retrieval process more intuitively and flexibly. Experimental example shows that the association feedback has a good applying future.

6 Acknowledgements

This work has been supported under grants NNSF-69672029 and done in Tsinghua-Packetvideo Multimedia United Laboratory.

References

1. Yong Rui et.al: Relevance Feedback: A Power Tool for Interactive Content-Based Image Retrieval. IEEE Trans. on Circuit and Systems for Video Technology. Vol.8, No.5, (1998) 644-655
2. Yong Rui et.al: Content-based image retrieval with relevance feedback in MARS, ICIP. (1997) 815-818
3. Yin Xu, Y. J. Zhang: Image retrieval framework driven by association feedback with feature element evaluation built in. SPIE Storage and Retrieval for Media Databases. Vol. 4315. (2001) 118-129
4. Androutsos, D, et.al: Vector Angular Distance Measure For Indexing And Retrieval of Color. SPIE. Vol. 3656. (1999) 604-613
5. Greg Pass, Ramin Zabih: Histogram Refinement for Content-Base Image Retrieval. IEEE Workshop on Applications of Computer Vision. (1996) 96-102
6. Huang, Jing et.al: Spatial Color Indexing and Applications. Proceedings of the IEEE International Conference on Computer Vision. (1998) 602-607
7. Irving Biederman: Recognition-by-components: a theory of human image understanding. Psychological Review. Vol. 94. No. 2. (1987) 115-147
8. Ruggero Milanese: Detecting Salient Regions in an Image: from Biological Evidence to Computer Implementation. Ph.D. thesis. (Geneva: Univ. of Geneva, 1993)
9. Shoji Tanaka et.al: Foreground-Background Segmentation Based on Attractiveness. International Conference on Computer Graphics and Imaging (CGIM). (1998) 191-194
10. Alejandro Jaimes, Shih-fu Chang: Model-Based Classification of Visual Information for Content-Based Retrieval. SPIE. Vol. 3656. (1999) 402-414
11. Vailaya, Aditya, Jain, Anil, Zhang, Hong Jiang: On image classification: City images vs. Landscapes. Pattern Recognition. Vol. 31. No. 12. (1998) 1921-1935
12. Krzysztof Cios, et.al: Data Mining Methods for Knowledge Discovery. Kluwer Acdemic Publishers. (1998) 27-71

Query by Visual Example: Assessing the Usability of Content-Based Image Retrieval System User Interfaces

Colin C. Venters[1], Richard J. Hartley[2], Matthew D. Cooper[1], William T. Hewitt[1]

[1] Manchester Visualization Centre, Manchester Computing, University of Manchester, Oxford Road, Manchester, M13 9PL, England, UK
{c.venters, matt.cooper, w.t.hewitt}@man.ac.uk
[2] Department of Information & Communication, Geoffrey Manton Building, Manchester Metropolitan University, Oxford Road, Manchester, M15 6LL, England, UK
r.j.hartley@mmu.ac.uk

Abstract. This paper reports a study designed to investigate the requirements of a user interface for a content-based image retrieval system, and presents the preliminary results of an inquiry into the usability of the query by visual example paradigm. Twenty eight evaluation sessions were conducted to test the usability of two user interfaces. The study was segmented by image type, user group and use function. Usability was measured using a combination of both objective and subjective measuring instruments: benchmark tasks, critical incidents, and the Questionnaire for User Interface Satisfaction (QUIS). Preliminary findings suggest that both user interfaces had an overall positive usability score, although there were a number of areas that would improve the overall score. The results also indicate that the efficacy of some currently used features are questionable.

1 Introduction

The field of image retrieval has been an active research area for several decades. In recent years, the field has been the focus of renewed interest as the dramatic and unparalleled swell in the volume of digital image data has exacerbated the problem of image retrieval [1]. Solutions to address this have resulted in the development of second-generation visual information systems that focus on the automatic indexing and retrieval of images by their visual characteristics. Content-based image retrieval is a general term used to describe the overall approach. This method permits the automatic, unsupervised extraction of perceptual information from raw sensory data, through the objective analysis of pixel distribution, and the derivation of visual similarity measures [2]. Supporters of the approach have hailed this technique as a powerful information retrieval tool, which can compliment the traditional information retrieval paradigm or be utilized as a novel query mechanism for the retrieval of images from large repositories of image data [3]. Nevertheless, the difficulties involved in developing effective and efficient image retrieval systems are problematic.

Little empirical or independent evidence exists to verify the effectiveness of this approach and the viability of applying the technology in real world applications, and there are still a significant number of open research issues to be addressed if this technique is to pay dividends [4]. Many research topics in this field, which have been suggested by several commentators as integral elements to the advancement of this approach as a creditable retrieval tool, have been largely ignored [5, 6]. One such area is the user interface and the tools necessary to express a visual query. This paper provides an overview of an investigation designed to examine the user interface to content-based image retrieval systems and presents the preliminary results of an evaluation that assessed the usability of the query by visual example paradigm.

2 Research Background

It is widely recognized that information seeking is a complex iterative process in which the information seeker, often for good reasons, may well be unable to specify an information need. Nevertheless the interface can have a significant impact upon search success [7]. One mode of interaction for content-based image retrieval systems allows end users to submit a query image as the basis of their search. This mode of interaction is commonly known as Query by Visual Example (QVE). Supporting the construction of image queries by this mode of interaction is a non-trivial problem. The more complex the query i.e. the shape and structure, the more difficult it is for the end user to express and produce a meaningful visual example. Several user interfaces and their features have been described in the literature, and these features have recently been summarized by Del Bimbo [8]. The query by sketch method is a common feature employed in several systems [9]. By this method users can sketch out their desired image by combining several features commonly found in computer graphic applications. The sketch represents a template of either a completed object or scene. However, Korfhage [10] indicates that queries formulated by this method are simplistic, relatively crude sketches of the desired query image, and that the tool has a limited functionality for expressing more complex image queries. Similarly, the effectiveness of shape matching features is influenced by noise and pixel arrangement in the query image. There is little evidence to support the usability of this query tool. However, it is highly probable that this method may ultimately result in end-user frustration if the retrieval output produced continued unexpected and unpredictable results. Gupta and Jain [11] note that most systems are limited in the query types they can handle and propose that image query specification should be extended through a range of different tools: query canvas, containment queries, semantic queries, object-related queries, spatio-temporal queries. Whether the current or proposed query tools are effective in aiding the process of visual query formulation and construction is unclear as there is little empirical evidence to date to support such claims. Research to date is contradictory and the validity of the interaction methods remains untested with real end-user populations [12, 13].

The literature suggests that there is no clear understanding of the user interface and tools to express a visual query, both in terms of the user design requirements and their existing level of usability. The user interface remains the least researched and developed element of content-based image retrieval systems.

3 User Requirements

The project was segmented by image type, user group, and use function. The image type consists of a set of device marks supplied by the UK Trademark Registry. A sizeable number of the dataset is made up of abstract geometric designs that have little or no representational meaning. Typical images for this class are monochrome, multi-component, with few textured areas. The following images are examples from the registry:

The dataset comprises ten thousand, two-dimensional, bi-level shapes, stored as files in the Xionics SMP format using CCITT Group 4 Fax compression. The sample population in the study was purposefully selected to produce a group who shared similar task orientation, motivation, systems expertise, and domain knowledge [14]. Dependent variables were determined by the user group, all are intermediaries performing a search for an external body with predefined boundaries. Independent variables were categorised from a phenomenological perspective, the users deciding on their own level of ability and determined by means of a questionnaire. Three user groups were selected to assist in the user requirements engineering process: patent information network libraries (PIN), patent services, and trademark agents. The rationale for targeting these specific groups was based on the premise that their primary business function involves the effective identification of similar images from the dataset and shared similar task orientation and motivation. The use function is restricted to the retrieval of images by shape similarity. The ARTISAN [15] shape retrieval system was used to demonstrate the novelty of content-based image retrieval technology to the end user population. ARTISAN is a similar-shape retrieval system. The system performs automatic shape analysis and provides both example-based similarity retrieval and partial shape matching facilities. Twenty three semi-structured interviews were conducted between August and September 1997 with individuals from the three selected groups. The aim of the interviews was to explore the user requirements for a content-based image retrieval system. A number of key areas were explored within the topics of system input, system output, and user interface issues. The data collected from the interviews was analysed using a constant comparative method [16]. The data suggests that a number of user interface features are required to support visual query construction.

The three user groups proposed several features including: a scanning tool, a sketch tool, a browsing tool, and a shape-building tool. This data suggests that end users have a range of query needs, which could be supported by several interface features, and that no single interface feature would support all the activities and tasks of this end user population. For known item queries, all twenty-three interviewees suggested a scanning tool as their primary and preferred tool. This feature should allow users to scan an image directly into the system to use as the basis of their search. This feature would also be used to scan in images to modify prior to its submission as a query. While the three end-user groups have a common interest in the effective identification of similar images from the dataset, the findings highlighted a dichotomy between the activities of trademark agents and those of PIN information officers and patent service personnel. This is reflective of the activities of the three user groups and can be attributed to the type of client and nature of the service they provide. For example, trademark agents have specific requests for known item queries. The data suggests that trademark agents would only currently require a scanning facility to accurately capture the client's proposed device mark. In contrast, PIN information officers and patent service personnel have a broader range of enquiries that encompass both known and partially known item queries. As a result, these two groups proposed a broader range of features to assist in image query construction: a shape-building tool, a browsing tool, and a sketch tool. The shape-building tool should allow end users to select from a range of predefined shape features to form the basis of their query e.g. circles, squares, triangles, and rectangles. These shapes should be based on the main categories defined in the Vienna classification scheme. The browsing tool should allow end users to browse through a hierarchy of visual surrogates and select an image to use as their query. The structure should be based on the Vienna classification scheme. The sketch tool should allow end-users to construct their queries by free-hand drawing, and utilize basic shape features and functions found in computer-based drawing applications e.g. MS Paint.

4. Design & Development

Potential designs were investigated by drawing upon two standard approaches: structured and holistic design. Based on the results of the design phase, two user interfaces were built for comparison purposes at the evaluation stage: a single feature browsing interface and the user-defined interface. The browsing interface allowed users to scroll through categories of visual surrogates and select an image(s) on the basis of their visual properties. Users are able to progressively move through the structure of the hierarchy to refine the search to one or two relevant surrogates. The hierarchy was based on the Vienna classification scheme. The user-defined interface reflected the proposed features identified during the user analysis stage: shape-building, browsing, sketching, and scanning tools. The shape-building feature allowed users to select a single image shape as the basis of their query or construct a query by combining different shape elements from a standard range of shape features e.g. circles, squares, triangles, rectangles.

Selection of the shape-building function spawned a new window within the main user interface to allow users to build their query. The integrated browsing feature performed the same functions outlined in the stand-alone visual-browsing user interface. The sketch tool allowed users to construct their queries by free-hand drawing. A new window and a drawing tool were spawned within the main user interface to allow users to draw their desired query image. The scanning feature allowed users to simulate the process of scanning an image directly into the system as no scanning hardware or software would be present during the evaluation. Analysis of a scanning procedure at the design stage provided a realistic simulation of the process. The simulation of scanning an image spawned a new window displaying the image within the main user interface. In addition, a set of standard image editing facilities enabled users to make modifications to images e.g. erase. The image editing facilities were present at all times during the input and output stages. To reduce programming and development overheads the decision was taken to build a horizontal prototype. Horizontal prototyping enables the illustration of the system without having to develop a fully functional system. The development work was undertaken on a PC within a Windows environment. Visual Basic was selected as the development environment to build the user interfaces.

5. User Interface Evaluation

Evaluation of information retrieval systems has traditionally focused on retrieval efficiency and effectiveness [17]. However, from an HCI perspective, evaluation is concerned with gathering data about the usability of a design or product by a specified group of users, for a particular activity, within a specified environment or work context. Usability is defined as a measure of the ease with which a system can be learned or used, its safety, effectiveness and efficiency, and the attitude of its users towards it [18]. The purpose of the evaluation was to assess the usability of the user interfaces and to determine whether the proposed user interface features improved the human-computer interaction. Twenty eight evaluation sessions were conducted to test the usability of the user interfaces. The evaluation was segmented by the same image type and use function employed in the user requirements analysis stage. However, this time participants were selected solely from the 14 UK PIN offices. Two separate sessions took place over the duration of the evaluation. The evaluation involved field-testing and took place on site within the participants' working environment. The overall evaluation session lasted three hours. A maximum thirty-minute time period was allocated for introductory remarks, discussions on the evaluation, participant questions and reassurances, and for participants to receive a tutorial on basic techniques for interacting with the system and executing the major interface functions. All participants were issued with introductory instructional remarks. These provided uniform instructions clarifying the purpose of the evaluation and removed some of the potential variance from the test sessions. All participants were required to read and sign an informed consent form.

Usability was measured using a combination of both objective and subjective measuring instruments: benchmark tasks, a concurrent semi-structured interview, and the Questionnaire for User Interface Satisfaction [QUIS] [19]. Benchmark tasks are representative tasks that a user will perform e.g. search. Specific, single interface tasks were selected to enable problems discovered during the evaluation to be traced to specific parts of the design. Intervening representative tasks were also included in the evaluation. These tasks were not tested quantitatively but were important in adding breadth and depth to the evaluation. Representative tasks are common tasks that users would be expected to perform on a regular basis e.g. print. Both benchmark and intervening representative tasks were based on activities identified during the user requirements analysis process. All tasks were solvable using either interface. The tasks were administered as a written list. Participants were required to read each task description aloud before beginning. Completion of this was used as a cue for the evaluator to start timing the task performance. All appropriate tasks were timed using a stopwatch and captured by means of a paper-based form. An audio taped, concurrent semi-structured interview was used to collect users' subjective responses to positive and negative critical incidents. Critical incidents may happen while a participant is working that have either a significant positive or negative effect on task performance or user satisfaction, and thus on usability of the interface. Critical incidents were noted on a paper-based form and discussed after completion of the appropriate task. The well-established QUIS questionnaire was used and adapted to provide a quantitative measure of a user's subjective satisfaction with various user interface features. QUIS is organized around general categories e.g. screen, terminology and systems information, and employs a ten point rating scale. The granularity of the QUIS rating scale was modified from its linear scale of 1-10 to a negative and positive scale as studies have suggested that negative and positive scale readings correspond more accurately to the negative and positive opinions of users e.g. –5 –4 –3 -2, -1, +1, +2 +3 +4 +5 and NA, [20]. The scale contained no neutral value in order to reduce the error of central tendency. The questionnaire was distributed to participants after the completion of each session. For the purpose of this evaluation two error types were operationally defined. Firstly, any time a participant cannot take a task to completion, Type I. Secondly, any time a participant takes action that does not lead to progress in performing the desired task, Type II. When a participant did something unexpected which lead to a different way of accomplishing a task it did not constitute an error but was considered as a critical incident.

6. Preliminary Results

The final results of the evaluation are still being analysed, but preliminary results of QUIS suggest that both user interfaces had an overall positive usability score. In general, user reaction to the interfaces was positive. All participants thought the user interfaces were quick and easy to learn. Participants commented that the simplicity of the interfaces was their major strength.

Functions were clear and led to predictable results. However, the data from QUIS also highlights several areas where the interfaces can be modified to improve the overall level of usability. For example, several participants indicated the position of a counter, which expressed the time remaining to search the database, could be moved from its current position. This feature was fixed on the screen until the database search had been completed and obstructed access to the retrieval results. Ideally participants would like to scroll through the results as they appear. Several participants also expressed this as a negative critical incident. The single feature interface was the preferred user interface of choice by the majority of participants. All participants felt comfortable with its functionality and were quick to settle into the set tasks. The set tasks were performed faster and easier with this interface. This interface produced an observed positive reaction in the participants who expressed that this interface would address their current working difficulties. Similarly, the browsing feature in the user-defined interface was also the preferred feature of choice. This supports evidence from previous studies [13]. However, we suggest that this is in part an intuitive display of their current information seeking behavior. Ultimately, the information seeking behavior of end users may impact on this technology being adopted. All participants completed the benchmark and representative tasks successfully. However, several participants produced a Type II error with the user-defined interface. This was prevalent with the sketch function. While participants were keen to exploit and test out the range of functions available several resorted to completing the sketch task by another function as they felt the sketch tool was inadequate for expressing the query. They felt they had little control over the tool and that it relied solely on their artistic ability. They suggested that some form of graphics tablet where they could draw with a pen and select shapes instead of using a mouse would be more natural. Many of the comments concerning this feature reiterated those expressed by Korfhage [10].

7. Summary

This paper provided an overview of a project designed to investigate the requirements of a user interface for a content-based image retrieval system, and presented the preliminary results of an evaluation that assessed the usability of the query by visual example paradigm. This work attempts to add to our existing knowledge and further our understanding of the content-based image retrieval system user interfaces. Our work suggests that this end user group had a range of query needs, which could be supported by the QVE paradigm. The preliminary results indicated that while both user interfaces had an overall positive usability score there were several areas where the interfaces could be improved. The results also imply that the efficacy of sketching tools is highly questionable. However, the data also suggests that a complete paradigm shift in user perception may be required if content-based image retrieval is to be adopted as a viable retrieval tool.

8. References

1 Fidel, R., Challenges in Indexing Electronic Text and Images. ASIS, 1994, p. 3.

2 Del Bimbo, A., Visual Information Retrieval, Morgan Kaufmann, 1999.

3 Eakins, J. P., and Graham, M. E., Content-Based Image Retrieval, JTAP. 1999, pp. 1-63.

4 Rui, Y. and Huang, T. S. Chang, S-F., Image Retrieval: Current Techniques, Promising Directions, and Open Issues. Journal of Visual Communication and Image Representation, 10, (1), 1999, pp. 39-62.

5 ibid, pp. 39-62.

6 Gudivada, V. N., and Raghaven, V. V., Content-Based Image Retrieval Systems, IEEE Computer, September, 1995, pp. 18-22.

7 Shaw, D., The Human-Computer Interface for Information Retrieval, ASIS, 1991.

8 Del Bimbo, 1999. op. cit.

9 Niblack, W., Barber, R., Equitz, W. Flickner, M. Glasman, E. Petkovic, D. Yanker, P. Faloutsos, C. Taubin, G. The QBIC Project: Querying Images By Content Using Color, Texture and Shape. In: Proceedings of Storage and Retrieval for Image and Video Databases. San Jose, California, USA, SPIE, 1993.

10 Korfhage, R., Information Storage & Retrieval. Wiley, 1997.

11 Gupta, A. and Jain, R.., Visual Information Retrieval, Communications of the ACM, 40 (5), 1997, pp. 71-79.

12 Batley, S. (1989) Visual Information Retrieval: Browsing Strategies in Pictorial Databases. In: Proceedings of the 12th Online Information Meeting, 6th-8th December 1989, London, England, p. 373-381.

13 Lai, T-S., Tait, J, and McDonald, S., A User-Centred Evaluation of Visual Search Methods for CBIR, CIR2000: The Challenge of Image Retrieval: 3rd UK Conference on Image Retrieval, Brighton, 4-5 May 2000

14 Ford, J., (1975) Paradigms and Fairytales: An Introduction to the Science of Meanings, Routledge & Kegan Paul, p.238.

15 Graham, M E & Eakins, J P. ARTISAN: A Prototype Retrieval System for Trademark Images. Vine, no.107, 1998, 73-80.

16 Bogdan, R., (1992) Qualitative Research for Education, 2nd edition, Simon & Schuster, pp. 72-75.

17 Salton, G., and McGill, M. J., Introduction to Modern Information Retrieval, Computer Science Series, McGraw-Hill Book Company, 1983

18 Nielsen, J., Usability Engineering, AP Professional, 1993.

19 Chin, J. P., et al. Development of an Instrument Measuring Satisfaction of the Human Computer Interface. Proceedings of CHI Conference on Human Factors in Computing Systems, New York, 1988.

20 Hix, D., and Hartson, H. R., Developing User Interfaces: Ensuring Usability Through Product & Process. Wiley, 1993.

Using Keyblock Statistics to Model Image Retrieval *

Lei Zhu, Chun Tang and Aidong Zhang

Department of Computer Science and Engineering
State University of New York at Buffalo
Buffalo, NY 14260, USA
{lzhu,chuntang,azhang}@cse.buffalo.edu,
WWW demo page: http://vangogh.cse.buffalo.edu:8080/

Abstract. Keyblock, which is a new framework we proposed for the content-based image retrieval, is a generalization of the text-based information retrieval technology in the image domain. In this framework, keyblocks, which are analogous to keywords in text document retrieval, can be constructed by exploiting a clustering approach. Then an image can be represented as a list of keyblocks similar to a text document which can be considered as a list of keywords. Based on this image representation, various feature models can be constructed for supporting image retrieval. In this paper, we will conduct keyblock statistic analysis and propose keyblock importance vector to improve the retrieval performance. The statistic analysis is based on the keyblock entropy as well as the keyblock frequency in the image database.

1 Introduction

With the advance of the multimedia technology, image data in various formats are becoming available at an explosive rate. The search and retrieval of images based on content are demanded to provide open access to relevant information and products. However, although content-based image retrieval (CBIR) using low-level features such as color [9], texture [6] and shape [10] extracted from the images has been well studied, effective and precise image retrieval still remains to be an open problem because of the extreme difficulty in image understanding. In contrast, many text-based information retrieval (IR) systems such as Yahoo, Lycos, and Google have achieved great success for indexing and querying web sites. Since both text and image retrieval are involved in information retrieval, the success of the text-based information retrieval motivates us to apply relatively mature theories and techniques of the text-based information retrieval to the image retrieval.

But the generalization of information retrieval from the text domain to the image domain is non-trivial. One of the greatest obstacles is the intrinsic difference between text and image as different media in representing and expressing information. With respect to representation, syntactically, a text document is 1-dimensional while an image is 2-dimensional. With respect to expression, semantically, the units (words) of a text document, especially those keywords, carry direct semantics which are related to the semantics of text documents. In contrast, the units of an image, either in the pixel level

* This research is supported by NSF and NCGIA at Buffalo.

or in the segment level after segmentation, provide generally no clue at all about the semantics of the image in the first case, or give unreliable object description in the second case. Thus the critical issue is how to construct feature segments in images which are similar to keywords in documents.

Keyblock [5] is such a new framework we proposed for this purpose. In our context, an image is defined as a set of feature segments such as pixels, blocks and regions, etc. In the keyblock framework, keyblocks, which are considered as the representative feature segments analogous to keywords in the text document retrieval, can be constructed by exploiting a clustering approach [3]. With a codebook of keyblocks, each image can be encoded as a list of index codes of the keyblocks in the codebook, which is similar to a text document that is considered as a linear list of keywords. With this new image representation, the retrieval can be done in the image domain by exploiting techniques in the text domain. This idea was explored and extensively tested in Zhu *et. al.* [5], where the histogram model, the vector model, and the boolean model used in the text retrieval [1] were generalized to image retrieval. It was demonstrated that all models out-perform the traditional image retrieval techniques. However, these models assumes that each keyblock has equal importance in describing image content and facilitating retrieval. This may not always be true. For example, keyblocks which occur too frequently in the images usually are not good discriminators for retrieval and their negative effects should be eliminated. In this paper, we will construct a keyblock importance vector which defines keyblock importance for retrieval based on the statistics of the whole image database, and use it to model image retrieval.

This paper is organized as follows. We will first briefly introduce the keyblock framework in Section 2. In Section 3, we will present the weighted histogram method which uses the keyblock importance vector. Two statistic measures, keyblock frequency and keyblock entropy will be used to define the keyblock importance vector. In Section 4, experimental results will be presented to demonstrate the effectiveness of the new model. The conclusion will be provided in Section 5.

2 Keyblock-based Image Retrieval

To generalize techniques of information retrieval from the text domain to the image domain, we proposed a practical framework called keyblock-based image retrieval in [5]. The approach, illustrated in Figure 1, includes the following main stages:

(1). *Keyblock generation*: generate codebooks which contain keyblocks of different resolutions. Although objects are good candidates to be considered as visual keywords in the images, object recognition for natural images is still an unsolved problem and may remain to be an open problem in the long term. With a limited degree of sacrificing the accuracy, one practical approach is to partition/segment the images into smaller blocks, and then select a subset of representative blocks using clustering algorithms. These representative blocks can be used as the keyblocks to represent the image contents. In [5], we have described how to construct keyblocks by applying clustering algorithms such as Generalized Lloyd Algorithm (GLA) and Pairwise Nearest Neighbor Algorithm (PNNA) to the segmented blocks in a training set from the images in a database. In [4], we have constructed keyblocks on the region level.

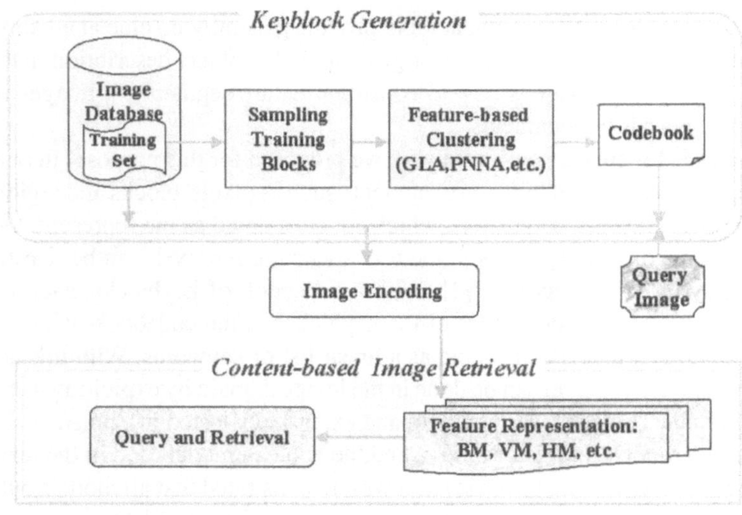

Fig. 1. Flowchart of the keyblock-based image retrieval.

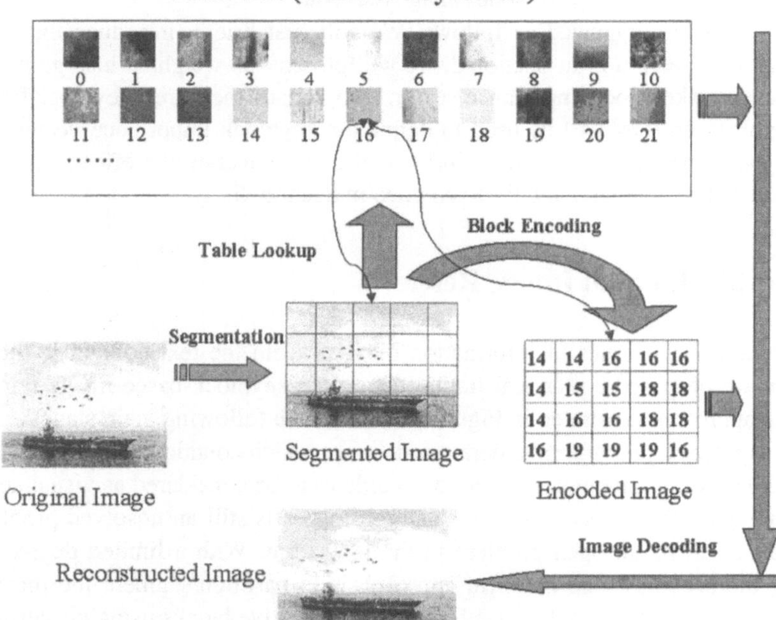

Fig. 2. The procedure of image encoding and decoding.

(2). *Image encoding*: for each image in the database as well as in the query, decompose it into blocks. Then, for each of the blocks, find the closest entry in the codebook and store the index correspondingly. Each image is then a matrix of indices, which can be treated as 1-dimensional codes of the keyblocks in the codebook. This property is similar to a text document which is considered as a linear list of keywords in text-based information retrieval. The image can also be re-constructed by using the codebook. Figure 2 illustrates the general procedure for image encoding and decoding.

(3). *Image feature representation and retrieval*: extract comprehensive image features, which are based on the frequency of the keyblocks within the image, and provide retrieval techniques to support content-based image retrieval. There are four main components in this stage: (a). Database $D = \{I_1, ..., I_j, ..., I_M\}$: a list of encoded images; (b). Codebook $C = \{c_1, ..., c_i, ..., c_N\}$: a list of keyblocks; (c). CBIR model $\varphi = (f, s)$: f is a feature extraction mapping which generates the feature vector for each image, and s is a similarity measure between the feature vectors of two images; and (d). Q: a set of visual queries, where each query q has a feature vector which is similar to the feature vector of an image.

2.1 Histogram Model

Given an encoded image which has similar representation as a text document, image features can be extracted based on keyblocks' frequency. Let $I_j = \{w_{1,j}, ..., w_{i,j}, ..., w_{N,j}\}$ be the feature vector for image I_j, and $q = \{w_1(q), ..., w_i(q), ..., w_N(q)\}$ be the feature vector for query q respectively. In the histogram model, $w_{i,j} = f_{i,j}$, where $f_{i,j}$ is the frequency of c_i appearing in I_j. Similarly, $w_i(q)$ equals the frequency of c_i appearing in q. Thus, the feature vectors I_j and q are the *keyblock histograms*. The similarity measure is defined as $s(q, I_j) = \frac{1}{1+dis(q,I_j)}$, where the distance function is

$$dis(q, I_j) = \sum_{i=1}^{N} \frac{|w_{i,j} - w_i(q)|}{1 + w_{i,j} + w_i(q)}.$$

The weighted sum is to remove the excessive influence of the frequently appearing keyblocks on the similarity.

The histogram model, as well as the boolean and vector models presented in [5], assumes that each keyblock has equal importance in describing image content and facilitating retrieval which may not always be true. In the following section, we will focus on a new model which considers different keyblocks' effects on image retrieval.

3 Weighted Histogram Model

In the text-based information retrieval, *stopword* [1] refers to words which occur frequently in the text documents. Examples of stopwords include articles, prepositions, and conjunctions such as 'a', 'the', 'by', etc. Since they are too frequent in the collection, they are usually lack of discrimination power. Thus they can be disregarded for the purpose of retrieval.

We generalize the concept of "stopword" to the keyblock-based image retrieval. Keyblocks which occur too frequently in the images usually are not good discriminators for retrieval and their negative effects should be eliminated. Furthermore, different importance of keyblocks for retrieval should be specified by defining a *keyblock importance vector* $K = \{k_1, ..., k_i, ..., k_N\}$, where each element $k_i (0 \leq k_i \leq 1)$ indicates the weight of keyblock c_i for image retrieval. With the keyblock importance vector, the distance function of the histogram model can be redefined by

$$dis(q, I_j) = \sum_{i=1}^{N} k_i * \frac{|w_{i,j} - w_i(q)|}{1 + w_{i,j} + w_i(q)}.$$

Thus we get a new model called *weighted histogram model.*

The general procedure for weight assignment is: (1) for each keyblock c_i, calculate its frequency F_i in the whole image database; and (2) use one of the weight assigning strategies listed below to assign k_i a value.

Strategy 1. Set up a threshold $A (0 < A < 100)$. If F_i is among the highest A percent keyblock frequencies, then c_i is assumed to be a "stopword", and set $k_i = 0$; else $k_i = 1$.

Strategy 2. Instead of abruptly setting weights to 0 or 1 in Strategy 1, we can set the weights from low to high in a gradual changing style according to F_i. For example, first, let $k_i = 1/log(F_i)$, then normalize k_i such that $0 \leq k_i \leq 1$. In this strategy, high-frequency keyblocks get lower weights while low-frequency keyblocks get higher weights.

However, since images are more complex than text documents for the task of retrieval, keyblock frequency may not be sufficient to determine "stopword". Other statistic metrics are needed. We propose *keyblock entropy* which is the Shannon entropy of the keyblock based on pixel values. For example, let X be a pixel in the keyblock c_i, and X is in the RGB space, $0 \leq R, G, B \leq 255$, then the keyblock entropy of c_i is defined as

$$E_i = -\sum_{R=0}^{255} \sum_{G=0}^{255} \sum_{B=0}^{255} P(R,G,B) * logP(R,G,B),$$

where $P(R,G,B)$ is the probability of pixel $X(R,G,B)$ appears in the keyblock c_i. The entropy measures color variability within the keyblock . If this entropy is low, the keyblock include a relatively uniform color information; in most cases, it appears in the background area. If the keyblock entropy is high, generally the region is foreground which is more important in capturing image content [8] [2]. Figure 3 presents two examples which show that the entropy information can be used for image segmentation. This hints us to use keyblock entropy to define keyblock importance vector. The intuition is: for images, the keyblocks in the part of background usually appear more frequently than those in the part of foreground; and background keyblocks are usually not good discriminators for retrieval because they are less effective in representing image semantics and more likely to be treated as "stopwords". Based on this assumption , there are two more strategies to define keyblock importance vector:

Strategy 3. Set $k_i = E_i$. In this strategy, lower entropy keyblocks get lower weights because they are more likely to be "stopword".

Strategy 4. Set $k_i = E_i/log(F_i)$. This strategy combines the effects of both keyblock frequency and keyblock entropy.

Fig. 3. Two images whose lower entropy regions are marked black by taking threshold at 3.7 and 2.5 respectively.

4 Performance Evaluation

Fig. 4. Retrieval results of different approaches on an animal image(109096.jpg) in COREL.

The experiments are conducted on a general-purpose image database (denoted COREL) which consists of 31646 color photos from CD7 and CD8 of *COREL Gallery 1,300,000*. These photos are stored in JPEG format with the sizes either 120×80 or 80×120. Since the content of these photos are so diverse and complex, accurate retrieval as well as the evaluation is non-trivial. Because the images are in favor of the color feature, we compare the performance of the weighted histogram model with the traditional color

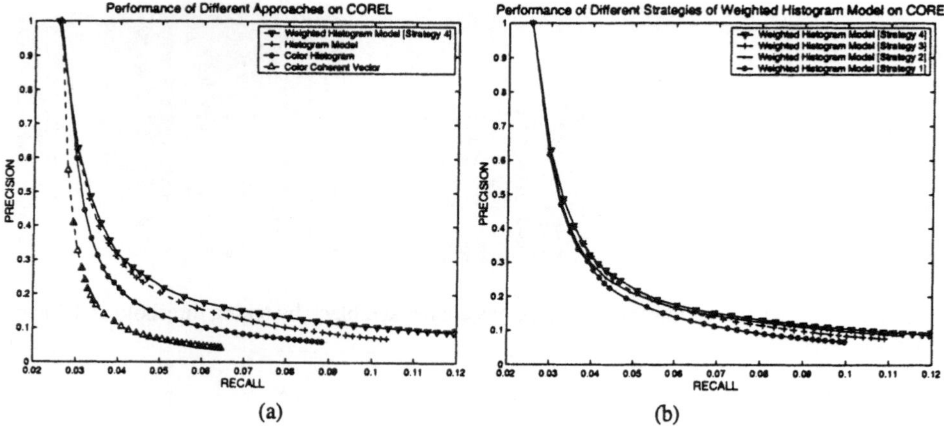

(a) (b)

Fig. 5. Average Precision-Recall on COREL: (a) performance comparison of the keyblock Approach with CCV and Color Histogram; (b) Performance comparison of different strategies for the Weighted Histogram Model.

histogram proposed by Swain and Ballard [9] and the color coherent vector (CCV) proposed by Pass and Zabih [7], as well as the histogram model [5] in the keyblock framework.

To generate the keyblocks, we selected 621 images as the training set. Three block sizes, 2×2, 4×4 and 8×8, are used. For each block size, experiments have been performed to generate the codebooks of three different sizes 256, 512 and 1024. So, the testing is conducted with 9 (3 block sizes $\times$ 3 codebook sizes) codebooks. After the codebooks are generated, each image in the database is encoded and feature vectors under each model are generated correspondingly. Due to the length limitation of the paper, we only report the best case under the condition of block size 2×2 and codebook size 256.

Figure 4 shows the retrieval results of different approaches on an animal image. For each approach, the query image is at the leftmost column. The two numbers below the images are the image ID and the similarity between the query and the matched image. The quality of the matched images from the keyblock approaches, especially from the weighted histogram model, is better because the semantics of the returned images are more related to the query image.

To evaluate the retrieval performance, we categorized 6895 images into 83 categories. These categories include human activities such as skiing and swimming, objects such as table and tools, animals such as goat and shark, landscapes such as beach and forest, etc. These 6895 images are also taken as the query set so that any bias in selecting the queries is avoided. For each query, only the images in the same category as the query are considered relevant, thus the precision and recall corresponding to the top 1, 2, ..., up to 100 retrieved images are calculated. Finally, the average precision and recall are calculated over all the 6895 queries.

Figure 5 (a) shows that the performance of the weighted histogram model outperform other approaches. For example, in the weighted histogram model, 12% of all the relevant images are among top 100 retrieved images, while only 10% are returned by the histogram model, 9% are returned by the color histogram and 6.5% are returned by CCV. At each recall level, the weighted histogram model achieves higher precision which further proves its effectiveness in image retrieval.

Figure 5 (b) compares the performance of different weight assignment strategies for the weighted histogram model proposed in Section 3. Strategy 1 ($A = 10$) performs not good because the weight assignment is too abrupt. Strategy 2 and 3 achieve similar performance while Strategy 4 is the best because it combines the effectiveness of both keyblock entropy and keyblock frequency.

5 Conclusion

In this paper, we have proposed a new model named weighted histogram model to represent image features for supporting the keyblock-based image retrieval. This new model generalizes the concept of stopword from text retrieval to image domain by defining a keyblock importance vector and use this vector to incorporate different representing power of keyblocks in representing image features. Experimental results have demonstrated that the weighted histogram model is effective in image retrieval compared with traditional techniques such as color histogram and color coherent vector as well as histogram model originally proposed for the keyblock-based image retrieval.

References

1. R. Baeza-Yates and B. Ribiero-Neto. *Modern Information Retrieval.* Addison Wesley, 1999.
2. C. Vertan and N. Boujemaa. Upgrading color distributions for image retrieval: can we do better? In *Proceedings of International Conference on Visual Information Systems Visual2000*, Lyon, 2-4 Nov. 2000.
3. A. Gersho and R. M. Gray. *Vector Quantization and Signal Compression.* Kluwer Academic Publishers, 1992.
4. Lei Zhu. *Keyblock: An approach for content-based image retrieval.* PhD thesis, Department of Computer Science and Engineering, State University of New York at Buffalo, July 2001.
5. Lei Zhu, Aidong Zhang, Aibing Rao and Rohini Srihari. Keyblock: An approach for content-based image retrieval. In *Proceedings of ACM Multimedia 2000*, pages 157–166, Los Angeles, California, USA, Oct 30 - Nov 3 2000.
6. B. Manjunath and W. Ma. Texture Features for Browsing and Retrieval of Image Data. *IEEE Transactions on Pattern Analysis and Machine Intelligence*, 18(8):837–842, August 1996.
7. G. Pass, R. Zabih, and J. Miller. Comparing images using color coherence vectors. In *Proceedings of ACM Multimedia 96*, pages 65–73, Boston MA USA, 1996.
8. Shu-Cherng Fang , J.R. Rajasekera and H.S.J. Tsao. *Entropy Optimization and Mathematical Programming.* Kluwer Academic Publishers, Boston, 1997.
9. M. Swain and D. Ballard. Color Indexing. *Int Journal of Computer Vision*, 7(1):11–32, 1991.
10. T. Syeda-Mahmood. Finding shape similarity using a constrained non-rigid transform. In *International Conference on Pattern Recognition*, 1996.

Pitch Tracking and Melody Slope Matching for Song Retrieval

Yongwei Zhu, Mohan S Kankanhalli[†], Changsheng Xu

RWCP[*] Information-Base Functions KRDL Laboratory, Kent Ridge Digital Labs
21 Heng Mui Keng Terrace, Singapore 119613
{ywzhu,xucs}@krdl.org.sg
[†]School of Computing, National University of Singapore
10 Kent Ridge Crescent Singapore 119260
mohan@comp.nus.edu.sg

Abstract. There have been several query-by-humming techniques developed for music retrieval. The techniques either are error-prone due to the inaccuracy of the hummed query or force the users to hum according to a metronome. This paper presents a new slope-based query-by-humming technique, in which the retrieval is robust to the inaccuracy in query and the use of metronome is eliminated. A pitch tracking method is developed to construct the *melody curve* from a user's humming. The method is robust to the noise in the humming. Users are even allowed to sing the melody with lyrics. We use *melody curve* to represent the melodies of the original songs and the hummed query. And curve features like *melody slope pitch range, time duration and note changes in the slopes* are extracted from the melody curves. A melody slope matching method has been developed to do music retrieval, in which the melody slopes from a query is matched with the melody slopes for the original songs in the database. Results have shown the pitch tracking method and slope-based feature matching algorithms are robust to humming inaccuracy.

1 Introduction

With the proliferation of Internet and standardization of audio compression technology, there has been a great growth in number and size of music collections or databases. The conventional fashion of organization of music collection using singer's names, album's name, or any other text-based manner is becoming inadequate for effective and efficient usage of the music collection for average users. People sometimes prefer to access the music database by its musical content rather than textual keywords. Content-based music retrieval has thus become an active research area in recent years.
Since humming is the most natural way to formulate music queries for people who are not trained or educated with music theory. Therefore many researchers have proposed techniques for query-by-humming.
There are basically two approaches. In [1-7], pitch contour of the hummed query is detected and pitch changes are then converted into strings according to the direction and/or magnitude of the pitch change. Similarly, the melody contour of the MIDI music is also converted into strings, which are stored in the database. String matching algorithms are employed to do the similarity retrieval. In [6], music melody is represented by 4 types of segments ac-

cording to the shape of the melody contour, and the associated segment duration and segment pitch. Song retrieval is done by matching segments of melody contour.

In [8,9], user's humming is transcribed into MIDI melody using commercial software, and statistical features, such as note distribution, are used to match the query to the MIDI music files in the database.

The string matching approach requires precise detection of individual notes (onset and offset) out of the hummed query. However, it is not uncommon that people substitute a long note with several short notes with same pitch value while humming a tune. And when there are tied notes in the melody, it is very likely wrong or incomplete notes are detected. The string matching result would suffer drastically when the error in note detection is not minor.

The second approach can cope with the above-mentioned issue. The query processing is done based on beats instead of notes. The statistical feature, such as tone distribution, is thus robust against erroneous query. This technique however requires the users to hum by following a metronome. Such requirement could be difficult for users sometimes. When a tune is hummed from memory, the user may not be able to keep in correct tempo. And different meters (e.g. duple, triple, quadruple meters) of the music can also contribute to the difficulty.

In this paper, we propose a new query-by-humming technique for musical song retrieval. The melodies of the musical songs are represented by melody curves and curve features are stored in the database. A user's hummed query is transcribed to a melody curve, and curve features are extracted. The retrieval is done by searching for similar occurrences of the query melody curve in the database. Algorithms have been developed to do pitch tracking in the humming and extract robust curve features for the curve searching. This technique has overcome the limitation of forcing user to hum according to a metronome. User's inability of accurately following the original music's tempo is also tolerated. The pitch tracking method can even allow a user to sing the melody with lyrics.

This paper is organized as follows. Section 2 describes how to represent music melodies by melody curves and what features to be extracted from the melody curves. In section 3, we present algorithms, by which a hummed query is pitch-tracked to form a melody curve and curve features are extracted. Section 4 presents a slope matching method, which is based on melody curve features. Section 5 presents experimental results. Section 6 concludes with a summary.

2 Melody Curve for Melody Representation

2.1 Melody Curve

Researchers have adopted melody contour to do music retrieval [1]. By melody contour, a melody is represented by a string with three alphabet symbols, such as "u" for up, "d" for down and "s" for same note, which correspond to the directions of the note changes. And music retrieval is conducted by doing string matching. Kosugi [8,9] utilized relative interval to increase the resolution of note changes.

We propose melody curve for melody representation and feature extraction. Melody curve is similar to melody contour in that, the horizontal dimension is time and vertical dimension is note/pitch value. The difference is that, there is no explicit note in melody curve and the

pitch values do not correspond to music keys. What is meaningful is the relative difference among the pitch values within one melody curve.
Construction of melody curve from music score or MIDI music file is straightforward. Each note in a music score corresponds to a piece of line in melody curve. Rests in music score are replaced by the last note's key value. The absolute pitch value in the melody curve is arbitrary. The lowest value is set above zero for convenience. An example of melody curve derived from music notes is shown in Figure 1(a).
On the contrary the construction of melody curve for a hummed query is much difficult, and the algorithms for doing this will be discussed in section 3.

2.2 Melody Curve Feature Extraction

The melody curve captures the main melodic information of the music. We believe that the shape features of the melody curve can help to do robust melody search. We have identified a few important curve shape features: peaks and valleys, and slopes.
A peak is a horizontal interval, at which the melody curve has a local maximum value. And a valley corresponds to a local minimum. They are shown in Figure 1(b).
We define the part of a melody curve from a peak to its next closest valley or from a valley to its next closes peak a *slope*. Each slope has a range value, which is the difference of the peak value and valley value. An up going slope has a positive range value and a down going slope has a negative range value.
Slope is the element that we used for curve matching. The value range of a slope and the time duration of a slope are thus important features that we will employ for doing curve matching. The pitch value changes within a slope depict the detailed melodic information and are also used in the retrieval process.

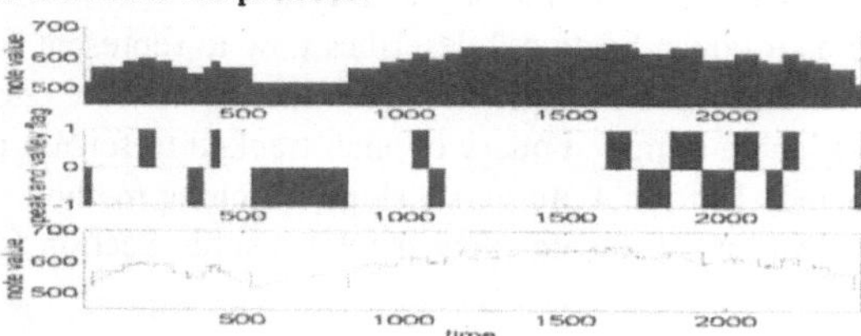

Figure 1. (a) Melody curve constructed from the music score; (b) the position of the peaks and valleys in the melody curve; (c) melody slopes.

3 Pitch Tracking and Melody Curve Processing for Hummed Query

In our query processing, the hummed query undergoes a few steps of processing:

- Pitch tracking and melody curve construction;
- Melody curve trimming and peak valley detection;
- Pitch change detection.

3.1 Pitch Tracking for Melody Curve Construction

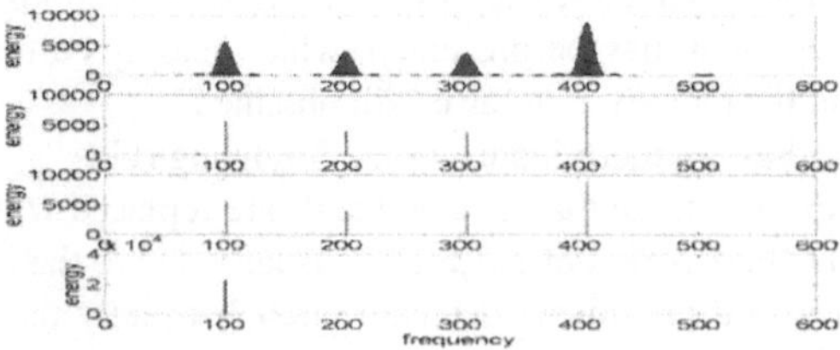

Figure 2: Pitch detection from humming

We have developed a new pitch tracking method, by which the pitch in a user's humming is stably estimated. This algorithm can help many pitch tracking applications, such as melody transcription, which is the first step for many query-by-humming techniques.

The sampled input humming is firstly windowed by a window size corresponding to 100 ms, which corresponds to 1/10 of a quarter note in a moderate slow tempo. This window size gives good time resolution for pitch tracking in music humming. The window shift step size is half of the window size.

The windowed values are transformed to frequency domain by FFT (Fast Fourier Transform). The energy $E_i(f)$ of the frequency sample at f for the ith window is calculated by taking the square of the frequency sample values. To increase the frequency resolution, zeros are padded before FFT.

Figure 2 (a) shows the spectrum of windowed samples from a humming. The pitch value is determined by the positions of peaks in the spectrum. An algorithm is developed to robustly locate the pitch in the signals.

1. Find the first 8 peaks with highest energy, and substitute each of them with a single point in frequency, and the energy is the height of the corresponding peak (top value of the peak minus the higher base value of the peak). See figure 2(b). 8 peaks are used here, because in most cases, the first 8 peaks contain more than 99% of the total energy in the spectrum.
2. Peaks with energy less than 1/9 of the max peak energy are removed. See figure 2(c).
3. The peak P_{ref} with highest energy is considered one of the harmonics of the desired pitch. So any peak that frequency is integer multiple of P_{ref} is merged with P_{ref} by shifting the energy of current peak to the energy of P_{ref}.
4. Since it is possible that the desired pitch is lower than P_{ref}, frequency that is ½, 1/3, ..., 1/8 of P_{ref} is examined. However, only candidates that have corresponding peaks in the spectrum are considered. For each candidate, the energy of all the peaks that are integer multiples of the candidate frequency are summed as E_p, and the energy of all other peaks are summed as E_n.
5. If for any candidate, the E_n is 0, then this candidate claims the pitch value. Because all the energy in the spectrum conform to this pitch value. If such candidate is found then go to step 7.
6. If for any candidate, the ratio E_n / E_p is smaller than threshold 1/3, then the pitch value is claimed by this candidate. Smaller frequency candidate has higher priority.
7. If a candidate is identified as desired pitch, but if the corresponding E_p is smaller than a threshold Te, then the pitch is declaimed. If no candidate is found, then no pitch is claimed. Figure 2(d) shows the detected pitch value.

This pitch tracking method can robustly detect the pitch in a user's humming. It can work when users hum with various syllables, such as with lyrics. In such kind of difficult cases, many small interval of no-pitch may be presented, which mainly correspond to the consonant in the humming. But the melody contour is still obtained.

The 0s in the detected pitches are modified using the following rules:

If the length of interval of 0s is small than 8, then the 0s are replaced with previous non-zero values. The reason is that short period of no-pitch is usually due to the impurity of the pitch in the windowed samples, and previously detected pitch is usually the desired pitch value for current samples. If the length of 0 interval is longer than 8, they are discarded and the previous and next values are joined together. The long period of no-pitch is usually the rest period in the melody. The positions of the discarded zeros are remembered and appropriate values are padded back when slope feature extraction is done.

The pitch values are then logarithmically scaled down to make the vertical distance proportional to the note distance used in melody curve, because human's perception of pitch difference is logarithmic to the frequency difference.

The pitch value is then quantized into integer values with one octave corresponding a value range of 120, which means the pitch resolution is 1/10 of a semitone, which is necessary for accurate feature processing and matching.

The double octave problem presents in this pitch tracking method only occasionally. We have used a simple heuristic rule to clear the double octave pitch values.

Figure 3(a) shows the pitch curve of a humming of the tune discussed previously.

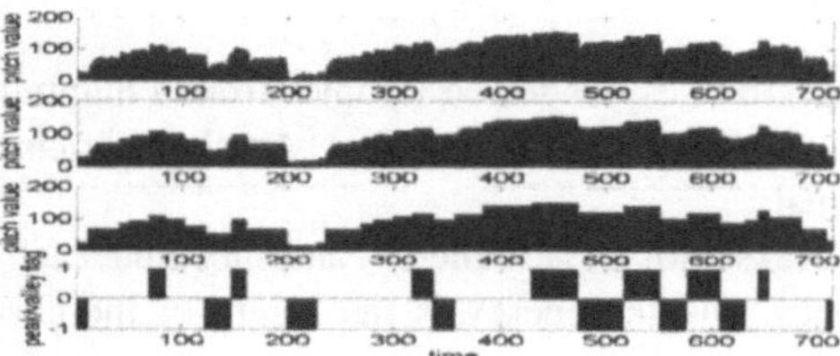

Figure 3: A pitch curve of humming by a male subject. (a) pitch curve after pitch tracking and zero removing, (b) pitch curve after peak and valley detection, (c) pitch curve after note detection within slopes, (d) positions of peaks and valleys in the pitch curve.

3.2 Melody Curve Trimming and Pitch Change Detection

After the previous step, a rough melody curve is obtained. But the ubiquity of small variation in the curve has made the curve features such as peaks and valleys difficult to be extracted. Thus a melody curve-trimming algorithm has been developed to make the desired peaks and valleys obvious. A pitch change detection algorithm is also developed to find the pitch changes in the melody curve. Details of the algorithms are presented in [10].

A result of above processing is shown in Figure 3. The result of (a) pitch tracking, (b) peak and valley detection, (c) note detection and (d) the positions of the peaks and valleys are shown respectively in the sub-plots.

The zeros discarded after pitch tracking are padded back to the pitch curve at their original positions. The values are the non-zero value that precedes the zero position. The result is shown in figure 4. Identified slopes are illustrated by straight lines connecting the beginning and end of each slope.

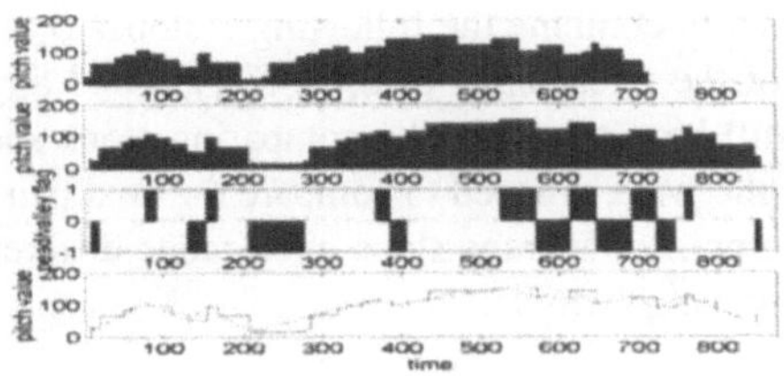

Figure 4: Pitch curve after padding of zero positions

4 Slope-Based Feature Matching for Retrieval

Each slope has a pitch range value, which is the difference between the peak value and valley value. An upward slope has a positive range value and a downward slope has a negative range value.

The duration of a slope is the time interval from the starting of the first note in the slope to the starting of the last note of the slope. The duration of the last valley/peak note is not included.

Pitch range value and duration are used for melody matching and alignment. For more accurate matching, the note information within a slope is also important. The note duration and changes between every two adjacent notes are stored as second part of the slope features and used for melody matching. Here one note is a virtual note, which may correspond to several consecutive notes with same note value in the original melody.

The slope feature for the melody curve shown in Figure 1 is illustrated as table 1.

Table 1: Slope feature for a melody curve

Slope	Notes
80 175	[(25)50(100)20(50)10]
-50 150	[(50)-10(50)-20(50)-20]
40 75	[(50)20(25)20]
-70 125	[(25)-20(100)-50]
100 500	[(300)50(100)20(50)10(50)20]

The slope feature for the pitch curve shown in Figure 4 is illustrated as table 2.

Table 2: Slope feature for a pitch curve for a humming.

Slope	Notes
83 68	[(10)41(30)18(9)9(19)15]
-55 53	[(15)-11(18)-19(20)-25]
45 24	[(24)45]
-82 53	[(14)-30(39)-52]
101 160	[(70)7(8)44(34)19(12)9(18)13(18)9]

We developed a dynamic matching algorithm to match the slope-based features of a humming $S_h(i)$ to those for the music in the database $S_n(j)$. Where $i = 1,..,N$ ($N = 4,5,6,7$) and $j = 1,\dots,M$ (M=number of slopes in the database). The matching algorithm has 3 steps.

In step 1, only the slope pitch range and time duration is used. The N slopes in $S_h(i)$ are firstly aligned with each candidate in $S_n(j)$ by comparing the pitch range values of the corresponding pairs of slopes. If the difference between a pair of corresponding slopes is smaller than a threshold T_s, then proceed to compare the next pair of slopes. If the difference is larger then T_s, then it is tried to combine the following 2 slopes $S_n(j+1)$ and $S_n(j+2)$ to current slope $S_n(j)$. The sum of the pitch range of $S_n(j)$, $S_n(j+1)$ and $S_n(j+2)$ is compared with $S_h(i)$. If the difference is still larger than T_s, the comparing stops and goes to compare the next sequence candidate. Otherwise, proceed to compare the next pair of slopes.

In step 2, two values are computed: average slope pitch range difference and slope duration correlation, as shown in following formula.

$$dist_{slope} = \left(\sum_{i=1}^{N} |(Rh(i) - Rn(i))| \right) / N \tag{1}$$

$$corr_{slope} = \sqrt{\sum_{i=1}^{n} (Dh(i) \times Dn(i)) / \left(\left(\sum_{i=1}^{n} (Dh(i))^2 \right) \left(\sum_{i=1}^{n} (Dn(i))^2 \right) \right)} \tag{2}$$

where N is the number of slope used for matching in $S_h(i)$. $R_h(i)$ is the pitch range of slopes for humming and $R_n(i)$ is the pitch range of slopes for original music. $D_h(i)$ and $D_n(i)$ is the respective slope duration after zero mean processing. Here $R_n(i)$ and $D_n(i)$ might be for a combined slope, which consists of 3 slopes.

$dist_{slope}$ measures the average distance of pitch range of the two slope sequences, and $corr_{slope}$ measures the similarity of the speed of the two melodies. The matching is done for all possible slope sequences. If $dist_{slope} < T_d$ and $corr_{slope} > T_c$, then a match is considered.

In step 3, the virtual notes of the two candidates are matched. The percentage of the pitch curve that have matches with a note curve are computed and used for the final similarity measure of the two melodies.

The note duration and note transition contains all information about the pitch values in the slopes. To do note matching, the pitch curve or note curve are constructed from the note information. All the notes of the considered slopes are matched together. The starting note value is set to 0.

The centroid note value can then be computed by:

$$note_m = \left(\sum noteval(i) \times duration(i)\right) / \left(\sum duration(i)\right) \tag{3}$$

The note duration are then normalized by:

$$duration_{normal}(i) = (duration(i)) / \left(\sum duration(i)\right) \tag{4}$$

For each note duration in humming, the note distance is computed by:

$$dist_{note}(i) = \min_j \left\| note_a(i) - note_{ma} - note_b(j) + note_{mb} \right\| \tag{5}$$

where $note_a(i)$ is a note duration in the query, $note_b(j)$ is a note durations in the note curve. The j are chosen from all note duration in the note curve that has overlap with $note_a(i)$ in the normalized duration.

The normalized durations, where $dist_{note}(i) < Tn$, are summed and set to SCORE

$$SCORE = \sum_{i: dist_{note}(i) < T_n} duration_{normal}(i) \tag{6}$$

The final similarity of the two candidates is SCORE, which characterizes how much percentage of the notes has matches with another candidate. Tn is usually set to about 10, which corresponds to 1 semitone.

5 Experimental Results and Discussion

We have collected music scores of 80 music melodies by manual entry. We also downloaded 1,070 Karaoke files in MIDI format from the web [11]. Note information of melody tracks are extracted from the MIDI files. The top notes are used whenever there are chords. Melody curve processing and slope-based feature extraction is then conducted. There are totally 149,555 slopes in the test set.
We have achieved over 90% retrieval accuracy in the top 5 rank list.

6 Conclusion

A novel query-by-humming technique has been presented in this paper. A slope-based representation of the music melody makes the matching more robust against the inaccuracies of the humming query. The melody curve for query is constructed by a robust pitch tracking method. This method does not require the user to hum at a certain tempo specified with a metronome. Our experiments also show that the method is effective for music retrieval by humming.

Reference

1. A. Ghias, J. Logan, and D. Chamberlin. "Query By Humming". *Proceedings of ACM Multimedia 95,* November 1995, pages 231-236.
2. S. Blackburn and D. DeRoure. "A Tool for Content Based Navigation of Music". *Proceedings of ACM Multimedia 98,* 1998, pages 361-368.
3. R.J. McNab, L.A. Smith, I.H. Witten, C.L. Henderson and S.J. Cunningham. "Towards the digital music library: tune retrieval from acoustic input". *Proceedings of ACM Digital Libraries'96*, 1996, pages 11-18.
4. P.Y. Rolland, G. Raskinis, and J.G. Ganascia. "Muisc Content-Based Retrieval: an Overview of the melodiscov Approach and System". *Proceedings of ACM Multimedia 99,* November 1999, pages 81-84.
5. A. Uitdenbogerd and J. Zobel. "Melodic Matching Techniques for Large Music Database". *Proceedings of ACM Multimedia 99,* November 1999, pages 57-66.
6. A. Chen, M. Chang, J. Chen, JL. Hsu, C.H. Hsu, and S. Hua, "Query by Music Segments: An Efficient Approach for Song Retrieval", *Proceedings of ICME 2000*, pages 873-876.
7. C Francu, C.G. Nevill-Manning, "Distance Metrics and Indexing Strategies for a Digital Library of Popular Music", *Proceedings of ICME 2000*, pages 889-892.
8. N. Kosugi, Y. Nishihara, S. Kon'ya, M. Yamanuro, and K. Kushima. "Music Retrieval by Humming". *Proceedings of PACRIM'99,* IEEE, August 1999, pages 404-407.
9. N. Kosugi, Y. Nishihara, T. Sakata, M. Yamanuro, and K. Kushima. "A Practical Query-By-Humming System for a Large Music Database". *Proceedings of ACM Multimedia 2000*, Los Angeles USA, 2000, pages 333-342.
10. Y. Zhu, M. Kankanhalli, C. Xu, "Music Retrieval by Humming: A Slope-based Approach", KRDL Technical Report 2001.
11. http://members.nbci.com/karaokefun/

Analysis of Environmental Sounds as Indexical Signs in Film

Simon Moncrieff[1], Chitra Dorai[2], and Svetha Venkatesh[1]

[1] Department of Computer Science, Curtin University of Technology, GPO Box U1987, Perth, 6845, W. Australia {simonm, svetha}@cs.curtin.edu.au

[2] IBM T. J. Watson Research Center, P.O. Box 704, Yorktown Heights, New York 10598, USA dorai@watson.ibm.com

Abstract. In this paper, we investigate the problem of classifying a subset of environmental sounds in movie audio tracks that indicate specific indexical semiotic use. These environmental sounds are used to signify and enhance events occurring in film scenes. We propose a classification system for detecting the presence of violence and car chase scenes in film by classifying ten various environmental sounds that form the constituent audio events of these scenes using a number of old and new audio features. Experiments with our classification system on pure test sounds resulted in a correct event classification rate of 88.9%. We also present the results of the classifier on the mixed audio tracks of several scenes taken from *The Mummy* and *Lethal Weapon 2*. The classification of sound events is the first step towards determining the presence of the complex sound scenes within film audio and describing the thematic content of the scenes.

1 Introduction

The sound track of a film enhances our enjoyment and understanding of the accompanying visual presentation. It consists of both literal sounds (e.g., dialog) and non-literal sounds (e.g., sound effects). Although dialog is the more powerful element in a movie, non-literal sounds are very useful indicators of scene content and drama. For example, sounds that are associated with car chases in a scene are trademark sound effects such as car horns, tires skidding, engines revving, etc. In this paper, we investigate audio features that best discriminate between sound effects that occur as acoustic (sound) events during car chase scenes and violent scenes in film. There is a great deal of literature on the analysis of audio tracks including systems proposed for segmenting the audio into silence, speech, music, noise [7], for detecting violent sounds [5], and more general systems for aural content based media indexing and retrieval [1, 3, 7]. Our work goes beyond the basic segmentation and classification of low level sounds, and analyses various sound events and presents what event classes reliably signal thematic content of a scene in film.

Sound event detection is analogous to object recognition in computer vision and thus, a broad task. Consequently, this paper focuses on a subset of sound events, e.g., sirens, gun shots, etc., that indicate specific indexical use. These sound events are semantically rich and compositionally form high level sound scenes that indicate particular dramatic purposes in film, in this case, violence and car chase scenes. Detecting the presence of the sound scenes enables both the analysis and characterisation of the film at a higher level of abstraction than is done currently. We propose some new audio features for sound event detection, and analyse the performance of classifiers such as decision trees and Support Vector Machines using these features on data containing both pure sounds and mixed movie sound tracks. Our results show that the new features enable a better discrimination between the sound events studied.

2 Sound Event Detection

Non-literal sounds form the trademark sounds for many types of scenes in film. For example car chases are characterised by the sounds of *engines revving*, *horns*, *sirens*, *tires skidding*, *car crashes*, and the *breaking of glass*. Violent sound scenes are characterised by *explosions*, both *single* and *multiple* occurrences of *gunfire*, and the aural impact of *people hitting each other*. These sounds form the 10 sound event classes studied to characterise car chase and violent scenes. In this paper, we propose a system that will detect these ten individual sound events which can then aid in characterising a scene depending on the sound events that compose the scene, as a *car chase scene* or *violent scene*.

Some of the experimental data used in this work, comprising of pure, homogeneous sound samples of the 10 event categories was obtained from the WWW. A total of 861 sound samples were collected, with each event class containing sounds of varying duration and occurrences in samples. All audio files were converted to 16-bit mono with a sampling rate of $22050Hz$ before being processed for features. When a feature was calculated and smoothed using a rectangular window, a window of size 512 frames, with an overlap of 256 frames was used. For the case where the audio features were calculated using the SFS [2] software, the default SFS window and window size values were used.

2.1 Audio Features for Sound Events

A number of low level psychoacoustical and physical audio features and other higher order features derived from the low level ones were used to to develop a comprehensive audio feature set for sound event discrimination. The large feature set was refined to create an optimal feature set according to the efficacy of each feature in classifying and discriminating between the sound event classes. The optimal feature set was determined so as to encapsulate the characteristics of an audio signal within a single vector.

To determine the effectiveness of a feature vector, the entire set of audio features and feature statistics were first calculated for each of the pure homogeneous audio samples. For each audio sample, the first 25 mel-frequency cepstral coefficients, averaged over the entire sound signal, were used as a baseline feature vector. The remaining feature values, or set of statistics computed, were appended individually to the base feature vector. The statistics determined for the temporal features to summarise the time-varying behaviour were the mean, standard deviation, skew, and kurtosis. The statistical autocorrelation, calculated for all lags without wrap around, was also determined for each temporal feature, again using the mean, standard deviation, skew, and kurtosis to summarise the autocorrelation. For each new feature vector set generated in this way from the audio samples, a decision tree was trained using a subset of the vectors, around 700. The tree was then tested using the remainder of the vectors. The same training and testing audio feature vectors were used for each feature vector set generated. The classification accuracy of each feature vector and its ability to distinguish between sound classes was compared with the classification accuracy of the baseline case, as determined by the baseline feature vector comprising of the first 25 mel-frequency cepstral coefficients. Using this method a suitable feature set was determined to distinguish between the sound classes by selecting the features and statistics with the highest classification rate and sound class discrimination. The resultant optimal feature set (N=33) included: the first 5 mel-frequency cepstral coefficients [1], the volume contour features [3], characteristics of the energy envelope and loudness, duration [6], the zero crossing rate [7], and the normalised fundamental frequency [6]. Included also were the new features we developed that characterise the amplitude boundary behaviour, the harmonicity and inharmonicity of a sound signal, and repetition within a sound sample.

2.2 New Audio Features

The new audio features are presented in detail here. Some of these features required thresholds, which were derived either based on empirical evidence shown by the data or using a simple percentage limit [4]. The graphs displayed depict the values for audio features computed across samples for each class. In each graph, the values are plotted after sorting them in ascending order against sample numbers. As different audio classes have different numbers of samples, the cutoff for each audio class on the graph corresponds to the number of samples in the audio class.

Boundary Behaviour *Loudness Minima and Maxima*: The raw loudness minima and maxima are determined by detecting the number of peaks and troughs present in the non-smoothed loudness of the signal in a sample. The loudness was determined directly from the signal without using a window for smoothing. The peak and trough values are again detected by using an upper and lower percentage limit. The number of peaks calculated using the raw loudness of the signal is a coarser feature than both repetition, which uses the smoothed energy envelope, and the smoothed loudness maxima, as the loudness was not smoothed by a window. This feature also differs from repetition as it reflects the number of peaks present in the sound. The feature also allows for comparison between maxima and minima as both peaks and troughs are calculated. Figure 1 shows the peaks detected for the sound samples in each class. The plot shows the feature trend for sound events such as single gun, multiple gun and glass breaking to have a low number of peaks, whereas engine and siren sounds have a relatively higher number of peaks. Siren sounds were also found to have a higher number of troughs.

The smoothed loudness maxima were similarly determined by calculating the number of peaks in the smoothed loudness of the signal. The smoothed maxima distinguishes repeated and single peak audio signals, which if correctly determined have a lower number of maxima. If the multiple occurrences of a sound event within an individual audio sample are sufficiently distinguishable this features also approximates the number of occurrences of the audio event present in the sample. This is possible if there is a clear distinction between the maximum amplitude of one occurrence of the event

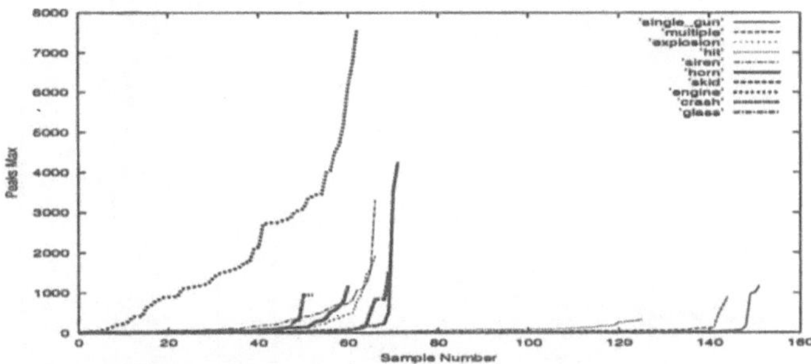

Fig. 1. Raw loudness peaks in the data set for each sound event.

to the next. Figure 2 shows the number of maxima detected for the sound samples, in ascending order for each class. The single gunshot generally has 0 maxima, when the first loudness value is a maximum due to smoothing, or 1, whereas multiple peaks are detected for multiple gunfire. This is displayed in Figure 2, where hit, single gun, and to a lesser extent glass breaking, have maxima concentrated in the lower valued regions.

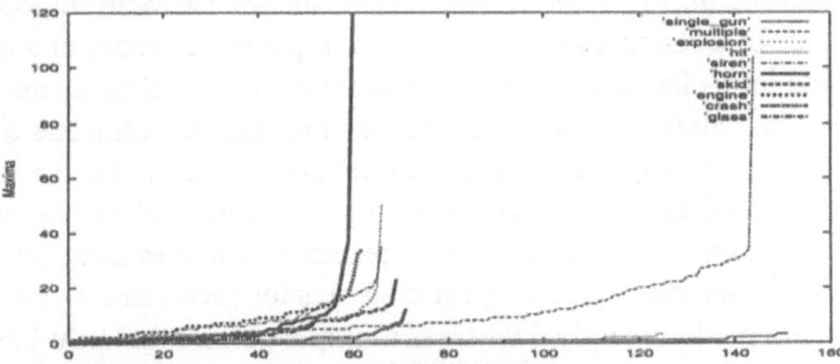

Fig. 2. Peaks in the smoothed loudness values of audio samples.

Extrema: This determines the proportion of the smoothed energy envelope that is in either a maximal or minimal energy region of the envelope. Two proportions were calculated, one for the minimal region of the envelope and one for the maximal region. The range between the maximum and minimum energy of the envelope was used to heuristically determine an upper and lower threshold which was used to detect regions of high and low energy respectively. This allows the determination of the regions of the energy envelope of the signal where the energy is concentrated, or diminished. For example, a sound with rapid attack and decay, but a longer sustained period, will have a majority of the energy in the higher energy regions of the signal. Figure 3 shows the maxima proportions for the samples in ascending order for each class. Glass breaking and car crash events have a high proportion of high energy, the remaining sound types have a lower maximum energy component, due either to repetition, multiple gunfire, or fast attack and decay, single gunfire. With energy minima, horn and hit have the largest proportion of minimal energy.

Repetition Repetition is a binary value feature that determines whether or not a sound is repeated. If there are multiple occurrences of a sound in a signal repetition is set to a value of 1, otherwise the value is set to 0. The smoothed energy envelope of the signal was used to determine whether or not a sound is repeated. The algorithm to determine repetition is as follows: Upper and lower thresholds are determined for the smoothed envelope using the mean, standard deviation, and minimum and maximum

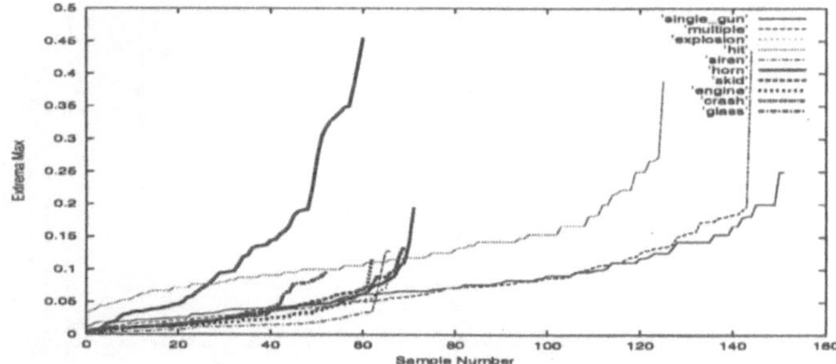

Fig. 3. Maxima proportion of smoothed energy envelope over data set.

values of the envelope. The thresholds for each signal are determined dynamically given the envelope of the sound. The sound is repeated if the energy envelope exceeds the upper threshold and subsequently descends below the lower threshold and then exceeds the upper threshold again. That is, there is a peak, a trough, and then another peak in the energy envelope.

Repetition allows the classifier to make the distinction between audio signals with a single occurrence of a sound and signals with multiple occurrences of a sound. This is both an inter and intra class distinction. For example, the interclass distinction between a single gunshot and multiple automatic weapons fire, and the intraclass distinction between a single occurrence of a horn and multiple horns. Figure 4 shows the repetition detected for the sound samples in ascending order for each class. As the values are shown in ascending order, the point at which repetition changes from 0 to 1 is an indication of how many samples exhibit repeated sounds for each class. For example single gun audio data are predominantly 0 whereas multiple gunfire has only 10% of the data as 0.

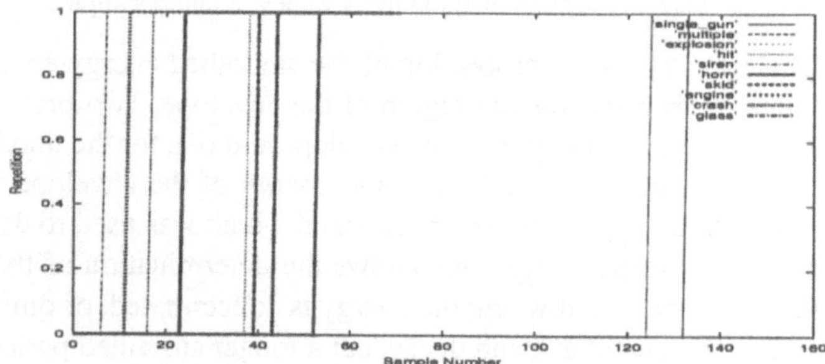

Fig. 4. Repetition detection on the data set.

Inharmonicity This measures the non-harmonic content of the signal. The fundamental frequency of the signal was determined by SFS using autocorrelation of the signal. If a segment of the signal was determined to be inharmonic, the fundamental frequency is set to a value of 0. Inharmonicity is calculated as the proportion of the fundamental frequency that is 0. For example, sirens are predominantly harmonic, gunfire is predominantly inharmonic, and sounds such as tires skidding contain harmonic portions. Figure 5 shows the inharmonicity for the sound samples in ascending order for each class, the harmonic sounds are concentrated at lower values and the inharmonic sounds at higher values. Siren, horn, and to a lesser extent skid and engine have lower values of inharmonicity.

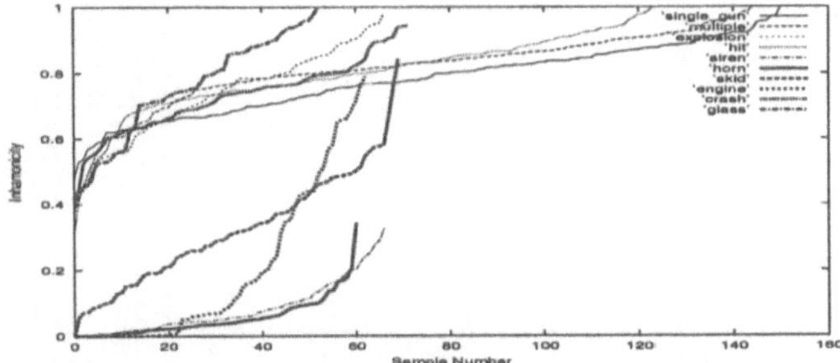

Fig. 5. Ascending values of inharmonicity over the data set.

Harmonicity Harmonicity is a measure of the stable harmonic content of the audio signal. The fundamental frequency of the sound signal was determined by the SFS using cepstral coefficients. The signal is harmonic at time t_i if the fundamental frequency is defined, that is, greater than 0. The fundamental frequency of the signal is stable if the frequency does not vary from time t_i to t_{i+1}. In order to determine the stability of the fundamental frequency, $\mathcal{F}$, the absolute first derivative was calculated.

$$\Delta\mathcal{F}_i = |\mathcal{F}_i - \mathcal{F}_{i-1}| \tag{1}$$

The stable and harmonic content, *content*, of the signal was then calculated by

$$content = \sum_{i=1}^{N} hs(\mathcal{F}_i). \tag{2}$$

$$\text{where } hs(\mathcal{F}_i) = \begin{cases} 1, & \text{if } \Delta\mathcal{F}_i = 0 \text{ and } \mathcal{F}_i > 0; \\ 0, & \text{otherwise.} \end{cases}$$

Two statistics were then derived from *content* to measure the harmonicity of the sound. The first is the ratio of the harmonic and stable fundamental frequency content to both harmonic and inharmonic content of the signal. The ratio of the harmonic and stable fundamental frequency content to just harmonic content of the signal determines the second harmonicity measure. Harmonicity detects portions of the sound signal that are harmonic and do not vary over time. For example, both horns and sirens contain periods of stable fundamental frequency, while gunfire has little detectable harmonicity, and even less stable harmonic content, as shown in Figure 6, which shows the first harmonicity measure for the sound samples in ascending order for each class. Siren and horn occur in the high ranges of the harmonicity measure, skid in the middle range, and multiple and single gunfire, and hit in the lower range for both harmonicity measures. Engine sounds, while relatively low in inharmonicity, also contain little stable and harmonic audio content.

3 Experimental Results

A decision tree classification system, trained using the optimal feature set described in Section 2.1, was used to study event detection with both pure audio samples and sound samples extracted from the the audio tracks of selected films. A Support Vector Machine (SVM) was also used for event classification, trained using the same data.

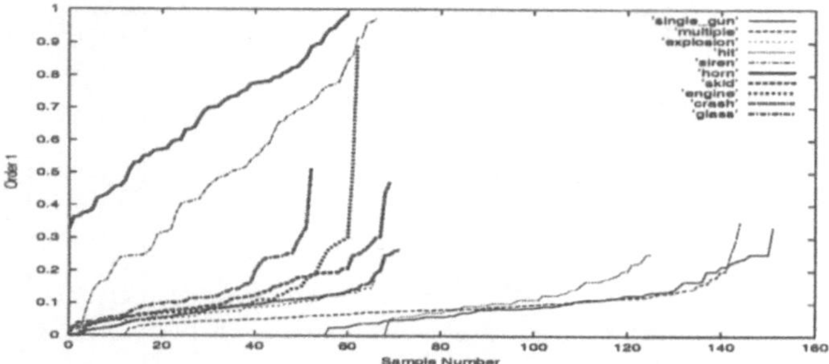

Fig. 6. Harmonicity measure 1 values in ascending order.

3.1 Event Classification of Pure Sounds

Pure audio sample event classification was studied to derive a reference performance mark to compare when real movie audio tracks, which contain mixed sounds, were used for testing. The features described in Section 2.1 were calculated for each pure audio sample. The resulting feature vectors were used to test classification performance for the homogeneous sound samples. The DT-based system was tested using a random selection of 65% of the pure sound samples from each class as training data and the remainder as test data. An average of 88.9% correct classification was achieved from 25 test trials. The general classification performance was good, with the exception of car crash events; this can be attributed to the lack of structure of the sounds associated with car crashes. With SVMs, a five fold cross-validation was performed on the data achieving an average of 87.7% correct classification.

3.2 Event Detection with Movie Audio Tracks

Sample scenes were extracted from two action movies, *Lethal Weapon* 2 and *The Mummy*. The DT and SVM, trained using the pure homogeneous audio samples, were used to classify the sound samples extracted from the movie scenes. Table 1 shows the confusion matrix for the combined DT classification results for 7 scenes, 2 of which consisted of car chases, and 5 of violence. The table shows the number of events from each class that were correctly classified and also how many from each class were incorrectly classified as instances of other classes. From the table it can be seen that the classification accuracy is lower compared with the classification of pure audio. This is due to the nature of the film audio data, which contains mixed sounds, including other low level sound events. However, the misclassifications largely occur within the subset of sounds that form the high level scene. For example, horn, skid and siren are misclassified as engine due to the presence of engines in the background of the sounds, but most of the misclassifications occurred within the broad category of car chase scenes. The DTs correctly recognised 93.8% of car chase events and 73.0% of violence events, while the correct detection rates for SVMs were 80.4% and 78.2% respectively. The low level of accuracy in classifying multiple gunfire is attributed to the semantic labelling of certain sound samples taken from *The Mummy*. Multiple simultaneous single occurrences of gunfire were labelled, for the purposes of classification, as multiple, or automatic, gunfire.

4 Conclusion

This paper proposes a method for analysing and classifying a set of non-literal film sounds, using signal features, *old and new*, into a number of semantic-rich sound classes

Table 1. Confusion matrix resulting from Decision Tree-based classification of car chase and violent scenes comprising of the ten sound events.

Class		a	b	c	d	e	f	g	h	i	j
Engine	a	38									
Horn	b	8		3							
Skid	c	15		5	1			1			
Siren	d	8		4	5						
Glass	e					3			1		
Car crash	f	1						2	2		
Explosion	g										
Single	h	4				1			28	8	1
Multiple	i	5				10	8	6	6	11	
Hit	j									1	4

that form the constituent audio events of certain high level sound scenes in cinema. The classification system was on the whole successful in classifying the 10 semantic audio event classes that serve as aural icons denoting the occurrence of car chase and violence in film using the pure audio samples. The classification accuracy of the audio obtained directly from film is lower due to the nature of the audio data, which rarely consists of pure distinct sounds. However, the misclassifications generally occur between the events within the sound scenes, which suggests that the classification system can be used to classify the film audio data according to higher sound scene type. The reliable classification of sound events is the first step in investigating the feasibility of sound scene detection in film for deducing thematic scene content.

References

[1] Foote, J. T.: Content-based retrieval of music and audio. Multimedia Storage and Archiving Systems II, Proceedings of SPIE. (1997) 138–147

[2] Huckvale, M.: Speech Filing System. Url: www.phon.ucl.ac.uk/resources/sfs/

[3] Liu, Z., Wang, Y., Chen, T.: Audio Feature Extraction and Analysis for Scene Segmentation and Classification. Journal of VLSI Signal Processing Systems for Signal, Image, and Video Technology, **20(1)** (1998)

[4] Moncrieff, S., Dorai, C., Venkatesh, S.: Detecting Indexical Signs in Film Audio for Scene Interpretation Tech Rep. 2001/1, Curtin University of Technology, W. Australia

[5] Pfeiffer, S., Fischer S., Effelsberg, W.: Automatic audio content analysis. Technical Report TR-96-008, University of Mannheim, April 1996

[6] Wold, E., Blum, T., Keislar, D., Wheaton, J Content-Based Classification, Search, and Retrieval of Audio. IEEE Multimedia, **3(3)** (1996) 27–36

[7] Zhang, T., Jay Kuo, C.-C.: Classification and retrieval of sound effects in audiovisual data management. 33rd Asilomar Conference on Signals, Systems, and Computers, Oct 1999.

A Low Missing Rate Audio Search Technique for Cantonese Radio Broadcast Recording

H.S. Lam, Tan Lee, and P.C. Ching
Department of Electronic Engineering
The Chinese University of Hong Kong

ABSTRACT

This paper describes a keyword spotting based audio searching engine that can browse through a long recordings of radio broadcast with a low missing rate. Both sub-syllable (*Initial-Final*) and base-syllable based keyword spotting strategies are investigated. The system can achieves a 20% missing rate with around 1.5 false alarm per keyword per hour (FA/KW/H) and the performance cam be further improved to near zero missing rate with as low as 0.5 FA/KW/H by incorporating better keyword specifications.

1. Introduction

In this study, we deal with radio broadcasting materials in Hong Kong. Archives of radio broadcast, recorded for monitoring purpose, usually last for many hours and contain heterogeneous sessions like news, phone-in sessions, music, DJ chattering, and frequently noises due to interference. There is no transcription or caption available to aid the searching. To locate interested sessions in such a huge amount of audio data requires the efforts of many hours of labour work in listening to the recordings manually. This is obviously a very boring job and is prone to missing of important messages.

There are various automatic methods to search for key sessions in audio archives, for example, using dynamic time warping between recognized inputs and a well-prepared index [1], pre-computed phonetic lattices [2][3], keyword spotting based on captions [4], or text search based on large vocabulary continuous speech recognition (LVCSR) result [5][6]. These approaches require significant efforts either to obtain an accurate transcription beforehand, to identify certain pattern existed in the broadcast, or to carry out real-time LVCSR on the huge amount of speech data.

The majority of radio broadcasts in Hong Kong are in Cantonese, one of the major Chinese dialects. Cantonese is a monosyllabic language in which each Chinese character is pronounced as a single syllable. A Chinese word is typically constituted by a couple of characters. Based on this special structure of Cantonese speech, we have designed a Cantonese Broadcasting Searching System (CBAS) to search very long recordings of radio broadcast without first converting them into phonetic lattices or LVCSR results. The system helps users to locate audio section(s) that contains his/her own selection of keywords quickly while ignoring those not falling into their interest.

CBAS is designed to have a low missing rate. This is required in many real-world applications, for example, automatic monitoring of phone-in to radio programs to remove obscene language, or searching for radio recordings of a major event, where losses due to missing may not be recoverable – once the system declared a session void of keywords, the session will not be further analyzed. On the other hand, false alarm may be tolerated because users can easily identify and dismiss the false alarms by actually listening to it. The worst condition for severe false alarm is that the user must spend as much time as without CBAS.

To achieve a low missing rate, the use of LVCSR is precluded because state-of-the-art LVCSR on broadcasting news reports an word error rate in the order of 30%-40% [5][6]. Thus, we decided to use keyword-spotting technique with null grammar to cover the vastly diverse languages encountered in regular radio broadcast. Both syllable and sub-syllable based keyword spotting techniques have been used in this work.

The technique for CBAS are not limited to radio broadcastings. It can be applied to long recording of audio data collected from investigation interviews, conference recordings, or voice messages [7] for easy searching and reference.

This paper is organized as follows. In Section 2 we discuss the system modeling employed by CBAS. Section 3 will address the system design. In Section 4 and 5 we will describe our testing system and present our test results. Conclusions will be given in Section 6.

2. Acoustic Modeling

2.1 Training Data

The speech corpora used for the training of our Cantonese speech recognition systems are CUWORD™ and CUSENT™ developed at the DSP Laboratory, Department of Electronic Engineering, the Chinese University of Hong Kong [8][9]. Although these corpora were designed mainly for dictation-like applications, they serve as a starting point for full Cantonese syllable coverage.

2.2 Modeling Strategies

Cantonese is a tonal language. However, we choose to ignore tonal information because tones are difficult to be accurately determined due to context variations. In addition, without considering the tonal variation, the number of models can be reduced so that the recognition system requires relatively less training data.

For open vocabulary keyword spotting without a language model, we must rely on accurate acoustic modeling for good performance. In this study, two types of acoustic models are investigated: (1) *Initial-Final* modeling (IF), and (2) Base syllable modeling (BS), in a view to address the concern of recognition technique and filler design in keyword spotting. In section 4 we will investigate the performance of the two modeling approaches and to verify whether our design can meet the low missing rate requirement on radio broadcast recordings.

The acoustic features used are the mel-frequency cepstral coefficients (MFCC) which include 12 cepstral coefficients together with the energy. The first and second derivatives of the parameters are also included in the final feature vectors, making the number of elements in the final feature vectors 39.

The training and testing are carried out with an HMM based speech recognizer. For initial-final modeling, 3 states per HMM model are used. For base syllable approach 11 states per model are used. All states contain four Gaussian mixtures.

In this paper, all phonetic units are labeled using the Linguistic Society of Hong Kong (LSHK) system [10].

2.2.1 Initial-Final modeling (IF)

Cantonese syllables have the general structure of $(C_1)V(C_2)$, where C_1 and C_2 are optional consonants and V can be either a simple vowel or a diphthong. Traditional Chinese phonology treats each syllable as the combination of an *Initial* (C_1) and a *Final* (VC_2) [11]. The total number of *Initials* and *Finals* are 19 and 53 respectively.

2.2.2 Base syllable modeling (BS)

Cantonese is a monosyllabic language. The number of different base syllables is about 580 [8][11]. We remove some rarely occurring syllables and retain only 459 syllables in our research. These are trained and served as a syllable pool for keyword construction. Keywords, once having been input by a user, are translated into this reduced syllable set. Fillers are based on Cantonese finals.

3. Keyword Spotting System Design

3.1 IF based keyword spotting system

Figure 1 shows the basic structure of the IF based keyword spotter. There are two parts. One is an IF-based large vocabulary continuous speech recognizer (LVCSR). The other part is a keyword spotter. After LVCSR outputs an IF sequence, a keyword spotter checks to see if the sequence contains keywords.

IF based keyword spotter takes two parameters that are the keyword list and filler list. When new keywords are defined, they are converted into IF transcriptions and added to the system straightforwardly.

With the IF acoustic models, there is no basic difference between keyword sequences and filler sequences at the acoustic level. The classification between keywords and fillers is done after IF sequences are determined. Any sequence that is not mapped into a keyword sequence is treated as filler.

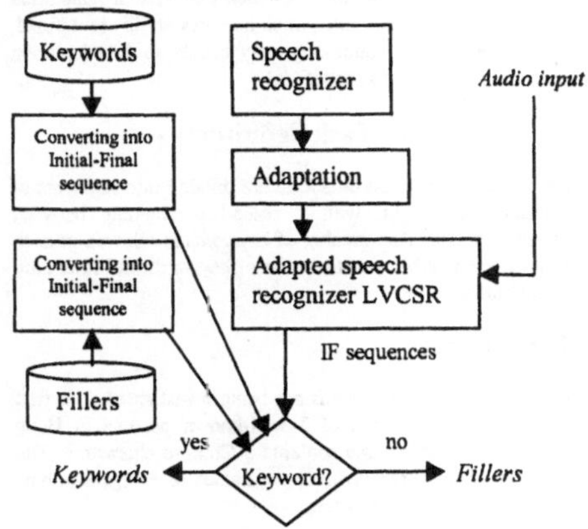

Figure 1 Keyword spotting using Initial-Final models

3.2 BS based keyword spotting system

Figure 2 shows the BS based keyword spotter. In this case, different keywords are modeled as the concatenations of base syllables. Using syllables as the basic recognition unit has the benefit of better modeling accuracy than IF models because syllables implicitly incorporate the intra-syllable co-articulation effects. However, the large number of models requires relatively large amount of data for training and adaptation and makes recognition speed rather slow.

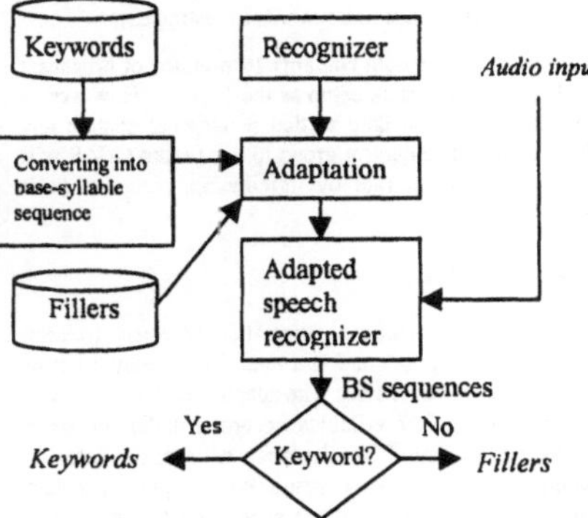

Figure 2. Keyword spotting using base-syllable models

However, if system adaptation is deferred to after keyword definition, we can reduce the number of models that need to be adapted. Although it has the drawback that system adaptation must be carried out each time when new keywords are defined, the reduction in model number greatly speeds up the adaptation process so the trade off is beneficial.

4. Task definition

Long recordings of radio broadcast are divided into segments of 10 seconds in length, with 1 second overlapping between adjacent segments. Any number of keywords is allowed in each recording segment because the order of keywords and fillers are not constrained.

4.1 Keywords

Two different sets of keywords are being investigated. The first set consists of the names of 3 well-known persons in Hong Kong. Each person's name contains 3 Chinese characters. The second set of keywords involves the names of 3 organizations, each containing 5 – 7 characters.

4.2 Test data

Two sets of test data are prepared. The first set contains 34 minutes of radio broadcasting covering different topics. They are randomly selected from a large collection of radio broadcast archives. Half of the recordings are news and the other half are mixtures of phone-in sessions, music and casual chatting among DJ's. The total number of syllable occurrences is about 10,000. Table 1 shows the coverage of these keywords in this set of testing data.

Keyword Set	Occurrence Count
Set 1: Person Names	19
Set 2: Organization Names	17

Table 1 Occurrence of keywords in testing data

The second set of testing data contains 10 minutes of broadcast data recorded under the same setup as the first set. However, it is chosen from a different date so that it does not contain any keywords. It is used as a control group to verify that CBAS will not produce low missing rate by introducing excessive false alarms.

4.3 Adaptation data

There is an obvious acoustic mismatch between training database (dictation purpose) and test data. Thus, adaptation of the acoustic models is carried out. The adaptation data consist of 21 sentences covering 257 syllables, recorded under the same conditions as the test data. The adaptation data set is chosen to not containing keywords. As a result our adaptation favors fillers rather than keywords, and we expect our test system to have a slightly higher missing rate than actual system because in actual system adaptation data containing keywords can be used.

5. Experimental Results

5.1 The effect of model adaptation strategy

Given the limited amount of adaptation data, we group similar models (IF or base syllable) into one cluster so that each model will be accessed to the same amount of adaptation data. When the number of clusters increases fewer models will be grouped together so that the adaptation will be more specific but the amount of adaptation data available to each model will decrease.

To determine the optimal number of adaptation clusters that we should use, we carry out Test 5.1 to search for the Keyword Set 1 in test data set 1.

Adaptation clusters	Performance			
	H	D	S	I
1	15	3	1	27
2	16	3	0	18
4	16	3	0	20
8	16	3	0	23
256	13	6	0	23

Table 2 Performance of IF based keyword spotter with different number of adaptation clusters

Adaptation clusters	Performance			
	H	D	S	I
1	14	5	0	24
2	15	4	0	20
4	1	18	0	2
8	0	19	0	0

Table 3 Performance of BS based keyword spotter with different number of adaptation clusters

Legends:

H: Hits (correct spotting)
D: Deletions/Missing
S: Substitutions
I: Insertions/False alarm

From the above results, we conclude that increasing adaptation clusters makes adaptation more specific. And because of insufficient adaptation data, performance of base-syllable based keyword spotter will drop sharply if more than 1 or 2 clusters are used. Compared with BS approach, IF modeling is less prone to the number of adaptation clusters, although the best performances of the IF and the BS approaches are quite similar.

5.2 The effect of keyword length

To increase the efficiency of searching, the user tends to use longer keywords that contain more specific information. This will alleviate the false alarm problem because it will be more difficult for a string of syllables other than the keywords to be mis-recognized as a keyword string. However, missing rate may also increase. We have carried out Test 5.2 using Keyword Set 2, which contains 5 to 7 characters, to verify that our system can cope with the requirement under different keyword lengths.

From the results of Test 5.1 we found that the optimal adaptation cluster number is 2. So we use 2 clusters in this test as well.

Keyword spotter	Performance		
	Missing rate	False alarm per keyword per hour	Occurrence count of keywords
IF with short keywords	16%	1.67	19
BS with short keywords	21%	1.86	19
IF with long keywords	18%	0.93	17
BS with long keywords	0	0.42	17

Table 4 Performance of keyword spotters under different keyword length on test data set 1

	No. of false alarms
IF with short keywords	2
BS with short keywords	2
IF with long keywords	0
BS with long keywords	0

Table 5 Performance of keyword spotters on test data set 2

6. Conclusions and future work

CBAS is designed to help users efficiently search archives of Cantonese radio broadcastings without the aid of transcripts or captions, with little missing rate. By utilizing special structure of Cantonese we tested the ability of sub-syllable based (initial-final) and syllable based (base-syllable) keyword-spotting system to fulfil the design criteria.

After a small amount of adaptation, both types of keyword spotters can achieve a missing rate close to 20% with reasonable false alarms. Initial-final based keyword spotter is more adaptable because initial-final models have relative simple structures. Base syllable based spotter is more sensitive to adaptation settings such as the number of adaptation clusters. The test result shows a lower bound rather than optimum system performance because the amount of adaptation data is kept to minimum and the keywords are chosen to not appear in the adaptation data. For more stable system performance, more adaptation data are required and user can be asked to provide audio samples of keywords at system startup.

When longer keywords are used, the false alarm rate drops as expected for both IF modeling and BS modeling. However, it is interesting to observe that for IF based keyword spotter there is a slight drop of missing rate, while BS based keyword spotter improves its performance greatly. The latter is quite unexpected. It may be due to the fact that the implicit intra-syllable constraints enjoyed by base syllable modeling helps to reduce false alarm to such a high degree that the system can afford a lower threshold for keywords,

In future work we would like to address the open vocabulary problem. Because each time the searching criteria is different, keyword changes must be handled effectively and efficiently.

There are limitations to our approach. We cannot find a consistent set of keywords that appear in everyday radio broadcastings. Thus our results may be prone to statistical variations. However, we believe that our findings serve as a basis for further investigation of efficient searching and browsing of long audio recordings.

7. References

[1] Philippe Gelin, Chris J. Wellekens, "Keyword spotting for video soundtrack indexing", *ICASSP'96*

[2] Alexander G. Haupmann and Howard D. Wactlar, "Indexing and search of multimodal information," *ICASSP'97*

[3] S. J. Young, M. G. Brown, J. T. Foote, G. J. F. Jones, K. Sparck Jones, "Acoustic indexing for multimedia retrieval and browsing," *ICASSP'97*

[4] Yasuo Ariki, Yoshiaki Sugiyama, "A TV News Retrieval System with Interactive Query Function", *COOPIS'97*

[5] Dave Abberley, Steve Renals and Gary Cook, "Retrieval of broadcast news documents with the THISL system", *ICASSP'98*

[6] Steven Wegmann, Puming Zhan, and Larry Gillick, "Progress in broadcast news transcription at Dragon Systems", *ICASSP'99*

[7] R. Rose, E. Chang and R. Lippmann, "Techniques for information retrieval from voice message," *ICASSP'91*

[8] W.K. Lo *et al.*, "Development of Cantonese spoken language corpora for speech applications," *ISCSLP'98*

[9] Tan Lee, W.K. Lo, P.C. Ching and Helen Meng, "Spoken language resources for Cantonese speech processing", to appear in *Speech Communications.*

[10] 《粤語拼音字表》, the Linguistic Society of Hong Kong, 1997.

[11] Tan Lee and P. C. Ching, "Cantonese Syllable Recognition Using Neural Networks", *IEEE Transactions on Speech and Audio Processing,* Vol. 7. No. 4, July 1999.

Emotion Detection from Speech to Enrich Multimedia Content

Feng Yu[1*], Eric Chang[2], Ying-Qing Xu[2], Heung-Yeung Shum[2]

[1]Dept. of Computer Science and Technology, Tsinghua Univ., Beijing 100084, P.R.C.
yufeng99@stumail.tsinghua.edu.cn
[2] Microsoft Research China, 3/F Beijing Sigma Center, Beijing 100080, P.R.C.
{ echang,yqxu,hshum}@microsoft.com

Abstract. This paper describes an experimental study on the detection of emotion from speech. As computer-based characters such as avatars and virtual chat faces become more common, the use of emotion to drive the expression of the virtual characters becomes more important. This study utilizes a corpus containing emotional speech with 721 short utterances expressing four emotions: anger, happiness, sadness, and the neutral (unemotional) state, which were captured manually from movies and teleplays. We introduce a new concept to evaluate emotions in speech. Emotions are so complex that most speech sentences cannot be precisely assigned to a particular emotion category; however, most emotional states nevertheless can be described as a mixture of multiple emotions. Based on this concept we have trained SVMs (support vector machines) to recognize utterances within these four categories and developed an agent that can recognize and express emotions.

1 Introduction

Nowadays, with the proliferation of the Internet and multimedia, many kinds of multimedia equipment are available. Even common users can record or easily download video or audio data by himself/herself. Can we determine the contents of this multimedia data expeditiously with the computer's help? The ability to detect expressed emotions and to express facial expressions with each given utterance would help improve the naturalness of a computer-human interface.

Certainly, emotion is an important factor in communication. And people express emotions not only verbally but also by non-verbal means. Non-verbal means consist of body gestures, facial expressions, modifications of prosodic parameters, and changes in the spectral energy distribution [12]. Often, people can evaluate human emotion from the speaker's voice alone since intonations of a person's speech can reveal emotions. Simultaneously, facial expressions also vary with emotions. There is a great deal of mutual information between vocal and facial expressions. Our own research concentrates on how to form a correspondence between emotional speech and expressions in a facial image sequence. We already have a controllable cartoon facial model that can generate various facial images based on different emotional state

---

* Visiting Microsoft Research China from Department of Computer Science and Technology, Tsinghua University, Beijing, China

inputs [14]. This system could be especially important in situations where speech is the primary mode of interaction with the machine.

How can facial animation be produced using audio to drive a facial control model? Speech-driven facial animation is an effective technique for user interface and has been an active research topic over the past twenty years. Various audio-visual mapping models have been proposed for facial animation [1..3]. However, these methods only synchronize facial motions with speech and rarely can animate facial expressions automatically. In addition, the complexity of audio-visual mapping relations makes the synthesis process language-dependent and less effective.

In the computer speech community, much attention has been given to "what was said" and "who said it", and the associated tasks of speech recognition and speaker identification, whereas "how it was said" has received relatively little. Most importantly in our application, we need an effective tool by which we can easily tell "how it was said" for each utterance.

Previous research on emotions both in psychology and speech tell us that we can find information associated with emotions from a combination of prosodic, tonal and spectral information; speaking rate and stress distribution also provide some clues about emotions [6, 7, 10, 12]. Prosodic features are multi-functional. They not only express emotions but also serve a variety of other functions as well, such as word and sentence stress or syntactic segmentation. The role of prosodic information within the communication of emotions has been studied extensively in psychology and psycholinguistics. More importantly, fundamental frequency and intensity in particular vary considerably across speakers and have to be normalized properly [12].

What kinds of features might carry more information about the emotional meaning of each utterance? Because of the diversity of languages and the different roles and significance of features in different languages, they cannot be treated equally [13]. It is hard to calculate which features carry more information, and how to combine these features to get a better recognition rate.

Research in automatic detection of expressed emotion is quite limited. Recent research in this aspect mostly focuses on classification, in the other words, mostly aims at ascertaining the emotion of each utterance. This, however, is insufficient for our applications. To describe the degree, compound and variety of emotions in speech more realistically and naturally, we present a novel criterion. Based on this criterion, emotion information contained in utterances can be evaluated well.

We assume that there is an emotion space corresponding to our existing facial control model. In [11] Pereira described his research on dimensions of emotional meaning in speech, but our emotion space is totally different from his ideas. The facial control model contains sets of emotional facial templates of different degrees drawn by an artist. Within this emotion space the special category "neutral" lies at the origin; other categories are associated with the axes directions in this space. With this assumption we correspond our cartoon facial control model with emotions. We also would like to determine the corresponding location in this emotion space of given emotional utterances, unlike other methods that simply give a classification result. This part of the investigation is confined to information within the utterance.

Various classification algorithms have been used in recent studies about emotions in speech recognition, such as Nearest Neighbor, NN (Neural Network), MLB (Maximum-Likelihood Bayes), KR (Kernel Regression), GMM (Gaussian Mixture

Model), and HMM (Hidden Markov Model) [5, 6, 9, 12]. Appropriate for our implementation we choose SVM as our classification algorithm.

In our investigation, we have captured a corpus containing emotional speech from movies and teleplays, with over 2000 utterances from several different speakers. Since we model only four kinds of basic emotions—"neutral", "anger", "happiness" and "sadness"—we obtain good recognition accuracy. A total of 721 of the most characteristic short utterances in these four emotional categories were selected from the corpus.

2 Experimental Study

Because in practice only the emotions "neutral", "anger", "happiness" and "sadness" lead to good recognition accuracy, we deal just with these four representative categories in our application even though this small set of emotions does not provide enough range to describe all types of emotions. Furthermore, some utterances can hardly be evaluated as one particular emotion. We still can find some utterances that can be classified solely as one kind of emotion, which we call pure emotional utterances.

We construct an emotion space in which the special category "neutral" is at the origin, and the other categories are measured along the axes; all pure emotions correspond to the points lying directly on an axis (or if we relax the restrictions, nearby an axis); the distance from these points to the origin denotes the degree of these emotional utterances. When the coordinates of a point have more than one nonzero value, the utterance contains more than one kind of emotion and cannot be ascribed to any single emotion category.

We further consider utterances whose emotion type is undoubtedly "neutral" as corresponding to the region closely surrounding the origin of the emotion space. For each of the other three categories, take "anger" for example, utterances which are undoubtedly "anger" have a strong correspondence with the anger axis.

Since people cannot express emotions to an infinite degree, we assume that each axis has an upper limit based on extraordinarily emotional utterances from the real world. So we choose extraordinary utterances for each emotion as our training data. Since people cannot measure the degree of emotions precisely, we simply choose utterances that are determined to portray a given emotion by almost 100% of the subjects to find the origin and the upper limits of the three axes.

Our approach is considerably different from those of other researchers. Other methods can only perform classification to tell which emotional category an utterance belongs to. Our method can handle more complicated problems, such as utterances that contain multiple emotions and the degrees of each emotion.

2.1 Corpus of Emotional Data

We need an extensive amount of training data to accurately estimate statistical models. So speech segments from Chinese teleplays are chosen as our corpus. By using teleplays (one film is still not long enough to satisfy our requirement), we were able to collect a large supply of emotional speech samples in a short amount of time. And previous experiments indicate that the emotions in acted speech could be consistently decoded by humans and automatic systems [6], which provided further motivation for their use.

The teleplay files were downloaded from Video CDs with audio data extracted at the sampling rate of 16 KHz and the resolution of 16 bits per sample. We employed three students to capture and segment these speech data files.

A total of more than 2000 utterances were captured, segmented and pre-tagged from the teleplays. The chosen utterances are all preceded and followed by silence with no background music or any other kinds of background noise. The expressed emotion within an utterance has to be constant.

All of these utterances need to be subjectively tagged as one of the four classes. Only pure emotional utterances are usable in accurately forming statistical models.

One of these students and a researcher tagged these utterances. They heard and tagged all these utterances several times. Each time, if the tag of an utterance differed from its previous designation, this utterance was removed from our corpus. The initial tags were those that the three students pre-tagged for all of the over 2000 utterances. Each tagging session was separated by several days.

After tagging several times, only 721 utterances remained. The numbers of waveforms which belong to each emotion category are shown in Table 1.

Table 1. Data sets

Anger	Happiness	Neutral	Sadness
215	136	242	128

All data files are 16kHz, 16bit waveforms.

2.2 Feature Extraction

Previous research has shown some statistics of the pitch (fundamental frequency F0) to be the main vocal cue for emotion recognition. Also, the first and second formants, vocal energy, frequency spectral features and speaking rate contribute to vocal emotion signaling [6].

In our study, evaluation features of voice are mainly extracted from pitch, and the features that we grasp from pitch are sufficient for most of our needs. The main means of choosing and drawing features is the method of [6].

First, we obtained the pitch sequence using an internally developed pitch extractor [4]. Then we smoothed the pitch contour using smoothing cubic splines. The resulting approximation of the pitch is smooth and continuous, and it enables us to measure features of the pitch: the pitch derivative, pitch slopes, and the behavior of their minima and maxima over time.

We have measured a total of sixteen features, grouped under the headings below:

- **Statistics related to rhythm:** Speaking rate, Average length between voiced regions, Number of maxima / Number of (minima + maxima), Number of upslopes / Number of slopes;
- **Statistics on the smoothed pitch signal:** Min, Max, Median, Standard deviation;

- **Statistics on the derivative of the smoothed pitch:** Min, Max, Median, Standard deviation;
- **Statistics over the individual voiced parts:** Mean min, Mean max;
- **Statistics over the individual slopes:** Mean positive derivative, Mean negative derivative.

All these features are calculated only in the valid region which begins at the first non-zero pitch point and ends at the last non-zero pitch point of each utterance.

The features in the first group are related to rhythm. Rhythm is represented by the shape of a pitch contour. We assume the inverse of the average length of the voiced part of an utterance denotes the speaking rate; the average length between voiced regions can denote pauses in an utterance.

The features in the second and third groups are general features of the pitch signal and its derivative.

In each individual voiced part we can easily find minima and maxima. We choose the mean of the minima and the mean of the maxima as our fourth group features.

We can compute the derivative of each individual slope. If the slope is an upslope, the derivative is positive; otherwise the derivative is negative. The mean of these positive derivatives and mean of negative derivatives are our features in the fifth group.

2.3 Performance of Emotion Evaluator

The classification algorithms used in this research section are mostly based on K-nearest-neighbors (KNN) or neural networks (NN). Considering our application, we need not only classification results, but also proportions of each emotion an utterance contains. After some experimentation, we chose the *support vector machine* (SVM) as our evaluation algorithm [8], because of its high speed and each SVM can give an evaluation to each emotion category. From training data, we can find the origin and the three axes.

Because different features are extracted from audio data in different ways and the relationships among these features are complex, we chose a Gaussian kernel $K(x_i, x_j) = e^{-\|x_i - x_j\|^2/2\sigma^2}$ to be our SVM kernel function.

For each emotional state, a model is learned to separate its type of utterances from others. We refer to SVMs trained in this way as 1-v-r SVMs (short for one-versus-rest). The scheme we adopted learns different SVM models for different categories that can distinguish this kind of emotion from others.

Our preliminary experimental results indicate that we can obtain satisfactory results only when there are at least 200 different utterances in each emotion category. While each SVM only deals with just a two-class problem and the performance of a SVM classifier is related to just these two classes, the boundary will tend to benefit the class that contains more data. To avoid this kind of skewing, we balance the training data set of the SVM. Taking "anger" as an example, we choose about 150 utterances in the "anger" state and also choose about 150 utterances from other emotion categories, with approximately the same number chosen from each of the other categories. In this way, the results are much better than those learned from imbalanced training data sets. Note that the training data can be replicated to balance the data sets.

The training data and performances for each SVM are shown in Table 2. The remainder of the data set not used during learning for each individual SVM are used as testing data for this SVM.

Table 2. SVM training data sets and performance

SVM \ Category	One	Rest	Accuracy on test set
Anger	162	147	77.16%
Happiness	102	94	65.64%
Neutral	194	193	83.73%
Sadness	96	96	70.59%

We obtain the given emotional utterance's feature vector by computation using each SVM and collecting each evaluation. We then have the emotional evaluation of the utterance. If only one evaluation is greater than 0, ($f_i(x)>0$, $0\le i\le 3$, $f_j(x)<0$, $i\ne j$), we label this utterance as this particular kind of emotional utterance; if more than one evaluation is greater than 0, ($f_i(x)>0$, $f_j(x)>0$, $0\le i,j\le 3$, $i\ne j$), we label the emotion of this utterance as a mixture of several kinds of emotions, each proportional to the emotion's SVM evaluation. If all evaluations are less than 0, ($f_i(x)<0$, $i=0..3$), we can say the emotion of this utterance is undefined in our system.

2.4 Comparison

We have also compared the effectiveness of the SVM classifier to the K-nearest neighbor classifier and the neural network classifier. One can observe that the SVM classifier compares favorably to the other two types of classifiers.

Table 3. Comparison of NN, KNN and SVM

Method	Accuracy (%)			
	A	H	N	S
NN	40.00	27.78	62.68	35.71
KNN	42.86	39.28	89.29	32.14
SVM	77.16	65.64	83.73	70.59

Remark: In each category there are 100 learning utterances, and all remaining utterances are used for testing.

3 Conclusions & Discussion

Compared with KNN, training an SVM model gives a good classifier without needing much training time. Even if we do not know the exact pertinences between each feature, we still can obtain good results. After we produce the SVM model from training data sets, these training data sets are no longer needed since the SVM model contains all the useful information. So classification does not need much time, and almost can be applied within real-time rendering. The KNN rule relies on a distance metric to perform classification, it is expected that changing this metric will yield different and possibly better results. Intuitively, one should weigh each feature according to how well it correlates with the correct classification. But in our investigation, those features are not irrelevant to each other. The performance landscape in this metric space is quite rugged and optimization is likely expensive. SVM can handle this problem well. We need not know the relationships within each feature pair and the dimensionality of each feature.

Compared with NNs, training a SVM model requires much less time than training an NN classifier. And SVMs are much more robust than NNs. In our application, the corpus comes from movies and teleplays. There are many speakers with various backgrounds. In these kinds of instances, NNs do not work well.

The most important reason why we chose SVMs is that SVMs give a magnitude for recognition. We need this magnitude for synthesizing expressions with different degrees. For our future work, we plan to study the effectiveness of our current approach on data from different languages and cultures.

References

1. Brand, M.: "Voice Puppetry", Proceedings of the SIGGRAPH, 21-28, 1999.
2. Cassell, J., Bickmore, T., Campbell, L., Chang, K., Vilhjlmsson, H., and Yan, H.: "Requirements for an architecture for embodied conversational characters", Proceedings of Computer Animation and Simulation, 109-120, 1999.
3. Cassell, J., Pelachaud, C., Badler, N.I., Steedman, M., Achorn, B., Beckett, T., Douville, B., Prevost, S. and Stone, M.: "Animated conversation: rule-based generation of facial display, gesture and spoken intonation for multiple conversational agents", Proceedings of the SIGGRAPH, 28(4): 413-420, 1994.
4. Chang, E., Zhou, J.-L., Di, S., Huang, C., and Lee., K.-F.: "Large vocabulary Mandarin speech recognition with different approaches in modeling tones", International Conference on Spoken Language Processing, 2000.
5. Roy, D., and Pentland, A.: "Automatic spoken affect analysis and classification", in Proceedings of the Sencond International Conference on Automatic Face and Gesture Recognition, pp. 363-367, 1996.
6. Dellaert, F., Polzin, T., and Waibel, A.: "Recognizing Emotion in Speech", Proceedings of the ICSLP, 1996.
7. Erickson, D., Abramson, A., Maekawa, K., and Kaburagi, T.: "Articulatory Characteristics of Emotional Utterances in Spoken English" , Proceedings of the ICSLP, 2000.
8. Joachims, T., Schölkopf, B., Burges, C., and Smola, A.(ed.): Making large-Scale SVM Training Practical. Advances in Kernel Methods - Support Vector Training, MIT-Press, 1999.
9. Kang, B.-S., Han C.-H., Lee, S.-T., Youn, D.-H., and Lee, C.-Y.: "Speaker Dependent Emotion Recognition using Speech Signals" , Proceedings of the ICSLP, 2000.
10. Paeschke, A., and Sendlmeier, W. F.: "Prosodic Characteristics of Emotional Speech: Measurements of Fundamental Frequency Movements", Proceedings of the ISCA-Workshop on Speech and Emotion, 2000.

11. Pereira, C.: "Dimensions of Emotional Meaning in Speech", Proceedings of the ISCA-Workshop on Speech and Emotion, 2000.

12. Polzin, T., and Waibel, A.: "Emotion-Sensitive Human-Computer Interfaces", Proceedings of the ISCA-Workshop on Speech and Emotion, 2000.

13. Scherer, K.R.: "A Cross-Cultural Investigation of Emotion Inferences from Voice and Speech: Implications for Speech", Proceedings of the ICSLP, 2000.

14. Li, Y., Yu, F., Xu, Y.-Q., Chang, E., and Shum, H.-Y.: "Speech-Driven Cartoon Animation with Emotions", to be appeared in ACM Multimedia 2001.

Proxy Caching Based on Patching Scheme and Prefetching

Yong Woon Park[1], Keon Hyo Baek[1], Ki Dong Chung[2]

[1]Department of Computer Science, Dong-eui Institute of Technology, San72, Yangjung Dong, Pusanjin Ku, Pusan, Rep. of Korea
ywpark@dit.ac.kr

[2]Department of Computer Science, Pusan National University, San 37, Keumjung Ku, Pusan, Rep. of Korea
kdchung@hyowon.pusan.ac.kr

Abstract. In this paper, we propose a proxy caching policy using both prefetching and patching technique for the efficient continuous media stream service on the network. In the proposed proxy caching policy, caching is done in two phases that in the first phase, the prefix of the requested object is cached when the requested object is not cached at all; this is done to reduce initial latency for future streams for that object. In the second phase, that object is cached stepwise based on the interval between the current and preceding streams for that object if the prefix of that object has already cached. Our experimental results show that our proposed proxy caching policy works better than existing ones in terms of network channel and read ahead buffer usage.

1 Introduction

Continuous media streams require lots of network bandwidth to transmit requested objects to the clients' nodes that the most expensive resource in transmitting continuous media is the network bandwidth[12]. Therefore, reducing the total bandwidth requirement of the backbone network should be an important objective in the design of a real time continuous media data delivery system. One way to improve performance of the network is using proxy server but current proxy caching policies do not consider the characteristics of the time constraint objects[9]. Moreover, current replacement algorithms make a binary decision on the caching of an atomic object, i.e., an object is cached or rejected in its entirety based on the popularity of that object. However, in case of continuous media data, streams are usually large in size, so prefetching the entire stream before playback is not desirable[6].

Therefore, to resolve network congestion problem, we propose a proxy space management policy using both prefetching and patching technique[5]. In the proposed proxy server management policy, other than the existing proxy caching policies where the caching scheme operates at the object level, the object is cached at the segment level based on the access patterns of the requested objects. With the proposed caching policy, some hot objects will be cached in their entirety while moderate objects are cached partially including their prefix part to reduce initial latency when they are requested again from other users. On the contrary, cold objects are serviced directly from the central server to keep them from being cached so as to reduce proxy space management overhead.

2 Related Works

So far, much research has been done to address network-IO bottleneck in the literature. With batching[1, 3], a group of requests for the same object in a given time interval are serviced with only one stream; only one disk fetch is needed for the group of users. While this method is simple, it causes as much initial latency as the length of time interval that the longer the service round, the longer the initial latency. Multicasting[10] can be a good solution to network congestion; it operates well on some real time applications such as Internet conferencing where the participants and their QoS are known in advance. With Patching[5], when a client requests an object, the client opens two channels concurrently; the one is the primary channel and the other is the secondary channel. With the primary channel, which is the multicasting channel currently transmitting the requested object, the client receives part of the requested object using his memory or disk. At the same time, with the secondary channel the client immediately contacts the server and then receives the initial part of the requested data, which cannot be serviced from the multicasting channel. The client reaches the point from which the primary channel has started to store the object; he stops receiving the data with the secondary channel and then consumes the stored data by the primary channel. Generally, proxy caching[2, 4, 11, 13, 14] has been widely known to reduce the Internet communication overhead but has mainly concerned with Web files such as images and text. It is not until recently that some proxy caching schemes for continuous media objects are introduced. However, they are focused on reducing the initial latency[7] or smoothing the burstiness of the VBR stream[12].

Table 1. Notations used in the proposed caching algorithm

Parameters	Description
o_i	Object i(i = 1, ..., n)
$S(o_i)$	Size of o_i
$S_{prefet}(o_i)$	Prefix portion of o_i
$d(p,f)_i$	Distance between two streams p & f for o_i
$S(d(p,f)_i)$	Data size amounting to $d(p,f)_i$
$S_{cache}^{d(p,f)}(o_i)$	Partially cached portion of o_i based on $d(p,f)_i$
$S_c^a(o_i)$	Already cached portion excluding $S_{prefet}(o_i)$
$S_c^a(o_i)^p$	Already cached portion of o_i after stream p

3 Two Phase Proxy Caching Algorithm

In this section, we introduce our proposed proxy caching policy where the requested object is cached gradually at the segment level starting from the prefix portion of that object. The main purpose of our proposed caching algorithm is to reduce proxy cache space management overhead and then exploit the network bandwidth resource efficiently. For this, in our proposed caching policy, caching is done in two phases. Before we are going into detail about our algorithm, we first explain some parameters used in our proposed proxy space management algorithm in Table 1.

3.1 Two Phase Caching Procedure

In the first phase, as shown in Fig. 1(a) and 1(b), assume that there is only one stream for object *i* or o_i and not any part of o_i is cached at all, only the prefix of o_i or $S_{prefet}(o_i)$ is prefetched in the proxy so that future streams for that object could reduce initial latency for the central server. More specifically, for o_i, $U_c(o_i)$, the caching unit of o_i in the first phase caching with a single stream is expressed as

$$U_c(o_i) = \begin{cases} none\ , & if\ already\ \ cached \\ S_{prefetch}(o_i) \end{cases} \tag{1}$$

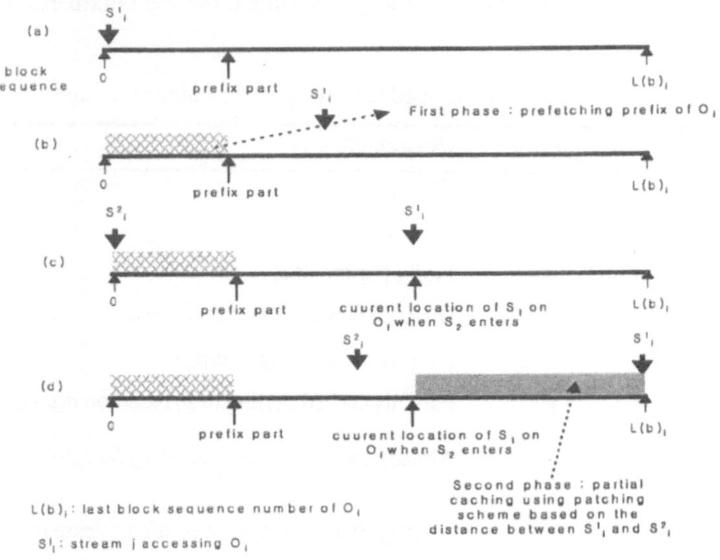

Fig. 1. Schematic explanation of our proposed caching policy

```
Proc. proxy caching(proxy v,stream f,node u,server s)
  Notations :
   f_u : stream  f  from u
   S(o_i)_s,S(o_i)_v  :  S(o_i) in s and v respectively
   S_prefet(o_i)_s,S_prefet(o_i)_v  :  S_prefet(o_i) in s and v respectively

  input : stream f requesting o_i
  output : caching status and service mode setting

  Procedure :
  ▶ o_i is not cached in v, prefetching prefix in v
    as much proxy space allocation as S_prefet(o_i);
    f_u ← S(o_i)_s && v ← S'_c(o_i)_s;
    set caching status of o_i to second phase;

  ▶ prefix of o_i has already cached in v
    // when entire blocks of o_i  is cached in v
    If (S(o_i)∈v) then f_u ← S(o_i)_v; return;

    // when partially cached
    if (preceding stream p exists) then
    {
      check distance between p and f;
      as much proxy space allocation as S_cache^{d(p,f)}(o_i);
      // caching based on the distance between p and f
      v ← S_cache^{d(p,f)}(o_i) by stream p;
      // streaming using both central sever and proxy
      f_u ← [{S(o_i)_v, S_cache^{d(p,f)}(o_i)_v}, S(S(o_i) - {S(o_i)_v, S_cache^{d(p,f)}(o_i)_v})_s]
    return;
    }
    else  f_u ← S'_c(o_i)_v

End of Proc:
```

Fig. 2. Proxy management algorithm

In the second phase, suppose that the requested object has already been cached in its first phase, i.e., the prefix portion of the requested object has already been cached by S_1 as shown in Fig. 1(c) and there are two streams S_1 (preceding stream *p*) and S_2 (following stream *f*) accessing the same object o_i, then caching is done partially using patching scheme based on the distance between two streams S_1 and S_2. Therefore, $U_c(o_i)$ in the second phase will be

$$U_c(o_i) = S_{cache}^{d(p,f)}(o_i) = \begin{bmatrix} S(o_i) - S_{prefet}(o_i) - S_c^a(o_i), S(d(p,f))_i \leq S_{prefet}(o_i) \\ S(o_i) - S(d(p,f)_i) - S_c^a(o_i)^p, S(d(p,f))_i > S_{prefet}(o_i) \end{bmatrix} \quad (2)$$

3.2 Proxy Space Allocation and Replacement

In the proxy caching algorithms, unlike conventional caching algorithms that are generally applied to the internal file caching, objects are cached in their entirety and are not necessarily of homogeneous in size. So, if two objects are accessed with equal frequency, the hit ratio is maximized when the replacement policy is biased towards the smaller document. Thus, while deciding which documents to replace when a new document enters, we must take into account not only the relative frequency, but also factors such as the sizes or transfer time savings[13]. According to [8], objects' popularity on the Internet follows a Zipf-like distribution, whereby the frequency of document access is proportional to the rank of the document. They also show the temporal locality of reference, i.e., the recently requested documents are likely to be requested again. Therefore, in our proposed caching algorithm, we take the long-term access frequency, recency and size of the requested object into consideration to generate a replacement function that for all $o_i \in O$, there exists *replacement function* $f_v^R(o_i)^k$ at the *k*th reference at proxy node *v*, which is given by dividing the weighted frequency by the cached portion of o_i, such that $f_v^R(o_i)^k$ is used as a replacement metric when cache replacement occurs.

$$f_v^R(o_i)^k = \frac{W_v^{freq}(o_i)^k}{S_{prefet}(o_i) + S_C^A(o_i)} \quad (3)$$

where $O = \{o_1, \ldots, o_n\}, W_v^{freq}(o_i)^k = k + \sum_{j=1}^{k} \left(\frac{AVG_v(I(s_i)_1^j)}{AVG_v(I(s_i)_1^{j-1})} \right)$

$AVG_v(I(s_i)_1^j)$:average arrival interval for o_i from 1st to *j*th reference at *v*

4 Experimental Results

In this section, the proposed caching algorithm will be evaluated through simulation. Through the simulation, it is checked to see how much performance gain the proposed proxy caching scheme shows. Some simulation parameters are explained in Table 2. According to [7], round trip delays vary widely, depending on the end-points and the degree of congestion in the network, but delays of several seconds are not uncommon. Therefore by building up proxy buffer that could store the prefix of the requested object as much as the size of several seconds' playback, the initial latency taken to access data from the central server will be hided.

Table 2. Simulation parameters

Parameter	Description
# of objects	300, 600,1200
Object length(sec)	30 – 180(sec)
# of proxy servers	8
Arrival rate(sec)	1,2,3,5
Playback rate/sec	4 Mbps
Cache's transfer rate/sec	10 Mbytes/sec
Cache's storage capacity	3 GB
Prefix size	5 secs of playback

4.1 Network Channel Usage with Different Arrival Rates

By the channel usage it means how many network channels are needed to service all requests without violating their real-time constraints in the delivery of the requested objects. The graphs in Fig. 3 present the experimental results for the network channel usage with different arrival rates. The *pure* policy means caching is not applied to service all users' requests at all. Each of three different caching algorithms is expressed as lru-size(LRU-SIZE algorithm), mru(MRU algorithm) and lfu(LFU algorithm). The proposed algorithm is denoted as *patch*.

Regardless of how many streams arrive except some cases, *pure* policy requires more network channels than other caching policies do. When caching is applied, the number of objects serviced from the central server also affect the number of channels required as the arrival rate increases(see the case with the arrival rate is 1 or 2). This is because how many network channels are required is heavily dependent on the capacity of proxy server such that as the number of objects serviced increases, the possibility of finding the requested object in the proxy server gets low. On the contrary, with *pure* policy, the number of network channels required is not dependent on the number of objects serviced because network channels from the central server to users' destination should be established per each stream regardless of which object is

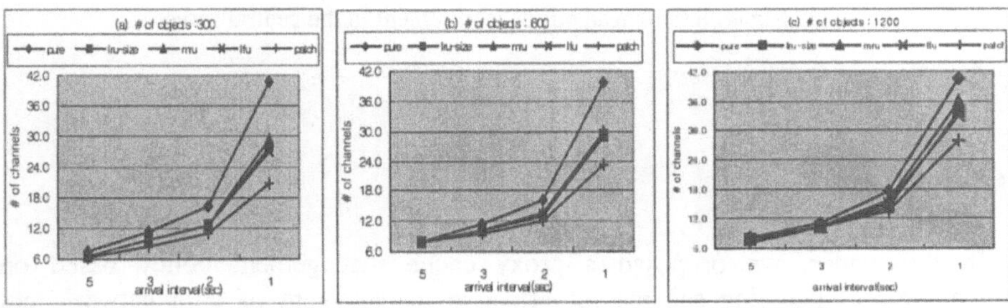

Fig. 3. Channel usage with different arrival rate

chosen to access. The proposed algorithm does not show any performance increase compared with other caching polices when the arrival rate is low. However, as the arrival rate goes up(in case of arrival rate of 1), the proposed algorithm shows better performance than other caching policies do.

4.2 Read-ahead Buffer Requirement in the Server with Different Arrival Rates

As the second performance metric, we checked how much read ahead buffer is required to service the maximum numbers of concurrent streams. It is imperative that to provide the users with continuous media delivery, each client session should need some amount of read ahead buffer memory to buffer the speed discrepancy between data retrieving speed from disk to buffer memory and data sending speed from buffer memory to the client.

As shown in the graphs in Fig. 4, regardless of the number of objects archived in the server, the proposed algorithm shows better performance than other caching policies. When the users' arrival rate is low, the performance gap among caching policies are not significant. However, when the users' arrival rate is high(say 1/sec), the performance gap between our proposed algorithm and others is significant that as the arrival rate gets low, it does not matter which caching algorithm a server adopts for stream service. On the contrary, the proposed alorithm works better than others when the users' arrival rate is high. Moreover, as the disk bandwidth the streams have reserved approaches its maximum point, the amount of read ahead buffer is increased abruptly that the performance gap between our proposed algorithm and others will be widening considering the abruptly increasing amount of read ahead buffer with the increasing numbers of streams.

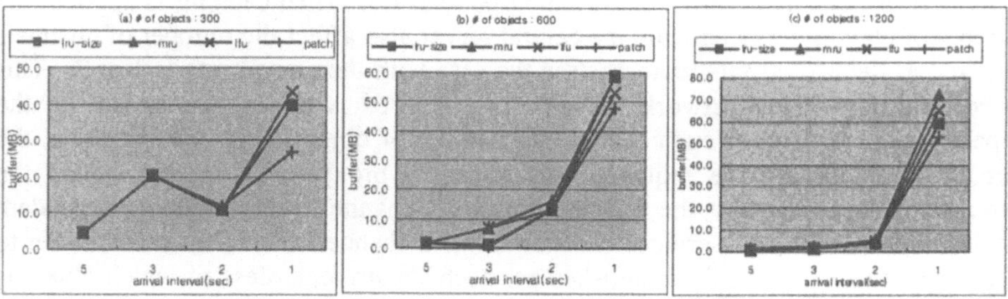

Fig. 4. Read-ahead buffer requirement in the central server

5 Conclusions

In this paper, we proposed a proxy cache management policy based on prefetching and patching scheme for effective management of both network and central server resources. With the proposed proxy server management policy, other than the existing proxy caching policies where caching scheme operates at the object level, the requested object is cached stepwise on the patch basis using access patterns of the requested object in the proxy server. Simulation results show that the proposed algorithm shows better performance than other caching algorithms do; the number of backbone network channels required could be reduced fairly compared with other caching polices and moreover, in terms of read ahead buffer requirement in the central server, our proposed algorithm also shows better performance result than other caching policies.

References

1. C.C. Aggarwal and J. L. Wolf and P.S. Yu, "On Optimal Batching Policies for Video-On-Demand Storage Server.", Proc. of the IEEE Int'l Conf. On Multimedia Systems. June 1996
2. Aggarwal C., Wolf J.L., Yu P.S., "Caching on the World Wide Web", Knowledge and Data Engineering, IEEE Transactions on Volume: 11 1 , Jan.-Feb. 1999 , Page(s): 94 –1
3. Asit Dan, D. Sitaram, and P. Shahabuddin, "Scheduling Policies for an On-Demand Video Server with Batching", In Proceedings of ACM Multimedia, pp 15-23, San Fransisco, California, Oct. 1994
4. Greg Barish and Katia Obraczka, "World Wide Web Caching: Trends and Techniques", Univ. of Southern California USC tech reports
5. Kien A. Hua Ying Cai Simon Sheu, "Patching : A Multicast Technique for True Video-on-Demand" , ACM Multimedia Bristol, 1997, UK 191 – 200
6. Reza Rejaie, Mark Handley, Haobo Yu, Deborah Estrin, "Proxy Caching Mechanism for Multimedia Playback Streams in the Internet",1999, USC tech reports
7. Rexford S., J. Towsley, "Proxy Prefix Caching for Multimedia Streams", INFOCOM '99. Eighteenth Annual Joint Conference of the IEEE Computer and Communications Societies. Proceedings. IEEE Volume: 3 , 1999 , Page(s): 1310 -1319 vol.3
8. Rizzo L., Vicisano L., "Replacement Policies for A Proxy Cache", Networking, IEEE/ACM Transactions on Volume: 8 2 , April 2000 , Page(s): 158 –170
9. R. Tewari, H.M. Vin, A. Dan, and D. Sitaram, "Resource-based Caching for Web Servers", In Proceedings of ACM/SPIE Multimedia Computing and Networking 1998 (MMCN'98), San Jose, pp. 191-204, January 1998
10. Viswanathan S. and T. Imielinski, "Metropolitan area video-on-demand service using pyramid broadcasting. Multimedia Systems, 4(4):197-208, Aug 1996
11. Wessels D., Claffy K, "ICP and the Squid web cache", Selected Areas in Communications, IEEE Journal on Volume: 16 3 , April 1998 , Page(s): 345 –357
12. Zhi-Li Zhang, Du, D.H.C., Dongli S, Yuewei Wang, "A network-conscious approach to end-to-end video delivery over wide area networks using proxy servers", INFOCOM '98. Seventeenth Annual Joint Conference of the IEEE Computer and Communications Societies. Proceedings. IEEE Volume: 2 , 1998 , Page(s): 660 -667 vol.2
13. Michael A. Goulde, "Network Caching Guide – Optimizing Web Content Delivery", March 1999/6/23 – White Paper , Inktomi Corp.
14. A. Chankhunthod, P. B. Danzig, C. Neerdaels, M. F. Schwartz, and K. J. Worrel, "A Hierarchical Internet Object Cache", In Proceedings of the 1996 USENIX Technical Conference, San Diego, CA, January 1996

A Stateless Active Queue Management Scheme for Approximating Fair Bandwidth Allocation and Stabilized Buffer Occupation

Hu Yan and Zhang Guangzhao

Department of Electronics and Communication Engineering, Zhongshan University
510275 Guangzhou, P. R. China
hu_yan@263.net, isszgz@zsu.edu.cn

Abstract. This paper proposes an active queue management algorithm we called "SCHOKe", which wants to address the problems of providing a fair bandwidth allocation and a stabilized buffer occupancy in congested routers. The scheme works in concert with a simple FIFO queue that is shared by all flows, so it is stateless and easy to implement. In the algorithm, unresponsive flows are punished effectively and buffer occupancy is stabilized by a "hit", which happens when an arriving packet's flow ID is the same as one of packets randomly chosen from the FIFO queue. Simulations of a TCP/IP network are used to illustrate the performance of the scheme.

1. Introduction

TCP flows are "responsive" to congestion signals (i.e., dropped packets) from the network [1]. It is primarily these TCP congestion avoidance algorithms that prevent the congestion collapse of today's Internet. However, there are a growing number of UDP-based applications running in the Internet, such as packet voice and packet video. The flows of these applications do not back off properly when they receive congestion indications. As a result, they aggressively use up more bandwidth than other TCP compatible flows. Therefore, it is necessary to have router mechanisms to shield responsive flows from unresponsive flows and to provide a good QoS to all users.

The traditional technique for managing router queue lengths is known as "tail drop", but it has two important drawbacks, i.e. "lock-out " and "full-queue" [1]. The solution to the full-queues problem is for routers to drop packets before a queue becomes full, so that end nodes can respond to congestion before buffers overflow. We call such a proactive approach "active queue management". By dropping packets before buffers overflow, active queue management allows routers to control when and how many packets to drop. The lock-out phenomenon is that a single connection or a few flows monopolize(s) queue space, preventing other flows from getting room in the queue. Active queue management is used to control the queue size for each individual class or queue. Because all flows in same class need a fair bandwidth allocation, a active queue management of the class must provide this function. So the fair bandwidth allocation is important to solution to the lock-out problem.The scheme in this paper, which wants to solve both problem listed above, is an active queue management algorithm.

The organization of this paper is as follows. In the next section we discuss related work where SRED and CHOKe schemes are highlighted. Our scheme is discussed in Section 3. Section 4 presents our simulation results. The paper's conclusions are summarized in Section 5

2. Related Work

In this section we briefly describe some existing router algorithms. In FQ [2], one of famous scheduling algorithms, packets are sent in the order in which the router would have finished sending them if it could send each packet one bit at a time. Deficit Round Robin (DRR) [3] differs from FQ in its implementation, but achieves a similar effect. Both of these algorithms offer an upper bound on extra delay introduced over a hypothetical fluid model scheme. Because both of these mechanisms also use per-flow queuing and maintain flow state information, packets belonging to different flows are essentially isolated from each other and one flow cannot degrade the quality of another. However, it is well known that they are somewhat expensive to implement. The goal of CSFQ [4] is to achieve fair queuing without using per-flow state in the core of an island of routers. On entering the network, packets are marked with an estimate of their current sending rate. A core router estimates a flow's fair share and preferentially drops a packet from a flow based on the fair share and the rate estimate carried by the packet. A key impediment to the deployment is that it would require an extra field in the header of every packet. Other drawbacks of CSFQ include the requirement that for full effectiveness, all the routers within the island need to be modified.

On the other hand, queue management algorithms have had a simple design from the outset. [1] suggests using the RED scheme proposed by Floy and Jacobson [5]. A router implementing RED maintains a single FIFO to be shared by all the flows, and drops an arriving at random during periods of congestion. The drop probability increases with the level of congestion. Since RED acts in anticipation of congestion, it does not suffer from the lock out and full queue problems. By keeping the average queue-size small, RED reduces the delays experienced by most flows. However, like Drop Tail, RED is unable to penalize unresponsive flows [6]. Another drawback of RED is that over a wide range of load levels it cannot stabilize its buffer occupation at a level independently of the number of active connecting [7]. Stabilized buffer occupation of routers is important to multimedia flows, because real-time multimedia flows that go though routers with variant buffer occupation will increase playback jitters. This paper proposes a scheme that wants to address synchronously both of the problems. To improve RED's ability for distinguishing unresponsive users, a few variants (like Flow Random Early Drop (FRED) [8])have been proposed. FRED is similar to CSFQ in that it uses FIFO scheduling, but instead of using information in packet headers, FRED constructs per-flow state at the router for those flows with packets currently in the queue. The dropping probability of a flow depends on the number of packets whose flow has buffered at the router. FRED's fair allocation of buffers can yield very different fairness properties from a fair allocation of bandwidth [4]. In addition, the results obtained by FRED are not predictable, as they depend on the packet arrival times of the individual flows.

The scheme called (Stabilized CHOKe) SCHOKe in the paper draws heavily from CHOKe and Stabilized RED (SRED), two approaches that both use packet hits in concert with FIFO scheduling.

2.1 SRED: Stabilized Buffer Occupation

SRED has an additional feature that over a wide range of load levels helps it stabilize its buffer occupation at a level independent of the number of active connections [7]. The main idea is to compare, whenever a packet arrives at some buffer, the arriving packet with a randomly chosen packet that recently preceded it into the buffer. When the two packets are "of the same flow", a "hit" is declared. The statistical sequence of hits is used to estimate the number of active flows and to find candidates for "misbehaving (unresponsive) flow". The hit frequency around the time of the arrival of the t-th packet at the buffer, denoted by $P(t)$, is estimated. As the authors say, $P(t)^{-1}$ is a good estimate for the effective number of active flows in the time shortly before the arrival of packet t. We can use $P(t)$ to update the candidate drop probability p_{zap}. When a packet arrives at the buffer, $P(t)$ is first estimated as described in (1).

$$P(t) = (1-\alpha)P(t-1) + \alpha Hit(t). \tag{1}$$

and let

$$Hit = \begin{cases} 0 & \text{if no hit,} \\ 1 & \text{if hit.} \end{cases} \tag{2}$$

with $0 < \alpha < 1$. If at the arrival instant the buffer contains q bytes, the packet is dropped with probability p_{zap}, which equals to

$$p_{zap} = p_{sred} \times \min(1, \frac{1}{(256 \times P(t))^2}) \tag{3}$$

The function p_{sred} is defined as equation (4).

$$p_{sred}(q) = \begin{cases} p_{\max} & \text{if } \frac{1}{3}B \le q \le B, \\ \frac{1}{4} \times p_{\max} & \text{if } \frac{1}{6} \le q < \frac{1}{3}B, \\ 0 & \text{if } 0 \le q < \frac{1}{6}B. \end{cases} \tag{4}$$

2.2. CHOKe: Fair Bandwidth Allocation

When a packet arrives at a congested router, CHOKe draws one (or several) packet(s) at random from the FIFO queue and compares it (or them) with the arriving packet. If they both belong to the same flow, then they are both discarded, else the randomly chosen packet is left intact and the arriving packet is admitted into the buffer with probability that depends on the level of congestion (this probability is computed exactly as in RED). Simulations in [6] suggest that it works well in protecting congestion-sensitive flows, such as TCP flows, from congestion-insensitive flows, like UDP flows.

Just as RED algorithm, the shortcoming is that the buffer occupancy of the router is not stabilized and depends on the number of active flows.

3. The algorithm: CHOKe with Stabilized Buffer Occupation

To approximate a fair bandwidth allocation and stabilize buffer occupation at a level independent of the number of active flows in congestion routers, we propose SCHOKe. It works in concert with a single FIFO buffer for queuing the packets of all the flows that share an outgoing link.

First, SCHOKe estimates the hit probability p_hit(t) when the t-th packet arrives at the buffer, just as SRED does(see equation (1)). When the two packets, in which one is a arriving packet and the other is a packet randomly chosen from the buffer, are of the same flow, a hit comes about. But we use a kind of flexible definition of a hit. SCHOKe compares the arriving packet with not one, but with some $K\geq 0$ randomly chosen packets from the queue. So as one of K packets and an arriving one belong to a same flow, we also can say that a hit happens. In this paper, we let K is dependent on the instantaneous buffer occupation q (see Table 1). We find that it is helpful to get stabilized buffer occupation.

q	$0\sim1/6*B$	$1/6*B\sim1/3*B$	$1/3*B\sim1/2*B$	$1/2*B\sim5/6*B$	$5/6*B\sim B$
K	2^0-1	2^1-1	2^5-1	2^6-1	2^7-1

Table 1. The Drop Times K (B is buffer capacity)

Secondly, p_hit(t) is used to update drop probability p_drop that is calculated using equation (3). Let B stand for the queue limit. If the instantaneous buffer occupation q is less than $1/6*B$, every arriving packet is queued into the FIFO queue. If the q is greater than $1/6*B$, SCHOKe choose K packets from the queue. As one or more packet(s) from the K packets is (are) hit by the arriving packet, we can drop the arriving packet and the chosen packet(s). When no hit happens, the arriving packet is dropped with the previous drop probability p_drop that is computed exactly as in SRED.

Like CHOKe, SCHOKe is a truly stateless algorithm. As in SCHOKe the K values is greater (see Table 1) than previous two algorithms, so we propose that the K packets can be chosen from the head (or tail) of the FIFO queue and mark every packet that is hit and the router can discard those marked packets when they depart from the FIFO queue.

4. Simulation Results for SCHOKe

In this section, we show by simulations that SCHOKe is indeed successful in a) penalizing misbehaving flows and thus approximating a fair bandwidth allocation and b) keeping the buffer occupancy close to a specific target and away from overflow or underflow. All of our simulations are conducted using NS software [9]. The results are presented in two parts: fair bandwidth allocation and buffer occupancy.

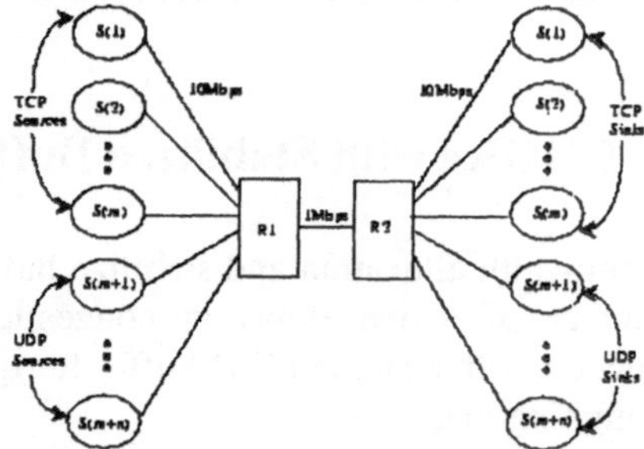

Fig. 1. Simulation Network Configuration

4.1 Fair Bandwidth Allocation

To illustrate SCHOKe's fair bandwidth allocation, we simulate it in a single congested link whose standard network configuration is shown in Figure 1. The congested link in this network is between the routers R1 and R2. The link, with capacity of 1 Mbps, is shared by m TCP and n UDP flows. An end host is connected to the routers using a 10 Mbps link, which is ten times the bottleneck link bandwidth. All links have a small propagation delay of 1ms so that the delay experienced by a packet is mainly cause by the buffer delay rather than the transmission delay. The maximum window size of TCP is set to 300 packets such that it does not become a limiting factor of a flow's throughput. The TCP flows are derived from FTP sessions that transmit infinite large size files. The UDP sources send packets at a constant bit rate (CBR) of *r* Kbps, where *r* is a variable. All packets are set to have a size of 1K Bytes.

In this simulation, we set up the following network configuration parameters: there are m = 32 TCP sources (Flow 1 to Flows 32) and n = 1 UDP source (Flow 33) in the network. 4 queue management algorithms (SCHOKe, RED, CHOKe and RED) are simulated using NS2 to study those algorithms' features of fair bandwidth allocation. Following [5,6], The minimum threshold min_{th} in the RED and CHOKe algorithm is set to 100 packets, allowing on average around 3 packets per flow in the buffer before a router starts dropping packets. The maximum threshold max_{th} is set to be twice the min_{th}, and the physical queue size limit B is fixed at 300 packets.

To gauge the degree to which SCHOKe achieves fair bandwidth, the individual throughput of each of the 33 flows in the simulation above is plotted in Figure 2 (left). The UDP source (Flow 33) sends packets at a rate r = 1Mbps, such that the link R1-R2 becomes congested. Figure 2 (left) shows that like CHOKe, SCHOKe can approximate a fair bandwidth allocation. All of TCP flows' throughputs are less than the fair bandwidth that they should be allocated (33.03Kbps). As we state in previous section, TCP flow is a responsive flow, while UDP flow is unresponsive flow because of r = 1Mbps bigger than 33.03Kpbs much more. In this network configure, the throughput of the UDP flow (Flow 33) is 266.79Kbps, which is a litte higher than those of the TCP flows.

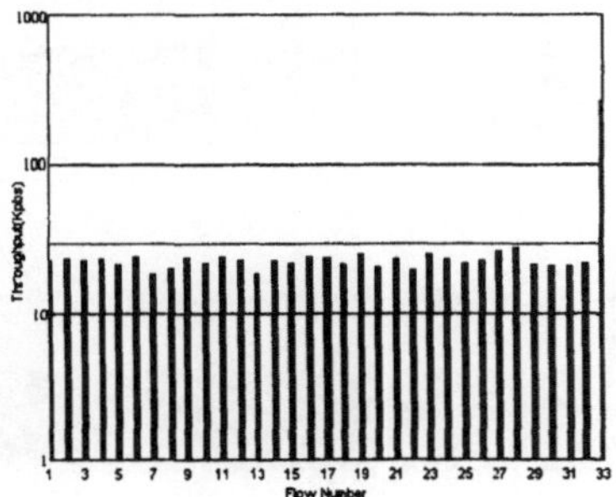

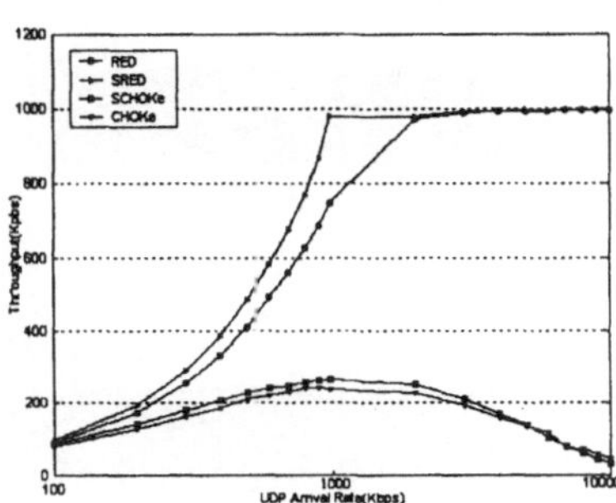

Fig. 2. (left) SCHOKe: Throughput Per Flow (TCP and UDP flow), (right) Throughput under Different Traffic Load

UDP(Kbps)	100	300	500	1000	3000	5000	10000
RED	13.0%	14.2%	16.0%	24.6%	66.9%	80.1%	90.0%
CHOKe	23.8%	45.4%	57.8%	75.9%	83.5%	97.4%	99.6%
SCHOKe	16.4%	39.9%	54.3%	73.0%	92.8%	97.2%	99.6%

Table 2. UDP Dropping Percentages at Different UDP Arrival Rate

We vary the UDP arrival rate r to study SCHOKe's performance under difference traffic load condition. Our simulation results are summarized in Figure 2 (right), where the UDP throughput versus the UDP arrival rate is plotted. In the contrastive experiment, we simulate 4 schemes under the same conditions. The min_{th} and the max_{th} of CHOKe and RED are respectively set to 30 and 60 packets. If $q \geq 1/6*B$, the K of SCHOKe is 1, else $K = 0$. For CHOKe, if average queue length $avg \geq min_{th}$, the K is set 1, else K = 0. The UDP drop percentages of the experiment are described in Table 2. From Figure 2 (right) and Table 2, we can see that SCHOKe approximates a fair bandwidth allocation as good as CHOKe and that UDP use up almost all of bottleneck link bandwidth when $r \geq$ 1M in RED and SRED. Table 2 shows that SCHOKe drops 16.4% of the UDP packets when its arrival rate is as low as 100 Kbps. As the UDP arrival rate increases, the drop percentage goes up as well. It drops almost all of the packets (99.6%) when the rate reaches 10 Mbps. In SCHOKe, UDP throughput increases as the arrival rate increases from 100 Kbps to 1 Mbps, but throughput decreases as the rate increases from 1 Mbps to 10 Mbps. In comparison, the performances of SRED and RED under different traffic load are illustrated in Table 2 and Figure 2 (right). It is obvious that SRED as well as RED can't provide protection against greedy flows. The unresponsive flows use up all the bottleneck bandwidth (996.11 Kbps as r = 10Mbps) and starve out the well behaving flows. Our simulation shows that SRED uses up more bandwidth of the congested link than RED does. So we can conclude that SRED and RED can't punish misbehaving connections and that our scheme can do it as well as CHOKe.

4.2 Buffer Occupancy

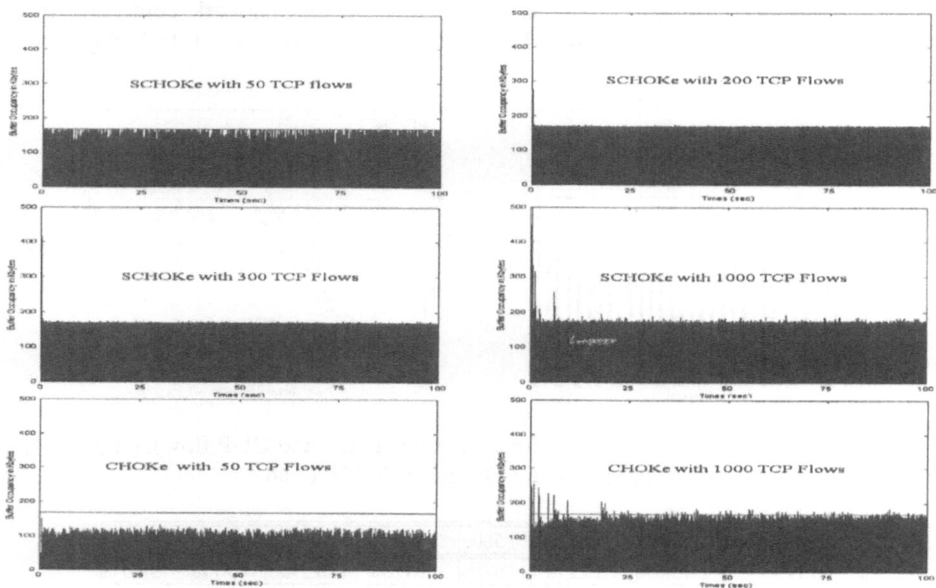

Fig. 3.SCHOKe and CHOKe with different TCP flows

The target of this simulation is to illustrate SCHOke's buffer occupancy. The network configuration used for this section is almost the same as above section (see figure 1). But some of parameters are different. The capacity of the bottleneck link between R1 and R2 is DS3 (45Mbps) and its propagation is 1 ms. The bottleneck link in R1 has a buffer of capacity 500 Kbytes. There are only m TCP flows and no UDP flows in this simulation. The m is variable. The links between the TCP source and the router are also DS3 links, which have a propagation delay of 10 ms. In that case the minimal possible round trip time (RTT) is 42 ms. All flows' packets have an size of 576 bytes which is the typical segment size for TCP. For the time being we assume a persistent source, i.e., a source will always send a packet whenever the congestion window permits transmission of a packet.

We have simulated to show buffer behavior for SCHOKe with p_{max} = 0.15 (see equation (3, 4)), for 50, 100, 200, 300, 500, 800, and 1000 persistent TCP sources (Figure 3). All of buffer occupancy figures are plotted using 10 ms samples. All sources start at time zero a file transfer of an "infinitely large" file. In the simulation of SCHOKe, the drop times K is set according to Table 1. We find that it is useful to keep buffer occupancy steady. Specially, when the number of TCP flows is close to or greater than 1000, the *K* is more important. It is the future work to study the influence of *K* on steady buffer occupancy. In a word, those figures illustrate that SCHOKe can stabilize the buffer occupation at a level independent of the number of active flows. To compare SCHOKe with CHOKe, the buffer occupancies of CHOKe are plotted in Figure 3. In the simulation of CHOKe, we let $min_{th} = 1/6*B$ and $max_{th} = 1/3*B$. For CHOKe, it is obvious that as the number of TCP flows increases, the buffer occupancy approaches the *1/3*B*, while for SCHOKe it is stabilized around *1/3*B* with independent of the number of TCP connections. Like SRED, the buffer occupancy of SCHOKe is independent of the number of connections from 50 to 300 connections, and increases only slightly if the number of connections increases to 1000. Then we can state that SCHOKe improves the performance of buffer occupancy of CHOKe, since above simulation has validated it.

5. Conclusions

We proposed a queue management algorithm, SCHOKe, which aims to a) approximating fair queuing at a minimal implement overhead and to b) stabilized buffer occupancy. Simulation suggests that it works well in protecting responsive flows from unresponsive ones and it is an ideal algorithm to stabilize the router buffer occupancy that is important factor to multimedia flows.

6. Acknowledgment

We thank Rong Pan of Stanford University for his CHOKe source code of simulation and advice of NS2 simulation.

Reference:

[1]B. Braden, etc. IETF RFC (Informational) 2309, April 1998.
[2]A. Demers, etc."Analysis and Simulation of a Fair Queueing Algorithm." In ACM SIGCOMM, September 1989.
[3]M. Shreedhar etc. "Efficient Fair Queuing using Deficit Round Robin." In ACM SIGCOMM, August 1995.
[4]I. Stoica, etc. "Core-Stateless Fair Queueing: Achieving Approximately Fair Bandwidth Allocations in High Speed Networks." In Proceedings of SIGCOMM, September 1998.
[5]S. Floyd, etc. "Random Early Detection Gateways for Congestion Avoidance Control." IEEE/ACM Transactions on Networking, 1(4): 397-413, July 1993.
[6]R. Pan, etc. "CHOKe, A Stateless Active Queue Management Scheme for Approximating Fair Bandwidth Allocation." In IEEE INFOCOM, March 2000.
[7]Teunis J Ott, etc. "SRED: Stabilized RED." In IEEE INFOCOM, March 1999.
[8]Dong Lin, etc. "Dynamics of Random Early Detection." In Proceedings of SIGCOMM' 97.
[9]ns – Network Simulator (Version 2.0), October 1998.

QoS-based Checkpoint Protocol for Multimedia Network Systems

Shinji Osada and Hiroaki Higaki
{shinji,hig}@higlab.k.dendai.ac.jp
Department of Computers and Systems Engineering
Tokyo Denki University

1. Introduction

Advanced computer and network technologies have lead to the development of computer networks. Here, an application is realized by multiple processes located on multiple computers connected to a communication network such as the Internet. Each process computes and communicates with other processes by exchanging messages through communication channels. Mission-critical applications are required to be executed fault-tolerantly. That is, even if some processes fail, execution of an application is required to be continued. One of the important methods to realize fault-tolerant networks is *checkpoint-recovery* [2,4,6,7,10–12,16,19–21]. During failure-free execution, each process takes local checkpoints by storing state information into a stable storage [14]. If a certain process fails, the processes restart from the checkpoints by restoring the state information from the stable storage. For restarting execution of applications correctly in conventional data communication networks, a set of local checkpoints taken by all the processes and from which the processes restart should form a *consistent global checkpoint* [3]. A global checkpoint is defined to be consistent if there is neither *orphan* nor *lost message*. However, in a multimedia communication network, applications require transmission of large-size multimedia messages and low overhead failure-free execution rather than complete consistency. Hence, this paper proposes a novel criteria for consistent global checkpoints based on properties of multimedia communication networks and applications.

The rest of this paper is organized as follows: In section 2, we review consistent global checkpoints in a conventional data communication network. In section 3, we discuss properties of a multimedia communication network and requirements for a consistent global checkpoint. Section 4 proposes a novel criteria for a consistent global checkpoint in a multimedia communication network. In section 5, we design a checkpoint protocol based on QoS for consistency and timeliness. In section 6, relation between required synchronization and achieved consistency in the conventional protocol and our proposed two protocols is evaluated. In addition, our protocol is applied to MPEG-2 data transmission for evaluate required synchronization.

2. Conventional Consistency

Let $\mathcal{N} = \langle \mathcal{V}, \mathcal{L} \rangle$ be a computer network where $\mathcal{V} = \{p_1, \ldots, p_n\}$ is a set of processes p_i and $\mathcal{L} \subseteq \mathcal{V}^2$ is a set of communication channels $\langle p_i, p_j \rangle$ from a process p_i to another process p_j. Execution of an application in p_i is modeled by a sequence of occurrences of *events*. p_i transits from one *state* to another by an occurrence of an event. There are two kinds of events; *local events* and *communication events*. At a local event, state transition in p_i is caused by local computation without exchanging a message. At a communication event, p_i communicates with another process by exchanging a message and the state of p_i is transitted. There are two kinds of communication events; a *message sending event* $s(m)$ and a *message receipt event* $r(m)$ for a message m. In order to realize a fault-tolerant network, there are two kinds of methods; checkpoint-recovery and *replication*. In replication [1,8,9,13,17], each process is replicated and placed on multiple computers. Even if a certain process fails, other replicated processes continue to execute an application. On the other hand, checkpoint-recovery is widely available [2,4,6,7,10–12,16,19–21].Here, during failure-free execution, each process p_i sometimes takes a *local checkpoint* c_i by storing state information into a *stable storage* [14]. After p_i fails and recovers, p_i restarts execution of an application from c_i by restoring the state information from the stable storage. If p_i restarts independently of the other processes, there may be two kinds of *inconsistent messages*; *lost messages* and *orphan messages* [3].

[Inconsistent message] Suppose that processes p_i and p_j take local check points c_i and c_j, respectively. A message m transmitted through $\langle p_i, p_j \rangle$ is *inconsistent* if m is a lost message or an orphan message for a set $C_{\{p_i, p_j\}} = \{c_i, c_j\}$ of local checkpoints. m is a *lost message* iff $s(m)$ occurs before taking c_i in p_i and $r(m)$ occurs after taking c_j in p_j. m is an *orphan message* iff $s(m)$ occurs after taking c_i in p_i and $r(m)$ occurs before taking c_j in p_j. □

In order to correctly recover from a process failure, there should be no inconsistent message in any communication channel in $\mathcal{L}$. Thus, in case of a failure in a process p_i, not only p_i but also other processes restart from local checkpoints. Hence, a *global check-*

point $C_{\mathcal{V}} = \{c_1, \ldots, c_n\}$ which is a set of local checkpoints of all the processes in $\mathcal{V}$ should be *consistent* [3].

[Consistent global checkpoint] A global checkpoint $C_{\mathcal{V}}$ in $\mathcal{S} = \langle \mathcal{V}, \mathcal{L} \rangle$ is consistent iff there is no inconsistent message in any communication channel in $\mathcal{L}$. □

3. Multimedia Networks

Recently, multimedia network applications such as distance learning, tele-conference, tele-medicine and video on demand have been developed on communication networks [15]. Here, messages with multimedia data including text, voice, sound, picture and video are exchanged among processes. These messages are larger than those with conventional data. Hence, it takes longer time to transmit and receive them. As shown in Figure 1, the following four *primitive events* are defined for a multimedia message m transmitted through a communication channel $\langle p_i, p_j \rangle$ [18]:

- $sb(m)$: p_i begins sending m.
- $se(m)$: p_i ends sending m.
- $rb(m)$: p_j begins receiving m.
- $re(m)$: p_j ends receiving m.

A message sending event $s(m)$ for m begins at $sb(m)$ and ends at $se(m)$ in p_i. A message receipt event $r(m)$ for m begins at $rb(m)$ and ends at $re(m)$ in p_j.

Computer network protocols, e.g. TCP/IP protocols [5], are hierarchically composed. A message transmitted through a communication channel $\langle p_i, p_j \rangle$ in an upper layer is decomposed into multiple *packets* in a lower layer in p_i and the packets are reassembled to the message in p_j. Thus, a multimedia message m is decomposed into a sequence $\langle pa_1, \ldots, pa_l \rangle$ of multiple packets as shown in Figure 1. Here, $s(pa_k)$ is a *packet sending event* and $r(pa_k)$ is a *packet receipt event* for a packet pa_k.

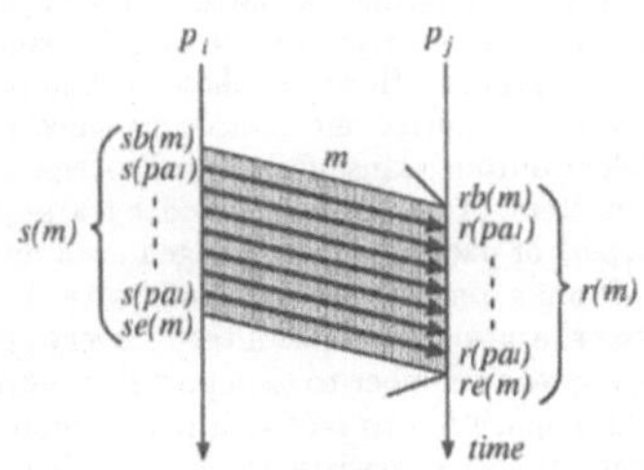

Figure 1. Multimedia message transmission.

For a message m with conventional data, communication events $s(m)$ and $r(m)$ are assumed to be atomic. Here, each local checkpoint c_i in a process p_i is taken only when no other event occurs in p_i. However, a multimedia message is so larger than a conventional data message that it takes longer time to transmit and receive the message. Thus, if a process is required to take a local checkpoint during a communication event, it has to wait until an end of the event. Hence, timeliness requirement in a checkpoint protocol is not satisfied and communication overhead in recovery is increased. Therefore, a local checkpoint should be taken immediately when a process is required to take it even during a communication event. That is, a process p_i sending $m = \langle pa_1, \ldots, pa_l \rangle$ takes a local checkpoint c_i between primitive events $s(pa_s)$ and $s(pa_{s+1})$ and another process p_j receiving m takes a local checkpoint c_j between primitive events $r(pa_r)$ and $r(pa_{r+1})$. In addition, a part of a multimedia message can be lost in a communication channel for an application, e.g. MPEG-2 data transmission. Such an application requires not to retransmit lost packets in recovery but to transmit packets with shorter transmission delay. Hence, an overhead for taking a checkpoint during failure-free execution is required to be reduced.

4. Novel Consistency

As discussed in section 2, since the conventional criteria of consistency for a global checkpoint is based on an architecture of conventional data communication networks, a novel criteria should be introduced into multimedia communication networks. *Global consistency* Gc for a global checkpoint $C_{\mathcal{V}} = \{c_1, \ldots, c_n\}$ denotes degree of consistency for $C_{\mathcal{V}}$ in $\mathcal{N} = \langle \mathcal{V}, \mathcal{L} \rangle$. In a conventional data communication network, Gc is defined as follows:

$$Gc = \begin{cases} 1 & \text{no inconsistent message in } \mathcal{L}. \\ 0 & \text{otherwise.} \end{cases} \quad (1)$$

In a multimedia communication network, a local checkpoint is taken even during a communication event and it is acceptable for an application to lose a part of a multimedia message. Hence, a domain of Gc is a closed interval $[0, 1]$ instead of a discrete set $\{0, 1\}$. Here, Gc should be compatible with the conventional criteria, i.e. (1) should be satisfied.

Gc is determined by timing-relation between local checkpoints and messages transmitted through communication channels. Thus, Gc is calculated by *channel consistency* Cc_{ij} for all the communication channels $\langle p_i, p_j \rangle \in \mathcal{L}$. Cc_{ij} is calculated by *message consistency* Mc^u_{ij} for all the messages m_u transmitted through $\langle p_i, p_j \rangle$. Finally, Mc^u_{ij} is induced by timing-relation between communication events for m_u and a set $C_{\{p_i, p_j\}} = \{c_i, c_j\}$ of local checkpoints.

4.1. Message Consistency

Message consistency Mc^u_{ij} is degree of consistency for a set $C_{\{p_i, p_j\}} = \{c_i, c_j\}$ of local checkpoints and a multimedia message m_u transmitted through a communication channel $\langle p_i, p_j \rangle$. Here, c_i and c_j are taken by processes p_i and p_j, respectively. We define an *inconsistent multimedia message.*

[Inconsistent multimedia message] A multimedia message m_u is inconsistent iff m_u is a *lost multimedia message* as in Figure 2 or an *orphan multimedia message* as in Figure 3. m_u is a lost multimedia message iff $se(m_u)$ occurs before taking c_i in p_i and $rb(m_u)$ occurs after taking c_j in p_j. m_u is an orphan multimedia message iff $sb(m_u)$ occurs after taking c_i in p_i and $rb(m_u)$ occurs before taking c_j in p_j. □

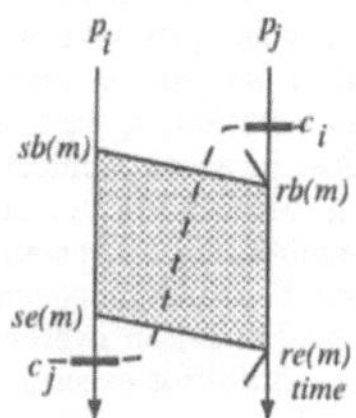

Figure 2. Lost multimedia messages.

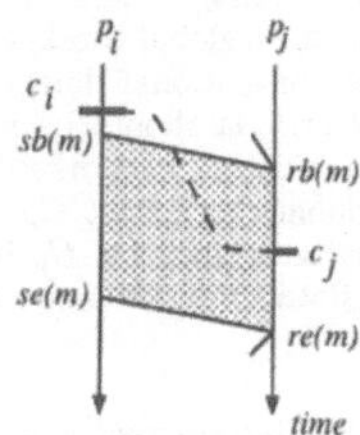

Figure 3. Orphan multimedia messages.

If m_u is a lost multimedia message, all the packets of m_u have been already sent by p_i but none of them is received by p_j in recovery. If m_u is an orphan multimedia message, m_u might not be retransmitted after recovery due to non-deterministic property of p_i even though p_j has already received a part of m_u. For compatibility with (1), $Mc_{ij}^u = 0$ for m_u.

[Consistency for inconsistent multimedia message] $Mc_{ij}^u = 0$ for an inconsistent multimedia message m_u. □

If c_i and c_j are taken before $sb(m_u)$ and $rb(m_u)$, $Mc_{ij}^u = 1$. In addition, if c_i and c_j are taken after $se(m_u)$ and $re(m_u)$, $Mc_{ij}^u = 1$. Thus, it is compatible with (1). As discussed in the previous section, a multimedia message m_u is decomposed into a sequence of multiple packets $\langle pa_1, \ldots, pa_l \rangle$. Thus, $s(m_u)$ is composed of a sequence $\langle s(pa_1), \ldots, s(pa_l) \rangle$ of packet sending events and $r(m_u)$ is composed of a sequence $\langle r(pa_1), \ldots, r(pa_l) \rangle$ of packet receipt events.

[Lost and orphan packets(Figures 2 and 3)] Suppose that local checkpoints c_i and c_j are taken between $s(pa_s)$ and $s(pa_{s+1})$ and between $r(pa_r)$ and $r(pa_{r+1})$ for a multimedia message $m_u = \langle pa_1, \ldots, pa_l \rangle$, respectively. pa_k is a *lost packet* iff $s(pa_k)$ occurs before taking c_i in p_i and $r(pa_k)$ occurs after taking c_j in p_j. pa_k is an *orphan packet* iff $s(pa_k)$ occurs after taking c_i in p_i and $r(pa_k)$ occurs before taking c_j in p_j.□

If $s = r$, there is no lost and orphan packet. Hence, $Mc_{ij}^u = 1$.

If $s > r$, $\{pa_{r+1}, \ldots, pa_s\}$ is a set of lost packets. These packets are not retransmitted after recovery. Lost packets in a conventional data communication network can be restored by logging them in failure-free execution [16]. However, in a multimedia communication network, less overhead in failure-free execution is required since applications require time-constrained execution. For example, storing a message log in a stable storage makes transmission delay and jitter in MPEG-2 data transmission larger. In addition, even if a part of a multimedia message is lost in recovery, an application accepts the message. The less packets are lost, the higher message consistency we achieve. A multimedia message is usually compressed for transmission. Thus, value of packets for a message is not unique. For example in an MPEG-2 data transmission, value of a packet for an I-picture is higher than value of a packet for a B-picture. Therefore, message consistency depends on total value of lost packets as follows:

$$\frac{\partial Mc_{ij}^u}{\partial lostvalue} < 0 \quad \text{where } lostvalue = \sum_{lost\ packets\ pa_k} value(pa_k). \tag{2}$$

Here, a domain of Mc_{ij}^u is an open interval $(0, 1)$.

If $s < r$, $\{pa_{s+1}, \ldots, pa_r\}$ is a set of orphan packets. An orphan multimedia message might not be retransmitted after recovery due to non-deterministic property of a process. However, these orphan packets are surely retransmitted after recovery since c_i and c_j are taken during transmission and receipt of m_u and the content of m_u being carried by a sequence $\langle pa_1, \ldots, pa_l \rangle$ of packets is not changed even after recovery. Orphan packets are received twice, once in failure-free execution and once after recovery. By assigning a sequence number to each packet, it never occurs for an application to receive a packet more than once. Hence, message consistency does not depend on orphan packets.

[Message consistency] Let $value(m_u)$ be total value of packets $pa_1, \ldots, pa_l$ of m_u.

$$\begin{aligned} Mc_{ij}^u &= 0 \quad \text{if } lostvalue = value(m_u). \\ Mc_{ij}^u &= 1 \quad \text{if } lostvalue = 0. \\ \frac{\partial Mc_{ij}^u}{\partial lostvalue} &< 0 \quad \text{otherwise.} \end{aligned} \tag{3}$$

□

[Example 1] In Figure 4, the reduction of message consistency is proportional to total value of lost packets. Here, message consistency is induced as follows:

$$\begin{aligned} Mc_{ij}^{u} &= 1 - \frac{lostvalue}{value(m_u)} \\ &= 1 - \frac{\sum_{lost\ packets\ pa_k} value(pa_k)}{value(m_u)} \end{aligned} \quad (4)$$

□

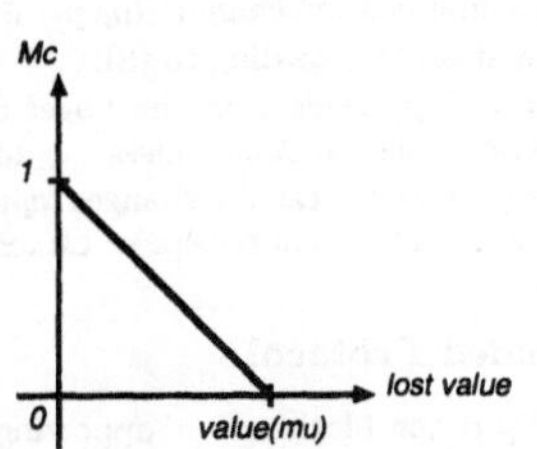

Figure 4. Message Consistency Example(1).

[Example 2] In Figure 5, if most of the packets of a

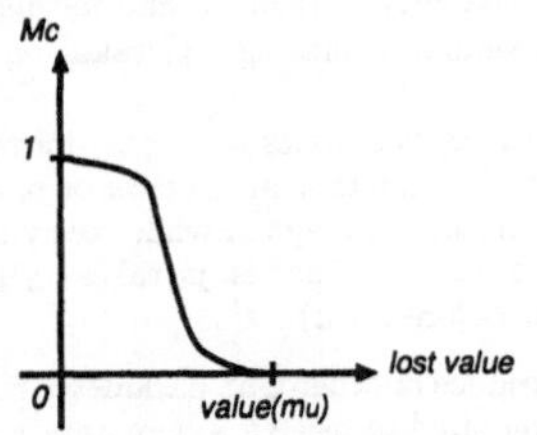

Figure 5. Message Consistency Example(2).

message m_u is not lost, message consistency is almost 1. On the other hand, if most of the packets of m_u is lost, message consistency is almost 0. For example in MPEG-2 data transmission, even if a small part of a message is lost, applications accept the message. On the other hand, if most part of a message is lost, applications does not accept the message. Hence, according to increasing total value of lost message, message consistency decreases first gradually, then rapidly and finally gradually. Hence, message consistency is induced as follows:

$$Mc_{ij}^{u} = \frac{\dfrac{\tan^{-1}(\frac{value(m_u)}{2} - lostvalue)}{\tan^{-1}(\frac{value(m_u)}{2})} + 1}{2} \quad (5)$$

□

4.2. Channel Consistency

Based on the message consistency for multimedia messages m_u and local checkpoints c_i and c_j in processes p_i and p_j respectively, channel consistency Cc_{ij} is defined as degree of consistency for a set $C_{\{p_i,p_j\}} = \{c_i, c_j\}$ of local checkpoints in a communication channel $\langle p_i, p_j\rangle \in \mathcal{L}$. Cc_{ij} is calculated by using message consistency Mc_{ij}^{u} for every message m_u transmitted through $\langle p_i, p_j\rangle$. For compatibility with (1), if message consistency for every message transmitted through $\langle p_i, p_j\rangle$ is 1, channel consistency is also 1. On the other hand, if message consistency for at least one message transmitted through $\langle p_i, p_j\rangle$ is 0, channel consistency is also 0. In addition, channel consistency monotonically increases for consistency of the messages transmitted through $\langle p_i, p_j\rangle$.
[Channel consistency] Let $\mathcal{M}_{ij}$ be a set of messages transmitted through $\langle p_i, p_j\rangle$.

$$\begin{aligned} &Cc_{ij} = 1 \quad \text{if } \forall m_u \in \mathcal{M}_{ij}\ \ Mc_{ij}^{u} = 1. \\ &Cc_{ij} = 0 \quad \text{if } \exists m_u \in \mathcal{M}_{ij}\ \ Mc_{ij}^{u} = 0. \quad (6) \\ &\forall m_u \in \mathcal{M}_{ij}\ \frac{\partial Cc_{ij}}{\partial Mc_{ij}^{u}} > 0 \text{ otherwise.} \ \square \end{aligned}$$

[Example 3] Cc_{ij} is calculated by multiplication of Mc_{ij}^{u} for all the messages m_u transmitted through $\langle p_i, p_j\rangle$. This satisfies (6).

$$Cc_{ij} = \prod_{m_u} Mc_{ij}^{u} \quad \square \quad (7)$$

4.3. Global Consistency

Based on the channel consistency for communication channels $\langle p_i, p_j\rangle \in \mathcal{L}$ and global checkpoint $C_{\mathcal{V}} = \{c_1, \ldots, c_n\}$, global consistency Gc is defined as degree of the global checkpoint. Gc is calculated by using channel consistency Cc_{ij} for every communication channel $\langle p_i, p_j\rangle \in \mathcal{L}$. For compatibility with (1), if channel consistency for every channel in $\mathcal{L}$ is 1, global consistency is also 1. On the other hand, if consistency for at least one communication channel is 0, global consistency is also 0. In addition, channel consistency monotonically increases for consistency of the communication channels in $\mathcal{L}$.
[Global consistency]

$$\begin{aligned} &Gc = 1 \quad \text{if } \forall\langle p_i, p_j\rangle \in \mathcal{L}\ \ Cc_{ij} = 1. \\ &Gc = 0 \quad \text{if } \exists\langle p_i, p_j\rangle \in \mathcal{L}\ \ Cc_{ij} = 0. \quad (8) \\ &\forall\langle p_i, p_j\rangle \in \mathcal{L}\ \frac{\partial Gc}{\partial Cc_{ij}} > 0 \text{ otherwise.} \ \square \end{aligned}$$

[Example 4] Gc is calculated by multiplication of Cc_{ij} for all the communication channels $\langle p_i, p_j\rangle \in \mathcal{L}$. For independence of system scale, normalization factor $|\mathcal{L}|$ is applied. This satisfies (8).

$$Gc = \left(\prod_{\langle p_i, p_j \rangle} Cc_{ij} \right)^{\frac{1}{|\mathcal{L}|}} \quad \square \tag{9}$$

5. Checkpoint Protocol

Here, we design a checkpoint protocol for a multimedia communication network according to the global consistency defined in (8). The protocol is based on a 3 phase coordinated checkpoint protocol [12]. In a data communication network, for avoiding inconsistent messages, each process is required to be blocked, i.e. suspend execution of an application for a certain period. However, for time-bounded failure-free execution of an application, our protocol does not require processes to suspend execution of an application during checkpoint protocol. Each process p_i takes a local checkpoint c_i immediately when p_i is required to take c_i. In this protocol, there is a ***coordinator process*** p_c. Here, we make the following assumptions:

- A sequence number $seq(m)$ is assigned to a message m when m is transmitted. $seq(m)$ is piggied back to each packet pa_k of m.
- $value(pa_k)$ and $value(m)$ are carried by each packet pa_k.

5.1. Basic Checkpoint Protocol

A basic checkpoint protocol $\mathcal{P}_{\mathcal{B}}$ is designed where global consistency is used as a QoS parameter. Though $\mathcal{P}_{\mathcal{B}}$ is designed based on a 3-phase coordinated checkpoint protocol, it is non-blocking. Each process is not required to suspend execution of an application as in a conventional protocol for data communication networks.

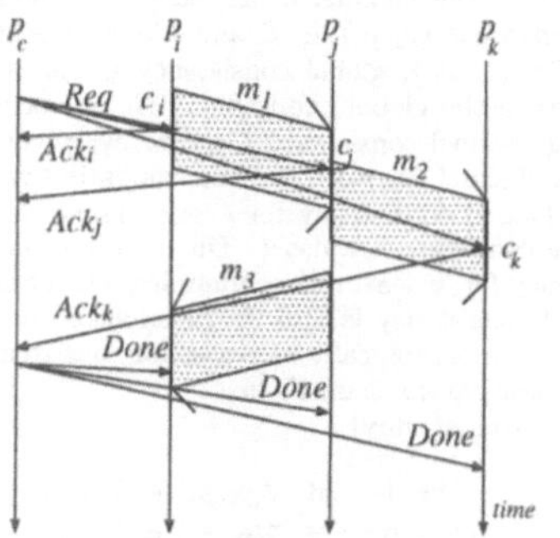

Figure 6. Basic protocol $\mathcal{P}_{\mathcal{B}}$.

[Basic protocol $\mathcal{P}_{\mathcal{B}}$ (Figure 6)]

1) Let RC be required global consistency. p_c sends a checkpoint request message Req to every $p_i \in \mathcal{V}$.
2) On receipt of the Req, each p_i takes a tentative local checkpoint tc_i.
3) Each p_i sends back an acknowledgement message Ack_i to p_c. For every communication channel $\langle p_i, p_j \rangle$ from p_i, $seq(m_{ij})$ and $tvalue(m_{ij}) = \sum value(pa_k)$ for pa_k of the last message m_{ij} sent before tc_i are piggied back to Ack_i. In addition, for every communication channel $\langle p_j, p_i \rangle$ to p_i, $seq(m_{ji})$ and $tvalue(m_{ji}) = \sum value(pa_k)$ for pa_k of the last message m_{ji} received before tc_i are also piggied back to Ack_i. That is, $seq_{ij} = seq(m_{ij})$, $tvalue_{ij} = tvalue(m_{ij})$, $seq_{ji} = seq(m_{ji})$ and $tvalue_{ji} = tvalue(m_{ji})$ are piggied back to Ack_i.
4) On receipt of all the Ack_i, p_c calculates Cc_{ij} for every communication channel $\langle p_i, p_j \rangle \in \mathcal{L}$.
5) p_c calculates Gc according to (8).
6) If $Gc > RC$, p_c sends $Done$ messages to $p_i \in \mathcal{V}$. Otherwise, p_c sends $Cancel$ messages to $p_i \in \mathcal{V}$.
7) On receipt of $Done$, each p_i changes tc_i to a stable local checkpoint c_i. On receipt of $Cancel$, each p_i discards tc_i. □

5.2. Extended Protocol

Though $\mathcal{P}_{\mathcal{B}}$ is non-blocking for supporting realtime multimedia applications, it is not certain to take $C_{\mathcal{V}}$ with required global consistency. According to the definition of global consistency, the less lost packets are, the higher global consistency we archive. Thus, the following modification in step 2) of $\mathcal{P}_{\mathcal{B}}$ is introduced for higher probability to take $C_{\mathcal{V}}$ and for higher Gc.

- If p_i is sending a message, p_i takes tc_i immediately.
- Otherwise, p_i postpones taking tc_i for ΔT_i. If p_i starts sending another message m or p_i starts receiving another message m while receiving a message, p_i takes tc_i. That is, p_i takes tc_i just after $sb(m)$ or before $rb(m)$.

Here, we introduce another QoS parameter τ for timeliness. p_c is required to receive Ack_i within τ since the transmission of Req. Thus, $\Delta T_i = \tau - 2\delta_i$ where δ_i is transmission delay between p_c and p_i.

[Extended protocol $\mathcal{P}_{\mathcal{E}}$]

1) Let RC and τ be required consistency and timeliness. p_c sends Req to every $p_i \in \mathcal{V}$. τ is piggied back to Req.
2) On receipt of the Req, each p_i takes tc_i as follows:
   - 2-1) If p_i is sending a message, p_i takes tc_i.
   - 2-2) Otherwise, p_i postpones taking tc_i for ΔT_i. During this period,
     - 2-2-1) if p_i is receiving a message and starts sending another message m, p_i takes tc_i just after $sb(m)$.
     - 2-2-2) if p_i is not communicating and starts sending a message m, p_i takes tc_i just after $sb(m)$.
     - 2-2-3) if p_i is not communicating and starts receiving a message m, p_i takes tc_i just before $rb(m)$.

On taking tc_i, p_i sends back Ack_i to p_c as in step

2) of $\mathcal{P}_B$.

Steps 3), 4), 5), 6) and 7) are the same as in $\mathcal{P}_B$. □

6. Evaluation

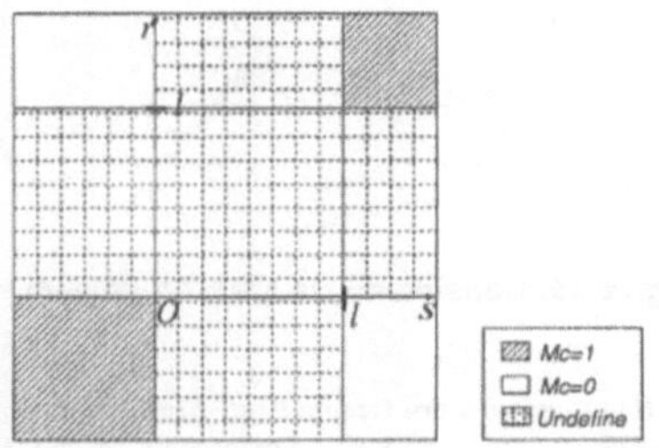

Figure 7. Message consistency in conventional protocol.

Here, we evaluate the proposed checkpoint protocols. First, the relation between required synchronization and achieved consistency is evaluated. Suppose a message m is transmitted through a communication channel $\langle p_i, p_j \rangle$ and local checkpoints c_i and c_j are taken by processes p_i and p_j,respectively. l is a number of packets consisting of m, i.e. $m = \langle pa_1, \cdots, pa_l \rangle$. p_i receives a *Req* message for c_i between $s(ps_s)$ and $s(ps_{s+1})$ and p_j receives a *Req* message for c_j between $r(pa_r)$ and $r(pa_{r+1})$. Here, $s \leq 0$ ($r \leq 0$) means that p_i (p_j) takes c_i (c_j) before $sb(m)$ ($rb(m)$) and $s > l$ ($r > l$) means that p_i (p_j) takes c_i (c_j) after $se(m)$ ($re(m)$). In the conventional checkpoint protocol for a data communication network, p_i has to wait until finishing transmission of m if $0 < s < l$ and p_j has to wait until finishing receipt of m if $0 < r < l$,. Hence, achieved message consistency is not defined in the area. Thus, higher synchronization overhead is required and message consistency is shown in Figure 7.

Next, message consistency $Mc(s,r)$ for a message m in $\mathcal{P}_B$ is shown in Figure 8.

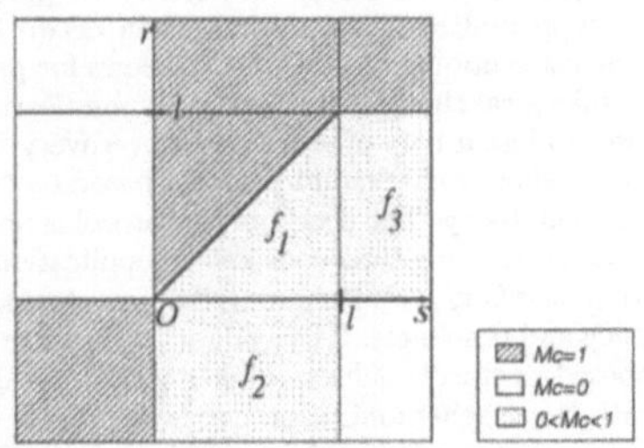

Figure 8. Message consistency in $\mathcal{P}_B$.

- $Mc(s,r) = 1$ if $s \leq 0$ and $r \leq 0$.
- $Mc(s,r) = 0$ if $s \leq 0$ and $r > 0$ since m is an orphan multimedia message.
- $Mc(s,r) = f_2(s)$ where $df_2(s)/ds \leq 0$, $\lim_{s\to 0} f_2(s) = 1$ and $\lim_{s\to l} f_2(s) = 0$ if $0 < s < l$ and $r \leq 0$.
- $Mc(s,r) = f_1(s,r)$ where $f_1(u,u) = 1(0 < u < l)$, $df_1(s,r)/ds \leq 0$ and $df_1(s,r)/dr \geq 0$, $\lim_{s\to l} f_1(s,r) = f_3(r)$ and $\lim_{r\to 0} f_1(s,r) = f_2(s)$ if $0 < s < l$ and $0 < r < s$.
- $Mc(s,r) = 1$ if $0 < s < l$ and $s \leq r$.
- $Mc(s,r) = 0$ if $l \leq s$ and $r \leq 0$ since m is a lost multimedia message.
- $Mc(s,r) = f_3(r)$ where $df_3(r)/dr \geq 0$, $\lim_{r\to 0} f_3(r) = 0$ and $\lim_{r\to l} f_3(r) = 1$ if $l < s$ and $0 < r < l$.
- $Mc(s,r) = 1$ if $l \leq s$ and $l \leq r$.

Clearly, message consistency in $\mathcal{P}_B$ is higher than that in the conventional protocol with lower synchronization overhead.

By introducing a delaying method, $Mc(s,r)$ in $\mathcal{P}_\mathcal{E}$ is modified as shown in Figure 9. Here, Δl represents a number of packets transmitted for ΔT_i.

- $Mc(s,r) = 1$ if $s \leq 0$ and $r \leq 0$.
- $Mc(s,r) = 0$ if $s < -\Delta l$ and $r > 0$.
- $Mc(s,r) = 1$ if $-\Delta l < s < 0$ and $r \geq 0$.
- $Mc(s,r) = g_2(s) = f_2(s)$ if $0 < s < l$ and $r \leq 0$.
- $Mc(s,r) = g_1(s,r) = f_1(s, r + \Delta l)$, if $\Delta l < s < l$ and $0 < r < s - \Delta l$.
- $Mc(s,r) = 1$ if $0 < s < l$, $r \geq s - \Delta l$ and $r \geq 0$.
- $Mc(s,r) = 0$ if $s > l$ and $r < 0$.
- $Mc(s,r) = g_3(r) = f_3(r + \Delta l)$ if $s > l$ and $0 < r < l - \Delta l$.
- $Mc(s,r) = 1$ if $s > l$ and $r \geq l - \Delta l$.

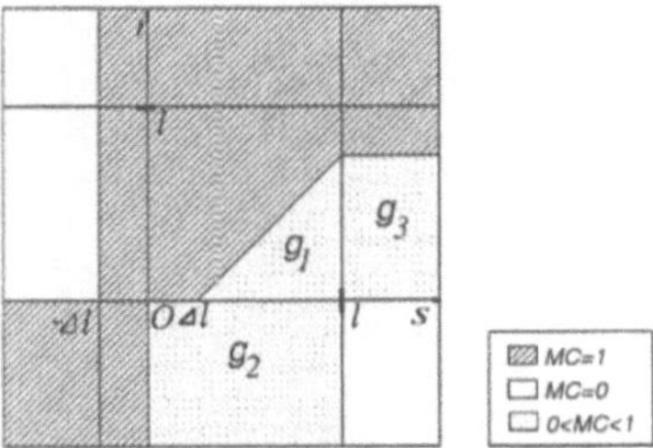

Figure 9. Message Consistency in $\mathcal{P}_\mathcal{E}$.

Comparing $\mathcal{P}_\mathcal{E}$ with $\mathcal{P}_B$, message consistency $Mc(s,r)$ changes from $Mc(s,r) < 1$ to $Mc(s,r) = 1$ in the following three domains:

- $-\Delta n < s < 0$ and $0 \leq r$
- $s > l$ and $l - \Delta n \leq r \leq l$
- $0 < s < \Delta n$ and $s > r + \Delta n$

Since $df_1(s,r)/dr \geq 0$ and $df_3(r)/dr \geq 0$, $Mc(s,r)$ in $\mathcal{P}_\mathcal{E}$ is always higher than or equal to that in $\mathcal{P}_\mathcal{B}$.

Finally, we apply $\mathcal{P}_\mathcal{B}$ to an MPEG-2 data transmission. MPEG-2 is a specification of video data compression [10]. The amount of an original video data is 720 × 480 dots/frame and 29.97 frames/sec [1]. Each frame is encoded to one of the following three kinds of pictures; an I-picture, a P-picture and a B-picture. An I-picture is achieved by encoding an original frame with DCT (Discrete Cosine Transform). An original frame is achieved by decoding an I-picture alone. A P-picture and a B-picture are achieved by using motion compensation. The sizes of a P-picture and a B-picture are about 1/3 and 1/6 of an I-picture, respectively. An original frame encoded to a P-picture is achieved by the P-picture and the previous frame encoded to an I-picture or a P-picture. If the previous I-picture or P-picture is lost, the original frame cannot be achieved. An original picture encoded to a B-picture is achieved by using bidirectional prediction. Here, the previous and the following I-pictures or P-pictures are used. Thus, if one of the pictures is lost, the original frame cannot be achieved.

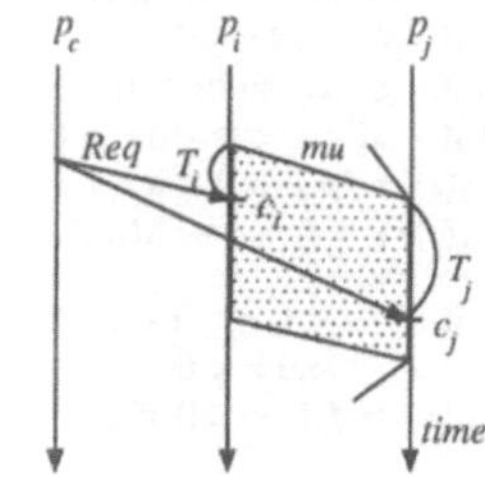

Figure 10. Evaluation parameters.

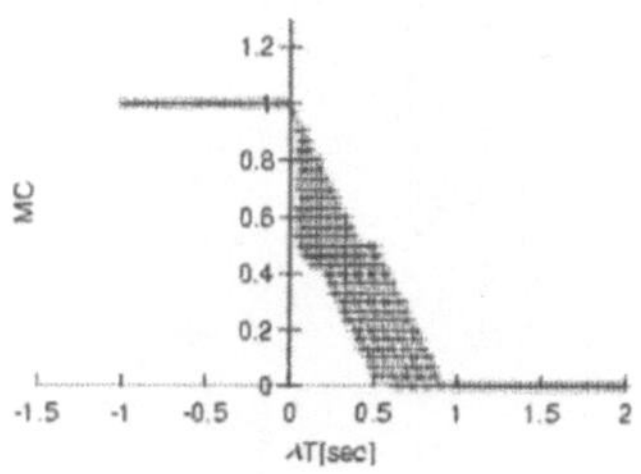

Figure 11. Consistency in MPEG-2 (1.0sec).

Suppose there are two processes p_i and p_j connected by a communication channel $\langle p_i, p_j\rangle$ and a multimedia message m_u is transmitted through $\langle p_i, p_j\rangle$ as shown in Figure 10. In the proposed checkpoint protocol, *Req* messages are transmitted from a coordinator process p_c to p_i and p_j. On receipt of the *Req* messages, p_i and p_j take local checkpoints c_i and c_j, respectively. Let T_i be time duration from $sb(m_u)$ to $r(Req)$, i.e. taking c_i in p_i, and T_j be time duration from $rb(m_u)$ to $r(Req)$, i.e. taking c_j in p_j. Here, message transmission delay of communication channels $\langle p_c, p_i\rangle$ and $\langle p_c, p_j\rangle$ are not the same. Let $\Delta T = T_i - T_j$.

[1]This encoding is called MP@ML (Main Profile, Main Level).

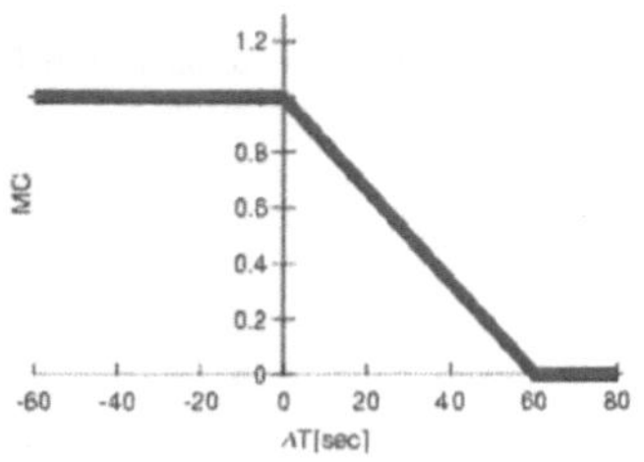

Figure 12. Consistency in MPEG-2 (60sec).

Figures 11 and 12 show relation between ΔT and $MC = Mc_{ij}^u$ for a message m_u which includes 1.0sec and 60sec MPEG-2 data. In MPEG-2, if a B-picture is lost, only one frame cannot be decoded. However, if an I-picture is lost, all the frames in the GOP (Group of Pictures) cannot be decoded. That is, $value(pa_k)$ is different for each pa_k. Thus, the mapping from ΔT to MC is not one-to-one but one-to-N as shown in Figure 11. According to Figure 12, $MC(5.52) = [0.900, 0.907]$ and $MC(5.90) = [0.894, 0.900]$. Hence, if required consistency is 0.9 and $\Delta T < 5.52$sec, a global checkpoint $\{c_i, c_j\}$ is consistent. In addition, if $\Delta T < 5.90$sec, $\{c_i, c_j\}$ might be consistent. This depends on which pictures are lost due to difference of transmission delay for *Req* messages. Therefore, even if p_i and p_j are not completely synchronized, we can achieve a QoS-based consistent global checkpoint.

7. Concluding Remarks

This paper proposes novel consistency of global checkpoints in multimedia communication networks. Unlike the conventional consistency, it allows for processes to take local checkpoints during communication events and to lose a part of a message in recovery. In addition, we show a checkpoint protocol based on the proposed consistency. The checkpoint protocol is non-blocking for supporting time-constrained applications. In addition, it is QoS-based where QoS parameters are consistency and timeliness. The evaluation shows that the proposed protocols achieve higher global consistency with lower synchronization overhead. Furthermore, the consistency and the protocol work well in the system transmitting an MPEG-2 data. In our future work, by introducing a new criteria for recovery time, based on a tradeoff between the criterias of consistency and recovery time, we will design an improved QoS based checkpoint protocol in a multimedia communication network.

References

[1] Bernstein, P.A. and Goodman, N., "An Algorithm for Concurrency Control and Recovery in Replicated Distributed Databases," ACM Trans. on Database Systems, Vol. 9, No. 4, pp. 1197–1207 (1984).

[2] Bhargava, B. and Lian, S.R., "Independent Checkpointing and Concurrent Rollback for Recovery in Distributed Systems," The 7th International Symposium on Reliable Distributed Systems, pp. 3–12 (1988).

[3] Chandy, K.M. and Lamport, L., "Distributed Snapshot: Determining Global States of Distributed Systems," ACM Trans. on Computer Systems, Vol. 3, No. 1, pp. 63–75 (1985).

[4] Cristian, F. and Jahanian, F., "A Timestamp-Based Checkpointing Protocol for Long Lived Distributed Computations," Reliable Distributed Software and Database Systems, pp. 12–20 (1991).

[5] Douglas, E.C., "Internetworking with TCP/IP," Prentice-Hall (1991).

[6] Elozahy, E.N., Johnson, D.B. and Wang, Y.M., "A Survey of Rollback-Recovery Protocols in Message-Passing Systems," Technical Note of Carnegie Mellon University, CMU-CS-96-181 (1996).

[7] Elnozahy, E.N., Johnson, D.B. and Zwaenepoel, W., "The performance of consistent checkpointing," The 11th International Symposium on Reliable Distributed Systems, pp. 39–47 (1992).

[8] Giffrod, D.K., "Weighted Voting for Replication Data, " The 7th ACM Symposium on Operating Systems, pp. 150–162 (1979).

[9] Higaki, H., Nemoto, N., Tanaka, K. and Takizawa, M., "Protocol for Groups of Pseudo-Active Replication Objects," International Workshop on Object Oriented Realtime Distributed Systems, pp. 35–41 (1999).

[10] Juang, T.T.Y. and Venkatesan, S., "Efficient Algorithms for Crash Recovery in Distributed Systems," The 10th Conference on Foundations of Software Technology and Theoretical Computer Science, pp. 349–361 (1990).

[11] Johnson, D.B., "Efficient Transparent Optimistic Rollback Recovery for Distributed Application Programs," The 12th International Symposium on Reliable Distributed Systems, pp. 86–95 (1993).

[12] Koo, R. and Toueg, S., "Checkpointing and Rollback-Recovery for Distributed Systems," IEEE Trans. on Software Engineering, Vol. SE-13, No. 1, pp. 23–31 (1987).

[13] Kumar, A., "Hierarchical Quorum Consensus: A New Algorithm For Managing Replicated Data," IEEE Trans. on Computers, Vol. 40, No. 9, pp. 996–1004 (1991).

[14] Lampson, B.W., Paul, M. and Siegert, H.J., "Distributed Systems - Architecture and Implementation," Springer-Verlag, pp. 246–265 (1981).

[15] Mathew, E. H. and Russell, M. S., "MULTIMEDIA COMPUTING - Case Studies from MIT Project Athena," Addison-Wesley (1993).

[16] Pankaj, J., "Fault Tolerance in Distributed Systems," Prentice Hall, pp.185–213 (1994).

[17] Pu, C.A., Noe, D.D. and Proudfoot, A., "Regeneration of Replicated objects: A Technique and its Eden Implementation," IEEE Trans. on Software Engineering, Vol. 14, No. 7, pp. 936–945 (1988).

[18] Shimamura, K., Tanaka, K. and Takizawa, M., "Group Protocol for Exchanging Multimedia Objects in a Group," 2000 ICDCS Workshop on Group Computation and Communications, pp. 33–40 (2000).

[19] Silva, L.M. and Silva, J.G., "Global Checkpointing for Distributed Programs," The 11th International Symposium on Reliable Distributed Systems, pp. 155–162 (1992).

[20] Venkatesh, K., Radhakrishnan, T. and Li, H.F., "Optimal and Local Recording for Domino-Free Rollback Recovery," Information Processing Letters, Vol. 25, pp. 295–303 (1987).

[21] Wood, W.G., "A Decentralized Recovery Protocol," The 11th International Symposium on Fault Tolerant Computing Systems, pp. 159–164 (1981).

An Interactive Audio and Video Station over Internet*

Chung-Ming Huang, Pei-Chuan Liu, and Pi-Fung Shih

Department of Computer Science and Information Engineering
National Cheng Kung University
Tainan, Taiwan 70101
{huangcm, liupc, shihpf}@locust.csie.ncku.edu.tw
http://bear.csie.ncku.edu.tw

Abstract. An Interactive Audio and Video Station named IAVS over Internet is presented in this paper. The IAVS system is a personal audio and video multicast transmission system and provides an interactive two-way communication over Internet. IAVS provides two features using the realtime multimedia interaction technique. The first one is that IAVS audience can transmit his voice to the IAVS server with a call-in operation. The second one is that IAVS offers the dual server mode to allow a secondary DJ, who is geographically separated from the main DJ, to join the program. That is, two geographically separated DJs cooperatively control the program. Many Internet entertainment applications, such as talk show and music station, can be constructed using IAVS. Related technique issues and the corresponding system development of IAVS are presented in detail in the paper. ...

1 Introduction

Today's people are becoming increasingly sophisticated, demanding richer and fully way of communication. This is evidenced by the fact that viewing video along with its associated audio becomes commonplace. Live call-in programs become popular and unavoidable because of their characteristics to allow interaction between the host and audiences. Based on these trends, we propose and develop an interactive audio and video multicast transmission system, which is called IAVS (Interactive Audio and Video Station), for possible entertainment applications over Internet. The IAVS system provides the capability of sophisticated communication for Internet users against traditional radio and TV stations.

An entertainment station over Internet is essentially a 1-to-n multipoint communication system, i.e., from a DJ server to n audiences [4]. One challenge that IAVS wants to overcome is to adopt the multicast technique [1] for enlargement

* The research is supported by the National Science Council of the Republic of China under the grant NSC 89-2219-E-006-019

of program scale and providing capacity of interaction at the same time. Consequently, the number of audiences becomes scalable and the quality of transmitted media is still maintained.

Interactive design plays an important role in IAVS. Audiences can try to make an interactive communication, which is called call-in in the current Radio and TV stations, if their machines have the sound recording capability. The key point is that when the call-in request is accepted, the response latency between the DJ server and the call-in audience should be limited to assure the conversation quality. Additionally, the IAVS system provides a nomadic server to improve the practicability. The secondary DJ, who is geographically separated from the main DJ server, can join the program by using the nomadic server. As a result, two geographically separated DJs can cooperatively control the program. Figure 1 depicts the abstract execution environment of IAVS.

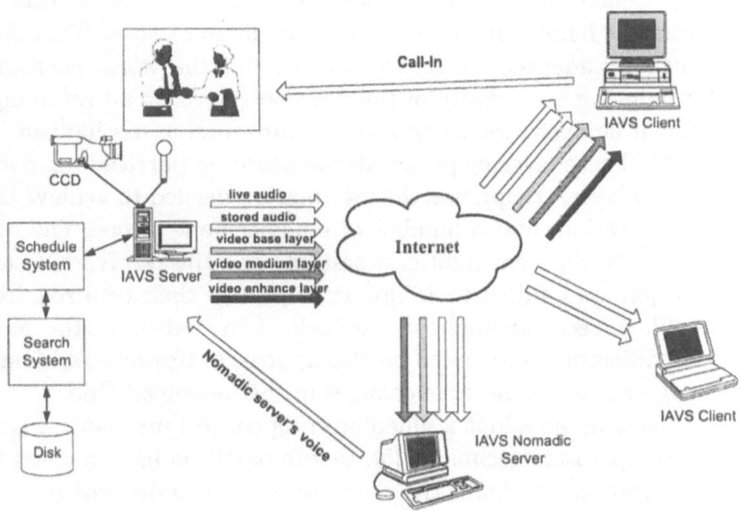

Fig. 1. The abstract execution environment of IAVS

In addition to the user interaction feature, IAVS supports multiple media sources, i.e., voice, music, and video. The feature of supporting multiple media sources makes IAVS to be able to perform as a radio station, a music station, or a TV station according to the preference of audiences. IAVS adopts the layered multicast mechanism to gain the feasible QoS for audiences connected in a heterogeneous network environment. Audiences can choose to watch the host's video if the required bandwidth is available, or only listen to the hosts audio if the network performance is not good enough to transmit video data. IAVS preserves the idea of live interactive communication and implements a graceful control scheme to maintain the real-time property. Consequently, the performance of the interaction between the host and the call-in audience is not degraded.

The remaining of the paper is organized as follow. Section 2 presents technique issues about audio and video transmission and its quality of service. Section 3 describes the system architecture of the IAVS system. Section 4 presents the presentation modes of the IAVS system. Section 5 concludes this paper.

2 Technique Issues

2.1 Live Layered Video Transmission

To improve the QoS of the best-effort based networks, many multimedia applications have the ability to adapt to fluctuations in the network conditions. Actually, various mechanisms have been proposed recently for adjusting the transmission rate of senders in accordance with the network congestion state [3, 8]. However, due to the heterogeneity of Internet, a single sender transmission rate cannot satisfy the conflicting bandwidth requirements at different sites. Therefore, the sender rate is usually adapted to the requirements of the worst positioned receiver, thereby reducing the quality of the data perceived at all receiving sites. This limitation can be overcome using layered transmission mechanisms as was proposed in [6, 10]. These layering proposals are based on partitioning a medium stream into a based layer, comprising the information needed to achieve the lowest quality representation, and a number of enhancement layers. The different layers are then sent to different multicast sessions and the receivers decide how many sessions to join and adjust their QoS in respect to their own requirements and capacities [9]. A receiver might dynamically join and leave the multicast sessions carrying different layers based on this approach. However, adding a new layer or removing one results in large changes in the perceived QoS.

In the IAVS system, we adopt a video layering control mechanism based on the Indeo video compression technique [5]. Before partitioning the video stream into layers, it is important to know the characteristics of Indeo video.

Characteristics of Indeo Video

Three types of frames in the Indeo video compression scheme are I, D, and P

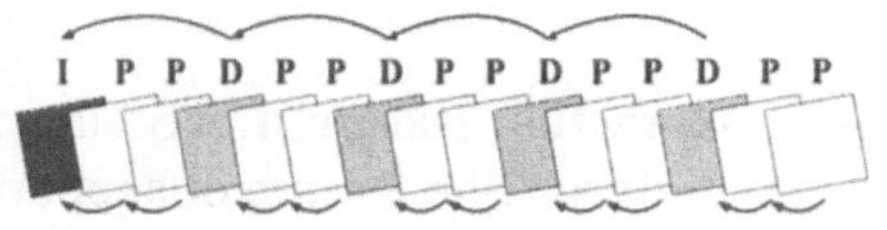

Fig. 2. The dependence relation of Indeo video frames

frames. I frames are independently decodable without referencing other frames. D frames are decoded by referencing leading I or D frames located before them. P frames are decoded by referencing any frames located in front of it. Figure 2 depicts the dependence relation of Indeo video frames with key frequency rate 15. The I frame occurs once for every 15 frames when the key frequency rate is 15. A group of frames from an I frame to the P frame right before the next I frame is named as Cycle of Pictures (COP). Actual Indeo video data are composed of a sequence of COPs. According to the dependence relation of Indeo video, a COP can be divided into five groups in which each group contains three consecutive frames. Each group starts with I or D frame and follows with two P frames. That is, the dependency relation can be divided into inter-group dependency (I and D frames) and intra-group dependency (P frames). If frame I or D is damaged, the error is propagated to related inter-group and intra-group dependent frames. If frame P is damaged, the error is only propagated inside intra-group and the inter-group dependency is hold. The layering mechanism is designed based on this group dependency and described as follow.

The Layering of Indeo Video

Figure 3 shows the three layers layering mechanism of Indeo video adopted in

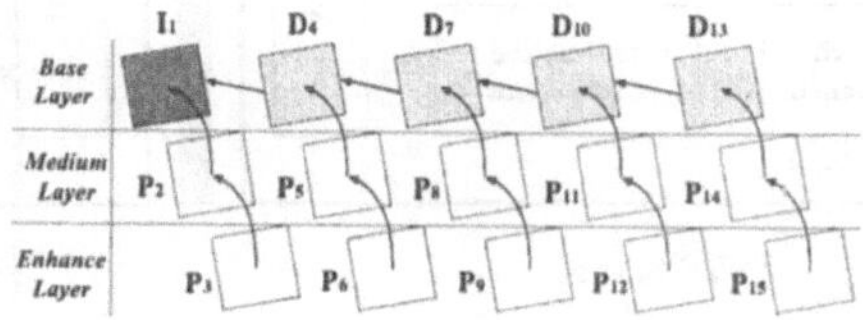

Fig. 3. The layering mechanism of Indeo Video

the IAVS system. The three layers are base layer, medium layer, and enhance layer. The base layer is composed of inter-group dependency, such as I and D frames, and has no reference to other layers. The medium layer is composed of the first P frame within intra-group dependency. The frames in the medium layer have to reference the I or D frames in the base layer before they are decoded. The enhance layer is composed of the second P frame within intra-group dependency. Decoding the frames of the enhance layer requires information from the P frames of the medium layer. Obviously, due to the dependence relation, the priority among the three layers is base layer ¿ medium layer ¿ enhance layer. According to the priority relation of the three layers, the receiver can subscribe layers cumulatively. That means the receiver can just subscribe the base layer for minimum requirement, subscribe the base layer and the medium layer for better presentation quality, or subscribe the base layer, the medium layer, and the enhance layer for full presentation quality. These three layers are sent to different multicast sessions and the receivers decide how many sessions to join. This layering mechanism and receiver subscribing scheme is called "Receiver-Driven Layered Multicast (RLM)" [6].

3 System Architecture

The abstract system architecture of IAVS is depicted in Figure 4. The IAVS system consists of the IAVS server part and the IAVS client part, both of which contain a presentation component, a synchronization component, an interactive component, and a network component. Two additional components in the IAVS server part are a schedule/authoring component and a search component.

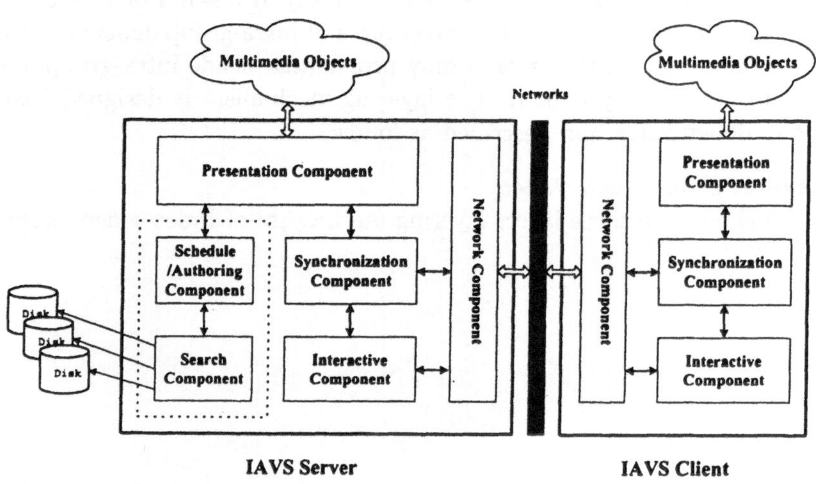

Fig. 4. The abstract system architecture of IAVS

Presentation Component

In a typical IAVS scenario, there can be one or more audiences connecting to IAVS service and harmonically presenting music and speech of the host through the presentation component. The GSM compression algorithm is adopted to achieve real-time voice transmission in IAVS. Besides, we adopt MP3 with the highest quality encoding rate, i.e., 128kbps, to have real-time music transmission in IAVS.

Synchronization component

The synchronization component achieves intra-media and inter-media synchronization [2], which are used to compensate for the temporal anomalies during media presentations. According to the specific communication model of IAVS, we select GSM live audio as the master stream, and MP3 stored audio and Indeo live video as the slave streams for the master-medium-based synchronization control scheme [7]. Besides, the inter-stream synchronization control is divided into live-stored synchronization and lip synchronization, which are described as follows.

(1) Live-Stored Synchronization: Synchronization between live and stored media is essential for IAVS system because the system has to perform the same section of MP3 music that DJ is talking about to audiences. We put the major work in

the server site to eliminate the time differences between live and stored media and to deliver media units on time according to the presentation program. In order to eliminate the time differences, we design a wait-for-send control method for the system. Using the wait-for-send method, the stored media is kept in the buffer to wait for the corresponding time to be sent, which is decided by the live media. Figure 5 depicts an example of using the wait-for-send method. The packet of the stored media is not sent out immediately after reading from the storage. The packet waits for D_S+D_L time interval and synchronizes with the packet of the live media. Then these two media packets are sent out in a timely manner.

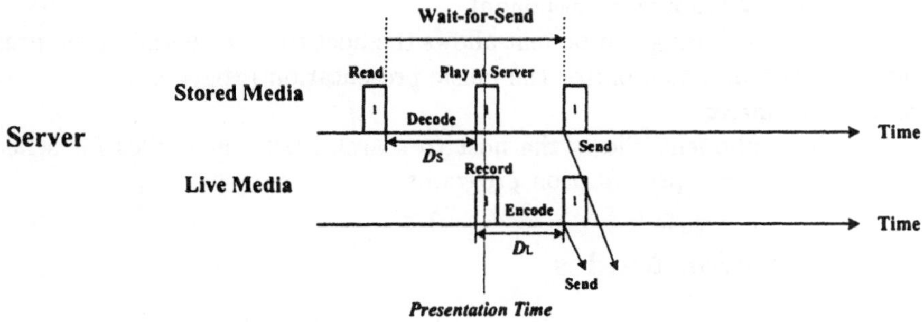

Fig. 5. The wait-for-send control

(2) Lip synchronization: The lip synchronization takes synchronization control between live audio and live video, which is the GSM audio and the Indeo video in IAVS. Based on the master-medium-based synchronization control scheme, the GSM audio is chosen as the master stream and the Indeo video is chosen as the slave stream.

Due to the video dependence properties, if an I frame is lost, the following frames of this COP have to be dropped and thus do not need to be synchronized with the audio stream. Therefore, if an I frame is received, we can at least decode one frame of the COP and synchronize with the audio stream. In IAVS, we choose the I frame to be the synchronization point of the slave medium. That is, the video medium process checks the synchronization information from the central process before playing back the I frame, and adjusts its presentation accordingly. The slave medium process will stop or resume the presentation, even drop some frames. Two synchronization situations may occur:

1. If video leads, the video medium process is forced to stop the video playback thread for a moment. When it reaches the synchronization point, the medium process resumes the playback thread.
2. If the video lags behind the audio, the video medium process is forced to drop some video frames according to the lag time. Assume the lag time is θ,

and the video frame display interval is 60 ms. Then, $\theta/60$ frames need to be dropped on the end of the COP.

`Interactive Component`
The major function of the interactive component is to provide interactive conversation, which is the call-in event between the host and the audiences. The interactive controller is responsible for processing call-in events.

`Network component`
The network component is in charge of multipoint communication, which is based on the IP-multicast environment. The network component is responsible for transmitting media packets and adapting client's presentation quality according to the network situation.

`Schedule and Authoring Component`
The schedule/authoring component allows the host to arrange the music presentation program and to monitor the music presentation program.

`Search Component`
The search component allows the host to search MP3 music files for scheduling/authoring music presentation programs.

4 Presentation Modes

In order to achieve smooth music presentation and flexible interaction between the host and audiences over Internet, IAVS supports three presentation modes, i.e., the listen mode, the call-in mode, and the dual server mode. In the listen mode, the IAVS server continuously multicasts MP3 music and speech of the host to all joined audiences. Interested audiences can listen to the music presentation program by joining the multicast group. In the call-in mode, the host schedules music programs for audiences and is able to invite one of the audiences to have a gossip with the host. The audiences, who want to give talks, simply click the call-in button via the user interface dialog and then send the call-in request messages to the host.

Three-party conversation may be needed in Internet multimedia applications. For example, the host invites a famous specialist to give a talk and have an interactive conversation with the host and audiences. In the past, the invitee may need to have a long journey in order to reach the radio station company. The dual server mode is provided to solve the time wasteness and the invitee inconvenience. In the dual server mode, the main host is able to cooperate with the nomadic server to host the program. The nomadic server can simply click the call-in button via the user interface dialog and then send the dual server mode request messages to the main host.

5 Conclusion

In this paper, we have proposed a feasible interactive entertainment station system, which is named IAVS, to provide simultaneous multimedia multicasting over Internet. Main features of the IAVS system are summarized as follows:

Interactive communication: The interactive communication between host and audiences can reduce the distance gap. Currently, a lot of traditional radio programs provide live Call-Ins from audiences through PSTN telephone services. The call-in capability is included in the IAVS system. The IAVS system also provides a nomadic server to support the dual server cooperation mode. In the dual server mode, the main host can cooperate with the nomadic server, who is geographically separated from the main server, to control the program.
Variety media source support: The IAVS system supports both live and stored media transmission. The server can broadcast live voice from the real time recording capability. The stored media, i.e., MP3, also can be directly broadcasted to audiences to provide high quality music presentations.
Authoring and searching functions: Nowadays, most of traditional radio stations prepare their programs before presentation time. The IAVS host system provides the same function to authoring programs. The authoring system helps the host to control its presentation sequence. Additionally, IAVS also provides a searching function to cooperate with the authoring function. The searching function gives the host an easy way to find the MP3 data from the storage media.

References

1. K. C. Almeroth, "The evolution of multicast: from the MBone to interdomain multicast to Internet2 deployment," IEEE Network, VOL. 14, No. 2, pp. 10-20, January/Feberuary 2000.
2. E. Biersack, W. Geyer, and C. Bernhardt, "Intra- and Inter-Stream Synchronization for Stored Multimedia Streams," Proceedings of the 3rd IEEE International Conference on Multimedia Computing and Systems, VOL. 12, No. 1, pp. 372-381, 1996.
3. I. Busse, B. Deffner, H. Schulzrinne, "Dynamic QoS control of multimedia applications based on RTP," Computer Communications, VOL. 19, No. 1, pp. 49-58, January 1996.
4. C. Diot, W. Dabbous, and J. Crowcroft, "Multipoint Communication: Survey of Protocols, Functions, and Mechanism," IEEE Journal on Selected Areas in Communications, VOL. 15, No. 3, pp. 277-290, 1997.
5. Intel Indeo Video Technical Overview, http://developer.intel.com/ial/indeo/video/overview.htm
6. S. McCanne, V. Jacobson, and M. Vetterli, "Receiver-driven layered multicast," Proceedings of ACM SIGCOMM, August 1996.
7. J. Sato, K. Hashimoto, M. Katsumoto, and Y. Shibata, "Performance evaluation of media synchronization for multimedia presentation," Proceedings of International Workshops on Parallel Processing, pp. 608-613, 1999.
8. D. Sisalem, "Fairness of adaptive multimedia applications," Porceedings of International Conference on Communications, June 1998.
9. L. Xue, M. H. Ammar, and S. Paul, "Video multicast over the Internet," IEEE Network, VOL. 13, pp. 46-60, March/April 1999.
10. Z. Wei, M. Willebeek-LeMair, and P. Tiwari, "Efficient adaptive media scaling and streaming of layered multimedia in heterogeneous environment," Proceedings of the 6th IEEE International Conference on Multimedia Computing and Systems, pp. 377-381, 1999.

Query by Tapping: A New Paradigm for Content-Based Music Retrieval from Acoustic Input

Jyh-Shing Roger Jang[1], Hong-Ru Lee[2], Chia-Hui Yeh[3]

Multimedia Information Retrieval Laboratory
Computer Science Department, National Tsing Hua University, Taiwan
jang@cs.nthu.edu.tw[1], khair@ms24.hinet.net[2]
beball@wayne.cs.nthu.edu.tw[3]

Abstract. This paper presents a query by tapping" system, which represents a new paradigm for CBMRAI (content-based music retrieval via acoustic input) systems. Most CBMRAI systems take the user acoustic input in the format of singing or humming, and the timing or beat information (durations of notes) is sometimes discarded during the retrieval process in order to save computation. Our query by tapping" mechanism, on the other hand, takes the user input in the format of tapping on the microphone and the extracted duration of notes is then used to retrieve the intended song in the database. Since there is no singing or humming, no pitch information is used in the retrieval process at all. Most people would think that it is hard to do music retrieval via beat information alone. However, our experiments demonstrate that beat information is also an effective feature in the sense that it can be used to retrieve the intended song from a large collection of music database with a satisfactory recognition rate.

1 Introduction

As there are more and more digital music files (such as MP3, MIDI, ASF, RM) being created over the Internet, the corresponding issue of music information retrieval [1][2] is becoming increasingly important. In particular, most people do not have professional music skills and the best way to specify an intended song is to sing or hum it. As a result, CBMRAI (content-based music retrieval via acoustic input) systems are the most natural tools for common people needs of music information retrieval. Application domains of CBMRAI are immense, such as

1. Internet music search engine
2. Query engine for digital music libraries/museums
3. Intelligent interface for karaoke bars (which are quite popular in China, Japan, Korea and Taiwan)
4. Song-activated interactive toys
5. Education software for music/vocal training

Most CBMRAI systems [3][13][12][11][14][4] take the user input in the format of singing or humming, and then transform the audio signal into a pitch vector for retrieval purpose. To save computation time, the pitch duration (or equivalent, beat or timing information) is sometimes discarded to have a more compact representation and a shorter computation time.

Unlike most CBMRAI systems, our music retrieval system, called Super MBox" [7][9][8], has a unique feature that can take the user input in the format of tapping on the microphone, which represents the beat or timing information of the intended song. The system then uses the beat information alone to identify the intended songs from a database of 11744 candidate songs. Most people would think that CBMRAI based on beat information alone can not have good performance since amateur persons cannot identify a song solely based on its beat information. However, our experiments indicate otherwise. In fact, we have applied a dynamic-programming-based comparison procedure to achieve a top-100 (or top 0.85% of all candidate songs) recognition rate of about 80%, which is considered satisfactory performance. We also did error analysis to demonstrate the causes of cases of failure.

The rest of the paper is organized as follows. Section 2 explains the feature extraction process, which transforms the user's tapping input into a timing vector. Section 3 describes the dynamic-programming-based procedure that we employ to compare the input timing vector with those of the songs in the database. Section 4 demonstrates the performance evaluation of the system and explores the causes that might degrade the performance. Section 5 gives conclusions and future directions.

2 Feature Vector Extraction

The feature vector used in our system is simply a time vector in which each element represents the duration of a note. To extract such information, the user is required to gently tap on the microphone to indicate the beat information of the intended song. The recording conditions are

- Sample rate of 11025
- 8-bit resolution
- Recording duration of 15 seconds
- Single channel (mono)

A typical waveform of the user's tapping input of the song "You Are My Sunshine" is shown in plot (a) of the following Fig. 1; the corresponding log energy profile is shown in plot (b). (The plots only show the first 10 seconds.)

From plot (a) of the below figure, it is obvious that the user has input 16 complete notes. To extract the duration of each note, we need to do frame blocking first and then find the energy of each frame. The circles in (b) indicate where local maxima of the log energy are located. The local maxima are legal only when their values are greater than a heuristically determined threshold (about –20 dB, indicated by the horizontal line in plot (b)).

Once the legal local maxima are found, the duration of each note is equal to the distance between two neighboring local maxima. The beat information is then represented as a timing vector in which each element is a note's duration. For example, the timing vector extracted from the above example would be [0.4180, 0.3715, 0.3831, 0.7314, 1.1262, 0.4063, 0.3599, 0.3715, 0.7779, 1.1610, 0.3947, 0.3483, 0.3715,

0.8127, 1.0797, 0.3715], in where there are 16 elements, representing durations of 16 notes in seconds.

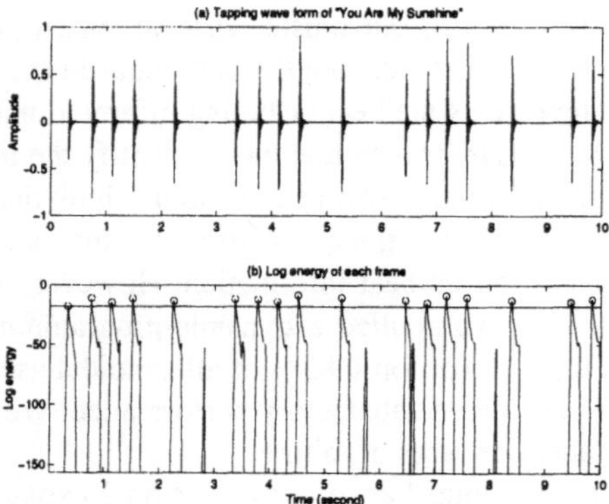

Fig. 1. (a) Tapping waveform of "You Are My Sunshine"
(b) Corresponding log energy plot.

The parameters of the feature extraction process can be listed as follows:

1. The frame size is 256 points.
2. The threshold for legal local maxima is equal to the fifth global maximum of log energy minus 7 dB.

Note that the frame size determines the resolution of the resultant timing information. In our case, the resolution is equal to 256/11025 = 0.0232 seconds, which is good enough for our comparison procedure. If the frame size is smaller, the timing resolution is higher, but the energy profile becomes jagged and the exact location of the desired local maxima would be difficult to find.

3 Comparison Procedure

Once the timing vector from a user's input is obtained, we need to compare it with those of the songs in the database. In this section we shall propose a comparison procedure based dynamic programming [15]. In fact, the concept is similar to dynamic time warping [6] used in our previous work [7]. In this paper, for simplicity, we assume that the user always taps from the beginning of the intended song. However, this is not an absolute requirement since the proposed method can still start matching at anywhere in a middle of a song.

To match the input timing vector against those of the songs in the database, we need to be aware of two things:

1. The tempo of the user's input is usually different from those of the candidate songs in the database.
2. The user is likely to lose notes instead of gaining notes.

To solve the first problem, we need to normalize the input timing vector and those of the candidate songs. Suppose that the input timing vector (or test vector) is represented by vector t of length m, and the reference timing vector (reference vector) by r with length n. Usually n is greater than m. Suppose that the user did not lose/gain any notes, so we only need to compare t with the first m elements of r. However, since the user might lose or gain notes, we need to compare t with a selection of different versions of r with different lengths. Suppose that the first q elements of r is selected for comparison, then the normalization step convert both vectors to a total duration of 1000:

$$\begin{cases} \tilde{t} = round(1000 * t / sum(t)) \\ \tilde{r} = round(1000 * r(1:q) / sum(r(1:q))) \end{cases} \tag{1}$$

In the above equations, $r(1:q)$ indicates a vector formed from the first q elements of vector r; $sum(t)$ indicates the summation of all elements in vector t. The operation of *round* rounds all elements of the vectors into integers. The purpose of multiplication by 1000 is to increase the precision since our comparison procedure is based on integer operations to save computation time. After the above normalization step, the subsequent comparison procedure is based on $\tilde{t}$ and $\tilde{r}$. Actually, we need to vary the value of q to get different versions of $\tilde{r}$; the distance between $\tilde{t}$ and $\tilde{r}$ is taken to be the minimum of distances between $\tilde{t}$ and all variants of $\tilde{r}$. In our system, the value of q is varied from $p-2$ to $p+2$, where p is the length of $\tilde{t}$.

The comparison procedure is based on the concept of dynamic time warping (DTW) [6]. For notation simplicity, we shall remove the "tilde" temporarily. Suppose that the (normalized) input timing vector (or test vector) is represented by $t(i), i=1,\ldots,m,$ and the (normalized) reference timing vector (reference vector) by $r(j), j=1,\ldots,n$. These two vectors are not necessarily of the same size and we can apply DTW to match each point of the test vector to that of the reference vector in an optimal way. That is, we want to construct a $(m+1)\times(n+1)$ DTW table $D(i,j)$ according to the following forward dynamic programming algorithm:

Optimal value function:

$D(i,j)$ is the minimum accumulated distance starting from **(0, 0)** of the DTW table to the current position (i,j).

Recurrence relation:

$$D(i,j) = \min \begin{cases} D(i-1,j-2) + |r(i-1)+r(i)-t(j)| + \eta_1 \\ D(i-1,j-1) + |t(i)-r(j)| \\ D(i-2,j-1) + |t(i-1)+t(i)-r(j)| + \eta_2 \end{cases} \tag{2}$$

where η_1 and η_2 are a small positive numbers. In the above equation, $|r(i-1)+r(i)-t(j)|+\eta_1$ represents the cost when the user mistake two note for one; $|t(i-1)+t(i)-r(j)|+\eta_2$ represents the cost when the user mistake a note for two.

Boundary conditions:

The boundary conditions for the above recursion can be expressed as

$$\begin{aligned} D(i,0) = 0, i = 0,\ldots,m, \\ D(0,j) = 0, j = 0,\ldots,n. \end{aligned} \tag{3}$$

After we have the boundary conditions, the recursion formula to fill the DTW table can be performed either row-wise or column-wise.

The cost of the optimal DTW path is defined as $D(m,n)$

After finding $D(m,n)$, we can back track to obtain the entire optimal DTW path and the corresponding alignments between the two vectors.

In summary, the whole comparison procedure can be listed as follows:

1. Extract the input timing vector from the user's acoustic input of tapping. Normalized the timing vector.
2. Find the DTW distance between the input timing vector and that of each candidate song in the database. Note that the timing vector of a song has to be compressed or extended to have 5 versions of different lengths. Then the distance between the input timing vector and that of a song is taken to be the minimum among all 5 distances between the input timing vector and 5 variants of that of the song.
3. List the results according to DTW distances.

Fig. 2 illustrates the flowchart of our query-by-tapping system.

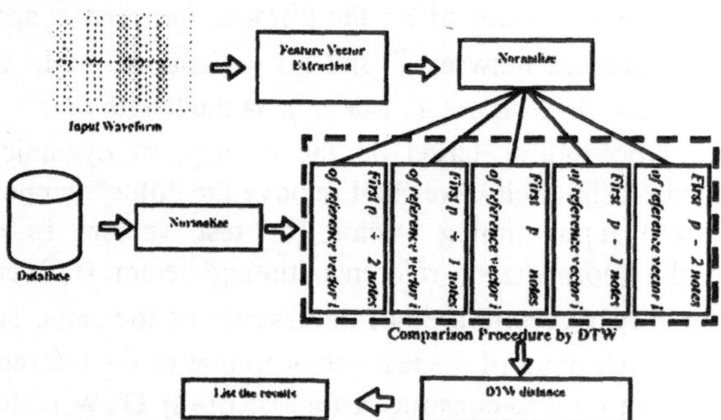

Fig. 2. Flowchart of our query-by-tapping system

4 Performance Evaluation

In this section we present the performance evaluation of our query-by-tapping system. We have a dataset of around 269 clips of tapping from by 9 persons (7 males, 2 females). Specs of the dataset are:

- No. of clips: 269
- Resolution: 8 bits
- Duration: 15 seconds
- Type: Single channel (mono)
- Sample rate: 11025 samples/second
- Start position: Beginning of a song

All of the recordings start from the beginning of a song. The specs of our platform and candidate songs are

- CPU: Pentium-III 800MHz
- No. of candidate songs: 11744
- RAM: 128 MB
- Match position: Beginning of each song

In the first experiment, we take all the tapping clips of 15 seconds to evaluate our system. The average response time of a query with 15-second tapping clip is about

3.42 seconds. In average, a 15-second tapping clip contains about 29.98 notes. The performance of the system can be viewed from the following pie chart:

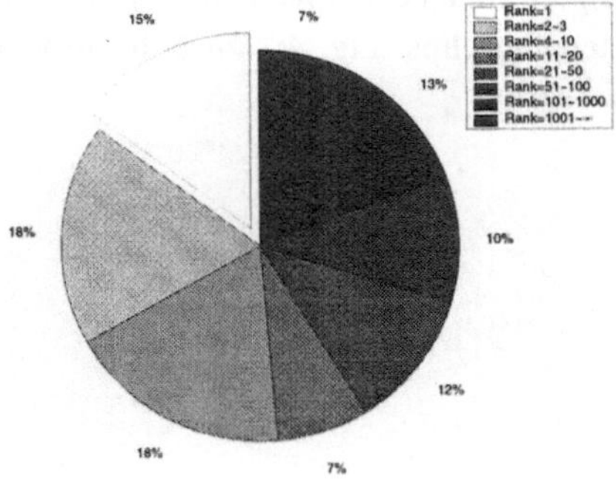

Fig. 3. The performance of our system

From Fig. 3, the top-1 recognition rate (percentage of recordings that Super MBox can find the intended songs in the top-1 ranking) is 15%, the top-10 recognition rate is 51%, and the top-100 recognition rate is 80%. Apparently it seems that these recognition rates are not so impressive. However, remember we are only using timing information to do the query, and there are 11744 candidate songs in the database (so top-100 is equivalent to top 0.85% of the whole candidate songs).

For those songs that fall below top-100, we performed an error analysis and found that most of the errors could be attributed to the following reasons:

1. Some users can only tap the songs correctly at the beginning but could not keep it through the whole recording duration of 15 seconds.
2. Some of the tapping clips are too noisy to extract the correct timing information.
3. Some MIDI files do not correctly represent the rendition of the original songs. This is mostly due to the fact that the composers of the MIDI files tried to add personal styles and made the rendition different from the original ones.
4. Some MIDI files include preludes. Since we match from the beginning of a song; the prelude will be matched incorrectly.

Reasons 3 and 4 are MIDI errors and can only be corrected manually. This MIDI correction task is very labor intensive and time consuming. What is worse is that the task can only be accomplished by someone familiar with the songs. Obviously it is impossible to find a person who knows all 11744 songs. Hence MIDI correction is a long-term task that plays a pivotal role to improve our system performance incrementally.

Reason 2 typically occurs when the user microphone has an abnormal high/low gain, or the sound card has a wrong driver. On the other hand, we can also improve our feature extraction procedure to make it more robust to adversary recording conditions.

Reason 1 demonstrates an interesting fact that some people cannot tap a song through 15 seconds. The reasons are two fold. First, the user might be familiar with only the first 10 seconds of the song, but not the whole 15 seconds. Second, the user might not be able to keep the same tempo through out 15 seconds. To have an in-depth evaluation, we perform an experiment that evaluation the system performance on the duration of tapping clips. Fig. 4 shows the results of recognition rates with respect to recording duration.

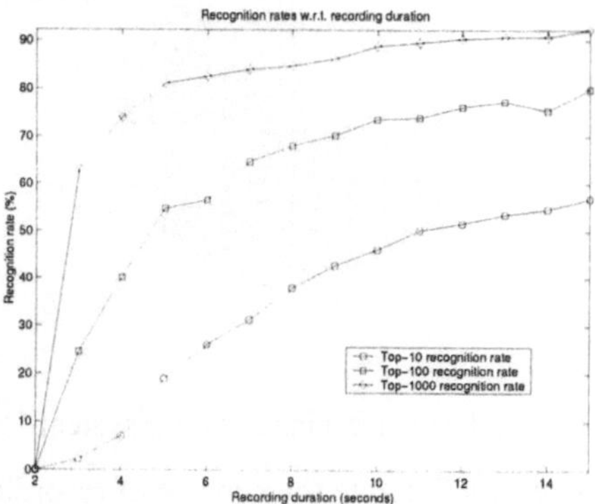

Fig. 4. Recognition rates with respect to recording duration

The above plot shows the curves of top-10 (top-0.085%), top-100 (top-0.85%), and top-1000 (top-8.5%) recognition rates with respect to tapping durations. It is observed that top-10 curve goes up with the increase of recording duration. On the other hand, top-100 and top-1000 curves level off at about 10 seconds. In particular, for the top-100 curve, the recognition rate for 14 seconds is even lower than those of 12 and 13 seconds. This indicates that a longer tapping duration does not imply a better recognition rate, which comes from the observation that some users can only tap the songs correctly at the beginning but could not keep it through the whole recording duration of 15 seconds.

5 Conclusions and Future Work

In this paper, we have presented a new paradigm for content-based music retrieval system via acoustic input. The new retrieval paradigm, called query by tapping", allows the user to query a music database by simply tapping on the microphone to input the durations of the first several notes of the intended song. Most people would think this retrieval paradigm is ineffective for large-scale music database. However, our experiments demonstrate that query by tapping" is not only interesting but also effective way of retrieving music from a large-scale music database. The top-10 and top-100 recognition rates of query by tapping" on a database of 11744 songs are about 51% and 80%, respectively. Moreover, we found that long tapping clips do not always lead to better performance due to the facts that most people cannot keep correct tapping or consistent tempo over the whole 15 seconds of recording.

We have implemented query by tapping" as a query method besides query by humming" and query by singing" to our content-based music retrieval system called

Super MBox". The online version of the system can be downloaded from the link n-line demo of Super MBox" at the author homepage at

http://www.cs.nthu.edu.tw/~jang

This is on-going research and our goal is to make Super MBox an intelligent content-based music retrieval system that allows as many different ways of music retrieval as possible. Future work involves the following tasks:

1. Allow the user to start tapping from the middle of a song.
2. Modify the feature extraction procedure to make it more robust to noisy environment.
3. Combine query by tapping" and query by humming" to have a multi-modal user interface for better performance.

6 References

[1] 1st International Symposium on Music Information Retrieval (MUSIC IR 2000), Plymouth, Massachusetts, Oct. 23-25, 2000. (http://ciir.cs.umass.edu/music2000/)

[2] 2nd Annual International Symposium on Music Information Retrieval (MUSIC IR 2001), Indiana University, Bloomington,Indiana, Oct.15-17, 2001.(http://ismir2001.indiana.edu/)

[3] A. J. Ghias, and D. Logan, B. C. Chamberlain, Smith, query by humming-musical information retrieval in an audio database", ACM Multimedia '95 San Francisco, 1995.

[4] A. Uitdenbogerd, and J. Zobel, "Melodic Matching Techniques for Large Music Databases", (http://www.kom.e-technik.tu-darmstadt.de/acmmm99/ep/uitdenbogerd/)

[5] B. Chen, and J.-S. Roger Jang, "Query by Singing", 11th IPPR Conference on Computer Vision, Graphics, and Image Processing, PP. 529-536, Taiwan, Aug 1998.

[6] J. R. J. G. Proakis, and J. H. L. Hansen, "Discrete-time processing of speech signals," New York, Macmillan Pub. Co., 1993.

[7] J.-S. Roger Jang, and Ming-Yang Gao, "A Query-by-Singing System based on Dynamic Programming", International Workshop on Intelligent Systms Resolutions (the 8th Bellman Continuum), PP. 85-89, Hsinchu, Taiwan, Dec2000.

[8] J.-S. Roger Jang, Hong-Ru Lee, and Ming-Yang Kao, "Content-based Music Retrieval Using Linear Scaling and Branch-and-bound Tree Search", IEEE International Conference on Multimedia and Expo, Waseda University, Tokyo, Japan, August 2001. (Submitted)

[9] J.-S. Roger Jang and Hong-Ru Lee, "Hierarchical Filtering Method for Content-based Music Retrieval via Acoustic Input", The ninth ACM Multimedia Conference, Ottawa, Ontario, Canada, September 2001.

[10] N. Y. Kosugi, Kon'ya, S. Nishihara, M. Yamamura, and K. Kushima, "Music Retrieval by Humming – Using Similarity Retrieval over High Dimensional Feature Vector Space," pp 404-407, IEEE 1999.

[11] R. J. McNab, and L. A. Smith, Melody transcription for interactive applications" *Department of Computer Science University of Waikato*, New Zealand.

[12] R. J. McNab, L. A. Smith, and Jan H. Witten, Signal Processing for Melody Transcription" *Proceedings of the 19th Australasian Computer Science Conference*, 1996.

[13] R. J. McNab, L. A. Smith, and Jan H. Witten, Towards the Digital Music Library: Tune Retrieval from Acoustic Input" ACM, 1996.

[14] R. J. McNab, L. A. Smith, I. H. Witten, and C. L. Henderson, "Tune Retrieval in the Multimedia Library,"

[15] Stuart E. Dreyfus, and Averill M. Law, The art and theory of dynamic programming", New York :Academic Press, 1977.

Multi-modal Sign Icon Retrieval for Augmentative Communication

Chung-Hsien Wu, Yu-Hsien Chiu, and Kung-Wei Cheng

Department of Computer Science and Information Engineering,
National Cheng Kung University, Tainan, Taiwan
{chwu, chiuyh, kungwei}@csie.ncku.edu.tw

Abstract. This paper addresses a multi-modal sign icon retrieval and prediction technology for generating sentences from ill-formed Taiwanese sign language (TSL) for people with speech or hearing impairments. The design and development of this PC-based TSL augmentative and alternative communication (AAC) system aims to improve the input rate and accuracy of communication aids. This study focuses on 1) developing an effective TSL icon retrieval method, 2) investigating TSL prediction strategies for input rate enhancement, 3) using a predictive sentence template (PST) tree for sentence generation. The proposed system assists people with language disabilities in sentence formation. To evaluate the performance of our approach, a pilot study for clinical evaluation and education training was undertaken. The evaluation results show that the retrieval rate and subjective satisfactory level for sentence generation was significantly improved.

1 Introduction

People with communication disabilities are unable to communicate with others naturally. Since 1970, developed countries have designed AAC technology to provide language learning and speech correction aids for improving the communication ability of individuals with language disabilities. Unfortunately these developed AAC technologies cannot be directly applied to people using Chinese languages. In Taiwan, TSL has been generally used in schools for the hearing-impaired. However, hearing-impaired students using TSL as their native language usually have difficulty constructing grammatical Chinese sentences.

Current research on augmentative communication technologies focuses largely on developing a more efficient user interface and extending accessibility [1], [2], ranging from unaided modes such as American Sign Language and the manual sign system to aided communication systems such as voice synthesis output systems and orthographic symbols. Due to the rapid advances in computer and Internet technologies, many human-computer interfaces (HCI) and natural language processing systems have the potential to integrate state of the art information retrieval [3] and speech technologies [4] into the development of AAC systems. This motivates us to explore the use of multi-modal technologies as communication aids for the hearing-impaired.

The purpose of this study was to investigate the methods for improving the input rate and accuracy for TSL AAC system communication aids. More specifically, this research focuses on: 1) developing an effective TSL icon retrieval method, 2) investigating TSL prediction strategies for input rate enhancement 3) and using the proposed PST tree for sentence generation. These interface strategies can in turn be used to achieve a wide range of functions for the disabled depending upon their specific needs.

2 AAC System for the Hearing and Speech Impaired

The proposed TSL AAC system, shown in Fig.1, is composed of three main components: 1). *Alternative multi-modal access with message prediction*, 2). *Message decoding and translation*, and 3). *Multi-sensory feedback*. Alternative access refers to how a person interacts with the system regarding message composition and selection techniques. For interactive purposes , a TSL virtual keyboard (VK), is proposed as an alternative interface for sign icon input. Furthermore, a speech keyword-spotting engine is integrated to provide a different sign icon mode for normal people. For quick retrieval from a large TSL icon database, a prediction strategy is used to enhance the accessibility. The PST tree is proposed to generate sentences from ill-formed sign icon input for the language disabled. Finally, the translated message is provided via speech synthesis and visualized icon sequences.

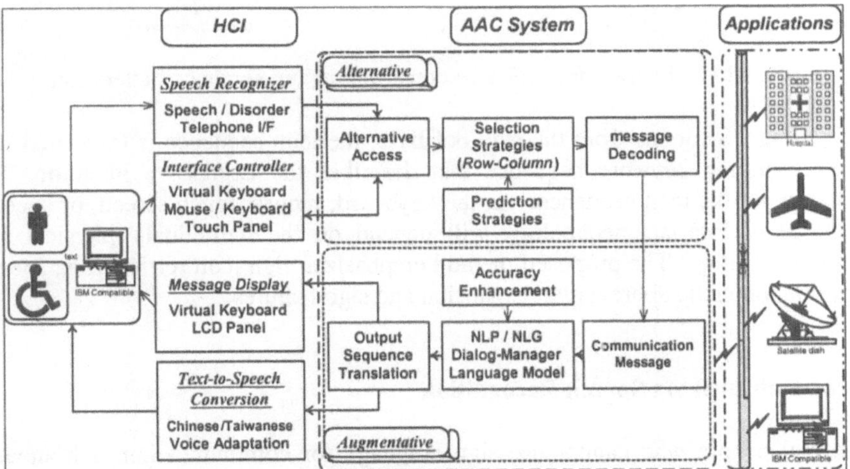

Fig. 1. AAC framework

3 Multi-Modal Sign Icon Retrieval

The sign language set used in our system is hierarchically categorized and recorded as an icon template tree structure. Each keyword (KP_i) consists of a part-of-speech feature (POS_i), a semantic feature (CF_i), an N-gram information (Ng_i), an inverted index (I_i), visualized features of sign typology ($SC_{i,j}$, for j=1,..,10), and Chinese phonetic symbols (CP_i) for retrieval from a large TSL vocabulary. Each leaf node/icon contains an ordered vertex list ($POS_i, CF_i, Ng_i, I_i, SC_{i,j}, CP_i$) named feature list sequence (FLS), from the root. This set of FLSs is converted into various structural forms such as a sub-tree or list, etc. A PST tree is proposed to deal with the ill-formed input. Fig. 2 shows the block diagram for PST tree construction and sentence generation.

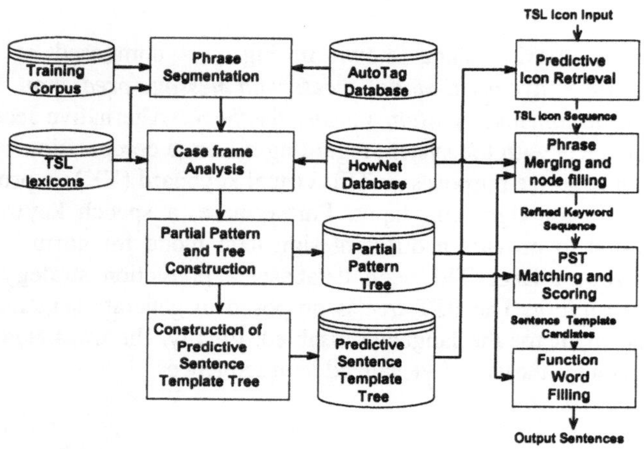

Fig. 2. Block diagram for PST tree construction and sentence generation

By retrieving TSL icons from the sign database, the icon sequence is translated into the corresponding keyword sequence that describes the expressive intention. The users can input the icon sequences via the keyboard, mouse, touch screen, or speech. The choice of interface technology will depend on the individuals' physical and language capability. The proposed method emphasizes sign icon retrieval via speech recognition, phonetic abbreviation expansion and sign features.

3.1 Icon Retrieval via Speech Recognition

For normal people who cannot use sign language for communication, a Mandarin speech keyword spotting system is proposed to retrieve TSL icons via speech. First, the acoustic features are extracted and fed to the syllable recognition models. The Viterbi algorithm generates the recognized syllable lattice and its corresponding state and mixture sequences for the N best paths. A keyword detection algorithm [4] is used to generate the possible keyword candidates. The pre-trained anti-models are then used for verification to output the verified keyword candidates. Finally, all of the candidates are further verified and scored using the PPT. The top 3 most probable candidates and their corresponding FLSs are used to retrieve the corresponding TSL icons.

3.2 Icon Retrieval via Abbreviation Expansion

The Chinese phonetic abbreviation expansion method was designed to limit the number of selected inputs necessary to access a particular sign icon from a large TSL icon database. This design concept is based on the characteristic that no two consecutive consonants can be mapped to any Chinese character. Fig. 3 shows the ATN-based approach. State 0 indicates the initial state of the ATN. The single circle represents the intermediate state and the dark circle indicates the accept stage. State 3 represents the accepting state and returns a word and State 7 returns a character. A phonetic symbol-matching algorithm is then used to iteratively match the icons from the rearranged CP_i set in a left-to-right mode using the phonetic rules such as the consonant is always followed by a vowel. Finally, all of the candidates with partially matched pairs are used to retrieve the TSL icons. This fast search method is integrated into the VK by providing a pop-up dialog window of the Chinese phonetic keyboard.

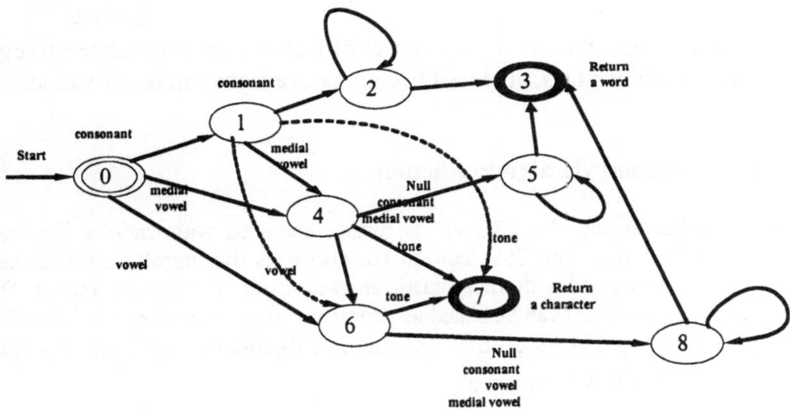

Fig. 3. ATN for abbreviation expansion

3.3 Icon Retrieval via Sign Features

Sign Language involves a manually produced, visually received signal. Three types of TSL behavior listed below are applied as the *aspects* of a sign to avoid unnecessary confusion [5]:

a. ***tab***: the location of the sign in relation to the body;
b. ***dez***: the handshape of the hand;
c. ***sig***: the movement executed by the hands.

According to Strokeo's analysis [5], 21 distinct locations, 50 distinct handshapes, and 12 distinct movements are used as the basic manual components of signs. Moreover, based on the topology of signs, two main configurations for signing formation are categorized as follows: 1). One-handed signs with/without contact to the body; 2). Two-handed signs with the same or different handshapes. Therefore, for the sign retrieval, 10 sign features, listed in Table 1, are proposed to record the signing information in detail.

Table 1. Data structure of 10 sign features

Initial Position				Final Position				Movement	
Left Hand	Right Hand	Left Hand	Right Hand	Left Hand	Right Hand	Left Hand	Right Hand	Left Hand	Right Hand
dez	tab	dez	Tab	dez	tab	dez	tab	sig	sig

In order to retrieve a TSL icon, the $SC_{i,j}$ set is organized into a *multilist* structure. When a feature is identified, the partially matched $SC_{i,j}$ is ordered and a pointer list can be followed using a list-merging algorithm. This pointer chain provides all secondary SC_i in addition to the primary feature attached to the record. To retrieve a sign from this *multilist* in answer to a conjunctive query feature, it suffices to find the shortest list using the combined indices, similar to the term phrase formation. The partial features chains can then be searched in parallel to reduce the search time and the needed number of combined indices for n features is equal to $\binom{n}{\lfloor (n+1)/2 \rfloor}$. While this number is much smaller than $n!$. If any subset of features appears consecutively in at least one of the combined lists, all possible conjunctive signs can be answered.

3.4 Rate Enhancement via Sign Prediction

For input rate enhancement, the TSL-VK is further endowed with various icon retrieval strategies and the PST tree. The TSL icon on the display is dynamically updated based on previous input and constrained with the syntactic characteristics of Chinese grammar. The task of predicting the next keyword can be stated as attempting to estimate the probability function $P(POS_n \mid POS_1 \cdots POS_{n-1})$. Using the maximum likelihood estimation, we can reformulate the probability function as

$$P_{MLE}(POS_n \mid POS_1 \cdots POS_{n-1}) = \frac{C(POS_1 \cdots POS_n)}{C(POS_1 \cdots POS_{n-1})} \qquad (1)$$

where $C(POS_1 \cdots POS_n)$ represents the frequency of sequence $POS_1 \cdots POS_n$. Using the statistical language model (LM), the icon sequence can be retrieved via TSL-VK with predictive capability. Fig. 4 shows an example for illustrating the PST tree with predictive capability using variable N-gram LM. The function words are excluded in the predictive process.

4 Sentence Generation

The Chinese sentences formed by people with hearing impairments are almost all ill formed or ungrammatical. For accuracy enhancement, the statistical-based bottom-up parsing with top-down filtering strategy is proposed to generate grammatical sentences from ill-formed TSL icon sequence inputs. Firstly, in bottom-up parsing stage, the POS and semantic features are used to merge possible phrases using partial patterns and concatenate the adjectives and quantifiers into a noun phrase segment based on the HowNet. All of the keyword candidates and the combined phrases are then aligned into a suitable node with POS constraint in the PST tree. For example, the user inputs the partial sentence *{紅/Na(red)->蘋果/Na(apple)->二/Neu(two)}*, to generate a new phrase *{二顆紅色的蘋果"/Na(two red apples)}*. In top-down filtering stage, the node-matching criteria are applied first to all of the templates. The matching criteria are defined as follows: 1) The number of verbs in the template is equal to the number of verbs in the phrase segment; 2). The number of nouns is smaller or equal to the number of nouns in the phrase segment; 3). The number of function words in the phrase segment should be smaller than 2. According to these three criteria, a PST syntactic score is used to retrieve the top-10 candidate paths. Finally, in function word filling stage, the function words are filled into the nodes with the POS of the function word, such as the node Dfa shown in Fig. 4. For example, the words "很"(very) and "非常"(greatly) are function words. The words "嗎" or "吧" can be inserted into the end of a sentence to form an interrogative sentence. Finally, the PST score and LM score are combined to rank the sentence candidates, which provide the user with a means to select and generate the voice output via a Chinese text-to-speech conversion system. This can take advantage of generating more sentences and speed up the rate of communication by skipping the input of function words.

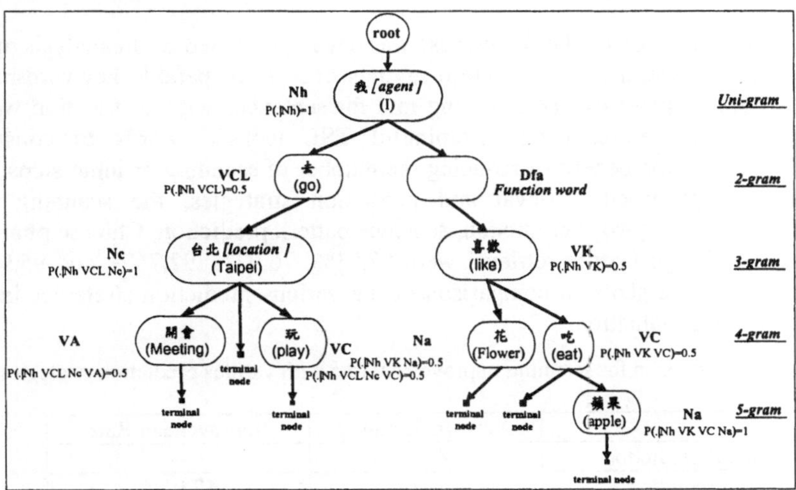

Fig. 4. An example using PST tree

5 Evaluation Results

In order to evaluate the performance of our approach, a case study for clinical evaluation and education training was undertaken. Three thousand forty-five commonly used TSL icons were adopted to investigate the effect of message expressive communication for 20 students with speech-hearing impairments. One thousand sixty-four Chinese sentences, in which the average utterance length is 4.9 words, were selected to develop the 491 sentence templates in the PST tree and partitioned into training and testing databases.

5.1 Evaluation of System Performance

In the practice evaluation, the usefulness of the proposed system is dependent on many factors, ranging from the user's cognition abilities to the interface design. Fig. 5 shows this intelligent TSL AAC system and the retrieval interface using the sign features. The evaluation focuses on the various strategies of rate enhancement.

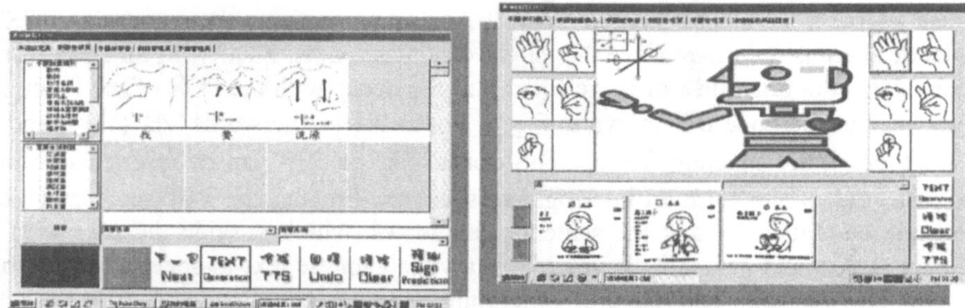

Fig. 5. TSL AAC system and Sign feature retrieval interface

An evaluation of the potential effectiveness was developed based on an analysis of the training corpus to estimate the selection savings over a comparable keyword-based system. A 26.25% keystroke (KS) saving rate for sentences without function words was achieved. Therefore, using meaningful TSL icons/keywords to construct sentences can have the benefit of reducing the number of scanning or input steps. For evaluating our proposed retrieval and prediction strategies, the scanning rate enhancement using keyword prediction, sentence pattern prediction, Chinese phonetic abbreviation and sign feature retrieval were 57.91%, 76.92%, 92.76%, and 95.93%, respectively. Table 2 shows a comparison of the various prediction strategies in the keyword selection evaluation.

Table 2. Comparison for scanning improvement rate with various prediction strategies

	Average Scanning	Improvement Rate
Without prediction	44.2	--
Word prediction	18.6	57.91%
Syntax prediction	10.2	76.92%
Abbreviation	3.2	92.76%
Sign feature	1.8	95.93%

5.2 Case Study

For the practical communication aid assessment, a special educator was asked to select suitable subjects meeting a predefined literacy and language learning capability requirement. Through the integration of clinical and educational evaluation, a single subject with hearing-impairment was asked to participate in these experiments. After the training (TP), adaptation (AP) and evaluation (EP) phases, the successful generation rates with respect to manual transcription were 47.4%, 65.0% and 68.2%, respectively. The generation rate and subjective satisfactory sentence generation level were significantly improved. Table 3 shows the practical evaluation results.

Table 3. Case study for evaluating practice communication aids and system performance

PHASE	TP	AP	EP
Number of Sentences	19	20	22
Average Keyword Number	6.1	5.5	4.2
Average Generation Time (sec/sentence)	191.7	114.6	68.4
Successful Generation Number	9	13	15
Successful Generation Rate (%)	47.4	65.0	68.2
Subjective Satisfactory Level (5 levels)	3.6	4.2	4.4

6 Conclusion

The proposed system applies TSL icon retrieval and prediction innovative design methodology to the development of a TSL AAC system for Chinese people in need of communication aids. The newly proposed sign feature indexing design takes more consideration of the human factors, visual concentration and eye-hand coordination. In addition to speeding up the sentence generation rate for individuals, the proposed system has the potential to assist people with language disabilities to form sentences. Evaluation results show that the generation rate and subjective satisfactory level for sentence construction were significantly improved. In the future, this system can be ported into a palm-sized platform and other multi-modal applications.

7 Acknowledgment

The authors would like to thank the National Science Council, Republic of China, for financially supporting this work, under Contract No. NSC89-2614-H-006-003-F20.

References

1. Demasco, P. and McCoy, K. F.: Generating Text from Compressed Input: An Intelligent Interface for People with Severe Motor Impairments. Communication of the ACM, Vol. 35. (1992) 68-78
2. Simpson, R. C. and Koester, H. H.: Adaptive One-Switch Row-Column Scanning. IEEE Transaction on Rehabilitation Engineering, Vol. 7. (1999) 464-473
3. Colombo, C.; Del Bimbo, A.; Pala, P.: Semantics in Visual Multimedia Information Retrieval. IEEE Multimedia, Vol. 63. (1999) 38-53
4. Wu, C.H., Yan, G.L. and Chen, Y. J.: Integration of Phonetic and Prosodic Information for Robust Utterance Verification. IEE Proceedings, Vision, Image and Signal Processing, Vol.147, pp.55-61. (2000)
5. Valli, Clayton and Lucas, Ceil: Linguistics of American Sign Language: An Introduction. Gallaudet University Press, Washington, D.C. (1996)

Comparison of Word and Subword Indexing Techniques for Mandarin Chinese Spoken Document Retrieval

Hsin-min Wang and Berlin Chen

Institute of Information Science, Academia Sinica
128 Academia Road, Section 2, Taipei 115, Taiwan
{whm, berlin}@iis.sinica.edu.tw

Abstract. In this paper, we investigate the use of words and subwords (including both characters and syllables) in audio indexing for Mandarin Chinese spoken document retrieval. Two retrieval approaches, including the well-known vector space model approach and the newly proposed HMM/N-gram-based approach, are used in the present work. We focus on the use of an entire Chinese textual story (from a newspaper) as a query to retrieve Mandarin Chinese spoken documents (from news broadcasts). Experiments are based on the Topic Detection and Tracking Corpora.

1 Introduction

Massive quantities of audio and multimedia content, such as broadcast radio and television programs, are becoming increasingly available in the global information infrastructure. Since users need to be able to search for desired information efficiently, there is increasing demand for multimedia information retrieval technologies. As a result, the spoken document retrieval (SDR) task has been extensively studied in recent years [1-2]. In the area of Mandarin Chinese spoken document retrieval, some research works have been conducted at Academia Sinica, Taipei [3], and at The Chinese University of Hong-Kong [4]. In addition, Mandarin-English Information (MEI), a research project conducted in the Johns Hopkins University Summer Workshop 2000, investigated the use of an entire English newswire story (text) as a query to retrieve relevant Mandarin Chinese radio broadcast news stories (audio) in the document collection [5].

In Mandarin Chinese, there exists an unlimited number of words, though only tens of thousands of them are commonly used. Each word is composed of from one to several characters. Each character is pronounced as a monosyllable and is a morpheme with its own meaning. As a result, new words are easily generated every day by combining a few characters or syllables. For example, the combination of 電 (electricity) and 腦(brain) gives a new word, 電腦(computer). Mandarin Chinese is phonologically compact; an inventory of about 400 base syllables provides full phonological coverage of Mandarin audio. On the other hand, an inventory of about 6,800 characters provides full textual coverage of written Chinese (in GB code), and one of about 13,000 characters does so for conventional Chinese (in Big5 code).

There is a many-to-many mapping between characters and syllables. For example, the character 乾 may be pronounced as /gan1/ or /qian2/ while all of the characters 甘干柑肝竿尷疳 are also pronounced as /gan1/ and all of 前錢潛黔虔掮 are pronounced as /qian2/. Consequently, a foreign word can very often be translated into different Chinese words. For example, "Kosovo" in "As the Kosovo peace talks in France..." may be translated into 科索沃/ke1-suo3-wo4/, 科索佛/ke1-suo3-fo2/, 科索夫/ke1-suo3-fu1/, 科索伏/ke1-suo3-fu2/, or 柯索佛/ke1-suo3-fo2/.

Word-level indexing features possess more semantic information than subword-level features; thus word-based retrieval enhances precision. On the other hand, subword-level indexing features are more robust against Chinese word tokenization ambiguity, Chinese homophone ambiguity, the open vocabulary problem, and speech recognition errors; thus, subword-based retrieval enhances recall. Consequently, there is good reason to study information fusion of indexing features of different levels. In this paper, we first investigate the use of words and subwords (including both characters and syllables) in audio indexing for Mandarin Chinese spoken retrieval and then explore information fusion.

In the following, all the experiments were conducted to study the use of an entire Chinese newswire story (text) as a query to retrieve relevant Mandarin Chinese radio broadcast news stories (audio) from the document collection. Such a retrieval context is termed *query-by-example*. The experiments were based on the Topic Detection and Tracking Corpora (TDT-2 and TDT-3). Two retrieval approaches were adopted in this work: the well-known vector space model approach and the HMM/N-gram-based approach that we recently proposed [6].

2 Experimental Corpora

We used two Topic Detection and Tracking (TDT) collections in this study. TDT-2 was taken as the development test set, while TDT-3 was used as the evaluation test set. Chinese news stories (text) from the Xinhua News Agency were used as our queries (or query exemplars). Mandarin news stories (audio) from Voice of America news broadcasts were used as spoken documents. All news stories were exhaustively tagged with event-based topic labels, which served as the relevance judgments for performance evaluation. Table 1 lists details of the corpora used in this paper.

The Dragon large-vocabulary continuous speech recognizer provided Chinese word transcriptions for our Mandarin audio collections (TDT-2 and TDT-3). We spot-checked a fraction of the TDT-2 development set (of 39.90 hours) by comparing the Dragon recognition hypotheses with the manual transcriptions and obtained error rates of 35.38% (word), 17.69% (character) and 13.00% (syllable). Spot-checking approximately 76 hours of the TDT-3 test set gave error rates of 36.97% (word), 19.78% (character) and 15.06% (syllable). Notice that Dragon's recognition output contains word boundaries (tokenizations) resulting from its language models and vocabulary definition, while manual transcriptions are running texts without word boundaries. Since Dragon's lexicon is not available, we augmented the LDC Mandarin Chinese Lexicon with the 24k words extracted from Dragon's word recognition output, and used the augmented LDC lexicon (about 51k words) to tokenize the manual transcriptions for computing error rates. We also used this augmented LDC lexicon to tokenize the text query exemplars in the retrieval experiments.

Table 1. Statistics of TDT-2 and TDT-3 collections used in this paper

	TDT-2 (Dev.) 1998, 02-06			**TDT-3 (Eval.) 1998, 10-12**		
# Spoken documents	2,265 stories, ~46hrs of audio			3,371stories, ~98hrs of audio		
# Distinct text queries	16 Xinhua text stories (Topics 20001~20096)			47 Xinhua text stories (Topics 30001~30060)		
	Min.	**Max.**	**Mean**	**Min.**	**Max.**	**Mean**
Doc. length (characters)	23	4841	287.1	19	3667	415.1
Query length (characters)	183	2623	532.9	98	1477	443.6
# relevant doc. per query	2	95	29.3	3	89	20.1

3 Retrieval Models

3.1 The Vector Space Model

In the vector space model approach, a document D can be represented by a set of feature vectors $\vec{d}_s$, each consisting of information for one type of indexing term [3], such as word unigrams or overlapping word bigrams (or called word pairs). Each component $g(t)$ of a feature vector $\vec{d}_s$ for a document D is associated with the statistics of a specific indexing term t:

$$g(t) = (1 + \ln(c(t))) \cdot \ln(N/N_t), \tag{1}$$

where $c(t)$ is the occurrence count of indexing term t within document D, and the value of $1+\ln(c(t))$ denotes the term frequency for indexing term t, where the logarithmic operation is used to condense the distribution of the term frequency. $\ln(N/N_t)$ is the Inverse Document Frequency (IDF), where N_t is the number of documents that include the term t and N is the total number of documents in the collection. A query Q is also represented by a set of feature vectors $\vec{q}_s$ constructed in the same way. The Cosine measure is used to estimate the query-document relevance for each type of indexing term:

$$\mathrm{R}_s(\vec{q}_s, \vec{d}_s) = (\vec{q}_s \bullet \vec{d}_s) / (\|\vec{q}_s\| \cdot \|\vec{d}_s\|). \tag{2}$$

The overall relevance is, then, the weighted sum of the relevance scores of all types of indexing terms:

$$\mathrm{R}(Q,D) = \sum_s w_s \cdot \mathrm{R}_s(\vec{q}_s, \vec{d}_s), \tag{3}$$

where w_s represents empirically tunable weights. We mainly use unigrams and overlapping bigrams (also called overlapping pairs) since previous works [3-5] indicated that they are most effective.

3.2 The HMM/N-gram-based Model

In the probability model approach, given a query Q and a set of documents, the retrieval system ranks the documents according to the probability that D is relevant, conditioned on the fact that query Q is observed; i.e., $P(D \text{ is } R|Q)$, which can be transformed into the following equation by applying Bayes' theorem:

$$P(D \text{ is } R|Q) = \frac{P(Q|D \text{ is } R)P(D \text{ is } R)}{P(Q)}, \tag{4}$$

where $P(Q|D \text{ is } R)$ is the probability of the query Q being posed under the condition that document D is relevant, $P(D \text{ is } R)$ is the prior probability that document D is relevant, and $P(Q)$ is the prior probability of query Q being posed. $P(Q)$ in Equation (4) can be eliminated because it is identical for all documents. Furthermore, because there is no general way to estimate the probability $P(D \text{ is } R)$, we can simply set it to unity for simplicity and approximate the probability $P(D \text{ is } R|Q)$ by means of the probability $P(Q|D \text{ is } R)$ for the problem studied here.

In the HMM/N-gram-based approach, a query Q is treated as a sequence of input observations (or indexing terms), $Q = q_1q_2..q_n..q_N$, where each q_n can be a word or a subword, while each document D is modeled by a single-state discrete HMM as shown in Fig. 1. The observation probabilities for this HMM are modeled by the weighted sum of N-gram probabilities of words or subwords. Therefore, the relevance measure, $P(Q|D \text{ is } R)$, can be estimated by means of the N-gram probabilities of the indexing term sequence for the query, $Q = q_1q_2..q_n..q_N$, predicted by document D. As mentioned earlier, in the present work, we mainly use unigrams and bigrams. Equations (5) and (6) illustrate, respectively, the estimation of $P(Q|D \text{ is } R)$ based on unigrams alone and based on both unigrams and bigrams:

Type I: Unigram-based (Uni)

$$P(Q|D \text{ is } R) = \prod_{n=1}^{N}\left[m_1P(q_n|D) + m_2P(q_n|Corpus)\right]; \tag{5}$$

Type II: Unigram-/Bigram-based (Uni+Bi)

$$\begin{aligned} P(Q|D \text{ is } R) = {} & \left[m_1P(q_1|D) + m_2P(q_1|Corpus)\right]\times \\ & \prod_{n=2}^{N}\left[m_1P(q_n|D) + m_2P(q_n|Corpus) + m_3P(q_n|q_{n-1},D) + m_4P(q_n|q_{n-1},Corpus)\right]; \end{aligned} \tag{6}$$

here, $P(q_n|D)$ is the unigram probability of a specific indexing term q_n within document D and $P(q_n|q_{n-1},D)$ is the bigram probability of a specific indexing term sequence $q_{n-1}q_n$ within document D. In order to model the general distribution of the indexing terms, both unigram and bigram parameters trained by a large text corpus, i.e., $P(q_n|Corpus)$ and $P(q_n|q_{n-1},Corpus)$, were also included in Equations (5) and (6). In addition, for Equations (5) and (6), the weights m_i were summed to 1 (e.g., $\sum_{i=1}^{4} m_i = 1$ in Equation (6)), and the weights were tied among all the documents. These weights can be optimized using the expectation-maximization (EM) algorithm given a training set of query exemplars and their corresponding query-document relevance

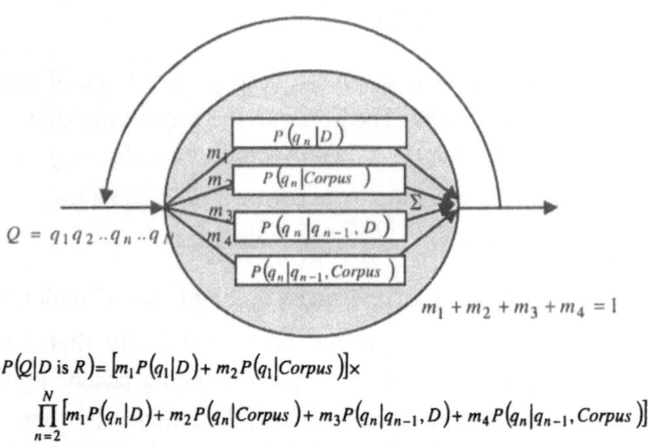

Fig. 1. The HMM structure for a specific document D.

information. For example, the weight m_1 of Equation (5) can be estimated using the following equation:

$$m_1 = \frac{\sum_{Q \in [TrainSet]_Q} \sum_{D \in [Doc]_{R \text{ to } Q}} \sum_{q_n \in Q} \left[\frac{m_1 P(q_n|D)}{m_1 P(q_n|D) + m_2 P(q_n|Corpus)} \right]}{\sum_{Q \in [TrainSet]_Q} |Q| \cdot |[Doc]_{R \text{ to } Q}|}, \tag{7}$$

where $[TrainSet]_Q$ is the set of training query exemplars, $[Doc]_{R \text{ to } Q}$ is the set of documents that are relevant to a specific training query exemplar Q, $|Q|$ is the length of query Q, and $|[Doc]_{R \text{ to } Q}|$ is the total number of documents relevant to query Q. Fig. 1 depicts the Type II (Uni+Bi) HMM structure for a specific document D.

4 Experiments

4.1 Experiment Setup

In the HMM/N-gram-based approach, the probabilities of $P(q_n|Corpus)$ and $P(q_n|q_{n-1}, Corpus)$ in Equations (5) and (6) were estimated using a general text corpus consisting of 40 million Chinese characters. The weights m_i were derived by means of the EM training formula as described in Equation (7) using an outside training query set consisting of 819 query exemplars and their corresponding query-document relevance information with respect to the development set of the TDT-2 document collection. These weights were applied to the evaluation set of the TDT-3 document collection. In the result tables below, the test results obtained for manual transcription of the spoken documents (denoted as TD) are also provided for comparison with the results obtained for erroneous transcription through speech recognition (denoted as SD). The test results are expressed in terms of the *mean non-interpolated average precision* (*mAP*) following the TREC evaluation [7], which is computed by the following equation:

$$mAP = \frac{1}{m}\sum_{i}^{m}\frac{1}{n_i}\sum_{j}^{n_i}\frac{j}{r_{i,j}}, \tag{8}$$

where m is the number of queries, n_i is the total number of documents that are relevant to query i, and $r_{i,j}$ is the position (rank) of the j-th document that is relevant to query i, counting down from the top of the ranked list.

4.2 Word- vs. Subword-level Indexing Using The Vector Space Model

Table 2 shows the retrieval results obtained by applying the vector space model retrieval approach to both the TDT-2 and TDT-3 collections. It can be found from the first two columns of Table 2 that, for the word-level indexing features, using unigram information alone achieved reasonable performance while including overlapping bigram information offered only limited improvement. On the other hand, for the subword-level indexing features, including overlapping bigram information always gave significant improvement, especially for the syllable-level indexing features (the last two columns). In other words, for the subword-level indexing features, using unigram information alone seemed inadequate. Comparing the best performance of the word-, character- and syllable-level indexing features, the word-level indexing features outperformed the character- and syllable-level indexing features in most cases, but the syllable-level indexing features (the Uni+Bi case) performed best when applied to the real, desired case, the erroneous speech transcriptions (SD) of the TDT-3 evaluation set. Another interesting observation is that, though the word error rates for both the TDT-2 and TDT-3 spoken document collections were higher than 35%, the performance for the SD cases was only slightly lower than that for the TD cases.

4.3 Word- vs. Subword-level Indexing Using The HMM/N-gram-based Model

The retrieval results obtained when the HMM/N-gram-based retrieval approach was applied are shown in Table 3. Several observations could be made based on these results. First, similar to the case with the vector space model approach, the word-level indexing features in general outperformed the character- and syllable-level features, but the syllable-level features (the Uni+Bi case) performed best when applied to the real, desired case of SD for TDT-3. Second, unlike the vector space model approach, for the word- and character-level indexing features, including bigram information for indexing always degraded the retrieval performance instead of enhancing it. Since the numbers of distinct words and characters (51k and 6.8k) are relatively large compared to the number of syllables (0.4k), the estimation of bigram probabilities for the word- and character-level indexing features inherently suffered from the sparse data problem. Obviously, in Equation (6), the smoothing terms obtained from the general text corpus did not work well. This needs further study. Third, using syllable unigram information alone for indexing in the HMM/N-gram-based approach always gave significantly better performance than did using syllable unigram information alone in the vector space model approach. Fourth, the HMM/N-gram-based approach achieved consistently better performance than the vector space model approach, and the difference between the two was is significantly larger for the TDT-2 development set from which the linear combination weights were trained.

Table 2. Retrieval results of the vector space model approach

		Word-level		Character-level		Syllable-level	
		Uni	Uni+Bi	Uni	Uni+Bi	Uni	Uni+Bi
TDT-2 (Dev.)	TD	0.5548	0.5623	0.5122	0.5441	0.3412	0.5254
	SD	0.5122	0.5225	0.4803	0.5176	0.3306	0.5077
TDT-3 (Eval.)	TD	0.6505	0.6531	0.6275	0.6373	0.3963	0.6502
	SD	0.6216	0.6233	0.5836	0.6106	0.3708	0.6353

Table 3. Retrieval results of the HMM/N-gram-based approach

		Word-level		Character-level		Syllable-level	
		Uni	Uni+Bi	Uni	Uni+Bi	Uni	Uni+Bi
TDT-2 (Dev.)	TD	0.6327	0.5427	0.5743	0.5204	0.4698	0.5697
	SD	0.5658	0.4803	0.5437	0.4804	0.4411	0.5305
TDT-3 (Eval.)	TD	0.6569	0.6141	0.6465	0.5843	0.5343	0.6544
	SD	0.6308	0.5808	0.6031	0.5309	0.5177	0.6413

4.4 Information Fusion

Word-level indexing features possess more semantic information than syllable-level features. On the other hand, syllable-level indexing features provide a more robust relevance measure between queries and documents when dealing with such problems as those arising from the flexible wording structure of Mandarin Chinese and speech recognition errors in spoken documents. This is shown by the above experimental results. It was believed that proper fusion of the word- and subword-level information would be useful in the retrieval task. As a result, fusion of the best approaches described in Sect. 4.3 and 4.4 using the following equation was tested:

$$\mathrm{R}(Q,D) = w_W \mathrm{R}_W(Q,D) + w_C \mathrm{R}_C(Q,D) + w_S \mathrm{R}_S(Q,D), \tag{9}$$

which is simply the weighted sum of the relevance scores obtained with the word-, character- and syllable-level indexing features.

The results are shown in Table 4, where for the vector space model (denoted as VSM) approach, all the indexing features include both unigram and bigram information, while for the HMM/N-gram-based (denoted as HMM) approach, the word-level and character-level features are based on unigrams only, while the syllable-level features use both unigrams and bigrams. Comparison with the results obtained using either word-, character- or syllable-level information alone shows that fusion was in general helpful for retrieval, though in some cases, it slightly degraded retrieval performance instead of enhancing it. We also combined the two approaches by using the weighted sum of their relevance scores, based in both cases on the S+C+W case. Fusion gave average precision results of 0.6218 and 0.5726 for TD and

SD for TDT-2, and of 0.6815 and 0.6650 for TD and SD for TDT-3. Based on the results shown in the last column of Table 4, fusion was indeed helpful with respect to the evaluation set (TDT-3).

Table 4. Retrieval results based on information fusion

			S+C	S+W	C+W	S+C+W
TDT-2 (Dev.)	TD	VSM	0.5620	0.5744	0.5619	0.5741
		HMM	0.5860	0.6264	0.6197	0.6254
	SD	VSM	0.5187	0.5293	0.5372	0.5397
		HMM	0.5302	0.5769	0.5664	0.5643
TDT-3 (Eval.)	TD	VSM	0.6605	0.6683	0.6540	0.6664
		HMM	0.6408	0.6545	0.6734	0.6697
	SD	VSM	0.6380	0.6447	0.6409	0.6456
		HMM	0.6210	0.6334	0.6471	0.6466

5 Concluding Remarks

In this paper, we have focused on the use of words, characters and syllables in audio indexing for Mandarin Chinese spoken retrieval. Though word-level indexing features outperformed character- and syllable-level features in most cases, syllable-level indexing features performed very well in the real, desired case of retrieval from the erroneous speech transcriptions (SD) of the evaluation set. We also found that information fusion of indexing features of different levels was, in general, useful for retrieval.

References

1. Jones, K. S., Jones, G. J. F., Foote, J. T., Young, S. J.: Experiments on Spoken Document Retrieval. Information Processing & Management 32(4) (1996) 399-417
2. Makhoul, J., Kubala, F., Leek, T., Liu, D., Nguyen, L., Schwartz, R., Srivastava, A.: Speech and Language Techniques for Audio Indexing and Retrieval. Proceedings of the IEEE 88(8) (2000) 1338-1353
3. Chen, B., Wang, H. M., Lee, L. S.: Retrieval of Mandarin Broadcast News Using Spoken Queries. Int. Conf. on Spoken Language Processing (2000)
4. Meng, H., Lo, W. K., Li, Y. C., Ching, P. C.: Multi-scale Audio Indexing for Chinese Spoken Document Retrieval. Int. Conf. on Spoken Language Processing (2000)
5. Meng, H., et al.: Mandarin-English Information (MEI): Investigating Translingual Speech Retrieval. Human Language Technology Conf. (2001)
6. Chen, B., Wang, H. M., Lee, L. S.: An HMM/N-gram-based Linguistic Processing Approach for Mandarin Spoken Document Retrieval. European Conf. on Speech Communication and Technology (2001)
7. Harman, D.: Overview of the Fourth Text Retrieval Conference. The Fourth Text Retrieval Conf. (1995)

Interactive Web Multimedia Search Using Query-Session-Based Query Expansion

Chien-Kang Huang[1], Lee-Feng Chien[2], Yen-Jen Oyang[3]

[1] Department of Computer Science, National Taiwan University, Taiwan.
ckhuang@mars.csie.ntu.edu.tw
[2] Institute of Information Science, Academia Sinica, Taiwan.
lfchien@iis.sinica.edu.tw
[3] Department of Computer Science, National Taiwan University, Taiwan.
yjoyang@csie.ntu.edu.tw

Abstract. The purpose of this paper is to deal with the query expansion problem of Web multimedia search. It will present an effective query expansion mechanism that expands users' queries by mining the associations among query terms in query session logs. Such a log-based mechanism has been proven effective to perform query expansion for short queries and increase the recall rate in Web multimedia search.

1 Introduction

Document-based query expansion techniques are commonly used in interactive information retrieval systems for increasing recall rate of retrieval [1]. For those low-recall queries that retrieve only a few relevant documents, such techniques can retrieve more relevant documents by expanding the queries with the terms extracted from the initial set of the retrieved relevant documents. Unfortunately, Web multimedia objects such as Web image, video and audio files most contain insufficient text descriptions to extract relevant query terms. The document-based query expansion techniques are, therefore, not appropriate to be applied to retrieving multimedia objects.

The purpose of this paper is to deal with the query expansion problem of Web multimedia search. It is going to present an effective query expansion mechanism that expands users' queries by the relevant terms extracted from users' *query session* logs rather than from the text descriptions of the retrieved multimedia objects. A query session log is defined as a sequence of consecutive search requests submitted by a user for a certain search subject. It was found in our research that the relevant terms extracted by mining the associations among the query terms in the query sessions with similar requests could be more precise and comprehensive than conventional document-based methods. The proposed log-based mechanism has been proven effective to perform query expansion for short queries and increase the recall rate in Web multimedia search.

Most of existing Web multimedia search engines rely much on text-based techniques including keyword indexing and metadata search. Unlike Web pages, Web multimedia objects are often lack of sufficient text descriptions as the surrogates for search. Although there are different textual resources such as surrounding texts, filenames, anchor texts that can be indexed, the searchable terms (keywords) associated with a multimedia object are less than that of a web page. Low-recall queries or failed queries, the queries that have no retrieved results, are easy to appear even in a Web multimedia search engine with a collection of millions of objects. Although it can combine with content-based multimedia retrieval and relevant feedback techniques [2,3] as a supplementary method to perform interactive search, it is in vain if there are no relevant objects can be retrieved by user's initial queries.

The proposed query expansion mechanism adopts a log-based relevant term extraction (RTE) method that makes the extraction of relevant query terms can be performed not limited in the retrieved document contents. Research on mining search engine logs is increasing and believed helpful in dealing with the considering problem [4,5,6]. Beeferman and Berger [4] proposed a relevant query clustering method based on "clickthrough data", to discover similarity between queries and clicked URLs. Silverstein et al. [5] performed a second-order analysis for a log with a huge number of Web query terms. Similar approaches were ever used for helping phrase recognition and query expansion [6]. Different from the previous works, the proposed mechanism extracts relevant terms from query session logs. In the following sections, the proposed mechanism will be described in details and the achieved performances on term extraction and query expansion for Web image search will be reported as well.

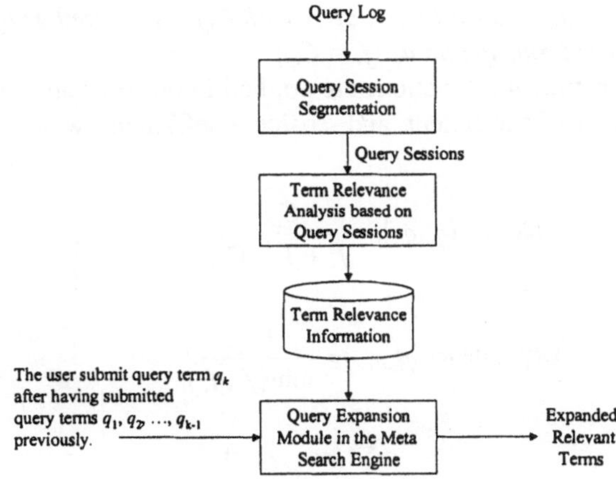

Fig. 1. The basic operations of the proposed query expansion mechanism.

2 Overview of The Mechanism

Fig. 1 depicts the basic operations of the proposed query expansion mechanism. The kernel query expansion module operates based on a term relevance analysis conducted in advance on a collected log of users' queries. The query log that collects the query transactions to search engines is first partitioned into a number of query sessions and relevance among the query terms in the log is computed based on how these query terms are clustered in query sessions. The result from the term relevance analysis is then exploited by the query expansion module on-the-fly. When a user submits a new query term q_k after having submitted a series of query terms $q_1, q_2, \ldots, q_{k-1}$ previously, the query expansion module will suggest terms that are not only relevant to the currently submitted term q_k but also the previously submitted terms $q_1, q_2, \ldots, q_{k-1}$.

The query expansion mechanism can be extended to be a meta-search engine. For those low-recall queries that have fewer retrieved results and failed queries that even have no results, it can trigger an automatic process to send the most relevant query terms as the next queries in sequence to some existing Web multimedia search engines. The process can be terminated until the number of the retrieved multimedia objects is sufficient enough.

3 Relevant Term Extraction

With the query sessions obtained from the query log, it is able to perform relevance analysis among query terms. The relevance analysis proposed in this paper is based on a term co-occurrence matrix defined as follows.

Definition: *The co-occurrence matrix* **C** *of the distinct query terms in a query log, denoted by* $q_1, q_2, \ldots, q_n$, *is an* n *by* n *matrix with* $C_{i,j}$ = *the number of query sessions containing both query terms* q_i *and* q_j. ($f_i = C_{i,i}$)

Three similarity estimation functions are applied in our relevant analysis – Jaccard coefficient, dependence coefficient and cosine coefficient, which are defined as follows.

$$\text{Jaccard}(q_u, q_v) = \frac{C_{u,v}}{f_u + f_v - C_{u,v}} \tag{1}$$

$$\text{Dependence}(q_u, q_v) = \frac{C_{u,v}}{\min(f_u, f_v)} \tag{2}$$

$$\cos(q_u, q_v) = \frac{\sum_{\forall q_j \in Q} (C_{u,j} \cdot C_{v,j})}{\sqrt{\sum_{\forall q_j \in Q} C_{u,j}^{\;2}} \cdot \sqrt{\sum_{\forall q_j \in Q} C_{v,j}^{\;2}}} \tag{3}$$

The relevance of each pair of query terms is then computed using the co-occurrence matrix. Fig. 2 shows the RTE method for computing the term relevance. For each given query term, its relevant query terms can be obtained with the method. One may note that the method does not apply a uniform formula to all the cases. The reason behind adopting this practice is due to some empirical experiences.

4 Query Expansion

Once the relevance between each pair of query terms in the query log has been computed in advance, the mechanism has all background information to start operating. This is an empirical query expansion method based on the term relevance computed in last section. As mentioned earlier, the major distinction of the proposed query expansion mechanism is that it exploits the contextual information embedded in the query session that is currently being handled.

```
function compute_relevant_term_set(qu, Q, C, R)
{
  Input:
    qu: the query term of concern
    Q: the set of all query terms in the log
    C: the co-occurrence matrix
  Output:
    R: relevant term set
  R = ∅
  For every qv in Q {
    if (C_{u,v} ≥ √f_u)
      R = R ∪ {qv}
    else if (⁴√f_u ≤ C_{u,v} ≤ √f_u)
      if (fu >> fv or fu << fv)
        if (Dependence(qu, qv) > threshold1)
        then R = R ∪ {qv}
      else
        if (Jaccard(qu, qv) > threshold2)
        then R = R ∪ {qv}
    else if (C_{u,v} ≤ ⁴√f_u) {
      If (cos(qu, qv) > threshold3)
      then R = R ∪ {qv}
  }
  return R;
}
```

Fig. 2. A procedure showing the RTE method for computing the relevant term set.

The method re-ranks and filters the relevant terms of the current query term q_k by estimating scalar-cluster-based relevance between each pair of the relevant terms and the previous query terms $q_1, q_2, \ldots, q_{k-1}$. The terms the method will expand are not only relevant to q_k but also relevant to some of the previous query terms. The procedure of the query expansion method is described as follows.

1. Assume that q_k is the current query term submitted by user, $q_1, q_2, \ldots, q_{k-1}$ are the previous query terms. S is the set of all clusters of relevant terms of q_k, which is generated with the above procedure, and q_r is a relevant term appearing in S.

2. For each q_r in S, calculate the contextual cosine coefficient. The contextual cosine coefficient is defined as equation (4) in which the cosine coefficients are defined similar to equation (3) in last section. If the contextual_cos(q_r, q_1, ..., q_{k-1}) < threshold$_4$, q_r is removed from S.

$$\begin{aligned} &\text{contextual\_cos}(q_r, q_1, q_2, \Lambda, q_{k-1}) \\ &= \cos(q_r, q_{k-1}) + \alpha \cos(q_r, q_{k-2}) + \Lambda + \alpha^{k-2} \cos(q_r, q_1) \end{aligned} \quad (4)$$

3. Re-rank the relevant terms in S as the expanded query term set according to their contextual cosine coefficients.
4. Send query terms in S in sequence to the selected Web multimedia search engine(s) to retrieve relevant multimedia objects, until the number of the retrieved objects is sufficient.

In the next section, we will discuss the effectiveness of the proposed query expansion mechanism.

5 Experiments

Performance on Relevant Term Extraction

To test the performance of the relevant term extraction method, several experiments have been performed with a query log obtained from a local proxy server in the campus of National Taiwan University. Some statistics of the test query log are listed in Table 1. The query log contains all of the search requests from 21,421 clients to the major search engines in Taiwan in 126 days.

Table 1. Some statistics of the test session log for relevant term extraction.

	All query sessions	Sessions with more than one unique query terms
1. Number of obtained sessions	615,634	160,180
2. Total query terms in the sessions	2,369,282	1,213,226
3. Number of unique query terms	218,362	177,324
4. Average unique query terms s per session	1.45	2.75

In our experiments, only the 160,180 sessions that contain more than one unique query terms were taken. Among the query sessions, there are 5,366 unique query terms with occurrences large than 10. We randomly selected 95 queries as the test set from the unique queries. The frequencies of the test queries are ranged from MP3's 1,054 times to a company name's 10 times. We adopted the F_b-measure in our evaluation process. The F_b-measure is defined as follows:

$$F_b = \frac{(b^2+1)pr}{b^2 p + r} \tag{5}$$

where p is precision, r is recall and b is a specified parameter which reflects the relative importance of recall and precision. Both F_1 (b = 1) and F_2 (b = 2) were applied in our evaluation, because we were more interested in precision than recall in the relevant term extraction process. The above metrics were used to observe if the extracted terms are relevant to the test queries. The recall set for each test query was obtained by manual analysis from all of its co-occurred terms and the terms occurred with the co-occurred terms. There were five volunteers joining the analysis. The terms taken as relevant were qualified by at least three of the volunteers. Since the log size is not large enough, the obtained recall sets are just taken as a reference.

The experiments were also performed to observe the performance of the three different similarity estimation functions: Jaccard coefficient, dependence coefficient and cosine coefficient. According to the experiments, the Jaccard coefficient is useful in dealing with normal co-occurrence cases. The use of the dependence coefficient is helpful to deal with the cases with medium co-occurrence frequencies that cannot be extracted by the Jaccard coefficient. With the estimation function of the cosine coefficient, some relevant terms that may not be extracted with the previous two functions can be found back for those low-frequency query terms, and many less-relevant query terms can be also extracted to increase recall rate. With extensive experiments, the most proper thresholds were obtained. Table 2 shows the recall and precision rates in the case of the highest value of F_1-measure and F_2-measure respectively. Though the test log size is small, the extracted terms especially for those high-frequency query terms are most relevant and hard to be obtained by manual analysis.

Table 2. The obtained recall and precision rates with the RTE method for the test query set.

	Recall	Precision
Best thresholds for F2-measure	0.648	0.890
Best thresholds for F1-measure	0.822	0.772

Using the proposed method to extract relevant query terms for the 5,366 unique query terms, it is found can successfully extract relevant terms for 3,330 of them. On average there are 9.28 extracted relevant terms for high-frequency terms, 4.82 for medium-frequency terms, and 2.77 for low-frequency terms. The achieved relevance between the query terms and extracted relevant terms is highly out of our expectation.

Comparison with the Document-based Method

In order to realize the performance of the proposed log-based RTE method compared with conventional document-based methods, some further experiments were performed. Conventional IR systems often rely on the keyterms extracted from the retrieved documents. In our experiments, a document-based method was implemented to combine with the Google Chinese search engine. The basic idea of the document-based method is to extract co-occurred keyterms for each test query from a set of Web documents D which are top-n documents retrieved from Google Chinese. It is supposed there exist a set of keyterms W which have been collected. The estimation of relevant terms is based on mutual-information-based association estimation between t and each term $w \in W$ where w is found appearing in D and satisfying the condition that $N(w,t)/N(w)+N(t)$ > a threshold value, in which $N(w)$, $N(t)$, $N(w,t)$ are the numbers of the Web documents in D containing term w, t, and both term w and t, respectively. In our experiments, we collected up to 100 search result entries for each test query term, and extracted each entry's title and description as the representation of the corresponding document containing the query term.

To further investigate the performance of the proposed RTE method, a query log from Dreamer a representative search engine in Taiwan was collected as the basis keyterm set for analysis. The Dreamer's log contains 228,566 distinct query terms with a total frequency of 2,184,256 within a period of over 3 months in 1998. We took the top 20,000 query terms as the basic keyterm set which represent fully 81% of the total number of query terms in the log. The test query set contains 100 queries randomly selected from the 3,330 queries whose relevant query terms have been extracted with the proposed log-based method. For each of the test queries, its document-based relevant terms were also extracted with the implemented document-based method for comparison. The relevant terms extracted with the two different methods were merged and inspected manually to judge the relevance between the test query terms. The terms really relevant were taken as the recall sets for the corresponding test queries. Table 3 shows the obtained recall and precision rates. It is clear that the proposed log-based method outperforms the document-based method in the precision rate. The low precision rate of the document-based method might be resulted from the poor relevance of the retrieved documents and the diversity nature of Web documents.

Table 3. The obtained recall and precision rates with the two different methods.

	Precision	Recall	Comments
The document-based method	0.25	0.66	Low precision Useful for low-frequency queries
The proposed log-based method	0.90	0.45	High precision, low recall More comprehensive Need sufficient log

Performance on Web Image Search

To realize the performance on Web multimedia search, an additional experiment was conducted. A representative Chinese Web image search engine namely eefind (http://www.eefind.com) which was developed by VisionNEXT Inc. was selected as the backend search engine. To seek for failed queries for evaluation, the 3,330 query terms whose relevant terms have been obtained with the proposed log-based method were submitted to eefind for image search test. Note that the query terms were obtained from the proxy server log described in Table 1, which might not all be submitted for image search purposes. Among the query terms, 556 queries (16.7%) were found failed queries. These failed queries were then performed with the proposed query expansion mechanism to retrieve relevant Web images through their relevant query terms.

The recall rate of Web image retrieval was shown can be effectively increased with the proposed query expansion mechanism. In fact the obtained experimental result shows that 47.4% of the failed queries can, therefore, retrieve relevant images and on average only 1.8 query terms need to be expanded to retrieve first relevant images. For example, for the failed query term like "Taipei Map" in Chinese, it can retrieve more than 50 relevant Web images through its most relevant query term "Taipei City Map" in Chinese. The relevant terms which can retrieve relevant images are called effective relevant terms. According to the analysis on the effective relevant terms, it was found that 7.8% of them are abbreviations of the corresponding test failed query terms, 21.5% are synonyms, 9.4% are translations, 11.0% are typo corrections, and 50.3% are other related terms. Since the utilized query session log was not for the purpose of image search, it is believed the achieved performance could be better if a log for Web image search can be adopted. Observing the results obtained from the above experiments, the proposed log-based mechanism is found effective to perform query expansion for short queries and increase the recall rate of retrieval.

References

1. J. Xu and W.B. Croft, "Query expansion using local and global document analysis", Proceedings of 19th International ACM SIGIR Conference on Research and Development in Information Retrieval (SIGIR-96), pp. 4-11, 1996
2. Y. Lu, C.-H. Hu, X.-G. Zhu, H.-J. Zhang and Q. Yang, "A Unified Framework for Semantics and Feature Based Relevance Feedback in Image Retrieval Systems", In Proceedings of 2000 ACM Multimedia Conference.
3. A. B. Benitez, M. Beigi, and S.-F. Chang, "Using Relevance Feedback in Content-Based Image Metasearch", IEEE Internet Computing Magazine, Vol. 2, No. 4, pp. 59-69, 1998.
4. D. Beeferman and A. Berger, "Agglomerative clustering of a search engine query log", Proceeding of International ACM SIGKDD Conference on Knowledge (KDD-00), pages, 2000.
5. C. Silverstein, M. Henzinger, H. Marais, and M. Morics, "Analysis of a very large AltaVista query log", Technical Report 1998-014, Digital Systems Research Center, 1998.
6. S. Jones and M.S. Staveley, "Phrasier: a system for Interactive Document Retrieval Using Keyphrases", Proceedings of 22nd International ACM SIGIR Conference on Research and Development in Information Retrieval (SIGIR-99), pp. 160-167, 1999.

Codec Schemes Selection for Wireless Voice over IP (VoIP)

Han-Chieh Chao, Y. M. Chu
hcc@mail.ndhu.edu.tw
Department of Electrical Engineering, National Dong Hwa University
Hualien, Taiwan, Republic of China
+886-3-8662500 ext. 17001 (O)
T. G. Tsuei
adttg@et4.thit.edu.tw
Department of Electronic Engineering, Ta Hwa Institute of Technology, Hsinchu, Taiwan, ROC.

Abstract With the maturity in mobile communication, the new mobile communication systems are shaped up gradually especially for the 3rd Generation. The next generation mobile communication, the 4th Generation wireless System, will be converged on Internet Protocol like wired environment. Although the traffic is not only voice, how the voice over IP in wireless environment can be accepted satisfactory, is still a very important issue. Besides the problems of VoIP in wired line, there are a lot of difficult issues and problems must be considered and solved. In this paper, three different VoIP schemes are simulated using OPNET for wireless LAN. From the results, the G723.1 is considered to be the most appropriate one for wireless environments.

1 Introduction

Due to the Internet is flourishing of recent years; there are a lot of good openings for business about every kind of Internet applications along with this Internet trend. In 1995, Vocaltec Ltd., a small company in Israel, developed Internet telephony software that can deliver the voice services provided originally other than traditional telephony networks. Although the quality is not acceptable at that time, the idea that delivering voice over Internet is still very demanding for people [1].

VoIP (Voice over IP), as its literal meaning, is a technology that transforming voice signal to IP packets and delivered by Internet protocol in networks. It has paved a way for a global approach to designing communication service platforms. But the real driver is the convergence between heterogeneous communication network technologies [2].

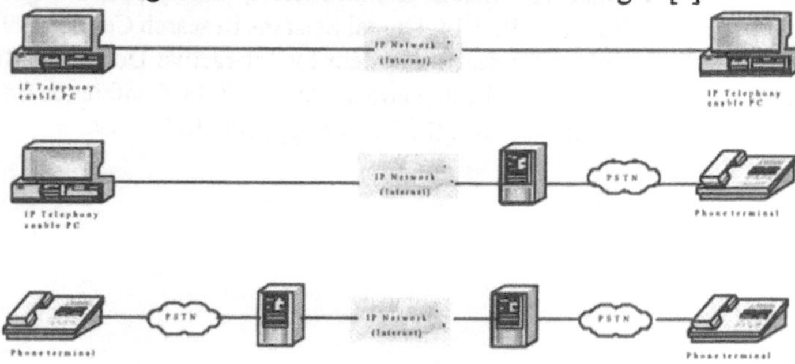

Fig. 1 : Three scenarios in VoIP.

There are three scenarios for using VoIP to deliver voice messages, PC-to-PC, PC-to-Phone, and Phone-to-Phone [3][4]. Figure 1 shows the three scenarios [3]. In scenario 1, the PCs are equipped with sound card and IP telephony software, etc. In scenario 2, there is a gateway that connects IP network to phone network. Scenario 3, there are more gateways that connect IP network to phone network.

Besides these three scenarios, some companies release a so-called IP-Phone terminal. It looks like a common telephone, but inside it is an IP-enable device [5]. We can find that this kind of product will be more popular and more convenient soon. Thus, we can predict that VoIP will be an irresistible general trend in the future. In particular, integrating wireless network with VoIP becomes an important issue [6][7].

The most important import of VoIP is "Multimedia on IP", or it may be nearer the truth to say that "Everything over IP". All application will be integrated into Internet.

In Internet, the delay can vary between milliseconds and almost infinity depending on the hop distance, network congestion, and geographical distance. The expected unidirectional propagation and queuing delay in Internet is assumed to be 30-100ms. However, the delays in the Internet have large variations and depend on many factors that make the analysis almost impossible. In this paper, we also exam the end-to-end delay of VoIP over an Internet cloud.

The main VoIP standard is recommended by International Telecommunication Union – Telecommunication Standardization Sector (ITU-T) as H.323 [8]. It was designed for multimedia communications systems and not that suitable for simpler voice applications. Thus, the Session Initiation Protocol (SIP) was developed as an alternative protocol offering less complexity and more flexibility [9]. H.323 is so far the most acceptable protocol suite in VoIP platform for it is the first available VoIP standard. It supports G.711, G.722, G.723.1, G.728, and G.729 for audio codecs.

VoIP over GPRS has also been studied thoroughly for its transmission error, background noise and delay recently [10][11]. G723.1, GSM, and G729 are currently widely used [12] and were shown to be the most appropriate codec schemes for GPRS [10]. Thus, in this paper, we choose these three schemes as the candidates for our simulation.

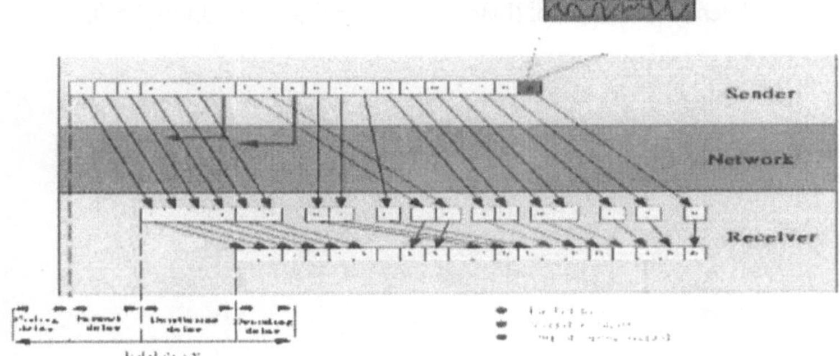

Fig2 : QoS issue in Real-Time IP service.

2 Performance issues of VoIP

There are often three factors on the performance issue of VoIP. There are packet loss, variable delay (jitter) and out-of-order arrival [1][8]. Fig. 2 shows the situation effected by them [3]. Packet 5 in Fig. 2 is "packet loss". Packet 9 and 10 are "out-of-order" caused by the "variable delay". VoIP communications is particularly sensitive to both packet loss and delay; 1% packet loss and 10-200 ms delay are typically considered the maximum acceptable values.

Table1 shows the various voice codec schemes for VoIP. Currently H.323 specifies G711 as the mandatory voice codec [9]. Other voice codecs are optional, but they are definitely needed to investigate in wireless environment.

Table1 : Codec Schemes for Voice over IP

Audio Codec	Technology	Bitrate Kbit/s	Frame size/ lookahead	Approval date	Complexity		
					MIPS	RAM	ROM
G.711	PCM	64	0.125ms	1972			
G.726	ADPCM	16,24,32,40	0.125ms	1990	2	<100W	1kW
G.728	LD-CELP	16	0.625ms/0ms	1992,1994	30	2.3kW	10kW
G.723.1	MPC-MLQ	5.3/6.3	30ms/7.5ms	Nov 95	16	2.3kW	10kW
G.729	CS-ACELP	8	10ms/5ms	Nov 95	20	2.3kW	10kW
G.729.A	CS-ACELP	8	10ms/5ms	Mar96	11	2.3kW	10kW
GSM	RPE-LTP	13	20ms/0ms	1987	4.5		
GSM-HR	VSELP	5.6		1994	30		
GSM-EFR	CD-ACELP	12.2		1997			
G.722	SB-ADPCM	48,56,64		1988	2	<100W	1kW

Assuming that G.723.1 is used as the encoder scheme. Its parameters are as follows:

Frame Size: 30 msec
Lookahead Size: 7.5 msec
DSP processing Ratio: 1.0
Coding Rate: 5.3 Kbps
Number of Frame per packet: 1
DSP Time = DSP ratio * Frame Size = 30 msec
Steady State packet inter-arrival time = DSP Time = 30
Number byte / Packet Size
= Number of Frame per packet * Coding Rate * Frame
= 1 * 5.3 Kbps * 30msec = 159 bytes/packet
Average Traffic Sent (packet/sec) = 1/30 msec = 33.33 packet/sec
Average Traffic Sent (byte/sec) = 159 * 33.33 = 5299.47 bytes/sec

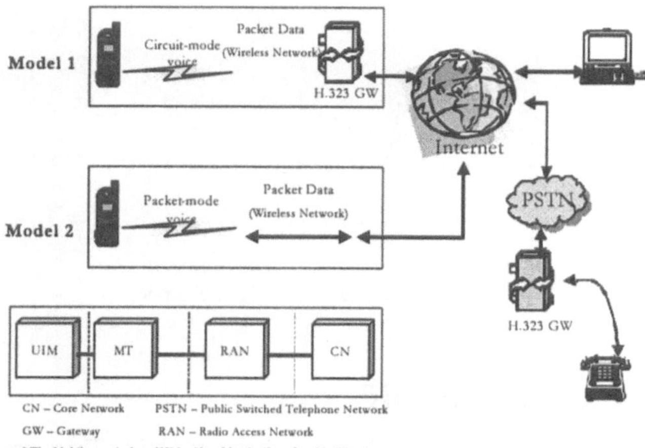

Fig3 : Models of the Wireless VoIP

3 The Model of Wireless VoIP

Figure 3 shows the models of wireless VoIP and their relation to the IMT-2000 network reference model [4]. It depends on whether IP packets are transmitted over the air (the "last hop") or not [4]. In model 1, we can find the VoIP only used on the backbone. It uses conventional circuit voice service over the air interface and employs a gateway like an H.323 within the wireless core network to convert the voice to IP packets, without requiring additional software for the mobile terminal. On the other hand, it is as the scenarios that Phone-to-Phone or PC-to-Phone as shown in Figure 1. In fact, there are many operating service systems using this architecture. In Model 2, the mobile itself is capable of supporting IP/TCP/UDP. Not only the backbone and core networks are IP-Based, but also voice is transmitted in IP packets over the air.

4 Simulation Tools

OPNET is a modeling and simulation tool that provides an environment for analysis of communication networks. OPNET provides the necessary simulation engine, the event-driven programming that are necessary to develop complete dynamic simulation, along with an efficient user interface. It provides a three layer modeling hierarchy. Network domain is the highest layer. It allows definition of network topologies. The second layer, node domain, allows definition of the node architecture (data flow within a node). The third layer, process domain, specifies logic or control flow among components in the form of a finite state machine. Thus, with this kind of capability, OPENT is capable of implementing this sophisticate simulation.

5 Voice over IP in Wireless Environment

In this section, we will make a simulation about the VoIP performance. The Figure 4 (a), (b) and (c) show the simulation network topologies. Subnet_1 is an IEEE 802.11 wireless LAN.

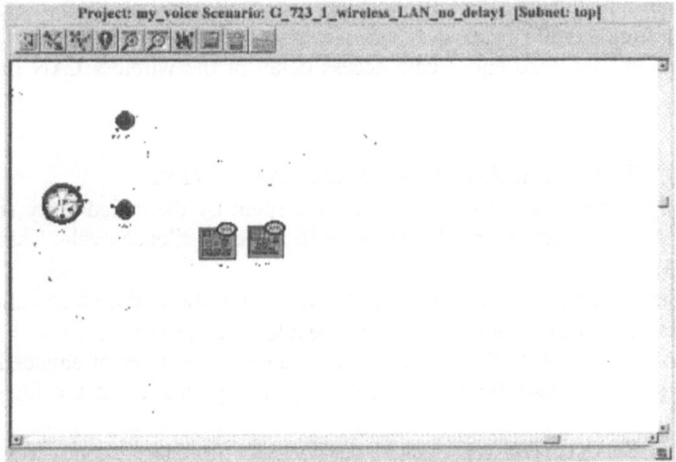

Fig4(a): The simulation network for VoIP

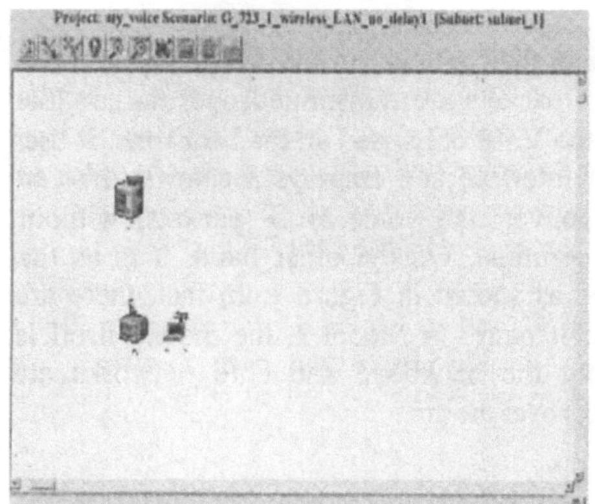

Fig4(b) : Subnet_1

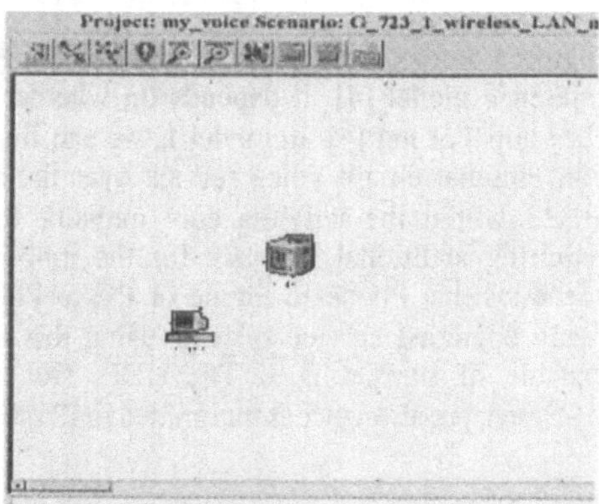

Fig4(c) : Subnet_0

5.1 The Simulation Attribute in the Internet Cloud

Packet Discard Ratio: It specifies the percentage of packets dropped (ratio of packets dropped to the total packets submitted to this cloud multiplied by 100.)
Packet Latency (secs): It specifies the average latency (in seconds) experienced by packets traversing through this cloud.
We will analyze the effect on the VoIP by using various packet latency.

5.2 Wireless LAN Parameters

Data Rate: 2Mbps; 11Mbps.Physical Characteristics: This flag is "1", Direct Sequence.
Buffer Size: This attribute specifies the maximum length of the higher layer data buffer. This value is 256,000 bits. Channel Settings: Bandwidth: This attribute specifies the bandwidth of the channel. The value is 10 KHz. Channel Settings: Min Frequency: This attribute specifies the operating frequency of the channel. The value is 30 Mhz.
Wireless LAN Range (meters): This attribute defines the range across which the station can communicate. This is the physical boundary beyond which the signal cannot be received. This value is 300 meters in this simulation.
We will analyze the load and media access delay of the wireless LAN in VoIP by this simulation.

5.3 The Simulation Attribute in the Application

Silence Length (seconds): It specifies the time spent by the called party (incoming) and the calling party (outgoing) in silence mode in a speech-silence cycle. This default value is Exp (0.65).

Encoder Scheme: Encoder Scheme to be used y the calling and called party. The details about the various encoder schemes can be referenced in Table 1.
Voice Framers per Packet: This attribute determines the number of encoded voice frames group into a voice packet before being sent by the application to the lower layers. The value is 1.

Type of Service: ToS assigned to packets sent from the client. This value is "6 ", Interactive Voice. The IP queues in the network use this attribute to determine the QoS to be provided to the packets.

In this simulation, we will analyze the received traffic, packet End-to-End delay and packet delay variation in various encoder schemes.

6 Results and Conclusions

6.1 Delay in Internet Cloud

Fig. 5 shows the performance affected by the latency in Internet using G.723_1. We assume the packet loss ratio is 5%. The expression for the Internet delay is as follows,

We can see the result can be accepted if the distribution of packet latency time in Internet is exponential 0.1 disregarding which codec schemes we were using.

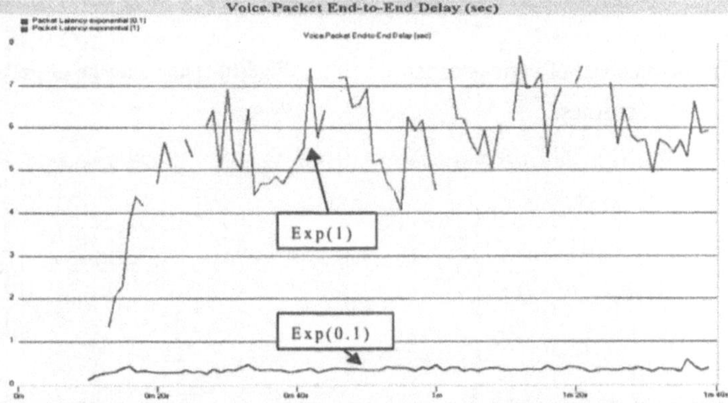

Fig5 : Voice packet end-to-end delay of various Internet cloud scenario.

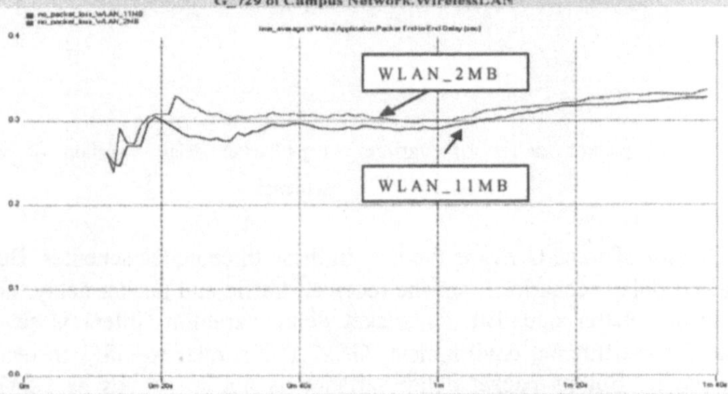

Fig6: G.729 codec scheme end-to-end delay over IEEE 802.11.

6.2 Wireless Environments

The Fig. 6 shows the performance affected by the various wireless environments. We can observe that the IEEE 802.11 11MB version provides smaller delay. If the number of mobile nodes increases, the performance of WLAN_11MB will be even better.

6.3 Various Encoder Scheme for WLAN_11MB

Fig. 7-9 show the performance affected by various codec schemes. Fig. 7 shows the traffic received of various codec schemes.

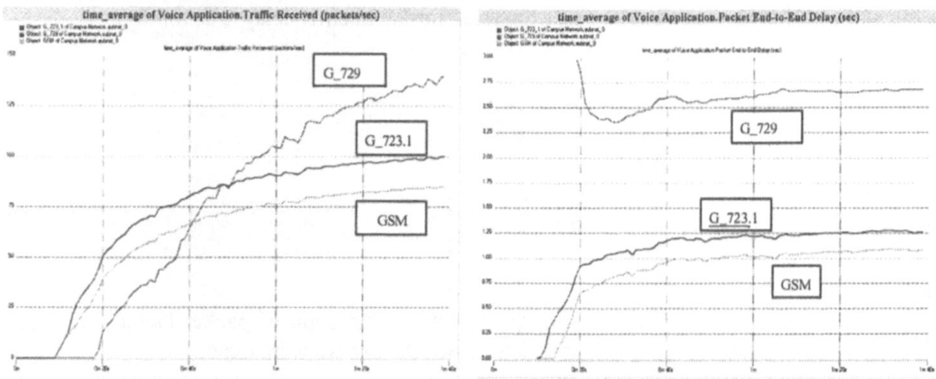

Fig7 :Traffic received of various codec schemes.

Fig8(b) :Time average of packet end-to-end packet delay

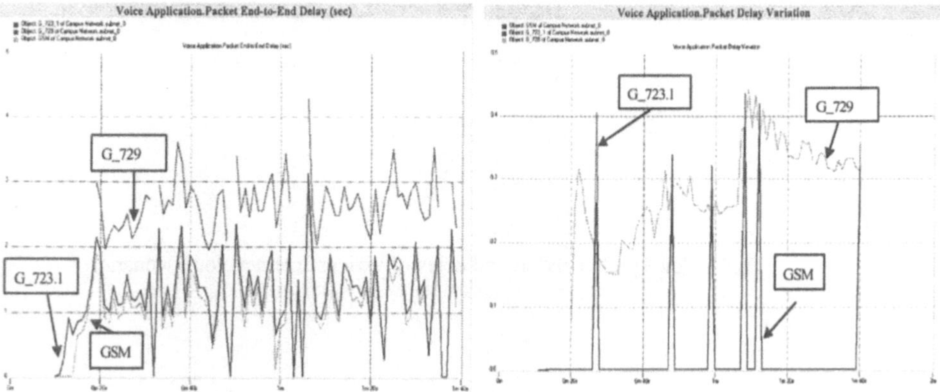

Fig8(a): End-to-End packet delay of various schemes.

Fig9:Packet delay variation of various Codec schemes

The Quality of voice G.729 is the best in these three codec schemes. But it appears to be a serious delay scenario. From the received traffic and packet delay, GSM scheme seems to be the better one. But its packet delay variation (jitter) is severe. This is unfavorable for the Internet environment. G.723.1 is similar to GSM in received traffic and packet delay. But its packet delay variation is not so serious as GSM. Therefore G723.1 should be the most appropriate scheme for wireless applications.

Acknowledgement

Authors wish to thank T. Y. Wu for his kindly assistance on this work. This paper is a partial result of project no. NSC 89-2119-E-259-004 conducted by National Dong Hwa University under the sponsorship of the National Science Council, ROC.

References

[1] H. Woomer and Anaed Zaragoza, "Voice over the Internet, Final Project", July 16, 1997.
[2] J. Wang etc., "Wireless Voice-over-IP and Implications for Third-Generation Network Design", Bell Labs Technical Journal, July-September 1998
[3] Patrick Frene, "Voice over IP and GPRS", GPRS 99-IBC Conference 99, 1999.
[4] D. Rizzetto and C. Catania, "A Voice over IP Service Architecture for Integrated Communications", IEEE INTERNET COMPUTING, May, June, 1999.
[5] Mark A. Miller, P.E. "Implementing IPv6", M&T Books, ISBN 155851-579-8.
[6] J. Feigin, K. Pahlayan, M. Ylianttila," Hardware-fitted modeling and simulation of VoIP over a wireless LAN", IEEE Vehicular Technology Conference, 2000. (VTC 2000). Volume 3, pp. 1431 -1438, 2000.
[7] Ai-Chun Pang; Phone Lin; Yi-Bing Lin, "Modeling mis-routing calls due to user mobility in wireless VoIP" IEEE Communications Letters, Volume 4, Issue 12, pp. 394 -397, December 2000.
[8] ITU-R Rec. H.323, "Packet-Based Multimedia Communications Systems," 1999.
[9] H. Handley et al, "SIP: Session Initation Protocol," IETF RFC 2543, Mar. 1999.
[10] A. Lakaniemi, J. Parantainen, "On voice quality of IP Voice over GPRS" 2000 IEEE International Conference on Multimedia and Expo (ICME 2000), Volume 2, pp. 751 -754, 2000.
[11] J. Parantainen and S. Hamiti, "Delay analysis for IP speech over GPRS" 1999 Vehicular Technology Conference, Volume 2, pp. 829 -833, 1999.
[12] Thuan Nguyen, Ferit Yegenoglu, and Agatino Sciuto "Voice over IP Service and Performance in Satellite Networks" IEEE Communications Magazine, Vol. 39, No. 3, pp. 164-171, March 2001.

On the Use of Error Correction Codes in Spread Spectrum Based Image Watermarking

T. Brandão, M.P. Queluz and A. Rodrigues

Instituto de Telecomunicações - Instituto Superior Técnico, Av. Rovisco Pais, 1049-001 Lisboa, Portugal

Abstract. This paper analyses and compares the influence of common error correction codes (BCH, Reed-Solomon with multilevel signaling, binary convolutional codes with Viterbi decoding) in spatial spread spectrum based image and video watermarking. In order to improve the results for video, diversity techniques are used together with channel coding. Three approches for diversity were implemented and compared. Besides a theoretical evaluation of the expected performance of the different codes, the effectiveness of the channel coding and diversity is also assessed under compression (JPEG for still images and MPEG-2 for video sequences).

1. Introduction

Most proposed watermarking methods use a so-called *spread spectrum* approach [1]: a narrowband signal (the watermark information) has to be transmitted via a wideband channel that is subject to noise and distortion (the multimedia host data, e.g., still images, video or audio). Under this approach, digital watermarking can be treated as a communication problem. In this line, some authors [3,4,6] have already shown that error protection techniques might be used advantageously in watermarking. However, it is a difficult task to perform a fair comparison between the results obtained, as they lack a common approach in the watermarking techniques, test conditions, and images/ video sequences used. This paper tackles this limitation by evaluating common error correction codes (BCH, Reed-Solomon with multilevel signaling, binary convolutional codes with Viterbi decoding) in equivalent conditions. A spatial spread spectrum based watermarking technique was chosen as embedding method. In order to improve the results for video sequences, the use of diversity techniques, together with channel coding, is proposed in this paper. This concept, well known from digital communication theory, is implemented by simultaneously considering a group of consecutive frames at the extraction procedure. Analytical expressions and bounds for the bit error rate are compared with empirical results, for different types of images. The effectiveness of the channel coding and diversity techniques is also assessed under compression (JPEG for still images and MPEG-2 for video sequences).

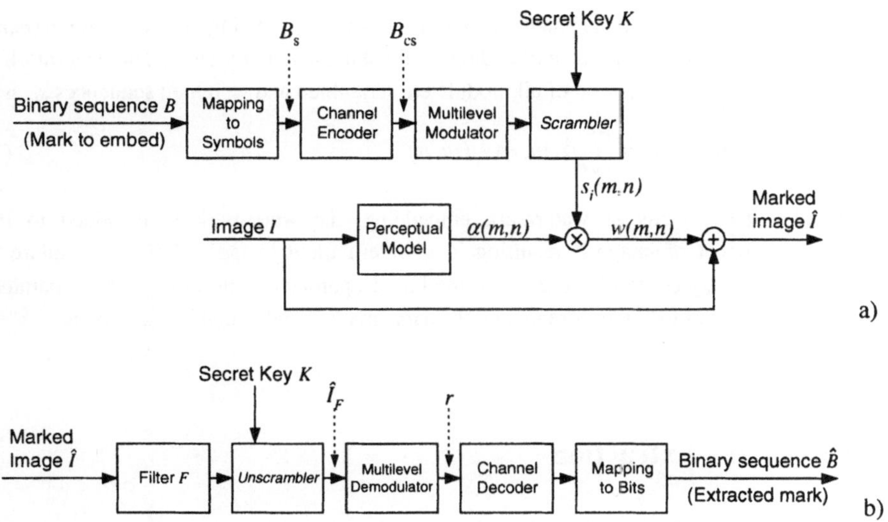

Fig. 1. Watermark embedding / extraction schemes. a) Embedding; b) Extraction.

2. Watermark Embedding

The watermark embedding system is depicted in fig. 1-a). The mark consists on a N_b bit long sequence $B=\{b_1, b_2,...,b_{Nb}\}$ and is embedded in the luminance component of the image. Before embedding, the binary sequence B is mapped to a symbol sequence – B_s – with length N_s. If M levels are used to perform multilevel signaling, then $N_s = N_b / \log_2 M$. In this case, there will exist M different symbols $-Y_1,...,Y_M-$ and each symbol will convey $l=\log_2 M$ bits.

The channel encoder performs error correction encoding over the symbol sequence B_s. Encoding is performed using either *binary block codes* (BCH codes) or *binary convolutional codes*, if M=2, and *non-binary block codes* (shortened Reed-Solomon codes), if M>2. If the selected code has code rate cr, the encoded symbol sequence – B_{cs} – will have N_c symbols, with $N_c = N_s / cr$.

For M>2 and following the approach proposed in [2], the symbol sequence B_{cs} is modulated using M bi-orthogonal sequences with zero mean and unitary variance, which assigns a modulating sequence s_i, $i=\{1...N_c\}$, to symbol i. The use of M bi-orthogonal sequences requires $M/2$ orthogonal sequences, which are used to modulate symbols Y_1 to $Y_{M/2}$. The remaining symbols – $Y_{M/2+1}$ to Y_M – are modulated using the antipodal sequences of the defined $M/2$ orthogonal sequences. For M=2, two antipodal sequences are used for modulating the two different symbols.

The modulating sequences – s_i – are then sent to a *scrambler* that maps each sequence to a sub-set of pixel positions. The mappings are non-overlapping and pseudo-randomly generated, being secret key dependent, and the inverse operation is only possible if the key is known. Symbol $s_i(m,n)$ designates the element of the sequence s_i that was mapped to image position (m,n).

After the spatial assignment, the values $s_i(m,n)$ are further weighted by a local factor $\alpha(m,n)$, the purpose of which is to adapt the embedding to the human visual system. The watermark w is then defined as the superposition of all modulated, scrambled and weighted sequences s_i, as:

$$w(m,n) = \sum_{i=1}^{N_c} \alpha(m,n) s_i(m,n) . \tag{1}$$

To complete the process of watermark embedding, the watermark w is added to the luminance component of image I, resulting in a watermarked image – $\hat{I}$. The procedure is extended to video sequences following a frame-based approach – the embedding separately processes each frame of the video stream and the same mark is embedded in each frame.

3. Watermark Extraction

Retrieving the watermark without any knowledge of the original image can be achieved using the system depicted in fig. 1-b). To reduce major components of the image signal, a receiver filter (filter F) is used. As shown in [5], it may significantly improve the performance of the watermark extraction system. After this pre-processing step is completed, the filtered image passes through the *unscrambler*. This block performs the inverse operation of the *scrambler* defined in previous section. Using the same key of the embedding, the *unscrambler* generates the image positions corresponding to each embedded symbol.

The demodulator consists in $M/2$ linear correlators where the received signal is correlated with each orthogonal sequence. The correlation exhibiting largest absolute value leads to the choice of two possible symbols: symbol Y_x, $x=\{1, .., M/2\}$, or its antipodal pair. The sign of the correlation completes this selection: if it is positive, then symbol Y_x is selected, otherwise the antipodal symbol is selected. To complete the watermark extraction algorithm, the received symbol sequence is decoded and mapped to a binary sequence. The resulting binary sequence – $\hat{B}$ – is the received watermark. For video sequences, the extraction algorithm operates over a group of J (*diversity window*) consecutive frames (see section 4.4).

4. Performance Analysis

4.1 Uncoded case

Expressions related to mean and variance of correlators' output – r_i – for any embedded symbol i, can be used to model channel parameters, assuming that filter F guarantees a valid Gaussian channel approach (F should be a whitening filter). The demodulator statistic of correlation r_i for watermark message symbol i given the modulating sequence s_i, can be written as:

$$r_i|s_i = \langle \hat{I}_F, s_i \rangle = \langle \hat{I} * F, s_i \rangle + \langle w * F, s_i \rangle , \tag{2}$$

where $\hat{I}_F$ is the marked and filtered image at the unscrambler output and <.> denotes the inner product operator.

Defining μ and σ as the expected value and the standard deviation of r_i, respectively, an approximation for these values can be written as [2]:

$$\mu \approx \frac{DHV}{N_c} E[\alpha(m,n)] \tag{3}$$

$$\sigma \approx \sqrt{\frac{DHV}{N_c}\left(E\left[\hat{I}_F^2(m,n)\right] + E\left[\alpha^2(m,n)\right]\right)}, \tag{4}$$

where D is the density of watermark embedding (the ratio between marked image locations and total number of image locations), N_c is the number of embedded symbols, H, V are, respectively, the horizontal and vertical image dimensions and $E[.]$ denotes expected value.

For uncoded *M-ary* bi-orthogonal signaling, the symbol error probability - P_M - is given by [2,6,7]:

$$P_M = 1 - \frac{1}{\sqrt{2\pi}} \int_{-\frac{\mu}{\sigma}}^{+\infty} e^{-\frac{v^2}{2}} \cdot erf\left(\frac{1}{\sqrt{2}}\left(v + \frac{\mu}{\sigma}\right)\right)^{\frac{M}{2}-1} dv, \tag{5}$$

and the bit error probability P_b is bounded by:

$$\frac{P_M}{2} < P_b \le P_M . \tag{6}$$

In the binary case, P_b matches the upper bound ($P_b = P_M$ with $M=2$) and with increasing number of levels, this probability approaches the lower bound (large M leads to $P_b \approx P_M / 2$).

4.2 Binary and Non-binary Block Codes

Let us consider the case in which binary antipodal signaling ($M=2$) is used in conjunction with a linear (n,k) binary block code with minimum distance $d_{min}=2t+1$, where t is the number of errors corrected by the code, and a bit-by-bit hard decision. Assuming that the bit errors occur independently, the probability of a decoded message bit-errors is upper bounded by [6,7]:

$$P_{db} \le \frac{1}{n} \sum_{i=t+1}^{n} \min(i+t, n) \cdot \binom{n}{i} P_b^i (1-P_b)^{n-i}, \tag{7}$$

where P_b stands for channel bit error rate. This probability is given by (5) using $M=2$ and μ/σ computed for $N_c=N_b\, n/k$ embedded bits.

For non-binary (N,K) linear block codes, with symbol-by-symbol hard decision, and considering P_M as the probability of symbol error in the channel (as defined in equation (5), but now computed for $N_c=N_b\, N/(K \log_2 M)$ inserted symbols), we get [6,7]:

$$P_{db} \le \frac{2^{l-1}}{2^l - 1} \cdot \frac{1}{N} \sum_{i=t+1}^{N} \min(i+t, N) \cdot \binom{N}{i} P_M{}^i (1-P_M)^{N-i} . \tag{8}$$

4.3 Convolutional Codes

With this class of codes, simple implementations of soft decision algorithms can be achieved, like the well-known Viterbi algorithm, case that will be considered in this paper. The code

Fig. 2. *Lena* (still image, 512×512 pixels); *Table-Tennis*; *Stefan*; *Mobile & Calendar* (CCIR-601 video sequences, with 300 frames each).

rate *cr* and the constraint length *L* usually characterize a convolutional code. The *minimum free distance* d_f is also an important parameter in the definition of the code performance. It can be defined as the resulting minimum distance when the constraint length goes to infinity. Its calculation involves the generating function of the convolutional code, *T(D,N)*. If transmission errors occur independently and with equal probability, the probability of a decoded message bit- error is upper-bounded by [8]:

$$P_{db} < Q\left(\sqrt{d_f}\,\frac{\mu}{\sigma}\right) e^{\frac{d_f \mu^2}{2\sigma^2}} \left.\frac{\partial T(D,N)}{\partial N}\right|_{D = e^{-\frac{\mu^2}{2\sigma^2}}}^{N=1} . \tag{9}$$

4.4 Diversity Techniques

Video watermark can be seen as a multi-channel system, since the same mark is embedded in each frame, and each frame can be considered as an independent channel. In this sense, results from diversity theory can be applied, and watermark extraction may be improved considering simultaneously a group of *J* (*diversity window*) consecutive frames. Three strategies of signal combination have been studied and implemented:

1 *Majority-logic* – The coded symbols (or the message symbols if channel coding is not used) are independently extracted for each frame, and the final symbol sequence is obtained by simple majority counting over the retrieved symbols. The resulting N_c symbol sequence is then applied to the channel decoder;

2 *Equal ratio combining* [7] – For each coded symbol, the correlation output obtained in each frame is summed-up along the group of frames. The resulting correlation value is used for the transmitted symbol decision;

3 *Maximal ratio combining* [7] – As the previous one, but the correlators output are squared before being summed.

5. Results

Figure 2 presents the still image and video sequences used in simulations. The bi-orthogonal sequences necessary for *M-ary* modulation were generated using Hadamard-Walsh functions. The *perceptual factor* – $\alpha(m,n)$ in eq. (1) – was obtained by filtering the image with a Laplacian high-pass filter and taking absolute values. The coefficients of the Laplacian filter

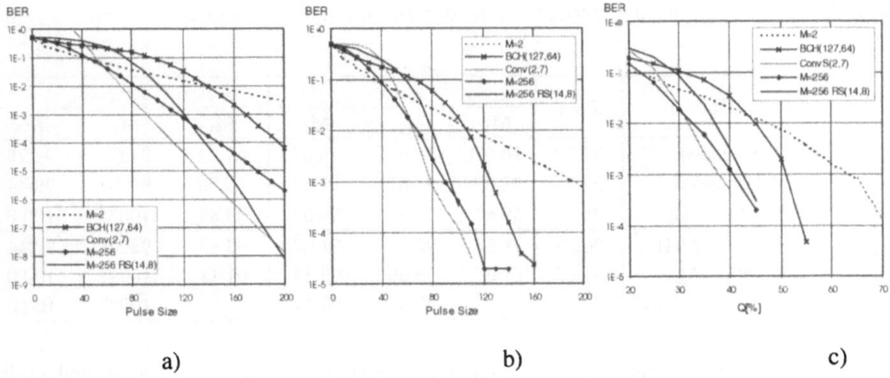

Fig. 3. BER for binary and non-binary codes: a) Theoretical; b) Empirical; c) Under JPEG compression.

were scaled by a factor β, which accounts for the watermark insertion strength. As pre-detection filter – filter F in figure 1-b) – a 3×3 cross-shaped high-pass filter has been used.

5.1 Results for Still Images

In the absence of JPEG compression, theoretical and experimental curves for the bit error rate (BER) were obtained as a function of the *pulse size*, defined as DHV/N_b, which accounts for the amount of pixels used to embed one information bit. For the theoretical plots, the statistical parameters μ and σ were estimated as described by equations (3) and (4). In the presence of JPEG compression, BER curves are plotted as a function of JPEG quality factor (Q).

The plots depicted in figure 3 show a comparison for the performance achieved with: multilevel signaling without channel coding and M=2 or 256; multilevel signaling with RS(14,8) codes and M=256; binary signaling with BCH(127,64) codes; convolutional coding with cr=1/2 and L=7 (Conv(2,7) in the plots). The soft decision of the Viterbi decoder uses 256 quantization levels.

Theoretical BER curves versus *pulse size* are represented in figure 3–a). Each point on these curves was obtained using 100 different insertion keys. In all tests, the embedded mark has a length of N_b=256 bits and is randomly generated. The parameter that regulates the watermark insertion strength (β) was set to 0.4, a value that guarantees the invisibility of the mark. For the *pulse size* range displayed in the figure, the performance achieved by convolutional codes is remarkable, but the curve corresponding to RS(14,8) codes with M=256 crosses it for a *pulse size* value of ≅190. Binary block codes exhibit poor performance compared to these cases.

Empirical BER curves are shown in figure 3–b). The number of tests for the uncoded binary case was 250, while for the remaining cases were 1000, due to an expected lower BER. Here, the best performance is achieved by RS encoding, which doesn't exhibit errors for *pulse size* values greater than 100. For the binary cases, convolutional encoding also performs well, and BCH encoding, again, exhibits poor performance. Some instability occurs for the lowest BER rates (below 10^{-4}) due to the limited number of tests.

Table 1. Percentage rates of watermark extraction success under MPEG-2 @ 4 Mbit/s.

Levels / Code	J = 1	J = 3			J = 5		
		M_1	M_2	M_3	M_1	M_2	M_3
M=2 / Uncoded	21.22	28.67	76.67	78.67	67.22	91.67	92.78
M=16 / Uncoded	27.55	32.67	93.67	91.33	85.00	99.44	99.44
M=256 / Uncoded	36.35	59.67	99.00	99.00	93.89	100.0	100.0
M=2 / BCH (127,64)	26.89	78.67	92.33	91.67	93.89	98.89	99.44
M=256 / RS (14,8)	31.22	61.67	99.00	98.33	91.11	100.0	100.0
M=2 / Conv. soft decision	38.89	–	99.67	94.67	–	100.0	100.0

As can be observed from fig. 3–c), under JPEG compression the convolutional coding performs better than the remaining codes. No errors were detected above a JPEG quality factor of 40%. Multilevel signaling with M=256, both coded and uncoded, leads to BER values below those obtained for BCH codes, and to BER curves with faster decay. JPEG tests have been performed using an insertion density of 100 % and randomly generated marks with a length of 64 bits.

5.2 Results for Video Sequences

Table 1 presents the percentage of frames (averaged over the three tested sequences and after MPEG-2 compression at 4 Mbit/s) in which the watermark was successfully retrieved, as a function of the signaling levels, error correction code, diversity technique and diversity window size (J). M_1, M_2 and M_3 represent *majority logic*, *equal gain combining* and *maximal ratio combining* methods, respectively. Each sequence was watermarked two times, using different embedding keys, and randomly generated watermarks with 64-bit length. The insertion strength (β) was set to 0.2, a value that guarantees that the watermark is far below visibility.

As sketched in table 1, an increase in the number of signaling levels brings an improvement in performance. The use of error correction is generally profitable. A significant increase in the detection rate is obtained by making decisions over a group of consecutive frames. For J=3 and J=5, with methods M_2 and M_3 the watermark was always extracted with success when using convolutional coding, or multilevel signaling with M=256 (uncoded or RS coded).

5.3 Processing Time

To get some insight into the decoding complexity we present, in table 2, the decoding times for the analyzed codes. For the normalized values, the minimum time was used has reference. As expected, the convolutional code is the highest time-consuming code, followed by the BCH code. We must however highlight that the different source codes are not equally optimized. Each correlation (at the demodulator) took, in average, 2.58 *ms*. If done in parallel, the total correlation time is independent of M, but $M/2$ different correlators are then required. The simulations were carried on a Pentium II @ 350 MHz, using as test conditions: *Lena* image; β=0.4; D=0.15; 256-bit watermark.

Table 2. Decoding times of the sudied codes.

	Decoding time [ms]			
	BCH (127,64)	**RS (14,8)** $M = 16$	**RS (14,8)** $M = 256$	**Conv.(2,7)**
Mean	2.413	0.162	0.368	4.922
Std.	0.047	0.025	0.005	0.017
Normalized	14.928	1.000	2.276	30.448

6. Conclusions

In this paper it has been confirmed, both theoretically and experimentally that, for still images, spread spectrum-based spatial watermarking can benefit from multilevel signaling and/or error correction coding. From the theoretical analysis, the best performance was expected for the binary convolutional codes and non-binary block codes. In the experiments, this was confirmed for the convolutional codes. The advantage in using RS codes is not so evident from the tests, a fact that may be justified by the uncertainty of the results for BER values below 10^{-4}. However, the slope of the experimental RS curves suggest that, for lower BER values, these codes may achieve the performance predicted theoretically. Better results can be expected from the use of *Turbo coding,* which may lead to a performance near to the Shannon limit. However, this possible improvement has to be balanced against the resulting increase in system complexity.

For video, under MPEG-2 compression, the relative behavior of the different codes is similar to the behavior observed for still images, under JPEG compression. The experimental results also show that a remarkable increase in performance can be achieved by retrieving the mark over a window of consecutive frames, using signal combination techniques.

References

1. I. J. Cox, J. Kilian, F.T. Leighton and T. Shamoon, "Secure spread spectrum watermarking for multimedia", *IEEE Trans. Image Processing*, vol. 6, pp. 1673-1687, Dec. 1997.
2. M. Kutter, "Performance improvement of spread spectrum based image watermarking schemes through *M-ary* modulation", in Andreas Pfitzmann (Ed.), *Proc. Information Hiding'99*, Vol. LNCS 1768, Sep. 1999, pp. 237-252.
3. J. Hernández, J.-F. Delaigle and B. Macq, "Improving data hiding by using convolutional codes and soft-decision decoding", in *Proc. SPIE/IST: Security and Watermarking of Multimedia Contents II*, San Jose, USA, pp. 24-47, Jan. 2000.
4. J. Hernández, J. Rodríguez and F. Pérez-González, "Improving the performance of spatial watermarking of images using channel coding", *Signal Processing*, no. 80, pp. 1261-1279
5. G. Depovere, T. Kalker and J.-P. Linnartz, "Improved watermark detection reliability using filtering before correlation", in *Proceedings of ICIP*, pp. 430-434, 1998.
6. T. Brandão, M.P. Queluz and A. Rodrigues, "Performance improvement of spatial watermarking through efficient non-binary channel coding", in *Proc. SPIE/IST: Security and Watermarking of Multimedia Contents III*, San Jose, USA, Jan. 2001.
7. J. G. Proakis, "Digital Communications", McGraw-Hill, 2nd edition, 1989.
8. A. J. Viterbi and J. K. Omura, "Principles of digital communication and coding", McGraw-Hill, 1979.

Correlation Detection of Asymmetric Watermark

Jin S. Seo and Chang D. Yoo

Korea Advanced Institute of Science and Technology, Department of EECS,
373-1 Kusong-dong, Yusong-gu, Daejeon 305-701, Korea
pobi@eeinfo.kaist.ac.kr, cdyoo@ee.kaist.ac.kr

Abstract. This paper proposes a novel method to detect Furon's asymmetric watermark by using a correlation detector that is mathematically tractable and simple. The performance of the proposed method is tested under various conditions. The experimental results matched the theoretical results well, showing that the correlation detector can indeed be used for the detection of asymmetric watermark. The proposed detector is applied to both single and multiple bit embedded watermark. Bit error rate (BER), obtained from the experiment, was compared to the one obtained from the theory.

1 Introduction

With the advent of Internet, there has been an explosive growth in the use of digital media. Since digital media is easily reproduced and manipulated, anyone is potentially capable of incurring considerable financial loss to the media producers and content providers. In this respect, digital watermarking is essential.

Most of the existing watermarking methods use symmetric key, that is to say the same key or pattern is used in the embedding and detection. Thus the secrecy of the key is shared by the embedder and detector. In situations where the detector must be available to the public, the secrecy can be divulged by tampering the detector. Based on public-key crypotography, T. Furon addresses this problem with asymmetric watermarking. In his work [1], the presence of filtered watermark that is considered as an output of a filtered random process is detected using only the knowledge of the magnitude of frequency response of the filter.

In this paper, a simple and mathematically tractable detection method is proposed for the detection of asymmetric watermark. It is based on the theory of detecting a known signal in noisy channel. The known signal is the power spectrum of the embedded watermark, and the noise is the estimation error. The estimation error of the power spectrum is assumed to be additive, uncorrelated and Gaussian noise. By using periodogram averaging in the power spectrum estimation, the assumptions are satisfied. The advantages of periodogram averaging over periodogram used in [1] are the reduction of the variance of the power specturm estimate and computational load in estimating the power spectrum. The optimum threshold of the correlator output is set using the Neyman-Pearson lemma that maximizes the probability of correct detection for a given false alarm probability.

Embedding one bit of information is not sufficient for the real application, such as DVD copy protection [2], thus we modified T. Furon's method to increase information rate. By using PN sequences in filter shaping, multiple bits of information can be conveyed. BER, obtained from the experiment, followed the one obtained from the theory favorably. The reliability of the correlation detector is verified by the experiment.

This paper is organized as follows. Section 2 explains the asymmetric watermark embedding. Section 3 describes the proposed detection method. Section 4 describes the multiple bit embedding and detection. Section 5 shows the experimental results.

2 Correlation detector

For asymmetric watermark embedding, filtered watermark pattern is embedded after interleaving. As in [3], the symmetric method given in [4] is translated into asymmetric method. The filtered watermark pattern is embedded into the interleaved DFT magnitude coefficients of the image as shown in Fig. 1. Details of embedding are in [1] and [3].

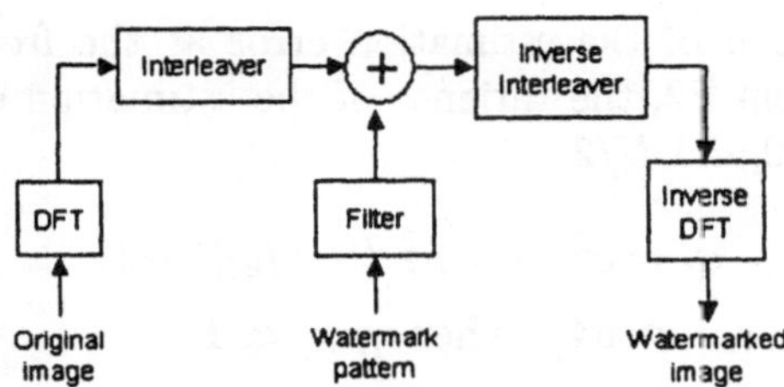

Fig. 1. Asymmetric watermark embedding in DFT domain

In order to detect the embedded watermark, the following binary hypothesis test was used in the interleaved domain as in [3]. The DFT magnitude coefficients of the received image are denoted by r_u. The interleaved signal of r_u is denoted by $\tilde{r}_u$. The Fourier transform of the filter used in the embedding is denoted by $H(f)$.

- H_0 : r_u is not watermarked, so $\tilde{r}_u$ is a white noise. The power spectrum of $\tilde{r}_u$ is as follows:

$$g_0(f) = \mu_{\tilde{r}_u}^2 \delta(f) + \sigma_{\tilde{r}_u}^2. \tag{1}$$

- H_1 : r_u is watermarked, so $\tilde{r}_u$ is a colored noise. The power spectrum of $\tilde{r}_u$ is as follows:

$$g_1(f) = \mu_{\tilde{r}_u}^2 \delta(f) + \sigma_{\tilde{r}_u}^2 + \gamma^2 \mu_{\tilde{r}_u}^2 (|H(f)|^2 - 1). \tag{2}$$

Under this hypothesis the power spectrum is shaped by $|H(f)|^2$.

The detection is formulated as detecting a known signal in noisy channel. The known signal is the power spectrum of the embedded watermark, and the noise is the estimation error. The power spectrum estimation error is assumed to be additive. First, we observe three properties of periodogram for the frequencies $\{f_k = k/N, 0 \le k \le N/2\}$ where N is the length of r_u [5].

P1) The mean of the periodogram is given by

$$\text{Mean}\{I_N(f_k)\} = P_{\tilde{r}_u}(f_k) + \mathcal{O}(N^{-1}) \tag{3}$$

where $I_N(f) = \frac{1}{N}|\sum_{k=0}^{N-1} \tilde{r}_u(k)e^{j2\pi kf}|^2$ which is the periodogram of $\tilde{r}_u$ and $P_{\tilde{r}_u}(f)$ is the true power spectrum of $\tilde{r}_u$.

P2) The variance of the periodogram is given by

$$\text{var}\{I_N(f_k)\} = \begin{cases} 2P^2_{\tilde{r}_u}(f_k) + \mathcal{O}(N^{-1}) & k = 0 \text{ or } \frac{N}{2} \\ P^2_{\tilde{r}_u}(f_k) + \mathcal{O}(N^{-1}) & \text{otherwise.} \end{cases} \tag{4}$$

P3) The covariance of the periodogram at different frequencies is given by

$$\text{cov}\{I_N(f_k), I_N(f_l)\} = \mathcal{O}(N^{-1}) \;\; k \neq l\,. \tag{5}$$

From P1, the mean of the estimation error at the frequencies f_k can be regarded as zero. From P2, the variance of the estimation error σ_e^2 is given by equation (7) for $k \neq 0$ and $N/2$:

$$\begin{aligned} \sigma_e &= \sigma^2_{\tilde{r}_u} + \gamma^2\mu^2_{\tilde{r}_u}(|H(f_k)|^2 - 1) \\ &\approx \sigma^2_{\tilde{r}_u} \quad \text{when } \gamma\mu_{\tilde{r}_u} \ll 1 \end{aligned} \tag{6}$$

when the watermark exists. In the case that the watermark does not exist, σ_e is also given by $\sigma^2_{\tilde{r}_u}$. From P3, the estimation error for the frequencies f_k is uncorrelated.

Second, the probability of distribution of the estimation error should be considered. Through the periodogram averaging, the distribution of the estimation error becomes Gaussian. Periodogram averaging consists of three steps. First, the N-length sequence $\tilde{r}_u$ is subdivided into K nonoverlapping segments, where each segment has length M. This results in the K data segments. For each segment, the periodogram is computed for the frequencies $\{f_k = k/M, 0 \le k \le M/2\}$. By averaging K data segments, the power spectrum estimate is obtained. The most important advantage of periodogram averaging is the distribution of the estimation error can be regarded as normal by the central limit theorem. Due to the averaging of K independent periodograms, the distribution of the estimation error approaches normal distribution. In practice, the normal approximation is good even for the small value of K. The second advantage of periodogram averaging is the reduced variance of the estimation error by the factor of K. Thus the variance of the estimation error is $\sigma_e^2 = \sigma^4_{\tilde{r}_u}/K$. But periodogram averaging reduces the resolution by the factor of K. There is a trade-off between the variance and the resolution of the power spectrum estimate. The required resolution is determined by the frequency response of the filter. The third advantage of periodogram averaging is the reduction of computational load by using K small size DFT (M point) instead of one large size DFT (N point).

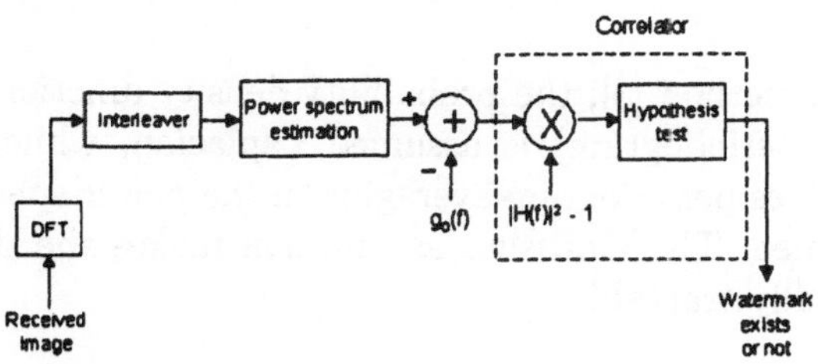

Fig. 2. Proposed correlation detector of asymmetric watermark

From the above, the estimation error can be regarded as additive, uncorrelated and Gaussian, then the detection problem can be transformed into the following hypothesis test shown in Fig. 2. A test function t, that can be modeled as some nominal value ρs plus noise with variance σ_e^2, is obtained by subtracting g_0 from the power spectrum estimation as follows:

$$t(f_k) = I_N^K(f_k) - g_0(f_k) = \rho s(f_k) + \sigma_e n(f_k) \tag{7}$$

where I_N^K is the averaged periodogram obtained from K data segments, $\{f_k = k/M, 1 \leq k \leq M/2 - 1\}$, $s(f_k) = |H(f_k)|^2 - 1$ and $n(f_k)$ is distributed as multivariate normal distribution $N(0, I)$. It needs to determine whether H_0 : $\rho = 0$ or $H_1 : \rho > 0$ from $t(f_k)$ that is distributed as $N(\rho s, \sigma_e^2 I)$. From the Fisher-Neyman factorization theorem, the sufficient statistic for the parameter ρ is

$$m = \frac{< s, t >}{\sigma_e(< s, s >)^{1/2}}. \tag{8}$$

The statistic m is distributed as $N(\frac{\rho\sqrt{E_s}}{\sigma_e}, 1)$ where $< s, t >= \sum_{k=1}^{M/2-1} s(f_k)t(f_k)$ and $E_s =< s, s >$ [6]. In communication theory, this hypothesis test based on m is known as correlation detector.

Let m_0 be the detection threshold in determining whether $\rho = 0$ $(m < m_0)$ or $\rho > 0$ $(m \geq m_0)$. By the Neyman-Pearson lemma, the false alarm probability P_{FA} is given by

$$P_{FA} = \int_{m_0}^{\infty} (2\pi)^{-1/2} e^{-x^2/2} dx = \frac{1}{2} erfc\Big(\frac{m_0}{\sqrt{2}}\Big). \tag{9}$$

For a certain value of P_{FA}, the threshold m_0 can be set by solving the above equation. The detection reliability is determined by the threshold m_0. The correct detection probability P_D is given by

$$P_D = \int_{m_0}^{\infty} (2\pi)^{-1/2} e^{-\left(x-\frac{\rho\sqrt{E_s}}{\sigma_e}\right)^2/2} dx$$
$$= \frac{1}{2} erfc\left(\left(m_0 - \frac{\rho\sqrt{E_s}}{\sigma_e}\right)/\sqrt{2}\right). \tag{10}$$

In the Furon's method [3], the probability density function of the estimated power spectrum (periodogram) is assumed Laplacian, while in the proposed method that involves periodogram averaging in the power spectrum estimation, Gaussian is assumed. The Gaussian assumption makes the detection problem more mathematically tractable.

3 Multiple bit embedding and detection

To increase information rate from a single bit to L bits, the frequency bins are divided into L bands; $(l-1)\frac{0.5}{L} < f < l\frac{0.5}{L}$ where $l = 1, 2, \cdots, L$. Each of the information bit is modulated by a PN sequence. In the l-th band, $|H(f)|$ is shaped as follows:

$$|H(f)|^2 = 1 + (-1)^{mes(l)} R_l(f) \tag{11}$$

where $R_l(f)$ is generated by a PN sequence with zero sum and $mes(l)$ is a information bit as shown in Fig 3. For the length of each PN sequence D, periodogram averaging factor K should satisfy the following inequality

$$K \leq \frac{1}{C}\left(\frac{N}{2LD}\right) \tag{12}$$

to meet the resolution requirement (experimental choice of C was 3).

In the detection, the power spectrum is estimated from K periodogram averaging and the sufficient statistic m_l of the l-th band is defined as follows:

$$t_l(f_k) = \rho R_l(f_k) + \sigma_e n(f_k) \tag{13}$$

where $(l-1)\frac{0.5}{L} < f_k < l\frac{0.5}{L}$.

$$m_l = \frac{\sum_k R_l(f_k) t_l(f_k)}{\sigma_e (\sum_k R_l^2(f_k))^{1/2}} \quad \text{for } l = 1, 2, \ldots, L. \tag{14}$$

For each band, the detection is performed by testing the three hypotheses:

- H_0 : The watermark does not exist. ($\rho = 0$)
- H_1 : The embedded information is 0. ($\rho > 0$)
- H_2 : The embedded information is 1. ($\rho < 0$)

in the model m_l is distributed as $N(\frac{\rho\sqrt{E_{R_l}}}{\sigma_e}, 1)$ where $E_{R_l} = \sum_k R_l^2(f_k)$.

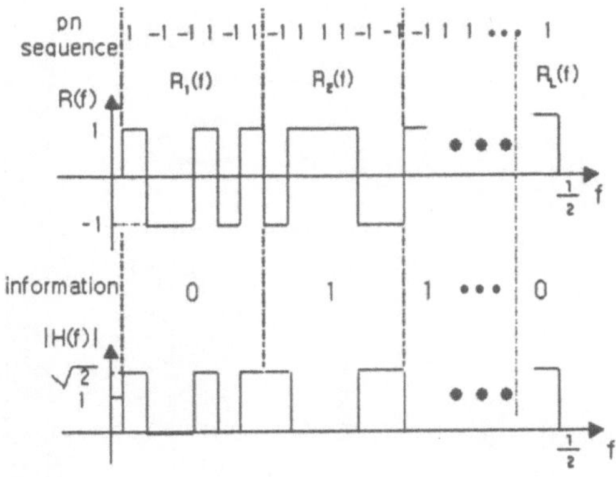

Fig. 3. Multiple bit embedding

4 Experimental results

In order to validate the proposed scheme, we tested our scheme on 512 by 512 "Lena" image. The embedding is the same as in [3] and [4] except that HVS (human visual system) was not used ($\gamma = 0.22$).

To show the validity of the proposed detection method, the outputs of the correlation detector, obtained from ten different interleavers and 100-tap FIR filters, were averaged. Fig. 4 shows the behavior of the statistic m versus the averaging factor K. On the whole, the correlation output was well-matched to the theoretical expectation. Even in the case of $K = 1$ (periodogram), the experimental correlator output followed the theoretical expectation. This result shows that the correlation detector can indeed be used for asymmetric watermarking. As K increases, the correlation output slowly decreases due to the reduced resolution. It was observed that the variance of m was a little higher than 1. This is attributed to the imperfection of the interleaver.

To compare the proposed method with that of Furon's [3], the performance of each method in detecting watermark from a JPEG compressed image is evaluated. Fig. 5 shows the averaged detection value normalized to the value obtained for uncompressed image. In the Furon's method, the normalized output varies roughly between -1 and 1, while in the proposed method the normalized output varies roughly between 0 and 1. Thus, we can conclude that the performances of two methods are similar. Robustness tests against other attacks, such as noise addition, enhancement filtering and malicious attacks, are required for more accurate comparison.

To investigate the possibility of embedding and detecting multiple bits, we calculated the bit error rate (BER) from the experiments using 20 different interleavers and PN sequences for a given false alarm probability. Fig. 6 shows the BER $(1 - P_D)$ versus the embedded bits L. BER, obtained from the experiment, was a little higher than that obtained from the theory. This is attributed to possible loss of information due to the quantization (256 levels) of watermarked

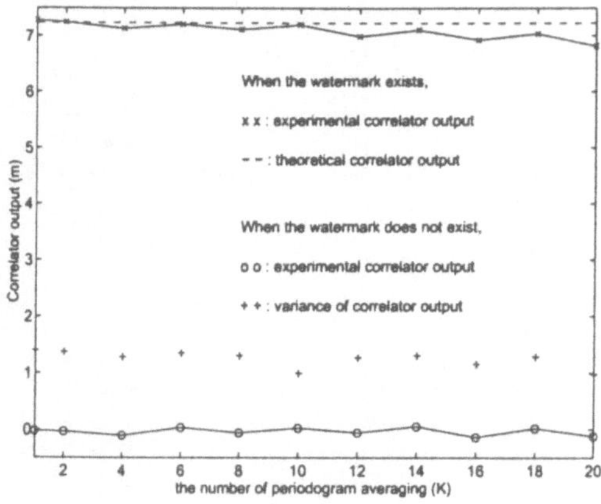

Fig. 4. Correlator output Vs. averaging factor

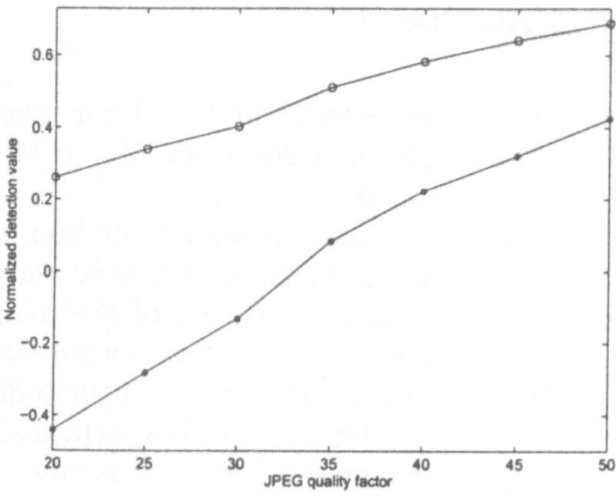

Fig. 5. Normalized detection value Vs. JPEG quality factor: o proposed detector, * Furon's detector [3]

image after watermark embedding and the imperfection of the interleaver. In the power spectrum estimation, periodogram averaging ($K = 8$) was used. As the embedded bits L increases, the number of DFT points allocated for each bit is decreased; thus the BER increases. Only several bits of information can be embedded without severe error rate for the data length $N = 16200$. The possible information rate is proportional to the data length N. To increase the information rate further, N must be increased.

5 Conclusion

A novel and simple detector for an asymmetric watermarking is proposed and tested. With certatin assumptions, a correlation detector is used in detecting

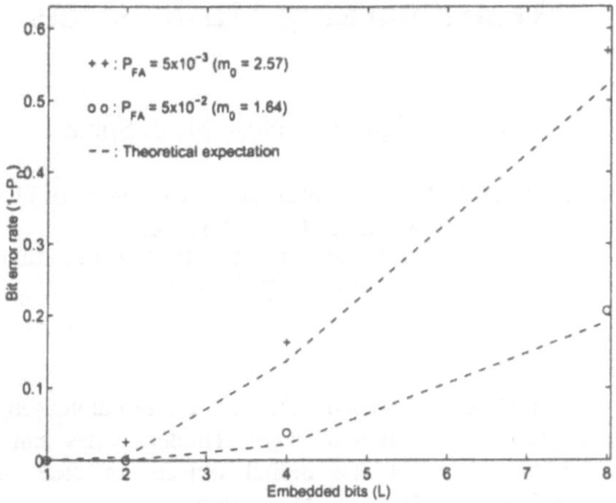

Fig. 6. Bit error rate Vs. Embedded bits

asymmetric watermark. It is based on the theory of detecting a known signal in noisy channel. The correlation detector output was well-matched to the theoretical expectation, showing that the correlation detector can indeed be used for the detection of asymmetric watermark. The proposed detector is applied to both single and multiple bit embedded watermark. Multiple bits of information are embedded by using PN sequence in filter shaping. From the experiment, several bits of information can be embedded without severe error rate. Testing the robustness of the proposed method and applying the detector to spatial domain additive watermarking remain as further works.

References

1. Teddy Furon and Pierre Duhamel, "An asymmetric public detection watermarking technique," in *Proc. of the 3rd Int. Work. on Infomation Hiding*, Dresden, Sept 1999.
2. J. A. Bloom, I. J. Cox, T. Kalker, J.-P. G. Linnartz, M. L. Miller, and C. B. S. Traw, "Copy protection for DVD video," *Proceedings of IEEE*, vol. 87, no. 7, pp. 1267–1276, July 1999.
3. Teddy Furon and Pierre Duhamel, "Robustness of asymmetric watermarking technique," in *Proc. IEEE Int. Conf. Image Processing*, Vancouver, Canada, Sept 2000.
4. A. De Rosa, M. Barni, V. Cappellini, and A. Piva, "Optimum decoding of non-additive full frame DFT watermarks," in *Proc. of the 3rd Int. Work. on Infomation Hiding*, Dresden, Sept 1999.
5. Boaz Porat, *Digital Processing of Random Signals: Theory & Methods*, Prentice Hall, 1994.
6. Louis L. Scharf, *Statistical Signal Processing: Detection, Estimation, and Time Series Analysis*, Addison-Wesley, 1991.

Watermarking Music Sheets

M. Monsignori, P. Nesi, M. B. Spinu

Department of Systems and Informatics, University of Florence
via. S. Marta, 3 50139 Florence, Italy
monsignori@hpcn.dsi.unifi.it, nesi@dsi.unifi.it,
spinu@dsi.unifi.it

Abstract. . Watermarking allows hiding information into digital objects such as images, videos, audio files and text pages. Hidden codes can be used to demonstrate the ownership of the digital objects in case of copyright infringement verification. Most of the commonly used applications of watermark are referred to color or b/w images. In this paper, an analysis of specific innovative techniques for watermarking music scores is presented. The analysis was performed on the basis of the requirements highlighted by the user group of the European Project WEDELMUSIC. The discussion reported in this paper has been performed taking into account the skills of musicians in detecting changes in the music sheets. This work can be useful for other researchers that would like to work in this area.

1. Introduction

Watermark techniques allow embedding information into digital distributed data (for example, images, videos, audio, or text files). The watermarking approach can be used to demonstrate the property of a given digital object and thus to require a non-recognized copyright fee [7]. In order to demonstrate the ownership of printed images (for example on a journal, poster, etc), the reading of the watermark code must be performed on an image acquired by using a scanner. Afterwards, specific image processing and analysis is needed to verify if the image contains the watermark. Typically, when an image is printed a significant decrement of information (in terms of color scale and/or dots per inch) and other deformations are operated. These operations make the watermark more difficult to recover, and thus the watermark itself has to be stronger and more intrusive to resists against these attacks bringing the data from digital format to analogue (on paper) to digital again. In the case of b/w images, most of the approaches used for color images became unusable. For example, for b/w pictorial images (as the method presented in [2]) it is unsuitable to work in the transform domain since it implies to generate a unacceptable noise for the musicians. Some other techniques proposed for watermarking text such as in [5] can be also considered as possible approaches in music scores watermarking.

The copyright owners (the music publishers) have in their archives high quantity music scores. In classical music, the original music is normally stored on paper since it was produced several years ago. Presently only new pieces of light and popular music are saved in symbolic notation format. Light and popular music have a limited life in terms of time duration in comparison with classical music pieces. Publishers keep their distance from transforming their classical music pieces in digital format for e-commerce purposes since whenever distributing in this way their copyright ownership is not protected. Therefore, classical music risks to remain in the archives of publishers and libraries since its distributed is too dangerous. The life of the copyrights for that music is close to 60-80 years. Current copyright infringement is only via photocopy process. The Internet distribution is presently considered an efficient vehicle to lose the control on this material. The situation is different for light and popular music where the copyright life itself is shorter. Also the interest on light music is in practice null after few years.

If a good protection is developed, many publishers could decide to publish their classical music pieces on Internet and this will have surely positive effects on the music market:

- The music should be bought in real-time
- The distribution will not be limited to geographical areas
- A further evolution of music software (editors, delivering systems, commercial tools, etc.) might be expected

2. Requirements & Problems

In this section, the identified requirements are exposed and discussed. They have been collected interviewing the experts of the WEDELMUSIC project user group. WEDELMUSIC information can be recovered on www.wedelmusic.org. The user group is mainly comprised of musicians, music copyists, music engravers, musicologists and music publishers. The major problem in music scores distribution is that a great part of music sheets are photocopied. In these cases, the copyright owner is not able to identify the source and the path of illegally distributed materials.

According to the previous analysis the identified requirements have been those reported in the following list.

- The embedded data has to contain the publisher identification, the music piece identification (watermark) and the music distributor identification (fingerprint[1]). Please note that several different meanings have been given to the term fingerprint. According to the CERTIMARK Project [9] 64 bits are enough to code both watermark and fingerprint. Please note that the code has to be repeated several times in the music sheet in order to make it enough robust and to ensure the watermark reading.
- The watermark inserted in the printed music sheet has to be invisible for musicians or at least it must not disturb or bother anyone during music playing.

[1] As defined in [7]: *fingerprints are like hidden serial numbers which enable the intellectual property owner to identify which customer broke his license agreement by supplying the property to third parties.*

- The watermark has to be present inside the music printed by the final users in any format. Subsequently, the watermark reading has not to depend on the availability of the music sheet's reference image.
- The attacks aimed at removing the watermark must be extremely expensive if compared to regular buying.
- The watermark must resist during sheet manipulation until the music printed becomes unreadable. Typically, 5 levels of photocopy are sufficient to make music unreadable (this depends obviously on the quality of both the copy machine and the original copy). In general, the watermark has to be readable after photocopies of music sheets until the music sheet you get is of a very low quality.
- The watermark should also be readable by processing a piece of music sheet (greater than ¾ of the whole music sheet page). A copy of a smaller part of the score does not present a commercial value
- In any case, once the music sheet is printed with the watermark, this has to be robust enough to resist against most common attacks.

In order to meet the above refereed user requirements several approaches have been considered.

Original music sheets as stored by the publishers may be available in two different digital formats: (i) images of music sheets acquired by a scanner (music produced 10 or more years ago is only available in this format), (ii) symbolic coding of the music sheet in terms of music notation. This last digital format is obtained by using computer music editors. They are typically used to produce modern music sheets. Music editors are used to produce PostScript or PDF outputs. These formats can be used for digital distribution of music. PostScript and PDF files of music sheets can be considered as images of music sheets.

Please note that from the point of view of robustness against the attack for removing watermark, the images are safer if compared with the PostScript or PDF codes that could contains graphical description of the music sheet. In fact, also the phase during which the watermark insertion is performed has to be considered. If the watermark is added while printing the music sheet, the source manipulation is normally easier but the techniques have to be different (it is difficult to recreate the original). For this reason, we assume that all-possible music scores formats are transformed in a common b/w image for printing them. This means that even in the case of watermarking while printing the produced output (for the printer) is a watermarked black and white image of the music sheet.

Please note that, if the watermark is included while printing the music sheet, this process can be performed in the computer of the final user. This also means that the final user may choose the final music sheet format. In this case, the music sheet original image is not available during the watermark reading.

3. Approaches

In general, the musicians appreciate to have high quality music scores thus the noise inserted with a classic image watermarking techniques disturbs the music reading. In fact, the watermark insertion using the frequency domain should not be considered as a valid approaches since it produces black pixels (points in the sheet) that can be interpreted as music notation elements (accents).

The most workable approaches for watermarking music scores are mainly related to geometric transformation and graphic element manipulations. They can be classified in two categories: (i) transformation of music elements, (ii) adoption of different fonts for the same music symbol.

There are different ways to apply the described approaches. A first possibility is to apply the algorithm to the images acquired by a scanner and the second one is to use a music editor and then generate an image including watermarked music.

An important part of the WEDELMUSIC project is dedicated to the implementation of such protection methods.

3.1 Transformation of music elements

In the approaches based on the transformation of music elements symbols such as staff lines, bar lines, beams, stem or slurs (ties) are manipulated. The most significant examples are:

- modifying the orientation of note stems,
- modifying the position of the notes in the staff,
- modifying the orientation of beam lines,
- adding white dots in the middle of other bigger music notation symbols,
- modulating staff lines by giving them different thickness, and considering thinner segments 0 and deeper as 1,
- modulating staff lines to give them a sort of sinusoidal behavior, etc.

In general, the information to be hidden can be included in the changes considering both their presence and absence, as 1 and 0 respectively. In some cases, the magnitude of the change can be used for hiding more bits, for example in the orientation the angle can be variable adding more bits.

3.2 Beam thickness modification

By modifying the orientation or thickness of beam lines it is possible to hide only few bits. The presence of beams is not guaranteed into the music page. Musicians easily detect the thickness variation when the beam is placed near to a staff line. This method requires the original music page in order to perform the watermark reading.

3.3 Stem rotation

The major problems of hiding information in the stem rotation [1] are the music score degradation and the low capacity in terms of hidden bits. As depicted in Fig.1, a non-expert musician is capable to identify that kind of changes into the music score. This method bothers the musicians when the music is read. In addition, it needs the original music page for watermark reading.

Fig. 1. Stem rotation approach

3.4 Noteheads shifting

The approach chosen in [8] consists in shifting note heads (see Fig.2). The distance between the notes has a musical significance so in several cases the approach may disturb the music reading. In the figure the second chords from the first and third staff was moved to left and the musicians may detect the missed alignment of the chords. The movement of notes may generate problems when the notes are marked with ornaments, accents, expressions, etc. The idea is good but unfortunately is feasible only for specific music score (with a large amount of notes).

Fig. 2. Shifting beamed notes

The idea is suitable to hide a significant code length if a sufficient number of noteheads are present in the score page. The number of notes in a score image is quite low, it ranges from 10 to 50 for each music staff. A score page may have from 7 to 15 music staffs. This solution requires the original music page for watermark reading.

If considering the main score, the shifted notes are quite easy to be detected by the musicians reading them (according to the needs of simultaneity among parts/layers/voices), while it turns out to be quite invisible in single parts. Such a watermark can be easily to detected by musicians in regular groups of notes when the insertion disturb the regular positioning of successive notes of the beam. If the shift is too evident, it may become a problem the musicians, since it might give the impression that some changes in the note duration were imposed (see Fig.2).

3.5 Adding white dots

This approach consists in adding small white dots into larger music notation symbols. The results can be quite easily detected by musicians and are not annoying while playing music. This approach is not robust, a mere photocopy may destroy the dots when they are smaller enough to be acceptable by musicians. The number of bits, which can be hidden in the music page, depends on the number of notes, which are on the same page. The approaches based on changing single music notation symbols are unsuitable since they do not allow hiding a high number of bits nor do they permit to replicate the code in a single score page.

3.6 Modulating the staff lines thickness

Fig.3 depicts an example of the line modulation approach. It consists in modifying the lines' thickness in order to insert a binary code made up of several bits [6]. Modulated lines can be easily noted if their presence is known whereas they are not perceived if the approach is unknown. This was confirmed during our validation phase by a group of experts (this resulted in a 45% of acceptance, [6]).

The proposed solution enables to hide a considerable number of bits in several instances. We have a code length of 120 bits and we repeat it 4 times in each staff. This makes the solution particularly suitable and robust to permit the watermark reading even from a small part of the music sheet.

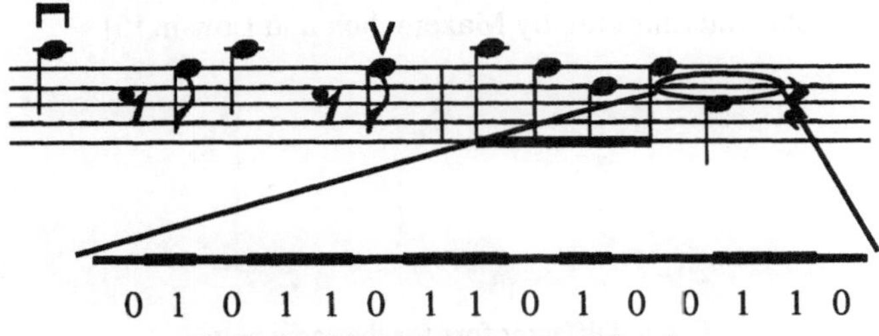

Fig. 3. Staff lines thickness modification

3.7 Adding lines mask

A possible approach consists on marking some points on the score based on a number of hidden lines that hide the watermark code. Different techniques to hide the information can be used. For example, the code can be associated with angles of the hidden lines or to their thickness (line can produce white or black dots in the image). In order to identify the points to be marked in the score, the hidden lines and part of music score are overlapped.

Fig. 4. Points to be marked on the music score

The points obtained by the intersection of the watermark lines with the staff lines are the points (or a part of them) that can be marked (see Fig.4). The points covered with a music symbol are eliminated from the group of "markable" points. More points are marked higher is the probability to retrieve the lines. For marking points different techniques can be used: cutting the staff line with a white line, modifying staff lines thickness and so forth. In the watermark reading process the identification of the marked points means finding the lines and subsequently the watermarked code.

3.8 Different fonts for the same music symbol

According to this technique (see Fig.5), different fonts for the selected music symbols are used to hide either 1 or 0, depending on the font used. This implies that the font has to be easily recognized in the phase of watermark reading. The approach was proposed for text watermarking by Maxemchuk and Low in [5].

Fig. 5. Different font for the same note

Fig.5 shows an example of possible font modification. The original character (on left) was changed by modifying flag thickness (on center) or length of the hook (on right). An undefined number of small changes can be performed on musical symbols in order to add the watermark. In some cases, the same character may present 4 different forms in order to hide 2 bits of the watermark code. The problem in using this technique is related to the channel capacity as well (since it is also a method based on symbol modification). The difference with respect to text watermark is that in music language the number of "characters" on a page is smaller. Therefore, it may became difficult to hide the whole code in a single music score page.

4 Conclusions

Music scores are very important for copyright owners. The lack of a functional tool to watermark music scores creates market inhibitions since the publishers have not the possibility to claim their property on that music.

This paper analyzed some possible approaches for watermark insertion in music scores. Some of them have been developed within the frame of the European project named WEDELMUSIC (Web Delivering of Music). Others are still under development and testing at the Department of Systems and Informatics (DSI) of the University of Florence.

The lines thickness and lines mask approaches were completely implemented and is under final test and application at DSI. Validation of the line thickness approach was done using metrics correlated with the Human Visual System (HVS) and based on Perceptual Quality Metrics as proposed in [3]. Validation results confirmed the validity of the approach. It is invisible until is unknown and it does not disturb the musicians since they do not notice it as long as they are not aware of its presence. In addition, it allows hiding a considerable number of bits with a reasonable robustness against photocopy.

References

1. C. Busch, E. Rademer, M. Schmucker, S. Wothusen, "Concepts for an Watermarking Technique for Music Scores" Visual 2000, 3rd International Conference on Visual Computing, New Mexico, 2000.
2. M. P. Deseilligny, H. Le Men, "An Algorithm for Digital Watermarking of Binary Images, Application to Map and Text Images", in Proceedings of International Workshop on Computer Vision, Hong Kong , September 1998.
3. M.Kutter and F.A.P. Petitcolas "A fair benchmark for image watermarking system" Proceedings of SPIE, vol.3657, January 1999
4. M.J.J.B Maes, C.W.A.M. van Overveld, "Digital Watermarking by Geometric Warping", in Proc. of IEEE Int. Conference on Image Processing, ICIP98, Vol.2, pp.424-426, 1998
5. N. F. Maxemchuk, S. Low, "Marking Text Documents" International Conference on Image Processing, Santa Barbara, Calif., October, pp.26-29, 1997.
6. M. Monsignori, P.Nesi, M. B. Spinu "Watermarking music scores while printing", Proc. of the International Conference on WEB Delivering of Music, in press, Florence, Nov. 2001.
7. F.A.P. Petitcolas, R.J.Anderson, M.G.Kuhn, "Information Hiding - A Survey", Proc. of the IEEE, special issue on protection of multimedia content, Vol.87, n.7, pp.1062-1078, 1999.
8. M. Schmucker, C. Busch, A. Pant, "Digital Watermarking for the Protection of Music Scores", in Proc. of IS&T/SPIE 13th International Symposium Electronic Imaging 2001, Conference 4314 Security and Watermarking of Multimedia Contents III, San Jose, California, January 2001.
9. Certimark Project, http://www.certimark.org/
10. Wedelmusic Project, http://www.wedelmusic.org

BCH Coded Watermarks for Error-Prone Transmission of MPEG Video

Shaou-Gang Miaou, Tzung-Shian Lee, and Chih-Ming Chen
Dept. of Electronic Eng., Chung-Yuan Christian Univ.
Chung-Li, 32023, Taiwan, R.O.C.
miaou@wavelet.el.cycu.edu.tw

Abstract. In this paper, BCH coding is integrated into a wavelet-based digital image watermarking technique. The resulting system is evaluated under an error-prone environment for MPEG transmitted video. First, a watermark is encoded by the BCH (31, 6) code. The encoded watermark is then embedded into each video frame using the watermarking technique. Next, the resulting frames are MPEG encoded and transmitted with 8.78% random macroblock loss in each P frame. In the proposed system, a simple temporal domain error concealment technique is also considered in the receiver end to reduce the visual degradation effect of transmission errors. MPEG compression and transmission errors can be treated as the attacking sources for the proposed watermarking system, and our simulation study confirms it. Error concealment may also be another attacking source. However, our experimental results show otherwise. In fact, the error concealment can slightly improve the robustness of the watermarking system. In addition, the experimental results show that BCH coding significantly enhances the robustness of the proposed watermarking system.

1 Introduction

The rapid growth of the Internet introduces a new challenge in multimedia data security problem, where unauthorized video, music, and image data are delivered. To protect the copyright of these media effectively in a ubiquitous network environment, one promising solution to this problem is digital watermarking, where a special identification symbol called watermark is hidden in multimedia data. It can be used to settle a copyright dispute by identifying the legal owner of the data.

Many watermarking techniques for various multimedia have been proposed [1]. In this paper, only video data are considered. Usually, a good digital watermarking technique must satisfy the following requirements:

(1) Low imperceptibility: The watermark must be hidden into video frames, and it should not present any visible artifact in the host image to maintain its visual quality.

The chance that attackers undermine a watermark may also be reduced if the trail of the watermark is hardly detectable.

(2) Non-removable watermark: The invisible watermark cannot be removed easily without seriously damaging the video frames.

(3) Robustness: The watermark technique should be robust against as many attacking methods as possible. These attacking operations include lossy compression (e.g., MPEG), and other video processing tasks.

Consider a wireless video broadcasting scenario, where MPEG compressed video data are transmitted via antennas in an error-prone environment. The program providers concern whether their copyrights are protected properly, whereas the end viewers care about the visual quality of the programs. The former concern can be resolved by embedding watermarks into video data. The later can be achieved using an error correcting and/or concealment technique. Both watermarking and error handling techniques are necessary in the scenario.

In the scenario above, a video watermarking system is under both man-made and natural attacks, where the attacks are coming from MPEG compression and transmission errors, respectively. The transmission error could result in packet losses or bits in error due to network congestion, packet collision, noises, strong fading, jamming, interference, etc. Some errors but may not be all can be recovered faithfully using a channel coding technique. More effective techniques such as the automatic repeat request (ARQ) scheme cannot be used in real time video. In this case, an error concealment technique can be used to improve the quality of damaged video. However, the concealment technique itself may also be a man-made attacking source on the embedded watermark. Thus, it is interesting to study how an error concealment technique affects (either positively or negatively) the robustness of video watermarking system in an error-prone transmission environment.

For an MPEG video compression system, we can embed watermarks in three places: original video source, MPEG encoding stage, and the MPEG compressed bit-stream, as shown in Fig. 1. Only the first case is considered here because many still-image based watermarking algorithms, including the one that we proposed in [2], can be applied easily. Our objective is to propose a watermarking system with high robustness and low perceptibility in an error-prone video transmission environment.

The paper is organized as follows. Section 2 describes the proposed system, including a simplified MPEG-based compression system, a wavelet-based watermark embedding technique, BCH encoded watermarks, and an error concealment technique. Experimental results are shown in Section 3. Finally, conclusions are given in Section 4.

2 The Proposed System

The block diagram of the complete system is shown in Fig. 2. More details will be given next.

2.1 Simplified MPEG Compression

In this paper, we use the MPEG-based compression, where DCT and motion compensation are used to compress watermark embedded video frames. DCT is used for the blocks in intra-frames (I frame) and motion compensation is used for the macroblocks (MB) in inter-frames (such as P frame). Only pure compressed data are generated and no header or other related data is attached.

2.2 Watermarking Method

Only a brief summary of our watermarking algorithm proposed in [2] is given here. The video frames are assumed to be gray-level frames and the watermark is a bipolar image (1's and -1). The block diagram of our watermark embedding process is shown in Fig. 3. The function of each block is explained as follows.

DWT of the host image: We perform a three level discrete wavelet transform (DWT) with 9-7 biorthogonal filters to obtain a multiresolution decompression of the host or original image [3]. The image size is $M \times N$. However only the highest two levels (the coarse approximations) of size $\frac{M}{2} \times \frac{N}{2}$ are used as the working matrix X, the other details are unchanged.

Wavelet based HVS: We implement the human visual system (HVS) given in [3] for the spatial frequency of 32 and obtain the visual threshold $t_{l,f}$ of X, where l and f denote the resolution level and orientation, respectively, l = 1, 2, and f = 1, 2, 3.

Pseudo-random permutation of watermark: A pseudo-random permutation is performed to disperse the spatial relation of the digital watermark W. The permutation makes the digital watermark look like a noise pattern which will be hard to detect or remove. The required pseudo-random sequences are generated using a system with delay elements and feedbacks. The sequences are then converted to coordinate pairs to obtain a fairly random pattern S from W .

Map of original wavelet coefficients: The visual threshold $t_{l,f}$ is used to obtain a coefficient map P as follows:

$$P_{m,n,l,f} = \begin{cases} 1, X_{m,n,l,f} \geq t_{l,f} \\ -1, otherwise \end{cases} \quad (1)$$

where (m, n) represents the position of a coefficient, $1 \leq m \leq \frac{M}{2}$, $1 \leq n \leq \frac{N}{2}$.

Key-watermark: We find that the elements in P still have some spatial relation. Hence, we introduce an intermediate result called key-watermark K, by performing the exclusive_OR (XOR) operation between S and P:

$$K = S \oplus P \quad (2)$$

where the $\oplus$ operation is defined as in Table 1. Hence, the matrix K would be a noise-like bipolar pattern with 1 and -1 . Finally, K will be kept to detect the watermark during the watermark detection process. The possible element permutation of K is $2^{\frac{M}{2} \times \frac{N}{2}}$, which is normally a very huge number. For example, for $M = N = 256$,

$2^{\frac{M}{2}\times\frac{N}{2}} = 2^{128\times128} \approx 10^{4932}$. In addition, the XOR operation is a one-way function between S and P. Thus, it is almost impossible or at least very difficult for an attacker trying to remove the watermark from the watermarked image.

Key-watermark insertion: For a level l and orientation f, this operation can be described as

$$\tilde{X}_{m,n,l,f} = X_{m,n,l,f} + t_{l,f} \times k_{m,n,l,f} \tag{3}$$

where $X_{m,n,l,f}$ refers to the original wavelet coefficient at position (*m*, *n*), $\tilde{X}_{m,n,l,f}$ represents the watermark inserted wavelet coefficient at the same location, and $k_{m,n,l,f}$ is the element of the key-watermark at position (*m*, *n*). Finally, we perform the inverse DWT (IDWT) on watermark- inserted wavelet coefficients and other unchanged details to obtain a watermarked image.

The watermarking extraction process is basically the reverse of the watermark embedding process. The popular similarity measurement, called normalized correlation (NC) [2], between an original watermark and its extracted version, is used.

2.3 BCH Encoded Watermark

Based on the watermarking method given in [2], we propose a modified version, where the watermark is encoded by the BCH code before it is embedded into video frames to enhance the robustness of the system. The idea of using error correcting codes to enhance the robustness of a watermarking system is relatively new [4][5]. This field is not matured and further study is necessary.

In the watermarking system proposed in [2], the embedded size for an original watermark is 256×256. To be compatible with that system and realize that BCH codes will generate redundant codewords, which will reduce the quality of extracted watermark and its embedding capacity, the watermark size must be much smaller than 256×256. In this study, we choose 64×48. The size-reduced watermark is obtained from the original watermark by downsampling and boundary line dropping. We use the BCH (31, 6) code, which can correct 7 single bit errors. Four same watermarks are encoded to obtain BCH coded watermarks with 4×64×48×31/6 = 63488 bits. It is then zero padded to reach the size of 256×256. In the watermark detection stage, the watermark with the highest NC value among the four will be extracted.

2.4 Error Concealment

Since neighboring MB in an image frame often belong to the same object and thus move together, their motion vectors are similar. This fact can be exploited to recover the lost motion vector. For example, we can take the averaging or median operation on the motion vectors of the MB that are around the lost MB. For a more accurate result, we can use an MB matching algorithm, such as the modified block-matching algorithm (MBMA) [6] that we use in this paper. With an estimated motion vector for a lost MB, the MBMA can recover the lost MB in a frame from the corresponding MB in the previous adjacent frame.

3 Experimental Results

Three well-known video sequences, i.e. Football, Flower garden, and Miss America, are used in our simulation study. The size of each image fame is 512×512. The size of group of picture (GOP) is 11, including one I-frame and 10 P-frames. Each sequence contains two sets of GOP, i.e., 22 frames. The MB lost rate is 8.78%, which is equivalent to about 3 slices in error per image frame. All the pixels in a lost MB are filled by the value of 255. Here we assume that each I-frame is heavily protected so that it is error free, and the concealment is performed only on P-frames. The error concealment technique indeed improves the signal quality significantly (about 15dB or higher in average PSNR per frame was obtained).

In Table 2 and Table 3, we show the average PSNR values of image sequence and the average similarity measures of watermarks for the 20 P-frames, respectively. Several interesting results can be observed from Table 2. The imperceptibility of watermark is great because the PSNR drop is fairly small regardless of the use of BCH code. In addition, the PSNR values for BCH encoded and not encoded cases are very close, which is reasonable because they have the same watermark embedding capacity.

From Table 3, we found that the BCH code increases the robustness of the watermarking system by making the watermark detection more reliable. Transmission errors can be treated as a form of cropping attack. Thus, the similarity measure is decreased if transmission errors occur. On the other hand, the error concealment can slightly increase the similarity measure. A possible explanation is given as follows. In the wavelet-based watermarking method, the watermark information is actually distributed all over the host image frame. The local MB loss does not seriously degrade the robustness of the watermark. Furthermore, any two similar adjacent frames contain similar watermark distribution in the corresponding position. Thus, the temporal domain error concealment may actually recover some lost watermark information.

4 Conclusions

In this study, we propose a DWT-based video watermarking technique in an error-prone MPEG transmission system, where MPEG compression and transmission errors are treated as attacks on the watermarked video. The MPEG compression can be treated as a low-pass filtering attack and the transmission errors can be treated as a cropping attack on watermarks. Although the error concealment is used to reduce the visual effect of transmission errors, it may be harmful for the embedded watermark. So in this sense, error concealment may also be an attacking source. However, our experiment shows otherwise. In fact, error concealment can enhance the robustness of the system rather than destroying it, at least in our wavelet-based watermarking system.

The BCH encoded approach effectively enhances the robustness of our watermarking system; whereas error concealment can enhance it slightly.

As a future work, the frame dependence of adjacent video frames can be exploited so that a watermark can be inserted in every two or three frames to reduce the complexity of the watermark embedding process.

References

1. Hartung, F., Kutter, M.: Multimedia Watermarking Techniques. Proc. IEEE. **87** (1999) 1079-1107
2. Miaou, S.-G., Chen, C.-M.: A Robust Image Watermarking Technique Based on Wavelet Transform and Human Visual Systems. J. of Computers. **13** (2001) 21-32
3. Watson, A. B., Yang, G. Y., Solomon, J. A., Villasernor, J.: Visibility of Wavelet Quantization Noise. IEEE Trans. Image Processing. **6** (1997) 1164 - 1175
4. Lee, J.,Won, C. S.: A watermarking Sequence Using Parities of Error Control Coding for Image Authentication and Correction. IEEE Trans. Consumer Electronics. **46** (2000) 313 – 317
5. Niu, X., Sun, S., Xiang, W.: Multiresolution Watermarking for Video Based on Gray-Level Digital Watermark. IEEE Trans. Consumer Electronics. **46** (2000) 375-384
6. Feng, J, Lo, K. T., Mehrpour, H.: Error Concealment for MPEG Video Transmissions. IEEE Trans. Consumer Electronics. **43** (1997) 183-187

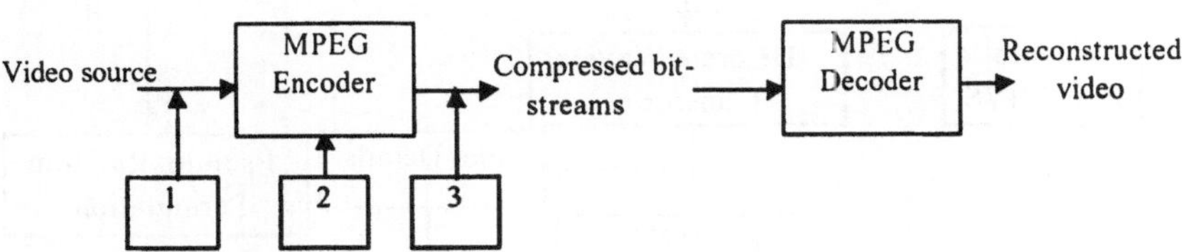

Fig. 1. Three embedding watermark occasions

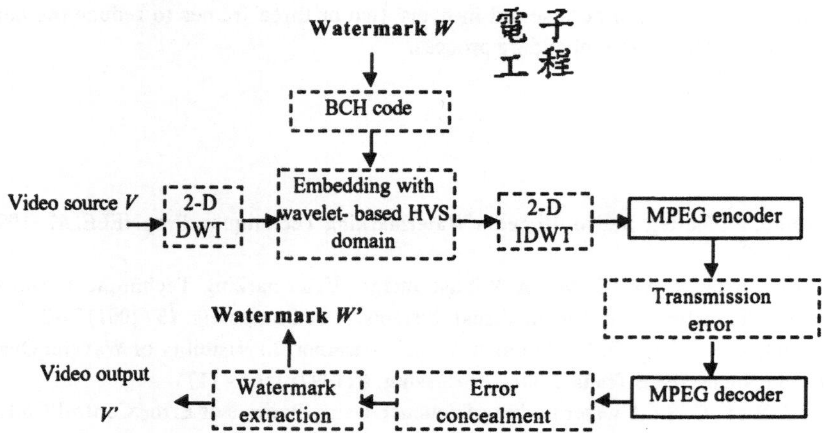

Fig. 2. The block diagram of the proposed system

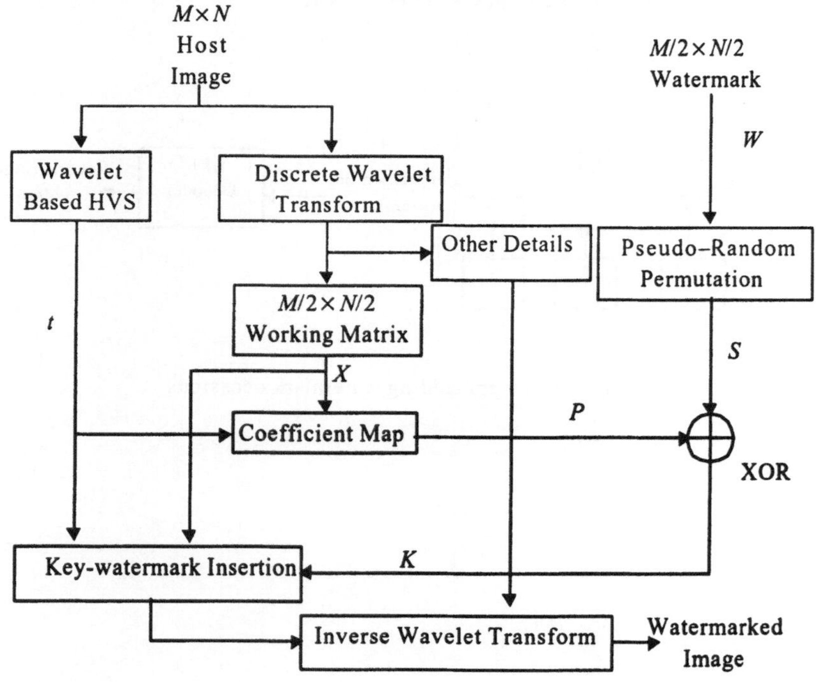

Fig. 3. The watermark embedding process

Table 1. XOR operation, $K = S \oplus P$

S	P	K
1	1	-1
1	-1	1
-1	1	1
-1	-1	-1

Table 2. Average PSNR performance of video frames

Transmission error	Watermark	Error concealment	BCH	PSNR Football	PSNR Flower garden	PSNR Miss America
No	No	No	No	30.4610	31.6509	37.7862
No	Yes	No	No	30.1778	31.2342	37.1773
			Yes	30.2644	31.3352	37.1434
Yes	Yes	Yes	No	27.7182	30.1842	36.8759
			Yes	27.7678	30.2545	36.8693

Table 3. Average similarity measure of extracted watermarks

Transmission error	Error concealment	BCH	Similarity Football	Similarity Flower garden	Similarity Miss America
No	No	No	0.8724	0.9155	0.9016
		Yes	0.9806	0.9934	0.9528
Yes	No	No	0.8331	0.8781	0.8456
		Yes	0.9469	0.9789	0.9241
Yes	Yes	No	0.8595	0.9104	0.9000
		Yes	0.9716	0.9914	0.9504

Smart Classroom - an Intelligent Environment for Tele-education

Weikai Xie[1], Yuanchun Shi[1], Guanyou Xu[1], Dong Xie[2]

[1] Dept. of Computer Science and Technology, Tsinghua Univ., Beijing, China
xwk@media.cs.tsinghua.edu.cn,{shiyc, xgy-dcs}@tsinghua.edu.cn
[2] IBM China Research Lab, Beijing, China
dongxie@cn.ibm.com

Abstract. The Smart Classroom project explores the challenges and potentials of the Intelligent Environment as a new human-computer interaction paradigm. By constructing an intelligent classroom for tele-education, we try to provide teachers the same experiences as in an ordinary classroom when giving tele-education lessons. The Smart Classroom could actively observe, listen and serve the teachers, and teachers can write on a wall-size media-board just by their hands, or use speeches and gestures to conduct the class discussion involving of the distant students. This paper discusses the advantages and main underlying technologies of this system.

1 Introduction

We are steadily moving into a new age of information technology named as ubiquitous computing (pervasive computing), where computation power and network connection will be embedded and available in the environments, on our bodies, and in the numerous handhold information appliances [1]. The human computer interaction paradigm we currently used on the desktop computers will not be sufficient [2]. Instead of operating on individual computers and dispatching many trivial commands to separated applications through keyboard and mouse, we should be able to interact with all related computation devices as a whole, and express our intended tasks in a high abstraction level and by ways as natural as we used to communicate with other people in everyday life.

The research of Intelligent Environment is just motivated by this vision. General speaking, an Intelligent Environment is an augmented living or working environment which could actively watch and listen to the occupants, recognize their requirements and attentively provide services for them. The occupants could use normal human-being interaction methods such as gesture and voice to interact with the computer system embedded in the environment. The researches in this filed are bring into mainstream in the late 1990's by several first-class research groups of the world such as AI Lab and Media Lab at MIT, Xerox PARC, IBM and Microsoft. Currently there are dozens of related projects carried out in research groups from all over the world. The most famous ones are Intelligent Room project from MIT AI Lab [3, 4], Aware Home project from GIT [5] and Easy Living project from Microsoft [6, 7].

The Smart Classroom project in our group is also a research effort on Intelligent Environment. It demonstrates an intelligent classroom for teachers involved in tele-educations, in which teachers could have the same experiences as in a real classroom.

This paper is organized as follows. In Section 2 we present the scenario of Smart Classroom. In Section 3 we discuss the main technologies involved in implementing the scenario. Finally we give a summary and outline the future work.

2 Teacher's Experience in Smart Classroom

2.1 Disadvantages of Desktop-Computing Based Tele-Education Systems

Almost all the tele-education systems developed today are desktop-computing based, where teachers are required to seat down in front of the desktop computer and use the keyboard or mouse to give a tele-education class. The teacher's experience is of much difference from teaching in an ordinary classroom, where the teacher could make handwriting on the blackboard, use speech and gesture to conduct the students to take part in the class discussions and other body languages like that. The different experience always makes the teacher feel uncomfortable and reduced the efficiency of the course as well.

2.2 Room Setup

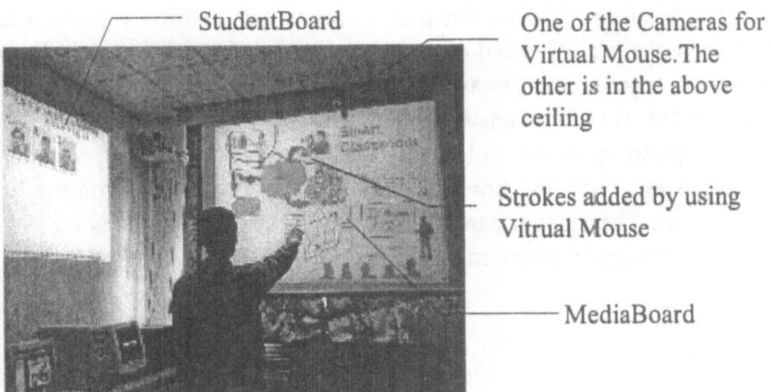

Fig. 1. The first author is using the Smart Classroom

A prototype of Smart Classroom is deployed in a room of our lab. Two wall-sized projector systems is equipped in it. One is used to display the courseware prepared by teacher - an analog of the blackboard in an ordinary classroom. We call it media-board [12, 13]). The media-board is synchronized with the display of the remote students' client software, i.e., whatever changes the teacher makes on the media-board will be reflected on the remote student's client software.

The other project system is used to display the portraits of remote students (we call it student-board). Each of attended remote students will have their portraits displayed on it. And if the teacher has given the floor to a remote student, the remote student's audio and video will be played here too. (also on other remote students' screen)

Several cameras and a wireless microphone system are installed in the proper positions to capture the teacher's video and voice. The captured audio and video are both sent to the remote students' sites by multicast and feed to the perception modules of the room such as hand-tracking module and speech recognition module.

All the computers running the room's software are deliberately hide out of sight, just to give the teacher a feeling that they are not using some computer programs but teaching in a real classroom. An illustration of the room setup can be seen in Fig. 1.

2.3 Interactivities in the Smart Classroom

The scenario might seem no significant differences from many other whiteboard based tele-education systems. However, the magic of the Smart Classroom is the way teachers using the system - teachers are no longer tied up to the desktop computer, nor cumbersome keyboard and mouse. Making annotations on the courseware is just as easy as writing on an ordinary classroom blackboard, i.e. the teacher only need to move his finger, then the stroke will be displayed on the media-board, overlapped with the displayed courseware. The teacher could also point to the object displayed on the media-board and say a predefined command to do what he wanted. For example, to following a hyperlink in the courseware, the teacher just need to point at the hyperlink and tell the Smart Classroom "follow this link". The way to enable a remote student to speak on the class is also intuitive and easy. It can be completed by speech. For example, let's suppose the teacher want to ask a student named Peter to answer a question. Then he can say "Peter, could you answer this question?" Whenever a student requires speaking, the corresponding image will start to blink to alert the teacher.

Actually, this system blurs the border between the ordinary classroom education and the tele-education. The teacher can give a class to the local students on the Smart Classroom and those remotely attended students at the same time.

3 Underlying Technologies in the Smart Classroom

3.1 Software Platform

The Smart Classrooms, just like many other similar Intelligent Environments, is an assembly of many different kinds of hardware and software modules such as projectors, cameras, sensors, face recognition module, speech recognition module and eye-gaze recognition module. It is unimaginable to install all these components in one computer due to the limited computation power and terrible maintenance requirements. Thus, a distributed computing platform is a must for an Intelligent Environment.

There are a handful of distributed computing platforms from commercial organizations or research groups. These distributed computing platforms can be classified into two different types according to their structure modal. One is called distributed-component- modal based system, such as CORBA from OMG and DCOM from Microsoft. The other is called multi agent system, such as OAA from SRI and Aglets from IBM. Although the distributed component modal is currently more prevalent and mature than the multi agent system modal, we considered the latter is more suitable for the Intelligent Environment system, including our Smart Classroom. The consideration is explained as following.

The distributed component modal implies monolithic control logic and tight-couple system structure. Put it another way, the software in a distributed-component-modal system is composed of a central logic and several other peripheral objects offer service to the central logic. There is only one execution process in the system and the objects run only when invoked by the central logic. On the contrary, the multi agent modal, which have been invented and used for years in the AI domain, implies a loose-couple system structure. According to this modal, a system is divided into many individual autonomous software modules called agent, which has its own executing process. Each agent has limited capabilities and limited knowledge of the functions of the whole system, but through communication and cooperation the agents' community will expose a high degree of intelligence and can achieve very complex functions.

A loose-couple system will be far more suitable than a tight-couple system in the Intelligent Environment.

1) The scenarios of an Intelligent Environment are usually very complex, so developing a central logic for it is very difficult even an unpractical matter.

2) The scenarios and configurations in an Intelligent Environment are often very dynamic. New functions will be added, old module will be revised, and all those things are happened frequently. The monolithic system structure is very inflexible under this situation, because any trivial modifications will require the whole system to shut down and all modules in the system should be re-linked.

3) The central logic is likely to be the bottleneck of the system.

After a survey of some multi agent systems, we finally adopted the OAA (Open Agent Architecture), a public available multi-agent system, as the software platform for the Smart Classroom. It was developed by SRI and has been used by many research groups [10]. (We fixed some errors of the implementation provided by SRI to make it more robust.)

All software modules in the Smart Classroom are implemented as OAA agents. At start up, they will register their capabilities in a central coordinating logic called "facilitator". When they want services from other agents they can just send a message encoded in the Inter Agent Language (ICL) to the facilitator, and need not to know which agent actually provided the services. The ICL is essentially based on an extension of the Prolog language.

3.2 Multi-modal Processing

People use multiple modalities to communicate with each other in everyday life, such as speaking, pointing and gesturing. The multi-modal interaction capability is a fundamental requirement of the Intelligent Environment, since any single modality is often semantic incomplete. For example, when one say "move it to right", without the recognition of the hand pointing modality we could not tell which object is referred by the speaker. Another benefit of the multi-modal processing is the information from other modalities often helps to improve the recognition accuracy of a single modality. For example, suppose in a noise environment, a not so smart speech recognition algorithm maybe has difficulty to decide what the user said is "move to right" or "move to left". But after referring the information from the hand gesture recognition module, the system could eventually make the correct choice. This also happens in Smart Classroom. In the scenario we designed, the teacher can use speech and hand gesture to make annotations on the media-board, to manage the content in the media-board and to pass floor to a remote student.

The formalization architecture we used to address this issue is based on the "unification based multimodal parsing" presented in [9]. It essentially takes the multimodality integration process as a kind of language parsing process, i.e., each separate action in a single modality is considered as a phrase structure in the multi-modal language grammar, they are grouped and induced to generate a new higher level phrase structure. The process is repeated until a semantic completed sentence is found. The process could also help to correct the wrong recognition result of one modality. If one phrase structure could not be grouped with any other phrase structure according to the grammar, it will be regarded as a wrong recognition result and will be abandoned.

3.3 Virtual Mouse

Several cameras installed on the room together with a skin color consistency based algorithm are used to recognize the 3D movement parameters of the teacher's hand, as well as some simple actions of the teacher's palm such as open, close and push [14]. These modules function as a virtual mouse for the teacher, i.e. the movement of the teacher's hand will be explained as dragging of the pointer on the screen and the actions of his palm will be explained as clicks of the mouse button. In this way, the teacher can easily make annotations on the media-board or select a remote student on the student-board just by his hand.

3.4 Flexible Speech Recognition Framework

Since we started to design the system structure, we have been keeping in our mind that the structure should be flexible enough to support gradually extending the scenario of the Smart Classroom. The speech recognition framework we developed is one of the examples.

In the core of the framework is an enhanced speech grammar, which could not only describe the syntax of legal phrases, but also mark the semantic effect of the phrase when recognized. Exactly, the semantic effect refers to an Inter-Agent-Language message that can trigger wanted actions of other agents in the system. Using this grammar, other agents could add vocabularies into the speech recognition agent on the runtime. Nevertheless, the vocabularies could be dynamically enabled and disabled by other agents according to their knowledge of current context in order to keep the effective vocabulary at a minimum size, which is very important to improve the recognition speed and accuracy rate.

3.5 Tele-education Supporting System

The tele-education system behind the scene is based on the Same View system from another group in our lab [11,12,13]. The system is constituted of three layers. The most upper layer is a multimedia whiteboard application we called media-board and associated floor-handling mechanism. As mentioned above, one interesting feature of the media-board is it can record all the actions on it, which could be used to aid the creation of the courseware. The middle layer is a adapting content transform layer, which could automatically re-authorizing or transforming the content sent to the user according to the user's bandwidth and device capability [11]. The media-board use this feature to ensure that students at different sites could get the contents on the media-board at a maximum quality according to their different network and hardware conditions. The lowest layer is a reliable multicast transport layer called Totally Ordered Reliable Multicast (TORM), which could be used in a WAN environment where sub-networks capable of or incapable of multicast coexist [12,13]. The media-board uses this layer to improve its scalability across large networks like Internet.

4 Future Works and Concluding Marks

In the next stage we want to introduce the acoustic-recognition and face-recognition capabilities into the Smart Classroom so that the classroom could automatically identify the teacher and provide better services for the teacher. For example the speech recognition module could use this information to load the specific voice model to improve the recognition accuracy. Another example is the classroom could automatically resume the context (such as the content on the media-board) where the teacher stopped at the last class.

We believe the Intelligent Environment will be the right metaphor for people to interact with the computer systems in the ubiquitous computing age. The Smart Classroom is our test-bed for the researches on the Intelligent Environment as well as an illustration of its application.

References

1. Weiser, M.: The Computer for the 21st Century. Scientific American, September (1991) 94–100
2. Weiser M.: The world is not a desktop. Interactions, January (1994), 7–8
3. Coen, M.: Design Principles for Intelligent Environments. In Proceedings of The Fifteenth National Conference on Artificial Intelligence, Madison, Wisconsin (1998)
4. Coen, M.: The Future Of Human鉀omputer Interaction or How I learned to stop worrying and love My Intelligent Room. IEEE Intelligent Systems, March/April (1999)
5. Kidd, Cory D., Robert J. Orr, Gregory D. Abowd and et al.: The Aware Home: A Living Laboratory for Ubiquitous Computing Research. In the Proceedings of the Second International Workshop on Cooperative Buildings, October (1999)
6. Shafer S. and et al.: The New EasyLiving Project at Microsoft Research. Proceedings of the 1998 DARPA/NIST Smart Spaces Workshop, July (1998) 127–130
7. Brumitt, B. L., Meyers, B., Krumm, J. and et al.: EasyLiving: Technologies for Intelligent Environments. Handheld and Ubiquitous Computing, 2nd Intl. Symposium, September (2000) 12–27
8. G. D. Abowd.: Classroom 2000: An experiment with the instrumentation of a living educational environment. IBM Systms Journal, Vol. 38. No.4
9. Johnston M.: Unification打ased multimodal parsing. In the Proceedings of the 17th International Conference on Computational Linguistics and the 36th Annual Meeting of the Association for Computational Linguistics, ACL Press, August (1998) 624–630
10. OAA web site: http://www.ai.sri.com/~oaa/
11. Liao, C.Y., Shi, Y.C., Xu, G.Y.: AMTM – An Adaptive Multimedia Transport Model. In proceeding of SPIE International Symposia on Voice, Video and Data Communication. Boston, Nov. (2000)
12. Pei, Y.Z., Liu, Y., Shi, Y.C. and et al.: Totally Ordered Reliable Multicast for Whiteboard Application. In proceedings of the 4th International Workshop on CSCW in Design, Compigne, France (1999)
13. Tan K., Shi, Y.C., Xu, G.Y.: A practical semantic reliable multicast architecture. In proceedings of the third international conference on multimodal interfaces, Beijing, China, (2000)
14. Ren, H.B., Zhu, Y.X., Xu, G.Y. and et al.: Spatio李emporal appearance modeling and recognition of continuous dynamic hand gestures. Chinese Journal of Computers (in Chinese), Vol 23, No. 8, Agu. (2000) 824–828

Movie Video Hypermedia Authoring System

Wenli Zhang[1] Yoshitomo Yaginuma[2] Masao Sakauchi[1]

[1]Institute of Industrial Science, the University of Tokyo4-6-1 Komaba, Meguro-ku, Tokyo 153-8505, Japan
{zhang, Sakauchi}@sak.iis.u-tokyo.ac.jp
[2]National Institute of Multimedia Education
2-12,WAKABA, MIHAMA-KU, CHIBA, 261-0014, Japan
yaginuma@nime.ac.jp

ABSTRACT. *The wider application of the Internet and digital broadcasting has brought about a dramatic increase in the amount of multimedia data in the last few years. For further use of the data in a more flexible way, the relevant reference information extracted from these multimedia sources will be very helpful. In order to better integrate and manage all the description information obtained in ways such as automatic or manual ones, we have begun and are still working on developing an XML-based framework. It is called as Movie Video Stream Description Language for TV Movie Show (VSDL-TV). In this paper, as an application based on VSDL-TV, the so-called "Movie Video Hypermedia Authoring System" will be introduced.*

1.Introduction

With the rapid development of digital broadcasting and the Internet, it has become imperative to develop a system in order to store, retrieve, and manipulate the huge amount of multimedia data. Different with the traditional databases that only handle the text or numeric data, a multimedia database should deal with video, image, sound and text documents and so on.

Video is a typical type of multimedia data. For a flexible use of the data, for example, in the case of movie video, the relevant reference information, such as titles, characters' names or program catalogs can be a quite helpful. In recent years, a lot of research work has been made on video description languages [1][2][3][4]. During the research [1][2][4], people mainly studied the general video media. As a would-be standard description language, ***MPEG-7*** [4] focuses on the criteria of the description, but pays little attention to the methods of video recognition. ***TV Program Making Language*** [3] is a language for producing TV programs in a simplified video processing. Video reorganization, for e.g., can be easily obtained by using the language.

Since a feature movie is typical of video data, with video, sound media and the script, so in our previous work, we proposed a movie video stream description language, called ***VSDL-TV*** [7]. In ***VSDL-TV***, we first define methods on how to describe video or the objects in it. Then, we prepare a set of fundamental operation methods. For further combination with these fundamental operation methods, we also define some application-oriented methods, which can be stored in the ***VSDL-TV***.

VSDL-TV now mainly deals with movie video data. It will be enhanced in the near future for developing various potential applications.

Based on the ***VSDL-TV***, we have established an application, called as *Movie Video Hypermedia Authoring System*, which alters the multiple movie video data into the hypermedia styles, namely XHTML, HTML and XML.
The rest parts of this paper are as follows: Section 2 is an outline of *Movie Video Hypermedia Authoring System*. Section 3 shows a frame-based hypermedia authoring method and its implementation. Section 4 presents an object-based hypermedia authoring method. In Section 4, an algorithm to specify a human object is also discussed. Finally, Section 5 gives a summary.

2. Movie Video Hypermedia Authoring System based on VSDL-TV

2.1 The Outline of VSDL-TV

In ***VSDL-TV*** [7], we treat the video data as a tree structure, which grows up from video, through scene(s), shot(s), frames(s), object(s) to section(s). Every node of every hierarchical level in the tree is taken as a ***VSDL*** class, which implants a ***JAVA*** class in ***VSDL-TV***.
The internal structure of a ***VSDL*** class consists of two parts: ***DESCRIPTION*** and ***METHOD***. There are default methods in ***VSDL*** classes; the user is given the freedom to define their default methods if necessary. *fClass parentID* and Class *childID* indicate the parent-child relationship within the "tree".
Furthermore, the ***VSDL*** class, once processed, can remain as a ***VSDL*** class ready for use in the next operation. When we define a new hierarchy class higher in the tree, the former lower processed class can be extended as the parent class of the new one.
In ***VSDL-TV***, we used ***DP Matching*** [6] to establish the linkage between the video and its text scripts. As a result, the video is annotated with its corresponding scripts. The higher layers of the video structure tree, like "scene" and "shot", consist of descriptions acquired by the ***DP Matching*** method. Descriptions are stored in XML format.
We also implant the fundamental operation methods in ***VSDL-TV*** to each video hierarchy. Among the methods, there are temporal operation, media analysis, media reorganization, description management and others.
The different combinations of fundamental operation methods make the different *application-oriented operation methods (AOOM)*. With *AOOM*, we can do the retrieval, query or other processes on the data. A set of application-oriented methods can further make up an application.
With the framework-***VSDL-TV***, we can implement TV Drama Management System, Cyber shopping and other potential applications.

2.2 Hypermedia Authoring System

The concept of hypermedia came with the wider application of digital technology and the Internet. Hypermedia is a text media, which is not constrained to linear form and contains links to other texts. Hypermedia is a term (Ted Nelson coined the term around 1965 [11].) used for hypertext, which is not constrained to text form: it can include graphics, video and sound. The huge amount of digital resource of video, sound, and text documents are stored in non-linear order. For retrieving and browsing the data at his will, the user should be able to use the information telling the relations between the various media data.
With the framework ***VSDL-TV***, we have focused on how to alter the multiple movie video data to hypermedia styles, which includes XHTML, HTML and XML.

As mentioned in *section 2.1*, the methods in ***VSDL-TV*** equip the user with a potential environment for implanting multimedia applications. A "*Movie Video Hypermedia Authoring System*" is one of these implanted applications.
In the next section, we will introduce two types of hypermedia authoring methods used in the system. One is frame-based; and the other is object-based. We use VisualCafe4.0 for software package development; Java Media Framework2.1(JMF2.1)[9] for media control management.

3 Hypermedia Authoring – Frame Based

Two elements will be used for this purpose, one is the image frame, and the other is the description on the image frame. However, we could not use all the descriptions concerned. That would be too big to manage. Therefore, we should know (1) what is the most important description and (2) on what conditions the next page is linked to the current one.
Partly, we make the descriptions manually, but the descriptions can be done with help of the results of *DP Matching* [6].
Video-to-hypermedia authoring methods *creatHyperDoc()* can be implemented by using the following fundamental operation methods,
getName() for extraction of actor's name
getlocation() for extraction of location name
getRelatedFrame() for getting the related frames
getTags() for extraction of the keywords for the descriptions.
In addition, *outputHyperFile()* can output the descriptions to the hypermedia file. We can choose one type among HTML, XHTML or XML for the format of the created hypermedia file.
Figure 1 shows the interface of the authoring system.

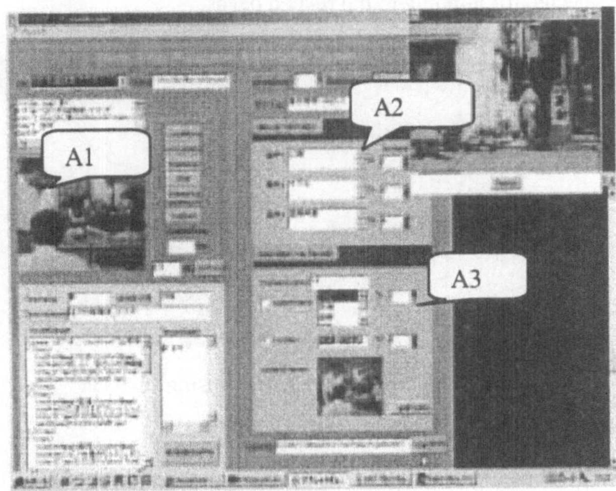

Figure 1 An Interface of System

By using this system, we can get a frame through text-based **retrieval** function and/or **capture** function from the video being replayed. Then the descriptions and the address of next linked page can be set manually or automatically. The information such as locations, character's names can be extracted automatically from the descriptions, which correspond to the selected frame. Finally, the hypermedia file can be made.

A1 in the Figure 1 shows the selected frame. A2 shows the manual input area, A3 shows the automatic results area.

Before the authoring, we should determine the scenario of the hyper linking. For example, we label the scene 2 is "who is the sufferer". First, by using "capture", "text-based retrieval", and/or "text-based edit" functions, one frame can be determined. Next, for the manual definition, the selection items are set as the scenario. For the automatic definition, the name of the actor and the location can be used as the selected items. For example, we can tell item4 is "morimura", and when it is selected, the link is "scene 1". The link page address (es) is (are) also necessary (Table 1).

A free software named as "Gassan"[8] can help us brows the authoring results. "Gassan" is a tool for creating the games that are like "Roles playing game". For example, the user clicks one item on the given selection list to jump to the specified linked page, then click there to select other items... and finally, arrives to the end of the game. Scenarios of such games can be described by using "Gassan Scenario Markup Language"(*GSML*), an XML-based description language. "Gassan" can brow the hypermedia file written in ***GSML*** format.

Table 1 -setting description manually and/or automatically

Item	Link page address
Item1: Keiko	Scene 6
Item2: Yumi	Scene 7
Item3: a young woman	Scene 8
Item4: Morimura	Scene 1

"Scene" + "number" indicates the link address.

"Gassan" uses two pages to browse one scene of "who is the sufferer". Figure 2(left) shows the scene title "who is the sufferer", if the user clicks this item, the location list (Figure 2(right)) will appear to be selected for jumping to the related pages.

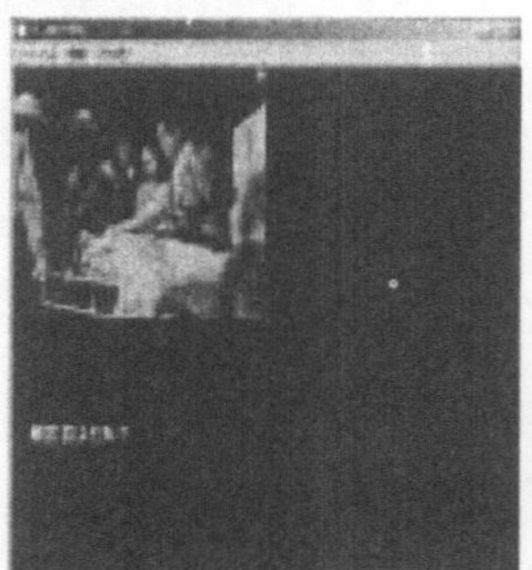

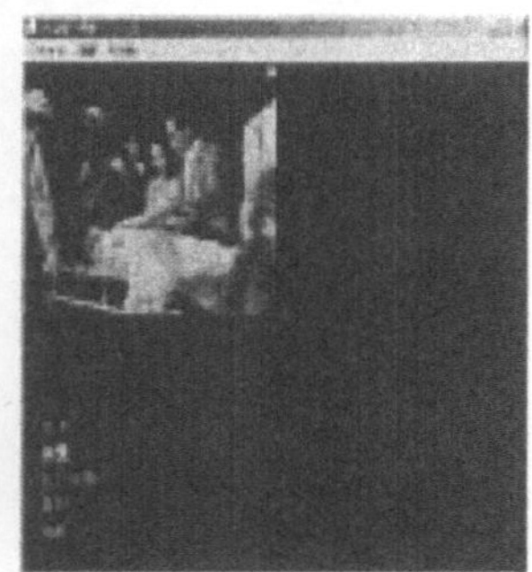

Figure 2 The browsing results by using "Gassan"

4 Hypermedia Authoring –Object based

In this section, we will discuss the hypermedia linking via the objects in the frames.

Index is added to the objects based on the information of segmentation, video analysis, and the information from the script.

In ***VSDL-TV***, the fundamental methods, such as location extraction, character extraction, lines extraction and motion extraction are implanted. All relevant information can be extracted from

the script. The object(s) extraction, such as character extraction, motion extraction can be obtained from the video media by using these implanted methods.
For integrating the above information, we suppose that there are the two types of the description-the descriptions of characters are attached to the video by using ***DP matching***, and the description(s) of the character(s) objects are not attached with the corresponding object(s). In this case, we will introduce that how to provide the description(s) of every object within the video though combining with the information from the script and from the result(s) of the video analyzing respectively.

4.1 Extraction of Character Objects

Since the movie video is about people, so to extract the character objects from it will help us further use the data in a flexible way. Usually, however, this necessary process can be very complicated by automatic methods.
For the extraction in our research, we first use the contrasting effect of characters' complexion in the movie due to the makeup and the light. Then, we use the characteristics of the faces' size (length) and their locations; colors of faces, hair, clothes and so on; the number of the people; and the action of the people in the scene.
To be more specific, we extract the characters by:

- Complexion of the face,
- Hair above the face,
- Torso part under the face.

Moreover, if the following conditions are met, we treat the part as non-face one. The conditions are
- The filling rate[1] of the minimum-bounding rectangle is smaller than a threshold.
- The vertical coordinate of the center of gravity of the minimum bounding rectangle is lower than a certain threshold, the ratio of the length to height does not belong to a certain range and etc.

4.2 Assumption for Specifying Character Object

In order to specify the character object, the following assumptions can be made.

- ***Assumption :***

By using the color information extracted from the character object from the two frames, we can get the similarity of the two character objects. In another words, by using the color information, we can assume the two objects are the same character.
However, since the character's presence information from the script is not always correct, the following two points are often assumed:

- ***Assumption 2:***

About the number of character, we assume the following formulae are satisfied.

The number of the presumed existence character>=
The number in the frame actually >=
One character = speaker

- ***Assumption 3:***

If there is only one-character object in the frame, it is the speaker.

---

[1] The filling rate: the ratio of the area of the object to the area of its minimum-bounding rectangle

By integrating the above assumptions, the character object can be specified. In the following session, a proposed algorithm will be discussed.

4.3 The Algorithm for Specifying A Character Object

The following is the explanation of the algorithm in detail.

- Step 1(generating an object):
  - First, extract the character object(s) from the frame. Assumption 2 sets the maximum number of the objects extracted out. And extracted objects are indexed as ***obj(k-l){l=1..N}***. So ***obj(k-l),*** for example, is the number **l** object in **k** Frame.
- Step 2(Setting the initial status):
  - If there is only one object was extracted, according to Assumption 3, we use the **name of the speaker** as the **label of the object**.
  - If there are more than two objects extracted, according to Assumption 2, the names of people presumed to be in the frame are used as the would-be labels of the objects. That is to say, the names of the characters are used as a kind of candidate labels, taking form as ***obj(k-l).name***.
- Step 3 (Setting the link between the objects):
  - According to Assumption 1, by using the color information obtained from the objects, do the retrieval process in all the objects in order to find those objects of higher similarity. Then, set the link between similar objects. The most similar object is shown as ***obj (m-n).***
- Step 4 (Deciding the candidate labels)
  - To ascertain the intersection set of the character's name of the two linked objects. If the intersection set is a null set, the names of the two character objects are treated as the intersection set.
- Step 5 (Deciding other remaining objects)
  - If there is only one element in the intersection set, this element will be removed from the set of the name description of the all objects, except ***obj(k-l)*** and ***obj(m-n)*** in the **k** and **m** frame.
- Step 6(Tracking the link):
  - Following the link history of obj(m-n), go back to Step 4. If there is no more link to be traced back, the process will stop at obj(k-l), and for obj(k-l+1), the process will start from the second step.

By following these steps, the links are set for all the objects in **k** Frame, and the process will go to the next frame after the final link has made in **k** Frame.

In order to estimate the algorithm for specifying a character object, we did an experiment on a workstation and JAVA language was used. The sample videotape was 15 minutes long. We used 136 frames in total, 320x240 pixel, RGB 24bit. The sampling interval of the frames was 8 frames per minute. For the estimation, we classified the frames by the number of the character(s) in them. Recall rate[2] was 92%.

4.4 The Link Between the Character Objects

In order to define the similarity between the character objects, we can use the information on the locations, size and colors of such parts as the nose, eyes, mouth in the face, or the outline of

---

[2] The recall rate = extracted objects/ the total objects in frames.

the face, or the color of the hair or hairstyles, etc. However, it is difficult to extract such kind of feature from the image frame automatically.

For this reason, we use the color information of the clothes to calculate the similarity of the objects. That is to say, we divide the section of the clothes to 6x6, register the 36 sections in order according to their degrees of the similarity to the corresponding sections in another fames, and then calculate the average value of the top 24. What we have done above is to reduce the influence of the object motion and the background. The similarities of the targeted sections are calculated by using the algorithm [2].

For the estimation, we used 136 frames, and classified the frames by the number of the character(s) in them. Recall rate shows the rate of correct extraction of character object. E1 shows the percentage of successful specification of the character object; E2, though not that certain, is the percentage of right guess on the character object. As a result of the estimation of E1 and E2, 78% human objects can be specified or singled out.

4.5 Establishing the Hyper Linkage

From now on, hyper linkage will become one of necessary functions used in a Multimedia database for enabling the user to have a direct interactive dialog with the video data.

With the above algorithms, we can specify the characters in the video. For example, when we click the video, if the clicked part is the character, we can get the character's name, and according to the name, we can go to the hyper page from which one may see the resume of that character, or other relevant information from WEB.

4.6 System Implement

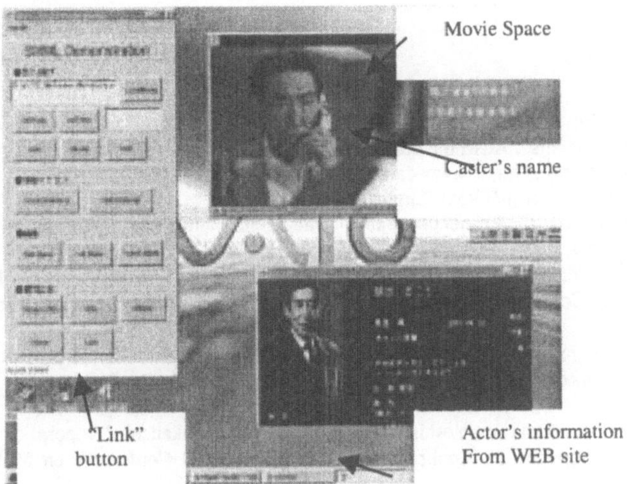

Figure 3an Interface for object-base linkage

VSDL-TV provides us with a library of powerful fundamental methods. By using these methods, the character specifying algorithm mentioned above could be made out.

For example, ***getColor(object)*** is the method for extracting the color information of the object.

getHistDistance(Image im1,Image im2) is a method for calculating *the similarity of the two frames* by using [2] Color histogram algorithm. ***getUpperOjbect(object1)*** is a method for getting the object2 superior

than object1.***getLowerOjbect(object1)*** is a method for getting the object2 lower than object1.For ***getUpperOjbect(object1)*** and ***getLowerOjbect(object1)***, the position managing of the objects and/or sections methods are also be used, such as: ***isupper(object1)*** or ***islower(object1)***. Combining the above methods, we implemented the object-base hypermedia authoring system shown as Figure 3.
While a movie is shown in the "Movie Space", when we click the face of a character, we may have the relevant information on his name. After the name has been shown out, for some further ready information on the character, we may access to a stars information database by clicking the [LINK] button. The URLs on the Web may also be used to help check out the relevant information on the Internet.

5. Conclusions

In this paper, for showing the potential ability of implementing the multimedia application based on our proposed ***VSDL-TV***, we have used an XML-based movie video description language—***VSDL-TV*** to introduce "*Movie Video Hypermedia Authoring System*".
In this system, we use two algorithms to realize the hypermedia authoring. One is frame-based and the other is object-based.
For the frame-based authoring, the results of ***DP matching*** between the video and the script are used.
For the object-based authoring, we provide the description (name) of the character object by combining the information from the script with that of video analysis. As a result, we can specify the character that is in the scene of the video being replayed, and find the linkage information from the Web site based on the character name. This algorithm can also be used as "Query and answer about the character in the video", and in a more flexible scene retrieval such as "find the scene that A is right to B".
This system can be used as a tool to produce games such as "love simulation" or "adventure game", and etc.
In the near future, we will focus on the object segmentation; find a good way to make out the description of an object. Meanwhile we will also focus on the completion of the framework ***VSDL-TV*** through adding more fundamental methods and application-oriented methods, such as auto linkage methods.

6. References

[1] Michael J. Hu, Ye Jian: "Multimedia Description Framework (MDF) for Content Description of Audio/Video Documents", ACM the 4th Conference on Digital Libraries Proc.
[2] MPEG-7 Main page, "http://www.darmstadt.gmd.de/mobile/MPEG7/"
[3] http://www.strl.nhk.or.jp/TVML/English/E01.html
[4] P. Senthil Kumar, G. Phanendra Babu, "Intelligent multimedia data: data + indices+ inference", Multimedia Systems, 6:395-407(1998).
[5] Sato, S., Kanade, T., "NAME-IT: Association of Face and Name in Video." In Proceedings of IEEE Computer Society Conference on Computer Vision and Pattern Recognition, San Juan, Puerto Rico, 17-19 June, 1997.
[6] Yoshitomo Yaginuma, Masao Sakauchi, "Content-Based Retrieval and Decomposition of TV Drama based on Inter-media Synchronization", First International Conference on Visual Information Systems.1996.
[7] Wenli Zhang, YunYun Cao, Yoshitomo Yaginuma, Masao Sakauchi, "Proposal of Movie Video Stream Description Language and its Application", IEEE International Conference on Multimedia and EXPO, Tokyo, Japan (2001-08)
[8] http://www.mars.dti.ne.jp/~y-sato/wffm/
[9] http://java.sun.com/products/java-media/jmf/index.html
[10] http://www.smi.co.jp/web-cm/smil/about.html
[11] http://www.w3.org/History.html
[12] http://www.cybercoaster.org/
[13] Wei-hsiu Ma, Yen-Jen Lee, David H.C.Du, and Mark P.McCahill."Video-based Hypermedia for Education-on-Demand", IEEE Multimedia, pp71-83, January-March, 1998.

Design Considerations for the Video Analyzer SDK

Frank Wang, Grace Lian, Jeff Zheng

Intel China Software Lab
22nd Floor, ShanghaiMart Tower, No.2299 Yan'an Road (West)
Shanghai 200336, P.R.C
{Frank.Wang, Grace.Lian, Jeff.Zheng}@intel.com

Abstract. Technology advances in video capture, storage, and distribution, give rise to the need for efficient video indexing, retrieval, editing and navigation. These applications often are built on top of video analyzers, which, up to present, are available only to high-end developers or professional uses. This paper presents our experience in developing a video analyzer tool kit (SDK) that will enable software vendors to develop easy to use video applications for the mass PC users. Our SDK creates video summary automatically using the state of the art shot detection algorithms. It is interactive, efficient, intuitive and easy to use. The SDK enables application areas ranging from PC users for customizing their home video, Internet content providers for publishing video summary, and researchers for advanced video content analysis. The SDK also contains user-friendly interfaces and APIs for performing cut, copy, paste, merge and split operations.

1. Introduction

Video is a natural and effective media for entertainment, advertising, presentation, training, and education. The rapid advances in video capture, storage, and distribution technologies, coupled with the ubiquity of PC, call for compelling applications that enable average PC users to create and manipulate video clips as easy as managing text documents. In addition, the vast amount of multimedia information available in the Internet demands intuitive and efficient indexing, searching, and browsing support

Unlike text documents, automatic search and navigation among vast volume and semantic-less video and audio information is a challenging task. Content-based retrieval and analysis is one possible way to tackle this problem. It however needs to extract knowledge from video and audio and transform them into semantic presentations that are effective for further analysis. This transformation is non-trivial and has not been proven capable of providing satisfactory performance on a PC if raw video is used as the only input.

Another way of resolving the problem evolves around video segmentations or shot detections. Algorithm based on compressed domain provides high performance and accurate detection results. These algorithms detect the effects of hard cut, fade, and dissolve, etc. in a video. Segmenting the raw video abstracts the video, which is the base of further complex video analysis algorithms. It also has the potential to reduce the bandwidth required by streaming and boost the interactivity because video can be streamed from any point. For home video users, the solution enables them to customize their favorite views. Combined with other technologies, video segmentation can play major roles in video editing, remote education, and training.

While there have been much research work reported in the video segmentation area based on various shot detection algorithms [1][2][3], commercial applications are limited mainly to high-end applications. In this paper, we attempt to report our efforts and experiences in developing such a product for PC platforms. Our video analyzer tool kit (SDK) enables application areas ranging from customizing home video for PC users, publishing video summary for Internet content providers, and advanced video content analysis for researchers. The SDK also contains user-friendly APIs for performing cut, copy, paste, merge and split operations.

The toolkit is powered by COM and ActiveX technologies and enables users to manage their MPEG1 and MPEG2 video assets through the concept of video summary, create their own applications capable of publishing, re-purposing and analyzing video. One of the key features is that it provides random access to any frame and is considerably faster than commercially available libraries.

The remainder of this paper is organized as follows. Section 2 discusses the governing architecture of the video analyzer SDK. It outlines the marketing requirements and presents the resulting architecture for accommodating the requirements. Section 3 provides detailed descriptions of all major components making up the SDK. Section 4 presents the performance number. We then summarize our key learning in section 5.

2. Architecture

Before describing the architecture design of our video summary SDK, we will first briefly list the major marketing requirements:

- Detect hard cut, fade in/out with the flexibility to add new scene events
- Edit video, such as copy, paste, etc, to create different views
- Flexible video playback for different views, not just a MPEG player
- Easy integration with MS environment
- Support Internet content provide
- Support third party decoder
- Support local and streaming video sources
- Support MPEG1 and MPEG2 video format

Traditional waterfall development life cycle and iterative and incremental development life cycle (such as Rational Unified Process) dominates the whole software development. Waterfall process is a top-down or bottom-up process and works well for procedure base development. Iterative and incremental process is neither strictly top-down nor bottom-up and works well for object-oriented, frequent requirements change and high-risk projects.

Our SDK follows the object-oriented development style. As a result we adopt the iterative and incremental development life cycle as our process. Due to the length limitation, we will focus our paper more on object-oriented analysis and design but little on implementation and deployment.

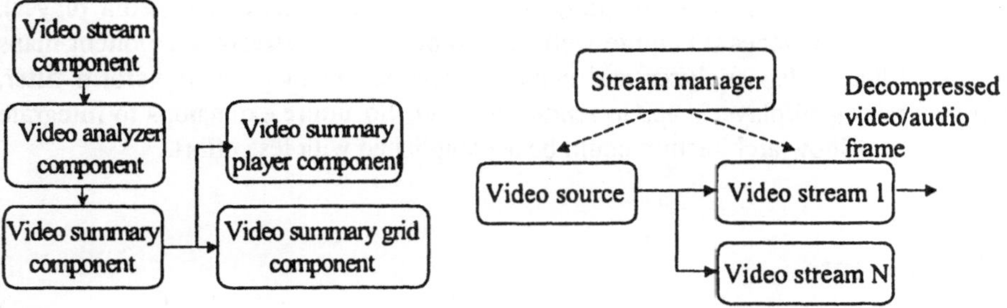

Fig. 1. Architectural view of our SDK

Fig. 2. Internal architecture of stream component

To define the architecture of our SDK, we need to describe the problem from the perspective of software engineering. The following description depicts a basic scenario to guide the design of the architecture:

The SDK reads different video sources, such as local MPEG video file, streaming MPEG video source and broadcast video source. The MPEG decoder decodes the video. We used MPL (Intel's MPEG decoding library) for that purpose. A third party decoder may be plugged in if needed. Decompressed video frames and audio frames will be rendered on display or analyzed by our algorithm. The algorithm currently shall support hard cut, fade in/out and dissolve detection algorithm. Future extensions to new algorithm shall also be easily achieved. When a frame is ready all the algorithms will be triggered. If the algorithm detects a segment, it sends out events. The event specifies the position where the event happened, and the event kind. These events are used to define shot and shot sequence, which are called video summary. User can access the shot and shot sequence, and use cut, paste, merge and split operations to edit the shot sequence. We shall also provide an API to customize shots and shot sequences. It's computationally intensive to create the raw shot sequence and hence it's useful to keep this information persistently and load it next time. The shot sequence is better displayed in a grid. The representative frame is a good method to represent a shot. A player renders the shot sequence in display. The play order of each frame in the video is defined by the shot sequence.

In the above scenario, we can discover these objects: video source, local/streaming/broadcast video source, decoder, MPL/third party decoder, decompressed video/audio frame, algorithm, shot detection algorithms (e.g. hard cut, fade in/out, dissolve), event, shot, shot sequence, permanent storage, representative frame, grid, and player. Here logically related objects shall be grouped and the dependencies among groups shall be minimized. The video source and decoder are closely related and the decompressed video/audio frame serves as the interface to other components. Algorithm, hard cut/fade in/out/dissolve detection algorithms are closely related and the event serves as the interface to other components. Shot, shot sequence and permanent storage are closely related. Representative frame and grid are closely related. Player is a separate group. Based on these analyses, we defined five cohesive and loosely coupled components. The five components constitute our architecture, and are defined as video stream component, video analyzer component, video summary component, video summary player component and video summary grid component respectively. Their relationships are described in Figure 1. Another consideration for the architecture design is to map it to Microsoft DirectShow. In Microsoft DirectShow architecture, connected filters are used to process the multimedia data. Typical filters include source filter (reading the source), transform filter (such as decoding, transforming) and rendering filter (such as media player). Our architecture matches this quite well, for example, video stream component maps to source filter, video analyzer and summary component maps to transform filter, video summary grid/player maps to rendering filter. So future extensions to integrate with the DirectShow architecture could be accomplished with less effort.

3. Components

3.1 Video Stream Component

The video stream component is tightly coupled with Intel Media Processing Library to provide the decoding service of MPEG1 and MPEG2 video. It provides decoding functions to all the other components.

From the above requirement description, we are required to provide abstractions for the video source. The video stream component is expected to read more than one kind of video source, such as local MPEG video, streaming video and broadcast video. As we investigated, we learned that different video sources have behaviors in common. All of them need to provide a way to notify the decoder to decode. However streaming video, real-time and rate control are the most important. The behavior of each video source is not trivial. So the abstraction of MPEG1/2 video source defines the crisp boundaries between the video source and the MPEG decoder. This division makes the design extensible to new video sources in the future. It reads the video source (reading ahead) and notifies decoder to decode. It's a kind of push model.

To consider the circumstance when the video source is real-time broadcast video, we need two components to process the video synchronously, one component to analyze the video and the other to play it. Instantiating two copies of this component is expensive. So we create the video stream sub-component. One or more video stream objects may exist in system and work synchronized to stream the video/audio frames downward. The role of video stream is to decode the video source and push the decompressed video/audio frame to the other components. We put the decoder in the video stream sub-component mainly because different users of the same video source have different decoding requirements. For example, the analyzer may only need the reduced-coefficient decoding while the player may need full decompression.

To support third party decoders in the future (for example, some decoders feature powerful error correction), it's helpful to provide an adaptation layer above all the decoders. So we use the abstract base class with the interfaces clearly defined for other decoders to use as an interface with. Our decoder is a derived class and provides all the detail implementations. Future extensions to third party decoder can be easily achieved.

Stream manager sub-component is relatively complex. It controls how, when and what to be delivered to other components. Below are two important design considerations for stream manager:

- Provide video/audio synchronization and real-time support. The advantage of putting them in stream manager is that it defines clear boundaries, and also encapsulates all decoder-related details. Synchronization is achieved by comparing timestamps attached to audio and video frames. To provide real-time support, we baseline the video present timestamp with a real-time clock, and if it's too slow we ask decoder to skip frames. To support non-real-time requirements, such as analyzer, stream manager can also deliver video/audio frames in maximized speed.

- Notification management. Notifications could be classified into two groups, one set comes from decoder (such as new video frame) and the other set comes from stream manager (such as state change). Because all the users are connected through the video stream, we propagate all the notifications through video stream sub-component. We therefore assume that direct users of this component are responsible to route notifications to their users. So this design enables all users, either direct or indirect, to receive the notifications.

So the internal architecture involves three major sub-components. Figure2 shows the internal architecture of this component.

3.2 Video Analyzer Component

The video analyzer component contains the shot detection algorithms (hard cut, fade in/out, dissolve) and is activated to work whenever an audio frame or video frame is decompressed. For details of these algorithms, please refer to reference [1][2][3]. We design the algorithms in object-oriented method, and make them work within our architecture. The video analyzer component contains mainly two modules, frame buffer and algorithm.

Providing abstractions for audio and video frame buffers encapsulates all the details of image operation. The above algorithm only needs the video frames buffer. The size of buffer is determined by the maximum value required by the algorithms to work properly. Intel Image Processing Library (IPL) is used for image operation for its optimized high performance on Intel CPU family.

The algorithm module contains three algorithm objects: hard cut, fade in/out and dissolve detection algorithm. We found these objects to have features, or behaviors in common. First, all the algorithms need to read data from frame buffer. Second, all the algorithms are segment detection algorithms. Third, all the algorithms need to send out events if their event of interest is detected. So we create an abstract base class that defines all these common behaviors, and from which all algorithms are derived. The derived class provides the actual detection algorithm and specifies which kind of event to fire. The video summary component receives these events to construct shot sequences. All algorithms are linked in a list and will be triggered in turn. To meet different requirements of performance and application, each algorithm could be disabled or enabled at run time. We can envision extending the system to support new segment detection algorithms, such as pan detection, etc. can be easily achieved.

3.3 Video Summary Component

We designed the video summary component as a medium component that processes the analyzer events, constructs different views, and notifies grid and player components to render them. Summary also provides persistent archive for the analyzed results. The design considerations mainly involve: multiple shot sequences, advise list, reference counting and persistence. Before we describe them, we would first go through two intuitive definitions:

– A ***Shot*** is a collection of consecutive video frames. Shots can be generated by the video analyzer in which case each shot is a sequence of frames that were shot contiguously in time by a single camera position, of a single subject. Shots have three kinds: transition (such as fade in/out, dissolve), non-transition and edited (not created by analyzer).
– A ***Shot sequence*** is an ordered list of shots, which can be represented as a sequence of still images (representative frames). The shots can be accessed directly and are played in a pre-determined order.

Video summary abstraction provides the interface, which lets user treat video from a different viewpoint. The most important is the multiple shot sequence support. Multiple shot sequences provide different views of a video. For different users, they probably hope to customize it according to their different experiences. Multiple shot sequences just provide such kind of support. At the very beginning, a raw shot sequence is created as the result of processing analyzer detection events. The sequence serves as the start point for future customization. Operations on raw shot sequence, such as cut, copy, paste, create a new one, etc. Multiple shot sequences could also be used for a hierarchical video summary. We could hope video summary to be analogous to table contents, then a shot sequence is a table of contents entry, and the shot is the page. At that time, video can be treated exactly as a well-organized document.

Event management and memory management are also two key points that especially need to be considered here. The video summary component may have more than one user at the same time, such as video grid, summary player or user application. So reference counting and an advice list are helpful for memory management and for event firing.

Video summary also loads or saves its state to persistent storage in a binary format, called summary file. The advantage of binary format is it's easy and efficient to parse and can't be accidentally changed. Next time, user can load the summary file and enjoy what's he created last time. Future extension to plain text (such as XML presentation) to open the interface and will provide more flexibility without impacting other components.

Easily porting components while keep it easy to use in Microsoft platform also needs consideration. Instead of using COM wizard to glue everything together, video Summary is implemented independently and wrapped with a COM wrapper outside. So in Microsoft environment, it's a COM component and can be easily worked with Visual C++, Visual Basic, etc. As you can see from here, video summary, video analyzer and video stream constitutes the basic workable unit and can all be ported to other platform easily.

3.4 Video Summary Player Component (VSPlayer)

The video summary player component plays the video according to the selected shot sequence in video summary. It's designed as an ActiveX control so it can be easily integrated into a Microsoft environment. VSPlayer implements the methods of a general MPEG player. But it also provides more elegant controls over the video playing. It plays the video according to the view (shot sequence) customized by user. User can easily navigate among the shots in a sequence by skipping forward or backward to next shot, selecting a particular shot to play, set the shot number range, skipping frame by frame, play in loop etc.

3.5 Video Summary Grid Component (VSGrid)

We designed a VSGrid component in order to have a static graphic view for video summary. It displays the representative frame of each shot, which is defined as the frame in the middle. For the same reason as VSPlayer, it is designed as a full ActiveX control. VSGrid component provides the user-friendly GUI to customize your view of a video. Cut, copy, paste, drag and drop, merge and split operations based on video summary interfaces, and performed through context menu. They are frame based to provide accuracy editing capability. The following is a screen shot of VSGrid.

It's important here to balance the performance and interactivity. It's our assumption that a user would be able to select an already detected shot in VSGrid and start to playback even though video analysis is not completed. We would use VSPlayer for the playback, but we also need to decide how and when to decode the representative frames. We have lots choices, and we selected the following as our final decision: open anther stream manager expressly for retrieving representative frames. This method is easy, clean and interactive, but it is inefficient and could have a long startup-time, use of more memory and CPU initialization. We selected the method, because the initialization of stream manager is only once and actually not too CPU/memory intensive.

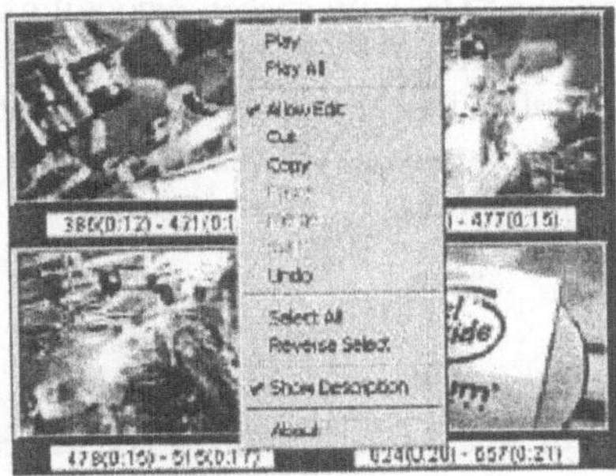

Fig. 2. Screen shot of VSGrid control.

4. Performance

The accuracy of hard cut detection is above 99%. The accuracy of fade in/out detection is near 95%. The following list shows the performances of our SDK with hard cut and fade in/out algorithms enabled. The data is based on Intel PIII 600 MHz CPU and Microsoft Window98. For 657M (01h-04min-57sec) MPEG1 file in local HD, it needs 02min-12sec to detect hard cut and fade in/out. For 657M (01h-04min-

57sec) MPEG1 file in local CDROM, it needs 7min-05sec to detect hard cut and fade in/out. We can see here that storage media is the bottleneck, so we suggest analyzing video from hard disk. Upgrading your hard disk to SCSI will also help performance.

5. Summary and Future Work

In this paper, we have reported our experiences in developing a video analyzer SDK product for PC platforms. We showed how we followed a rigorous software engineering process and devised an SDK that forms a solid and extensible foundation for many potential video application products. The SDK has been released to several multimedia application vendors to be included in their commercial products.

In addition to working with ISVs to roll out more products based on the SDK, we are working toward expanding the tool kit on three fronts. First, we will support more elaborate shot detection techniques as well as content-based analysis algorithms. Examples of algorithms we are currently pursuing include audio analysis, color/texture analysis, scene detection, text extraction, etc. Audio analysis could be used to detect the commercials in a video. Scene detection is based on shots and links the shots by semantics. Text extraction could be useful especially if the video contains captions, such as MTV. The combined capability will enable more elegant and effective navigation across a long video.

Second, we are extending video streaming capability to enable efficient video contents consumption over the Internet. The random video access advantage provided by our SDK coupled with streaming will provide rich interactive experience and conserve precious bandwidth. Furthermore, by combining transcoding technology, video clips processed through our SDK could be conveniently accessed by all kinds of embedded devices.

Third, we are combining our SDK with speech recognition, text to speech, and natural language processing technologies to form an intelligent multimedia foundation to enable a richer class of applications. Remote education and interactive multimedia training are a few among many possible application areas for this technology.

6. Reference

[1] R. Lienhart. Comparison of Automatic Shot Boundary Detection Algorithms. In Storage and Retrieval for Image and Video Databases VII, SPIE Vol. 3656, pp. 290 –301, Jan. 1999

[2] B. Davies, R. Lienhart and B. -L. Yeo. The Video Document. Multimedia Storage and Archiving Systems IV, SPIE Vol. 3846, pp. 22-34, 20-22 September 1999

[3] B. -L. Yeo and B. Liu. Rapid Scene Analysis on Compressed Video. IEEE Transactions on Circuits and Systems for Video Technology, Vol. 5, No. 6, pp. 533-544, December 1995

[4] Booch. G. Object-Oriented Analysis and Design. Addison-Wesley

Network-Adaptive Cache Management Schemes for Mixed Media

Fang Yu Qian Zhang Wenwu Zhu Ya-Qin Zhang

Microsoft Research, China
No. 49, Zhichun Road, Haidian District
Beijing, 100080, P.R. China

ABSTRACT

For efficently caching mixed-media, this paper discusses several network-adaptive cache management schemes. Considering the characteristics of different types of media, we first proposed a multi-level page-size management scheme. Then, a media-characteristic-weighted replacement policy is presented to improve the hit ratio of mixed media including continuous and non-continuous media. Lastly, a network-condition- and media-quality-adaptive resource management mechanism is described to dynamically re-allocate cache resource for different types of media according to their request patterns. Simulation results demonstrate effectiveness of our propsoed approaches.

I. INTRODUCTION

With the popularity of the World Wide Web, web proxy caching has become a useful approach for it can alleviate network congestion and reduce latency through distributing network load. Traditional proxy servers were designed to serve web requests for non-continuous media, such as textual and image objects [1]. With the increasing advent of video and audio streaming applications, continuous-media caching has been studied in [2, 3]. Most recently, there has been interest in caching both continuous and non-continuous media [4].

Replacement policy is one of the key components in the proxy design. The existing caching replacement policies for Web data can be roughly categorized as recency-based and frequency-based. Recency-based algorithms, e.g., LRU (Least Recently Used) [5], exploit the locality of reference inherently in the programs. While frequency-based algorithms, e.g., LFU (Least Frequently Used) [6], are suited for skewed access patterns in which a large fraction of the accesses goes to a disproportionately small set of hot objects. To balance frequency- and recency-based algorithms, several improved algorithms named LRU-k and LRFU are proposed in [7].

For most of the data accessed on the web today, which contain text and static images, the above algorithms seem adequate. As streaming of continuous media data becomes popular, different media characteristics and access patterns need to be considered. To the best of our knowledge, to date fewer works have clearly addressed how to efficiently cache mixed media, especially for multimedia streaming applications. In [5], a cache replacement algorithm for mixed media according to media's bandwidth and space requirement is proposed. However, the bandwidth resource considered therein is the fixed bandwidth of the disk, rather than the varying network-bandwidth from client to proxy and from proxy to server.

Considering the heterogeneous network conditions and characteristics of mixed media, we proposed an end-to-end caching architecture for multimedia streaming over the Internet [8]. This paper addresses cache-management issue and proposes several network-adaptive cache management approaches. First, a multi-level page-size management scheme is introduced to satisfy the different size requirement of mixed media. Secondly, a media-characteristic-weighted replacement policy is proposed to improve the hit ratio of mixed media. Lastly, a network-condition- and media-quality-adaptive resource management mechanism is presented to dynamically re-allocate cache resource for mixed media according to their request patterns.

II. CACHE RESOURCE MANAGEMENT

Figure 1 illustrates architecture of our network-adaptive caching for mixed media. The *cache resource allocation* module periodically re-allocates the current resource according to the media characteristics, the access frequencies of different types of media, and the varying network conditions of client-proxy and proxy-server. In this section, we address several issues of cache resource management such as page size management, cache replacement policy, and cache resource re-allocation by considering the media characteristics and network conditions.

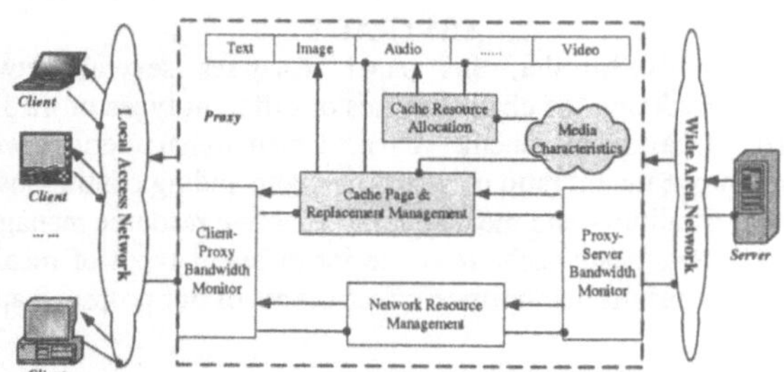

Figure 1. The diagram of our proposed network-adaptive caching scheme for mixed media.

2.1 Multiple-level Page-size Management Scheme

It is known that different types of media have different sizes. For example, text object may have the smallest size, image object may have medium size, audio object may have medium high size, and video object may have the largest size. For video object, each frame (e.g., I, B, and P) also has different sizes. In the case of multi-layer scalable video, it assumes that base layer has the smallest size, and the sizes of enhancement layers are increased gradually. As we know, the traditional proxy server supports fixed page size. It, however, may not be suited for mixed media caching. If the page size is large, it is not good for caching text object since the resource is wasted. On the other hand, if the page size is small, video object may have a large index. Considering the variable bit rate (VBR) nature of the continuous media, one may naturally consider to assign unequal page sizes to each different frame. However, it may be complex and difficult in terms of the cache management.

Considering both the complexity and efficiency of page management, we propose a multiple level page size management scheme, which adopts different page sizes for different types of media. To be specific, for the same type of media, the page size is fixed. For instance, we may have the following page size relation, $S_1 < S_2 < S_3 < S_4 < S_5 < S_6$, where S_1 is for text, S_2 is for image, S_3 is for audio, S_4 is for video B frame, S_5 is for video P frame, and S_6 is for video I frame. In the cache we store the objects of the same level together, as shown in Figure 2. Our proposed scheme works as follows. We first divide psychical cache into several parts. Each part stores a specified type of media and the page size of each part is equal. However, different parts have different page sizes. Specifically, the two adjacent parts have different page sizes, and the latter one is multiple of the former one. The space each type of media occupies is variable and adaptively changes according to the hit/miss ratio. After the specific period of time, we enlarge the space of the media with high hit-ratio and decrease the one with high miss-ratio. The details will be discussed later.

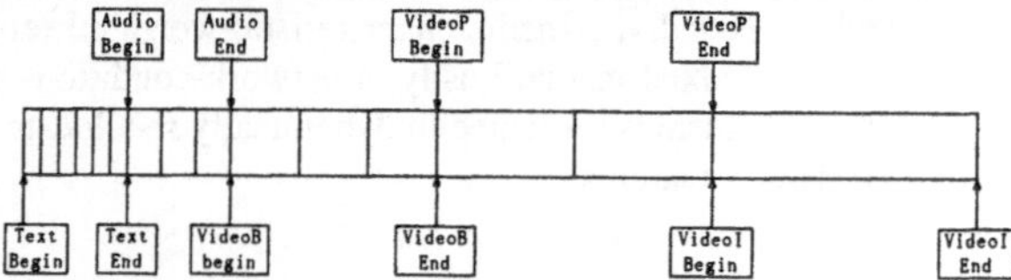

Figure 2. A multiple-level page size management scheme.

2.2 Media-characteristic-weighted Cache Replacement Policy

In general, a proxy server has a fixed amount of storage. When the storage fills up, the proxy must choose one or more media objects based on a certain caching replacement policy. The goal of the replacement policy is to make the best use of available resources, including disk and memory space as well as network bandwidth. To achieve this goal, the cache replacement policy should be able to accurately predict future popularity of objects and determine how to use its limited space in the most advantageous way.

Media characteristics could significantly affect the performance of the caching replacement algorithm. Specifically, first, different types of media have different request patterns. For continuous media, it has tendency to be sequentially accessed; in the meanwhile, there exists certain reference relation among media objects (e.g., the P and B frames in a video sequence highly depends on the I frame). As for non-continuous media objects, they are usually randomly and independently accessed. Secondly, different types of media have different quality impacts, e.g., audio object may have higher quality impact than that of video object. Thirdly, different types of media have different sizes. Taking network bandwidth, storage space, and media characteristic into consideration, we propose a media-characteristic-weighted replacement policy (MCW-n) for mixed media caching.

In our scheme, each object in the cache has a weight as a measure for replacement. When a new object comes in, if there is no free space in the cache, the proxy flushes out the object with the lowest weight. As discussed above, the value of the caching gain not only depends on the estimation of the time-to-reaccess (TTR) or the access probability of the object, but also depends on the importance of the object. Therefore, the weight function is defined as follows:

$$W = Priority \times (\beta \times Tendency + (1-\beta) \times Frequency), \quad (1)$$

where *Priority* represents the importance of an object. The proxy can assign different priorities to different types of objects. The priority assignment may depend on different applications. *Tendency* indicates the impact of the current request on the following requests according to the continual characteristic of the media. *Frequency* represents the popularity of the object to be accessed. β is the control parameter balancing the impact between *Tendency* and *Frequency*.

Tendency shows the probability of the following requests' hitness. For text and images, we may use data mining rule to calculate probability of the following requests' hitness. As for the continuous media such as audio and video, *Tendency* essentially represents continuity of the continuous media in the time scale. Because the continuous media is usually highly correlated, one can infer the future events from the past ones. Upon receiving a request of the video or audio object in the proxy, the weights of objects residing within the pre-determined window are enhanced according to the weight calculation function. There are several approaches for calculating *Tendency* of a certain media. One way is to use a mathematical distribution such as Gaussian distribution to represent *Tendency*.

We can use the method proposed in [9] to calculate *Frequency*, which is described as follows.

$$Frequency = 1 / MTTR, \quad (2)$$

where *MTTR* (mean time-to-re-access) is measured as the weighted sum of the inter-arrival times between the previous accesses. Denote the access times of the last *n* accesses as t_n, $t_{n-1}, \ldots, t_0$, where t_i is the time of the last i^{th} access. Let the weighting function, *w(i)*, satisfy

$$w(i) = \alpha \times w(i-1), \alpha \le 1 \text{ and } w(0) = 1 - \alpha . \quad (3)$$

Then we have

$$MTTR = \sum_{i \ge 0} (t_i - t_{i-1}) \times w(i) \cdot \quad (4)$$

Thus, for a given time t_0, $MTTR(t_0) = (1-\alpha)(t_0 - t_1) + \alpha \times MTTR(t_1)$. Note that the averaging factor α can be tuned to a bias for or against recently.

In summary, our proposed caching replacement policy (MCW-n) has the following characteristics:

- It can store the media objects hierarchically based on their priorities. For example, enhancement layer alone is not useful if the base layer or the lower layers are missed. Our algorithms ensure that we drive out the higher layers (less important layers) first by setting their priorities.
- Since tendency, frequency and priority are used to determine the weight of each object, we can increase the hit ratio for continuous media and non-continuous media simultaneously.
- It supports VCR functions of video. To be specific, I frame has higher priority and thus has higher weight. When a VCR function (e.g., forward) is triggered, though the media of that part is not fully in the cache, we can still send back some related I frame. In the case of scalable video, lower layer has higher priority, thus it has lower probability to be driven out.

2.3 Network-condition- and Media-quality-adaptive Resource Re-allocation Scheme

As discussed above, we adopted the multiple-level page size management approach for caching mixed media. We divide the physical cache into several parts. Each part stores a specified type of media with fixed page size. Moreover, two adjacent media have different page sizes, one is multiple of the other. Based on media characteristics, different types of media need to occupy different cache resource. That is, larger resource is usually allocated to continuous media, such as video and audio, than non-continuous media such as text and image. Note that in our scheme cache is not divided based on a fixed proportion. In addition, with the varying network conditions and media request patterns in mind, we periodically re-allocate the cache resource to dynamically match the present condition.

To efficiently re-allocate the cache resource, several issues are addressed in our scheme. First, we take the priorities of different media into account. For example, text's priority is usually very high. As a result, text will be replaced last. In the case of scalable media such as video, the priority of base layer should be set higher than that of enhancement layers so that relatively more objects of base layer can be kept in the cache. Secondly, the size that each media currently occupies is considered. Thirdly, the miss ratio, which shows how often the cache cannot meet client requests, is considered.

Ideally, the optimal solution can be achieved by establishing the relation between miss-ratio gain and cache resource requirement for each type of media. For the sake of simplicity, here we present a simple criterion for resource re-allocation. Let S_i represent the size that the media i currently occupies, P_i denote the priority of the media i, and MR_i represent miss ratio for the ith media. Then, the re-allocation demand D_i for the ith media can be calculated as:

$$D_i = P_i \times MR_i \Big/ S_i \,. \qquad (5)$$

The re-allocation demand for each type of media, D_i , is calculated and sorted as $D_1' < D_2' \ldots < D_m'$. The threshold value δ is introduced to determine whether it is necessary to re-allocate cache resource among different types of media. If $D_m' - D_1' < \delta$, then all the media are in a similar condition and no cache resource should be moved. This can reduce the possibility of thrashing.

Suppose *video* media has the highest *re-allocation demand* and *text* media has the lowest *re-allocation demand*. The number of pages the text media occupies should be reduced and the number of pages the video object occupies should be increased accordingly. Even if the pages that are required to move are not adjacent, proxy can move page pointer, as illustrated in Figure 3, using the scheme described as follows.

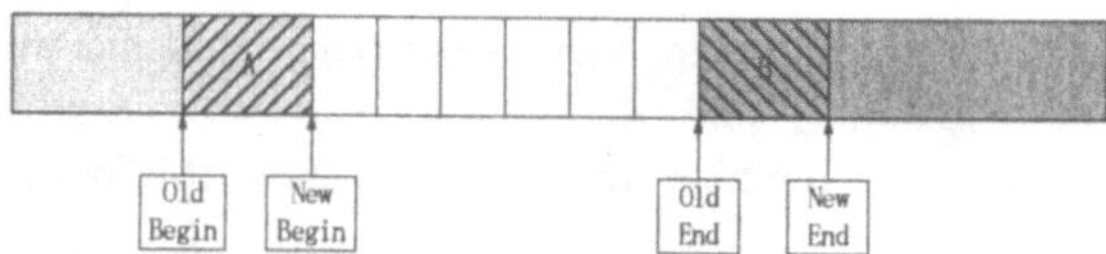

Figure 3. Caching resource re-allocation.

If $D_m' - D_1' \geq k \times \delta$ *for* $k > 1$, Then, re-allocate some resource from media m to media 1. More specifically,

$$\left| \frac{\sqrt{PageSize_m \times PageSize_1}}{Max_{pagesize}} \times k \right| \times \frac{Max_{pagesize}}{PageSize_m} \qquad (6)$$

pages are moved from media *m* to media *1*. Repeat the above procedure until $D_{m-i}' - D_{i+1}' \leq \delta$.

Since the page size of media *m* may differ greatly from the one of media 1, $\sqrt{PageSize_m \times PageSize_1}$ is calculated as the average page size from media *m* to media 1. In addition, we should move *m* times the predefined moving page number if the difference of $N_m' - N_1'$ is *k* times δ. Furthermore, we want to re-allocate the cache resource as multiple of largest page size in the cache, $Max_{pagesize}$, so that it is easy to re-allocate the cache resource and no fragment in the cache occurs. Note that because the two media have different page sizes and the current one is multiple of the precious one, page movement can be achieved by just moving the pointer of the previous one's *end* and that of the current one's *begin*.

III. SIMULATION RESULTS

The purpose of our simulation is to demonstrate the effectiveness of our media-characteristic-weighted replacement policy, MCW-2, and our dynamic cache resource re-allocation scheme.

Client requests follow Zipf distribution with the ON/OFF behavior in our simulation [7]. The following Pareto probability distribution is adopted to model ON/OFF behavior:

$$\Gamma_w(t_w) = 1 - e^{-(\frac{t_w}{a})^b}, \qquad (7)$$

where $a = 0.328$ and $b = 1.47$.

Table 1 depicts the distribution pattern of client requests among different media shown in [10]. We use the average distribution of those data to generate requests in our simulation.

Table 1. Breakdown of document types and sizes for all data sets

Web Server	HTML (%)	Images (%)	Sound (%)	Video (%)	Dynamic (%)	Formatted (%)	Other (%)
Waterloo	38.7	50.1	0.01	0.006	0.3	3.7	7.184
Calgary	47.1	50.3	0.1	0.3	0.04	1.0	1.16
Saskatchewan	55.6	36.5	0.1	0.004	6.7	0.02	1.076
NASA	30.7	63.5	0.2	1.0	2.6	0.01	1.99
ClarkNet	19.9	78.0	0.2	0.007	1.2	0.01	0.683
NCSA	51.1	48.1	0.2	0.1	0.01	0.006	0.484

The generated requests under different distributions for different types of media are shown in Figure 4. Note that we do give large variation to the requests of continuous media, but because the number of requests for continuous media is rather small compared to that of other media, it can't be shown proportionally in this figure. In fact, even a very small variation in continuous-media requests will affect the caching performance greatly, because the huge amount of data needs to be transferred for one request.

A layered scalable codec, PFGS [11], is used as video object. PFGS encodes input video into two layers: one is the base layer (BL) that carries the most important information; the other is the enhancement layer (EL) that carries less important information. Different priorities are assigned for BL and EL.

We conducted simulations under different kinds of network conditions. The bandwidth between clients and proxy varies from 100kb/s to 1100kb/s, and varies from 800kb/s to 3000kb/s between proxy and server.

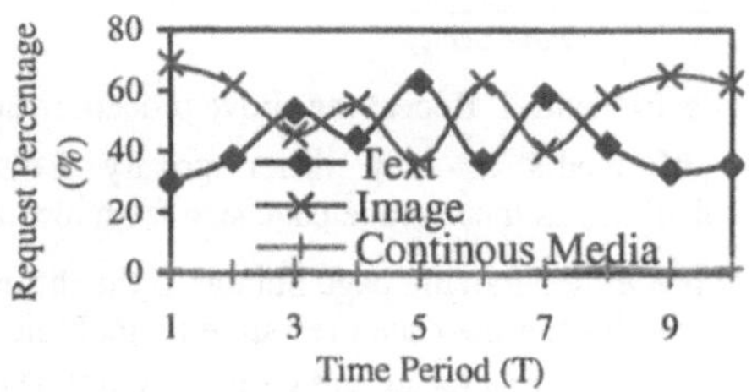

Figure 4. The variation of requests from different types of media.

A. Performance of replacement policy

This simulation is to demonstrate effectiveness of our media-characteristic-weighted replacement policy, MCW-2. The MCW-2 algorithm is compared with the recency-based replacement policy using LRU-2. The total caching size varies from 3M to 21M (Bytes).

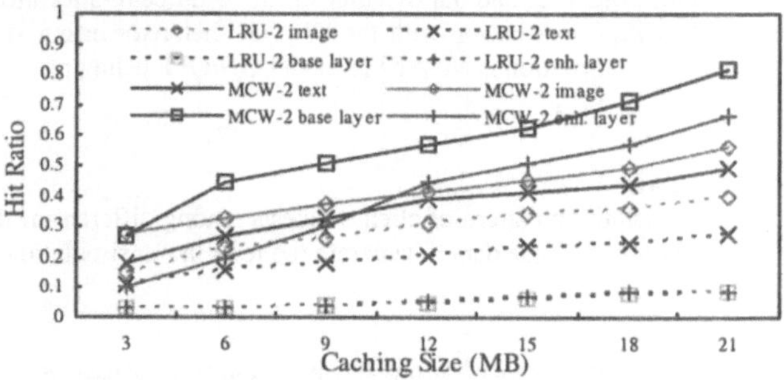

Figure 5. Comparison of MCW-2 and LRU-2 for all types of media.

Figure 5 shows comparison results of hit ratio for mixed media using MCW-2 and LRU-2. It can be seen that MCW-2 outperforms LRU-2 for all types of media. Having considered the tendency and priority of continuous media in MCW-2, the hit ratio of continuous media, especially for the base layer of the media, is significantly higher than the one obtained by LRU-2.

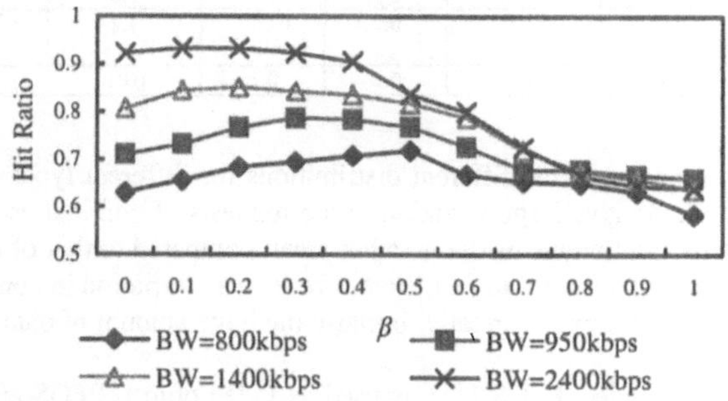

Figure 6. Performance of parameter β in the weight function under different conditions.

Next, we analyze the cache performance under different β values in the weighting function. If parameter β is 0, we use the tendency as the only criterion for weight. If the parameter β is set to 1, the frequency is used as the only criterion for weight. Figure 6 shows the performance of hit ratio in the weight function under different situations. It can be seen from Figure 6 that combining the frequency and tendency can outperform either one alone.

If the bandwidth from proxy to server is low, the highest hit ratio occurs when β is relatively large. Because under such a condition, the probability of being pre-fetched is relatively low. To combat this, one intends to increase the *Tendency* impact on weight calculation, which can be achieved by choosing a larger β. Vice verse in the high bandwidth case.

B. Performance of dynamic cache resource re-allocation

This simulation is to show the performance of our dynamic cache resource re-allocation scheme. Note that in this experiment, to reduce the influence of pre-fetch and to show the effectiveness of dynamic resource re-allocation alone, the hit ratio of continues media we studied here is the one without using pre-fetching. In the simulation, we assign different importance levels for different types of media. More specifically, we assume the priorities of text, image, audio and video are ranked in the listed order.

Figure 7 shows the hit-ratio comparisons with and without cache resource re-allocation scheme. As shown in Figure 7, with the dynamic resource re-allocation, better performance can be achieved. We obtain higher hit ratios for those four types of media since we take the request patterns into account. Note that the hit-ratio's increment of important media is higher than those of unimportant ones. In real applications, these priorities can be set by users or the cache manager.

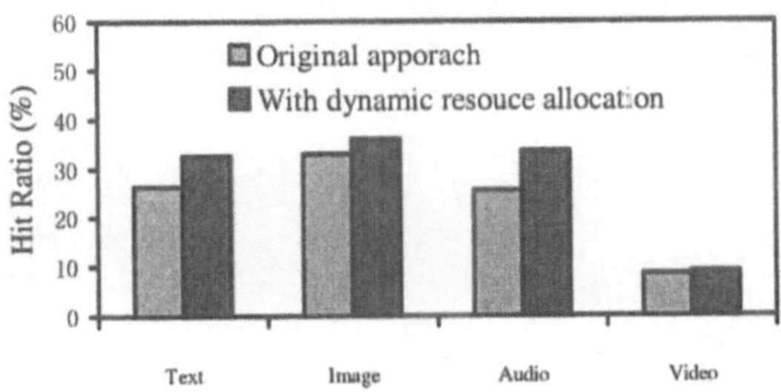

Figure 7. Performance of cache resource re-allocation scheme.

IV. CONCLUSION

This paper addresses how to cache mixed media in a proxy server for multimedia streaming over the Internet. The main contributions of this paper are summarized as follows.

- The client-proxy and proxy-server bandwidth monitors that dynamically estimate the available network bandwidth from client to proxy and from proxy to server;
- A replacement policy considering the characteristics of different types of media and different request patterns;
- A network-condition- and media-quality-adaptive resource management mechanism to dynamically allocate cache resource among different types of media.

Simulations using mixed media with multiple priorities and different request patterns demonstrated that our proposed caching scheme adapts fairly well to network bandwidth variations and high hit ratio is achieved using our caching scheme.

REFERENCES

[1] A. Ortega, F. Carignano, S. Ayer, and M. Vetterli. "Soft caching: Web cache management techniques for images," *IEEE Multimedia Signal Processing*, pp. 475-480, 1997.

[2] S. Sen, J. Rexford, D. Towsely. "Proxy prefix caching for multimedia streams", *IEEE INFOCOM*, 1999.

[3] E. Bommaiah, K. Guo, M. Hofmann, and S. Paul, "Design and implementation of a caching system for streaming media over the Internet", *IEEE Real-Time Technology and Applications Symposium (RTAS'2000)*, May, 2000.

[4] R. Tewari, H. M. Vin, A. Dan, D. Sitaram. "Resource-based caching for web servers", in *Proceedings of SPIE/ACM Conference on Multimedia Computing and Networking (MMCN)*, San Jose, 1998.

[5] A. Dan, and D. Towsley, "An approximate analysis of the LRU and FIFO buffer replacement schemes," in *ACM SIGMETRICS*, pp. 143-152, May, 1990.

[6] H. Chou and D. DeWitt, "An evaluation of buffer management strategies for relational database systems," *Proceedings of the 11th VLDB Conference*, 1985.

[7] E.J.O'Neil, P.E.O'Neil, and G. Weikum, "The LRU-k page replacement algorithm for database disk buffering," in Proceedings of International Conference on Management of Data, May, 1993.

[8] F. Yu, Q. Zhang, W. Zhu, and Y.-Q. Zhang, "QoS-Adaptive Proxy Caching for Multimedia Streaming over the Internet", *IEEE PCM'2000.*

[9] R. Rejaie, M. Handley, H. Yu, and D. Estrin. "Proxy caching mechanism for playback streams in the internet," *IEEE INFOCOM*, 2000.

[10] M. F. Arlitt, C. L. Williamson, "Web Server Workload Characterization: The search for invariants", A*CM SIGMETRICS*.

[11] S. P. Li, F. Wu, and Y.-Q. Zhang, "Study of a new approach to improve FGS video coding efficiency," ISO/IEC JTC1/SC29/WG11, MPEG99/m5583, December 1999, Maui.'96, PS, USA 5/96, pp 126-137.

Robust Scalable Image Transmission over Wireless Fading Channel*

GuiJin Wang, and Xinggang Lin

Department of Electronic Eng., Tsinghua University, Beijing, P. R. China

Abstract. With the emerging of the third generation (3G) wireless technology, image over wireless has been received much attention recently. In this paper, we present a framework for scalable image over wireless fading channel, combining the UEP with FEC, hybrid ARQ and error resilience. Rate-Distortion based scheme is presented to allocate bits between the source coding and the channel coding. Simulation results show that our scheme can achieve rather good reconstructed image with shorter delay under different channel conditions. Furthermore, the energy consumed at the receiver, can also be reduced.

1 Introduction

With the emerging of the third generation (3G) wireless technology, wireless image/video transmission has been received much attention recently. However, this is a very challenging task due to the inherent unreliability of the wireless channel, which suffers from fading or shadowing effects. To cope with errors in the wireless channel, there are two approaches: error resilient techniques and error control techniques. Error resilient techniques at the source coding level can detect and locate errors, support resynchronization, and prevent the loss of entire information [1]. With the aids of error resilient tools, like *Data Partition (DP), Resynchronize Mark (RM), and etc.*, acceptable video/image quality can be obtained at error rate of 10^{-5} or lower [2]. But sometimes BER in the wireless channel can be high as much as 10^{-2}[3], which results in severely bad reconstructed quality only with error resilient tools. Thus error control techniques such as Forward Error Correction (FEC) and Automatic Repeat reQuest (ARQ) are necessary to ensure robust image/video transmission. FEC transmits the original data with some redundant ones, called parities, to allow reconstruction of corrupted data at the receiver. But varying channel conditions limit its effective use, since a bad design may lead to a large amount of overhead. ARQ has been shown to be more effective than FEC [4]. But as each incremental transmission requires a feedback and hence a decoding process, additional delay and computation are

*This work was partially supported by National Science Foundation of China under Grant No. 60072009 and was done in Tsinghua-PacketVideo Multimedia United Laboratory

introduced at the receiver, which are critical for the service on hand-held units where power is at a premium.

Scalable image coding is of great interest recently because it is capable of coping with variability of bandwidth gracefully. Furthermore, scalable stream representation naturally fits unequal error protection (UEP), which can effectively combat transmission errors induced by the wireless network. Joint work on scalable coding with error protection for image transmission over wireless channel has been studied recently [5,6]. Fixed Unequal Error Protection (UEP) and Error Resilient Entropy Code (EREC) are adopted in [5]. However, how to determine the error protection rate is not addressed in [5]. In [6], *Chanade* allocated the transmission budget between the source coding rate and channel coding rate by maximizing the correctly received bits at the receiver, which cannot reflect different priority nature of the multimedia stream. Additionally, it is assumed that the source can get the feedback instantly, which may be not true for the practical transmission.

In this work, we propose a framework to deliver JPEG-2000 images over the wireless fading channel, combining the UEP with FEC, hybrid ARQ and error resilience. More specifically, based on the channel conditions, error control is adopted to ensure high quality image transmission. Meanwhile Rate-distortion based scheme is presented to allocate bits between the source coding and the channel coding.

The rest of this paper is organized as follows. The framework for scalable image over wireless is described in Section 2. Section 3 presents our error control strategies, where the rate-distortion based bits allocation is also proposed. Simulation results are given in section 4. Finally, Section 5 gives the concluding remarks.

2 System Description

2.1 The end-to-end architecture of the scalable image over wireless

In this work, we use JPEG-2000 as an example for demonstration of our scheme. Figure 1 depicts our proposed end-to-end architecture. On the sender side, JPEG-2000 encodes raw image data into embedded stream with quality scalability. According to channel conditions and the media characteristics, each priority layer of JPEG-2000 is packetized and UEP is applied. On the receiver side, the channel decoder reconstructs packets through channel decoding. If any residual error exists, receiver sends a request to the sender for retransmission of the corrupted packet. Meanwhile, some related channel parameters, such as bit error rate and the transmission delay, are collected in the *Channel Monitor* module and fed back to the sender. Upon receiving these feedbacks, *Channel Estimation* Module in the sender estimates the channel conditions. Under the constraint of the available bandwidth, the *Bit Allocation* module on the sender side allocates the bits budget between the source coding and the channel coding.

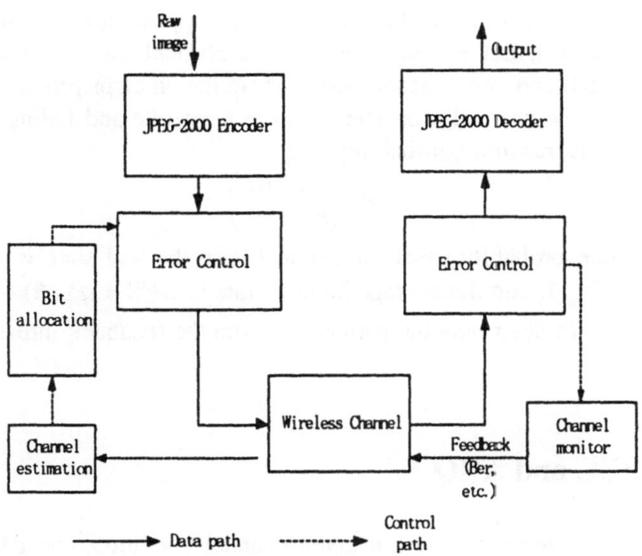

Figure 1. Architecture of the scalable image over wireless

2.2 Scalable Image Coding

JPEG-2000 is an emerging wavelet-based image-coding standard. The error resilient tools introduced in the JPEG-2000 VM consist of hierarchical resynchronization combined with data partitioning and error detection. The resynchronization approach adopted is a source packet approach. The hierarchical structure of the source packets follows the hierarchical structure of the data introduced by the wavelet-based bit-plane entropy coder [1]. Each source packet consists of a header followed by the payload data. The source packet header has the highest priority, including control information such as the length in bytes of all the bit-stream segments contained in the source packet as well as information regarding from which blocks and which bit-plane they come from. The payload part consists of bit-stream segments from individual blocks. Since each block is encoded independently, the bit error from one block will not propagate to the next block. With the header control information, we can rearrange the bit-stream properly in the receiver. This property significantly improves the error robustness of the JPEG-2000 bit-stream.

2.3 Channel Model

Feedback information from several layers can be used to estimate and model the wireless channel. Channel BER, fading depth, and mobility speed can be fed back by the physical layer. Error type and transmission delay can be fed back by the data link layer. Based on these feedback information, a proper model is adopted to accurately estimate the channel conditions.

It has shown that two-state Markov model can approximate the wireless fading channel accurately [7]. Let B and G denote bad channel state (where the bit error probability is Pe(B)) and good channel state (where the bit error probability is Pe(G)), respectively. Then the channel properties, such as error rate and fading depth, can be characterized by the transition probability matrix

$$P = \begin{pmatrix} P_{BB} & P_{BG} \\ P_{GB} & P_{GG} \end{pmatrix}. \tag{1}$$

The steady-state probability that the channel is in the bad state is then given by $\varepsilon = P_{GB} / (P_{BG} + P_{GB})$, and the average bit error rate is $BER = \varepsilon P_e(B) + (1-\varepsilon) P_e(G)$. The details of how to determine the parameters from the feedback information can be referred to [7].

3 Hybrid FEC and ARQ

It can be observed that under a given channel condition, the additional FEC increases the error robustness, but on the other hand reduces the available rate for source coding. Thus there is a trade-off between source rate and FEC rate. Furthermore, considering the hand-held receiver becomes increasingly common and popular, the energy of the receiver should be consumed as small as possible. It is known that excessive retransmission and acknowledgements will consume additional energy, because the transmission of these extra messages increases the energy consumption of the wireless network interface device [8]. Therefore, we argue that the objective during image transmission is to obtain higher quality reconstructed image with shorter delay and less energy consumed in the hand-held device.

Now let us describe our error control strategies. To ensure high quality image transmission, we present the rate-distortion based bits allocation scheme for the first transmission. Let R, R_S, and R_{FEC} denote the available rate, JPEG-2000 source rate, and FEC rate, respectively. Then the problem becomes to allocate the available bit rate such that the optimal R_S, and R_{FEC} are respectively achieved by minimizing the end-to-end expected distortion under the constraint $R_S + R_{FEC} \le R$.

It is known that the end-to-end distortion, $D(R)$, is composed of the source distortion, D_s, and the channel distortion, D_c. Assuming that D_s and D_c are uncorrelated, the end-to-end distortion can be represented as

$$D(R) = D_s(R_s) + D_c(R_{FEC}). \tag{2}$$

Source distortion is the sum of the residual quantization distortion in each code block. On the other hand, the channel distortion resulted from the transmission errors can be formulated as follow

$$D_c(R_{FEC}) = \sum_{i=1}^{R} (D_e(i) \times P(i)), \tag{3}$$

where $D_e(i)$ is the distortion due to the error at the i_{th} position, and $P(i)$ is the probability that i_{th} byte is corrupted while the corresponding information is error-free.

After the above discussion, the optimal FEC rate and source rate for each layer can be obtained through searching the possible rate. This can be formulated as follows:

$$\min_{R_s} [D_s(R_s) + D_c(R_{FEC})]$$
$$s.t.\ R_s + R_{FEC} \le R\,. \tag{4}$$

Next, the ARQ strategy is presented. On the receiver side, if residual errors exist in the packet after channel decoding, the receiver will require the sender for the retransmission. In our scheme, to reduce the amount of the retransmission data, only the higher protection part of the corrupted packet is sent. Suppose N_{RT} is the retransmission times, the expected bits budget consumed by one packet can be calculated as follows:

$$R_{total} = L_{packet} + \sum_{n=1}^{N_{RT}} \left(\prod_{m=1}^{n-1} P_{corrupt}(m)\right) \times P_{correct}(n) \times L(n)\,, \tag{4}$$

where L_{packet} is the length of the packet, $P_{corrupt}(m)$ and $P_{correct}(m)$ are the corrupt probability and correct probability at the m_{th} retransmission respectively, and $L(n)$ is the bits delivered at the m_{th} retransmission.

4 Simulation Results

For simulations, we chose one gray-scale test image, hotel, with dimensions 720×576, from the set of JPEG-2000 test images [9] as original image. Reed-Solomon (RS) codes [10] were used for error protection of each layer. RS codes are a well-known class of block codes with good error-correction properties, especially for burst errors. An RS code is denoted as *RS (n, k)*, where *k* is the length of source symbols and *n-k* is the length of protection symbols.

We conducted simulations under wireless fading channels with the average BER from 10^{-3} to 10^{-2} and the average burst length is 16 bits. We tested three schemes in this section: (1) pure ARQ scheme, that is, for the source packet header, strong RS code (255,123) is applied; while for the payload, if the error exists in the packet, the corrupted packet is retransmitted. This is similar to the TCP, or ATM directly used in the wireless environment. (2) Equal Error Protection (EEP), 4% overhead for each quality layer. This scheme is similar to that in [6], where each layer is assumed to be equally important. The protection degree is the average of our scheme at BER 5×10^{-3}. (3) Our error control scheme. The following results are all obtained by averaging over 30 Monte Carlo simulations.

Figure 2 shows the results of average PSNR under different BER with the total bits budget 200kbit with no retransmission. The experimental results demonstrate that our scheme is much better than the compared schemes under different BER, the higher BER, the more gain our scheme obtained. We can make several conclusions: (1) the error resilient techniques within the source coding cannot guarantee the high quality of wireless image. (2) Comparing the performance between the EEP and our scheme, the priority of the data has the much influence to the reconstructed quality.

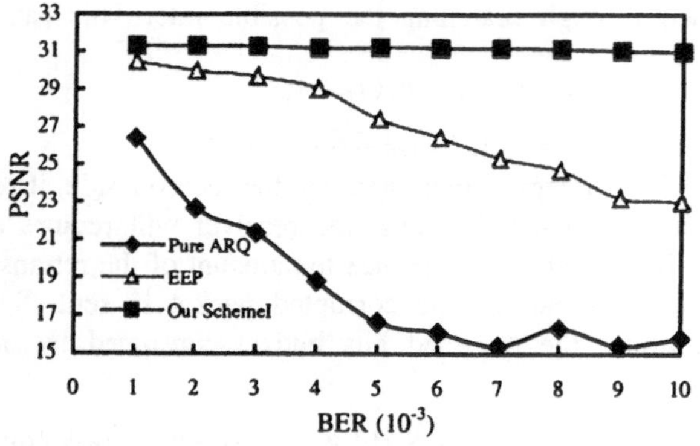

Figure 2. Average PSNR under different BER.

Table 1 tabulates the average PSNR for the image *hotel* over wireless channel with BER 5×10^{-3}, where the retransmission times allowed is from 1 to 4. It can be observed that our scheme can reach the steady performance through 1 retransmission, although the reconstructed image without retransmission are very good. While for the compared scheme, the accepted quality cannot be got until 3 or 4 retransmissions, which prolongs the image service time and may consume more energy at the receiver. Additionally, the compared scheme needs more bits budget to obtain the same quality of our scheme, which aggravates the limit wireless resources.

Table 1. PSNR of image *hotel* over wireless with BER 5×10^{-3}

Retransmission times	0	1	2	3	4
Pure ARQ	16.67	23.19	25.94	28.32	30.23
Our Scheme	31.20	31.37	31.37	31.37	31.37

5 Conclusions

In this work, we presented a framework to deliver JPEG-2000 over the wireless fading channel, combining the UEP with FEC, hybrid ARQ and error resilience. More specifically, after the channel conditions are estimated based on feedback information, error control is adopted to ensure high quality image transmission. Rate-distortion based scheme is proposed to allocate bits between the source coding and the channel coding. Several conclusions can be drawn by observing simulation results. First, the error resilient techniques are not sufficient to ensure high quality image transmission. Secondly, the priority of the data has much influence on the reconstructed quality. Thirdly, our approach can maintain high image quality under different BER from 10^{-3} to 10^{-2}. Fourthly, our scheme can reach very good performance with at most 1 retransmission is allowed, which shorten the multimedia service time and power can be saved.

References

[1] I. Moccagatta, S. Soudagar, J. Liang, and H. Chen, "Error-Resilient Coding in JPEG-2000 and MPEG-4", *IEEE Journal on Selected Area in Communications,* Vol. 18, No. 6, JUNE 2000.

[2] S. Gringeri, R. Egorov, K. Shuaib, A. Lewis, and B. Basch, "Robust compression and transmission of MPEG-4 video," *ACM MM 2000 Electronic Proceedings*, June 2000, http://wood-worm.cs.uml.edu/rprice/ep/gringeri.

[3] 3G TS 23.107: "Qos Concept and Architecture", http://www.3gpp.org

[4] M. Khansari, A. Jalali, E. Dubois, and P. Mermelstein, "Robust low bit-rate video transmission over wireless access systems," *Proceedings of International Conference on Communication (ICC)*, New Orleans, May 1994.

[5] T. Yang and C. C. Jay Kuo, "Error Correction for Wireless Image Communication with A Rate-Distortion Model." *the 31st Annual Asilomar Conference on Signals, Systems, and Computers*, Pacific Grove, CA, Nov. 2-5, 1997

[6] V. Chande, N. Farvardin, and H. Jafarkhani, "Image Communication over Noisy Channels with Feedback." *Intl. Conf. Image Proc.* , Kobe, Oct. 99.

[7] Q. Zhang, W. Zhu, G. J. Wang, Y. Q. Zhang, "Resource Allocation with Adaptive Qos for Multimedia Transmission over W-CDMA Channels," *IEEE WCNC*, Chicago, Sept. 2000.

[8] M. Stemm and R. Katz, "Reducing power consumption of network interfaces in hand-held devices," in *International Workshop on Mobile Multimedia Communication (Momuc-3)*, 1996.

[9] ISO/IEC JTC 1/SC 29/WG 1 (ITU-T SG8). *JPEG 2000 test images.* ISO/IEC JTC,1997.

[10] R.E.Blahut, Digital Transmission of Information Reading, MA:Addison-Wesley, 1990.

A Dynamic Regulation with Scheduler Feedback Information for Multimedia Networks

Hsiang-Ren Shih, Chun-Liang Hou, I-Chieh Lin, and Shie-Jue Lee

Department of Electrical Engineering
National Sun Yat-Sen University
Kaohsiung 80424, Taiwan
leesj@ee.nsysu.edu.tw

Abstract. We propose a dynamic regulation scheme which makes use of scheduler feedback information to reduce the mean delay of multimedia traffic. Traditional methods do not consider the state of a scheduler and a cell will wait in the regulator even when the queue of the scheduler is empty, resulting in a long delay of the involved cells. We use a dynamic scheme whose regulation function is modulated by both the tagged stream's characteristics and the state of the scheduler. As a result, the mean delay of the traffic can be controlled. In particular, the mean delay can be greatly reduced in the case when the scheduler's queue is empty. Simulation results have shown that the mean delay of our dynamic scheme is less than that of other methods.

Keywords: ATM networks, regulator, scheduler, probability mass function, mean delay.

1 Introduction

A major challenge in the design of multimedia networks is to be able to provide the quality of service (QoS) guarantees [1]. These guarantees are usually in the form of bound on end-to-end delay, bandwidth, delay jitter, cell lose rate, or a combination of these parameters. Regulation and scheduling are key factors for the fulfillment of QoS guarantees. Many regulation and scheduling schemes have been proposed, such as Packet by packet Generalized Processor Sharing (PGPS) [4], Rate Controlled Static Priority (RCSP) [7], Carry Over Round Robin (CORR) [5], Traffic Controlled Rate Monotonic (TCRM) [3], the two-class paradigm [6], and Dynamic Regulation and Scheduling (DRS) [2]. Some deadline service disciplines like PGPS have good performance, but it was argued because of its high complexity. Other simpler service disciplines like RCSP utilize a traffic regulator to control the source traffic rate, and then send these regulated traffic streams to a scheduler. RCSP uses a FCFS queue, the simplest one, for its scheduler. CORR uses a round-robin scheduler to achieve fairness. TCRM uses a rate-monotonic priority queue for its scheduler. DRS is basically a dynamic version of RCSP.

An apparent drawback of the rate-based schedulers is that regulation and scheduling functions are separated. These schemes will waste bandwidth when they are used in conjunction with regulators. That is, cells may be queued in the buffers of the regulators even though the buffer of the scheduler is empty. This is very possible since the traffic streams can have a much higher arrival rate than the reserved rate of the corresponding regulator during a short interval of time. To overcome the drawback, the DRS scheme [2] proposed a dynamic scheme whose regulation function is modulated by both the tagged stream's characteristics and information capturing the state of the coexisting application as provided by the scheduler. However, this scheme focuses on the reduction of delay jitter. Although the mean delay is better than RCSP, it can be improved.

We propose another scheme which dynamically adjust the behavior of the regulators based on the state information fed back from the scheduler. In addition to adopting the regulating policy used in DRS, the release of cells from the regulators is solicited when the scheduler is idle. In this way, the mean delay of multimedia traffic can be reduced. Simulation results have shown that the mean delay of our scheme is less than that of other methods.

2 Our scheme

The architecture of our scheme with N connections is shown in Figure 1. The

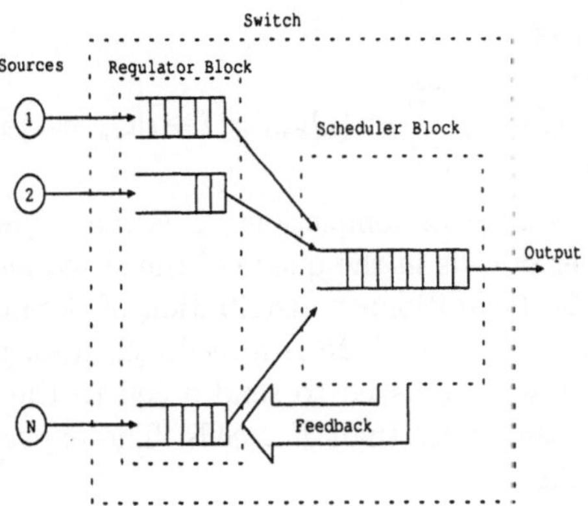

Fig. 1. Architecture of our scheme

traffic streams from sources will be regulated by regulators to control the instantaneous rates. The eligibility time of the kth cell on connection i, ET_k^i is defined to be

$$ET_k^i = \begin{cases} AT_k^i & \text{if } k = 1 \\ \max(ET_{k-1}^i + T^i, AT_k^i) & \text{if } k > 1 \end{cases} \tag{1}$$

where AT_k^i is the arrival time of the k-th cell on connection i and T^i is the expected inter-departure time of two cells from regulator i. Each regulator controls its output such that the eligibility time of each cell is honored. Then all the regulated traffic streams from the regulators are sent to a first-come-first-serve (FCFS) scheduler.

The scheduler will feed back state information to the regulators. Normally, each regulator regulates its output according to the cell eligibility time shown in Eq.(1). As in DRS [2], a regulator will be asked to send a cell to the scheduler when the cumulative number of cells released from the other regulators to the scheduler following the last cell released from the regulator exceeds T-2. However, when the queue of the scheduler is empty, the scheduler will urge regulators to send cells as follows. First, the scheduler finds out the regulator whose queue is not empty and its next cell eligibility time is the smallest away from the present time. Let ΔT be the difference between this eligibility time and the present time. The scheduler feeds back ΔT to all the regulators. Each regulator then adjusts its next cell eligibility time by $-\Delta T$. In this way, cells will come to the scheduler and the likelihood of the scheduler being idle will be decreased. Therefore, the mean delay of all connections will be reduced.

We give a discussion on mathematical analysis for our scheme, RCSP, and DRS. For RCSP, there is no feedback from the scheduler to the regulators. The eligibility time of a cell is similar to the form of Eq.(1), but it cannot be adjusted by the scheduler. Let X_k denote the inter-departure time between the $(k+1)$th cell and the kth cell leaving from the scheduler. Then the expected value of X_k for RCSP can be expressed by [2]:

$$E\{X_k^s\} = \sum_{l=-i}^{(N-1)T} (T+l) \sum_{i=0}^{\infty} Pr\{Q_{k+1} = i + l | Q_k = i\} \pi_q(i) \tag{2}$$

where N is the total number of connections, T is the expected inter-departure time, Q_k is the number of cells in the queue of the scheduler when the k-th cell is released, and $\pi_q(i)$ is the stationary distribution of the number of cells in the queue of the scheduler. In DRS, there is a feedback from the scheduler to the regulators. A regulator will be asked to send a cell to the scheduler when the other regulators have sent more than T-2 cells. The expected value of X_k for DRS can be expressed as:

$$E\{X_k^d\} = \sum_{l=-(T-1)}^{N-2} (T+l) Pr\{X_k^d = T+l\}. \tag{3}$$

For our scheme, if the network utilization is ρ, the scheduler's queue will be empty with a probability of $(1-\rho)$. Let $Pr\{\Delta T = j\}$ denote the probability of $\Delta T = j$. The expected value of X_k of all connections can be decreased by

$$\sum_{j=1}^{T_{max}} j(1-\rho) Pr\{\Delta T = j\} \tag{4}$$

from that of DRS, where $T_{max} = \max T^1, \ldots, T^N$. Therefore, the expected value of X_k for our scheme can be expressed as:

$$E\{X_k^o\} = E\{X_k^d\} - \sum_{j=1}^{T_{max}} j(1-\rho)Pr\{\Delta T = j\}. \quad (5)$$

Apparently, the expected X_k of our scheme is less than that of DRS.

3 Simulations

We present some experimental results here and give a comparison between our scheme, RCSP [7], and DRS [2]. A system with $N = 7$ *ON-OFF* Markov sources were simulated using OPNET. Let P_{on} denote the probability that the current state is *ON* and the next state is still *ON*, P_{off} denote the probability that the current state is *OFF* and the next state is still *OFF*. The state transition graph of each *ON-OFF* Markov source is shown in Figure 2. Also, let P_{arr} denote the

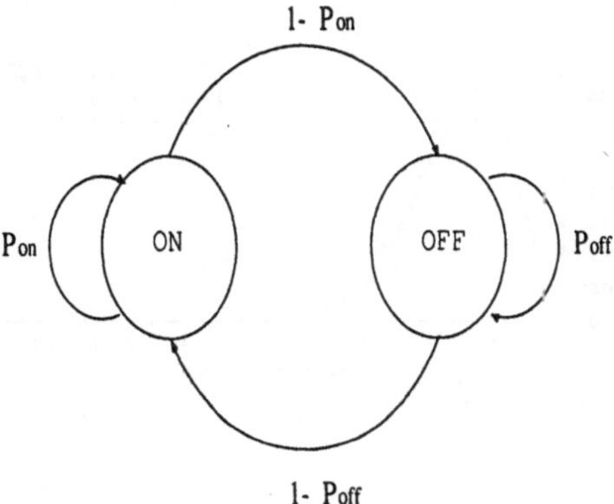

Fig. 2. State Transition of a source

cell arrival rate for a source when the source is in the *ON* state, and no cells are generated when the source is in the *OFF* state. Two traffic conditions were simulated, one in lower traffic loading and the other in higher traffic loading. The parameters and results of the first scenario are shown in Table 1. Note that P_{on}=0.8 and P_{off}=0.9 for src_0, src_1, and src_2, P_{on}=0.8 and P_{off}=0.85 for src_3 and src_4, P_{on}=0.8 and P_{off}=0.75 for src_5 and src_6, and $P_{arr}[0]$–$P_{arr}[6]$ are 0.5, 0.4, 0.4, 0.1, 0.1, 0.2, and 0.2, respectively. For each source, the value of T and the measured average source rate λ_{ave} are shown in the table. The sources with $T = 1$ are unregulated, implying that they are allowed to release their cells to the scheduler as soon as the cells are generated.

The system utilization, ρ, of the first experiment is equal to 0.7530. Therefore, the probability that the scheduler's queue will be empty is equal to 0.247. For

Table 1. Simulation parameters for the first experiment, with $\rho = \sum_i \lambda_{ave,i} = 0.7530$.

Source	T	λ_{ave}	X^o_{ave}	X^d_{ave}
0	1	0.1733	2.2508	2.3878
1	1	0.1354	2.7768	2.8971
2	1	0.1379	2.6978	2.8249
3	10	0.0429	3.9011	9.5227
4	10	0.0430	3.8600	9.5571
5	5	0.1111	2.6330	4.7870
6	5	0.1094	2.6316	4.7683

unregulated sources, src_0, src_1, and src_2, the effect of our scheme on the mean delay is not significant. Figure 3 shows the probability mass function (PMF) of the delay obtained from our scheme, RCSP, and DRS, respectively, for source 1. From this figure, it is apparent that the improvement on the mean delay is not

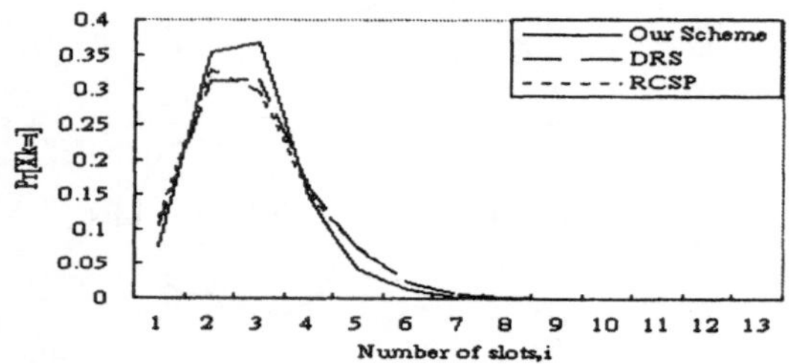

Fig. 3. Delay PMF for experiment 1: Source 1

much. However, the improvements on the regulated sources, src_3, src_4, src_5, and src_6, is clearly observed in Table 1. Comparisons between our schemes and the other two methods for the regulated sources are shown in Figure 4 to Figure 7. Apparently, the mean delay resulted from our scheme, (X^o_{ave}), is substantially smaller than the mean delays X^s_{ave} and X^d_{ave} obtained from RCSP and DRS, respectively.

The parameters and results of the second scenario are shown in Table 2. Note that P_{on}=0.8 and P_{off}=0.8 for src_0, src_1, and src_2, P_{on}=0.8 and P_{off}=0.85 for src_3 and src_4, P_{on}=0.8 and P_{off}=0.75 for src_5 and src_6, and $P_{arr}[0]$–$P_{arr}[6]$ are 0.5, 0.4, 0.4, 0.1, 0.1, 0.2, and 0.2, respectively. In this case, the system utilization, ρ, is equal to 0.9492. Since the network is under heavy loading, the scheduler's queue is hardly empty. Therefore, our scheme is only of slight contribution to reducing the mean delay, as shown in Figure 8.

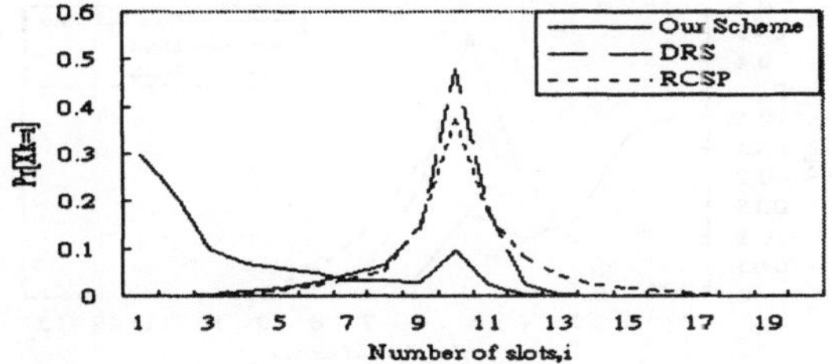

Fig. 4. Delay PMF for experiment 1: Source 3

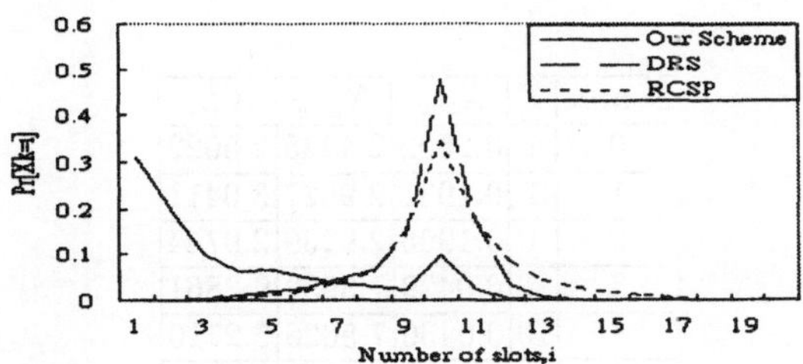

Fig. 5. Delay PMF for experiment 1: Source 4

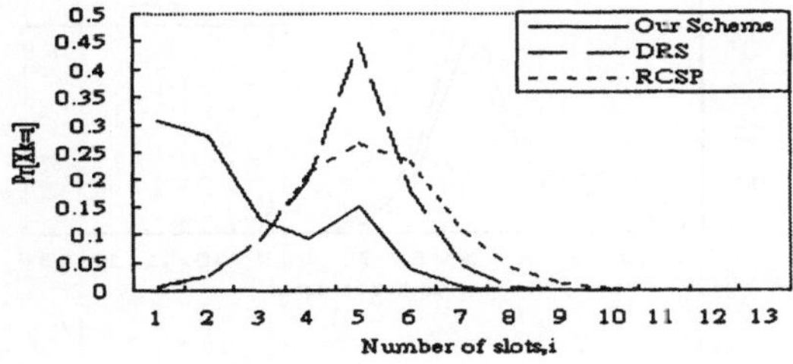

Fig. 6. Delay PMF for experiment 1: Source 5

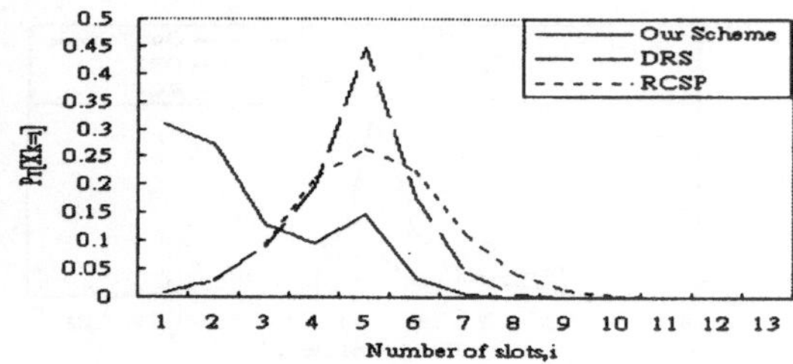

Fig. 7. Delay PMF for experiment 1: Source 6

Table 2. Simulation parameters for the second experiment, with $\rho = \sum_i \lambda_{ave,i} = 0.9492$.

Source	T	λ_{ave}	X^o_{ave}	X^d_{ave}
0	1	0.2502	2.4445	2.5022
1	1	0.1931	2.9827	3.0411
2	1	0.1995	2.9209	2.9744
3	10	0.0429	7.3932	9.2861
4	10	0.0430	7.5026	9.2710
5	5	0.1111	4.1060	4.7010
6	5	0.1094	4.0800	4.6979

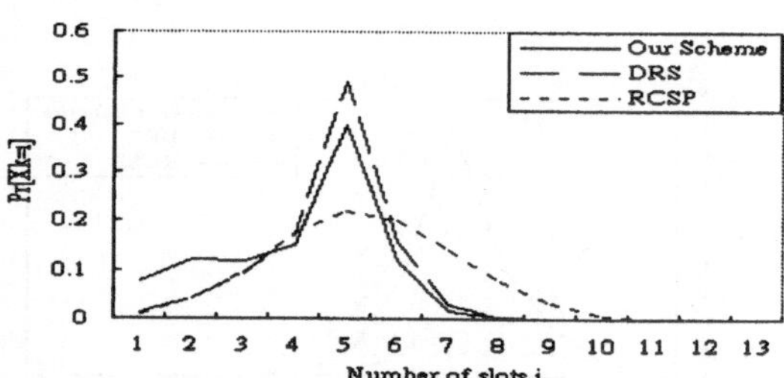

Fig. 8. Delay PMF for experiment 2: Source 5

4 Summary

We have described a dynamic regulation scheme for multimedia networks. The scheme makes use of scheduler feedback information to accelerate the release of cells from regulators when the scheduler is idle. We have also shown that the scheme can help to reduce the mean delay of multimedia traffic. Our scheme does not increase the buffer size required for the scheduler. Statistically speaking, the buffer demand is even reduced by our scheme for both regulators and the scheduler.

A simpler scheme might be used: When the queue of the scheduler is empty, the scheduler notifies all the regulators to send a cell. However, if all connections send cells at the same time, the connections might suffer a delay equal to the total number of connections, N. When N is much smaller than the delay bounds of most connections, this drawback can be ignored. But in a large network system, there could be thousands of connections, then this simpler scheme would not work satisfactorily.

References

1. A. Hać, *Multimedia Applications Support for Wireless ATM Networks*, Prentice Hall PTR, Upper Saddle River, NJ, 2000.
2. S. Iatrou and I. Stavrakakis, "A dynamic regulation and scheduling scheme for real-time traffic management," *IEEE/ACM Transactions on Networking*, vol. 8, pp. 60–70, February 2000.
3. S.K. Kweon and K.G. Shin, "Providing deterministic delay guarantees in ATM networks," *IEEE/ACM Transactions on Networking*, vol. 6, pp. 838–850, December 1998.
4. A.K. Parekh and R.G. Gallager, "A generalized processor sharing approach to flow control in integrated services networks: The single-node case," *IEEE/ACM Transactions on Networking*, vol. 1, pp. 344–357, June 1993.
5. D. Saha, S. Mukherjee and S.K. Tripathi, "Carry-over round robin: A simple cell scheduling mechanism for ATM networks," *IEEE/ACM Transactions on Networking*, vol. 6, pp. 779–796, December 1998.
6. J. Soldatos, E. Vayias and N. Mitrou, "CAC and traffic shaping for performance control in ATM: the two-class paradigm," *Computer Networks*, vol. 34, pp. 65–83, July 2000.
7. H. Zhang and D. Ferrari, "Rate-controlled static-priority queuing," *Proceedings of IEEE INFOCOM'93*, pp. 227–236, September 1993.

A New Scheduling Scheme for Multicast True VoD Service *

Huadong Ma[1] and Kang G. Shin[2]

[1] College of Computer Science & Technology,
Beijing University of Posts and Telecommunications, Beijing 100876, China
mhd@bupt.edu.cn

[2] Real-Time Computing Lab., EECS Depart.,
The University of Michigan, Ann Arbor, MI 48019-2122, USA
kgshin@eecs.umich.edu

Abstract. Multicast Video-on-Demand (VoD) has excellent performance, but it is very difficult to equip such a system with full support for interactive VCR functions. In this paper, we propose a new scheme, called the *Best-Effort Patching* (BEP), that offers a TVoD service in terms of both request admission and VCR interaction for multicast VoD system. Moreover, by using a novel dynamic merging algorithm, BEP significantly improves the efficiency of TVoD interactivity, especially for popular videos. Our extensive simulation results show that BEP outperforms the conventional multicast TVoD interaction protocols.

1 Introduction

A VoD service allows remote clients to play back any video from a large collection of videos stored at one or more video servers at any time. VoD service is usually long-lived and real-time, and requires high storage-I/O & network bandwidths, and needs to support VCR-like interactivity. TVoD service supports all of the control functions such as Play/Resume, Stop/Pause/Abort, Fast Forward/Rewind, Fast Search/Reverse Search and Slow Motion, and is an ideal service for consumers. The conventional TVoD system uses one dedicated channel for each service request, which offers the client the best QoS and interactive service. However, it incurs high system costs, especially in terms of storage-I/O and network bandwidth. One efficient solution to these problems is to use multicast. Multicast VoD has excellent scalability and cost/performance efficiency.

There are several approaches for multicasting VoD service. One approach is to multicast each popular video at fixed intervals. In order to eliminate service latency, patching [8] was proposed to enable an existing multicast to serve new additional clients, but the conventional patching is suitable only for TVoD admission control. The other approach is to use a fixed number of multicast

* The work reported in this paper is partly supported by the US NSF under Grant EIA-9806280 and the NNSF of China under Grant 69873006. The work was done when Huadong Ma visited EECS Depart., the University of Michigan.

channels to periodically broadcast video objects to a group of subscribers [2,9, 12]. This periodic broadcast is efficient in transmitting popular videos from one server to many clients, but it is difficult to support VCR interactivity.

In order to provide TVoD service, we propose a new patching scheme, called the *Best-Effort Patching* (BEP). Like the conventional patching, BEP multicasts a popular video via regular channels at fixed intervals. Requests between two consecutive regular channels will share the latest regular stream by patching the missed leading segment. Moreover, patching is used to support the user interaction in BEP. Once a client interaction exceeds the capability of his CPE buffer, BEP dispatches a patching channel to support the client's interaction and its merging into the nearest multicast channel. Further, BEP uses a novel dynamic merging scheme, thus offering TVoD service efficiently.

2 Background

To eliminate the service latency, patching was proposed in [8] by enabling each multicast session to dynamically add new requests. An important objective of patching is to increase the number of requests each channel can serve per time unit, thereby reducing the per-customer system cost. A new service request can exploit an existing multicast by buffering the video stream from the multicast while playing a new catch-up stream (via a patching channel) from the beginning. Once the new catch-up stream is played back to the skew point, it can be terminated and the new client can join the original multicast. Allowing clients to dynamically join an existing multicast improves the multicast efficiency. Moreover, requests can be honored immediately, achieving zero-delay VoD service.

In the patching scheme, channels are often used to patch the missing portion of a video, or deliver a patching stream. The time period during which patching must be used, is referred to as the *patching window* [4]. Two simple approaches to setting the patching window are discussed in [8]: greedy patching and grace patching. An improved patching technique, called as the *transition patching* [5], has better performance without requiring any extra download bandwidth at the client site. Other optimal patching schemes were presented in [6, 11].

In order to implement the interactivity of multicast VoD service, some efficient schemes have been proposed. For example, the SAM protocol [10] offers an efficient way for TVoD interactions, but it requires many I-Channels, thus resulting in a high blocking rate. The authors of [1] improved the SAM protocol by using the CPE buffer. Other researchers, such as those of [3], focused on interactions without picture. In this paper, we present an efficient approach to the implementation of the continuous TVoD interactions.

3 Best-Effort Patching for TVoD Interactivity

3.1 Basic Idea

Continuous service of VCR actions can be supported in multicast VoD systems by employing the CPE buffer, but this support is limited by the size of CPE buffer (see Fig. 1). Initially, the play point corresponds to the most recent frame and the CPE buffer is progressively filled in with past frames as the playback continues. The *Play* operation doesn't change the relative position of the play point with respect to the most recent frame. When forward/backward interactions are performed, the play point will eventually be near the most recent frame/the oldest frame. The displacement of the play point depends on the speedup factor *SP* or the slow motion factor *SM*. For example, the Fast Forward spanning over time t will cause an actual displacement of $(SP-1)t$. Suppose d_r (usually equals $d/2$) is the displacement between the play point and the most recent frame, then Fast Forward will continuously be supported if $t \leq \frac{d_r}{SP-1}$ (e.g. A is the desired play point). A similar observation can be made for a backward interaction.

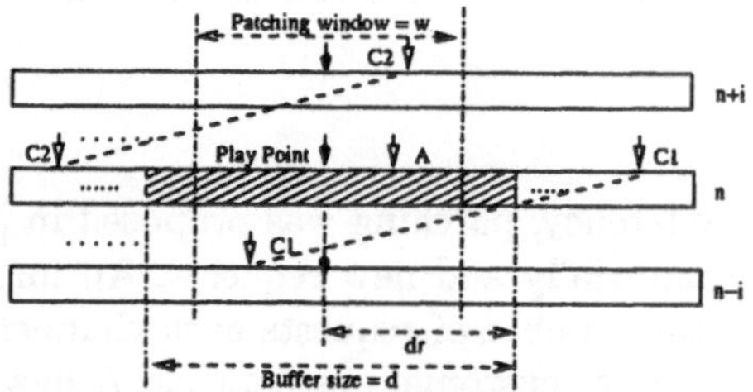

Fig. 1. The CPE buffer and VCR actions

Now, let's consider another situation when a Fast Forward interaction was performed over time $t \geq \frac{d_r}{SP-1}$, or Rewind interaction took place over the time allowed by the CPE buffer. The CPE buffer can't guarantee a smooth transition between adjacent multicast groups, i.e., a discontinuous VCR interaction may take place. The interaction can't always join an existing channel immediately because there isn't always a channel with the desired playback time.

BEP eliminates discontinuity so that customers may enjoy zero-delay VCR interactions. The main idea behind BEP is as follows. In executing VCR interactive operations, once the interaction time exceeds the capacity of the CPE buffer, BEP dispatches a patching channel to transmit the video from the desired time point, and supports the interaction and its merging into the latest multicast channel. For an interaction without picture, such as Fast Forward, Rewind, Pause, Stop, BEP only needs to dispatch a patching channel for its merge into an existing channel after the interaction, where the client downloads the video from both the patching channel and the closest multicast channel simultaneously. The video from the patching channel is played back immediately, and the video from the closest multicast channel is buffered in the CPE buffer. For merging, the patching channel is required only for the displacement between the play point of the closest channel and the desired play point, and then the patching channel is released. This way, the customer seamlessly joins an existing multicast group. It doesn't incur any additional CPE cost because it just makes use of the CPE buffer required by the conventional patching.

We can further illustrate BEP by Fig. 2. Once the interaction time exceeds the CPE buffer capacity, BEP will assign a channel to the customer. The channel is used during both the interaction and merging phases. In the interaction phase, the channel acts like an I-Channel in the SAM protocol [10], while it is used as a patching channel in the merging phase. For the forward interaction shown in Fig. 2(a), such as Fast Search, the interaction takes t units of time, and the customer's desired play point is A. P0 is the original play point. Upon completion of the interaction, the normal play point of the multicast group n that the customer shares, becomes $P(n)$. The interaction phase uses the channel for a period of $t - t_0$ $(t > t_0)$, where t_0 is the duration the CPE buffer can support Fast Search without an additional channel, and $t_0 = \frac{d_r}{SP-1}$. The length of the patching channel for the merging is $|P(n - i - 1) - A|$. For the backward interaction shown in Fig. 2(b), such as Reverse Search, one can give a similar illustration.

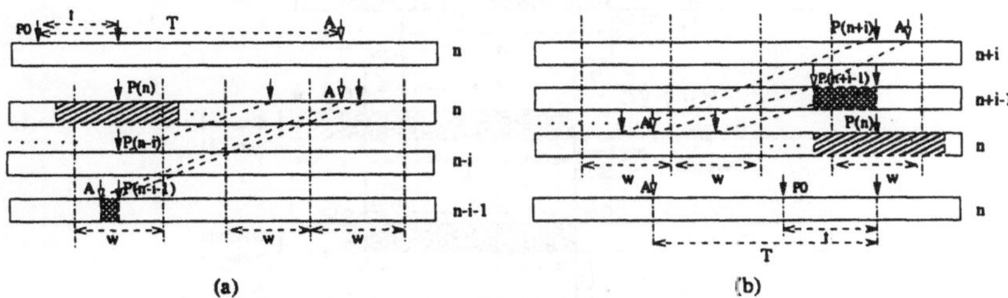

Fig. 2. Forward/Backward interactions

3.2 The Dynamic Merging Algorithm

To improve the merging of interaction and multicast streams, BEP uses a novel dynamic merging approach as described below.

Let $P(n)$ be the play point of multicast group n. After completing an interaction, A is the desired play point in Fig. 3. Thus, the client needs to use a patching channel to catch up with the multicast stream of group n. The patching stream for A is denoted as *Stream A*, and its *lifetime* is the same as its group offset $a = |P(n) - A|$. When the merging is going on, say t_1 minutes later, the other interaction completes and its stream also needs to be merged into that of group n, and its desired play point is B behind A in the relative offset of the stream. The group offset of B is $b = |P(n) - B|$. If t_1 is less than the lifetime of Stream A and $a - t_1 > b - a$, we can make the patching stream for the second interaction (denoted as *Stream B*) share the grid part of Stream A so that the need/use of patching channels can be reduced. In this situation, Stream A will be extended so that its lifetime is b, and the lifetime of Stream B is set to $b - a$. The new client downloads the video segment from Stream A and B simultaneously, and begins downloading of the video from the stream of multicast group n after using up Stream B. Such merging of patching channels can go on, and the merged clients can be recorded in a *merging queue*.

Assume that q is a merging queue for multicast group n, the offset of q is the group offset of its first client, and the head record of q is the client patching stream initiating this queue, and the lifetime of q is initially set to the offset of its head and will possibly be changed when a new client joins it. A merged client patching stream is called as an *element* of the queue. If t is the time when the latest client joins, the queue will be released when the time is t plus its lifetime. A merging queue has the following data structure:

```
struct MQueue {
   element *head; /*the head record*/
   int offset,lefetime; /*the offset and lifetime of queue*/
   int latime; /*joining time of the latest client*/
   }
```

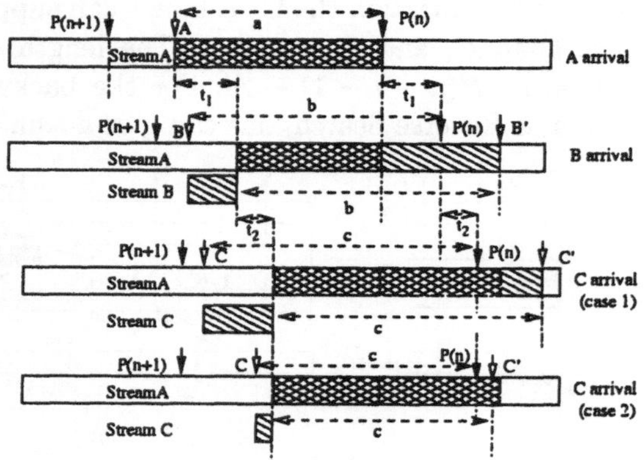

Fig. 3. Dynamic merging

When a new client C wants to join this queue that holds a merging stream A, given that c is C's group offset and the arrival time of C is $t+t_2$. We also assume that $c \geq q.offset$ and $c < q.offset + q.lifetime - t_2$; otherwise, C shouldn't join q. We can manage this queue for C to join in the two cases shown in Fig. 3.

Case 1: $c > q.lifetime - t_2$, meaning that the lifetime of the queue q is not enough to merge C, so *q.lifetime*, also equal to the lifetime of Stream A, must be extended. That is, after C is merged, the lifetime of Stream C, the patching stream for the missing leading segment of C, is set to *c-q.offset*, *q.lifetime=c*, $q.latime = t + t_2$. The client downloads the video segments from Stream A and C simultaneously. After *c-q.offset* time units, the client begins to download the video from the stream of group n. In this case, the usage time of a patching channel that our algorithm can save is $q.offset + q.lifetime - t_2 - c$ time units.

Case 2: $c <= q.lifetime - t_2$, meaning that *q.lifetime* is enough to merge C, so the lifetime of Stream A need not be extended. After C is merged, the lifetime of Stream C, the patching stream for the missing segment of C, is set to *c-q.offset*, $q.latime = t+t_2$, *q.lifetime* is unchanged. The client downloads the video segments from Stream A and C, and the stream of group n in the same way as in Case 1. In this case, the usage time of a patching channel that our algorithm can save is *q.offset* time units.

If C can't be merged into the existing queues, a new queue will be initiated. Because there are probably many merging queues, C will be merged into the queue which saves the maximum usage time of channel.

The dynamic merging algorithm is described below.

Algorithm DMA(Q, C, n, t)

```
/*Q is a set of merging queues, C is an interaction client*/
/*n is the group number, t is the arrival time of C*/
c = offset(C,n); /* get the offset of C in group n*/
q0 = max_{q∈Q}{min{q.offset + q.lifetime − c − (t − q.latime), q.offset}
        |q.offset ≤ c < q.offset + q.lifetime − (t − q.latime)}
if (q0 = null) { /* generate a new merging queue*/
  Genqueue(q0); /*generate a new queue*/
  q0.head is set to C; q0.offset = c;
  q0.lifetime = c; q0.latime = t; }
else { /* merging C into q0*/
  delta = t − q0.latime; q0.latime = t; lifetime(C) = c − q0.offset;
  /* the lifetime of patching stream C is changed*/
  if (c > q0.lifetime − delta) q0.lifetime = c;
  }
```

3.3 Discussion

BEP differs from the SAM protocol in at least three aspects. First, BEP aims to offer a zero-delay (or continuous) service for both request admission and VCR interactions. Thus, patching channels are used to patch all of the segments that can't be provided by regular multicast channels for TVoD service, whereas I-Channels in the SAM protocol are used only for VCR interaction service. Second, the SAM protocol uses *synchronization buffer* to merge I-Channels and regular multicast channels, whereas BEP uses a patching channel to patch the missing segments of multicast VoD and merge it with regular multicast channels using the client's CPE buffer. Of course, use of the CPE buffer can also improve the efficiency of the SAM protocol [1]. Third, BEP uses a dynamic technique to merge interaction streams with regular multicast streams, significantly improving the efficiency of multicast TVoD service.

4 Performance Evaluation

4.1 Client's Interaction Model

We use the interaction model proposed in [1] to evaluate our approach. In this model, a set of states corresponding to different VCR actions are designed durations and probabilities of transitions to neighboring states. If the initial state is Play, then the system randomly transits to other interactive states or remains at Play state according to the behavior distribution. As shown in Fig. 4, transition probabilities P_i ($i = 0, \ldots, 9$) are assigned to a set of states corresponding to different VCR actions. For tractability, we divide customers into two types: *Very Interactive (VI)* or *Not Very Interactive (NVI)*. Our simulation assumes $P_8 = 0$, and $P_9 = 0.5$. The other transition possibilities are summarized as Table 1.

Assume that BEP serves each state for an exponentially-distributed period of time, and d_i ($i = 0, 1, 2, \ldots, 8$) are the mean durations for the corresponding interaction states ($d_1 = 0$), and their default values are given in Table 2. Meanwhile, the speedup factors of Fast Forward/Rewind and Fast Search/Reverse

Search are defined as K_0, K_1, respectively, and the speeddown factor of Slow Motion is defined as K_2. Our simulation used $K_0 = 10$, $K_1 = 3$, and $K_2 = 2$.

Fig. 4. VCR interactive model

Table 1. Transition probabilities from Play/Resume

Behavior	P_0	P_1	P_2, P_3	P_4	P_5	P_6, P_7
VI	0.50	0.04	0.08	0.06	0.08	0.08
NVI	0.75	0.02	0.04	0.03	0.04	0.04

Table 2. Mean interactive durations

Parameter	d_0	d_1	d_2, d_3	d_4, d_5	d_6, d_7	d_8
Default	10	0	0.5	5	2.5	2

4.2 The Simulation Results

We compare BEP with the SAM protocol [10], and the SAM protocol improved by the CPE buffer (abbreviated as BSM) [1]. Because the latter two schemes also achieve the same admission performance as that of BEP by transition or grace patching, we focus only on the comparison of their TVoD interactivities, especially for the merging performance. For a video of 90 minutes, requests arrive according to a Poisson process with rate λ ranging from 0 to 10 per minute. The patching window size w is varied from 1 to 25 minutes, and the CPE buffer size d is ranging from 0 to 30 minutes. Two types of interactive behaviors, VI and NVI, are simulated. The results are collected from 10-hour simulations.

Fig. 5(a) shows the merging channel requirement while varying the request rate. The merging channel requirement for SAM is significantly greater than that for both BSM and BEP. When the request rate is low, there is not a big difference between the merging channel requirements for BSM and BEP. The higher the request rate is, the bigger their difference is. Fig. 5(b) indicates that the patching window will greatly affect the merging channel requirement. When the patching window size is small, there is not a big difference between the merging channel requirements for BSM and BEP. When the patching window size is large, BEP significantly outperforms BSM. Note that BEP and BSM can work only if the patching window size is less than or equal to the CPE buffer size.

5 Conclusion

Multicast is shown to be a good remedy for improving the performance of VoD system. In this paper, we proposed a new multicast TVoD approach called the

Best-Effort Patching. This scheme supports both continuous VCR interactions and zero-delay requests admission. Moreover, a novel dynamic merging algorithm improves the efficiency of merging interaction and regular streams. Our simulation results indicate that BEP can achieve significantly better performance than the conventional multicast TVoD protocols, especially for popular videos. BEP supports TVoD service with less bandwidth requirement.

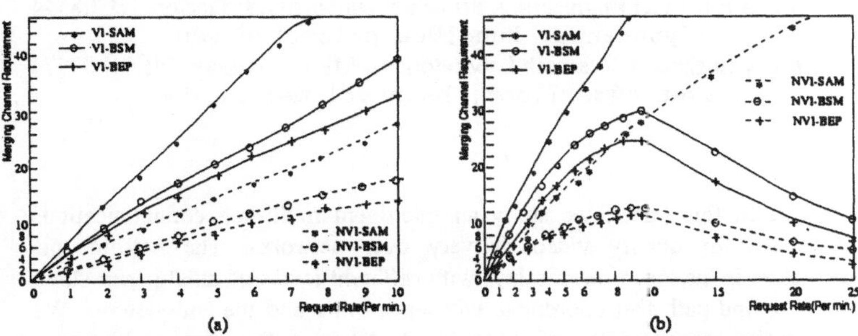

Fig. 5. (a) Effect of request rate λ ($w = d = 5$ min.); (b) Effect of patching window w ($\lambda = 5$, If $w \leq 5$ min. then $d = 5$ min., if $w > 5$ min. then $d = w$)

References

1. E. L. Abram-Profeta and Kang G. Shin, Providing unrestricted VCR capability in multicast video-on-demand systems, Proc. of IEEE ICMCS'98, Austin, June 1998.
2. C.C. Aggarwal, J.L. Wolf, and P.S. Yu, A permutation-based pyramid broadcasting scheme for video-on-demand systems, Proc. of IEEE ICMCS'96, pp.118-126, Hiroshima, Japan, June 1996.
3. K.C. Almeroth and M.H. Ammar, The use of multicast delivery to provide a scalable and interactive video-on-demand service, IEEE Journal of Selected Areas in Communications, Vol.14, No.6, pp. 1110–1122, Aug.1996.
4. Ying Cai and K.A. Hua, Optimizing patching performance, Proc. of SPIE Conf. on Multimedia Computing and Networking, pp.204-216, San Jose, Jan. 1999.
5. Ying Cai and K.A. Hua, An efficient bandwidth-sharing technique for true video on demand systems, Proc. of ACM Multimedia'99, pp.211-214, Orlando, Nov.1999.
6. D.L. Eager, *et al.*, Optimal and efficient merging schedules for video-on-demand servers, Proc. of ACM multimedia'99, pp.199-202, Orlando, Nov.1999.
7. L. Gao and D. Towsley, Supplying instantaneous video-on-demand services using controlled multicast, Proc. of IEEE ICMCS'99, pp.117-121, Florence, June 1999.
8. K.A. Hua, Y. Cai, and S. Sheu, Patching: A multicast technique for true video-on-demand services, Proc. of ACM Multimedia'98, pp. 191–200, Bristol, U.K., Sept. 1998.
9. K.A. Hua and S. Sheu, Skyscraper broadcasting: A new broadcasting scheme for metropolitan video-on-demand systems, Proc. of ACM SIGCOMM'97, pp.89-100, Sept. 1997.
10. W. Liao and V.O.K. Li, The split and merge protocol forinteractive video-on-demand, IEEE Multimedia, Oct.-Dec. 1997, pp.51-62.
11. S. Sen, L. Gao, J. Rexford, D. Towsley, Optimal patching schemes for efficient multimedia streaming, Proc. of IEEE NOSSDAV'99, Basking Ridge, NJ, June 1999.
12. S. Viswanathan and T. Imielinski, Pyramid broadcasting for video on demand service, Proc. of SPIE MMCN'95, Volume 2417, pp.66–77, San Jose, 1995.

Intelligent Multi-hop Video Communications

Yunnan Wu[1], Anthony Vetro[2], Huifang Sun[2], S.-Y. Kung[1]

[1] Dept. of Electrical Engineering, Princeton University, Princeton, NJ, 08544
{yunnanwu, kung}@ee.princeton.edu
[2] Mitsubishi Electric Research Laboratories – MERL, Murray Hill, NJ 07974
avetro@merl.com, hsun@atl.meitca.com

Abstract. In this paper, we study an intelligent multi-hop communications architecture for quality video delivery over networks. The key to this architecture is the insertion of relays with different levels of intelligence along the end-to-end path that coordinate with each other and the end-systems. We study traffic management and content adaptation within this architecture. Compared with the end-to-end model, the multi-hop model can achieve higher throughput without increasing the risk of overloading the network and the end-to-end delay. Experimental results show a throughput gain of 19.3% on a concatenation of two best-effort networks, and 37.8% for a concatenation of a best-effort network and a guaranteed service network. With the error withdrawal feature at the relay, abrupt quality drops are avoided. Analysis and simulations suggest that the multi-hop traffic management can gain high throughput, and the content adaptation should be sender-centric with occasional relay supports.

1 Introduction

Multimedia transmission over today's Internet is a challenging problem. The present Internet suffers from two aspects for multimedia: (1) the core is stateless in nature, and inadequate for guaranteed QoS, and (2) the existing end-system software cannot be readily tailored to individual access link characteristics, especially for heterogeneous networks. As a remedy, several recent research efforts[1]-[5] propose to place proxy servers (or filters) in the Internet. Filters can be used to combat the path heterogeneity in the wireless-Internet[3], accommodate end-systems with different link bandwidths for efficient multimedia multicast[2][5], implement distributed caching[4], place user-defined computations into the network[1], and etc.

The idea of using filters has long existed. However, the collaboration among the filters and end-systems has not been well solved so far. We may require these filters to operate on their own and appear transparent from other filters and end-systems. But the lack of collaboration may result in inefficiency, duplication, and/or negative interaction. Furthermore, the achievable performance gains are not well understood.

To combat this problem, this paper investigates the configuration, coordination, and performance issues of an intelligent multi-hop video communications architecture, where *smart relays* are added to the end-to-end path to *coordinate* with each other and the end-systems. The main objective is to achieve a synergy among these strategically deployed control points to optimize the end-to-end performance.

Toward that end, we study the design of traffic management and content adaptation in the multi-hop architecture. Traffic management determines *how fast* to send, and content adaptation determines *what* to send. Intuitively, the unique problem for the multi-hop model is "what to know and what to do at each control point?"

This paper is organized as follows. In section 2, we introduce the multi-hop architecture. The two major components, traffic management and content adaptation are discussed in detail in section 3 and 4. Simulation results are presented in section 5. Finally, conclusions are given in section 6.

2 The Multi-hop Architecture

Fig. 1 illustrates the multi-hop communications architecture. In contrast to the traditional end-to-end model, where intelligence is only present at the sender and the receiver, we consider the inclusion of smart relays to assist the transmission. Note that each pipe between two intelligence points is an abstraction as there may be several intermediate routers in between.

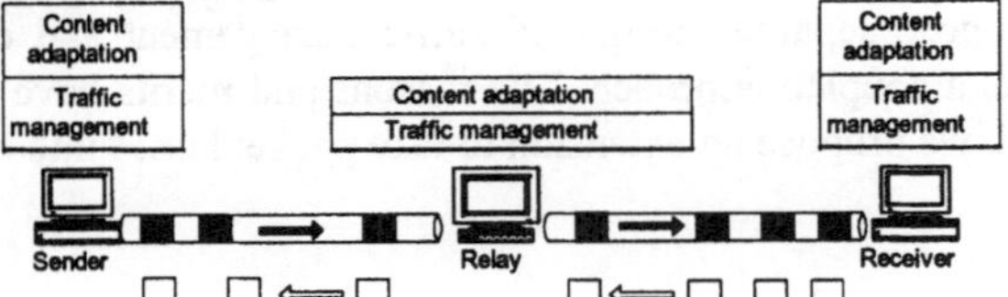

Fig. 1. The multi-hop communications architecture

Depending on the positions and affordable system resources, the network relays can be configured with different intelligence levels: (1) Observer: lightweight agent to collect QoS information for either the link to which it is directly attached, or the flow it is monitoring. (2) Advisor: agent to provide adaptation suggestions based on information from one or many observers. For example, packet coloring can be used to assess priority relations. (3) Controller: agent that performs content adaptation, taking into consideration the resource tradeoff of multiple competing connections.

From the perspective of network layering, the relay has a distinct internal view as shown in Fig. 1. For simplicity, only the upper layers, namely the transport layer and the application layer, are shown. Unlike a router, which commonly performs only per-packet processing, the relay is assumed to be able to identify flows. Also, the upper layers are intentionally shown to be *thinner* to emphasize that they should be lightweight compared to the full-blown end systems.

The most powerful smart relay, namely the controller mentioned above, consists of two modules: traffic management and content adaptation. While it may be possible to couple the two parts, we propose a separate design and clear interface. The reasons are as follows. First, multiple peer connections at a relay may share the traffic management module. In [6], the authors propose to share the congestion control among connections with identical source and destination pairs at the end host. Here, we propose to extend its use to the relays in the network, where sharing can happen more frequently. Second, many network QoS provisioning schemes assume traffic shaping at entrances, hence traffic management may have to be policed by the service provider, while the content adaptation program should be *uploaded* by the application. Finally, the layering principle in network design supports such a separation.

With the multi-hop architecture, the QoS problem is accounted for by coordinating the traffic management and content adaptation at both the end systems and the relays. To begin with, we only consider the case of a single unicast connection, leaving the multi-connection case as a future work.

3 Traffic Management

In this section, we study the end-to-end multimedia traffic management and the strategies in the multi-hop model. The two main requirements for multimedia traffic management are responsiveness to network condition and smoothness in sending rate. Our end-to-end traffic management falls into the category of *congestion avoidance*, i.e. trying to prevent congestion in the first place. This category is to observe, predict and control the network state, as exampled by [7][8]. This study differs from [7] by several important aspects. First, we don't assume the routers can give any system state information. Instead, we estimate the state through end-to-end feedbacks only. Second, we propose separate design of traffic management and content adaptation while [7] adopts a coupled approach. The reasons and merits have been discussed in section 2. Third, we propose an extension to take packet losses into consideration.

3.1 End-to-end Traffic Management

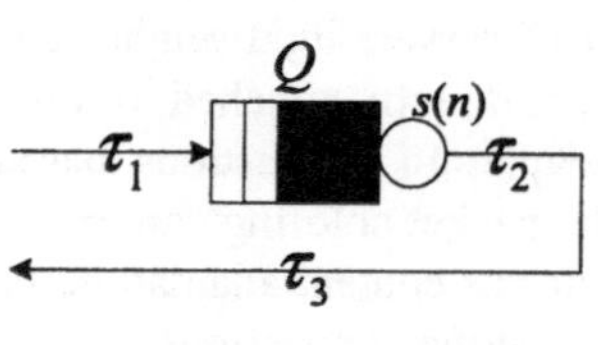

Fig. 2. A single queue model

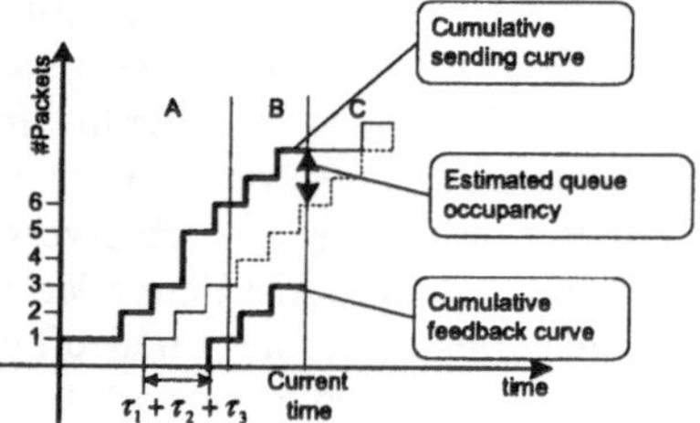

Fig. 3. Illustration of the traffic management

We model a network as a simple FIFO queuing model with one server (Fig. 2). Although there can be many intermediate routers, as far as the connection performance analysis is concerned, we can simplify the model by examining the bottleneck router only and treat other routers as delay elements. We model the packet service time for the current connection as a random process *s(n)*, where *n* represents the packet number. In this work, we take the simplistic view that the service time process is unaffected by the adaptations of the single user under consideration. This may be justifiable in a large network and is in part due to the difficulties in modeling the complicated multi-connection interactions in sharing the bottleneck bandwidth. We assume the random process is stationary, at least locally.

Fig. 3 illustrates the traffic management process at the sender. By the current time, the sender maintains the cumulative packet sending curve and the cumulative feedback curve. In order to evaluate the input and output rate at the queue, we shift the cumulative feedback curve back in time by $\tau_1+\tau_2+\tau_3$. Now the time axis is divided into three parts, shown as A, B, and C in Fig. 3. Part A corresponds to the packets sent and acknowledged by the receiver, Part B the packets sent by not acknowledged, and Part C the packets not yet sent. At a certain time, the vertical difference between the cumulative sending curve and the cumulative feedback curve is the queue occupancy. For a particular packet, the horizontal difference between the two curves is the time spent in the queue, i.e. the waiting time plus the service time.

From Part A, we are able to collect the samples for the service time process *s(n)* as the following equation:

s(n) = departure time of packet n - max(departure time of packet n-1, arrival time of packet n) (1)

In order to estimate the most recent queue occupancy and regulate further packets, we need to predict the time series *s(n)* some steps ahead. As we predict longer, the local details become less and less important. So we use a multi-timescale linear prediction by doing decimation, linear prediction and interpolation in a series with the decimation factor 2^k in the *k*-th timescale. In this way, at any timescale, we only predict two steps ahead. The prediction FIR filter taps can be obtained by the Yule-Walker equation or using an adaptive filtering algorithm such as LMS[9].

Applying the predicted service time series to the cumulative sending curve yields the estimated cumulative feedback curve for all the packets sent. We then regulate the sending of the next few packets to gradually drive the queue occupancy to the desired value. A simple analysis[10] with the M/M/1 queue model suggests setting the queue length to be 1.

Although the above algorithm strives to avoid congestion, congestion loss can happen due to errors in prediction. Since a packet is dropped when there is no room in the shared queue, congestion loss signals the size of the available queue space for the connection. For example, in Fig. 3, suppose we learn that packet 2 is lost when the feedback of packet 3 arrives, we can infer the *trouble-making* queue occupancy when packet 2 arrived at the queue and update the estimated available queue space. Similarly, when a packet gets through, we collect another sample of the available queue space. The available queue space information can be incorporated in the estimation for the queue occupancy in Part B. When it estimates the queue occupancy is too large when a packet arrives, it can predict the packet is to be lost. The available queue space can also be used to control the speed the queue occupancy is driven to the desired value.

3.2 Multi-hop Traffic Management

In the multi-hop model, there are two or more *local* traffic management loops. So every relay can keep track of two curves, one for the cumulative arrival, and the other for the cumulative departure. Because the loop is shortened, each local loop can track the network condition better and react to changes more quickly.

There are three phases in the traffic management in the system: learning phase, speed-up phase, and steady phase. During the initial phase, the entire system transmits packets slowly to learn the network characteristics. After that, each local loop runs at maximal speed to best utilize the available bandwidth without congestion. Because of the mismatch in the throughput of the different loops, the buffers at the relays before the bottleneck are built up. In the long run, the faster loops should be constrained by the bottleneck. Such a constraint can be applied to the traffic management module by estimating the throughput at the receiver and try to keep the total outstanding packets in the system roughly at a constant value. That corresponds to the steady phase.

4 Content Adaptation

Given the available bandwidth determined by the traffic management module, the content adaptation module schedules the data to be transmitted. This is often formulated as a rate-distortion optimization problem. A recent work[11] considers the optimized video adaptation with playback time constraints for variable bit-error-rate wireless channel. They show that the delay constraints are equivalent to bit budget constraints from *future* channel rates. Here we extend their work to the multi-hop network scenario for the adaptation procedures at a control point.

In the multi-hop model, both the sender and the relay are candidates to do content adaptation. From Fig. 1, since the data packets flow from the sender to the receiver and the feedback packets goes the opposite way, the sender has better content knowledge while the relay has better network knowledge. It is possible for the relay to acquire future content knowledge. When a high bandwidth pipe is feeding a low bandwidth one, we can devote a large buffer at the relay and let the previous link run at high speed. However, it is expensive in system resources and consumes additional bandwidth than necessary. Consequently we propose to adopt a sender-centric adaptation, and we show that we can use the content adaptation at relay to "withdraw" erroneous over-allocation at sender when there is a sudden decrease in the available bandwidth.

4.1 Adaptation Procedure

In this section we explain the sliding window content adaptation procedure for rate-distortion optimized resource allocation with delay constraints. The procedure is applicable to both the sender and the relay. Existing approaches for sender adaptation can be adapted to work at the relay. Two new requirements are: (1) the relay should assume passing-by data streams that may be subject to packet loss, bit error, delay jitter, (2) the relay should be very efficient in order not to add too much latency.

The throughput curve fed back from the final receiver maps the playback time constraints into bit budget constraints. We illustrate this with Fig. 4. The current time is T. Because the adaptation refers to future throughput, the throughput curve has to be predicted by the traffic management. The playback times are shown as vertical dashed lines. Each frame, denoted by a dot, must arrive before its playback time. This would mean equivalently the cumulative bits used must be less than a bound at the intersection between the throughput curve and the frame playback time.

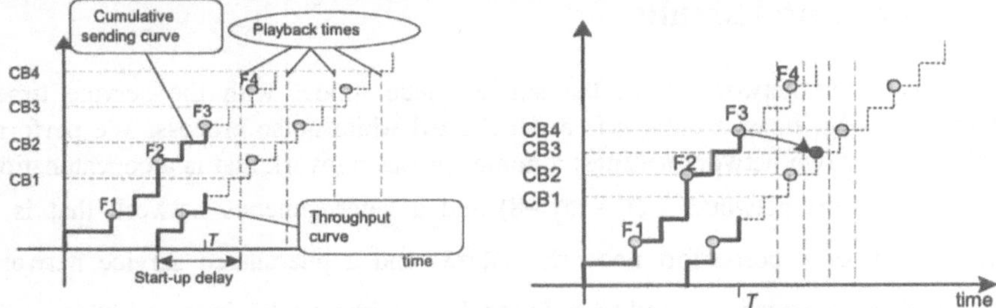

Fig. 4. The adaptation procedure

Fig. 5. Over-allocation withdrawal

The adaptation procedures are as follows:

1. For all the frames in the buffer, collect the rate-distortion characteristics.

2. Partition the available bandwidth into shares for each frame, minimizing the received distortion under the bit budget constraints. This optimization problem can be solved with dynamic programming or Lagrange multiplier[11].

3. If the buffer is full while there are some arriving data, apply a similar rate-distortion based discarding/compression on the buffered data.

4. When the determined frame finishes transmission, the window slides forward and the process is applied again.

4.2 Over-allocation Withdrawal

The relay can be more than just a buffer if appropriate coordination is established with the sender. The sender knows the source characteristics better and hence can do long-term planning in bit allocation. However since it may wrongly estimate the future throughput, it may end up over-allocating bits for some frames and having few or no bits left for later frames. This could lead to abrupt drops in the image quality.

When the sender realized the over-allocation, it has no way to withdraw the previously made decisions. For example, F3 was over-allocated in Fig. 5. However when the relay sees the same amount of feedback information, it may only need to determine the bit allocation for F2. Thus the relay can realize the over-allocation of F3 before it is sent out from the relay. This would lead to the bit reduction for F3, shown with an arrow in Fig. 5.

Consequently, if the relay can notify the sender the reduction, the sender can perform allocation assuming some previous over-allocation has been withdrawn. This is equivalent to *pulling* back the starting point for current allocation, namely the total bits consumed by all the previous frames. Signaling overhead can be reduced if the sender predicts the reduction behavior at the relay. Note that the sender doesn't need to predict *what* will be reduced, but to predict *how much* will be reduced only. The sender can check all the frames that has been sent but not acknowledged by the final receiver from the oldest to the newest. If a frame exceeds the frame playback time, the sender assumes the relay can reduce it to the frame playback time and adjusts the total bits consumed.

5 Experimental Results

We simulate the networks with the single queue model with the service times generated by Fig. 6, where the n is a normalized white noise process. We perform simulation over two network settings: a homogeneous network that is a concatenation of two best-effort networks ($\sigma_1 = \sigma_2$ =8) and a heterogeneous network that is a concatenation of a best-effort network (σ_1 =8) and a guaranteed service network (σ_2 =1). The reference is the end-to-end model, i.e. without relay in the middle.

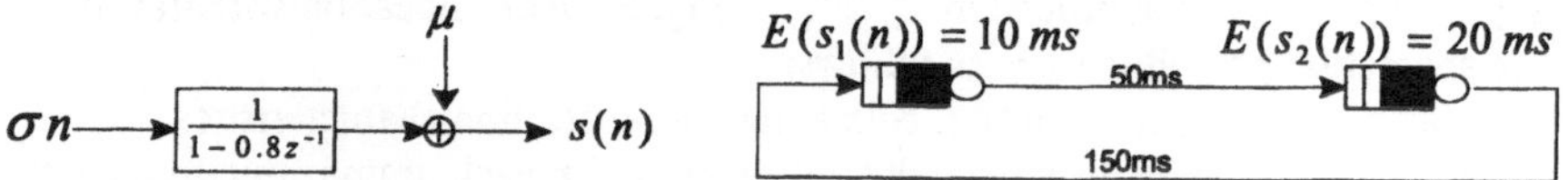

Fig. 6. Generation of *s(n)* **Fig. 7.** Simulation network

Using the proposed traffic management, we obtain the cumulative traffic curves for both networks, with and without relay. Due to limitations in space, we cannot show these curves, but we maintain that the sending and arrival curves are closely matched, hence achieving low delay and low delay jitter. For the traffic curves with relay, the two local loops maintain a constant vertical difference in a large timescale, hence the buffer at the relay is kept at a constant level. The slope of the curves corresponds to the bandwidth utilization. Comparing the homogeneous traffic simulations, the multi-hop model gains 19.3% in throughput. Comparing the heterogeneous traffic simulations, the multi-hop model gains 37.8% in throughput. Although the service time process is randomly generated, due to congestion avoidance, the sender can't always keep the queue non-empty. The mean and standard deviation of the two queues are shown in Table 1 to give a rough idea of the probability that the queue length exceeds a threshold. We note that the standard deviations for the bottleneck queue Q_2 are roughly the same for both schemes. Thus the multi-hop model didn't increase the risk of overloading the bottleneck queue much.

We use FGS (Fine Granularity Scalable) codec for the simulation of content adaptation. The decision is then the number of enhancement layer bit planes for each frame. The R-D function in the optimization is an approximate equation: $D=(Q_b 2^{-l})^2$, where l is the number of bit planes, and Q_b is the base layer quantization step size.

Table 1. (mean, std) of queue length

	Ref-Q_1	Relay-Q_1	Ref- Q_2	Relay-Q_2
Hom.	0.44,0.61	1.07,1.87	1.10,1.17	1.55,1.27
Het.	0.50,0.72	1.65,2.22	0.73,0.53	1.09,0.40

The test sequence is 10 second *Akiyo* CIF at 15fps, with 1 I-frame every 30 frames. The decoder startup delay is 0.5s. The packet size is 400bytes. So the bandwidths for the two links are roughly 320kbps and 160kbps. Applying the content adaptation algorithm gives the decoded PSNR results in Table 2. For initialization simplicity, the first 20 frames are fixed to operate at 7 bit planes. We can see that the content adaptation translates the throughput gain into 0.6dB for the homogeneous network and

1.2dB for the heterogeneous network. The gain would be more obvious if we were operating at lower bit rate because of the relatively flat video rate-distortion at high bit rate. The third column Relay-OW stands for over-allocation withdrawal. In the heterogeneous network, the bottleneck throughput is highly predictable. So the relay adaptation never reduces bit rate. For the homogeneous network, the average PSNR gain with over-allocation withdrawal is small. This is because the over-allocation withdrawal is called for only when there is a sudden decrease in throughput. In comparing frame-by-frame PSNR results, we observe that the over-allocation withdrawal eliminates all the sudden drops in PSNR.

Table 2. Average decoded PSNR results (dB)

	Ref.	Relay	Relay-OW
Hom.	35.58	36.24	36.30
Het.	35.96	37.19	37.19

6 Conclusion

In this paper, we study the design of the traffic management and the content adaptation in the intelligent multi-hop video communications architecture. The gains with the relay can be summarized in the following: 1) timely reaction to changing network condition, 2) separating different channel characteristics, 3) content specific operations moved into the network. Analysis and simulations suggest that the multi-hop traffic management can gain high throughput, and the content adaptation should be sender-centric with occasional relay supports.

References

1. Amir, S. McCanne and R. Katz, "An Active Service Framework and its Application to Real-time Multimedia Transcoding", Proc. SIGCOMM, 1998
2. E. Amir, S. McCann, and H. Zhang, "An Application Level Video Gateway", Proc. ACM Multimedia'95, Nov. 1995.
3. H. Balakrishnan, "Challenges to Reliable Data Transport over Heterogeneous Wireless Networks", Ph.D dissertation, U.C.Berkeley, May 1998.
4. Z.-L. Zhang, Y. Wang, D. H. C. Du, and D. Su, "Video Staging: A Proxy-Server-Based Approach to End-to-End Video Delivery over Wide-Area Networks", IEEE/ACM Trans. on Networking, vol.8, no.4, pp.429-442, Aug. 2000.
5. N. Yeadon, F. Garcia, D. Hutchison, and D. Shepherd, "Filters: QoS support mechanisms for multipeer communication", IEEE JSAC, vol. 14, no. 7, pp. 1245-1262, Sept. 1996.
6. H. Balakrishnan, H. Rahul, and S. Seshan, "An Integrated Congestion Management Architecture for Internet Hosts", Proc. ACM SIGCOMM, Sept. 1999.
7. H. Kanakia, P. P. Mishra, and A. Reibman, "An adaptive congestion control scheme for real-time packet video transport", Proc. ACM SIGCOMM, Sept. 1993.
8. L. Brakmo and L. Peterson, "TCP Vegas: End-to-End Congestion Avoidance on a Global Internet", IEEE JSAC, vol. 13, No. 8, pages 1465-1480, Oct. 1995.
9. S. Haykin, "Adaptive Filter Theory", Third Edition, Prentice-Hall, 1996.
10. M. Schwartz, "Broadband integrated networks", Prentice-Hall, 1996.
11. C.-Y. Hsu, A. Ortega, and M. Khansari, "Rate control for robust video transmission over burst-error wireless channels", IEEE JSAC, vol. 17, no. 5, May. 1999.

Classification of Facial Images Using Gaussian Mixture Models

Pin Liao [1,2], Wen Gao [1,2,3], Li Shen [2], Xilin Chen [1,2,3], Shiguang Shan [1,2], Wen-bing Zeng [4]

[1] ICT-YCNC FRTJDL, [2] Institute of Computing Technology, Chinese Academy of Sciences, Beijing 100080,China
[3] Department of Computer Science, Harbin Institute of Technology, Harbin, 150001, China
[4] YCNC Co. Chengdu, SiChuan Province, 610016, China

Abstract. We present a new technique for face recognition. Two distinct and mutually exclusive classes of difference between two facial images are defined: within-class differences set (differences in appearance of the same individual) and between-class differences set (differences in appearance between different individuals). Then Gaussian mixture models (GMMs) are used to estimate the eigenspace densities of the two classes. And subsequently a matching similarity measure is computed based on the maximum likelihood (ML) method. The new method achieved as much as 45% error reduction compared to the standard eigenface approach on the ORL database.

1 Introduction

As one of the most active areas of research in computer vision and pattern recognition, face recognition has recently received significant attention, especially during the past few years. There are at least two reasons for this trend: the first is the wide range of commercial and law enforcement applications and the second is the availability of feasible technologies after 30 years of research [1].

A family of subspace methods for face recognition is popular currently, originated by Turk and Pentland's "eigenfaces"[2], which has become a common baseline for comparison in the area. Those approaches often make use of simple image similarity metrics such as Euclidean distance or normalized correlation, which correspond to a standard "template-matching" approach, i.e. nearest-neighbor-based classification.

In a canonical face recognition method, each individual is a class and the distribution of each face is estimated or approximated with many samples per class. However, face recognition is different from some classical pattern-recognition problems such as OCR on that there are usually only a few images per person. In fact, it is not uncommon to have only a single training example for each person. Therefore there is no enough information to estimate the distribution of each class, and then the standard Euclidean nearest-neighbor matching technique is often adopted. Such a matching technique suffers from a major drawback: it does not exploit knowledge of which type of variations are critical (as opposed to incidental) in expressing similarity [3].

Accordingly a novel classification modeling method was proposed [3][4][5], that the differences between facial images are modeled as two mutually exclusive classes: within-class differences (differences in appearance of the same individual relating, for example, to facial expression variations, illumination variations, pose variations according to the same person) and between-class differences (differences in appearance between different individuals corresponding to variation in identity).

Moghaddam et al. assumed the both classes as Gaussian distributions and obtained two probabilistic similarity measures using the Bayes (maximum a posteriori, MAP) rule and the maximum likelihood (ML) rule respectively [3][4]. Philips directly applied support vector machines (SVMs) to the two classes problem. Those approaches all achieved much better performances than the standard eigenface matching.

Considering that it is usually difficult to provide a good representation of practical distributions by common typical distribution forms of parametric functions in statistics, there are inevitably some inaccuracy and limitation with the approach of Moghaddam et al., simply using normal density to approximate the eigenspace distributions of the two kinds of differences. Therefore, we propose a technique to estimate the two densities using Gaussian mixture models (GMMs) instead of using normal density. Note that GMMs have also been used, in a different manner, for maximum likelihood detection of faces by Moghaddam and Pentland [9]. The experimental results show that our method outperforms those above-mentioned approaches.

2 Within-class Difference and Between-class Differences

As for a conventional face recognition algorithm in which each individual is a class, the classification problem is a K class problem for a gallery of K individuals. However, the K classes problem can be reduce to a two classes problem by modeling the differences of facial images.

The difference between two facial images I_1 and I_2 is denoted by $\Delta = I_1 - I_2$. Then two mutually exclusive classes are defined: within-class differences Ω_I and between-class differences Ω_E.

In terms of the within-class a posteriori probability as given by Bayes rule, the similarity measure between two facial images can be directly defined as:

$$\begin{aligned} S(I_1, I_2) &= P(\Delta \in \Omega_I) \\ &= P(\Omega_I|\Delta) \\ &= \frac{P(\Delta|\Omega_I)P(\Omega_I)}{P(\Delta|\Omega_I)P(\Omega_I) + P(\Delta|\Omega_E)P(\Omega_E)} \end{aligned} \tag{1}$$

where the priors $P(\Omega_I)$ and $P(\Omega_E)$ can be set to reflect some sources of a priori knowledge concerning the images being matched, and a defaulting setting of equal priors, $P(\Omega_I) = P(\Omega_E) = 1/2$, is often used.

It is the representation of the within-class differences subspace that is the critical part of formulating the probabilistic measure of facial similarity. Then, an alternative probabilistic similarity measure can be defined in simpler form using the ML rule instead of the MAP rule, only exploiting the within-class likelihood,

$$S(I_1, I_2) = P(\Delta|\Omega_I) \tag{2}$$

Moghaddam et al. modeled each of the classes as Gaussian density [3][4], and then the class-conditional densities were defined as

$$P(\Delta \mid \Omega_I) = \frac{1}{(2\pi)^{d/2}|\Sigma_I|^{1/2}} \exp\left(-\frac{1}{2}\Delta^T \Sigma_I^{-1} \Delta\right) \tag{3}$$

$$P(\Delta \mid \Omega_E) = \frac{1}{(2\pi)^{d/2}|\Sigma_E|^{1/2}} \exp\left(-\frac{1}{2}\Delta^T \Sigma_E^{-1} \Delta\right) \tag{4}$$

Therefore, when in identification there is a gallery $\{g_j\}$ of K known individuals and a probe p is to be identified, the similarity score between p and each g_j is $S(p, g_j)$. Accordingly the probe is identified as person k with the maximum similarity score, e.g.

$$k = \arg\max_j S(p, g_j) \tag{5}$$

3 Gaussian Mixture Models

Gaussian mixture models (GMMs) are a semi-parametric approach to density estimation, combining the advantages of both parametric and non-parametric methods. GMMs are not restricted to specific functional forms, and yet where the size of the model only grows with the complexity of the problem being solved, and not simply with the size of the data set.

GMMs are defined as a linear combination of M component normal densities $p(x \mid j)$:

$$p(x) = \sum_{j=1}^{M} p(x \mid j) P(j) \tag{6}$$

where the number M of components is typically much less than the size N of the training data set $\{x^n\}$. Such a representation is called a mixture distribution [6] and the coefficients $P(j)$ are called the mixing parameters.

$P(j)$ can be regarded as the prior probability of the data point having been generated from component j of the mixture. These priors are chosen to satisfy the constraints

$$\sum_{j=1}^{M} P(j) = 1 \quad \text{and} \quad 0 \le P(j) \le 1 \tag{7}$$

In addition, the component density functions $p(x \mid j)$ are normalized so that

$$\int p(x \mid j)\, dx = 1 \tag{8}$$

and hence can be regarded as class-conditional densities.

Each component distribution $p(x \mid j)$ is Gaussian with a covariance matrix Σ_j and a mean μ_j. The parameters of a GMM, such as Σ_j, μ_j and $P(j)$, can be achieved in a maximum likelihood framework by the well-known expectation-maximization (EM) algorithm. The mean μ_j and the covariance Σ_j for each Gaussian component is initialized using the K-means algorithm, and $P(j)$ is initialized as $1/M$. The determinants of covariance matrices and the inverse covariance matrices have to be computed at each iteration of the EM algorithm to evaluate the new value of the log likelihood.

However, the covariance matrices are often ill-conditioned. The problem can be resolved by multiplying the off-diagonal elements of the covariance matrices by a number, $0 \le f < 1$, to reduce their influence [8].

4 Combination of Multiple Gaussian Mixture Models

Although GMMs are a popular tool for density estimation, choosing the number of mixture components is notoriously difficult. There are many approaches to this problem, but our intention here is to investigate the basic effectiveness of the GMMs approach. So we adopt a simple classifier combination approach based on the mean rule, partly for it is well known that a combination of many different classifiers can lead to significant improvements in the predictions on new data and in fact it's performance can be better than the performance of the best single classifier used in isolation [7].

By setting various number M components of GMMs, different GMMs are produced to approximate the eigenspace densities of the two kinds of differences between facial images, and then different classifiers are yielded.

It is supposed that we have obtained a set of L various classifiers C_l where $l = 1,\ldots,L$ based on different GMMs. Then for a gallery $\{g_j\}$ of K known individuals, the similarity score between a probe p and each g_j presented by a classifier C_l is $S_l(p, g_j)$.

The similarity scores are firstly normalized as

$$S'_l(p, g_j) = \frac{S_l(p, g_j)}{\sum_{i=1}^{K} S_l(p, g_i)} \tag{9}$$

and then the mean combination rule is introduced:

$$S_{mean}(p, g_j) = \frac{1}{L} \sum_{l=1}^{L} S'_l(p, g_j) \tag{10}$$

Consequently the probe is identified as person k with $k = \arg\max_j S_{mean}(p, g_j)$.

5 Experiments

Fig. 1. Some examples from the ORL database

5.1 Data

We have used the ORL database from the Olivetti Research Laboratory in Cambridge, U.K. There are ten different images of each of 40 distinct subjects. For some subjects, the images were taken at different times, varying the lighting, facial expressions (open/closed eyes, smiling/not smiling) and facial details (glasses/no glasses). All the images were taken against a dark homogeneous background with the subjects in an upright, frontal position, with tolerance for some tilting and rotation of up to about 20 degrees. There is some variation in scale of up to about 10%. The images are grayscale with a resolution of 92×112. Some examples from the database are shown in figure 1.

The 400 images are divided into disjoint training and testing sets. Each set consists of 10 images of 20 people. Accordingly 900 ($C_{10}^2\times20$) with-class difference samples and 19000 ($C_{20}^2\times10\times10$) between-class difference samples corresponding to the classes Ω_I and Ω_E respectively are created from the training set, while PCA analysis is performed.

Moghaddam et al. have showed that the distributions of the two classes appear to be two enmeshed distributions, differing primarily in the amount of scatter, with Ω_I displaying smaller differences as expected [3][4].

In this paper the two distributions are investigated further. Visualizations of the distributions are shown in Fig.2 and Fig.3, which are approximative 3-D plots and contour plots of the distributions of the two classes respectively in the first two principal components based on the training samples. From the plots it can be seen that the relative orientation and scatter of the distributions are considerably different. And we can also observe that it is not quite precise to simply assume either the distribution of the within-class differences or the one of the between-classes differences as Gaussian density.

A gallery was built by randomly selecting 20 images from the testing set, with one image per person, and the remaining 180 images made up of a probe set. This random selection was repeated 100 times to create 100 different galleries and 100 different probe sets accordingly. All recognition techniques to be evaluated below were assessed over these 100 testing subsets.

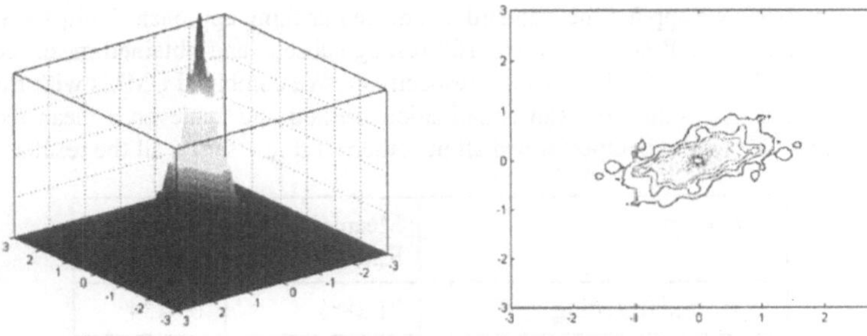

Fig. 2. Approximative 3-D plot and contour plot of the distribution of the within-class differences class Ω_I in the first two principal components

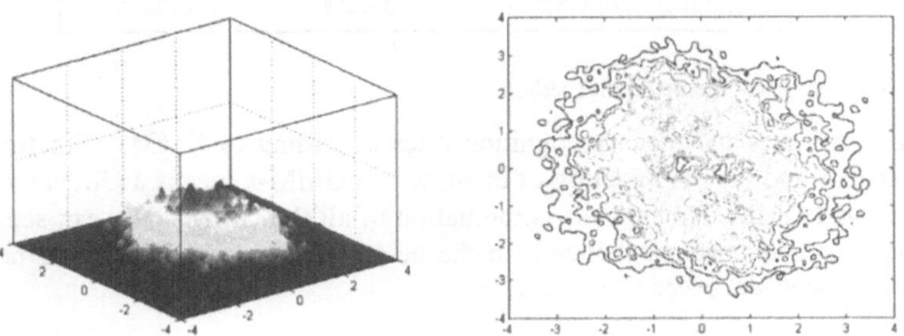

Fig. 3. Approximative 3-D plot and contour plot of the distribution of the between-class differences class Ω_E in the first two principal components

5.2 Experimental Results

We modeled the two distributions using GMMs with different number of components and obtained two kinds of similarity measures based on the MAP rule and the ML rule respectively. Surprisingly, in our experiments the ML approach outperformed the MAP approach with a minor (2%) increase in the recognition rate over the testing set, contrary with the experimental results of Moghaddam et al [3][4]. And on the training set the MAP method excelled the ML method with an addition of 3-4% to the recognition rate. It can be explained that, the theoretically optimal Bayes classifier is sensitive to density estimation errors, and it is considerably difficult to obtain an estimation of the distribution of the between-class differences, which relevant to variations in identity, with desirable generalization over a training set consisting images of only 20 individuals. We therefore show only the ML results in this paper.

For comparisons we applied the standard eigenface matching approach, Philips's SVM, and Moghaddam et al.'s MAP and ML to the 100 testing subsets, and obtained mean recognition rates of 71.38%, 77.78%, 79.87%, 81.68% respectively. We combined GMMs with from 1 to 8 Gaussian components using the mean combination method and achieved a mean recognition rate of 84.25%. Our method outperformed all the others. Table 1 shows all the results.

Approach	Mean Recog. Rate	Variance
Eigenface matching	71.38%	0.0434
Philips' SVM	77.78%	0.0384
Moghaddam et al.'s MAP	79.87%	0.0237
Moghaddam et al.'s ML	81.68%	0.0323
Combination of GMMs	84.25%	0.0275

Table 1. Results by the different methods

Fig.4 illustrates the mean recognition rates according to GMMs with from 1 to 8 components and the combination of them, where GMM-x means a GMM with x components and GMM-C means the combination of all the GMMs. We can see the combination method performs better than the best of the individual models, providing a solution to the model selection problem.

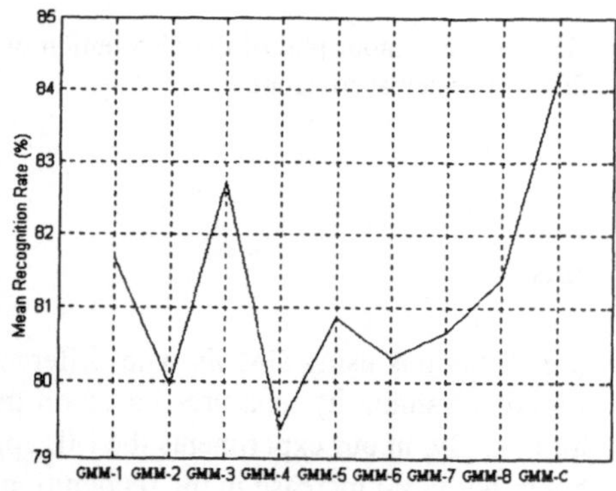

Fig. 4. Results according to GMMs with from 1 to 8 components and the combination of them

6 Conclusions

It has been suggested that the differences between facial images can be modeled as two mutually exclusive classes: within-class differences and between-class differences. In this paper we investigated replacing normal density with GMMs to estimate the distributions of the two classes, which consequently resulted in significant reduction in the error rate up to 45% compared to the standard eigenface approach. The better performance of our method than the others indicates that GMMs can make more efficient use of the information in face space.

Acknowledgment

This research is sponsored partly by Natural Science Foundation of China (No.69789301), National Hi-Tech Program of China (No.863-306-ZD03-01-2), and 100 Talents Foundation of Chinese Academy of Sciences.

References

1. W. Zhao, R. Chellappa, A. Rosenfeld, P.J. Phillips. Face recognition: a literature survey, Technical Report, University of Maryland at College Park, the Computer Vision Laboratory, 2000.
2. M. Turk, A. Pentland, Eigenfaces for recognition, J. Cognitive Neuroscience, 3, pp. 71-86, 1991.
3. Baback Moghaddam, Tony Jebara, Alex Pentland, Bayesian face recognition, Pattern Recognition, 33, pp. 1771-1782, 2000.
4. Baback Moghaddam, Alex Pentland, Beyond Euclidean eigenspaces: Bayesian matching for visual recognition, in H. Wechsler, V. Bruce, T. Huang, J. P. Phillips, eds., *Face Recognition: From Theories to Applications*, Springer-Verlag, Berlin, 1998.
5. P. Jonathon Philips, Support vector machines applied to face recognition, in M.J. Kearns, S. A. Solla, and D. A. Cohn, eds., Advances in Neural Information Processing Systems II, MIT Press, 1999.
6. A. N. Titterington, A. F. M. Smith, and U. E. Makov, Statistical analysis of finite mixture distributions, New York: Jonhn Wiley, 1985..
7. C. M. Bishop, Neural Networks for Pattern Recognition, Oxford University Press, Oxford, 1995.
8. Steve Lawrence, Peter Yianilos, Ingemar Cox, Face recognition using mixture-distance and raw images, 1997 IEEE International Conference on Systems, Man, and Cybernetics, IEEE Press, Piscataway, NJ, pp. 2016-2021, 1997.
9. Baback Moghaddam, Alex Pentland, Probabilistic visual learning for object detection, in International Conference on Computer Vision, pp. 786-793, 1995.

A Fast Descriptor Matching Algorithm for Exhaustive Search in Large Databases

B. C. Song, M. J. Kim, and J. B. Ra*

Dept. of EECS, KAIST

373-1 Kusong-dong, Yusong-ku, Taejon, 305-701, Republic of Korea

Abstract

In order to find the best match to a query image in a database, conventional content-based image retrieval schemes need the exhaustive search, where the descriptor of the query, e.g., histogram, must be compared with literally all images in the database. However, the straightforward exhaustive search algorithm is computationally expensive. So, fast exhaustive search algorithms are demanded. This paper presents a fast exhaustive search algorithm based on a multi-resolution descriptor struc[1]ture and a norm-sorted database. First, we derive a condition to eliminate unnecessary matching operations from the search procedure by using a norm-sorted structure of the database. Then, we propose a fast search algorithm based on the elimination condition, which guarantees an exhaustive search for either the best match or multiple best matches to a query. With a luminance histogram as a descriptor, we show that the proposed algorithm provides a search accuracy of 100% with high search speed.

1. Introduction

Since the amount of multimedia data such as video and image is drastically increasing, it is very difficult to explore a particular data on the internet or a large database. Thus, it is strongly demanded to develop efficient techniques to store, browse, index, and retrieve multimedia data [1]. Especially, an effective data management technique for image databases is very challenging because it is not only a key element to general multimedia management systems, but also has abundant applications such as digital museum, entertainment, internet shopping, and medical image retrieval systems. Therefore, active research has recently focused on the indexing and retrieval of image databases. To quickly retrieve a desired image among all images in a database, they have to be manually annotated by keywords or automatically indexed by visual cues or visual features extracted from them, in advance. However, the efficiency of text-based retrieval dramatically decreases for large image databases, because a prohibitive amount of labor should be involved for the annotation of all images and a limited number of keywords is insufficient to describe details in a content-abundant image.

Due to the above-mentioned deficiency of text-based retrieval, content-based image retrieval (CBIR) is preferred. Conventional CBIR schemes such as QBIC [2] are tightly coupled with a similarity measure, which rates the similarity of two images according to image contents, and they usually employ a similarity measure based on low-level features, e.g., color, texture, and shape. On the other hand, MPEG-7, which is being standardized currently, defines the descriptors based on low-level features, e.g., color histogram and edge histogram.

---

* B. C. Song is now with Digital Media R&D Center, Samsung Electronics Co., Ltd, 416 Maetan-3 dong, Paldal-gu, Suwon, Korea.

If images are indexed by high-dimensional descriptors, the best match(es) to a query image can be searched by examining the similarity between the query descriptor and descriptors from database images, in high-dimensional space. A brute-force way to perform similarity matching is to read all candidate descriptors in the database, compute their distances from the given query, and select the closest match(es). This is called the exhaustive search algorithm (ESA). However, the running time of ESA is proportional to the dimension (B) and size (N) of the dataset, or $O(BN)$, which can be very large. A logical way to improve the search speed of ESA is to reduce the search space. Hence, a lot of tree-like structures such as R-, R*-, SS-, and SR-trees have been developed for search space reduction. However, recent studies point out that these tree-like structures suffer from the *curse of dimensionality* in that the time to traverse the index structure to find the adjacent blocks (e.g., by using the branch-and-bound algorithm) and the number of the adjacent blocks to look for the best match(es) grow explosively with data dimension [3]. Kleinberg theoretically showed that ESA is faster than these indexing schemes when $B \geq \log N$ [4]. It is also commonly known that even efficient data structures for data indexing like R*-trees [5], work well only up to the dimension of 20.

To overcome the demerit of tree-based approaches in high-dimensional descriptor matching, several fast exhaustive search algorithms have been developed recently [6]-[8]. Hafner *et al.* proposed a novel fast exhaustive search algorithm based on the color histogram distance of quadratic form [6]. However, this algorithm may have limits in further improving speed performance since it filters out unnecessary matching processes only in a single step. On the other hand, Berman and Shapiro employed the concept of triangle inequality to avoid full-resolution matching of unreliable candidate descriptors with the query descriptor, and reduced a great deal of computation [7]. However, its speed performance highly depends on the choice of key images, and is not satisfying in large image databases. So, they employed a data structure known as the Triangle Trie [8]. But, the speed performance of the algorithm still depends on key images, Trie depth, and the threshold.

On the other hand, Li and Salari proposed a fast motion estimation algorithm for video coding, which is called the successive elimination algorithm (SEA) [9]. The SEA eliminates unreliable candidates by using the fact that the lower bound of the distance between the current block and the candidate block in the previous frame can be derived from the simple difference of their L_1-norms. Therefore, it can achieve very fast motion estimation with the same accuracy as that in ESA.

In this paper, we extend SEA to a general multi-resolution case, and propose a fast exhaustive image search algorithm by applying the multi-resolution concept to descriptor matching and sorting the candidates in the image database in ascending order of their descriptor-norms. The norm-sorted database brings out an additional computation reduction since it achieves a half-way-stop without loss of search accuracy. The proposed algorithm provides not only faster search ability than existing algorithms, but also the same search results as the ESA. In addition, the proposed algorithm can rapidly provide multiple best matches in an efficient way. Through experiments, the proposed algorithm has proven to be a credible solution for fast exhaustive search in large image databases.

2. The Proposed Algorithm

2.1 Brief Review of SEA

In this section, we will introduce SEA for descriptor matching in image search rather than block matching in motion estimation. Suppose that an image descriptor is a B-dimensional vector (B=2^L). Then, the L_1-norm of a descriptor $\mathbf{X}$, $\|\mathbf{X}\|$ is represented as

$$\|\mathbf{X}\| = \sum_{n=1}^{B} X(n), \qquad (1)$$

where $X(n)$ denotes the n-th bin value. And the following inequality is obtained [9]:

$$d(\mathbf{X},\mathbf{Q}) \geq \left| \|\mathbf{X}\| - \|\mathbf{Q}\| \right|, \tag{2}$$

where $d(\mathbf{X}, \mathbf{Q})$ denotes the L_1-distance between two descriptors **X** and **Q**. Therefore, for a given query descriptor **Q**, it is possible to eliminate any candidate whose descriptor **X** satisfies $\left| \|\mathbf{X}\| - \|\mathbf{Q}\| \right| \geq d_{\min}$, without the time-consuming calculation of $d(\mathbf{X}, \mathbf{Q})$. Here, $d_{\min}$ means the "so far" minimum distance.

2.2 Inequality Property Based on Norm Pyramid

We extend the inequality property in Eq. (2) to a multi-resolution case, so that tighter decision boundaries for decreasing search operations can be obtained in a multi-level manner. For each descriptor **X**, an L_1-norm pyramid can be defined as a sequence of descriptors $\{\mathbf{X}^0, \ldots, \mathbf{X}^l, \ldots, \mathbf{X}^L\}$, where $\mathbf{X}^L = \mathbf{X}$, and $\mathbf{X}^l$ has a dimension of 2^l and is a lower resolution version of $\mathbf{X}^{l+1}$ reduced by half. A pyramid data structure can be formed by successively summing two neighboring element values at the higher level. $X^l(n)$ can be obtained as follows:

$$X^l(n) = X^{l+1}(2n-1) + X^{l+1}(2n) \quad \text{for } 1 \leq n \leq 2^l. \tag{3}$$

Then, we can derive the following inequality for a given query descriptor **Q**.

***Property*:**

$$d(\mathbf{X},\mathbf{Q}) \equiv d^L(\mathbf{X},\mathbf{Q}) \geq \ldots \geq d^l(\mathbf{X},\mathbf{Q}) \geq \ldots \geq d^0(\mathbf{X},\mathbf{Q}), \tag{4}$$

where $d^l(\mathbf{X},\mathbf{Q})$ denotes $d(\mathbf{X}^l,\mathbf{Q}^l)$.

***Proof*:**

$$\begin{aligned} d^{l+1}(\mathbf{X},\mathbf{Q}) &= \sum_{n=1}^{2^{l+1}} \left| X^{l+1}(n) - Q^{l+1}(n) \right| \\ &= \sum_{n=1}^{2^l} \left\{ \left| X^{l+1}(2n-1) - Q^{l+1}(2n-1) \right| + \left| X^{l+1}(2n) - Q^{l+1}(2n) \right| \right\}, \end{aligned} \tag{5}$$

From Eq. (3),

$$\begin{aligned} d^l(\mathbf{X},\mathbf{Q}) &= \sum_{n=1}^{2^l} \left| X^l(n) - Q^l(n) \right| \\ &= \sum_{n=1}^{2^l} \left| X^{l+1}(2n-1) - Q^{l+1}(2n-1) + X^{l+1}(2n) - Q^{l+1}(2n) \right|. \end{aligned} \tag{6}$$

Since $|A| + |B| \geq |A + B|$,

$$\begin{aligned} &\sum_{n=1}^{2^l} \left\{ \left| X^{l+1}(2n-1) - Q^{l+1}(2n-1) \right| + \left| X^{l+1}(2n) - Q^{l+1}(2n) \right| \right\} \\ &\geq \sum_{n=1}^{2^l} \left| X^{l+1}(2n-1) - Q^{l+1}(2n-1) + X^{l+1}(2n) - Q^{l+1}(2n) \right|. \end{aligned} \tag{7}$$

From Eqs. (5), (6), and (7),

$$\begin{aligned} d^{l+1}(\mathbf{X},\mathbf{Q}) &= \sum_{n=1}^{2^l} \left\{ \left| X^{l+1}(2n-1) - Q^{l+1}(2n-1) \right| + \left| X^{l+1}(2n) - Q^{l+1}(2n) \right| \right\} \\ &\geq \sum_{n=1}^{2^l} \left| X^{l+1}(2n-1) - Q^{l+1}(2n-1) + X^{l+1}(2n) - Q^{l+1}(2n) \right| \\ &= d^l(\mathbf{X},\mathbf{Q}), \end{aligned} \tag{8}$$

which coincides with Eq. (4).

2.3 The Proposed Algorithm

We propose a fast exhaustive search algorithm based on Eq. (4). Assume that N denotes the total number of images in a database. Multi-resolution descriptors of all images are pre-computed and stored. Prior to the search procedure, all the descriptors and images are stored in ascending order of their L_1-norm values (see Fig. 1).

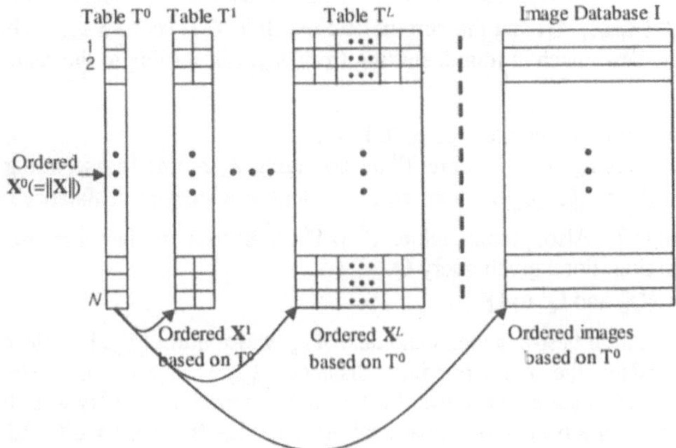

Fig. 1. Ordering of ordinary descriptors $\mathbf{X}^L$ and their L_1-norm-based multi-resolution descriptors according to the ordering of $\|\mathbf{X}\|$.

Note in the figure that all the elements of tables (T^0, T^1, ..., T^L) and image database (I) are arranged in the same order as Table T^0. In the search process, a proper selection of the starting candidate to compare is important in improving search speed. In this scheme, we select $\mathbf{X}_{ibm}$ whose norm $\|\mathbf{X}_{ibm}\|$ is the closest to the query norm $\|\mathbf{Q}\|$, and consider it the initial best match. To obtain $\mathbf{X}_{ibm}$, the binary search can be performed in $\log_2 N$ steps since Table T^0 has been sorted in advance. Then, the "so far" minimum distance $d_{\min}$ is set to $d(\mathbf{X}_{ibm}, \mathbf{Q})$.

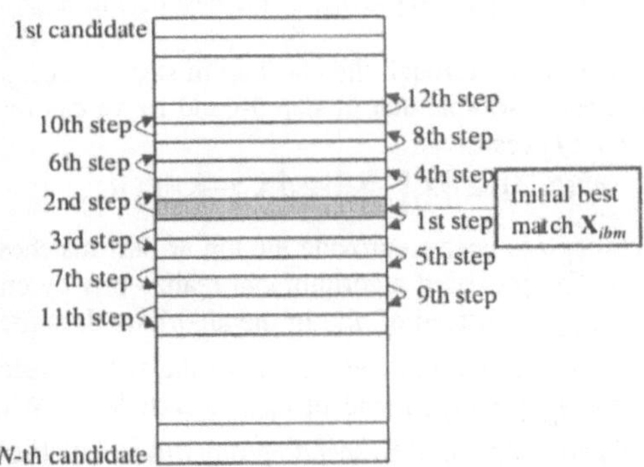

Fig. 2: Search order in the database.

The searching proceeds in alternating order starting from $\mathbf{X}_{ibm}$ as depicted in Fig. 2. To determine whether the next candidate $\mathbf{X}_{ibm+1}$ is closer to $\mathbf{Q}$ than the current best match $\mathbf{X}_{ibm}$, we examine $\mathbf{X}_{ibm+1}$ starting from the top level of its L_1-norm pyramid. First, $d^0(\mathbf{X}_{ibm+1}, \mathbf{Q})$ is computed, and is compared with $d_{\min}$. If it is larger than or equal to $d_{\min}$, $d^L(\mathbf{X}_{ibm+1}, \mathbf{Q}) \geq d_{\min}$ from Eq. (4). Thus, $\mathbf{X}_{ibm+1}$ cannot be the closest one and is rejected. Otherwise, $d^1(\mathbf{X}_{ibm+1}, \mathbf{Q})$

is calculated and compared with $d_{\min}$. If $d^1(\mathbf{X}_{ibm+1}, \mathbf{Q}) \geq d_{\min}$, $\mathbf{X}_{ibm+1}$ is rejected due to the same reason as above. Otherwise, the next level is evaluated. This process is repeated until $\mathbf{X}_{ibm+1}$ is rejected or the bottom level is reached. If the bottom level is reached, $d^L(\mathbf{X}_{ibm+1}, \mathbf{Q})$ is computed and compared with $d_{\min}$. If $d^L(\mathbf{X}_{ibm+1}, \mathbf{Q}) \geq d_{\min}$, $\mathbf{X}_{ibm+1}$ is rejected. Otherwise, $d_{\min}$ is replaced with $d^L(\mathbf{X}_{ibm+1}, \mathbf{Q})$ and the current best match to $\mathbf{Q}$ is set to $\mathbf{X}_{ibm+1}$. This procedure is repeated until the best match is found, starting from $\mathbf{X}_{ibm-1}$ according to the search order shown in Fig. 2.

The proposed algorithm is summarized as follows:

a) Off-line preprocessing: Build Table T^0 by arranging L_1-norms in ascending order so that $\|\mathbf{X}_1\| \leq \|\mathbf{X}_2\| \leq \ldots \leq \|\mathbf{X}_{N-1}\| \leq \|\mathbf{X}_N\|$. Then, sort the candidate images in database I in the same order as in Table T^0. Also, prepare tables T^1 to T^L for $\mathbf{X}^1$ to $\mathbf{X}^L$ in the same order.

b) On-line processing: For a given query $\mathbf{Q}$,

1. Evaluate $\|\mathbf{Q}\|$ and $\mathbf{Q}^1$ to $\mathbf{Q}^L$.
2. Select the initial best-matched candidate $\mathbf{X}_{ibm}$ whose norm $\|\mathbf{X}_{ibm}\|$ is closest to $\|\mathbf{Q}\|$, and then calculate the corresponding distance $d_{\min} = d(\mathbf{X}_{ibm}, Q)$. Here, to reduce computational burden, the initial best match is found via binary search within $\log_2 N$ steps since T^0 has been sorted in ascending order. Let $\mathbf{R} = \{\mathbf{X}_i \mid \mathbf{X}_i \in T^L, \mathbf{X}_i \neq \mathbf{X}_{ibm}\}$.
3. Go to step 8 if $\mathbf{R}$ is empty.
4. Choose the current candidate $\mathbf{X}_j$ from $\mathbf{R}$ according to the search order shown in Fig. 2.
5. If $d^0(\mathbf{X}_j, \mathbf{Q}) \geq d_{\min}$, then go to either the following step i or ii. Otherwise, set $l = 1$.
   i. If $(\|\mathbf{X}_j\| \geq \|\mathbf{Q}\|)$, then delete all $\mathbf{X}_i$ from $\mathbf{R}$ whose $i \geq j$, and go to step 3.
   ii. If $(\|\mathbf{X}_j\| \leq \|\mathbf{Q}\|)$, then delete all $\mathbf{X}_i$ from $\mathbf{R}$ whose $i \leq j$, and go to step 3.
6. Evaluate $d^l(\mathbf{X}_j, \mathbf{Q})$. If $d^l(\mathbf{X}_j, \mathbf{Q}) \geq d_{\min}$, delete $\mathbf{X}_j$ from $\mathbf{R}$ and go to step 3. Otherwise, set $l = l + 1$. If $l = L$, go to step 7, otherwise, repeat step 6.
7. Evaluate $d^L(\mathbf{X}_j, \mathbf{Q})$, i.e., $d(\mathbf{X}_j, \mathbf{Q})$. If $d(\mathbf{X}_j, \mathbf{Q}) < d_{\min}$, update the "so far" minimum, i.e., $d_{\min} = d(\mathbf{X}_j, \mathbf{Q})$. Delete $\mathbf{X}_j$ from $\mathbf{R}$ and go to step 3.
8. Select the candidate corresponding to $d_{\min}$ as the best match, $\mathbf{X}_{bm}$.

Note that significant time is saved through the checkup in step 5, because the following steps will then rarely be executed. Also note that in step 5-i and ii, we can remove not only $\mathbf{X}_j$ but also all $\mathbf{X}_i$ from $\mathbf{R}$ whose $i \geq j$ because

$$d^L(\mathbf{X}_i, \mathbf{Q}) \geq (\|\mathbf{X}_i\| - \|\mathbf{Q}\|) \geq (\|\mathbf{X}_j\| - \|\mathbf{Q}\|) \geq d_{\min}. \tag{9}$$

In general, image search engines need to provide the top M best matches for the query rather than a single best match. The proposed algorithm can realize this by employing a minimum distance array of size M, $d_{\min}[\cdot]$, instead of $d_{\min}$ in the algorithm described above. Let $d_{\min}[m]$ denote the $(m+1)$-th shortest distance. In other words, for the M best matches, all distances are compared with the largest $d_{\min}[M-1]$ instead of $d_{\min}$ at each level. Whenever $d_{\min}[M-1]$ is updated, $d_{\min}[\cdot]$ is sorted and ranked in the ascending order (a simple bubble sorting algorithm is used in this paper.) for the next candidate evaluation. After repeating the procedure for all probable candidates, the proposed algorithm can provide the top M best matches by choosing the images corresponding to the final $d_{\min}[\cdot]$, without any false misses. Here, initial values of $d_{\min}[\cdot]$ are computed around $\mathbf{X}_{ibm}$.

3. Experimental Results

For performance evaluation, we use a database containing 10,000 still images (N = 10,000), which are composed of 7,000 images from an MPEG-7 content set [10] and 3,000 images from an ftp site. The database includes various types of images such as natural scenes, architectures, and people so as to prevent a bias to a particular type of image. Besides database images, 100 test images having very different characteristics from one another are adopted. We use the luminance histogram with a bin-size of 256 as an image descriptor, and adopt the L_1-norm distance as a distance measure. Histograms of all images are normalized with their respective image size so that histograms at level 0 (or 1 bin-histograms) may always have the value of 1. Hence histograms at level 0 are not subject to comparison, and Table T^0 in Fig. 2 cannot be obtained directly.

Therefore, in this experiment, histograms in the database are sorted in the ascending order of the second bin-values of their histograms at level 1, i.e., $X_i^1[1]$ for $1 \le i \le N$. Note that the ascending order of $X_i^1[1]$ is equivalent to the descending order of $X_i^1[0]$ since $X_i^1[1] = 1 - X_i^1[0]$. Even though the tables and image database are sorted in this alternative way, we can still achieve the half-way-stop effect as in Section 2.3. If $|X_j^1[1] - Q^1[1]| \ge d_{\min}$, $d(\mathbf{X}_j, \mathbf{Q}) \ge d_{\min}$ since $d(\mathbf{X}_j, \mathbf{Q}) \ge d^1(\mathbf{X}_j, \mathbf{Q}) \ge |X_j^1[1] - Q^1[1]|$. Here, we can derive a removal condition that if $X_j^1[1] \ge Q^1[1]$, all $\mathbf{X}_i$ from $\mathbf{R}$ whose $i \ge j$ can be deleted without any loss. This condition can be easily proved. Similarly, even in the case that $X_j^1[1] < Q^1[1]$, if $|X_j^1[1] - Q^1[1]| \ge d_{\min}$, we can delete all $\mathbf{X}_i$ from $\mathbf{R}$ whose $i \le j$ without any loss. Thus, step 5 of the proposed algorithm can be modified as follows:

5'. If $|X_j^1[1] - Q^1[1]| \ge d_{\min}$, then go to either the following step i or ii. Otherwise, set $l = 2$.

i. If $(X_j^1[1] \ge Q^1[1])$, then delete all $\mathbf{X}_i$ from $\mathbf{R}$ whose $i \ge j$, and go to step 3.

ii. If $(X_j^1[1] < Q^1[1])$, then delete all $\mathbf{X}_i$ from $\mathbf{R}$ whose $i \le j$, and go to step 3.

We choose a speed-up ratio (SUR) as the evaluation measure, which is defined as follows:

$$\mathrm{SUR} = \frac{O_{\mathrm{ESA}}}{O_{\mathrm{COMP}}}, \qquad (10)$$

where O_{ESA} and O_{COMP} are the number of operations for ESA and the algorithm to be compared with, respectively. In the proposed algorithm, the computational cost for preparing the L_1-norm pyramid is also included. The number of operations is obtained by adding two dominant operations: addition and absolute operations. For fair comparison, we examine three kinds of SUR for 100 test images, i.e., the average SUR ($\mathrm{SUR}_{\mathrm{AVG}}$), maximum SUR ($\mathrm{SUR}_{\mathrm{MAX}}$), and minimum SUR ($\mathrm{SUR}_{\mathrm{MIN}}$). We compare the proposed algorithm with an existing triangle-inequality-based algorithm (TIA) [7]. In implementing TIA, we select 50 key images at random.

To examine the performance of the proposed algorithm, we investigate four cases: M = 1, 5, 10, and 20. As shown in Table I, the proposed algorithm is about 61 times faster than ESA on average when producing a single best match, i.e., M = 1. It is also noted that SUR tends to decrease as M increases. For M of 20, we obtain only about 18 times faster speed than ESA on average. This is because more distances at each level should be computed since $d_{\min}[M-1]$ increases in proportion to M. However, the proposed algorithm is still much faster than ESA even when producing multiple best matches. On the other hand, we notice that our algorithm outperforms TIA by about 5.9~12.6 times depending on M. The fact that $\mathrm{SUR}_{\mathrm{MAX}}$ of our algorithm is about 1100 for M of 1 is very noticeable. This is because all the descriptors are sorted according to their L_1-norms in advance.

Table I: Comparison of SURs. All available levels of 8 are used here.

M	The proposed algorithm			TIA		
	SUR_{AVG}	SUR_{MAX}	SUR_{MIN}	SUR_{AVG}	SUR_{MAX}	SUR_{MIN}
1	60.5	1098.5	30.8	4.8	8.4	1.8
5	33.5	261.1	16.5	3.8	6.7	1.4
10	24.6	121.5	12.3	3.3	6.3	1.3
20	17.7	65.8	9.5	3.0	5.8	1.2

Table II shows how many candidates the proposed algorithm examines at each level. According to this table, for M of 1, the proposed algorithm statistically examines only 0.1% of the candidates at level 8. In other words, the remaining candidates of 99.9% are eliminated at the lower levels with significantly less computational burden. Therefore, the proposed algorithm can achieve very high search speed.

Table II: Percentages of candidates examined at each level.

Level		1	2	3	4	5	6	7	8
M	1	60.9	34.1	9.09	2.14	0.61	0.28	0.19	0.11
	5	71.0	41.7	14.0	4.42	1.69	0.94	0.68	0.45
	10	75.1	45.1	16.6	5.90	2.53	1.52	1.15	0.80
	20	78.6	48.2	19.4	7.72	3.71	2.41	1.91	1.38

4. Conclusions

We propose a fast descriptor matching algorithm for exhaustive image search in a large database, where the multi-resolution descriptor structure is used and the descriptors are sorted in ascending order of their norms. In the proposed algorithm, the distance at each level is computed and compared with the latest minimum distance, starting from the low-resolution level. Due to this multi-resolution structure and norm-sorted database, we can dramatically reduce the total computational complexity by eliminating improper candidates with much less computation at lower levels. The proposed algorithm provides the same retrieval results as the exhaustive search, with a much faster searching ability than the existing fast exhaustive algorithm, TIA. Through experiments, we show that the proposed algorithm is a credible solution for fast exhaustive search in large image databases.

References

[1] J. R. Smith and S. F. Chang, "Exploring image functionalities in www applications-development of image/video search and editing engines," in *IEEE Proc. ICIP*, pp. 1-4, Oct. 1997.

[2] M. Flicker, H. Sawhney, W. Niblack, J. Ashley, Q. Huang, B. Dom, M. Gorkani, J. Hafner, D. Lee, D. Petkovic, D. Steele, and P. Yanker, "Query by image and video content: the QBIC system," *IEEE Computer*, vol. 28, no. 9, pp. 23-32, 1995.

[3] R. Weber, H. Schek, and S. Blott, "A quantitative analysis and performance study for similarity–search methods in high-dimensional spaces," in *Proceedings of the 24th VLDB*, pp. 194-205, 1998.

[4] J. M. Kleinberg, "Two algorithms for nearest-neighbor search in high dimensions," in *Proceedings of the 29th STOC*, 1997.

[5] M. Otterman, "Approximate matching with high dimensionality R-trees," MSc scholarly paper, Dept. of Computer Science, Univ. of Maryland, College Park, Md., supervised by C. Faloutsos, 1992.

[6] J. Hafner, H. S. Sawhney, W. Equitz, M. Flickner, and W. Niblack, "Efficient color histogram indexing for quadratic form distance functions," *IEEE Trans. Pattern Analysis and Machine Intelligence*, vol. 17, no. 7, pp. 729-736, July 1995.

[7] A. P. Berman and L. G. Shapiro, "Efficient image retrieval with multiple distance measures," in *SPIE Proc. Storage and Retrieval for Image and Video Databases*, vol. 3022, pp. 12-21, Feb. 1997.

[8] A. P. Berman and L. G. Shapiro, "Triangle-inequality-based pruning algorithms with triangle tries," in *SPIE Proc. Storage and Retrieval for Image and Video Databases*, vol. 3656, pp. 356-365, Jan. 1999.

[9] W. Li and E. Salari, "Successive elimination algorithm for motion estimation," *IEEE Trans. Image Processing*, vol. 4, no.1, pp. 105-107, Jan. 1995.

[10] ISO/IEC JTC1/SC29/WG11/N2466, "Licensing agreement for the MPEG-7 content set," Atlantic City, USA, Oct. 1998.

FBCC: An Image Similarity Algorithm Based on Regions

Fang Qian[1,2], Lei Zhang[1,2], Fuzong Lin[1,2] and Bo Zhang[1,2]

[1]State key laboratory of Intelligent Technology and Systems, Tsinghua University
[2]Department of Computer Science and Technology, Tsinghua University
Beijing, 100084, China
qf@s1000e.cs.tsinghua.edu.cn

Abstract. Region-based image retrieval has been an active research area for the past few years. A good similarity measure that combines information from all regions is very important for region-based retrieval systems. In this paper, we propose FBCC (Foreground-Background Corresponding Comparison), a novel image similarity measure based on region comparison. The basic idea is comparing query foreground regions with database foreground regions and query background regions with database background regions. Three factors have been considered in the algorithm: the comparable credit between two regions, the significance of each region and the difference of total number of regions between two images. Experimental results on a testbed of 10.000 general-purpose images show that this approach is effective for center-surround images.

1 Introduction

Content-based image retrieval (CBIR) becomes more and more important in this multimedia age. Many general-purpose image search engines, both commercial and research, have been developed, such as IBM QBIC [8], MIT Photobook [2], Columbia VisualSEEK [4], UCSB Netra [9], UIUC MARS [11] and so on. The usual approach of early systems is to represent each image as a feature vector and to assess similarity between images by way of a metric function. Many low level features have been explored to describe the color, texture or shape of an image. However, their usefulness is limited by the gap between low-level features and high-level concepts. The global feature cannot sufficiently capture the important properties of individual objects, therefore, the methods usually fail when images contain similar objects, but at different locations or in varying sizes or under different background. Relevance feedback is a powerful tool to bridge the gap [11], however, in this paper we will focus on another way: region segmentation.

Region-based image retrieval systems attempt to overcome the drawbacks of global features by representing the image at object-level. If objects can be identified in an image, it would be easy for system to recognize similar objects at different locations and with different orientations or sizes, even under different backgrounds. However, extracting objects from an image is still a hard problem in image processing field.

Only in ideal case, an object corresponds to a region, but in most cases, an object is split into several regions or a region contains more than one object, as shown in Figure 1. Inaccurate segmentation brings the difficulty for region-based matching.

VisualSEEK [4] is an early region-based system. The similarity between two images is computed by taking into account colors, sizes and spatial layouts of color regions. Later, UCSB NeTra [9] and Berkeley Blobworld [3] were developed, with more emphasis on region segmentation results. Both the two systems compare images based on individual regions. However, it is often difficult for users to decide which regions or features should be used for retrieval. Some overall image-to-image similarity measures are given to provide users a simple interface, e.g. the WALRUS system [1], the Windsurf system [7] and the SIMPLIcity system [5]. Although each has its own advantages, the common drawback of them is that they consider the sizes of regions instead of the significance of regions in region comparison. In WALRUS system, the similarity measure between a pair of images is defined to be the fraction of the area of the two images covered by matching regions from the images. When Windsurf system defines similarity coefficients, it only takes into account the sizes of regions. The SIMPLIcity system defines the significance of a region as its area percentage. How to define a good similarity measures that combine information from all regions is still an open problem. We conclude that there are three main problems in defining an image similarity measure based on region comparison:

- How to decide the comparable region pairs between two images?
- How to decide the significance of each region?
- How to compute the differences when two images have different numbers of regions?

We are not aiming to solve all problems perfectly in this paper; instead, we propose a novel image similarity measure designed specifically for center-surround images. We named it FBCC (Foreground-Background Corresponding Comparison), because its basic idea is comparing query foreground regions with database foreground regions and query background regions with database background regions. Since center-surround images have a large fraction in image database and they are most suitable for region-based retrieval, our method does not lose generality.

This paper is organized as follows. In Section 2 the segmentation method is introduced first, and then the region similarity and image similarity measure are described. In Section 3, experimental results are given. Finally we conclude and outline our future work.

2 Region-based image retrieval

2.1 Image Segmentation (JSEG Algorithm)

The image segmentation method we used is JSEG algorithm [10]. To make the paper self-contained, we introduce it briefly in this subsection. First, image pixel colors are replaced by their corresponding quantized colors, thus forming a class-map of the image. Let Z be the set of all N image data points in the class-map, let $z = (x, y)$, $z \in Z$, and m be the mean,

$$m = \frac{1}{N} \sum_{z \in Z} z \tag{1}$$

Suppose color has been quantized into C levels, thus Z is classified into C classes, $Z_i, i = 1, \cdots, C$, let m_i be the mean of the N_i image points of class Z_i,

$$m_i = \frac{1}{N_i} \sum_{z \in Z_i} z \tag{2}$$

Let

$$S_T = \sum_{z \in Z} \| z - m \|^2 \tag{3}$$

and

$$S_W = \sum_{i=1}^{C} \sum_{z \in Z_i} \| z - m_i \|^2 \tag{4}$$

Define a criterion for "good" segmentation as follows:

$$J = S_B / S_W = (S_T - S_W) / S_W \tag{5}$$

It measures the distances between different classes S_B over the distances between the members within each class S_W. A higher value of *J* indicates that the classes are more separated from each other and the members within each class are closer to each other, and vice versa. Applying the criterion to local windows in the class-map results in the "J-image", in which high and low values correspond to possible region boundaries and region centers, respectively. Finally, a region growing method is used to segment the image based on the J-image.

In the original JSEG algorithm, image is segmented on multiple scales, and different local window sizes are applied at different scale. In our implementation, for computational reasons, the image size is regularized to a fixed scale, and only 9*9 local window is used. Figure 1 shows some segmented images.

(a) (b) (c)

Fig. 1. Examples of image segmentation using JSEG. (a) ideal segmentation; (b) one object corresponds to several regions; (c) one region contains several objects.

2.2 Region similarity

We choose the color histogram in the HSV color space to represent each region. The HSV color space has de-correlated and uniform coordinates, which better matches the human perception of color. Also the color histogram is easy to compute. Suppose R_i and R_j are regions in query image Q and database image T respectively, f_i and f_j are their corresponding features. The distance between R_i and R_j is measured as follows:

$$d(R_i, R_j) = d(f_i, f_j) + \frac{|sig(R_i) - sig(R_j)|}{(sig(R_i) + sig(R_j))} \tag{6}$$

where $d(f_i, f_j)$ use the L1distance, $sig(R_i)$ represents the significance of R_i in Q and $sig(R_j)$ represents the significance of R_j in T. Their computation will be described in next subsection.

2.3 Image similarity

Given a query image $Q = \bigcup_{i=1}^{m} R_i^Q$ and a database image $T = \bigcup_{i=1}^{n} R_i^T$, how to estimate the distance between Q and T? We think there are three problems need to consider. First, how to decide the comparable region pairs between two images? Obviously, comparing two non-corresponding regions is meaningless and it will give incorrect result if they have similar features. Second, how to compute the significance of each region? The significance of a region not only lies on its size but also its location. Generally speaking, the region near the center attracts more attention. Third, How to measure the distance between two images when they have different region numbers?

We define a parameter for each region to describe the probability of being foreground. The image is divided into 4*4 equal blocks. The center 2*2 blocks are regarded as foreground window, as Fig. 2 shown. Define the probability of being foreground for R_i:

$$P_{fore}(R_i) = \frac{size(R_i \text{ fall in the foreground window})}{size(R_i)} \tag{7}$$

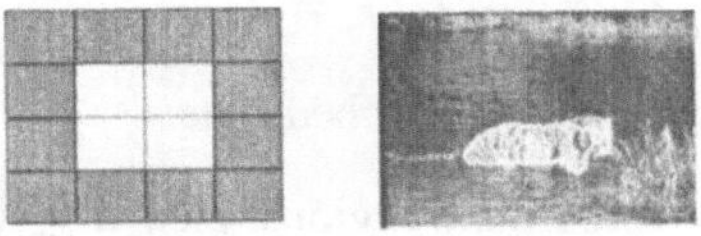

Fig. 2. Foreground Window

We classify regions to three types according to the foreground probability:

$$\begin{cases} R_i \text{ is foreground, } & \text{if } P_{fore}(R_i) > \theta_f \\ R_i \text{ is background, } & \text{if } P_{fore}(R_i) < \theta_b \\ R_i \text{ is both foreground and background, } & \text{otherwise} \end{cases} \quad (8)$$

where θ_f and θ_b are two thresholds. In our experiment, we let $\theta_f = 0.6$ and $\theta_b = 0.4$. Now we give the following definition of comparable region pair:

Definition: (comparable region pair) Two regions are comparable region pair only when they belong to the same type.

The significance of a region is not only related to its size but also its location. The region near the center should be given more significance. We define the significance of R_i as

$$sig(R_i) = \begin{cases} \max(2 * a, 1), \text{if } P_{fore}(R_i) > \theta_f \\ a, \text{otherwise} \end{cases} \quad (9)$$

where $a = \frac{size(R_i)}{size(I)}$ represents the area percentage of R_i in the image I. In our experiment, for the simplicity reason, only the most 5 important regions were stored for an image. Formula (9) guarantees the priority for a foreground region to be stored.

Suppose the query image Q is decomposed into m regions, the target image T is decomposed into n regions. The actual number of matching regions is k. Let $d_{fore}(Q,T)$ represents the foreground distance between Q and T, $d_{back}(Q,T)$ represents the background distance between Q and T. The FBCC algorithm can be described as follows. Note that one region of an image is allowed to match only one region of another image.

Step0: At beginning, let k=0, $d_{fore}(Q,T) = 0$, $d_{back}(Q,T) = 0$.

Step1: Choose the most important and unmatched region R_i from Q. If all the regions of Q have been visited, then go to step 7;

Step2: Choose an unmatched region R_j from T. If all the regions of T have been visited, then go to setp1;

Step3: if R_j and R_i are not comparable, then go to step 2;

Setp4: compute $d(R_i, R_j)$ according to formula (6). Go to step 2 to find R_j satisfying $d(R_i, R_j) < d(R_i, R_{j'})$, $R_{j'} \in T, j' \neq j$

Step5: $k = k+1$, mark R_j and R_i be matched state.

If both R_j and R_i are the foreground regions, then $d_{fore}(Q,T)$ += $d(R_i, R_j)$; if both are the background regions, then $d_{back}(Q,T)$ += $d(R_i, R_j)$; otherwise, $d_{fore}(Q,T)$ += $P_{fore}(R_i) * d(R_i, R_j)$, $d_{back}(Q,T)$ += $(1 - P_{fore}(R_i)) * d(R_i, R_j)$.

Step6: go to step 1;

Step 7: compute the overall distance between Q and T according to formula (10).

$$d(Q,T) = w_{fore} d_{fore}(Q,T) + w_{back} d_{back}(Q,T) \quad (10)$$

where the weights w_{fore} and w_{back} satisfying $w_{fore} + w_{back} = 1$. Adjusting them can provide users more flexible query. The larger w_{fore} is, the foreground is considered more, and the larger w_{back} is, the background is considered more.

The last but not least important question is how to eliminate the affect that two images have different region numbers? In case of a perfect match, the actual number of matching regions k is equal to m, the number of regions of Q, and the distance vector will be a zero vector. But if a perfect match cannot be established, an additional penalty will be added. Since color histogram is used as region signature, the maximal distance between two regions is 2, thus the penalty item is set equal to $2(m-k)$. Formula (10) is modified as

$$d(Q,T) = \left(w_{fore} d_{fore} + w_{back} d_{back} + 2(m-k)\right)/m \quad (11)$$

Note (11) is not a symmetric distance function. There are two reasons: one is Q and T may have different numbers of regions, so the penalty item is different; the other is the matching process prefer to the important regions. In order to get a symmetric function, we define the distance between Q and T as

$$dist(Q,T) = \left(d(Q,T) + d(T,Q)\right)/2 \quad (12)$$

In our experiment, formula (12) achieved better result than formula (11).

3 Experiments

3.1 Data Sets and performance measure

In order to evaluate the effectiveness of FBCC, we compared it with color autocorrelagram [6], a very effective global color feature. The image database is downloaded from James Wang's website (http://wang.ist.psu.edu/). It contains 10,000 images stored in JPEG format, each of whose sizes is 85 * 128, 96*128 or 128*85.

The retrieval performance is measured by the recall vs. scope. Let $T_1, T_2, \ldots, T_t$ be the top t retrieved images based on the query image Q. The recall r at a scope s is then defined as

$$r(s) = \left|\{T_i \mid \text{relevant}(T_i) = true, 1 \le i \le s\}\right|, \ s \le t \quad (13)$$

where $|\{\ \}|$ is the number of relevant images. This measure is simpler than the conventional recall vs. precision, but is effective in evaluating the retrieval performance.

3.2 Experimental Results

We randomly choose five query images from flower category and five query images from butterfly category, calculating the recall vs. scope. Fig. 3 is the average recall vs. scope results. It shows that FBCC retrieved more relevant images than autocorrelagram in the same scope. The query example in figure 4 shows while the autocorrelagram have six irrelevant images in the top sixteen, the FBCC only have two. Experimental results support the hypothesis that FBCC yields good results when querying center-surround images.

4 Conclusion

In this paper, we have proposed a novel similarity measure of images based on region representation, which is called FBCC algorithm here. It has several advantages: only comparable region pair is contribute to the distance; the central region can get larger significance; the different numbers of regions between two images are considered; foreground and background distance weights can be adjusted; more important region has more priority. Experiments show it is suitable for center-surround images. In the future work, better foreground/background detection method can be used; region can be represented by more effective color and texture features; and the significance parameter for each region can be learned from user feedback. Other planned work includes the comparison to other region-based approaches.

Acknowledgement

This work was supported by Natural Science Foundation of China (69823001) and Doctoral Program Foundation of State Ministry of Education (98000335)

References

1. Natsev, A., Rastogi, R., Shim, K.: WALRUS: A similarity retrieval algorithm for image databases. Proc. 1999 ACM SIGMOD International Conference on Management of Data, Philadelphia, PA, June (1999)
2. Pentland, A., Picard, R.W., Sclaroff, S.: Photobook: tools for content-based manipulation of image databases. Proc. SPIE, vol. 2185, 34-47, San Jose, February 7-8, (1994)
3. Carson, C., Belongie, M. S., Hellerstein, J. M., Malik, J.: Blobworld: a system for region-based image indexing and retrieval. Third Int. Conf. On Visual Information Systems, (1999)
4. Smith, J.R., Chang, S.-F.: VisualSEEk: a fully automated content-based image query system. ACM Multimedia, Boston, MA, Nov. (1996)
5. Wang, J. Z., Li, J., Wiederhold, G.: SIMPLIcity: Semantics-sensitive Integrated Matching for Picture Libraries. IEEE Transactions on Pattern Analysis and Machine Intelligence, vol. 23, (2001). to appear.

6. Huang, J., Kumar, S. R., Mitra, M., Zhu, W., Zabih,R.: Image indexing using color correlograms. In IEEE Conference on Computer Vision and Pattern Recognition, (1997) 762~768.

7. Ardizzoni, S., Bartolini, I., Patella, M.: Windsurf: Region-Based Image Retrieval Using Wavelets. IWOSS'99, Florence, Italy, September (1999) 167-173

8. Niblack, W., Barber, R., Equitz, W., Flickner, M., Glasman, E., Petkovic, D., Yanker, P., Faloutsos, C., Taubin, G.: The QBIC project: querying images by content using color, texture, and shape, Proc, SPIE, vol. 1908, San Jose, February, (1993) 173-187

9. Ma, W. Y., Manjunath, B. S.: NETRA: A toolbox for navigating large image databases. Proc. IEEE International Conference on Image Processing, Santa Barbara, California, Vol. I, Oct (1997) 568-571

10. Deng, Y., Manjunath, B. S., Shin, H.: Color Image Segmentation. Proc. IEEE Computer Society Conference on Computer Vision and Pattern Recognition, Fort Collins, CO, vol.2, June (1999)

11. Rui, Y., Huang, T. S., Ortega, M., Mehrotra, S.: Relevance feedback: A power tool in interactive content-based image retrieval. IEEE Tran on Circuits and Systems for Video Technology, Special Issue on Segmentation, Description, and Retrieval of Video Content, September 8(5), (1998), 644-655.

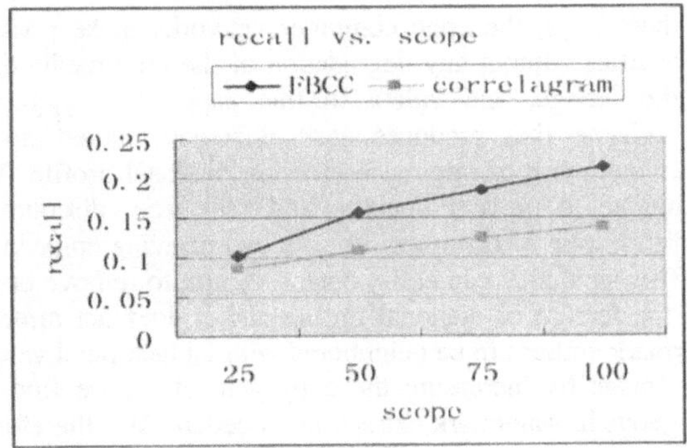

Fig. 3. Recall vs. scope comparison between FBCC and autocorrelagram

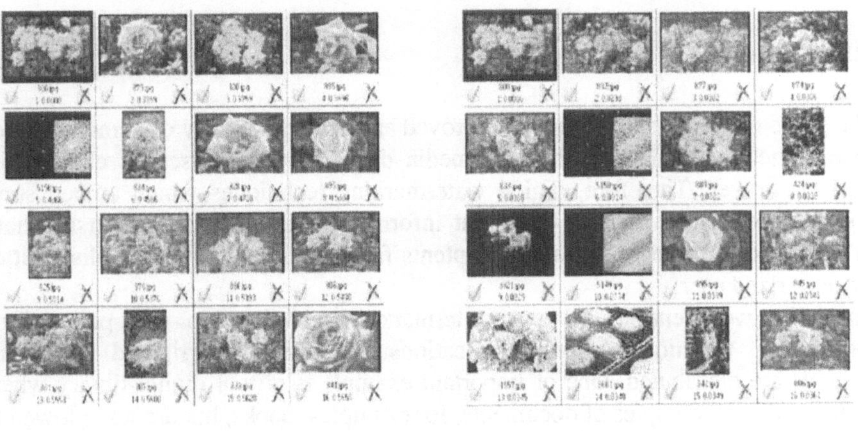

(a) FBCC (b) autocorrelagram

Fig. 4. A query example (the top left image is query)

A New Digital Watermarking for Text Document Images Using Diagonal Profile

Ji Hwan Park[1], Sook Ee Jeong[2] and Young Huh[3]

[1] Div. of Elec., Computer, and Telecommu. Eng., Pukyong Nat'l Univ.
599-1, Daeyeon3-dong, Nam-gu, Busan, 608-737, Korea
jpark@pknu.ac.kr
[2] Dept. of Computer Science, Pukyong Nat'l Univ.
599-1, Daeyeon3-dong, Nam-gu, Busan, 608-737, Korea
waterpur@unicorn.pknu.ac.kr
[3] Applied Imaging Research Group, Korea Electrotechnology Research Ins.
665, Naeson2-dong, Euwang, Keonggi-do, 437-808, Korea
yhuh@keri.re.kr

Abstract. In these days, the open computer networks make possible to use intellectual properties without any degradation of the multimedia data such as document, audio, image, and video. In this paper, we suggest a digital watermarking scheme that produces each different marked document by embedding a unique mark of original user using diagonal profile. This can be applied a technique to prevent unauthorized user from discouraging illicit copying or redistribution of document images by retrieving embedded mark of original user. This technique can easily detect attempt to remove or change the watermark by the feature of diagonal profile and it does not affect the skew since the watermark embeds to be neighbored with a black pixel value. And we produce noisy image by increasing the copy generation, we find out that it occurs unambiguous in watermark extraction procedure. We, therefore, propose a tip to extract the watermark after removing produced noise by copying.

1. Introduction

As the speed of computer network is improved and the high quality of communication service come into wide use, the multimedia data can be accessed or changed by unauthorized user. Therefore, digital watermarking techniques which embed some important information such as copyright information, expire date, ownership have been proposed to protect multimedia contents from illegal copying or redistribution by unauthorized user.

Specially, we mention the text watermarking technique in this paper. Text watermarking techniques have applications wherever copyrighted electronic documents are distributed. One of important example is virtual digital library where users may download copies of documents, for examples, books, but are not allowed to further distribute them or to store them longer than for a certain predefined period. In this type of application, a requested document is watermarked with a requester specific watermark before releasing it for download. If illegal copies are discovered later, the embedded watermark can be used to determine the original ones.

At first, we briefly review the text watermarking techniques in section 2. And we propose a embedding and extraction process of the watermark using diagonal profile in section 3. Then we present experimental results, conclusion and further works in section 4 and 5.

2. Digital Watermarking for Text Documents

Digital watermarking technique for text document image is mainly classified two categories as follows. Spatial domain technique by Brassil *et al.*[2][3][4][8] and Low *et al.*[6][7] slightly moves the location of words or lines, this is perceptually invisible even after embedding the marks.

According to this, embedded watermark can be detected using feature detection, correlation detection, centroid detection even though it has been corrupted by copying, scanning, fax transmission. Feature detection, so called baseline detection, is attempted to locate the position of the text baseline in line-shifted documents. Correlation detection is a well-known result from communication theory tells us that a correlation detector optimally detects signals in the presence of additive white Gaussian noise. Centroid detection is used when the effect of translation cannot be compensated for accurately. Feature detection is most directly applicable for detecting line shifting, it has an advantage that does not require any information on the original unmarked document, but it also has a disadvantage of relatively poor performance on documents that have suffered significant distortions. Although centroid detection can be applied to detect both line and word spacing, its performance in the presence of noise is satisfactory only for line spacing. It is more reliable but requires centroid of original unmarked document profile. Correlation detection performs much better than centroid detection on word spacing, but its performance is sensitive to how accurately can be compensate for the translation of the profile. This method requires the profile of original unmarked document.

On the contrary to digital watermarking in spatial domain, frequency domain digital watermarking technique by Y. Lui *et. al*[8] uses the original Cox *et al.* algorithm[5] as a representative transform domain technique. This technique marks using word or line shifting algorithm by Brassil *et al.* which is mentioned above, then measures the similarity in Cox et al. algorithm between original watermarked document image and corrupted watermarked document image to detect watermark. This technique has an advantage of robustness against noise like Cox et al. algorithm.

3. The Marking and Identification Scheme Using Diagonal Profile

At first, we assume that the image of the one page is represented as follows.

$$f(i,j) \in \{0,1\}, \quad i \in [0, n-1], \quad j \in [0, m-1] \tag{1}$$

where, *n* and *m*, whose values depend on the scanning resolution, are the height and width of the page, respectively.

The image of a text line is simply the function restricted to the region of the text line

$$f(i,j) \in \{0,1\}, \quad i \in [t_t, b], \quad j \in [0, m-1] \tag{2}$$

where, t_t and b are the top and bottom boundaries of the text line, respectively. And the image of a word can be represented as follows.

$$f(i,j) \in \{0,1\}, \quad i \in [t_t, b], \quad j \in [s, e] \tag{3}$$

where, s and e are the start and end of the word in the text line.

Diagonal profile[1] of the text image is a projection of two-dimensional array. To making the diagonal profile is to compute a index for the histogram bucket for the current row and column. Let the row and column be noted by i and j, respectively. Suppose that the dimensions of the image are n row and m columns, so i and j range from 0 to n-1 and 0 to m-1, respectively. And we assume that the index k for the diagonal can be computed by an affine transformation of the row and column. The index k can be described as Eqn(4). Therefore, the diagonal profile will be required n+m-1 buckets.

$$k = i - j + m - 1, \qquad 0 \le k \le n + m - 2 \tag{4}$$

Figure 1 is an example of diagonal profile. Since the affine transformation should be mapped the upper right pixel into the first position, and the lower left pixel into the last position. Therefore, the index k is produced from right side to left side direction.

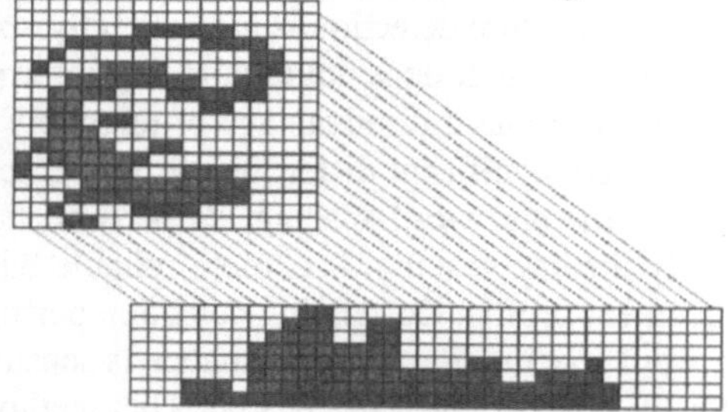

Fig. 1. An Example of Diagonal Profile

3.2 Watermark Embedding Procedure

In this method, the watermark embedding algorithm to generate copyright information for original owner of text document is described as follows. Figure 2 illustrates this process.

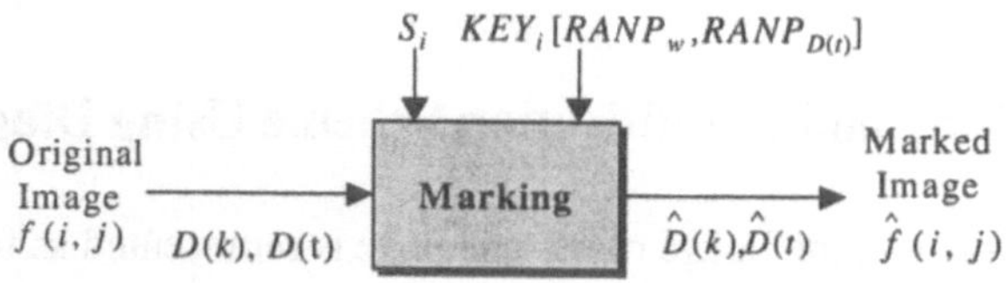

Fig. 2. Watermark Embedding Procedure

[Step1] Generate diagonal profile $D(k)$ of the entire document image $f(i, j)$.

$$D(k)=\begin{cases} D(k)+1, & if\ f(i,j)=1 \\ D(k), & otherwise \end{cases} \quad (5)$$

where, $k = i - j + m - 1$ $(0 \le k \le n + m - 1)$, $0 \le i \le n - 1$, $0 \le j \le m - 1$

[Step2] Randomly choose a word to embed $S_i \in \{0,1\}$, then generate diagonal profile $D(t)$ of the randomly chosen word $f(i, j)$.

$$D(t)=\begin{cases} D(t)+1, & if\ f(i,j)=1 \\ D(t), & otherwise \end{cases} \quad (6)$$

where, $t = x - y + p - 1$ $(0 \le t \le (e\text{-}s)+(b\text{-}t_t)+1)$, $t_t \le i \le b$, $s \le j \le e$, $0 \le x \le p$, $0 \le y \le q$, $p = e - s + 1$, $q = b - t_t + 1$

[Step3] Embed S_i on selected $D(t)$ as following conditions

$$\hat{D}(t) = D(t) + W(S_i) \quad (7)$$

- Divide $D(t)$ into two blocks b_l, b_r
  S_i = '0' (white pixel value) : embed one pixel on randomly chosen position of b_l.
  S_i = '1' (black pixel value) : embed one pixel on randomly chosen position of b_r.
- Randomly selected position is a pixel adjacent to the black pixel value, which has same index on text document image.
- Maintain corresponding embedded position of the word on a table to prevent from reselecting of embedded position.
- Avoid the word that doesn't have plenty of width because an embedded watermark should not be visible under normal observation.

[Step4] Repeat Step[2]~[3] until S_i finish to embed.

[Step5] Reconstruct document image $\hat{f}(i, j)$.

[Step6] Produce diagonal profile $\hat{D}(k)$ of the watermarked page $\hat{f}(i, j)$.

For line or word shifting, the change of the particular region with the intentional attacks by someone only results in changing of the corresponding region. But, for this proposed method, it can be resulted in changing the entire profile of document, not some particular region because of the feature in [Step1] and [Step2]. We, therefore, can easily detect the modification of document image.

3.3 Watermark Extraction Procedure

3.3.1 Watermark Decoding Model I

Before mentioning specific algorithm, this scheme has an advantage as follows. If you only want to detect the change of the watermarked document, you can easily detect whether the document has been changed or not by comparing the number of vertical strip between the diagonal profile $\hat{D}(k)$ of watermarked document and the diagonal profile of $D^*(k)$ of possibly corrupted or changed document $f^*(i, j)$.

Now, let's look into the watermark detection procedure. This procedure is shown in Figure 3.

[Step1] Generate digitalized document $f^*(i, j)$ which is possibly corrupted.
[Step2] Generate $D^*(k)$ of $f^*(i, j)$.
[Step3] Generate a corresponding $D^*(k)$ using the position $KEY_i[RANP_w]$ of a randomly selected word, detect S_{i_D} using Eqn(8) .

$$S_{i_D} = D^*(t) - \hat{D}(t) \quad \textbf{(8)}$$

[Step4] Detect S_i using the randomly chosen position $KEY_i[RANP_{D(t)}]$ on $D^*(t)$ which is used to embed S_i
[Step5] Repeat step[3]~[4] until detecting S_i.

3.3.2 Watermark Decoding Model II

In decoding Model I, we first detect S_{i_D}, then we can detect S_i using $KEY_i[RANP_{D(t)}]$. Actually S_{i_D} include the watermark S_i and noise N. Therefore, we can just detect whether the watermark information exist or not using $KEY_i[RANP_{D(t)}]$. To acquire the watermark without noise, we propose a tip to remove the noise N as follows. Figure 4 illustrates the extraction process of the watermark after removing the noise N using Eqn (9) and (10).

$$D^*(t) - \hat{D}(t) = N \quad \textbf{(9)}$$

$$S_{i_D} = D^*(t) - D(t) - N \quad \textbf{(10)}$$

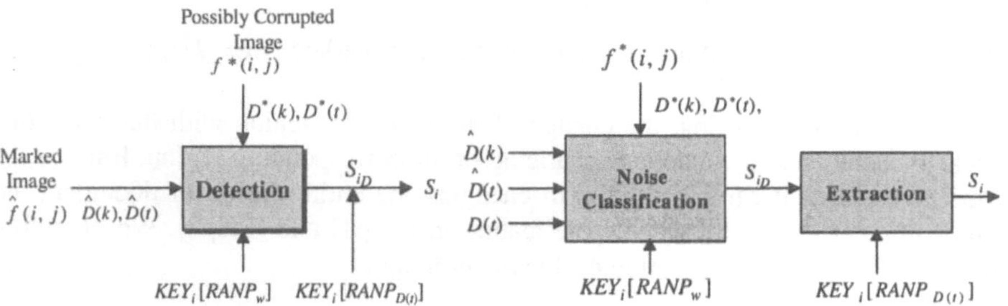

Fig. 3. Watermark Decoding Model I   **Fig. 4.** Watermark Decoding Model II

4. Experimental Results

To test how well marked documents could be decoded after passing through noise, we performed the following experiments. The original and the watermarked document were printed on HP Laser Jet 6P. And then the original image is used size with 901×622(13 lines and 87 word, 10 Times New Roman) scanned 300dpi on HP5200C. And we also use the binary image size with 50×33 which consists of the initial of name for the secret information, i.e. watermark. We sequentially read the watermark, then randomly embedded on the document image using diagonal profile. To be satisfied the condition of perceptual transparency, we embedded the watermark on the word composed over 60 pixels of width. Figure 5 and 7 show the original text document and the result of watermark embedding. Figure 6 and 8 show the diagonal profiles of Figure 5 and 7, respectively.

We also experiment to extract the watermark by increasing the copy generation of marked document. We produce noisy images by increasing the copy generation of marked document image on Zerox 330 from 1st to 10th. We could get reasonable detection response to 5th copy generation for both of decoding Model I and II. As you may know in Fig. 12~15 and Fig. 18~21, the extracted watermarks for decoding Model I include additional noises and the results for decoding Model II show us the watermark information only. And this technique dose not has influence on skewing of words or lines because the watermark embeds to be neighbored with a black pixel value.

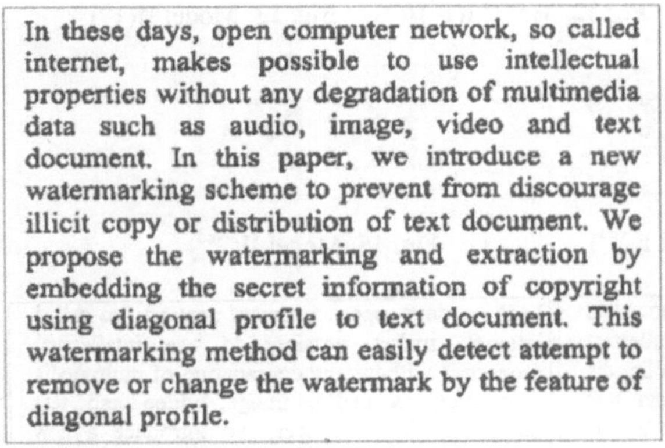

In these days, open computer network, so called internet, makes possible to use intellectual properties without any degradation of multimedia data such as audio, image, video and text document. In this paper, we introduce a new watermarking scheme to prevent from discourage illicit copy or distribution of text document. We propose the watermarking and extraction by embedding the secret information of copyright using diagonal profile to text document. This watermarking method can easily detect attempt to remove or change the watermark by the feature of diagonal profile.

Fig. 5. Original Unmarked Document(901×662, 10font)

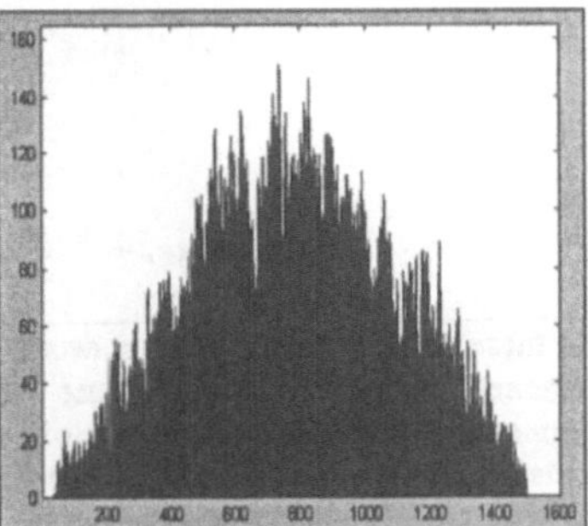

Fig. 6. Diagonal Profile of Fig. 5

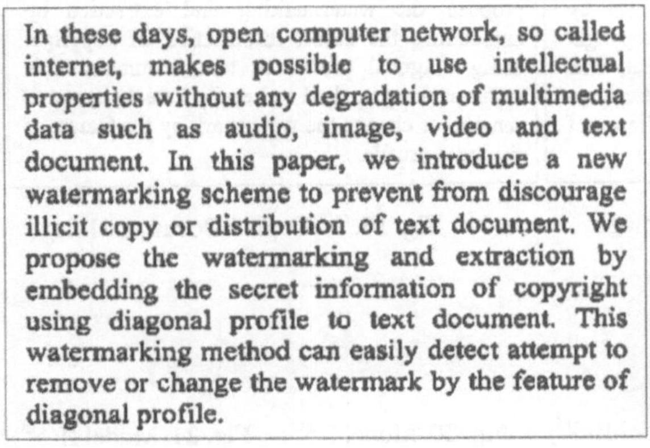

In these days, open computer network, so called internet, makes possible to use intellectual properties without any degradation of multimedia data such as audio, image, video and text document. In this paper, we introduce a new watermarking scheme to prevent from discourage illicit copy or distribution of text document. We propose the watermarking and extraction by embedding the secret information of copyright using diagonal profile to text document. This watermarking method can easily detect attempt to remove or change the watermark by the feature of diagonal profile.

Fig. 7. Watermarked Document Image

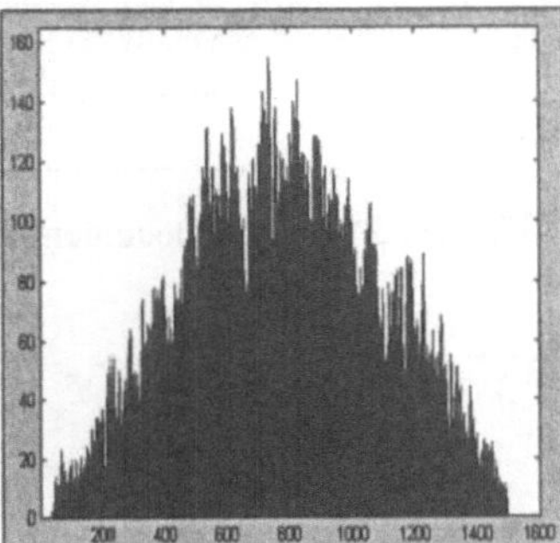

Fig. 8. Diagonal Profile of Fig.7

In these days, open computer network, so called internet, makes possible to use intellectual properties without any degradation of multimedia data such as audio, image, video and text document. In this paper, we introduce a new watermarking scheme to prevent from discourage illicit copy or distribution of text document. We propose the watermarking and extraction by embedding the secret information of copyright using diagonal profile to text document. This watermarking method can easily detect attempt to remove or change the watermark by the feature of diagonal profile.

Fig. 9. 1st Copied Document Image

In these days, open computer network, so called internet, makes possible to use intellectual properties without any degradation of multimedia data such as audio, image, video and text document. In this paper, we introduce a new watermarking scheme to prevent from discourage illicit copy or distribution of text document. We propose the watermarking and extraction by embedding the secret information of copyright using diagonal profile to text document. This watermarking method can easily detect attempt to remove or change the watermark by the feature of diagonal profile.

Fig. 10. 2nd Copied Document Image

Fig. 11. Watermark(50×33)

Fig.12. Model I(1st)

Fig. 13. Model II(1st)

Fig. 14. Model I(2nd)

Fig. 15. Model II(2nd)

In these days, open computer network, so called internet, makes possible to use intellectual properties without any degradation of multimedia data such as audio, image, video and text document. In this paper, we introduce a new watermarking scheme to prevent from discourage illicit copy or distribution of text document. We propose the watermarking and extraction by embedding the secret information of copyright using diagonal profile to text document. This watermarking method can easily detect attempt to remove or change the watermark by the feature of diagonal profile.

Fig. 16. 3rd Copied Document Image

In these days, open computer network, so called internet, makes possible to use intellectual properties without any degradation of multimedia data such as audio, image, video and text document. In this paper, we introduce a new watermarking scheme to prevent from discourage illicit copy or distribution of text document. We propose the watermarking and extraction by embedding the secret information of copyright using diagonal profile to text document. This watermarking method can easily detect attempt to remove or change the watermark by the feature of diagonal profile.

Fig. 17. 5th Copied Document Image

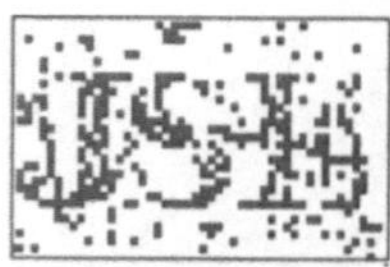

Fig. 18. Model I(3rd)

Fig. 19. Model II(3rd)

Fig. 20. Model I(5th)

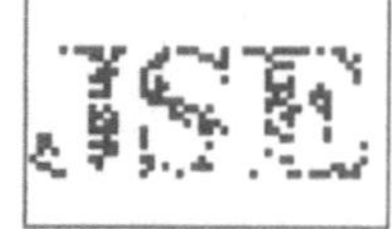

Fig. 21. Model II(5th)

5 Conclusions and Further Works

Document delivery by computer network offers information providers the opportunity to reach a large audience more quickly and cheaply than does media-based distribution. To facilitate the transition to network distribution, we proposed a new watermarking algorithm that embeds secret information of original owner on text document using diagonal profile. If the watermarked image has been changed or deleted on arbitrary position of text document by an attacker, the original owner of that document can easily detect the difference by comparing each diagonal profiles.

And we have shown two different decoding Models. Model I needs small amount of side information in detection procedure as compared with Model II, but also has a disadvantage that we can't exactly separate between the watermark and the noise. On the other hand, Model II can get exact watermark information without any noise, but it has a disadvantage the need of original image to decode the watermark.

For further research, we will present for the next paper on a watermarking technique using bi-directional diagonal profiles to reduce the side information in decoding Model II. It is only needed the indexes of the embedded watermarks on each diagonal profiles to extract the watermark. And it also can be applied fragile watermarking technique.

References

[1] R. Jain, R. Kasturi, B. G. Schunck, "Machine Vision", MaGraw-Hill, 1995.

[2] J. T. Brassil, S. H. Low, N. F. Maxemchuk and L. O'Gorman, "Hiding Information in Document Images", in Proc. 1995 Conf. Information Sciences and Systems, pp.482-489, March 1995.

[3] J. T. Brassil, S. H. Low, N. F. Maxemchuk, J. T. Brassil, and L. O'Gorman, "Document Marking and Identification using both line and word shifting", in Proc. Infocom '95, pp. 853-860, April, 1995.

[4] J. T. Brassil, S. H. Low, N. F. Maxemchuk, L. O'Gorman, "Electronic Marking and Identification Techniques to Discourage Document Copying", IEEE J.Setected. Area Commun. Vol. 13, pp. 1495-1504, Oct. 1995.

[5] I. Cox, J. Killian, T. Leighton and T. Shamoon, "Secure Spread Spectrum Watermarking for Multimedia", Proc. of First Int. Workshop of Informaiton Hiding, pp 183-206, May. 1996.

[6] S. H. Low, N. F. Maxemchuk and A. M. Lapone, "Document Identification for Copyright Protection using Centroid Detection", IEEE Trans. Commun. Vol. 46, pp. 372-383, March 1998

[7] S. H. Low, A. M. Lapone, N. F. Mexemchuk, "Performance Comparison of Two Text Marking and Detection Methods", IEEE J. Selected Areas Communication, Vol. 16, No. 14, May 1998.

[8] Y. Lui, J. Mant, E.Wong, S. H. Low, "Marking and Detection of Text Documents Using Transform-domain Techniques", SPIE Vol.3657, Jan. 1999.

[9] J. T. Brassil, S. H. Low, N. F. Maxemchuk, "Copyright Protection for the Electronic Distribution of Text Documents", Proc. of the IEEE, Vol. 87, No. 7, July 1999.

Gesture Classification and Recognition Using Principal Component Analysis and HMM

Hyun-Ju Lee, Yong-Jae Lee, Chil-Woo Lee

Department of Computer Engineering, Chonnam National University
{leehj, skleeyj}@image.chonnam.ac.kr, leecw@chonnam.ac.kr

Abstract. In this paper, we describe the method that can automatically compose gesture models and recognize those gestures using 2D features extracted from gesture image sequences. In the conventional gesture recognition algorithms, previously well-known patterns are introduced by the hand or the model indexing algorithm. However, our method automatically composes the model space by clustering arbitrary input image sequences. The models are recognized as gesture using probability calculation of HMM. Our method can compose the models fast and robustly and is easy to learn on new image sequences.

1 Introduction

Humans frequently use gestures to communicate information among one other. Considering the fact, it is necessary to develop efficient and fast gesture recognition algorithms for more natural human-computer interaction. In recent years, gesture recognition has become an increasingly important topic in the computer vision field, with the construction of massive video databases, surveillance systems, and highly-compressible communication systems.

Briefly speaking, gesture recognition means automatically knowing how a human's parts temporally change. However, it is difficult to recognize temporal changes automatically because a human body is a three-dimensional object of a very complex structure.

In early works, many researchers tried to measure the configuration of the human body with sensors attached to the joints of limbs and to recognize gesture by analyzing the variation of joint angles. However, this requires the user to wear cumbersome devices such as a data glove and a data suit, and usually long cables connect the device to computers. So, it hinders the ease and natural quality of the user's motion.

As a non-tactile method, recently a very accurate gesture recognition method using Moving Light Displays (MLD) was developed. In the MLD method, various bright markers are attached to the joints of a moving articulated body, and the lighting conditions are designed such that only the markers are visible against a black background. However, for this method, it is necessary to arrange the camera in advance and to illuminate the environment, so that it is very expensive and real-time processing is difficult.

Any awkwardness in wearing devices can be dissolved by using video-based *noncontact* recognition techniques. One approach adopts a set of video cameras and computer vision techniques to interpret gestures. We call the method "appearance-based gesture recognition" since only the visual appearance is used in the recognition process.

Appearance-based gesture recognition approaches are different depending on whether they use a 3D model or a 2D model of the human body. 3D model has difficulty for modeling and matching because the joints connecting the bones naturally exhibit different degrees of freedom (DoF). Furthermore, the 2D model requires complex calculations since appearances are different according to the position of cameras.

In this paper, we describe the method that can extract multi-dimensional features from gesture image sequences and project these images into the parametric eigen space with PCA (Principal Component Analysis). The projected models are recognized as gestures using the probability calculation of HMM. Our method can detect the key frame that shows how the configuration of the human body is abruptly changed in fixed backgrounds and that frame is used in constructing models and recognizing gestures.

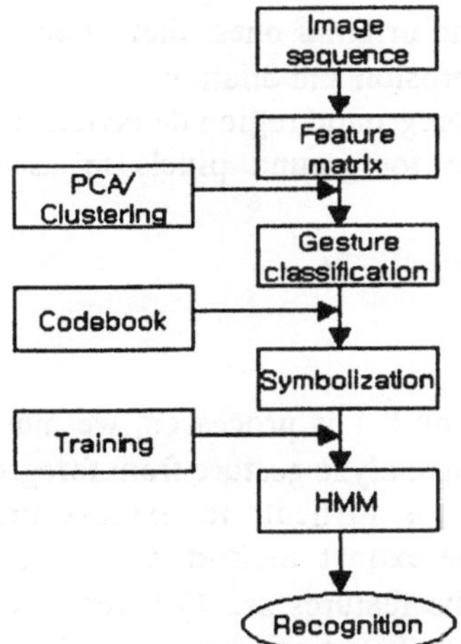

Fig. 1. Block diagram of gesture recognition

2 Automatic Model Composing

2.1 Segmentation

Gesture refers to the human body movement, hand movement and a means of expression. So, gesture recognition needs a process in which the person who is performing the gestures is extracted from the rest of the visual image. Therefore, we must model a background scene. It is modeled by representing each pixel by three values, its minimum and maximum intensity values and the maximum intensity difference between the consecutive frames observed during this training period.

Foreground objects are segmented from the background in each frame of the video sequence by a four stage process: thresholding, noise cleaning, morphological filtering and object detection.

Each pixel is first classified as either a background or a foreground pixel using the background model[1]. Giving the minimum (M), maximum (N) and the largest interframe absolute difference (D) images that represent the back-ground scene model, pixel x from image I is a foreground pixel if:

$$|M(x,t)-I(x,t)| OR |N(x,t)-I(x,t)| > D(x,t)+C \qquad (1)$$

where C is the constant.

Thresholding alone, however, is not sufficient to obtain clear foreground regions since it results in a significant level of noise, for example, due to illumination changes. We use region-based noise cleaning to eliminate noise regions. After thresholding, one iteration of erosion is applied to the foreground pixels to eliminate one-pixel thick noise. Then, a fast binary-connected component operator is applied to find the foreground regions, and small regions are eliminated. Since the remaining regions are smaller than the original ones, they should be restored to their original sizes by processes such as erosion and dilation.

As the final step of the foreground region detection, a binary-connected component analysis is applied to the foreground pixels to assign a unique label to each foreground object.

2.2 Feature extraction

Once segmentation in section 2.1 is processed, we must extract the features of the body configurations that can analyze gesture from foreground region. However, if we use an abstract feature, it is difficult to express the complex configuration or movement. Furthermore, we extract multi-dimensional features from gesture image sequences. In this paper, the features are 1) Feret ratio, the dimension ratio of the human body in horizontal and vertical directions, 2) the x position, the center of gravity, 3) the y position, the center of gravity, 4)compactness, 5) the angle at which a blob has the least moment of inertia, 6) the angle perpendicular to 5). Also, because the interpretation of gestures requires dynamic configurations of the human body, we acquire the movement information from the subtraction operation on the consecutive frames. Therefore, multi-dimensional features are calculated from equation (2) as shown in Figure 2.

$$I_t^{t+n} \quad (1 \le t \le T-5, 0 \le n \le 5) \qquad (2)$$

In equation (2), each image (I) is a binary image described in section 2.1 and T is the total length of the image sequence. Consequently, the temporal body's movements are configured by features.

The features must be normalized to the same weight because those have a numerically different unit.

Let N (= $T - 5$) be the number of the group which is composed of 6 features. The normalized feature set x is shown in equation (3).

$$x = [x_1, x_2, \cdots, x_N]^T \tag{3}$$

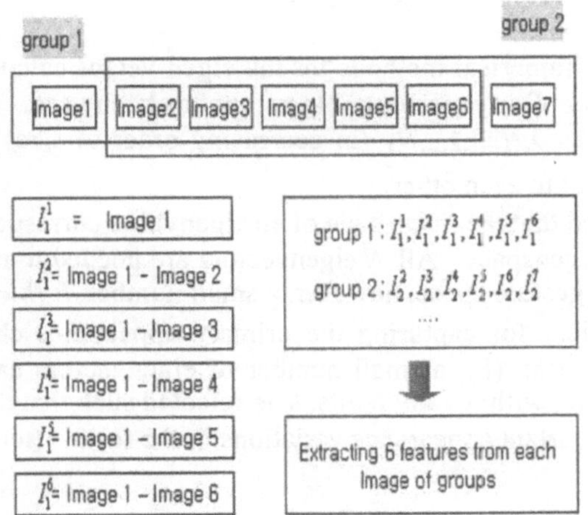

Fig. 2. Temporal image grouping

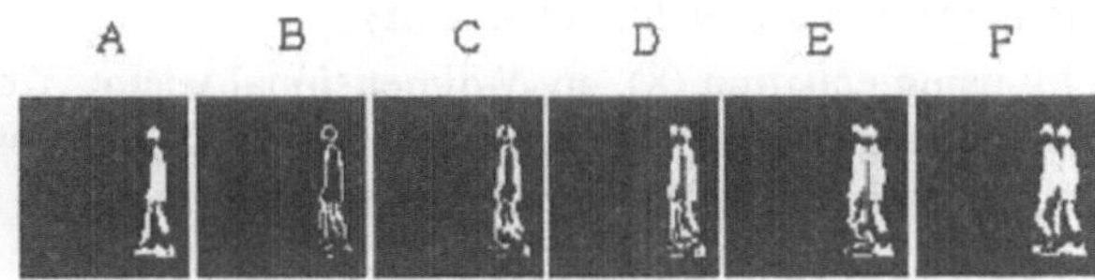

Fig. 3. Example of temporal image grouping (group 1 of walking)

2.3 Principal Component Analysis

Constructing a gesture space, we apply *principal component analysis* to the normalized gesture features as described in section 2.2.

Each feature set has been scanned into a column vector x of length *36*. By subtracting the average vector, c, of the all features, as in equation (5), the new feature matrix X is obtained, where the size of the matrix X is 36 x N. The covariance matrix, Q, of gesture features can be obtained from equation (6). Then, the PCA is straightforward requiring only the calculation of the eigen vectors satisfying equation (7).

$$c = (1/N)\sum_{i=1}^{N} x_i \tag{4}$$

$$X \stackrel{\Delta}{=} [x_1 - c, x_2 - c, \ldots\ldots, x_N - c]^T \tag{5}$$

$$Q \stackrel{\Delta}{=} X \cdot X^T \tag{6}$$

$$\lambda_i \cdot e_i = Q \cdot e_i \tag{7}$$

There are many numerical methods for the eigen vector calculation, however, the SVD (*Singular Value Decomposition*) algorithm has been used. The SVD provides a series of eigenvalues $\lambda_i (i = 1,2,..,N)$ (in decreasing order of size) and eigenvectors e_i, which are orthogonal to each other.

It should be noted that the magnitude of an eigenvalue corresponds to the weight of that vector in the eigenspace. All N eigenvectors are needed to represent the feature sets accurately in a gesture space, however, a small number, k ($k \ll N$), of eigenvectors is generally sufficient for capturing the primary appearance characteristics of the gestures. From equation (8), a small number of eigenvectors can be chosen which span the whole space, without any faults. k is selected such that the first eigenvectors of Q capture the important appearance variations in the feature sets.

$$\frac{\sum_{i=1}^{k} \lambda_i}{\sum_{i=1}^{N} \lambda_i} \geq T \tag{8}$$

where the threshold T_1 is close to, but less than, unity.

Consequently, by using equation (8), an N-dimensional vector X can be projected to a low k-dimensional eigenspace. An input feature, set x, is subtracted from an average vector c, and projected into the eigenspace as in equation (9).

$$m_i = [e_1, e_2, \ldots\ldots, e_k]^T (x_i - c) \tag{9}$$

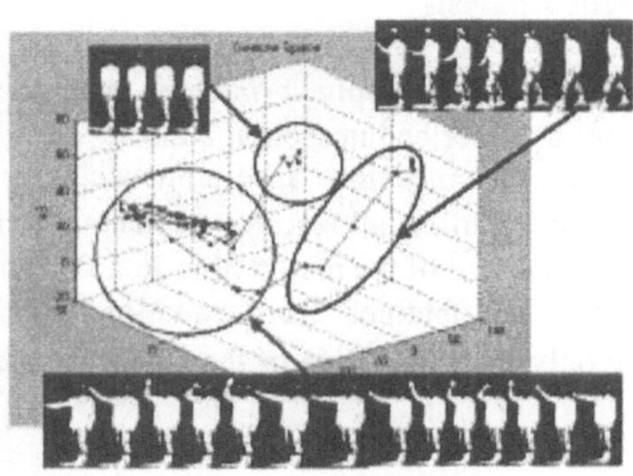

Fig. 4. Projection of model sequence into the gesture space

2.4 Clustering

To automatically detect the frames that show how gesture is abruptly changed on image sequences and to interpret models, a process which can group frames so that the frames are similar within each group is required. These groups are called clusters. However, we don't know how many clusters exist in gesture spaces. Therefore, it is necessary to determine the number of clusters. In this paper, we can overcome this problem using a multi-variable variance decomposition algorithm. This approach assumes that the number of clusters g that the between-class scatter $\boldsymbol{B}$, is much lager than the total within -class scatter $\boldsymbol{W}$.

$$B = \sum_{i=1}^{g} N_i(\overline{X_i} - \overline{X})(\overline{X_i} - \overline{X})^T \tag{10}$$

$$W = \sum_{i=1}^{g}\sum_{j=1}^{N} N_i(X_{ij} - \overline{X_i})(X_{ij} - \overline{X_i})^T \tag{11}$$

where N_i is the number of points included in cluster i and $\overline{X_i}$ means the average of cluster i. $\overline{X}$ is the total average of points in a gesture space. The total variation $\boldsymbol{T}$ and the between-class variation $\boldsymbol{B}$ ratio to the total variation are calculated by equation (12) and (13).

$$T = B + W = \sum_{i=1}^{g}\sum_{j=1}^{N} N_i(X_{ij} - \overline{X_i})(X_{ij} - \overline{X_i})^T \tag{12}$$

$$\Lambda = \frac{|B|}{|B + W|} \tag{13}$$

In equation (13), the small Λ means that change within clusters is relatively small compared to that between clusters. Determining the number of clusters, gesture images are classified by a hierarchical clustering algorithm.

$$J = \{j_i\} \quad (1 \le i \le g) \tag{14}$$

3 Gesture Recognition Using Hidden Markov Model

3.1 Hidden Markov Modeling

HMM is a stochastic process, a probabilistic network with *hidden* and *observable* states. A time domain process demonstrates a Markov property if the conditional probability density of the current event, given all present and past events, depends only on the jth most recent events. If the current event depends solely on the most recent past event, then the process is a first order Markov process. The initial topology for an HMM can be determined by estimating how many different states are involved in specifying a sign. Fine tuning this topology can be performed empirically.

If image sequences are classified with several gesture patterns using the clustering algorithm used in section 2.4, each cluster J_i is converted into a symbol by a codebook and this sequence is used with the input of HMM.

HMM λ is represented by the following variables. The state transition probability a_{ij} indicates that state of HMM will change from i to j. The probability $b_{ij}(y)$ indicates that the output symbol y will be observable in the transition of state j from state i. Also, π_i is the initial state probability. Learning of a HMM is equal to estimating the parameters $\{\pi, A, B\}$ of the HMM. The algorithm which we use for estimation of the HMM parameters is the *Baum-Welch Algorithm*[2].

$$\xi_t(i,j) = \frac{P(s_t = i, s_{t+1} = j, Y \mid \lambda)}{P(Y \mid \lambda)} \tag{15}$$

$$= \frac{\alpha_t(i) a_{ij} b_{ij}(y_{t+1}) \beta_{t+2}(j)}{\sum_{i=1}^{N} \sum_{j=1}^{N} \alpha_t(i) a_{ij} b_{ij}(y_{t+1}) \beta_{t+2}(j)}$$

$$\gamma_t(i) = \sum_{j=1}^{N} \xi_t(i,j) \tag{16}$$

Where $\xi_t(i,j)$ is the probability of being in state s_i at time t and in state s_j at time $t+1$, and $\gamma_t(i)$ is the probability of being state s_i at time t. From equation (15) and (16), the gesture model is estimated.

3.2 Gesture Recognition

Given the observation sequence (Y), the model λ can be calculated using the forward variable $\alpha_t(i)$ and backward variable $\beta_t(i)$ by the following equation. It is recognized as a model which has the maximum value of equation (17).

$$P(Y \mid \lambda_i) = \sum_i \sum_j \alpha_t(i) a_{ij} b_{ij}(y_{t+1}) \beta_{t+1}(j) \tag{17}$$

4 Experiments and Conclusion

The gesture images used in the experiment consist of 13 kinds, including walking, sitting, exercising the legs and so on. These were captured by a video camera with a resolution of 320*240 pixels. The total 8 gesture sequences were composed to models. In the experiment, the method we used has been shown to accurately analyze gestures by using the gesture information of the input action obtained through the analysis of specific motion information. However, there are some problems to be solved.

One problem to be solved is that the gesture cannot be recognized when the gesture that moves an arm and the gesture that moves a leg are classified to the same posture, since we use features described the total body' s configurations. In the future, a plan to develop a robust recognition algorithm by adding features classifying movements of the body' s region is required.

Now, it is difficult to classify all images with the models used in the experiment. So, in order for our method to have general applicability, we must gather all gesture images and analyze these.

In this paper, a gesture recognition method has been proposed that uses not the geometric features of edges and corners, but uses very abstract and simple features such as moment, and ratio of body region. Therefore, the detail motion information cannot be fully recognized, but brief actions or gestures in a specific area can be analyzed.

References

1. Ismail Haritaoglu, David Harwood and Larry S. Davis, "W4: Who? When? Where? What? A Real Time System for Detecting and Tracking People", *International Conference on Face and Gesture Recognition*, 1998, pp.14-16
2. Yoshio IWAI, Tadashi HATA, and Masahiko YACHIDA, "Gesture Recognition based on Subspace Method and Hidden Markov Model", *IEEE*, 1997, pp. 960-966
3. Ismail Haritaoglu, Ross Cutler, David Harwood and Larry S. Davis, "Backpack: Detection of People Carrying Objects Using Silhouettes", *IEEE International Conference on Computer Vision (ICCV)*, 1999
4. Takahiro Watanabe and Masahiko Yachida, "Real Time Recognition of Gesture and Gesture Degree Information Using Multi Input Image Sequence", *ICPR*, 1998
5. Shigeyoshi Hiratsuka, Kohtaro Ohba, Hikaru Inooka, Shinya Kajikawa, and Kazuo Tanie, "Stable Gesture Verification in Eigen Space", *LAPR Workshop on Machine Vision Application*, 1998, 17-19
6. D.M. Gavrila, L.S. Davis,"Towards 3D model-based tracking and recognition of human movement: a multi-view approach", *Int. Workshop on Face and Gesture Recognition*, 1995
7. Christian Vogler, Dimitris Metaxas, "ASL Recognition Based on a Coupling Between HMMs and 3D Motion Analysis", *ICCV*, 1998
8. Andrew D. Wilson, Aaron F. Bobick, "Parametric Hidden Markov Models for Gesture Recognition", *IEEE Transaction on PAMI*, Vol. 21, No. 9, September 1999

A Robust Line-Feature-Based Hausdorff Distance for Shape Matching

Wai-Pak Choi, Kin-Man Lam, and Wan-Chi Siu

Centre for Multimedia Signal Processing
Department of Electronic and Information Engineering
The Hong Kong Polytechnic University, Hong Kong
enkmlam@polyu.edu.hk

Abstract. The Hausdorff distance can be used to measure the similarity of two point sets. In matching the two point sets, one of the point sets is translated, rotated and scaled in order to obtain an optimal matching, which is a computationally intensive process. In this paper, a robust line-feature-based approach for model-based recognition is proposed, which can achieve a good performance level in matching, even in a noisy environment or with the existence of occlusion. The method is insensitive to noise and can find the rotation and scale of the image point set accurately and reliably. For this reason, instead of 4D matching, a 2D-2D matching algorithm can be used. This can greatly reduce the required memory and computation. Having rotated and scaled the image point set, the difference between the query point set and the model point set can be computed by considering translation only. The performance and the sensitivity to noise of our algorithm are evaluated using simulated data. Experiments show that our 2D-2D algorithm can give a high performance level when determining the relative scale and orientation of two point sets.

1 Introduction

Object matching is an important task in computer vision, model-based recognition and content-based retrieval [1,2]. The algorithms used usually analyze the object contours in computing the similarity of the objects, forming an essential part of the retrieval or recognition systems. One of the critical problems is how to match two objects efficiently and accurately with the existence of noise, partial occlusion or spurious parts, and under different translations, orientations and scales. In terms of comparing the shapes of two objects, it is well known that moments [1] and Fourier coefficients [3] can provide invariant features with respect to the affine transformation. However, both the high-order moments and the Fourier descriptors of two-dimensional images for shape matching are sensitive to noise, and produce a significant degree of error when an object is occluded.

Hausdorff Distance [4] has been used for matching two point sets because of its simplicity and relatively insensitivity to noise, requiring no explicit correspondence between the two point sets. Different Hausdorff distance measures [5] for object matching have been investigated while Takács *et. al.* [6] applied the modified

[1] This work is supported by HKPolyU research grant G-V596.

Hausdorff distance in human face recognition. Most of the Hausdorff distance algorithms can find the best match for translation only. A huge amount of computation is required for matching objects of different orientations and scales. In [7], a line-based Hausdorff distance based on 4D matching was proposed. A line segment formed by two consecutive points along a contour is represented by its mid-point (x, y), the logarithm of its segment length, and its orientation. However, this approach is sensitive to noise, so 4D matching must be used. This approach requires a large memory and is computationally intensive. In this paper, we propose a robust line-feature-based approach for object matching. A segment formed in our algorithm is obtained by joining a point and its corresponding farthest point in a point set when extracting the feature. We will prove that this arrangement can make the extracted features robust to noise and occlusion, so 2D-2D matching algorithm can be used. The first 2D matching is to determine the relative scale, s, and orientation, ϕ, while the second 2D matching is based on the traditional Hausdorff distance.

2 Hausdorff Distance for Shape Matching

The Hausdorff distance is a kind of metric measurement used to measure the degree of mismatch between all possible relative positions of two point sets. The definition of Hausdorff distance between two point sets, A and B, is:
Given two finite point sets $A = \{a_1, a_2, \ldots, a_m\}$ and $B = \{b_1, b_2, \ldots, b_n\}$, the Hausdorff distance $H(A,B)$ for these two point sets is defined as follows:

$$H(A,B) = \max(h(A,B), h(B,A)) \tag{1}$$

$$h(A,B) = \max_{a_i \in A} \min_{b_j \in B} d(a_i, b_j), \tag{2}$$

where $h(A,B)$ is the directed Hausdorff distance and $d(a,b)$ is the Euclidean distance between two points a and b.

The relative position between the two point sets can be calculated by searching a minimum value of the HD on the (x,y)-plane. If a translation transformation t applied to the point set B is best matched with the point set A, a minimum value of the Hausdorff distance $H(A,t(B))$ for point set A and its transformed point set $t(B)$ can be obtained. The searching function for matching can be written as follows:

$$H_{\min} = \min_t H(A, t(B)) \tag{3}$$

where $t(.)$ represents the translation transformation function. For a specific transformation t, the minimum value of the Hausdorff distance, H_{min}, represents the similarity between the two point sets. Different Hausdorff distance measures have been proposed for shape matching. The M-Estimation Hausdorff distance [8] (ME-HD) has been proposed; it is insensitive to noise. This distance measure only requires the comparison and summation operations. The definition of ME-HD is:
Given two finite point sets $A = \{a_1, a_2, \ldots, a_m\}$ and $B = \{b_1, b_2, \ldots, b_n\}$, the M-Estimation HD $H_M(A, B)$ for the point sets A and B is defined as follows:

$$H_M(A,B) = \max(h_M(A,B), h_M(B,A)) \tag{4}$$

and the directed ME-HD, $h_M(A,B)$, is

$$h_M(A,B)=\frac{1}{N_A}\sum_{a\in A}\rho(d_B(a)) \tag{5}$$

where $\rho(x)=\begin{cases}|x|, & |x|<\tau\\ \tau, & |x|\geq\tau,\end{cases}$

$d_B(a)$ represents the minimum distance value from point a to the point set B, and N_A is the number of points in the point set A. The threshold τ is used to eliminate outliers. This distance measure can therefore eliminate those outliers yielding large errors.

3 A Robust Feature For Shape Matching

Feature selection is an important issue for object matching. The selected features should be robust to noise and invariant to position, scale and orientation. In this paper, a robust feature for shape matching using HD is proposed such that 2D-2D matching can be adopted instead of 4D matching. The feature is based on the line segments formed between each point and their corresponding farthest point in a point set. The orientation and length of each of the line segments are then used to form points in the (θ, log l)-plane. The features used are robust to noise and partial occlusion, so 2D matching can be used to determine the scale and orientation between the point sets accurately. Having rotated and scaled the query point set, the relative position between the point sets is computed in the second 2D matching in the (x, y)-plane.

Robust Features for matching with different orientation and scale

Suppose that we have a model object, S_m. A query object, S_q, is obtained by rotating and scaling the object S_m by an angle ϕ and a scaling factor s, respectively, as shown in Fig. 1(a) and (b). Robust line-features are extracted by considering line segments formed by joining each contour point and its corresponding farthest point in the point set. Consider two points, z_m and z_q, which are the corresponding farthest points from the contour points, c_m and c_q, of the two shapes. Two line-segments, z_mc_m and z_qc_q, for the two objects are therefore formed. These two line segments are converted to feature points, (θ_m, log l_m) and (θ_q, log l_q), in the (θ, log l)-feature plane, which can then be used to measure the relative scale and orientation of the objects. Since c_m and c_q are the corresponding points in the two objects, the lengths and the orientations of the line-segments have the following relationship:

$$\log(l_q)=\log(l_m)+\log(s) \tag{6}$$

$$\theta_q=\theta_m+\phi \tag{7}$$

where the parameters ϕ and s represent the orientation and the scaling factor, respectively.

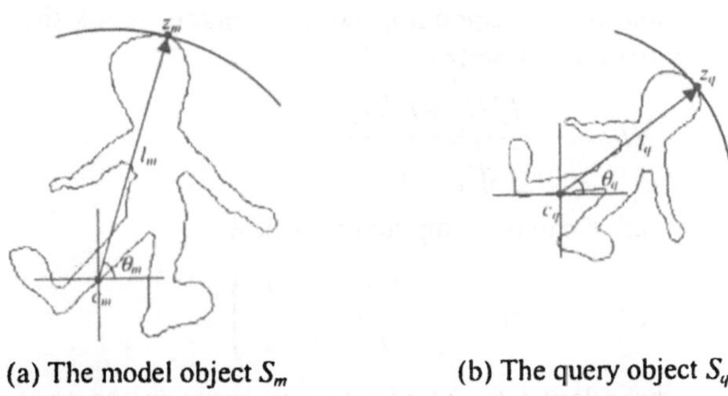

(a) The model object S_m (b) The query object S_q

Fig. 1. A model and a query object under different translations, orientations and scales.

A set of feature points can be extracted for each object to form a feature pattern in the (θ, log l)-feature plane. Figure 2 shows an object and its rotated and scaled versions with and without additional distortion. By projecting the logarithmic lengths and the orientations of the longest line segments of these three objects into their corresponding feature planes, as shown in Fig. 2(b), the scale s and the orientation ϕ can be obtained by means of the ME-HD. In order to find their relative orientation within the range of 0° to 360°, the feature pattern of the model object is duplicated to the range of 360° to 720°, as shown in the first feature plane in Fig. 2(b). The feature patterns of these shapes in the (θ, log l)-feature plane are similar, but are translated relative to each other. By using the ME-HD, the minimum value can be obtained at a specific relative position. The orientation and the scaling factor can then be computed based on equations (6) and (7).

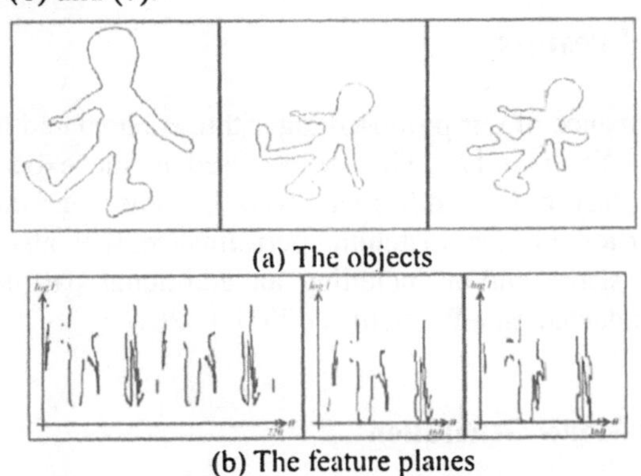

(a) The objects

(b) The feature planes

Fig. 2. The objects and their corresponding (θ, log l)-feature planes.

3.2 Robustness with respect to noise and occlusions

Considering the feature pattern of an object, the effect of noise and occlusion can be minimized since the feature pattern is extracted based on the line segments formed by each contour point and its corresponding farthest contour point along the boundary. Since the line segments considered are the longest segments, the extracted features, the orientation and the logarithm of their lengths, are affected to a lesser extent than other possible line segments formed by the contour points. Suppose that noise is added to a contour point and its corresponding farthest contour point, the length of the line segment formed by these two points is as follows:

$$\nabla l \approx \frac{l_x \nabla l_x + l_y \nabla l_y}{\sqrt{l_x^2 + l_y^2}} \tag{8}$$

The change in orientation can be computed as follows:

$$\nabla \theta \approx \arctan\left(\frac{l_y \nabla l_x - l_x \nabla l_y}{l_x^2 + l_y^2} \right) \tag{9}$$

where (l_x, l_y) are the relative (x, y)-coordinates between the contour point and its farthest contour point along the boundary and $(\nabla l_x, \nabla l_y)$ are the resultant shift of the points. Since the line segment is the longest line-segment that can be formed in the point set and the displacement, ∇l_x and ∇l_y, are small compared to l_x and l_y, the values of ∇l and $\nabla \theta$, i.e. the deviations of the length and orientation of the line segment, are the smallest compared to other possible line segments in the point set.

If an object is distorted or occluded in some parts, only the corresponding parts of the feature pattern are affected, as shown in the third column in Fig. 2(a) and (b). The feature pattern is still similar to the original one. By using the ME-HD, the effect of changes to the feature pattern due to noise, distortion or occlusion can be minimized. If more feature points are considered, the scaling and orientation factors between two objects can be obtained more accurately. Consequently, matching based on the feature pattern using the ME-HD can achieve robustness in comparing two shapes, even in the presence of noise, distortion or occlusion.

4 Experimental results

The matching performance of our proposed algorithm is compared to the line-segment feature proposed by Yi *et. al.*[7]. The shapes used in the experiment are closed-contour, which are distorted by different levels of noise variance. The effect of occlusion and distortion on the matching performance will also be evaluated by removing part of a shape and/or including an additional part to the shape. The experiments were conducted on a Pentium II 400MHz PC.

Noise and Distorted Model Generation

The images used in the experiments are sized 640×480. The shapes of the objects in the images are extracted using the adaptive snake method [9]; the shapes then form the model set. The extracted shapes are rotated and scaled, and distorted by different levels of noise to form a set of query shapes.

In the experiment, 10 different shapes are adopted to form the model set. These 10 model shapes are first rotated by an angle of 37° and scaled by a factor of 0.7. These transformed shapes are then distorted by noise levels from 2.0 to 20.0 in a step size of 2.0. A query set containing 100 shapes is therefore generated by applying different noise levels. Another query set is also generated by arbitrarily removing and/or adding parts of contours to the shapes.

The effect of noise levels and distortion

Figure 3 illustrates the effect of noise added to a shape on the feature pattern generated. The rotated and scaled objects with or without noise added are shown in the first row. Their corresponding feature patterns based on the line-segment features and our approach, robust line-segment features, are then matched by using the ME-HD. The scale and orientation of a transformed shapes relative to the original shape can therefore be computed. Having transformed the shapes accordingly, the ME-HD is applied again to match the shapes in the (x, y)-plane. The matching results based on the line-segment features and our approach are illustrated in the second and third rows. As the noise level increases, our approach will result in only minimal change to the feature patterns. However, using the line-segment approach will cause a significant change in the feature patterns. Consequently, our approach can provide a good matching performance even when the noise level is high. The line-segment approach will fail to match the shapes in a high noise level.

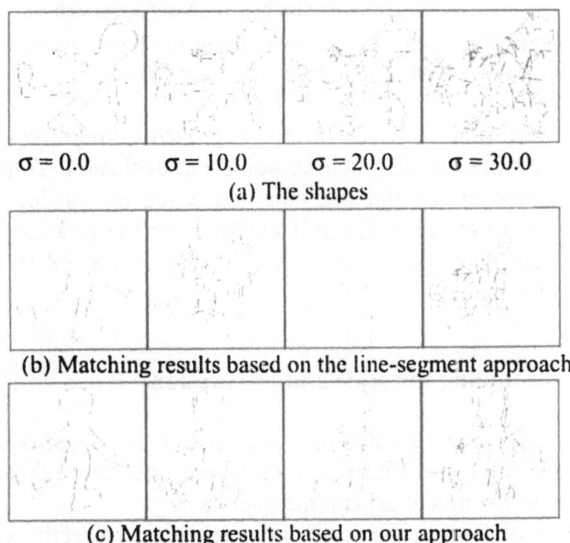

Fig. 3. The comparison of matching performance using the line-segment and the robust line-segment features with different levels of noise.

Similarly, Fig. 4 illustrates the effect of distortion or occlusion on the feature patterns. The rotated and scaled shapes with and without distortions are shown in the first row. Their corresponding feature patterns and the matching results based on the line-segment approach and our approach are illustrated from the second row to the third row. As parts are added or removed, the feature patterns generated using our approach are affected to a lesser extent than the line-segment approach. Consequently, our approach can also achieve a better matching performance than the line-segment approach.

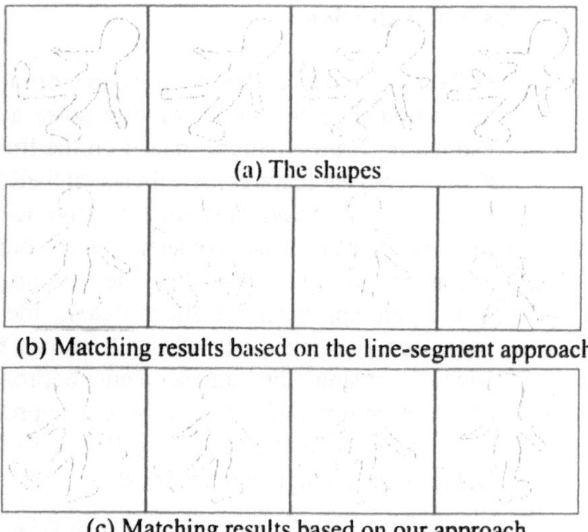

(a) The shapes

(b) Matching results based on the line-segment approach

(c) Matching results based on our approach

Fig. 4. The comparison of matching performance using the line-segment and the robust line-segment features with occlusion and additional parts to the shapes.

The matching performance based on our approach outperforms the line-segment approach when the shapes are distorted by noise and occlusion. This is mainly due to the fact that the extracted features are obtained based on the longest possible line segments formed in a point set. Noise or disturbance on the contour points will have a relatively lesser effect when compared to the features extracted from other possible line segments of the point set.

The performance of finding the scale and orientation

To evaluate the performance of computing the relative scale and orientation between two shapes, the probabilities of finding the scale and orientation factors are measured based on the shapes in the model set and the query set.

The probabilities of finding the scale and orientation correctly within a threshold to the true value against the level of noise variance using the line-segment approach and our approach are plotted in Fig. 5. According to the results, we can observe that the probabilities drop rapidly when the noise level is higher than 4.0 for the line-segment approach. Our proposed feature can be used to find these two factors accurately even if the noise is increased to 20.0.

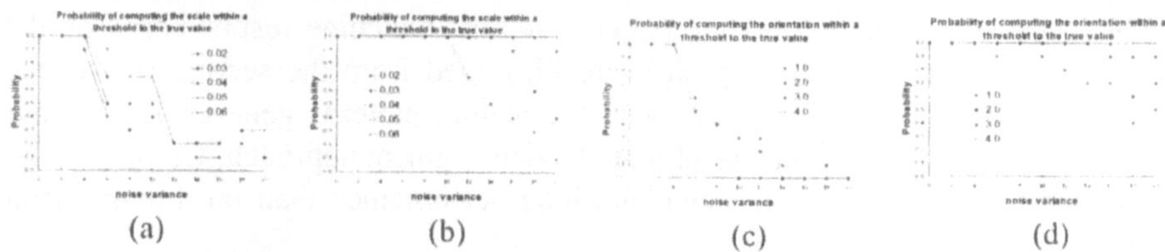

(a) (b) (c) (d)

Fig. 5. The probabilities of finding the scaling factor by the (a) line-segment approach, and (b) robust line-segment approach, and the probabilities of finding the orientation by the (c) line-segment approach, and (d) robust line-segment approach.

Figure 6 illustrates some more matching results, where the solid line represents the model shape, while the dotted line represents the query shape. A query shape is the affine transformation of the original shape, distorted by noise on the contour points and by occlusion. The results show that our proposed algorithm can be used for matching even when the objects are distorted, rotated and scaled.

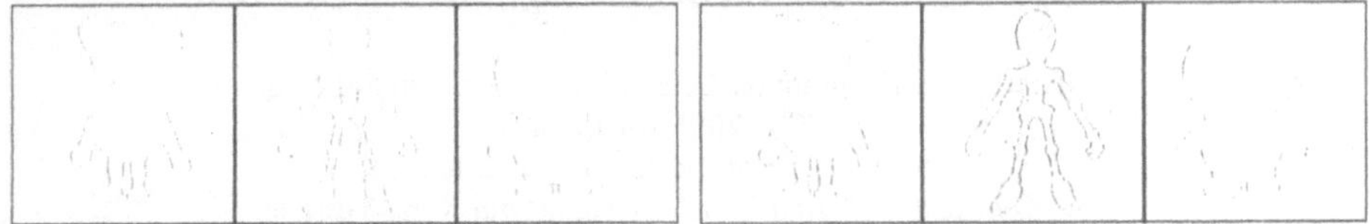

(a) The model shapes and the query shapes (b) The matching results

Fig. 6. The matching of the model shapes and query shapes.

5 Conclusions

In this paper, a robust line-feature-based approach for model-based recognition is proposed. It can provide a good performance level in a noisy environment or with the existence of occlusion. This new approach is insensitive to noise, and can find the rotation and scale of the image point set more accurately and reliably than other approaches. It solves the problems of determining the translation, rotation and scale between two objects. The feature points are generated based on the line segments formed by each contour point and its corresponding farthest point in a point set. The robustness and performance of our method have also been addressed. Experiments show that our approach can achieve an accurate result and is robust to noise. Consequently, 2D-2D matching can be used instead of 4D matching. This can greatly reduce the memory requirement and the required computation.

References

[1] Y. S. Kim, W. Y. Kim, "Content-based trademark retrieval system using a visually salient feature", Image and Vision Computing, Vol. 16, pp. 931-939, 1998.

[2] B. Günsel and A. M. Tekalp, "Shape similarity matching for query-by-example", Pattern Recognition, vol. 31, no. 7, pp. 931-944, 1998.

[3] A. Blumenkrans, "Two-Dimensional Object Recognition using a Two-Dimensional Polar Transform", Pattern Recognition, vol. 24, no. 9, pp. 879-890, 1991.

[4] D. P. Huttenlocher, G. A. Klanderman, and W. J. Rucklidge, "Comparing Image Using the Hausdorff Distance", IEEE Transactions on PAMI, vol. 15, no. 9, pp. 850-863, 1993.

[5] M. Dubuisson and A. K. Jain, "A modified Hausdorff distance for object Matching", Proc. 12th Int. Conf. on Pattern Recognition (ICPR), Jerusalem, Israel, pp. 566-568, 1994.

[6] B. Takács, "Comparing Face Images Using the Modified Hausdorff Distance", Pattern Recognition, vol. 31, no. 12, pp. 1973-1881, 1998.

[7] X. Yi and Octavia, "Line-Based Recognition Using A Multidimensional Hausdorff Distance", IEEE Transactions on Pattern Analysis and Machine Intelligence, vol. 21, no. 9, pp. 901-916, September 1999.

[8] D. G. Sim, O. K. Kwon, and R. H. Park, "Object Matching Algorithms Using Robust Hausdorff distance Measures", IEEE Transactions on Image Processing, vol. 8, no. 3, pp. 425-429, March 1999.

[9] W. P. Choi, K. M. Lam, and W. C. Siu, "An adaptive active contour model for highly irregular boundaries", Pattern Recognition, vol. 34, pp. 323-331, 2001.

Copyright Protection for WAV-Table Synthesis Audio Using Digital Watermarking

Changsheng Xu[1,2], David Dagan Feng[1], and Yongwei Zhu[2]

[1] Department of Computer Science, The University of Sydney, NSW 2006 Australia
{xucs, feng}@cs.usyd.edu.au
[2] Kent Ridge Digital Labs,, 21 Heng Mui Keng Terrace, Singapore 119613
ywzhu@krdl.org.sg

Abstract. In this paper, we present a novel audio watermarking method for WAV-table synthesis audio (Downloadable Sounds - DLS) copyright protection. In order to guarantee the inaudibility and robustness, we embed watermark both in sample data and in articulation parameters. For sample data, we propose an adaptive low-bit coding method based on finite automaton. For articulation parameters, we generate a virtual instrument and use its parameters to hide watermark information. We also discuss the watermark detection and give the experimental results of watermarked DLS to the listening and robustness tests.

1 Introduction

As the rapid development of the computer network and the increased use of multimedia data through the Internet, digital information exchange gets fast and convenient. However, the open environment of Internet causes a problem of illegal distribution of privately owned multimedia products. To prevent digital media from illegal copying, there is a need for the copyright protection. Digital watermarking is such a technique to solve this problem. It directly embeds the copyright information into the original media and keeps the information present in the media after all kinds of manipulations. Generally, a watermark should be inaudible or invisible and robust to different attacks and collusion. Furthermore, watermark detection should identify the ownership and copyright unambiguously. A variety of digital watermarking techniques has been widely investigated in the last few years. These techniques mainly focus on spatial domain[1,2] and transformation domain[3,4,5]. In the meantime, many watermarking products are developed and embedded into some popular software such as Photoshop and Digimarc. Most importantly, digital watermarking technology has been considered as an integral part of some international standard contributions such as JPEG 2000 and MPEG 4.

Downloadable Sounds (DLS) is a synthesizer architecture specification which requires a hardware or software synthesizer to support all of its components[6]. It will become a new standard in musical industry because of its specific advantages. Compared with MIDI, it can provide a common playback experience and an unlimited sound palette for both instruments and sound effects. Compared with sampled digital audio, it has true audio interactivity and smaller storage requirement. One of the objectives of DLS design is that the specification must be open and non-proprietary. Therefore, how to effectively protect its copyright becomes an important problem.

In this paper, we proposed a novel watermarking scheme for DLS audio files. In our method, inaudibility and robustness of watermarked DLS are fully taken into consideration. The general watermarking method including embedding and extracting schemes is introduced in section 2. In section 3, the strategy of low-bit coding based on Finite Automaton (FA) is described in details. Preliminary experimental results are shown in section 4. Finally, section 5 illustrates the concluding remarks.

2 Watermarking Scheme

Comparing with digital video and image watermarking techniques, digital audio watermarking techniques provide a special challenge because the human auditory system (HAS) is extremely more sensitive than the human visual system (HVS). A perfect watermark should be inaudible and robust. For the inaudible, we mean the digital audio signal with and without watermark should be same in the listening test. For the robust, we mean the watermark should be difficult to be removed or detected without destroying the host audio signal. However, there is always a conflict between the inaudibility and the robustness existing in current audio watermarking methods. In this section, we will provide a solution to solve the conflict between the inaudibility and the robustness in embedding and extracting watermarks, based on the characteristics of DLS.

2.1 Embedding Scheme

A DLS file contains two parts: articulation parameters and sample data. Unlike traditional sampled digital audio, the sample data in DLS are not the prevalent components. On the contrary, it is the articulation parameters in DLS that control how to play the sounds. Therefore, in our embedding scheme we not only embed watermarks into sample data but also into articulator parameters. The embedding scheme is shown in Fig.1. Firstly, original DLS is divided into sample data and articulation parameters. Then, we use two different embedding schemes to process them respectively and form the relevant watermarked outputs. Finally, the watermarked DLS is generated by integrating the watermarked sample data and articulation parameters.

For sample data of DLS, we employ a low-bit hiding method based on Finite Automaton (FA) to embed watermark. This will be described in section 3. In order to guarantee the robustness of watermarked DLS, we also embed the watermark and watermarked sample data into articulation parameters. This process is called information hiding and shown in Fig.2. Watermark and watermarked low-bit sequence are encrypted and form a data stream. In the meantime a virtual instrument is generated.

We use these data as the parameters of this virtual instrument and then embed these parameters into the DLS articulation parameters. Because the locations of the parameters belonging to the virtual instrument are not known by attackers, they are difficult to be detected in the presence of attacks. On the other hand, it can ensure the correction of detection if the watermarks in DLS sample data are distorted.

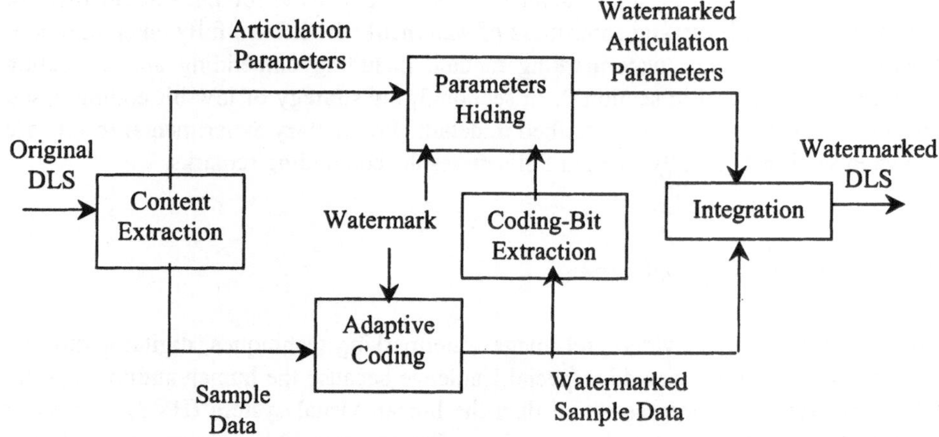

Fig.1 Watermark embedding scheme

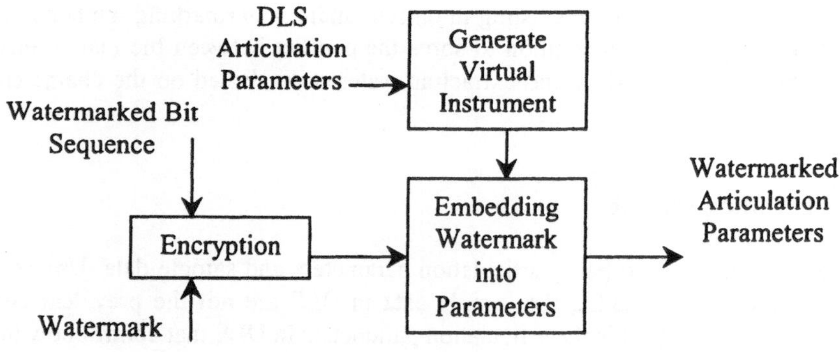

Fig.2 Information hiding scheme

2.2 Extraction Scheme

In the extracting process, the original DLS is not needed. For a watermarked DLS, it is also divided into sample data and articulation parameters at first. Then we will detect the watermark sequence in the low-bits of the sample data and the encrypted watermark information in the articulation parameters of the virtual instrument. If the watermark sequence in sample data is obtained, it will be compared with the watermark in articulator parameters to make the verification. If the sample data suffered from distortions and the watermark sequence can not be detected, we will use the watermarked low-bit sequence in the articulation parameters to restore the low-bit information in the sample data and make the detection in the restored data. Similarly, the detected watermark will be verified by comparing with that embedded in articulation parameters. The whole watermark extracting scheme is shown in Fig. 3.

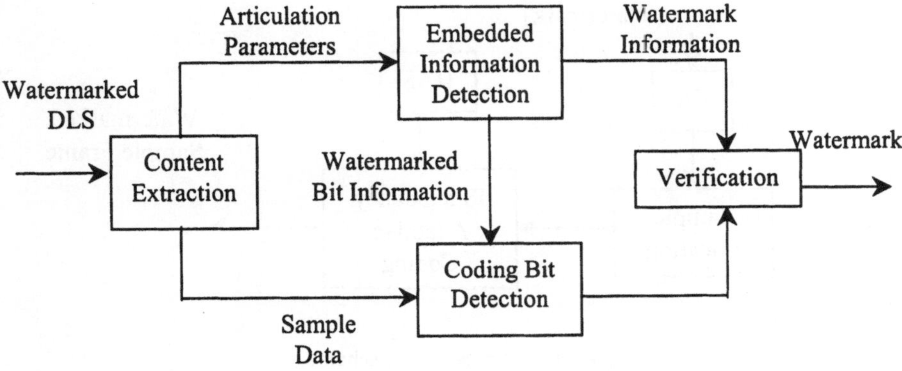

Fig.3 Watermark extracting scheme

3 Low-Bit Coding Based on FA

The basic idea in low-bit coding technique is to embed the watermark into an audio signal by replacing the least significant bit of each sampling point by a coded binary string corresponding to the watermark. For example, in a 16-bits per sample representation, the least four bits can be used for hiding watermark. The hidden data detection in low-bit coding is done by reading out the value from the low bits. The stego key is the position of altered bits. Low-bit coding is the simplest way to embed data into digital audio and can be applied in all ranges of transmission rates with digital communication modes. Ideally, the channel capacity will be 8kbps in an 8kHz sampled sequence and 44kbps in a 44kHz sampled sequence for a noiseless channel application.

The major disadvantage of low-bit coding is its poor immunity to manipulations. Embedded information can be destroyed by channel noise, re-sampling, and other operations. The reason why we choose low-bit coding technique in our watermarking scheme is based on several considerations. Firstly, unlike any sampled digital audio, DLS is a parameterized digital audio, so it is difficult to attack it using the typical signal processing methods such as adding noise and re-sampling. Secondly, the size of wave sample in DLS is so much small that it is unsuitable to embed watermark in the frequency domain. Finally, in order to guarantee the robustness, the watermarked low-bit sequence of sample data will be embedded into the articulation parameters of DLS.

If the sample data are distorted, we can use the embedded information to restore the low-bit of sample data. Fig. 4 shows the scheme of low-bit data hiding. In this scheme, we proposed two techniques (finite automaton and redundancy) to improve the robustness. The watermark message is converted into a string of binary sequence. Each bit of the sequence will replace the corresponding bit of the sample points. The location of sample points will be determined by finite automaton and the number of sample points will be calculated according to the redundancy technique.

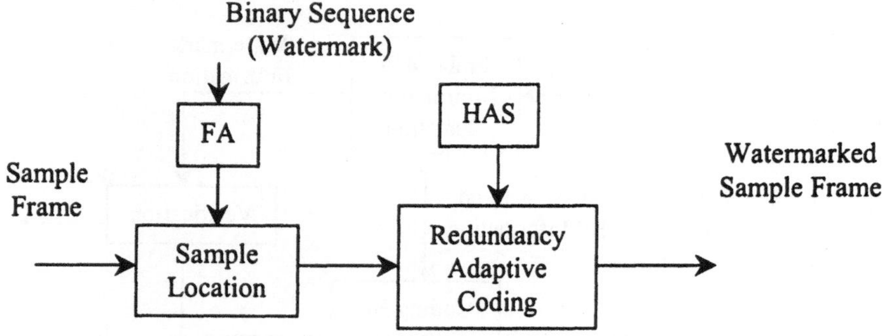

Fig.4 Low-bit data coding scheme

A finite automaton M can be described as a quintuple:

$$M = < X, Y, S, \delta, \lambda > \tag{1}$$

where X is a non-empty finite set (the input alphabet of M), Y is a non-empty finite set (the output alphabet of M), S is a non-empty finite set (the state alphabet of M), $\delta : S \times X \to S$ is a single-valued mapping (the next state function of M) and $\lambda : S \times X \to Y$ is a single-valued mapping (the output function of M).

In our method, X, Y, S, δ, λ are expressed as follows:

$$X = \{0,1\} \tag{2}$$

$$Y = \{y_1, y_2, y_3, y_4\} \tag{3}$$

$$S = \{S_0, S_1, S_2, S_3, S_4\} \tag{4}$$

$$S_{i+1} = \delta(S_i, x) \tag{5}$$

$$y_i = \lambda(S_i, x) \tag{6}$$

where y_i $(i = 1,2,3,4)$ is the number of sample points which will be jumped off when embedding bit corresponding to relevant states, and S_i $(i = 0-4)$ is five kinds of states corresponding to 0, 00, 01, 10 and 11 respectively and S_0 is to be supposed the initial state. The state transfer diagram of finite automaton is shown in Fig.5.

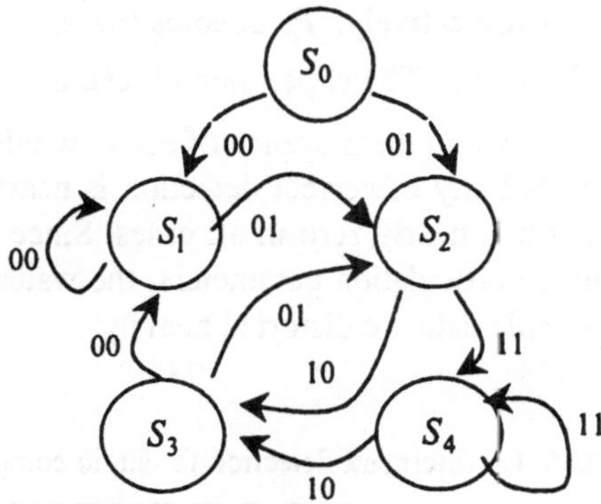

Fig.5 Finite automaton

4 Experimental Results

In order to further illustrate the performance of our DLS watermarking scheme, we took several different DLS Level 1 audio files to make both inaudible and robust test. In DLS Level 1 audio file, the maximum sampling rate of wave data is 22.05kHz and it only supports mono data. In our watermarking scheme, we try to get a trade-off between the inaudibility and robustness of the embedded files.

4.1 Inaudible

The inaudible means the additional information to the audio file must not affect the sonic quality of the original sound recording. In DLS audio, only the modification of wave sample can affect the audible quality. However, in our method we only use watermark bits to replace the low-bits of sample data. Since low-bit coding method will generate imperceptible disturbances, the inaudibility in watermarked DLS can be guaranteed. On the other hand, we invite four "golden ears" to listen the original and the watermarked DLS audio respectively. None of them can point out any difference between the original and watermarked DLS.

4.2 Robust

Since it is difficult to attack DLS without the specific tools. In order to illustrate the robustness of our watermarking scheme, we segment the sample data in DLS by using DLS Synth/Author v1.0 for Windows 95. These sample data will be processed by common signal manipulations and then will be embedded in the DLS files.

We studied the robustness of the watermark to audio compression, re-sampling and adding noise. The watermark detection results only due to sample data are shown in

Tab.1, Tab.2 and Tab.3 respectively. P_c denotes the probability of correct detection and P_f denots the false alarm. The experimental results indicate that it is possible to reliably detect the watermark in the presence of above manipulations. From the tables, we can see that the probability of correct detection is nearly one in all cases and the probability of false alarm is nearly zero in all cases. Since we also embed the watermark information into the articulation parameters, the watermark can be still detected correctly in case the sample data are distorted heavily.

Table 1. Watermark detection for audio compression

DLS	1	2	3	4	5
P_c	1	0.9989	1	1	0.9993
P_f	0	0	0	0	0

Table 2. Watermark detection for re-sampling

DLS	1	2	3	4	5
P_c	0.9991	0.9988	1	1	0.9974
P_f	0.0015	0	0	0	0.0016

Table 3. Watermark detection for adding noise

DLS	1	2	3	4	5
P_c	1	0.9979	1	1	0.9994
P_f	0	0	0	0	0.0009

5 Summary

DLS is a new standard of musical industry. Compared with traditional sample audio, it has its own special format. In view of this format, we proposed a new watermarking scheme for DLS. The watermark information is embedded both in sample data and in articulation parameters. This scheme can not only guarantee the inaudibilty but also the robustness in watermarked files. Furthermore, it is no need to use original file when doing watermark detection.

References

1. Wolfgang, R.B., Delp, E.J.: A Watermark for Digital Images, *Proc. of IEEE Int. Conf. On Image Processing*, Vol.3, (1996) 219-222
2. Cox, I.J., Miller, M.L.: A Review of Watermarking and the Importance of Perceptual Modelling, *Proceedings of SPIE Human Vision and Electronic Imaging*, Vol.3016, (1997) 92-99
3. Cox, I.J., Kilian, J., Leighton, T.: Secure Spread Spectrum Watermarking for Multimedia, *IEEE Trans. on Image Processing*, Vol.6, No.12, (1997) 1673-1687
4. Kundur, D., Hatzinakos, D.: A Robust Digital Image Watermarking Method Using Wavelet-Based Fusion, *Proc. of IEEE Int. Conf. On Image Processing*, Vol.1, (1997) 544-547
5. O'Ruanaidh, J., Pun, T.: Rotation, Scale and Translation Invariant Digital Image Watermarking, *Proc. of IEEE Int. Conf. On Image Processing*, Vol.1, (1997) 536-539
6. Downloadable Sounds Level 1, Version 1.0, *The MIDI Manufacturers Association*, CA, USA, (1997)
7. Bender, W., Gruhl, D., Morimoto, N., Lu, A.: Techniques for Data Hiding, *IBM Systems Journal*, Vol.35, No.3-4, (1996) 313-336.

Sign Correlation Detector for Blind Image Watermarking in the DCT Domain

Xiaochen Bo, Lincheng Shen, Wensen Chang

Institute of Automation, National University of Defense Technology,
Changsha 410073, P.R.CHINA
boxiaoc@163.com

Abstract. Digital watermarking is a key technique for protecting intellectual property of digital media. Due to the ability to detect watermark without the original image, blind watermarking is very useful if there are too many images to be authenticated. In this paper, we pose the difference on mathematical models between private watermark detection and blind watermark detection, and then point out the limitation of linear correlation detector (LCD). After reviewing some statistical models which have been proposed to better characterize the DCT coefficients of images, we deduce a new blind watermark detector — sign correlation detector (SCD) based on the Laplacian distribution model. Computing result of asymptotic relative efficiency demonstrates the effectiveness of the detector. A series of experiments show its robustness.

1 Introduction

Digital watermarking, which has been proposed as a solution to the problem of copyright protection of multimedia data, is a process of embedding signature directly into the media data by making small modifications to them. With the detection/extraction of the signature from the watermarked media data, it has been claimed that digital watermark can be used to identify the rightful owner, the intended recipients, as well as the authenticity of media data. In general, there are two most common requirements of invisible watermark. The watermark should not only be perceptually invisible, but also be robust to common signal processing and intentional attacks.

Watermarking schemes can be classified into two categories by watermark detection process. One is called "private watermarking" and the other is "public watermarking" (also referred to as blind watermarking). Blind marking systems can detect the watermark without the original image, while the private marking systems have to access the original. The ability to access the original image limits the use of private watermarking systems, since if there are too many images to be authenticated, it must be difficult to find the original image according to a watermarked image. As a matter of fact, it becomes a special case of content based image retrieval. More serious, Craver [6] reported a counterfeit attack to private watermarking system, which is called "IBM attack". Most of current private watermarking systems could not resist this attack. We notice that more and more blind watermarking schemes have been proposed recently.

Since Cox et al. [1] proposed a global DCT-based spread spectrum approach to hide watermark, a lot of watermarking schemes in the DCT domain have been presented. Barni [2] improved Cox's algorithm, and made it a blind watermarking scheme by embedding the signature in the fixed position. But the watermark detection algorithm in [2] is based on the calculation of the correlation coefficient between the image and the watermark in the DCT domain. As shown in this paper, this correlation structure, which has been somewhat taken for granted in the previous literature in the DCT domain watermarking, would be optimal only if the DCT coefficients followed Gaussian distribution. However, as many authors have pointed out, the popular Gaussian distribution is not accurate enough to model the peaky, heavy-tailed marginal distribution of DCT coefficient [3, 4, 5, 7]. In this paper, based on the Laplacian distribution model of DCT AC coefficients, we deduce a sign correlation detector (SCD) for blind watermarking. Computing result of asymptotic relative efficiency demonstrates the effectiveness of the detector. A series of experiments show its robustness.

The rest of this paper is organized as follows: Section 2 reviews watermarking scheme proposed by Cox [1] and Barni [2], discusses why Barni's watermark detection algorithm is not appropriate. Section 3 briefly describes statistical models which have been proposed to better characterize the DCT coefficients of common images. In section 4, we deduce the sign correlation watermark detector and compute its asymptotic relative efficiency. Section 5 illustrates experimental results. Section 6 draws some conclusions.

2 Blind Image Watermarking in the DCT Domain

Due to the ability to access the original image, Cox inserted the watermark in the 1000 largest DCT coefficients. But for Barni 's blind watermark detector, it is impossible to determine the position of coefficients with the largest magnitude, so the watermark has to be inserted in the fixed position of DCT spectrum. To achieve both perceptual invisibility and robustness against JPEG compression, the watermarking algorithms always select host coefficients in the low-middle frequency band.

Like [1] and [2], watermark $X = \{x_1, x_2, \cdots, x_n\}$ consists of a pseudo-random sequence of length n , each value x_i, $i = 1,2,\cdots,n$, is a random real number with a normal distribution having zero mean and unity variance. What changes in this paper is that we use the 8×8 block-wise DCT coefficients to embed watermark, not the full frame DCT coefficients, so that our algorithm can adapt to JPEG standard. Given an Image I, the 8×8 block-wise DCT transform $D = DCT\ (\ I\ )$ is computed. Some low-frequency coefficients of each block are then extracted and reordered into zig-zag order. Thus we obtain the host sequence $V = \{v_1, v_2, \cdots, v_n\}$. The watermarked sequence $V' = \{v'_1, v'_2, \cdots, v'_n\}$ is obtained according to

$$v'_i = v_i + \alpha x_i\,,\ i = 1,2,\cdots,n \tag{1}$$

where α is the scaling parameter. Finally, V' is reinserted in the zig-zag scan and the inverse 8×8 block-wise DCT is performed, thus we obtain the watermarked image $I' = DCT^{-1}(D')$. To detect certain watermark X in possible distorted image I^*, Cox extracted the estimation of watermark X^* using both I^* and the original image I, the similarity is measured by computing standard correlation coefficient

$$sim(X, X^*) = (X^* \cdot X) / \sqrt{X^* \cdot X^*} \tag{2}$$

To decide whether X and X^* match, one determines whether $sim(X, X^*) > T_g$, where T_g is some threshold.

In fact, $X^* \cdot X$ is the inner product between X and X^* from the mathematical view, it can be also regarded as metric of distance in R^n space. So the watermark "detection" in [1] is not detecting weak signal in noise, but comparing watermark signal and its estimation. To detect watermark without the original image, Barni [2] embedded the signature in the $(l+1)$th to $(l+n)$th full frame DCT coefficients in zig-zag order. The watermark casting rule is similar to (1). Given a possible corrupted image I^*, the $(l+1)$th to $(l+n)$th full frame DCT coefficients of I^* are selected to generate a vector V^*, then the correlation between V^* and X

$$T = \frac{1}{n} V^* \cdot X = \frac{1}{n} \sum_{i=1}^{n} v_i^* \cdot x_i \tag{3}$$

can be used to determine whether watermark X is present or not.

We notice that Barni [2] did not take into account the difference between (2) and (3). In (3), V^* must be viewed as the mixture of watermark X (which is the weak signal) and the channel noise V, therefore (3) is so-called linear correlation detector (LCD). As is well known, linear correlation detector can be optimal only if the noise follows a Gaussian distribution. But as many authors have pointed out, the Gaussian distribution is not accurate enough to model the peaky, heavy-tailed marginal distribution of DCT coefficients. It is pointed out in [8] that linear correlation detector works badly in non-Gaussian noise. These analyses reveal that (3) is not appropriate for blind watermarking in the DCT domain. In the following sections, we will deduce a new watermark detector — sign correlation detector (SCD) based on the non-Gaussian statistical model of DCT coefficients.

3 Statistical Modeling of the DCT Coefficients

As we will see in the following sections, the use of these models in designing the watermark detector will lead to considerable improvements in performance. Over the past two decades, there have been various studies on the distributions of the DCT coefficients for images. Early on, Pratt [9] conjectured that the ac coefficients follow a zero-mean Gaussian distribution. By using the Kolmogorov-Smirnov test, Reininger and Gibson verified that the ac coefficients had a Laplacian distribution [4] , defined as

$$f_L(x) = (1/\sqrt{2}\sigma)\cdot \exp(-\sqrt{2}\cdot|x|/\sigma) \tag{4}$$

Joshi and Fischer modeled the ac coefficients with a General Gaussian density function [5], defined as

$$f_{GGD}(x) = \frac{\gamma\alpha(\gamma)}{2\sigma\Gamma(1/\gamma)}\cdot \exp\{-[\alpha(\gamma)\,|\,x/\gamma\,|]^{\gamma}\} \tag{5}$$

where $\alpha(\gamma) = \sqrt{\dfrac{\Gamma(3/\gamma)}{\Gamma(1/\gamma)}}$, $\Gamma(\cdot)$ denotes the usual gamma function, γ is the shape parameter of the pdf. describing the exponential rate of decay, and σ is the standard deviation. The shape of the $f_{GGD}(x)$ for some shape parameters is depicted in figure 2.

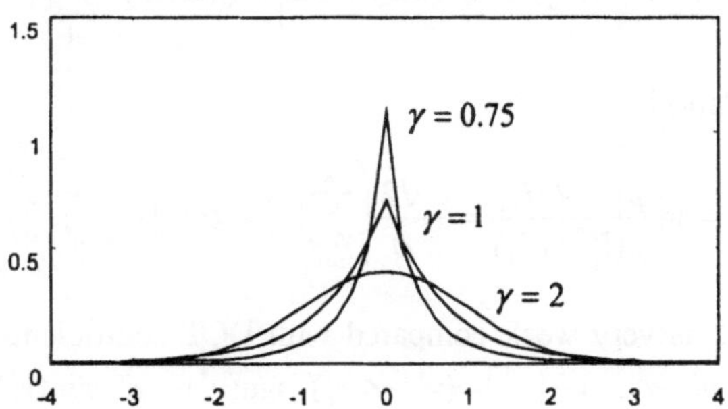

Fig. 1. Shape of the $f_{GGD}(x)$ for some shape parameters. The Gaussian and Laplacian distribution as special cases, using $\gamma = 1$ and $\gamma = 2$, respectively.

According to the maximum likelihood criterion, Barni [3] evaluated the shape parameter using 170 natural images, the experimental results demonstrate that ac coefficients can be effectively modeled by Laplacian density function. In [7], Lam and Goodman offered a comprehensive mathematical analysis of the DCT coefficient distributions of natural images, they demonstrated that Laplacian distribution of the coefficients can be derived by using a doubly stochastic model. In this paper, we deduce the blind watermark detector on the assumption that the ac coefficients of natural images follow Laplacian distribution.

4 Sign Correlation Detector

Detection of the watermark is accomplished via the hypothesis testing:

H_0: $v_i^* = v_i$, $i = 1,\cdots,n$ not contain the watermark

H_1: $v_i^* = v_i + a x_i$, $i = 1,\cdots,n$ contain the watermark

According to the assumption that v_i follows Laplacian distribution, the conditional probability densities can be written as

$$p(v_i^* / H_0) = (1/\sqrt{2}\sigma)\cdot \exp\left(-(\sqrt{2}/\sigma)\cdot |v_i^*|\right) \tag{6}$$

$$p(v_i^* / H_1) = (1/\sqrt{2}\sigma)\cdot \exp\left(-(\sqrt{2}/\sigma)\cdot |v_i^* - \alpha x_i|\right) \tag{7}$$

Since DCT is a quasi-optimal transform, we can assume coefficients $\{v_i^*\}$ to be statistically independent, then

$$p(V^* / H_0) = \prod_{i=1}^{n} p(v_i^* / H_0) = (1/\sqrt{2}\sigma)^n \cdot \exp\left(-(\sqrt{2}/\sigma)\cdot \sum_{i=1}^{n} |v_i^*|\right) \tag{8}$$

$$p(V^* / H_1) = \prod_{i=1}^{n} p(v_i^* / H_0) = (1/\sqrt{2}\sigma)^n \cdot \exp\left(-(\sqrt{2}/\sigma)\cdot \sum_{i=1}^{n} |v_i^* - \alpha x_i|\right) \tag{9}$$

the loglikelihood ratio is

$$\ln\Lambda(V^*) = \ln\frac{p(V^* / H_1)}{p(V^* / H_0)} = -\frac{\sqrt{2}}{\sigma}\left(\sum_{i=1}^{n} |v_i^* - \alpha x_i| - \sum_{i=1}^{n} |v_i^*|\right) \tag{10}$$

Since watermark is very weak compared with DCT coefficients, we can approximately assume $|v_i^* - \alpha x_i| - |v_i^*| = (v_i^* - \alpha x_i)\cdot \mathrm{sgn}(v_i^*) - v_i^* \cdot \mathrm{sgn}(v_i^*) = -\alpha x_i \cdot \mathrm{sgn}(v_i^*)$, where sgn(•) is sign function. Then (10) can be rewritten as

$$\ln\Lambda(V^*) = \frac{\sqrt{2}\alpha}{\sigma}\sum_{i=1}^{n} x_i \cdot \mathrm{sgn}(v_i^*) \tag{11}$$

Thus, we obtain the new detector $T = \sum_{i=1}^{n} x_i \cdot \mathrm{sgn}(v_i^*)$. If $T > T_g$, we shall decide that the image contains watermark X, where T_g is the decision threshold.

As one of non-parameter detection, the performance of sign correlation is characterized by asymptotic relative efficiency (ARE). Asymptotic relative efficiency of sign correlation detector is

$$ARE = \frac{1 - 4v_0 p(0) + 4\sigma^2 p^2(0)}{1 - (v_0 / \sigma)^2} \tag{12}$$

where σ is the standard deviation of {vi* }, v0 is the first-order absolute moment of DCT coefficients, $p(0)$ is the value of probability density function $p(x)$ when $x = 0$. Based on the Laplacian distribution model, we get $ARE = 2$. This result suggests that the efficiency of sign correlation detector is much greater than that of linear correlation detector on the assumption that DCT coefficients follow Laplacian distribution.

5 Experimental Results

In order to test the new detector, 1000 watermarks are randomly generated. Among them, only the 300th match the watermark embedded in the standard image "cameraman" shown in Fig.2 (Left). Selecting the first five DCT coefficients in zig-zag order in every blocks as the host sequence, we sign the original image with scaling parameter $\alpha = 0.02$. The watermarked copy shown in Fig.2 (Right). Fig.3 shows the response of the line correlation detector (Above) and sign correlation detector (Below). It can be seen that sign correlation detector outperforms linear correlation detector at least ten times.

Fig. 2. Original standard image "cameraman" (left) and its watermarked (right) version.

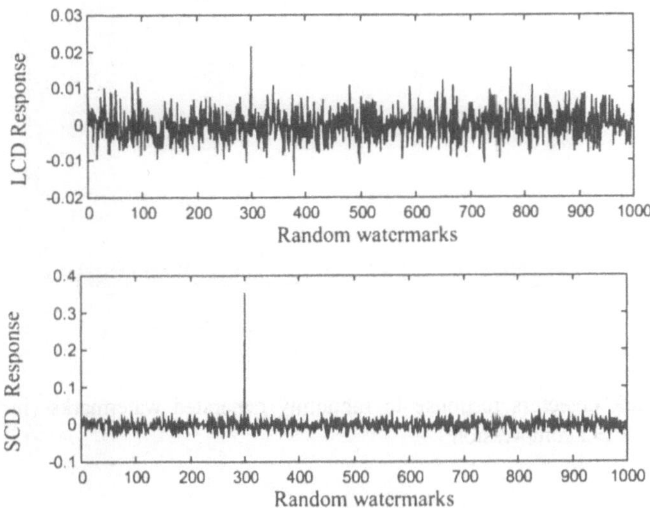

Fig. 3. Watermark detectors response to 1000 randomly generated watermarks (including the real watermark) without attacks

To test the robustness of the detector, we compress the watermarked image using JPEG standard with 75% quality, illustrated in Fig.4 (Left), the response of linear correlation detector (Above) and sign correlation detector (Below) are shown in Fig.5. In another experiment, we filter the watermarked image three times using 3×3 median filter, illustrated in Fig.4 (Right), the corresponding response of linear correlation detector (Above) and sign correlation detector (Below) are shown in Fig.6. From these results, we can see that linear correlation detector can not detect correctly after these attacks, while sign correlation detector still outputs satisfactorily.

Fig. 4. Watermarked image after JPEG compression (Left) and low pass filtering (Right)

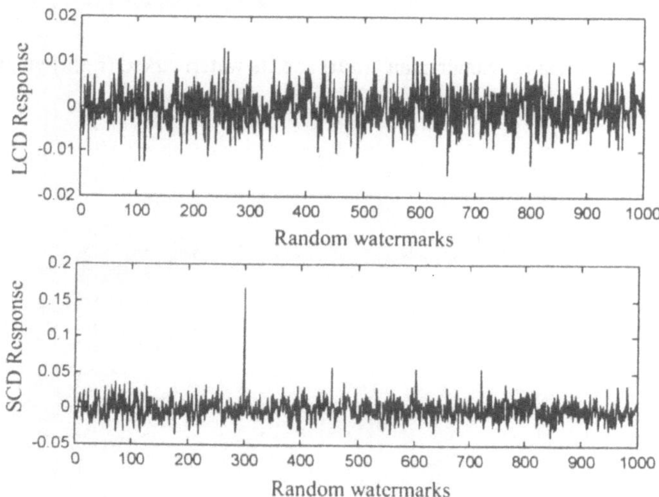

Fig. 5. Watermark detectors response to randomly generated watermarks (include the real watermark) after JPEG compression

6 Conclusion

In this paper, we begin our research by posing the difference on mathematical models between [1] and [2], then present a new blind watermark detector — sign correlation

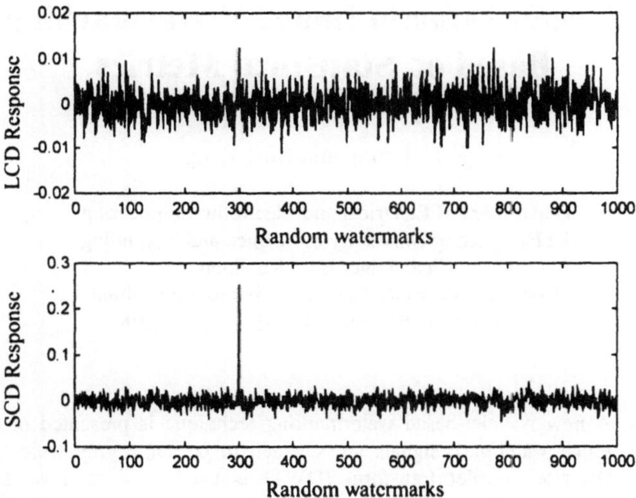

Fig. 6. Watermark detectors response to randomly generated watermarks (including the real watermark) after median filtering

detector based on statistical model of DCT coefficients. A series of experiments show that it is more robust than linear correlation detector used in [2]. Computing result of asymptotic relative efficiency also demonstrates the effectiveness of the detector theoretically.

References

1. Cox, I.J., Kilian, J., Leighton, T., Shamoon, T.: Secure Spread Spectrum Watermarking for Multimedia. IEEE Trans. on Image Processing. 6 (1997) 1673–1687
2. Barni, M., Bartolini, F., Cappellini, V., Piva, A.: A DCT-Domain System for Robust Image Watermarking. Signal Processing. 3 (1998) 357–372
3. M.Barni, F.Bartolini, V.Cappellini, A.Piva: Statistical Modeling of Full Frame DCT Coefficients". Proceedings of EUSIPCO'98 , Rhodes, Greece, 1998.
4. Reininger, R.C., Gibson, J.D.: Distributions of the two-dimensional DCT Coefficients for Images. IEEE Trans. on Communications, 6 (1983) 835–839
5. Joshi, R.J., Fischer, T.R.: Comparison of Generalized Gaussian and Laplacian Modeling in DCT Image Coding. IEEE Signal Processing Letters, 5(1995) 81–82
6. Craver, S., Memon, N., Yeo, B., Yeung, M.: Resolving Rightful Ownerships with Invisible Watermarking Techniques: Limitations, Attacks, and Implication, IEEE Journal on Selected Areas in Comm., 4 (1998) 573–586
7. Lam, E.Y., Goodman, J.W.: A Mathematical Analysis of the DCT Coefficients Distributions for Images, IEEE Trans. on Image Processing, 10 (2000) 1661–1666
8. Chen, B.H., Random Signal Processing, Publishing House of National Defense Industry, Beijing (1996)
9. Feng, Y.M., Shao, Y.M., Zhang, X.: Digital Image Compression and Coding, Chinese Publishing House of Railway, Beijing (1993)

Wavelet-Domain Image Watermarking Based on Statistical Metrics

K.H. Leung and Bing Zeng

Department of Electrical and Electronic Engineering
The Hong Kong University of Science and Technology
Clear Water Bay, Kowloon
Hong Kong Special Administrative Region, China
Email: {eehang, eezeng}@ust.hk

Abstract. A new wavelet-based watermarking technique is presented in this paper, in which watermark signals are selected to be some gray-scale logo image(s). Discrete wavelet transform (DWT) is used to decompose each original image first, whereas the selected watermark logo is decomposed into bit-planes at the same time. In the embedding process, the wavelet coefficients of an original image are divided into blocks. The energy and standard deviation of these blocks are computed and used to control the inserting process. Significant bits of the watermark logo are embedded first in order to have more protection. Original image is necessary in the recovering process, and the differences of the energies and standard deviations between individual blocks in the original image and the watermarked image are used to determine the embedded bit being 1 or 0. Experiment results show that our new method yields quite good visual quality in watermarked images, and is robust to typical signal processing attacks such as compression and filtering.

1. Introduction

Internet technology has been developed rapidly in the past decade. It is now a very common exercise that users connect into Internet to obtain multimedia information, particularly audio-visual contents. Meanwhile, unfortunately, it is also very easy to distribute and duplicate these digital contents illegally (i.e., without approval or authorization of original authors). Therefore, there is an urge need to provide copyright protection to these digital data. Digital watermarking is one of the copyright protection techniques. So far, a lot of different kinds of schemes have been proposed for watermarking, including spatial-domain embedding methods [1,6] and frequency-domain embedding methods [2-5]. For the spatial-domain watermarking, we embed a watermark signal by modifying the pixel values of the original image. Usually, error-correcting code such as Hamming code is used to protect data bits. In the frequency-domain watermarking, we insert a watermark signal in the frequency domain of the original image.

Most of frequency domain watermarking methods uses the discrete cosine transform (DCT) or a discrete wavelet transform (DWT). Some recent papers showed that embedding watermark in the DWT domain could have better results. In the meantime, it is widely believed that the frequency-domain watermarking is more robust to typical signal processing attacks, as most spatial-domain watermarking schemes are pretty easy to be destroyed by lossy compression or filtering.

The watermark recovering process is also divided into two categories: using the original image (destination-based) or not (source-based). In this paper, a destination-based watermarking technique is proposed, i.e., we will use the original image in the recovery process. In fact, many research papers showed that using the original image in the recovering could make the scheme more robust.

There are two main properties that we have to pay special attentions when designing a watermarking scheme: robustness and invisibility. Good watermarking schemes should be robust to any types of attacks (intentional or unintentional), and watermarking signal should be perceptually invisible in the watermarked image. However, these two properties often conflict each other. In most of currently existing watermarking methods, watermarking signals are usually chosen to be a Gaussian noise or 1-bit (binary) image. In our work, a gray-scale logo image is used to be the watermarking signal, as its commercial value is obviously much higher. In this scheme, watermarking information is embedded into an original image according to the block-wise energy and standard deviation of the wavelet coefficients of the original image.

In the next section, we will introduce the embedding process. Then, the recovering process will be described in Section 3. Some experiment results are presented in Section 4, and finally some conclusions are drawn in Section 5.

2. Embedding Process

In our watermarking method, the watermark signal is selected to be an 8-bits gray-scale logo image with size that is typically (much) smaller than that of the original image. Firstly, the original image undergoes through a 3-level wavelet decomposition using the 9/7-tap bi-orthogonal filters. Then, the resulting wavelet coefficients are divided into 2 by 2 blocks. In the meantime, the logo image is decomposed into bit planes by using the following equation:

$$B_i(m,n) = (floor(|\, X(m,n)/2^i \,|))Mod_2 \tag{1}$$

where $X(m,n)$ is the pixel values of watermark, B_i is the i-th bit plane, Mod_2 is module 2 operation and *floor* is the floor operation.

All resulting bit planes are re-ordered into a 1-D binary sequence: starting from the most significant bit plane and ending at the least significant bit plane.

Figure 2.1 shows the ordering of embedding the resulting 1-D binary sequence into the wavelet coefficients of an original image. It is seen from this figure that the most significant bits of the watermark signal are embedded into the highest scale of the original image first. This is because that the most significant bits of the watermark signal need to have more protection and we find that less error bits happen in the higher level(s). The wavelet coefficients in the lowest level are not used to embed the watermarking bits, as these coefficients are very sensitive to attacks. In our scheme,

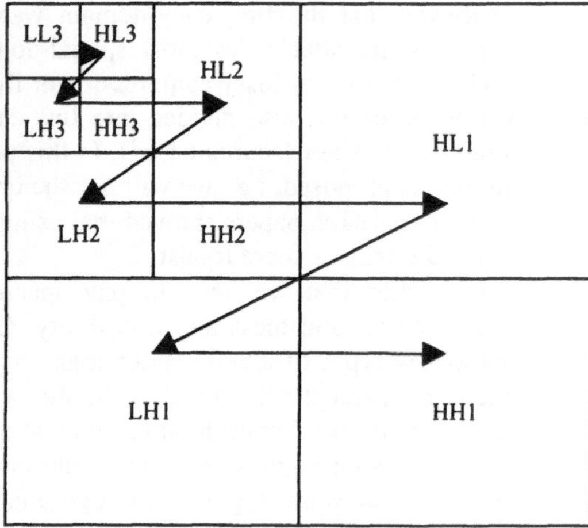

Fig. 2.1. Embedding process

we thus propose that only the wavelet coefficients at level 2 and level 3 are considered in the embedding process.

For level 2 and level 3, we further propose to use different embedding mechanisms to insert the watermark bits. For wavelet blocks in level 3, we add watermark bits by the following equations if the watermark bit is 1:

$$G_i(x,y) = F_i(x,y) + sign(F_i(x,y)) * \alpha \quad (2)$$

where $F_i(x,y)$ is the wavelet coefficients for block i, $G_i(x,y)$ is the watermarked wavelet coefficients, $sign$ is the sign function that obtained the sign of the wavelet coefficients, and α_s is the constant values that are embedded into the coefficients with sub-bands.

It is seen from Eq. (2) that we changed the energy value of one wavelet block only if the watermark bit is 1; we otherwise kept everything unchanged. In order to achieve a good balance between the quality of watermarked image and the robustness, we propose that different orientations at level 3 use different α_s 's. Their values would be determined through extensive simulations (as described in Section 4).

For wavelet coefficients at level 2, we do not use the energy to control the watermark embedding process, as the energy at this scale becomes significantly smaller. Using the energy to do the embedding at this level is thus unlikely to be robust. Instead, we use the standard deviation of each wavelet coefficient block to embed the watermark bits. That is, we try to increase the standard deviation of each wavelet coefficient block i by using the following equation if the corresponding watermark bit is 1:

```
While Std(G_i(x,y)) - Std(F_i(x,y)) < T_s
    Max(G_i(x,y)) <= Max(G_i(x,y)) + β_s * g
  if Std(G_i(x,y)) - Std(F_i(x,y)) < T_s
    Min(G_i(x,y)) <= Min(G_i(x,y)) - β_s * g
    end
  end
```

where Std is to compute the standard deviation of the block i, Max and Min are to obtain the maximum and minimum values of the block i, β_s and g are positive constant values, and T_s is a positive thresholds that can be defined by user. The value g can be calculated by this equation:

$$g = \sum_{U \in (x,y)} | F_i(x,y) | / 4 \tag{3}$$

where U is the pixel set inside block i. If data bit is 0, we do nothing to that block.

Obviously, this is an iterative operation. At each iteration, we just change the maximum value and the minimum value of block i in order to minimize the number of coefficients needed to modify. After the embedding process, we can then perform inverse discrete wavelet transform (IDWT) to the modified wavelet coefficients to obtain the watermarked image. The whole embedding process is shown in Fig. 2.2.

3. Recovery Process

Simply speaking, the recovering process just reverses the whole embedding process described in the last section. Firstly, we perform three-level wavelet decomposition on the testing image. We then divide the resulting wavelet coefficients into 2 by 2 blocks. Finally, we retrieve the watermark bits that are embedded inside the wavelet coefficient blocks. Notice that the retrieving is different in level 2 and level 3. For each level, we need first to compute:

For level 3,

$$R(i) = \sum_{U \in (x,y)} (| Y_i(x,y) |) - \sum_{U \in (x,y)} (| F_i(x,y) |) \tag{4}$$

For level 2,

$$R(i) = Std(Y_i(x,y)) - Std(F_i(x,y)) \tag{5}$$

Then, the embedded watermark bit can be extracted as follows:

```
If  R(i) > T_s',
        Watermark bit = 1;
Else,
        Watermark bit = 0;
```

where $R(i)$ is the recovered values and $T_s^{'}$ is the threshold for sub-bands, $Y_i(x,y)$ is the tested wavelet coefficient and $F_i(x,y)$ is the original wavelet coefficient inside the block i.

To recover the watermark image, we need to re-order all data bits into bit planes; while the logo image is finally generated by the following equation:

$$W = \sum_{n=0}^{7} B(n) * 2^n \tag{6}$$

where $B(n)$ means all the pixels in bit plan n and W is the recovered watermark.

4. Experiment Results

Three testing images, Lena, Baboon, and Airplane, each with size 512 by 512, are used in our simulations. We choose to use HKUST's logo to be the watermark image. The size of watermark image is 64 by 32 and its bit depth is 8.

We examined different values for α_s and β_s in Eq. (2). Then, we set them at values as follows: α_s is 30 for sub-band LL3 and 24 for all other sub-bands (at level 3); while β_s is 0.5 for all sub-bands in level 2. The threshold T_s for sub-bands HL2, LH2, and HH2 would be 11, 11, and 9, respectively. We also tested different thresholds $T_s^{'}$ in the recovery process. The threshold $T_s^{'}$ for sub-band LL3 and other sub-bands in level 3 is set to 34 and 32, respectively. The threshold $T_s^{'}$ is set to 4 for all sub-bands in level 2. The threshold $T_s^{'}$ is a little bit smaller than T_s so that small changes in recovered values would not affect the recovering bits.

Figures 3.1-3.3 show three watermarked images. From these figures, we can see that the quality of three watermarked images is good, as it is hard to distinguish any visual difference between the original image and the corresponding watermarked image. We also measured the peak signal-to-noise ratio (PSNR) of three watermarked images, with the results listed in Table 3.1. It is seen that the resulting PSNR is around 32 dB, which is fairly high.

We also examined the robustness of the proposed watermarking method against JPEG compression, lowpass filtering, median filtering, and SPIHT. The bit rate of JPEG compression is selected at 0.88 bit per pixel (bpp) and 1.08 bpp, respectively. The low-pass filter is chosen to be a 3-by-3 triangular filter. The size of the median filter is also 3-by-3. The bit rate of SPIHT is selected at 0.8 bpp and 1 bpp, respectively.

Simulation results of the robustness testing are shown in Figs. 3.4-3.10. Figure 3.4 shows the original watermark logo and the rest of figures show the testing results. From these figures, we see that our new method is quite robust to the various attacks examined here, especially for lossy compressions, as we are still able to see the logo image clearly even after the watermarked image being attacked. Table 3.2 summarizes numerically the robustness results of our watermarking method, in which we also used the PSNR for the measurement. The percentage of error bits shows that most of the recovered watermarks have less than 10% error bits. Both the PSNR numbers and error-bit percentages show that our method is rather robust.

5. Conclusions

A new wavelet-domain watermarking method was presented in this paper, where the watermark signal is chosen to be an 8-bit gray-scale logo image, instead of a commonly used Gaussian noise or binary sequence. We proposed to use different metrics (energy and standard deviation) for embedding watermark bits at different wavelet decomposition levels. We performed extensive simulations to determine the various parameters that are involved in the embedding process as well as the recovering process. We also preformed lots of simulations in order to examine the robustness of the proposed watermarking method. Overall, we found that the proposed method yields a quite good compromise between the robustness and the invisibility (of watermarking signal).

	Lena image	Baboon image	Airplane image
PSNR (dB)	32.45	31.87	32.37

Table 3.1. PSNR of watermarked image

	JPEG 0.88 bpp	JPEG 1.08 bpp	Lowpass filtering	Median filtering	SPIHT (0.8 bpp)	SPIHT (1 bpp)
PSNR (dB)	34	39.7	19.57	22.07	24	28
Percentage of error bits (%)	2.29	0.85	8.08	7.83	9.22	3.82

Table 3.2. Robustness results of watermarked Lena image.

6. References

1. P. M. Chen, "A robust digital watermarking based on a statistic approach," *IEEE Trans. on Information Technology: Coding and Computing,* pp.116-121, 2000.
2. I. Cox, J. Kilian, T. Leighton, and T. Shamoon, "Secure spread spectrum watermarking for multimedia," *NEC Research Inst. Tech. Report*, pp. 95-10, 1995.
3. M. George, J. Y. Chouinard, and N. Georganas, "Digital watermarking of images and video using direct sequence spread spectrum techniques," *IEEE Conf. on Electrical and Computing Eng.*, pp. 116-121, 1999.
4. D. Kundur, and D. Hatzinakos, "Digital watermarking using multiresolution wavelet decomposition," *IEEE Trans. on Acoustic, Speech and Signal processing,* vol. 5, pp. 2969-2972, 1998.
5. Z. H. Wei, P. Qin, and Y. Q. Fu, "Perceptual digital watermark of images using wavelet transform," *IEEE Trans. on Consumer Electronics*, vol. 44, no. 4, pp. 1267-1272, 1998.
6. M. S. Hwang, C. C. Chang, and K. F. Hwang, "A watermarking technique based on one-way hash function", *IEEE Trans. on Consumer Electronics*, vol. 45, no. 2, pp. 286-294, 1999.

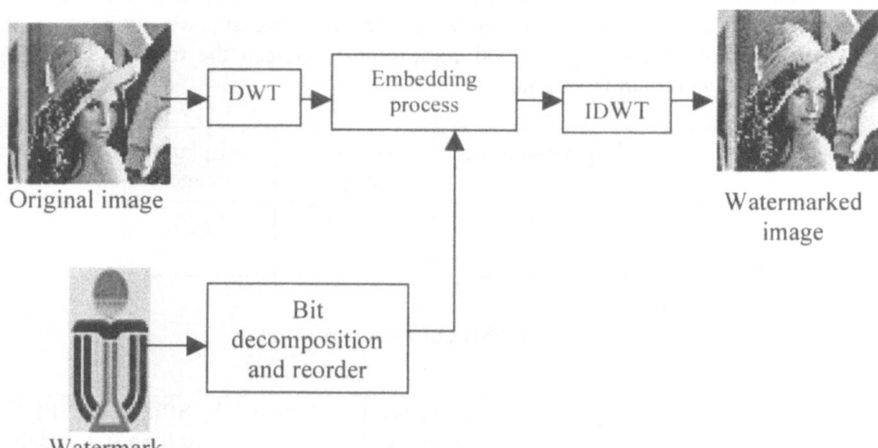

Fig. 2.2. Embedding process.

Fig. 3.1. Watermarked Lena image.

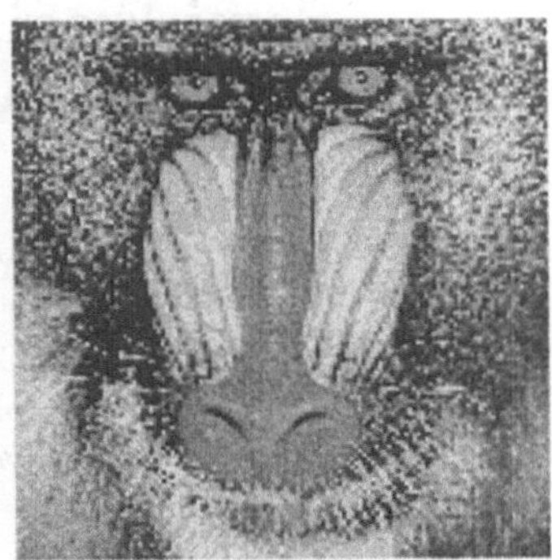

Fig. 3.2. Watermarked Baboon image.

Fig. 3.3. Watermarked Airplane image.

Fig.3.4. Watermark.

Fig.3.5. Recovered watermarked attack by JPEG compression with 0.88 bpp.

Fig.3.6. Recovered watermarked attack by JPEG compression with 1.08 bpp.

Fig.3.7. Recovered watermarked attack by median filtering.

Fig.3.8. Recovered watermarked attack by lowpass filtering.

Fig.3.9. Recovered watermarked attack by SPIHT with 0.8 bpp.

Fig. 3.10. Recovered watermarked attack by SPIHT with 1 bpp.

Semi Fragile Watermarking Based on Wavelet Transform

Yuichi Nakai

Akashi College of Technology
679-3 Uozumi-cho Nishioka, Akashi, Hyogo 674-8501, JAPAN
ynakai@akashi.ac.jp

Abstract. Watermarking schemes are traditionally classified into two classes, robust watermarking and fragile watermarking. Recently a third type of watermarking called semi fragile watermarking has been proposed. Using semi fragile watermarking a user can determine whether the image is tampered with or not for individual applications. For this purpose semi fragile watermarking should indicate the degree of tampering correctly. Most semi fragile watermarking schemes can indicate the position of tampering for localized alteration. Most of them, however, cannot indicate the degree correctly for lossy compression such as JPEG, since lossy compression changes almost all pixels' values. In this paper we will propose a new semi fragile watermarking technique based on the wavelet transform. The proposed scheme embeds multi-valued watermarks to wavelet coefficients for evaluating the degree of tampering for each pixel. It is proven that the proposed scheme can evaluate the degree of JPEG correctly for a wide range of SN ratios.

1 Introduction

Digital image watermarking techniques play an important role in protecting copyright of digital contents these days. Digital images are easily copied by third parties and they can obtain identical copies. This is the reason why watermarking techniques are needed. Watermarking used to protect copyright is called robust watermarking. Another type of watermarking scheme, used for image authentication, is called fragile watermarking. For example, fragile watermarking techniques are used for a digital photograph which is intended to use as evidence in court. In such cases it should be proven that the photograph has not undergone any kind of operation. Therefore fragile watermarking should ideally detect even a one bit change in a digital image. Many previously proposed fragile watermarking techniques can detect small changes in digital images with high probability. Moreover most fragile watermarking schemes can detect the tampered regions.

However, fragile watermarking techniques cannot accommodate lossy compression. Since image data is usually huge, image compression is applied innocently when it is stored or transmitted. In that situation we cannot distinguish between the compressed image and the original image; most fragile watermarking techniques claim that the entire image has been tampered. This is not desirable for most people who are interested in the "contents" of the image. So a third type of watermarking technique is proposed. This type of watermarking is called semi fragile watermarking. Ideally semi fragile watermarking should distinguish attacks which preserve image contents from attacks which alter image contents. Most semi fragile watermarking schemes decide whether there has been tampering or not using the degree of tampering. Some semi fragile watermarking techniques have been previously proposed [1] [2][3].

Most fragile and semi fragile watermarking schemes divide images into small sub-blocks to detect the tampered regions. Kundur and Hatzinakos [4] proposed a semi fragile watermarking scheme based on the wavelet transform. Unlike other fragile or semi fragile watermarking schemes their scheme does not need a block division process due to the localization ability of wavelet transform. In their scheme the user can evaluate the degree of tampering using an index called TAF (Tamper Assessment Factor). If the value of TAF is greater than a user-defined threshold, the user considers that the image has been tampered with. It can detect the tampered regions, like locally low pass filtered regions. However for lossy compression like JPEG, their scheme does not work well. Like other semi fragile watermarking schemes, they embed binary watermarks and TAF is defined as the number of different bits between original watermarks and extracted ones. TAF can only show whether a pixel has been tampered with or not (yes or no). Since lossy compression changes most of the original pixel values, their scheme shows high TAF values even in light grade lossy compression.

In this paper, we propose a new semi fragile watermarking technique which can evaluate the degree of tampering for each pixel. The proposed scheme embeds watermarks in wavelet coefficients and each watermark can take multiple values. It is proven that it can evaluate the degree of tampering for each pixel successfully. As a result the proposed scheme can evaluate the degree of lossy compression.

In Section 2 the process of embedding multi-valued watermarks is described. In Section 3 we present some experimental results to demonstrate the validity of the proposed scheme.

2 Proposed System

We use the wavelet transform for embedding watermarks because of its localization ability. Unlike Kundur-Hatzinakos's scheme or most previously proposed schemes, the proposed scheme embeds multi-valued watermarks. We call this type of watermarks q-ary watermarks where q is any integer greater than 2. When we use binary watermarks, we can only detect the positions or the number of positions which have been tampered with. However using q-ary watermarks we can evaluate not only the positions or the number of positions but also the degree of tampering for each pixel. As a result, for lossy compression like JPEG which operates on entire pixels, we can evaluate the degree of tampering more precisely than any previously proposed schemes. In this paper we use eight valued watermarks (8-ary watermarks).

The wavelet transform decomposes an image into several frequency subband levels. Most lossy compression first removes higher frequency components not to degrade image quality. If higher compression ratio is needed, it gradually removes lower frequency components. In this case image quality is degraded.

Therefore we have to embed watermarks reflecting this feature. We embed MSB of 8-ary watermarks in lower frequency components and embed LSB of watermarks in higher components to reflect the effect of lossy compression. Fig. 1 shows this concept applied to three level wavelet transform. We embed MSB to level 3 subband, second bit to level 2 and LSB to level 1 subband. In principle we can use any combination of frequency subbands. In the remainder of this paper, we assume that HH_1, HH_2 and HH_3 are used to embed watermarks. When another combination is selected, only that part of the coefficients selection need be changed.

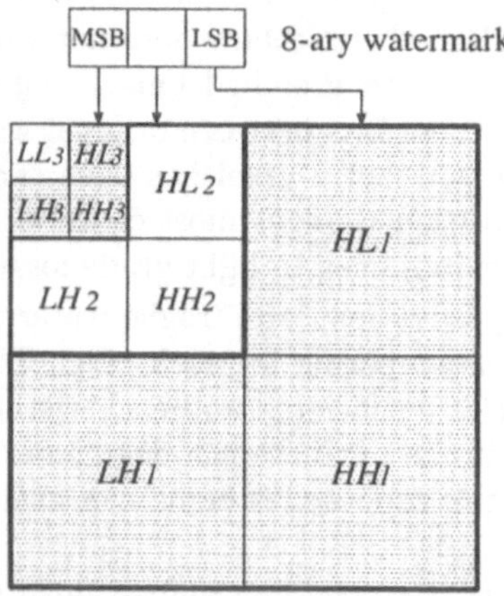

Fig. 1. Embedding 8-ary watermarks in several wavelet coefficient levels

2.1 Embedding Watermarks

We make some assumptions in describing the embedding algorithm.

1. The size of the original image is $N \times N$ pixels.
2. We use three level Haar wavelet transform.
3. To detect the tampered regions, we use all coefficients in HH_3 for embedding.

In this case the number of embedded watermarks is $(N/8)^2$. First we define embedding squares to determine which wavelet coefficients are selected for embedding. Embedding squares consist of 12 patterns shown in Fig. 2.

Since we need the position of embedding squares, let

$$sq_i(m,n) \quad (i = 1, 2, \ldots, 12, \quad m, n = 1, 2, \ldots, N)$$

be i-th embedding square at position (m, n). The position is specified by its upper left pixel and origin $(1, 1)$ is upper left of wavelet coefficients. Although we use only two components in each embedding square, we still use squares, since it is easy to specify their position. In Fig. 2 shaded squares are only dummy (don't care).

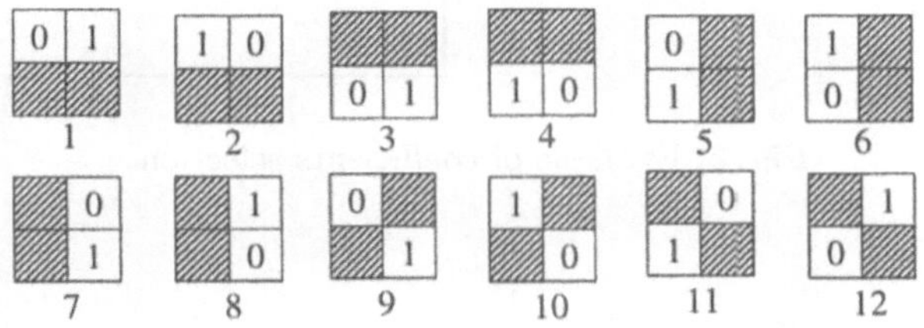

Fig. 2. Embedding Squares

The following algorithm is used for embedding 8-ary watermarks. The bit embedding method is the same as Kundur-Hatzinakos's scheme.

1. Generate random 8-ary watermarks $x_i \in \{0, 1, \ldots, 7\}$ $(i = 1, 2, \ldots, (N/8)^2)$.
2. For each x_i, select two embedding squares sq_{i_1}, sq_{i_2} randomly. The triples $(x_i, sq_{i_2}, sq_{i_1})$ are the key information for embedding.
3. For each coefficient in HH_3, do
   (a) Embed MSB of x_i to $HH_3(m_3, n_3)$ $(m_3, n_3 = N/8 + 1, \ldots, N/4)$.
   (b) For each $HH_3(m_3, n_3)$, locate $sq_{i_2}(2(m_3 - 1) + 1, 2(n_3 - 1) + 1)$. Find the component which has equal value to second bit of x_i in the sq_{i_2}. Let (m_2, n_2) be the position of the component where $m_2 = 2(m_3-1)+1+\alpha_2$, $n_2 = 2(n_3 - 1) + 1 + \beta_2$ $(\alpha_2, \beta_2 = 0, 1)$. Embed second bit of x_i to $HH_2(m_2, n_2)$.
   (c) Locate $sq_{i_1}(2(m_2 - 1) + 1, 2(n_2 - 1) + 1)$. Find the component which has equal value to LSB of x_i in the sq_{i_1}. Let (m_1, n_1) be the position of the component where $m_1 = 2(m_2-1)+1+\alpha_1$, $n_1 = 2(n_2-1)+1+\beta_1$ $(\alpha_1, \beta_1 = 0, 1)$. Embed LSB of x_i to $HH_1(m_1, n_1)$.

Fig. 3 shows an example of above algorithm. In this example we assume that the image size is 32×32 and $(2, 3, 11)$ is generated as the key information for coefficient $HH_3(7, 6)$. For $HH_3(7, 6)$ locate $sq_3(13, 11)$ and select coefficient $HH_2(14, 12)$ since second bit of "2" is equal to $sq_3(14, 12)$. Similarly we can select $HH_1(27, 24)$. Shaded coefficients are used for embedding.

2.2 Extracting Watermarks

Extract watermark bits using key information as follows.

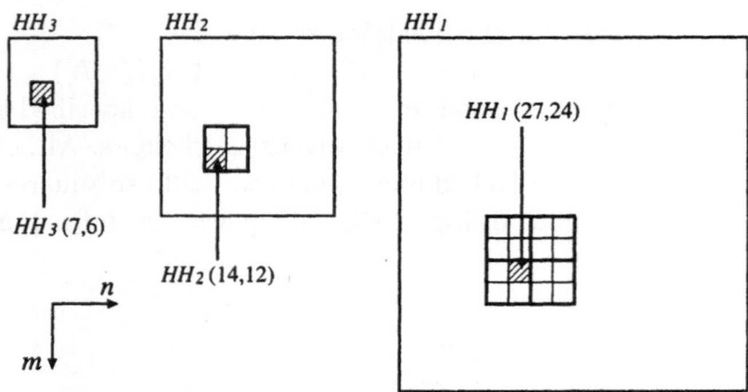

Fig. 3. Example of coefficients selection

1. Select wavelet coefficients using the same process as in embedding.
2. Extract watermark bits from these coefficients.
3. Reconstruct 8-ary watermark x'_i from extracted bits.

In the above process the extraction method is also the same as Kundur-Hatzinakos's scheme. We define a new evaluation index MTAF (Multi-valued TAF) which can evaluate the degree of tampering as follows:

$$\mathrm{MTAF} = \sum_{i=1}^{(N/8)^2} |x_i - x'_i| \ . \tag{1}$$

3 Experimental Results

In this section we show some experimental results of the proposed scheme on sample images. We use two sample images, "lenna" and "goldhill". Both are 512×512 pixels, 256 gray level image. In this case we can embed $(512/8)^2 = 4096$ 8-ary watermarks.

For "lenna" SN ratio of 8-ary watermarked image is 49.9(dB), while SN ratio of image applied Kundur-Hatzinakos's scheme is 46.4(dB). The reason for this result is that the number of watermarks which are embedded by the proposed scheme is less than Kundur-Hatzinakos's scheme.

We evaluate MTAF/TAF values for lossy compressed images. Because the number of watermarks which can be embedded is different for TAF and MTAF, we should normalize the results using maximum number of watermarks which can be embedded. These are given by the following equations.

$$\mathrm{TAF}_{max} = \frac{N^2}{6}\left(1 - \frac{1}{4^3}\right) , \tag{2}$$

$$\mathrm{MTAF}_{max} = \frac{N^2}{2^4}\left(1 - \frac{1}{2^4}\right) , \tag{3}$$

where N denotes the size of image. In our simulation $N = 512$.

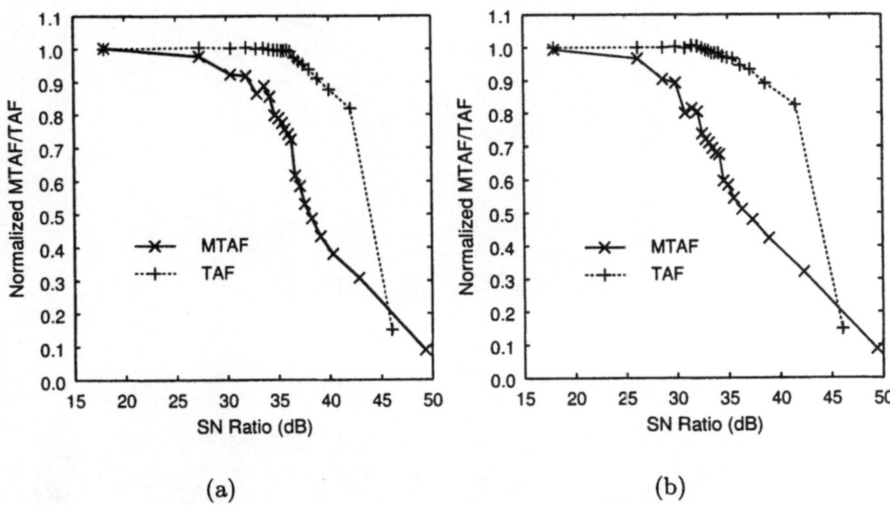

Fig. 4. Normalized MTAF/TAF value of JPEG image: (a)lenna. (b)goldhill.

Fig. 4 shows results for JPEG compressed image. In these figures the x axis is SN ratio of compressed image, and the y axis is normalized MTAF/TAF values. As can be seen from these results, 8-ary watermarking scheme MTAF values decrease slowly and linearly except in very low SN ratio. On the other hand in Kundur-Hatzinakos's scheme TAF values are saturated in the low SN ratio range and decrease above 40 (dB) very steeply.

Generally speaking no one can distinguish images with quality of over 40 (dB) and original images. Therefore using Kundur-Hatzinakos's TAF values we can only identify very good quality images as credible. In practical meaning the range which we are interested in is middle quality range. As MTAF decreases slowly and linearly, we can use it to assess the degree of JPEG compression properly for that range.

In Fig. 5 we show detection result for localized image tampering. The image is locally low pass filtered. Low pass filter is applied inside the black frame. Although the number of embedded watermarks is less than Kundur-Hatzinakos's scheme, the proposed scheme can detect the tampered region properly.

4 Conclusion

In this paper we have proposed a new semi fragile watermarking scheme using q-ary watermarks which can evaluate the degree of tampering for each pixel. We have shown that the degree of JPEG compression can be evaluated appropriately

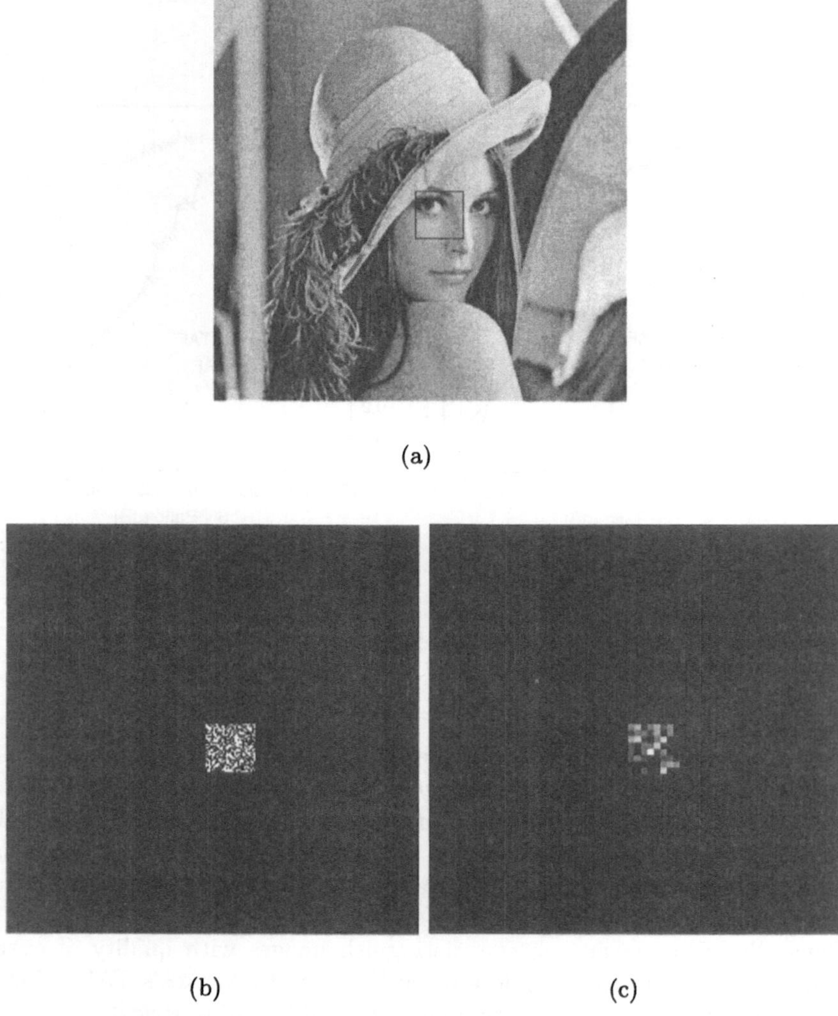

Fig. 5. Detection of localized tampering: (a)Filtered image. (b)Kundur-Hatzinakos's scheme. (c)Proposed scheme.

using the proposed scheme. We can easily specify the threshold which determines the allowable degree of tampering based on MTAF for a wide range of JPEG compression.

Although we fix the number of wavelet transform levels and combination of using subbands in this paper, investigation of other combinations remains for further work. Applying other wavelet kernels is also an interesting option.

Acknowledgement

I wish to thank Dr. Colin Boyd and Dr. Wageeh Boles of Queensland University of Technology for encouraging the work presented here. I also would like to thank Prof. Ed Dawson of Information Security Research Centre of QUT for giving me a chance to stay at ISRC.

References

1. S. Bhattacharjee, M. Kutter: Compression Tolerant Image Authentication. *Proc. of IEEE Int. Conf. On Image Processing*, Chicago, Illinois, Vol. 1, pp. 435-439, October 1998.
2. E. T. Lin, C. I. Podilchuk, and E. J. Delp: Detection of Image Alterations Using Semi-Fragile Watermarks. *Proc. of the SPIE International Conference on Security and Watermarking of Multimedia Contents II*, Vol. 3971, January 23 - 28, 2000, San Jose, CA.
3. R. B. Wolfgang and E. J. Delp: Fragile Watermarking Using the VW2D Watermark. *Proc. of the SPIE/IS&T International Conference on Security and Watermarking of Multimedia Contents*, Vol. 3657, January 25 - 27, 1999, San Jose, CA, pp. 204-213.
4. D. Kundur and D. Hatzinakos: Towards a Telltale Watermarking Technique for Tamper-Proofing. *Proc. IEEE Int. Conf. On Image Processing*, Chicago, Illinois,Vol. 2, pp. 409-13, October 1998.

A Novel Scheme for Securing Image Steganography

*Chin-Chen Chang, *Jyh-Chiang Yeh, and **Ju-Yuan Hsiao

*Department of Computer Science and Information Engineering
National Chung Cheng University
Chiayi, Taiwan 621, R.O.C.

**Department of Information Management
National Changhua University of Education
Changhua, Taiwan 500, R.O.C.

Abstract. In this paper, we shall propose a more secure scheme with a larger embedding capacity for image steganography based on vector quantization and discrete cosine transform. Instead of encrypting the whole secret image, our method only encrypts the important features extracted from a secret image and then embeds the encrypted features into a cover image for producing a stego-image. During the work of data encryption and embedment, we introduce the data encryption standard cryptosystem and a pseudo random mechanism to ensure the security of the secret image. Besides, the distortion between the cover image and the stego-image is also imperceptible by the human eye, even when the size of the secret image is as large as that of the cover image. According to the substantial experimental results we shall give later, we can demonstrate the applicability of our method.

1 Introduction

A conventional cryptosystem has long been one kind of technique used to ensure the security of important information, but the main purpose of most cryptosystems today is only to encrypt text data only. Because the size of an image is usually much larger than that of a piece of text data, general cryptosystems designed for text data processing are not suitable for encrypting image data. Moreover, for text data, the decrypted text must be exactly the same as the original one; however, for image data, it is not necessarily required that the quality of a decrypted image must be identical to that of the original one without any distortion. This is because the limited sensitivity of the human eye to detect tiny changes in the decrypted image. So, a decrypted image with little distortion is still acceptable for us.

To our knowledge, several previous works based on general cryptosystems have been offered to protect the security of a secret image during data transmission [2, 4, 6, 10, 13]. However, these methods have some drawbacks. Since most of them encrypt the secret image directly, it means that the encryption process is usually inefficient and time-consuming. In addition, we can obtain an encrypted image after the process of encryption, but its form is mostly rambling and meaningless. As a result, illegal users may very easily fix their eyes upon the encrypted result due to the fatal attraction the obviously strange form of the encrypted image, which of course means that the probability for the encrypted image to be attacked will race high.

In the later literature concerned, the appearance of image steganography has lessened the problems caused by traditional cryptosystems. Image steganography provides an additional kind of protection on a secret image. It introduces a cover image to camouflage a secret image. In an image steganographic system, a secret image is hidden in a cover image, and this joint image is called a stego-image. Since the distortion between the cover image and the stego-image is so small as not to be noticed by the human eye, the security of the secret image can be guaranteed through the use of camouflage. As we know, some image steganographic methods have been discussed in recent years [1, 3, 4, 7, 11]. These steganographic methods can be classified into two categories. In the first category, a secret image is hidden in the spatial domain of a cover image [1, 3, 4]. In the second category, a secret image is hidden in the frequency domain of a cover image [7, 11]. However, there still exists a fatal drawback for these methods. In order to achieve the effect of camouflage, the amount of the hidden data must be constricted, which means that the size of the secret image must be much smaller than that of the cover image. In other words, if we try to hide a secret image whose image size is equal to or even larger than that of the cover image, the distortion caused by data embedment between the cover image and the stego-image may very probably be perceptible to the human eye.

Hence, we conclude that cryptography can be considered as one kind of technique which attempts to conceal the content of the secret information itself, while the main purpose of steganography is to conceal the existence of the secret information. Thus, we can distill the distinct benefits from cryptography and steganography to overcome the drawbacks mentioned above. In this paper, we shall propose a new scheme for image steganography. In our method, we only need to encrypt the important features extracted from the secret image instead of encrypting the whole secret image. It is more efficient and timesaving. Besides, in order to camouflage the secret image, we also introduce a cover image and then hide the encrypted result in the cover image for producing a stego-image. Since we just hide in the cover image the important features extracted from the secret image, the size of the secret image can be as large as that of the cover image itself. During the process of data embedment, we also apply a pseudo random mechanism to enhance the security of the hidden data. Through the use of camouflage, most illegal users will consider the stego-image an ordinary image and let it go without smelling any abnormality about the stego-image. Even if any illegal user were to detect that there is something going on in the stego-image, it is still difficult to decrypt the secret image from the stego-image because the secret image inside has been encrypted via the data encryption standard (DES) [8] cryptosystem.

The rest of this paper is organized as follows. We shall discuss our new method in detail in Section 2. In addition, the security of our method will be analyzed in Section 3. In Section 4, we shall show our experimental results to prove the applicability of our method. Finally, the conclusions will be given in Section 5.

2 The Proposed Scheme

This section will propose a novel scheme for securing image steganography. This scheme can be divided into two modules: image embedding and image extracting. Assume that we want to embed a secret image S into a cover image C and produce a stego-image C'. In the image embedding module, we apply VQ [5, 9] to compress the secret image S and then generate a set of indices for S after the process of image compression. Then, we encrypt the set of indices by DES and apply DCT [12] on the cover image C. Finally, we embed the set of encrypted indices into the DCT coefficients of the cover image C for obtaining a stego-image C'. On the other hand, in the image extracting module, at first, we extract the set of encrypted indices from the DCT coefficients of the stego-image C'. Next, we decrypt the set of encrypted indices and then apply VQ on the set of decrypted indices to decompress the secret image S. In the following, we are going to state the details of these two modules.

2.1 Image Embedding Module

In this section, let us see how we can embed a secret image S into a cover image C to obtain a stego-image C'. Note that the image embedding module is composed of two phases: index encrypting and index hiding. In the index encrypting phase, at first, we divide the secret image S with the image size being $M_1 \times M_2$ pixels into blocks of 4 × 4 pixels each. Here we take a pixel block for an image vector. Then, we compress these image vectors following the lead of a VQ codebook with 256 codewords and then generate the corresponding index for each image vector. So, there is a set of $\frac{M_1 \times M_2}{4 \times 4}$ indices for the secret image S. In addition, we also divide the cover image C, whose image size is the same as that of the secret image S, into blocks of 4 × 4 pixels each. Next, we apply DCT on these pixel blocks and then generate the corresponding DCT block for each pixel block. Hence, there is a set of $\frac{M_1 \times M_2}{4 \times 4}$ DCT blocks for the cover image C, too. Finally, we can encrypt the set of indices via DES using a private key K as its secret key.

In the index hiding phase, at first, we randomly select a DCT block from the cover image C and then embed an encrypted index of the secret image S into the DCT block. Here we use a key K_s as the seed of a pseudo random number generator to perform the DCT block selection. We must do this block selection $\frac{M_1 \times M_2}{4 \times 4}$ times in order to embed a set of $\frac{M_1 \times M_2}{4 \times 4}$ encrypted indices into a set of $\frac{M_1 \times M_2}{4 \times 4}$ DCT blocks. Before the process of index hiding, we need to encode an encrypted index into binary form with eight bits. Next, we select eight DCT coefficients from the middle frequency area of a DCT block. After the action of coefficient selection, we repeatedly embed one bit of an encrypted index into one coefficient of a DCT block and another bit into another coefficient until all are done. According to the definition of JPEG DCT, the value of a DCT coefficient (AC coefficient) can range from –1023 to 1023. Hence, we can encode a DCT coefficient into binary form with eleven bits. The binary form of a selected coefficient D can be denoted as $d_{10}d_9,\ldots,d_0$, where the value of d_i can be either zero or one, and $i = 0,1,\ldots,10$. If the value of a selected coefficient D is positive, the value of its MSB d_{10} must be zero. On the other hand, if the value of the selected coefficient D is negative, the value of its MSB d_{10} must be one. Thus, we can take the MSB d_{10} for the sign bit, which cannot be used for bit embedding.

In addition, there is something worthy of paying attention here. Since there is a difference about ± 1 for a DCT coefficient between DCT and inverse DCT (IDCT), we need to modify the two LSBs d_1 and d_0 into 1 and 0 to prevent the distortion caused by DCT and IDCT. Thus, the two LSBs d_1 and d_0 are not suitable for bit embedding, either. Due to the reason we mentioned above, we decide to use the other eight bits $d_9 d_8, \ldots, d_2$ as the positions of a DCT coefficient for bit embedding.

Besides, we shall use another key K_p as the seed of the pseudo random number generator to select one position from the eight bits $d_9 d_8, \ldots, d_2$, in which we embed one bit of an encrypted index. After the action of bit embedding, we must adjust the value of the DCT coefficient toward its original value without affecting the embedded bit. After applying IDCT on the modified cover image C, we can obtain a stego-image C'. Finally, because the three keys K, K_s, and K_p are the most important issue to extract the secret image S from the stego-image C', we must send them to a legal receiver through a secure channel.

2.2 Image Extracting Module

In this section, we shall explain in detail how to extract the secret image S from the stego-image C' via the three keys K, K_s, and K_p. Note that the image extracting module contains two phases: index extracting and index decrypting. In the index extracting phase, at first, we divide the stego-image C' into blocks of 4 × 4 pixels each. We apply DCT on each pixel block to obtain the corresponding DCT blocks. Then, we use the two keys K_s and K_p as the seeds of the pseudo random number generator to extract the encrypted indices of the secret image S from the DCT coefficients of the stego-image C'.

In the index decrypting phase, we use the secret key K as the key of DES to decrypt the set of encrypted indices. After we obtain the set of decrypted indices, we can decompress the secret image S by applying VQ on the set of decrypted indices.

3 Security Analysis

The security of our method comes from both the camouflage of steganography and the encryption of the DES cryptosystem. In addition, a pseudo random mechanism that has been applied to the process of data embedment also helps with protecting our method from being broken. Assume that we have embedded a secret image into a cover image and produced a stego-image. In our method, illegal users won't pay special attention to the stego-image, since they don't smell anything fishy about it. Even if they should detect that the stego-image is the camouflage of a secret image, it would still be difficult for them to get the encrypted secret. This is because we have employed the DES cryptosystem and a pseudo random mechanism to enhance the security of the secret image. No illegal users can decrypt the secret image from the stego-image without the three keys K, K_s, and K_p in hand concurrently. If they tried to guess these keys by using brute force attack, they would have to spend much longer time than they would be willing to. Thus, the security of our method can be guaranteed.

4 Experimental Results

In our experiments, an 512 × 512 gray-level image "Airplane" is used as the secret image which is shown in Figure 1(a). In Figure 1(b), we use another gray-level images "Lenna" as the cover images. We embed the secret image "Airplane" into the cover images "Lenna" and then obtain its corresponding stego-images in Figure 2(b). The *PSNR* values of the stego-images "Lenna" is 33.80 *dB*. Note that the distortion between the cover image and the stego-image is really small; therefore, it is difficult for us to detect the abnormality with our eyes. This is the effect of camouflage in display. In Figure 2(a), we show the extracted secret image "Airplane" from the stego-images "Lenna" with a *PSNR* value of 30.12 *dB*. Due to the reason that we have compressed the original secret image before hiding it in the stego-image, the *PSNR* value of the extracted secret image is not as high as that of the original one. However, it is still a clear picture for us.

Additionally, we also conduct an experiment in comparison with the method proposed by Wu and Tsai [14]. Their method is based on the similarity among the gray values of consecutive image pixels and the variation insensitivity of the human visual system from smooth to contrastive. Following their method, we can produce a stego-image by replacing the gray values of a differencing result obtained from a cover image with those of a differencing result obtained from a secret image. Their method keeps the secret image with no loss and preserves the stego-image with low distortion.

In Table 1, we embed three secret images "Peppers", "Airplane" and "Lenna" into three different cover images "Peppers", "Airplane" and "Lenna", respectively. We show the *PSNR* values of the corresponding stego-images. We also show the *PSNR* values of the three extracted secret images "Peppers", "Airplane" and "Lenna" in Table 2. Please notice that the image size of these secret images and stego-images used here are all 512 × 512 pixels. Since Wu and Tsai's method cannot tolerate a secret image with size more than half that of a cover image to be embedded in the cover image, the *PSNR* values of the stego-images based on their method are not available. After we embed the three secret images "Peppers", "Airplane" and "Lenna", 256 × 256 pixels each, into three different cover images "Peppers", "Airplane" and "Lenna", also 512 × 512 pixels each respectively, we show the *PSNR* values of the corresponding stego-images in Table 3. As you can see, our method is better than Wu and Tsai's method according to the performance comparison. Although Wu and Tsai's method allows an outstanding secret image size of about half that of the cover image, our method outperforms theirs by allowing a secret image as big as the cover image.

5 Conclusions

In this paper, we present a more secure and efficient scheme for image steganography. In particular, our scheme allows the size of the hidden secret image to be as big as that of the cover image. The embedding capacity our method offers is much larger than those of traditional image steganographic methods. On the other hand, instead of encrypting the entire secret image directly, our method only encrypts the important image features extracted from the secret image. We hide the encrypted features in a cover image and generate a stego-image. According to the experimental results, we can show that the distortion between the cover image and the stego-image is so little that the human eye cannot detect the difference. Hence, the purpose of camouflage is achieved. In addition, we apply the DES cryptosystem and a pseudo random mechanism during the process of data encryption and embedment, which makes our method more secure than traditional image steganographic methods.

(a) (b)

Figure 1. (a) The secret image "Airplane" (b) The cover image "Lenna"

(a) (b)

Figure 2. (a) The extracted secret image "Airplane" (*PSNR*=30.12*dB*)

(b) The stego-image "Lenna" (*PSNR*=33.80*dB*)

Table 1. The *PSNR* values of the stego-images of 512×512 pixels each with the secret images being also 512×512 pixels each

Secret image	Stego-image *PSNR (dB)*					
	Peppers		Airplane		Lenna	
	Our method	Wu's method	Our method	Wu's method	Our method	Wu's method
Peppers	30.07	N/A	32.56	N/A	33.67	N/A
Airplane	30.50	N/A	32.79	N/A	33.80	N/A
Lenna	29.91	N/A	32.69	N/A	33.58	N/A

Table 2. The *PSNR* values of the extracted secret images sized 512×512 pixels

Secret image	Peppers	Airplane	Lenna
PSNR (dB)	31.21	30.12	31.57

Table 3. The *PSNR* values of the stego-images of 512×512 pixels each with the secret images being also 256×256 pixels each

Secret image	Stego-image *PSNR (dB)*					
	Peppers		Airplane		Lenna	
	Our method	Wu's method	Our method	Wu's method	Our method	Wu's method
Peppers	40.02	39.80	42.33	40.05	42.46	39.44
Airplane	40.03	38.81	42.35	40.19	42.52	38.99
Lenna	38.91	39.09	42.35	39.76	42.46	39.17

References

1. R. Anderson, and F. Petitcolas, "On the limits of steganography," *IEEE Journal on Selected Areas in Communications*, Vol. 16, No. 4, 1998, pp. 471-478.
2. Bourbakis, and C. Alexopoulos, "Picture data encryption using scan patterns," *Pattern Recognit.*, Vol. 25, 1992, pp. 567-581.
3. Bender, D. Gruhl, N. Morimoto, and A. Lu, "Techniques for data hiding," *IBM System Journal*, Vol. 35, 1996, pp. 313-336.
4. K. Chang, and J. L. Liou, "An image encryption scheme based on quadtree compression scheme," *Proc. Int. Computer Symp.*, Vol. 1, 1994, pp. 230-237.
5. Cziho, B. Solaiman, I. Lovanyi, G. Cazuguel, and C. Roux, "An optimization of finite-state vector quantization for image compression," *Signal Processing: Image Communication*, Vol. 15, 2000, pp. 545-558.

6. T. S. Chen, C. C. Chang, and M. S. Hwang, "A virtual image cryptosystem based upon vector quantization," *IEEE Transactions on Image Processing*, Vol. 7, No. 10, October 1998, pp. 1485-1488.
7. J. J. Chae, and B. S. Manjunath, "A robust embedded data from wavelet coefficients," *Proc. SPIE-Int. Soc. Opt. Eng.*, Vol. 3312, 1998, pp. 308-317.
8. D. E. R. Denning, *Cryptography and Data Security*, Reading, MA: Addison-Wesley, 1983.
9. A. Gersho, and R. M. Gray, *Vector Quantization and Signal Compression*, Kluwer Academic Publishers, Boston, 1992.
10. C. J. Kuo, "Novel image encryption technique and its application in progressive transmission," *J. Electron. Imag.*, Vol. 2, 1993, pp. 345-351.
11. L. M. Marvel, C. G. Boncelet, Jr., and C. T. Retter, "Spread spectrum image steganography," *IEEE Transactions on Image Processing*, Vol. 8, No. 8, August 1999, pp. 1075-1083.
12. K. R. Rao, and P. Yip, *Discrete Cosine Transform – Algorithms, Advantages, Applications*, Academic Press, 1990.
13. C. Schwartz, "A new graphical method for encryption of computer data," *Cryptologia*, Vol. 15, 1991, pp. 43-46.
14. D. C. Wu, and W. H. Tsai, "Spatial-domain image hiding using image differencing," *IEE Proc.-Vis. Image Signal Process.*, Vol. 147, No. 1, February 2000, pp. 29-37.

A Synchronous Fragile Watermarking Scheme for Erroneous Q-DCT Coefficients Detection*

Minghua Chen and *Yun He*

State Key Lab on Microwave and Digital Communications
Department of Electronic Engineering, Tsinghua University, Beijing, 100084, China
{chen, hey}@video.mdc.tsinghua.edu.cn

Abstract

In video communications over error prone channels, error concealment techniques are widely applied in video decoder for good subjective image output. However, a damaged MB could be concealed only after it is detected as erroneous. Because of the poor performance of the traditional syntax based error detection schemes, the error concealments thereafter show bad results. Our previous work explored the potential of transmission error detection by *fragile* watermarking. In this paper, a synchronous fragile watermark based transmission error detection scheme for hybrid decoder is proposed. By watermarking, we enforce a synchronization signal like correlation on Q-DCT coefficients. Thus the decoder *could* use this pre-forced information for detecting errors. The simulation results show that the erroneous Q-DCT coefficients detection capabilities are largely improved compared to syntax-based scheme.

Keywords: watermarking, fragile watermark, error detection, error resilience, video communication

1. Introduction

In video communication system, due to Motion Compensated (MC) Inter Frame Prediction and Vary Length Coding (VLC) techniques employed by many highly efficient video coding standards, such as H.26x [1] and MPEG-x[2], the compressed video streams are highly sensitive to channel errors. While in many cases, the real channels do introduce vast errors; the correct video transmission will crash if no protection against errors is applied.

There are many error resilience techniques designed for resolving that challenging problem. Other than error correction and interleaving techniques, error detection and error concealment techniques are usually employed in video decoders. When a Macro-block (MB) is damaged due to channel degradations, if the video decoder detects this erroneous MB, the content- dependent concealment actions, such as resynchronization or temporal interpolation, so as to make the decoded video look more comfortable. Clearly, the efficiency and results of the error concealment rely on the error detection performance. Typically, error concealment techniques are applied at MB level. So, in this paper, we only concern the error detection at MB level.

In a typical system that employed DCT transform, MC and VLC, following syntax checks are often applied in video decoders to detect bit stream error.

- Motion vectors is out of range
- DCT coefficients is out of range
- Invalid VLC table entry is found
- The number of DCT coefficients in an 8x8 block exceeds 64
- Quantizer scale factor is out or range

Due to the bits to represent Q-DCT coefficients is normally significantly more than the bits to represent the header information and motion vector (MV) information, the Q-DCT coefficients are much easier to be damaged by channel bit errors. So, the error detection scheme should have the ability to well detect erroneous Q-DCT coefficients. Error detection by these syntax checks, however, has inevitable disadvantages on detecting erroneous Q-DCT coefficients, namely low error detection rate (E.D.R.) and low error correctly located rate (E.C.L.R.). Those disadvantages are showed in [3]. Besides the discussions in [3], it is also difficult for syntax checks to detect shift phenomenon and thus difficult to conceal it. A shift phenomenon is shown below.

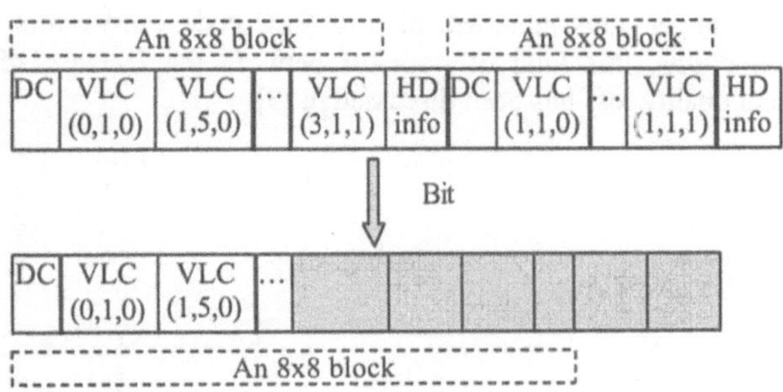

Figure 1. A *Shift phenomenon: An 8x8 block is "removed"*

When a bit error happens in a VLC code word, it may cause the code word changes to a new one with the same length, run and level value but different last value. In such case, an 8x8 block is "inserted" into the bit stream if the last value changes from zero to one; an 8x8 block is "removed" if the last value changes from one to zero. This phenomenon is called shift. In the particular case that the bit error only results in combining two 8x8 blocks and keeping data in other 8x8 blocks untainted, the bit stream may be correct in syntax but will cause MB shift all over a slice. Consider the MC used in video decoder, unacceptable reconstructed images would be produced.

In summary, to detect transmission error only by syntax checks is not good enough. Recent contributions [3]-[6] explore the potential of detecting transmission error by watermarking. The idea in [5] and [6] is to employ robust watermarking into error detection. In this paper, followed the basic idea in [3] that introduce fragile watermarking into error detection, we propose a synchronous signal like fragile watermarking scheme for detecting erroneous quantized DCT (Q-DCT) coefficients, namely FZW. Analysis on the PSNR loss due to watermarking is also provided in section 2. Section 3 gives out simulation results, followed by a summary in section 4.

2. Force Zero Watermarking (FZW) Scheme

2.1 Description of the technique

The scheme proposed here follows the work in[4], and it fragile watermarking the 8x8 blocks to improve error detection capabilities of video decoder. The watermarking makes a zero coefficients sequence in Q-DCT coefficients before they are passed to VLC, this zero sequence can serve as a synchronous signal when decoding the streams. Since error in VLC code words would cause the *run/last* value to change, the synchronous signal may be damaged if a non-zero coefficient exists in the sequence. Hence, by checking this signal, the video decoder could detect the error happened at 8x8 block level. The description of the scheme is:

- ***On encoder side***, a special watermark is forced into Q-DCT coefficients of any coded 8x8 blocks, before these coefficients are passed to VLC. To avoid drift, the watermarking procedure is included in MC loop.

- ***On decoder side,*** after an 8x8 block is decoded, the synchronous signal (zero sequence) is checked on Q-DCT coefficients. An error is reported if the signal is damaged; otherwise, current 8x8 block is assumed to be correct. A MB is assumed to be a correct one only if all 8x8 blocks inside are detected as correct.

For the 64 Q-DCT coefficients in an 8x8 block, the watermarking procedure force zero on the coefficients from AC_{pos} to AC_{64} (Fig. 2). Clearly, the parameter *pos* control the visual quality loss due to watermarking, and it could vary due to intra-/inter- block or Y/C block. The *pos* also determine the fragility of the watermark. The decrease of the *pos* makes the zero coefficients sequence longer, thus more sensitive to VLC code word errors. It is a trade-off when select parameter *pos*, this kind of trade-off between the increase of error detection capabilities and visual quality loss has been discussed in [3].

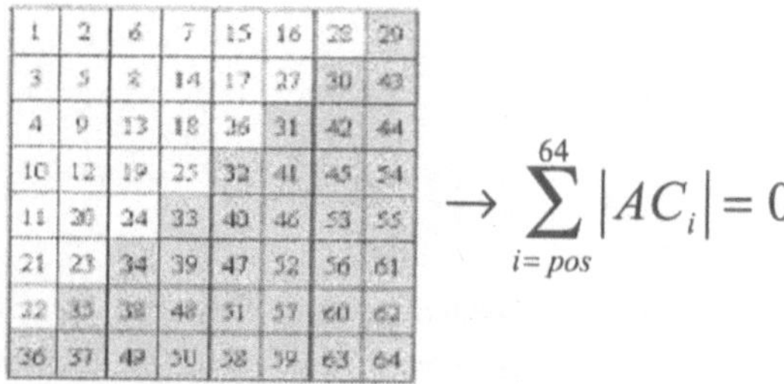

Figure 2. FZW *Watermarking illustration*

In the case that most Q-DCT coefficients in an 8x8 block are zeroes, the watermarking procedure may affect no coefficient. This 8x8 block is then thought as "originally watermarked" since it fits the forced correlation the watermarking procedure want to cast on it. So not surprising, the error detection procedure works well under such situation.

Due to cutting off some coefficients, the quality of the frame under consideration is decreased a little after watermark embedding, thus the prediction for the next frame may be affected negatively, increasing the required bit rate under a given quality level. Yet, the simulation results show that the select watermark would not increase the coded bit rate to an unacceptable level, which is important in video transmission over band-limit channels. For the proposed scheme, it is a trade-off between the increase in probability of transmission error detection and the decrease of visual quality, similar to the one noted in [3].

2.2 Analysis on *PSNR* loss after watermarking

In this section, we consider the visual quality loss on the images due to watermarking as a function of system parameters. We firstly explore the relationship between the expectation of Mean Square Error of DCT coefficients, namely $E(MSE_{DCT})$ and watermarking parameters *pos* and quantization parameter QP. Then with the acknowledgement that DCT is a linear orthogonal transformation, we know the MSE_{DCT} is exactly the MSE on spatial domain. Hence, we can calculate the *PSNR* between quantized but unwatermarked images and quantized and watermarked images using $E(MSE_{DCT})$.

In [7], it is shown that the non-dc DCT coefficients in intra- blocks could follow Laplacian distribution. From section 2.1, we know after watermarking, all non-zero coefficients after zig-zag index *pos* are forced to zero. If we only concern the quantization function using in intra-block in TMN8[8], the expectation of square error between quantized coefficient AC_i and quantized- watermarked coefficient AC_i^w ($i \geq pos$) is:

$$E\left(\left|AC_i - AC_i^*\right|^2\right) = E\left(AC_i^2\right)$$

$$= 2\sum_{k=0}^{\infty}\int_{2kQP}^{2(k+1)QP}(k)^2\frac{\lambda_i}{2}e^{-\lambda_i x}dx \quad (1)$$

$$= e^{-2QP\lambda_i} + \frac{3e^{-4QP\lambda_i}}{1-e^{-2QP\lambda_i}} + \frac{2e^{-6QP\lambda_i}}{\left(1-e^{-2QP\lambda_i}\right)^2}$$

where $\lambda_i \quad i = pos, pos+1, \ldots 64$ are the parameters of Laplacian distributions of different index unquantized AC coefficients. Hence, the $E(MSE_{DCT})$ could be calculated as (2):

$$E(MSE_{DCT}) = \frac{1}{64}\times$$

$$\sum_{i=pos}^{64}\left[E\left(4QP^2AC_i^2\right) + 4QP^2E\left(\left|AC_i\right|\right) + p\{AC_i \neq 0\}QP^2\right] \quad (2)$$

$$= \frac{1}{8}QP^2\sum_{i=pos}^{64}\left[e^{-2QP\lambda_i} + \frac{2e^{-4QP\lambda_i}}{1-e^{-2QP\lambda_i}} + \frac{e^{-6QP\lambda_i}}{\left(1-e^{-2QP\lambda_i}\right)^2}\right] + \frac{1}{64}QP^2e^{-2QP\lambda_i}$$

Then as mentioned above, the MSE_{DCT} is equal to MSE on spatial domain; hence, the PSNR between quantized- unwatermarked images and quantized-watermarked images due to watermarking can be calculated as below:

$$PSNR = 10\log_{10}\left[\frac{255^2}{E(MSE_{DCT})}\right] \quad (3)$$

To verify the correctness of formula (3), the relationship between *PSNR* and the watermark parameter *pos*, a result is given by using TMN8 codec to encode Cost Guard CIF sequence. In experiment, the *PSNR* between quantized-unwatermarked and quantized-watermarked intra frames are calculated, with watermarking parameter *pos* varies from 24 to 44. Then, with the parameters $\lambda_i \quad i = pos, pos+1, \ldots 64$ by statistics, a theoretic curve is provided using formulas (2) and (3). From Fig. 3, it is shown that these curves are quite match. While for the sequence that its DCT coefficients are not strictly follow the Laplacian model, it is possible for the curves do not match well. In those case, better result could be retrieved if more sophisticated model is applied, Generalize Gaussian Distribution for example, however the method here to calculate the visual quality loss is making sense. With (2) and (3), if all the parameters in the formulas are known, we can evaluate the visual quality loss performance of

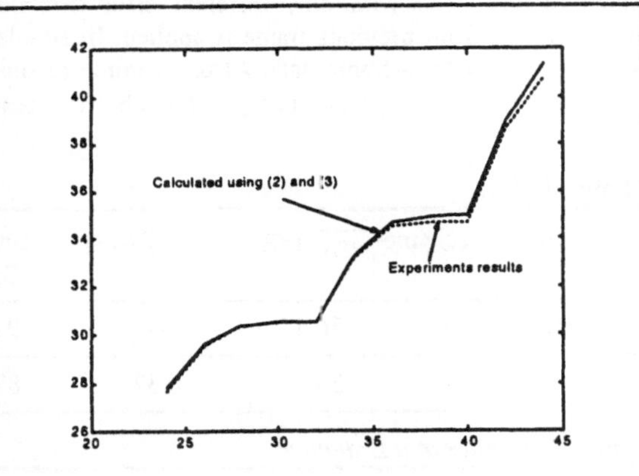

Figure 3. *Visual quality loss due to watermarking (QP=10), horizontal: pos, vertical: PSNR*

the watermarking. At the same time, if the *PSNR* is pre-set, we can get the minimum value that the watermarking parameter *pos* could be set under the constrain, which is exciting when designing the watermark.

3. Simulation Results

In simulation, we choose modified TMN8 as video codec. In encoder, watermarking module is included follow the structure shown in [3]. In decoder, the corresponding watermark-detecting module and syntax based error detection module are implemented. After video sequence is encoded, the coded stream is sent to a Binary Symmetric Channel (BSC) with a random bit rate $5e^{-4}$ and then arrived at the decoder. BSC is applied here because we assume under protection of error correction techniques and interleaving, a real channel can be equivalent to a BSC channel. We assume the remaining random bit error rate for steams is 10^{-3}~10^{-4}. We select QP as 10 for both intra-/inter- blocks; coding frame rate is 30 frames/s. For watermarking, the parameter *pos* is select as 44 for intra-Y-blocks, 29 for inter-Y-blocks, 29 for intra-C- blocks or 16 for inter-C-blocks. To focus on erroneous Q-DCT coefficients detection ability, we only cast bit error on those bits that represent Q-DCT coefficients, and leave motion vectors and header information untainted. The frames are coded in IPPPP... format.

In order to test the robustness of the proposed scheme, three standard video test sequences with different complexity are used in simulation. These sequences are 240 frames Akiyo, Mother and Daughter and Car Phone, all in CIF format. For different schemes, Error Detection Rate (E.D.R.), Error Correctly location Rate (E.C.L.R). and *encoding PSNR* without/after watermarking are listed in Table 1-3. And Fig. 4 shows the error detection rate distribution graph as the error detected relative position varies. From Fig. 4, it is shown that by detecting the forced synchronous signal, the decoder significantly improved the E.C.L.R.. So it is expected that the proposed scheme could detect the kind of bit error mention in Fig. 1 and avoid shift phenomena to exist.

From the results, it is shown the FZW scheme can improve the E.D.R. with an extra 52%~95%, the E.C.L R. with an extra 270%~700%, comparing with the syntax based error detection scheme. While *PSNR* loss is minor, complexity is low and coded bit rate does not increase. Figure 5 show the *Y-PSNR* comparison of the reconstructed images on encoder/decoder side with only different error detection schemes. For error concealment, simple copying from previous frame is applied. In simulation, no error is cast on the bits that represent the first intra-frame data. Also, a sample reconstructed frame applied different error detection scheme only is shown in Fig. 6 for subjective results comparison.

Table 1. *Akiyo*

Error detection scheme	$\overline{PSNR}$ (dB)	$\overline{PSNR}$ (dB)	Bit rate (Kbits/s)	E.D. rate (%)	E. C. L. rate (%)
Syntax based	36.45	--	92.56	28.9	11.3
FZW	35.82	0.37	87.29	55.04	42.64

Table 2. *Mother and Daughter*

Error detection scheme	$\overline{PSNR}$ (dB)	$\overline{PSNR}$ (dB)	Bit rate (Kbits/s)	E.D. rate (%)	E. C. L. rate (%)
Syntax based	34.95	--	158.14	31.1	6.0
FZW	34.62	0.31	155.20	60.62	44.02

Table 3. *Car Phone*

Error detection scheme	$\overline{PSNR}$ (dB)	$\overline{PSNR}$ (dB)	Bit rate (Kbits/s)	E.D. rate (%)	E. C. L. rate (%)
Syntax based	35.36	--	333.76	37.0	4.9
FZW	34.08	0.67	291.22	56.29	39.77

4. Summary

In this paper, a synchronous fragile watermarking scheme, namely FZW, for detecting erroneous Q-DCT coefficients is proposed. We also provide analysis for visual quality loss due to watermarking under some assumptions. With the expression derived, the value range that the watermarking parameter could choose can be calculated when visual quality loss is pre-defined. A more precise result could be derived using more sophisticated model (GGD for example), thus it can be applied in wider range. The simulation results show that less than 0.7 dB loss is reported while the error detection capabilities gain are 52%~95% for the error detection rate and 270%~700% for the error correctly located rate, comparing to the syntax based scheme. Thus would improve the efficiency and results of the error concealment techniques.

Though the FZW scheme now works with Q-DCT coefficients only, future work would explore the ability of detect erroneous header information and MV information by fragile watermarking. At current time, the FZW scheme can work with syntax check for detecting all these kinds of error. Under a pre-defined visual quality loss requirement, the watermarking parameter *pos* may vary when QP changes. Hence, a look up table for these two elements should be applied in the applications that employ bit rate control scheme.

5. References

[1] "Video coding for low bitrate communication", ITU-T Rec. H.263, Mar. 1996

[2] "Coding of moving pictures and associated audio for digital storage media at up to about 1.5Mbit/s", ISO/IEC 11172, Aug. 1993

[3] Minghua Chen, Yun He and Reginald L. Lagendijk, "Error detection by fragile watermarking", *Proceeding of PCS2001*, pp. 287-290, Seoul, April, 2001

[4] Minghua Chen, Yun He, "A watermark based transmission error detection scheme for hybrid decoder", *Journal of Tsinghua University Science and Technology*, to appear

[5] Teng Sing Wang, Pao-Chi Chang, Chih-Wei Tang, Hsueh-Ming Hang and Tihao Chiang, "An Error Detection Scheme using Data Embedding for H.263 Compatible Video Coding", *ISO/IEC JTC1/SC29/WG11 MPEG99/ N6340* July 2000

[6] Chih-Wei Tang, Hsueh-Ming Hang, and Tihao Chiang, "A Proposal for Some Non-Security Watermarking Applications ", ISO/IEC JTC1/SC29/WG11, MPEG99/N6339, July 2000

[7] Keith A. Birney, Thomas R. Fischer, "On the modeling of DCT and subband image data for compression", *IEEE transaction on image processing*, vol. 4. No. 2, Feb. 1995

[8] ITU-T Study Group 16. TMN8 video codec test model near-term version 8. *Q15-B-46*. Sunriver; ITU-T, 1997,09

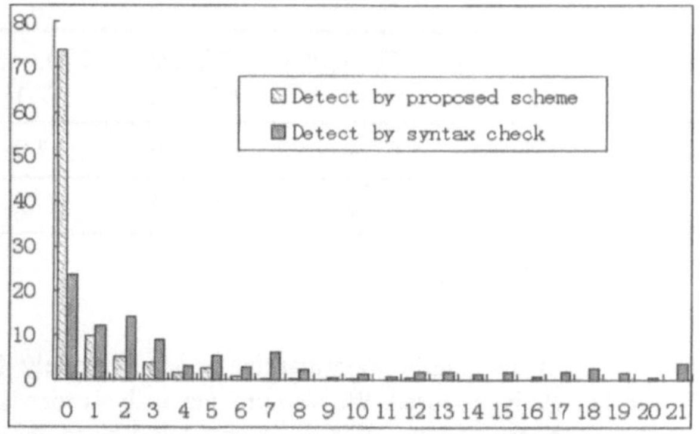

Figure 4 *Horizontal: relative position between error detected position and error occurred position. Unit: MB. Vertical: ratio of error detected at current relative position divided by total error detected. Unit: %*

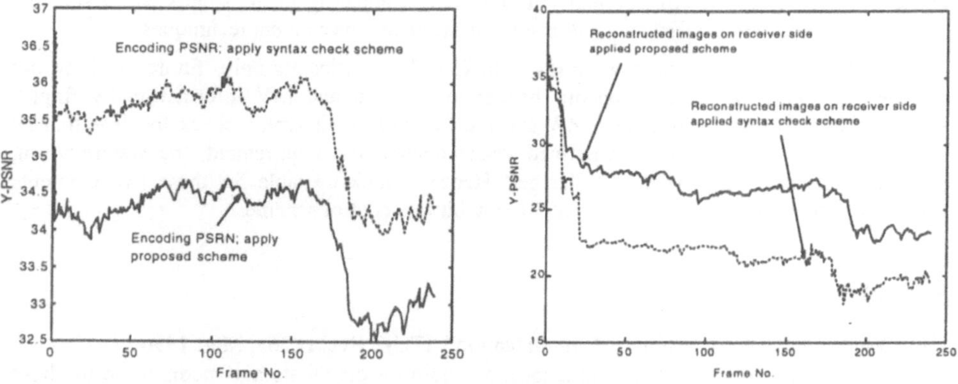

Figure 5. *Encoding/reconstructed Y-PSNR comparison under different error detection scheme*

a) Apply syntax based scheme b) Apply proposed scheme

Figure 6. *The 180th reconstructed frames applied different error detection scheme only*

Shot Change Detection
Based on the Reynolds Transport Theorem

C. C. Shih*, H. R. Tyan**, and H. Y. Mark Liao*

*Institute of Information Science, Acadmeia Sinica, Taipei, Taiwan
**Department of Information and Computer Engineering
Chung-Yuan Christian University, Chung-Li, Taiwan

e-mail: liao@iis.sinica.edu.tw

Abstract. Most of the conventional gradual shot change detection algorithms are heuristics-based. Usually, a general shot transition detection algorithm which can deal with different kinds of situations may be very tedious and complicated if it is heuristics-based. Under the circumstances, a general detection algorithm which has a solid theoretic ground is always preferrable. In this paper, we propose a general shot change detection algorithm which is able to achieve the above mentioned goal. The proposed algorithm consists of two major stages: the modeling stage and the detection stage. In the modeling stage, we model a shot transition by calculating the change of color/intensity distribution corresponding to the shots before and after a transition. In the detection stage, we consider a video clip as a continuous "frame flow" and then apply the Reynolds Transport Theorem to analyze the flow change within a pre-determined control volume. Using the above mentioned methodology, the shot change detection problem becomes theoretically analytic. Experimental results have proven the superiority of the proposed method.

1. Introduction

In the past decade, shot change detection has been extensively explored[1-5]. In the first few years, the focus was put on abrupt change detection. The techniques adopted included: histogram difference, frame difference, motion vector, compression difference, etc. Some good surveys with regard to abrupt change detection techniques can be found in [1,2]. In recent years, the research focus on shot change detection has been shifted to gradual change detection [3-5]. Conventional gradual shot change algorithms usually have a common drawback, i.e., they are usually designed for solving some specific gradual shot changes only. In other words, these algorithms are most of the time heuristics-based. In [4], Bescos et al. proposed a new shot change detection algorithm and they claimed that their approach could detect any kind of gradual transitions. However, their method was not analytic at all. In Yu and Wolf [3], shot transition was judged by calculating a characteristic function which was a function of intensity change. Since their approach was pixel-based, only the gradual transitions such as fade and dissolve could be detected. In this paper, we shall devise a more general shot change detection algorithm which can detect most of the existing gradual shot transitions.

The proposed approach consists of two major stages, i.e., the modeling stage and the detection stage. In the modeling stage, we model a shot transition by calculating the change of color/intensity distribution that correspond, respectively, to the shots before and after a transition. We assume during a shot transition, the histogram of any frame located within a transition section can be derived by a linear combination of the average histograms of the two shots located at both sides of the transition section. With this reasonable assumption, the histogram of any frame located within a transition section must be an intermediate state of the histograms of the two shots located at both sides of the transition section. In the detection stage, we consider a video clip as a continuous ``frame flow" and then use the ``Reynolds Transport Theorem" [6] which is commonly used in the field of fluid mechanics to analyze the flow change within a pre-determined control volume. Through this mechanism, we successfully model the shot change detection problem and make it become analytic.

2. Generalized Modeling and Detection of A Shot Transition

2.1. A Generalized Shot Transition Model

Let a video be composed of L_s consecutive frames. Let the video sequence located from frame 1 to frame t_a be shot **A** and that located from frame t_b to the last frame be shot **B**. Therefore, the ordering for the critical frames should be $1 < t_a < t_b < L_s$. As to the sequence of frames located between t_a and t_b, we call them the frames in a shot transition. Let **I**(i) be the ith frame of the video and $\vec{H}^R(i)$、$\vec{H}^G(i)$、and $\vec{H}^B(i)$ be the histograms of the **R** channel, **G** channel, and **B** channel, respectively, of the frame i. Based on the above mentioned assumption, i.e., the histogram of those frames located within the same shot are very homogeneous, we can use a set of representative RGB histograms to represent a shot.

Let $\mathbf{H_A}=(\vec{H}_A^R \quad \vec{H}_A^G \quad \vec{H}_A^B)$ and $\mathbf{H_B}=(\vec{H}_B^R \quad \vec{H}_B^G \quad \vec{H}_B^B)$ be the set of representative **RGB** histograms that correspond to shot **A** and shot **B**, respectively. For the ith frame in the video, its potential **RGB** histograms, $\mathbf{H}(i)=(\vec{H}^R(i) \quad \vec{H}^G(i) \quad \vec{H}^B(i))$, can be analyzed as follows:

(a) if $0 \le i < t_A$, then $(\vec{H}^R(i) \quad \vec{H}^G(i) \quad \vec{H}^B(i)) \approx (\vec{H}_A^R \quad \vec{H}_A^G \quad \vec{H}_A^B)$;

(b) if $t_B < i \le L_S$, then $(\vec{H}^R(i) \quad \vec{H}^G(i) \quad \vec{H}^B(i)) \approx (\vec{H}_B^R \quad \vec{H}_B^G \quad \vec{H}_B^B)$;

(c) if $t_A \leq i \leq t_B$, then $\vec{H}^R(i)$, $\vec{H}^G(i)$, and $\vec{H}^B(i)$ can be represented, respectively, as follows:

$$\vec{H}^R(i) = \Gamma^R(i) \cdot \vec{H}_A^R + \bar{\Gamma}^R(i) \cdot \vec{H}_B^R , \quad (1)$$

$$\vec{H}^G(i) = \Gamma^G(i) \cdot \vec{H}_A^G + \bar{\Gamma}^G(i) \cdot \vec{H}_B^G , \quad (2)$$

and $$\vec{H}^B(i) = \Gamma^B(i) \cdot \vec{H}_A^B + \bar{\Gamma}^B(i) \cdot \vec{H}_B^R . \quad (3)$$

$\Gamma^k(i)$ and $\bar{\Gamma}^k(i)$ (where k can be R, G, and B) are two 256x256 matrices and can be represented as follows :

$$\Gamma^k(i) = \begin{bmatrix} \alpha_1^k(i) & 0 & \cdots & 0 \\ 0 & \alpha_2^k(i) & \cdots & \vdots \\ \vdots & \vdots & \ddots & 0 \\ 0 & \cdots & 0 & \alpha_{255}^k(i) \end{bmatrix},$$

$$\bar{\Gamma}^k(i) = \begin{bmatrix} 1-\alpha_1^k(i) & 0 & \cdots & 0 \\ 0 & 1-\alpha_2^k(i) & \cdots & \vdots \\ \vdots & \vdots & \ddots & 0 \\ 0 & \cdots & 0 & 1-\alpha_{255}^k(i) \end{bmatrix}.$$

α is a decreasing function with respect to i and it can be formally defined as $0 \leq \alpha_j^k(i) \leq 1$, for $0 \leq j \leq 255$. Let $\| \vec{H}^k(i) \|$ represent the norm of $\vec{H}^k(i)$, it is apparent that the value of $\| \vec{H}^k(i) \|$ should fall in between those of $\| \vec{H}_A^k \|$ and $\| \vec{H}_B^k \|$. This relation can be formally represented as:

$$min(\| \vec{H}_A^k \| , \| \vec{H}_B^k \|) \leq \| \vec{H}^k(i) \| \leq max(\| \vec{H}_A^k \| , \| \vec{H}_B^k \|) . \quad (4)$$

The inequality shown in Equation (4) means during the transition from shot **A** to shot **B**, the histograms of those transitional frames won't exceed the extreme values defined by the average histograms of shot **A** and shot **B**. The above inequality holds for most of gradual shot transitions. However, for a few cases such as fade-out-then-fade-in, Equation (4) does not hold.

2.2. Shot Transition in a TCV

In Section 1 we have mentioned that the Reynolds transport theorem can be used to analyze the characteristics of a fluid material. In this section, we shall use the theorem to analyze the shot transition problem in a video.

Assume a frame flow only moves in the positive x-axis direction. Figure 1 shows how a video clip changes dynamically with respect to time. Let x_p be a stationary spot, and $x_a(t_o)$ and $x_b(t_o)$ be the positions of the ending frame of shot **A** and that of the starting frame of shot **B**, respectively, at time t_o. Figure 1(a) shows that $x_b(t_o) < x_a(t_o) < x_p$. This means when one looks at x_p, the corresponding frame belongs to shot A. When $t = t_1 >$ to, as indicated in Figure 1(b), the frame corresponding to x_p belongs to shot transition. When time goes on and $t=t_2 > t_1 > t_o$, as indicated in Figure 1(c), $x_p < x_b(t_2)$ and the frame located at x_p at time t_2 belongs to shot **B**. In what follows we shall define a control volume which will be used to detect shot change. We call a control volume of this kind a transition control volume (TCV). Let the locations of the entrance and the exit of a TCV be X_{in} and X_{out}, respectively. Having a TCV and a video as a control volume and a frame flow, respectively, we are able to apply the Reynolds transport theorem to analyze the frame flow and see how it changes within the predefined TCV.

Since there is no external energy introduced into a frame flow during the observation process, we can easily measure the energy change within a TCV based on the Reynolds transport theorem. According to the theorem, if there is no external energy introduced in, then the energy change within a TCV at a specific moment is equal to the amount of difference between the energy flow out and flow in at that moment. Therefore, if one would like to know the energy change within a TCV at a specific moment, then what he/she has to do is to calculate the energies of the frames at X_{in} and X_{out} at that moment, respectively, and then compute their difference.

3. Experimental Results

In the experiments, we used two real videos to test the effectiveness of our algorithm. Figures 2 and 3 were the interfaces of our system as well as an instance of the shot transition detection process. The result shown in Figure 2 was obtained by using a shuttle launching video as the test video. The video was composed of four different shots and three cut-type transitions. The top diagram of the right column of Figure 2 was the curve on the calculated $|\Delta\Re(t)|$ vs. time. The middle diagram of the right column showed the detected transition durations in white stripes and complete shots in black blocks. Since in most applications the transition sections won't play any role, we can eliminate these components and then perform higher level analysis or processing on the pure shot sections. The bottom diagram of the right column of Figure 2 showed the overlapped RGB histograms at a specific instance (or frame). The test video used in another experiment was ``The introduction of London." The total number of frames contained in this video was 760, and the total number of shots included in the video was 18. Among the 17 shot transitions, six were abrupt changes and the rest were the dissolve-type transitions. The results of this experiment is shown in Fig. 3. It is apparent that our algorithm could detect all of them accurately.

4. Conclusion

In this paper we have proposed a general video shot transition detection methodology. We have applied the Reynolds transport theorem borrowed from fluid mechanics to calculate the locations of potential video shot transitions. The experimental results obtained by applying our algorithm to a set of synthetic and real videos turned out to be very good. In this work, we didn't consider the case when there were significant motions contained in a video. Our system may detect false shot transition boundaries when the above mentioned condition happens. We shall work on this kind of problem in the future.

Reference

[1] H. Jiang, A. Helal, A. K. Elmagarmid, and A. Joshi, "Scene Change Detection Technique for Video Database systems", Multimedia Systems, Vol. 6, pp. 186-195, 1998.

[2] R. M. Ford, C. Robson, D. Temple, and M. Gerlach, "Metric for Shot Boundary Detection in Digital Video Sequences", Multimedia Systems, Vol. 8, pp. 37-46, 2000.

[3] H. Yu and W. Wolf, "A Hierarchical Multiresolution Video shot Transition Detection Scheme", Computer Vision and Image Understanding, Vol. 75, Nos. 1/2, Jul./Aug., pp. 196-213, 1999.

[4] J. Bescos, J. M. Menendez, G. Cisneros, J. Cabrera, and J. M. Martinez, "A Unified Approach to Gradual Shot Transition Detection", Proc. Int. Conf. on Image Processing, Vo. III, pp. 949-952,. 2000.

[5] H. J. Zhang, A. Kankanhalli, and S. W. Smoliar, "Automatic Partitioning of Full-Motion Video", ACM Multimedia Systems 1, pp. 10-28, 1997.

[6] I. Shames, "Mechanics of Fluids," McGRAW-HILL Book Company, Inc., 1962.

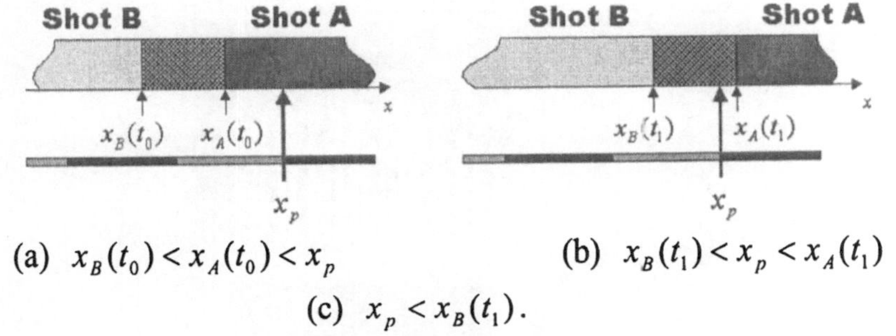

(a) $x_B(t_0) < x_A(t_0) < x_p$ (b) $x_B(t_1) < x_p < x_A(t_1)$

(c) $x_p < x_B(t_1)$.

Figure 1: Frame flow during a shot transition.

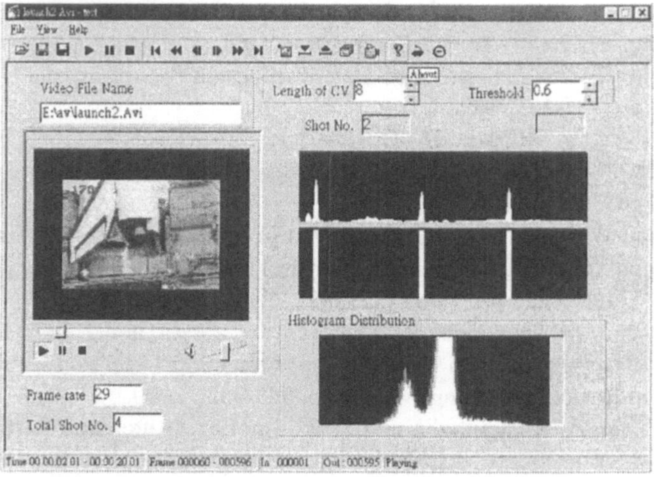

Figure 2 : A real test sample : The video of "Shuttle launching."

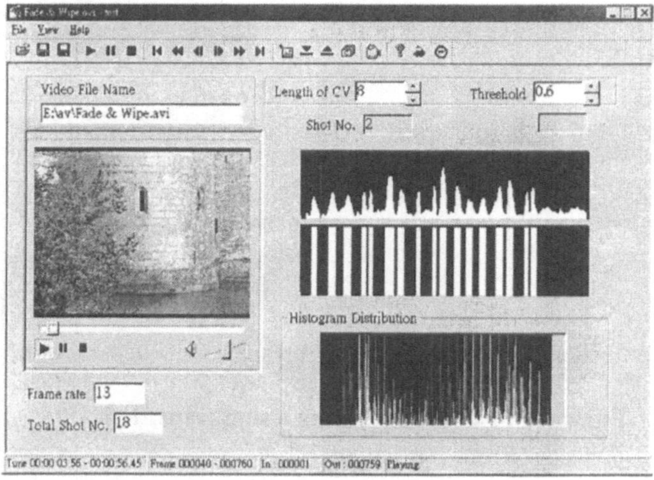

Figure 3 : Another real test sample : The video of "The introduction of London."

Automatic Subject Categorization of Query Terms for Filtering Sensitive Queries in Multimedia Search

Shui-Lung Chuang[1], Lee-Feng Chien[1], and Hsiao-Tieh Pu[2]

[1] Institute of Information Science, Academia Sinica, Taiwan
slchuang@iis.sinica.edu.tw, lfchien@iis.sinica.edu.tw
[2] Department of Library & Information Studies, Shih Hsin University, Taiwan
htpu@cc.shu.edu.tw

Abstract. The purpose of this paper is to deal with Web query categorization problem. It will present a feasible approach to categorizing Web query terms into pre-defined subject categories based on their supposed search interests. With the approach, a successful application that can filter out users' sensitive queries such as pornographic-related terms in multimedia search will be introduced.

1 Introduction

In some cases, it is necessary for a Web multimedia search engine to understand the corresponding subject domains of users' queries. For example, to prevent from providing some inappropriate information to certain users like children, a multimedia search engine needs to know whether the query terms are pornographic-related. Manually collecting and organizing such term vocabularies is really inapplicable due to the rapidly variable nature of the Web environment.

The purpose of this paper is to deal with the problem of categorizing Web queries. We are interested in developing an automatic approach for organizing users' query terms into pre-defined subject categories. Our considering problem is: given a pre-defined subject taxonomy and a users' query log, the proposed approach should be able to assign users' query terms into proper subject categories, such as determining the appropriate categories "Computer/Company" or "Computer/Software Download" for the query term "Real Player".

In fact, a well-organized subject taxonomy on Web query terms can be helpful in many Web information retrieval tasks, including observing Web users' search interests, collecting domain-specific query terms, filtering sensitive queries, and organizing Web multimedia resources. Unfortunately, the Web query term categorization problem as known was little directly investigated in the literature. Some early researches on term clustering are in certain degree related to our research, such as works on latent semantics, SVD, term relationship analysis etc [2,4,3]. A recent similar work is the clustering of Web queries [1], in which queries are statistically grouped to find out similar queries. The clustered queries can then be used for term suggestion to help users on forming their search requests. Our research differs from these works in that we try to structure each unknown query term into appropriate and meaningful subject categories, and provide possible corresponding subject domains for each unknown term.

In the rest of this paper, we first introduce the details of the proposed approach. Next, the working environment in which we carried out the research is introduced. Finally, the conducted experiment and its application to sensitive query filtering are presented.

2 The Approach

Query categorization is the problem of automatically assigning pre-defined categories to query terms according to their supposed search interests. More formally, let C be a pre-defined taxonomy and $V = \{w_1, w_2, \ldots, w_n\}$ be the set of all query terms that have been categorized into C properly. Query categorization is to determine a category set $C(t) \subseteq C$ for a given unknown query term $t \notin V$, so that each $c \in C(t)$ is considered as a possible category t is related to.

Since a query term, usually containing 1-2 words in English [5] or 2-3 characters in Chinese, is too short to convey enough information in itself, some extra useful information is required to assist the determination of the corresponding categories. In our considering problem, a query term is the string submitted to a search engine to express certain search request(s). Although the user's original search interest for a query term is hard to be judged, the retrieved documents are believed containing helpful information about the unknown query term. Collecting the required documents for each candidate query term can be easily performed by submitting the query string to on-line search engines. Thus we assume there exists virtually a document collection D and let D_t denote the set of documents that can be retrieved by query term t.

The basic idea of our work is to represent the feature vector of the candidate query term t by the term features extracted from t's retrieved document set D_t. The feature space is defined by the pre-categorized query term vocabulary set V in which each term has already been associated with proper category information. The ranking scheme to estimate the confidence of a query term t belonging to a category c is to use the information of term frequency (tf) and document frequency (df) to give a weighted value for each occurred feature term. The intuition is that the degree of the query term t being categorized into the category c is determined by whether there are many feature terms appearing in D_t with category c and the number of times these feature terms appear.

Let n_w be the number of documents in D_t that the feature term $w \in V$ appears in and f_w be the raw frequency of term w in D_t (i.e., the summation of the number of times the term w is mentioned in the text of each document $d_i \in D_t$). The ranking function based on *tf-df* information is given by

$$R(t,c) = \sum_{w \in W_{t,c}} \frac{f_w}{\max_{k \in W_t} f_k} \log(n_w + 1)$$

where W_t is the set of total feature terms in D_t and $W_{t,c}$ is the set of those feature terms regarding category c. The computation of the maximum frequency over all feature terms is only for beautifying and making more reasonable the formula, and doesn't have any effect if we only use the formula to rank a set of categories based on the same document set D_t. Adding a count of one to n_w is to avoid logarithm value of zero.

3 Working Environment

In this section, we describe the environment in which the research was carried out. The diagram depicted in Figure 1 shows the overall concept of the proposed approach, which is composed of three computational processes: query term log analysis, relevant document retrieval, and subject categorization. The function of the query term log analysis is to obtain the subject taxonomy and the categorized term set through the analysis of the search-engine logs. The relevant document retrieval process is to retrieve the most relevant document sets by combining with the search process of real-world engines. And finally, the categorization method is applied to determine the appropriate subject categories for each query term.

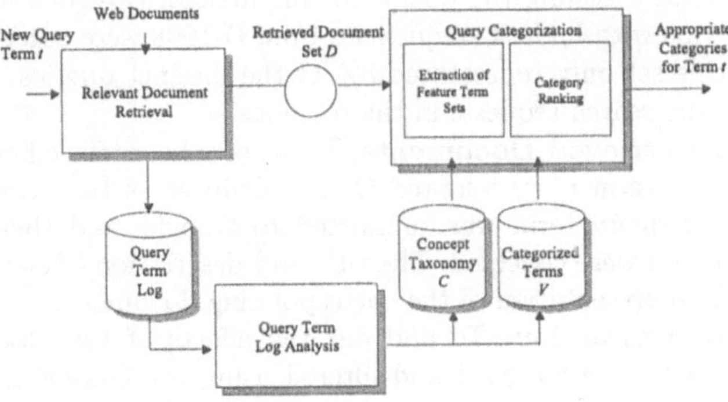

Fig. 1. An abstract diagram showing the concept of the proposed approach.

Analysis on Two Log Data Sets. To instantiate the research, two query logs from Dreamer (D-1998) and GAIS (G-1999) search engines in Taiwan were collected as the basis for our analysis. The query logs contain a series of request entries, and each entry contains a query term, the IP address of the machine that sent the request, the corresponding timestamp etc. Since we were only interested in the query terms themselves in our research, only the query-term parts of the logs were extracted. Table 1 shows these data sets by the collected time periods, counts of distinct query terms, and the total query frequencies. In our research design, we focus on analyzing D-1998 and let G-1999 be the cross-reference set.

Structuring a Subject Taxonomy. To advance the study of the considering problem, we structured a popular subject taxonomy to describe the subjects

Table 1. Statistics of three log data set

Data Set Name	D-1998	G-1999
Year	1998	1999
Period	3 months	2 weeks
# distinct queries	228,566	114,182
# total queries	2,184,256	475,564

on users' search interests. We quickly reviewed the top 5,000 query terms from D-1998 and then constructed the hierarchy mainly based on the analysis of human observations. The intention and information requests of each query term was estimated by several people with substantial experiences of surfing the Internet. Finally, a two-level hierarchical structure, consisting fourteen major categories together with one hundred sub-categories, was developed.

Manually Categorizing High-frequency Terms. The categorization of high-frequency terms was performed manually by five Library & Information Science students together with a professional reference librarian for three months. In the whole process, each query term was examined, and the corresponding categories were determined according to subjective estimation for the information requests of the users issuing the query. In this manual categorization process, total 18,017 terms with highest-frequencies from D-1998 were categorized properly. Though this set only represented 8% of the distinct queries, they totally formed 81% of the search requests in the test logs.

Collecting Retrieved Documents. To collect the retrieved document set D_t for each query term t, we adopted Google Chinese as the backend engine. Each categorized query term was submitted to Google, and then up to 100 search result entries were collected. The title and description of each entry were extracted as the representation of the corresponding document.

Core Term Extraction. To find out the effects of time locality, query terms from D-1998 were matched and filtered using the G-1999 log to have a comparison of the coverage. It was found that near 77% of D-1998's top 20,000 query terms still existed in G-1999's two weeks randomly-selected log, which indicates many core or important information requests are not much affected by time and worthy of further study.

To obtain the seed feature terms, the query terms without the effects of time, so-called "core terms," are extracted. Except some proper nouns like names of famous Web sites and people, an interesting finding is that the core terms like "movie," "baseball," or "flight ticket" are found mostly subject terms. Using the core terms as the features in the categorization process is believed to be more effective than just using common words.

4 Experiment and Application

An experiment was performed to evaluate the performance achieved in categorizing the test query terms into the pre-defined second-level 100 categories of our taxonomy. The 9,709 core terms were taken as the feature term set V. Then 1,000 non-core terms, which were randomly selected from the categorized high-frequency terms in D-1998, were treated as the test term set. In addition, in order to reveal the effects of variant size of core term set as the feature set for categorization, we ran the experiment with different core term sets: top 100, 200, ..., 900, 1,000, 2,000, ..., 9,000, and 9,709 terms from the seed feature term set, in accordance with the frequency of the core terms. The obtained accuracy curve is depicted in Figure 2, where top n means the highly ranked n candidate categories contain the appropriate category.

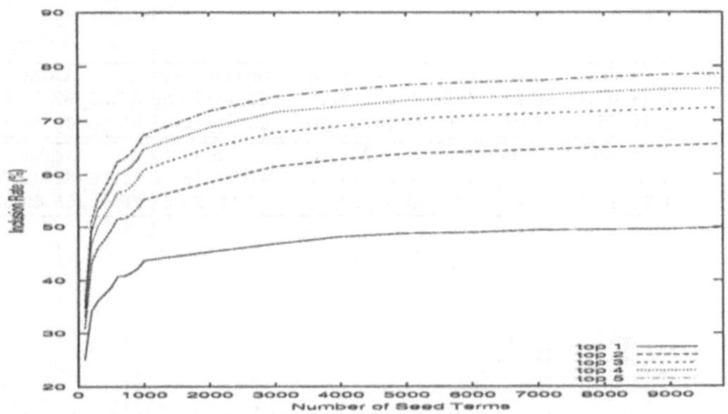

Fig. 2. Top 1-5 inclusion rate with core term set.

Even with the proposed approach, the performance seems to be acceptable. Considering only the top one categorization result, the average top-1 inclusion rate, i.e., the rate the obtained top one categories contains the most appropriate categories assigned by human indexers, is 49.83%. If we consider the performance of the top five categories, the inclusion rate can be up to 78.64%. The achieved performance is assumed nearly competitive with human indexers. Human indexers normally assign one or two categories for each test query term due to the difficulties of complete analysis.

Sensitive Query Filtering

To prevent search engines from providing some inappropriate information to certain users like children, it is necessary to have a query term filter for filtering out sensitive query terms such as pornographic-related terms. The problem of the query term filter is similar to the query term categorization problem: whether the term can be categorized as porn-related or not. Our approach directly provides a possible solution to this problem. Table 2 shows some other statistics about the categorization with the first-level 14 major categories from our previous experiment described previously. Each table cell shows for one category the precision, the correct rate that the terms been categorized in the category really belong to that category, and the recall, the correct rate that terms in the category are correctly categorized. The result shows the possibility in applying the proposed method to query term filtering within some categories such as Adult, Computer, etc. With the proposed approach, it is useful in collecting users' query terms in these domains. Combining with some human efforts for final examination, the collection of the query terms can be incrementally updated. A real-world query term filter in filtering out pornographic-related terms for Web image search has been successfully developed, in which more than 20,000 sensitive query terms have been collected based on the concept of the proposed approach.

Table 2. Recall-precision rates about the categorization with the first-level 14 major categories.

	Humanities	Business	Computer	Education	Entertainment	Chat	Game
top 1	43.41/70.10	70.38/62.41	80.11/53.29	72.28/76.48	55.36/75.86	57.35/63.71	65.51/77.07
top 3	71.26/40.39	91.81/28.15	96.07/22.35	92.16/43.06	80.44/46.61	85.60/30.81	87.69/51.66

	Health	Science	Shopping	Media	Society	Adult	Travel
top 1	70.07/77.22	43.10/43.43	60.60/60.95	54.74/49.87	41.21/78.75	51.26/81.02	74.51/56.63
top 3	86.98/54.41	74.20/12.07	91.45/21.58	83.03/20.86	78.17/38.61	75.92/65.49	90.40/21.53

5 Conclusion Remarks

In this paper, we have presented an approach which is able to categorize query terms, obtained from on-line search engine logs, into a hierarchical structure of popular search interests. The experiment shows the promising results that various new terms given by users could be categorized automatically, and one possible application that can benefit from our work is also pointed out.

References

1. D. Beeferman and A. Berger. Agglomerative clustering of a search engine query log. In *Proceedings of the Sixth ACM SIGKDD International Conference on Knowledge Discovery and Data Mining*, pages 407–416, 2000.
2. G. W. Furnas, S. Deerwester, S. T. Dumais, T. K. Landauer, R. A. Harshman, L. A. Streeter, and K. E. Lochbaum. Information retrieval using a singular value decomposition model of latent semantic structure. In *Proceedings of the 11th ACM International Conference on Research and Development in Information Retrieval (SIGIR'88)*, pages 465–480, 1988.
3. R. Mandala, T. Tokunaga, and H. Tanaka. Combining multiple evidence from different types of thesaurus for query expansion. In *Proceedings of the 22th ACM International Conference on Research and Development in Information Retrieval (SIGIR'99)*, pages 191–197, 1999.
4. M. Sanderson and B. Croft. Deriving concept hierarchies from text. In *Proceedings of the 22th ACM International Conference on Research and Development in Information Retrieval (SIGIR'99)*, pages 206–213, 1999.
5. C. Silverstein, M. Henzinger, H. Marais, and M. Moricz. Analysis of a very large altavista query log. *DEC SRC Technical Note*, 1998.

A Color Image Retrieval Method Based on Local Histogram

*Chin-Chen Chang, *Chi-Shiang Chan, and **Ju-Yuan Hsiao

*Department of Computer Science and Information Engineering
National Chung Cheng University
Chiayi, Taiwan 621, R.O.C.

**Department of Information Management
National Changhua University of Education
Changhua, Taiwan 500, R.O.C.

Abstract. In this paper, we shall propose a color image retrieval method. Among the methods of color image retrieval, the histogram technique only captures the global properties so that it cannot effectively characterize an image. To overcome this drawback, we propose a scheme to capture local properties so that it can do retrieval more accurately. In our method, we segment the original image into several subimage blocks, and we do color histogram with every subimage block. After combining color histogram vectors into a multi-dimensional vector, we use this multi-dimensional vector to search the database for similar images. The experimental results show that our method gives better performance than the original color histogram technique.

1 Introduction

In recent years, color image retrieval has become an interesting research field in application. At the present time, there are many techniques available for image retrieval. Most of these techniques use perceptual features such as color [1], shape [3] and spatial relations [10] to do similar image retrieval. We usually want to find several images that are close to the query image if there is not any identical image in the database. Therefore, similar images retrieval is essential for image databases. However, it is really time-consuming when we have to extract the shapes or spatial relations of perceptual features to build up a merely adequate database. That is the reason why we use the color feature to do similar image retrieval. As a matter of fact, the use of the color feature for image processing has become a major research topic in the past years. Color histogram [7, 8] is the most commonly used color feature in those researches. In the method released by Mehtre *et al.* [4], they make up a color table and do color histogram according to the color table. They then use this color histogram to do image search in the database. However, a feature of color cannot effectively characterize an image, since it only captures the global properties. Here, we propose a scheme that captures not only the global properties but also local properties, and it can make retrieval more accurate. To arrive at capturing local properties, image segmentation and histogram techniques are used to extract features from images. We first segment the original image into several subimage blocks and then do color histogram to every subimage block. The next step is to combine all the color histogram parts of the subimage blocks into one multi-dimensional histogram. We use this multi-dimensional histogram to retrieve images from the database.

The rest of this paper is organized as follows. We shall describe the related works first in Section 2. To be more exact, we shall have, the conversion of RGB color space into YUV color space [6] in Section 2.1 and similar images measurement [5] in Section 2.2. After that, we shall portray the details of our method in Section 3. In Section 4, the experimental results will show how our method performs. Finally, the conclusions will be presented in Section 5.

2 Related Works

In this section, the related works are introduced. We will first look at the method of converting RGB color space into YUV color space. After transforming, we will move on to the similarity measurement between two images.

2.1 Color Space Transform

The RGB color space is represented with the three primary colors red (R), green (G) and blue (B). Mixing red, green and blue in a certain ratio, every color image can be displayed in RGB color space.

The YUV color space is the standard color space for color TV broadcast [6]. The color TV broadcast combines two image transmissions. One is the brightness level (luminance) defined by the Y component, and the other is the color level (chrominance) defined by the U component and the V component. As surveys have revealed, the human eye is more sensitive to changes in luminance than to changes in chrominance, and that is a good reason for us to use only the Y component as an index to characterize the feature of image. Any color pixel in the RGB color space can be converted into the YUV color space through the three-by-three transform matrix. The formula for converting is as follows [6]:

$$\begin{bmatrix} Y \\ U \\ V \end{bmatrix} = \begin{bmatrix} 0.299 & 0.587 & 0.114 \\ 0.596 & -0.275 & -0.321 \\ 0.212 & 0.523 & 0.311 \end{bmatrix} \times \begin{bmatrix} R \\ G \\ B \end{bmatrix}. \qquad (1)$$

2.2 The Similar Images Measurement

In this section, we shall introduce how to measure the distance between two multi-dimensional vectors.

Let's first look at the normalization of a multi-dimensional vector. The total sum of a vector is defined as $SUM(I)$, where I is a multi-dimensional vector. First of all, we must normalize every element in a vector because it may cause miscarriage if $SUM(I)$ and $SUM(I')$ in two multi-dimensional vectors I and I' are different, which means that the corresponding images I and I' have different sizes. After that, we assume that there are exactly n elements in each vector. The process of normalization goes on as we divide each element in I by $SUM(I)$ and then put it back to the original position in vector I. After doing so, the elements in the vector are in the range of 0 to 1, and the total sum is equal to 1. We use $Dim(j,I)$ to represent the jth element of a multi-dimensional vector I which has already been normalized.

We measure and decide whether or not the two multi-dimensional vectors, I and

I', are similar using Formula (2) defined by Swain and Ballard [9]. The formula is presented as follows:

$$DIS(I,I') = \sum_{j=1}^{n} \left| Dim(j,I) - Dim(j,I') \right|. \quad (2)$$

In this paper, we will use this formula to measure the distances and decide which image in the database is the most similar to the query image.

3 The Proposed Method

In this section, we shall first introduce how to build a multi-dimensional vector with the histogram from an image. In the beginning, we get a color image and use Formula (1) to convert RGB color space into YUV color space. Then we eliminate the U component and the V component directly and use the Y component only to build the histogram.

In the process of histogram extraction, we set the number of bits, called ***bit_number***, as a variable and define ***max_bit_number_valu*** $= 2^{bit\_number}$. For example, if we set ***bit_number*** to be 2, then the value of ***max_bit_number_value*** is equal to 4. Accordingly, we cut the range of the Y component into equal parts whose number is ***max_bit_number_value***. Namely, if we continue with the example and segment the Y component, we get four segments. The first segment of the Y component is the range from 0 to 63; the second segment is the range from 64 to 127, and so on. We can build a 4-dimensional vector to gather statistics for every segment, namely $DIM = < d_0, d_1, d_2, d_3 >$. It means that we first scan all the pixels in an image and determine which segment they fall in. If one of them falls in the first segment, we increase d_0 by one; if another falls in the second segment, we increase d_1 by one; and so on. After doing so, we can get the ***DIM*** finally and normalize this ***DIM*** in the way described in Section 2.2. We can use this 4-dimensional vector as an index to retrieve the image from the database. It is clear that the dimensions of ***DIM*** correspond to the value of ***max_bit_number_value.***

In our method, we first segment an image into non-overlapping subimage blocks and the number of subimage blocks is 4*4. All the blocks are the same size and are taken as independent subimages. We build a histogram vector for every subimage through the histogram and normalization process. Finally, we combine all the histogram vectors to form a single histogram vector. This single histogram vector, namely $INDEX = <DIM_0, DIM_1, DIM_2, .., DIM_{15}>$, is taken as an index to retrieve the image from the database. We derive this DIM_i pretty much the same way as we do ***DIM*** above with one difference being that DIM_i is created from the ith subimage block while ***DIM*** is created from the original image. Each dimension of every DIM_i is identical to the others and is controlled by the variable of ***bit_number***. For an original image of any size, we segment it into the same number of subimage blocks. After normalizing all the blocks, what is recorded is the distribution of the pixels in this subimage block. There is no problem at all if we want to search similar images of different sizes.

It is easy to see that every element of DIM_i falls in the range from 0 to 1 after they are normalized. However, it causes a waste of storage to put ***INDEX*** into disk. To overcome this drawback, we need to do some work to reduce the space occupied by ***INDEX***. First of all, we use the value of the variable, ***max_bit_number_value*** to extend the values of the elements in $\boldsymbol{DIM_i}$. In order to save storage, we want to change the values of the elements in $\boldsymbol{DIM_i}$ from decimal fractions to integers. We multiply the value of every element in $\boldsymbol{DIM_i}$ by ***max_bit_number_value*** and eliminate the decimal fraction part. It means that it only costs the bits of ***bit_number*** to store each element of $\boldsymbol{DIM_i}$ into disk. Of course, the storage of ***INDEX*** corresponds to that of $\boldsymbol{DIM_i}$. If we want to have a more accurate result, then the value of ***bit_number*** must be set larger; on the contrary, if we want to save storage, then the value of ***bit_number*** must be set smaller. In our experiments, whose results are soon to come, we will try different ***bit_number*** values and see how the results will be.

The query image goes through the same procedure to get its histogram vector so that we can search the database for similar images. Now, the remaining work is how to determine which image is similar to the query image. We use Formula (2) described in Section 2.2 to measure the distance of vectors and determine the degree of similarity between images. We compare the ***INDEX*** of the query image to every ***INDEX*** in the database. Then we pick out the image with its ***INDEX*** giving the smallest outcome in Formula (2) as the most similar image to the query image.

4 Experimental Results

With the results of our experiments, we can compare the accuracy of the original histogram-based method with that of our method. Our method is also compared with the reference color table method [4]. There are 400 color images used as database images. There are also 400 color images used as query images. Let $\boldsymbol{D_i}$ denote the $\boldsymbol{i}$th database image and $\boldsymbol{Q_i}$ denote the $\boldsymbol{i}$th query image. Modifying the $\boldsymbol{i}$th image in the database derives the $\boldsymbol{i}$th query image. The variance between $\boldsymbol{D_i}$ and $\boldsymbol{Q_i}$ may be in the brightness, noise or rotation. All of them are 128 pixels * 128 pixels. We get those images from [2]. In our experiments, we segment the original image into several non-overlapping subimage blocks. The size of those subimage blocks are 32 pixels * 32 pixels. It means that we can get the number of 4 * 4 block subimages for each original image. We, then, do color histogram to every block to get $\boldsymbol{DIM_i}$. After combining these 4*4 $\boldsymbol{DIM_i}$'s into ***INDEX***, we use it to search the database for similar images. Although there are no identical images between database images and query images, there exist similar images between the two groups. That means, for query image $\boldsymbol{Q_i}$, there is one most similar image $\boldsymbol{D_i}$ among the database images.

In the experiments, if the system responds that $\boldsymbol{D_i}$ is an answer to the query image $\boldsymbol{Q_i}$, we say the system gets an accurate answer to our query. In the original histogram-based method, we set the range of ***bit_number*** to be from five to eight, while in our result, we set the range of ***bit_number*** to be from two to five bits. We do not show values of ***bit_number*** in our tables of experimental data but their corresponding storages instead. We give simple examples to calculate the requisition of storage both in the original histogram-based method and in our method.

1. In the original histogram-based method, if the ***bit_number*** is equal to 8, then the ***max_bit_number_value*** is equal to 256. The number of dimensions of ***DIM*** is equal to 256, and that means every element costs ***bit_number***, that is 8 bits. The storage of every ***DIM*** is 256*8 = 2048 bits. It is the storage of an image index in the database. We know that there are 400 color images in the database, and the

total storage of database indexing is (2048*400)/8=102400 bytes. That is the storage of requisition in the last column of Table 1.

2. In our method, if the ***bit_number*** is equal to 5, then the ***max_bit_number_value*** is equal to 32. For every $\boldsymbol{DIM_i}$ that has 32 dimensions, every element costs ***bit_number*** bits, which is 5 bits. The storage of every $\boldsymbol{DIM_i}$ is 32*5 = 160 bits. The storage of ***INDEX*** is the total sum of the number of 16*$\boldsymbol{DIM_i}$, which is 16*160=2560 bits. It is the storage of an image index in the database. For 400 color images in the database, the total storage of database indexing is (2560*400)/8=128000 bytes. That is the storage of requisition in the last column of Table 2.

The number-of-respondents list shows the number of similar images as answers to each query. The meaning of "accuracy ratio" in all tables is the percentage of the query image that has accurate answers in the respondent list. The result of the original histogram-based method is shown in Table 1, and that of our new method is shown in Table 2. After that, the accuracy ratio of the method proposed by Mehtre *et al.* [4] is illustrated in Table 3, whose data comes from [2].

From the experimental results, we know that our method gets a better accuracy ratio than the original histogram-based-method and Mehtre *et al.* [4]'s method in most of the cases. Two different images may have the same ***DIM*** if the distribution of color in two images is the same. It goes without saying that the method of original histogram cannot recognize them, but our method can tell the difference between them. The reason why our method can recognize them is that our method can characterize the local features. However, if the rotation or shift of the object between two related images goes too far, our method would also fail.

5 Conclusions

Color histogram has its advantage in image retrieval. The computation of histogram is very easy and simple. However, it may cause miscarriage of justice because of the same distribution of color. It is because the method of histogram does not take into consideration the characteristics of local information. Consequently, the color histogram cannot effectively distinguish two distinct images even if they have quite different appearances. To make the retrieval more accurate, we introduce the method that can capture the local features. Therefore, our image retrieval method can give us better performance of accuracy in most cases of recognition than the original histogram-based method and Mehtre *et al.* [4]'s method.

Table 1: Accuracy ratio (%) of the original histogram-based method

Accuracy Ratio(%)	Space (bytes)			
Number of Respondent List	8000	19200	44800	102400
1	57.40	79.82	83.86	86.10
2	64.80	82.96	88.79	90.58
3	67.71	85.43	91.26	92.15
4	69.51	86.10	92.15	93.72
5	71.08	87.00	92.60	94.17

Table 2: Accuracy ratio (%) of the proposed method

Accuracy Ratio(%)	Space (bytes)			
Number of Respondent List	6400	19200	51200	128000
1	67.94	82.74	88.57	89.91
2	72.42	88.57	92.15	93.50
3	76.01	90.13	92.60	93.50
4	77.13	91.48	92.60	93.72
5	79.37	92.15	92.83	93.95

Table 3: Accuracy ratio of the method proposed by Mehtre et al. [4] (Data from [2])

Accuracy Ratio (%)	Space (bytes)
Number of Respondent List	43200
1	85.33
2	89.39
3	91.65
4	92.55
5	93.90

References

1. E. Binaghi, I. Gagliardi and R. Schettini, "Image Retrieval Using Fuzzy Evaluation of Color Similarity, " *Int. J. Pattern Recognit. Artif. Intell.*, vol. 8, no. 4, 1994, pp 945-968.

2. Y. K. Chan, " Image Matching Using Run-Length Feature, " *Similar Image and Video Retrieval Systems Based on Spatial and Color Attributes*, Ph. D. thesis, Department of Computer Science and Information Engineering, National Chung Cheng University, Republic of China, December 2000

3. B. Huet and E. R. Hancock, "Line Pattern Retrieval Using Relational Histograms," *IEEE Transactions on Pattern Analysis and Machine Intelligence*, vol. 21, no. 12, December 1999, pp. 1363-1370.

4. B. M. Mehtre, M. S. Kankanhali, A. D. Narasimhalu and G. C. Man, " Color Matching for Image Retrieval, " *Pattern Recognition Letter*, vol. 16, March 1995, pp. 325-331.

5. D. S. Park, J. S. Park, T.Y. Kim and J. H. Han, "Image Indexing Using Weighted Color Histogram, " *Proceedings of International Conference on Image Analysis and Processing,* 1999, pp. 909 –914.

6. D. H. Pritchard, " U. S. Color Television Fundamentals – A Review, " *IEEE Transactions on Consumer Electronics*, vol. CE-23, no 4, 1977, pp. 467-478.

7. H. S. Sawhney and J. L. Hafner, " Efficient Color Histogram Indexing, " *Proceedings of IEEE International Conference on Image Processing*, vol. 2, Austin, Texas, November 1994, pp. 66-70.

8. B. Shahrary, " Scene Change Detection and Content-Based Sampling of Video Sequence, " *Proceedings IS&T/SPIE, Conference on Storage and Retrieval for Image and Video Databases*, San Joe, CA, February 1995.

9. M. J. Swain and D. H. Ballard, "Color Indexing, " *International Journal of Computer Vision*, vol. 7, no. 1, 1991, pp. 11-32

10. H. Tagare, F. M. Vos, C. C. Jaffe and J. S. Duncan, "Arrangement: A Spatial Relation between Parts for Evaluating Similarity of Tomographic Section, " *IEEE Transactions on Pattern Analysis and Machine Intelligence*, vol. 17, no. 9, September 1995, pp. 880-893.

Seeded Semantic Object Generation Toward Content-Based Video Indexing

Jianping Fan[1], Xingquan Zhu[2], Lide Wu[3]

[1]Department of Computer Science, University of North Carolina at Charlotte, USA
fanj@cs.uncc.edu
[2]Department of Computer Science, Purdue University, W. Lafayette, 47907, USA
zhuxq@cs.purdue.edu
[3]Department of Computer Science, Fudan University, Shanghai, 200433, China
ldwu@fudan.edu.cn

Abstract. A novel semantic object generation algorithm is proposed by collaborative integration of a new feature-based image segmentation technique and a seeded region aggregation procedure. The homogeneous image regions with closed boundaries are obtained by integrating the results of color edge detection and seeded region growing procedures. The object seeds are then distinguished from these homogeneous image regions. The semantic objects are finally generated by a seeded region aggregation procedure. The extracted semantic objects can then be tracked along the time axis. The video objects can then be used as the basic units for content-based video indexing.

1 Introduction

Recent development of video object segmentation leads to two types algorithms, i.e. automatic segmentation [1,2] and semiautomatic segmentation [3,4]. Generally, the automatic feature-based video object segmentation algorithms can only provide the homogeneous regions according to some criteria of the selected features such as motion, color or both of them. On the other hand, the semiautomatic algorithms can provide the semantic objects, but human interaction is needed.

Automatic semantic object extraction is still a very challenging problem in computer vision domain, but the automatic semantic video object generation is becoming possible for content-based video database accessing applications. First, the users of video database system are not interesting on all video objects in the videos, thus the videos can be indexed by some semantic video objects in their interest such as human being, cars, airplanes. Second, these semantic objects in user's interest have their special region constraint graphs and these region constraint graphs can be exploited for object extraction. Therefore, several independent functions can be defined for semantic object generation according to their special region constraint graphs, each function can only provide one special type of semantic object in user's interest if the videos include the corresponding type of objects.

Based on the above observations, a novel seeded semantic object generation technique is proposed. This paper is organized as follows. In Section 2, a novel seeded semantic object extraction algorithm is proposed. Experimental results are given in Section 3. Section 4 contains concluding remarks.

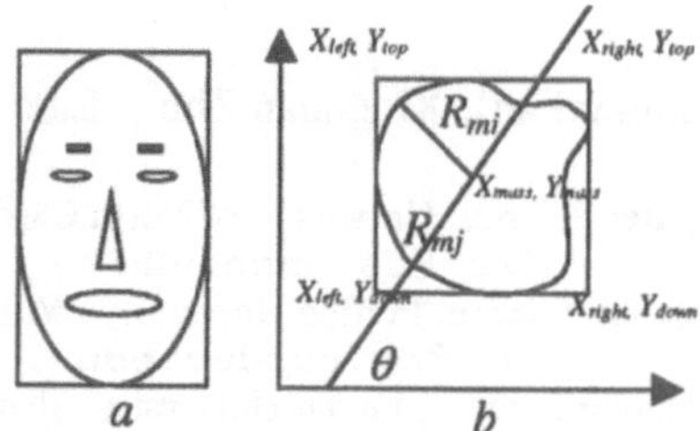

Fig. 1. The relation ship constraints for face detection

Fig. 2. The edge detection results: original images *vs* color edge

2 Semantic Object Generation

The major steps of this proposed semantic object generation technique include: (a) feature-based image segmentation for providing the accurate homogeneous regions; (b) object seed extraction from these obtained homogeneous color regions; (c) model-based automatic region classification and aggregation according to some perceptual models of the semantic objects of interest such as human beings, cars, planes etc.

2.1 Color Image Segmentation

The simplified geometric structures of the image regions can be provided by a color edge detection procedure, however, these color edges are normally discontinuous or over-detected as shown in Fig.2, thus they can not be used as the image content descriptor directly. At the same time, a region growing procedure is used for providing the homogeneous image regions with closed boundaries as shown in Fig.3. However, these region boundaries may not be very accurate. In this paper, we try to exploit the advantages of the boundary-based and region-based approach while avoiding the complex post-procedures required by the boundary-based approach. Therefore, the results of color edge extraction and region growing are integrated for providing more accurate segmentation of the images. Moreover, a minimum spanning tree of region relationship graph can be used to manage this fusion procedure. The region boundaries (boundary pixels) are determined as the first and last pixels of each row and column of the corresponding homogeneous image region.

2.2 Object Seed Detection

Object seeds, which are used for generating the semantic objects in this work, should be the intuitive, understandable, and representative parts of the corresponding semantic objects. The faces, which can be taken as the seeds of human objects, are first distinguished from these obtained homogeneous regions [5,6]. An automatic skin color map generation algorithm is suggested and a set of training face images are

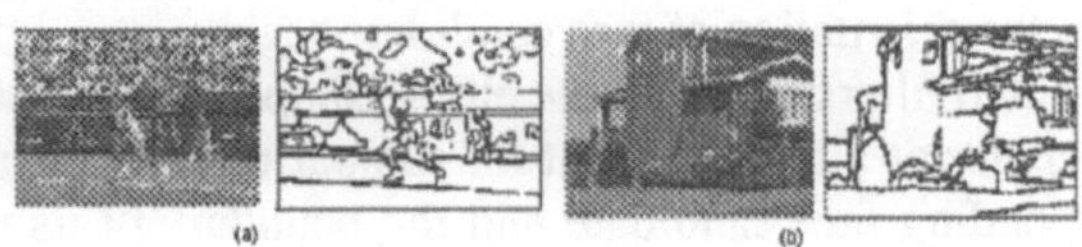

Fig. 3. The region growing results

selected for generating the skin color map for automatic face detection. The generated skin color distribution model (*skin color map*) is used to detect the homogeneous color regions that can be taken the skin color regions by testing their *skin color likeness* (SCL). Homogeneous color regions which have higher skin color likeness should be taken as the skin color regions.

$$\begin{cases} \beta_i \geq \overline{S}, & skin \quad color \quad region \\ \beta_i < \overline{S}, & non\_skin \quad color \quad region \end{cases} \tag{1}$$

Where $\overline{S}$ is the pre-defined threshold generated by the training procedure, β_i is the average skin color likeness of region R_i. In our experiments, $\overline{S}$ should be in [0.68, 0.81] range. After the skin color region detection procedure takes place, the homogeneous image regions can be further classified into two opposite classes: *skin color regions* and *non-skin color regions*.

The identified skin color regions are taken as the candidates of human faces because face regions should be included in the skin color regions; human faces are verified by a set of facial filters. Locating the skin color region that resembles a face region is an important first step in facial feature extraction. The rectangular box of each face candidate region can be determined automatically as shown in Fig.1. Since the aspect ratio of the human face should be distributed in a narrow range, an aspect ratio filter must first be performed. The *aspect ratio* of the corresponding region can be defined in Eq. 2.

$$Aspect\_ratio = \frac{|X_{right} - Y_{left}|}{|Y_{down} - Y_{top}|} \tag{2}$$

Where (X_{left}, Y_{top}) indicate the coordinates of the boundary pixel with the smallest values on both the *x* and *y* directions as shown in Fig.1(b), respectively. (X_{right} , Y_{down}) indicate the coordinates of boundary pixel with the largest values both on *x* and *y* directions, respectively. In our experimental procedure, the aspect ratio of the face candidates should be in [0.4, 0.85] range.

As shown in Fig.1(a), the *density ratio* (Eq. 3) of face region to its rectangular box should be distributed in a special range because the face region contains several small white regions for eyes, nose, and mouth with special size ratios.

$$Density\_ratio = \frac{N\_fact\_pixel}{|Y_{down} - Y_{top}| \cdot |X_{right} - X_{left}|} \tag{3}$$

Where *N_face_pixel* indicates the total number of *skin color pixels* within the rectangular box of the corresponding face candidate region. In our experimental procedure, the density ratio of the face candidate region should be in [0.65, 0.8] range and also depends on the orientation of face candidate region.

After two ratio-based filters are used, the ellipse shape filter is performed. We use the kth Hausdorff distance as a measurement for comparing the similarity between the shape of the corresponding face candidate and the boundary of its ellipse mode [2]. These detected face candidates are further verified by searching for facial features in the interior of the face. A set of face detection results are shown in Fig.4.

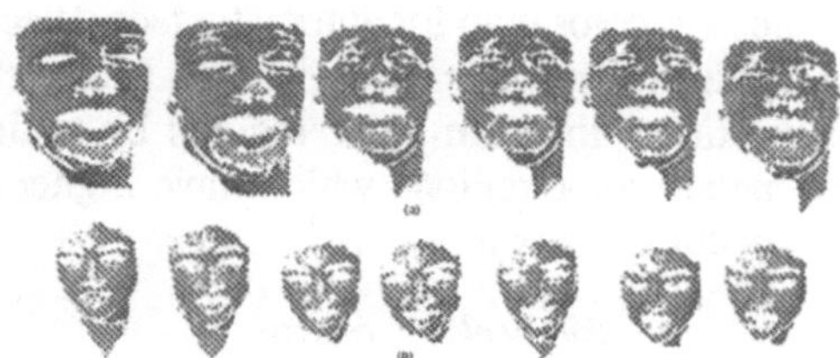

Fig. 4. The face detection results

2.3 Semantic Object Generation

It is very difficult to design an universal semantic object generation technique which can provide variant semantic objects by using the same function. However, semantic object generation for content-based video database application becomes possible because the videos in database can be accessed through some semantic objects of interest to users, such as human being, cars, airplanes. This interest-based video database accessing approach is reasonable because users do not focus on all the objects in the video. Hence, the difficulties of automatic object generation for content-based video indexing application is reduced [7].

Since the relationships among the adjacent homogeneous regions have been determined by the image segmentation procedure and represented by a minimum spanning tree, the semantic object generation function first tries to find the object seed from the obtained homogeneous image regions, and then match the region constraint graph (used for designing the corresponding function) with the minimum spanning tree (determined by the image segmentation procedure) of the detected object seed. If the object seed is detected and its minimum spanning tree also matches well with the corresponding region constraint graph, a *seeded region aggregation* procedure is used for merging the adjacent regions of the object seed as a semantic object.

Since the presence or absence of people usually provides important clues about the video content, human object extraction is especially interesting for content-based multimedia database applications. For this reason, a novel human being generation scheme is proposed and its major steps are given in Fig.5. These obtained semantic objects can then be tracked along the time axis for exploiting their temporal relationship [2].

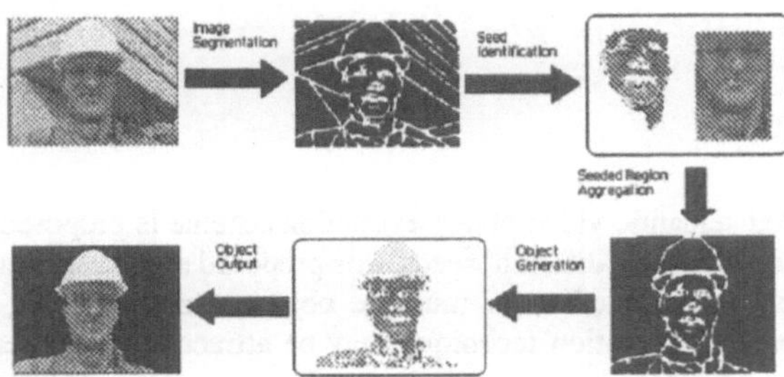

Fig. 5. The major steps for human object generation

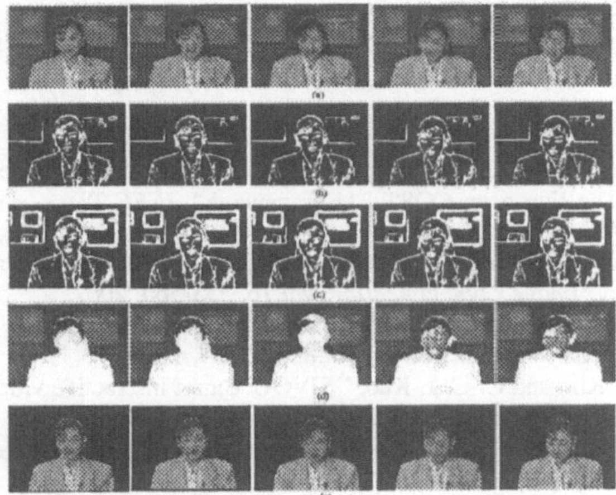

Fig. 6. Semantic object generation results: (a) original images; (b) corresponding luminance edges; (c) color edges; (d) objects obtained by ratio-based method; (e) refined objects.

Fig. 7. The experimental results for "News"

3 Experimental Results

For evaluating the real performance of this proposed video object generation algorithm, we have tested many video sequences, where the segmentation results for ``Akiyo", ``News" are given in Fig.6 and Fig.7. One can find the performance of this proposed semantic object generation scheme is reasonable. Since different semantic objects have different seeds, this proposed seeded semantic object generation technique is very suitable for multiple object extraction. These extracted semantic video objects can be used as the basic content units for accessing video database through a set of representative visual features [8-9].

4 Conclusion

An automatic seeded semantic video object extraction scheme is proposed in this paper. Since different semantic objects have different seeds, this proposed seeded semantic object generation technique might be very attractive for multiple object extraction. This proposed automatic seeded semantic object generation technique may be attractive for current research topic on content-based video databases.

Lide Wu was supported by NSF of China under contract 69935010.

Reference

1. A. Alatan et al., ``Image sequence analysis for emerging interactive multimedia services-The European COST 211 framework", *IEEE Trans. on CSVT, vol.8, 802-813, 1998.*
2. J. Fan et al., ``Spatiotemporal segmentation for compact video representation", *Signal Processing: Image Communication, vol.16, 553-566, 2001.*
3. C. Gu and M.C. Lee, ``Semantic segmentation and tracking of semantic video objects", *IEEE Trans. on CSVT, vol.8, 572-584, 1998.*
4. J. Guo, J. Kim and C.-C. J. Kuo, ``SIVOG: Smart interactive video object generation system", *ACM Multimedia'99, Orlando, Fl., USA, 13-16.*
5. G. Yang and T.S. Huang, Human face detection in a complex background, *Pattern Recognition, vol.27, 53-63, 1994.*
6. D. Chai and K.N. Ngan, Face segmentation using skin-color map in videophone application, *IEEE Trans. on CSVT, vol.9, 551-564, 1999.*
7. S.-F. Chang, W. Chen and H. Sundaram, ``Semantic visual templates: linking visual features to semantics", *ICIP'98, Chicago, 1998.*
8. S.F. Chang et al., ``A fully automatic content-based video search engine supporting spatiotemporal queries", *IEEE Trans. on CSVT, vol.8, 602-615, 1998.*
9. H.J. Zhang, J. Wu, D. Zhong and S. Smoliar, ``An integrated system for content-based video retrieval and browsing", *Pattern Recognition, vol.30, 643-658, 1997.*

Automatic Scene Detection in News Program by Integrating Visual Feature and Rules

Xingquan Zhu[1], Lide Wu[2], Xiangyang Xue[2], Xiaoye Lu[2], Jianping Fan[3]

[1]Department of Computer Science, Purdue University, W. Lafayette, IN, 47907, U.S.A
{zhuxq}@cs.purdue.edu
[2]Department of Computer Science, Fudan University, Shanghai, 200433, China
{ldwu,xyxue,980015}@fudan.edu.cn
[3]Department of Computer Science, University of North Carolina at Charlotte, U.S.A
{fanj}@cs.uncc.edu

Abstract. Organizing video sequences from shot level to scene level is a challenging task, however, without the scene information, it will be very hard to extract the content of the video. In this paper, a visual and rule information integrated strategy is proposed to detect the scene information of the News programs. First, we extract out the video caption and anchor person (*AP*) shots in the video. Second, the rules among the scene, video caption, *AP* shots will be used to detect the scenes. Third, the visual features will also be used to analysis the scene information in the region which can not be covered by the rules. And experimental results based on this strategy are provided and analyzed on broadcast News videos.

1 Introduction

Browsing and querying video data requires to first extract and organize video information from the visual and other features' analysis and organization. The first is to segment the video sequence into shots. However, shots are the physical units of the video sequence, it can not express any semantic information of the video. A video scene consists of a sequence of semantically correlated shots, with only the scene information, a structured video content will be available for hierarchical browsing, video abstraction, etc. So, how to extract the scene information beyond the shots level has becoming a new research direction of video processing.

A number of algorithms have been developed to detect scene boundaries in video sequences via merging similar and consecutive shots into scenes [1,2,3,4]. However, shot similarities defined by frames in the shot do not represent the temporal information completely, and what needed is a quantitative measure of semantic correlations between shots. According to this problem, [2] used the motion information in the shot to find out the correlation between shots, and [1] developed a new method to extract video scene unit via shot correlation and dominant color grouping and tracking, both of them use only the visual features correlations between shots to organize scene information. Due to the inherent insufficiency of low-level features, the correlations among the shots are not always can be found via visual feature similarity. [4] presented a News story units segmentation method, however, not all the TV signal can provide close caption text which is used to extract semantic information in this paper.

A scene unit of the News programs means a semantic independent News item which can express a whole single semantic event in the video. Most of the other scene detection methods put much emphasis on color, motion and other visual information in the shot. In our algorithm, we want to integrate the visual information and rule information of the video to detect the scene unit. After we browse and statistic tens of *CCTV* News and *SHTV* News, we found out the common rules among all these News programs:

- The *AP* shot always act as the boundary of scenes, that means, wherever we find out a *AP* shot in the News, the shot succeed and precede always belong to different scenes. The *AP* may make some comments about the last scene, however, it will always present an overview information of the scene succeed.
- In each scene of News programs, there always has at least one video caption to express the semantic content of the current News item. Since, comparing with sound and image information, the text will be more simple in presenting the overview of the video content, it can also be used to help the people with obstacle in hearing.
- The shots in the same scene are not always similar in visual information, however, since all the shots in one scene are semantic related. These visual features will be helpful in determining the content and boundary of the scene.

With all the common features of the News programs, a visual feature and rules integrated strategy will be used to detect the scene information of the broadcast News.

The paper is organized as follows. Section 2 will describe our video caption detection method. Section 3 specifies the *AP* shot detection technology. Then, Section 4 will describe the scene detection strategy. Experimental results and conclusion are reported in Section 5, and 6 respectively.

2 Video Caption Detection

According to the resolution of TV signal, only those caption information will be most valuable for understanding and recognition. Consideration the huge information of the video, what we most concern is to develop an efficient and fast video caption detection method.

Assuming there are n shots $(S_0, S_1, \ldots, S_{n-1})$ in current video V with shot S_i is composed with M_i frames $[F_{i,0}, F_{i,1}, \ldots, F_{i,Mi-1}]$. A boolean variant *Is_Caption* will be used to indicate the state of current frame with value 1(true) means a caption emerging. Since the video caption may cross several shots, this indicator will also be used to indicate whether there is a video caption emerged in last shot which will also cross current shot. In general, there is no caption at the beginning of the whole video, so it will be set to zero initially.

1. According to the location and the size of the common video caption, a rectangle area W for detection is defined.
2. For any frame in current shot, the distance of the rectangle area between current frame and the frame with step m (m=5 in our system) will be calculated. If the distance is smaller than threshold T_1, then go to step 3. If not, step 2 will be used to calculate next frame's distance.
3. If the variant *Is_Caption* equal to zero, that means current frame is the starting of a video caption, set the variant with value 1, if not, it means current frame is the ending of a caption, value 0 will be set to *Is_Caption*. And, in both of the situation, a binary search scheme will be used to find out the exact staring or ending frame of the current caption.
4. Go to step 1 to examine all other shots or other frames in the current shot.

3 *AP* Shot Detection

An template based *AP* shot detection method has be proposed in [5], this method seeks the shot with certain kind of feature in the first part of the video, then takes it as the template to find out other *AP* shots in the video. However, if there are more than one *AP* shots appear in the current video, or if the *AP* not always appear in the first part of the video, the method will not work well. In this section, we will present a new *AP* shot detection method which can overcome such kinds of limitations.

3.1 The Common Features of *AP* Shots

In common situation, *AP* shots have almost all the features below:

- In order to express the content of the News clearly, the *AP* shot will last for a rather long time (300 frames or more to speak about 25 words).
- Almost all the *AP* shots are similar in both background and dominant color, even there are more than one *AP* appear in current video.
- The camera motion in the *AP* shots are almost all still.
- As the most important feature of the *AP* shots, they can be found in most parts of the News program.

With the common features above, a cluster process can be used to detect those *AP* shots. However, if there are a lot of shots in the video, it will be a time consumptive operation. So, we use Eq. (1) to erase most of non-*AP* shot at first.

$$G(S_i) = \frac{[1 - Dis(F_i^S, F_i^E)] * e^{\frac{A-300}{1000}}}{\log(M + \delta)} \quad (1)$$

Assuming *N* means the number of shot in current video, S_i means any shot *i* in current video $i \in [0, N-1]$, F_i^S and F_i^E means the start and end frames of shot *i* respectively. $Dis(F_i^S, F_i^E)$ means the visual feature distance between these two frames. *A* means the total frame number of the current shot, and *M* means how many kinds of camera motion in the shot, δ is an adjust operator define by the system, we set it to be 3 in our system.

With Eq. (1), only those kinds of shots which last for a rather longer time, with a still camera motion, and appear in almost all the video stream will result in a large value in $G(S_i)$, and are reserved to take part in the cluster process below.

3.2 Shot Cluster and Classification

As we mentioned in section 3.1, almost all the *AP* shots in the same News program are similar in background and dominant color. So, an *ISODATA* cluster method based on color histogram and dominant color (in *HSV* color space) is used to merge those AP shots into one cluster.

After the cluster processing has been finished, those clusters with only several members will be erased at first. Then, with Eq. (2), we can find out which one is the *AP* shot cluster.

$$F(C) = \sqrt{(ST_{C,S} - F_S)^2 + (ST_{C,E} - F_E)^2} \quad (2)$$

where F_S and F_E means the start and end frame of the whole video respectively. *C* means the Cth cluster of the shot, and $ST_{C,S}$ means the start frame of the shot which is nearest to the beginning of the video in cluster *C*, and $ST_{C,E}$ means the end frame of the shot which is nearest to the end of the video in cluster *C*. Since the *AP* shot always appear in the different part of the video, they should both near to the beginning and the end of the video, then, the cluster which consists with *AP* shot will be ranked with the smallest value in *F(C)*.

After we find out the *AP* shot cluster, three shots which most near to the cluster center will be selected as the templates. All other shots in this cluster will be taken as the *AP* shots. Since the filter operation in section 3.1 may fail in erasing some *AP* shot as non-*AP* shot, we will use the templates to calculate the similarity between all the shots in the video and the templates. If the distance is smaller than a threshold, it will also be taken as the *AP* shot.

4 Scene Detection

Our News scene detection strategy can be described as steps below:

- Detect all *AP* shots and video captions at first.
- If there is only one video caption between each two *AP* shots, then, group the shots between these two *AP* shots as one scene, and, take the first *AP* shot as the first shot of this scene. Such as *AP* shot 3 in Fig. 1(A).
- In very rare situation, there may have no any video caption between each two *AP* shots, then, take the shots between this area as one scene. Such as *AP* shot 2 in Fig. 1(A).
- If there are more than one video captions between two *AP* shots, such as *AP* shot 1 in Fig. 1(A), this may be caused by several scene or one scene with several video captions. Visual feature will be used to detect the scene information in this region.

Since the shots in the same scene always have some correlations in semantics and visual features, in order to determine whether there is any scene segmentation, any current shot will be compared with the shots precede and succeed (no more than 3 shots) to find out the correlation between them [1,2]. Because the first 3 shots after the first *AP* shot are always in the same scene, we will group them as the first scene, then start our procedure:

Suppose $Dis(S_i,S_j)$ means the distance between shot i and j.

1. From left to right, for each shot i (except the first three shots since they have been grouped into the first scene) such as in Fig. 1(c), it's correlation with the shots on both left and right will be calculated with the equations below.
   $CL_i = min\{Dis(S_i,S_{i-1}), Dis(S_i,S_{i-2}), Dis(S_i,S_{i-3})\}$
   $CR_i = min\{Dis(S_i,S_{i+1}), Dis(S_i,S_{i+2}), Dis(S_i,S_{i+3})\}$
2. If CL_i is smaller than $1.25*CR_i$, then take shot i into current scene and go ahead (return to step 1), otherwise, the correlation of the shot i+1 will be calculated with the equations below.
   $CL_{i+1} = min\{Dis(S_{i+1},S_{i-1}), Dis(S_{i+1},S_{i-2}), Dis(S_{i+1},S_{i-3})\}$
   $CR_{i+1} = min\{Dis(S_{i+1},S_{i+2}), Dis(S_{i+1},S_{i+3}), Dis(S_{i+1},S_{i+4})\}$
3. If CL_{i+1} is smaller than $1.25*CR_{i+1}$, then we will take both shot i and i+1 into current scene and go ahead (return to step 1), however, if $1.25*CR_{i+1}$ is still smaller than CL_{i+1}, we will claim that there is a new scene segmentation in shot i, then, shot i and i+1 and i+2 will be grouped into a new scene and start a new seeking (return to step 1).

After all these shots have been grouped successfully, the number of scene in this region may be much larger than the number of video caption. However, in common situation, there is only one video caption in each scene. Hence, a visual feature based group correlation method will be used to remerge these scenes into a certain number of groups.

Assume G_i means any video group i, with N_i means the number of shot in it and $S_{i,k}$ $(k\in[1,N_i])$ means the shot k in G_i. Given a threshold T_2 (we set T_2=0.3 in our system) and two groups G_i or G_j in neighbor, for any shot in G_i (or G_j), the maximal similarity between it and all the shots in the other group G_j (or G_i), $Max\{1-Dis(S_{i,k},S_{j,l}),\ l=1,..N_j\}, \forall k,\ k\in[1,N_i]$, will be calculated at first. If this value is larger than T_2, these two shots will be claimed as similar shots, if not, non-similar shots. After all shots in G_i and G_j have been processed in this way, the rate between average similarity of similar shots and non-similar shots and the rate between the number of similar shots and non-similar shots will be obtained as two factors to reflect the relationship between G_i and G_j. The groups with larger rates will have a higher probability to be merged into one group. A pair of threshold τ_1, τ_2 of the rates will be found to remerge those groups into a certain number which is almost the same as the number of video caption in this region.

In our system, *NFL* method is used to evaluate the distance between shots, since it has been shown to yield good results in face recognition and video retrieval [6]. Assuming $K_{i,S}$, $K_{j,E}$ means the start and end frames of the shot *i*, for sake of simplicity, we only take the first and end frame as the keyframs of each shot. Then, $\overline{K_{i,S}K_{i,E}}$ means the feature line of the shot *i*, $dis(p, \overline{K_{i,S}K_{i,E}})$ means the distance between frame *p* and feature line $\overline{K_{i,S}K_{i,E}}$, hence, the distance between shot *i*, *j* can be calculated with Eq. (3):

$$Dis(S_i, S_j) = \arg\{\min\{\ \min\{dis(p, \overline{K_{i,S}K_{i,E}}), \forall p=\{K_{j,S}, K_{j,E}\}\ \},\ \min\{dis(q, \overline{K_{j,S}K_{j,E}}), \forall q=\{K_{i,S}, K_{i,E}\}\ \}\}\} \tag{3}$$

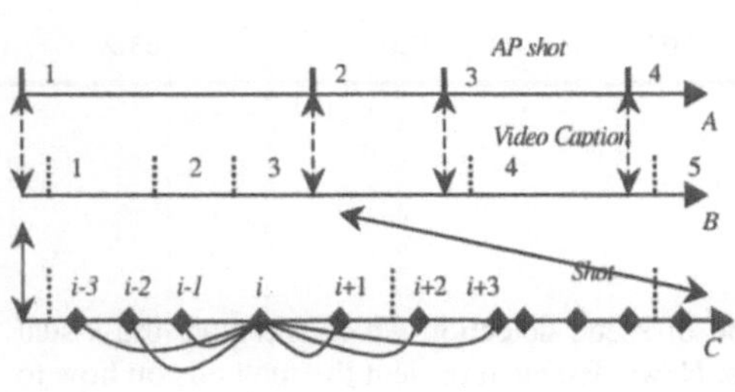

Fig. 1. Visual Feature and Rules Integration

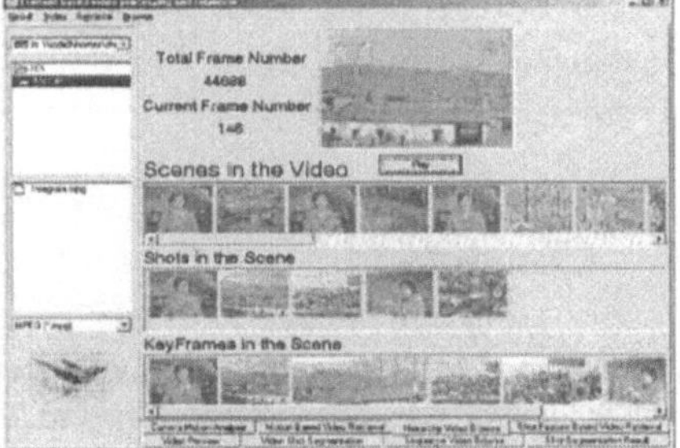

Fig. 2 Scene Detection Result

5 Experimental Results

Three kinds of experimental results are presented in this paper, video caption detection, *AP* shot detection and News scene detection. All the experiments are implemented on Pentium III 500Mhz with 4 *CCTV* and *SHTV* News programs, with *P* and *R* in tables means precision and recall respectively. Fig. 2 also shows the system interface of the scene detection result.

Table 1 presents the results of our video caption detection and *AP* shot detection strategies. Since only the motif captions are taken as correct ones. When the there are several kinds of superimposed icons or texts in the video, the precision ratio is unsatisfactory, however, the recall is high. The results of *AP* shot detection with *CCTV* News is better than the *SHTV* News, that because there are some Tag images which have almost the same features as the *AP* shot in *SHTV* News programs, it makes the algorithm take both of them as *AP* shots.

Table 2 presents the scene detection results with our visual feature and the rule information integrated method (*VRM*). In order to compare with other method uses only visual feature correlation (*VCM*), the visual feature correlation scheme introduced in section 4 is also used to process all videos. It can be seen from the results that, with the rule information, our method makes a better achievement both in precision and recall.

Table 1. Video Caption Detection and *AP* Shot Detection Results.

Video Type	*Frames*	*AP shot*	*Video Caption Detection*		*AP Shot Detection*	
			P	*R*	*P*	*R*
CCTV	44638	15	89.2	96.2	94.7	100.0
SHTV1	30312	10	74.7	100.0	88.2	91.0
SHTV2	35281	12	78.0	100.0	79.0	93.5
SHTV3	24220	9	80.1	93.7	85.4	92.2

Table 2. Scene Detection Results.

Video Type	*Scene*	*VRM* *P*	*VRM* *R*	*VCM* *P*	*VCM* *R*
CCTV	32	59.1	83.2	32.1	43.2
SHTV1	26	66.7	81.0	22.4	52.5
SHTV2	30	71.0	78.5	35.5	47.8
SHTV3	19	67.1	80.7	41.0	53.2

6 Conclusion

In this paper, we have presented a new method of scene detection which integrate the visual feature and the rule information of the broadcast News. We even present the methods on how to detect the video caption and *AP* shot in News Program. Since it is really hard to determine the scene segmentation via natural eyes without any audio or text information, our method can prove that there is a long way to go in common video scene segmentation, however, in certain kind of video, some of the rule information can give us a great help in video analysis and retrieval.

Reference

1. T. Lin, H.J. Zhang "Automatic Video Scene Extraction by Shot Grouping", *Proc. ICPR 2000.*
2. C.W. Ngo, T.C. Pong, H.J. Zhang, R.T. Chin "Motion-based Video Representation for Scene Change Detection", *Proc. ICPR 2000.*
3. Y. Rui, T.S. Huang, S. Mehrotra "Exploring Video Structure Beyond The Shots", *Proceedings of the IEEE International Conference on Multimedia Computing and Systems1998,*
4. Hauptmann, A., Witbrock, M. "Story Segmentation and Detection of Commercials in Broadcast News Video", *ADL-98 Advances in Digital Libraries Conference, Santa Barbara, CA., April 22-24, 1998*
5. Alan Hanjalic, Reginald L. Lagendijk, Jan Biemond, "Template-based Detection of Anchorperson Shots in News Program", *In: ICIP 1998, Chicago.*
6. L. Zhao, W. Qi, S.Z. Li, S.Q. Yang, H.J. Zhang "Key-frame Extraction and Shot Retrieval Using Nearest Feature Line (NFL)", *Proceedings on ACM multimedia 2000 workshops*, 2000, p.217-220.

Shape Retrieval by Hierarchical Evolution

Hans Shui-Hua, LU Zheng-Ding

Institute of Computer Science and technology
Huazhong University of Science and Technology
Wuhan , 430074, PR.CHINA
hxsui@sina.com

Abstract

A robust shape matching approach should be invariable to rotation、 transition and scale. In this paper, a multiscale shape matching approach is presented based on discrete curve evolution. Given different maximum transform error, using haar transform, we can not only decompose 2D object into polygonal curve but also induce a hierarchical structure of shape. Combining "Coarse level" with "fine level" in hierarchical similarity matching, the retrieval of shape image can be effective for both retrieval accuracy and efficiency.

1 Introduction

Object recognition is an important problem in computer vision and has received considerable attention.[1, 2] there have been many approaches to solve the problem, such as template matching, string matching, feature point matching, dynamic programming, graph matching and relax matching. Most approaches are model-based, they are limited to specific image types. However , the increasing amounts of image data in many application domains has generated additional interest for real-time management and retrieval of shape[3].
In this paper, we present a shape matching approach based on discrete curve evolution. Using Haar transform and different transform errors, we can not only decompose 2D object into polygonal curve but also induce a hierarchical structure of polygonal shape. Combing "Coarse level" with "fine level" in similarity matching, the retrieval of shape image can be effective and efficient.

2 Hierarchical Shape Evolution

Now, we are interested in representing the perimeter of a feature in a digital image as a connected series of line segments. The motivation lies in the fact that the shape of a feature can be compactly represented as a polygon which can be compared with a set of perimeter templates for shape recognition. Here, we decompose the digital curve into a series of orthogonal basis function., these basis functions are determined by our desire to smooth parts of the perimeter that are almost linear while preserving sharp changes in direction.

To detect linear segments in the perimeter P, we use coordinate differences:

$$P=\{(\triangle x_n, \triangle y_n)=(x_n - x_{n-1}),(y_n - y_{n-1})\} \quad \cdots\cdots \cdots\cdots (1)$$

Where the coordinate of nth point on the perimeter of a feature in digital image is (x_n, y_n)。We assume that these coordinates are complete and ordered, in the sense every point on the perimeter is represented by a coordinate pair and that adjacent points have coordinate indices n that differ by 1, this means $\triangle x_n$ and $\triangle y_n$ take values from {-1, 0, 1}. If we think of representation (1) in term of graphs as $\triangle x_n$ and $\triangle y_n$ plotted against n, then line segments in the perimeter have constant slopes and appear in graph as horizontal line. At joint between line segments, there are abrupt changes in direction that are represented by discontinuities in the graphs. Thus we decompose the perimeter into a connected series of straight line segments have appearance of square -wave。By choosing basis functions to preserve the discontinuities , then we naturally maintain sharp angle between line segments.

Haar function [4] was first proposed by Haar in 1910, it forms a complete set of orthogonal functions. On a set of N equally spaced points, the discrete forms of the Haar functions and their transforms are as following:

$$h_{0,n}=1 \quad \text{for } 0 \leqslant n < 2^p$$

$$h_{i,j,n}=\begin{cases} 2^{i/2} & \text{for } 2^{p-i} j \leqslant n < 2^{p-i}(j+1/2) \\ -2^{i/2} & \text{for} 2^{p-i}(j+1/2) \leqslant n < 2^{p-i}(j+1) \\ & \text{otherwise} \end{cases} \quad \cdots\cdots (2)$$

where $N=2^p$, i,j are integers, $0<i<p$, $0<j<2^i$, these function represent asymmetric square pulse with pulse widths related by a power of two to the number by data points. The first eight Haar function show as Figure 1.

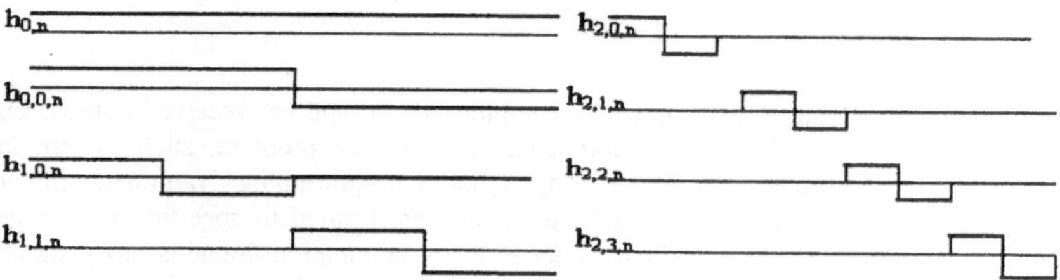

Figure 1 the first eight Haar function

Haar functions form natural groups, labeled by I, with each function within the group labeled by j , every group divided the group into 2^i distinct regions, with each range covered by one and only one Haar function.

Haar function satisfy an orthonormality condition:

$$1/N \sum h_{i,j,n} h_{k,l,n} = \begin{cases} 1 & i=k \text{ and } j=l \\ 0 & i \neq k \text{ or } j \neq l \end{cases} \quad \cdots\cdots (3)$$

Because the functions form a complete set , an arbitrary function on the interval $0 \leqslant n<N$ can be presented as a sum of Haar function.

$$fn=\sum a_{i,j} h_{i,j,n} \cdots\cdots (4)$$

where the expansion coefficients are given by

$$a_{i,j}=1/N \sum f_n h_{i,j,n} \cdots\cdots (5)$$

Each $\triangle x_n$ and $\triangle y_n$ are thought as fn function of n, and the expansion coefficients are computed by representation (5). let some coefficients be zero, therefore form an approximate polygon. For three equally spaced points in perimeter, their x coordinates are xa, xb, xc whose indices satisfy c-b=b-a. By choosing these points, make one of the Haar function $h_{i,j,n}$ start edge align with n=a, mid point with n=b, tail edge with n=c, which is illustrated as Figure 2. the x coordinate difference for Haar function is $\triangle x_n= a_{i,j} h_{i,j,n}$

therefore:

$$x_n=\begin{cases} a_{i,j}2^{i/2}(n-a) & a\leqslant n<b \\ a_{i,j}2^{i/2}(2b-n-a) & b\leqslant n<c \\ 0 & n<a \text{ or } n\geqslant c \end{cases} \qquad (6)$$

From equation (6) , we see the x coordinate formed by Haar function locate between two line, one connects start point n=a with midpoint n=b, the other one connect midpoint with end point n=c. Therefore the Haar functions decompose a curve into two line among these points

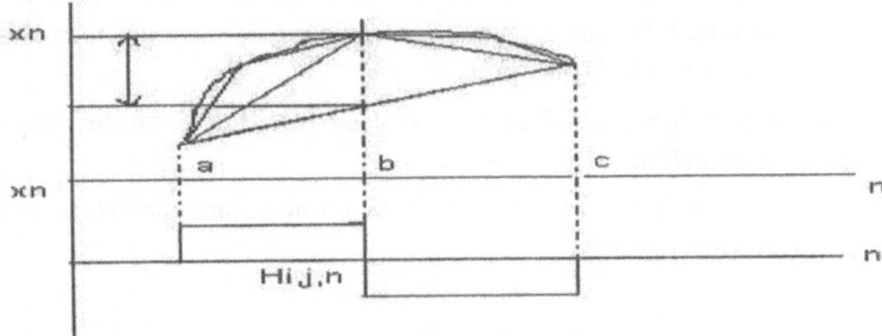

Figure 2 shape transform and its haar function

Now we consider the expansion coefficients $a_{i,j}$ determined by Haar functions. The sum extent of equation (5) is $a\leqslant n<c$, while $h_{i,j,n}=0$ out of the extent. Therefore

$$a_{i,j}=1/N\Sigma^{c}_{n=a}\triangle x_n\, h_{i,j,n}=2^{-p+i/2}(\Sigma^{b}_{n=a}\triangle x_n-\Sigma^{c}_{n=b}\triangle x_n)=2^{-p+i/2}(xb-(xa+xc)/2) \cdots\cdots (7)$$

The last term in equation (7) is the distance between the midpoint in curve and line connected xa with xc, show as figure 2. So the coefficients in equation (4) is related with the error caused by which line segments replace with the curve along midpoint. We can explain the equation (4) as the approximate result using finer line segment to replac curve perimeter, which every line segment separate front line into two line segment along the midpoint.

Using equation (7) as filter rule, assume we have given the maximum allowed error ξ which midpoint in line segment far from the curve, then one by one examine every expansion coefficient from highest order (maximum I and j) to lowest order. If the i and jth coefficient satisfy:

$$|ai,j|\geqslant 2^{1-p+i/2}\,\xi \cdots\cdots (8)$$

then keep the coefficients, otherwise the coefficient are not important, let it be zero. Such can be effective to remove Haar functions from the series

By filtering the expansion coefficients, we can use expansion (4) to compute the coordinate difference $\triangle x_n^F$ 和 $\triangle y_n^F$ in curve , therefore get the value of start point and end point in approximate line of curve.

Algorithm 1: curve evolution with hierarchical polygons

Step 1:separate the curve into N equally spaced points ($N=2^P$) ,choose one point as reference, represent curve using the coordinate difference.

Step 2: the coordinate differences of curve is described by Haar functions $\triangle x_n= a_{i,j}h_{i,j,n}$ where$0<i<p$, $0<j<2^i$

Step 3: given the maximal allowed error ξ from the line mid to curve, then test every Haar expansion coefficients from high to lower order, if $|ai,j|\geqslant 2^{1-p+i/2}\,\xi$, then keep the expansion coefficients otherwise $h_{i,j,n}=0$.

Step 4:By filtering the expansion coefficients, we get the approximate polygon representation of curve.

3 Shape Similarity Measure

After such evolution transform, any digital curve C can be interpreted as a polygonal curve with a possibly large number of vertices. Suppose digital curve C is a polygonal curve with vertices $v_0v_2\cdots\cdots v_{m,,}$ then curve C is decomposed into digital line segment D (C) $=S_0\cdots\cdots S_{m,}$ where S_i is line which connect V_i with V_{i+1}. Assume length $S(V_k)$ represents the distance from V_0 to V_k along clock direction. When the length of curve C is rescaled to 1, then we get $S(V_m)=1$。 Reference by start line segment S_0 of polygon. we can get reference angle $\delta(s)$ of line segment along reverse clock direction.

Definition 1: turning function $\Theta(s)$ is a relation function between reference angle and length along clock direction.

A closed polygon shape S can be represented as turning function $\Theta(s)$。 A polygon and its turning function show as figure 3。

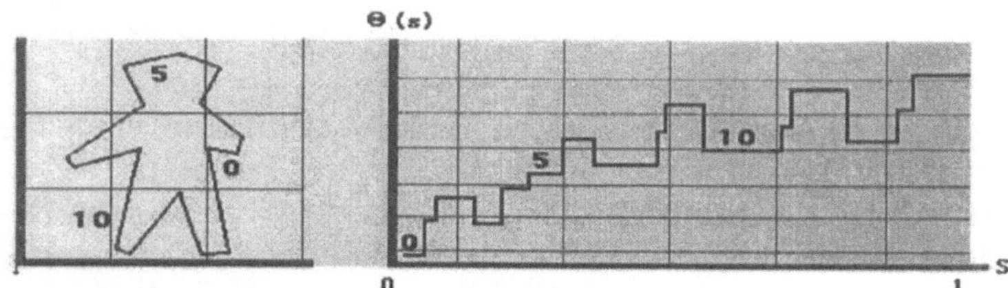

Figure 3 a close curve and its turning function

Now we define the similarity measure between object and model curves. Let A and B be simple closed polygons. We denote by $\Theta_a(s)$ and $\Theta_b(s)$ their turning function uniformly scaled, the curve similarity measure is given by distance between two turning function $\Theta_a(s)$ and $\Theta_b(s)$. If we let reference point move distance t along curve A, $t\in[0,\ 1]$, then turning function turns into $\Theta_a(s+t)$. Find the minimal distance for all value of t, which is just the similarity measure of these two curves. such as:

$$D(A, B)= \min_{t\in[0,\ 1]} \left(\int_0^1 |\Theta_a(s+t)-\Theta_b(s)|^2 ds\right)^{1/2} / 2\pi \cdots\cdots\cdots\cdots\cdots\cdots (9)$$

When move along curve A for $\Theta_a(s)\rightarrow\Theta_a(s+t)$, $t\in[0,1]$, then the break in curve A will meet the break in curve B. Define value t as key value when A meets B. If A have m breaks, B have n breaks, then there possibly have mn key values. Assume $S_0S_1\cdots S_N$ be N key values, when $t=S_0, S_1, \cdots S_N$, compute all distances between A and B, the minimal value is the final similarity measure.

Algorithm 2:similarity measure between two curves A and B

Step 1: Using algorithm 1, curve A and B is evolved into two approximate polygons。

Step 2: make the length of curve C rescale to 1.

Step 3: turn two approximate polygons into turning function $\Theta_a(s)$和$\Theta_b(s)$。

Step 4: Suppose S[0],S[1]···S[n] to be key values of $\Theta_a(s)$, where S[0]=0

```
    For j=1 to m do
        For i=1 to n do
        t= S[i]
         D (i)= ( ∫₀¹|Θa(s+t)− Θb(s)|²ds)^(1/2)/ 2 π
        end do
        d(A,B)= d(A,B)+ min_i D (i)
    end do
```

Step 5: the final similarity measure $S_c(A,B)= 1-d(A,B)$

4 Hierarchical Retrieval

4.1 hierarchical shape retrieval

In general, single level shape representation is not enough. Using Haar transform, from initial contour, a group of hierarchical polygons with decreasing edge number is generated, they construct hierarchical two- dimension shape representation. The key level representation with prominent error is "Coarse level"; the non-key level with ordinary error is "fine level". A hierarchical shape evolution process is shown as Figure 4.

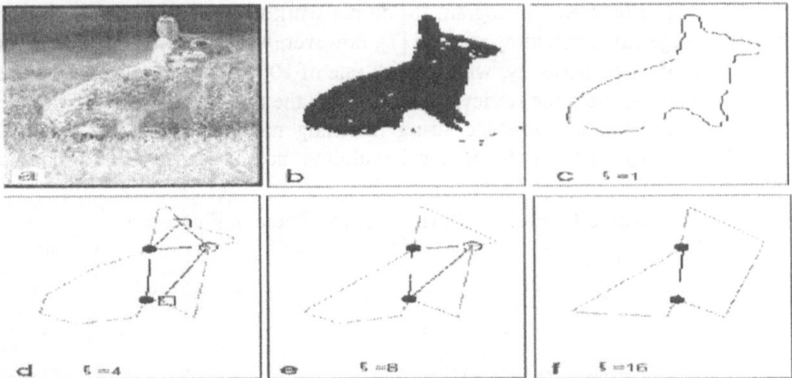

Figure 4 hierarchical evolution of curve

The object for shape retrieval is to find high efficiently images that users need. The accuracy and efficiency for retrieval are constrained by each other, in order to make high efficiency, cost for distance measure must be low, however accurate distance measure has high computing cost. Here we retrieve shape from coarse level to fine level using a series of hierarchical shape features. Using coarse level method, compute the distance in key level, filter not similar images to decrease the indexing size; then using fine level method, compute the distance in fine level. The cost of this method can be lower than that of thorough fine level method.

Assume the user want to query k images, he can compute the distance using coarse level method, if the result number less than k then the querying process is end; Otherwise he can farther compute the distance using fine level. Once the last level reaches, and the result number still bigger that k, it shows that these images are very similar, and return the result for the user choice.

4.2 Experiment Evaluation

A robust shape matching approach should be invariable to rotation、 transition and scale. we choose 9 kinds of different model for experiment which are illustrated as figure 5.Given 8 kinds of sample with different position, meanwhile the sample image was zoomed by 90%, 80%, 70% along X and Y coordinate, each model has 8×4 kinds of sample, they form an image database size of 256.

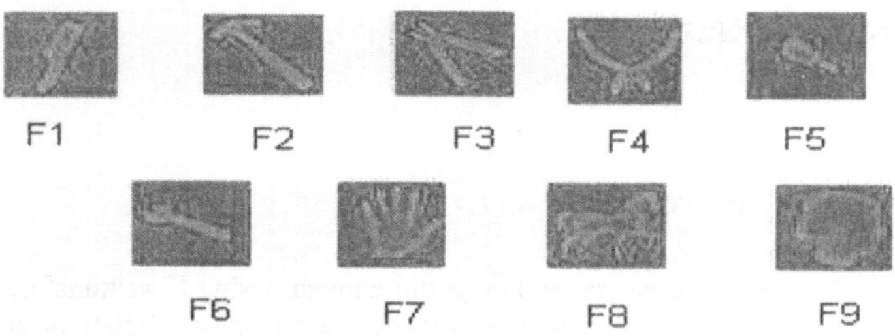

Figure 5 Database with 9 kinds of shape

Table 1 shows retrieval result using different matching approaches. From table 1, we find the string matching [5] or relational histogram [6] do not work well individually in discriminating shape. The two-stage string matching method [7], however, works well, being able to recognize all the same kind of shape perfectly, with a recall rate of 100% (or 0% false alarm rate)。 The hierarchical method has the same retrieval perform with the two-stage string matching method, but is much faster than the two-stage string matching method. The result shows that the retrieval of shape image using the hierarchical evolution method is effective for both accuracy and efficiency.

Table 1 Result of Retrieval of the Shape in Figure 5

Method	F1	F2	F3	F4	F5	F6	F7	F8	F9	Time (ms)
String Matching	96.1%	100%	100%	98.6 %	100%	100%	92.4%	73.4 %	87.8 %	0.10
Histogram	83.5%	92%	73.6 %	65%	100%	92%	87.2%	43.1 %	82%	0.10
Two-stage Matching	100%	100%	100%	100%	100%	100%	100%	100%	100%	0.20
ierarchical Matching	100%	100%	100%	100%	100%	100%	100%	100%	100%	0.12

5 REFERENCES

[1] E.M.Arkin, L.P.chew etc, an efficiently computable metric for comparing polygonal shape. IEEE Trans on Pattern Analysis and Machine Intelligent Vol 13, No3, pp209-216, 1991

[2] F.Stein , Structural Indexing: Efficient 2-D object Recognition. IEEE Trans on Pattern Analysis and Machine Intelligent Vol 14, No12, pp1855-1870, 1992

[3] R.Horaud and H.Sossa, Polyhedral Object Recognition by indexing. Pattern Recognition, Vol 28, No12, pp1855-1870, 1995

[4] K.G.Beauchamp, Walsh function and their Applications. New York Academic Press,1975

[5] S.W.Chen , S.T.Tung and C.Fang , Extended attributed string matching for shape recognition. Computer Vision and Image Understanding Vol 70, No1 pp36-50 1998

[6] Benoit Huet and Edwin R. Hancock, Line pattern retrieval using Relational histogram. IEEE Trans on Pattern Analysis and Machine Intelligent Vol 21, No12, pp1363-1370, 1999

[7] Wen-Yen Wu and Mao-Jian J, Two-dimensional object recognition trough two-stage string matching. IEEE trans on Image processing Vol 8 No 7 pp978-981 1999

A Comparison of Shape Retrieval Using Fourier Descriptors and Short-Time Fourier Descriptors

Dengsheng Zhang and Guojun Lu

Gippsland School of Computing and Information Technology
Monash University
Churchill, Victoria 3842
Australia
dengsheng.zhang, guojun.lu@infotech.monash.edu.au
http://www-mugc.cc.monash.edu.au/~dengs
http://www.gscit.monash.edu.au/~guojunl

Abstract. Shape is one of the primary features in Content Based Image Retrieval (CBIR). Many shape representations and retrieval methods exist. However, most of those methods either do not well capture shape features or are difficult to do normalization (or matching). Among them, methods based Fourier descriptors (FDs) achieve both good representation and easy normalization. FDs is often blamed for not being able to locate local shape features. Methods are proposed in attempt to overcome this drawback. These methods include short-time Fourier transform and wavelet transform. In this paper, we make a study and a comparison of shape retrieval using FDs and short-time Fourier descriptors (SFDs). Query data is given to show the retrieval performance of this two descriptors on a standard database.
Keywords: Fourier descriptors, CBIR, shape, retrieval.

1 Introduction

Recently, due to the tremendous increase of multimedia information and the emerging multimedia applications such as Digital Library, image search engine, there is urgent need of image retrieval tools. Recent researches on image retrieval focus on content based image retrieval (CBIR). Shape is one of the primary low level image features of image. Varieties of shape representations and retrieval methods exists. However, most of those methods either do not well capture shape features or are difficult to do normalization (or matching). Among them, methods based on FDs achieve both good representation and easy normalization.

FDs is often blamed for not efficient in capturing local shape features. Recently, several researchers have proposed methods attempting to overcome this drawback, they include short-time Fourier transform [1] and multi-resolution approach using wavelet [7], [8]. Although wavelet transform has the advantage over Fourier transform and short-time Fourier transform in that it is multi-resolution in spatial space, the complicated matching scheme of wavelet representation makes it impractical for online shape retrieval. In this paper we make a study and comparison between FD and SFD using a standard shape database.

The rest of the paper is organized as following. In Section 2, we introduce FD. In Section 3 SFD is described. Section 4 gives the retrieval performance of the two descriptors and Section 5 concludes the paper.

2 Fourier Descriptors

For a given shape defined by a closed curve C. At every time t, there is a $u(t), 0 \leq t < T$. $u(t)$ is called shape signature which is any one dimensional function representing shape boundary. The discrete Fourier transform of $u(t)$ is given by

$$a_n = \frac{1}{N} \sum_{t=0}^{N-1} u(t)\ exp(-j2\pi nt/N) \quad n = 0, 1, \ldots, N-1 \tag{1}$$

It has been shown in [10] that FDs derived from centroid distance function outperforms FDs derived from other shape signatures. The centroid distance function $r(t)$ is expressed by the distance of the boundary points from the centroid (x_c, y_c) of the shape

$$r(t) = ([x(t) - x_c]^2 + [y(t) - y_c]^2)^{1/2} \tag{2}$$

where

$$x_c = \sum_{t=0}^{N-1} x(t), \qquad y_c = \sum_{t=0}^{N-1} y(t) \tag{3}$$

and N is the number of boundary points. An example of $r(t)$ is given in Fig. 1.

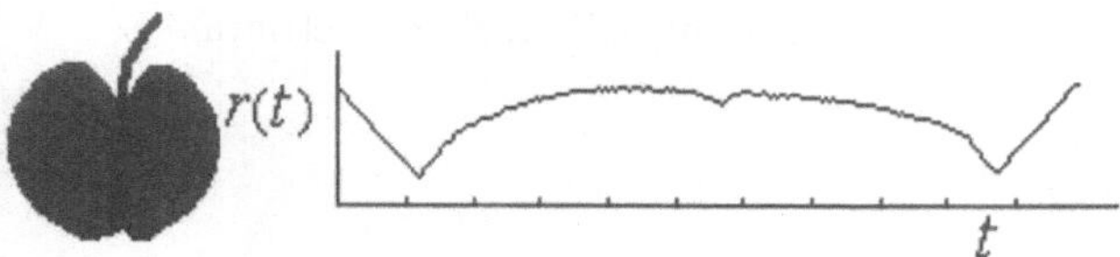

Fig. 1. An apple and its centroid distance function $r(t)$

Since shapes generated through rotation, translation and scaling of a same shape are similar shapes, shape descriptors should be invariant to these operations.

The general form of the Fourier coefficients of a contour generated by translation, rotation, scaling and change of start point from an original contour is given by:

$$a_n = exp(jnt) \cdot exp(j\phi) \cdot s \cdot a_n^{(o)} \tag{4}$$

Now considering the following expression

$$b_n = \frac{a_n}{a_0} = \frac{exp(jn\tau) \cdot exp(j\phi) \cdot s \cdot a_n^{(o)}}{exp(j\tau) \cdot exp(j\phi) \cdot s \cdot a_0^{(o)}} = \frac{a_n^{(o)}}{a_0^{(o)}} = b_n^{(o)} exp[j(n-1)\tau] \tag{5}$$

where b_n and $b_n^{(o)}$ are normalized Fourier coefficients of the derived shape and the original shape respectively. The normalized coefficient of the derived shape b_n and that of the original shape $b_n^{(o)}$ have only difference of $exp[j(n-1)t]$. If we ignore the phase information and only use magnitude of the coefficients, then $|b_n|$ and $|b_n^{(o)}|$ are the same. In other words, $|b_n|$ (denoting as $\{FD_n, 0 < n < N\}$) is invariant to translation, rotation, scaling and change of start point. The similarity between the query shape Q and the target shape T is given by the Euclidean distance d between their FDs. Since $r(t)$ is real, only half of the FDs are distinct, therefore

$$d = (\sum_{i=1}^{N/2} |FD_i^Q - FD_i^T|^2)^{\frac{1}{2}} \tag{6}$$

3 Short-Time Fourier Descriptors

In the short-time Fourier transform, the signal is multiplied with a window function (called analysis filter) that is typically nonzero only in the region in which we're interested, that is

$$a_{nm} = \frac{1}{T}\int_0^T u(t) \cdot g(t - nt_0) \cdot exp(-j2\pi nt/T)\, dt \tag{7}$$

where t_0 is the filter step size. This is effectively equivalent to projecting the signal $u(t)$ into new family of basis functions: $g(t-nt_0) \cdot exp(-j2\pi mt/T)$ dependent on t_0 and $w_0 = 2\pi/T$ and parameterized by n and m [3].

The window function $g(t)$ is usually a Gaussian function or a rectangular function. The Gaussian function used in this paper is given

$$g(t) = (\frac{\sqrt{2}}{t_0})^{\frac{1}{2}} \cdot e^{(-\pi t^2/t_0^2)} \tag{8}$$

and the rectangular function is defined as

$$rect(t) = \begin{cases} 1 & -t_0/2 < t < t_0/2 \\ 0 & elsewhere \end{cases} \tag{9}$$

The main difference between a $g(t)$ and $rect(t)$ is that $g(t)$ has infinite support and $rect(t)$ has finite support. The normalization of the coefficients within each window is the same as that of FDs described in Section 2. After the normalization, a set of SFDs $\{SFD_{nm}, n = 0, \ldots, N-1; m = 0, \ldots, M-1\}$ is generated, where N is the spatial resolution and M is the frequency resolution. To eliminate the dependency of SFDs on starting point, all the indexed shapes are normalized to the same starting point, that is, the point with the largest $r(t)$ is select as the starting point. Since the SFDs are not rotation invariant, the similarity measurement needs shift matching between the SFDs of the query shape Q and those of the target shape T, that is

$$d = \min_{0 \le k < N} \{d_k\} \quad and \quad d_k = (\sum_{n=0}^{N-1} \sum_{m=0}^{M-1} |SFD_{nm}^Q - SFD_{(n+k)m}^T|^2)^{\frac{1}{2}} \tag{10}$$

4 Experiments

To evaluate the retrieval performance of the FDs and SFDs described in Section 2 and 3, we created a standard shape database and a Java retrieval framework to compare the retrieval results. Online information of this paper can be accessed by visiting the following sites using Java appletviewer:
http://www-mugc.cc.monash.edu.au/ dengs/Contour/gabor/query.html.

In the experiments, a database consisting of 2700 shapes is created from Set B and Set C of MPEG-7 contour shape database. MPEG-7 contour shape database consisting of set A, B and C. Set A has 420 shapes, set B has 1400 shapes which are generated from set A through scaling, affine transform and arbitrary deformation. Set C has 1300 shapes, it is a database of marine fishes. Set B is grouped into perceptually similar shape classes. Set C is not grouped, most members in set C are similar. All the shapes in the database are indexed using FDs and SFDs separately. For FDs indexing, the first 60 FDs are used to generate the feature vector representing the indexed shape. For SFDs indexing, two window functions (Gaussian and rectangular) and two spatial resolution (8 and 16) are tested. The frequency resolutions corresponding to the two spatial resolutions are 32 and 16 respectively. This creates four indexing methods for SFDs. 15 groups of shapes are selected as queries (Fig. 2(d)). Except KK-748, the ray fish (10th query shape), all the other 14 shapes have 20 similar shapes in the database, the ray fish has 61 similar shapes in the database. The precision and the recall of the retrieval are used as the evaluation of the query result. Precision P is defined as the ratio of the number of retrieved relevant shapes r to the total number of retrieved shapes n. Recall R is defined as the ration of the number of retrieved relevant shapes r to the total number m of relevant shapes in the whole database. The average recall and precision from the 15 groups of queries using the four set of SFDs are shown in Fig. 2(a).

It is found that SFDs derived using rectangular function with spatial resolution 16 has the best retrieval performance. The retrieval performance of SFDs and that of FDs is shown in Fig. 2(b). Although SFDs performs better than FDs on some particular shapes such as the butterfly shape and the tree shape (3rd and 14th query shape), it is clear from Fig. 2(b), that overall FDs performs better than SFDs. The reason for this result is that while SFDs captures the local information of the shape, it fails to capture the global structure of the shape. For this reason, the first 30 FDs corresponds to lower frequency features of the shape are added to the SFDs in the purpose of capturing both global and local information. The performance of this new set of descriptors and that of FDs is shown in Fig. 2(c). Although the retrieval performance of SFDs is improved with the addition of low frequency FDs, SFDs still performs lower than FDs.

It indicates that the local information captured by SFDs is not as effective in helping increasing shape discriminability as higher frequency FDs.

5 Conclusions

In this paper, we have made a study and comparison between Fourier descriptors (FDs) and short-time Fourier descriptors (SFDs). It has been found that FDs outperforms SFDs in terms of retrieval performance. Although local distortions can affect the entire set of FDs, significant affect is mainly on the very higher frequency FDs. The lower frequency FDs which are usually employed as shape representation is robust to local distortions (FDs' robustness has also been enhanced by the use of centroid distance r(t) which is very robust to local distortions). To capture more local features of the shape, relatively higher frequency FDs can be added to increase the discriminability. It has been proved in this paper that it is more effective to add higher frequency FDs than to use SFDs for higher discriminability. The SFDs which only captures local shape features is subject to noise disturbance due to its fixed spatial resolution. Furthermore, the recognition performance of SFDs can also be affected by the inaccurate location of starting point. Wavelet is not a desirable solution due to its high cost of matching. The application of boundary curvature on scale space will be a possible alternative.

References

[1] G. Eichmann et al. Shape representation by Gabor expansion. SPIE Vol.1297, Hybrid Image and signal Processing II, 1990, pp.86-94.

[2] G. Granlund. Fourier Preprocessing for hand print character recognition. IEEE Trans. Computers, 21: 195-201, 1972.

[3] A. S. Glassner. Principles of Digital Image Synthesis (I) Morgan Kaufmann Publisher Inc. 1995.

[4] C. Huang and D. Huang. A Content-based image retrieval system. Image and Vision Computing, 16:149-163, 1998.

[5] H. Kauppinen, T. Seppanen and M. Pietikainen. An Experimental Comparison of Autoregressive and Fourier-Based Descriptors in 2D Shape Classification. IEEE Trans. PAMI-17(2):201-207, 1995

[6] E. Persoon and K. Fu. Shape Discrimination Using Fourier Descriptors. IEEE Trans. On Systems, Man and Cybernetics, Vol.SMC-7(3):170-179, 1977.

[7] Q. M. Tieng and W. W. Boles Recognition of 2D Object Contours Using the Wavelet Transform Zero-Crossing Representation IEEE Trans. on PAMI 19(8):910-916, 1997.

[8] H. S. Yang, S. U. Lee, K. M. Lee. Recognition of 2D Object Contours Using Starting-Point-Independent Wavelet Coefficient Matching. Journal of Visual Communication and Image Representation, 9(2): 171-181, Jun 1998.

[9] C. T. Zahn and R. Z. Roskies. Fourier Descriptors for Plane Closed Curves. IEEE Trans. Computer, 21(3):269-281, 1972.

[10] D. Zhang and G. Lu. Shape Retrieval Using Fourier Descriptors. Submitted to ACM Multimedia'01

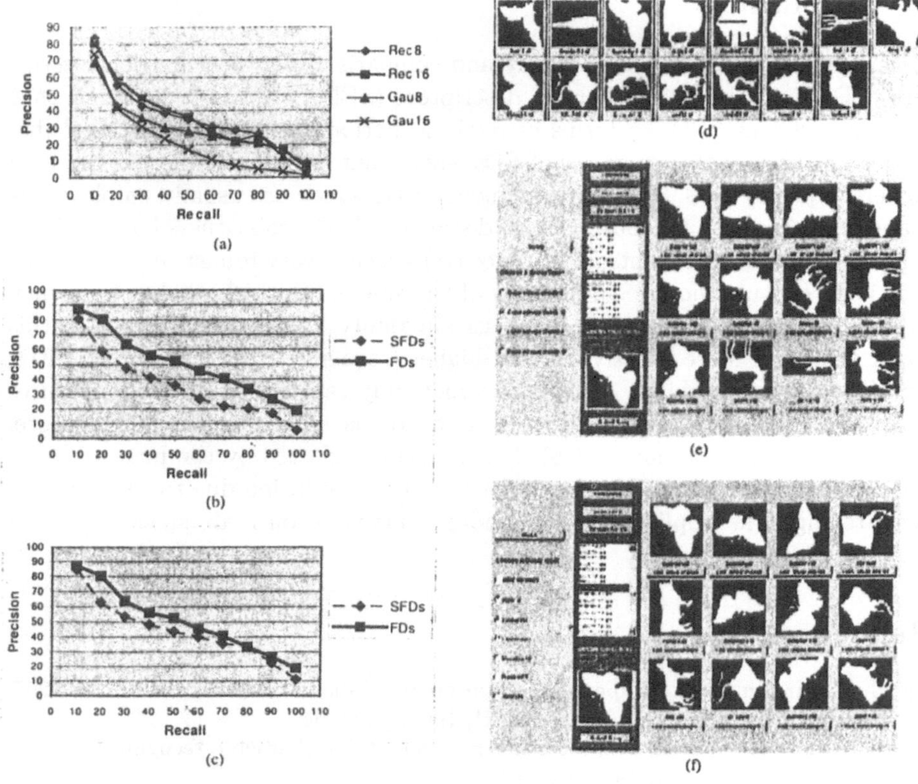

Fig. 2. (a) Precision-recall chart of SFDs; (b) Precision-recall chart of SFDs v FDs; (c) Precision-recall chart of combined SFDs v FDs; (d) 15 groups of query shapes; (e)(f) sample screen shots of shape retrieval using SFDs and FDs respectively.

A SMIL Browser with an Enhanced Image, Audio and Video Effect Library for Multimedia Rich Presentations

Kathy Cheung, Cindy Hung, Chi-Wah Kok and Mansun Chan

Department of Electrical and Electronic Engineering
Hong Kong University of Science & Technology
Clear Water Bay, Kowloon, Hong Kong
E-mail: mchan@ee.ust.hk

Abstract. This paper describes the enhancement of SMIL 2.0 through the inclusion of a comprehensive set of multimedia processing effects that can be described through XML alike syntax. The enhancements are fully integrated with the time control module in SMIL 2.0 which provides the necessary object synchronization. Such enhancement not only results in better quality Internet presentation, the text based, XML alike syntax also improved the editing environment of the presentation. Furthermore, it improves the reuseability, and partial extraction of the Internet presentation.

1. Introduction

With the rapid development of the Internet, online document in plain form with static objects become unattractive. A number of technologies have been proposed to enhance both visual and audio effects for online documents. Some examples are streaming video through RealPlayer by RealNetwork [1] and FLASH by Macromedia [2], etc. However, both approaches do not conform to the text based Internet presentation platform as defined by XML [3]. Furthermore, those commercial products do not support open source architecture, which has imposed subsequent difficulties in editing and maintaining the Internet documents. The non-text based approach also limited the document or object reusability through concatenating contents from various sources.

To enable user-friendly authoring of an immersive multimedia presentations such as training courses on the Web, W3C has designed the Synchronized Multimedia Integration Language (SMIL) under the XML standard [4]. The SMIL language is an easy-to-learn HTML-like language. Thus, SMIL presentations can be written using a simple text-editor. Following the conventional HTML concept, the components of the presentation document can be located at various servers and linked together by hyperlinks. The existing SMIL 1.0 standard, however, is very primitive which only support simple manipulation of web objects. The result is far more inferior to the competing technologies, such as FLASH from macromedia. To enhance the quality of SMIL based presentations, a working draft of a new SMIL 2.0 is has been released [5]

In this paper, we will describe the development and implementation of a SMIL 2.0 based browser. In addition, an Enhanced Multimedia Processing Effect Library (EMPEL) has been developed to enhance the multimedia object manipulation capability beyond that specified in the SMIL 2.0 working draft. The new functionalities can be invoked by a new set of directives that follow the XML definitions and fully compatible with existing SMIL specifications.

The EMPEL is implemented with ActiveX control on Microsoft Window platform. The SMIL scene description language together with the EMPEL extensions are used to compose the internet document. The browser will retrieve the required contents from various locations and compose it at client's display. As the servers only need to transmit the components and instructions to compose the final presentation at the client side, this approach can also reduce the required transmission bandwidth. The browser also supports various audio and image processing effects on the retrieved objects used for the presentations.

The enhanced effects provided by the EMPEL includes:

1) Audio Effects: Volume control, Fading, Echo, Reverberation, Panning, Surround Sound, Time Stretching, Time Shrinking, etc.
2) Image Filtering Effects: Fading, Brightness Control, Blurring, Embossing, Sharpening, Feathering etc.
3) Text Animations: Curving, Free Rotation, Directional-Scrolling, Shooting, Flashing, Spotlighting, Blinking, Cinema-Scrolling, etc.
4) Video Effects: Successive filtering, Stretching, Shrinking, Background color removal, transitions etc.
5) Scene Object Interactivities: Overlapping, Diffusing, Synchronization etc.

The improved presentation quality with the enhanced effect provided through the EMPEL will be demonstrated.

2. Implementation

As a result of the different nature of audio, image, video and text objects, each category of the multimedia objects is first processed on the client's machine. Afterward, synchronization and interaction between objects are derived dynamically during execution.

2.1 Audio Processing Effects

The audio effects can be categorized into four main categories: amplitude based effects, time delay effects, waveform distortion effects and frequency response effects. Representative effects in all categories have been implemented. The block diagram for implementing the audio effects is given in figure 1. The 'unprocessed buffer' buffer the input samples while the output samples buffer is known as 'processed buffer'. The sizes of the two buffers are determined by user for performance optimization. In case the output sample rate is faster than input sample rate, multiple unprocessed buffers can be created to acquire input through multiple channels.

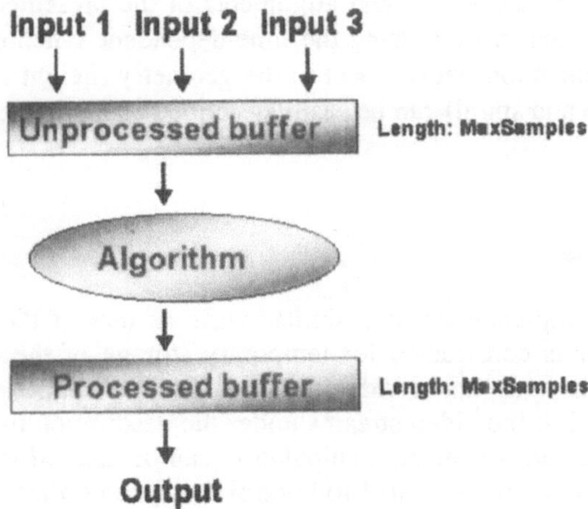

Fig. 1. Implementation of audio processing effects in the SMIL browser

After acquiring the audio samples in the unprocessed buffer, the EMPEL routines will be invoked to generate the desired audio effect. The audio effects applied to an audio clip can be specified by a set of attribute that consists of audio-delay, audio-volume, audio-max-samples and duration.

2.2 Image Manipulations

In addition to the image manipulation methods allowed by SMIL and DHTML such as motion and resizing, the EMPEL extension provides image filtering and background removal features similar to that found in photo editing software. The new features significantly enhance the capability to combine multiple image objects into a single scene. The current implementation will download the document description to locate various images required in the presentation. The subroutines that have been implemented in EMPEL will then be invoked to perform all the necessary image transformation and filtering required to produce the desired effect while the image are being downloaded from the Internet. Time synchronization modules are being implemented to synchronize the image with other streaming media for smooth presentation.

The special effects for images are specified together with a set of attributes for both filtering and orientation techniques which includes image-back-color, image-x-value, image-y-value, image-tilting, filtering effects and duration.

2.3 Text Manipulations

The enhancements in text manipulation can be classified into motion and distortion effects. The position, orientation and alignments of the presented text object can be precisely synchronized in time using the time-dependent synchronization module in SMIL. Font customization with respect to the geometry (height and width) and trace line (curve, incline and spiral) can be easily described using the new scene description language.

2.4 Video Effects

Video effects are implemented in a similar ways as that of the audio effects. An unprocessed buffer is constructed for temporary storage of the input video stream. Successive filtering and other video processing algorithms implemented in the EMPEL are applied to the video streams under the description of the new directives. All filters implemented for image manipulation can be applied to video. A separate time control module is implemented to control the synchronization of varies effects. In particular, gradual transition is implemented as in-between frame transition for two given keyframes using one of the transition algorithm defined by EMPEL.

3. Runtime Examples

A screen capture of the SMIL browser with the EMPEL extension is given in figure 2. The current browser implementation and the EMPEL plug-in, include a presentation window and a source window to display the SMIL codes that composes the document. The source window can be minimized if desired. A large number of effects have been implemented through the EMPEL extension. The following sections will describe some of the representative algorithms in EMPEL. Audio and video effects will be demonstrated in the conference section

3.1 Image Effects

Showing in figure 3 is the result of fading by random pixel implemented in EMPEL when browsed through the enhanced SMIL browser. The rate of fading can be synchronized with other clips (such as audio) to generate non-linear disappearance. This capability significantly enhances rhythmic property of a presentation. Figure 5 is a snapshot of feathering. A smooth transition has been observed which is the result of the time-dependent synchronization of multiple objects (the two images).

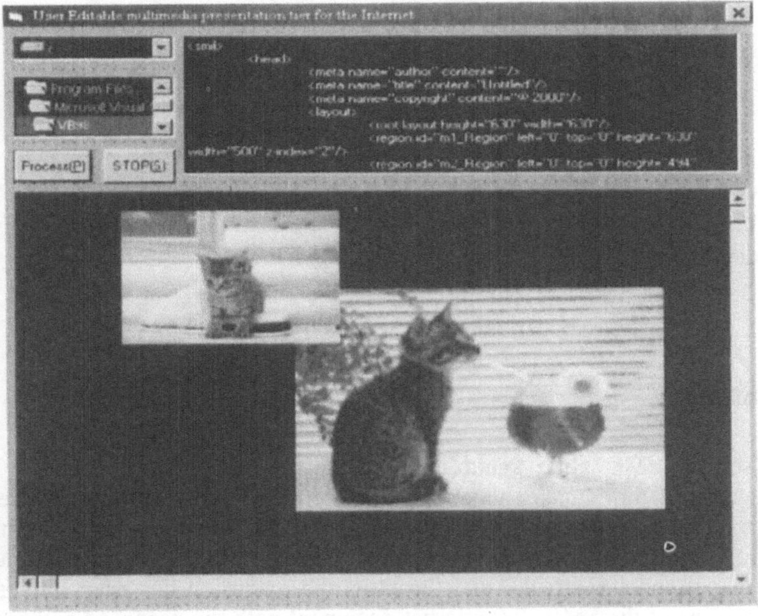

Fig. 2. Runtime appearance of the SMIL browser with the EMPEL enhancement

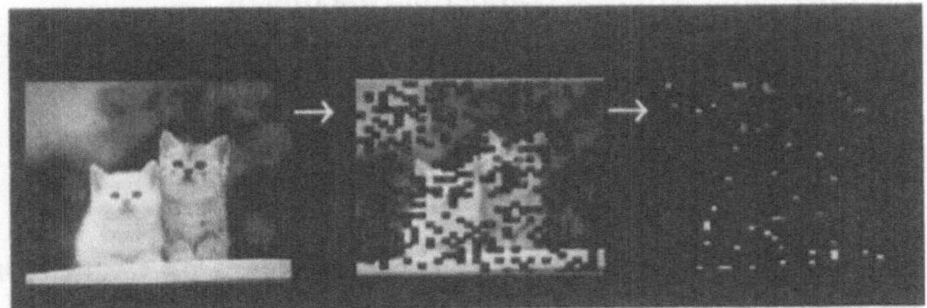

Fig. 3. Example of fading using random selection of disappearing pixels

3.2 Text Effects

Showing in figure 4 is an example of text effects in EMPEL, which includes curved trace line, rotation and fading. The freedom to provide text animation with arbitrary orientation and alignment can significantly enhance the dynamic annotation capability for online animations.

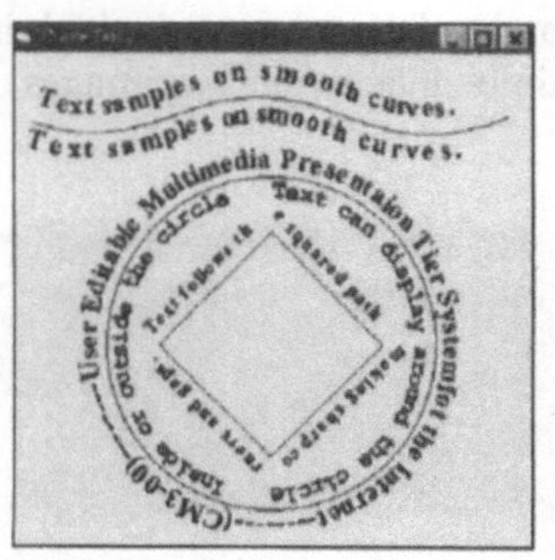

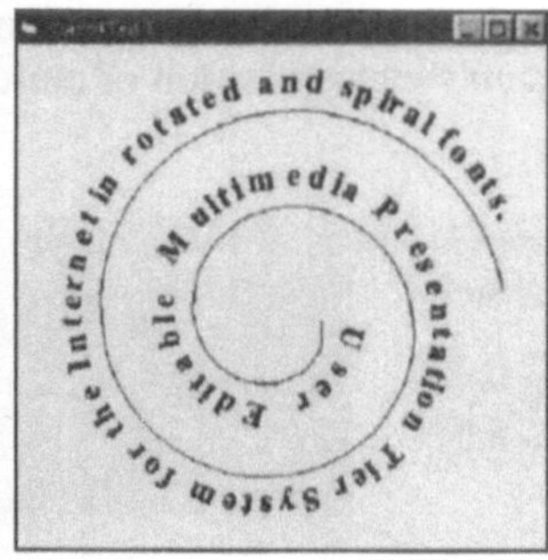

Fig. 4. Example of the text effect (rotation and curving)

4. Summary

A new set of XML alike syntax is defined for document description with a comprehensive audio, image, video and text effects. The multimedia effects are grouped to form an effect library known as EMPEL which can be invoked in SMIL enable browser that support the proposed multimedia object description language. A browser that support SMIL 2.0 and the proposed extension has been implemented. Screen captures of the SMIL 2.0 internet document with the proposed extensions are presented. A user-friendly GUI is proposed for authoring SMIL 2.0 document with the proposed extension. An example editing tool using the proposed GUI has been developed, where a SMIL document compiler is provided to convert the user input captured from the GUI into SMIL 2.0 compatible document.

Acknowledgement

This work is sponsored by a Competitive Earmarked Research Grant from Research Grant Council of Hong Kong

References

[1] http://www.real.com/playerplus
[2] http://www.macromedia.com/software/flash
[3] http://www.w3c.org/xml
[4] http://www.w3c.org/AudioVideo
[5] http://www.w3.org/TR/2001/WD-smil20-20010301

A Method for Photograph Indexing Using Speech Annotation

Jiayi Chen[1], Tele Tan[1], Philippe Mulhem[2]

[1] Information-Base Functions Lab, Real World Computing Partnership,
Kent Ridge Digital Labs, 21 Heng Mui Keng Terrace, Singapore, 119613
{jiayi, teletan}@krdl.org.sg
[2] IPAL-CNRS, 21 Heng Mui Keng Terrace, Singapore, 119613
mulhem@krdl.org.sg

Abstract. We explore the feasibility of using speech input to perform the task of indexing a large volume of digital photographs. As a natural medium for image communication, speech can be used to complement existing content-based techniques thereby promoting the reliability and use-ability of image retrieval systems. We introduce a methodology for image indexing using speech annotation technique. Speech recognition tools, like *Dragon NaturallySpeaking* can be adapted to perform the main role of speech-to-text transcription. The use of structured speech as opposed to free form speech in a limited system can further boost the transcription accuracy. We also introduce the idea of using N-best lists from the speech recognition output to improve the recognition performance. The transcribed text is used to populate the metadata of the corresponding photograph. A photo query strategy is implemented to affirm the performance of proposed technique for photo indexing and retrieval.

1 Introduction

1.1 Motivation

With the advent of low cost and high quality digital cameras, the pervasive use of digital photography is expected to cause a phenomenon increase in the quantity of photos stored in a typical digital collection. This drives the demand for an effective and efficient system for the index, storage and retrieval of a large collection of digital photographs. Content-based image retrieval (CBIR) systems have been developed for over a decade to address the indexing aspect [1,2,3]. As its name implies, in a CBIR system attribute properties derived from the content of image signal are used to describe the content essence. Some commonly used physical properties like colour, texture and shapes are particularly effective in providing the content information according to a genre of objects like sky, water, building, foliage, rock and mountain. Such features are also useful for implementation in a query by examples situation.

In the last couple of years, face recognition technology has been applied to index human faces in photographs [4]. In such content rich environment, different modes of information can be harnessed together to enhance the indexing accuracy.

To further improve the performance of image indexing, we explore the feasibility of making image annotation by speech since speech is a natural medium for image communication. The work is primarily motivated by the following development:

- The commercial success of speech recognition technology in domain specific applications like navigating mobile devices, voice activated command interfaces.
- The introduction of new generation of digital cameras with built-in microphone for speech storage by many vendors such as Sony, Fujifilm and Kodak.

Besides, making speech annotation immediately after taking a photograph is more effective since information about the photo is still fresh in the mind of cameraman.

We explore here the use of a COTS speech recognition engine; namely *Dragon NaturalSpeaking* to perform the transcription. Engine customisation of user training and dictionary control was implemented to improve accuracy in real application. An N-best formalism to enhance the photo query and retrieval task is also adopted.

In Section 2, we introduce the methodology of our speech annotation approach, the selection criteria for the speech recognition engine and the use of N-best lists from the recognition process. Results and assessment are presented in Section 3. Section 4 concludes this paper by detailing the future work of the research.

1.2 Related Work

Recently, a lot of efforts have been concentrated on handling personal collections of still images and video by integrating speech recognition with information technology [5]. Show&Tell by the State University of New York at Buffalo uses speech annotations to index and retrieve both personal and medical images, while FotoFile at HP Labs extends to more general multimedia objects [6,7]. AT&T Laboratories Cambridge works out a tool called Shoebox to apply audio annotations to home photo collections for text retrieval, which is to some extent similar to our work [8].

2 Underlying Methods

2.1 Integration of Image Retrieval and Speech Recognition with N-Best Lists

The mechanism of a typical speech recognition engine can be explained briefly as follows. The engine extracts acoustic features from the input speech signal, searches through a number of different lattices in the space using evidence from both acoustic and language models, then scores nodes and paths in the lattice and ranks a subset of possible word sequences. The one with the highest score is chosen as the final recognition output, while a list of N most likely paths is also generated as the engine's next N best guesses, which is usually known as the N-best list.

Currently, many systems that incorporate speech recognition for text retrieval only take the top1 results into consideration, which may lead to performance degradation due to uncertainties in the recognition process. A natural and practical solution is to make use of the additional information of probability features provided by the N-best lists. In our structured way of image description, since each speech annotation is short in length and each word is rich in information bearing, it is even more effective to exploit the N-best lists for individual 'nodes' than for the whole 'path'.

2.2 Our approach

The speech recognition engine used in this project is *Dragon NaturallySpeaking* (DNS) Preferred version 5.0 by Dragon System (now L&H, www.dragonsys.com). DNS is selected in comparison with other products for its following features:

1. Good recognition accuracy.
2. Flexibility in vocabulary editing, word training and enrollment customising.
3. Compliance with Microsoft SAPI4 based programming.

System training is completed in two steps. The first step is implemented by DNS whenever a new user is created. The user is required to read a selection of documents. The second one is done through a custom document designed to bias the language model in order to meet the syntactic requirement of our proposed annotation structure.

Here we adopt a structured syntax for the speech input. Structured speech has been used extensively in speech-activated devices like mobile phones and palms. The high recognition accuracy of these applications is assured by restricting the dictionary of commands and words. In our implementation, 4 fields are defined to represent the speech structure, i.e., ***People***, ***Place***, ***Date*** and ***Event***. Following each field is a list of elements or description of the field. To ensure the utterance of these field names can always be correctly recognized, those words are trained with the word-level training feature by DNS. The same can be done for the elements in the ***People*** and ***Date*** fields. The system can prompt the user to register names of family members and friends that appear frequently in the albums, using the same word-level training to enhance the recognition. For the ***Date*** elements, the day, month and year can also be trained in this manner. However, elements in ***Place*** and ***Event*** fields cannot be determined *a priori* since there is no specific form to describe the content. In this case, the embedded dictionary of DNS is expected to contain these elements. But we must be aware that there will be certain situations when the elements are not found in the dictionary. For example the name of addresses or venues of local flavor are most likely unavailable in

Original Speech Annotation:

PEOPLE David Tom *PLACE* Beijing *DATE* 18th April 1995 *EVENT* traveling around China

Typical Transcription (Misrecognised words are underlined):

people dated town place 18 date 18th April 1995 event traveling around China

N-best list for misrecognised names of people and places
(Top-1 hypotheses in boldface):

N-best rank

1	**dated**	**town**	**18**
2	stated	from	taking
⋮	⋮	Tom	⋮
⋮	David		Beijing
N	⋮	⋮	⋮

Fig. 1. A Simple Representation of Annotation Structure and N-best List

the dictionary. While one possible solution is to include names of local places in a secondary dictionary, it is not in the scope of present research to deal with.

Fig.1 illustrates a typical annotation structure of our system, its transcription produced by DNS and the correct names of people and places appearing in the N-best lists at different ranks. Because 4 field names are pre-trained with particular emphasis and expected to always occur, the whole annotation sentence can then be divided into different segments according to the structure, with one segment corresponding to one field. Hence for simplicity we can discuss a single field as representative of others.

Suppose that there are n_k names of people pre-registered in the dictionary and n_t transcriptions from the engine for n_t photos. Since one person cannot appear twice in one photo, term count $c_{t,k}$ for a keyword k in transcription t can be Boolean-valued like term presence $i_{t,k}$. Particularly, with a priori knowledge of the structure and the introduction of N-best list, $i_{t,k}$ can even be set to 1 as long as it appears in the N-best list of a recognized word w in t. Then we apply the standard TFIDF relevance

$$\hat{rel}(q,t) = (\sum_k b_{q,k} c_{t,k} idf_k) / l_t \ , \tag{1}$$

$b_{q,k}$ is term count of k in query q. The inverse document frequency idf_k is defined as

$$idf_k = \log_2 (\sum_t i_{t,k} / n_t) \ , \tag{2}$$

with t=1,...,n_t, k=1,...,n_k and q=1,...n_q.

Furthermore, we also find that the speech engine tends to make similar mistakes. For example, 'Ben' is often recognized as 'been' or 'then'. While sometime the correct word appears in the N-best list, sometime it doesn't. If we assign a value $R_{w,t,k}$ for the word w when a pre-registered word k is found in its N-best list at rank $r_{w,t,k}$

$$R_{w,t,k} = (N - r_{w,t,k} + 1) / N \ , \tag{3}$$

we may re-determine the presence of k instead of w when k is not in w's N-best list. A straightforward decision rule can simply be based on

$$P_{w,k} = \sum_t R_{w,t,k} \Big/ \sum_t i_{t,w} \ , \tag{4}$$

where $i_{w,t}$ is the word presence of w in t and $P_{w,k}$ can be regarded as a measure of relationship between w and k. More work needs to be done to further explore this feature and results will be addressed elsewhere.

3 Experiments

3.1 Experimental Settings

Our experimental collection database contains 200 photographs of a family taken in several countries spanning a few years. Speech description of each photograph using the structure shown in Fig.1 is recorded into a wave file in the lab environment. Each

Speech Annotation

PEOPLE David Mary *PLACE* Goodwood Park Hotel Singapore *DATE* 23rd December 1994 *EVENT* Christmas time

Transcription

people David marrying place Hollywood Park Hotel Singapore date 23rd December 1994 event Christmas time

Fig. 2. A Example of the ground truth description and corresponding transcription

annotation is both manually indexed to generate the ground truth and transcribed by the DNS engine. The N-best lists are generated to produce the metadata for the photographs. Fig.2 shows an example of the photographs with the ground truth description and the transcribed text from the Top-1 hypothesis result.

We then launched 16 queries selected randomly. The keywords in the queries are different combinations of names of people, place, date and event. On average, the number of keywords per query is 3.6 and each query has 17.5 relevant photos. The top 10 choices of possible words and phrases are searched in N-best lists, i.e., N=10. Fig.3 shows the precision and recall from Top-1 hypotheses and N-best lists, together with those from the manual transcriptions at 5, 10, 15, 20, 25, 30, and 35 images.

3.2 Evaluation and discussion

From Fig.3 we obtain an average of 50.3% and 72.1% improvement in precision and recall respectively, consistent with the findings at CMU [8]. Although the size of test collection is quite small, the use of speech annotations for retrieving home photos is very encouraging. The potential in further improving the overall system through the N-best list from the speech recognition can also be seen.

At present our segmentation strategy is based on the high recognition accuracy of field names. In order to have a relaxed annotation style and more robust segmentation, a method for direct audio search from the angle of signal processing is being studied.

The practicality of speech annotation technique will be evaluated next by using the actual speech recorded by the built-in microphone of a digital camera under different acoustic conditions. Speech pre-processing techniques will be applied to counter the problem of acoustic degradation. Further exploring the known structure of the speech annotations and constructing a better relevance evaluation for the free-form event descriptions are also under development to improve the average precision and recall.

Our goal is to extend this speech annotation system to multiple users, integrate it with content-based image retrieval and face recognition technique to provide a full suite of functionality to implement a practical photo indexing and retrieval system.

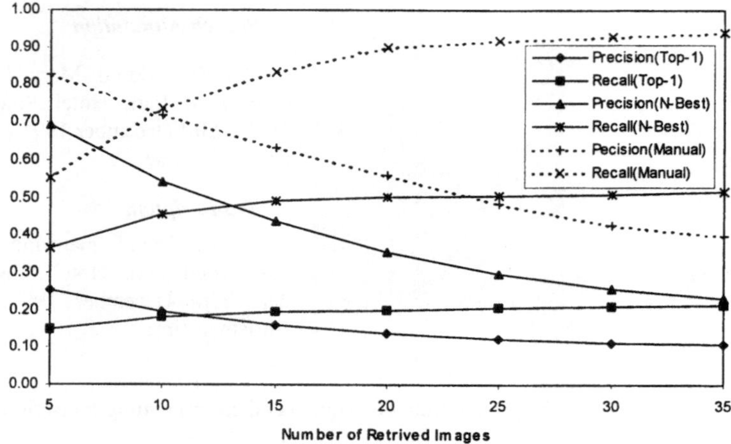

Fig. 3. Precision and Recall

4 Conclusions

We have introduced a method for photograph indexing using speech annotation. It has been shown that upon the use of structured speech together with a training strategy to bias the language model, improvements on the recognition and retrieval results are very encouraging, suggesting the speech annotation scheme can be finally applied to improve the performance of content- and semantic-based retrieval systems.

References

1. Flickner, M., Sawhney H., Niblack, W., Ashley J., Huang Q. and Dom B.: Query by Image and Video Content: The QBIC System. IEEE Computer, Vol. 28(1995) 23-32
2. Wu J.K.: Content-based Indexing of Multimedia Databases. IEEE Trans. on Knowledge and Data Engineering, Vol. 9(1997) 978-989
3. Tan T., Mulhem P.: Image Query System using Object Probes. Submitted to ICIP 2001, Thessaloniki, Greece, 2001
4. Satoh S., Nakamura Y., and Kanade T.: Name-It : Naming and Detection Faces in News Videos. IEEE Multimedia (1999) 22-35
5. Siegler M.A.: Integration of Continuous Speech Recognition and Information Retrieval for Mutually Optimal Performance," *Ph.D. Thesis*, Carnegie Mellon University, U.S.(1999)
6. Srihari R.K. et al: Multimedia Indexing and Retrieval of Voice-Annotated Consumer Photos. Proceedings of the Multimedia Indexing and Retrieval Workshop, SIGIR '99, University of California, Berkeley, U.S (1999) 1-16
7. Kuchinsky A. et al: FotoFile: A Consumer Multimedia Organization and Retrieval System. Proceedings of the CHI 99 Conference on Human Factors in Computing Systems, Pennsylvania, U.S. (1999) 496-503
8. Mills T.J., Pye D., Sinclair D. and Wood K.R.: Shoebox: A Digital Photo Management System. AT&T Labs Cambridge Technical Reports, UK (2000)

A Fast Anchor Shot Detection Algorithm on Compressed Video

WeiQiang Wang[1] Wen Gao[1,2]

[1](Institute of Computing Technology, Chinese Academy of Sciences, BeiJing, 100080)
[2](Department of Computer Science, Harbin Institute of Technology, 150001)
Email: {wqwang, wgao}@ict.ac.cn

Abstract. Detecting anchor shots accurately is very important for automatically parsing news video and extracting news items. The paper presents a fast anchor shot detection algorithm, based on background chrominance and skin tone models. The algorithm involves only simple computation, but robust. Moreover it operates in MPEG compression domain, which makes the detection speed very fast. The algorithm was evaluated on a big test set containing more than 480000 frames and news video from two different TV stations. More than 98.9% accuracy and 100% recall have been obtained. The experiment results also show the system has an average detection speed of 77.55 f/s. The statistics indicates the algorithm is fast and effective.

1. Introduction

To index, browse and retrieve increasing audio-visual information available, parsing tools are required to automatically extract structure and content features of the audio-visual data. Then description of content is generated. Owing to the-state-of-arts of computer vision and audio signal analysis techniques, parsing general video automatically has not yet been well realised to date. In almost all research on parsing news video, the technique of detecting anchor shots is studied as an integral topic. Identification of anchor shots is crucial for extracting news items, since the items are often introduced and/or concluded by anchor shots. Merlino [1] detects some text tags in a broadcast's closed-caption transcript, such as '>>' (speaker change), "I'm" <Anchor Name>, et. al., as a textual cue. Combining with a priori model about news structure, anchor shots are located. Zhang et.al. [2] exploit image analysis techniques to identify anchor shots. For each shot generated by the shot segmentation module, the parser exploits histogram and pair-wise pixel metrics to find candidates of anchor shots, and further verifies them based on region models. Qi et.al. [3] integrate audio and visual cues to detect anchorperson shots. After audio segments characterized by different speakers and shots represented by key frames are clustered, anchorperson candidates are selected based on the following heuristics, that the proportion of the anchorperson speech/image is higher and the distribution is more disperse. Then integration of audio and visual channels is imposed to identify the true ones.

This paper presents a fast anchor shot detection algorithm, which is based on background chrominance and skin tone models. Compared with the forementioned algorithms, the whole detection process can run online, and shot segmentation is not required. The speed is very fast since the algorithm operates in compression domain.

The rest of the paper is organized as follows. In section 2, our algorithm is presented in detail. Section 3 gives the results of evaluation experiments, over CCTV and JXTV news. Section 4 concludes the paper.

2. Anchor Shot Detection Algorithm

In news video produced by different broadcast corporations, an anchorperson frame always has the similar structure, made up of anchorperson and background, as in Fig. 1. Anchorpersons may differ, or are in different dresses on different days, but some region B in the background usually keeps unchanged for a long period and has distinct content. We assume there exists a sub-region T, which has consistent color texture, in the region B. We call it a feature region. Then the region T's color model can be constructed through statistics approaches, and be exploited to locate start frame and end frame positions of anchor shots in news video.

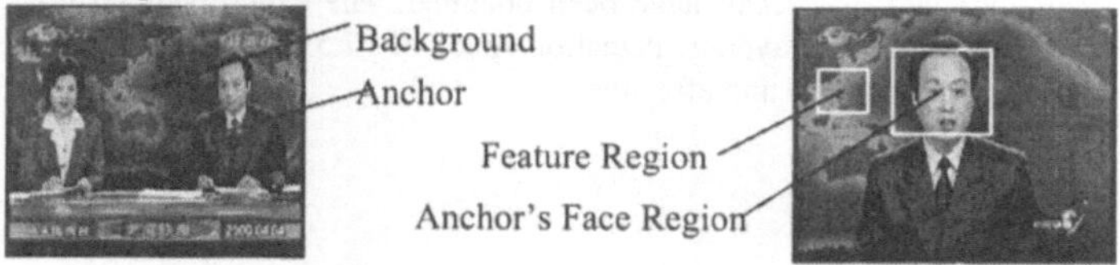

Fig. 1. Typical anchor shots in CCTV news

2.1 Model Construction

Before detection, the system needs to construct models for all types of anchor shots in advance. It can be implemented through a semi-automatic tool. Each model is formalized as a 3_tuple G=$<L,D,F>$, where L is the feature region, D is dynamic distribution of DC in L, and F is an anchorperson's face region. D is formalized as a 6_tuple $< rv^{cb}$, $ravg^{cb}$, rsd^{cb}, rv^{cr}, $ravg^{cr}$, $rsd^{cr} >$, where rv^{cb} is the distribution interval of DC values in L for the component Cb, $ravg^{cb}$, rsd^{cb} are the distribution intervals of average and standard variance of all the DC values in L. rv^{cr}, $ravg^{cr}$ and rsd^{cr} have the consistent meanings, for the component Cr. The frames in anchor shots can be labeled manually through a learning tool. Then the regions L and F are chosen visually. Let f_i $(i=1,2,\ldots M)$ represent the frames in the training set, D_{ij} $(j=1,2,\ldots N)$ represent DC values in the region L, and rv^{cb} = $[v_s^{cb}, v_e^{cb}]$, then

$$v_s^{cb} = \min_i \{\min_j D_{ij}\} - \tau_v^{cb}, \qquad v_e^{cb} = \max_i \{\max_j D_{ij}\} + \tau_v^{cb} \tag{1}$$

Define $ravg^{cb}$ =$[avg_s^{cb}, avg_e^{cb}]$ and rsd^{cb}= $[sd_s^{cb}, sd_e^{cb}]$, then

$$E_i = \frac{1}{N}\sum_{j=1}^{N} D_{ij} \tag{2}$$

$$avg_s^{cb} = \min_i\{E_i\} - \tau_{avg}^{cb}, \quad avg_e^{cb} = \max_i\{E_i\} + \tau_{avg}^{cb} \tag{3}$$

$$V_i = \sqrt{\frac{1}{|N|}\sum_{j=1}^{N}(D_{ij}-E_i)^2}, \quad sd_s^{cb} = \min_i\{V_i\} - \tau_{sd}^{cb}, \quad sd_e^{cb} = \max_i\{V_i\} + \tau_{sd}^{cb} \tag{4}$$

Where τ_v^{cb}, τ_{avg}^{cb} and τ_{sd}^{cb} are different relaxation factors. Similarly, for the component Cr, the intervals rv^{cr}, $ravg^{cr}$ and rsd^{cr} can be calculated out based on the data in the training set. Experiment can help to select an appropriate model.

2.2 Algorithm Description

The algorithm in [4] can extract a DC image for each frame in MPEG compressed video with minimal decoding. A DC in each block is equal to the average of the pixels in that block. Through interactively choosing a feature region T (Fig.1 (b)), we can construct the region T 's color model through statistics. Since anchor shots generally last more than three seconds, the algorithm exploits two different resolution granularities to increase the detection speed. First, all I frames in display order are checked. Once frames in an anchor shot are found, the start and end frame positions of the anchor shot are refined in the resolution of frames. The detailed description of the detection algorithm is given as follows.

① Initialization. Open a video stream file fp , obtain the sequence number $CurFrmNum$ of the first I frame, and the GOP length gl of the MPEG stream.

② For chrominance components Cb and Cr, extract DC images $X_{cb} = \{x_{ij}^{cb}\}$ and $X_{cr} = \{x_{ij}^{cr}\}$ from the frame with the sequence number $CurFrmNum$.

③ Suppose T represents the feature region, b_{ij} is the corresponding region for the element whose index is (i, j) in DC image X_{cb} and X_{cr} . Let $C_{cb}=\{c_{ij}^{cb} \mid c_{ij}^{cb}=x_{ij}^{cb}, b_{ij}\in T\}$, $C_{cr}=\{c_{ij}^{cr} \mid c_{ij}^{cr}=x_{ij}^{cr}, b_{ij}\in T\}$. Calculate a feature vector $Q=(r_s^{cb}, r_e^{cb}, avg^{cb}, sd^{cb}, r_s^{cr}, r_e^{cr}, avg^{cr}, sd^{cr})$, where $r_s^{cb} = \min_{d\in C_{cb}} d$, $r_e^{cb} = \max_{d\in C_{cb}} d$, $r_s^{cr} = \min_{d\in C_{cr}} d$, $r_e^{cr} = \max_{d\in C_{cr}} d$, $avg^{cb} = \frac{1}{|C_{cb}|}\sum_{d\in C_{cb}} d$, $avg^{cr} = \frac{1}{|C_{cr}|}\sum_{d\in C_{cr}} d$, $sd^{cb} = \sqrt{\frac{1}{|C_{cb}|}\sum_{d\in C_{cb}}(d-avg^{cb})^2}$, $sd^{cr} = \sqrt{\frac{1}{|C_{cr}|}\sum_{d\in C_{cr}}(d-avg^{cr})^2}$, where $|C|$ represents cardinal number of a set C .

④ If $[r_s^{cb}, r_e^{cb}] \subseteq [v_s^{cb}, v_e^{cb}]$, $avg^{cb} \in [avg_s^{cb}, avg_e^{cb}]$, $sd^{cb} \in [sd_s^{cb}, sd_e^{cb}]$, $[r_s^{cr}, r_e^{cr}] \subseteq [v_s^{cr}, v_e^{cr}]$, $avg^{cr} \in [avg_s^{cr}, avg_e^{cr}]$, $sd^{cr} \in [sd_s^{cr}, sd_e^{cr}]$ all hold, then the frame $CurFrmNum$ is an anchorperson frame, where $[v_s^{cb}, v_e^{cb}]$, $[avg_s^{cb}, avg_e^{cb}]$, $[sd_s^{cb}, sd_e^{cb}]$, $[v_s^{cr}, v_e^{cr}]$,

$[avg_s^{cr}, avg_e^{cr}]$, $[sd_s^{cr}, sd_e^{cr}]$ are the dynamic ranges of different components in the feature vector F, which are obtained through the model construction process aforementioned. Besides the features in Q, relation features can also be found and utilized, to improve the detection accuracy. For example, we observed there is such relation feature $avg^{cb} \geq avg^{cr}$ in CCTV news.

⑤ To eliminate noises, the system declares an appearance event of anchor shots, if and only if it consistently detects existence of anchorperson frames in W_s consecutive I frames. Similarly, Only when the system cannot detect existence of anchorperson frames in W_e consecutive I frames, a disappearance event will be declared. W_s and W_e are system parameters. Define *SAnchorFrmNum* and *EAnchorFrmNum* as the start and end frame of the anchor shot in the resolution of GOP.

⑥ Refine the start and end position of the anchor shot in the resolution of frames, by the similar computation described by step ③ and ④, between the frames $SAnchorFrmNum - gl$ and $SAnchorFrmNum$, as well as between $EAnchorFrmNum$ and $EAnchorFrmNum + gl$.

⑦ $CurFrmNum = CurFrmNum + gl$. If the end of the stream is not reached, then go to ②; else the stream file fp is closed, and the whole detection process ends.

Through above computation, some false anchor shots may appear in the resultant clip set. To filter them out, a face skin tone model is exploited to refine the results. Though skin tone differs among different persons, different peoples, it distributes in a specific region on the plane Cb-Cr. The fact has been applied by many systems [5-7]. Our system exploits it in a more simple form to help filter the false claims. As in Fig.1 (b), define F a anchorperson face region, and dc_{mn}^{Cb}, dc_{mn}^{Cr} are the DC values of the blocks in the region F, respectively for Cb and Cr, where m, n are position index of the blocks in the region F. We define a function to examine skin tone.

$$Skin(m,n) = \begin{cases} 1 & \text{if } dc_{mn}^{Cb} \in [s\min Cb, s\max Cb] \\ & \text{and } dc_{mn}^{Cr} \in [s\min Cr, s\max Cr] \\ 0 & \text{else} \end{cases} \tag{5}$$

Where $[s\min Cb, s\max Cb]$, $[s\min Cr, s\max Cr]$ are the distribution ranges of face skin tone in the plane Cb-Cr, constructed by us through sampling 80 different faces. If

$$\sum_{block\,(m,n) \in regionF} Skin(m,n) \Big/ BlockNum > \mu \tag{6}$$

then the region F contains a face and the clip is declared as an anchor shot clip, where $BlockNum$ is the number of blocks in F and μ is a predefined threshold.

3. Evaluation Experiment

We random choose 11 days' CCTV news from video database as test data to evaluate the algorithm. Three of them are used to construct the background model and the face skin tone model. The remaining data forms a test data set. Before testing, we label manually all the anchor shots as a standard reference. Tab. 1 tabulates the experiment results, when only background chrominance model is used in identifying anchor shots. The detection accuracy is derived, i.e., $P = 1 - \frac{E}{D} = 1 - \frac{8}{96} = 91.7\%$ and the recall $R = 1 - \frac{U}{S} = 1 - \frac{0}{88} = 100\%$. Eight false claims occur in the experiment result. Our observation implies their blue tone in the feature region is very similar with that of the anchor shots, which confuses the system.

Table 1. the Experiment Results only Using Background Model ($W_s = W_e = 3$)

Video	Frames	Anchor shots (S)	Output (D)	Error (E)	Missed (U)
News0	44965	9	9	0	0
News1	44770	11	15	4	0
News2	45106	15	17	2	0
News3	44913	13	15	2	0
News4	36339	13	13	0	0
News5	59610	12	12	0	0
News6	44447	10	10	0	0
News7	49775	5	5	0	0
Total	369925	88	96	8	0

For the obtained results, the face skin tone model is further applied to refine them. Keeping the recall 100%, the system filters out seven false claims and the accuracy increases to 98.9%, with μ equal to 0.17. The statistics indicates the algorithm is very effective. Additional experiment is done to measure detection time to reflect the fastness of the algorithm. The results are tabulated in Tab. 2. Though the decoding engine embedded in the system has only the performance of 8 f/s for the MPEG-2 streams in the test set, Tab. 2 indicates the algorithm has a average detection speed of 77.55 f/s, faster than real time. It results from several factors. Firstly, the algorithm completely operates in compression domain, involving very simple computation. Secondly, two different resolutions is applied and a large number of P, B frames are skipped in the state of coarse resolution.

Table 2. detection time for the programs in the test set

News ID	0	1	2	3	4	5	6	7
Time(m:s)	9: 40	8: 44	9: 20	9: 39	8: 28	12: 36	9: 22	11: 41

Table 3. the experiment results for JiangXi Satellite TV news

Video	Frames	Anchor shots(S)	Output (D)	Error (E)	Missed (U)
JXTV0210	29600	9	9	0	0
JXTV0212	29484	9	9	0	0
JXTV0213	25990	8	8	0	0
JXTV0214	29500	8	8	0	0
Total	114574	34	34	0	0

To evaluate the validity and robustness of the algorithm further, 4 days of JiangXi

Satellite TV news are chosen as another group of test data, to make sure the algorithm can also be applied to other TV stations' news. The corresponding experiment results are tabulated in Tab. 3. The accuracy and the recall are calculated out as follows. $R = 1 - \frac{U}{S} = 1 - \frac{0}{34} = 100\,\%$, $P = 1 - \frac{E}{D} = 1 - \frac{0}{34} = 100\,\%$. The very high accuracy and recall demonstrate the algorithm can be applied to news programs of different TV stations. High accuracy and recall are the prominent advantage of the algorithm.

4. Conclusion

The paper presents a fast anchor shot detection algorithm, based on the background feature region's color model and face skin tone models. We evaluate it on a large data set of two TV stations 's news. The experiment results indicate it has an ideal performance, and achieve the 100% recall and more than 98.9% accuracy, as well as average detection speed of 77.55 f/s. Therefore it is a fast and effective algorithm and can be applied to not only CCTV news, but also other TV news, if the anchorperson frames in news video satisfy the assumptions mentioned in section 2. What need to be done is to choose the background feature region and construct its color model again, as well as specify the anchorperson face region. These can be finished semi-automatically through an interactive tool.

Acknowledgment

This work has been supported by National Science Foundation of China (contract number 69789301), National Hi-Tech Development Programme of China (contract number 863-306-ZD03-01-2), and 100 Outstanding Scientist foundation of Chinese Academy of Sciences.

References

[1] A. Merlino, D. Morey and M.Maybury, "Broadcast News Navigation Using Story Segmentation," Proc. ACM Multimedia 97, Seattle ,USA, Nov. 1997, pp 381-391.

[2] H. J. Zhang, S.Y. Tan, S. W. Smoliar and Y. Gong, "Automatic Parsing and Indexing of News Video", Multimedia Systems, 2: 256-266, 1995

[3] W. Qi, L. Gu, H. Jiang, X.R. Chen and H.J. Zhang, " Integrating Visual, Audio and Text Analysis for News Video", IEEE ICIP-2000, Vancouver, Canada, Sept., 2000.

[4] B.L. Yeo and B. Liu, "Rapid Scene Analysis on Compressed Videos", in IEEE Transactions on Circuits and Systems for Video Technology, Vol. 5, No. 6, December 1995 (Transactions Best Paper Award). pp. 533-544.

[5] H. Wang and S.-F. Chang, "A Highly Efficient System for Automatic Face Region Detection in MPEG Video," IEEE Transactions on Circuits and Systems for Video Technology, Special Issue on Multimedia Technology, Systems, and Applications, Vol. 7, No. 4, August 1997

[6] K. Sobottka, I. Pitas, "A Novel Method for Automatic Face Segmentation, Facial Feature Extraction and Tracking", Signal Processing: Image Communication, vol.12, No.3, pp263-281, June, 1998

[7] H.M. Zhang, D.B. Zhao, W. Gao and X.L. Chen, "Combining Skin Color Modal and Neural Network for Rotation Invariant Face Detection", Int. Conf . Multimodal Interface 2000, Beijing, 2000.

Content-Based News Video Retrieval with Closed Captions and Time Alignment

Young-tae Kim, Jae-Gon Kim, Hyun Sung Chang,
Kyeongok Kang, and Jinwoong Kim

Broadcasting Media Technology Department
Electronics and Telecommunications Research Institute
161 Gajeong-Dong, Yuseong-Gu, Daejeon, 305-350, Korea
{kytae, jgkim, chs, kokang, jwkim}@etri.re.kr

Abstract. In this paper, we propose a new method for searching and browsing news videos, based on multi-modal approach. In the proposed scheme, we use closed caption (CC) data to index the contents of TV news articles effectively. To achieve time alignment between the CC texts and video data, which is necessary for multi-modal search and visualization, supervised speech recognition technique is employed. In our implementations, we provide two different mechanisms for news video browsing. One is to use a textual query based search engine, and the other is to use topic based browser which acts as an assistant tool for finding the desired news articles. Compared to other systems mainly dependent on visual features, the proposed scheme could retrieve more semantically relevant articles quite well.

1 Introduction

As more and more audiovisual information becomes available, the main concern has been moved from compression for efficient storage and transmission to efficient access on the basis of content [1], [2].

In this aspect, we propose a method that can retrieve the desired news articles among large amounts of news videos as fast as possible. For the past few years, a number of methods have been proposed for content-based retrieval of news video [3]-[6]. In [3], Bertini *et al.* exploited a shot based descriptor which comprises the words obtained from caption OCR and speech recognition in anchorperson's shots to retrieve news videos. Although it presents semantic information, its drawback is that each shot detected by visual features might not be a desirable unit for news video browsing. Q. Huang *et al.* [4], [5] proposed an automated method to generate news content hierarchy. In this method, several levels of abstraction can be established for an interesting news program to satisfy diverse requirements from many users.

In this paper, we propose a new method for news video indexing based on multi-modal feature analysis. To retrieve news video in semantically meaningful unit, it should be firstly structurized. In general, video structuring methods using visual features such as shot boundary detection might be undesirable, because they do not completely present semantic information in each unit. Therefore, we employ sub-natural language processing (sub-NLP) technique to partition a CC document into semantically meaningful units. If the CC document has the information about synchronization to the video, it is possible to structurize the video directly from the CC partitioning results. The generation of this synchronization information is one of the significant contributions made in our proposal. Also, we utilize the CC text for cross modal retrieval, not just for video structurization.

The merits of the proposed approach are: 1) it can retrieve the semantically relevant news videos because it is based on the CC analysis, 2) it operates very reliably because it is mainly dependent on sub-NLP of a CC document that is more stable than visual feature processing in performance.

The rest of this paper is organized as follows. We will overview the proposed system in Sect. 2, and then present the process of the database construction with multimodal features in Sect. 3. In the next section, an explanation will be made on how the relevant news materials can be retrieved. In Sect. 5, the feasibility of the proposed system will be verified through implementations and experiments. Finally, conclusions are made in Sect. 6.

2 System Architecture

The overall procedure of our proposal for a multi-modal database construction and retrieval of news video is shown in Fig. 1. Multi-modal database means that each record item contains audio, video, text data and also the information about the synchronization among them.

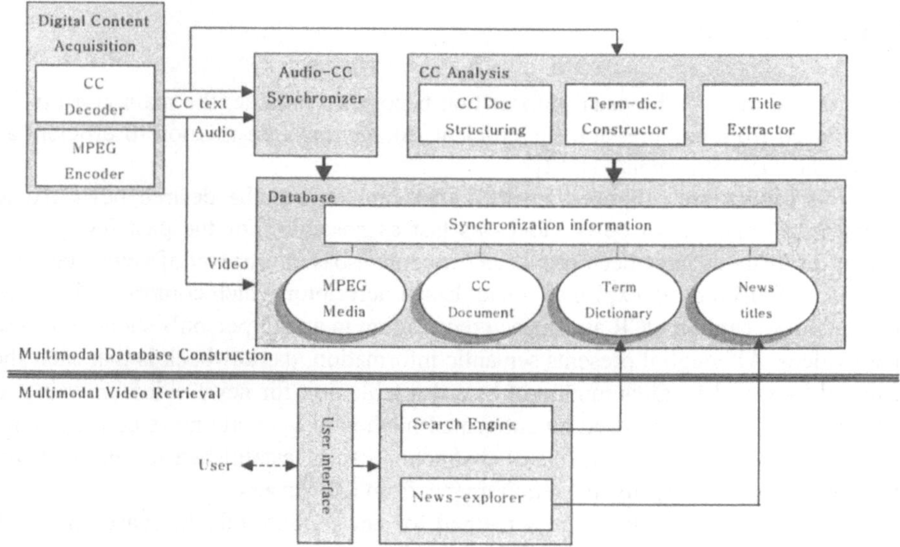

Fig. 1. The overall process of database construction and retrieval for news videos

Multi-modal retrieval means that the multi-modal components in the searched items are retrieved and presented in synchronized ways.

To construct a database with multi-modal features, in first, we should have the news videos in digital formats. In our implementation, the digital content acquisition module that comprises a commercial MPEG encoder and a developed CC decoder converts the incoming NTSC TV signal into the MPEG-1 systems streams and ASCII files, for audiovisual data and CC document, respectively [8].

Generally, there is no time code in CC document itself. Therefore, it is necessary to align between the words in CC document and those in the audio tracks of the video for synchronized presentation. CC analysis module comprises three sub-modules of CC document structuring, term-dictionary constructor, and title-extractor. CC document structuring is to partition a CC document into semantically meaningful units. At this stage, keywords are also extracted from the CC document using noun-extractor for the later use as elements constructing term-dictionary. The term-dictionary may be searched for the text queried by user. In title extractor, we select some keywords that well represent the article and combine them to make the title of article systematically. It may be used by news-explorer in the retrieval process. The detailed process will be explained in Sect. 3.

3 Multi-modal Feature Analysis

3.1 Audio-CC Synchronization

The synchronization between CC text and video is achieved by supervised speech recognition that works on the audio track in the video signal with a roughly time-aligned CC text stream. From an MPEG systems stream, we extract an audio stream by demultiplexing, and then uncompress the MPEG audio file as PCM wave file.

As feature parameters for speech recognition 12-th order MFCC (Mel-Frequency Cepstral Coefficient) and signal energy were used every 10 millisecond. A context dependent semi-continuous HMM (Hidden Markov Model) is used for each phoneme-liked unit HMM [9].

3.2 CC Document Structuring

Since each CC document contains the whole daily news reports, the first thing to do is to partition it by semantically meaningful unit. It may be used as a retrieval unit in the retrieval process. A CC document consists of many articles on political, economic, social and cultural affairs, etc. Each article can be further decomposed into several speakers' dialogues such as anchor, reporter, and interviewee. We partition a CC document into several articles and again each article into several clips on the basis of speaker. In the process of CC production, speaker tags are also inserted to the CC document, which make it very straightforward to separate between clips. Each article boundary can be detected by exploiting typical patterns of speaker transition and sub-NLP. The speaker transition patterns can be modeled by finite state automata [8]. In sub-NLP, some specific words that lead to next article are analyzed. Article boundaries may be adjusted by means of shot boundary detection.

3.3 Indexing

In general, indexing means extraction of the keywords and some additional information of document unit. In the indexing process, we use a noun extractor. It finds a matched word by consulting built-in dictionaries such as biographical, geographical dictionary, and auxiliary word's dictionary. To search those keywords efficiently in the retrieval process, we make a term-dictionary that consists of the extracted keywords and added information. In the dictionary, keywords are arranged in alphabetical order. Detailed specification of added information is represented in Fig. 2.

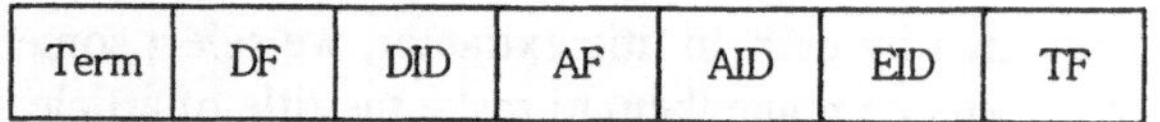

Term	DF	DID	AF	AID	EID	TF

Fig. 2. The composition of term's added information

DF (Document Frequency) means the number of the documents containing the term. DID is a numeric identifier of the document containing the term. DIDs are needed as many as DF. Similarly, AF (Article Frequency) and AID denote the occurrence frequency of the articles containing the term and a numeric identifier of the article, respectively. Likewise, AIDs are needed as many as the AF value. EID (Element ID) represents information on the speaker such as anchor, reporter, and interviewee.

EID may be used to limit the search range of term-dictionary in the process of retrieval. TF (Term Frequency) is a measure of how many times the term occurred in an article. So term's frequency is increased, as the amount of added information is increased. It is used as a weighting factor for ranking the searched articles.

3.4 Article Title Extraction

Several approaches are possible to extract an article title. In this paper, we combine some keywords that are extracted in the process of indexing to make article titles. In doing so, we consider keyword's weight that is the degree of article characterization. The weight $w(a_i)$ of a keyword i in an article a is calculated by the parameters of TF and inverse DF (IDF) as shown in (1).

$$w(a_i) = \log(tf + 1.0) \cdot \log(N/n)\,, \tag{1}$$

where

tf term frequency of the keyword i within the article a;
N the total article number in the entire database;
n the number of articles containing the keyword i.

Compared to manual extraction, sometimes it does not represent well the article's content but is very simple, reasonable approach.

4 Multi-modal News Retrieval

To retrieve news articles to be viewed, we approach in two ways. The first one is to search the term-dictionary for keyword queried by users, and the other is to utilize a topic-based browser called news-explorer.

4.1 Multi-modal News Retrieval by Text Query

The kernel of this method is a text search engine. When a user submits a keyword to find some relevant news articles, it searches the term-dictionary for that keyword. As a result, it retrieves the relevant news articles in a ranked order. In general, the article of the highest rank is shown on top row of the retrieval result panel. Among the list of retrieved news articles, a user can select one so that its multi-modal components, CC texts and the associated video clips, may be displayed together synchronously.

4.2 Multi-modal News Retrieval by News-Explorer

We also provide a news-explorer as another way of news video searching. It displays the titles of news articles in the database in the form of a table of contents. So hierarchical directory structure in a computer acts a guide to find a file, as the news-explorer acts as a guide to find a specific news article to be viewed. In other words, the news-explorer is designed to have hierarchical structure of year-month-day-event titles. View depth and range displayed on the user interface are controllable by users.

5 Implementation

We implemented the proposed scheme as an application with sever-client structure as

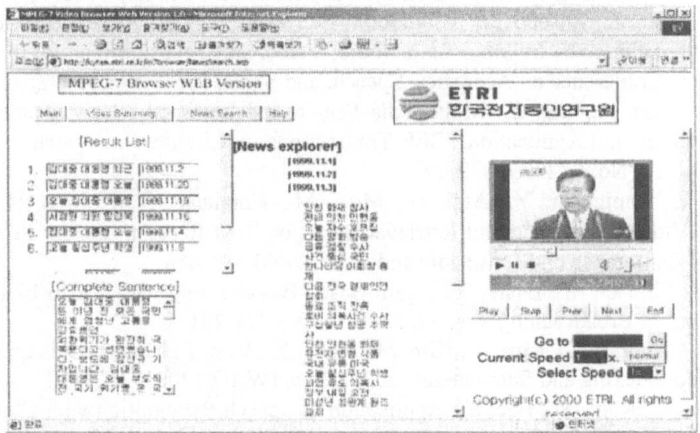

Fig. 3. The implementation of proposed method.

shown in Fig. 3. The data used in the experiments consist of seven daily news broadcasts of KBS (Korean Broadcasting System) on the air during November 1999. The term-dictionary has about six thousand keywords. A user can submit a textual query to search the desired news clips. As a result a list of searched articles' titles and date are shown to the user, as illustrated in Fig. 3. Also, we can find the article to be viewed by means of news-explorer. By selecting an article in the search list or news-explorer, the very news clips are displayed synchronized with the corresponding CC texts.

6 Conclusions

In this paper, we proposed a new method for searching TV news articles based on multi-modal approach. We utilized CC text data, which are the valuable sources of semantic information, to index the contents of TV news articles effectively. For multi-modal search and visualization, time alignment between CC text and video data was performed using a supervised speech recognition technique. Compared to other systems mainly dependent on visual features, the proposed method could retrieve well more semantically relevant articles.

Acknowledgement

This work was supported by the Ministry of Information and Communication (MIC) of Korean government.

References

1. MPEG Requirements Group: Introduction to MPEG-7. ISO/IEC JTC1/SC29/WG11 N3751 (2000)
2. Kim, J.-G., Chang, H. S., Kim, M., Kim, J., Kim, H.-M.: Summary Description Schemes for Efficient Video Navigation and Browsing. In: Proc. IS&T/SPIE Visual Communications and Image Processing (2000) 1397-1408
3. Bertini, M., Bimbo, A. D., Pala, P.: Content Based Annotation and Retrieval of News Videos. In: Proc. IEEE International Conference on Multimedia and Expo (2000) 483-486
4. Huang, Q., Liu, Z., Rosenberg, A., Gibbon, D., Shahraray, B.: Automated Generation of News Content Hierarchy by Integrating Audio, Video, and Text Information. In: Proc. IEEE International Conference on Acoustics, Speech, and Signal Processing (1999) 3025-3028
5. Huang, Q., Puri, A., Liu, Z.: Multimedia Search and Retrieval : New Concepts, System Implementation, and Application. IEEE Transactions on Circuits and Systems Video Technology, Vol. 10, No. 5 (2000) 679-692
6. Kuwano, H., Taniguchi, Y., Arai, H., Mori, M., Kurakake, S., Kojima, H.: Telop-on-Demand : Video Structuring and Retrieval Based on Text Recognition. In: Proc. IEEE International Conference on Multimedia and Expo(2000) 483-486
7. Kim, Y.-B., Shibata, M., Ehara, T.: Agent-Based Broadcasting with Video Indexing. IEEE Transactions on Broadcasting, Vol. 42, No. 3 (1996) 215-221
8. Kim, J.-G., Chang, H. S., Kim, Y., Kim, M., Kang, K., Kim, J.: Multimodal Approach to the News Video Indexing and Summarization. In: Proc. IWAIT (2001) 187-192
9. Son, J., Kim, J., Kang, K., Bae, K.: Application of Speech Recognition with Closed Caption for Content-Based Video Segmentation. In: Proc. IEEE Digital Signal Processing Workshop (2000)

Query Similar Music by Correlation Degree

Feng Yahzong, Zhuang Yueting, Pan Yunhe

Institute of Artificial Intelligence

Zhejiang University, Hangzhou 310027, P. R. China

Abstract. We present in this paper a novel system for query by humming, our method differs from other ones in the followings: Firstly, we use recurrent neural network as the index of music database. Secondly, we present correlation degree to evaluate the music matching precision. We now hold a database of 201 pieces of music with various genres. The result of our experiment reports that the successful rate is 63% with top one matching and 87% with top three matching. Future work will be on melody extraction technique from popular formats of music and on-line music retrieval.

1. Introduction

Booming digital audio information in digital library and on the internet demand efficient retrieval tools. Query music by humming is a content-based music retrieval approach. Imaging that you whistle to your PC the tone of a piece of music that you can not recall its title, its author or even its lyrics, your PC will play that music for you automatically! We will be able to find more and more applications for query by humming. For example, it helps CD vendor to find the CD that customer wants to buy, musician can find out if his work is of originality by humming the tune of his composition, copyright agency can determine whether an opus is really new by humming to its music database.

2. Related Work

We will review the related research about music retrieval in the following. With regard to the input of music retrieval system, some format, such as sound file, MIDI file, string representing pitch direction and hummed tune are used as queries to retrieval music from music database [3][6][7][11][12]. Most music databases are in MIDI format only because melody information can be extracted exactly and easily form music in this format. Although, MPEG-7 and XML query language are used to describe musical resources, we will not discuss them here. As for music matching, it is usually converted to string matching procedure [3][11][12] for the reason that music is a sequence of notes, which can be converted to a string of letters when pitch contour [3] instead of exact pitch is used to construct the string. Some practical music retrieval systems are available now, such as [3][7][9][10][11]. Our work differs from other ones in two facets. Firstly, we use recurrent neural network as the index of music database, after extracting melody from MIDI format music, we train a respective recurrent neural network to remember this piece of music, the weight matrices of the network are used as the indices of music database. Secondly, we present correlation degree to evaluate the music similarity matching.

3. System Sketch

Our system is, to some extent, the same as other system [3][7] in its components, users hum the tune of music via microphone to the system, the pitch tracking component extracts pitch to generate pitch contour, the system holds a MIDI music database, or the music database sits on server, the string matching component executes matching of input with stored music to generate scored music list, the most similar music in database with hummed tune is listed on the top. Fig. 1 describes our system. You will find some unique components in it. MIDI format music usually arranges its melody in channel 1 of all its 16 channels [8], so we can extract the melody manually or automatically, we change the melody into a string of three letters [-1, 0, 1], this string is used as the input of a recurrent neural network, in our approach we call the networks that express the strings *Music Nets*. Our approach for making index on music database is to train the neural network, after the training terminate, the convergent weights are used as indices of the corresponding piece of music. Obviously, the weight space is much smaller than music data space. *String Matching* component in our system calculates the output of recurrent neural network and evaluate the similarity of the output string with the stored strings. The time cost is $O(n)$, n is the number of piece of music in database. In our system, we do not concern fast matching ability of the system, which is necessary in some system because of our unique indexing and matching method. The detailed approach will be explained in the following sections.

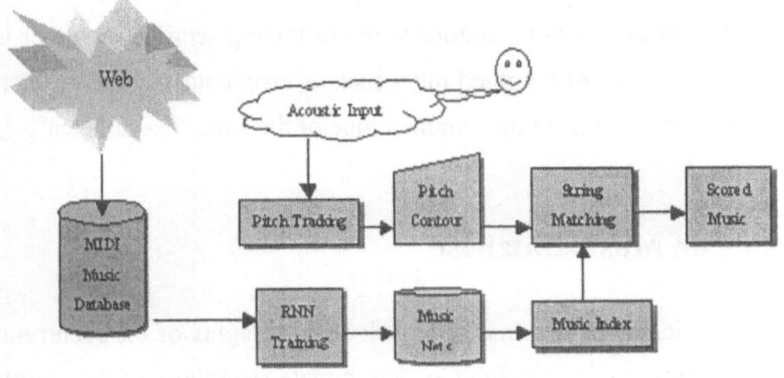

Fig. 1. System Sketch

4. Notes Segmentation from Acoustic Input

Our goal is to build an interactive music retrieval system, which demands real time response to the inputs, we do not adopt commercial software to convert user's humming into MIDI format data, instead, we segment notes from acoustic input directly. Users hum via microphone to the computer, the acoustic inputs are processed to estimate the pitch period by Rabiner's technique [4]. We adopt this technique for the reason that it is well documented and studied.

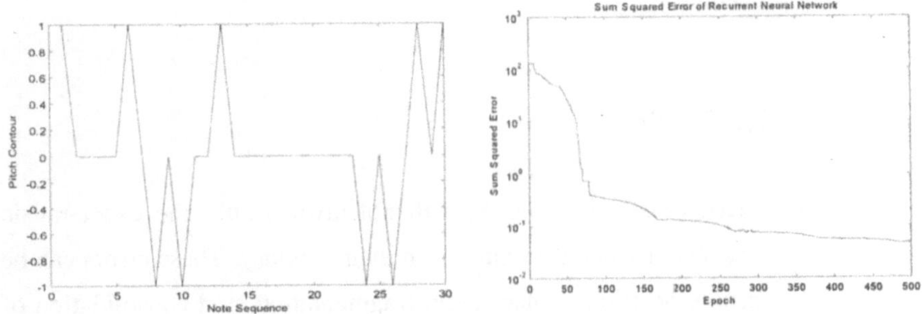

Fig. 2. Pitch Contour(Casablanca) **Fig. 3.** SSE of The Recurrent Neural Network

Pitch contour is a string of three letters [-1, 0, 1]. It records the relative relationship between two adjacent notes in a piece of music instead of the exact frequency of the note, 1, 0, -1 stand for that note is higher than, the same as, or lower than the previous one respectively [3]. Pitch contour is adopted for two reasons: one is that it is in the same format as the note contour which is derived from a piece of music in the database, we will discuss the note contour in the following section, the other is that it helps eliminate some error of hummed tune, such as erroneous in tone or tempo. Fig. 2 is a pitch contour derived from the hummed tune of the song "Casablanca".

5. Indexing on Music Database

The indices of music database in our approach is the weights of the recurrent neural networks, the dimension of the weights is determinate regardless of the length of the music in database. We get note contour directly from MIDI format music in music database. We change the melody into a three letters string just as the one in pitch contour. Obviously, we do not know in advance that which part of a piece of music users will hum, so the system must be robust enough for users to hum any part of the music. Recurrent neural network is of strong ability in time series prediction [2], if a neural network remembers a note contour, it will be able to recall any part of the note contour. There is four layers in this structure: input layer, output layer, hidden layer and context layer, the weights between different layers stores information the network remembers. The neural network is trained by means of BP algorithm with adjustable learning rate and momentum item, the note contour is fed into the neural network one letter at a time, and the desired output is the next letter in it. Fig.3 describes the neural network training procedure.

6. Similarity Evaluation

It is obvious that users, mostly lay people, will not always hum the exact music melody, errors will also occur when they sing from their memory. These errors can be categorized into insertion, deletion, replacement, fragmentation, and consolidation of notes. Errors in a hummed tune may also include variations in tone and tempo [7]. Even if people is apt to these errors, they seem to be able to hum some part of a piece of music exactly, we present correlation degree [1] to evaluate the similarity of two strings, the pitch contour and the note contour:

Let X be correlation factor set, $x_0 \in X$ be reference sequence, $x_i \in X$ be related sequence, $x_0(k), x_i(k)$ are the value at k point of x_0, x_i respectively. If $\gamma(x_0(k), x_i(k))$ is a real number, then define

$$\gamma(x_0, x_i) = \frac{1}{n}\sum_{k=1}^{n}\gamma(x_0(k), x_i(k)) \tag{1}$$

If the following four axioms are satisfied:

- Regularity.

$$\forall k, 0 < \gamma(x_0, x_i) \le 1, \ \gamma(x_0, x_i) = 1 \Leftrightarrow x_0 = x_i, \gamma(x_0, x_i) = 0 \Leftrightarrow x_0, x_i \in \Phi . \tag{2}$$

- Even symmetry.

$$\text{If } x, y \in X \text{, then } \gamma(x, y) = \gamma(y, x) \Leftrightarrow X = \{x, y\} . \tag{3}$$

- Integrality.

$$x_j, x_i \in X \doteq \{x_\delta \mid \delta = 0, 1, \ldots, n\}, n \ge 2, \gamma(x_j, x_i) \overset{often}{\neq} \gamma(x_i, x_j) . \tag{4}$$

- Adjacency.

$$\text{The less } |x_0(k) - x_i(k)| \text{ is, the bigger } \gamma(x_0(k), x_i(k)) \text{ is.} \tag{5}$$

We call $\gamma(x_0, x_i)$ the correlation degree of x_i with x_0, $\gamma(x_0(k), x_i(k))$ is the correlation parameter of x_i with x_0.

When $X = \{x_i \mid i \in I\}$, let $\gamma(x_0(k), x_i(k)) = \dfrac{\min\limits_{j \in I}\min\limits_{k}|x_0(k) - x_j(k)| + \xi \max\limits_{j \in I}\max\limits_{k}|x_0(k) - x_j(k)|}{|x_0(k) - x_i(k)| + \xi \max\limits_{j \in I}\max\limits_{k}|x_0(k) - x_j(k)|}$, $\xi \in (0,1)$ is a real number, we select $\xi = 0.5$. We can prove that $\gamma(x_0, x_i) = \frac{1}{n}\sum_{k=1}^{n}\gamma(x_0(k), x_i(k))$ satisfies the four axioms. Correlation degree is more indicative then Euclidean distance of two strings when only part of them is matched or they are of only different phase. Our matching procedure is a monophonic to monophonic one, because pitch contour and note contour are all monophonic, it works in this way: input the pitch contour to all recurrent neural networks, which are used as the indices of music database, then calculate the output of them. The pieces of music in database are ranked according to the correlation degree with hummed tune, the most similar three songs are displayed for users to select and play.

7. Experimental Results

We test our approach on a music database of 201 songs. We found that the size of recurrent neural network with 1 input node, 1 output node and 5 hidden nodes is proper for our music database. We will test in the future if this network size is also enough for a larger music database. The query result is as following:

Matching Resolution	Successful Rate
Top 1	63%
Top 3	87%

Future work will focus on melody extraction technique from most formats of music and on-line music retrieval. More attention will be paid to MPEG-7 to develop more practical music query approach.

References

1. Deng J. L.: Control problems of Grey System. Syst. Contr. Let..vol. 5(1982) 288-94
2. Elman, L. J.: Finding Structure in Time. Cognitive Science, 14(1990) 179-211
3. Ghias, A., Logan, J., Chamberlin, D., and Smith, B. C.: Query by Humming-Musical Information Retrieval in an Audio Database. In Proc. of ACM Multimedia'95(1995)
4. Gold, B. and Rabiner, L. R.: Parallel Processing Techniques for Estimating Pitch Periods of Speech in the Time Domain. J. Acou. Soc. of Am., Vol. 46, No.2, Part 2, August (1969) 442-48
5. Kosugi, N.: A Practical Query-By-Humming System for a Large Music Database. In Proc. ACM Multimedia'2000(2000)
6. Kosugi, N., Nishihara, Y., Kon'ya, S., Yamamuro, M., and Kushima K.: Music Retrieval by Humming. In Proc. PACRIM'99(1999) 404-407
7. McNab, R. J., Smith, L. A., Bainbridge, D. and Witten, I. H.: The New Zealand Digital Library MELody inDEX. Technical Report, D-Lib(1997)
8. MIDI information. http://www.midi.org
9. Muscle Fish LLC. http://www.musclefish.com/
10. OMRAS(Online Music Recognition And Searching). http://www.omras.org
11. Sonoda, T., Goto, M., Muraokal Y. : A WWW-based Melody Retrieval System. ICMC98
12. Uitdenbogerd, A. and Zobel, J.: Melodic Matching Techniques for Large Music Database. In Proc. of ACM Multimedia'99(1999) 57-66

Color Content Matching of MPEG-4 Video Objects

Berna Erol and Faouzi Kossentini

Department of Electrical and Computer Engineering, University of British Columbia
2356 Main Mall, Vancouver, BC, V6T 1Z4, Canada
e-mail: {bernae, faouzi}@ece.ubc.ca

Abstract. Color histogram is one of the most widely used visual feature representations in content-based retrieval. When processing the image/video data in the JPEG/MPEG compressed domains, the DC coefficients are used commonly to form the color histograms without fully decompressing the image or the video bit stream. In this paper, we address the issues arising from the adaptation of DC based color histograms to the arbitrarily shaped MPEG-4 video objects. More specifically, we discuss the color space selection, quantization, and histogram computation with the consideration of the specific characteristics of the MPEG-4 video objects. We also propose a method for reducing the chroma keying artifacts that may occur at the boundaries of the objects. The experimental results show that great retrieval performance improvements are achieved by employing the proposed method in the presence of such artifacts.

1. Introduction

Color histograms are commonly used for image and video retrieval, as they are relatively easy to extract, not much sensitive to noise, and invariant to image scaling, translation, and rotation. Because digital image and video is available mostly in the compressed formats, several researchers suggested methods for obtaining the color histograms from the coded bit stream without requiring full decompression and reconstruction of the visual data [1]. In most of the current image and video coding standards, such as JPEG, MPEG-1/2/4, and H.263, each frame is divided into 8x8 blocks, followed by DCT, quantization, zigzag scan, and run length coding. The quantized DC coefficient of each 8x8 block could be easily extracted from the bit stream by only performing parsing of the headers and run length decoding. In the intra coded frames, with a simple scaling, the DC coefficient is equal to the mean value of the corresponding block. Therefore, the DC coefficients of the Y, C_b, and C_r components can be simply employed to extract color features, including color histograms, as presented in the literature [1]-[3].

The most recent MPEG video coding standard, MPEG-4, supports the representation of arbitrarily shaped video by allowing the coding of the shape information of the video objects along with their texture. In this paper, we look into selection of color space, the number of quantization bins, and the histogram computation for the arbitrarily shaped MPEG-4 video objects, which generally have lower resolutions than that of frame based video and have consistent color throughout their lifespan.

Chroma keying is one of the most popular methods to obtain arbitrarily shaped video objects. If the video object shape is not accurately extracted prior the MPEG-4 encoding and/or the MPEG-4 encoder does not employ the LPE padding technique described in the MPEG-4 verification model [4], the chroma key value of the background could contribute to some color artifacts that would eventually affect the color histogram of the video object. In this paper, we also propose a method to detect and compensate for such artifacts in order to obtain a more accurate color histogram representation.

The remainder of the paper is as follows. In the next section, we discuss the extraction of the DC coefficients from the MPEG-4 bit stream. In Section 3, we address the issues rising from the use of DC based color histograms to represent the MPEG-4 video objects. In Section 4, our proposed method for reducing the chroma keying artifacts in histogram computation is presented. Experimental results and conclusion are given in Section 5 and Section 6, respectively.

2. DC Coefficient Extraction in the MPEG-4 Bit Stream

Intra (I) frames are commonly used to obtain color histograms from the video sequences, as they are not predicted from any other frames. In MPEG-1/2 and H.263 I-frames, the DC coefficient can be obtained simply by parsing of the headers and run length decoding. On the other hand, in the MPEG-4 intra coded Video Object Planes (IVOPs), the reconstruction of the DC coefficient is required as the DCT coefficients of macroblocks can be predictively coded (either from the left or above block). After the DC coefficients are extracted from the MPEG-4 bit stream, reconstructed, and dequantized, the mean Y, C_b, and C_r values of the corresponding blocks are obtained by

$$M_Y = \frac{DC_Y}{8}, \quad M_{Cb} = \frac{DC_{Cb}}{8} - 128, \quad M_{Cr} = \frac{DC_{Cr}}{8} - 128,$$

where DC_Y, DC_{Cb}, and DC_{Cr}, are the DC coefficients of the luminance, chrominance b, and chrominance r blocks, respectively.

Parsing of the MPEG-4 bit stream in order to extract the DC information is also more complex than parsing of the MPEG-1/2 and H.263 bit streams. In MPEG-4, the shape information is placed before the texture information in the bit stream [4]. Therefore, arithmetic decoding of the shape is required before obtaining the DC coefficient. Nevertheless, reconstruction of the shape is not necessary.

3. Video Object Retrieval Using Color Histograms

Video objects, different than frame based video sequences, generally have low resolution, less variation in color, and their color content usually remains consistent unless there is occlusion by a large object or the video object is entering to or exiting from the scene. Therefore, a color histogram representation that is optimal for the frame based video is not necessarily optimal for the object based video.

Here, we address the problems of color space selection, quantization of colors, and histogram computation for arbitrary shaped video objects. In order to justify our particular color space and quantization parameter selections, we evaluate the retrieval results based on a measure used during the MPEG-7 standardization activities: Normalized Modified Retrieval Rank (NMRR) and Average NMRR (ANMRR). NMRR and ANMRR values are in the range of [0, 1] and the lower values represent a better retrieval rate. The specific formulas of these measures are given in Section 5.1.

3.1 Color Space and Histogram Size Selection

Video in MPEG-4 domain is represented in YC_bC_r color space, as in MPEG-1/2. While YC_bC_r representation is good for efficient compression, it is not a desirable representation in visual retrieval as it is not a perceptually uniform color space. HSV (Hue, Saturation, Value) color space, which is adopted for the MPEG-7 color histogram descriptor, more closely resembles to human perception, but it is also a non uniform space [5]. MTM (Mathematical Transformation to Munsell) is a perceptually uniform color space that very closely represents the human way of perceiving colors [5]. In the MTM space, the colors are represented by Hue (H), Value (V) and Chroma (C) components [6].

Table 1 presents the video object retrieval performance comparison employing three different color spaces. The results are obtained by querying MPEG-4 video object planes in a database of more than a thousand VOPs. Uniform quantization is employed to reduce the number of histogram bins. Employing YC_bC_r color representation does not require conversion to another color space, however it gives the lowest retrieval performance. Using the MTM representation clearly offers a superior retrieval performance. Table 2 shows the retrieval results when different number of quantization bins used to represent the color components of the MTM space. As can seen from the table, employing a 128-bin histogram offers the best tradeoff between the retrieval performance and the memory requirements.

query video object plane	**HSV** H:8 S:4 V:4	**MTM** H:8 V:4 C:4	**YC_bC_r** Y:5 C_b:5 C_r:5
bream	0.0007	0.0004	0.0097
fish	0.0876	0.0249	0.2400
stefan	0.0116	0.0208	0.1303
singing girl	0.2686	0.2006	0.2715
Average NMRR	**0.0912**	**0.0617**	**0.1629**

Table 1. NMRR values obtained by querying the first video object planes of the various video objects, employing color histograms computed in three different color spaces.

query video object plane	256 bins: H:16 V:4 C:4	128 bins: H:8 V:4 C:4	64 bins: H:4 V:4 C:4	32 bins: H:4 V:2 C:2
bream	0.0003	0.0004	0.0728	0.0202
fish	0.0411	0.0249	0.0425	0.0194
stefan	0.0302	0.0208	0.1841	0.1900
singing girl	0.0666	0.2006	0.3349	0.3812
Average NMRR	**0.0346**	**0.0617**	**0.1586**	**0.1527**

Table 2. The retrieval performance results (in NMRR) for using different number of quantization bins for the H, V, and C components of the MTM color histograms.

3.2 Histogram Computation for Video Objects

We obtain the color histograms of individual VOPs by using only the color components that correspond to the blocks that are either completely inside (i.e., opaque) or on the boundary (i.e., intra) of the video object planes. This information is directly available in the MPEG-4 bit stream. In average, only half of the pixels in a boundary block lie in a video object. Therefore, when computing the color histograms for individual VOPs, we count the color components of the boundary blocks as half of the color components of the opaque blocks.

After constructing the histograms for the individual VOPs, the video object histogram can be formed by using one of the following techniques used for frame based video [7].

- Average histogram: It is obtained by accumulating the histogram values over a range of frames and normalizing that by the number of frames.
- Median histogram: The bin values of this histogram is computed by taking the median values of each corresponding histogram bin of the individual frames.
- Intersection histogram: This histogram contains only the colors that are common to all the frames.

It is presented in the literature that employing average histogram yields the best results for frame based video retrieval [7]. Video object color generally remains consistent during its lifespan, therefore, in most cases, an average histogram represents the video object color content accurately. Median histogram is most useful if some frames in a video sequence differ in color significantly than the others, which is usually not the case for video objects. Also, there is an increased computational cost associated with the median operation because of the sorting performed for each bin. Intersection histogram is also not very suitable for video object color representation: When the objects are entering to/exiting from a scene or when they are occluded, only a small part of their color range is visible, which would be the only colors represented by an intersection histogram. In conclusion, considering the characteristics of the arbitrarily shaped video objects, the average histogram is clearly the most appropriate choice to represent the color histogram of video objects.

Average histogram can be computed using the individual histograms of all the IVOPs in an MPEG-4 video object. A better alternative that reduces the computational requirements would be computing the histogram on a temporally sampled subset of IVOPs or on key VOPs that represent the salient content of the video object [8].

4. Compensation for the Chroma Keying Artifacts

Chroma keying remains one of the most popular methods to obtain semantic video objects. In chroma keying, the foreground object is separated from the background by placing the object in front of a color screen that has a unique chroma key value (typically blue or green) and defining the pixels that belong to the screen as outside the video object. Ideally, the coded video object should not contain any pixels from the background. However, if an MPEG-4 encoder does not approximate the video object shape very accurately and/or it does not perform low pass extrapolation (LPE) padding technique prior to DCT, which is defined in the MPEG-4 verification model [4] but not part of the MPEG-4 standard, the boundary blocks of the video object could contain some severe chroma keying artifacts. These artifacts could result in the chroma DC values (DC_{Cb} and DC_{Cr}) of the boundary blocks include the chroma key color along with the actual video object color, resulting in an inaccurate computation of the color histogram. In order to overcome this problem, we propose to first detect the existence of such artifacts and then compensate for them accordingly.

Our experiments show that, if a video object plane has any chroma artifacts, it is likely to affect all the blocks on the video object boundary. Therefore, if such effects are detected in one or several boundary blocks, it is reasonable to assume that the most of the boundary blocks of the video object have such artifacts. We propose to detect the chroma artifacts at the decoder, assuming no apriori information about the encoder, by decoding the texture and the shape of the first boundary block of the video object plane and then computing the mean chroma values (C_b and C_r) for the pixels that are inside and outside the video object area using the shape mask for that particular block. If the difference between the chroma values corresponding to the inside and outside of the video object is very small, than it could be concluded that the segmentation was done properly and the LPE technique was employed prior to encoding. Therefore, the DC values of the boundary blocks correctly reflect the real video object color and no further processing is required. However, if the inside and outside chroma mean values differ significantly, then we define the chroma key values (K_{Cb}, K_{Cr}) as equal to the mean chroma values of the outside pixels.

After chroma keying artifacts are detected and the chroma key values are determined, then the scaled DC coefficients (M_{Cb} and M_{Cr}) of the boundary blocks are adjusted to reduce the chroma artifacts. Considering that, in average, half of the pixels in a boundary belongs to the inside the object and the other half belongs to the outside the object, the following approximations can be made to find actual mean value of the pixels inside the video object.

$$M_{Cb} \approx \frac{V_{Cb} + K_{Cb}}{2}, M_{Cr} \approx \frac{V_{Cr} + K_{Cr}}{2} \Rightarrow V_{Cb} \approx 2M_{Cb} - K_{Cb}, V_{Cr} \approx 2M_{Cr} - K_{Cr},$$

where the M_{Cb} and M_{Cr} are the scaled chrominance DC coefficients extracted from the bit stream, K_{Cb} and K_{Cr} are the approximated chroma key values, and V_{Cb} and V_{Cr} are the mean chrominance values of the pixels that belong to the video object in a boundary block. Video object color histogram is computed by using the approximated V_{Cb} and V_{Cr} values of the chrominance components, along with the unmodified luminance component, M_Y.

5. Experimental Results

Here, we demonstrate the performance of our proposed technique in the presence of chroma keying artifacts. We present retrieval results for some individual VOPs as well as some video objects. Our database consists of over 20 arbitrarily shaped video objects, coded in 2 to 3 different spatial resolutions each, resulting in an MPEG-4 database of over 50 bit streams and over 1500 intra coded VOPs. We utilize the MTM color space and 128-bin uniform quantization for the color histograms of the VOPs. Video object histograms are formed by histogram averaging on their key VOPs. The key VOPs are found by the algorithm described in [8]. The color histogram distances between two VOs or two VOPs are computed using the L1 norm, which was demonstrated to have a superior performance for measuring the histogram distances [7][9].

5.1 Performance Evaluation Criteria

We present our retrieval results by utilizing the Normalized Modified Retrieval Rank (NMRR) measure used in the MPEG-7 standardization activity. NMRR not only indicates how much of the correct items are retrieved, but also how highly they are ranked among the retrieved items. NMRR is given by

$$NMRR(n) = \frac{\left(\sum_{k=1}^{NG(n)} \frac{Rank(k)}{NG(n)} \right) - 0.5 - \frac{NG(n)}{2}}{K + 0.5 - 0.5 * NG(n)},$$

where NG is the number of ground truth items marked as similar to the query item, Rank(k) is the ranking of the ground truth items by the retrieval algorithm. K equals to min(4*NG(q), 2*GTM), where GTM is the maximum of NG(q) for the all queries. The NMRR is in the range of [0 1] and the smaller values represent a better retrieval performance. ANMRR is defined as the average NMRR over a range of queries.

5.2 VO Retrieval Results

Table 3 demonstrates the retrieval results for several video object (VO) queries. The first column shows the results when there are no chroma keying artifacts. The second column gives the retrieval performance when the query VO and several VOs in the database are coded by simulating chroma keying artifacts. Simulation of such artifacts are done by simply imposing a blue background to the objects and encoding the video objects with no LPE padding. As seen from the Table 3, chroma keying artifacts results in a poor retrieval performance. After applying the proposed technique to reduce these effects, the retrieval performance improves significantly.

query video object	Without artifacts	With artifacts	With reduced artifacts
children 1	0. 0000	0. 6396	0. 3333
stefan	0. 0741	0. 0410	0. 0370
hall monitor 2	0. 0250	0. 4250	0. 1500
Average NMRR	**0. 0330**	**0. 3685**	**0. 1734**

Table 3. Video object retrieval results (in NMRR) without any chroma artifacts, with chroma artifacts, and after compensation of the artifacts with the proposed method.

6. Conclusions

In this paper, we discussed the issues arising from employing the DC based color histogram technique in the MPEG-4 compressed domain and proposed a method to compute color histograms for the arbitrarily shaped MPEG-4 video objects. We also proposed a technique for reducing the chroma keying artifacts that may occur at the boundaries of these video objects. Our experimental results show that great retrieval performance improvements are obtained by employing our method in the presence of such artifacts.

References

[1] R. Chang, W. Kuo, and H. Tsai, "Image Retrieval on Uncompressed and Compressed Domains", IEEE ICIP, 2000.

[2] J. Lay and L. Guan, "Image Retrieval Based on Energy Histograms of Low Frequency DCT Coefficients", IEEE ICASSP, vol. 6 , pp. 3009 –3012, 1999.

[3] M.Shneierand and M.Abdel-Mottaleb "Exploiting the JPEG Compression Scheme for Image Retrieval", IEEE Trans. on Pattern Anal. and Machine Intelligence, pp. 849-853, 1996.

[4] ISO/IEC JTC1/SC29/WG11, "MPEG-4 Video VM 12.2", doc no. M4576, March 1999.

[5] Del Bimbo, A., "Visual Information Retrieval", Morgan Kaufmann Publishers, 1999.

[6] M. Miyahara and Y. Yoshida, "Mathematical transform of (R,G,B) color data to Munsell (H,V,C) color data," in SPIE Visual Com. and Image Proc., vol. 1001, pp. 650-657, 1988.

[7] M. Ferman, S. Krishnamachari, M. Tekalp, M. Abdel-Mottaleb, and R. Mehrotra, "Group of Frames Color Histogram Descriptors for Multimedia Applications", IEEE ICIP, 2000.

[8] B. Erol and F. Kossentini, "Automatic Key Video Object Plane Selection Using the Shape Information in the MPEG-4 Compressed Domain", IEEE Trans. on Multimedia, June 2000.

[9] R. Brunelli and O. Mich, "On the Use of Histograms for Image Retrieval", Proceedings of ICMCS, vol. 2, pp. 143-147, 1999.

Multiple-Person Tracking System for Content Analysis

Jun-Wei Hsieh [1], L.W. Huang [2], and Yea-Shuan Huang [2]

[1] Department of Electrical Engineering
YuanZe University, Taoyuan, Taiwan
shieh@saturn.yzu.edu.tw
[2] Advanced Technology Center,
Computer and Communication Laboratories
Industrial Technology Research Institute, HsinChu, Taiwan

Abstract. This paper presents a framework to track multiple persons in real-time. First, a method with real-time and adaptable capability is proposed to extract face-like regions based on skin, motion, and silhouette features. Then, a two-stage face verification algorithm is proposed to quickly eliminate false faces based on the face geometries and the Support Vector Machine(SVM). In order to overcome the effect of lighting changes, a method of color constancy compensation is applied. Then, a robust tracking scheme is applied to track multiple persons based on a face-status table. With the table, the system has extreme capabilities to track different persons at different statuses, which is quite important in face-related applications. Experimental results show that the proposed method is much robust and powerful than other traditional methods.

1 Introduction

With the advent of computer technologies, real-time face tracking has become an important issue in many applications include video surveillance, teleconference, video retrieval, virtual reality, and so on. However, it is difficult to track faces well in real-time since faces are highly complex due to variations in illumination, races, background, hair styles, orientations and so on. In order to track a human face well, there are two important issues: what to track and how to tack. For the first issue, Rowley *et al.* [1] proposed a neural network based algorithm, where a face region is verified with a neural network after light correction and histogram equalization. While the approach provides satisfying detection rate, its heavy computation has become a burden for real-time applications. For the second issues, Yang *et al.* [2] proposed a tracking framework to track single face in real time based on color and motion information. The limit of this approach is to assume the initial face to be tracked is the largest moving skin region appearing in the whole video sequence. Later, Wang *et al.*[3] used several cameras to track single person based on motion information and region boundary. Anyway, those methods permit that only one face can be tracked in the whole video sequence. A successful surveillance system should have enough capabilities to detect and track multiple persons simultaneously.

In this paper, a simple but effective method is proposed to track multiple faces in real time. Before tracking, all the face-like regions are extracted from images based on the skin color, motion, and silhouette features. Here, silhouette feature is used to separate two face-like regions from one connected skin region if they connect together. Then, a two-stage face verification algorithm is proposed to eliminate false faces quickly for real-time tracking. At the first stage, based on the face's shape geometry, we can eliminate most of false face candidates. Then, only few regions are survived and then further verified with the SVM approach. At this stage, a color constancy compensation method is proposed to overcome the lighting changes during verification. When tracking, a so-called face status table is created based on skin region and a face history. With this table, different tracking strategies can be applied to handle different tracking conditions. More importantly, the next positions of the tracked faces can be decided without using the correlation technique, which will often fail when the lighting condition is poor. Compared with other methods, the proposed scheme is a great improvement in terms of accuracy, efficiency as well as reliability for tracking persons in real time.

The paper is organized as follows. Section 2 is the details of face region extraction. Section 3 is the two-stage face verification procedure and Section 4 discusses the details of multiple face tracking. Experimental results will be discussed in Section 5.

2 Multiple Face-Like Region Extraction

The following is the details of interesting face region extraction as the key to track multiple persons based on skin color, motion, and silhouette information (see Fig. 1).

2.1. Skin Color Model and its Adaptation

For a given pixel (R,G,B), the chromaticity transformation is defined as: $r = R/(R+G+B)$ and $g=G/(R+G+B)$. Then, a pixel in an image is classified into skin-pixel and non-skin-pixel by the Gaussian model: $gau(r,g) = \exp[-(g-u_g)^2/2\sigma_g^2 - (r-u_r)^2/2\sigma_r^2]$, where u_r, u_g σ_r and σ_g are the means and variances of the r and g components, respectively. To overcome the lighting changes, an adaptive skin mode $gau^{j,k}(r,g)$ for each tracked face is proposed to fitting such conditions, where $gau^{j,k}(r,g)$ is the skin model for the kth tracked face in the jth frame. If previous M frames are used, the linear skin model to predict the new model is: $\hat{u}^{j,k} = \sum_{l=0}^{M-1} w_l u^{j-l,k}$ and $\hat{\sigma}^{j,k} = \sum_{l=0}^{M-1} w_l \sigma^{j-l,k}$, where $\hat{u}^{j,k}$ and $\hat{\sigma}^{j,k}$ is the adapted mean and variance of the kth tracked face at the jth frame, respectively. w_l is a weight defined as follows: $w_l = (1-l/M)(1+|u^{j,k} - u^{j-l,k}|)^{-1}\Omega^{-1}$, where $\Omega = \sum_{l=0}^{M-1} (1-l/M)(1+|u^{j,k} - u^{j-l,k}|)^{-1}$.

2.2 Skin Region Isolation with Motions and Silhouette

For a real-time face tracking system, motion information is a good cue to effectively distinguish a human face from the background. For each segmented skin region, if there are more than 20% pixels classified as moving pixels, this region is labeled as a possible face region. Based on the motion information, interesting regions can be extracted from background.

On the other hand, different faces will connect together due to clothes or naked body. Fig. 2 shows two faces connect together after skin color detection. Therefore, a method is then proposed to separate two different face-like regions from silhouettes. Basically, the contour of a face region looks like the symbol 凸. The following is a method presented to extract such symbol. Let *v(x)* denote the vertical position of the first touched pixel of the connected region *R* when we track all pixels along the *x*th column from top to down. Then the position difference *d(x)* can be obtained as follows: $d(x)=v(x-1)-v(x+1)$. If the absolute value of *d(x)* is larger than a threshold, then there exists a vertical edge E_i. Let *e(i)* denote the edge response of E_i. If there exists a face-like region between two edges E_i and E_j, the following rules should be satisfied: $e(i) > w$ and $e(j) < -w$, where $w = 0.5 * (p(j)-p(i))$ and E_i and E_j are neighbors.

3. Face Verification

The following section describes a two-stage verification algorithm to efficiently eliminate impossible face regions for further tracking.

3.1 Rule-based Face Verification Algorithm

At the fist stage, non-face regions are removed according to their shape geometries and texture information. There are five decision criteria used to verify a face region *R*. The first decision criterion is the compactness of the region *R*: $c = A / r^2$, where *A* and *r* are the area and perimeter of *R*, respectively. The second criterion is the ratio between the height and width of a face. The third criterion is the statistic variance of a face. All components with a lower variance are removed since a face is not a flat plane. The fourth criterion is the number of holes existed in the region. If the number of holes in the region is less than two, the region will not be considered as a face since the eyes and month will occupy three holes if the region is a face. The last criterion is the convexity of a face. In practice, a hand region would satisfy all above four criteria but cannot satisfy the requirement of the convexity of a face.

3.2 Color Constancy Compensation and the SVM Verification Algorithm

Before applying the SVM method, it is noticed that the image color is very sensitive to the lighting variation. Therefore, the following is a color constancy compensation procedure to reduce the lighting effect into the minimum. Assume *X* is a skin region, where $\bar{m}$ and σ are the mean and the variance of *X*, respectively. Let *I(i)* mean the intensity of the *i*th pixel in *X*. The intensity *I(i)* is compensated into $\bar{I}(i)$ according to the form: $\bar{I}(i) = 128 + (I(i) - \bar{m})\sigma^{-1}\beta$, where β is a scale factor.

Once the region *X* has been compensated, the SVM approach is then applied to verify the region *X*. It is known that the SVM has extreme capabilities in solving two-class classification problems [4][5]. The goal in training a SVM is to find the separating hyper-plane with the largest margin. If the radial basis function is used in training the SVM, finding the optimal separating hyper-plane amounts to maximizing

$$W(\alpha)=\sum_{i=1}^{N}\alpha_i-\frac{1}{2}\sum_{i,j=1}^{N}\alpha_i\alpha_j y_i y_j \phi(X_i)\phi(X_j),$$

where $\alpha_i \geq 0$, $\phi(X)$ is a radial basis function, and $y_i \in \{-1,1\}$, the label of X_i. Such criterion leads to the optimal separating hyper-plane solution:

$$f(X)=\mathrm{sgn}(\sum_{i=1}^{N}\alpha_i^0 y_i K(X_i,X)+b_0), \tag{1}$$

where $K(X_i,X)=\phi(X_i)\phi(X)$ is a kernel function, α_i^0 a coefficient and b_0 a constant. The kernel K used here has the form $K(X_i,X)=X_iX+1$. $f(x)\in\{-1,1\}$ is a sign function to decide the binary class of the data point X_i. To train the optimal SVM model, we begin with a face database of 2000 images to calculate the separating hyper-plane. The negative examples are taken from scenes that do not contain any faces. Then, given a skin color region X, the likelihood of X being a face can be verified based on Eq. (1). Since most false-face regions have been filtered out at the first pass, the second pass is applied only to a small number of connected skin areas.

4. Multiple Face Tracking

In the past, the common approach to track faces is through the correlation technique. However, this technique is time-consuming and often fails when the environment lighting condition changes or the objects move much. Therefore, in this paper, a method is proposed to solve the above problems based on skin color and a face history.

During tracking, different tracking strategies should be used to deal different tracking conditions; that is, people leaving, entering, and staying. The key contribution in this paper is that we use a "face-status" table to track multiple peoples in real time. Let *H(i)* denote the *i*th face in the history list and *S(j)* denote the *j*th skin region extracted from the current frame based on the information of skin, motion, and silhouette. Then the face status table (*FST*) is built as follows:

Step 1: Set FST*(i,j)* to be one if there exists more 10% overlapped area between the face *H(i)* and the region *S(j)*; otherwise, set FST*(i,j)* to be zero.

Step 2: Calculate $FST(i,0)=\arg\max_j \mathrm{size}(S(j))$ if $FST(i,j)>0$ for all $i>0$, where *size(S(j))* is the area of *S(j)*. Besides, $FST(0,j)=\sum_{i>0}FST(i,j)$ for $j>0$.

The details of the whole tracking procedure are shown in Fig. 1. For the *j*th skin region in *S*, if *FST(0, j)* is larger than zero, the skin region is labeled as an old face; that is, the face has been tracked in the previous frame. Its position is directly updated. Otherwise, the region is labeled as a new face that needs to be further verified with the proposed verification approach. In this way, without using the correlation technique, the next positions of most tracked faces can be found. Furthermore, for the *i*th face in the list *H*, if *FST(i,0)* is larger than zero, the face has its corresponding face in current frame, i.e., *S(FST(i,0))*. Otherwise, the *i*th face probably seems disappeared in the current frame. For the case, the correlation technique is then applied for getting its next position. If the correlation value is less than a threshold, label the face as "disappeared". Otherwise, the tracked face is correctly tracked. Without involving much correlation computation, the proposed method can track all the faces in real -time.

4. Experimental Results

The proposed method has been tested by many people under different conditions. For all the experiments, the average frame rate is about 20 fps with the dimension 320×240. Fig. 3 shows the example of two peoples being tracked. Due to the clothes with skin color, some non-face skin regions still exist. However, the proposed verification method with color constancy compensation still can eliminate them and exactly locate and track the faces. Fig. 4 shows three persons being tracked under a complex background and a complex lighting environment. Due to poor lighting condition, the face regions couldn't be well segmented even though using an adaptive skin model. That will lead to the confusion of the tracking system to judge whether the tracked faces have left or not. However, the proposed method still can work well to locate them. Furthermore, for comparisons, the CMU face tracker [2] and the Harvard hybrid tracking system [3] are discussed. The CMU system assumed the tracked face is the one who area is the largest one for all the moving objects with skin colors in the sequence. For the latter system, the face is located based on the neckline extracted from the head boundary. Such approach will fail if the head boundary cannot be well extracted due to noises. Therefore, our method can achieve better accuracy of locating and tracking the true faces than both methods. Of course, both methods cannot track multiple persons especially. The details of comparisons are listed in Table 1. Compared with other methods, the proposed scheme is a great improvement in terms of accuracy, efficiency and ability for tracking multiple-persons.

5. Conclusions

In this paper, we have presented a SVM-based approach to track multiple persons in real time. This method provides quite flexibility and robustness in tracking different persons at different statuses under an unconstrained environment. Before tracking, all the interesting face-like regions are extracted based on skin, motion, and silhouette features. Then, a two-stage verification algorithm is proposed to quickly eliminate false faces. During tracking, a face-status table is created based on skin color and a face history. With the table, it is easy to identify different statuses of tracked persons so that different strategies can be used to tackle all the tracking conditions. Experimental results show that the proposed method is much powerful than other methods.

Acknowledgement

This paper is a partial result of the project no. 3XS1B11 conducted by the ITRI under sponsorship of the Minister of Economic Affairs, Taiwan, R.O.C.

References

1. H. A. Rowley, S. Baluja, and T. Kanade, "Neural network-based face detection," *IEEE transactions on PAMI.*, vol. 20, no. 1, pp. 22-38, Jan. 1998.
2. J. Yang and A. Waibel, "A real-time face tracker," *International Workshop on Automatic Face and Gesture Recognition, pp. 142-147*, Sarasota, FL, 1996.
3. C. Wang and M. S. Brandstein, "A hybrid real-time face tracking system," Proceedings of ICASSP 1998, Seattle, WA, May, 1998.

4. E. Osuna, R. Freund, and F. Girosi, "Training Support Vector Machines: an Application to Face Detection", *CVPR* 97, pp. 130-136.
5. C. Papageorgiou and T. Poggio, "A general framework for object detection", *Int'l J. Computer Vision*, vol. 38, no. 1, pp. 15-33, 2000.

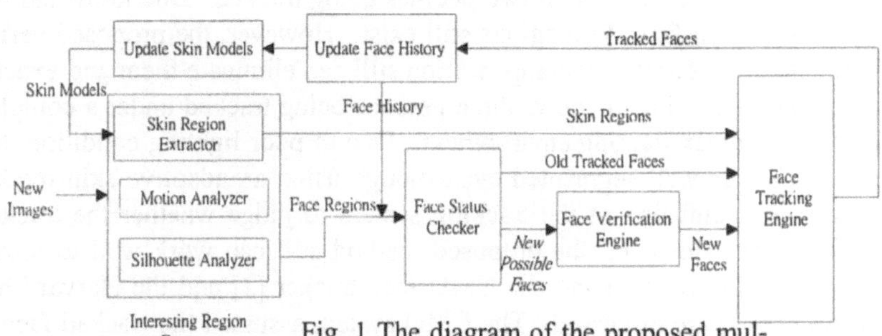

Fig. 1 The diagram of the proposed multiple-person tracking system

Fig. 2 The face regions still connect together even using color and motion information.

Fig. 4 Three girls walking under a noisy environment. (a) Tracking result. (b) Skin region extraction under bad lighting condition.

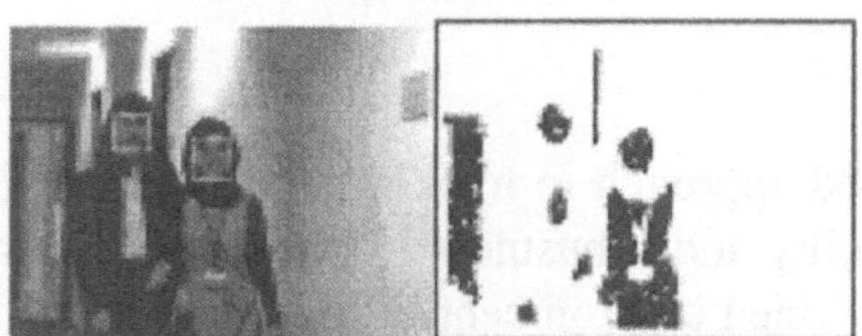

Fig. 3 Two walking girls. (a) The result; (b) Skin region extraction.

	CMU System	Harvard System	Proposed system
Capability to track multiple persons	No	No	Yes
Sensitive to Head Orientation	Yes	No	No
Face detection	the largest region	Based on neckline	Rule + SVM
Accuracy of tracking	Low	Low	High
Image Size	192 × 144	192 × 144	320 × 240
Frame Rate	15 fps at 0.5 m 30 fps at over 2m	25 fps for 0.5 ~5m	20 fps

Table 1 Comparisons among the CMU system, the Harvard system, and the proposed system. Only the proposed method can track multiple persons.

Motion Segmentation with Census Transform

Kunio Yamada [1], Kenji Mochizuki [1], Kiyoharu Aizawa [1, 2] and Takahiro Saito [1, 3]

[1] Multimedia Ambiance Communication Project,
Telecommunications Advancement Organization of Japan (TAO)
4F, Hortensia Hakusan, 1-33-16 Hakusan, Bunkyo-ku, Tokyo 113-0001, Japan
{ymdkn, mochi}@hrc4.tao.go.jp
[2] Department of Information and Communication Engineering,
The University of Tokyo
7-3-1, Hongo, Bunkyo-ku, Tokyo 113-8656, Japan
aizawa@hal.t.u-tokyo.ac.jp
[3] Department of Electrical, Electronics and Information Engineering,
Kanagawa University
3-27-1, Rokkakubashi, Kanagawa-ku, Yokohama 221-0802, Japan
saitot01@kanagawa-u.ac.jp

Abstract. This paper presents a new approach to motion segmentation. Unlike most other methods, the proposed approach relies on summarized local image structure obtained by census transform, and not on absolute luminance values. We apply census transform for two frames from the sequence which are registered to the sub-pixel accuracy regarding to the moving target object. The registration is carried out by estimation of affine parameters. The two sets of resulting local image structures, in the forms of bit strings, give good and dense correspondence on the object to segment the region. We study the effectiveness of the sub-pixel registration compared to the pixel unit registration. We show segmentation results for natural scenes.

1 Introduction

Multimedia Ambiance Communication Project of TAO (Telecommunications Advancement Organization of Japan) has been researching and developing an image space, that can be shared by people in different locations and can lend a real sense of presence. The image space is mainly based on photo-realistic texture. We aim to accomplish shared-space communication by an immersive environment consisting of the image space stereoscopically projected on an arched screen. We refer to this scheme as "ambiance communication" [1], [2]. In the ambiance communication natural moving objects are synthesized with other natural or CG objects on large screens. Accordingly motion segmentation with accurate contour is more important than in applications such as object based coding (e.g., MPEG-4) and video surveillance.

Many of conventional motion segmentation approaches are based on dense motion. The motion is estimated by correspondence search of the luminance values or by calculating optical flows. In either case, it is very difficult to segment the object under such conditions as: 1)luminance values of the object and the back ground are close, and 2) global luminance values of the object change slightly between the frames. Even if the condition is not so critical, the dense motion model does not give very accurate contours.

In this paper, we describe a segmentation technique based on census transform [3]. We first register the two frames in the sequence to the sub-pixel accuracy regarding the moving target object by affine transform. The affine parameters are estimated through the steepest decent algorithm. The reason for the accurate registration is studied theoretically in 2.2. Then the two frames are census transformed. Census transform gives the summarized image structure at a pixel in the form of a bit string. The pixel with good correspondence of bits, i.e. short Hamming distance, is regarded as a candidate for a part of the object region. Since our approach rely on local image structure and not on absolute luminance values, it enables segmentation of the object whose background is close in luminance, robustness in luminance change and accurate contours.

2 Proposed Approach

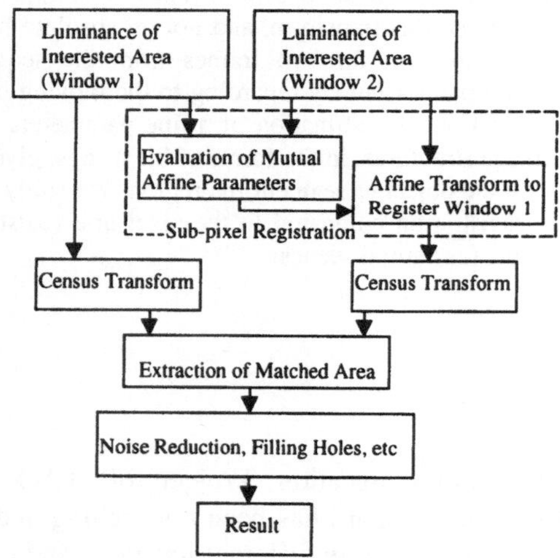

Fig. 1. Flow Diagram of the Algorithm

Fig. 1 shows the overall flow of the method. The algorithm is quite simple. The target object is cut out from the original frames so that the object is prominent in the windows. We call the windows Window 1 and Window 2. Window 2 is affine transformed to register Window 1 to the sub-pixel accuracy. The affine parameters are estimated through the steepest decent algorithm. The two frames are census transformed. The transformed area is a 9*9 block. Then the correspondence is estimated for each pixel, and the area dense with good matching pixels are regarded as the object area. After noise reduction and filling holes, the segmentation mask is obtained.

2.1 Census Transform [3]

Census transform is a kind of non-parametric local transform, which summarizes local image structure as a bit string representing the set of neighboring pixels whose intensity value is less than the pixel considered. Fig. 2 shows an example with 3*3 block transform area. The pixel has 8 bit data of summarized image data. In case of 9*9 block the data length for each pixel is 9*9-1=80 bits.

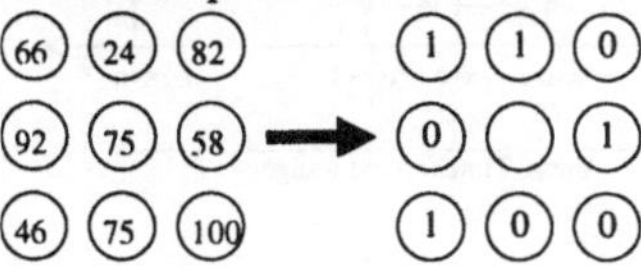

Fig. 2. Example of census transform

Census transform is an excellent tool for stereo correspondence problems [3], [4], [5]. However, in case that translation is not in the pixel unit and includes sub-pixel shift, which is more general a case, some of corresponding pairs give different summarized local image data. Accurate registration is the solution to the problem. In the next subsection, we study the effectiveness of the accurate registration.

2.2 Sub-pixel Registration and Census Transform

In this subsection we treat images as one dimensional pixel strings for the sake of simplicity. We assume that Frame 2 is a translated image of Frame 1 by $(P+\alpha)$ pixels, where P is an integer and α is a decimal ($0<\alpha<1$). And values on Frame 2 are assumed to be able to be linearly interpolated by the sample values on Frame 1. We call an image which Frame 2 is registered to Frame 1 to the pixel accuracy (α shift is left) α *shifted Frame* 2, and one registered to the sub-pixel accuracy *registered Frame* 2 (no shift is left). We compare the census transformed results of α *shifted* and *registered Frame* 2 with the results of Frame 1. Assuming that the odd integer m is the transformed range, m=2n+1 (n: integer), and $-n \le c \le n$ (c: integer), Frame 1 and α *shifted Frame* 2 can be expressed as vertical solid and dotted lines on Fig. 3. α *shifted Frame 2* is interpolated as follows.

$$f(x+c+\alpha)=(1-\alpha)f(x+c)+\alpha f(x+c+1) \tag{1}$$

Then *registered Frame* 2 is obtained by linearly interpolating the α shifted sample data given by

$$f_{reg}(x+c)=\alpha f(x+c-1+\alpha)+(1-\alpha)f(x+c+\alpha) \tag{2}$$

Equations (1) and (2) yield

$$\begin{aligned} f_{reg}(x+c)&=\alpha f(x+c-1+\alpha)+(1-\alpha)f(x+c+\alpha) \\ &=(\alpha-\alpha^2)f(x+c-1)+(1-2\alpha+2\alpha^2)f(x+c)+(\alpha-\alpha^2)f(x+c+1) \end{aligned} \tag{3}$$

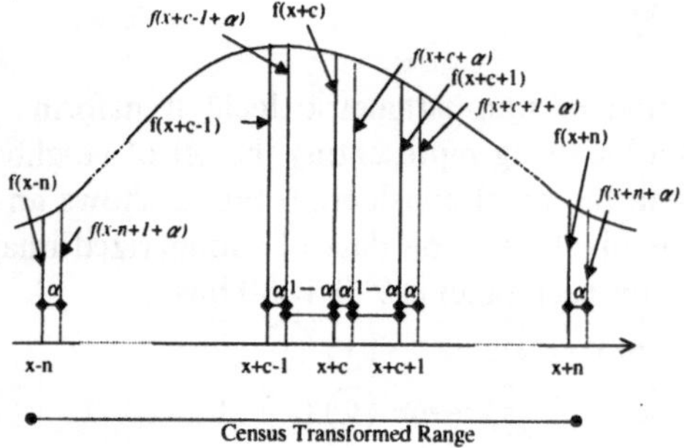

Fig. 3. Frame 1 and α *shifted Frame 2*

This equation indicates that *registered Frame 2* can be regarded as FIR filtered Frame 1 whose characteristics depend on the shift α.

We now compare the census transformed results. Let function U(a),

$$U(a)=\begin{cases}0(a\geq 0)\\1(a<0)\end{cases} \tag{4}$$

The census transformed results for Frame 1 is

$$U(f(x+c)-f(x)) \tag{5}$$

where and hereinafter c$\neq$0. For α *shifted Frame 2,*

$$\begin{aligned}&U(f(x+c+\alpha)-f(x+\alpha))\\&=U(f(x+c)-f(x)+\alpha(f(x+c+1)-f(x+c)-f(x+1)+f(x)))\end{aligned} \tag{6}$$

For registered Frame 2,

$$\begin{aligned}&U(f_{reg}(x+c)-f_{reg}(x))\\&=U(f(x+c)-f(x)+(\alpha-\alpha^2)(f(x+c-1)-2f(x+c)+f(x+c+1)\\&-f(x-1)+2f(x)-f(x+1)))\end{aligned} \tag{7}$$

Comparing equations (5) and (6), the sufficient condition for them to give the same results is that the first order differential values around x and x+c equal zero or the same. And comparing equations (5) and (7), the sufficient condition for them to give the same results is that the second order differential values at x and x+c equal zero or the same. The latter condition is much more commonly satisfied on generic images. Consequently *registered Frame 2* gives much better correspondence than α *shifted Frame 2* in census transformed results.

3 Experimental Results

The proposed method is applied for two frames in the sequence shown in Fig. 4. The mountain is still, the water moves to the left, and the boat (the target object) moves to the right.

Fig. 4. Considered frames in the sequence

For each frame, the target object is cut out so that the object is prominent in the windows. The windows are named Window 1 and Window 2 as mentioned earlier. Fig. 5 shows Window 1 and Fig. 6 shows Window 2. The window size is 290*100.

Fig. 5. Window 1 **Fig. 6.** Window 2

Then Window 2 is affine transformed to align Window 1 regarding the boat to the sub-pixel accuracy and bi-linearly interpolated as shown in Fig. 7.

Fig. 7. *Registered Window* 2

Both Window 1 and *registered Window 2* are census transformed and matched bits are counted for each pixel. Luminance values in Fig. 8 indicates the matched bit number multiplied by 3, accordingly 240 is perfect match. The brighter the pixel, the better the correspondence of the local image structure.After gaussian filtering and threshold discrimination, Fig. 9 is obtained. And choice of large areas, and filling of holes, the segmentation mask is obtained as shown in Fig. 10. Then, Window 1 is segmented by the mask and the segmentation result is given as shown in Figure 11.

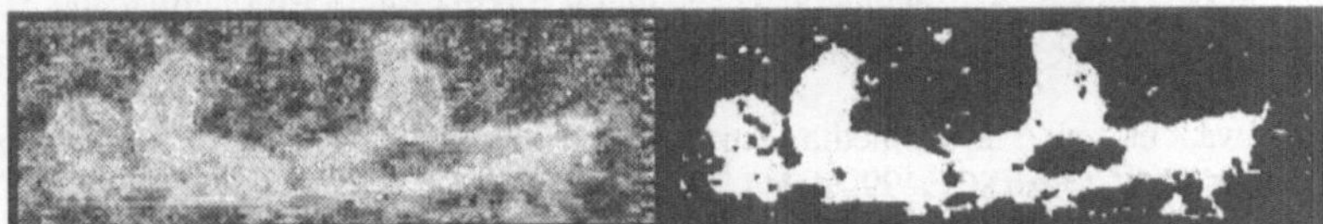

Fig. 8. Correspondence of the local structure **Fig. 9.** Regions of high correspondence in local structure

Fig. 10. Segmentation mask **Fig. 11.** Segmentation result

Subsequent results are comparisons by two existing approaches. Fig. 12 is the corresponded areas by luminance block (9*9) matching between Window 1 and Window 2, with the same block shift of the blocks as the boat movement. Fig. 13 is the area with little difference of luminance values between Window 1 and *registered Window 2,* which aims separation of the target (usually little difference) from the background (usually large difference). Comparing the images with Fig.9, block matching gives worse contour accuracy and object subtraction does not enable segmentation.

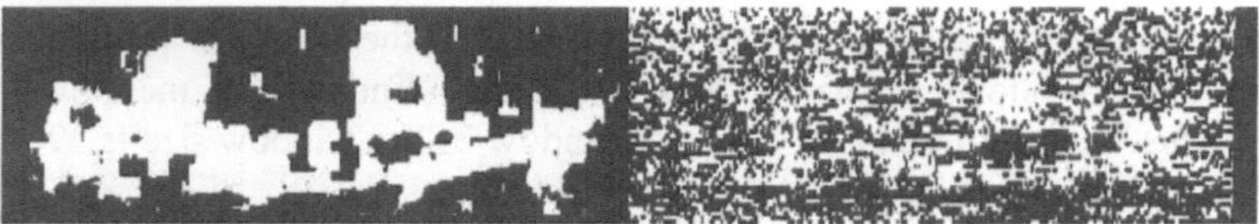

Fig. 12. Corresponded areas by luminance block matching **Fig. 13.** Corresponded areas by object subtraction

4 Conclusion

We have developed a motion segmentation technique, which relies on summarized local image structure given by census transform, and not on absolute luminance values. Applying census transform for two images registered to the sub-pixel accuracy regarding to the moving target object, resulting local image structures, in the forms of bit strings, give good and dense correspondence on the object to segment the region. The effectiveness of the sub-pixel registration is theoretically studied. The method provides the capability to segment the object on the background close in luminance, robustness in luminance change and accurate contours.

References

1. T. Ichikawa, K. Yamada, T. Kanamaru, T. Naemura, K. Aizawa, S. Morishima, and T. Saito: "Multi-media Ambiance Communication", IEEE Signal Processing Magazine, vol.18, no.3, pp.43-50, May 2001.
2. T. Ichikawa, et. al: "Multimedia Ambiance Communication Using an Immersive Environment", MICC & ISCE '99, Vol. 1, 18, Nov. 1999
3. Ramin Zabih and John Woodfill: "Non-parametric Local Transforms for Computing Visual Correspondence", LNCS, Vol. 801, Computer Vision – ECCV '94.
4. K. Yamada, T. Ichikawa, T. Naemura, K. Aizawa and T. Saito: "Generation of Disparity Panorama using a 3-camera Capturing System", IEEE ICIP 2000, TP08.09, Sep. 2000.
5. K. Yamada, T. Ichikawa, T. Naemura, K. Aizawa and T. Saito: "Structure Analysis of Natural Scenes using Census Transform and Region Competition", SPIE VCIP 2001, 4310-22, June 2000.
6. M. Hotter: "Object-Oriented Analysis-Synthesis Coding Based on Moving Two-Dimensional Objects", Signal-Process.: Image Commun., 2, 4, pp.409-428, Dec. 1990.
7. N. Diel: "Object-Oriented Motion Estimation and Segmentation in Image Sequences", Signal-Process.: Image Commun., 3, 1, pp23-56, Feb.1991.

Efficient Algorithms for Motion Based Video Retrieval

Jong Myeon Jeong* and Young Shik Moon**

*Broadcasting Media Technology Department, ETRI, Daejon, Korea
jmjeong@etri.re.kr
**Dept. of computer science & engr., Hanyang University, Ansan, Korea
ysmoon@cse.hanyang.ac.kr

Abstract. In this paper, efficient algorithms for content-based video retrieval using motion information are proposed. We describe algorithms for a *temporal scale invariant and spatial translation absolute* retrieval using trail model and a *temporal scale absolute and spatial translation invariant* retrieval using trajectory model. In the retrieval using trail model, the Distance transformation is performed on each trail image in database. Then, from a given query trail the pixel values along the query trail are added in each distance image to compute the average distance between the trails of query image and database image. For the *spatial translation invariant* retrieval using trajectory model, a new coding scheme referred to as Motion Retrieval Code is proposed, which is suitable for representing object motions in video. Since the Motion Retrieval Code is designed to reflect the human visual system, it is very efficient to compute the similarity between two motion vectors, using a few bit operations.

1 Introduction

Most existing content-based video retrieval systems use the color, texture, shape, and motion features. However, the motion information has not been widely used for the video retrieval, since it is difficult to extract and match the feature set, and it is not easy to find good matching measures for motion information which properly reflect user's requests. Some motion-based retrieval schemes have been proposed [1]-[8], where it is difficult to efficiently search database due to the enormous computation time[1], or it often produces inaccurate results[2],[3],[6] or it is not easy to retrieve with flexibility[4].

In this paper, we propose an efficient method for motion based video retrieval using motion trajectory.

2 Temporal Scale Invariant Retrieval

Temporal scale invariant retrieval is the video retrieval scheme, which does not consider the speed of moving objects, but only considers the path of the object's motion. To retrieve video clips independent of their temporal scale, we use a trail model which captures the path of moving objects over a sequence of frames. The object trail is equivalent to taking the mosaic image of the object's trajectory, and the temporal characteristics of the video clip are ignored. To efficiently compute the average distance between the trails of query image and database image, we use the Distance transformation of database images[9].

2.1 Distance Transformation

The Distance transformation converts a binarized edge image into a distance image whose pixel represents the spatial distance to the nearest edge pixel[9]. Figure 1 shows an example of Distance transformation. In figure 1(b), the intensity of each pixel represents the distance from that pixel to the nearest edge pixel in figure 1(a). The distance image is computed by the approximate Euclidean distance referred to as Chamfer 3/4 distances.

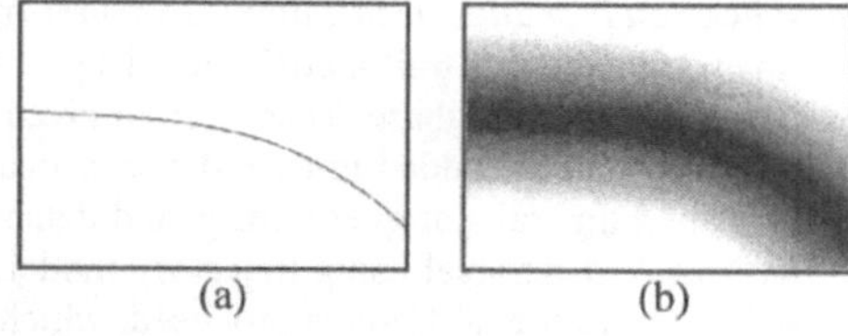

Fig. 1. An example of Distance transformation: (a) Edge image, and (b) Distance image for (a).

2.2 Similarity Measure

In order to perform *spatial translation absolute* retrieval based on trail model, the distance image for the trail image for each video clip is stored in database. Then, from a given query trail the pixel values along the query trail are added in each distance image to compute the average distance between the trails of query image and database image. The query can be given by an example or by a sketch.

The query trail can be represented by the following equation:

$$Q^* = [q_x^*(i), q_y^*(i)]^t, \quad i=1, 2, \ldots, k, \tag{1}$$

where Q^* is a query trail and $(q_x(i), q_y(i))$ represents the coordinate of a point in the query trail Q^*. The dissimilarity between two trails is computed by equation (2).

$$Dist(Q^*, D^{j*}) = \frac{\sum_{i=1}^{k} I^{D^{j*}}(q_x(i), q_y(i))}{k}, \tag{2}$$

where D^{j*} is the distance image for the *j*-th trail in database, $Dist(Q^*, D^{j*})$ denotes dissimilarity between Q^* and D^{j*}, $I^{D^{j*}}(x,y)$ is the intensity value of D^{j*} at pixel coordinate (x, y) in D^{j*}, and k is the number of points in Q^*.

3. Temporal scale Absolute Retrieval

In order to retrieve video clips dependent of their temporal scale, we use a trajectory model which represents the motion vector of moving object at each frame of the sequence. Previous works on *temporal scale absolute* retrieval include [1],[4]-[8]. As a matching measure, Dagtas *et. al.*[1] and Chang *et. al.*[4] use the Euclidean distance between two points and Panchanathan *et. al.*[5] and Dimitrova *et. al.*[6] use the Euclidean distance between two chain codes. However, the Euclidean distance metric often produces incorrect results from the viewpoint of human visual system, since it does not properly reflect motion characteristics. In the human visual system, two motion vectors in figure 2(a) are more similar than those in figure 2(b), but the Euclidean distance metric produces the opposite result.

For the *spatial translation invariant* retrieval based on trajectory model, we propose a new coding scheme referred to as Motion Retrieval Code, which is suitable for representing object motions in the human visual sense.

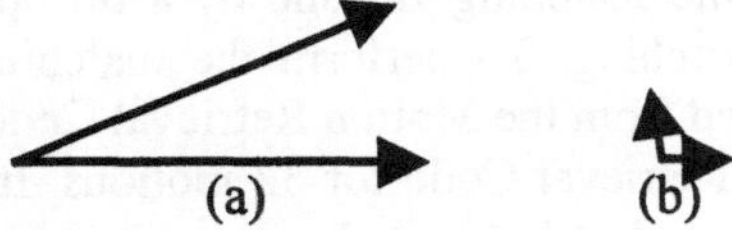

Fig. 2. Problem involved in Euclidean distance metric.

3.1 Motion Retrieval Code

As shown in figure 3, we first quantize the object's motion into 32 vectors by considering moving direction and speed. In the Motion Retrieval Code proposed in this paper, 4 bits for 8 directions and 3 bits for 4 motion magnitude are allocated to represent the total 32 motion vectors. Table 1 shows the Motion Retrieval Code. It is noted that for two motion vectors the number of bit positions with different values represents the difference in direction(magnitude) of those two vectors. For example, vector 0(0000 000) and vector 14(0111 011) are different by 3 quantized steps in direction and by 2 quantized steps in magnitude.

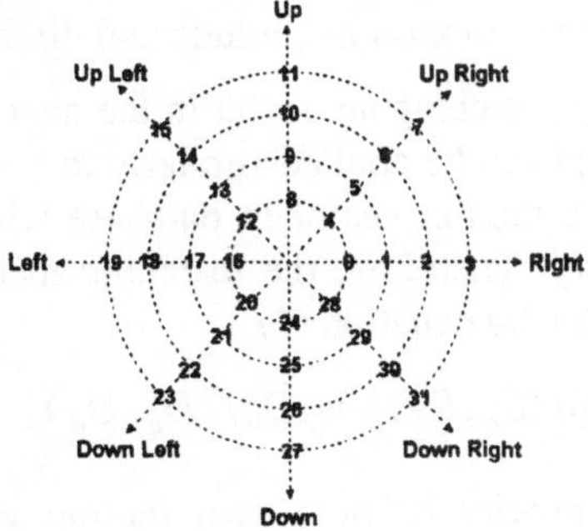

Fig. 3. Quantized object's motion.

Table 1. Motion Retrieval Code.

ID	Dir.	Mag.	ID	Dir.	Mag.	ID	Dir.	Mag.	ID	Dir.	Mag.
0	0000	000	8	0011	000	16	1111	000	24	1100	000
1	0000	001	9	0011	001	17	1111	001	25	1100	001
2	0000	011	10	0011	011	18	1111	011	26	1100	011
3	0000	111	11	0011	111	19	1111	111	27	1100	111
4	0001	000	12	0111	000	20	1110	000	28	1000	000
5	0001	001	13	0111	001	21	1110	001	29	1000	001
6	0001	011	14	0111	011	22	1110	011	30	1000	011
7	0001	111	15	0111	111	23	1110	111	31	1000	111

If the object motion is represented by the Motion Retrieval Code, the matching for retrieval is performed by counting the number of different bits between the Motion Retrieval Code of the given query trajectory and the Motion Retrieval Codes for each trajectory in database. Since the matching is done by a bit operation, the proposed algorithm can achieve fast matching. To perform the matching more efficiently, a look-up table can be constructed from the Motion Retrieval Code.

Table 1 shows the Motion Retrieval Code for 32 motions. It is noted that if more bits are allocated to the Motion Retrieval Code, more precise quantization can be obtained.

3.2 Justification of Motion Retrieval Code

Many researchers have used the small velocity change constraint for motion analysis and correspondence search. Equation 3 is an example of matching measure which is commonly used in correspondence search to reflect the small velocity change constraint[10]-[11].

$$E = w_1 \frac{dS}{dt} + w_2 \frac{dD}{dt}, \tag{3}$$

where w_1, w_2 are the weights for the motion magnitude and direction, and dS/dt, dD/dt are the deviations of motion magnitude and direction, respectively.

The object tracking is done by searching an object in the next frame which has the minimum value of E. This concept can be applied similarly to the motion based video retrieval because we search for a motion vector in database which is similar to the motion vector for the given query. Therefore, the matching measure for the motion based video retrieval can be written by equation (4).

$$Diff(Q,D) = w_1 Diff(S_q, S_d) + w_2 Diff(D_q, D_d), \tag{4}$$

where, $Diff(Q,D)$ is the dissimilarity between two motion vectors in the query trajectory and the trajectory stored in database, $Diff(S_q, S_d)$ is the dissimilarity of magnitude, $Diff(D_q, D_d)$ is the dissimilarity of direction, and w_1 , w_2 are the weights.

The Motion Retrieval Code is appropriate for the video retrieval, since it consists of the magnitude and direction of a motion, and exactly reflects the concept of equation (4).

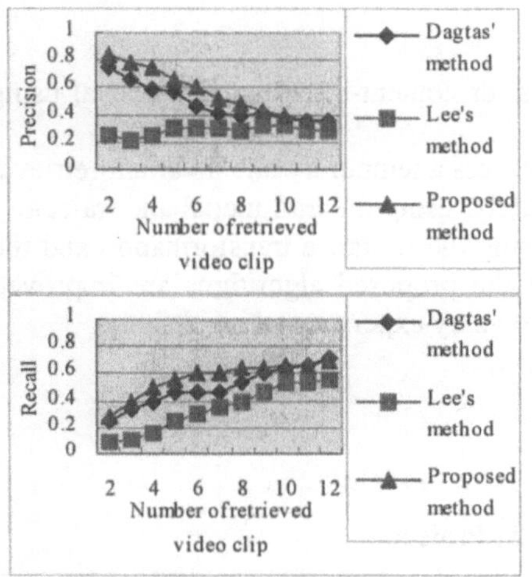

Fig. 4. Performance evaluation of spatial translation absolute retrieval using the trail model.

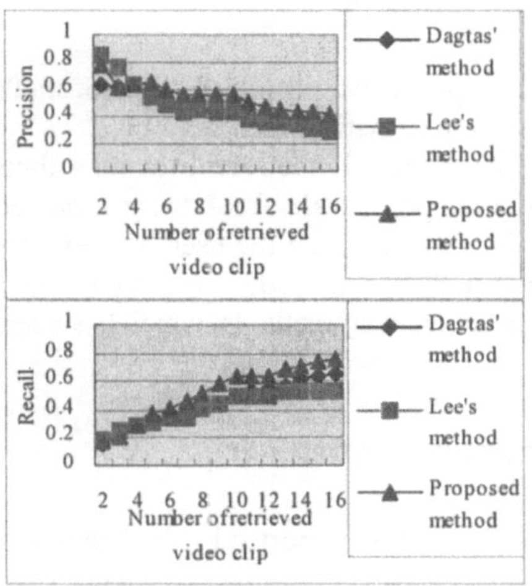

Fig. 6. Performance evaluation of spatial translation invariant retrieval using the trajectory model.

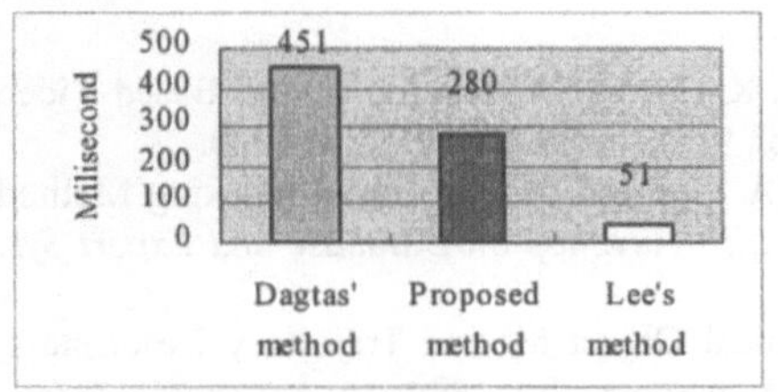

Fig. 5. Execution time for spatial translation absolute retrieval using the trail model.

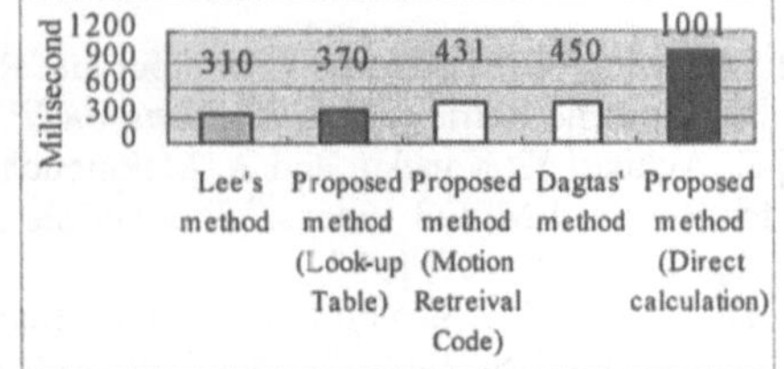

Fig. 7. Execution time for spatial translation invariant retrieval using the trajectory model.

4. Performance Evaluation

The simulations have been performed on 3 video sequences, including Che, Yard, and Walkmen sequences which are the MPEG-7 test sequences. The trajectories stored in database consist of 68 moving objects with 13309 frames. To evaluate our methods, precision-recall metrics are computed. The performance results for the proposed methods are presented in figure 4 through figure 7. Figure 4 shows that the precision and recall are respectively improved by 17 % and 14 %(in maximum) over the existing *temporal scale invariant and spatial translation absolute* methods, and figure 5 shows the comparative result in terms of computational cost. Figure 6 shows that precision and recall are improved by 14 % and 15 %(in maximum) respectively over the existing *temporal scale absolute and spatial translation invariant* methods, and figure 7 shows the comparison of the execution time. It is noted that the computation time is reduced considerably by using the Motion Retrieval Code instead of direct calculation and it is further reduced by using look-up table.

5. Conclusion

In this paper, we proposed efficient methods for content-based video retrieval using motion information.

The proposed video retrieval algorithms process a temporal scale invariant retrieval and a temporal scale absolute retrieval separately, using the trail model and trajectory model depending on the users request. By using the Distance transformation and the Motion Retrieval Code, the performance of the proposed algorithms are improved over the existing methods, which has been shown by experimental results.

Acknowledgment

This work was supported by the Brain Korea 21 Project.

References

[1] S. Dagtas, W. Al-Khatib, A. Ghafoor and R. L. Kashyap, "Models for Motion-Based Video Indexing and Retrieval," *IEEE Trans. on IP.*, vol. 9, no. 1, pp. 88-101, Jan. 2000.

[2] Z. Aghbari K. Kaneko, and A. Makinouchi, "A Motion-Location Based Indexing Method for Retrieval MPEG Videos," *Proc. of the 9th Int. Workshop on Database and Expert Sys. Appli.*, pp. 102-107, 1998.

[3] K. W. Lee, W. S. You and J. Kim, Hierarchical Object Motion Trajectory Descriptors, ISO/IECJTC1/SC29/ WG11/MPEG99/M4681, Vancouver, Jul. 1999.

[4] S. F. Chang, W. Chen, H. J. Meng, H. Sundaram, and D. Zhong, "A Fully Automated Content-Based Video Search Engine Supporting Spatiotemporal Queries," *IEEE Trans. on CSVT.*, vol. 8, no. 5, pp. 602-615, Sep. 1998.

[5] S. Panchanathan, F. Golshani, and Y. C. Park, "VideoRoadMap : A System for Interactie Classification and Indexing of Still and Motion Pictures," *Proc. of IEEE Instrumentation and Measurement Tech. Conf.*, pp. 18-21, 1998.

[6] N. Dimitrova, and F. Golshani, "Motion Recovery for Video Content Classification," *ACM Trans. on Info. Sys.*, vol. 13, no. 4, pp. 408-439, Oct. 1995.

[7] K. W. Lee, W. S. You and J. Kim, "Video Retrieval based on the Object's Motion Trajectory," *Proc. of SPIE*, vol. 4067, pp. 114-124, 2000.

[8] W. Chen, S. F. Chang, "Motion Trajectory Matching of Video Objects," *Proc. of SPIE*, vol. 3972, pp. 544-553, 2000.

[9] G. Borgefors, "Distance Transformations in Digital Images," *CVGIP*, vol.34, no. 3, pp. 334-371, 1986.

[10] D. H. Ballard, C. M. Brown, Computer Vision, Prentice-Hall, 1982.

[11] I. K. Sethi and R. Jain, "Finding Trajectories of Feature Points in an Monocular Image Sequence," *IEEE Trans. on PAMI.*, vol. 9, no. 1, pp. 56-73, Jan. 1987.

Content-Based Retrieval on the Compressed Domain of 2nd Generation Image Coding

G. Qiu

School of Computer Science, The University of Nottingham
Jubilee Campus, Nottingham NG8 1BB, UK
qiu@cs.nott.ac.uk

Abstract. The so-called 2nd generation image coding methods segment images into homogenous regions of various sizes adaptively. Each region is then coded with an appropriate method according to its perceptual characteristics. One of our research aims is to extend 2nd generation image coding methods to meet not only the traditional rate distortion criterion but also the new "easy content access" criterion [6] of image coding. Towards this end, we introduce the region and colour co-occurrence matrix (RACOM), an image content description feature easily computable directly (without decoding) from the compressed domain of 2nd generation image coding methods, and use it for content-based image retrieval from large image databases. We show that RACOM is a very effective image content descriptor and has a comparable performance to state of the art techniques for content-based image retrieval.

1 Introduction

Image coding is the key enabling technology in the current digital media revolution. Traditionally, rate distortion criterion was the goal of image coding. Over the past several decades, much effort has been spent on reducing the bit rate and improving the distortion performances. It can be argued that to a certain extent, the rate distortion criterion has been met by many modern image-coding techniques. In the author's view, trying to improve bit rates by a fraction of bit per pixel and distortion by a fraction of a dB on existing image coding frameworks is not the best use of resources. With the explosive increase in visual data (image and video), the new challenge faced by the research community is how to make the vast collection of images and video data easily accessible.

Content-based image indexing and retrieval is a promising technology for managing large image/video databases [1]. Research in this direction has been actively pursued in different disciplines for over a decade. Well-known techniques such as colour histogram [2] and textures descriptors [3], newer methods such as color correlogram [4] and blobworld [5], and many others variations [1] have been developed. In terms of image retrieval accuracy and relevance, all these methods have different strengths and weaknesses. In the present paper, we attempt to address a common weakness associated with traditional approaches to content-based image indexing and retrieval.

Naïve approaches to content-based image indexing store images using standard compression techniques and store low-level image features as explicit side information as indices. However, these methods are unsatisfactory because extra side information leads to data expansion; the use of pre-computed indexing features restricts the flexibility of retrieval methods; and computing new indexing features requires either partial or full decompression, which demands extra computation. Since image coding is an essential component of an imaging system, what would be better, is to make the coded bits accessible "midstream" without the need to decompress the image. Making image data accessible in the compressed domain, or midstream, has been advocated as an extra criterion for image coding, the so-called "4th criterion" [6].

Segmentation based image coding, also known as the second generation image coding, was once regarded as a very promising image compression method and was actively pursued by researchers in the 1980s [7]. However, its full potential was never realized due to the algorithmic and computer hardware limitations of the time. We believe this line of research will be useful in managing large image databases. In particular it can be used to compress images to moderate bite rates and to enable fast processing in the compressed domain for easy content access. Completely unconnected to image coding and compressed domain content access, the blobworld system [5] has demonstrated the advantages of segmenting images into meaningful regions for content-based retrieval. In this paper, we present the region and color co-occurrence matrix (RACOM) easily computable from the compressed domain of an adaptive segmentation based image coding method [8]. Using the RACOM as image content descriptor we have successfully applied it to content-based image retrieval from large image databases

This paper is organized as follows. In Section 2, we briefly review a variable block size segmentation based image compression method and describe an adaptive image segmentation algorithm. In Section 3, we present the region and colour co-occurrence matrix (RACOM). Section 5 presents experimental results and concluding remarks are given in Section 6.

2 Segmentation-based Image Compression

Broadly speaking, segmentation based image methods are often classified as 2nd generation image coding [7]. The idea behind this scheme is that if we can classified image regions into different classes, then we can allocate different number of bits to different regions according to the properties of the region thus achieving optimality in rate-distortion performance. However, in unconstrained image segmentation, both the numbers of the regions and their shape are determined solely by the image being examined. This fact implies that a very large number of bits may be needed to represent the shape and location information. Therefore, certain constraints have to be imposed in segmenting the image into regions for efficient coding. Many methods based on this principle have been developed over the years. One such technique, which represents one of the most promising segmentation-based approaches to image coding was the variable block size segmentation technique developed by Vaisey and Gersho [8]. As has been reported in [8] excellent rate distortion performance can be achieved by such a method. For details of coding methods and achievable bit rates, readers are referred to [8]. Of particular interest to our current project is the way in which each variable size block is coded. In particular, the average colour of the block is coded separately which implies it is readily available with minimal computation. Although many other properties of each variable size block are computable also, we shall only exploit the mean colour and study the use of other properties in the future.

Following the essential idea of [8], we have developed our own implementation of the variable block size segmentation method, and we will not repeat the original implementation (the complete coder) in full. Instead, our interest is to demonstrate that image content description features can be easily computed from the compressed bit streams (the block mean colour) of this type of image coding techniques for content-based image retrieval. The constraints we used in this work were as follows: 1) the shapes of the regions were restricted to be square; 2) the maximum size of the regions must not exceed N x N; 3) within each region, the pixels must have similar colours. Therefore an image is segmented into squared regions of sizes 1 x 1, 2 x 2, 3 x 3, 4 x 4, ..., N x N. The procedures is as follows.

Step 1. Scan the image from left to right top to bottom direction. If the current pixel p(x, y) has been assigned a region label, then move to the next pixel. Notice we are working on colour images and p(x, y) is a vector.

Step 2. If p(x, y) has not been assigned a region label, then do the following

2.1. Set S = 1

2.2. Calculate

$$e(x,y)=\sum_{i=0}^{S-1}\sum_{j=0}^{S-1}\left\|p(x+i,y+j)-m(x,y)\right\|,\ \text{where}\ m(x,y)=\frac{1}{S^2}\sum_{i=0}^{S-1}\sum_{j=0}^{S-1}p(x+i,y+j)$$

2.3. If e(x, y) < EL; where EL is a pre-set error limit value, and p(x+S, y) and p(x, y+S) have not been assigned a region label, and S < = N, where N is a pre-set maximum region size, then increase S by 1 and go to 2.2, otherwise go to 2.4

2.4 Label all p(x + i, y +i), i = 0, 1, ..., S-1, with the next available region label.

Step 3. If not reach the end of the image go to 1. Otherwise stop.

As an example, Fig. 1 shows an image segmented by the algorithm. Notice that we have not implemented the full coder, because the mean colour of each block will be readily available in a real coder [8] we shall use the mean colour of the segmented blocks directly to derive image content description features in the next section.

3 Region and Colour Co-occurrence Matrix

For the compressed bit streams of the variable block size segmentation based colour image coding, the average colours of the blocks are readily available [8], so are the sizes of the blocks. It is based on the block mean colours and the block sizes we construct the region and colour co-occurrence matrix (RACOM). The RACOM is a two-dimensional array. Each cell, RACOM (m, n), records the probability that a segmented region (SR) of size n x n having an average colour C_m. We know that the number of block sizes are fixed by the coding algorithm, in order to keep the size of

RACOM small, we have to restrict the number of possible colours. Similar to colour correlogram [4], we use a colour table $CT_g = \{C_g(0), C_g(1), \ldots, C_g(M)\}$ (used by all images) to quantize the mean colours in each region to a small fixed set of colours. Notice that the colour table has not been used to code the image but used only for the construction of RACOM. Formally, the RACOM is constructed as

$$RACOM(m,n) = \Pr\{Size(SR) = n \mid Q(C_{SR}) = m\}, \forall m,n \tag{1}$$

where C_{SR} is the mean colour of the region and Q is the colour quantizer with a codebook CT_g. The size of RACOM is O(M x N). Since the number of regions in a typical image will be small and it may be possible to construct RACOM on the fly. In addition, we found that RACOM is very sparse and can therefore be stored very efficiently.

4 RACOM for Content-based Image Retrieval

Using RACOM described in the last section as image index, we can perform content-based image retrieval from image databases. To construct the image data database, we can store the RACOM or compute it on-line. Content-based retrieval can be performed by comparing the query image's RACOM with those of the images in the database use an appropriate distance measure. We have found that the following L_1 norm distance measure worked well. Let $RACOM_q$ and $RACOM_d$ be the RACOMs of the query and database images respectively. The similarity of the two images can be measured as the L_1 distance as follows:

$$D(q,d) = \sum_{m=1}^{M}\sum_{n=1}^{N} \frac{\left|RACOM_q(m,n) - RACOM_d(m,n)\right|}{1 + RACOM_q(m,n) + RACOM_d(m,n)} \tag{2}$$

5 Experimental Results

We have tested the RACOM's performance in content-based image retrieval using a database of 20,000 photography color images from the Corel Photo collection. We collected 96 pairs of similar images from various sources as query ground truth. The query images were embedded in the database. The goal was to use one image as query to retrieve the corresponding target image from the database. A subset of the query images is shown in Fig. 2.

In the results presented below, EL = 15, N = 8 and M = 64 (the number of colours). As a comparison we have also implemented the color correlogram of [4] (4 distances and 64 colors). In total, 192 queries were performed, and for majority of the queries, the target image was returned in the first few positions for both colour correlogram (CC) and RACOM. This is in agreement with similar studies by other groups. The cumulative retrieval rate, i.e., the number of retrieved target images above a certain rank, of the CC and RACOM method is shown in table 1. As can be seen, both methods have very similar performance. The average rank of all target images for the

CC method was 265 and for the RACOM method was 129. The average rank was high because a few queries returned their targets in positions greater than 1000. If we consider a query which returned its target at a position higher than 30 as failure, then CC had a success rate of 169/192 (88%) and RACOM had a success rate of 168/192 (87.5%). Examples of retrieved images are shown in Fig. 3.

Fig. 1. Images segmented using different values of EL.

	Cumulative Retrieval Rate		
Method	<= 10	< = 30	<= 100
CC	163	169	174
RACOM	157	168	174

Table 1. Cumulative retrieval rate performances

6 Concluding Remarks

In this paper, we have introduced an effective image content descriptor easily computable from the compressed domain of 2nd generation image coding methods. We demonstrated its usefulness in content-based retrieval of colour images in large image database. It is fair to say that 2nd generation coding methods were not favored based on the traditional rate distortion only criterion of image coding. However, with the new demand for easy content access, this type of image coding techniques may have overall advantage over current MPEG and JPEG frameworks in developing image coding and representation methods which will not only satisfy the traditional rate distortion criterion but also the new easy content access criterion of image coding.

References

1. 1. Y. Rui et al, "Image retrieval: current techniques, promising directions, and open issues", Journal of Visual Communication and Image Representation, Vol. 10, pp. 39-62, 1999
2. M. Swain and D. Ballard, "Color indexing", International Journal of Computer Vision, Vol. 7, pp. 11-32, Year 1991
3. B. S. Manjunath and W. Y. Ma, "Texture features for browsing and retrieval of image data", IEEE Trans Pattern Analysis and Machine Intelligence, vol. 18, pp. 837 – 842, 1996

4. J. Huang, et. al., "Image indexing using color correlogram", Proc. CVPR, pp. 762-768, 1997
5. C. Carson et al, “Blobworld: A system for region-based image indexing and retrieval”, Proc. Int. Conf. Vis. Inf. Sys. 1999
6. R.W. Picard, "Content Access for Image/Video Coding: "The Fourth Criterion"", MIT Media Lab TR No. 295. 1994
7. M. Kunt et al, “Second generation image coding”, Proc. IEEE, vol. 73, pp. 549 –574, 1985
8. J. Vaisey and A Gersho, “Image compression with variable block size segmentation, IEEE Trans Signal Processing, vol. 40, pp. 2040 – 2060, 1992

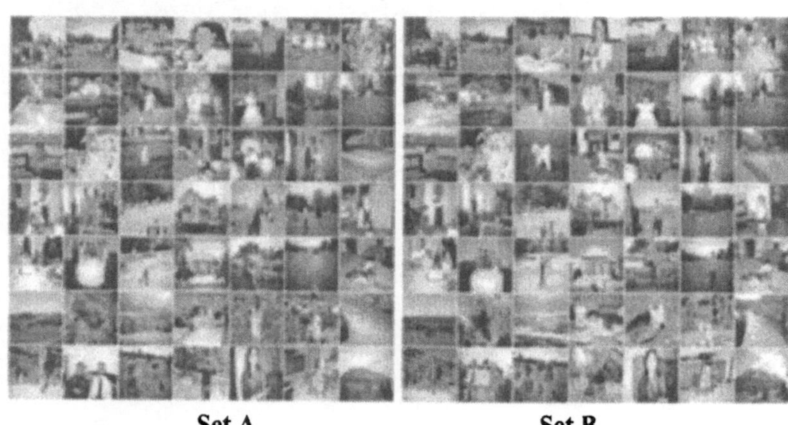

Set A **Set B**

Fig. 2. .Query image pairs. For each image in **Set A,** there is a target image in **Set B**

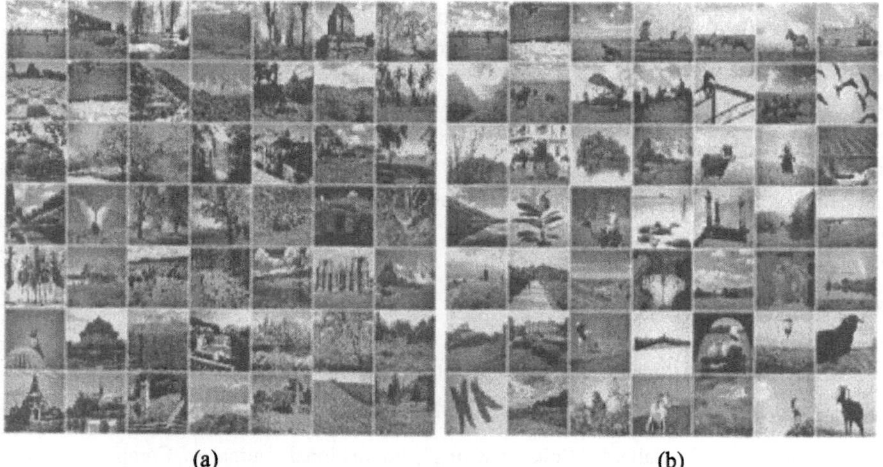

(a) (b)

Fig. 3. , Examples of retrieved images. The top-left corner image is the query and subsequent ones from left to right top to bottom are returned images ordered according to their similarity to the query. (a) results of colour correlogram. (b) results of RACOM.

Retrieving Landscape Images Using Scene Structural Matrix

G. Qiu and S. Sudirman

School of Computer Science, The University of Nottingham
Jubilee Campus, Nottingham NG8 1BB, UK
{qiu,sxs}@cs.nott.ac.uk

Abstract. In this paper, we present Scene Structural Matrix (SSM) and apply it to the retrieval of landscape images. The SSM captures the overall structural characteristics of the scene by indexing the geometric features of the image. A binary image tree (bintree) is used to partition the image and from which we derive multi-resolution geometric structural descriptors of the image. It is shown that SSM is particularly effective in retrieving images with strong structural features, such as landscape photographs. We show that SSM is robust against spatial and spectral distortions thus making it superior to current state of the art techniques such as color correlogram in certain applications. We will also show that images retrieved by the SSM are more relevant than those returned by color correlogram and color histogram.

1 Introduction

Content-based indexing and retrieval [1] have attracted extensive research interests in recent years. Traditional methods use global statistics of local image features, e.g., color histogram [2], color correlogram [3] and their variance as image indices. These methods have been shown to be very successful in retrieving images with similar local feature distributions. However, since these measures do not take into account the locations of the local features, the retrieved results often do not make a lot of sense. For example, using a landscape image with blue sky on top and green countryside at the bottom as query example and trying to retrieve images with similar structures, i.e., blue sky on top and green countryside at the bottom, methods based on global statistics of local features often give very unsatisfactory results. Another scenario is one in which two or more images of the same scene photographed under different imaging conditions, e.g., images of a countryside taken at dusk or dawn under a clear or a cloudy sky. Using one of these images as a query example often fails to retrieve other images of the same scene taken under different time or conditions. In yet another situation maybe one in which a same scene imaged by different, uncalibrated devices. Using one image taken by one device may fail to find the same scene taken by other devices.

In this paper, we present a method which uses a binary image tree [8] to partition an image recursively into hierarchical sub-images and introduce the Scene Structural Matrix (SSM), a 2-dimensional table to summarize the geometric structures of the

partitioned image. We use the SSM as image indices for content-based image retrieval. Experiments have been performed on an image database consisting of over 7000 high-resolution photographic color images. It is shown that the SSM is particularly effective in retrieving images with strong structural features such as landscape images. It is also shown that the SSM is more robust to spatial and spectral distortions than traditional color histogram and state of the art color correlogram methods and therefore is advantageous in applications such as retrieving images of the same scene imaged at different time and under different imaging conditions.
The organization of the paper is as follows. Section 2 describes the scene structural matrix. Section 3 presents the application of SSM to content based image retrieval. Section 4 presents experimental results and section 5 concludes the paper

2 Scene Structural Matrix

To construct the SSM, we first segment the image using a simple, easy to implement, binary image tree (bintree) adaptive image segmentation method [8], which can be regarded as a much simplified version of binary space partitioning tree image segmentation method [4-6]. An image (assumed rectangular in shape) is first cut into two equal sized sub-images by either a vertical or a horizontal straight line. Each of the resulting two sub-images is again cut into two equal sized sub-images by either a vertical or a horizontal straight line. The process is repeated for each of the subsequent sub-images until a stopping criterion (e.g., when the pixel value variation in the sub-image falls below a preset value) is reached. Figure. 1 illustrates such a scheme.

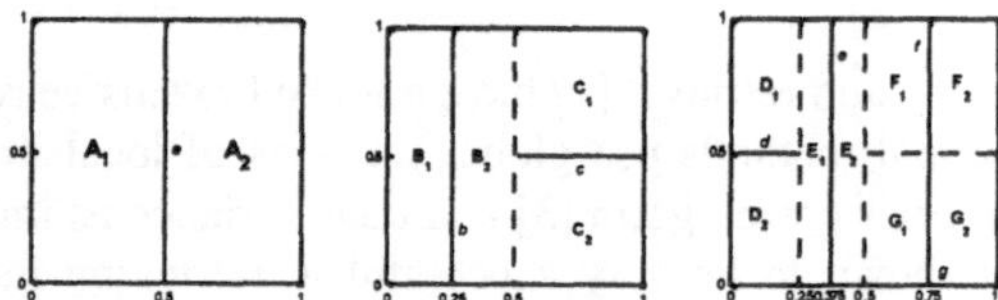

Fig. 1. The bintree adaptive image segmentation scheme. The original image is partitioned by the vertical line a into two equal sized halves (left); Lines b and c partition the resulting two halves (middle); and the resulting four sub-images are partitioned by the lines d, e, f and g (right). The capital letters denote the characteristics of the corresponding region. They might represent the region average color, the distribution of color or even textures.

Whether a sub-image (including the original) is cut by a horizontal or a vertical line depends on the structure of the sub-image (hence the segmentation is adaptive), and there are many criterion can be used. One method is to cut the sub-images based on the predominant edge orientations. In this method, the horizontal and vertical gradients are first calculated and the sub-image is cut based on the magnitudes of the directional gradients. If the vertical gradient dominates, then the sub-image is cut horizontally, otherwise vertically. Some edge detection operators [7] may be used to calculate the directional gradients. Let $G_h(i, j)$ and $G_v(i,j)$, $i = 0, 1, \dots M-1$, $j = 0, 1, \dots, N-1$, be the horizontal and vertical gradients respectively, of an M x N sub-image to be partitioned. We calculate

$$G_h = \frac{1}{M \times N} \sum_{i=0}^{M-1} \sum_{j=0}^{N-1} |G_h(i,j)| \quad G_v = \frac{1}{M \times N} \sum_{i=0}^{M-1} \sum_{j=0}^{N-1} |G_v(i,j)|$$

If $G_h > G_v$, the sub-image will be cut vertically otherwise horizontally. Figure 2 shows an example of the segmentation.

Fig. 2. From left to right: Original landscape image, 1st, 4th, 7th and 12th level partition. Each sub-image is painted by its average color

Based on the bintree segmented image, we construct a table termed scene structural matrix. The rationale for building the SSM is that because the reconstruction are perceptually similar to the original, then the features from the reconstruction can be used to recognize the original. The fact that we recursively cut the image with only horizontal and vertical lines means that there are some very simple geometry structures can be extracted. When a line partitions a sub-image, it intersects with the two borders of the sub-image which are perpendicular to it forming a T shape structure at different resolutions (refer to Figure 1, the dash and solid lines). It is based on this T shape structure we build our scene structural matrix. The SSM is a two dimensional array indexing the T shape structures of the bintree segmented image. There are only two types of T shape structures and their conjugates. Therefore only the + and the - structures need to be indexed since (+ and ¦) and (- and -) will always appear in pairs. It is clear, at different level and depending on how a sub-image is cut, the two arms of the T-shape features will have different length. The SSMs capture this fact by indexing the T-shape features of various sizes. There are two SSMs, SSM^+ and SSM^- indexing the two unique T-shape features. Each cell in the matrix corresponds to the T-shape with a certain arm lengths. The values of the cells in SSM^+ are the accumulated average color difference across the horizontal arm, and the values of the cells in SSM^- are the accumulated average color differences across the vertical arm. The formal description of the SSM is as follows: Let $h_i = H/2^i$, $v_j = V/2^j$, where $i, j = 0, 1, 2, \ldots$ are two integers, H is the horizontal dimension of the image and V is vertical dimension of the image.

Let h_a and v_a be the lengths of horizontal arm and vertical arm of the T shape features. We have

$$SSM^+(i,j) = SSM^+(h_a = h_i \text{ and } v_a = v_j) = ACC\,|C_{top} - C_{bottom}|$$
$$SSM^-(i,j) = SSM^-(h_a = h_i \text{ and } v_a = v_j) = ACC\,|C_{left} - C_{right}|$$

where ACC denotes accumulation, and C_{top} is the average color of the top half and C_{bottom} is the average color of the bottom half of the partition. Similarly, C_{left} is the average color of the left half and C_{right} is the average color of the right half of the partition. As an example, Table 1 shows the SSMs of the scene partitions of Figure 1.

SSM^+

0	0	0
$\|C_1-C_2\|$	0	x
$\|D_1-D_2\|$	x	x

SSM^-

$\|A_1-A_2\|$	$\|B_1-B_2\|$	$\|E_1-E_2\|$
0	$\|F_1-F_2\| + \|G_1-G_2\|$	x
0	x	x

Table 1. The Scene Structural Matrices (SSM) of the segmentation of Figure 1. The capital letters denote the average colour vectors of their corresponding sub-images

3 Content-Based Image Indexing and Retrieval Using SSM

We can use the SSMs as image indices for content-based indexing and retrieval in image database application. The SSMs for each image in the database are constructed and image retrieval can be based on comparing these SSMs with that of the query image. It is worth noting that only a few (5 to 8) levels of partition suffice, hence the size of SSM is very small. Let SSMq(i, j) and SSMd(i, j) be the SSMs of the query image and the database image respectively. The similarity of the two images can be calculated by

$$D(q, d) = \min \{ D1(q, d), D2(q, d) \}$$
$$D2(q, d) = \Sigma_i \Sigma_j \left(W(i,j)(|SSM^+ q(i, j) - SSM^+ d(i, j)| + |SSM^- q(i,j) - SSM^- d(i,j)|)\right)$$
$$D2(q, d) = \Sigma_i \Sigma_j \left(W(i,j)(|SSM^+ q(i,j) - SSM^- d(i,j)| + |SSM^- q(i,j)\ SSM^+ d(i,j)|)\right)$$

The min {} operator guarantees a zero difference between identical images rotated by 90°. The matrix W(i,j) allows us to use different weights to the contribution of coarse and detail features of the image. Intuitively we would like global features to be more dominant than detail features. A typical weight matrix is

	0	**1**	**2**
0	1	½	1/3
1	½	1/3	x
2	1/3	x	x

Based on the image similarity measures, images that have smaller distances are considered more similar to the query and are returned to the user.

4 Experimental Results

We have implemented the SSM method for image indexing and retrieval using an image database of 7400 high-resolution color photographic images, a subset of the commercially available Corel Photo collection widely used by other research groups. From the database, we randomly chose 50 landscape images. In the experiment, each of these images was subjected to various spatial and spectral processing before being used as query image. The aim was to use the distorted (processed) image as query and retrieve the original image from the database. The processing performed include spectral (color) modification, spatial resolution scaling, and spatial filtering. As a comparison, we have also implemented color histogram (CH) [2] (4096-bin) and color correlogram (CC) [3] (4 distances, 64 colors) methods. For the results presented, the SSMs were built based on 7 level bintree partitions. The cumulative recall rate, i.e., the number of retrieved original images above a certain rank, of various processed images as queries and using different query methods are shown in Table 2.

The results show that SSM method is more robust to color alteration than the other two methods. It is also far more robust to scaling than color correlogram method and relatively stable to spatial smoothing. Furthermore, SSM retrieved far more relevant images than the other two methods. Figure 3 shows some examples. It is clearly seen that CC returns completely irrelevant images while CH despite being able to retrieve the original image the other returned images have little relevance to the query. On the other hand, the SSM method not only successfully found the original image using the distorted version as query, it also returned much more relevant images. These results clearly demonstrate the superiority of SSM method as compared to the others.

5 Concluding Remarks

We have presented an image content descriptor which captures simple geometrical structures within an image and indexes them efficiently into two relatively small matrices. It has been shown that this method has good performance in retrieving the original image when the same image having undergone substantial spatial and spectral processing was used as query. Furthermore, the method has been shown to return much more relevant images than state of the art methods when applied to landscape image retrieval. The concept of SSM is unique in the literature. It is worth pointing out that in the current paper only one of many possible image features was used to fill the contents of SSM.

6 References

[1] Y. Rui et. al., "Image Retrieval: Current Techniques, Promising Directions, and Open Issues", J. Visual Comm. Image Representation, vol.10, pp.39-62, 1999.

[2] M. J. Swain et. al., "Color Indexing", Int. J. Computer Vision, Vol. 7, no. 1, pp.11-32, 1991.

[3] J. Huang, et.al., "Image indexing using color correlogram", Proceeding of Computer Vision and Pattern Recognition, pp.762-768, 1997.

[4] H. Radha et. al., "Image compression using binary space partitioning tree", IEEE Trans. on Image Processing, vol.5, pp.1610-1624, 1996.

[5] G. Qiu and S. Sudirman, "Representation and Retrieval of Color Image Using Binary Space Partitioning Tree", Proceeding of 8th Color Image Conference, pp.195 - 201, 2000.

[6] X. Wu, "Image Coding by Adaptive Tree-Structured Segmentation", ", IEEE Trans. on Image Processing, vol.38, pp.1755-1767, 1992.

[7] R. C. Gonzalez et. al., Digital Image Processing, Addison-Wesley, 1992

[8] H. Samet, Applications of spatial data structures: computer Graphics, image processing, and GIS, Addison Wesley, 1989

		Ranks											
		1			< =10			< = 20			< =50		
Distortion		C	S	F	C	S	F	C	S	F	C	S	F
Method	SSM	2	37	47	23	46	50	38	49	50	46	49	50
	CC	0	0	49	0	1	50	0	2	50	0	3	50
	CH	0	50	50	0	50	50	0	50	50	1	50	50

Table 2. Cumulative Recall Rate (out of 50) when the query images were subjected to various distortions. Method codes: SSM-Scene Structural Matrix; CC-Color Correlogram; CH-Color Histogram. Distortion codes: C-color modification (-80% of overall hue and saturation, and +30% of overall intensity); S-spatial scaling (reduced to 1/16 in size); F-Filtering processing (7x7-neighborhood averaging). The table should be interperated as for example: when the query images were subjected to colour distortion (C), SSM retrieved 2 (out of 50) target images in the 1st rank, CC and CH retrieved none in the 1st rank etc.

Original image (left) and its 1/16th scaled version (right) which is used as query

The first 10 returned images by using **SSM** method

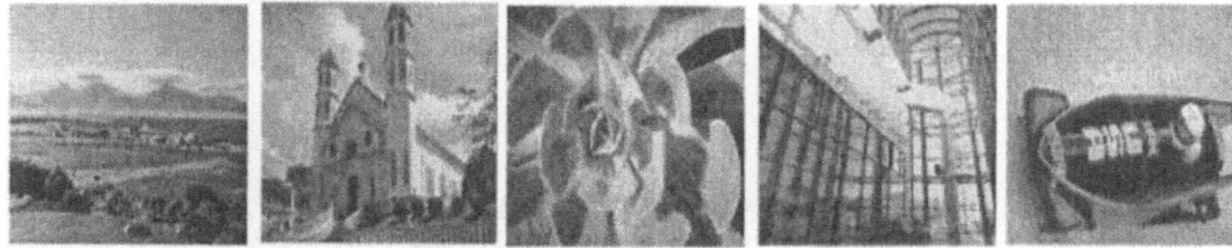

The first 5 returned images by using **Color Histogram** method

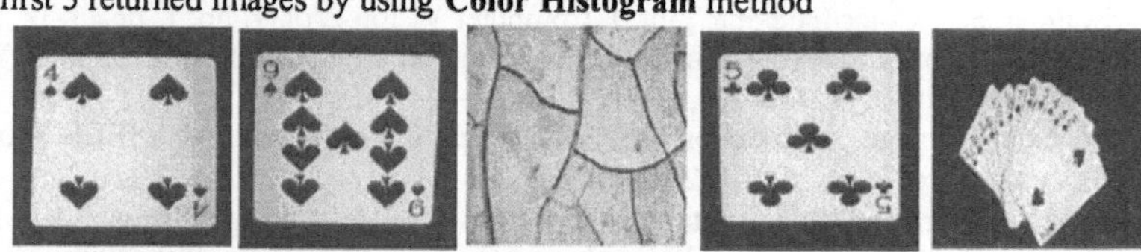

The first 5 returned images by using **Color Correlogram** method

Fig. 3. The first few returned images by using three retrieval methods when the target image is scaled down to $1/16^{th}$ of its original size. The images are displayed as square for convenience

Digital Watermarking: A Communications with Side Information Perspective

Chun-Shien Lu and Hong-Yuan Mark Liao

Institute of Information Science, Academia Sinica,
Taipei, Taiwan
{lcs, liao}@iis.sinica.edu.tw

Abstract. This paper discusses digital watermarking from the viewpoint of communications with side information (SI) since SI may be quite informative from a watermarking perspective. We survey several watermarking methods that were developed by utilizing the SI concept. We further classify these SI-based methods into two categories according to where the SI is available and where it comes from. We believe that incorporation of multiple side information might be helpful in developing a better watermarking scheme, i.e., a system with capabilities of blind detection, robustness (resistant to both removing and geometric attacks), and correct recovery of multiple-bit message.

1 Introduction

Digital watermarking [9] has received much attention for intellectual property protection. Typically, a watermarking system is composed of an embedder and a detector. At the embedder side, a watermark is concealed into the cover data and makes the combined data become a stego data. After the transmission of stego data, the hidden watermark is detected at the detector side. Under this paradigm, embedder and detector in watermarking correspond to transmitter and receiver in communication (see Fig. 1).

Conventionally, watermarking is proposed to be a spread spectrum-based style [1] by regarding both the cover data and the hidden watermark as noises. That is, the information about the cover data are not utilized. Furthermore, some environmental factors that may be available during watermark embedding are not used also. Therefore, conventional watermarking scheme is limited in its capability of robustness and/or detection.

Recently, some researchers have begun to explore the relationship between watermarking and communications. They tried to find a new way to connect both watermarking and communications to further improve the robustness. Cox *et al.* [2] were the first ones who explicitly proposed to view watermarking as communications with side information. Their idea was to use cover data as SI to enhance robustness.

In this paper, we survey state of the art watermarking methods involving the concept of communications with side information. In particular, those watermarking methods which originally do not explain their ideas from the aspects

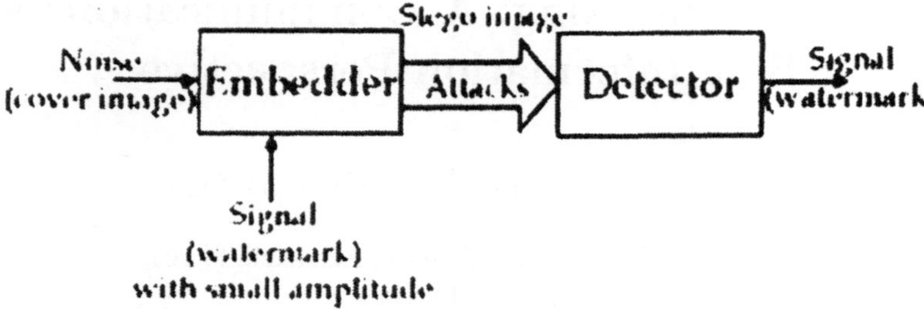

Fig. 1. A common watermarking system composed of an embedder and a detector.

of side information in communications will be re-interpreted. We will explicitly point out what available information could be used as prior knowledge for watermarking. We also examine from which the prior knowledge comes.

2 Communications with Side Information (SI)-based Watermarking

Some kinds of side information (SI) used in the existing watermarking methods will be discussed.

2.1 SI: Available at Detector and Comes from Pilot

In order to resist against geometric attacks, calibration signal might be embedded and then extracted to recovery the effects caused by geometric attacks. For this situation, a reference watermark (or a key-dependent pilot) [3] which can be known at the detector plays the role of watermark recovery (see Fig. 2). A reference watermark is a synchronization pattern which can be easily generated by a key and is able to detect affine transformation at the detector. Although reference watermark is helpful to resist geometric attacks, it is easy to be destroyed when geometric attacks are combined with removing attacks (such as compression or filtering).

2.2 SI: Available at Embedder and Comes from Channels

For copyright protection, robustness is a critical requirement. In order to resist various attacks, the behaviors of attacks should be taken into consideration to design a more robust watermark embedding technique. In [5], we have observed the importance of the behaviors of attacks and proposed the so-called "cocktail watermarking" approach. In fact, we have found that the behaviors of attacks either increase or decrease most of the transformed coefficients (DCT or wavelet). This prior knowledge available at the *channels* (attacks) are, thus, utilized at the *embedder* side to design a new modulation strategy (see Fig. 3). To my knowledge, this might be the first paper that takes the prior information about attacks into consideration in watermarking.

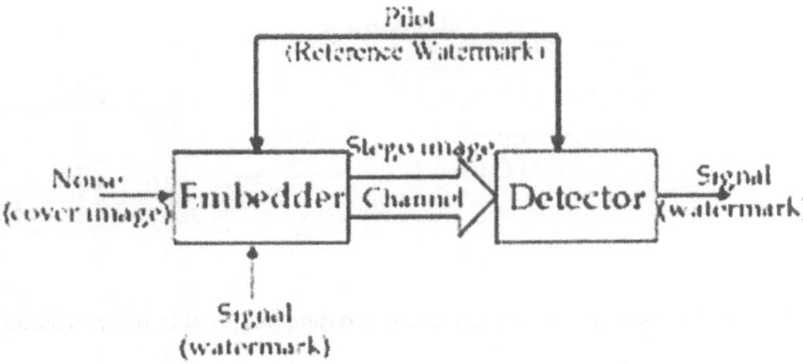

Fig. 2. Watermarking system using a reference watermark as side information.

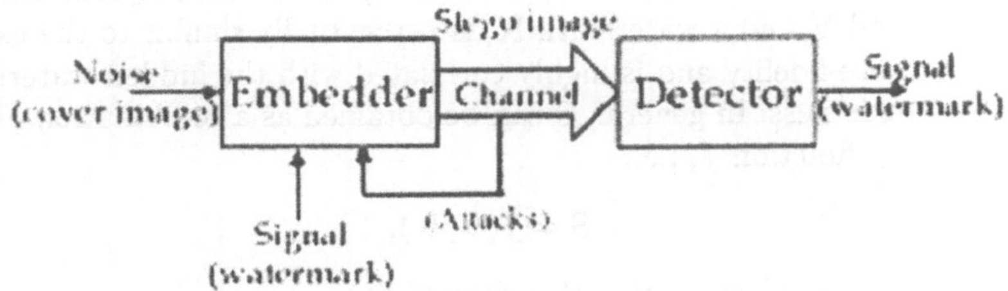

Fig. 3. Watermarking system using channel's behaviors as side information.

2.3 SI: Available at Embedder and Comes from Detector

Attackers are always smarter and one step ahead. Therefore, newly generated attacks may defeat the current watermarking methods. For example, the "copy attack" [4] and the "denoising and perceptual remodulation attack" [10] are two denoising-based attacks that will crack many watermarking methods. Basically, the above two mentioned attacks used denoising-like technique to predict the hidden watermarks, which were then used smartly to create the false negative or the false positive problem. Owing to the denoising-based watermark prediction could be used to extract the watermarks, this prior knowledge available at the detector can also be used at the embedder (see Fig. 4) to design a new modulation strategy to resist various attacks including the two denoising-based attacks. In [7], we have proposed a shrinkage-based image watermarking scheme, which can achieve both oblivious and robustness requirements. Especially, denoising-based attacks [4, 10] can be tolerated. The major drawback of [7] is that each image should be associated with a secret key.

2.4 SI: Available at Embedder and Comes from Cover Data

In [2], Cox *et al.* were the first ones who explicitly introduced the concept of viewing watermarking as communications with side information (see Fig. 5). More

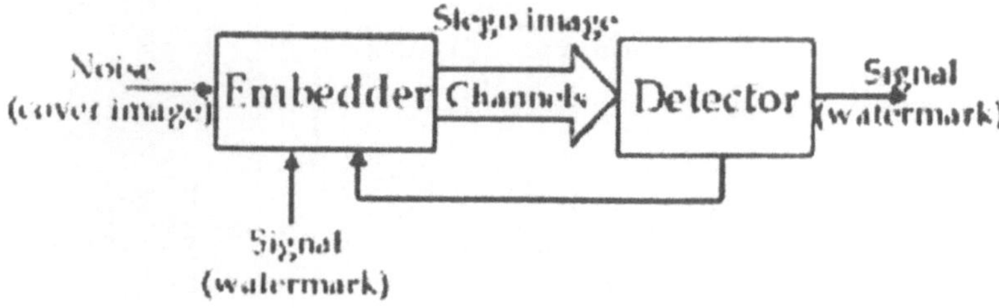

Fig. 4. Watermarking system using the detector as side information.

specifically, they used the cover data as the prior information which was available at the embedder such that a new watermarking scheme could be designed (see Fig. 6). In their scheme, the embedded signal **S**, which is composed of an extracted signal **V** and a watermark **K**, is perceptually similar to the extracted signal to achieve fidelity and is highly correlated with the hidden watermark **K** to achieve robustness. In general, **S** can be obtained as a combination of **V** and **K** by a mixing function f, i.e.,

$$\mathbf{S} = f(\mathbf{V}, \mathbf{K}). \tag{1}$$

A sub-optimal way of computing **S** is defined as

$$\mathbf{S} = \mathbf{V} + \omega \cdot \mathbf{K}, \tag{2}$$

where ω is a weight. However, there is no practical method proposed by them. Recently, we have proposed a watermarking scheme [6] based on the concept of [2] but with a new embedding strategy design.

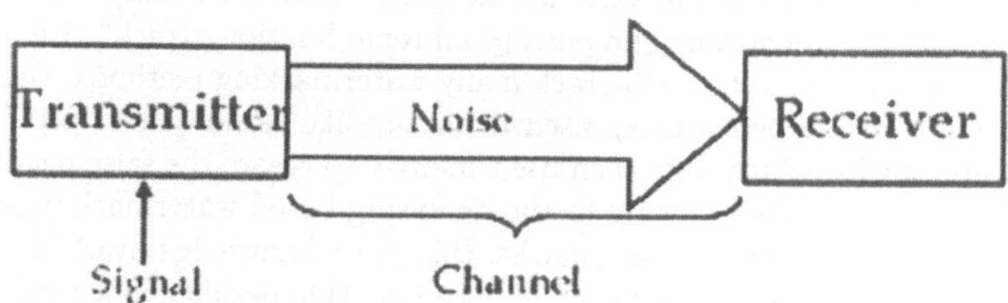

Fig. 5. Watermarking as communications with side information.

2.5 SI: Available at both Embedder and Detector and Comes from Cover Data and Pilot

In [11], the authors used more than one side information for watermarking (see Fig. 7). The stochastic model was used to derive an image-dependent noise visibility function (NVF) for content adaptive watermarking. That is, cover data

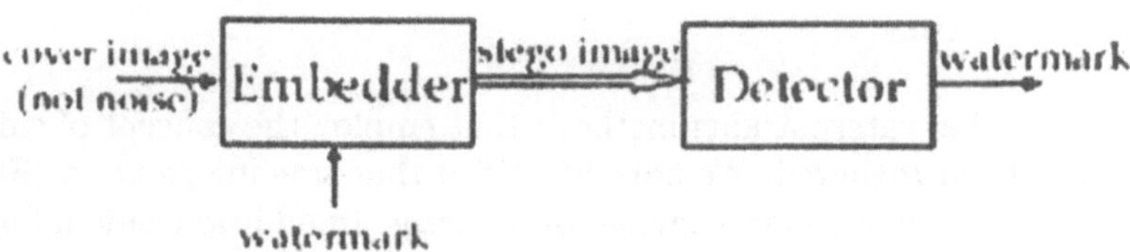

Fig. 6. Watermarking with side information available at the embedder and coming from cover data.

is used for channel state estimation at the embedder. In addition, in order to achieve reliable watermark detection both geometric attacks and removing attacks have been considered. For geometric attacks, the authors propose to allocate a watermark in a periodical block in order to improve the robustness over the autocorrelation function of the watermark itself [3]. For removing attacks such as compression, they took into account the channel that can be modeled as generalized fading plus generalized noise. The above results implied that their watermark was finally determined after the affine estimation and the channel estimation (fading+noise) at detector. Such a "channel state estimation" determines the robustness capability. This approach is intrinsically better than the ones described in the above in terms of robustness. However, it is still not clear whether the embedded watermark could still survive under combinations of geometric attacks and removing attacks or denoising-based attacks [4, 10].

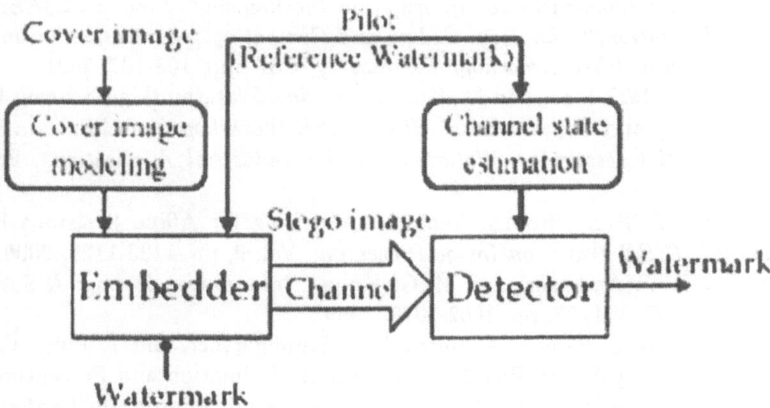

Fig. 7. Watermarking system using cover data, reference watermark, and channel as side information.

3 Conclusions

In this paper, the watermarking methods that employ the concept of side information have been reviewed. We have identified that side information (SI) could be available at the embedder, channel, or detector. In addition, side information can come from the cover data [2, 6], channel [5, 11], pilot [3, 8, 11] or detector [7]. It has been confirmed that side information-based watermarking methods are better since more requirements of watermarking can be achieved.

At present, it is still not possible for a watermarking scheme to resist all attacks because attackers are always smarter and one step ahead. In addition, it is also challenging for a watermarking scheme to satisfy all the requirements of watermarking. We believe that the uses of different types of side information might significantly help us develop a complete watermarking scheme.

References

1. I. J. Cox *et al.*, "Secure Spread Spectrum Watermarking for Multimedia", *IEEE Trans. on Image Processing*, Vol. 6, pp. 1673-1687, 1997.
2. I. J. Cox, M. L. Miller, and A. McKellips, "Watermarking as Communications with Side Information," *Proc. of the IEEE*, Vol. 87, No. 7, pp. 1127-1141, 1999.
3. M. Kutter, "Watermarking Resistant to Translation, Rotation, and Scaling", *Proc. SPIE Int. Symp. on Voice, Video, and Data Communication*, 1998.
4. M. Kutter, S. Voloshynovskiy, and A. Herrigel, "The Watermark Copy Attack", *Proc. SPIE: Security and Watermarking of Multimedia Contents II*, Vol. 3971, 2000.
5. C. S. Lu, S. K. Huang, C. J. Sze, and H. Y. Mark Liao, "Cocktail Watermarking for Digital Image Protection", *IEEE Trans. on Multimedia*, Vol. 2, No. 4, pp. 209-224, 2000.
6. C. S. Lu and H. Y. Mark Liao, "An Oblivious and Robust Watermarking Scheme Using Communications-with-Side-Information Mechanism," *Proc. 2nd IEEE Int. Conf. on Information Technology: Coding and Computing (special session on Multimedia Security and Watermarking Techniques)*, USA, pp. 103-107, 2001.
7. C. S. Lu, H. Y. Mark Liao, and M. Kutter, "A New Watermarking Scheme Resistant to Denoising and Copy Attacks", *Proc. IEEE Workshop on Multimedia Signal Processing: special session on Watermarking for Industrial Applications*, France, 2001.
8. S. Pereira and T. Pun, "Robust Template Matching for Affine Resistant Image Watermarks", *IEEE Trans. on Image Processing*, Vol. 9, pp. 1123-1129, 2000.
9. F. Petitcolas, R. J. Anderson, and M. G. Kuhn, "Information Hiding: A Survey", *Proc. of the IEEE*, Vol. 87, pp. 1062-1078, 1999.
10. S. Voloshynovskiy, S. Pereira, A. Herrigel, N. Baumgartner, and T. Pun, "Generalized Watermarking Attack Based on Watermark Estimation and Perceptual Remodulation", *Proc. SPIE: Security and Watermarking of Multimedia Contents II*, Vol. 3971, USA, 2000.
11. S. Voloshynovskiy, F. Deguillaume, S. Pereira, and T. Pun, "Optimal Adaptive Diversity Watermarking with Channel State Estimation", *Proc. SPIE: Security and Watermarking of Multimedia Contents III*, Vol. 4314, USA, 2001.

Adaptive Video Watermarking Scheme

Xiangwei Kong, Yu Liu, Huajian Liu

Department of Electronic Engineering, Dalian University of Technology, Dalian, 116023, China
Email: kongxw@dlut.edu.cn;liuyu@student.dlut.edu.cn;liu_hj@126.com

Abstract. In this paper, a new adaptive watermarking scheme for uncompressed and compressed video is presented. The proposed method embeds the watermark in DC components by quantizing DC coefficients to reference values, instead of embedding the watermark in AC components. To increase robustness and perceptual invisibility, adaptive quantization control strategy (AQCS) and error compensation strategy (ECS) are introduced. Experimental results demonstrate the proposed watermarking scheme is robust and invisible, and is feasible for real time system implementation.

1 Introduction

With the rapid growth of multimedia application including digital broadcasting and digital versatile disk (DVD), there has been significant recent interest in copyright protection of digital multimedia data such as video, audio and images. As a potential and effective way, digital watermarking becomes a very active research area of signal and information processing. Watermarking embeds an invisible signal into multimedia products and authenticates the ownership or other available information [1][2].

Watermarking scheme for digital video should include the capability to support following requirements [3][4][5]:

- **Invisibility**: The watermark in video data should be invisible or imperceptible.
- **Robustness**: The watermark should be difficult to remove without degrading the perceived quality of the video so much that it is of no commercial value any more.
- **Real time processing**: The watermarking scheme should guarantee the real-time embedding and extraction process when considering a large amount of video data.
- **Interoperability**: Although most video applications call for watermarking of compressed video, the scheme for watermarking of compressed video should be compatible with the scheme for watermarking of uncompressed video.

The purpose of this paper is to develop a digital watermarking scheme that is suitable for the requirements mention above. We first present a basic watermarking scheme for uncompressed video. Then we extend the scheme to the domain of MPEG-2 compressed video. To increase robustness and perceptual invisibility, an adaptive quantization control strategy (AQCS) based on visual masking is proposed to avoid visible artifacts and an error compensation strategy (ECS) is introduced to avoid drift due to motion compensation. Experimental results demonstrate the proposed watermarking scheme is robust and invisible, and is feasible for real time system implementation.

2 Scheme for Watermarking of Uncompressed Video

Our watermarking scheme is based on two properties. The first property is that more robustness can be achieved if watermarks are embedded in DC components since DC

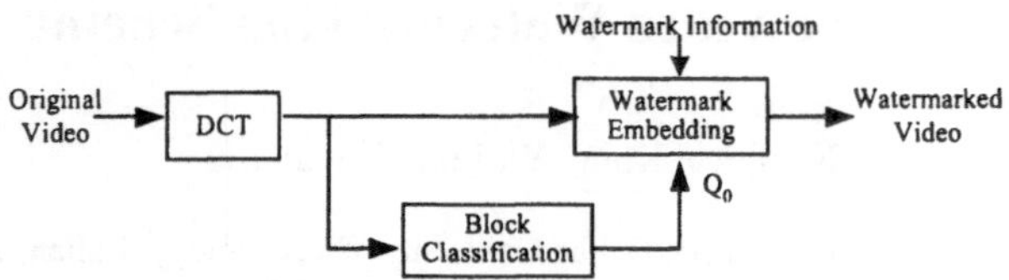

Fig. 1. Scheme for watermarking of uncompressed video

components have much larger perceptual capacity than AC components. The second one is that when we quantize a DCT coefficient to a reference value, this pre-quantized coefficient can be exactly reconstructed after subsequent MPEG compression if the original quantized step is larger than the one used in the MPEG compression. This property had been used for image authentication by Lin, and the proof of the property was presented in literature [2]. We utilize the two properties to embed the watermark information.

Fig. 1 shows the basic steps of watermark embedding of uncompressed video. To develop a reliable technique, we introduce adaptive quantization control strategy (AQCS) based on visual masking to watermark embedding and extraction process. First, original video sequences are divided into 8x8 blocks and each divided block is transformed to DCT domain. Then, each block is classified with respect to the *smoothness* and *edge* character of the block. Although sophisticated techniques were developed for HVS-characteristics, the calculation of the *smoothness* and *edge* character of the block is kept quite simple. This is due to the fact that in the following section this calculation has to be done in the MPEG2-stream domain and hopefully in real-time.

The parameter *smoothness* is simple the number of DCT coefficients which are not zero after quantization with the quantization matrix Q_m. The parameter *edge* is calculated as simple as smooth: *edge* is the sum of the absolute values of DCT coefficients 1,2,3,4,5,6,9,12,24 after quantization. The quantization matrix Q_m and the edge mask matrix are shown in Fig. 2. Block classification is performed as follows:

$$T = \frac{\sum_{i=0}^{7}\sum_{j=0}^{7}\tilde{C}(i,j)\cdot EdgeMask(i,j)}{\sum_{i=0}^{7}\sum_{j=0}^{7}\operatorname{sgn}(|\tilde{C}(i,j)|)} \rightarrow \begin{array}{ll} if\ (T \le T_0) & class = flat\ \ block \\ else & class = detailed\ \ block \end{array} \tag{1}$$

where $\tilde{C}(i,j) = Integer\ \ Round(C(i,j)/Q_m(i,j))$, and sgn(x)=1 if x>0, otherwise sgn(x)=0. T_0 is experimentally determined threshold value. Our experimental threshold value T_0 is 3.

After the block classification, we embed the watermark information in DC coefficient of each block. To embed a watermark information bit w_k (bipolar binary bit) in DC coefficient $C_k(0,0)$, we have to calculate:

16	11	10	16	24	40	51	61
12	12	14	19	26	58	60	55
14	13	16	24	40	57	69	56
14	17	22	29	51	87	80	62
18	22	37	56	68	109	103	77
24	35	55	64	81	104	113	92
49	64	78	87	103	121	120	101
72	92	95	98	112	100	103	99

(a)

0	1	1	1	0	0	0	0
1	1	0	0	0	0	0	0
1	0	1	0	0	0	0	0
1	0	0	1	0	0	0	0
0	0	0	0	0	0	0	0
0	0	0	0	0	0	0	0
0	0	0	0	0	0	0	0
0	0	0	0	0	0	0	0

(b)

Fig. 2. (a)Quantization matrix Q_m, (b) Edge mask matrix

$$\tilde{C}_k(0,0) = Integer\ \ Round(\frac{C_k(0,0)}{Q_0}) \tag{2}$$

Then we embed the watermark information bits by modifying $C_k(0,0)$ to $C'_k(0,0)$ as follows:

$$C'_k(0,0) = \begin{cases} \tilde{C}_k(0,0) \cdot Q_0, & if\ LSB(\tilde{C}_k(0,0)) = w_k \\ (\tilde{C}_k(0,0) + \mathrm{sgn}(\frac{C_k(0,0)}{Q_0} - \tilde{C}_k(0,0)) \cdot Q_0, & if\ LSB(\tilde{C}_k(0,0)) \neq w_k \end{cases} \tag{3}$$

where Q_0 is reference quantization step of DC coefficient. For watermarking, we quantize DC component using a pre-determined quantization step Q_0 that is larger than 8, the maximal quantization step of DC component that is used in MPEG compression. In our experiment, Q_0 take value as follows: if a block is a flat block, then $Q_0=12$; otherwise $Q_0=16$. If $C_k(0,0)$ is modified to the reference coefficient $C'_k(0,0)$, s.t. $C'_k(0,0)/Q_0 \in Z$, then this reference coefficient could be exactly reconstructed after MPEG compression according to the second property. In addition, this method can also resist these attacks whose distortion is smaller than half of Q_0.

The recovery of the embedded watermark information is easily accomplished without knowledge of the original video. Given the watermarked video, we first divide it into 8x8 blocks and for each block, we perform DCT. Then we perform the block classification, which is the same as the method used in embedding process of Eq.(1). From the result of block classification, the reference quanitization step Q_0 is obtained. Then the watermark information w'_k will be extracted as follows:

$$w'_k = LSB(Integer\ \ Round(\frac{C'_k(0,0)}{Q_0})) \tag{4}$$

3 Scheme for Watermarking of Compressed Video in MPEG-2 Bitstream Domain

In practical video storage and distribution systems, the video sequences are stored and transmitted in compressed format. Therefore, it must be possible to embed the watermark into the bitstream directly, instead of decoding and re-encoding the bitstream for the purpose of watermarking it. In the following, we present a scheme for watermarking of compressed video in MPEG-2 bitstream domain that is compatible with the scheme for watermarking of uncompressed video given in previous section. Fig. 3 shows an according watermarking scheme.

The principle of MPEG-2 video compression is motion-compensated hybrid coding. I-frames are split into blocks of 8x8 pixels that are compressed using the DCT, quantization, zig-zag-scan, run-level-coding and entropy coding. P- and B- frames are motion compensated and the residual prediction error signal frames are split into blocks of 8x8 pixels which are compressed in the same way as blocks from I-frames.

In I-frames, the watermark embedding method is similar to the method for watermarking of uncompressed video given in previous section. In Fig. 3, on the left side, the incoming MPEG-2 bitstream is split into DCT encoded blocks and other information. The DCT encoded signal blocks are represented by a sequence of Huffman codes. Each incoming Huffman code is decoded (VLC^{-1}) and inversely quantized (Q^{-1}). After inverse quantization, we have DCT coefficients of the current block. Then we embed the watermark information into the DC coefficient of the current block in the same way as embedding method of uncompressed video. We then quantize (Q), Huffman encode (VLC) the watermarked coefficients, and output the watermarked MPEG-2 bitstream.

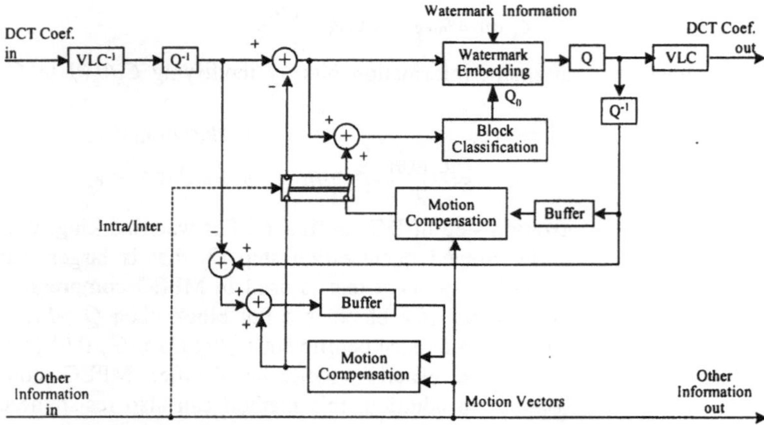

Fig. 3. Scheme for watermarking of MPEG-2 compressed video

Since P- and B- frames are motion compensated, only the residual prediction error signal frames are encoded. To embed the watermark information into P- and B- frames, we extract, for each encoded 8x8 residual prediction error block of P- and B- frames, the corresponding block from previous reference frames. We then add the two blocks in the DCT domain to get the DCT coefficient block of decoded P- and B- frames. In addition, adding a watermark in previous frame results in degradation that will propagate and accumulate in the following frames. To avoid this problem, we introduce error compensation strategy (ECS) to watermark embedding process of P- and B- frames. Before watermark embedding process of P- and B- frames, we add a drift compensation signal in P- and B- frames that compensates for watermark signal from previous frames. Finally, we recover the DCT coefficient blocks of decoded P- and B- frames without drift. Then the DCT coefficient blocks without drift are classified and the reference quantization step Q_0 is obtained. We embed the watermark information into P- and B- frames as follows:

$$B_k'(0,0) = \begin{cases} B_k(0,0) + \tilde{C}_k(0,0)\cdot Q_0 - C_k(0,0), & if \;\; LSB(\tilde{C}_k(0,0)) = w_k \\ B_k(0,0) + (\tilde{C}_k(0,0) + \mathrm{sgn}(\frac{C_k(0,0)}{Q_0} - \tilde{C}_k(0,0))\cdot Q_0 - C_k(0,0), & if \;\; LSB(\tilde{C}_k(0,0)) \neq w_k \end{cases} \quad (5)$$

where $C_k(0,0)$ is DC coefficient without drift, $\tilde{C}_k(0,0) = Integer \;\; Round(C_k(0,0)/Q_0)$, and $B_k(0,0)$ is DC coefficient of prediction error block.

There are two methods of watermark extraction, one to extract the watermark from the reconstructed video at the output of MPEG-2 video decoder and the other to analyze MPEG-2 compressed video directly. The former is the same as the watermark extraction method of uncompressed video given in previous section, the reconstructed video data is used as the input source data for the watermark extraction. Alternatively, we may also analyze MPEG-2 compressed video directly. Watermark detector takes the watermarked MPEG-2 bitstream as its input, parses the bitstream and extracts the watermark information in bitstream domain.

In order to detect the extracted watermark w', we calculate the similarity of w and w': $sim(w', w) = w'\cdot w/(w\cdot w)$, then compare it with a threshold T_l to decide whether the test video is watermarked. Our experimental threshold T_l is chosen around 0.1. The watermark is considered to be present if $sim>T_l$ and absent if $sim>T_l$.

4 Experimental Results

The scheme of Fig. 3 has been implemented and computer simulation is used to evaluate the performance of the proposed method. Video sequences used for this experiment are 120 frames of Mobile & Calendar and Flower. Each test sequence is encoded at bitrate 4Mbps using MPEG-2 TM5 algorithm [6]. Each frame is of size 704x480. Each GOP (Group of Pictures) includes 15 frames and I/P frame distance is 3.

Fig. 4 shows the example frames for the evaluation of the subjective quality of video. On the left side, the MPEG-2 encoded video frames without the embedded watermark are displayed, and on the right side, the compressed video frames with the embedded watermark are displayed. As can be seen, the MPEG-2 coded frame with watermark appears visually identical to the MPEG-2 coded frame without watermark. And perceptual degradation of video quality caused by the embedded watermark is evaluated by objective quality measurement. Table 1 shows the average PSNR results of MPEG-2 coded video with/without the embedded watermark at bitrate 4Mbps. The corresponding watermark extraction similarity values are shown in Fig. 6, and the presence of the watermark is easily observed. The embedded watermark can be extracted from the watermarked video without knowledge of the original video and is robust against frame cropping, low-pass filtering, and other. Cropping stands for cutting of one or more parts of the video frames, and Fig. 5(a) shows the resulting frame cropped for 30%. Fig. 5(b) shows the watermarked frame after low-pass filtering. The embedded watermark survived all those attacks.

5 Conclusions

In this paper, we first present a basic scheme for watermarking of uncompressed video. Furthermore, a scheme for watermarking of MPEG-2 compressed video in the bitstream domain has been presented. The latter is fully compatible with the scheme for uncompressed video. To increase robustness and perceptual invisibility, an adaptive quantization control strategy (AQCS) based on visual masking is proposed to avoid visible artifacts and an error compensation strategy (ECS) is introduced to avoid drift due to motion compensation. The watermark can be extracted from the reconstructed video or the MPEG-2 compressed video without knowledge of the original video.

References

1. Cox I.J., Kilian J., Leighton T. and Shamoon T.: Secure Spread Spectrum Watermarking for Multimedia. *IEEE Trans. on Image Processing.* 6 (1997) 1673-1687,.
2. LIN C.Y. and CHANG S.F.: Semi-fragile Watermarking for Authenticating JPEG Visual Content. *SPIE Security and Watermarking of Multimedia Contents II,* EI '00, San Jose, CA.(2000) 140-151
3. Hartung F. and Girod B.: Digital Watermark of Raw and Compressed Video. *Proceedings SPIE 2952: Digital Compression Technologies and Systems for Video Communication.* (1996) 205-213
4. Hsu C. and Wu J.: DCT-based Watermarking for Video. *IEEE Trans. on Consumer Electronics.* 44 (1998) 206-216
5. Hartung F. and Girod B.: Fast Public-key Watermarking of Compressed Video. *Proceedings IEEE International Conference on Image Processing (ICIP 97),* Santa Barbara. 1 (1997) 528 -531
6. ISO/IEC 13818-2, Generic Coding of Moving Pictures and Associated Audio, Recommendation H.262 (MPEG-2), 1995, International Standard

Fig. 4. Frames from MPEG-2 coded videos with/without watermark at 4Mbps. (a) Mobile & Calendar without watermark, (b) Mobile & Calendar with watermark, (c) Flower without watermark, (d) Flower with watermark

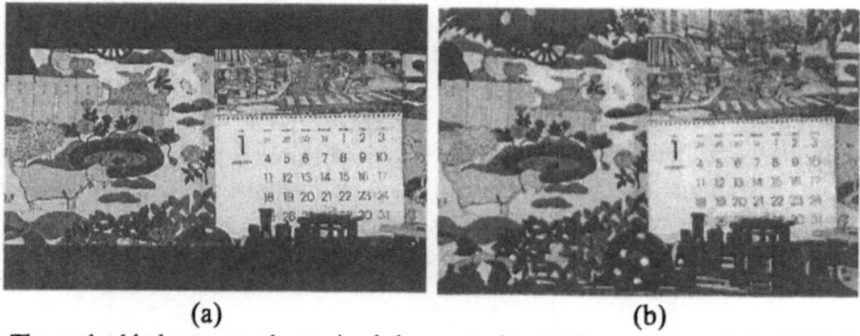

Fig. 5. The embedded watermark survived these attacks. (a) Frame cropped for 30%, (b) low-pass filtering

Table 1. The average PSNR results of reconstructed video with/without watermark

Test Sequence	I Frames	P Frames	B Frames
Mobile	28.54dB	27.93dB	27.15dB
Mobile^{w}	28.13dB	27.21dB	26.58dB
Flower	33.75dB	32.79dB	32.14dB
Flower^{w}	33.35dB	32.28dB	31.66dB

Note: Mobile and Flower are reconstructed sequences without watermark, but Mobile^{w} and Flower^{w} are reconstructed sequences with watermark

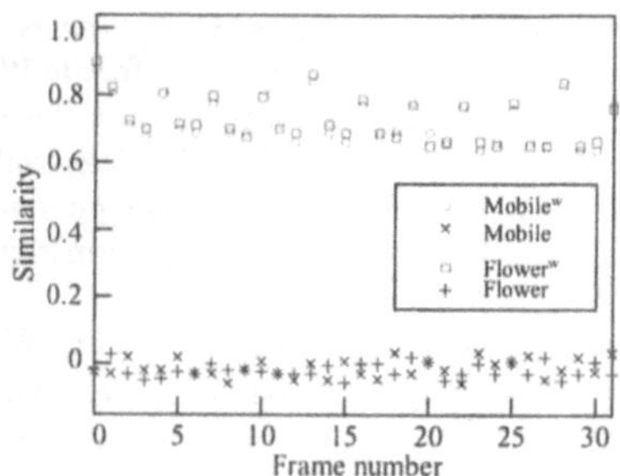

Fig. 6. Similarity values at MPEG-2 bitrate 4Mbps

An Error Resilience Algorithm for H.263++ Based Video Coding

Li Qiang[1], Cui Huijuan[1], Tang Kun[1]

[1] State Key Lab on Microwave and Digital Communications, Department of Electronic Engineering, Tsinghua University, Beijing, China
Liq99@mails.tsinghua.edu.cn,{cuihj,tangk}@mail.tsinghua.edu.cn

Abstract. Error resilience techniques have already been an important part of video coding in error prone environments. In this paper, an error resilience algorithm is proposed for compressed video sequences based on H.263++. It applies several techniques including data partitioning, reversible variable length coding (RVLC) etc. Compared with H.263++ Data Partitioned Slice Mode (DPS Mode), our proposed coder can be fully bi-directional decodable with more RVLC words as well as data partitioned packets introduced in the bitstream. In addition, a decoding model has been presented for it. Simulations show that the proposed method outperforms the conventional ones (H.263++ DPS Mode and H.263) in terms of PSNR under various error conditions, which significantly improves the quality of the reconstructed images.

1 Introduction

Current video compression algorithms (H.263, MPEG4...)[1][2] used in real time communications have achieved efficient compression by using techniques of prediction, transform coding and variable length codes etc. But in error prone environments, variable length codes are highly susceptible to the errors introduced in the bitstream, predicative coding algorithm makes things worse since the errors in one frame may be propagated to the future predicted images and rapidly degrade the reconstructed image quality.

Error resilience techniques have been employed to reduce the effect of channel errors. The syntax and structure of compressed video stream have been modified to get more adaptive to the error prone environments. So far, error resilience[3] includes the following stages: error detection and localization, resynchronization, data recovery and error concealment[4].

To lessen the effect of error propagation in variable length codes, RVLC[5] has been proposed which can be bi-directional decoded. If an error is detected and localized between two resynchronization markers, the decoder can decode the erroneous bitstream backward and reduce losses of information. Corresponding to it, data partitioning[6][7] makes full use of macroblock(MB) information and puts motion vector and DCT data together to further improve the resistance of channel errors. Position markers are used to localize the positions of synchronization codes of bitstream, once an error occurs in the data partitioned packet, the decoder can simply find the corrupt position and use a backward decoding algorithm to recover the residual information.

Though many video compression codecs have adopted data partitioning and RVLC techniques to improve their performance in error prone environments, they have only partly introduced or realized them. In this paper, a fully bi-directional coding algorithm based on the two techniques mentioned above is proposed, and a complete decoding process model has also been accomplished for it.

This paper is organized as following. Section 2 describes the syntax and structure of proposed video coding algorithms based on H.263++. Section 3 shows the decoding process model. Simulation results are given in Section 4, and conclusions are presented in Section 5.

2 Structure of Proposed Video Coding Algorithm

In this section, we will propose a novel structure of a video coding algorithm based on H.263++. As we know, DPS mode[7] in H.263++ demonstrates a hybrid of data partitioning and RVLC model, which shows good performance in erroneous environments. But it considers more P-Frame coding than I-Frame coding, only motion vectors and some header information for each of the macroblock unit are put together. However if an error occurs in the bitstream of I-Frame, the residual data of the total slice will be discarded, which will result in bad visual effects or even make the decoder failure to work properly.

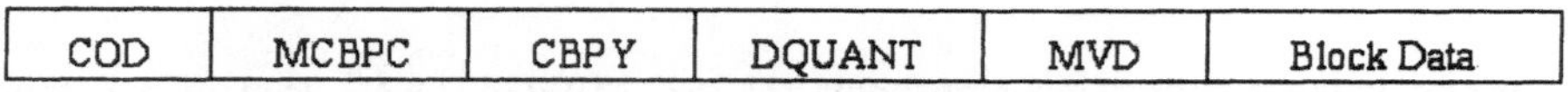

COD	MCBPC	CBPY	DQUANT	MVD	Block Data

Fig. 1 Structure of macroblock layer

Header	Header Marker	Motion Vectors	Motion Marker
CBPY	Coeff (DC)	Coeff (AC)	Resync Marker

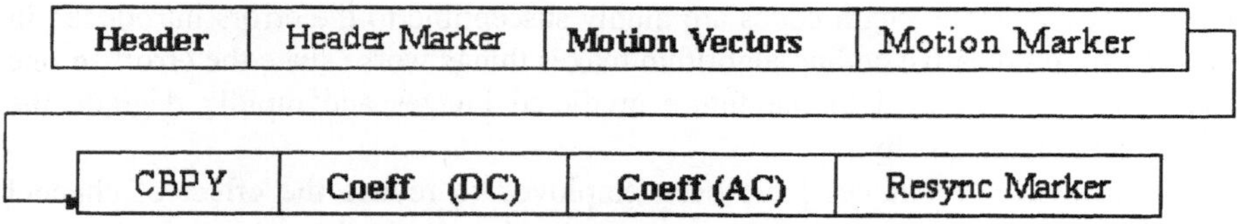

Fig. 2 Data Partitioning in Slice

Hence we propose a new coding structure which can be bi-directional robust-decoded both in I-Frame and P-Frame coding modes, it can be fully reversible decoded at any position of the bitstream. Fig1 shows the original structure of macroblock layer of H.263 and the syntax elements of our proposed method are illustrated in Fig2, where a slice we defined here presents one group of blocks (GOB).

Compared with original syntax of H.263, our proposed coder partitions a slice into four different packets separated by various position markers. The header, motion vector and coefficient packets are employed with RVLC, while the CBPY packet is assigned with constant length code words. Furthermore, the coefficient packet in P-

Frames can select VLC or RVLC mode so as to make a tradeoff between compression efficiency and error resilience performance.

The header and CBPY packets contain COD, MCBPC as well as CBPY information for all the MBs in a slice. The DC coefficients have been united together to separate from AC ones, since they are more important than AC coefficients. .

There are four types of position markers used here. The header marker separates the header and motion vector packets, the motion marker separates the motion vector and CBPY packet, and the resynchronization marker presents the start code of a new slice. In order to avoid the start code emulation, a CBPY marker is inserted in the bitstream to distinguish the CBPY codes from the start code.

From the syntax of the bitstream, we can see in all the partitioned packets, the data can be fully bi-directional decoded, which will facilitate the decoding process and give a better performance of reconstructed images in the erroneous environments.

3 Decoding Process Model

The decoder comprises three phases: error detection, error localization and error concealment phase. In the next paragraph we will show the three phases in detail.

3.1 Error Detection

Error detection is used to find errors from the received video bitstream. Because no FEC is employed, the decoder must comply the syntactic and logic constraints of H.263++ and our coding rules. If one of the following instances occurs, an error code is declared:

1. A codeword whose pattern is not listed in the VLC or RVLC table;
2. Motion vectors are out of range;
3. DCT coefficients are out of range;
4. More than 64 DCT coefficients are decoded in one block;
5. Conflict with the position markers declared in the encoder

Here we declare 5 patterns of error: resynchronization marker error (RSE), position markers error (PME), header error (HE), motion vector error (MVE) and coefficient error (CE). Once an error is detected, error pattern analysis and corresponding decoding strategy will be applied to it. Due to the decoder, the resynchronization marker is most important of all since it provides the resynchronization information for a whole slice, the slice information will be totally lost if RSE occurs. PME, HE, MVE are less important than RSE, they imply the damage of head information within a slice. HE and MVE can be solved through backward decoding strategy, but if PME is detected, the rest part of a slice is considered to be corrupt and must be discarded. CE is the least important of all, which can also be handled with reversible decoding. Though the coefficient packet is much less important than the other three packets in a slice, it plays an important role in I-Frame coding. If we use common VLC words in I-Frame coding, the occurrence of the transmission errors will cause the residual coefficients no use any more and the decoder must pause the VLC decoding and look for the next resynchronization marker. Therefore, the MBs between the error code and the next resynchronization marker are lost. RVLC provides the reversible decoding path and make the losses to minimum, which dramatically improves the decoded I-Frame quality.

3.2 Error Localization

At the first stage, various error patterns are found and the proximate error positions are located. In fact perhaps they are not the real positions where errors occur, sometimes error occurs far before we have detected it. In such a case, we must obtain the true position of the corrupt MB. Based on such an assumption that natural video signals vary little in adjacent pixels, the statistical properties of the corrupt MB and its correct neighboring MBs are calculated to find their differences. In our decoder model, the similarity of left and top border edge pixels of the adjacent MBs is employed as the rule for error localization. Assuming that MB_i is an error MB we have detected, MB_{i-1} is its left neighboring MB. The whole process can be described in three steps:

1. If MB_i is located at the top edge of the frame, calculate the absolute sum of difference between the pixels of left row of MB_i and right row of MB_{i-1}, in case that the sum is less than the predetermined threshold, then MB_{i-1} is declared to be corrupt. In this case, step 2 will be skipped.
2. Calculate the absolute sum of difference between the pixels of top row of MB_{i-1} and bottom row of its above adjacent MB. In case that the absolute sum is greater than the predetermined threshold, then we assume MB_{i-1} is damaged.
3. If MB_{i-1} is corrupt, then go back to step 1 and replace MB_i with MB_{i-1}, otherwise MB_i is considered to be the beginning corrupt MB. Following this strategy we can also find the final position of corrupt MB in the reverse direction.

3.3 Error concealment

After the corrupt MBs are determined by the error detection and error localization phase, we can apply error concealment algorithms to the corrupt MBs.

In I-Frame, the damaged MB is reconstructed by the correct top and bottom neighboring MBs, where the gradual interpolation method is used. In P-Frame, the decoder uses the following error concealment schemes:

1. If an error occurs in the header partitions (RSE, PME, HE, MVE), then the decoder uses its correct neighboring MBs to recover the motion vector information. Furthermore, temporal predictive compensation algorithm is used and the corrupt MB can be reconstructed from the previous frame through the recovered motion vectors.
2. If an error occurs in the coefficient partition, the decoder simply set all the corrupt DCT coefficients to be zero and apply the correct motion vector information to reconstruct the corrupt MB.

4 Simulation Results

In our simulation, we assume that the channel is a binary symmetric channel, and the transmission error is random error. Two test sequences are used for simulation, whose conditions are listed in Table 1:

Table1 Simulation Sequence Conditions

Sequence	Size	Frame Rate	Bit Rate
Foreman	QCIF	10fps	64kbit/s
Miss America	QCIF	20fps	64kbit/s

For the sake of comparing, we introduce another two robust video coders based on H.263 and H.263++ DPS mode. The three schemes are marked with "Proposed Method", "H.263 Normal Method" and "H.263++ DSP Mode" respectively. Different BERs are evaluated on the video sequences list in Table1. Fig3 shows the final result.

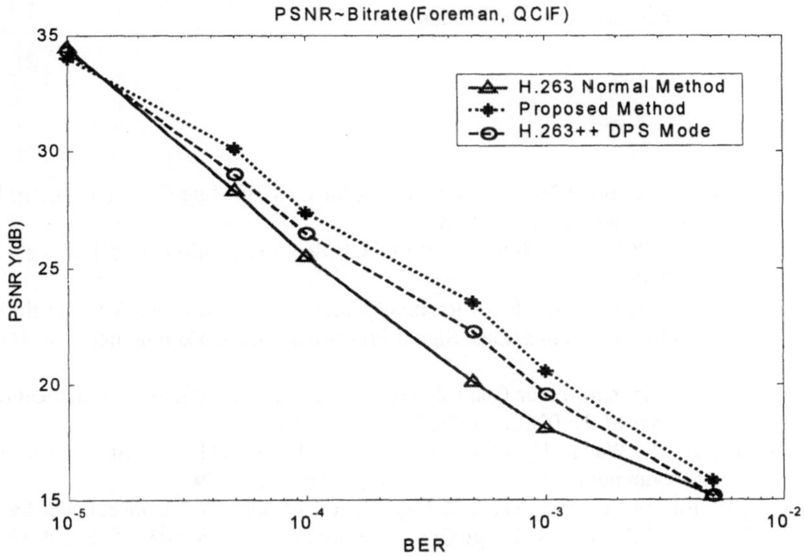

Fig 3. Performance Comparison of Foreman Sequence

It is obvious that the proposed coding scheme has provided a graceful degradation upon the occurrence of transmission errors in objective quality, which provides robust error resiliency better than the original methods in most cases, especially when BER varies from 5.00E-05 to 2.00E-3. In the error free environment, our proposed coder may not be as efficient as the original ones due to the use of RVLC. However, with the careful selection of RVLC words, we can reduce this effect to minimum. In the other hand, once BER increases, the original coders deteriorate much faster than our proposed one, for they can only partially obtain information within a slice, the rest parts are discarded and must be reconstructed from their neighboring MBs. On the contrary, with data much packed and separated with each other, our proposed decoder can use the information from both directions within a slice, which may not be destroyed easily when the transmission error occurs.

5 Summary

This paper has presented an error resilience algorithm based on H.263++. The codec has employed several error resilience techniques including data partitioning, RVLC etc. Within this scheme, the structures of the bitstream are rearranged to improve the resistance against the channel errors. It has been shown that the proposed algorithm outperforms the conventional ones under various error conditions. In addition, we also have shown a decoding model for the scheme, which gives a full solution to deal with various patterns of the errors.

In the future, we will carry out experiments on best slice segmentation method and mode selection algorithm between RVLC and VLC. It is a challenging and meaningful work for us, and our future work will focus on it.

References

1. ITU-T Recommendation H.263 – Video Coding for Low Bit Rate Communication. Draft Recommendation H.263 version 2, 1998
2. ISO/IEC JTC1/SC29/WG11 14996-2, MPEG-4 Video Verification Model version 16.0, N3312, March 2000
3. Koji Imura*, Yutaka Machida, Error Resilient Video Coding Schemes for Real-time and Low-bitrate Mobile Communications. Signal Processing: Image Communication 14(1999) 513-530
4. Yao Wang, Qin-Fan Zhu, Error Control and Concealment for Video Communication: A Review, Proceedings of the IEEE, vol.86, No.5, May 1998
5. Y. Takishima, M. Wada, H. Murakami. Reversible Variable Length Codes. IEEE Transactions on Communication. Vol.43, no. 4, pp158 ~ 162, 1995
6. Raj Talluri*, Iole Moccagatta, Yashoda Nag, Gene Cheung. Error Concealment by Data Partitioning. Signal Processing: Image Communication, vol.14, pp 505 ~ 518, 1999
7. John D. Villasenor, Proposed draft text for H.263 Annex V Data Partitioned Slice Mode, ITU-T document Q15-I-14, 1999

A Predictive Connection Admission Control Scheme for QoS Improvement

Bin Qiu and Xiaoxiang Guan
School of Computer Science and Software Engineering
Monash University, P O Box 26, Victoria 3800, Australia
bq@csse.monash.edu.au

Abstract. This paper proposes a based Call Admission Control (CAC) scheme which is based on measurement of past traffic situation and prediction of future sources. The scheme is presented by introducing an algorithm for prediction of the Cell Loss Probability (CLP). A free buffer threshold parameter is used together with the CLP to carry out the CAC. Unlike other CAC schemes[1-2], the proposed scheme does not rely on any existing traffic modeling, instead, a variable length history of input is used to compute the CLP and then compares the CLP with the required Cell Loss Ratio (CLR). By using the free buffer threshold parameter with the CLP, a good balance between the QoS requirements and the system efficiency is achieved. Simulation results are included in the discussion of this paper.

1. Introduction

Asynchronous Transfer Mode (ATM) has used as a major transport technology for broadband internet and multimedia services [3-4]. ATM networks provide inherent QoS guarantee for connections and achieve high system utilization. One of the most significant missions of traffic control in ATM is the Connection Admission Control (CAC). CAC is the control mechanism at the end of call requests to determine whether to admit or reject the call [5].

This paper presents a predictive, measurement-based CAC scheme that achieves better results in terms of efficiency and QoS compared with existing schemes.

2. CLP Prediction

The CLP prediction algorithm relies mainly on a period of history data. A certain warming up period is required. During the warming up period a connection request is admitted according to its peak cell rate (PCR). That is, if the PCR for this connection is less than the available bandwidth, the call is accepted, otherwise rejected.

A connection request can be admitted if the request can be served without excessive cell loss by the switch which consists of buffer and outgoing link capacity. Our algorithm attempts to make full use of the buffer and outgoing link capacity. When a call request arrives, it checks, by using the predicted CLP, if the buffer can be used to allocate the amount of work in the call. The following is the description of the CLP calculation and buffer allocation.

As shown in Figure 1, a connection request arrives at time t_j and we want to predict the cell loss probability for this connection request. Our algorithm for the prediction is specified as follows.

1) A certain period of time from t_j backwards that may include the warming up period is divided into equal intervals shown in Figure 1.
2) We calculate the amount of work arrived between t_{i-1} and t_i, where i = 2, 3, …, j as:

$$W_{i-1,i} = \begin{cases} A_i - A_{i-1} - \mu * T, & A_i - A_{i-1} \geq 0 \\ \mu * T - |A_i - A_{i-1}|, & A_i - A_{i-1} < 0, \end{cases} \quad (1)$$

where A_i denotes the amount of work available in the buffer waiting to be served at t_i time, μ is the service rate, and T represents the equal time interval.

3) The predicted cell loss probability is:

$$CLP = \frac{\forall \{W_{i-1,i} > B_j\}}{j} \quad (2)$$

where $1 \leq i \leq j$, and B_j is the free buffer at time t_j. $\forall \{W_{i-1,i} > B_j\}$ represents the number of intervals in which amount of work arrived that is greater than the current free buffer size at time t_j. The parameter j is an important criterion in this algorithm. Depending on the CLR specified by the user, j can be selected according to the following:

$$j \geq \frac{1}{\min\{CLR\}} \quad (3)$$

Formula (3) is the number of intervals used as the history data to calculate the CLP. However, the greater the total number of intervals is, the longer the warming up period will be. To reduce the warming up period, in the next section, we present a free buffer threshold parameter. Adjusting this parameter can achieve overall improvement in efficiency while the QoS is remained.

The free buffer threshold together with CLP also forms the CAC scheme.

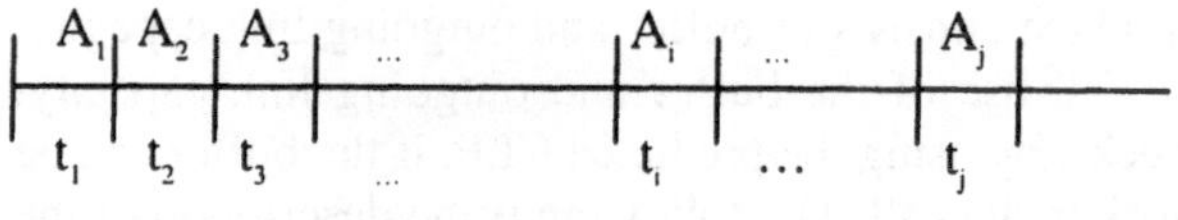

A_1 A_2 A_3 … A_i … A_j

t_1 t_2 t_3 … t_i … t_j

Figure 1. Available amount of work in the system

3. The CAC Scheme

The reasoning used to perform the CAC control is as follows. If estimated CLP > CLR (cell loss rate as given by the user), it will reject the call, otherwise rather than accept the call straight away, we introduce the ***free buffer threshold*** parameter to avoid some unnecessary cell loss.

The possible situation that causes cell loss is described here. When the free buffer size is very low and CLP is expected to be greater than CLR, then the call requests are rejected. However, after a certain period of time, the free buffer size will become larger due to the pass through of the admitted calls. At this point of time the CLP may become smaller. However, if we accept a call now, we may still face unnecessary cell loss because of insufficient free buffer size.

This is the reason for us to introduce the *free buffer threshold* to make sure that the free buffer size is large enough so the call request can be accepted when CLP is smaller than CLR. The free buffer threshold is the minimum and mandatory free buffer size before further call requests can be accepted. As specified above, the number of intervals can be calculated by formula (3). By adjusting the free buffer size threshold, we can actually vary the total number of intervals, aiming at reducing the length of warming up period. Basically, the bigger the free buffer threshold, the smaller the total number of intervals.

In summary, our CAC conditions are as follows:

- if CLP > CLR, the call request is rejected;
- if CLP ≤ CLR and free buffer size ≥ free buffer threshold, the call request is accepted.

4. Simulation Results and Performance Comparison

The simulation model consists of three major parts: the connection request queue, buffer capacity and link capacity, as shown in Figure 2.

Connection requests are generated as a Poisson process with independent exponentially distributed holding time for VBR sources, feeding into a service queue. Once a connection request is generated, the relevant parameters to the request are randomly created (except CLR). The parameters include QoS criteria (i.e. CLR that is fixed at 10^{-6}), traffic parameters like PCR (Peak Cell Rate) and amount of work, etc..

Upon the arrival of a new connection request, the decision process is triggered to see if the connection request can be accepted, based on the above algorithm.

If the call request is accepted, the amount of work will be put into the buffer. The buffer departure process adopts first-in-first-out discipline (FIFO).

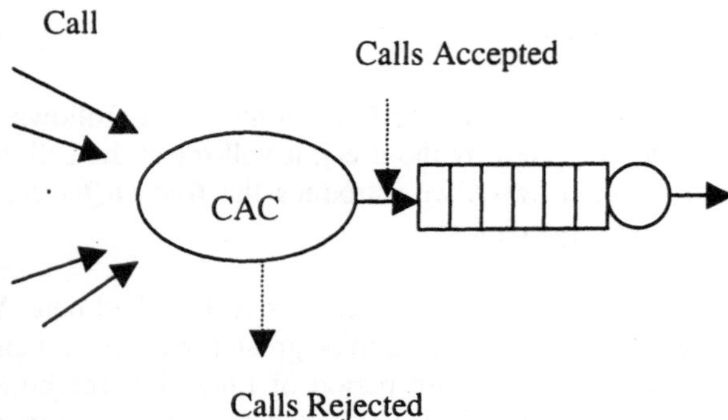

Figure 2. Simulation System Model

The user interface of the simulation system allows us to specify service rate, buffer size, and control data such as total cells to be simulated and other parameters. The simulation results are stored into a database which includes the source data, service data and statistical results. The source data mainly consist of CLR, PCR, connection start time, connection duration and amount of work generated. The service data are composed of service rate, buffer size, free bandwidth, free buffer, CLP, accepted or rejected status, and cell loss ratio. The statistical results include service rate, buffer size, interval, number of intervals, total cells to simulate, buffer utilization and cell loss, etc. Table 1 illustrates some of typical simulation conditions.

Table 1. Simulation conditions

Service rate	155 - 622 Mbps
Cell loss Rate	10^{-3} - 10^{-9}
Total cell simulated	0.5 -5 million
Free buffer threshold	1/10 -1/3 of total buffer
Buffer size	100-1000
Simulation interval size	20-40 cells
History interval	1000-10000

The comparison with other CAC schemes is based on the efficiency or utilization. Figure 3 illustrates the utilization achieved by different CAC schemes using various buffer size in terms of cells.

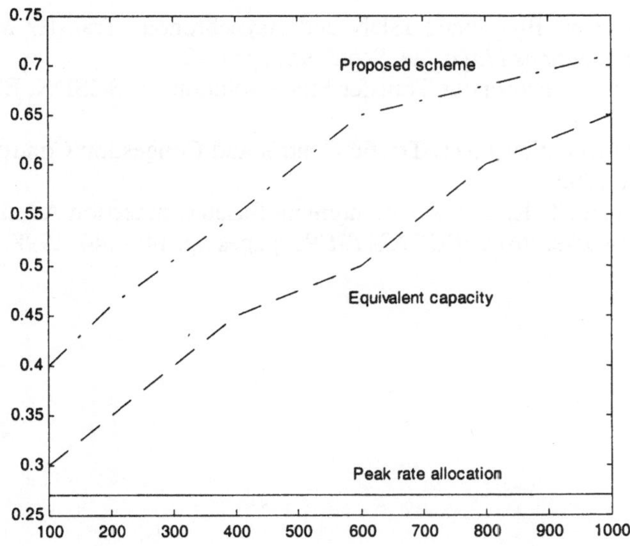

Figure 3. Comparison of CAC schemes

The result of the proposed scheme shown in Figure 3 has not experienced any cell loss.

In the simulation, the free buffer has been adjusted. Without cell loss, by changing the free buffer threshold, the following buffer utilization is achieved with two different buffer size, as shown in Figure 4.

From Figure 4 we can see that if better utilization is to be achieved, adjustment to lower free buffer threshold will help. It is obviously a trade-off between the efficiency and the level of cell loss.

5. Conclusions

In this paper, a noval CAC scheme based on the prediction of cell loss probability and free buffer threshold has been presented. The simulation results show better performance of the proposed CAC algorithm. Apart from a comparison between the proposed scheme and the other shemes, the simulation is also run by using different free buffer threshold values to illustrate how the balance between utilization and quality can be better achieved.

References

1. H. G. Perros and K. M. Elsayed. Call Admission Control Schemes: A Review. *IEEE Comunications Magazine*, vol. 34 (no. 11):pp. 82-91, Nov 1966.
2. K. Shiomoto, N. Yamanaka, and T. Takahashi. Overview of Measurement-Based Connection Admission Control Methods in ATM Networks. *IEEE Communications Surveys*, pages 2-13, First Quarter 1999.

3. Steven E. Minzer. Broadband ISDN and Asynchronous Transfer Mode (ATM), *IEEE Communications Magazine*, Sept. 1989, pp17-24.
4. M. De Prycer. Asynchronous Transfer Mode Solution for B-ISDN, Ellis Horwood, Second Edition, 1993.
5. ITU: Recommendation I.371, Traffic Control and Congestion Control in B-ISBN, Geneva, May 1996.
6. M.Zukerman and T. K. Lee. A measurement Based Connection Admission Control for ATM Networks. *Proc. IEEE ICATM'98*, pages pp. 140-144, 1998.

A Multiresolutional Coding Method Based on SPIHT

Keun-hyeong Park [*], Chul Soo Lee, and HyunWook Park

Dept. of Electrical Engineering, Korea Advanced Institute of Science and Technology
373-1 Guseong-dong, Yuseong-gu, Daejeon 305-701, Republic of Korea
{charlie, hwpark}@athena.kaist.ac.kr

[*] Hanaro Telecom Inc., Seoul, Korea
khpark@hanaro.com

Abstract. In this work, we incorporate a multiresolutional coding functionality into the SPIHT algorithm [1]. The multiresolutional coding can be considered as a kind of the region of interest (ROI) coding with multiple regions of interest. Therefore, the ROI coding proposed by authors can be extended for the multiresolutional functionality without any cost in performance. The parent of ROI (PROI) and the multiple lists for insignificant sets and pixels, which were proposed for the ROI coding, are also used for the multiresolution coding.

1. Introduction

The image coder should provide a good rate-distortion performance. In addition, several functionalities become important when we consider various applications. One of the most important functionalities is the capability to encode various resolution images in a single bit stream. The functionality gives us the flexibility in using the network resources. While users with a narrow bandwidth can reconstruct a low resolution image by decoding a small fraction of the bit stream, other users with a wider bandwidth can reconstruct a high resolution image by decoding the whole bit stream. It would be desirable to incorporate such a feature into an image coding system without incurring heavy cost such as increased computational complexity or reduced rate-distortion performance. Xiong et al. proposed a multiresolutioal image decoding method [2]. They selected necessary coefficients to reconstruct various resolution images. It is difficult to use the multiresolution method in the low bit rate environment.

In this work, we adopt the scheme of the region of interest (ROI) coding and slightly extend it in order to incorporate multiresolutional coding functionality into the SPIHT algorithm. The multiresolutional coding can be considered as a kind of the ROI coding with multiple regions of interest.

This paper is organized as follows: The following section describes the SPIHT algorithm briefly. Section 3 presents the ROI coding and the proposed multiresolutional coding. Experimental results are given in section 4. Finally, we conclude this paper in section 5.

2. SPIHT

The SPIHT algorithm is one of the most efficient algorithms for still image compression. This algorithm was designed to transmit images progressively. Using wavelet transform, images are decomposed into subband images and the SPIHT algorithm arranges the wavelet coefficients in the magnitude order and transmits them from the most significant bit plane.

When a threshold is given, the algorithm partitions the coefficients or the sets of coefficients into significant ones and insignificant ones. Significant coefficients are added to the list of significant pixels (LSP) and insignificant coefficients are to the list of insignificant pixels (LIP) or the list of insignificant sets (LIS). While the LIP contains the insignificant pixels, the LIS contains the sets that include at least four insignificant pixels. An entry of the LIS, that is a set, is partitioned into several significant pixels, insignificant pixels, and insignificant sets when it contains one or more significant pixels. Whenever the algorithm determines whether the coefficient or the set is significant or not, it produces one bit for the information. The resultant bits from significant tests are generated as many as the number of entries in the LIP and the LIS, and the sign bits are produced as many as the number of entries that are added to the LSP. Once a pixel is added to the LIP, the pixel generates a bit in every bit plane to show whether it is significant or not. Therefore, it is impossible to reduce the number of bits caused by such pixels after they are added to the LIP. To reduce the bit generation, we must keep the LIS from partitioning. This property is essential in adding functionalities to the SPIHT algorithm.

3. Multiresolutional Coding

In the previous work [2], they decoded the whole bit stream and selected the necessary coefficients to reconstruct an image they wanted. It is difficult to use this function in the narrow bandwidth environment because the whole bit stream should be transmitted to reconstruct even a small image. If we rearrange coefficients at the encoder, several decoders with different bandwidths can receive enough coefficients to reconstruct images with the corresponding resolution. This is the purpose of multiresolutional coding.

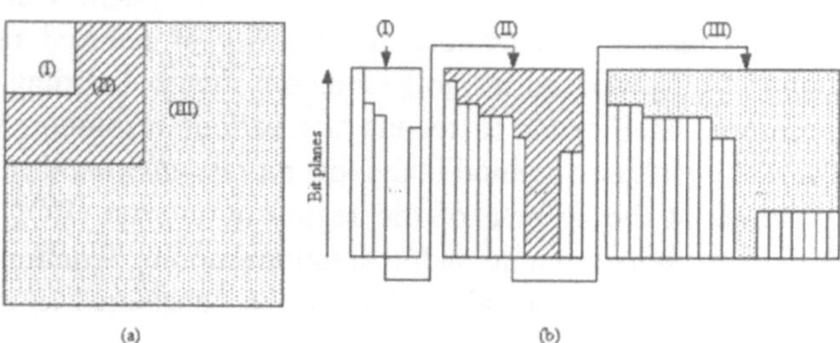

Fig. 1. (a) After wavelet transform, an image is decomposed into several subbands. (I) ROI for the quarter resolution image. (II) ROI for the half resolution image with (I). (III) ROI for the full size image with (I) and (II). (b) A coding sequence of the proposed multiresolutional coding.

If the encoder puts the bit stream for a low resolution image at the front part, a decoder can reconstruct the low resolution image with only the small fraction of the bit stream. If some decoders with wider bandwidth receive more bits, they can reconstruct a higher resolution image with them. Therefore, we can consider each part of coefficients as ROIs for reconstructing images. In Fig. 1 (a), we can think of the part (I) as an ROI for the quarter resolution image, and we can reconstruct the half resolution image from the coefficients of the part (I) and (II). Thus we can apply the ROI coding scheme into the multiresolutional coding. After describing the ROI coding in section 3.1, we present the multiresolutional coding in section 3.2.

3.1 ROI Coding

The ROI coding is a method to code images with an emphasis to regions of interest. Usually an encoder allocates more bits to coefficients of the ROI in order to emphasize the ROI. We proposed an algorithm that incorporated this functionality into the SPIHT algorithm [3].

```
a) Modified Sorting Pass:
      a.1) for each entry (i,j) in all the LIP(p) for n≤p≤n_max do:
    if (i,j) is one of the ROI coefficients, do:
      a.1.1) output S_n(i,j);
      a.1.2) if S_n(i,j) = 1, then move (i,j) to the LSP and output the sign of c_i,j;
   a.2) for each entry (i,j) in the LIS(p) for n≤p≤n_max do:
   a.2.1) if the entry is of type A, then
         if (i,j) is one of the PROI coefficients, do:
            output S_n(D(i,j));
            if S_n(D(i,j)) = 1, then
            for each (k,l) ∈ O(i,j) and it belongs to the ROI, do:
                  output S_n(k,l)
                  if S_n(k,l) = 1, then add (k,l) to the LSP and output the sign of c_k,l;
                  if S_n(k,l) = 0, then add (k,l) to the end of the LIP(n);
                  if L(i,j) ≠ Ø, then move (i,j) to the end of the LIS(n) as an entry of type B, and goto
                     Step a.2.2); otherwise, remove entry (i,j) from the current LIS(p);
                  if (k,l) doesn't belong to the ROI coefficients, do:
                     move (k,l) to the end of the LIP(n);
   a.2.2) if the entry is of type B, then
         if (i, j) is one of the PROI coefficients, do:
            output S_n(L(i,j));
            if S_n(L(i,j)) = 1, then
               add each (k,l) ∈ O(i,j) to the end of the LIS(n) as an entry of type A;
               remove (i,j) from the LIS(p);
b) Refinement Pass: for each entry (i,j) in the LSP,
      except those included in the last sorting pass (i.e., with same n),
         if (i,j) belongs to the ROI coefficients, do:
         - output the n-th most significant bit of | c_i,j |;
c) Quantization-Step Upgrade : decrement n by 1 and go to Step a) if n ≥ R
```

Fig. 2. Modified procedure for the ROI

In the ROI coding algorithm, coders perform the node test only when the node is in the ROI mask, and also perform the descendant test only if the node is in the PROI mask [3]. Then the LIP contains three types of coefficients: significant and non-ROI coefficients; insignificant and non-ROI ones; insignificant and ROI ones. At the following bit plane, sorting pass checks only the last ones and non-ROI coefficients stay in the LIP unrelated to thresholds.

After coding the ROI, the coder must deal with coefficients that are excluded in the ROI coding procedure. Then, the coder performs the node test for the entries in the LIP from the large threshold. However, the LIP contains lots of entries that are added to the LIP with relatively small thresholds. To reduce the bit generation, we partition the LIP into multiple LIP(n), and the LIS into LIS(n).

When we divide the LIP into several LIP(n) during the ROI coding procedure, the LIP(n) is a list of pixels that enter the list at the threshold of 2^n. After the ROI coding procedure, coders perform the node tests only the entries in the LIP(k), where k is greater than n. From this division, we can save lots of significant tests of the nodes in the LIS or the LIP. The modified coding procedure of the ROI is shown in Fig. 2 and we underlined the modified parts of the algorithm. During the procedure of the non-ROI coefficients, the coder concatenates the divided lists into each list, i.e., LIS and LIP. We omit the procedure for the non-ROI because it can be easily deduced.

3.2 Multiresolutional Coding

In the previous section, we reviewed the ROI coding method. We apply the concept of the ROI coding to multi-resolutional coding. As mentioned before, the multiresolutional coding is an ROI coding with multiple ROIs. In addition, the degree of interest is different among the regions. In Fig. 1(a), the region (I) is the most interesting and the region (II) is the second interesting. Therefore, we first encode the region (I) with the ROI coding method. During the ROI coding, both the region (II) and (III) are unrelated to the ROI. After completing the coding at the user-defined bit plane (R in Fig. 2), the region (II) becomes the second ROI. After coding of the region (II), the region (III) becomes the final ROI. Figure 1(b) shows such coding order, and the narrow bars in each region are the sorted coefficients.

Let us consider the bit plane where coders finish the ROI coding procedure. As the value of R is smaller, more bits are allocated to the corresponding ROI. On the contrary, a higher value of R supports wider regions. If the bit budget remains after encoding all of the regions, it is possible to code all coefficients in the whole regions ((I), (II), and (III) in Fig. 1(a)) using the original SPIHT algorithm.

4. Experiment Results

The following results were obtained from the Lena image with monochrome and 512×512 with 8 bpp for fixed rate coding. We used the 9/7-tap biorthogonal wavelet filters [5] to decompose the image.

Figures 3 (a) and (b) show the layered bit streams generated by the previous multiresolutional encoding [2] and the proposed multiresolutional encoding at 1 bpp and 0.1 bpp, respectively. In the figures, we can see that the first layer of the bit stream generated by the previous multiresolutional encoding method is much longer than the first layer of our algorithm. This result shows that the number of coefficients for low resolution image is very small. In addition, 'R' indicates a user-defined threshold – how many bit planes the coders must deal with. With a high bit rate, encoder can deal with many bit planes (small R) as well as various resolution images. However, a low bit rate limits the available bit planes and resolutions of support. This is coincident with our intuition.

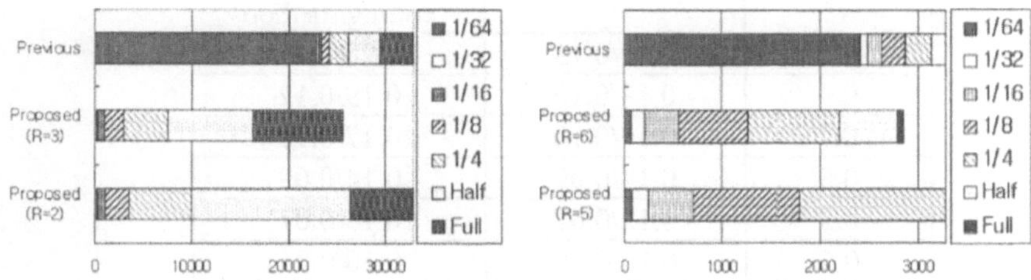

Fig. 3. (a) Left - Comparison of bit streams when the image is compressed with one bpp bit rate. (b) Right - Comparison of bit streams when the image is compressed with 0.1 bpp bit rate and with different thresholds.

Fig. 4. Reconstructed images with the proposed multiresolutional coding method (bit rate = 1 bpp) from a single bit stream. (a) 1/8 resolution. (b) Quarter resolution. (c) Half resolution. (d) Full resolution.

Figure 4 shows the images reconstructed at different resolutions with the proposed multiresolutional coding method. These images are reconstructed from a single encoded bit stream with the bitrate being set at one bpp.

Table 1 shows the computation times for encoding and decoding processes with the original SPIHT algorithm and the proposed algorithm. We applied the proposed method to the Lena image with 256×256 resolution. We got the results under a Pentium III (550 MHz) with Windows 2000. The computation time of the proposed algorithm is almost similar to that of the original algorithm. This fact shows that there is a little overhead for the additional functionality.

bpp	SPIHT	Proposed multiresolutional coding method
1.0	0.19/0.13	0.20/0.13
0.9	0.18/0.12	0.19/0.12
0.7	0.16/0.10	0.17/0.10
0.5	0.14/0.09	0.14/0.09
0.3	0.12/0.07	0.13/0.07
0.1	0.10/0.05	0.10/0.05

Table 1. Comparison of computation times of the original SPIHT algorithm and the proposed algorithm for encoding/decoding. (unit: sec)

5. Conclusions

We extended the ROI coding algorithm to incorporate a multiresolutional coding functionality, which can decode multiresolution images from a single embedded bit stream. By moving the ROI from the highest tree level to the lowest level, we can obtain the multiresolutional coding functionality easily. The greatest advantage of the proposed multiresolutional coding algorithms is that we can incorporate a new function into the SPIHT algorithm without cost loss in the performance. This multiresolutional coding has many applications in network communications such as scalable multicast transmission in heterogeneous network, fast decoding, image database browsing, telemedicine, multipoint video conferencing, and distance learning, etc.

References

1. Said and Pearlman, "A new, fast, and efficient image codec based on set partitioning in hierarchical trees," *IEEE Trans. Circuits and Systems for Video Technology*, Vol. 6, pp. 243-250, June, 1996.
2. Z. Xiong, B.J. Kim and W. A. Pearlman, "Multiresolutional encoding and decoding in embedded image and video coders," *Proceedings of the 1998 IEEE International Conference on Acoustics, Speech and Signal Processing*, Vol. 6, pp.3709-3712, 1998.
3. K. H. Park, C. S. Lee and H. W. Park, "Region-of-interest coding based on set partitioning in hierarchical trees," to be presented in *IEEE International Conference on Image Processing (ICIP-01)*, Thessaloniki, Greece, Oct. 2001.
4. E. Atsumi and N. Farvardin, "Lossy/lossless region-of-interest image coding based on set partitioning in hierarchical trees," *International Conference on Image Processing (ICIP-98)*, October 4-7, 1998 Chicago, Illinois, USA.
5. M. Antonini, M. Barlaud, P. Mathieu, and I. Daubechies, "Image coding using wavelet transform," *IEEE Trans. Image Processing*, Vol. 1, pp. 205-220, April, 1992.

LLEC: An Image Coder with Low-Complexity and Low-Memory Requirement

Debin Zhao[1], Wen Gao[1,2], Shiguang Shan[2] ,Y. K. Chan [3]

[1] Department of Computer Science, Harbin Institute of Technology, Harbin, 150001, China
{dbzhao,wgao}@vilab.hit.edu.cn
[2] Institute of Computing Technology, CAS, Beijing 100080,China
{wgao,sgshan}@ict.ac.cn
[3] Department of Computer Science, City University of Hong Kong
csykchan@cityu.edu.hk

Abstract: A Low-complexity and Low-memory Entropy Coder (LLEC) for image compression is proposed in this paper. The two key elements in LLEC are zerotree coding and Golomb-Rice codes. Zerotree coding exploits the zerotree structure of transformed coefficients for higher compression efficiency. Golomb-Rice codes are used to code the remaining coefficients in a VLC/VLI manner for low complexity and low memory. The experimental results show that the compression efficiency of DCT- and DWT-based LLEC outperforms baseline JPEG and EZW at the given bit rates, respectively. When compared with SPIHT, LLEC is inferior by 0.3 dB on average for the tested images but superior in terms of computational complexity and memory requirement. In addition, LLEC has other desirable features such as parallel processing support, ROI (Region Of Interest) coding and as a universal entropy coder for DCT and DWT.

1. Introduction

Recent impressive advance in image compression is mainly attributed to two aspects: these are transform techniques followed by entropy coding of transformed coefficients, respectively. Discrete Cosine Transform (DCT) and Discrete Wavelet Transform (DWT) are still the dominant transform techniques applied to current applications although LPPRFB (Linear Phase Perfect Reconstruction FilterBanks) [1] is sometimes used. On entropy coding, static Huffman codes have been essentially used in most popular compression standards such as JPEG [2], MPEG-1/2 [3], [4], MPEG-4 [5]-[7] and H261/3 [8], [9]. In the quest for higher compression efficiency, arithmetic coding has been app`lied to DCT and DWT. There are several representatives of such state of the art coders, namely EZDCT (Embedded Zerotree DCT coding) [10], [11], EZHDCT (Embedded Zerotree coding in Hierarchical DCT) [12], EZW (Embedded Zerotree Wavelet coding) [13], SPIHT (Set Partition In Hierarchical Trees) [14], ZTE (ZeroTree Entropy coding) [15], and EBCOT (Embedded Block Coding with Optimized Truncation) [16]. These coders provide very high compression efficiency in terms of Peak Signal-to-Noise Ratio (PSNR) versus required bits-per-pixel (bpp). The disadvantage of these coders is higher computational complexity and additional memory requirement. The higher computational complexity and additional memory requirement of arithmetic coder over the Huffman entropy coder is an extra burden when it has been pointed out that even static Huffman tables can be a bottleneck in hardware implementation [17]. It is the intention of this paper to propose the LLEC coder that has competitive compression efficiency and yet requires lower computational complexity and lower memory than most coders resulting in lower cost implementation.

2. Detailed Description of LLEC

2.1 Zerootree Coding

ZTC is a proven technique for coding DCT/DWT coefficients because of its superior compression performance [10]-[15]. In LLEC, the significant/insignificant decision is made depending on whether a quantized coefficient is zero or non-zero. All zerotrees are extracted and coded by ZTC. The coefficient scanning, tree growing and coding are done in one pass instead of multiple passes on a bit-plane-by-bit-plane basis as used in EZW and SPIHT.

2.2 Coding of Remaining Coefficients

2.2.1 Coefficient Bucketing: One of the most efficient techniques as used in JPEG is to partition the quantized coefficients into different buckets resulting in JPEG VLC/VLI [2]. Coefficient separation into two components enables higher compression efficiency to be achieved than the straightforward coding of quantized coefficients alone. Table I is an example of the bucketing strategy used in JPEG. In JPEG, *Category* is coded using Huffman tables and it is known as JPEG-VLC. This coefficient bucketing technique is also used in LLEC for coding the remaining coefficients. However, JPEG-VLC part is replaced by G-R codes resulting in lower complexity and lower memory, and LLEC-VLI part is still the same as JPEG-VLI.

Table I: Coefficient buckets

Category	Coefficient values
0	0
1	-1, 1
2	-3~-2 , 2~3
3	-7~-4 , 4~7
4	-15~-8 , 8~15
5	-31~-16 , 16~31
6	-63~-32 , 32~63

2.2.2 Category Statistical Characteristics: As stated in the previous paragraphs, the remaining coefficients are decomposed into two separate components as *Category* and

VLI. It is intended to show in here that *Category* has a very desirable probability distribution that is closely approximated by the probability distribution 2^{-i} ($i = 1,2,...,n$) regardless of quantization step and transform scheme (DCT or DWT) used.

The following two experiments attempt to show that the probability distribution of *Category* is highly invariant to different quantization steps and across transform schemes by a small standard deviation (σ) of its entropy (H). Furthermore, the resulting probability distribution from test images approximates closely to 2^{-i} ($i = 1,2,...,n$). In both experiments, the test image is grayscale 512×512 Lena image. The uniform+deadzone quantization is applied. The deadzone width is set to be 40% larger than that the regular stepsize .

Experiment One (DCT): Do 8×8 DCT on Lena; Using different quantization steps to quantize the DCT coefficients; the bucketing strategy showed in Table I is applied to the remaining coefficients. The probability distribution of *Category* is listed in Table II(a). The resulting average entropy of *Category* is 1.88 and the standard deviation is $\sigma = 0.057$.

Experiment Two (DWT): Do six-scale wavelet decomposition on Lena using 9-7 biorthogonal spline filters of Daubechies; Using different quantization steps to quantize the DWT coefficients; the same bucketing strategy is applied to the remaining coefficients. The probability distribution of *Category* is listed in Table II(b). The resulting average entropy of *Category* is 1.81 and the standard deviation is $\sigma = 0.050$. It can be seen that the entropy of *Category* both for DCT and DWT is only a few percent difference to the entropy of 2^{-i} ($i = 1,2,...,n$) when $n = 8$.

Table II: Probability distrubution of category

(a) DCT with uniform+deadzone quantization

DCT Category	Quantization step				
	10	15	20	30	50
0	49%	47%	47%	47%	49%
1	28%	30%	28%	28%	29%
2	13%	13%	15%	15%	14%
3	6%	6%	6%	6%	5%
4	3%	3%	3%	3%	2%
5	1%	1%	1%	1%	0.3%
6	0.6%	0.4%	0.3%	0.1%	0
7	0.01%	0	0	0	0
Entropy	1.91	1.91	1.92	1.91	1.77
G-R_FS Code Length	1.93	1.94	1.95	1.94	1.81

(b) DWT with uniform+deadzone quantization

DWT Category	Quantization step				
	10	20	30	40	50
0	52%	49%	50%	50%	51%
1	27%	28%	29%	29%	29%
2	13%	15%	14%	14%	13%
3	5%	5%	5%	5%	4%
4	2%	2%	2%	1%	1%
5	1%	1%	1%	0.7%	0.7%
6	0.3%	0.4%	0.3%	0.2%	0.2%
7	0.2%	0.1%	0.1%	0.1%	0.1%
Entropy	1.82	1.87	1.85	1.78	1.73
G-R_FS Code Length	1.85	1.90	1.89	1.81	1.75

2.2.3 G-R Codes: The two major components of G-R codes are the fundamental sequence (FS) and sample splitting [18], [19]. FS is a comma code with the property that a value *m* has a corresponding codeword that is made up of *m* zeros followed by a "1". *FS is optimal for coding source with the probability distribution of* 2^{-i} ($i = 1,2,...,n$).

From the statistical characteristics of *Category* in *Experiment One and Two*, it can be easily found that G-R_FS can be applied to code *Category* efficiently without the need to further use sample splitting or parameter estimation.

2.3 Algorithmic Description of LLEC

Before performing LLEC, a simple DPCM scheme (Relative DC = Current DC - Previous DC) is applied to decorrelate the neighboring DC coefficients or LL subband. The detailed algorithmic description of LLEC encoder operating on a transformed block is given in Fig. 1.

```
(1)  Initialization: k = relative DC;
(2)  G-R_FS(k);
(3)  ZeroTree_Coding(k) {
         if all k's descendants are zeros, then
             Output 0 in 1 bit;
         else {
             Output 1 in 1 bit;
             for every k's son:s,G-R_FS(s);
             if k's indirect descendants are zeros,
                 then Output 0 in 1 bit;
             else {
                 Output 1 in 1 bit;
                 for every k's son:s,ZeroTree_Coding(s);
             }
         }
     };
(4)  End.

G-R_FS(k){
    caculating its category C(k) and P(k);
    Output 1 in C(k)+1 bits;
                         //Golomb-Rice codes FS output;
    if (C(k) != 0) then Output P(k) in C(k) bits;
                         //output VLI;
}
```

Fig. 1. Algorithmic description of LLEC

2.4 Computational Complexity and Memory Requirement

In terms of computational complexity, LLEC is similar to JPEG entropy coding and lower than EZW and SPIHT. In LLEC, ZTC's computational complexity is comparable to JPEG run length coding. For the remaining coefficients, LLEC performs straightforward coding by G-R_FS/VLI while as JPEG needs to concatenate continuous zeros with a subsequent nonzero coefficient and then perform Huffman table lookup. When comparing with EZW and SPIHT, LLEC has lower computational complexity. This is because that the coefficient scanning, tree growing and coding in LLEC are done in one pass instead of multiple passes on a bit-plane-by-bit-plane basis as used in EZW and SPIHT and some of their versions involved in extra arithmetic coding.

When comparing memory requirement, we know that in JPEG or MPEG-1/2, there are at least two 16×11 Huffman tables (for luminance and chrominance, respectively) with the longest codeword length of 16-bit. This longest codeword length has been reduced to 12-bit in MPEG-4 and H.263+. For EZW and SPIHT, even without arithmetic coding and coding a grayscale image, memory requirement doubling the image size is necessary for saving significant/insignificant lists. If arithmetic coding or color image coding is needed, extra memory will be necessary. However, LLEC does not require any Huffman table, significant/insignificant list or arithmetic coding both for grayscale image and color image compression. So its memory requirement is minimized.

In terms of uniformity in processing logic, LLEC deals with relative DCs and ACs in a uniform manner. Furthermore, this uniform manner is maintained for coding chrominance components. In comparison, JPEG deals with relative DCs and Acs in different passes. The number of passes is further compounded for coding color images.

3. Experimental Results

LLEC has been tested on standard grayscale 512×512 Lena and 512×512 Barbara images with DCT and DWT. The size of DCT block is set to 8×8. In DWT, 7/9 Daubechies filters with six-scale decomposition are utilized resulting in reorganized DWT coefficient block size of 64×64. The uniform+deadzone quantization is applied to both DCT and DWT. The deadzone width is set to be 40% larger than that the regular stepsize.

3.1 LLEC with DCT

The PSNR results of DCT-based LLEC at different bit rates for Lena and Barbara images are given in Table III. For comparison purpose, LLEC versus baseline JPEG (using default Huffman table) and JPEG-O (using adaptive Huffman coding) are also tabulated. JPEG and JPEG-O are taken from http://www.ijg.org/.

In Table III, it can be seen that DCT-based LLEC consistently outperforms JPEG and JPEG-O. It is superior to JPEG by 1.0 dB on Lena image and 2.2 dB on Barbara image on average. Comparing to JPEG-O, LLEC gains an average of 0.6 dB on Lena image and 1.7 dB on Barbara image.

3.2 LLEC with DWT

The coding performance of DWT-based LLEC at different bit rates for both Lena and Barbara is listed in Table IV. In Table IV, LLEC is compared with EZW (with arithmetic coding) and SPIHT (six-scale decomposition with binary output).

Table IV shows that LLEC exceeds EZW by an average of 0.2 dB for Lena and 0.1 dB for Barbara, respectively. When compared with SPIHT, LLEC is inferior by 0.3 dB on average for both Lena and Barbara images.

Table III: DCT-based LLEC performance comparision (PSNR)

(a) LENA

bpp	LLEC	JPEG	JPEG-O
0.25	31.80	30.40	31.60
0.50	35.39	34.63	34.90
0.75	37.40	36.52	36.60
1.00	38.76	37.81	37.90

(b) BARBARA

bpp	LLEC	JPEG	JPEG-O
0.25	26.10	24.26	25.20
0.50	30.17	27.81	28.30
0.75	33.02	30.72	31.00
1.00	35.24	33.04	33.10

Table IV: DWT- based LLEC performance comparision (PSNR)

(a) LENA

bpp	LLEC	EZW	SPIHT
0.0625	27.83	27.54	28.00
0.125	30.51	30.23	30.71
0.25	33.43	33.17	33.70
0.50	36.44	36.28	36.73
1.00	39.42	39.55	39.91

(b) BARBARA

bpp	LLEC	EZW	SPIHT
0.0625	22.98	23.10	23.12
0.125	24.44	24.03	24.47
0.25	26.92	26.77	27.22
0.50	30.60	30.53	31.00
1.00	35.18	35.14	35.94

References

1. T. Tran and Q. Nguyen, "A Progressive transmission image coder using linear phase uniform filterbanks as block transform," *IEEE Trans. image Processing*, vol. 8, no. 11, pp. 1493-1507, 1999.
2. W. Pennebaker and J. Mitchell, *JPEG Still Image Data Compression Standard*. New York: 1993.
3. "Coding of moving pictures and associated audio for digital storage media up to about 1.5 Mbit/s," Tech. Rep., ISO/IEC IS 11172(MPEG-1), 1993.
4. "Generic coding of moving pictures and associated audio," Tech. Rep., ISO/IEC DIS 13818(MPEG-2), 1994.
5. L. Chiariglione, "MPEG and multimedia communications," *IEEE Trans. CSVT.*, vol. 7, no 1, pp. 5-18, 1997.
6. T. Sikora, "The MPEG-4 video standard verification model," *IEEE Trans. CSVT.*, vol. 7, no 1, pp. 19-31, 1997.
7. F. Pereira and T. Alpert, "MPEG-4 video subjective test procedures and results," *IEEE Trans. CSVT.*, vol. 7, no 1, pp. 32-51, 1997.
8. "Video codec for audiovisual services at $p \times 64$ kb/s," ITU-T Rec. H.261, 1990.
9. "Video coding for low bit rate communications," ITU-T Draft Rec. H.263, Dec. 1995.
10. Z. Xiong, O. Guleryuz, and M. Orchard, "A DCT-based embedded image coder," *IEEE Signal Processing Letters*, vol. 3, no. 11, pp. 289-290, 1996.
11. Z. Xiong, K. Ramchandran, M. Orchard, and Y. Zhang, "A comparative study of DCT- and wavelet-based image coding," *IEEE Trans. CSVT.*, vol. 9, no 5, pp. 692-695, 1999.
12. D. Zhao, W. Gao, and Y. K. Chan, "An embedded image coder based on hierarchical DCT," *Proc. Picture Coding Symposium*, pp. 425-428, Portland, USA, 1999.
13. J. Shapiro, "Embedded image coding using zerotree of wavelet coefficients," *IEEE Trans. Signal Processing*, vol. 41, no. 12, pp. 3445-3463, 1993.
14. A. Said and W. Pearlman, "A new, fast, and efficient image codec based on set partitioning in hierarchical trees," *IEEE Trans. CSV T.*, vol. 6, no 3, pp. 243-250, 1996.
15. A. Martucci, I. Sodagar, T. Chiang and Y. Zhang, "A zerotree wavelet video coder," *IEEE Trans. CSVT.*, vol. 7, no 1, pp. 109-118, 1997.
16. D. Taubman, "High performance scalable image compression with EBCOT," *IEEE Trans. Image Processing*, vol. 9, No. 7, pp. 1158-1170, July 2000.
17. N. Memon, "Adaptive coding of DCT coefficients by Golomb-Rice codes," *Proc. ICIP*, vol. 1, pp.516-520, Chicago, Illinois, USA, 1998.
18. S. Golomb, "Run-length encodings," *IEEE Trans. Inform. Theory*, vol. IT-21, pp. 399-401, July 1966.
19. R. Rice, "Some practical universal noiseless coding techniques--Part I-III," Tech. Rep. JPL-79-22, JPL-83-17 and JPL-91-3, Mar. 1979, Mar. 1983, Nov. 1991.

A Generalized Secret Image Sharing and Recovery Scheme

Chwei-Shyong Tsai and Chin-Chen Chang

Department of Computer Science and Information Engineering
National Chung Cheng University, 621, Chiayi, Taiwan, R.O.C.
{tsaics, ccc }@cs.ccu.edu.tw

Abstract: The secret sharing is an important issue in confirming the security of confidential information. This paper proposes a generalized sharing and recovery scheme suitable for secret images. The scheme coalesces vector quantization (VQ) compression technique and conventional generalized secret sharing scheme to produce pseudo codebooks out of the secret codebook used for compressing the secret image. Every pseudo codebook is held by a participant of the generalized access structure for secret sharing. On the other hand, the secret image can be only recovered by all participants, who belong to the same qualified subgroup of the generalized access structure, to work together with their possessed pseudo codebooks

1 Introduction

Till now, through Internet people easily reach to quickly exchange multimedia data between each other. However, Internet is a highly open environment. How to carry out secret communication becomes overemphasized. In general, cryptosystems can provide encryption and decryption procedures to protect secret information. When the sender wants to transmit the secret information, the secret information (plaintext) is first converted to be encrypted information (ciphertext) by encryption procedure and secret key, and then the ciphertext is transmitted on Internet. The receiver recovers the original secret information by employing the corresponded decryption procedure and secret key to the received ciphertext.

The security of cryptosystems mainly bases on the secret key. Even the encryption and decryption procedures are opened, the security of cryptosystems is still safe. However, consider the situation that only one participant possesses the secret key. Once the participant holds secret key has been missing, the secret may not be recovered. A more proper scheme is secret sharing which can distribute the access control of security among several participants. The secret sharing scheme provides increased control of the secret and decreased risk of its security.

The secret sharing schemes proposed by Blakely [2] and Shamir [6], respectively, are (t, n)-threshold scheme. In a (t, n)-threshold scheme, the secret holder (called dealer) shares a secret among n participants of a group such that each participant holds a partial secret (called shadows), respectively. To recover the secret, only t or at least t participants have to hand out their owned shadows and reconstruct the secret, however, any t-1 or less participants can not reveal any knowledge of the secret.

In a threshold secret sharing scheme, each participant has equal priority to each other. In 1987, Ito *et al.* [3] introduced a more generalized approach for secret sharing. In a generalized secret sharing scheme, it specifies which subgroups of participants can share a secret and which should not. The family of the subgroups of participants who can recover the secret forms an access structure, and the subgroup in the access structure is called the qualified (or authorized) subgroup. The number of participants in each subgroup need not be equal. Therefore, a secret can be shared among participants without being limited to a fixed threshold. Moreover, every participant could hold different number of shadows in such a way the different participant can own different access privilege and the secret can be shared according to any access structure. This generalized concept is more flexible and practice. This paper proposes a generalized secret sharing scheme which fits secret images.

The proposed generalized secret sharing scheme coalesces the techniques of VQ [4] image compression and conventional generalized secret sharing scheme. To share the secret image to participants in a group, the dealer first applies VQ compression technique to compress the secret image into a sequence of indices by using a pre-selected codebook. For the codebook used during the compression process, the utilization of conventional generalized secret sharing scheme produces corresponded pseudo codebook for each participant. On the other hand, the conventional generalized secret sharing scheme is also applied to the secret key, used to encrypt the produced indices, to generate key shadow for each participant. With the technique of the proposed scheme, the pseudo codebook and key shadows held by the participants of a qualified subgroup can reconstruct the secret image cooperatively.

2 The Proposed Scheme

The proposed generalized secret sharing scheme, a combination of VQ image compression technique and the concept of conventional generalized secret sharing scheme, has its pride of secret control of a secret image to be effectively distributed to many participants in a group. Let the gray-scale secret image X with $M \times N$ pixels be defined in Equation (1). Assume X will be shared among participants corresponding to the access structure A, where $A=\{G_1, G_2, \ldots, G_g\}$ such that each participant may appear in several subgroups G_k . First of all, dealer has to select a codebook C, which can be generated by LBG algorithm [4] and is defined in Equation (2), as the specified codebook. The proposed scheme, in the following subsections, constructed by secret sharing phase and secret recovery phase, can product a Pseudo Codebook

PCB_t for each participant t and reconstruct X through those pseudo codebooks held by the participants in a qualified subgroup G_k.

$X=\{X_{ij}| 0\leq X_{ij}\leq 255, 1\leq i\leq M \text{ and } 1\leq j\leq N\}$. (1)

$C=\{C_r|C_r=(V_{r,1}, V_{r,2}, \ldots, V_{r,u}), 0\leq V_{r,q}\leq 255, r=1,2,\ldots,n \text{ and } q=1,2, \ldots, u\}$, where C_r is the r-th codevector. (2)

2.1 Secret Sharing Phase

According to the selected codebook C, and through VQ compression encoding method, X is compressed into a sequence of indices. Let the produced index sequence be I. By the following processes, I will be encrypted and C will be used to generate the corresponding pseudo codebooks, respectively.

About using VQ technique, under only having knowledge of the produced index sequence I but in the absence of C, a participant who belongs to a qualified subgroup can recover extremely lossy version of X alone and can try to guess the content of X. One possible way is that the participant may randomly assign a different block (or codevector) to each index in I, individually, and then can obtain a reconstructed image with significant distortion. Through human eyes still can tell some degrees of information from the reconstructed image and the secret image may be revealed. Thus, to enhance the security, the index sequence I will not be distributed to each participant directly. The proposed scheme first chooses a secret key K_1 to be the seed of Pseudo Random Number Generator (PRNG). Next, PRNG(K_1) is performed to produce a sequence of distinct random numbers such that each random number as the permuted position of the corresponding index in I , respectively. Let I' be the permuted index sequence. At this moment, dealer can choose another secret key K_2 to encrypt I' by utilizing DES-like encryption procedure. Let the encrypted index sequence be EI.

Let $K=K_1||K_2$, where || represents the concatenation symbol. Through a conventional generalized secret sharing scheme, such as Benalon and Leichter method [1], K is shared by the participants and a key shadow $KS_{t,k}$ is generated for each participant t in the qualified subgroup G_k .

The secret image can not be decompressed without having codebook C. Therefore, each component $V_{r,q}$ of the codevector C_r is considered to be secret and is shared by participants in each subgroup G_k. Through a conventional generalized secret sharing scheme, a corresponding shadow $SV_{t,k}^{(r,q)}$ could be generated for each participant t in G_k such that $0\leq SV_{t,k}^{(r,q)}\leq 255$. However, in such a way, participant t can try to determine the shadows held by other participants in G_k by exhaustively guessing the values between 0 and 255-$SV_{t,k}^{(r,q)}$. In order to eliminate this dependency of shadows, $V_{r,q}$ and its corresponding $SV_{t,k}^{(r,q)}$ must follow Equation (3). Let all $SV_{t,k}^{(r,q)}$ compose a codebook shadow $CS_{t,k}$.

$$\sum_{participant\ t\in G_k} SV_{t,k}^{(r,q)} \bmod 256 = V_{r,q}. \quad (3)$$

The proposed scheme will then create a pseudo codebook for each participant. Here, the concept of solving simple Knapsack problem is utilized to generate a pseudo codebook PCB_t for each participant t to reach to the purpose of sharing of C. Without loss of generality, we assume that participant t holds codebook shadows $CS_{t,1}$, $CS_{t,2}$, ..., $CS_{t,w}$ and each $CS_{t,i}$ is composed by $SV_{t,i}^{(r,q)}$ ' s.

Knapsack problem [5], defined as follows, has been proven to be an NP-complete problem. However, this problem can be solved if some specific sequence exists in it. The Super-increasing sequence [5] is a famous one. When Super-increasing sequence is involved, 0/1 Knapsack problem, as defined in the following, can be easily solved.

Definition 1. [Knapsack problem]

Given a natural number sequence $B=(b_1,b_2,\ldots,b_n)$ and a number S, does there exist a subsequence $B' \subseteq B$, where $B'=(b_1',b_2',\ldots,b_m')$ such that $\sum_{i=1}^{m} b_i'=S$?

Definition 2. [Super-increasing sequence]

A Super-increasing sequence $B=(b_1,b_2,\ldots,b_n)$ satisfies that $b_j > \sum_{i=1}^{j-1} b_i$, $\forall j>1$.

Definition 3. [0/1 Knapsack problem]

Given a Super-increasing $B=(b_1,b_2,\ldots,b_n)$ and S, there exists a vector $X=(x_1,x_2,\ldots,x_n)$, $x_i \in \{0,1\}$, $i=1,2,\ldots,n$ such that $S=\sum_{i=1}^{n} b_i x_i$.

In the proposed scheme, shadows $SV_{t,1}^{(r,q)}, SV_{t,2}^{(r,q)}, \ldots, SV_{t,w}^{(r,q)}$ are used to generate $P_{r,q}^{(t)}$ according to Equation (4). Then all $P_{r,q}^{(t)}$ produce a pseudo codebook PCB_t.

$$P_{r,q}^{(t)} = \beta_1^{(t)} SV_{t,1}^{(r,q)} + \beta_2^{(t)} SV_{t,2}^{(r,q)} + \ldots + \beta_w^{(t)} SV_{t,w}^{(r,q)} \tag{4}$$

, where $\beta_1^{(t)} = 1, \beta_i^{(t)} = \sum_{j=1}^{i-1} \beta_j^{(t)} a_j^{(t)} + 1$ for each $i > 1$ and $a_j^{(t)}$ is the maximum of $SV_{t,j}^{(1,1)}, SV_{t,j}^{(1,2)}, \ldots, SV_{t,j}^{(n,u)}$.

It is easily to observe that $(\beta_1^{(t)}, \beta_2^{(t)}, \ldots, \beta_w^{(t)})$ is a Super-increasing sequence.

In the recovery phase, participant t can reconstruct each $SV_{t,i}^{(r,q)}$ with $P_{r,q}^{(t)}$ and $\beta_1^{(t)}, \beta_2^{(t)}, \ldots, \beta_w^{(t)}$ and then recovers the codebook shadows $CS_{t,i}$.

Finally dealer distributes EI publicly while transmits a key shadow $KS_{t,k}$, all $\beta_i^{(t)}$ and a pseudo codebook PCB_t surreptitiously through secret channel to each participant t like conventional generalized secret sharing scheme.

2.2 Secret Recovery Phase

If all participants $U_1, U_2, \ldots, U_y$ in a qualified subgroup G_k, expect a cooperation to recover the secret shared image, every one of them must first compute his own codebook shadows $CS_{t,k}$ by the codebook shadow reconstruction process now presented. When y codebook shadows go through the secret shared image reconstruction phase, the secret shared image can be therefore recovered.

When participant t expects to cooperate with the others in the qualified subgroup G_k to recover the secret image, he/she must obtain the corresponded codebook shadow $CS_{t,k}$ from PCB_t. Here, the principle that a Super-increasing sequence can solve the simple Knapsack problem is used. With $P_{r,q}^{(t)}$ in PCB_t and $\beta_1^{(t)}, \beta_2^{(t)}, \ldots, \beta_w^{(t)}$, the participant t can obtain each $SV_{t,i}^{(r,q)}$, i=1,2,...,w and then recovers the codebook shadows $CS_{t,i}$. The following algorithm shows the computing procedure.

Algorithm [Computing $SV_{t,i}^{(r,q)}$]
For r=1 **to** n **do**
For q=1 **to** u **do**
Begin
$SV_{t,w}^{(r,q)} = \mathrm{INT}(P_{r,q}^{(t)} / \beta_w^{(t)})$
$L = P_{r,q}^{(t)} - SV_{t,w}^{(r,q)} \times \beta_w^{(t)}$
For $i = w$-1 **downto** 1 **do**
Begin
$SV_{t,i}^{(r,q)} = \mathrm{INT}(L/\beta_i^{(t)})$
$L = L - SV_{t,i}^{(r,q)} \times \beta_i^{(t)}$
End
End.

Since $(\beta_1^{(t)}, \beta_2^{(t)}, \ldots, \beta_w^{(t)})$ is a Super-increasing sequence and $\beta_i^{(t)}$ are linear independent, we can find the unique solution of $SV_{t,i}^{(r,q)}$ for the equation $P_{r,q}^{(t)} = \sum_{i=1}^{w} \beta_i^{(t)} SV_{t,i}^{(r,q)}$.

After every participant t in a qualified subgroup G_k has handed in his/her own corresponding codebook shadow $CS_{t,k}$, the original codebook C can then be recovered.

Each component $V_{r,q}$ in the codevector C_r can be compute by Equation (5).

$$V_{r,q} = \sum_{z=1}^{y} SV_{z,k}^{(r,q)} \bmod 256 . \qquad (5)$$

On the other hand, the recovery method of conventional generalized secret scheme can be manipulated y corresponding key shadows to recover the secret key K.

In the mean time, K_1 and K_2 can thus be obtained (i.e. $K=K_1||K_2$). Next, DES-like decryption procedure with K_2 is applied to decrypt EI to recover the permuted index sequence I'. PRNG(K_1) is then performed to re-shuffle I' to obtain the original index sequence I. Finally, the proposed scheme utilizes the decoding method of VQ with the recovered C and I to reconstruct the secret image X'. Although inevitable result is little distortion, fortunately, human eyes will not detect any tiny difference between X' and X. This is the property of VQ.

3 Conclusions

To prevent the secret images from being either lost or destroyed, this paper presents an effective generalized secret sharing scheme. The proposed scheme coalesces VQ image compression technique and conventional generalized secret sharing scheme. Using VQ compression technique can extract the important secret information from the huge secret image and reduce the transmission amount of data. Using conventional generalized secret sharing scheme produces key shadows of the secret key, utilized to encrypt the generated compression index sequence, and codebook shadows of the codebook used for VQ encoding and decoding phases. What this does is that it distributes the access control privilege of the secret image to all participants. Finally, the principle of solving simple Knapsack problem is applied to generate a pseudo codebook for each qualified participant.

References

1. Benaloh, J., and Leichter, J.: Generalized Secret Sharing and Monotone Functions. Advances in Cryptology – CRYPTO '88, Vol. 403. Springer-Verlag, (1989) 27-35
2. Blakey, G.R.: Safeguarding Cryptographic Keys. Proceedings of National Computer Conference, Vol. 48. AFIPS Press, Montvale, New York (1979) 313-317
3. Ito, M., Saito, A., and Nishizeki, T.: Secret Sharing Scheme Realizing General Access Structure. Proceedings of IEEE Globecom'87, Tokyo (1987) 88-102
4. Linde, Y., Buzo, A., and Gray, R.M.: An Algorithm for Vector Quantization. IEEE Transactions on Communications, Vol. 28. (1980) 84-95
5. Merkle, R.C. and Hellman, M.E.: Hidding Information and Signatures in Knapdoor Knapsacks. IEEE Transactions on Information Theory, Vol. IT-24. (1978) 525-530
6. Shamir, A.: How to Share a Secret. Communications of the ACM, Vol. 22. No.11 (1997) 612-613

New Semi-fragile Authentication Watermarking

Jiaoying Shi, Kaixiang Yi

State Key Laboratory of CAD&CG at Zhejiang University, Hangzhou, 310027
{jyshi,kxyi}@cad.zju.edu.cn

Abstract. In this paper we propose a semi-fragile watermarking scheme, which can be used for image authentication. Let the original image be performed by the l-level discrete wavelet transformation. Then the approximate wavelet coefficient matrix of the original image and the real-value chaotic sequences are used to generate the content-based and secure watermark. The watermark is embedded into original image by using the technique of HVS. The tamper detection can identify the tampered region of the received watermarked image which may be undergone tamper attacked. Experimental results are excellent.

1. Introduction

Digital watermarking technique is one of the most effective methods for copyright protection and integrity authentication and is widely studied and used practically in recent years. Two primary types of digital watermarking have been studied: robust watermarking and fragile watermarking.

Robust digital watermarks[1] are designed for copyright protection and content tracking. But the robust watermarking can't answer the question whether the watermarked image is changed. Unlike robust watermarks, fragile watermarks[2] are designed for integrity authentication. In the past, many fragile watermark methods have been introduced. They can be classified into two primary categories: fragile watermarks and semi-fragile watermarks. Fragile watermarks are designed to detect every possible change in pixel values. They can provide a very high provability of tamper detection. At the same time, it means that any manipulations upon the fragile watermarked image including lossy compression are not allowed. Semi-fragile watermarks[3~5] combine the properties of fragile and robust watermarks. A semi-fragile watermark can tolerate some degree of changes to the watermarked image and also can localize regions of the image that have been tampered

Image authentication techniques can be classified into three categories: complete authentication, robust authentication and content authentication. Complete authentication refers to techniques that deal with the whole piece of image and any manipulation upon watermarked image is not allowed. The fragile watermarks techniques may be used for this authentication. Robust authentication techniques can tolerate some degrees manipulation upon watermarked image. Content authentication are designed to authenticate image content in a semantic level. So the semi-fragile may be used for robust authentication and content authentication.

In this paper we propose a content-based semi-fragile digital watermarking. Let the original image be performed by the l-level discrete wavelet transformation. Then the approximate wavelet coefficient matrix of the original image and the chaotic sequences are used to generate the content-based and secure watermark. Finally the watermark is embedded into the original image in DWT domain by utilizing the technique of HVS. The tamper detector generates a new content-based watermark W' for the received watermarked image using the real-value chaotic sequences. The original watermark, denoted as W^*, is extracted too. The place where the value of W^* is not equal to the value of W', is tampered. So we can identify the tampered region.

2 New Semi-Fragile Watermarking

2.1 HVS Model

Assume the original image is $I_{M \times N}$, M and N represent the height and width of the image respectively. Let the original be performed by l-level DWT. We can get $3*l+1$ different sub-band wavelet matrices.

So we choose to set the HVS threshold function T_l^θ as[9]:

$$T_l^\theta(i,j) = \lambda(l,\theta)\Lambda(l,i,j)\Xi(l,i,j) \tag{1}$$

where the first term

$$\lambda(l,\theta) = \begin{Bmatrix} \sqrt{2} & if \quad \theta = HH \\ 1 & otherwise \end{Bmatrix} \begin{Bmatrix} 1.00 & if & l=0 \\ 0.32 & f & l=1 \\ 0.16 & if & l=2 \\ 0.10 & if & l=3 \end{Bmatrix} \tag{2}$$

takes into account how the sensitivity to noise changes depending on the band that is considered . The second term:

$$\Lambda(l,i,j) = \frac{1}{256} I_3^{LL}(1+\frac{i}{2^{3-l}}, 1+\frac{j}{2^{3-l}}) \tag{3}$$

estimates the local brightness based on the graylevel values of the low pass version of the image. Finally. The third term:

$$\Xi(l,i,j) = \sum_{k=1}^{3-l} \frac{1}{16^k} \sum_{\theta \in \{LH,HL,HH\}} \sum_{x=0}^{1} \sum_{y=0}^{1} \left[I_{k+l}^\theta(y+\frac{i}{2^k}, x+\frac{j}{2^k}) \right]^2 + \frac{1}{16^{3-l}} Var\left\{ I_3^{LL}(1+y+\frac{i}{2^{3-l}}, 1+x+\frac{j}{2^{3-l}}) : \; x=0,1; y=0,1 \right\} \tag{4}$$

gives a measure of the activity of texture in the neighborhood of the pixel. In particular, this term is composed by two contributions: the first one is the local mean square value of the DWT coefficients in all detail sub-bands at the coarser levels, while the second is the local variance of the low-pass sub-band, both contributions are computed in a small 2x2 related corresponding to the location (i, j) of pixel.

2.2 Generation of content-based watermark

We generate our watermark, W, using the following steps. Assume the original image is $I_{M\times N}$, M and N represent the height and width of the image respectively:

First, let the original image be performed by l-step DWT. This generates the DWT coefficient matrices of the level-l approximation and horizontal, vertical and diagonal details. For any image, the approximation coefficient matrix contains almost all energy of image. So we can get the content-based tag matrix (WT) by using formula:

$$wt_{i,j} = \begin{cases} 1 & ll_{i,j} \geq T_l \\ 0 & ll_{i,j} < T_l \end{cases} \tag{5}$$

Where $wt_{i,j} \in$ WT, $ll_{i,j} \in LL_L$, i=0,1,2, ..., $M/2^l - 1$, j=0,1,2, ...,$N/2^l - 1$, T_l is threshold value.

Second, the masking matrix M must be generated in order to assure security of watermark.The chaotic sequences have many advantages. So, we choose chaotic sequences to modulate the WT in order to satisfy the secret requirements. We choose following two ways to generate the real-value sequences and binary sequences[1]:

1) Real-Value sequences, it is generated using the formula:

$$x_{k+1} = \mu x_x (1 - x_x) \tag{6}$$

2) Binary sequences, it is generated using above chaotic real-value sequences:

$$\Gamma(x) = \begin{cases} 0 & 0 \leq x < 0.5 \\ 1 & 0.5 \leq x \leq 1 \end{cases} \tag{7}$$

In this paper, we generate the real-value sequences x_k (k=0,1,2,...) using the formula (6). Then select $(M/2^l)*(N/2^l)$ elements from the sequences x_k and use formula (7) to generate the masking matrix M. So the M only contains 0 and 1, but it has the same advantages as chaotic sequences.

Lastly, modulate the tag matrix WT. Assume W represent the modulated watermark. For any $w_{i,j}$:

$$w_{i,j} = wt_{i,j} \oplus m_{i,j} \tag{8}$$

Where, $w_{i,j} \in$ W, $wt_{i,j} \in$ WT, $m_{i,j} \in$ M, I=0,1,2,..., $M/2^L - 1$, j=0,1,2, ..., $N/2^L - 1$, $\oplus$ represents the exclusive-or operation.

2.3 Watermark embedding and retrival

Figure 1 is the scheme of watermark embedding and retrieval.

We use the following step to construct the watermarked image:

1) Let the original image be performed by l-level discrete wavelet decomposition. Then generate the content-based tag matrix WT using formula (5).
2) Generate the masking matrix M. Then we can get the watermark W according to the formula (8).
3) Compute the values of HVS, T_l^θ (l=2,θ=LH,HL).
4) Embed the watermark into the LH2 and HL2 sub-band, for any $w_{i,j} \in W$,

if $w_{i,j} = 1$, then let $def_{il} = lh_{2i,2j} - hl_{2i,2j}$,

if $def_{i,j} < tl_{2i,2j}$, then let

$$lh_{2i,2j} = lh_{2i,2j} + (tl_{2i,2j} - def_{i,j})/2 \qquad (9)$$
$$hl_{2i,2j} = hl_{2i,2j} - (tl_{2i,2j} - def_{i,j})/2$$

if $w_{i,j} = 0$, then let $def_{li} = hl_{2i,2j} - lh_{2i,2j}$,

if $def_{i,j} < th_{2i,2j}$, then let

$$lh_{2i,2j} = lh_{2i,2j} - (tl_{2i,2j} - def_{i,j})/2 \qquad (10)$$
$$hl_{2i,2j} = hl_{2i,2j} + (tl_{2i,2j} - def_{i,j})/2$$

Where, $lh_{2i,2j} \in LH_2$, $hl_{2i,2j} \in HL_2$, $tl_{2i,2j} \in T_2^{LH}$, $th_{2i,2j} \in T_2^{HL}$, I=0,1,2,...,M/2^3 – 1, j=0,1,2, ...,N/2^3 – 1. T_2^{LH} and T_2^{HL} are the threshold matrix (see section 2.1).

5) Perform inverse DWT, we can get the watermarked image.

Also, we can retrieve the watermark information from the watermarked image:

Let the watermarked image be performed by the l-level decomposition.

For LH_2 and HL_2 sub-bands,

If $lh_{2i,2j} - hl_{2i,2j} \geq T$, then $w^*_{i,j} = 1$,

If $lh_{2i,2j} - hl_{2i,2j} \leq -T$, then $w^*_{i,j} = 0$,

If $-T < lh_{2i,2j} - hl_{2i,2j} < T$, then $w^*_{i,j} = -1$

It means the region has been tampered.

Where, $lh_{2i,2j} \in LH_2$, $hl_{2i,2j} \in HL_2$, i=0,1,2,...,M/2^3 – 1, j=0,1,2, ...,N/2^3 – 1, $w^*_{i,j}$ is the retrieval watermark sequences, T is threshold value

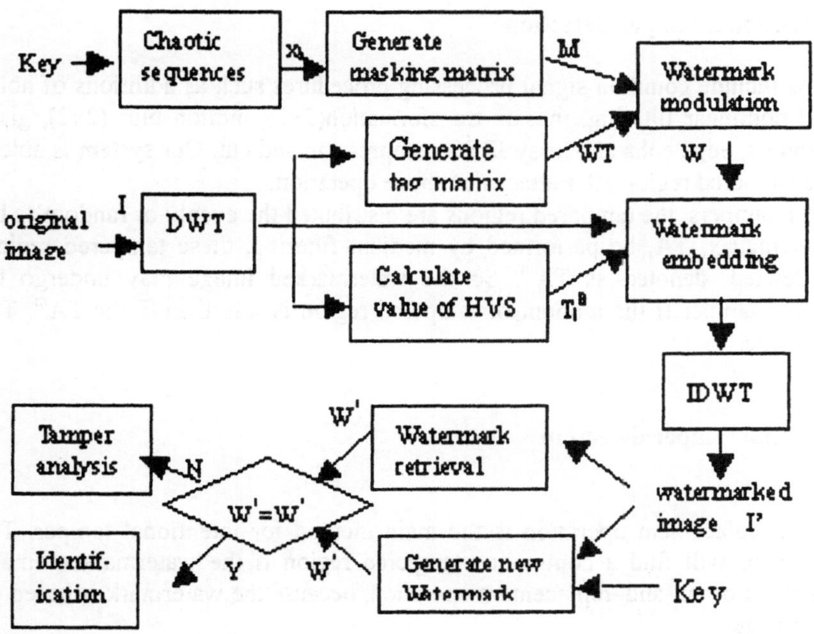

Fig. 1. The scheme of watermark embedding and identify authentication

3 Experimental results and Analysis for tamper

We have implemented the above system (l = 3) and tested it with standard test images for tamper detection. The original image is lena (256x256x8). The formula (2) is used to generate the initial chaotic sequences (the initial value of the iteration is the secret key, K=0.60773, and the parameter, μ , is 3.995)

Watermarked image may undergo two types tamper. One is unintentional, such as lossy compression. The other is intentional, such as cut-and-replacement operation. How can we identify the tampered region and distinguish this two types tamper.

The tamper detector scheme operates on the received watermarked image, denoted as I^* which may have been distorted and tampered. From I^* the original watermark, W^*, is extracted. A new content-based tag matrix, WT^*, is created from received watermarked image and then the new watermark, W', is generated by modulating the tag matrix WT^*. The tamper matrix, TA, is generated using following formula:

$$ta_{i,j} = \begin{cases} 0 & if \quad w^*_{i,j} = w'_{i,j} \\ -1 & else \end{cases} \tag{11}$$

Where $ta_{i,j} \in TA, w^*_{i,j} \in W^*, w'_{i,j} \in W'$,I=0,1,2,…,M/$2^3$ – 1, j=0,1,2,…,N/2^3 – 1.

The region where the $ta_{i,j}$ is equal to –1 means it may have been tampered.

3.1 Unintentional tamper detection

These tests include common signal processing procedures such as additions of noise, linear and nonlinear filtering, mosaic transformation(2x2), motion blur (2x2), gauss blur, sharpness, edge enhance, lossy JPEG compression and cut. Our system is able to locate the tampered region after attacks of above operation.

For these tampers, the tampered regions are distributed the evenly or randomly. Let the tamper matrix, TA, be performed by medium filtering, these tampered regions may be deleted, denoted as TA^m. So the watermarked image may undergo the unintentional tamper if the amount of tampered region is less than T for TA^m. T is threshold value.

3.2 Intentional tamper detection

The cut-and-replacement operation is the main method for intentional tamper. The tamper detector will find a continuous tampered region if the watermarked image undergo the cut or cut-and–replacement operation, because the watermark is based on content of image.

We have tested these operations: including cut, cut-and-replacement or cut, cut-and-replacement and then let intention image undergoes some signal processing operation such as addition of noise, JPEG compressing. For these tamper attack, our detector can accurately identify the tampered region.

4 Conclusion and Future Work

In this paper, We focus our discussion on how to generate the content-based watermark and embed the watermark into the original image by using the technique of the HVS. In order to increase the security of the system, the real-value chaotic sequences are used to modulate the watermark. Experimental results are excellent. Future works should include: increasing the robustness of the semi-fragile watermarking, applying our system for other kinds of media including video and audio.

Reference

1. Hui Xiang, et al. Digital Watermarking Systems with Chaotic Sequences. In: Proceeding of SPIE conf. San Jose, CA, USA, 1999, 3657:449-457
2. R. B. Wolfgang and E. J. Delp, "Fragile Watermarking Using the VW2D Watermark", *Proc.* SPIE conf., San Jose, California, Jan 25–27, 1999, pp. 204–213.
3. Eugene T. Lin, et al. Detection of Image Alterations Using Semi-Fragile Watermarks. In: Proc. of the SPIE Conf., San Jose, CA., 2000,Vol.3971
4. C.-Y.Lin and S.-F.Chang. Semi-Fragile Watermarking for Authenticating JPEG Visual Content. In: Proc. Of SPIE conf., San Jose, California, 2000, vol. 3971
5. M. Schneider and S.-F. Chang, "A Content-Based Approach to Image Signature Generation and Authentication", *Proc. ICIP '96* vol. III, pp. 227–230, 1996.
6. A.S.Lewis and G.Knowles. Image compression using the 2-D wavelet transformation. IEEE Trans. Image Processing 1,pp 244-250,April 1992

Performance Analysis of Video Storage Based on Clustered NAS Architecture

Yong Hu , Chang-sheng Xie

National Storage System Laboratory,
Huazhong University of Science and Technology, Wuhan 430074 ,
fox1019@263.net

Abstract

Previous studies on video storage servers focused on improving the disk throughput and reducing the server buffer size. In this paper, we propose a novel clustered NAS architecture to store the video files so as to improve the users supported and reduce the reponse time that clients have to wait. One performance model is presented to give the relationship among the factors that will affect the system performance. Through the model we can get the method to determine the size of data block that video file stripe to and allocate the requests arrived.

1. Introduction

Recently, the video-on-demand(VOD)system has been widely applied to entertainment and education. The most important issue of a video storage server design is to provide enough utilizition of the storage bandwidth to accommodate more usres. Disk array system which stripes video on several hard disks is a common approach to increase the space and bandwidth capacities and to support a large number of usres accessing a huge amount of video content from the video storage server. Two basic data striping techniques, fine-grain and coarse-grain, have been employed on a disk array. For fine-grain striping a video file is divided into access blocks,and each block is further striped into a number of hard disks.Here,an access block is defined as the total amount of data retrieved one time by the storage server for particular read request.Therefore,the hard disk can serve a single read request parallel to their bandwidths.On the other hand, for coarse-grain striping,each access block is completely stored on a hard disk in order to increase the number of concurrent users served by the storage server.In general,coarse-grain striping has a higher concurrency but a poorer parallelism than fine-grain striping.

Research on data striping techniques for VOD applications concluded that coarse-grain

---

This paper is supported by National Natural Science Foundation of China under the Grant No. **69873017**, also supported by State Ministry of Education for the "Distinguished Teacher" Project.

striping is more suitable for the VOD system than fine-grain striping due to its low buffer requirement and high disk throughput[1]. Similar to the Disk Array system we propose a novel architecture based on the clustered NAS. NAS, Network Atteched Storage, is one kind of the network storage. There are two true network standards for accessing remote data that have been broadly implemented by virtually all UNIX and Windows NT system vendors[3]. Developed and put into the public domain by Sun Microsystems, Network File System(NFS) is the defacto standard for all flavors of the Windows operating system. As a result of these broadly accepted standards for network data access, storage devices that serve data directly over a network are far easier to connect and manage than other devices. NAS devices support true file sharing between NFS and CIFS computer. The architecture of clustered NAS can make good effect on the scalability, and storage performance.

2. System architecture

Our video server system is based on the clustered NAS architecture. Each NAS can have disk array system. In figure1, arbitrating server is used to do the arbitrating work. Any request to video server must be submitted to arbitrating server first, then arbitrating server will decide which NAS sever will provide video stream for clients. The NAS clusters and the arbitrating server is connected to a switch. The switch provide private comunication channel for the clusters[4]. The arbitrating server will mirror the video file on several video server when one film is very popular. And the index information of the video files stored on the NAS servers can be found on the arbitrating server. When the request arrived at the arbitrating server, arbitrating server will make certification first, and then the location of the video file will be indexed on the arbitrating server. When the location is found, then the arbitrating server will let the NAS server communicate to the clients directly. When too many users like to enjoy the same film, arbitrating server will mirror the video file on other NAS servers to make the load on the NAS servers balanced.

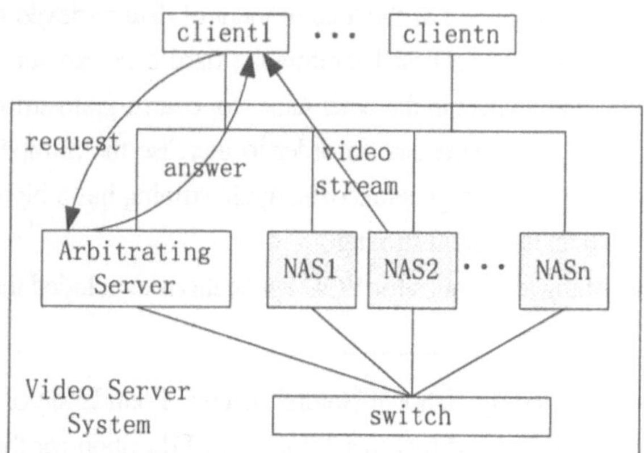

Figure1. video server architecture based on NAS clusters

3.Working scheme of video server

3.1user-level-parallelism

In this way, one video file will be integratedly stored on one NAS server. But the popularity of each video file will be recorded on the arbitrating server. The arbitrating server will mirror the video film which is often on demand on several NAS servers. Through this way the bottleneck problem when many users want to enjoy one particular film can be solved. The work of the mirroring video file will go through the switch, the private channel for the NAS clusters. This will keep enough bandwidth for the mirroring work.

3.2request commincation

When clients submit to the video server, the request will be send to the arbitrating server first. Then the arbitrating server will check the certification of the client. If the certification can be passed, the conditions of the film will be indexed in the arbitrating server. The conditons include the location of the film and the popularity of the video film, and next the NAS server that include the video file will comminicate with the client directly.

3.3mirroring procedure

The popularity of the video files is different one from another. When some video files are often visited, the bottleneck of one NAS server comes into being. In order to solve this problem, mirroring policy is executed. The popularity of every video file will be recorded on the arbitrating server. When the popularity is high than *Wp*, the video file will be mirrored on another NAS server. When the populariry of one video file is *n*Wp*, the total number of NAS server that include the video file will be: *X(n,Wp,Nmax,q)*, *q* is the additional parameter that is determined by the bandwidth of network..

4.Performance analysis

In this paper we focus on the performance analysis to the bandwidth of the video server. The number of NAS servers and the size of data block of each NAS server can greatly affect the performance of the video server.

The queue model is used to describe the relationship between the request and the video server[5]. Through the model, we get the result to analyze.

4.1Queue modeling

Queue model is used to describe the relationship between the server and requester. According to queue theory[6],we treat each NAS system as M/M/1 model. We take the system reponse time as the performance indicator. For one NAS server, the whole system can be treated as a M/M/1 queue to the client.

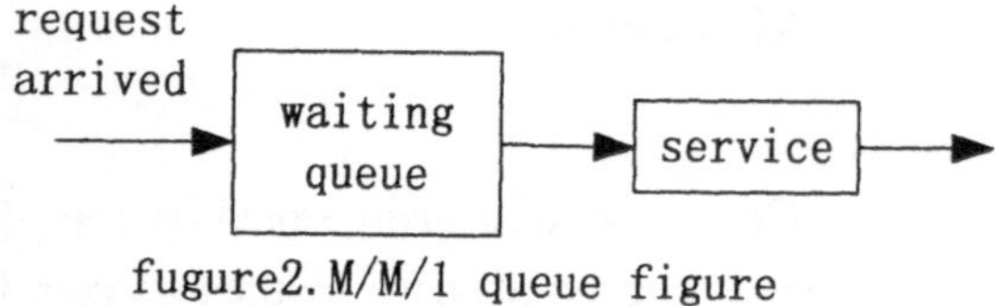

fugure2. M/M/1 queue figure

we assume that requests arrive with a negative exponential interarrival time distribution with rate λ .Furthermore, the job time service requirements are also negative exponentially distributed with mean Tserver=1/μ .Queueing model M/M/1 theory gives the following formula for mean response time, provided that the system is in stable state:

$$E[T_{system}] = \frac{1}{\mu - \lambda} \qquad (1)$$

The mean number of users in the system ,E[N] can give us the conditions of users of the whole system.Though the maxium number of users surpported is certain, which will be introduced later, we can get the conclustion about the number of users according the two kinds of conditions.

$$E[N] = \frac{\lambda}{\mu - \lambda} \qquad (2)$$

In the clustered NAS architecture, each NAS server can be treated as a queue model M/M/1. The arbitrating server will allocate the requests arrived to the NAS servers. The simplest way is to keep the load in every NAS server equal. That means the rate of request arrived is:

$\lambda_i = \lambda/n$, i=1…n, λ is the rate of total request arrived. Mirroring the video file will change the rate of the requests arriving at each NAS server.

4.2 The system response time

From the formula above, we get the relationship between the size of request arrived and the mean system response time. The result can be found in figure1. To the certain request arriaval rate, the mean system reponse time will increase with the increase of the request size, and to the certain request size, the mean system reponse time will accelerate with the acceleration of the request arrival rate.

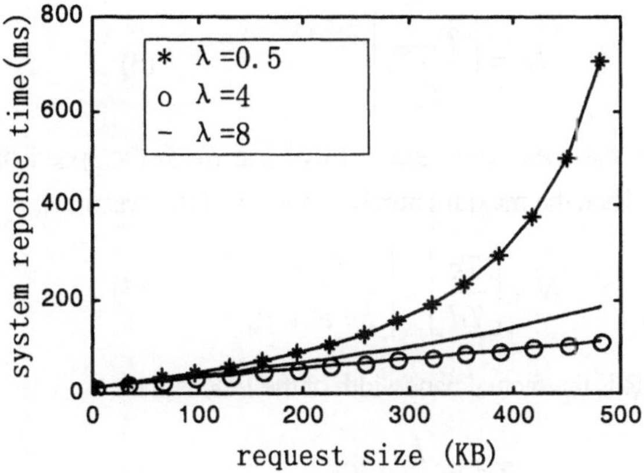

fugure3. the relationship between request size and system response time

So if we wants to reduce the mean sytem response time,two ways can be implemented.One

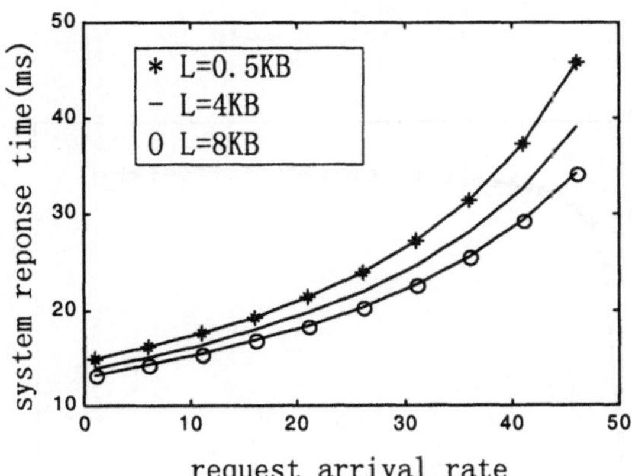

figure 4. the relationship between request arrivalrate and response time

is to reduce the request arrival rate,the other is to reduce the size of the request arrived. Reducing the rate of the request arrived will involve declination of the system performance. The more ideal way is to reduce the request size. That means we must try to reduce the buffer size of video file. The maxium number of users to the NAS video server is certain.

4.3Maxium number of users surpported

If the hardware of a NAS video server is certain,the maxium number of users surpported by the video server system will be certain.

Assume that *Trans* is data block transferring time, *Td* is the time for data to get out from the disk. From the theory of waterflow, the maxium number of users of the whole system is:

$$N = \left\lfloor \frac{T_{trans}}{T_d} \right\rfloor \qquad (3)$$

Assume that *Ta* is the mean disk access time, and *Rc* is the speed of the continous media flow playback. Then the maxium number of users of the system is:

$$N = \left\lfloor \frac{Tc}{Td} \right\rfloor = \left\lfloor \frac{L/R_c}{L/R+T_a} \right\rfloor \qquad (4)$$

In the formula above, R is the factual bandwidth of the I/Ochannel:

$$Td = \frac{L}{R} + Ta \qquad (5)$$

In order to estimate the relationship between the maxium number of users and the length of data block L, we had an experiment. In this experiment,
Ta=0.4ms,Rc=1.5Mbps, R=33.3MB/s(DMA mode). Then we can get the relationship below now.

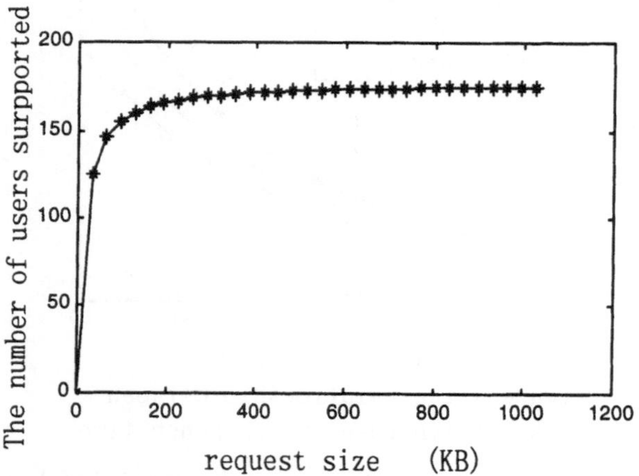

figure 5. the relationship between request size and the number of users

From the figure above, we can see that the number of users surpported by the system will increase with the increase of the size of request arrived. But the tendency of increase is obvious when the size of request is between 0KB and 256KB.When the size of request arrived continues to increase, the tendency of the acceleration of the number of users surpported is not obvious.

4.4 Fitable size of data block

The size of data block can affect the number of users. From the figure we can see that the mean number of users increases with the increase of the size of request arrived. The

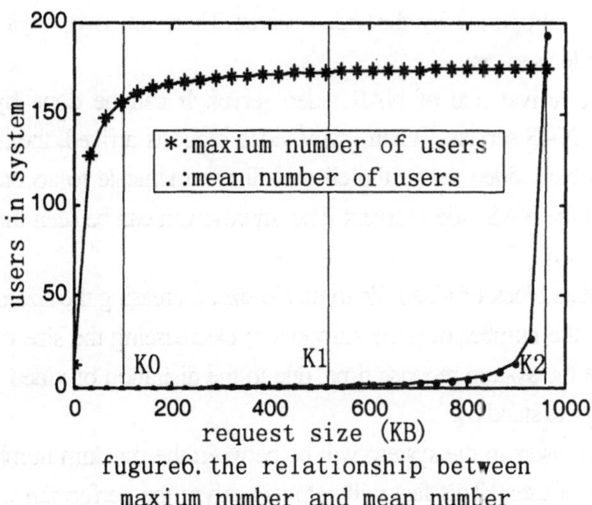

fugure6. the relationship between maxium number and mean number

number of users surpported by the video server sytem may be between the maxium number and the mean number of users.

In figure 6, the area surrounded by the curve of maxium number of users and mean number of users is the work area of our video server. When the size of data block is less than K0, the performance of system can not be shown. When the size of data block is between K0 and K1, the clients will wait for a long time, where the performance of system can be shown. When the size of data block is between K1 and K2, the performance of whole system will be the best, where the number of users can be enough, and client can get satisfied with the waiting time. When the size is more than K2, the performance of the system will decline instantly.

The maxium number of users is determined by the hardware of the video servers, and the mean number of users is determined by the queue model M/M/1. The model we used assumes that there is only one service window. We can add some service window in the system to increase the number of users by software designing, but the number of users after software improving will not be more than the maxium number of users before software improving. This will help us ananlyze the performance of one video server sytem.

5.Conclusions

In this paper, we proposed one video server architecture based on NAS architecture. The NAS architecture has excerlent scabality and data sharing capability. The characteristic will help the NAS system provide good performance of the video server. Then we dicussed two factors that will affect the performance of thevideo server, the system response time and the numbers of usrers surpported by the video server. There are two ways to improve the performance of video servers:

1. Reducing the arrival rate of NAS video server. It can be done by providing the clustering of NAS servers. When many video requests arrived, the arbitrating server will locate which video server the client will communicate to according to the load conditions of the NAS video servers. The improvment can be seen through the results of the simulation.
2. Change the data block of video file to fitable size. Increasing the size of the data block will increase the number of users surpported; Decreaseing the size of the data block will decrease the system reponse time, due to the disiration of video server to decide which strategy to stand by.

The number of users in the system will be between the maxium number of users and the mean number of users. This fact will help us analyze the performance of video server system.

References

[1]S.-L.Tsao,J.-W.Ding,Y.M.Huang,On cost-effevtive analysis of disk layout scheme for continuous media servers under bounded initail delay,*IEEE* Pacific Rim Conference on Communication,Computer and Signal Processing,Canada,
August 1997.

[2]D.Venkatesh,T.D.C.Little,Ion cost-performance characteristics of disk storage systems supporting continuous media , NOSDAV'96,1996.

[3]c.Ruemmler,J.Wilkes,An introduction to disk drive modelling,IEEE Computer 27 30 (1994) 17

[4]J.Gsoedl,Video on NT windows NT system,February 1998,pp.32-42.

[5]G.R.Ganger et al..,Disk arrays high-performance,high-relia-
bility storage systems,*IEEE* computer,March 1994.

[6]F.A.Tobagi,"Distance Learing with Digital Video",*IEEE* Multimedia Magazine,pp.90-94,Spring 1995.

Modeling Video-on-Demand System in Temporal Logic *

Weimin Liu[1,2] and Huadong Ma[1,2]

[1] College of Computer Science & Technology,
Beijing University of Posts and Telecommunications, Beijing 100876, China
mhd@bupt.edu.cn
[2] Computer Science Lab.,
Institute of Software, Chinese Academy of Science, Beijing 100080, China

Abstract. Based on the temporal logic language XYZ, this paper proposes a specification model of Video-on-Demand (VoD) system. By this model, we specify the behaviors of VoD system and discusses the features of VoD system. The advantages of this method are formal, and easy to transform the specification into implementable code.

1 Introduction

A VoD service [1, 2] allows remote users to play back any one of a large collection of videos at any time. Typically, these video files are stored in a set of central video servers, and distributed through high-speed communication networks to geographically-dispersed clients. In general, the VoD service can be characterized as follows: long-lived session, real-time service response, high storage-I/O and network bandwidth requirements, support for VCR-like interactivity, and QoS sensitive service. Thus, the VoD system is very complex in the resource and user management. In order to understand the architecture and features of the VoD system, it is necessary to use formal description technique to specify the system. A few works have been done in this aspect. For example, automata are used to specify DAVIC standard [2]. But these works are limited to description without analysis. This paper focuses on the specification model of the VoD system, and discusses the important properties of VoD system.

XYZ System designed by Zhisong Tang is a temporal logic based CASE environment [8]. Its kernel is a temporal logic language XYZ/E. XYZ System has the following functions: abstraction specification, concurrency specification, fastrapid prototyping, specification and verification for stepwise refinement design, etc.. Some attempts [3–6, 9] of applying it for specifying multimedia systems have been successful. This paper proposes a specification model of VoD system based on temporal logic language XYZ. This model can be used as the basis of the further property verification, and provides the guide for the design and implementation of VoD system.

* The work reported in this paper is partly supported by the NNSF of China under Grant 69873006 and Computer Science Lab., Institute of Software, CAS.

2 The Architecture of VoD system

Considering the universality, we analyze a typical DAVIC-based VoD system which consists of the following components: *Video Sever* (VS) composed of huge storage, high-performance CPU and high I/O bandwidth; *Management System* responsible for connecting the user and the server by two levels of gateway, i.e., L1GW and L2GW; *Backbone Network* supporting high speed video transmission; *Access Network* connecting the user device and the backbone network; *Set-Top Box* (STB) located at the user-end. For specifying the architecture of VoD system formally, we simplify the system as the structure shown in Fig. 1.

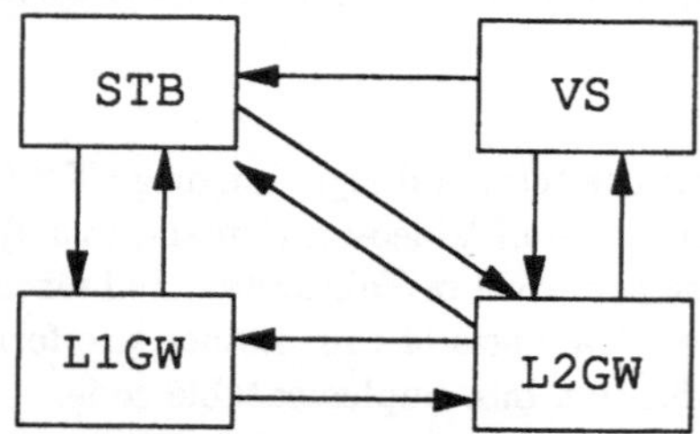

Fig. 1. The structure of VoD system

The user request is served as follows: (1). The user sends a request to L1GW; (2). L1GW sends back the user a welcome page and all services it can provide; (3). The user selects a service, such as playing a movie; (4). L1GW parses the user's selection, and transfers it to L2GW and returns a program menu to the user; (5). The user hits the title he/she likes to watch; (6). L1GW analyzes the required resource for this service, and creates the connection for it. L2GW transfers the user's request to VS which offers the program for the user; (7). Once the session between the user and VS is set up, the playing begins. When the user wants to change the program she/he is watching, L1GW needs to change/recreate the session according to the resource requirements; (8). After the service is finished, the session is disconnected, and the occupied resource is released.

3 Specification Model of VoD System

3.1 Temporal Logic and XYZ System

Based on the theory of linear temporal logic created by Manna and Pnueli [7], Zhisong Tang designed XYZ System [8], which supports various ways of programming. In other words, XYZ System is a family of programming languages extended by XYZ/E. In XYZ/E, the statement is called condition element (c.e.). The form of c.e. is defined as follows:

$LB = S_i \wedge P => \$O(v_1, ..., v_k) = (e_1, ..., e_k) \wedge \$OLB = S_j$

or $LB = S_i \wedge P => @(Q \wedge LB = S_j)$

where @ is "O","<>" or "[]". P and Q represent the part of condition and the part of actions, respectively.

The message passed from one process to another is implemented by using channel operations. In XYZ/E, channel can be dynamically determined. There are two channel operation commands: output command *Ch!y* and input command *Ch?x*, where *Ch* is the name of channel from the input process to the output process, y is an output expression of the output process, x is an input variable of the input process.

XYZ/RE is a sub-language for specifying real-time system. The condition element in XYZ/RE is as follows:

$LB = y \wedge R => @\{l,u\}(Q \wedge LB = z)$

where temporal operator @{l,u} indicates the low time delay l and the upper time delay u of a state transition.

3.2 Specification Model of VoD System

There are two types of concurrent behaviors in a VoD system: (1) the concurrent behaviors of different users; (2) the concurrent behaviors of different entities. The former behaviors have no direct dependency except for competing sharable system resources. The concurrency between the functional entities has strong temporal relation. A behavior of the entity usually triggers the behavior of other entity, and at that time the messages are exchanged. By a sequence of such behaviors, the system provides the service to the user. Thus, we first consider the concurrency between entities to specify the system (in single user mode).

Definition 1. Q is a set of system entities, Q={STB, L1GW, L2GW, VS}.

Definition 2. P is a set of channels, P={ch-s-l1, ch-l1-s, ch-s-l2, ch-l2-s, ch-l1-l2, ch-l2-l1, ch-v-l2, ch-l2-v, ch-v-s}, where ch-s-l1 is the channel between STB and L1GW, and ch-v-l2 is the channel between VS and L2GW, etc..

Definition 3. E is a set of events, E={Apply, Order, Quit, AssignResource, ReleaseResource, SendProgram}. The first three events are triggered by the user and the last three events are triggered by the system.

Definition 4. M is a set of messages between entities. M = {ClientConfigReq, ClientConfigConfirm, ClientSessSetupReq, ClientSessSetupConfirm, ServerSessSetupInd, ServerSessSetupAck, ServerAddResReq, ServerAddResConfirm, ProgramOver, ClientReleaseReq, ProgramName}.

Definition 5. S is a set of state transitions, $S \subset \Sigma \times T \times E \times \Sigma$, where Σ is a set of process states, Σ={Idle, Connect, Order, Watch, Disconnect}; T is a set of transition time, $T = R^+$; E is a set of events.

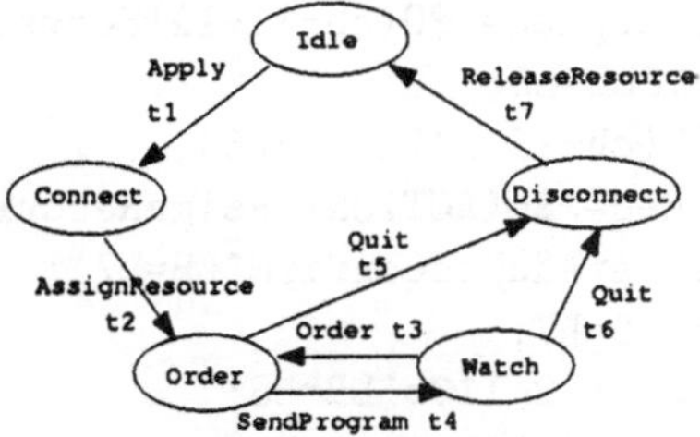

Fig. 2. State transitions

In Fig. 2, an ellipse represents a process state, and an event is the precondition of a state transition. A state transition is triggered by event, and a message is for an event. For the convenience, we assume that the system will set the corresponding boolean variable *apply, order, quit* to true when Apply, Order or Quit occurs. The state transitions are specified as the condition elements in XYZ/E, e.g., the transition from Idle to Connect can be specified as:

$LB = Idle \wedge apply => \$OLB = Connect$

Considering the time factor, we have

$LB = Idle \wedge apply => \$O(DELAY(t1) \wedge LB = Connect)$

Definition 6. A VoD system can be modeled as a five tuple, TLDM-VOD $=< Q, P, E, M, S >$.

In the above model, Q and P specify the entities of VoD system which represent its static features; E, S and M specify the relations between the entities and the behaviors which shows its dynamic feature. By combining the events between the functional entities, we can specify both the specific behaviors and the transition relations of the system. As a case study, we will discuss their cooperation relations for a user service, including establishing connection, watching program, quitting and etc.. We define the predication $ACTION$ as an external event, e.g., $ACTION(AssignResource)$ denotes the event "system assigns resources for establishing connection".

```
%SERVING Order==[
PSTB: [] [LB=START-stb=>$OLB=Waiting;
  LB=Waiting^apply=>$Oapply=FALSE^$OLB=SendReq;
  LB=SendReq=>$Och-s-l1!ClientConfigReq^$OLB=Wait1;
   ......
  LB=Wait4^j=ClientSessSetupConfirm=>$OLB=Order;
  LB=Order^order=>$Oorder=FALSE^$Och-s-l2!ProgmName^$OLB=Watch;
   ......
  LB=Warch1^k=ProgramOver=>$OLB=Order;
  LB=Order^quit=>$Oquit=FALSE^$Och-s-l1!ClientReleaseReq^$OLB=Stop]
PL1GW: [] [LB=START-l1gw=>$OLB=L1;
  LB=L1^~ch-s-l1?=>$OLB=L1;
  LB=L1^ch-s-l1? =>$O(ch-s-l1?l^LB=L2);
  LB=L2^l=ClientConfigReq=>$O(ch-l1-s!ClientConfigConfirm^LB=L3);
  LB=L3^~ch-s-l1? =>$OLB=L3;
  LB=L3^ch-s-l1? =>$O(ch-s-l1?m^LB=L4);
  LB=L4^m=ClientSessSetupReq=>$O(ch-l1-l2!ServerSessSetupInd^LB=L5);
  LB=L5^~ch-l2-l1? =>$OLB=L5;
  LB=L5^ch-l2-l1? =>$O(ch-l2-l1?n^LB=L6);
  LB=L6^n=SeverAddResReq=>$O(ACTION(AssignResourse)
         ^ch-l1-l2!ServerAddResConfirm^LB=L7);
  LB=L7^~ch-l2-l1?=>$OLB=L7;
  LB=L7^ch-l2-l1? =>$Och-l2-l1?o^LB=L8;
  LB=L8^o=ServerSessSetupAck=>
         $O(ch-l1-s!ClientSessSetupConfirm^LB=L9);
  ......
  LB=L10^ch-s-l1=>$O(ch-s-l1?p^LB=L10);
  LB=L11^p=ClientReleaseReq=>$OACTION(ReleaseRes)^LB=Stop)]
```

```
PL2GW: [] [LB=START_12gw=>$0LB=B0;
  ......
  LB=B2^q=SeverSessSetupInd=>$0(ch-12-11!ServerAddResReq^LB=B3);
  ......
  LB=B4^r=ServerAddResConfirm=>$0(ACTION(BuildConnection)
        ^ch-12-11!ServerSessSetupAck^LB=B5);
  LB=B5^ch-s-12? =>$0(ch-s-12?s^LB=B6);
  LB=B6^s=ProgramName=>$0(ACTION(SendProgram)^LB=STOP)]
```

PSTB, PL1GW and PL2GW represent STB, L1GW and L2GW in the system, respectively. An entity receives the input and then activates corresponding events as a response and outputs the messages. All entities exist concurrently, and cooperate to offer the service. For simplicity, we ignore VS when specifying the system. We also omit the interactions between L2GW and VS.

4 The Analysis of VoD System Features

In order to evaluate the features of VoD system, we extend the above model to specify the case of multi-users. Assume U be a set of user processes $U=\{U_1, U_2, U_3, ...\}$, the extended model is a six tuple $< Q, P, E, M, S, U >$.

(1) Safety and Liveness The liveness of VoD system means that the system should reach Order state finally after a user submits a request, except the user aborts his request. i.e.

$LB = Idle \wedge apply => <> LB = Order$

The safety of VoD system means that the system should provide the service and should not deprive the resources occupied by the user in Order state or Watch state. The safety is specified as follows:

$$\Box\neg((LB = Order \wedge ACTION(ReleaseResourse)) \\ \vee(LB = Watch \wedge ACTION(ReleaseResourse)))$$

(2) Real-time We can consider the real-time requirements in the specification of VoD system, for example, if the shortest expectation time from submitting request to watching program is T1, the longest delay the user can endure is T2. Then we can specify the procedure as follows:

$LB = Idle \wedge apply => <> \{T1, T2\}(LB = Watch)$

Similarly, we can assign the time restriction to the specific steps, such as:

$LB = Idle \wedge apply => <> \{T3, T4\}(LB = Order)$

$LB = Order \wedge order => <> \{T5, T6\}(LB = Watch)$

where $T3, T5 < T1$ and $T4, T6 < T2$.

XYZ/RE supports the above step-wise refinement design. The time of every transition can be assigned eventually, e.g., we can specify the transition from Order state to Watch state as follows:

$LB = Order \wedge Order => \$O(Delay(t4) \wedge LB = Watch)$

If $T5 \leq t4 \leq T6$, the system meets the requirements. If $t4 > T6$, the system needs to be improved or the time restriction needs to be assigned again.

(3) Fairness Due to limited resources, if the VoD system can not offer services for many users at the same time, some users have to wait, but the scheduling mechanism must guarantee that no user will wait forever and could not get the service. Fairness means that no user service will be postponed forever because of waiting for the resource. The fairness is specified in temporal logic:

$init \rightarrow \Box \bigvee_i (at(L_i) \wedge \Box\Diamond y_i > 0 \rightarrow \Diamond\neg at(L_i))$

It means that whenever the user process i reaches label L_i for requesting resource, then it has infinite chances to get the resource ($\Box\Diamond y_i > 0$), and it could finally get the resource ($\Diamond\neg at(L_i)$).

(4) Mutex In a VoD system, some resources can be shared by many processes. The processes impropriate the resource in turn, such as the I/O bandwidth and buffer. VoD system divides the available bandwidth into many channels and assign a logic channel for each user request. Any channel can be used by only one user at the same time. In other words, the channel is used in mutex. This property can be specified as follows:

$\Box\neg(A(s) \wedge B(s))$

where $A(s)$ and $B(s)$ means the user A and B use the channel s, respectively.

5 Conclusion

The VoD system is a complex multimedia system, so formally modeling this system is meaningful for its design, implementation and analysis. This paper proposes a specification model of VoD system based on temporal logic language XYZ. The formal specification based on XYZ supports stepwise refinement design, and easy to transform the specification to executable code. Furthermore, we will study the verification of features for VoD system.

Acknowledgment Authors thank Dr. Chen Zhao and Dr. Guangyuan Li for their helpful suggestions on this paper.

References

1. Reuven Cohen, Yee-Hsiang Chang, Video-on-Demand session management, IEEE Journal on Selected Areas in Communication, 1996, 14(6).
2. Digital Audio-Visual Council, DAVIC Specifications 1.0-1.4, www.davic.org.
3. Huadong Ma, Shenquan Liu, Multimedia data modeling based on temporal logic and XYZ System, J. Computer Science & Technology, 1999.14(2).
4. Huadong Ma and Xiaoping Tang, Design and implementation of multimedia authoring language. Journal of Software, 1998, 9 (12): 889-893 (in Chinese).
5. Huadong Ma and Shenquan Liu, Temporal logic based animation description model. Chinese Journal of Computers, 1995,18(11):814-821.
6. Huadong Ma, et al., The design and implementation of animation script description language SDL/A. Journal of Software, 1996,7(7):385-393 (in Chinese).
7. Z. Manna, A. Pnueli, The Temporal Logic of Reactive and Concurrent System: Specification, Springer-Verlag, NY, 1992.
8. Zhishong Tang, Temporal Logic Programming and Software Engineering (Vol.1). Science Press, Beijing, 1999 (in Chinese).
9. Chen Zhao, Zhishong Tang, Huadong Ma. A methodology for automatically constructing a multimedia synchronizer in XYZ/RE. Journal of Software, 2000,11(8): 996-1002 (in Chinese).

Adaptive Processing of Tree-Structure Image Representation

Zhiyong Wang, Zheru Chi, Dagan Feng and S. Y. Cho

Center for Multimedia Signal Processing
Department of Electronic and Information Engineering
The Hong Kong Polytechnic University
Hung Hom, Kowloon, Hong Kong
Email Address: enzheru@polyu.edu.hk

Abstract. Much research on image analysis and processing has been carried out for the last few decades. However, it is still challenging to represent the image contents effectively and satisfactorily. In this paper, a segmentation-free tree-structure image representation is presented. In order to learn the structure representation, a back-propagation through structure (BPTS) algorithm is adopted. Experiments on plant image classification and retrieval refining using only six visual features were conducted on a plant image database and a natural scene image database, respectively. Encouraging results have been achieved.

1 Introduction

Demands on content-based image retrieval have been increasing rapidly in the areas such as trademarks, digital library and geographic information systems(GIS) due to the great explosion of image generating sources and the disadvantages of capturing the image contents using textual annotations. On the other hand, content-based image retrieval allows a user to search the wanted images in terms of its true contents, which has become a promising and active research area. Some retrieval prototypes such as QBIC [1] and PhotoBook [2] were developed and performed well in certain way. Most of them represented the images only using the low level visual features such as color, texture, shape and spatial layout either globally or locally. However, global visual features cannot represent the image contents accurately and are not efficient for image retrieval, whereas, local visual features sometimes depend on the image segmentation result, and are lack of global information. Consequently, the retrieval performance of these systems may produce the results which are very different from those of human perception. In human sense, the image contents include the objects itself and their attributes, unfortunately, it is very difficult to segment the image well into object by object or region by region. Moreover, it is very difficult to integrate different domain visual features reasonably. In this paper, we propose a segmentation-free method to represent an image with tree-structure to characterize image contents at different levels, which is suitable for image classification in terms of their true contents. Recently Goller [3] and Sperduti [4] proposed to process data structure with neural networks. The BPTS algorithm can be adopted to learn the tree-structure representation. Relevance feedback is adopted in text information retrieval as well as content-based image retrieval [5] efficiently. We can also apply BPTS algorithm together with tree-structure representation to image retrieval refining, since the retrieval result can be labelled as a class either relevance or irrelevance according to user's feedback information.

2 Tree-structure Image Representation

Most of the images are stored in pixel map format, however, the pixel value has insignificant meaning to the users. Generally, the image consists of different objects with spatial relationship between them and the objects can be described in certain order. Unfortunately, it is very difficult to segment the image into individual object or homogeneous region ideally although lots of research was investigated on image segmentation using color, texture or both. The segmentation can be avoided by decomposing the image block by block. This idea has been used for color-mosaic based image retrieval. Its disadvantages are that the image is represented with only one resolution and it is not easy to select the block size properly. Therefore, we intend to decompose the subblocks further. This representation can characterize the global image features at the top level as well as local features at the bottom level. As Figure 1 shown, the image is represented with a quad-tree structure. The attributes of the root node are the global features of the original image, and the attributes of the leaf nodes characterize the local features of the image. We also observe that the layout information is encoded in the tree-structure if the node number is labelled orderly.

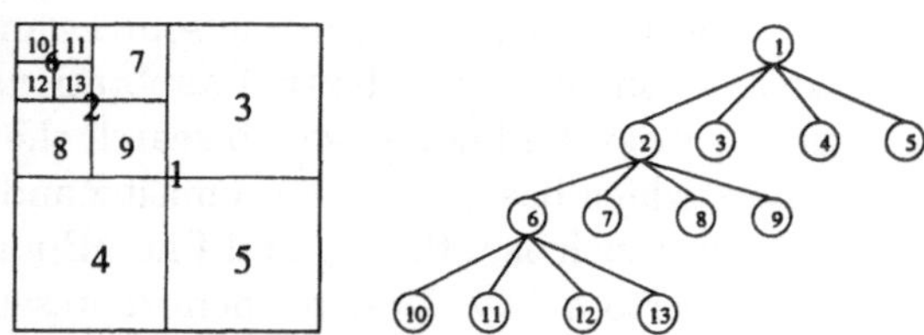

Fig. 1. A quad-tree representation of an image

It is well known that visual features, color, texture and shape are very important to characterize the image contents. Each node of the tree can be considered as an image and visual features will be extracted from it. So far, there are many approaches to extract these visual features in the literatures. In our experiments, only four color attributes and two texture attributes are extracted to characterize the block contents. The color attributes are the number of color as well as the percentages of the most three dominant colors in RGB color space. The average pixel value and the standard variance of the block pixels are used to characterize the block texture simply.

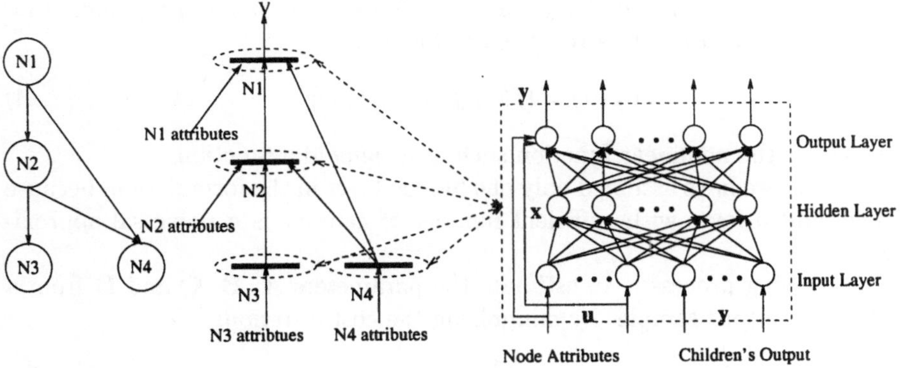

Fig. 2. An illustration of a tree-structure encoding network with a single hidden layer.

3 Adaptive Processing of Data Structure

Connectionlist models have been successfully employed to solve learning tasks characterized by relatively poor representations in data structure such as static pattern or sequence. Most structured information presented in real world, however, can hardly be represented by simple sequences. Although many early approaches based on syntactic pattern recognition were developed to learn structured information, devising a proper grammar is often a very difficult task because domain knowledge is incomplete or insufficient. On the contrary, the graph representation varies in the size of input units. Its encoding process shown in Figure 2 is independent on the classification task and it is not necessary to pay attention specifically to their nodes. Recently, neural networks for processing data structures have been proposed by Sperduti [4]. It has been shown that they can be used to process data structures using an algorithm namely back-propagation through structure(BPTS). The algorithm extends the time unfolding carried out by back-propagation through time(BPTT) in the case of sequences. A general framework of adaptive processing of data structures was introduced by Tsoi [6]. Considering a generalized formulation of graph encoding shown in Figure 2, we have

$$\mathbf{x} = \mathbf{F}_n(\mathbf{A}q^{-1}\mathbf{y} + \mathbf{B}\mathbf{u}) \tag{1}$$

$$\mathbf{y} = \mathbf{F}_p(\mathbf{C}\mathbf{x} + \mathbf{D}\mathbf{u}) \tag{2}$$

where $\mathbf{x}$, $\mathbf{u}$ and $\mathbf{y}$ are respectively the n dimensional output vector of the n hidden layer neurons, the m dimensional inputs to the neurons, and the p dimensional outputs of the neurons. q^{-1} is merely a notation to indicate that the input to the node is taken from its children. The $\mathbf{A}$ matrix is defined as follows:

$$\mathbf{A} = [\mathbf{A}^1 \mathbf{A}^2 ... \ \mathbf{A}^c] \tag{3}$$

where c is the maximal out degree of the graph. $\mathbf{A}^i, i = 1, 2, ..., c$ is an $n \times p$ matrix, and is formed from the vector a_j^i, $j = 1, 2, ..., n$. $\mathbf{A}$ is a $c \times (n \times p)$ matrix.

And $\mathbf{B}$, $\mathbf{C}$, and $\mathbf{D}$ are respectively matrices of dimensions $n \times m$, $p \times n$ and $p \times m$. $\mathbf{F}_n(.)$ is an n dimensional vector given as follows:

$$\mathbf{F}_n(\alpha) = [f(\alpha)\ f(\alpha)\ ...\ f(\alpha)]^T \tag{4}$$

where $f(.)$ is the nonlinear function such as a sigmoidal function.

Note that we have assumed only one hidden layer in the formulation, because a single hidden layer with sufficient number of neurons is a universal approximator [7].

The training process is to estimate the parameters $\mathbf{A}$, $\mathbf{B}$, $\mathbf{C}$ and $\mathbf{D}$ from a set of input/output samples by minimizing the cost criterion:

$$J = \frac{1}{2}||\mathbf{d} - \mathbf{y}||^2 \tag{5}$$

where $\mathbf{y}$ denotes the output of the root of the current sample, $\mathbf{d}$ denotes the desired output of the current sample.

The derivation of the training algorithm minimizing the cost criterion (5) will follow a fashion similar to gradient learning by computing the partial derivation of the cost J with respect to $\mathbf{A}$, $\mathbf{B}$, $\mathbf{C}$ and $\mathbf{D}$.

4 Experiments and Discussions

Fig. 3. Ten plant images used in our experiments.

We conducted several experiments including classifying images of ten different plants and content-based image retrieval with relevance feedback on 200 natural scene images. The tree-structure of each image is built with quad-tree decomposition and the six visual features mentioned in Section 2 are extracted as attributes for each node. The network of each node is a single hidden layer neural network. Note that, the hidden layer is with 10 neurons in our experiments.

In the experiments for the plant image classification, a training set and a test set for each plant image were generated by masking the image contents with the random size region in black color or clipping the subimage from the original image.

In Experiment 1, we simulated the information losing by masking the original image with random size block in black color and the training set and the test set of the same number of samples are generated. The size of the random block did not exceed 1/4 of the image size. In order to reduce the correlation among the images in both training and test set, the overlap between the samples was not more than 75%. If a block had at least 1/2 area in black color, no more decomposition was carried out in that block. That is, some of the nodes in the original tree would disappear. For example, in Figure 1, if region 6 was in black(missing information), nodes 6 and 11 to 13 would disappear. As a result, the generated trees had various sizes. They might have different number of nodes which were connected differently. The maximum depth of the tree in this experiment is 3. In Experiment 2, the masking block size grew up to 1/2 of the original image, which is the only difference from Experiment 1.

In Experiment 3 and 4, the training set and the test set were generated by clipping the subimage from the original image. The size of subimage was not less than 1/2 of the original image, and the overlap between them was not more than 90%. The only difference between Experiment 3 and 4 was the depth of the tree-structure. The depth of the tree-structure used in Experiment 3 and 4 was set at 3 and 4 respectively. The latter leaded to more tree nodes.

As Table 1 shows, very high classification accuracy even 100% can be achieved with our representation and BPTS neural network learning. In both Experiment 1 and 2, the classification accuracy is 100%, such that, the original image can be learned with sufficient training samples provided although the information in each training sample was partly incomplete. Experiment 3 and 4 indicate that main information of the image can be learned from its subimage set. Too many nodes are not certainly useful to improve the classification performance but increase the computational demand greatly.

Table 1. Classification Performance.

	Training Samples	Test Samples	Classification Accuracy(%)	
			Training Set	Test Set
Experiment 1	2000	2000	100.00	100.00
Experiment 2	741	741	100.00	100.00
Experiment 3	1430	1430	99.58	99.58
Experiment 4	1427	1427	99.58	98.88

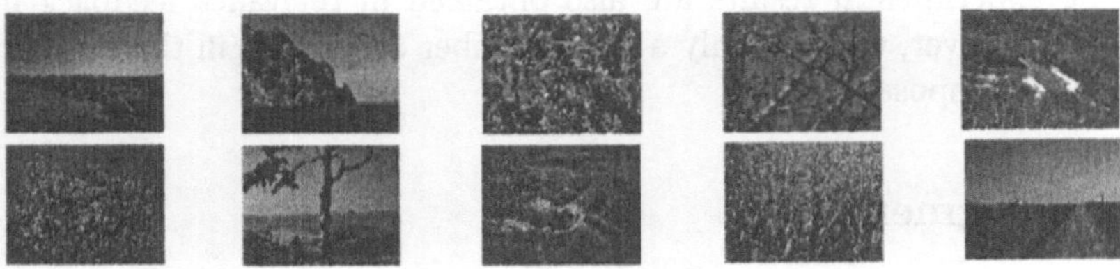

Fig. 4. The top ten retrieval images for the top-left query image without refining.

Fig. 5. The top ten retrieval images for the top-left query image after one iteration refining.

The representation scheme and BPTS learning algorithm were also applied to relevance feedback image retrieval on an image database with 200 natural scene images. At first, some images are returned in terms of distance between the feature vectors of the query image and the database image. In the second step, user will select the similar images relevant to the query image among the returned results. Therefore, there are two classes images, relevant and irrelevant images in user's subjective opinion. The system will learn these two classes images by adjusting the network parameters **A**, **B**, **C** and **D** in a similar way introduced in Section 3. Some images are retrieved in terms of distance between the graph output vector of the query image and the database image. Note that the second step can be performed repeatedly. A retrieval example for a query image with blue sky and green grass is presented in Figure 4 and Figure 5. Comparing between Figure 4 and Figure 5, we observe that the retrieval performance is improved greatly only after one iteration refining. Furthermore, the retrieval results presented the similar layout of the query image contents although there was no layout information to be extracted.

5 Conclusion and Future Work

A segmentation-free tree-structure image representation and the combination with adaptive processing of data structure are presented in this paper. The tree-structure can present the image features both globally and locally with nodes at different levels. It is also flexible and shows certain tolerance to the missing information. Adaptive processing of data structure with the BPTS algorithm is used to learn the image representation. Good classification accuracy is achieved when experiments are conducted on the images of ten different plants, and encouraging experimental results are also obtained in relevance feedback image retrieval. Moreover, we need only a small number of features in the experiments by using our proposed method.

Acknowledgment

The work described in this paper was supported by two research grants from the Hong Kong Polytechnic University (Project codes: G-V780 and G-T228).

References

1. M. Flickner, H. Sawhney, W. Niblack, J. Ashely, Qian Huang, B. Dom, M. Gorkani, J. Hafner, D. Lee, D. Petkovic, D. Steele, and P. Yanker. Query by image and video content: The qbic system. *IEEE Computer*, 28(9):23 - 32, Sept. 1995.
2. A. Pentland, R. Picard, and S. Sclaroff. Photobook: Cotent-based manipulation of image databases. *International Journal of Computer Vision*, 18(3):233 - 254, 1996.
3. C. Goller and A. Kuchler. Learning task-dependent distributed representations by backpropagation through structure. In *IEEE International Conference on Neural Networks*, pages 347 - 352, 1996.
4. A. Sperduti and A. Starita. Supervised neural networks for the classification of structures. *IEEE Trans. on Neural Networks*, 8(3):714–735, 1997.
5. Y. Rui, T. S. Huang, M. Ortega, and S. Mehrotra. Relevance feedback: a power tool for interactive content-based image retrieval. *IEEE Transactions on Circuits and System for Video Technology*, 8(5):644–655, 1998.
6. A. C. Tsoi. Adaptive processing of data structures:an expository overview and comments. Technique report, Faculty of Informatics, University of Wollongong, Australia, 1998.
7. F. Scarselli and A. C. Tsoi. Universal approximation using feedforward neural networks: a suervey of some existing methods, and some new results. *Neural Networks*, 11(1):15–38, 1998.

Blind Watermarking Algorithm Using Complex Block Selection Method

Yongwon Jang, Intaek Kim, Hwan Il Kang, Kab Il Kim, and Seung-Soo Han

Myongji University
Division of Electrical and Information Control Engineering
San 38-2, Namdong, Yongin Kyunggido 449-728, South Korea
Jang122@orgio.net, {kit, hwan, kkl, shan}@mju.ac.kr

Abstract. Digital watermarking is the technique, which embeds an invisible signal including owner identification and copy control information into multimedia data such as audio, video, images for copyright protection. A new watermark embedding algorithm is introduced in this paper. In this algorithm, complex 8×8 DCT blocks are selected by calculating the AC coefficients of the DCT blocks, and watermark information is embedded into the selected complex blocks using quantization and modulus calculation. This algorithm uses a blind watermark retrieval technique, which detects the embedded watermark without using the original image. The experimental results show that the proposed watermark technique is robust to JPEG compression with 90% of compression ratio and has an excellent PSNR. With the fast watermark extraction property, this algorithm is suitable for real-time watermark extraction applications such as compressed video watermark.

1 Introduction

With the rapid spread of computer networks and the further progress of multimedia technologies, security and legal issues of copyright protection have become important. Digital watermark is one promising technique for effectively protecting the copyright of digital contents[1]-[6]. The important properties of the embedded watermark are the quality of the contents having embedded watermark data, the robustness of the watermark against modification of the contents, resistance to intentional removal of or tampering with the watermark, and the reliability of extracted watermark data.

The watermarking techniques can be classified into two classes depending on the domain of watermark embedding, i.e. the spatial domain and frequency domain. Among the spatial domain watermark embedding methods, Schyndel *et al.* proposed a watermark embedding technique by changing the least significant bit of some pixels in an image [2]. Bender et al. described a watermarking approach by modifying a statistical property of an image called 'patchwork' [3]. The spatial domain watermarking techniques, however, are not robust to attacks such as compression, clipping, cropping, etc. On the other hand, there are many algorithms for watermark embedding in frequency domain. Cox *et al.* described a method where the watermark is embedded into the large discrete cosine transform (DCT) coefficients using ideas borrowed from spread spectrum in communications [4]. Xia *et al.* proposed a frequency domain method of embedding the watermark at all the subbands except LL subband, using discrete wavelet transform (DWT)[5].

In this paper, we introduced new watermark embedding/retrieving algorithm using complex block selection method. An image is divided into 8×8 blocks and the discrete cosine transform (DCT) is performed at each block. A block with largest AC coefficients is defined as a 'complex block.' The watermark is embedded only into the selected complex blocks using quantization and modulus calculation. The watermark information, which is pseudorandom binary sequence ('0' or '1'), is embedded only into the greatest AC component of the complex block. After embedding watermark, the PSNR is calculated to give the index of the image quality, and attacked the watermarked image using JPEG compression to verify the robustness of the algorithm. The watermark retrieving procedure of the embedded watermark doesn't require any prior information such as original image or key, and finds watermark embedded complex blocks to retrieve the hidden watermark information. Such a blind watermark retrieval technique is important for applications in huge image databases. To give an example, for archived movie films, art libraries and Internet image distributors, it may not be convenient to search the original image from a huge database for watermark detection [1]. The results show that the watermarked image has at least 40 dB in PSNR, and the extraction ratio of the watermark more than 100% even if we compress the watermarked image with 90% of compression ratio.

2 Proposed Watermarking Method

Inoue, *et. al.* proposed quantization based watermarking technique using discrete wavelet transform (DWT) for video [6], but with the complex calculation within DWT, this method is not suitable for the real-time watermark extraction. For the real-time processing in video such as MPEG, an efficient and less complex algorithm is required. The algorithm developed in this paper is based on the DCT, which is used in MPEG video decoding, and can reduce computation time. Embedding watermark into all area of an image degrades the picture quality and resulted in lower PSNR. To

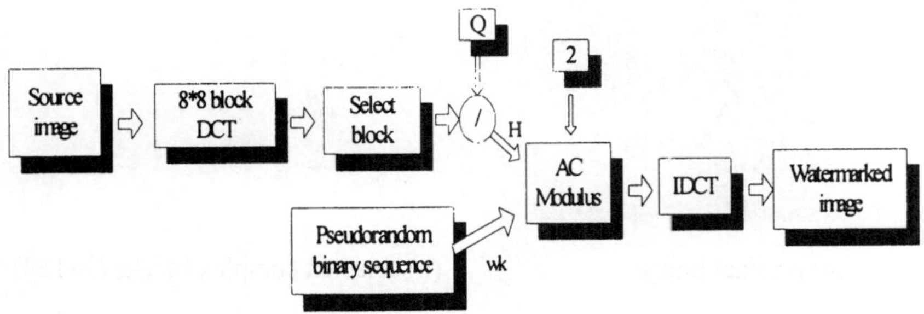

Fig.1 Watermark embedding procedure

improve PSNR, special DCT block selection algorithm is needed. In the proposed watermarking algorithm, the watermark embedding DCT blocks are selected based on the complexity of the image. A block with large AC coefficients is defined as a 'complex block.' The watermark is embedded only into those complex blocks to enhance the picture quality and reduce the calculation complexity. To embed the watermark information into an image, a quantization and modulus method is used. When extracting embedded watermark, the same complex block selection, quantization, and modulus calculation are processed and no prior information, such as original image, is required. This blind watermark extraction feature becomes more important because of the difficulties in keeping the huge amount of original images.

2.1 Watermark Embedding Algorithm

The watermark embedding procedure is as follows (See Fig. 1):

Step 1: Break up an image into 8×8 blocks and computes the DCT coefficients of each block.

Step 2: Select the complex blocks by comparing the magnitudes of the AC coefficients. The watermark information is embedded only into those complex blocks. Fig 2 shows the complex blocks. In this figure, the number of the complex blocks (k) is 128.

$$\mathrm{Max}(AC_i) \quad i=1,2,\ldots,n$$

where n is block number

Step 3: Select an AC component (AC) with the greatest magnitude in the selected complex block. The watermark will be embedded into this component.

Step 4: Generate the pseudorandom k binary sequence ('0' or '1'), which is used as watermark.

$$w_k=\{r_k\},\ r_k \in \{0,1\}$$

where k is the number of the complex blocks.

(a) original image

(b) selected complex blocks (k=128)

Fig. 2 Original image and selected complex blocks

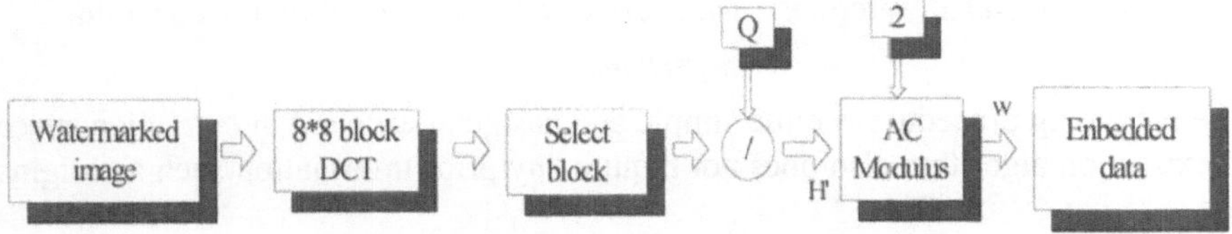

Fig.3 Watermark extraction procedure

Step 5: Quantize that *AC* value using the following equation.

$$H = round\,[max\,(AC)\,/\,Q]$$

where Q denotes the quantization step-size, which decides the embedding intensity.

Step 6: Calculate q_k according to the following condition.

$$\begin{aligned}&If\,(w_k == mod\,(H,2))\\&\quad q_k = H+2;\\&else\\&\quad q_k = H+1\end{aligned}$$

Step 7: From the calculated value q_k , compute new AC value (AC') using the following equation.

$$AC' = q_k \times Q$$

And replace the *AC* coefficient with the *AC'*.

Step 8: Watermarked image is constructed using inverse discrete cosine transform (IDCT).

2.2 Watermark Extracting Algorithm

The embedded watermark information, w_k, can be extracted using the following simple steps (see Fig. 3):

Step 1: Break up an image into 8×8 blocks and computes the DCT coefficients of each block.

Step 2: Find complex blocks and select the AC component with greatest magnitude (AC')

Step 3: Compute $H' = round\,[max\,(AC')\,/\,Q]$,

(a) Original image Lena

(b) Logo(size 8×16)

Fig.4 Test original image and logo

Step 4: The embedded watermark, w_k, is extracted using the following equation.

$$w_k = H' \bmod 2$$

The extracting procedure is quite simple and has great efficient in extraction speed. This extraction algorithm also does not require any prior information such as original image.

2.3 Correlation Quality

The correlation between the original watermark and the extracted watermark is calculated to detect the existence of the watermark.

The Correlation Quality function (CQ) is defined as follows :

$$CQ = \frac{\sum w_k \cdot w}{\sum w_k \cdot w_k}$$

where w_k is the original watermark data and w is the extracted watermark data.

3 Experimental Results

We utilized an 8 bit gray level, 256×256 size, Lena image as an experimental image and use an 8×8 block DCT to decompose the image into 64 sub-pixels. Fig 4 (a) shows the original Lena image, and (b) shows the logo image, which is used as watermark. The size of the logo image is relatively small because of the number of the selected complex is small. Fig.5 shows the relationship between the embedding quantization step-size Q and the peak signal-to-noise ratio (PSNR). We can see that the PSNR of the watermarked image is decreasing with increasing Q value, but in any case the PSNR is above 40dB. This shows that the embedded watermark doesn't degrade the original image quality. Selecting less than 30 as a Q factor, the watermarked image has a good PSNR. Fig.6 show the relationship between the

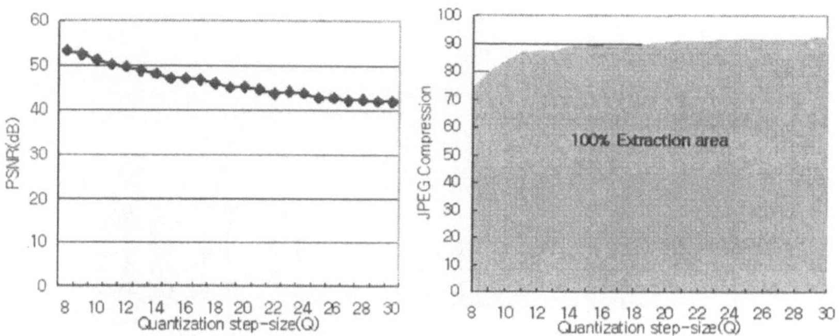

Fig.5 The relationship between Q and PSNR

Fig. 6 The relationship between Q and JPEG compression ratio for 100% logo extraction

embedded quantization step-size Q and the JPEG compression ratio. The 100% extraction area in the graph means that the correlation quality (CQ) is 1, which is the perfect extraction of the embedded watermark data. This graph shows that selecting large number as Q factor resulted in better robustness to the higher compression ratio. However, the larger Q value also degrades the PSNR, and we have to select Q number properly. If we want a watermark robust to higher compression up to 93%, the Q factor should be larger than 30, but in this case the PSNR of the watermarked image is less than 42dB.

4 Conclusions

In this paper, we proposed a new blind digital watermarking algorithm, in which the watermark information is embedded only into the selected complex blocks of a still image using quantizationa and modulus calculation. Experimental results demonstrate that the proposed watermarking method is robust to JPEG compression attack with higher watermarked image quality. Because of the simple and fast watermark extraction procedure, this algorithm is suited for real-time watermark applications such as MPEG video watermark.

Acknowledgment

The authors would like to thank the MarkAny for their support of this research.

References

1. Wang, H. M., Su, P.-C., Kuo, C.-C. J., :Wavelet-based digital image watermarking. Opt. Express, Vol.3, **12** (1998) 491-496
2. Schyndel, R. G., Tirkel, A. Z., Osborne, C. F., :A Digital Watermarking. Int. Conf. on Image Processing, **2** (1994) 86-90
3. Bendor, W., Gruhl, D., Morimoto, N., Lu, A., :Techniques for Data Hiding. IBM Systems Journal, Vol.38, **3&4** (1996) 313-336
4. Cox, I. J., Kilian, J., Leighton, T., Shamoon, T., :Secure spread spectrum watermarking for multimedia. IEEE Trans. on Image Processing, Vol.6, **12** (1997) 1673-1687
5. Xia, X., Boncelet, C. G., Arce, G. R., :A Multiresolution Watermark for Digital Images. Proc. IEEE ICIP, **3** (1997) 548-551
6. Inoue, H., Miyazaki, A., Araki, T., Katsura, T., :A Digital Watermark Method Using the Wavelet Transform for Video Data IEICE TRANS. FUNDAMENTALS, **E83-A** (2000) 90-95, 2000

MTEACH: A Language-Based Framework for Didactic Multimedia Production

P.L. Montessoro[1], D. Pierattoni[1], D. Cortolezzis[2]

[1] Dept. of Electrical, Management and Mechanical Engineering, University of Udine
I-33100 Udine, Italy
{montessoro, pierattoni}@uniud.it
[2] INSIEL – University of Udine, I-33100 Udine, Italy
Daniele.Cortolezzis@insiel.it

Abstract. Multimedia production is generally considered to be an expensive task. This is true when dealing with complex graphics, animation, artistic effects, music and high quality video editing, but didactic applications do not require such advanced features. A conventional lesson can be effectively reproduced in a multimedia environment using a small set of multimedia features and a simple, regular structure. However, didactic application often consists of a huge amount of multimedia material and logical interconnections. The MTEACH approach is based on a methodology supported by a language and a compiler, and allows the author of a didactic multimedia production to work at a higher level than conventional authoring tools. The "running code" of the multimedia application is generated in standard formats starting from a formal description of the lessons, providing a consistent and easy-to-navigate hypermedia structure.

1 Introduction

Didactic represents a natural application field for multimedia systems and authoring techniques. Traditional live lessons are basically "multimedia": the teacher talks, while explaining slides and pictures, showing objects and so on. With some improvements and adaptations, live lessons can be placed on an interactive CD-ROM or a Web site, as a support in media-based training and distance learning courses. Unfortunately, a well-known effect is that even few hours of teaching generate a huge amount of material (texts, audio, video, pictures, etc.). Thus, managing and handling large files and ramified data structures become a difficult task for both users and producers.

Common authoring tools, like ToolBook [1] and Macromedia Director [2], offer powerful functions for animation controls, programming and graphics. Authors that are not highly skilled at dealing with multimedia production are able to obtain a simple result with a limited effort. Advanced functions exceed the requirements of basic end users, which are often disoriented by an enormous choice of commands and low-level instructions.

Moreover, a considerable amount of manual work is necessary to collect the various features, especially because these tools are designed for the largest number of authors, including those for which the artistic aspect is the main part of the product. However this fact could not be a constraint in professional multimedia publishing, where authors are experienced programmers and work often in concurrent engineering teams, it often represents an unpleasant overload in case of simpler approaches for less skilled users. Another consequence is that multimedia production costs are often a big problem for high level didactic, such as for university or professional courses that cannot count on the profits of massive sells.

Further, reusability of parts of the final product is limited and additional manual work is necessary to restore all the links, in order to preserve the consistency of the multimedia data structure. This limitation descends from the strict embedding of the original data sources (audio, video and image files) inside the code generated by the authoring tool.

Cross-portability between different production environments, for example merging ToolBook and Director files, is nearly impossible, since each tool uses an internal coding system for the project description and generates archives with different formats. Working at a higher level would instead require a tool that describes the structure of the hypermedia, instead of directly implementing it.

Web-oriented authoring tools, like Microsoft FrontPage, provide some functions to preserve link consistence when the Web content is modified, or when a part of it is moved in a different context. However, considerable work is still required to create links, to fill template pages with the available material, and to check the logical correctness and consistence of the links in the final product.

Nevertheless, the total freedom left to the author when creating the outline and assembling the collected material can lead to a hypermedia not homogeneous in its parts. This makes navigation difficult and integration between different products almost impossible. Many authors do not recognize these aspects as disadvantages, being more interested in the artistic aspects of the work. Anyhow, this is not generally true for didactic productions, where lucidity and uniformity of style are key factors to gain the end user's comprehension.

2 Main Requirements

When handling multimedia-teaching material, reusability of modules is one of the most important features. For example, advanced courses can recall parts of basic courses, or smaller courses can be rearranged out from more extended ones, regarding the same subjects but modifying their order and/or the details of the treatment.

Most lessons are modularly organized in chapters and arguments, which are accompanied with a store of scheduled pictures, schemes and practical examples that enrich the explanation. We think that the teacher's approach to multimedia production would be easier, if the methodology for the hypermedia description offered a set of rules as coherent as possible with the structural elements of a common lesson.

Facing the design of a didactic-oriented authoring framework, software developers should identify the correct guidelines for the final success of the project. These are strictly dependent from the target of the authoring tool; both author's and end user's needs have thus to be satisfied, starting from an investigation on their practical requirements.

From the author's point of view, low production cost and skill, easiness of usage and a short hypermedia production time are key factors for a successful didactic multimedia production environment. A recognizable modularity is further essential to obtain a faster reusability of the parts of a final product.

On the other side, end users are commonly accustomed to the learning method imposed by the traditional didactic approach, i.e., live lessons which are normally accompanied by papers, books and personal notes. This fact imposes still didactic multimedia products to strictly respect the logical organization that characterizes traditional courses and lessons. It is likely that in a few years this constraint will not be present anymore. The increasing diffusion of personal and mobile computing devices, such as e-books, palmtops etc., will allow computer-based training sessions to reach a larger application field. As consequence, this will radically transform the way of teaching and, thus, the concept of learning.

3 A New Approach To Didactic Multimedia Design

Graphic environments are the most common user interface for authoring tools. This allows authors to develop their projects in a friendly workspace, and often simplifies the identification of a large variety of toolkit features. Models and templates enhance the visibility of the available instruments; on-line preview areas on the workspace can also present the direct effects of certain modifications on the final product.

A language-based approach could not offer the same helpful features. Although for less experienced authors the difficulty of learning a structured language could seem larger than discovering the instructions of a graphical tool, the value of a language-based hypermedia description is evicted when recursive procedures have to be applied on large hypermedia products. Reproducibility of operations is easier when dealing with a plain text source: text editors have a set of macros and automation features that are more powerful than repeating sequences of visual commands on a GUI.

This fact represents a common issue of most graphic-based applications: system administrators, for example, encounter some difficulties in automating procedures, when related commands are sequences of actions on graphical elements that are neither mapped on nor manageable at a lower level of abstraction.

Further, the regularity of the hypermedia data structure and the reusability of the teaching material are often issues which are difficult to be solved, if artistic features are complex and variously mixed in a high-level graphical authoring tool.

A language that makes the hypermedia project very similar to the index of a book will achieve this target; nevertheless, it allows keeping the project development at a higher level, not depending from toolkit's internal representation schemes. A simplified tool also requires an automated creation of links between data sources and the output, and their dynamic adaptation if some changes are made in the given description: both activities should be transparent to the author, in order to minimize the manual work and restrict the focus on the main activity.

On the other hand, such requirements imply a set of technical issues regarding both data sources and hypermedia description format. In order to obtain the full modularity at each layer, starting from data up to the project schema, the original multimedia sources should preserve their own identity in the output data structure.

Open data formats should be preferred for both sources and generated output. This assumption achieves the full cross-platform compatibility and allows to collect, modify and reuse the teaching material at any time and with the lowest conversion cost. It gets also through the disadvantages of most proprietary file formats, which require their own runtime libraries and are often platform-dependent.

Nevertheless, the hypermedia project structure should be based on a plain, portable, editable, source file (ASCII): such an open format would represent a common base for the interoperability between different production environments and could also stimulate further implementations of enhanced authoring tools.

4 MTEACH

The MTEACH authoring framework is based on automated code generation, starting from a structured language which describes the content of each lesson in terms of "primitive" multimedia elements: audio, video graphics, text, etc. These primitive elements are not related to any particular authoring system and are thus reusable in different contexts.

The lesson description also contains the logical connections between its various parts in terms of keywords (flat links) and hierarchical structure. In respect of commonly used authoring tools, this approach produces a more rigid, and therefore more regular, multimedia structure. Navigation becomes easier this way for both authors and end users.

MTEACH provides an effective methodology to build very large didactic multimedia products following as close as possible the normal activity of a teacher. The MTEACH language allows the teacher to describe the hierarchical structure of the lesson in the same way the index of a book is written; the keywords list associated to each element represents the logical interconnections of the arguments that will become glossary entries and hyper textual links.

From the technical point of view, the system can be easily extended to several different platforms and operating system environments, only by adding new interface modules to the code generator of the compiler. In particular, if an authoring tool provides application interfaces to external hi-level programs, it can be controlled by MTEACH to reduce or eliminate the need for manual work.

5 The MTEACH Methodology

One of the main purposes of MTEACH is to reduce the hypermedia production time. To achieve this goal, the first step consists in defining a methodology that preserves most of the normal preparation and teaching activity of the author and that leads to a straight sequence of tasks.

Firstly, the teacher prepares slides, pictures and animations to be used during the lesson; most of the didactic material should be ready before the lesson starts. Anyhow, the teacher can hand-draw pictures during the class, if exercises or detailed clarifications are needed.

The structure of the lesson is then described in the MTEACH language. This step provides a guide for the following production phases and guarantees that the audio and video recordings will match the logical flow defined by the lesson's schedule. Late modification of the structure of a didactic multimedia product often requires re-recordings of the teacher's speech to fit the new order of the arguments.

After that, the lesson is audio/video recorded, possibly live with students, in order to make the recording as natural as possible. If studio recording is preferred, the arguments can be individually recorded, possibly following the same order they will appear in the final product.

Audio/video recording is further digitized and edited, so that live recordings are splitted into the elementary modules (clips) defined by the structure of the lesson. Slides, pictures and animations are modified, if necessary, according to the actually recorded talk; for example, new slides can be prepared to reproduce additional drawings, which could have been added on the fly during live lessons.

At this point, all the elements needed for the code generation are ready. The structure described in the MTEACH language contains all the information necessary to build the links of the hypermedia structure. Compiler's template files will be used as definition of the graphical aspect of the output, as explained in the following section.

6 The MTEACH Language

MTEACH provides a very simple language to describe the structure of the hypermedia. The formal description of the MTEACH language, regarding the detailed explanation of syntax, lexical conventions and data types, would go beyond the purpose of this presentation paper. Nevertheless, current implementation is under development, application fields are getting larger, and new elements are to be added, according to the experimental results. Thus, a formal scheme would not still offer a complete and stable rule set for every kind of hypermedia description.

As said before, the description resembles the hierarchical index of a book. Traditional chapters become "lessons" and the sections within each chapter are called "arguments". The analogy with the book simplifies the description of the logical schema, which can be written with little effort directly from the teacher, not necessarily from a multimedia-authoring expert.

Each argument is a module that groups a collection of different types of documents together. "Clips", the most important type, are made of audio/video tracks and several synchronized images, or "slides". Synchronization is not obtained during the audio/video editing sessions; instead, it is featured by the automatic code generation. The way synchronization is achieved depends on the target operating environment; in current implementation, for example, the Real Media [3] synchronization capability is used.

The kernel of the MTEACH language definition.

```
keyword_list  ::=  <identifier>
                   [ , <keyword_list> ]

lesson        ::=  LESSON <identifier>
                   ( [ <keyword_list> ] )
                   { arguments }

arguments     ::=  argument [ arguments ]

argument      ::=  ARGUMENT <identifier>
                   ( [ <keyword_list> ] )
                   { contents }

contents      ::=  clip [ clip ]
```

```
clip           ::=  CLIP <identifier>
                         <filename>
                    ( [ <keyword_list> ] )
                    { slides }

slides         ::=  slide [ slide ]

slide          ::=  SLIDE <identifier>
                          <filename>
                    ( [ <keyword_list> ] )
                    AT <time>
```

The MTEACH language requires that timing information is associated to each slide related to the starting point of the audio/video track. A textual description of timing information could appear more complex and less effective than a graphical interface, but plain ASCII format still allow easy editing and manipulation when the description regards a large tree structure. Interactive graphical interfaces do not scale equally well, even though an additional program (with its own graphical interface) could be used to compute and insert timestamps into the source file.

An example of the MTEACH language.

```
lesson "Ulnar nerve exposure at the elbow"
       ("Ulnar","Exposure")
{
   argument "Sites of entrapment"
            ("Entrapment", "Elbow")
   {  clip "Sites of entrapment" "sites.rm" ()
      {  slide "View of the elbow" "elbow1.gif"
               ("Anatomy", "Elbow") at 01
         slide "Inside the elbow" "elbow2.gif"
               ("Anatomy", "Elbow") at 10
      }
   }
   argument "Surgical steps"
            ("Operating techniques")
   {  clip "Skin incision" "incision.rm" ()
      {  slide "Starting the incision",
               "skin_incision.gif"
              ("Skin incision", "Elbow") at 01 . . .
```

The lesson could be enriched by other documents, such as texts, animations and images not linked to any audio/video track. The language is currently being extended to include more data types.

A key feature of MTEACH is the automated generation of the several links, which are needed to logically interconnect topics. A list of keywords (such as "Ulnar", "Exposure", etc. in the example) is associated to each element in the description: this additional information will be used to build a multi-linked glossary during the code generation.Each keyword (it can be a word or a phrase) in the glossary will show the lists of related topics in the hierarchical index, i.e., the whole set of arguments in which the keyword is recalled.

Another set of automatically generated links provides a sequential visit of clips of the multimedia lessons.

7 The MTEACH Compiler

Automatic link generation makes MTEACH different from the conventional authoring tools and provides reusability of the multimedia material after it is organized in the lesson structure. Moving a part of a lesson description (clips, slides, timing, keywords, etc.) to another project does not lose the structural information. All the links are rebuilt when the new code is generated: this is a nice feature, since even very short lessons may contain hundredths of links.

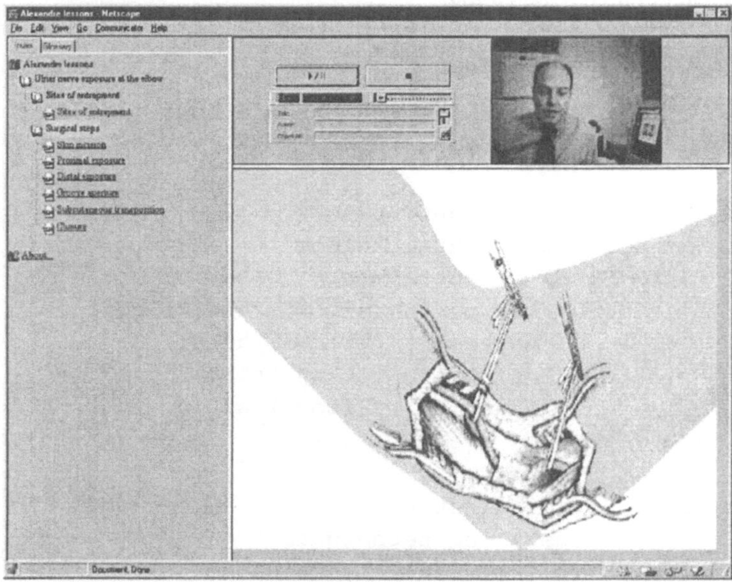

Fig. 1. Shot of a microneurosurgery application.

The MTEACH compiler has been developed using lex and yacc [4]. A data structure is built to internally describe the hypermedia structure and is visited during the code generation phase.

During the code generation phase, the compiler reads a set of template files and inserts into them the actual information described by the internal data structure. This approach allows the use of conventional editing and authoring tools to build and test the templates. Of course, this is possible only if the internal structure of the file of the chosen authoring system is known, or at least some APIs (Application Programming Interfaces) are accessible to control the editing feature of the authoring tool. Fig. 1 shows a shot of the final product in a microneurosurgery teaching application.

Code generation in the current prototype is targeted for HTML files with JavaScript procedures and RealMedia [5] audio/video encoding and synchronization. Animations use the animated GIF format [6] with timing information.

8 Summary

A simple and regular structure is suitable for most didactic applications of the multimedia technologies. Their value resides in contents and in richness of links to better describe the relationship between the topics, rather then in artistic and graphical effects.

MTEACH is limited to didactic or didactic-like productions based on a regular structure. The language is still being extended and some new features are being added, but a running prototype is already available and it is being used to understand the needs for future extensions.

To test the easiness of usage by users without specific knowledge in computer science, MTEACH is currently being used to produce some lessons in the field of microneurosurgery, whose examples appear in the pictures of this paper.

Another direction of development regards the creation of interfaces to other authoring tools, including ToolBook, Macromedia Director and Shockwave.

9 Acknowledgements

Authors wish to thank dr. Alberto Alexandre from EUNI (Treviso, Italy) and from the Microneurosurgery Service of Policlinico S. Giorgio, Pordenone, Italy, for his interest in this project and for his collaboration in the making of the didactic microneurosurgery application.

References

1. Asymetrix Learning Systems Asymetrix ToolBook web page: http://www.click2learn.com/products/
2. Macromedia Director Technotes web page: http://www.macromedia.com/support/director/
3. Real Networks Real Media File Format web page: http://www.real.com/devzone/documentation
4. Schreiner, A.T., Friedman, H.G. Jr.: Introduction to Compiler Construction with UNIX. Prentice Hall, Upper Saddle River, New Jersey (1985)
5. Real Networks Synchronized Multimedia web page: http://service.real.com/help/library
6. Compuserve Graphics Interchange Format, Version 89a. ftp://ftp.ncsa.uiuc.edu/misc/file.formats/graphics.formats/

Protocol and Buffer Design for Multimedia-on-Demand System

Siu-Ping CHAN, and Chi-Wah KOK

Department of Electrical and Electronic Engineering, Hong Kong University of Science and Technology, Clear Water Bay, Kowloon, HONG KONG

Abstract. A multimedia-on-demand system provides real-time playback of multimedia data transferred over UDP on IP is presented. Data buffer is allocated to overcome multimedia dropout problem. A flow control system is presented which constantly maintains the buffers at or near maximum capacity. Rate adaptation is employed which results in an overall improvement of the quality of the multimedia playback. Analytic analysis of the buffer design problem is presented to minimize startup delay and media quality fluctuation. Other system maintenance protocol is incorporated to minimize the effect of packet lost and nonuniform arrival. Simulation results are presented to demonstrate the efficiency of the developed system.

1. Introduction

A multimedia-on-demand system provides real-time playback of multimedia data transferred via an IP network is considered in this paper. At the request of a client (subscriber), a server transmits the compressed multimedia data over the network. The client receives and decompresses the transmitted data for playback. Real-time playback can be achieved by compressing the multimedia data to a rate lower than the channel rate. Otherwise multimedia dropout will be observed which is a phenomena wherein the multimedia playback terminates for some noticeable time period and resumes after this delay.

The internet is an unreliable network in that it has a high rate of packet loss and nonuniform packet arrival. To overcome these network difficulties, data buffers of reasonable size should be allocated with the client's system in order to avoid deleterious effect on network performance. If the multimedia data is transmitted and received within the data buffer at too fast a rate, the buffers would overflow causing loss of significant portions of data and multimedia dropout. On the other hand, if data was transmitted too slowly, the buffers would empty out and again resulting in significant dropout. As a result, a second system which run concurrently with the multimedia-on-demand system will monitor and regulate the flow of data. The main difference between the proposed flow control system and the current known systems is that now the client is responsible for the decision of bitstream quality adaption. The client can desire and achieve the best quality for his network environment. Simulation results showed that the designed adaptive buffer can efficiently store sufficient playtime than that of traditional buffer with the same buffer size. Sufficient buffer storage is to ensure a continuous multimedia playback for the client. This flow regulation system constantly maintains the buffer at or near maximum capacity so that, in the event of network delay, the client system continues to play the multimedia data stored in the buffers until new multimedia data begins to arrive again. Further quality improvement can be achieved by using variable rate data stream. Rate adaptation adds another dimension to the flow regulation system that maintains the highest quality bitstream in the buffer. Thought analyzing the experimental results, an optimal initial buffer design algorithm is presented to minimize the startup delay and fluctuation the media quality during playback.

Sequence Number	Bit Rate	Frame size		Multimedia Data (Frame size)

Fig. 1 UDP/IP Data Packet Format

1.1 System Model

A request from the client will initiate a connection using TCP/IP flow regulation in the multimedia-on-demand system. The server responses by transmitting a packet using TCP/IP that inform the client on the availability of the requested multimedia stream and the available bit rates, frame-sizes and other information required to decompress and playback the bitstream. The server starts streaming the data using UDP/IP right after the initial information packet. Showing in Figure 1 is a typical data packet of the streamed media. The sequence number indicates the sequential order of the packet being sent out. The bitrate shows the multimedia bitstream bitrate in the current period. The frame size is the size of each packet. The size of the UDP packet is pre-assigned for each stream. Specifying the packet size in advance of transmission allows the file to be encoded in accordance with a suitable frame size that overcome the error propagation effect due to packet loss. Such that loosing a packet will not affect the playback of neighboring packets. Buffer will be allocated to temporary store the received UDP packet which will then playback in according to the sequence number.

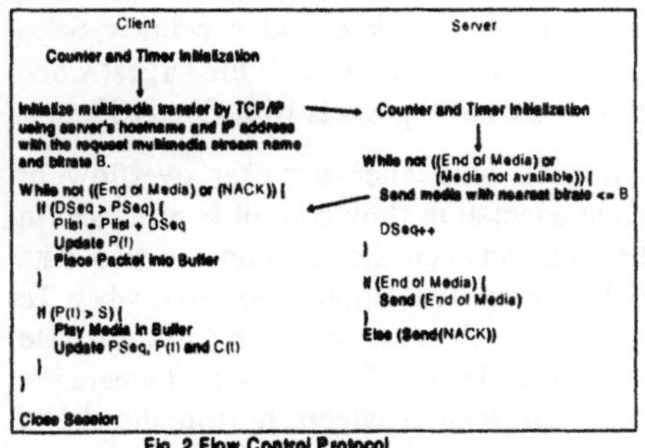

Fig. 2 Flow Control Protocol

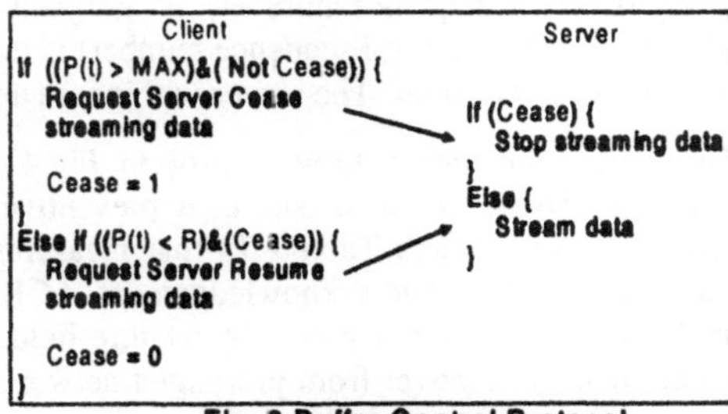

Fig. 3 Buffer Control Protocol

2. Protocol

2.1 Flow Control

UDP is a 'Connectionless' protocol. Unlike TCP and HTTP, when a UDP packet drops out, the server keeps sending information, causing only a brief glitch instead of a huge gap of silence for real-time playback of the media stream. To regulate the flow of the UDP packets, sequence numbers DSeq (Data Sequence number) are assigned to each data packet. The client maintains a PSeq (Play sequence number) counter, such that out-of-sequence data packet arrival is allowed onlyif the PSeq of the packet has been decompressed and played is smaller than the received DSeq. Otherwise, out-of-sequence arrival data packet will be discarded. Figure 2 details the flow control using these 2 counters plus two time dependent variable over UDP/IP. The stored bitstream will be played when buffered packet has a play time (P(t)) greater than a given start time (S). The playback will be continued until the client receives NACK or End Of Media where the communication session will be closed.

2.2 Buffer Control

When the bitrate, B, of the compressed media stream is lower than that of the network, the flow control will send a control sequence to request the server to suspend from streaming the data when the buffer is 'full', i.e. P(t)>MAX. The streaming will be resumed when the buffer content falls below a pre-assigned threshold R, i.e. P(t)<R. Due to the high packet loss rate of the internet, the effective bitrate of the network is substantially lower. Which in turn constrained the bitrate of the streaming media to be much lower than the channel capacity. In

much of the time, the channel bandwidth is wasted. The situation is worsen when the server cease data streaming due to client buffer overflow. Bitrate adaptation is therefore proposed.

2.3 Bitrate Adaptation

As normal quality data packets are transmitted at rate, B, faster than real time, the buffer begins to fill up and approach maximum capacity, MAX. Once the buffer has remained at maximum capacity for a predetermined amount of time, γ, the client's flow control system will request the server to transmit data with higher quality, e.g. $B \rightarrow B+\Delta$. High quality data takes more time to transmit since more data is required to be transmitted at the same baud rate. Furthermore, high quality data has a high consumption rate. Once the buffer falls beneath a minimum capacity, MIN, for the predetermined amount of time, γ, a low quality data packet request will be issued, e.g. $B \rightarrow B-\Delta$. The process is repeated such that high quality data will be combined with normal quality data resulting an overall improvement of the playback quality.

Because more than one blocks will typically be present on the IP network at a time. Once a "rate adaptation" request issued, the data packets still on the network will be received and stored in the buffer before the rate adapted packets. Such that the buffer overflow or underflow condition will remain for certain time, until previously received packets are consumed. Having a bitrate adaptation time threshold γ minimizes unnecessary rate changes request. Furthermore, CSeq (Control sequence number) is assigned to each control packet, and a counter SSeq (Server received control sequence number) is maintained in the server to store the largest CSeq number received so far. The server will ignore any received control packets with CSeq<SSeq.

The bitrate adaptation flow control in Fig.4 is effective only after a buffer overflow or underflow condition has occurred. A preventive bitrate adaptation flow control is proposed in Fig.5 with two timers Tc and Ts that measures the time between the reception of two data packet in the client and acknowledgement, ACK, in the server. The bitrate is lowered when Tc or Ts is greater than a pre-assigned threshold, TIMEOUT. Because streaming low bit rate packet helps to recover from prolonged network congestion. Tc and Ts is reset to 0 whenever the client receive a valid data packet or the server receive an acknowledgement from the client. The acknowledgement is sent to the server when the number of packet received by the client is greater than a pre-assigned threshold, δ, such as to minimize the amount of communications.

2.4 Loss Packet Recovery

A timer Td is maintained in the client system such that loss packet resent request is made periodically whenever Td > Tr (the resent timeout). Due to network delay, it is possible to have the resent packet arrived later than the current play time C(t). In that case, the received resent packet will waste bandwidth. The return path delay of the network can be measured as Tx. To account for further network congestion, only those lost packets with play time greater than 1.5 Tx should request resent. Changing the overhead from 50% Tx to a higher value will conserve the bandwidth, but will also increase the packet lost rate, hence glitch and dropout in playback.

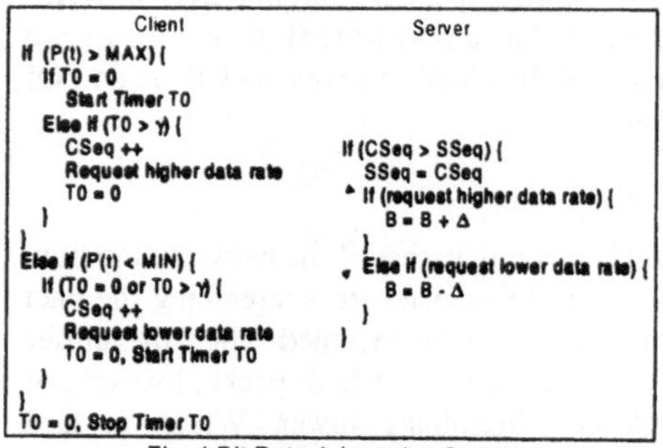

```
Client                                  Server
If (P(t) > MAX) {
   If T0 = 0
      Start Timer T0
   Else If (T0 > γ) {
      CSeq ++                           If (CSeq > SSeq) {
      Request higher data rate             SSeq = CSeq
      T0 = 0                               If (request higher data rate) {
   }                                          B = B + Δ
}                                          }
Else If (P(t) < MIN) {                     Else If (request lower data rate) {
   If (T0 = 0 or T0 > γ) {                    B = B - Δ
      CSeq ++                              }
      Request lower data rate           }
      T0 = 0, Start Timer T0
   }
}
T0 = 0, Stop Timer T0
```

Fig. 4 Bit Rate Adaptation Protocol

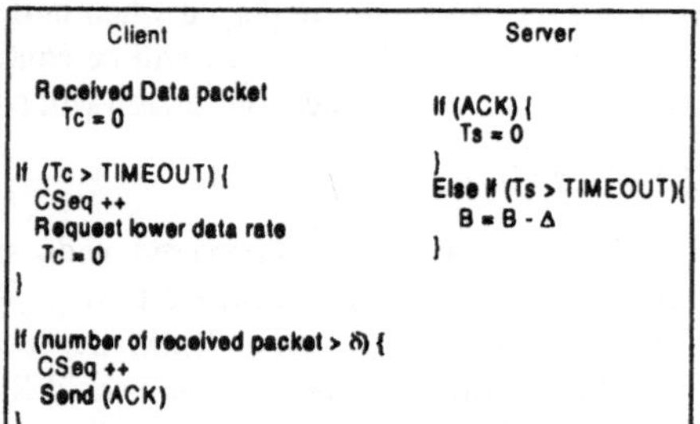

```
Client                                  Server
   Received Data packet
      Tc = 0                            If (ACK) {
                                           Ts = 0
If (Tc > TIMEOUT) {                     }
   CSeq ++                              Else If (Ts > TIMEOUT){
   Request lower data rate                 B = B - Δ
   Tc = 0                               }
}

If (number of received packet > δ) {
   CSeq ++
   Send (ACK)
}
```

Fig. 5 Bitrate Adaptation by Timeout Protocol

```
Client                                        Server

 Start Td                                     If (CSeq > SSeq) {
 Empty Rlist, Plist                             SSeq = CSeq
                                                If (Received Resent)
 Received Data packet                             Resent packets in Rlist
   Plist = Plist + DSeq                       }

If ((Td > Tr) && (P(t) > Resent)) {
  Empty alist
  For i = PSeq to RSeq {
    If (Playtime (i - C(t)) > 1.5 Tx)
      Break
  }
  For j = i to DSeq {
    If ( j != Plist & Rlist )
      alist = alist + j
  }
  CSeq++
  Rlist = alist
  Request resent of Rlist
}
```

Fig. 6 Loss Packet Recovery Protocol

```
Client

If (DSeq < RSeq){
  Droput --
  If (Dropout < 0)
    Dropout = 0
}
Else if (DSeq > RSeq + 1){
  Dropout = Dropout + DSeq - RSeq - 1
  If (Dropout > λ) {
    CSeq++
    Request lower data rate
    Dropout = 0
  }
```

Fig. 7 Nonuniform Arrival Protocol

A list Plist that stores the received packet numbers and a counter RSeq that stores the largest received packet number are used to identify the lost packet number. Another list, Rlist, will store the packet numbers in the resent request. In order to avoid wasting bandwidth due to multiple resent request in congested network, lost packet number in the previous resent request will not be considered in the current resent request.

2.5 Nonuniform Packet Arrival

The out-of-sequence packet arrival problem can be resolved by playing the buffered packets in the order of their sequence number. Such scheme will introduce glitch and dropouts in play back. To minimize the dropout rate, a count "Dropout" is maintained in the client to measure the dropout rate in the unit of packets. Bit rate adaptation should be performed when Dropout > λ, a predetermined dropout threshold. Fig.7. details the proposed protocol.

3. Buffer Design

3.1 Initial Buffer

The success of the presented flow control algorithm heavily depends on S, the initial buffer size. When S is too large, unnecessary startup delay will be resulted. If S is too small, the system will be subjected to a high dropout rate. Although the flow control system will minimize the dropout rate by adapting the bitrate of the streamed data, it also cause fluctuation in the quality of the playback. Since fluctuation in the quality of the playback is annoying and should be avoided. Experiments have been performed to determine a method to design the initial buffer size. The experimental results in Fig. 8 showed that the packet receive rate against time is exponentially asymptotic to a steady rate, C. Assume the play back time for each received packet is F, the buffered play time at time P(t) is given by

$$P(t) = F\int_0^t (1 - e^{-\lambda t})dt \text{ ,}$$

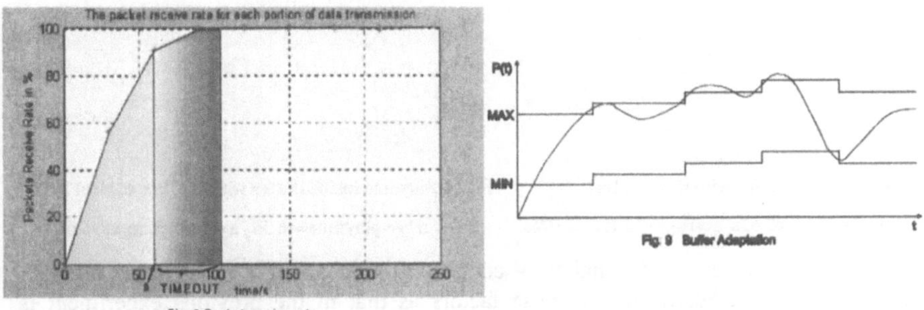

Fig. 8 Packet receive rate

Fig. 9 Buffer Adaptation

where λ is the packet arrival rate. The start time S should be large enough, such that the initial buffer will buffer data with P(t) larger than that can be received in one TIMEOUT period, T. Such that the buffer will start to fill up after the media data starts to playback,

$$\int_0^s (1-e^{-\lambda t})dt = \int_s^{s+T} (1-e^{-\lambda t})dt$$

Since there does not exist an analytical solution for S of the above equation for a given T and λ, a numerical solution can be obtained. A 50% safe margin is usually added to S to avoid unnecessary fluctuation of media quality.

3.2 Adaptive Buffer

The MAX and MIN parameters should be adjusted every time a bit rate adaptation request is issued such as to minimize unnecessary fluctuation of the quality of the streamed data. One basic criteria in adapting the MAX and MIN size of the buffer is to maintain the playtime between MAX and MIN to be a constant, i.e. MAX – MIN = constant, such as to minimize the dropout rate after adapting the margin of the buffer. Secondly, MAX should be increased to MAX + b(t), where b(t) is the playtime difference for the data packets before and after bitrate adaptation with higher bit rate bitstream request.

Similarly, MIN should be decreased to MIN – b(t) when a low bitrate request is issued. Concerning about the initial MAX buffer size, it can be set to the play time generated by the number of packet received within the time period (TIMEOUT+2*Tx) under the initial bitrate B. Similarly, the initial MIN buffer size is set to the play time generated by the number of packet received within the time period (2*Tx), such that there are enough time for the client to request bitrate adaptation. As a result, the initial buffer size can be determined with a given TIMEOUT which is determined by the tolerance of the user.

4. Results

Simulation results of the playtime stored in the proposed buffer had shown the effectiveness of the proposed flow control. The first experiment focused on exponential arrival of the multimedia packets. The initial bitrate is set to 132kbps. The targeted bitrate equals to the channel bandwidth which is set to 300kbps. The simulated network condition includes packet loss, network congestion and nonuniform packet arrival, and impulsive network noise at 150s, 200s, 225s, 250s, 300s and 700s. The impulsive network noise will stress the recovery ability of the flow control system. The Timeout constant is set to 20s and the round-trip delay Tx at 10s. Fig.10 shows the playtime stored in the buffer and the changes in playtime under the proposed flow control. The average stored playtime and the maximum buffer time are also shown.

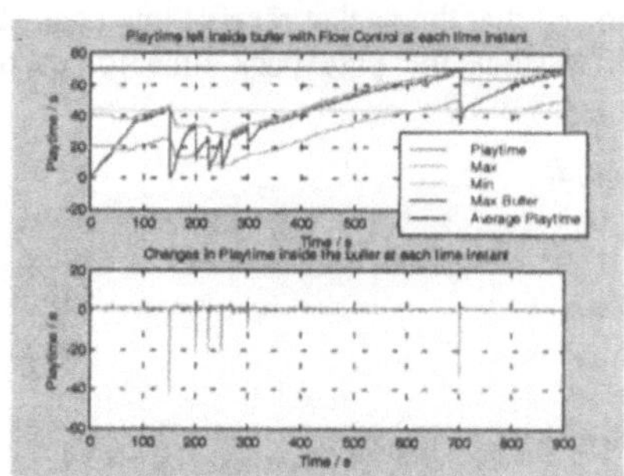

Fig.10 Playtime inside buffer with flow control with average playtime=43.52s, average changes=0.076s

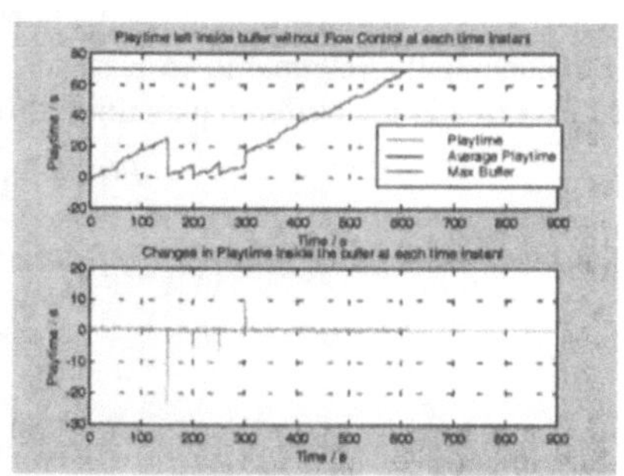

Fig.10 Playtime inside buffer without flow control with average playtime=40.3s , average changes=0.082s

Another simulation that use traditional flow control is also performed. The same network environment, multimedia bitstream and noise factors as that in the previous experiment is applied in the simulation. Fig.11 shows the playtime stored in the buffer and the changes in playtime of traditional flow control. The average playtime stored inside the buffer and the maximum buffer time are also shown. The simulation results showed that the proposed flow control with adaptive buffer can achieve longer stored average playtime in the buffer and higher average bitrate of the multimedia bitstream than that of system without flow control mechanisms. This result implies that more efficient utilization of the allocated buffer memory can be achieved with the proposed flow control algorithm. Furthermore, better streaming quality, as reflected by the higher average multimedia bitrate of the playback media can be achieved. Less changes in playtime stored in the adaptive buffer also demonstrate the proposed algorithm is more stable to various network condition than traditional methods.

5. Summary

The design of a multimedia-on-demand system over UDP on IP that provides real-time playback of multimedia data has been discussed. Data buffer is allocated to overcome multimedia dropout problem and minimize the startup delay. A flow control system is presented which maintains the buffers at near maximum capacity. Furthermore, bit rate adaptation system is discussed for media playback quality improvement. Other system maintenance protocol that minimizes the effect of packet loss and nonuniform arrival was also presented. An optimal buffer design method has been presented. The system's infrastructure has been implemented. Other experimental results on the packet size vs packet loss rate, and the packet receive rate vs time have been reported that helps to confirm our buffer design algorithm. The results show that the adaptive buffer design can store longer playtime than that of traditional buffer with the same buffer size. Besides, the proposed system can achieve a higher quality playback than that of traditional buffer with simple flow control mechanisms.

Reference

[1] A.Xu, W.Woszczyk, Z.Settel, B.Pennycook, R.Rowe, P.Galanter, J.Bary, G.Martin, J.Corey, J.R.Cooperstock, "Real-time streaming of multichannel audio data over Internet," Journal of the Audio Engineering Society, vol.48, no.7-8, July-Aug. 2000, pp.627-41.

[2] E.Bommaiah, K.Guo, M.Hoffmann, S.Paul, "Design and implementation of a caching system for streaming media over the Internet," Proc. Sixth IEEE Real-Time Technology and Applications Symposium. RTAS 2000, pp.111-21.

[3] L. Fang, S. Jitae, C-C J. Kuo, A.G. Tescher, "Streaming of MPEG-4 speech/audio over Internet," International Conference on Consumer Electronics 1999, pp.300-1.

[4] R.D. Gloser, M. O'Brien, T.B. Boutell, R.G. Goldberg, "Audio-on-demand communication system" US Patent no. 6151634.

[5] M. Hofmann, K. Sabnani, "Streaming and broadcasting over the Internet," Proc. IEEE Conf. on High Performance Switching and Routing 2000, pp.251-6.

[6] A. Mena, J. Heidemann, "An empirical study of real audio traffic," Proc. IEEE INFOCOM 2000, vol.1, 2000, p.101-10.

[7] R. Rejaie, Y. Haobo, M. Handley, & D. Estrin, "Multimedia proxy caching mechanism for quality adaptive streaming applications in the Internet," Proc. IEEE INFOCOM 2000, vol.2, 2000, pp.980-9.

[8] J. Rexford, S. Sen, & A. Basso, "A smoothing proxy service for variable-bit-rate streaming video," Proc. GLOBECOM'99. vol.3, 1999, pp.1823-9.

[9] S. Schmid, A. Scott, D. Hutchison, & K. Froitzheim, "QoS based real time audio streaming in IPv6 networks," Proc. SPIE, vol.3529, 1998, pp.102-13.

[10] D.A. Turner, & K.W. Ross, "Continuous media e-mail on the Internet: infrastructure inadequacies and a sender-side solution.," IEEE Network, vol.14, no.4, July-Aug. 2000, pp.30-7.

[11] S. Tasaka, M. Kato & K. Nakamura, "TCP versus UDP for media synchronization in PHS Internet access," IEICE Transactions on Communications, vol.E83-B, no.3, March 2000, pp.713-20.

Quality Weighted Bit Allocation for Smoother Streaming of Stored FGS Video

Zhibo Chen Yun He
State Key Lab on Microwave & Digital Communications
Dept. of Electronic Engineering, Tsinghua University, Beijing, 100084
{chenzb, hey}@video.mdc.tsinghua.edu.cn

Abstract

In this paper, a Fine Granularity Scalability (FGS) streaming framework together with a Quality Weighted Bit Allocation scheme for enhancement-layer is first proposed to achieve smooth video quality even under channel conditions with a wide range of bandwidth variation. PSNR is used as a quality metric and a theoretical analysis on how to maintain a smooth quality is given. We will show, however, taking advantage of the priori information of the PSNR value of the base-layer reconstructed frames will help in providing a consistent video quality. Simulations show that variance of the PSNR of decode frames decreased a lot with the average PSNR increased.

Keywords: Fine Granularity Scalability (FGS), video streaming, Quality Weighted Bit Allocation, smooth quality

1. Introduction

Transmission of video signal over Internet has enabled a wide range of multimedia applications. In recent years, streaming stored video has become a popular Internet application where stored video is streamed from the server to a client on-demand. And how to achieve a smoother playback quality with constraints on resources such as network bandwidth and delay makes video delivery a challenging task.

Typically the control schemes of streaming stored video could be broadly classified into receiver-driven, transcoder-driven, and sender-driven according to different protocol model. **Receiver-driven** scheme (also named pull-model) controls the flow of the stream at the client side by sending request to the sender [1] or joining different multicast group [2]. **Transcoder-driven** scheme addresses the problem inside the network by assigning transcoder [3] or priority based dropping technique [4] at routers in case of congestion, at the same time introduces some additional complexity at core routers. **Sender-driven** scheme (also named push-model) requires the sender to adjust its transmission schedule according to fluctuations of network bandwidth, and **prefetching** technique which sends video data ahead of schedule (with respect to its playback time) is often used to smooth the short time variance of bandwidth. Sender-driven scheme has achieved more attention [5][6][7][8] for its relative simplicity, stability and manageability without much impact on the current network structure.

Generally these traditional sender-driven control schemes of streaming stored video are all based on video coding standard such as MPEG-1 [6], MPEG-2 or Motion-JPEG [5]. These standards are for storage, broadcasting, or editing, not for streaming application, especially streaming over unreliable channel conditions. And this constraint has made the streaming schemes more complex, less efficient and limited applicability. Scalable coding is also proposed to provide finer and flexible control on video quality [7][8]. It is assumed that the frame size is equal and every layer are coded with CBR and in the same bit-rate in [7] which is unpractical for existent video coding standard, and [8] assumed that the client buffer is unlimited and an optimal allocation of bandwidth between base and enhancement layer is studied. Both [7] and [8] have to deal with each layer as a whole with limited flexibility on providing a smooth quality, and the complexity also arises with the number of layers.

Alternatively, Fine Granularity Scalability (FGS) has been recently developed [9] as a new MPEG-4 version to fulfill the fundamental requirements for video streaming which could provide the bit level bit-rate regulating stream with fine bandwidth-scalability and also some resilience to packet-loss. Usually the base layer is coded in CBR to minimally acceptable quality and the base-layer bit-rate R_{BL} must be chosen to be less than the minimal available bandwidth at all times ($R_{BL} \leq R_{\min}$). The enhancement-layer is over-coded using a bit-rate ($R_{\max} - R_{BL}$), $R_{\max}$ and $R_{\min}$ can be determined off-line. Generally based on the network feedback, we can estimate the available bandwidth $R_{ES}(t)$, and then the server transmits the enhancement-layer using a bit-rate as [10] describes:

$$R_{EL}(t) = \min(R_{\max} - R_{BL}(t), R_{ES}(t) - R_{BL}). \qquad (1)$$

Because of the fine granular characteristic of the enhancement-layer, an efficient usage of the bandwidth can be achieved by simple control in the server. And the more FGS enhancement-layer bits are received, the better the reconstructed video quality is [9].

However definitely, it is generally agreed that it is visually more acceptable to watch a video with consistent quality, though lower, than one with higher varying quality. Because the base-layer is coded in CBR and the quality of base-layer decoded frames maybe varied widely from scene to scene due to the VBR nature of compressed video, a simple control like (1) couldn't provide a smoother transmission quality under neither CBR nor VBR channels. Fig.1 shows the quality variation of the decoded frames using (1) as the bit allocation scheme under a variable channel (with scene changes).

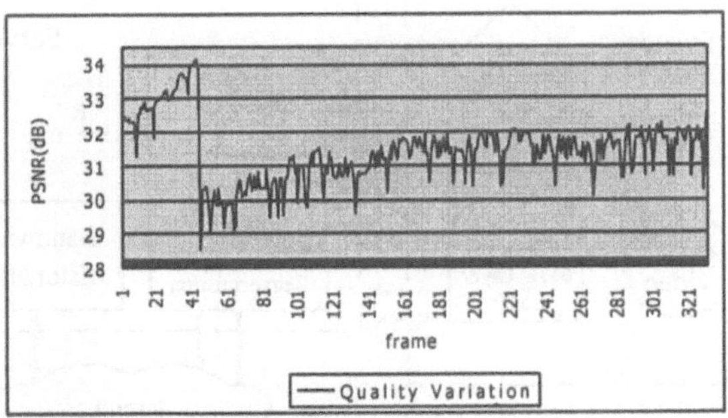

Fig.1 Quality Variation without optimal bit allocation

So an optimal bit allocation on the enhancement-layer bits should be investigated to get a generally consistent playback quality.

Considering the characteristic of the stored video, we can take advantage of some priori information to allocate different amount of bits to different enhancement layer. And prefetching technique [7] which send video data ahead of schedule is also used to smooth the short time variance of bandwidth. In this paper, Peak Signal Noise Ratio (PSNR) is used as the quality metrics. And a Quality Weighted Bit Allocation (QWBA) scheme is described in the next section and a theoretical analysis will be given.

The organization of this paper is as follows: in section 2 we give an FGS video transmission framework together with a QWBA scheme; section 3 presents some simulation results; the conclusion is provided in section 4.

2. Streaming of Stored FGS Video

Fig.2 shows the overall framework of the FGS video streaming system with two separate parts: encoder and server. Original video sequence is coded by the base-layer encoder with a constant bit rate $R_{BL} \le R_{\min}$ in the encoder side and the PSNR value of each decoded base-layer frame are stored as side information. Then the FGS encoder codes the residues of DCT coefficients by bit-plane coding. In our experiment, FGS encoder is lossless coded with bit rate $R_{\max}$.

When transmitting the stored FGS video, a simple prefetching scheme is used in our system because our focus is on the optimal allocation of enhancement-layer bits. The time is considered to be divided into intervals of T seconds and it is supposed that at the beginning of each interval the server reads $R_{BL} * T$ base-layer bits, $R_{\max} * T$ enhancement-layer bits together with the side information in this T seconds to the server application buffer. Then in our FGS streaming system, a QWBA scheme is performed based on smooth quality criteria. After that in each T second interval, the base-layer bits is first written to the network from the application buffer for its relative importance, and then followed by the enhancement-layer bits after QWBA. At the end of the interval, the buffer is flushed and the processing for next interval continues.

Simulations show that our streaming system could achieve smoother playback quality at the client side.

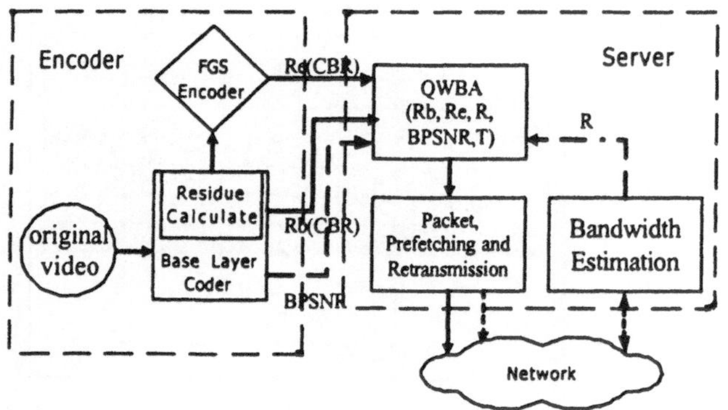

Fig.2 Framework of stored FGS video streaming system

2.1 Quality Weighted Bit Allocation (QWBA)

2.2 Problem formulation

The aim of the QWBA scheme is to minimize the variance of the quality of the decoded video sequence, subject to a bit rate constraint on the enhancement-layer. Then first we should define a metric to measure the smoothness of a decoded video sequence. It can be imagined that if all the PSNR values of the decoded frames are the same, the quality should be the most smoothness, and the smaller the scope of the variance, the smoother the quality is. So we choose PSNR as the quality metric, then the optimal bit allocation can be formulated as the following constrained optimization problem:

$$\begin{gathered} \min Var(DPSNR), \\ s.t. \sum_{i=1}^{N} R_{Ei} = R_E, and, R_{Ei} \geq 0, i = 1,\dots,N \end{gathered} \tag{2}$$

Where $DPSNR$ denotes the PSNR value of the decoded frames, and $Var()$ is to calculate the variance of this stochastic variable. Let N denotes the number of frames in the prefetching interval T, R_{Ei} denote the bits allocated for the enhancement-layer in the frame and R_E is the given total number of bits used for enhancement-layer in the prefetching interval T. In real system, R_E can be estimated by using a weighted exponential moving average (WEMA) of the past and current bandwidth observations as [8] described. For simplicity, we assume a considerable precise estimation of R_E in our simulations.

By doing unbiased estimation, we could change (2) to (3):

$$\begin{gathered} \min \frac{1}{N-1} \sum_{i=1}^{N} (DPSNR_i - DPSNR_{avg})^2, \\ s.t. \sum_{i=1}^{N} R_{Ei} = R_E, and, R_{Ei} \geq 0, i = 1,\dots,N \end{gathered} \tag{3}$$

Where $DPSNR_i$ is the corresponding PSNR value of decoded i th frame, which is the sample sequence of $DPSNR$, $DPSNR_{avg} = \frac{1}{N} \sum_{i=1}^{N} DPSNR_i$. Because N could be taken as a constant value, the optimization problem is equally formulated as:

$$\begin{gathered} \min \sum_{i=1}^{N} (DPSNR_i - DPSNR_{avg})^2, \\ s.t. \sum_{i=1}^{N} R_{Ei} = R_E, and, R_{Ei} \geq 0, i = 1,\dots,N \end{gathered} \tag{4}$$

2.3 Result and complexity

In order to solve this problem, two assumptions are made to simplify the bit allocation problem:

- $BPSNR_i$, PSNR value of i th frame decoded only by base-layer bits, can be achieved as priori information.
- R_{Ei} is in proportion to $\Delta PSNR_i$ (the increase of PSNR value) of the i th frame after enhancement-layer is decoded, formulated: $\Delta PSNR_i = DPSNR_i - BSPNR_i = \alpha * R_{Ei}$.

For the first assumption, $BPSNR_i$ is able to be obtained by the base-layer encoder, the computation load is very low and the storage space for $BPSNR_i$ is also negligible compare with the video streams, so this assumption is tenable in this case.

The second assumption is reasonable in FGS coding if only SNR scalability is considered as this paper do, because the enhancement-layer are all coded corresponding to the base layer of the same frame and from residues of the original frame and the reconstructed current frame. To be convinced, our experiments also validate an approximately linear relationship between R_{Ei} and $\Delta PSNR_i$, as Fig.3 shows.

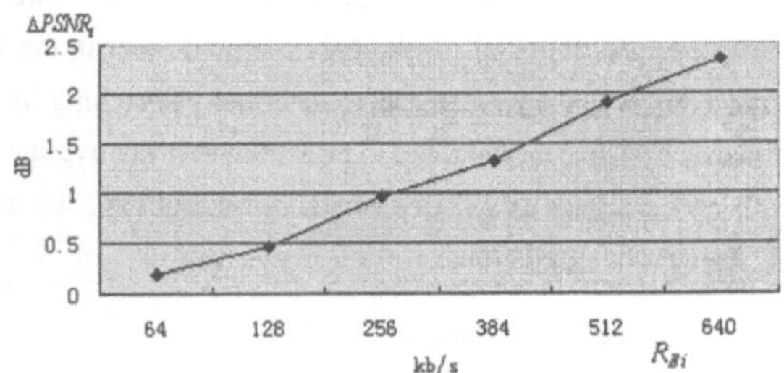

Fig.3 Relationship between R_{Ei} and $\Delta PSNR_i$

With these two assumptions, we can convert formulation (4) into the following problems:

$$\min \frac{1}{N-1}\sum_{i=1}^{N}(\Delta PSNR_i + BPSNR_i - BPSNR_{avg} - EPSNR_{avg})^2, \qquad (5)$$
$$s.t. \sum_{i=1}^{N} \Delta PSNR_i = \Delta PSNR, \Delta PSNR_i \geq 0 (i = 1,\ldots,N)$$

where $\Delta PSNR = \alpha * R_E$, $BPSNR_{avg} = \frac{1}{N}\sum_{i=1}^{N} BPSNR_i$, $\Delta PSNR_i = \alpha * R_{Ei}$ and

$EPSNR_{avg} = \frac{1}{N}\sum_{i=1}^{N}\Delta PSNR_i$.

In order to solve this non-linear programming problem, an iterative algorithm should be used and the computation load is increased with larger N.

For simplicity, we use a sub-optimal result after only once iteration like this:

$$R_{Ei} = 0 \qquad \text{if } p_i < 0$$

$$= p_i + \frac{1}{N'}(R_E - P) \qquad \text{if } p_i \geq 0 \qquad (6)$$

where $p_i = \frac{R_E}{N} + \beta * [BPSNR_{avg} - BPSNR_i]$, $\beta = \frac{1}{\alpha}$, P is the sum of those p_i with the constraint $p_i \geq 0$, and N' is the number of frames with $p_i \geq 0$, so $N' \leq N$. It should be noted that (6) couldn't ensure $R_{Ei} \geq 0$, we will set $R_{Ei} = 0$ in the case when $R_{Ei} < 0$ and allocate the bits according to (6) until all R_E bits are allocated. Our simulations show that this sub-optimal allocation scheme is both simple and effective in real application.

And it should be indicated that the performance of the proposed QWBA algorithm is related to the proportion of the base-layer bits and enhancement-layer bits, the more enhancement bits could be used, the better smoother quality could be achieved.

3. Simulation Results

In this paper, five CIF MPEG-4 video clips (Mother-Daughter, Hall-man, Akiyo, Container-Ship, News) of 300 frames, 30f/s each are cascaded to form a single test sequence. And our encoder is based on a TMN H.263 encoder which produces the base-layer stream with a constant bit rate at 64kb/s by TMN8 rate control, and DCT residues of each frame is coded by the bit-plane coding proposed in [11] to achieve a fine grained enhancement-layer. A Markov chain is used to model the channel bandwidth variation, and the mean bandwidth is 300kb/s in our experiments. The resulting bandwidth in our experiments is shown in Fig.4.

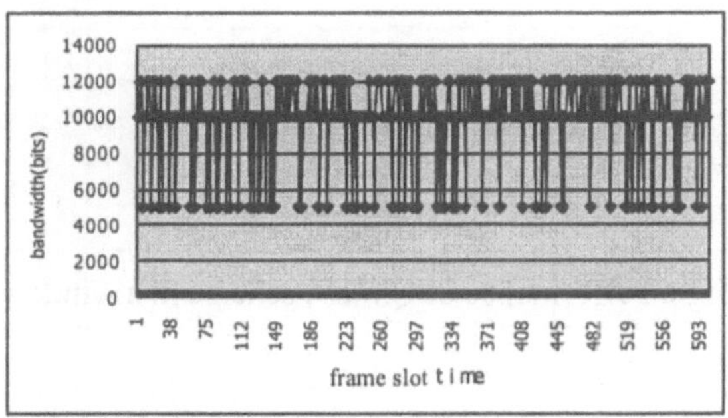

Fig.4 Varying Channel Bandwidth

Fig.5 shows the performance of our QWBA scheme ($\beta = 700$ is used) when the prefetching time T is set to the length of the whole sequence, where No-QWBA scheme means the bit allocation scheme without any optimization as (1) described. It can be seen clearly that QWBA scheme has a very good performance in achieving more smooth quality at the client side, especially during scene changes. The variance of decoded frame's PSNR has been decreased from 6.54dB to 3.72dB, and the average PSNR is increased about 0.1dB, in some cases such as scene changes the PSNR value increased up to 4 dB.

It can be imagine that the longer the prefetching time T is, the better the performance of the playback quality is achieved, but at the same time the more buffer is needed and the longer delay is. While in real system, constraints on client buffer and delay should be taken into account. Definitely for streaming of stored video, several seconds of delay is often sustainable in real application. So we can set the prefetching time $T = 4s$ without much delay and demands on the buffer, and the quality within this interval will keep smooth by prefetching the enhancement-layer stream after QWBA. Fig.6 shows the result of a window when $N = 120$ ($T = 4s$), the quality in each window with a length N keeps smooth. By moving the sliding window along the sequence, a rather smooth quality can be achieved.

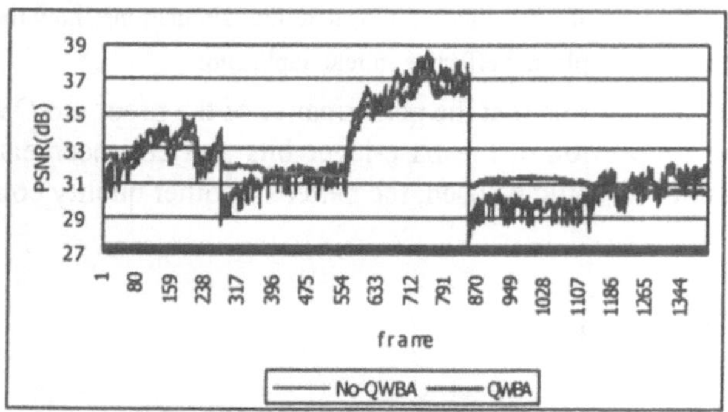

Fig.5 Performance of QWBA scheme

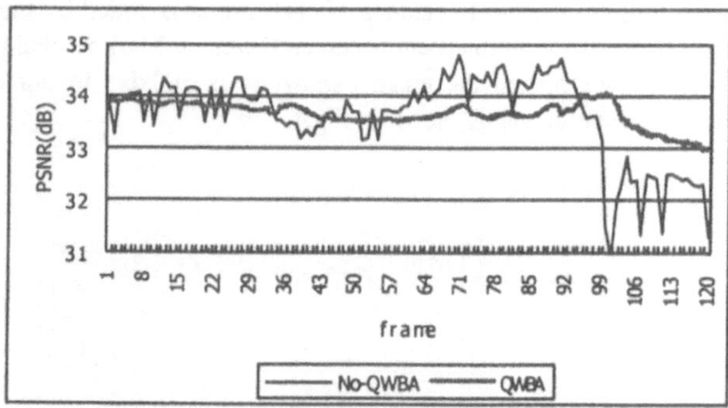

Fig.6 Performance of QWBA scheme in a window

Conclusion

In this paper, a complete video streaming system is presented based on an FGS encoder and a quality weighted bit allocation scheme in the server side. By taking advantage of the priori information of the PSNR values from the base-layer encoder, the Quality Weighted Bit Allocation scheme can keep more visually smooth video quality based on solid theoretical analysis; it is also simple and practical enough in the real system. There are also some simplifying assumptions made in this preliminary work such as no packet loss by precise bandwidth estimation, no rigid constraints on buffer, and only SNR scalability is considered. For future work, the tradeoff between retransmission of lost packets and prefetching of new streams should be investigated, temporal scalability and rigid buffer control should also be taken into account.

Reference

1□ Poon, S.M.; Jie, Song; Lee, B.S.; Yeo, C.K , "Performance of buffer-based request-reply scheme for VoD streams over IP networks", Computer Networks, Volume: 34, Issue: 2, August, 2000, pp. 229-240

2□ S.MacCanne, V.Jacobson, and M.Vetterli. "Receiver-driven layered multicast", Proc. ACM SIGCOMM'96, Oct 1996

3□ Jianzhong Zhou□"Heterogeneous multicasting based on RSVP and QoS filters", ICCT '98. 1998 International Conference on Volume: vol.2 , 1998 , Page(s): 8. vol.2

4□ S.Bajaj, L.Breslau, and S.Shenkar, "Uniform versus Priority Dropping for layered video", Proc. ACM SIGCOMM'98, Sep.1998

5□ Wu-Chi Feng, "Critical bandwidth allocation techniques for stored video delivery across best-effort networks ", Distributed Computing Systems, 2000. Proceedings. 20th International Conference on, 2000, Page(s): 56 –63

6□ Salehi, J.D.; Zhi-Li Zhang; Kurose, J.; Towsley, D. "Supporting stored video: reducing rate variability and end-to-end resource requirements through optimal smoothing" Networking, IEEE/ACM Transactions on Volume: 6 4 , Aug. 1998 , Page(s): 397 -410

7□ Srihari Nelakuditi, Raja R Harinath, Ewa Kusmierek, and Zhi-Li Zhang, "Providing Smoother Quality Layered Video Stream", NOSSDAV, North Carolina, USA, 2000

8□ Despina Saparilla, "Broadcasting and streaming of stored video", Ph.D thesis, University of Pennsylvania, 2000, http://www.eurecom.fr/saparill.

9□ Weiping Li, Fan Ling, Xuemin Chen, "Fine Granularity Scalability in MPEG-4 for Streaming Video", ISCAS 2000□pp.299-302

10□ M.van, and H.Radha, "Fine Grained Loss Protection for Robust Internet Video Streaming", San Jose, VCIP, pp.533-545, Jan, 2001.

11□ FGS verification model version 4.0. ISO/IEC JTC1/SC29/WG11 N3317, April, 2000

A Content-Based Multimedia Database Engine: MIR

Guohui Li, Jun Zhang, and Defeng Wu

Multimedia Laboratory
National University of Defense Technology,
Changsha, 410073, China
guohli@nudt.edu.cn

Abstract. Content management of multimedia information is an important foundational technology for information society. Content-based multimedia database engine: MIR is a prototype that can be embedded into object-relational DBMS. In this paper, we present the architecture of MIR that integrates information retrieval with data retrieval into database query, supporting content-based populating, manipulating and maintenances for multimedia database system. Then the data model describing visual features, content clues and spatio-temporal characteristics of multimedia data types is introduced, which provides an interval content-compression for multimedia data in database system. Finally, some content-based query schemes implemented in MIR are given.

1 Introduction

The researches on multimedia data management have been carried on more then ten years[1], for instance, from early extended-relational model to object-relational model and object-oriented model. In addition, hypermedia model is a navigation model of multimedia data organization.

At present, with great evolution in object-relational model, object-oriented model and associated database products, the researches of multimedia information management have been put emphasis on structural content management for multimedia data. Although a lot of researches have been done in content-based multimedia information retrieval [2],[3],[4], fewer works has been taken in integrating content-based methods into database system to manage multimedia data by content. "Multimedia Information Retrieval MIR" is prototype system designed and implemented as a multimedia database engine. This MIR project explored new architecture for multimedia database system with a content-based database engine, which integrating information retrieval with data retrieval in traditional database system, efficiently support populating, query, browsing and maintenance for multimedia database based on content. A data model describing visual features, the content clue and spatio-temporal characteristics for multimedia data was designed to support content-level data management, including content-based query and browsing.

In this paper, we will describe unique MIR architecture and its data model of content description from systematic perspectives. Some of the user query schemes designed and implemented as interfaces in MIR are given.

This paper is organized as follows. In Section 2 we present MIR architecture and its components. In Section 3 we then describe MIR's content model. Some query schemes are given in Section 4, and finally we summarize our works and make a conclusion.

2 MIR's Architecture

In order to manage multimedia data effectively according to multimedia content characteristics, integration of data query with content-based information retrieval in a database management system are mandated, which forms a new architecture of multimedia database. MIR database engine is composed of the following five modules, or components. As illustrated in Figure 1, the shaded parts of the figure are the components of MIR engine.

- Media Preprocessing
- Content-based Search Engine
- User Manipulation Interface
- High-dimensional Index
- Media Database

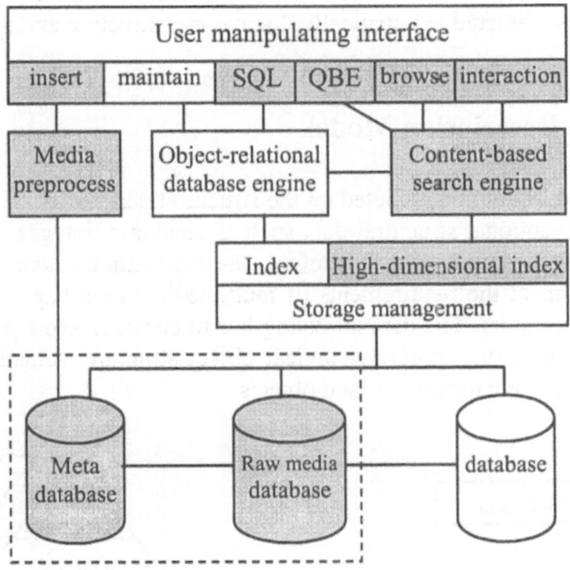

Fig. 1. The architecture of MIR engine

The preprocessing for media, such as structuring and feature extraction, was implemented in automatic or semi-automatic style. With this preprocessing component, visual physical features are extracted, logical relations are built, and objective attributes are assigned with regard to images, image objects, video representative frames, camera operations, and motion objects. As for audio, the script, aural features and audio segmentations are extracted via sound recognition and audio signal analysis [5].

The search process is similarity matching between feature vectors measured with a set of distance functions, which imitating human perceiving behavior to get ranking of returned query results according to similarity. There is a set of corresponding algorithms of similarity measuring in the search engine with respect to various media.

The visual query form such as QBE is used to provide query interface for a user. A delivered query can be based on an entire image, an image area, a video shot, and combination of various features. Browsing is a kind of new manipulation for database system, which especially useful for time-based media, such as video and audio. The interactions with query results are used to form relevance feedback for refining query results. MIR provides extended-SQL query interface to support data query and content-based query in one query delivery.

The search engine achieves fast searching through the database with index mechanism, thereby it can be used to large scale of multimedia database. MIR uses a clustering method on the media collections to form n clusters dividing the feature vector space, saving a lot of search time.

The features, logical-unit structures and their relations that were extracted in preprocessing components are inserted in meta database associated with raw media data. The media database established is composed of raw media database and meta database. The raw media databases contain multimedia data, such as image, video and audio etc.; while the meta databases contain objective attributes assigned by user, content features extracted automatically, logical-unit structure and their relations.

3 Content Description Model

Multimedia data should be modeled on the structural description of the content. Compared with conventional structural data such as character, integer, etc., raw multimedia data is non-structural data. Therefore, the conventional data modeling used in RDBMS can't meet the requirements of multimedia data modeling, and we need to derive new data model. The data modeling has to consider about audiovisual characteristics, spatio-temporal structure, logical object structure, semantics, and relationship between those characteristics and objects.

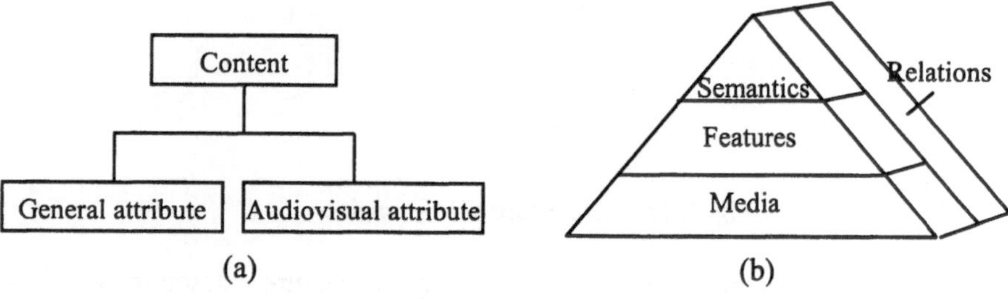

Fig. 2. HCM content model in MIR. (a) Content for multimedia; (b) Audiovisual content model

In MIR, we use attributes to describe content characteristic for multimedia data, which keep consistent with the scheme used in database system. Multimedia content is divided into general attributes and audiovisual attributes from a perspective of full content. The audiovisual attributes are the important information clues for content-based query. Further, the audiovisual attributes can be described with three layers: semantics, audiovisual characteristic and media data. The general model describing multimedia content is shown as figure 2. This is a pyramidal Hierarchical Content Model, called HCM.

A formal description of the HCM model is given in equations (1), (2) and (3), where A_g and A_{av} denote general content and audiovisual content of multimedia data respectively. S_L , F_L and M_L denote semantics layer, feature layer and media layer respectively, while $\leftarrow$ denotes "abstracted from". The Φ is media description model, where M, F and D respectively denote media (and its objects), feature and description of feature (feature and its value), $\propto$ means "by multiple". $\Re$ denotes the relations among media attributes, where R_{st}, R_s, R_{av} denote spatio-temporal relation, semantics relation and audiovisual relation respectively.

$$HCM = \Lambda\{A_g, A_{av}(S_L \leftarrow F_L \leftarrow M_L) \mid \Phi, \Re\} \tag{1}$$

$$\Phi(M \propto F \propto D) \tag{2}$$

$$\Re(R_{st}, R_s, R_{av}) \tag{3}$$

Content model in figure 2 indicates that multimedia content not only contain audiovisual content, but also contain general attribution from the common meaning. However, audiovisual content is primarily and special characteristics with respect to multimedia.

4 Query Schemes

Multimedia query should be a combination of various query schemes, such as query by example, SQL, keywords query, and browsing. The query result is a multimedia presentation to user, not only a simple display of database tables. Mainly query schemes in MIR as follows.

4.1 Query by Example

The example used to form audiovisual query can be an image, a video representative frame, or an audio segment. Figure 3 shows the query interface of MIR engine running on the Internet browser, on which returned images by query are ranked in turn according to similarity, by the example of the first image to form query with layout feature of the image. The user also can use a mouse to draw an area as example [6].

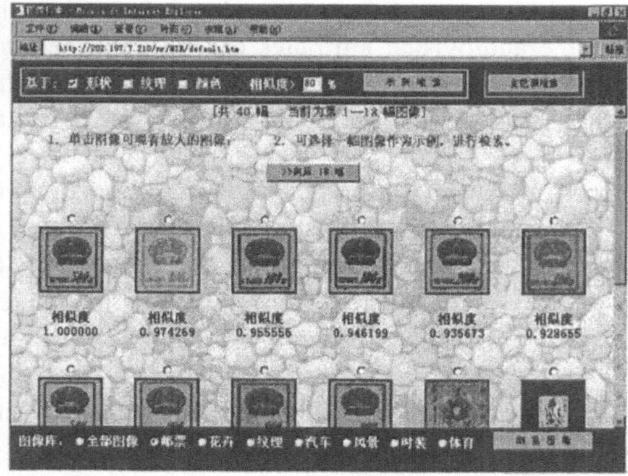

Fig. 3. One of query interface running on browser (*based on layout features*)

4.2 Query by Color Specified by User

MIR designs an algorithm making a Gaussian-distribution analog to extension of dominant-color [7], with which user can delivery a query based on visual subjective impression on color. User can set and adjust color fuzzy range to extend hue in the query. The query scheme implemented in MIR can use one dominant color or multiple dominant colors to form a query in color panel. Figure 4 shows the interface of multiple-dominant colors selection and fuzzy adjustment.

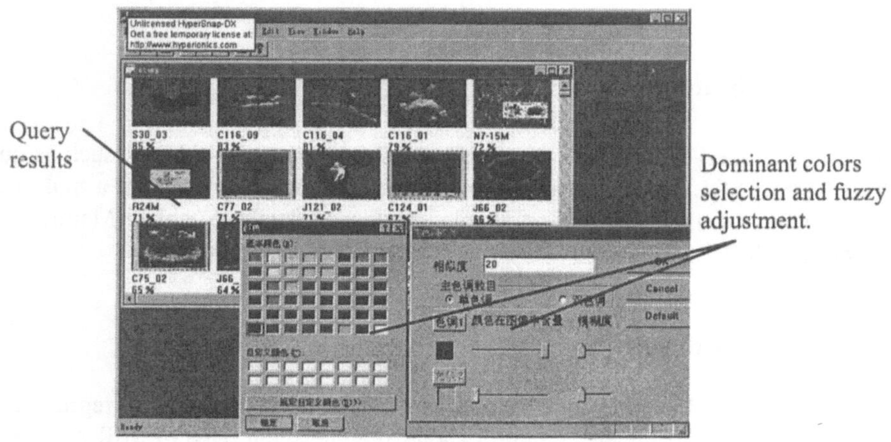

Fig. 4. Query by multiple dominant colors

4.3 Structural Browsing for Video

MIR browses video in three levels [8]: The video-level V_i is video records in video database, such as a film; the scene-level S_i represents story units under the video-level, which is composed of many shot groups. The shot-level R_i is the smallest browsing element. User can browse each element through the tree-like hierarchy.

In addition, MIR system provides the ability of classification and query based on the subjects of image and video. Audio signal associated with video is identified by voice recognition technique into script text, which used to describe corresponding scenes and shots. Therefore user can use conceptual keywords to query video segments.

MIR embeds the above query functions into extended-SQL, enabling database system to integrally process data query and content-based information query.

5. Summary

The MIR explored an engine-embedded approach that integrates content-based information retrieval with data query in the DBMS. Now we embed MIR engine into popular DBMS to manage multimedia data, such as image database managing scenery, stamp, fashionable dress, and flower photos, and video database managing film, MTV, news, documentary, and advertisement video. We will investigate more effective multiple-dimensional index mechanism integrated with DBMS to improve query effectiveness, and further explore query integration of batch, interactive, browsing and QBE with SQL into DBMS to implement a full information access interface.

References

1. Setrag Khoshafian, Brad Baker. “Multimedia and image database”. Morgan Kaufmann, 1995
2. Venkat N. Gudivada, Vijay V. Raghavan. “Content-Based Image Retrieval System”. IEEE Computer, Sept, (1995) 19-22
3. H.J. Zhang. “Video parsing, retrieval and browsing: a integrated and content-based solution. ACM Multimedia’ 95, (1995) 15-24
4. Myron Fliekner, et al. “Query by Image and Video Content: The QBIC system”. IEEE Computer, (1995) 23-32
5. G. Li and A. A. Khokhar, Content-based indexing and retrieval of audio data using wavelet, The IEEE international conf on multimedia and expro(ICME), New York (2000)885-888
6. G. Li, W. Liu and L. Chao. “A image retrieval approach based on color perception features”. Journal of Image and Graphics, 1999,4(3),248-251
7. L. Chao, W. Liu and G. Li. “Research and implementation of an image retrieval algorithm based on multiple dominant colors”. Journal of Computer Research and Development, 1999,36(1), 96-100
8. Lingqi Wu, G. Li. “Video structural browsing and querying system: Videowser”, Mini-micro System, 2002,22(1), pp112-115

A Flexible Access Control Model for Multimedia Medical Image Security

Sofia Tzelepi, and George Pangalos

Informatics Laboratory, Computers Division, General Department, Faculty of Technology, Aristotelian University, Thessaloniki 54006, Greece
{tzelepi, gip}@eng.auth.gr

Abstract. Most of the work on multimedia medical images security until now has focused on cryptographic approaches. While valuable, cryptography is not enough to control access to images. Therefore additional protection approaches should be applied at a higher level. Role-based access control (RBAC) is a good candidate to provide access control in a multimedia medical image DBMS. However, in a multimedia medical image DBMS, specifications of image access rights are often based on the semantic content of the images, the attributes of the user accessing the image, the relationship between the user and the patient whose images are to be accessed and the time. Unfortunately, RBAC cannot be used to handle the above requirements. In this paper we describe an extended RBAC model by using constraints in the specification of the Role-Permission relationship. The proposed access control model preserves the advantages of scaleable security administration that RBAC-style models offer and yet offers the flexibility to specify very fine-grained, flexible, content, context and time-based access control policies.

1 Introduction

Most of the work on multimedia medical images security until now has focused on cryptographic approaches [1]. While valuable, cryptography is not enough to control access to medical images [2]. Therefore additional approaches should be applied at a higher level. Role-based access control (RBAC) is a good candidate to provide access control, since roles accurately describe which types of people need access to certain types of objects.

The notion of roles is an important factor in authorization rules, but in a multimedia medical image database system context in order to be effective it has to be used in conjunction with the following information:

- Content of the images: image access is naturally described in terms of its semantic contents, for example, all images presenting a cancer of the lung must not be made available to physicians who are accessing information from no trust domain.
- Domain: what domain of the health system a particular caregiver works for. For example, medical images belong to certain departments and are not accessible by certain physicians, or a physician may be permitted to access only medical images of his/her subordinates and their subordinates, recursively.
- Location: where the user is accessing information services from. Location information is used in several types of authorization rules. One type uses location to identify the trust domain where the user is accessing information services from. Location can also be used to derive the emergency level of access. A policy can allow read access to all images of all patients for any user assigned to the role physician and accessing the information from an emergency room.
- Time: time constraints specify the validity periods for a policy.
- Relationship: what is the relationship between the user and the patient whose images are to be accessed (e.g. patient's primary care provider, part of the patient care team; healthcare staff explicitly assigned to take care of the patient, ..).

Unfortunately, RBAC cannot be used to handle the above requirements [3]. In order to overcome this problem, in this paper we propose an extended RBAC by using constraints in the specification of the Role-Permission relationship. The use of constraints allows RBAC to be tailored to specify very fine-grained, flexible, content and context-based access control policies. The proposed access control model preserves the advantages of scaleable security administration that RBAC-style models offer and yet offers the flexibility to specify complex access restrictions based on the semantic content of the images, the attributes of the user accessing the image, the relationship between the user and the patient whose images are to be accessed and the time. In the development of content-based constraints a simplified medical image model for describing the semantic content of a medical image is used.

The rest of this paper is structured as follows. Section 2 introduces related work and contrasts it with our work. The proposed RBAC and the detailed specification of its components are described in section 3. Section 4 introduces the medical image data model. Section 5 presents the access control mechanisms and the algorithm proposed in this paper. Section 6 introduces the access control architecture and section 7 concludes the paper.

2 Related Work

As mentioned above, one of the problems of applying RBAC to multimedia medical image DBMS is the specification and enforcement of fine-grained access control at the level of individual users and specific images [3]. For example, just because the doctor's role enables a set of accesses to medical images does not mean that the doctor's role should provide access to all medical images. A doctor can only access the medical images for those patient currently assigned to this doctor. There have been several approaches for creating an instance level policy for roles by using the notion of team-based access control (TMAC) [3] or by introducing parameterized roles to RBAC models [4], [5].

An alternative approach to specify and enforce fine-grained access control at the level of individual users and specific images is proposed in this paper by using constraints in the specification of the Role-Permission relationship. Constraints have also been addressed in [5]. In [5] content-based access control is enforced by simply specifying some constraints against attribute values of data objects. In contrast, due to the nature of images, content-dependent access control for a medical image DBMS must be based on the semantics of the medical images, rather than on the attributes characterizing them. Medical image attributes often only deal with physical characteristics of the medical images (for example, acquisition device, direction, format,...) and therefore are not significant for access control. In the development of content-based constraints specification a simplified medical image model for describing the semantic content of a medical image is described in the next section.

3 The Underlying Medical Image Data Model

For content-based access control, medical image databases must have capabilities to recognize and quantitate image content and merge the quantitated image data with textual patient data into a common data model [6]. Established algorithms can be readily integrated into a multimedia medical DBMS for image segmentation, texture analysis, content extraction and image registration. We use in the development of our content-based access control model a simplified medical image model introduced in [7]. In [7] a medical image usually is considered as an organic structure, where pathological signals can be detected in special places. Therefore, the semantic content of a medical image can be described in terms of iso-semantic regions and signals. In our proposed access control model, the content-based constraints we are concerned with deal with the presence or absence (and eventually with the characteristics) of a referenced object in a particular location of the image.

4 An Extended Role-Based Access Control Model for Multimedia Medical Image Databases

The basic components of a simplified RBAC model are Users, Roles, Permissions, User-Role (U-R) relationship and Role-Permission (R-P) relationship [8]. In this paper, an extended RBAC model for multimedia medical image database systems is presented. Two major extensions to the model are introduced. The first extension introduces the notion of user attributes (e.g. user name, his domain in the management hierarchy and his location). As mentioned above, there is a need to use user attributes for providing access control. The second extension concerns the Role-Permission relationship. In this case, each Role-Permission relationship is a decision rule, which specifies, besides the access modes the holder s of the permission is authorized for on object(s) o, also the constraints to be satisfied in order for s to exercise the access modes. In a multimedia medical database context, the general form of a Role-Permission relationship is 5-tuple

<identifier, s, r, {action}, t: target, constraints(s, t)>, where

- identifier: it is used to identify uniquely the permission,
- s: subject to which the permissions apply,
- r: role which can process this permission. Subject s is authorized for role "r",
- action: it is the operation, which is to be processed by role,
- t: object on which actions are to be performed,
- target: it is the object type,
- constraints(s, t): limit the applicability of the permission. Constraints must be satisfied by s and t.

A subset of Object Constraint Language (OCL) [9] is used for specifying constraints which limit the applicability of the permission, for example to a particular time interval or according to the state of the system. The following are some examples of constraint expressions:

- "left ventricle" $\in$ regions(x) $\wedge$ "tumor" $\in$ signals(x, "left ventricle") $\wedge$ height(x, "left ventricle", "tumor") $\geq$ 1cm.

This expression denotes all images (x) that present a tumor with a height of more than 1 cm on the left ventricle.

- time.between("1600", "1800")

This expression limits the policy to apply between 4:00pm and 6:00pm.

Application example: In the following example we consider a health-care organization security policy. In this example we have a health-care organization composed of several hospitals, and each hospital is structured into some divisions. A primary physician is assigned to a division and he/she can only access medical images for those patients currently assigned in that division and to this doctor. In order to achieve such policy, we define the following role-permission relationship:

{dp1, s: Primary_Physician, {view}, t: Image,
domain_user(s) = domain(t) $\wedge$ s $\in$ carrying_physicians(t)}

5 Access Control

The main goal of the access control mechanism is to verify whether user u, trying to access image i, using a privilege p, under a certain role r, is authorized to do so, according to access control restrictions enforced by that role. The access control algorithm is specified in Figure 1.

6 System Architecture

The complete system architecture is depicted in Figure 2. Through the *authorization manager*, the security administrator can add, modify, or delete User-Role relationships, Role-Permission relationships and User attributes. The *access control manager* implements the access control algorithm in section 5. The *image data manager* is responsible for handling of images. Each time a new image is acquired by the medical image database system, it is first processed by the *image postprocessing manager*, which extracts the semantic content from this image. Information on the semantic content are then stored and used to perform content-based access control restrictions. We used an RDBMS to implement our image model as described in section 3 and to store all necessary data.

ALGORITHM 1. **Access control Algorithm**
INPUT: [1] An access request (u, r, i, p), [2] The User-Role relationship set, [3] The Role-Permission relationship set, [4] The user attributes set
OUTPUT: [1] ACCEPT, [2] REJECT otherwise
METHOD:

```
If (Is_role_members(u, r) ∧ Is_role_operations(p, r)) then
    If (evaluation_constraints(u, i, p, r, cn)) then Return (ACCEPT)
   Else Return (REJECT)
Else Return (REJECT)
```

The function Is_role_members(u, r) returns TRUE if user u is authorized for role r, else return FALSE. The function Is_role_operations(p, r) returns TRUE if operation p is associated with role r, else return FALSE. The function evaluation_constraints(u, i, p, r, cn)) returns TRUE if image i and user u satisfies the constraints cn that are associated to the role r, else return FALSE

Fig. 1. Access control algorithm

7 Conclusions

In this paper, we have presented an extension of a generic RBAC model where role-based access decisions includes other factors beyond roles (e.g. the semantic content of the images, ..). The above factors are expressed using constraints in the specification of the Role-Permission relationship. Constraints offer the ability to specify complex access restrictions. From our development and implementation experience we are convinced that the proposed model provides significant capabilities to model and implement access control restrictions in a flexible manner, so as to meet the needs of healthcare multimedia medical image DBMS.

References

1. R. B. Wolfang and E. J. Delp, "Overview of image security techniques with applications in multimedia systems", SPIE Conf. on Multimedia Networks: Security, Displays, Terminals and Gateways, Vol. 3228, November 2-5, 1997, Dallas, Texas, pp:297-3308.
2. E. B. Fernandez and K. R. Nair, "An Abstract Authorization System for the Internet", in Proc. of the 9th International Workshop on Database and Expert Systems Applic., 1998.
3. R. K. Thomas, "Team-based access control (TMAC): A primitive for applying role-based access controls in collaborative environments", ACM RBAC'97, 1997.
4. L. Giuri and P. Iglio, "Role templates for content-based access control", in Proc. of the Second ACM RBAC Workshop, November 1997.
5. E. C. Lupu and M. Sloman, "Reconciling role-based management and role-based access control", in Proc. of the Second ACM RBAC Workshop, November 1997.
6. S. T. C. Wong and H. K. Huang, "Design methods and architectural issues of integrated medical image data based systems", Computerized Medical Imaging and Graphics, Vol 20, No 4, pp. 285-299, 1996.
7. A. Tchounikine, "Creation and content-based retrieval in a radiological documentary record", in Proc. of the 3rd Basque International Workshop on Information Technology, 1997.
8. R. Sandhu, E. J. Coynee, H. L. Feinsteinn, and C. E. Youman, "Role-based access control models", IEEE Computer, 29(2), February, 1996.
9. Rational Software Corporation, Object Constraint Language Specification, Version 1.1, Available at http://www.rational.com/uml/, September 1997.

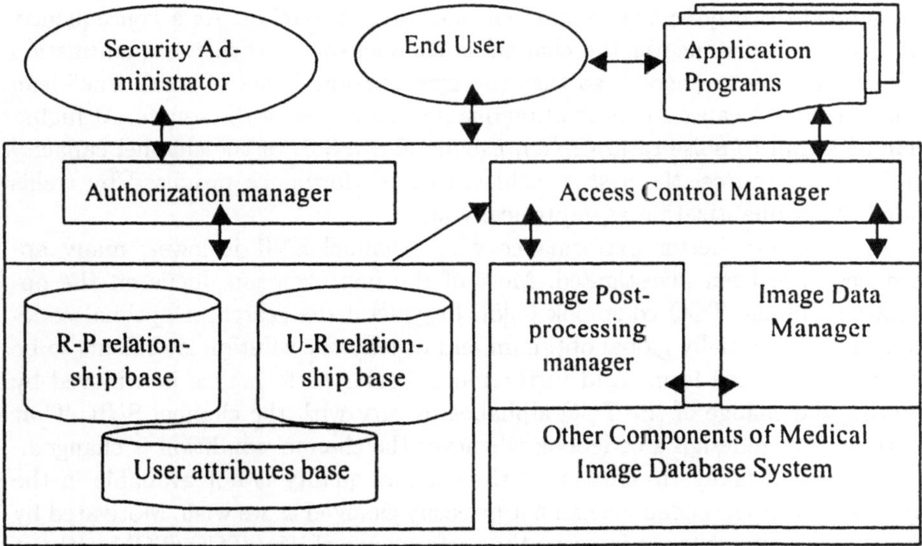

Fig. 2. System architecture for a secure multimedia medical image DBMS

Joint Source/Channel Coding Using Turbo Trellis Codes

Zhaohui Cai, T. H. Cheng, and Chao Lu

Nanyang Technological University, Singapore 639798
ezhcai@ntu.edu.sg,
WWW home page: http://www.ntu.edu.sg/home/ezhcai

Abstract. In this work we present a joint source/channel coding scheme TCQ/TTCM. Compared with its codebook-optimized variations, the scheme can achieve satisfying performance without the modifications of source codebooks. Simulation results show the new scheme can achieve the performance promised by trellis-coded scalar quantization at SNR slightly above the Shannon channel capacity bound.

1 Introduction

Exploiting the duality between modulation for digital communications and source coding, Trellis-coded quantization (TCQ) of memoryless sources is developed for transmmision over the additive white Gaussian noise (AWGN) channel [1]. Fischer and Marcellin further introduce the idea of combining TCQ with trellis-coded modulation (TCM) [2] for joint source/channel coding [3]. The trellis structures for TCQ and TCM are identical and the source encoded output can be mapped directly to the channel encoder output symbol. As a consequence, the Euclidean distance in the channel is commensurate with the quantization noise of the source encoder so that the transmission errors of small Euclidean distance tend to cause small addition quantization noise of the source. At higher channel signal-to-noise ratio (SNR), usually above 3dB of the channel capacity for Guassian source, the system achieves the performance promised by trellis coded scalar quantization asymptotically [3].

To achieve a better performance when channel SNR is lower, many approaches have been investigated. Most of the improvements focus on the optimization of the TCQ codebook [4][5]. In general the search of optimal codebook is not essentially global optimum and usually the solution is difficult to be expressed in closed form. And furthermore, better performance is achieved by allowing the change of the TCQ alphabet to vary with the channel SNR. That is, we have to redesign a codebook whenever the channel condition is changed.

However in many circumstances the channel quality is not available in the encoder side, or the codebook can not be easily changed as we wish. Motivated by this, in this work we try to improve the performance of joint TCQ/TCM without redesign the source codebook. Instead, we propose a joint TCQ/TTCM system which applies turbo trellis-coded modulation (TTCM) [6] to replace the TCM scheme. TTCM is a combination of TCM and turbo codes [7], which retains the important advantages of both schemes. Simulation results on memoryless Gaussian source show that at a moderate channel signal-to-noise ratio (SNR), the overall system performance can be significantly improved: the gap reported in [3] can be reduced to about 1.5dB.

This paper is organized as follows. In section 2 we first discuss the turbo TCM, which is proposed as a natural extension of turbo codes to achieve better bandwidth efficiency; then introduce the joint TCQ/TTCM scheme. The system performance is discussed in section 3 and section 4 gives the conclusion.

2 Joint TCQ/TTCM Scheme

2.1 Turbo TCM

Turbo codes are originally proposed for power-limited channels and apply binary modulation (BPSK) [7]. Since the constituent codes that make up turbo codes are always convolutional codes, a natural extension of these codes is to combine them with Trellis-Coded Modulation schemes, which is so-called TTCM.

Many extensions exist [6][8][9]; here we consider the scheme proposed in [6], which can be easily utilized in higher multi-dimension/higher constellation cases with minor modifications [8]. The 2-D TTCM scheme is depicted in Fig. 1. Please refer to [6][7] for detail description on turbo codes and turbo TCM.

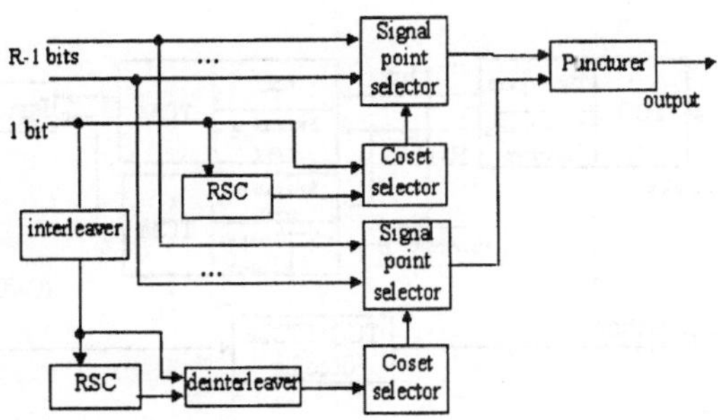

Fig. 1. 2-D Turbo TCM

TTCM retains the advantages of both turbo codes and TCM systems. It can achieve high bandwidth efficiency and the bit-error-rate (BER) performance is close to turbo codes. The gap is within the 1dB of the Shannon capacity limit. With this TTCM channel coding scheme, we will be able to get better source/channel system performance by integrating the TTCM into our joint TCQ/TCM coding scheme.

2.2 Joint TCQ/TTCM Scheme

As in usual joint TCQ/TCM system, our TCQ and TTCM scheme share the same symbol rate. The structure of TCQ/TTCM scheme is shown in Fig. 2. The TCQ source sampling rate is assumed equal to the TTCM symbol rate, i.e., the encoding is at a rate of R bits/sample and transmission is at source rate R bits/symbol. For this purpose, Ungerboeck codes [2] are employed as building blocks in the modulation part in a similar way as binary codes are used in [7]: the two TCM encoders are linked by the interleaver. 2D square constellation (QAM) is used for TTCM coding. To achieve the desired modulation performance, the puncturing of the parity information is carried out symbol-by-symbol, which is not quite straightforward as in the binary turbo codes case.

Compared with TCQ/TCM, an important difference in TCQ/TTCM is the utilization of the convolutional codes. In TCQ/TCM classical non systematic codes are used. To accommodate the natural requirement of turbo codes, rate 1/2 Recursive Systematic Codes (RSC) [7] are used in both TCQ and TTCM.

The trellis structures in TCQ and TTCM may be identical, as in TCQ/TCM. If they do share the same trellis, the upper part of the TTCM encoder in Fig. 2 can be merged into TCQ module except the signal constellation mapping (modulation).

Viterbi algorithm is used in TCQ encoder to determine the minimum distortion path through TCQ trellis [3]. In the decoder, modified Bahl-Jelinek algorithm is used to decode TTCM sequences [6], which is also a symbol-by-symbol maximum a posteriori probability (MAP) decoding algorithm. Of course it can be replaced by some faster algorithms with minor performance degradation, such as iterative soft-output Viterbi algorithm (SOVA) proposed in [10].

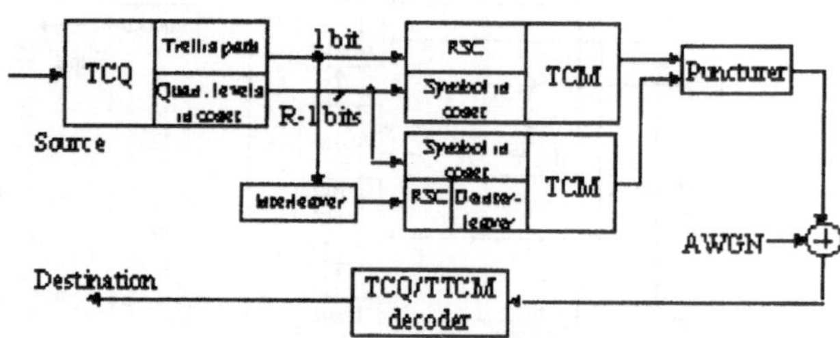

Fig. 2. Proposed joint TCQ/TTCM system, RSC is used in both TCQ and TTCM encoder

2.3 Performance Bound

The signal-to-quantization noise ratio (SQNR) performance bound of the joint TCQ/TTCM system can be determined as follows. For a memoryless zero-mean Gaussian source $N(0, \sigma_x^2)$,

$$D(R) = 2^{-2R}\sigma_x^2 \tag{1}$$

where R is desired coding rate. The capacity for a memoryless, discrete-valued input and continuous-valued output AWGN channel is

$$C = \max_{Q(0),\ldots,Q(N-1)} \sum_{k=0}^{N-1} Q(k) \int_{-\infty}^{\infty} P(z|a_k) \log_2 \frac{P(z|a_k)}{\sum_{i=0}^{N-1} Q(i)P(z|a_i)} dz \quad (2)$$

in bits/symbol [2]. N is the number of discrete input signals $\{a_0, ..., a_{N-1}\}$, $Q(k)$ is the a prior probability of the input a_k; $P(z|a_k)$ is the conditional pdf of received channel output. The value is difficult to calculate directly, usually it can be evaluated by Monte Carlo averaging.

Thus the SQNR performance bound can be evaluated through these two equations by setting $R = C$. The bound here is tighter than the one proposed in [3].

The performance of this joint TCQ/TTCM scheme is discussed in the next section. Our numerical simulation shows significant performance improvement compared with the conventional joint TCQ/TTCM even with a fixed source codebook.

3 Simulation Results

BER performance of TTCM scheme discussed in section 2.1 with $R = 3$ is shown in Fig. 3. The RSC we used here is the one with $G(D) = [1, (1 + D2 + D3 + D4)/(1 + D + D4)]$. The size of the "average" interleaver is $N = 2048$.

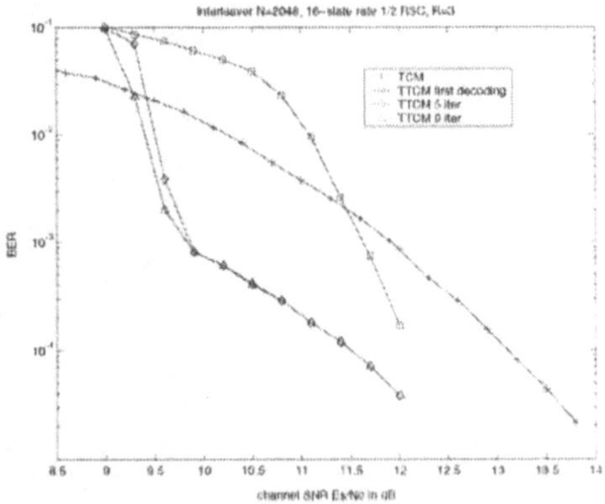

Fig. 3. BER for 2D-TTCM at 3 information bits/symbol

For comparison, TCM case with the same trellis structure is also diagrammed. The simulations show that there always exists a precipitous drop on the BER curve in a SNR region just about 1 dB higher than the channel capacity bound.

Fig. 4 and 5 summarize the performance of the joint TCQ/TTCM system for memoryless Gaussian source with $R = 3$ and 1, respectively. The TCQ reconstruction alphabet is doubled and optimized [3]. Also shown in those figures are the performance bounds and TCM cases with the same trellis. Please note that the performance bounds plotted here are determined by equation (1) and (2); they don't coincide with those in [1], where the channel capacity is determined by $C = \frac{1}{2}\log_2(1 + \frac{S}{N})$ for 1-D modulation. The encoder memories for TCQ and TTCM are both 4.

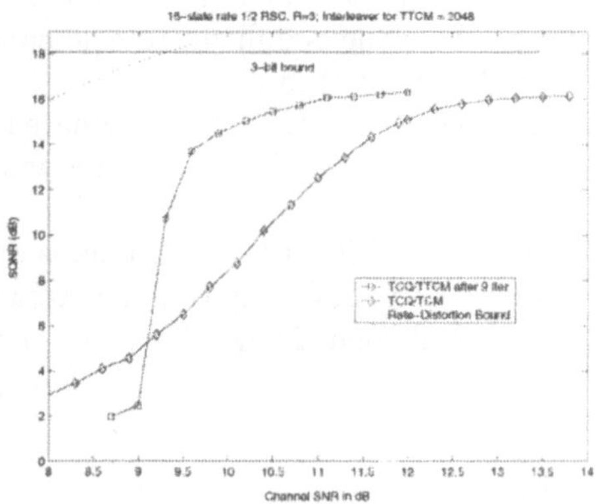

Fig. 4. System performance for a memoryless Gaussian source, R=3

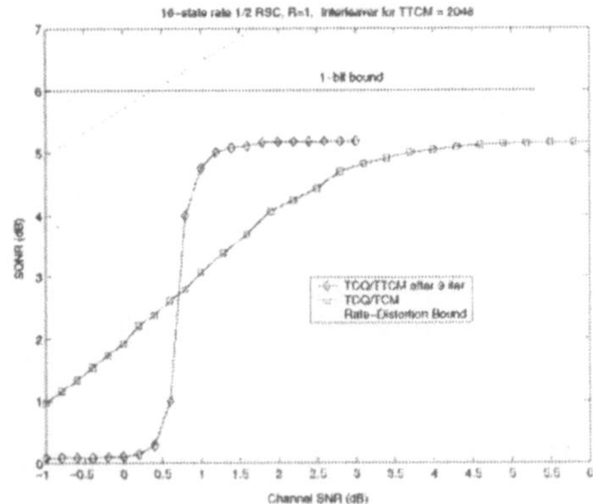

Fig. 5. System performance for a memoryless Gaussian source, R=1

As one might expect, the SQNR increases steeply in a SNR region slightly higher than the channel capacity bound. Compared to TCM case, the improvement is significant when SNR is above the capacity bound. About 3dB gap was reported in [1] for 1D channel. While in this scheme, the gap can be reduced to about 1.5dB for 2D channel when $R = 1$.

4 Summary

In this work we present a joint source/channel coding scheme TCQ/TTCM. Compared with the conventional TCQ/TCM and its codebook-optimized variations, TCQ/TTCM can achieve satisfying performance without the modifications of source codebooks. The overall system performance (SQNR) of this joint TCQ/TTCM is significantly improved at SNR slightly above the Shannon channel capacity bound.

References

1. Marcellin , M.W., Fischer, T.R., "Trellis coded Quantization of Memoryless and Gauss-Markov Sources," IEEE Trans. Commun. **38** (1990) 82–93
2. Ungerboeck, G., "Channel Coding with Multilevel/Phase Signals," IEEE Trans. Inform. Theory **28** (1982) 55–67
3. Fischer, T.R.,Marcellin , M.W., "Joint Trellis Coded Quantization/Modulation," IEEE Trans. Commun., **36** (1991) 172–176
4. Aksu, H. A. and Salehi, M., "Joint Optimization of TCQ-TCM Systems," IEEE Trans. Commun., **44** (1996) 529–533
5. Wang, M. and Fischer, T.R., "Trellis-Coded Quantization Designed for Noisy Channels," IEEE Trans. Inform. Theory, **40** (1994) 1792–1802
6. Robertson, P. and Worz, T., "Bandwidth Efficient Turbo Trellis-Coded Modulation Using Punctured Component Codes," IEEE J Select. Areas Commun., **16** (1998) 206–218
7. Berrou, C., Glavieux, A., and Thitimajshima, P., "Near Shannon Limit Error-Correcting Coding and Decoding: Turbo Codes," Proc. 1993 Int. Conf. Comm., (1993) 1064–1070
8. Cai, Z. H., Subramanian, K.R., and Zhang, L., "DMT Scheme with Multi-dimensional Turbo Trellis Code," Electronics Letters, **36** (2000) 334–335
9. Goff, S. L., Glavieux, A., and Berrou., C., "Turbo Codes and High Spectral Efficiency Modulation," Proc. ICC'94, (May 1994) 645–649
10. Hagenauer, J., Offer, E., and Papke, L., "Iterative Decoding of Binary Block and Convolutional Codes," IEEE Trans. Inform. Theory, **42** (1996) 429–445

An Adaptive Optimal Multimedia Network Transmission Control Scheme

Mei-Ling Shyu[1], Shu-Ching Chen[2], and Hongli Luo[1]

[1] Department of Electrical and Computer Engineering,
University of Miami, Coral Gables, FL 33124, USA
{shyu, hluo}@miami.edu
[2] Distributed Multimedia System Laboratory,
Florida International University, School of Computer Science,
Miami, FL 33199, USA
chens@cs.fiu.edu

Abstract. In this paper, we present a sender-driven adaptive optimal multimedia network transmission control scheme, which takes into account the buffer occupancy and network delay to maximize the utilization of network resources. For this purpose, adaptive network resource optimization with quadratic costs is used in the proposed scheme to provide the minimal allocation of the bandwidth and achieve the maximal utilization of the client buffer. Simulation results show that the transmission rate can be dynamically adjusted at the server according to the changing network delays and buffer packet sizes at the client to avoid the loss of packets, and at the same time to achieve the minimal bandwidth allocation at maximal utilization of the client buffer.

1 Introduction

The development and use of distributed multimedia applications are growing rapidly. Some applications are video-conferencing, video-on-demand, and digital library. To provide cost-effective multimedia services and satisfy the quality-of-service (QoS) of different applications, efficient utilization of network resources is essential. Some dominating parameters for QoS are reliability, bandwidth, packet loss, and jitter [2][5][10]. In general, multimedia applications have highly time-varying bandwidth requirements. These are the requirements that the special characteristics of multimedia applications place on the network.

There are several approaches to address the requirements of multimedia transmission. One approach is the static resource reservation [3][6] schemes based on fixed resource allocation at the connection stage. With large variations in bandwidth requirements, static allocation usually results in considerable wastage of network resources. Another approach is rate adaptation that adjusts the bandwidth used by a transmission connection according to the existing network conditions [11]. Compared with resource reservation, the adaptive approach can better utilize the available network resource that changes with time. There are several types of adaptive control schemes, namely sender-driven, receiver-driven and transcoder-based. Sender-driven schemes require the server to adjust the transmission rate according to changes of the network resources. The most commonly used sender-driven schemes are buffer-based adaptation schemes and loss-based adaptation schemes [8]. Receiver-driven schemes require the receiver to select the transmission according to the network condition [9]. Transcoder-based mechanism requires a gateway at suitable locations to perform different types of transmission [1]. Though much work has been done in the area of adaptive rate control mechanisms [7], the provision of adaptive transmission scheme from the point of view of providing optimal network resource utilization is still a challenge.

In this paper, a sender-driven adaptive optimal multimedia network transmission control scheme is designed. The server can dynamically change the transmission rate according to the occupancy of the buffer along the transmission path. Here we only consider the buffer at the client. At the same time, the bandwidth allocation can be minimized and the utilization of client buffer can be maximized.

The organization of this paper is as follows. Section 2 describes the proposed adaptive network framework. Simulation results are given in Section 3. Conclusions are presented in Section 4.

2 The Proposed Transmission Control Scheme

Fig. 1 gives the proposed adaptive network framework. Let k be the time interval, $Q(k)$ be the packet size in buffer at time interval k, $R(k)$ be the packets transmitted from the server at time interval k, $P(k)$ be the packets arriving at the client buffer at time interval k, $L(k)$ be the packets used for playback at time interval k, and Q_r be the allocated client buffer size at the setup of the connection. Because of the network delay, it is obvious that $P(k)$ is not equal to $R(k)$.

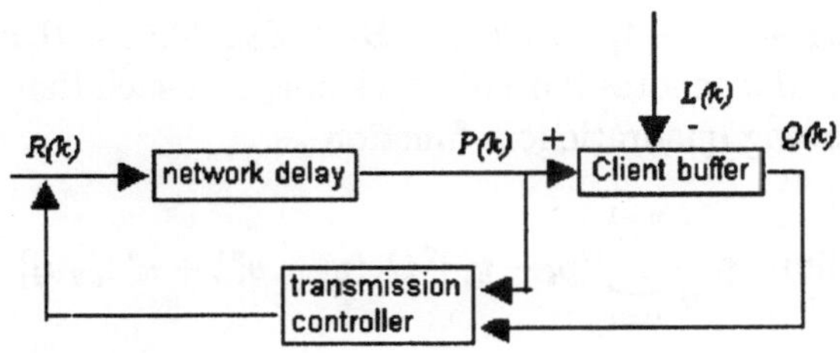

Fig. 1. The proposed adaptive network framework

In order to maximize buffer utilization, $Q(k)$ should be close to Q_r. For simplification, $R(k)$ is referred to as the transmission rate and $L(k)$ as the playback rate at interval k. The optimization goals for the proposed framework are to minimize Q_r-$Q(k)$ and the bandwidth requirements (i.e., to minimize the transmission rate $R(k)$).

Our approach is to design a transmission controller that provides high network resource utilization and good QoS. In this paper, packet loss and delay parameters for QoS are considered. Transmission rates can be changed automatically according to the existing network conditions such as the occupancy of client buffers and network delays, to maximize the buffer utilization and minimize the bandwidth allocation. Because the network delay is irregular due to the unpredictable network traffic, it is not possible to describe it with an exact mathematical model. Therefore, the modeling of network delays is considered as a stochastic process, and adaptive control for quadratic costs is used to design the transmission controller to obtain the optimal transmission rate.

2.1 Optimal Control for Quadratic Costs

For stochastic adaptive control, an ARMAX (autoregressive-moving average with exogenous input) process [4] that models the stochastic input-output feedback control system in discrete time is mainly considered. We can describe its multidimensional version as follows.

Let $A_1, A_2, \ldots, A_p, C_1, C_2, \ldots, C_r$ be m by m matrices and $B_1, B_2, \ldots, B_q$ be m by l matrices. We denote by y_k the m-dimensional output, u_k the l-dimensional control (input), and w_k the m-dimensional driven noise. The ARMAX system is in fact a stochastic difference equation:

$$\begin{cases} y_n + A_1 y_{n-1} + \ldots + A_p y_{n-p} & \\ = B_1 u_{n-d} + B_2 u_{n-d-1} + \ldots + B_q u_{n-d-q+1} & \\ \quad + w_n + C_1 w_{n-1} + \ldots + C_r w_{n-r} & n \geq 0 \\ y_n = w_n = 0, u_n = 0 & n < 0 \end{cases} \tag{1}$$

where $p \geq 0$, $r \geq 0$, and $d \geq 1$. The above equation can also be written in a compact form as follows.

$$A(z)y_n = B(z)u_{n-d} + C(z)w_n \tag{2}$$

where $A(z) = I + A_1 z + \ldots + A_p z^p$, $B(z) = B_1 + B_2 z + \ldots + B_q z^{q-1}$, $C(z) = I + C_1 z + \ldots + C_r z^r$, and z denotes the shift-back operator such that $zy_n = y_{n-1}$.

Consider the following quadratic loss function

$$J(u) = \limsup_{n\to\infty} \frac{1}{n} \sum_{i=0}^{n-1} [(y_i - y_i^*)^\tau Q_1 (y_i - y_i^*) + u_i^\tau Q_2 u_i] \tag{3}$$

where $Q_1 \geq 0$ and $Q_2 \geq 0$ are the weighting matrices and $\{y_i^*\}$ is a bounded deterministic reference signal. The control $\{u_i\}$ is designed to minimize $J(u)$.

2.2 Adaptive Optimal Transmission Controller

Consider the relationships among *Q(k)*, *R(k)*, *P(k)* and *L(k)* (defined earlier). Let *Q(k+1)* denote the buffer packet at the time interval *k+1*. We have the following buffer equation

$$Q(k+1) = Q(k) + P(k) - L(k) \tag{4}$$

P(k) can be represented as a function of the transmission rate *R(k-i)* of the source.

$$P(k) = B_1R(k) + B_2R(k-1) + \ldots + B_dR(k-d+1) \tag{5}$$

where $0 \leq B_i \leq 1$. The value of B_i depends on the percentage of those packets arriving at the kth interval to the packets transmitted at k-i time interval. The value for d can be determined by the timeout limit set by the transmission protocol. In order to catch the unknown network delay, the following model is introduced. With the knowledge of the incoming packets, the parameters of the model are updated at each time interval. That is, the vector $B = [B_1B_2 \ldots B_d]$ is updated. So we have

$$Q(k+1) = Q(k) + B_1R(k) + B_2R(k-1) + \ldots + B_dR(k-d+1) - L(k) \tag{6}$$

In order to maximize the utilization of client buffer and minimize the allocated bandwidth, the function J is set as the optimization index function.

$$J(u) = \limsup_{n\to\infty} \frac{1}{n} \sum_{i=1}^{n} [(Q(i) - Q_r)^2 + R(i)^2] \tag{7}$$

where n is the total number of time intervals. In addition, the proposed transmission controller runs at a discrete time interval of T, which means the feedback information is sent back to the server every T seconds.

3 Simulation Results

In order to evaluate the effectiveness of the proposed framework, different playback rates are generated randomly between 0.1MB per second (MBps) and 1MBps to simulate the actual playback scenario. Fig. 2 shows the changes of the transmission rates, packet sizes in the client buffer, playback rates, and network delays. Assume the allocated client buffer size is 2MB and it is run within the interval [1, 100] with the increment of one interval. Since there is no accurate function to describe the network delays, a function of the vector $B = [B_1B_2 \ldots B_i \ldots]$ is selected to roughly indicate the network delays. B_i is generated randomly to simulate the changing network delay. When B_i is increasing, more packets are arriving, which indicates the network delay at that time is decreasing. On the other hand, when B_i is decreasing, fewer packets are arriving indicating the network delay is increasing. The network delay displayed in Fig. 2

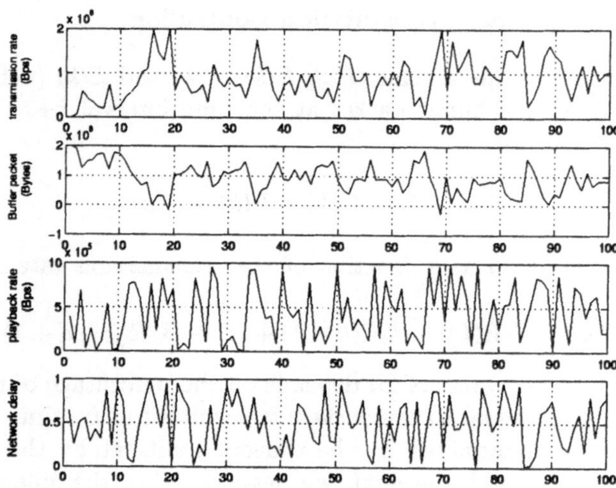

Fig. 2. Various transmission rates with different packet sizes in client buffer, playback rates, and network delays. The network delay is displayed as a weight value in the range of (0,1].

is a weight value in the range of (0,1], and a large value indicates large network delay.

The transmission rate for the next time interval is calculated based on the buffer packet, playback rate, and network delay information at the current time interval. In Fig. 2, the transmission rate displayed at a certain time interval is calculated at the end of this time interval and is actually the rate for the next time interval. The buffer packet displayed is the value when the current time interval is over.

As can be seen from this figure, the transmission rate is adjusted according to the buffer occupancy. When the buffer begins to fill up, the transmission rate is reduced. When the buffer turns to empty, the transmission rate is increased. Moreover, the transmission rate also changes with the network delay. For example, at the time interval 40, the playback rate is relatively high, buffer packet is medium, and the network delay is small, the transmission rate for the next interval (i.e., at time interval 41) is relatively low. The reason is that it takes a relatively short time for the packets to arrive at the client buffer to satisfy the playback requirement and not to overflow the buffer due to the small network delay. At the time interval 90, playback rate is low, buffer packet is low, and network delay is large. Therefore the transmission rate for the next time interval is high so that the packets can still arrive at the client buffer in time after a large network delay to satisfy the playback requirement.

The advantage of the proposed transmission control scheme is that the transmission rate of the server is dynamically adjusted according to the unpredictable network delay. The client buffer can be fully utilized under limited bandwidth requirement to provide jitter free playback. In our approach, the packet size in the buffer will never exceed the allocated buffer size, thus avoiding the overflow in client buffer and the loss of packets. In addition, the proposed transmission control scheme is easy to implement.

4 Conclusions

In this paper, a sender-driven adaptive optimal multimedia network transmission control scheme is presented. Under the proposed scheme, the server can dynamically adjust the transmission rate according to the buffer occupancy and network delay. An adaptive network framework is introduced to capture the changing network delays and adaptive optimal control with quadratic costs is used to achieve the maximal utilization of client buffer and the minimal allocation of bandwidth. Instead of giving a fixed transmission rate, the transmission rate can be determined dynamically to achieve the optimal utilization of network resources. The simulation results show that the proposed transmission control scheme can maintain high buffer utilization and minimum bandwidth allocation, and at the same time avoid buffer overflow.

References

1. Amir E., McCanne S., and Katz R.: An Active Service Framework and its Application to Real-time Multimedia Transcoding. SIGCOMM Symposium on Communications Architecture and Protocols, Vancouver, BC, Canada (1998)
2. Blakowski G. and Steinmetz R.: A Media Synchronization Survey: Reference Model, Specification, and Case Studies. IEEE Journal on Selected Areas in Communications, **14(1)** (1996) 5-35
3. Braden R., Zhang L., Herzog S., and Jamin S.: Resource Reservation Protocol (RSVP) - Version 1 Functional Specification. Internet Engineering Task Force, Internet Draft (1997)
4. Chen H. and Guo L.: Identification and Stochastic Adaptive Control. Birkhauser Boston (1991)
5. Grosky W., Jain R., and Mehrotra. (eds): The Handbook of Multimedia Information Management. Prentice-Hall Professional Technical Reference (1997) 335-363
6. Hui J. Y.: Resource Allocation for Broadband Networks. IEEE Journal on Selected Areas in Communication, **6(9)** (1988) 1598-1608
7. Jain, R.: Congestion Control and Traffic Management in ATM Networks: Recent Advances and a Survey. Computer Networks & ISDN Sys., **28(13)** (1996) 1723-1738
8. Kanakia H., Mishra P., and Reibman A.: An Adaptive Congestion Control Scheme for Real-time Packet Video Transport. SIGCOMM Symposium on Communications Architecture and Protocols, San Francisco, California (1993) 20-31
9. Mcanne S., Jacobson V., and Vetterli M.: Receiver-driven Layered Multicast. SIGCOMM Symposium on Communications Architectures and Protocols, Stanford, CA (1996)
10. Roberts, J., Mocci, U., and Virtamo, J. (eds.): Broadband network Teletraffic. Final Report of Action Cost 242, Springer (1996)
11. Wang X. and Schulzrinne H.: Comparison of Adaptive Internet Multimedia Applications. IEICE Trans. Commun., **E82-B(6)** (1999) 806-818

Effects of Sampling Rate and Pose Error on Volume Reconstruction by Space Carving

Alireza Nasiri Avanaki, Babak Hamidzadeh, and Faouzi Kossentini

University of British Columbia
Department of Electrical and Computer Engineering
Vancouver, BC, Canada V6T 1Z4
{alin, babak, faouzi}@ece.ubc.ca

Abstract. Effects of sampling rate and pose error on silhouette-based volume reconstruction are addressed in this paper. An account of importance of choosing silhouette samples (viewpoint distribution) is given. A new viewpoint distribution method is introduced and its performance is compared to a traditional method empirically. We also investigate effects of sampling rate variation and different levels of pose error on silhouette-based reconstruction quality. We observed that in presence of considerable pose error, increase of sampling rate cannot enhance reconstruction quality. We also observed that reconstruction process in higher sampling rates is more sensitive to pose error.

1 Introduction

Reconstruction of a three-dimensional (3-D) object from monocular video (frames are images of the object taken from different viewpoints), requires: (1) Estimation of the viewpoint for (or pose of the object in) each image. (2) Fusion of those images into a 3-D model. The quality of reconstruction in this paradigm depends on several factors, namely:

1. Pose error.
2. Volume quantization.
3. Image quantization.
4. Spatial sampling rate.
5. Choice of viewpoints.
6. Object concavity.

The system we proposed for 3-D information retrieval from monocular video [1], uses a pose estimator and a silhouette-based volume reconstruction method. For quality assessment of reconstructed 3-D models, in this paper we address sensitivity of this volume reconstruction method to choice of viewpoints, spatial sampling rate and pose error.

Some of the factors given above are discussed in the literature. Recent studies on sampling requirements of the Light Field Rendering [2], a method for fusion of images into a 3-D profile of the object, is given in [3] and [4]. To the best of authors' knowledge there is no similar work for sampling requirement of silhouette-based volume reconstruction method, although a class of studies (e.g. [5]) address the problem of camera viewpoint control for optimization of some local quality criterion.

Object concavities are a source of reconstruction error, since silhouette-based reconstruction methods are inherently able to make a model of the object up to the visual hull of the object only [6].

Our literature search for other issues of reconstruction quality assessment failed to produce any result. From the above mentioned issues of silhouette-based volume reconstruction quality analysis, we will explore effect of pose error, spatial sampling rate and viewpoint selection/distribution in this paper.

To this aim, we first introduce a new uniform viewpoint distribution scheme and demonstrate its good functionality by few experiments with different sampling rates. We then investigate variation of reconstruction quality with changes in spatial sampling rate and levels of pose error. We show that in presence of considerable pose error, sampling rate increase can result in inferior reconstruction quality. In the last section we mention a number of concluding remarks and some ways to extend this work.

2 Viewpoint Distribution

The capture phase of 3-D volume reconstruction consists of taking images of the subject from different viewpoints. In this section we introduce a new uniform distribution of viewpoints for 3-D volume reconstruction and compare it to traditional viewpoints distribution through an experiment.

Consider the object is located at the center of a large sphere. And each viewpoint is corresponding to a point on that sphere. We call this sphere the "focal sphere". Note that for each viewpoint on focal sphere, there is another viewpoint so that the segment connecting these two viewpoints is a diameter of the focal sphere. Assuming orthographic projection, the silhouette of the object is the same from these two viewpoints, i.e. one of these viewpoints is redundant as long as silhouette-based volume reconstruction is concerned. So all of the information of object's silhouette can be captured from viewpoints located on only half of the focal sphere, which we call "focal hemisphere".

In previous works ([7] and [8]), the object is placed on a turn table. While the table is turning, images are taken by a stationary camera. Changes in camera elevation result in viewpoint distribution depicted in Fig. 1 (left). Note that this sampling scheme is denser near the pole of the focal hemisphere, so it is not uniform.

To distribute the viewpoints evenly, one should have the same density of viewpoints on different spots of the focal hemisphere. To this aim, we first flattened a differential surface element of the focal hemisphere. Viewpoints are taken as nodes of a grid projected onto the flattened hemisphere. In other words, the angular distance of neighboring viewpoints should be scaled by $1/\cos x$; x denotes the latitude on which the viewpoints are placed. Thus less number of viewpoints

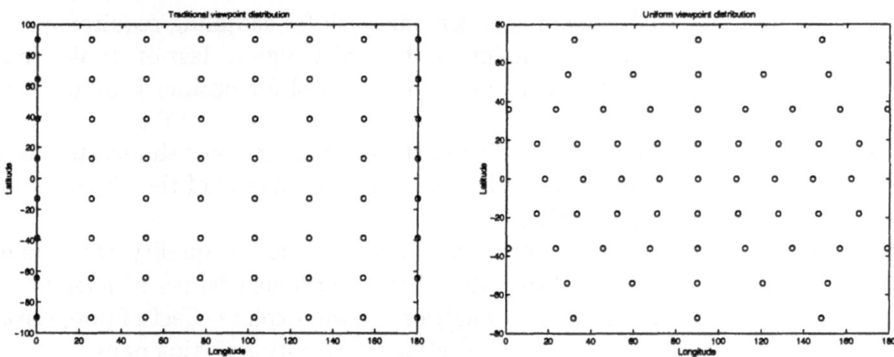

Fig. 1. Viewpoint distributions: traditional (left) and uniform (right).

can be inserted near the pole, giving almost uniform viewpoint distribution all over the focal hemisphere. An example of such viewpoint distribution is depicted in Fig. 1 (right).

To show better performance of the new sampling scheme, we used both traditional and the new sampling scheme to take samples for silhouette-based reconstruction of a sphere. The outcome is given in Fig. 2 (left). As shown in the graph, for a certain reconstruction quality, considerably fewer samples are needed using our proposed sampling scheme. Reconstruction quality is taken as the volume difference between reconstructed and the ideal sphere normalized by the volume of the reconstructed sphere. The metric is estimated by a function of standard deviation and mean value of the radius of reconstructed sphere.

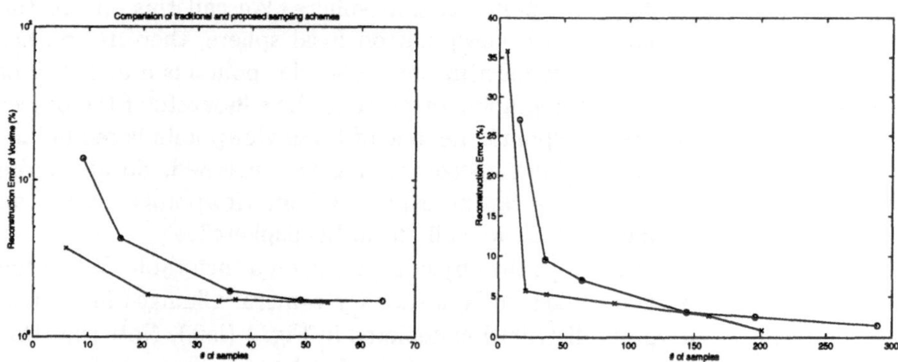

Fig. 2. Comparison of reconstruction quality using traditional ('o') and uniform ('x') distribution of viewpoints in reconstruction of a sphere (left) and a prism (right).

We ran the experiment again using a prism as the object. In this experiment reconstructed volumes are XORed with the representation of the object in the same voxelized space (a view of that is given in Fig. 3) where the experiment is performed. The result (Fig. 2 (right)) is taken as the number of voxels remained after XOR operation, normalized by the number of voxels comprising the object.

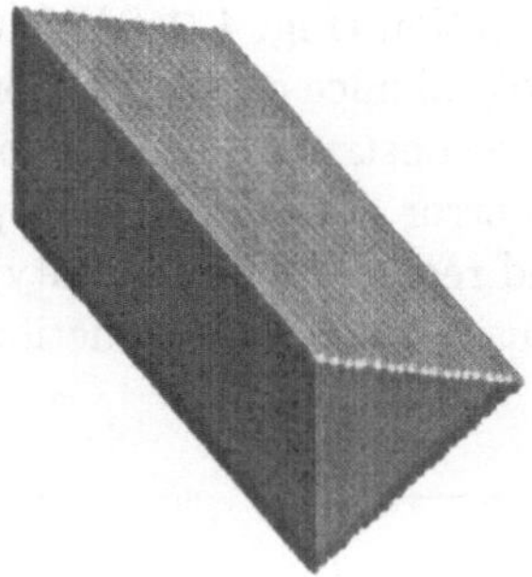

Fig. 3. The prism used in experiments in voxelized space.

Please note that reconstruction of a sphere and a prism are different [1] since sphere is a smooth object (i.e. infinite number of samples is required for exact reconstruction), while a prism is not. The interesting point is that new sampling scheme outperforms traditional scheme in both situations.

3 Effects of pose error and sample rate

In this section we discuss effect of pose error and sampling rate variation on silhouette-based reconstruction quality. We modeled error of the pose estimator under study [1] by a white random process with uniform distribution ranging from ± 0.2 to ± 10 degrees, depending on working condition of pose estimator (e.g. grid size, image resolution, depth quality/resolution, etc.). We also vary sampling rate to see how many samples are sufficient for a specific level of pose error and reconstruction quality.

Uniform sampling scheme is used, since we proved its superior performance over traditional sampling (see Section 2). The object used is a prism (Fig. 3). We compared reconstructed volume with the prism itself in voxel space and took the normalized difference as the measure for reconstruction error. While this metric is performing well, comparison of silhouettes of the reconstructed object and the original object from several (a random set for example) viewpoints can be another metric subject to test in future experiments. The carving is performed over a cube of $201 \times 201 \times 201$ by silhouettes of size 512×512. The same pseudo-noise pattern is used in all of the experiments (i.e. only noise level is changed) to limit random effect of noise on the results.

The result is given in Fig. 4 (left). For small levels of pose error i.e. ± 0.2, ± 0.5 and ± 1 degrees (the lines stick together on the graph), the effect of pose error is negligible (comparing to error-less pose graph in Fig. 2 (right)). That means errors of less than ± 1 degrees are tolerable by silhouette-based volume reconstruction, at least for simple rough objects like prisms. The reason is that the factors affecting reconstruction process (see Section 1) dominate pose error when it is small.

For higher values of error, firstly we see deviation from small error level curves. The interesting observation (Fig. 4 (left)) is that in high noise levels, increase of sampling rate cannot enhance reconstruction quality. For example, with error of ±10 degrees in pose, reconstruction quality becomes almost independent of sampling rate, while with error of ±5 degrees in pose an inverse relation between number of samples and reconstruction quality is observed, although some increase in sampling rate caused some reconstruction degradation.

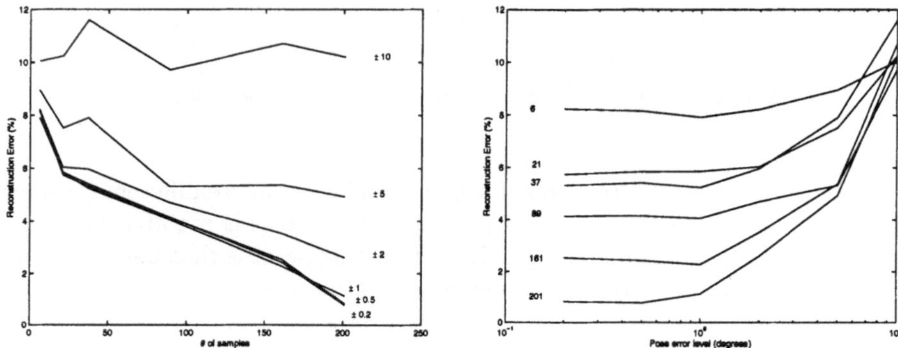

Fig. 4. Comparison of reconstruction quality in various levels of pose error and sampling rates. Left: pose error (degrees) used as parameter. Right: number of samples used as parameter.

The result is also depicted in Fig. 4 (right) from another point of view. Here we observe that reconstruction with large number of samples is more sensitive to pose error, i.e. reconstruction degradation with increase of pose error level is faster for large number of samples. That is, since the total error of reconstruction is small, a small error in pose degrades the quality considerably. Also it can be seen when pose error is large enough (±10 degrees), quality is degraded regardless of the sampling rate: all curves approach a point with increase of pose error. Small and local deviation of some of curves from the trend of quality degradation by error increase is because of random nature of pose error.

4 Conclusions

In this paper we introduced a new sampling scheme for silhouette-based volume reconstruction. For the same number of samples, we had better reconstruction quality when we took samples using new sampling scheme. We investigated effects of spatial sample rate (number of silhouettes used for reconstruction) and pose error (amount of deviation between estimated pose for a silhouette used for reconstruction and its real pose). We demonstrated that (see Section 3): (1) Low levels of pose error (up to ± 1 degree) are tolerable by silhouette-based reconstruction for simple rough objects. (2) High levels of pose error cannot be compensated by increase in sampling rate. (3) Reconstruction with high sample rate is more sensitive to error in pose.

Some ways to extend this work are studies on: (1) Effect of random sampling scheme. (2) Effect of silhouette quantization. (3) Effect of volume quantization. (4) Other metrics for reconstruction quality.

References

1. A. Nasiri Avanaki, B. Hamidzadeh, and F. Kossentini, "Multi-objective retrieval of object pose from video," in *Proc. of IEEE Conf. on Tools with Artificial Intelligence*, November 2000, pp. 242–249.
2. M. Levoy and P. Hanrahan, "Light field rendering," in *Computer Graphics Proceedings*, 1996, pp. 31–42.
3. S. C. Chan and H.-Y. Shum, "A spectral analysis for light field rendering," in *Proc. of International Conf. on Image Processing*, September 2000, vol. 2, pp. 25–28.
4. Z. Lin and H.-Y. Shum, "On the number of samples needed in light field rendering with constant-depth assumption," in *Proceedings of Computer Vision and Pattern Recognition*, June 2000, pp. 588–595.
5. W. Niem and M. Steinmetz, "Camera viewpoint control for the automatic reconstruction of 3d objects," in *Proc. of International Conf. on Image Processing*, 1996, pp. 655–658.
6. A. Laurentini, "The visual hull concept for silhouette-based image understanding," *IEEE Trans. on Pattern Recognition and Machine Intelligence*, vol. 16, no. 2, pp. 150–162, 1994.
7. E. E. Hemayed and A. A. Farag, "Object modeling using space carving," in *Proc. of International Conf. on Image Processing*, September 2000, vol. 2, pp. 760–763.
8. R. Szeliski, "Rapid octree construction from image sequences," *CVGIP: Image Understanding*, vol. 58, no. 1, pp. 23–32, 1993.

A Tree-Based Model of Prosodic Phrasing for Chinese Text-to-Speech Systems

Weijun Chen[1,2], Fuzong Lin[1,2], Jianmin Li[1,2], and Bo Zhang[1,2]

[1] Department of Computer Science and Technology, Tsinghua University, 100084 Beijing, China
{cwj, lfz, ljm, zb}@s1000e.cs.tsinghua.edu.cn
[2] State Key Laboratory of Intelligent Technology and Systems, Tsinghua University, 100084 Beijing, China

Abstract. This paper describes a tree-based model of prosodic phrasing for Chinese text-to-speech (TTS) systems. The model uses classification and regression trees (CART) techniques to generate the decision tree automatically. We collected 559 sentences from CCTV news program and built a corresponding speech corpus uttered by a professional male announcer. The prosodic boundaries were manually marked on the recorded speech, and word identification, part-of-speech tagging and syntactic analysis were also done on the text. A decision tree was then trained on 371 sentences (of approximately 50 min length), and tested on 188 sentences (of approximately 28 min length). Features for modeling prosody are proposed, and their effectiveness is measured by interpreting the resulting tree. We achieved a success rate of about 93%.

1 Introduction

Assigning appropriate phrasing in TTS systems is very important both for naturalness and for intelligibility, particularly in longer sentences. Generally speaking, fluent spoken language is not produced in a smooth, unvarying stream. People tend to group words into phrases and place short pauses between them. Furthermore, variation in phrasing can change the meaning hearers assign to the utterances of a given sentence. Researchers have shown that the relative size and location of prosodic phrase boundaries provides an important cue for resolving syntactic ambiguity [1].

Traditional research on the location of phrase boundaries has focused primarily on the relationship between prosodic structure and syntactic structure, and uses some sort of syntactic information to predict prosodic boundaries (often in the form of heuristic rules) [2-3]. However, such hand-crafted rules systems are notoriously difficult to write, maintain and adapt to new domains and languages. To avoid these problems, recently efforts have been concentrated on acquiring phrasing rules automatically by training self-organizing procedures on large prosodically labeled corpora. For these data-driven methods, the prediction of boundary location is seen as a classification problem, and the main differences between them lie in two aspects: the learning model and the feature set. The primary learning techniques currently used include hidden markov models [4], neural networks [5], classification and regression trees (CART) [6-8] and transformational rule-based learning (TRBL) [9]. And although a good feature set can help to improve the performance, finding suitable features is work intensive and language dependent. There are three types of features commonly used: part-of-speech (POS) sequences, temporal information, and syntactic information.

For Chinese, we know that precise syntactic analysis of the sentence structure is difficult and large amount of computation required. So most of the previous TTS systems just identify the words in the input texts and no more prosodic information is extracted for further processing [10]. In this paper, we describe a tree-based model of prosodic phrasing for Chinese TTS systems. CART techniques are used to construct the decision trees automatically from sets of continuous and discrete feature variables. Compared with others, the greatest advantage of CART is thought to be its high comprehensibility in the prediction process. The aim of this paper is twofold. First, we construct a large speech corpus and annotate the transcribed text for modeling Chinese prosody. Especially we annotate not only part-of-speech information, but also syntactic information. Second, we propose linguistic features which seem to affect Chinese prosody, and evaluate them by interpreting the resulting tree. We believe that these evaluation will help us better understand the relationship between syntax and prosody.

2 CART Techniques

In recent years CART techniques [11] have gained in popularity due to their straightforward interpretation of the resulting trees. By exploring the questions used in the nonterminal nodes, we can evaluate the effectiveness of the features, and get some insight into a given problem. The basic principle of CART is summarized as follows:

The training set is defined as $L = \{(\boldsymbol{x}_n, y_n), n = 1, 2, \ldots, N\}$, where $\boldsymbol{x}_n$ is the feature vector of a data point, y_n is the class label, and N is the total amount of the data. Note that the component x_i of a feature vector $\boldsymbol{x}$ can be M-valued categorical or real-valued. And the construction of a CART decision tree depends on four fundamental elements:

- A set of binary questions. For a real-valued feature variable x_i, questions take on the form "Is $x_i \leq c$?"; For a M-valued categorical variable x_i, and if it takes values in a set Q, questions take on the form "Is $x_i \in S$?", where S is a subset of Q. This set of questions generates a set of splits for each node t. Those sample cases in t answering "yes" go to the left descendant node and those answering "no" to the right.
- A splitting rule for finding an optimal split at any node. An impurity function is defined which describes the class probability distribution of the node, and the optimal split is the one that maximizes the reduction in the node impurity over all the possible binary splits.
- A stop-splitting rule. The simplest rule is to set a threshold $\beta > 0$, and declares a node t terminal if the optimal split results in a decrease in impurity less than β.
- A prediction rule for assigning every terminal node to a class. The rule simply chooses the class that occurs most frequently among the sample cases in the node.

The initial stopping rule is simple and unsatisfactory, generally some more sophisticated techniques are used, such as V-fold cross-validation. And then the typical procedure of constructing a tree can be divided into four steps: First, an overly large tree T_{max} is grown on the entire training data L by using a greedy algorithm that associates subsets of L with each node in the tree and successively partitions the data into finer and finer subsets with corresponding optimal splits. Second, a sequence of subtrees is formed from T_{max} using the cost-complexity pruning method, $T_0 = T_{max}, T_1, \ldots, T_k, \ldots, T_K = \{t_1\}$, ranging from the full tree to just the root node. Third, V auxiliary trees are grown on different portions (90%, if $V = 10$) of the data, and they are also pruned and tested on the remaining portions (10%). Last, two methods are proposed to select the final subtree. Under the 0SE (0 standard error) rule, the subtree with the minimum cross-validation error estimate $R^{cv}(T_k)$ is selected, while under the 1SE rule, the preferable one is the minimum-size tree whose estimate is less than $R^{cv}(T_k) + \mathrm{SE}(R^{cv}(T_k))$.

3 Experiments and Results

3.1 Corpus

For a data-driven method, the scale and quality of the corpus is important. Since there is no suitable corpus available for modeling Chinese prosody, we collected 559 sentences (of approximately 78 min length) from CCTV news program and built a corresponding speech corpus uttered by a famous male announcer. We found that the transcription of punctuation did not seem to exactly match the original written text, and the punctuation information is also used in some models [7][8], so we collected the original script of each piece of news from newspapers and other sources. And then, the annotation of this data for analysis was conducted in the following steps:

First, although a Chinese word is composed of one to several characters, a Chinese sentence is in fact a string of characters without blanks to mark the word boundaries. Therefore the first step is to identify the words in the text corpus. This task was accomplished by using a simple segmentation algorithm and the errors were corrected.

Second, we obtained the part-of-speech information of each word via Bai's POS tagger [12], whose output had been modified to adapt to the characteristic of prosody. We elaborately designed 72 POS's which belong to 20 word classes,

Third, the syntactic analysis was done manually. To describe the structure of a sentence, we propose a simplified Chinese grammar. The grammatical functions we considered include subject, predicate, object, modifier and complement. The syntactic phrasal units include noun phrases, prepositional phrases, adjectival phrases, etc.

Lastly, we labeled the speech prosodically by hand, noting location and type of boundaries and accents. We labeled two levels of boundary, major and minor; in the analysis presented below, however, these are collapsed to a single category.

3.2 Prosodic Phrasing Using CART Techniques

We define the problem of prosodic phrasing as follows [4]: the input sentence consists of a sequence of words and between each pair of adjacent words is a word juncture

$<w_i, w_{i+1}>$, where w_i represents the word to the left of the juncture and w_{i+1} represents the word to the right. There are a number of juncture types and the task of a phrasing model is to assign the most appropriate type to each juncture. The experiments in this paper use two types of juncture, boundary and non-boundary.

We selected 17 features which seem to affect Chinese prosody, most of them are from [6][7].

- *Pos*{1-4}: A part-of-speech window of four around the juncture, $<w_{i-1}, w_i, w_{i+1}, w_{i+2}>$. Note that we have 72 POS's, and the number of possible splits for such a variable is 2^{71}-1, thus, examining all the splits becomes computationally prohibitive. Our simple solution is that only the POS's belonging to the same word class are allowed to combine together. Another method is proposed latter in this paper;
- *Sbs*: The smallest syntactic constituent dominating both w_i and w_{i+1};
- *Sll*: The largest syntactic constituent dominating w_i, but not w_{i+1};
- *Srl*: The largest syntactic constituent dominating w_{i+1}, but not w_i;
- *Ltw, Ltc*: Total words and characters in the sentence;
- *Lsw, Lsc*: Distance from start to w_i, in words and characters;
- *Lew, Lec*: Distance from w_{i+1} to end, in words and characters;
- *Lllw, Lllc*: The size of *Sll*, in words and characters;
- *Lrlw, Lrlc*: The size of *Srl*, in words and characters.

3.3 Improvements

We try to improve the performance of our method in two aspects.

First, we added five more features. (1) *Acc*{0-1}: whether w_i or w_{i+1} bear an accent or not. (2) *Gbipos*: the probability of a boundary occurring within a POS bigram. Our previous experiments had confirmed its effectiveness in predicting the location of prosodic boundaries [13]. (3) *Lrrw, Lrrc*: the size of *Sbs* minus the size of *Sll*.

Second, we propose a simple and straightforward method to solve the problem of handling the categorical variable with a large number of categories (72, in our case). This algorithm can find the optimal split in polynomial time.

- Suppose the POS's of the sample cases at a node t consist of $P_1, P_2, \ldots, P_m$, and their corresponding cases are in $C_1, C_2, \ldots, C_m$.
- Calculate the probability of a boundary occurring among C_i (i = 1, 2,..., m), sort these probabilities in ascending order and rearrange the order of P_i (i = 1, 2,..., m), then we get a new POS sequence $P_1', P_2', \ldots, P_m'$.
- Select an optimal split from $\{P_1'\}, \{P_1', P_2'\}, \ldots, \{P_1', P_2', \ldots, P_{m-1}'\}$.

We trained the trees on 371 sentences (8170 word junctures) and tested on 188 (4084 junctures). The experimental results under the 1SE rules are summarized in Table 1. The results reported in [6-8] are also presented for comparison. In the table, N is the total amount of the training data, $|\tilde{T}_k|$ is the number of terminal nodes in T_k, $R^{cv}(T_k)$ is the cross-validation misclassification estimate and $R^{ts}(T_k)$ is the error rate on the test data.

Table 1. Performance of CART-based model of prosodic phrasing

	N	$\|\widetilde{T}_k\|$	$R^{cv}(T_k)$ (%)	$R^{ts}(T_k)$ (%)
Basic CART	8170	28	10.7	11.1
Improvements	8170	22	6.9	7.2
Wang	3677	6	10	-
Hirschberg	19473	14	5.8	-
Lee	2286	8	13.9	15.2

Table 1 shows that the new measures improved the performance remarkably, and the result of our experiment, 93.1% cross-validated accuracy and 92.8% accuracy on the test data, is competitive with that for Spanish prosodic phrasing where the average cross-validated accuracy is 94.2% [7]. Furthermore, our experiment did not include the boundaries between sentences because virtually there is always a boundary at the end of a sentence. If these boundaries were also excluded in [7], the baseline accuracy, i.e. the accuracy using the initial rule that assigns "non-boundary" to each word juncture, would be 92.7%, which is much higher than ours (77.6%).

Part of the decision tree by 1SE rule is illustrated in Fig. 1. The notion u / v by nodes denotes that v is the total amount of data arriving at the node and u is the amount of data corresponding to the label (YES or NO) of the node. The arcs linking nodes are labeled with the questions selected for splitting.

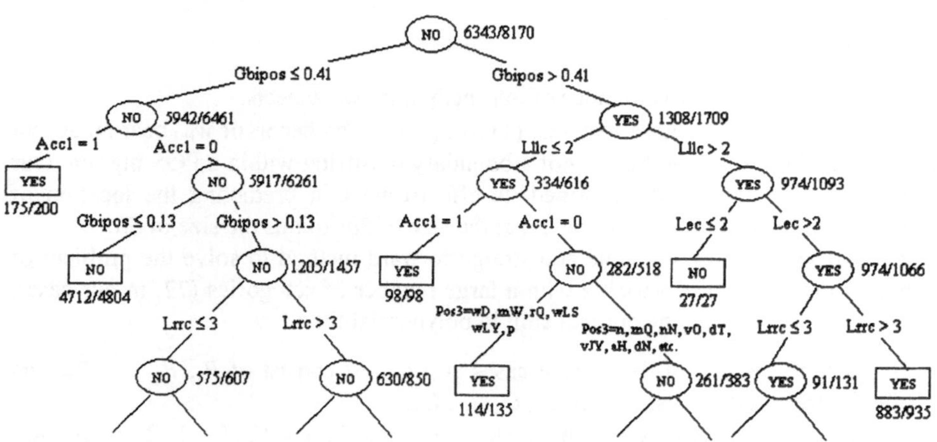

Fig. 1. Decision tree for prosodic phrasing under the 1SE rule

Taking a look at the decision nodes (nonterminal nodes) of the tree, we immediately note that five features are principally used: *Gbipos*, *Lllc*, *Acc*1, *Lec* and *Lrrc*. Especially *Gbipos* is the single best predictor of phrase boundaries, the word junctures with a *Gbipos* less than 0.13 tend overwhelmingly (4712/4804) to be correctly predicted as not containing boundaries. At the nodes that use *Lllc* and *Lrrc*, the boundaries occur more frequently when the value is large. This phenomenon is consistent with our intuition that people tend to pause for a short interval before and after a long syntactic constituent is encountered. At the node that use *Lec*, it is less likely that boundary will occur if the value is small enough. Furthermore, we find that accent location is also used in phrase boundary prediction, which is different from the result reported in [9], but we think this may be due to the difference in the language.

4 Conclusion

We have described a tree-based model of prosodic phrasing for Chinese TTS systems. The model uses CART techniques to generate the decision trees automatically. we collected 559 sentences and built the speech corpus. The prosodic boundaries were manually labeled, and word identification, POS tagging and syntactic analysis were also done on the text. Then we proposed 22 features and measured their effectiveness by interpreting the resulting tree. We found that the probability of a boundary occurring within a POS bigram, the size of syntactic constituents and the accent location are more effective than others. For ongoing research to further improve the performance in modeling prosody, we are experimenting to investigate the effectiveness of other learning techniques such as TRBL and SVM (Support Vector Machine).

References

1. Ostendorf, M., Wightman, C.W.: Parse Scoring with Prosodic Information: an Analysis/Synthesis Approach. Computer Speech and Language, 7 (1993) 193–210
2. Bachenko, J., Fitzpatrick, E.: A Computational Grammar of Discourse-Neutral Prosodic Phrasing in English. Computational Linguistics, 16 (1990) 155–170
3. Willemse, R., Boves, L.: Context Free Wild Card Parsing in a Text-to-Speech System. In: ICASSP, (1991) 757–760
4. Taylor, P., Black, A.W.: Assigning Phrase Breaks from Part-of-Speech Sequences. Computer Speech and Language, 12 (1998) 99–117
5. Muller, A.F., Zimmermann, H.G., Neuneier, R.: Robust Generation of Symbolic Prosody by a Neural Classifier Based on Autoassociators. In: ICASSP, (1996) 1285–1288
6. Wang, M.Q., Hirschberg, J.: Automatic Classification of Intonational Phrase Boundaries. Computer Speech and Language, 6 (1992) 175–196
7. Hirschberg, J., Prieto, P.: Training Intonational Phrasing Rules Automatically for English and Spanish Text-to-Speech. Speech Communication, 18 (1996) 281–290
8. Lee, S., Oh, Y.H. Tree-Based Modeling of Prosodic Phrasing and Segmental Duration for Korean TTS Systems. Speech Communication, 28 (1999) 283–300
9. Fordyce, C.S., Ostendorf, M.: Prosody Prediction for Speech Synthesis Using Transformational Rule-Based Learning. In: ICSLP, (1998) 682–685
10. Chou, F.C., Tseng, C.Y., Chen, K.J.: A Chinese Text-to-Speech System Based on Part-Of-Speech Analysis, Prosodic Modeling and Non-uniform Units. In: ICASSP, (1997) 923–926
11. Breiman, L., Friedman, J., Olshen, R., Stone, C.: Classification and Regression Trees. Belmont, CA: Wadsworth (1984)
12. Bai, S.H.: The Study and Realization of Statistics Based Approach to Tagging Chinese Corpus. Master thesis, Tsinghua University, (1992) (In Chinese)
13. Chen, W.J., Lin, F.Z., Li, J.M., Zhang, B.: Prosodic Phrase Analysis Based on Probability and Statistics. Computer Engineering and Applications, 37 (2001) 10–12 (In Chinese)

Detecting Facial Features on Image Sequences Using Cross-Verification Mechanism

Peng Zhenyun[1], Hong Wei[1], Liang Luhong[1],Xu Guangyou[1] and Zhang Hongjian[2]
[1] Dept. of Computer Science & Technology, Tsinghua University, Beijing, 100084, China
{xgy-dcs@mail.tsinghua.edu.cn}
[2] Microsoft Research, China, 5F, Beijing Sigma Center, No.49, Zhichun Road, Haidian District, Beijing, 100080, China

Abstract: An approach is presented to detect facial features on image sequences. Face regions are first detected across the sequence, then a PCA-based feature detector for still images is used to detect facial features on each single frame until the resulted features of three adjacent frames don't change significantly. Given a frame with correct features, the features of its neighbor frames are first detected by the still-image feature detector, then verified and corrected by using the smoothness constraint and the planar surface motion constraint. Experiments have been performed on image sequences taken under different environments, and prove the presented method to be quite robust and efficient over variable poses, ages and illumination conditions.

1 Introduction

Most of the existing facial feature detection methods[1][2][3] are performed on single frame images. Because one single frame cannot provide enough information on changes of poses, lightning conditions, background and expressions, these feature detectors likely lose features or extract false features. The key problem is that once the features are detected, no enough evidence can be got from the one single image to verify the results.

The presented approach targets to detect two irises, two nares and two mouth corners on video segments using the cross-verification mechanism over frames. Faces are first detected by using template matching and artificial neural network (ANN). On the resulted face regions, a PCA-based feature detector for still images is then used to detect facial features on each single frame until the resulted features of three adjacent frames don't change significantly. These three frames are defined as base frames whose features are considered to be correct. Given a base frame, the features of its neighbor frames are first estimated according to the known features, then detected by the still-image feature detector, finally verified and corrected by using the smoothness constraint and the planar surface motion constraint.

2 Facial Feature Detection on Still Images

2.1 Face Detection

As presented in [4], the face detection algorithm consists of two parts (Fig.1): template matching and ANN. Two types of templates - eye-pair and face itself, are used one by one in searching for face candidates. To verify the resulted faces, two three-layer perceptrons (MLPs) are used independently so as to exclude most of the false alarms.

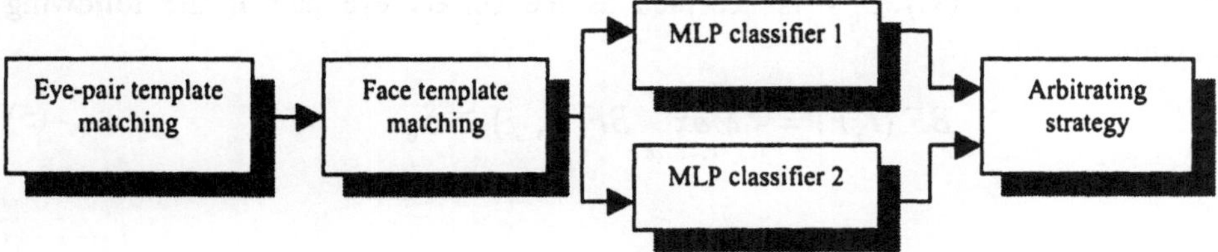

Fig.1. Flow chart of the face detector

2.2 Representation of Eyes in Eigen-eye Space

As stated in [5], eyes in the training set and the target image are first calibrated using the homogenous transform so that all eye regions under consideration have the same position and size. Then a total of l eigen vectors $(u_1, u_2, \ldots, u_l)$ are calculated from training set $\{i_1, i_2, \ldots, i_m\}$ based on the Singular Vector Decomposition theorem.

Let $p \in R^n$ be the normalized input eye pair of size $w \times h$. It can be projected onto the eigen-eye space as:

$$p = \sum_{i=1}^{l} c_i u_i = U(c_1, c_2, \ldots, c_l)^T \quad . \tag{1}$$

Because U is orthogonal, we have,

$$(c_1, c_2, \ldots, c_l)^T = U^T p \quad . \tag{2}$$

Therefore, p is mapped to the eigen-eye space as $p' = \sum_{i=1}^{l} c_i u_i$. The representation error is measured by the correlation between p and p' :

$$\delta(p, p') = \frac{E(pp') - E(p)E(p')}{\sigma(p)\sigma(p')} \quad . \tag{3}$$

2.3 Eyes Detection

By using the Hough transform-based eyes detection algorithm we presented in [6], k candidate irises $C_1, C_2, \cdots, C_k$ can be first found. Let $C_1, C_2, \cdots, C_k$ be the nodes of a complete graph G. A benefit function $BF(i,j)$ for the edge between C_i and C_j is defined as following:

$$B(i,j) = (k_1\delta(p_{ij}, p'_{ij}) + k_2\gamma(p_{ij}, p'_{ij}))*D(i,j)*A(i,j)\ . \tag{4}$$

The iris pair (C_l, C_r) is accepted as the correct eye pair if the following condition holds.

$$BF(l,r) = \underset{i,j=1,2,\ldots k}{Max} BF(i,j) \geq \delta_0\ . \tag{5}$$

2.4 Moth and Nose Detection

First, the mouth region can be roughly bound from the eye positions according to the anthropometrical measurements. Then the integral projection method is used for locating both the mouth corners and nares.

3 Facial Feature Detection in Image Sequences

3.1 Overview of the Cross-verification Mechanism

The process of feature detection in an image sequence is carried out as following:

1. Find three adjacent frames such that the features detected using the above method don't change significantly over these 3 frames. The features of these frames are considered as correct. A frame is defined as a base frame if its features have been correctly detected.
2. Given a base frame, features of its neighbor frame are detected in the following way:
   (1) Detection is only performed within the regions estimated according to the known features;
   (2) The resulted features are verified using the motion smoothness constraint; and,
   (3) If the resulting features don't comply with the smoothness constraint, new features are estimated using the planar surface motion constraint.

3.2 Motion Smoothness Constraint

Because the motion of the head is very smooth in the vedio segments, distances among features in two adjacent frames are constrained in a small range. The distances among features we used are shown in Fig. 2.

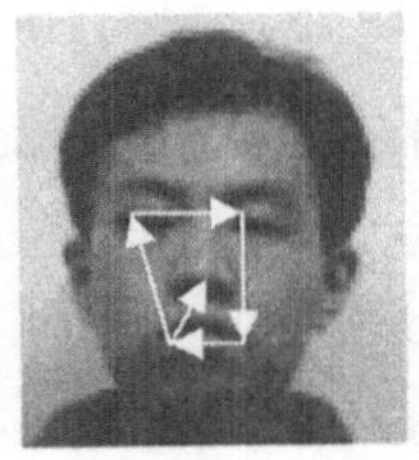

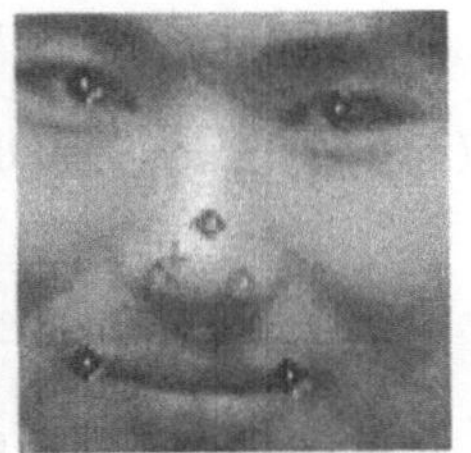

Fig.2. Distance between features **Fig.3.** An example of the estimated features

3.3 Planar Surface Motion Constraint

If the resulting features don't follow the smoothness constraint, new features have to be estimated using the planar surface motion constraint. Even if the resulting features can follow the smoothness constraint, these features might not be acurately. We use planar surface motion constraint to locate the features accurately.

The six features – 2 irises, 2 nares and 2 mouth corners can be considered as on a planar surface. Under perspective projection, these feature points satisfy a parametic 2-D motion model. Suppose $x=(x_1,x_2)$ be a feature point of the base frame, $x_0=(x_{01},x'_{02})$ to a feature point of the target frame, and $x'=(x'_1,x'_2)$ be the estimated corespondent feature point of the target frame. Then, we have:

$$x'_2=\frac{a_4 x_1+a_5 x_2+a_3}{a_7 x_1+a_8 x_2+1}\ . \tag{6}$$

$$x'_1=\frac{a_1 x_1+a_2 x_2+a_3}{a_7 x_1+a_8 x_2+1}\ . \tag{7}$$

Where, $a_1,\ldots,a_8$ are pure parameters. They can be estimated by the following equation:

$$\begin{bmatrix} x_1 & x_2 & 1 & 0 & 0 & 0 & -x_1x'_1 & -x_2x'_1 \\ 0 & 0 & 0 & x_1 & x_2 & 1 & -x_1x'_2 & -x_2x'_2 \end{bmatrix} A=\begin{bmatrix} x_1' \\ x_2' \end{bmatrix}\ . \tag{8}$$

$$A=[a_1\ \ a_2\ \ a_3\ \ a_4\ \ a_5\ \ a_6\ \ a_7\ \ a_8]^T\ . \tag{9}$$

To solve this equation, there must be at least 4 correspondent points. In the face feature case, there are 6 correspondent points between the base frame and the target frame. To select 4 correspondent points from 6 correspondent points, we have $C_6^4=15$ different combinations of 4 correspondent points. In order to obtain the most optimized combination, A is calculated under each combination of 4 correspondent points. The 15 different A are A1....A15.

Using each A, all the 6 feature point x' can be estimated from base frame using (6) and (7). The optimized pure parameters Aopt can be obtained by the following rule.

$$A_{opt} = \{A_i \mid Min(Err(A_i))\}, i = 1-15 \quad . \tag{10}$$

Where Err(Ai) is the error of this estimation that can be obtained by the follow formula.

$$Err(A_i) = Max(| x'^j (A_i) - x_0^j |), j = 1-6 \quad . \tag{11}$$

After obtaining Aopt, we can estimate the more accurate feature points by the parametic 2-D motion model. Fig. 3 shows an example. In this example, the nares are initially located at the positions of red cross, then which are corrected to the more accurate locations (indicated by diamonds) by using planar surface motion constraint.

4 Experimental Results and Conclusion

30 image sequences are tested for evaluating the performance of the presented algorithm. Each sequence contains of 50 frames. The training set includes 80 sample images. By using the PCA method, 55 eigen eye pairs are remained as the base of the eigen-eye space. All tested images are not included in the training set. The experimental results are concluded in table 1. The average computation time is 5 sec./frame. Fig. 4 shows part of the experimental results of two image sequences.

In our early work with still images [5][6], there are two kinds of errors: (1) eyes cannot be found because of false segmentation; and (2) mouth or nose are detected wrongly even if the eyes position is correct. By introducing the cross-verification mechanism, 80% of these kinds of errors are corrected.

The above study shows that cross-verification based on multiple threads is crucial to feature detection tasks in computer vision. One single thread, such as gray distribution or frequency spectrum, can only provide identical evidences, which cannot be used to verify the results. In our further research, we will try to use the cross-verification in each step of the whole detection process.

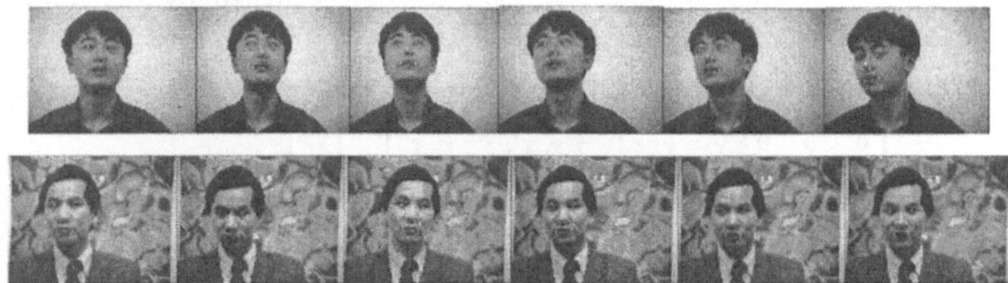

Fig.4. Part of the experimental results of an image sequence

No.	Correct Ratio of Irises	Correct Ratio of Nares	Correct Ratio of Mouth Corners	Overall Correct Ratio	No.	Correct Ratio of Irises	Correct Ratio of Nares	Correct Ratio of Mouth Corners	Overall Correct Ratio
1	97.62%	100.00%	100.00%	97.62%	16	100.00%	96.55%	100.00%	96.55%
2	94.74%	100.00%	100.00%	94.74%	17	93.10%	100.00%	96.55%	93.10%

3	93.33%	93.33%	93.33%	93.33%	18	100.00%	97.50%	100.00%	97.50%
4	96.97%	96.97%	96.97%	93.94%	19	100.00%	100.00%	100.00%	100.00%
5	97.37%	92.11%	92.11%	89.47%	20	100.00%	100.00%	100.00%	100.00%
6	92.00%	96.00%	96.00%	88.00%	21	100.00%	100.00%	100.00%	100.00%
7	96.00%	92.00%	96.00%	92.00%	22	100.00%	93.75%	100.00%	93.75%
8	95.35%	100.00%	95.35%	95.35%	23	100.00%	100.00%	100.00%	100.00%
9	100.00%	94.29%	100.00%	94.29%	24	100.00%	100.00%	100.00%	100.00%
10	100.00%	97.44%	100.00%	97.44%	25	100.00%	92.31%	100.00%	92.31%
11	95.35%	100.00%	100.00%	95.35%	26	90.48%	97.62%	92.86%	90.48%
12	100.00%	100.00%	100.00%	100.00%	27	100.00%	100.00%	100.00%	100.00%
13	100.00%	100.00%	100.00%	100.00%	28	100.00%	100.00%	100.00%	100.00%
14	100.00%	100.00%	100.00%	100.00%	29	97.83%	100.00%	97.83%	97.83%
15	100.00%	100.00%	97.62%	97.62%	30	100.00%	100.00%	100.00%	100.00%
Average						**98.00%**	**98.00%**	**98.49%**	**96.36%**

Table 1. Detection results of 30 image sequences

Reference

1. D. Reisfeld and Y. Yeshuran, "Robust detection of facial features by generalized symmetry," Proc. 11th Int. Conf. on Patt. Recog., 1992, pp. 117-120.
2. A. L. Yuille, D. S. Cohen and P. W. Halinan, "Feature extraction from faces using deformable templates," Proc. IEEE Computer Soc. Conf. on computer Vision and Patt. Recog., 1989, pp.104-109.
3. C. L. Huang and C. W. Chen, "Human facial feature extraction for face interpretation and recognition," Pattern Recognition, Vol. 25, No. 12, 1992, pp. 1435-1444.
4. Ai Haizhou, Liang Luhong and Xu Guangyou, "A General Framework for Face Detection, " Proc. 3rd Int. Conf. on Multimodal Interfaces, Vol.1948, 2000, pp.119-126.
5. Peng Zhenyun, Xu Guangyou and Zhang Hongjiang, "Detecting Facial Features on Images with Multiple Faces," Proc. 3rd Int. Conf. on Multimodal Interfaces, Vol.1948, 2000, pp.191-195.
6. Peng Zhenyun, You Suya and Xu Gunagyou, "Locating facial features using thresheld images," in the Third Int. Proc. of Signal Processing, Vol.2, 1996, pp.1162-1166

Rapid Object Tracking on Compressed Video

Hanfeng Chen, Yiqiang Zhan, Feihu Qi

Department of Computer Science & Engineering, Shanghai Jiao Tong University
Huashan Rd. 1954 Shanghai, 200030 P.R.China
Tel(Fax): (86-21)62932089
E-mail: chf011@mail1.sjtu.edu.cn

Abstract. Rapid object tracking algorithm is proposed in this paper. The algorithm operates on the DC sequence and motion vectors. Full-frame decompression is not necessary to extract the DC sequence and motion vectors from compressed video sequence, which speeds up the tracking process remarkably. More than one moving objects can be tracked in a video sequence simultaneously. Global motion compensation based on compressed streams is applied to track moving objects whenever there is global motion. Experimental results show that the proposed algorithm is effective in real-time object tracking on MPEG-2 video sequence.

1 Introduction

Object tracking means tracing the progress of objects (or object features) as they move about in a visual scene [1]. There is an urgent need of object tracking on video sequence for monitoring, video retrieval and scene analysis. Real-time operation is a major requirement in many object tracking applications. For compressed video, processing typically starts with decompression which is time consuming.

In this paper, a rapid object tracking algorithm which operates on compressed video sequence is proposed. Thresholded difference images of neighboring DC images [7] are obtained before tracking. Based on these difference images and block motion vectors which can be extracted conveniently from MPEG-2 compressed video sequence without full-frame decompression, moving objects are segmented and tracked through region growth and merging. Global motion compensation based on compressed video is processed to track moving objects in videos from mobile camera.

The paper is structured as follows. Section II introduces previous works on object tracking. Section III describes the DC sequence extracted from MPEG-2 compressed video sequence. The object segmentation algorithm is presented in section IV, while the tracking algorithm is described in section V. The experimental results are shown in Section VI. Finally, section VII draws the conclusions.

2 Review

There have been considerable work reported on object tracking [2-6, 8]. Soon and Kwang [3] present a method of tracking multiple objects of known geometry using multiple cameras. In their paper, multiple cameras are used to improve the accuracy of the estimated posture parameters. Philippe and Andre [2] propose a method to track a rigid object whose geometry is known.

Fabrice and Frederic [4] use spatio-temporal segmentation technique to get moving objects in the scene. In [5], absolute differencing and thresholding detect motion regions in the image. By tracking individual objects through the segmented data, a symbolic representation of the video is generated in the form of a directed graph describing the objects and their movement. Jakub and Sarma [6] describe a system for real-time tracking of people in video sequences, where the input is video data acquired by a stationary camera.

Our approach is most closely related to the work of Yeo and Liu [7], but their main concern is detecting scene changes on compressed video. Lorenzo and Alessandro [8] describe a tool for object tracking, notes insertion, and information retrieval, applicable to MPEG-2 sequences. In such a system, the images areas corresponding to the tracked objects should be identified manually by the information creator (called marker).

3 DC Sequence from MPEG-2 Coded Sequence

Images of MPEG-2 are divided into blocks of 8×8 pixels. *DC image*[8] is a spatially reduced image in which intensity of pixel (i, j) is the average intensity of the (i, j) block of the original image. Sequence formed in such manner is called *DC sequence*. For a block, the DC coefficient of its 2-D Discrete Cosine Transform (DCT) is related to the average intensity. I-frames and P-frames should be considered respectively to get the DC coefficients.

I-frames are intra-frame DCT encoded. From the definition of DCT, we have the relation[10]:

$$DCT(0,0) = \frac{1}{8}[\sum_{i=0}^{7}\sum_{j=0}^{7} f(i,j)] \tag{1}$$

That is, intensity of pixel (i,j) of DC image from I-frame is one eighth of the DC coefficient *DCT*(0,0) of the (i,j) block of the I-frame.

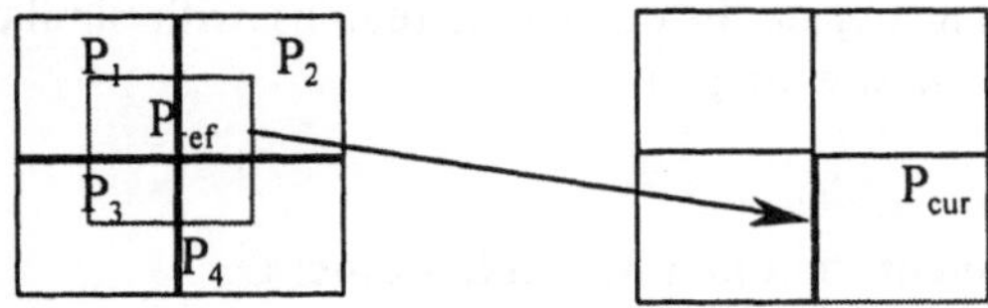

Fig,1. The sketch map of the reference block and current block

P-frames allow motion-compensated forward predictive coding with reference to a previous I- or P-frame. Fig,1 illustrates the block matching between neighboring P-frames. Thus, DC-image of current P-frame can be estimated from that of reference frame. The relation between DC coefficient of current block P_{cur} and those of $P_1,\ldots, P_4$ can be approximated as [7]

$$[DCT(P_{cur})]_{00} \approx \sum_{i=1}^{4} \frac{h_i w_i}{64} [DCT(P_i)]_{00} \tag{2}$$

where h_i and w_i are the height and width of the overlap of P_{ref} with P_i. Experimental results show that the approximation is reasonable.

4 Object Segmentation

Moving objects should be segmented firstly from the background to track them. In the case that the camera is stationary, the background does not change. The regions belongs to moving objects can be signed by thresholding the difference of neighboring DC images. Then, moving objects can be detected through regions merging technique. However, camera motions exist in many cases. Then, global motion compensation is necessary to detect the regions belongs to moving objects.

4.1 Object Segmentation in a Stationary Camera

The object segmentation algorithm in this paper includes three steps. Firstly, the difference images of temporally neighboring DC images are thresholded and a series of binary images are obtained throughout the video stream. The fact that value of pixel (i,j) in current binary image equals to 1 means that block (i,j) of current frame is a probable part of a moving object. The second step is region growing in the binary images. The growing starts at pixels with the value of 1. The value of pixel (i,j) is set as 1 if one of its spatially neighboring pixels has been set as 1. The *neighboring* here is defined as left, right in row and top, bottom in column. The result of region growing is a series of interconnected regions in the DDC image. Then, a series of rectangles are used to locate these regions. A rectangle of an interconnected region is defined as the minimal rectangle which can hold the interconnected region. The third step of region segmentation is region merging. A moving object may be divided into several moving regions in one frame because of noise and similarity between the background and moving objects. It is necessary to merge these regions into one region to track the moving object. In our work, regions with similar motion vectors and spatially close regions are merged.

4.2 Object Segmentation in a Movable Camera

Camera motion causes global motion in the frames which will lead to illusive moving objects (Fig.4(b)). Thus, global motion compensation is performed before the difference image of two neighboring DC images is gotten. A lot of wok has been done in global motion parameters estimation. Our work adopts the four parameters camera motion estimation model presented by [9]. Camera motion is modeled as

$$\begin{pmatrix} V_X \\ V_Y \end{pmatrix} = \begin{pmatrix} a_1 & -a_2 \\ a_2 & a_1 \end{pmatrix} \begin{pmatrix} X \\ Y \end{pmatrix} + \begin{pmatrix} a_3 \\ a_4 \end{pmatrix} \tag{3}$$

where (X,Y) is the locate of a pixel in the previous frame and (V_X, V_Y) is the associated motion vector caused by the global motion over one frame period and the parameters a_1, a_2, a_3 and a_4 are related to the camera motion zoom, roll, tilt and pan. Parameter a_1 can be estimated from block motion vectors extracted from MPEG-2 compressed video by

$$a_1 = \frac{1}{K_X + K_Y}\left[\sum_{\left|\frac{\partial}{\partial X}V_X - \overline{m}\right| < T+1} \frac{\partial}{\partial X}V_X + \sum_{\left|\frac{\partial}{\partial Y}V_Y - \overline{m}\right| < T+1} \frac{\partial}{\partial Y}V_Y\right] \tag{4}$$

where K_X and K_Y are the numbers of the $\frac{\partial}{\partial X}V_X$ and $\frac{\partial}{\partial Y}V_Y$ satisfying $\left|\frac{\partial}{\partial X}V_X - \overline{m}\right| < T+1$ and $\left|\frac{\partial}{\partial Y}V_Y - \overline{m}\right| < T+1$ respectively and

$$\overline{m} = \frac{1}{2K}\sum_{(X,Y)\in\Omega}\left(\frac{\partial}{\partial X}V_X + \frac{\partial}{\partial Y}V_Y\right) \tag{5}$$

Threshold T is an experiential parameter which can be set as

$$T = \frac{1}{2K}\sum_{(X,Y)}\sqrt{\left(\frac{\partial}{\partial X}V_X - \overline{m}\right)^2 + \left(\frac{\partial}{\partial Y}V_Y - \overline{m}\right)^2} \tag{6}$$

where Ω is the set of block centers and K is the number of blocks. a_2 can be estimated on the same way. From (3), a_3 and a_4 can be obtained.

5 Object Tracking

The result of object segmentation is a serial of moving objects located by respective rectangles. It is necessary to analysis the trajectories of segmented moving objects to track them. In our work, directed graph [6] is adopted to describe the trajectories. In Fig,2, an undirected line is related with a frame, a node represents a moving object in the frame and a directed edge describes the motion information. In creating the directed graph, a directed edge is created between two nodes if two objects represented by the two nodes in neighboring frames hold similar numbers of pixels and centers of them have similar positions in the same reference frame. In the directed graph, then, several directed path representing the trajectories of moving objects can be obtained.

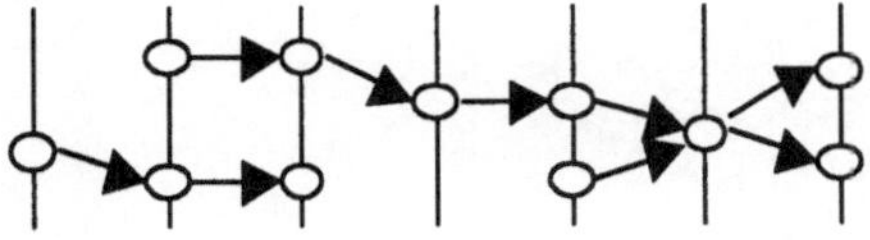

Fig.2. Directed graph

6 Experimental Results

A one minute MPEG-2 compressed sequence from stationary camera is used in object segmentation experiment fistly. Object segmentation is performed with the algorithm mentioned on section IV-A not only on compressed video but also on decompressed video. The experimental results are listed on **Table.1**, which shows that performing of object segmentation on compressed video is much faster than on decompressed video. Fig,3. displays several frames in which moving objects are noted with rectangles.

Table.1 Object segmentation on compressed video and decompressed video

	Video length (frame)	Speed (frame/s)
Compressed Video	1514	42.8
Decompressed Video	1514	12.5

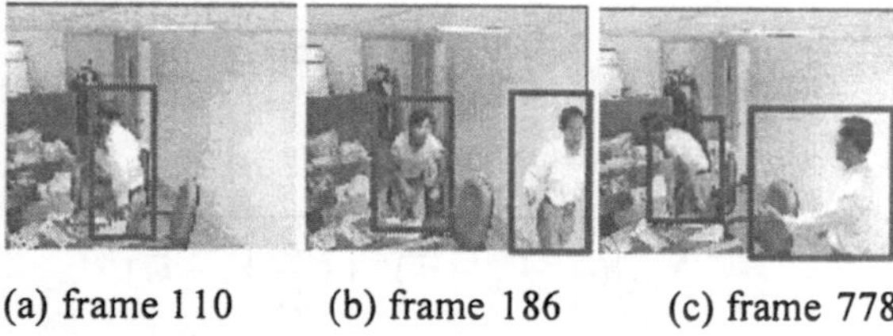

(a) frame 110 (b) frame 186 (c) frame 778

Fig.3. Moving objects tracking in a stationary camera

In global motion compensation experiments a one minute MPEG-2 compressed sequences are used. The camera pans from right to left and one people moves from right to left. Experimental results of compensation obtained by the method showed in section IV-B are displayed in Fig.3. Global motion compensation is performed in Fig.4(c) but not in Fig.4(b). The results indicate that illusive moving objects can be reduced greatly by global motion compensation.

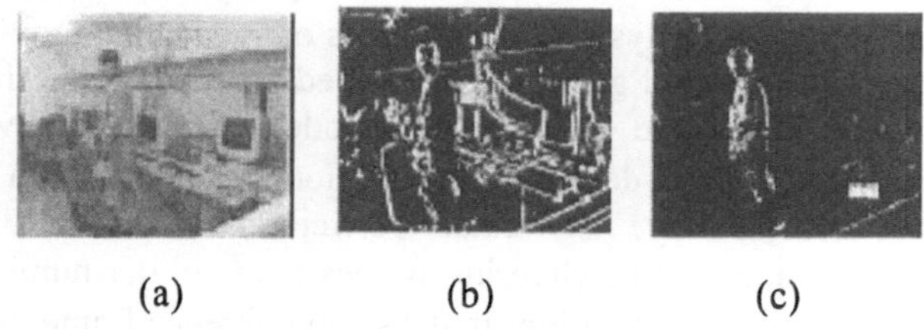

(a) (b) (c)

Fig,4. Global motion compensation

Fig,5. Trajectories of moving objects

We perform the object tracking on a one minute MPEG compressed sequence. Fig.5. shows the tracking results. The trajectories are presented on the top-right corner of the interface, where trajectories with different colors are related to different moving objects. What lie on the bottom-left corner are stations of moving objected. Three moving objects are tracked on this sequence.

7 Conclusion

We have shown in this paper how moving objects can be segmented and tracked on MPEG-2 compressed video sequence. Only DC coefficients and block motion vectors of compressed video are used in the segmentation and tracking. The processing is real-time because of the small data size and no necessary of full-frame decompression. Moving objects can be tracked not only in case that the camera is stationary but also in case that there is global motion. Multi-objects can be tracked simultaneously since object segmentation is performed by regions merging and directed graph is adopted in tracking the trajectories of moving objects.Many thresholds used in this paper are obtained manually by experiments. In future work, adaptive methods should be developed to setup these thresholds for unsupervised object tracking. Further more, morphological image processing methods could be introduced before region growing in section IV-A to reduce the effect of noise.

Reference

[1] Ziad M.Hafed: Object Tracking, IEEE Potentials, Aug./Sep. 1999, pp.10-13.

[2] Philippe Gerard, Andre Gagalowicz: Three dimensional model-based tracking using texture learning and matching, Pattern Recognition Letters 21 (2000), 2000,1095-1103.

[3] Soon Ki Jung, Kwang Yun Wohn: A model-based 3-D tracking of rigid objects from a sequence of multiple perspective views, Pattern Recognition Letters 19(1998) 499-512, 1998.

[4] Fabrice Moscheni; Frederic Dufaux; Murat Kunt: Object Tracking Based on Temporal And Spatial Information, IEEE International Conference on Acoustics, Speech and Signal Processing - Proceedings v4(1996), May 1996, pp.1914-1917.

[5] Jonathan, D.Courtney: Automatic Video Indexing Via Object Motion Analysis, Pattern Recognition, Vol. 30, No.4, 1997, pp.607-625.

[6] Jakub Segen, Sarma Pingali: A Camera-Based System for Tracking People in Real Time, Proceedings of ICPR '96, 1996, pp.63-67.

[7] Boon-Lock Yeo, Bede Liu: Rapid Scene Analysis on Compressed Video, IEEE Transactions on Circuits and Systems for Video Technology, Vol.5, No. 6, Dec. 1995, pp.533-544.

[8] Lorenzo Favalli, Alessandro Mecocci, Fulvio Moschetti: Object Tracking for Retrieval Application in MPEG-2, IEEE Transactions on Circuits And Systems for Video Technology, Vol.10, No.3, April 2000.

[9] H.Nicolas, C.Labit: Global Motion Identification For Image Sequence Analysis And Coding, IEEE International Conference on Acoustics, Speech and Signal Processing v4(1991), May 1991,pp. 2825-2828.

[10] A.Murat Tekalp: Digital Video Processing, Tsinghua University Press, 1998, pp.380.

Design and Implementation of the Multimedia Cluster System Based on VIA

Si-Yong Park Seung-Ho Park Ki-Dong Chung

Department of Computer Science, Pusan National University
{sypark, shpark, kdchung}@melon.cs.pusan.ac.kr

Abstract. We have designed and implemented Multimedia Cluster System based on VIA(VMCS). VMCS is 2-layered architecture consisting of a control server and storage servers. The control server manages the multimedia data, processes user requests and controls VIA. Storage servers store and manage the multimedia data. In particular, it is based on the novel VIA(Virtual Interface Architecture) protocol to reduce the message transmission overhead that is the general drawback in the cluster systems.

1. Introduction

As the distributed computing has developed with high performance hardware and network, operating system has been added the functions for distributed computing. For this trend, cluster system has also developed. Cluster system can distribute and process user's request but has the drawback of message processing overhead between the cluster nodes [1]. Existing network protocols such as TCP/IP have very heavy software protocol stack because they have the flow control, error recovery, and other several functions to contact to computers which connected to various network types in LAN or WAN. The overhead of this heavy protocol stack results in the long transfer latency between cluster nodes. Actually, TCP/IP protocol stack has latency more than 100μsec while network hardware for the high-speed networks such as ATM (Asynchronous Transfer Mode), Myrinet, Gigabit Ethernet and Compaq Servernet has latency less than 10μsec [2]. And, the TCP/IP protocol is not proper for the cluster system that is based on the high-performance network such as SAN (System Area Network) guaranteeing the low error rate[6].

2. Related works

Cluster system requires fast message passing protocol to enhance its performance. Commonly used message and data transferring methods are message passing , distributed shared memory, U-Net , VIA and so on[3].

This work was supported by Pusan National University Research Grant.

• MPI (Message Passing Interface) and PVM (Parallel Virtual Machine)

Since existing high-performance servers had their own message passing libraries, there was not enough portability between the heterogeneous systems. To deal with this problem, PVM and MPI have been developed[4].

• U-Net

U-Net was developed by Cornell University. To remove the operation of kernel, protocol processing had performed in kernel and end-point storing the message are positioned in user-level. It provides Virtual view for network adapter to directly access network adapter from the user-level[5].

• VIA

VIA is a new protocol for SAN. It reduces overhead of context switching occurred in heavy software protocol stack such as TCP/IP and data copy overhead from user-level to kernel-level. TCP/IP performs data copy from user area to kernel area to protect system and to share resources for reliable data transmission. In this case, context switching and data copy from user-level buffer to kernel-level system buffer cause large overhead. As a result, transmission latency occurred by the heavy protocol stack which can be reduced and the high-performance communication is possible [6]. But, VIA has some drawbacks. Because VIA provides a few simple transmission functions to reduce the message passing overhead caused in heavy software protocol stack, application programmer should add the control modules such as the flow control and the error checking modules that is contained in TCP/IP protocol stack for the stable network[6][7].

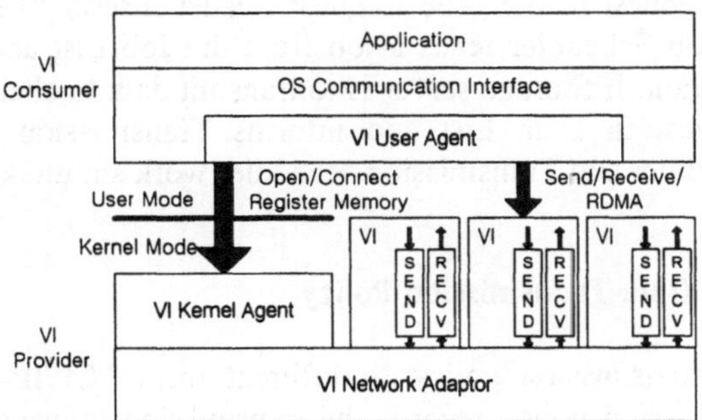

Fig. 1. VI architecture model

3. VIA based Multimedia Cluster System(VMCS)

3.1 VMCS Architecture

VMCS is 2-tired architecture consisting of a control server and storage servers. The control server manages the multimedia data, processes user requests and controls VIA. Storage servers store and manage the multimedia data.

3.1.1 Control Server Architecture

The Control server consists of Request Manage Group that process user requests and VI Manage Group that controls the messages and data transfer. Request Manager Group reads user requests through the Request reader and then inserts them to the Request List. Request List is similar to general queue and based on the FCFS (First Come First Served policy. Request Manager reads user requests from the Request List and then gets the reference information about the user request from the Meta data table.

Request Manage Group gets requiring buffer space from the Buffer Scheduler and sends the information about the user requests to VI Manager. VI Manager creates VIs of the storage servers sending messages and then requests connections to each storage server. VI Manager registers the allocated buffer on VI kernel agent, makes descriptor and then transmits the control messages to each storage server.

When VI Manager creates VIs, a VI can not communicate with multiple storage servers, because a VI is created with the address of a destination control server to communicate. Therefore, if VI Manager is to communicate with N storage servers, VI Manager should create N VIs.

3.1.2 Storage Server Architecture

Storage server architecture is similar to that of control server. Storage server consists of a VI Manager and Request Processing Group. After Control Server receives message through the VI Manager, VI Manager sends information about the buffer and message to the Request reader. The Request Reader inserts received information in the Job List. A job Scheduler reads a job from the Job List and processes that job from job information. If Storage server is to transmit data to client, the Job scheduler inserts data request in Data List and informs Transmission Scheduler. Request Reader, Job Scheduler and Transmission scheduler work simultaneously by thread.

3.2 Message and Data Transmission Policy

VIA-based data transmission policy is different from TCP/IP-based transmission. VIA-based transmission policy records the transmission information in a descriptor and the descriptor is inserted in the send or receive queue of VI. We refer to the procedure of inserting descriptor in the send or receive queue of VI as posting. After posting has completed, VI User Agent notifies VI NIC that the descriptor posing has completed with doorbell mechanism. Then, data sending or receiving starts. After sending or receiving has completed, VI Kernel Agent records a send or receive completed mark on the control segment in the descriptor and sends the address and the handle of descriptor to the process which posted the descriptor. And then message or data transmission is completed.

3.2.1 Message Transmission including Data

Transmission of messages including data is different from the message without data transmission in two aspects. First, to access the user memory space storing the data,

data segment should be set. Second, to store the data received from sender, memory space should be pre-allocated.

To set up data segment in the descriptor, we should notice the maximum numbers of data segments, maximum memory space and maximum transfer data size. In particular, our VMCS can transfer large size data, because it is designed and implemented for the multimedia data. In VMCS, VI Kernel Agent provides the data structure, VIP_NIC_ATTRIBUTES containing the information such as maximum numbers of data segments, maximum memory space and maximum transfer data size.

To transfer a message with including data, we should check the data size. If it is acceptable maximum, then the data can be transferred by one transmission with one descriptor. On the other hand, if it exceeds the maximum transfer able size, several transmission are required. After estimating the number of descriptors, sender should transfer a control message to a receiver. If the sender does not transfer the control message, the receiver could not know the number of data will be transferred from the sender, the number of receive descriptors and the required buffer size. Therefore receiver requires control message before receiving the data. After the receiver received the control message, receiver posts the required descriptors in receive queue and reserves memory space for data. Then the receiver sends an ACK message to sender and sender posts send descriptors in send queue of sender's VI .

VMCS has multiple storage servers. VMCS stripes multimedia data and stores them on disks of multiple storage servers. To stripe and store multimedia data on multiple storage servers, the equal numbers of VIs with the storage servers are required. And, to store every block on its respective storage server, we have to decide how many descriptors should post on each VI which associated with its respective storage server. The method to get the numbers of descriptors for each VI is following.

$$N = Total\_Trans\_Size / Max\_Trans\_Size \qquad (1)$$

N : Total number of blocks included in a descriptor

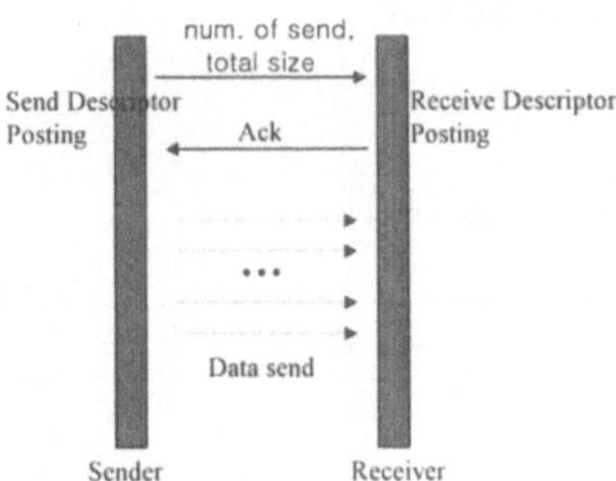

Fig. 2. Data Transmission flow

We calculate the number of total blocks to transfer and the number of descriptors for each VI by dividing the number of total blocks by the number of VIs. Each of remaining blocks are then stored its respective VI by ascending in term of the block number.

$$\begin{cases} V\_num_i = N/M & (i > N\%M) \\ V\_num_i = N/M + 1 & (i \le N\%M) \end{cases} \quad (2)$$

where,

V_num_i : the number of descriptors for ith VI

M : the number of VIs to attend for transmission

4. Performance Evaluations and Analysis

We experimented by varying the size of transmission data to prove whether VIA is an appropriate protocol to serve multimedia data or not. We compared VIA with TCP/IP. In the case of multimedia data transmission based on VIA, the main issues are the optimal size of buffer and the optimal number of posting of descriptors. Therefore, we evaluated the system performance for the fixed size transmission data by varying the size of the buffer and the number of posting of descriptors.

Table 1. Experiment Wnvironment

CPU	Intel Pentium 166MHZ
Main Memory	32Mbyte
Operating system	Linux Kernel 2.2.15
VIA	M-VIA 1.0

4.1 Comparison of VIA with TCP/IP

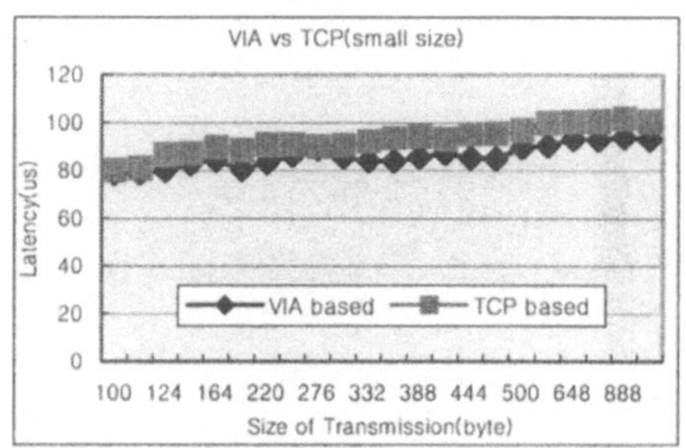

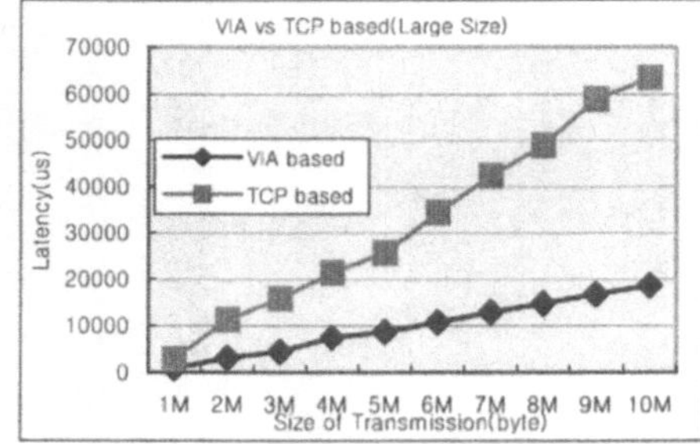

Fig. 3. Performance comparison according to the transmission data size

We experimented in two cases with the small size data of 100bytes~1Kbytes and the large size data of 1Mbytes~10Mbytes, because generally, multimedia server system transfers small size control messages and the large size multimedia data. As a result, in case of transferring the small size messages, transfer latency of VIA is similar to that of TCP/IP. In this case, if the additional functions for supporting the stable network are added to VIA, TCP/IP may have better performance than VIA. On the other hand, when transferring the large size multimedia data, transfer latency of VIA is smaller than that of TCP/IP. As show in Figure 9, VIA is three times better than TCP/IP in terms of transfer latency.

5. Conclusions and Future works

In this paper, we designed and implemented a multimedia cluster system, VMCS. In particular, it is based on the novel protocol VIA (Virtual Interface Architecture) to reduce the message transmission overhead that is the general drawback of the cluster systems.

Experimental results show that VMCS performs better than the TCP/IP-based system for transferring the large data. Therefore, it is clear that the VMCS is proper for the multimedia data services.

VMCS is a multimedia system to serve the multimedia data to the clients and the two-layered distributed cluster architecture. It is based on VIA that can reduce the message passing overhead between the cluster nodes. VIA outperforms significantly to traditional protocol like TCP/IP in terms of latency. And it is advantages that VIA can be supported in both hardware and software.

While the current VMCS is a specialized system for multimedia data service, it can also be used for traditional text and image data in the future. To do this, the studies for additional control mechanisms such as flow control for the small size data are required in order to modify the VMCS to perform well for the small size data transmission. Moreover, the studies about the various real-time scheduling policies are needed for the multimedia data services.

Reference

1. Jonathan Kay and Joseph Rasquale, "Profiling and Reducing Processing Overheads in TCP/IP," IEEE Transactions on Networking, vol.4, (1996)
2. S. Mukherjee and M. D. Hill, "A Survey of User-Level Network Interfaces for System Area Networks," UWCS TR@1340, University of Wisconsin-Medison, Feb (1997)
3. John Gustafson, "Pentium®Pro Cluster Workshop," http://www.scl. ameslab.gov /~workshops/PPCworkshop.html, (1997)
4. http://www.epm.ornl.gov/pvm
5. Aninya Basu, Vineet Buch, Werner Volgels, Thorsten von Eicken, "U-Net: A User-Level Interface for Parallel and Distributed Computing," SOSP, Dec. (1995)
6. Compaq, Intel, Microsoft, "Virtual Interface Architecture Specification Version 1.0," Dec. (1997)
7. M-VIA Documents, http://www.nersc.gov/research/FTP/via

A Fuzzy Inference System for Simplifying Surfaces with Color

Chin-Chen Chang [1], Shu-Kai Yang [2], JunWei Hsieh [3], Ding-Zhou Duan [2], and Ming-Fen Lin [2]

[1] Computer & Communications Research Laboratories, Industrial Technology Research Institute, Chutung, Hsinchu, Taiwan, R.O.C.
chinchen@itri.org.tw
[2] Opto-Electronics & System Laboratories, Industrial Technology Research Institute, Chutung, Hsinchu, Taiwan, R.O.C.
[3] Department of Electrical Engineering, Yuan Ze University, Taoyuan, Taiwan, R.O.C.

Abstract. A fuzzy inference system is presented in this paper for simplifying surfaces with color. We first propose a fuzzy surface position uncertainty, a fuzzy surface curvature uncertainty and a fuzzy surface color uncertainty to respectively measure the variations of surface position, surface curvature and surface color while simplifying surfaces. We then utilize the TSK fuzzy inference system integrating the proposed fuzzy uncertainties to determine the cost as the criteria of removing a portion of surface models. Experimental results show that our approach does produce high quality approximations of surfaces.

1 Introduction

Many computer graphics applications require complex models with fine details to construct realistic environments. Consequently, these complex models becomes very expensive to render, store and transmit since the rendering cost, the memory requirement and transmit through network are directly proportional to the number of polygons in a model. However, the complex models with high details are not always required and it is enough to use simpler versions of original models to achieve the realism in many situations. Surface simplification technique provides a solution to generate simpler versions of a model.

There has been much research in recent years in surface simplification [1,2,3,4,6,7,8,9,10]. The key to producing good approximations is to produce an approximation that will cause the smallest variation to the model. Hoppe et al. [6,7] proposed an approach to minimize an *energy function* that measures the competing desires of conciseness of representation and fidelity to the data. Klein et al. [9] used the *Hausdorff distance* between the original and the approximation as the geometrically error. This approach can reduce the number of triangles of a mesh without exceeding a user-specified Hausdorff distance between the original and the approximation. The approach can reduce the number of vertices in a dense mesh of triangles. Ronfard and Rossignac [10] proposed a method to iteratively collapse edges based on a measure of the geometric deviation from the initial shape. When edges are merged in the right order, this strategy produces a continuum of valid approximations of the original models. Garland and Heckbert [3,4] developed quadric error metrics for surface simplification to maintain surface error approximations and used iterative contractions of vertex pairs to simplify models. Ciampalini et al. [1] presented a surface simplification approach based on the mesh decimation method, has been designed to provide both increased approximation precision, based on global error management, and multiresolution output. Kase et al. [8] proposed an interactive quality evaluation of reduction polygon model to improve drawing speed without degrading image quality in computer graphics.

Since the visual quality of a model is subjective and uncertainty abounds in simplification process, it is hard to provide the complete solutions to measure the variation of a model when simplifying surfaces. In this paper, we propose a fuzzy inference system for simplifying surfaces with color since fuzzy set theory [5,11,12,13] can model non-statistical imprecision and the fuzzy inference system can integrate the concepts of fuzzy sets, fuzzy if-then rules and fuzzy reasoning. We first present a fuzzy surface position uncertainty, a fuzzy surface curvature uncertainty and a fuzzy surface color uncertainty to respectively measure the variations of surface position, surface curvature and surface color [2] while simplifying surfaces. We then utilize the TSK fuzzy inference system integrating the proposed fuzzy uncertainties to determine the cost as the criteria of removing a portion of surface models.

The rest of this paper is organized as follows. In Section 2, we simply describe the basic concept of fuzzy sets [5,13] and the TSK fuzzy inference system [11,12]. In Section 3, we present the fuzzy inference system for simplifying surfaces with color. The implementation and results are given in Section 4. Finally, conclusions are presented in Section 5.

2 Fuzzy Inference System

Let X be the universal set. In classical set theory, given a subset A of X, each element $x \in X$ satisfies either x belong to A, or x does not belong to A. However, in fuzzy set theory [5,13], an element may belong partially to a set. A fuzzy set A is usually defined as

$$\mu_A(x): X \rightarrow [0,1] \qquad (1)$$

where μ_A is the membership function indicating the membership grade of an element x in the universal set X.

The TSK fuzzy inference sytem [11,12], as proposed by Takagi, Sugeno and Kang (TSK), uses a typical fuzzy if-then rule as the following form:
Rule: if x is A and y is B then $z = f(x,y)$

where x and y are input variables, A and B are fuzzy sets in the antecedent part and z is the output which is a function of the input variables in the consequent part. Generally, $f(x,y)$ is a polynomial function of input variables x and y. If multiple fuzzy if-then rules are considered, then the final output is taken as the weighted average of each rule's output. The weight of each fuzzy if-then rule is computed by the minimum of the membership grades of input variables in the antecedent part.

3 The Proposed Approach

Without loss of generality, we assume the surfaces consist of triangles only. Basically, our approach is based on a cluster collapse algorithm simplifying models by repeated use of the simple cluster collapse operation, depicted in Figure 1. A *cluster* $C(u)$ is a vertex tree of a root vertex u consisting of a set of vertices and edges of a model along with u itself. Two clusters are adjacent if there exists an edge connecting the two clusters. In the cluster collapse operation, two adjacent clusters $C(u)$ and $C(v)$ are selected and all vertices in $C(u)$ and $C(v)$ are collapsed onto v. At each step, our approach first evaluates the cost of every adjacent clusters for collapsing and then selects the adjacent clusters with the minimal cost to collapse.

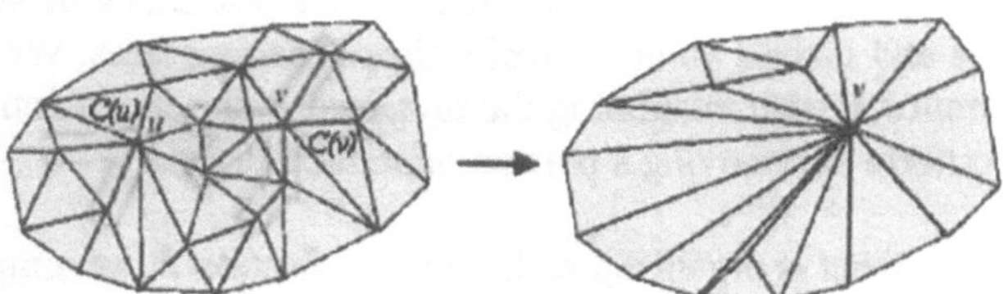

Fig. 1. Cluster collapse

We first define a *fuzzy surface position uncertainty*, a *fuzzy surface curvature uncertainty* and a *fuzzy surface color uncertainty* to respectively measure the variations of surface position, surface curvature and surface color [2] of the cluster collapse operation. Then, we utilize the TSK fuzzy inference system integrating the proposed three fuzzy uncertainties to determine the cost as the criteria of collapsing the clusters.

For the fuzzy surface position uncertainty, we measure the variation of surface position by calculating the maximal value among the distances of vertices in $C(u)$ and vertex v. The fuzzy surface position uncertainty of $C(u)$ to $C(v)$ is defined as

$$\mu_{pos}(C(u),C(v)) = \max_{x_i \in C(u)} \left\{ \left\| x_i.{}_{position} - v.{}_{position} \right\| \right\} \tag{2}$$

The fuzzy position uncertainty is normalized into [0,1] for the cluster collapse algorithm at each step. Let *LARGE* and *SMALL* be two fuzzy sets on [0,1] used to describe the fuzzy surface position uncertainty.

For the fuzzy surface curvature uncertainty, we measure the variation of surface curvature by computing the minimal value among dot products of normals of a triangle in *T(C(u))* and a triangle in *T(C(u),C(v))*, where *T(C(u))* is a set of triangles adjacent to *C(u)* and *T(C(u),C(v))* is a set of triangles adjacent to both *C(u)* and *C(v)*. The fuzzy surface curvature uncertainty of *C(u)* to *C(v)* is defined as

$$\mu_{cur}(C(u),C(v)) = \min_{f_i \in T(C(u)), f_j \in T(C(u),C(v))} \{ f_{i \cdot normal} \cdot f_{j \cdot normal} \} \quad (3)$$

The fuzzy surface curvature uncertainty is normalized into [0,1] for the cluster collapse algorithm at each step. Let *ROUGH* and *SMOOTH* be two fuzzy sets on [0,1] used to describe the fuzzy surface curvature uncertainty.

For the fuzzy surface color uncertainty, we measure the variation of surface color by calculating the maximal value among the differences of colors of vertices in *C(u)* and vertex *v*. The fuzzy surface color uncertainty of *C(u)* to *C(v)* is defined as

$$\mu_{col}(C(u),C(v)) = \max_{x_i \in C(u)} \{ \| x_{i \cdot color} - v_{\cdot color} \| \} \quad (4)$$

The fuzzy surface color uncertainty is normalized into [0,1] for the cluster collapse algorithm at each step. Let *DIFFERENT* and *SIMILAR* be two fuzzy sets on [0,1] used to describe the fuzzy surface color uncertainty.

For the purpose of the TSK fuzzy inference system for simplifying surfaces with color, the fuzzy if-then rules are defined as follows:

Rule 1: if *x* is *LARGE* and *y* is *ROUGH* and *z* is DIFFERENT then o_1 is $x^{p_1} y^{q_1} z^{r_1}$

Rule 2: if *x* is *LARGE* and *y* is *ROUGH* and *z* is SIMILAR then o_2 is $x^{p_2} y^{q_2} z^{r_2}$

Rule 3: if *x* is *LARGE* and *y* is *SMOOTH* and *z* is DIFFERENT then o_3 is $x^{p_3} y^{q_3} z^{r_3}$

Rule 4: if *x* is *SMALL* and *y* is *ROUGH* and *z* is DIFFERENT then o_4 is $x^{p_4} y^{q_4} z^{r_4}$

Rule 5: if *x* is *LARGE* and *y* is *SMOOTH* and *z* is SIMILAR then o_5 is $x^{p_5} y^{q_5} z^{r_5}$

Rule 6: if *x* is *SMALL* and *y* is *ROUGH* and *z* is SIMILAR then o_6 is $x^{p_6} y^{q_6} z^{r_6}$

Rule 7: if *x* is *SMALL* and *y* is *SMOOTH* and *z* is DIFFERENT then o_7 is $x^{p_7} y^{q_7} z^{r_7}$

Rule 8: if *x* is *SMALL* and *y* is *SMOOTH* and *z* is SIMILAR then o_8 is $x^{p_8} y^{q_8} z^{r_8}$

where *x* is the fuzzy surface position uncertainty, *y* is the fuzzy surface curvature uncertainty and *z* is the fuzzy surface color uncertainty. The functions o_1, o_2, ..., o_8 are outputs of the fuzzy if-then rules, respectively, as costs for collapsing clusters.

4 Implementation and Results

Our experimental platform is a PC with an Intel® Pentium® III 733MHz CPU and 256 Mbytes of memory running Microsoft® Windows 2000 Professional OS.

The *S*-function [5] is a valuable tool in defining a fuzzy set which encodes words like tall and large. We apply the *S*-function to define the fuzzy sets *LARGE, SMALL, ROUGH, SMOOTH, DIFFERENT and SIMILAR*. The membership functions of *LARGE, ROUGH, DIFFERENT* are defined as S(x;0,1) and the membership functions of *SMALL, SMOOTH, SIMILAR* are defined as 1 - *S*(*x*;0,1), respectively.

For efficiency, we make a discretization of the membership functions of *LARGE*, *SMALL*, *ROUGH*, *SMOOTH*, *DIFFERENT* and *SIMILAR*. We first take 101 samples (100 intervals) uniformly over the domain [0,1] and then the corresponding values of selected samples are pre-calculated and stored in a lookup table. The parameters p_1, q_1 and r_1 are, respectively, assigned 0.2, 0.2 and 0.2 indicating that the cost of the clusters to collapse is very high. The parameters p_2, q_2 and r_2 are, respectively, assigned 0.5, 0.5 and 0.5 indicating that the cost of the clusters to collapse is high. The parameters p_3, q_3 and r_3 are, respectively, assigned 0.5, 0.5 and 0.5 indicating that the cost of the clusters to collapse is high. The parameters p_4, q_4 and r_4 are, respectively, assigned 0.5, 0.5 and 0.5 indicating that the cost of the clusters to collapse is high. The parameters p_5, q_5 and r_5 are, respectively, assigned 2, 2 and 2 indicating that the cost of the clusters to collapse is low. The parameters p_6, q_6 and r_6 are, respectively, assigned 2, 2 and 2 indicating that the cost of the clusters to collapse is low. The parameters p_7, q_7 and r_7 are, respectively, assigned 2, 2 and 2 indicating that the cost of the clusters to collapse is low. The parameters p_8, q_8 and r_8 are, respectively, assigned 5, 5 and 5 indicating that the cost of the clusters to collapse is very low.

We test our approach to a teapot model. Figure 2 shows the results of a sequence of approximations produced by our method on the teapot model. Figure 2(a) shows the original model has 16256 polygons and Figures 2(b)-2(d) show the approximations have 3008, 1435, and 449 polygons, respectively. The entire sequence of teapots was calculated in about 10 seconds. Features such as geometry and color are well preserved through many simplifications and they begin to disappear only at very low levels of detail.

Fig. 2. A sequence of approximations produced by our method on the teapot model

5 Conclusions

A fuzzy inference system for simplifying surfaces with color was studied in this work. We have proposed the fuzzy surface position uncertainty, the fuzzy surface curvature uncertainty and fuzzy surface color uncertainty to respectively estimate the variations of surface position, surface curvature and surface color while simplifying surface models. Then, we have utilized the TSK fuzzy inference system integrating the proposed fuzzy uncertainties to determine the cost as the criteria of removing a portion of surface models. With the proposed approach, we can iteratively simplify surface models and generate high quality approximations.

Acknowledgements

This work is a partial result of the project number 903XS18F4 conducted by ITRI under sponsorship of the Ministry of Economic Affairs, R.O.C.

References

1. Ciampalini, A., Cignoni, P., Mantani, C., Scopigno, R.: Multiresolution Decimation Based on Global Error. The Visual Computer **13** (1997) 228-246
2. Cohen, J., Olano, M., Manocha, D.: Appearance-Preserving Simplification. Computer Graphics (SIGGRAPH'98 Proceedings) (1998) 115-122
3. Garland, M., Heckbert, P.S.: Surface Simplification Using Quadric Error Metrics. Computer Graphics (SIGGRAPH'97 Proceedings) (1997) 209-224
4. Garland, M., Heckbert, P.S.: Simplifying Surfaces with Color and Texture Using Quadric Error Metrics. IEEE Visualization'98 Proceedings (1998) 263-269
5. Giarratano, J., Riley, G.: Expert Systems: Principles and Programming. PWS-KENT Publishing Company (1989)
6. Hoppe, H.: Progressive Meshes. Computer Graphics (SIGGRAPH'96 Proceedings) (1996) 99-108
7. Hoppe, H., DeRose, T., Duchamp, T., McDonald, J., Stuetzle, W.: Mesh Optimization. Computer Graphics (SIGGRAPH'93 Proceedings) (1993) 19-26
8. Kase, D., Hamamoto, T., Hangai, H.: An Interactive Quality Evaluation of Reduction Polygon Model. 2000 International Conference on Image Processing Proceedings **2** (2000) 879-882
9. Klein, R., Liebich, G., Strasser, W.: Mesh Reduction with Error Control. IEEE Visualization'96 Proceedings (1996) 311–318
10. Ronfard, R., Rossignac, J.R.: Full-Range Approximation of Triangulated Polyhedra. EUROGRAPHICS'96 Proceedings **15** (1996) 67-76
11. Sugeno, M., Kang, G.T.: Structure Identification of Fuzzy Model. Fuzzy Sets and Systems 28 (1988) 15-33
12. Takagi, T., Sugeno, M.: Fuzzy Identification of System and Its Applications to Modeling and Control. IEEE Trans. SMC **3** (1985) 116-132
13. Zadeh, L.A.: Fuzzy Sets. Inf. Control **8** (1965) 338-353

Demosaic : Color Filter Array Interpolation for Digital Cameras

Suk-Han Lam and Chi-Wah Kok

Department of Electrical and Electronic Engineering, Hong Kong University of Science and Technology, Clear Water Bay, HONG KONG

Abstract. Classical linear signal processing techniques when applied to color demosaic tends to over smooth the color signal, resulting in noticeable artifacts along edges and color features. We proposed in this paper to let the color channels support the edges and the edge support the interpolation of missing color, and thus achieve demosaic full-color image with better perceptual quality. The computational complexity of the proposed algorithm is compatible with other fast demosaic algorithms.

1 Introduction

Digital camera uses an array of light sensor to collect image scene information. The information provided by each sensor forms the pixels of the image scene. Due to the trichromatic nature of human visual system, a *full-color* image requires more than light intensity information. To obtain full-color images, each pixel has to carry at least three pieces of information, such that intensity of three independent colors (i.e. red, green and blue) can be deduced. To reduce the cost of the digital cameras, color filter arrays (CFA) are typically used. Such that each light sensor is covered by one filter. As a result, each pixel will sample the intensity of one of the trichromatic color. Although the resulting image is not full-color, the CFA can be arranged in such a way that the missing color information can be inferred with a reasonable degree of accuracy. Such inference, commonly known as color interpolation or demosaic, is not perfect, but neither is the human visual system to see small discrepancies.

Obviously, the demosaic algorithm depends on the CFA arrangement. In this paper, we'll concentrate on the Bayer pattern [1], which uses the three additive primary colors, red, green and blue (RGB), for the filter elements as shown in Figure 1(a). The presented algorithm can be easily extended to other CFA patterns. A benchmark rose image together with its Bayer pattern sampled image are shown in Figure 3(a) and (b) respectively.

2 A Simple Color Model

A simple model for color images is the Lambertian non-flat surface patches [35]. The color signal received by the sensor is the reflected signal of the surface patch

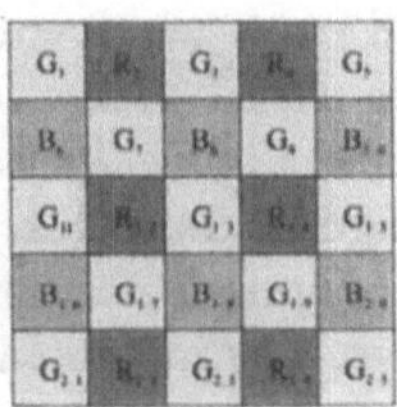

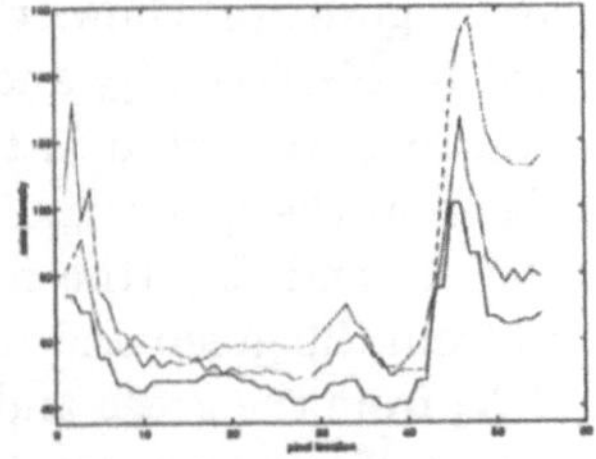

Fig. 1. (a) Bayer color filter array pattern. (b) The and colors of the 124th horizonal scan line of *rose* image from pixel number 160-214 in Figure 3a.

from a light source at direction ℓ. Assume the reflective surface is homogeneous. The received signal at spatial location (x, y) can be written as

$$I_R(x,y) = c_R(x,y)\mathbf{N}(x,y) \cdot \ell, \quad (1)$$

$$I_G(x,y) = c_G(x,y)\mathbf{N}(x,y) \cdot \ell, \quad (2)$$

$$I_B(x,y) = c_B(x,y)\mathbf{N}(x,y) \cdot \ell, \quad (3)$$

where $\mathbf{N}(x,y)$ is the surface normal. $c_i(x,y)$ (i stands for R, G, B) is the albedo capturing the characteristics of the reflective materials. Since the surface is assumed to be homogeneous, therefore, $c_i(x,y) = c_i$.

$$\frac{I_i(x,y)}{I_j(x,y)} = \frac{c_i(x,y)}{c_j(x,y)} = \frac{c_i}{c_j} = \text{constant}. \quad (4)$$

That is, the color ratio in a localized area is constant. This is an oversimplified assumption for color image analysis. It has shown to be consistent with natural scenes. Showing in Figure 1(b) is the color intensity plot of a typical scan line of the rose image (the 124th horizontal scan line from pixel number 160 to 214).

3 Proposed Demosaic Algorithm

A novel color demosaic algorithm is proposed which let the color channels support the edges and the edge support the interpolation of missing color. From eq.(4), G_i can be interpolated from R_i by

$$G_i = \frac{\bar{G}R_i}{\bar{R}}, \quad (5)$$

where $\bar{G}$ and $\bar{R}$ are the average green color and red color in a localized region. A localized region of minimum size is formed by neighboring pixels of the same color. Showing in Figure 2(a) is the windows used to compute eq.(5). Similarly, G_i can be estimated from B_i and $\bar{B}$ as in eq.(5) by replacing R_i and $\bar{R}$ with B_i and $\bar{B}$. The corresponding windows is shown in Figure 2(b).

The window is designed to maximize the overlap of neighbouring windows. The windows used to interpolate R_i and B_i are formed similarly as shown in

Figure 2, where Figure 2(a) shows the interpolation of G_{12} from the green color window formed by G_7, G_{11}, G_{13} and G_{17} and the red color window formed by R_2, R_4, R_{12}, and R_{14} were used in the estimation. Figure 2(b) shows the interpolation of G_5 from the green and blue color windows. Figure 2(c) shows the interpolation of R_9 and R_{11} (the red circles in the figures indicates the pixels consideration) from the green and red color windows. Figure 2(d) shows the interpolation of R_6 from the green and red color windows. The interpolation of B_i and the formation of windows are done similarly.

Figure 2(b) also shows the possible boundary problem of the demosaic problem. In such case, the color window may extended beyond pixel boundary, e.g. as in Figure 2(b). Symmetric extension is adopted to preserve the linearity of the color signal. The symmetric extension is modified such that the extended image follows the Bayer CFA pattern as shown in Figure 2(e).

Figure 2 exhausted all the possible local window formation for interpolating the missing color. The localized window is formed by the nearest neighbor pixels of the pixel under consideration. In case there are multiple windows that have the same overlap, the one at the upper top right corner of the pixel under consideration will be used in the estimation. Noted that eq.(5) actually computes the weighted average ratio of the color intensities for different color channels of the overlapped windows. While the average color intensities will results in smoothing artifact, the average ratio will be supported by the difference in intensity if there is an edge within the window under consideration. Furthermore, the average ratio will be weighted by the color value of a different color channel at the pixel under consideration. Which will further provide the necessary edge support in the estimation of missing color when the pixel under consideration contributes to an edge. As a result, compatible demosaic results in the reconstruction of full-color image with color edges are observed in the proposed algorithm when compared to other algorithms reviewed in this paper. The last but not the least, it can be shown that eq.(5) has limited variation. As a result, the hue transition from pixel to pixel will be limited, thus results in visually natural color in the same way as smooth hue transition interpolation algorithm [3, 6].

4 Simulation Results

We tested the proposed method on benchmark images (rose, lily and BMW) that were sampled with Bayer CFA pattern. Since there exist no known image quality measure that incorporates the characteristics of human visual system, the presented results are compared by subjective quality with visual observation alone. Noted that the simulation results are *full-color* images. As a result, for better color view, we refer to http://home.ust.hk/~ee_lshaa/result.html.

With reference to the images presented in the above website, all the reviewed demosaic algorithms as cited in our references and the proposed demosaic algorithm are capable of producing full-color image with reasonable quality. However, careful observation revealed that the full-color image produced by nearest neighbor algorithm [2–5] has the worst resolution and has roughness object edges. The bilinear interpolation algorithm [3–10] tends to over smooth the color image, resulting in an artifact similar to out-of-focus image. The smooth hue algorithm [3, 11, 12], smooth log hue algorithm [3, 11, 13], edge sensing interpolation algorithm [4, 5, 15], and log edge sensing interpolation algorithm [17] perform badly in fine details of the color image. This is especially true in the zoomed "lily" image from (d) to (g) in the provided wedsite, where dark dots are observed in small feature areas of the lily image. Such results indicate that the algorithms tend to over estimate the color value in fine detail areas. The variable number gradient interpolation algorithm [21] produces visually pleasing results but imposes a huge computation penalty. The pattern recognition interpolation algorithm [3, 10, 16, 34] is capable to produce good quality full-color image. However the resulting full-color image has diffused color, which results in lost of color contrast. The full-color image resulted from the proposed algorithm is shown to have good color contrast, and able to retain small features, including color edges. Visually pleasing results are observed which is comparable or even better than that of variable number gradients algorithm. However, the computational complexity of the proposed algorithm is much lower when compared to that of variable number gradients algorithm, and is considered to be comparable to that of bilinear interpolation algorithm.

5 Conclusions

In this paper, we have proposed a novel color demosaic algorithm which was shown to produce full-color image from Bayer CFA pattern encoded image. Various color demosaic algorithms are reviewed and their results are reproduced in this paper, which is compared with that obtained by the proposed algorithm. Based on a simple color model, the proposed demosaic algorithm was derived to let the color channels to be supported by the color edges of the image, and the edge will support the interpolation of the missing color. Visually pleasing results are observed in simulation which are shown to outperform other color demosaic algorithms. At the same time, the proposed algorithm has very low computational complexity, which is comparable to that required by bilinear interpolation. All the simulation results are available to be viewed in the website http://home.ust.hk/~ee_lshaa/result.html.

References

1. B.E.Bayer, "Color imaging array", *U.S. Patent* 3971065, 1976.
2. N.Ozawa, "Chrominance signal interpolation device for a color camera", *U.S. Patent* 4716455.
3. J.E.Adams, "Interactions between color plane interpolation and other image processing functions in electronic photography," *Proc. of SPIE*, vol. 2416, pp.144-151.
4. T.Sakamoto, et.al., "Software pixel interpolation for digital still cameras suitable for a 32-bit MCU", *IEEE Trans. Consumer Electronics*, pp.1342-1352, Nov. 1998.
5. Z.Hidemori, et.al., "A New digital signal processor for progressive scan CCD", *IEEE Trans. Consumer Electronics*, pp.289-295, May 1998.

6. D.R.Cok, "Single-Chip electronic color camera with color-dependent birefringent optical spatial frequency filter and red and blue signal interpolating circuit", *U.S. Patent* 4605956.
7. K.A.Parulski, "Color Filters and Processing Alternatives for one-chip cameras", *IEEE Trans. Electron Devices,* Aug. 1985.
8. W.H.Chan et.al, "A Mega-Pixel resolution PC Digital Still Camera", *Proc. SPIE,* vol.2654, pp.164-171.
9. Y.T.Tsai, "Optimized Image Processing Algorithms for a Single Sensor Camera", *1997 IEEE Pacific Rim Conf. Communications, Computers and Signal Processing,* vol.2, pp.1010-1013, 1997.
10. X.L.Wu, et.al., "Color Restoration from Digital Camera Data by Pattern Matching", *Proc. SPIE,* vol.3018, pp.12-17.
11. D.R.Cok, "Signal processing method and apparatus for producing interpolated chrominance values in a sampled color image signal", *U.S. Patent,* 4642678.
12. K.A.Parulski, et.al., "A High-Performance Digital Color Video Camera", *Proc. SPIE,* vol.1448, pp.45-48.
13. J.A.Weldy, "Optimized design for a single-sensor color electronic camera system," *Proc. SPIE* vol.1071, pp.300-307.
14. R.H.Hibbard, "Apparatus and method for adaptively interpolating a full-color image utilizing luminance gradients," *U.S. Patent* 5382976.
15. J.E.Adams, "Color processing in digital cameras," *Eastman Kodak Company.*
16. D.R.Cok, "Signal processing method and apparatus for sampled image signals," *U.S. Patent* 4630307.
17. C.A.Laroche, "Apparatus and method for adaptively interpolating a full color image utilizing chrominance gradients," *U.S. Patent* 5373322.
18. Hamilton Jr. et.al., "Adaptive color plane interpolation in single sensor color electronic camera," *U.S. Patent,* 5629734.
19. J.E.Adams et.al., "Adaptive color plane interpolation in single color electronic camera," *U.S. Patent* 5506619, 1996.
20. J.E.Adams et.al., "Design of practical color filter array interpolation algorithms for digital cameras," *Proc. SPIE,* vol.3028, pp.117-125, 1997.
21. E.Chang, et.al., "Color filter array recovery using a threshold-based variable number of gradients," *to be published in Proc. SPIE,* Jan 1999.
22. R.G.Keys, et.al., "Cubic convolution interpolation for digital image processing", *IEEE Trans on ASSP,* pp.1153-1160, 1981.
23. K.W.Simons, "Digital image reconstruction and resampling for geometric manipulation," *Proc. IEEE Symp. Machine Processing of Remotely Sense Data,* p.3A1-3A11, 1975.
24. D.P.Mitchell, et.al., "Reconstruction filters in computer graphics," *Computer Graphics, (Proc. SIGGRAPH'88),* vol.22-no.4, pp.221-228, Aug. 1988.
25. W.F.Schreiber, et.al., "Transformation between continuous and discrete representations of image: A perceptual appraoch," *IEEE Trans. PAMI,* pp.178-186, Mar. 1985.
26. H.S.Hou, "Cubic splines for image interpolation and digital filtering," *IEEE Trans. ASSP,* pp.508-517, 1987.
27. W.T.Freeman, "Method and apparatus for reconstructing missing color samples," *U.S. Patent* 4663655.
28. W.T.Freeman, "Median filter for reconstructing missing color samples," *U.S. Patent* 4724395, 1988.
29. M.A.Wober, "Method and apparatus for recovering image data through the use of a color test pattern," *U.S. Patent* 5475769.

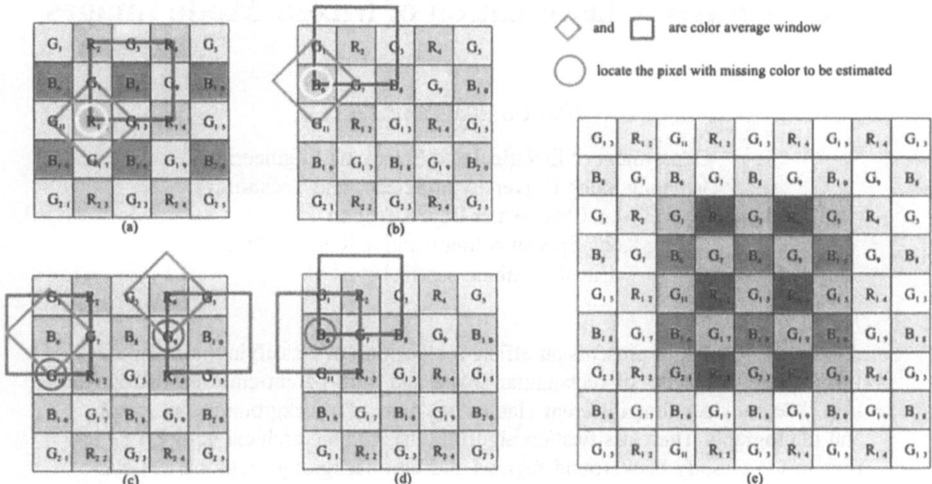

Fig. 2. (a) Red and green window location for the estimation of $G12$. (b) Blue and green window location for the estimation of $G5$. (c) Red and green window location for the estimation of $R11$. (d) Red and blue window location for the estimation of $R5$. (e) Bayer CFA constrained Symmetric extension for boundary pixels.

30. T.A.Matraszek, et.al. "Gradient based method for providing values for unknown pixels in a digital image," *U.S. Patent,* 5875040.
31. D.H.Brainard, et.al., "Bayesian method for reconstructing color images from trichromatic samples," *IS&T 47th Annual Conference*, pp.375-380, 1994.
32. E.Shimizu, et.al., "The digital camera using new compression and interpolation algorithm," *IS&T 49th Annual Conference*, pp.268-273, 1996.
33. C.H.Wu, et.al., "Reconstruction of color images from a single-chip CCD Sensor based on markov random field models," *Proc. SPIE*, vol.2564, pp.282-288.
34. D.R.Cok, "Reconstruction of CCD images using template matching," *Proc. IS&T Annual Conf. ICPS*, pp.380-385, 1994.
35. B.A.Wandell, *Foundations of Vision,* Sinauer Associates, Inc., 1995.

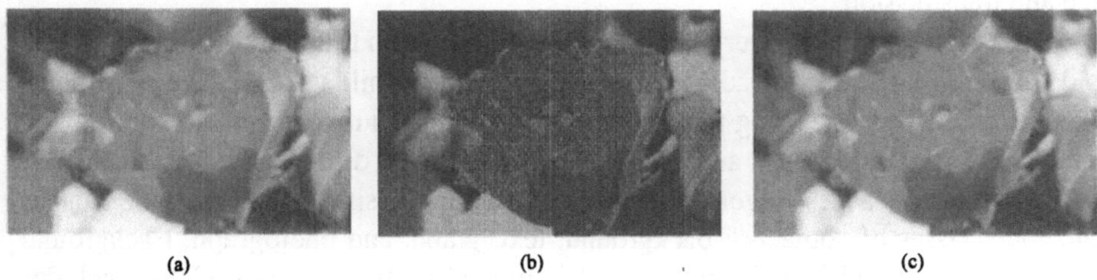

Fig. 3. (a)Original rose image, (b) Sampled with Bayer color filter array pattern, (c) Demosaic image with proposed algorithm.

Object-Based Classification of Mixed-Mode Images

Hua Cai and Bing Zeng

Department of Electrical and Electronic Engineering
The Hong Kong University of Science and Technology
Clear Water Bay, Kowloon
Hong Kong Special Administrative Region, China
Email: {caihua, eezeng}@ust.hk

Abstract. This paper presents an efficient algorithm of classifying mixed-mode images into "objects" of rectangular shape and with parent-children relationship. We consider four different classes of "objects": background, text, graph, and photograph. The classification algorithm has the hierarchical nature, i.e., it tries to (1) classify background regions and non-background regions, (2) classify bi-level objects and multi-level objects (in non-background regions), and (3) classify graph and photograph (in multi-level objects). During the classification, a merging-and-splitting refinement is used for boundaries and small fragments. Excellent classification results have been observed in all experimental tests.

1 Introduction

With the increase of bandwidth and computing power, multimedia applications are becoming more and more popular. Applications such as color fax, scanned documents, educational videos, and WebPages may not only contain continuous-tone images, but also contain texts and graphs. We call this kind of images as mixed-mode images. However, all current image compression standards, such as JPEG and JBIG, are tailored for certain type of images only, and therefore cannot work at all (such as JBIG) or cannot achieve acceptable quality (such as JPEG) for mixed-mode images. On the other hand, for transmission over a noisy channel, different error protections are typically required for different types of images. For such reasons, the classification of mixed-mode images becomes an important part of image processing systems for storage and transmission.

There have been a number of works trying to deal with this classification problem, and some of them have already achieved good quality while using different methods. These methods include using thresholds [1] to distinguish text and non-text, applying the Bayes VQ algorithm [2], and using wavelet coefficient distributions [3], etc.

In this paper, a new algorithm is developed for classifying mixed-mode images into four classes of "objects": background, text, graph, and photograph. Background refers to smooth and blank regions. Text is limited to bi-level texts. Graph includes artificial or computer generated graphs. Photograph refers to continuous-tone images.

This work has been supported by a grant from the Research Grants Council of the Hong Kong Special Administrative Region, China.

This new classification is done based on a principle that all classified objects are of rectangular shape and with parent-children relationship. Constraining each classified object being of rectangular shape would be rather beneficial to subsequent coding (compression) that could follow in many applications. Meanwhile, defining the parent-children relationship among classified objects makes the classification to be a hierarchical process (i.e., the classification is done through a layered structure).

We also develop a merging-and-splitting technique for boundary refinement during the classification. This refining process is controlled by several parameters. Selection of these parameters determines the number of fragments in the final classified image as well as the classification accuracy.

The rest of the paper is organized as follows. The next section introduces the "object" concept and the overall system. Section 3 presents the algorithm for classifying non-background objects from background region. Section 4 presents the algorithm of classifying bi-level objects and multi-level objects in a non-background parent object. The method of boundary refinement is introduced in Section 5. In Section 6, we present some experimental results. Finally, some conclusions are drawn in Section 7.

2 Object Concept and Overall System

It has been observed that an image can be thought of as a combination of "objects" with parent-children relationship. Here, we define an "object" as follows: (1) the shape of an object is always rectangular; (2) each object can contain background, text, graph, photograph, and other objects; and (3) a parent object can be further decomposed into children objects if it either contains more than one type of contents or contains only one type of content but with different properties.

According to these definitions, we can then denote each rectangular "object" as $O\{(x_1, y_1), (x_2, y_2)\}$, where (x_1, y_1) and (x_2, y_2) are the coordinates of its top-left and bottom-right corners, respectively. In this paper, we use $p(x, y)$ to denote the gray-value of the pixel at location (x, y), and assume that the horizontal axis increases from left to right and the vertical axis increases from top to bottom.

Figure 1 gives an example to demonstrate that an image can be divided into a number of objects. For instance, "Object A" represents the whole image; whereas "Object B" is one of the children decomposed from "Object A".

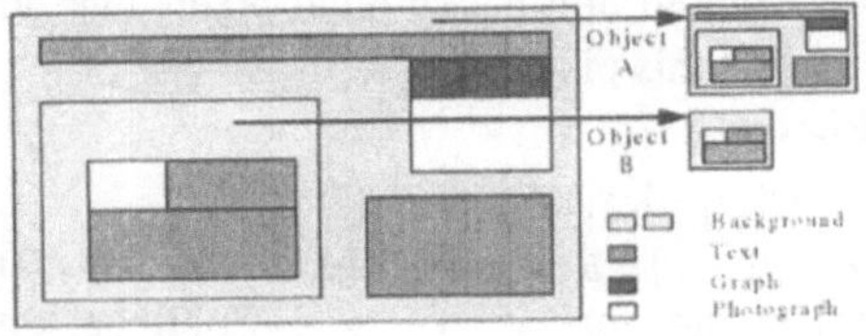

Fig. 1 An example of "Object"

Figure 2 shows the overall system. In the beginning, each whole image, treated as an initial object, is inputted to the system. Then, the system needs to determine whether or not to decompose the input object further. If the input object can be decomposed further, the system goes into the decomposition stage until no further decomposition can be done; otherwise, the system goes into the classification stage.

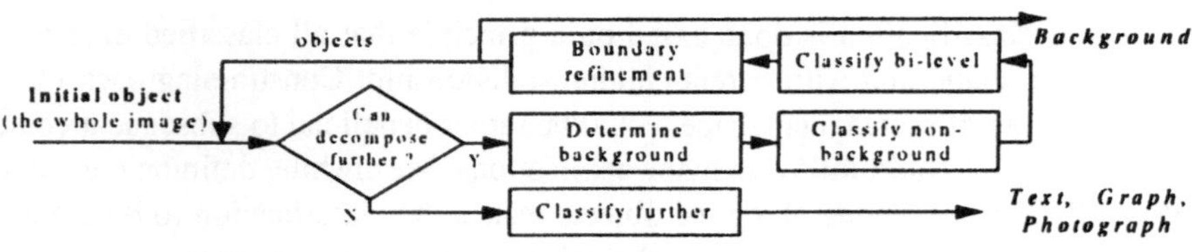

Fig. 2 Overall system

In fact, the decomposition process also does a classification, with an objective to classify the whole non-background region into two classes: bi-level and multi-level. After this, it would become easier to do further classifications within the bi-level class or the multi-level class.

The decomposition stage is composed of several steps. In the first step, the system needs to determine the background of a parent object. In this paper, we propose to calculate the histogram of the parent object and then select the value at the histogram peak as its background. After finding the background, the system needs to classify all non-background pixels into children objects in the second step. Since these children objects involve bi-level or multi-level contents, it is necessary to classify bi-level objects by using some robust and precise algorithm. In the last step, boundary refinement is carried out.

Normally, further classifying of bi-level objects does not help for any subsequent coding. On the contrary, it is highly necessary to classify between graphs and photographs for the subsequent coding. It has been shown that use the distribution of wavelet coefficients in high frequency band can successfully classify the graph and photograph [3], this method is used in our system for the further classification.

3 Classifying Non-background Objects

After knowing the background of an object, the system needs to continue classification on non-background objects. In principle, this can be done by locating a single non-background pixel first, and then letting this single pixel to grow until reaching its bounding size. The details are summarized in the following algorithm.

Non-background object growing algorithm

Step 1) Find the background value of the input parent object O_p and denote this value as b_p; select one pixel from all non-background pixels that do not belong to any of O_p's child objects and set this pixel as O_{nb}.

Step 2) O_{nb} grows as follows:

$$x_1 \leftarrow x_1 - 1 \quad \text{if} \quad \exists (x, y) \in O\{(x_1 - 1, y_1), (x_1 - 1, y_2)\}$$

$$\text{s.t.} \quad p(x, y) \neq b_p \quad \text{and} \quad p(x_1 - 1, y_1 - 1) = p(x_1 - 1, y_2 + 1) = b_p$$

Repeat the same processing for y_1, x_2, y_2. Continue this step if any of x_1, x_2, y_1, y_2 changes.

Step 3) Go to *Step 1)* if there still exists any non-background pixel in O_p that has not been classified.

The outputs of this classifying process contain many bi-level and multi-level objects. However, many of these objects (especially those with a small size) will be merged after the processing presented in the next two sections.

4 Classifying Bi-level Objects

Since texts may be mixed with multi-level parts and different texts may use different bi-level values, a robust algorithm of bi-level object classification is thus extremely important. Below is a robust and efficient algorithm that is adopted by this system.

Bi-level object growing algorithm

Step 1) Take a bi-level object O_{bi} from the classifying results of section 3, determine its background and foreground according to the histogram, and denote these two values as b and f, respectively; and also denote the background value of O_{bi}'s parent object as b_p, which has already been found in section 3.

Step 2) O_{bi} grows as follows:

$x_1 \leftarrow x_1 - 1$ if $\forall(x,y) \in O\{(x_1 - 1, y_1),(x_1 - 1, y_2)\}$ s.t. $p(x,y) = b$ or $p(x,y) = f$ Repeat the same processing for y_1, x_2, y_2. Continue this step if any of x_1, x_2, y_1, y_2 changes.

Step 3) Edges are refined as follows (only when $b = b_p$):

$x_1 \leftarrow x_1 + 1$ if $\forall(x,y) \in O\{(x_1, y_1),(x_1, y_2)\}$ s.t. $p(x,y) = b_p$. Repeat the same processing for y_1, x_2, y_2. Continue this step if any of x_1, x_2, y_1, y_2 changes.

Step 4) Go to *Step 2)* if any of x_1, x_2, y_1, and y_2 changes after *Steps 2) and 3)*.

Step 5) Merge all objects overlapped by O_{bi}.

Step 6) Go to Step 1) if there exists any bi-level object that has not been processed.

In *Step 2)*, an object's edge increases according to its boundary testing results. However, this increasing strategy, though quite simple and effective, may become non-optimal, as it would end up with some unsatisfactory results when it encounters a "reef" in a particular direction. Then, *Steps 3)* and *4)* will try to get across that "reef" by shrinking edge first and increasing it again. Meanwhile, *Step 3)* also makes the edge of O_{bi} as efficient as possible if both O_{bi} and its parent object have the same background, because it has thrown away all redundancy information.

5 Boundary Refinement

After the previous two classifications, we have found out all bi-level and multi-level objects. However, the results are far from optimal since there are too many neighboring objects and fragments remaining. In order to improve the goodness of classification, the following method is proposed to refine the boundary.

This boundary refinement process tries to do two jobs: (1) to merge some fragments with the same constant level and (2) to merge some neighboring multi-level objects. In some very special cases, several fragments with the same constant level (that is not equal to the background value of their parent object) will co-exist. Although all pixels in these fragments have the same value, it is often very inefficient to treat them as individual objects because they are too small in size. A much more efficient way to handle them is to merge them together. To this end, let us assume that each such fragment is bi-level (defining the second level as the background value of its parent object), and then we can just use the bi-level object growing algorithm to find new objects.

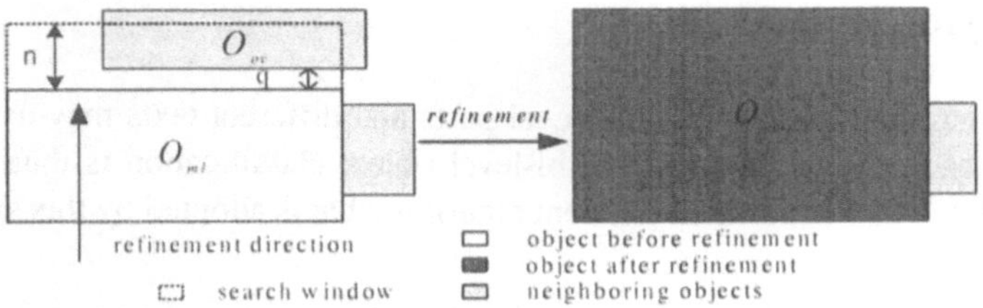

Fig. 3 An example of boundary refinement

On the other hand, it is more complicated to merge neighboring multi-level objects. For each multi-level object O_{ml}, we totally define four search windows for the upper, lower, left, and right directions, respectively. A search window's location is determined by both the object O_{ml} and parameter n: e.g., O_{ml}'s upper search window is $S_u\{(x_1, y_1 - n), (x_2, y_1)\}$ (Fig. 3). We then scan all other multi-level objects within the same parent object and try to find an object (denoted as O_{ov}) that overlaps with the search window. Finally, we will decide whether to combine these two objects (O_{ml} and O_{ov}) to form a new (and larger) object O_{new} which fully covers O_{ml} and O_{ov} with a minimal size. Since we use a larger object O_{new} to replace O_{ml} and O_{ov}, we may introduce some extra pixels that do not belong to any of the existing non-background objects. Thus, overall classification accuracy decreases. In order to control this accuracy, we use the following formula to determine whether to merge them or not:

$$f(M, q) = \frac{M_0\left(1 + \frac{n - q - 1}{n}\beta\right)}{M}$$

where M is the number of extra pixels; q is the distance between O_{ml} and O_{ov}. The pre-defined parameters M_0, n, and β, are all very important for the classification and also for the possible subsequent coding. M_0 determines how strict the merging algorithm is; n is the width of the search window, large n means that we consider more candidate objects for merging; and the non-negative parameter β determines the merging strictness related to the distance q.

If $f(M, q) \geq 1$, we use O_{new} to replace O_{ml}, O_{ov} and (possibly) other objects covered by O_{new}; and we do not merge them otherwise.

6 Results

Two mixed-mode images downloaded from Internets are used in testing of our proposed algorithm, and both of them achieved excellent results. In order to give a clear explanation about how this algorithm works, we provide two kinds of results, that is, the classification results after decomposing the initial object and the final classification results. The parameters n, M_0 and β used here are 8, 64, and 0.1 respectively.

Two examples are shown in Fig. 4: one in English with size 640x431 and the other in Chinese with size 775x410. From the partial classifying results, we can see that each initial object has already been decomposed into bi-level and multi-level classes. However, this decomposition is not complete yet, and both of them can be decomposed further. After completing the decomposition stage and classification stage, we finally get some very excellent results, as shown in Parts (e) and (f) of Fig. 4.

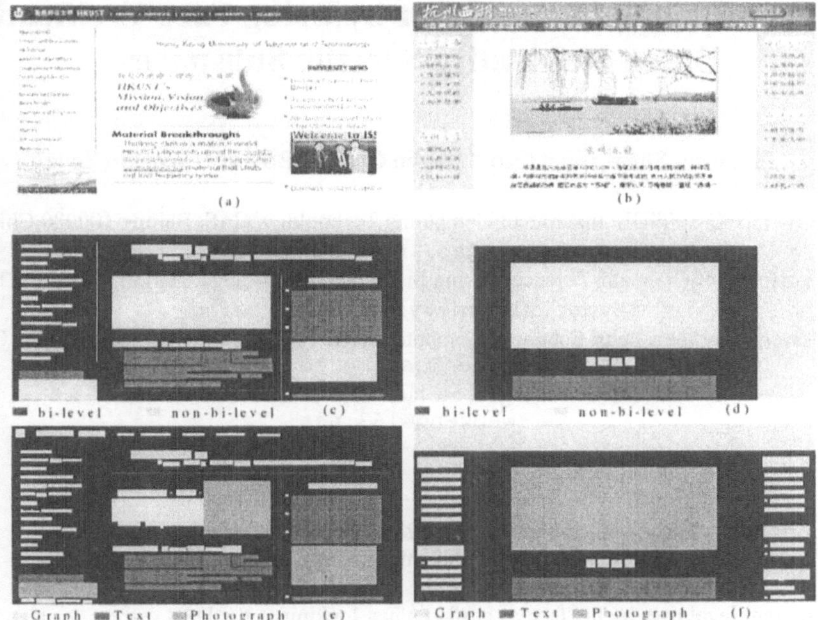

Fig. 4 Results: (a) and (b) show the original images; (c) and (d) show the partial classification results after the initial decomposition; and (e) and (f) show the final classification results.

7 Conclusions and Future Work

We developed a new classification system for classifying mixed-mode images into four classes of objects: background, text, graph, and photograph, where the classified objects are always of rectangular shape and with parent-children relationship. Excellent classification results have been observed in all of our testing experiments.

We believe that our developed algorithm can be improved further by defining a goodness measurement (for classification) based on three numbers: (1) number of objects, (2) number of misclassification pixels, and (3) number of total pixels in non-background objects; and perform optimization based on this measurement.

References

[1] N. Chaddha, *et. al.*, "Text Segmentation in mixed-mode images," in *Proc. Asilomar Conf. Signals, Systems, Computers*, vol. 2, Nov. 1994, pp. 1356-1361.

[2] K. O. Perlmutter, *et. al.*, "Text segmentation in mixed-mode images using classification trees and transform tree-structured vector quantization," in *Proc. of ICASSP*, vol. 4, Atlanta, GA, May 1996, pp. 2231-2234.

[3] J. Li and R. M. Gray, "Context-based multiscale classification of document images using wavelet coefficient distribution," *IEEE Trans. on Image Processing*, vol. 9, no. 9, Sep. 2000, pp. 1604-1616.

A Face-Unlock Screen Saver by Using Face Verification Based on Identity-Specific Subspaces

Shiguang Shan[1], Wen Gao[1,2], Xilin Chen[2,3], Bo Cao[1], Wenbin Zeng[4]

[1] ICT-YCNC FRTJDL, Institute of Computing Technology, CAS, Beijing 100080,China
{sgshan, wgao, bcao}@ict.ac.cn
[2] Department of Computer Science, Harbin Institute of Technology, Harbin, 150001, China
{wgao,xlchen}@vilab.hit.edu.cn
[3] Interactive Systems Labs, School of Computer Science, CMU, Pittsburgh, PA15221, USA
xlchen@cs.cmu.edu
[4]YCNC Co. Chengdu, SiChuan Province, 610016, China
webzeng@163.net

Abstract: A face-unlock screen saver prototype system is presented by using face verification technique based on identity-specific subspace. Instead of using password to unlock the screen saver, the proposed system can only accept the current legal user by his face as easily as just looking at the USB camera for a second, meanwhile refusing any other faces. The core techniques of the system are the proposed novel face verification algorithm based on identity-specific subspace and the maximum likelihood (ML) rule. Choosing these techniques is based on the fact that, for a task as screen saver, sufficient training facial images can be easily acquired. To achieve real-time verification, robust real-time facial feature localization and face normalization is presented, based on which an automatic samples collection tool is implemented. Practical experiments have shown the effectiveness of our proposed approaches.

1. Introduction

Traditional screen savers are based on passwords to prevent illegal users from accessing the personal computer locked by the current user. It is inconvenient for the legal user to unlock the screen saver, and there exists the risks that illegal users crack or steal the password to access the computer illegally. Faces are exclusive character for specific subjects, which provide a convenient and reliable way to prevent illegal access. In this paper, we present such a prototype by designing a face-unlock screen saver based on face verification techniques. The core technique in the system is face recognition. Face recognition is an important task in Human Computer Interface (HCI) and has significant applications for building more intelligent and intuitive HCI. Furthermore, tremendous potential applications in commerce and law enforcement have attracted more and more attention in the area.

While automatic face identification remains a great challenge, it does have a long history going as far back as the work in the 1960s [1]. It is believed that the most promising techniques should be the perfect combination of all kinds of information including shape, local appearance features and holistic appearance feature etc. In recent years, Eigenface [2], Elastic Bunch Graph Matching (EBGM) technologies [3], flexible models [4], and Fisherface [5]/LDA [6] based approaches have attracted much attention. FERET evaluation provided extensive comparisons of these algorithms [7]. More recently, SVM have been successfully applied to face recognition [8]. For detailed survey of FRT, [1] should be referred to.

Among the current state-of-the-art techniques, "eigenface" methods originated by Turk and Pentland's [2] are the most distinguished. In this paper, we extend Eigenface in an essentially different way by representing each face by using one face subspace private to the corresponding subject. Based on the identity-specific subspaces and maximum likelihood rules, a face verification technique is derived and applied to a practical face-unlock screen saver system with corresponding facial feature localization and face normalization techniques.

2. Identity-Specific Subspaces

"Eigenface" method [2] is PCA or KLT essentially, belonging to a kind of linear projection transform. The face subspace captures the common information of human faces, while the "noise" subspace contains three kinds of information: between-person variance, interpersonal variance and stochastic noise, among which between-person difference is essential for distinguishing different individuals. Unfortunately, the between-person difference crucial for recognition is blended inseparably with the within-person difference and noise information in the "noise" subspace. So we argue that "eigenface" technique might be more appropriate for face detection rather than distinguishing different faces. Based on the notion, we proposed the concept of identity-specific subspace.

Facial images, with the same specific identity, have similar appearance, for which they can be regarded as a stochastic observed signal. So one private signal subspace can be used to model them, by which the invariant facial feature belonging to the same person is mostly remained as the expected signal, while most of the within-class variance useless for classification is thrown away in the "noise" subspace.

For any specific person with an identity K denoted by Ω_k as a class, it can be analyzed by using eigenvalue decomposition as: $R_k = \sum_{i=1}^{d_k} \lambda_i^{(k)} v_i^{(k)} v_i^{(k)H} + \sigma_k^2 \sum_{i=0}^{M_k} v_i^{(k)} v_i^{(k)H}$. Then the signal subspace and corresponding noise subspace for the specific identity are $S_{face}^{(k)} = Span\{U_{face}^{(k)}\} = span\{v_1^{(k)}, v_2^{(k)}, \ldots, v_{d_k}^{(k)}\}$, $S_{noise}^{(k)} = Span\{U_{noise}^{(k)}\} = span\{v_{d_k+1}^{(k)}, v_{d_k+2}^{(k)}, \ldots, v_{M_k}^{(k)}\}$. They are K-identity-specific subspace and K-identity specific noise subspace respectively. Then any face image Γ can be projected to the K-identity-specific subspace $S_{face}^{(k)}$ by a matrix transform $W^{(k)} = U_{face}^{(k)\,T} \Phi^{(k)}$, in which $\Phi^{(k)} = \Gamma - \Psi^{(k)}$ is the difference image and $\Psi^{(k)}$ is the mean image obtained from the training images of the K-identity. And the input image can be reconstructed by $\Phi_r^{(k)} = U_{face}^{(k)} W^{(k)}$.

Then the distance between any input face image and the K-identity-specific subspace can be calculated as follows: $\varepsilon^{(k)} = \left\| \Phi^{(k)} - \Phi_r^{(k)} \right\|$. We denote the distance by DFISS to measure the similarity between the input image and the K-identity.

3. Face Verification Based on ISS and Maximum Likelihood Rules

As a two-class problem, face verification can be resolved by using the Bayesian method based on the maximum a posteriori (MAP) rule: $x \in \Omega_k$ if $P(\Omega_k \mid x) > P(\overline{\Omega}_k \mid x)$, where $P(\Omega_k \mid x) = \dfrac{P(x \mid \Omega_k) * P(\Omega_k)}{P(x \mid \Omega_k) * P(\Omega_k) + P(x \mid \overline{\Omega}_k) * P(\overline{\Omega}_k)}$ and $P(\overline{\Omega}_k \mid x) = \dfrac{P(x \mid \overline{\Omega}_k) * P(\overline{\Omega}_k)}{P(x \mid \Omega_k) * P(\Omega_k) + P(x \mid \overline{\Omega}_k) * P(\overline{\Omega}_k)}$, with $\overline{\Omega}_k$ the class containing the non-k-identity faces, which can be learned by using similar analysis as Ω_k.

For general face verification problem, equal probability $P(\Omega_k) = P(\overline{\Omega}_k) = 1/2$ is satisfied, so we only need to estimate class conditional probability density $P(x \mid \Omega_k)$, by which the rules converted to the maximum likelihood rule. While it is not an easy work to estimate $P(x \mid \Omega_k)$ since face images are hi-dimensional data with much variance due to the 2D appearance deformation caused by 3D facial pose and lighting changes. Fortunately, ISS we proposed provides a simple and convenient method to estimate the density. Since a Gaussian model can be used to approximately model a specific identity's distribution, the class conditional probability density corresponding to the K-identity is: $P(x \mid \Omega_k) = \dfrac{\exp[-\frac{1}{2}(x - \overline{x}_k)^T \Sigma_k^{-1}(x - \overline{x}_k)]}{(2\pi)^{N_k/2} \left|\Sigma_k\right|^{1/2}}$. And $P(x \mid \overline{\Omega}_k)$ can be estimated similarly. Then, base on the ISS we proposed in section 2, we adopt the algorithm in [3] to estimate $P(x \mid \Omega_k)$ as:

$$\hat{P}(x \mid \Omega_k) = \left[\frac{\exp[-\frac{1}{2}\sum_{i=1}^{M} \frac{(y_i^{(k)})^2}{\lambda_i^{(k)}}]}{(2\pi)^{M/2} \prod_{i=1}^{M} \lambda_i^{(k)}} \right] \cdot \left[\frac{\exp(-\frac{\varepsilon_{(k)}^2(x)}{2\rho^{(k)}})}{(2\pi\rho^{(k)})^{(N_k - M)/2}} \right].$$

Where: $\lambda_i^{(k)}, i = 1,2,\ldots,N_k$ are the eigenvalues calculated from training data of k-identity and ordered non-increasingly. M is the truncated dimension of eigenvalues. And $[y_1^{(k)}, y_2^{(k)}, \cdots, y_M^{(k)}]^T = Y^{(k)} = U_{face}^{(k)\,T} x$ is the transformed vector when x is projected to the k-ISS. $\varepsilon_{(k)}^2(x)$ is the DFISS. $\rho^{(k)} = \dfrac{1}{N_k - M}\sum_{i=M+1}^{N_k} \lambda_i$ is the optimal weight coefficient. Refer to [3] for details.

Using the similar algorithm $\hat{P}(x \mid \overline{\Omega}_k)$ can be estimated. So we get the following for k-identity face verification rule: $x \in \Omega_k$ if $\hat{P}(x \mid \Omega_k) > \hat{P}(x \mid \overline{\Omega}_k)$.

4. Face-Unlock Screen Saver Based on Face Verification

4.1 Localization of the Facial Features, Face Normalizations and Masking

In our system, based on the results of our face detection system [9] and the observations that the two irises are the most salient features, the two irises are localized first. Then other organs are localized by integral projection. Please refer to [10] for details.

To eliminate the effect of the hair and the background, normalization is necessary in order to achieve robust identification. In our system all faces are normalized as those in Fig.3, by face warping, affine transformation, luminance and scale normalization, and masking. After normalization, the eyes are positioned at fixed locations to achieve a certain extent of shape-free appearance. The normalized faces are 32x32 pixels in size. Some normalized faces are shown in Fig.2. In our system, no less than 25 samples for a specific user are needed.

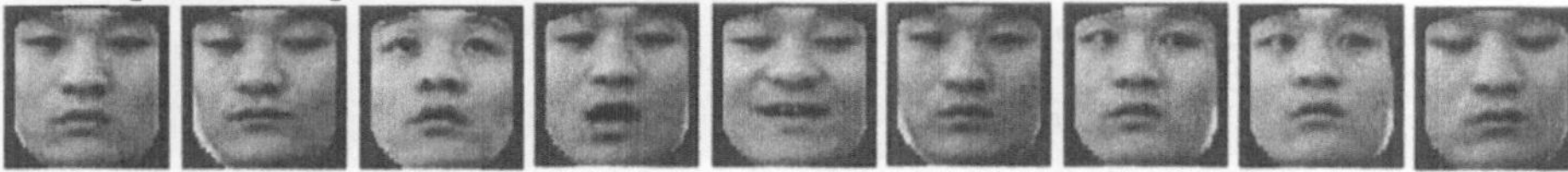

Fig.2 Normalized Facial Images

4.2 Automatic Training Samples Collecting Tool

To learn a new face automatically and conveniently, an automatic training sample collecting tool is designed, which can automatically capture enough samples (normalized facial images) needed to train the ISS for the specific identity by just requiring the user to sit before the USB camera and move his head for about tens of seconds. "Bad" samples, derived from occasional errors of features localization, are automatically deleted based on the quality of the sample as a normalized face. And the administrator is allowed to further check all the samples by deleting visually bad samples.

4.3 ISS Training

After collecting enough samples of the specific user, ISS of the specific face is trained by the eigen-analysis algorithm. In our system, $P(x \mid \overline{\Omega}_k)$ is trained by an independent face set containing 1000 faces. Then the two class conditional probability density functions are estimated, where the dimension of the principal subspace is set to 25 as an experiential choice. And eigenfaces specific for the first author of the paper (so called eigen-SGSHAN-faces) are illustrated in Fig.3, from which the main characteristics of the first author's face can be seen.

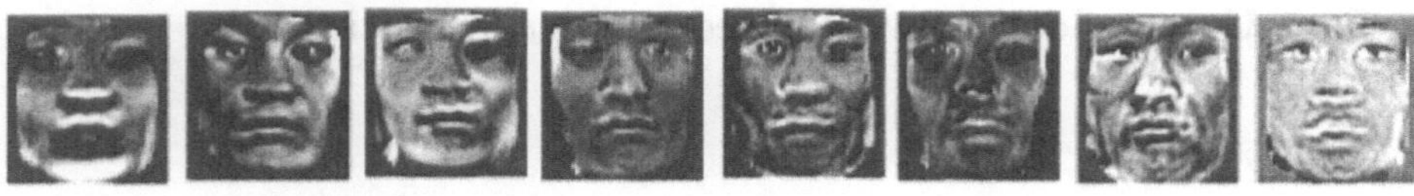

Fig.3 Top Eigen-SGSHAN-faces

4.4 System Setup and Experiments

The overall architecture of the face-unlock screen saver system is illustrated in Fig.4. Please note that, to reduce the occurrence of the occasional false acceptance, a strategy is designed to accept one user only when he passes the verification more than one time in a given time slot.

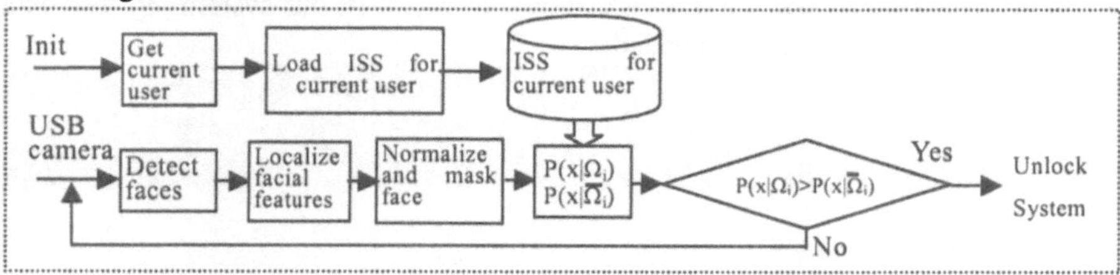

Fig 4. Architecture of the Face-Unlock Screen Saver

Using ordinary USB camera, under 320x240 image size, our system can verify a face (including the whole process from face detection, feature localization, normalization and verification finally) in less than 200 milliseconds, that it, about frames can be verified in one second. Practical experiments are conducted on legal user's unlocking and imposter's attempts to login. The legal user can always unlock the saver successfully during the experiments, with average time needed to unlock the saver less than two seconds under relatively uniform illumination and less than four seconds under poor lighting conditions. The system refused all the imposters among all the 50 attempts.

5. Conclusion and Future Works

Unlocking screen saver by the user's face is an interesting application of face recognition technology. Based on the fact that, for such kind of tasks, sufficient facial images can be easily obtained, the proposed algorithm can model the distribution of every person based on the identity-specific subspaces. And the verification is completed by the maximum likelihood rule based on the estimation of the distribution of the corresponding ISS private for the person. Related techniques to localize facial features and normalize facial images are proposed, which could work well in real-time. Practical experiments have shown effectiveness and excellent performance of our screen saver system.

Though we have failed to unlock the system by photos of the legal user, no techniques are adopted now to prevent this kind of cheats. Future work includes the discrimination between a live face and a photo of the legal user.

Acknowledgment

The research is sponsored partly by National Science Foundation of China (No.69789301), National Hi-Tech Program of China (No.863-306-ZD03-01-2), 100 Talents Foundation of Chinese Academy of Sciences, and all the researches are done under the sponsor of the YCNC Co. Chengdu, Sichuan, China.

References

1. R. Chellappa, C. L. Wilson, and S. Sirohey, Human and Machine Recognition of Faces: A Survey, Proceedings of the IEEE, Vol.83, No.5, pp. 705-740,1995
2. M. Turk, and A. Pentland, Eigen-faces for Recognition, Journal of Cognitive Neuroscience, Vol. 3, No. 1, pp. 71-86, 1991
3. L Wiskott, J.M.Fellous, N.Kruger and C.V.D.Malsburg, "Face Recogniton by Elastic Bunch Graph Matching", IEEE Trans. On PAMI, 19(7), pp775-779, 1997.7
4. Lanitis A. Taylor CJ. Cootes TF. Automatic interpretation and coding of face images using flexible models. IEEE Trans. on Pattern Analysis & Machine Intelligence, vol.19, no.7, July 1997, pp.743-756
5. P.N.Belhumeur, J.P.Hespanha and D.J.Kriegman. "Eigenfaces vs Fisherfaces: recognition using class specific linear projection". IEEE trans. on PAMI, vol.20, No.7, 1997.7
6. W.Zhao and R.Chellappa, "Robust Image-Based 3D Face Recognition", CAR-TR-932, N00014-95-1-0521, CS-TR-4091, Center for Auto Research, UMD, 2000.1
7. P.J.Phillips, H.Moon, etc. "The FERET Evaluation Methodology for Face-Recognition Algorithms", IEEE Transactions on PAMI, Vol.22, No.10, pp1090-1104, 2000
8. G.Guo, S.Z.Li and K.Chan, "Face Recognition by Support Vector Machines", Proc. of the 4th Int. Conf. on Auto. Face and Gesture Recog., pp.196-201, Grenoble, 2000.3
9. Baback Moghaddam, Tony Jebara, Alex Pentland, Bayesian Face Recognition, Pattern Recognition Vol.33, pp1771-1782, 2000
10. Wen Gao, Mingbao Liu. A hierarchical approach to human face detection in a complex background. Proceedings of the First International Conference on Multimodal Interface, pp.289-292, 1996
11. S.G. Shan, W.Gao, J.Yan etc. Individual 3d face synthesis based on orthogonal photos and speech-driven facial animation. Proceedings of the International Conference on Image (ICIP'2000), Vol. III, pp238-242, 2000

Analysis of Camera Operations in MPEG Compressed Domain Based on Generalized Hough Transform

Won-Young Yoo[1], and Joonwhoan Lee[2]

[1] Virtual Reality Center, Electronics and Telecommunications Research Institute, Korea
Zero2@etri.re.kr
[2] Department of Electronic Engineering, Chonbuk National University, Korea
chlee@moak.chonbuk.ac.kr

Abstract. In this paper, we propose a simple and efficient method to estimate the camera operations using MVs(Motion Vectors), which is extracted directly from MPEG-2 video stream without complete decoding. In the method, MVs in the compressed video stream are converted into approximated OF(Optical Flow). And the approximated OF is used to estimate the camera operations including pan, tilt and zoom based on the generalized Hough transform technique. The method provided better results than the conventional least square method for video streams of basketball and soccer games including captions. And these camera operations can be used in constructing a key frame as a mosaics image or making features for content-based video retrievals.

1 Introduction

For content-based video services, it is inevitable to analyze huge video stream and make index for the analyzed video. The automatic analysis of video data can be done in the uncompressed domain or compressed domain. But it is not difficult to expect all the video data in the future will have compressed format such as MPEG2 or MPEG4 and the analysis process in the compressed domain is more efficient. Therefore, there are a lot of efforts of analysis in the frame-based video streams [1]~[5]. MPEG4 is very nice features for content-based video services, because video stream itself contains a lot of information without additional efforts of video analysis. But, it is not completely available because the object segmentation is still problem in natural video. Therefore, MPEG2 will be used for a while in many applications like digital TV. That is why we take MPEG2 domain rather than MPEG4.

This paper proposes a method of the analysis of camera operations using the MVs without complete decoding of MPEG2 video stream. Because MVs involved in MPEG2 video stream is to enhance the efficiency of compression and the sequence of frames is not the same order as display, they cannot be used directly as sequential OF. Especially in the low-textured or uniform areas, there may be the noisy MVs because MPEG2 uses area-correlation method to extract the MVs. Therefore proper interpretation of MVs contained in different types of frames is needed and should be converted them to approximated OF according to the interpretation. As it is pointed out, the estimated OF may be noisy especially in the low textured area. We use the spatiotemporal vector median filter to remove the noisy. Once the OF is reconstructed, the parameters of camera operation is estimated by the generalized Hough transform in this paper. Least square method is usually used to extract the camera parameters. However, it has a problem, which is sensitive to noise due to the caption flow in the news video or motion of objects in video source because they could be considered as outliers. Since the generalized Hough transform technique is mode(maximum value) estimator, it can produce robust estimation results. Generally it works better in terms of robust estimation than least square method [6].

The proposed method performed the overall successful interpretation of camera operation with the accuracy of 93.75% at soccer and basketball sequences compressed in MPEG2 format. The estimated parameter was sufficiently exacted to construct mosaic images to represent key frames for content-based video retrievals. [7].

2. Construction of approximated OF

2.1 Approximate OF from MVs

The MV in MPEG video cannot be treated as the OF, because they are not arranged in sequential order and they have a different magnitude scale from frame to frame according to the distance of each reference frame. Also, it is impossible to get sequential motion flow directly between compressed B frames (see Fig. 1)[8]~[11].

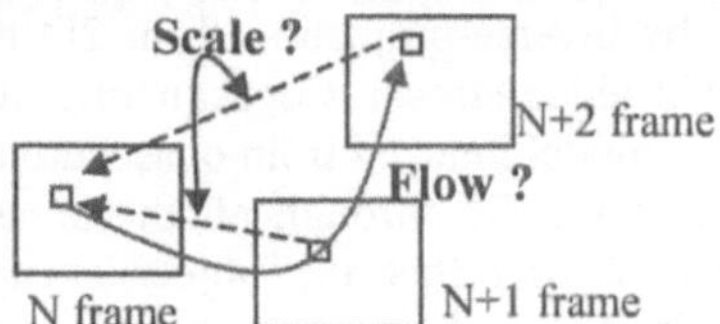

Fig. 1. Necessity of Scale Adjustment

In these reasons, we have to convert MVs with the same magnitude scale and to arrange them in sequential order [12].

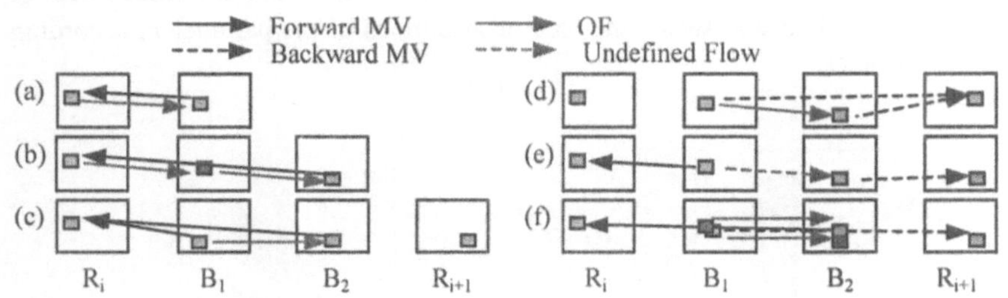

Fig. 2. OF Estimation between Frames

For the calculation of OF, Fig.2 shows the method to estimate the OF in each case.

Note that the OF cannot be defined form the MVs in the case of (e) in Fig. 2. In the case of (f) in Fig.2, OF is taken by the half of average vector of two MVs, backward one and the reverse of forward one. Also, in the case of OF estimation with opposite direction of MV, the OF of nearby MB(MacroBlock) pointed by forward MV is taken as the reverse of the MV.

2.2 Spatiotemporal filtering of OF

As MVs in MPEG are estimated by area-correlation method in order to enhance the compression efficiency, OF that we have estimated before is a lot different from an ideal OF. So, filtering is needed. In this paper, reconstructed OF is filtered in the spatial and temporal domain using vector median filter. This filter has a window of size 3*3*3 for the (x,y,t) domain. Vector median filter is nonlinear filter that choose a median vector of MVs that are participated in the filtering process. This filter works not only conserving the discontinuity of vectors but also removing the noisy vectors. That is, the goal of this filtering in the spatiotemporal domain is to remove the noisy vectors and to preserve the meaningful real motion.

3. Estimation of camera operation using the generalized Hough transform technique

The camera model is a transform projecting 3D space to 2D image. But conversely the 3D parameter extraction by inverse-projection from 2D image plane cannot be obtained only with the MPEG2 video stream. Consequently, this paper does assume the approximated pan-tilt-zoom model induced from consecutive image coordinates.

The camera operation affects the OF through all the areas of a frame, and the object motion influences only a part that the object occupies. In other words, calculated OF includes not only the camera motion, but also a moving caption or an object motion. The parameters of pan-tilt-zoom model are t_x(the amount of pan), t_y(the amount of tilt) and s(the amount of zoom). t_x and t_y are equal to Δx_0 and Δy_0 in the OF, respectively. s can be indirectly identified by the rate of increase or decrease in magnitudes of OFs as the distance from zoom center is increasing. In this paper, the amount of increase or decrease is defined as α. Fig. 3 shows the definitions of Δx_0, Δy_0, α with their signs and shows the ideal distributions of the parameters according to their frequencies.

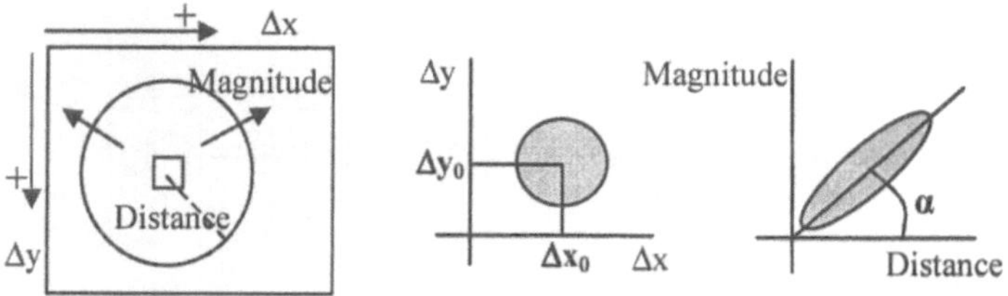

Fig. 3. An assumption & ideal distribution of parameters

The method used for estimation of the amount of pan-tilt using Δx and Δy can be treated as a generalized Hough transform. That is, in the parameter space consisted of Δx and Δy, and the parameters that has the largest population are taken as the amount of pan and tilt. Even if distance-magnitude space is not a parameter space exactly, the slope(magnitude/distance) can be regarded as 1D parameter space. Because the parameter space (Δx,Δy) can be separated two 1D accumulators using projections, the required memory space in this general Hough transform is not necessarily huge, and the amount of calculation is comparable to the least square method.

In order to estimate the α, it is needed to predict the zoom center, because α is calculated by the distance from the zoom center point and the magnitude of OF. In this paper, zoom center is calculated by the following manner. In each row(column), the consecutive MBs whose signs of MVs are changing in both sides or changing in a side with some thread number and which do not have MV are counted. And we take the inverses of the counts as the weights assigned to the consecutive MBs. The weights are summed in the column(row)-wise direction and treat the MB position having the maximum value as column(row) of the zoom center. For example, Fig.4 shows distribution of OF and method of finding center in the case of zoom-in.

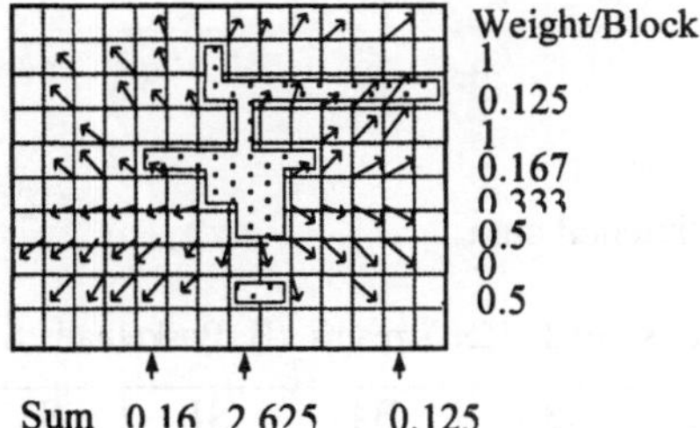

Fig. 4. Calculation of the zoom center

4. Experimental Results

We compared the result of proposed method with the result of least square method. In the case that only camera operation occurred in a frame(no object motion), both methods showed the similar results. However, the proposed Hough transform method provided the robust estimation when the camera operation occurred with a caption or partial motion of objects in frame as Fig.5. As a result, the estimation by the proposed method provides the similar results to the conventional least square without outliers such as moving captions and objects.

To annotate the camera operations using estimated parameters, we calculated Δx_0, Δy_0, and α of about 1000 frames as in Fig. 6 (704*480 size of basketball game compressed by MPEG2). In the Fig 6, section **a** represents zoom-in because α is positive, section **b** represents the pan-tilt operation that the camera is moving in to up and left directions with positive Δx_0 and Δy_0. Also, section **c** represents the pan operation that the camera is moving in to left direction with positive Δx_0.

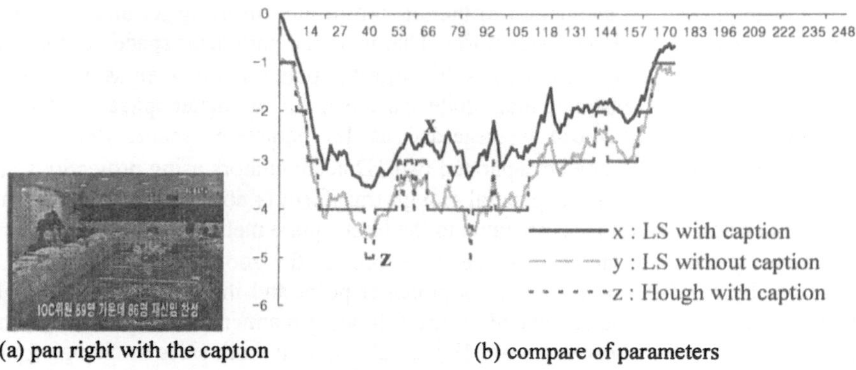

(a) pan right with the caption (b) compare of parameters

Fig. 5. Compare of experimental results

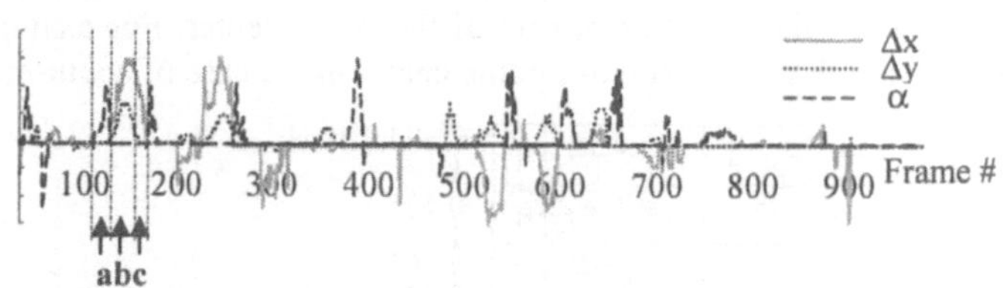

Fig. 6. Δx_0, Δy_0, α of experimental data

Table 1. Experimental results of several video streams. (B: Basketball , S: Soccer)

	B1	B2	B3	B4	S1	S2	S3	S4
Total	1121	1208	885	1691	1829	946	2379	1470
Original	618	318	485	995	938	250	762	493
Correct	575	289	447	948	856	217	682	429
Miss	61	36	54	73	103	43	106	92
False Alarm	18	7	16	26	21	10	26	29
%	92.95	96.44	92.09	94.15	93.22	94.40	94.45	91.70

Table 1 represents the experimental results of other basketball and soccer video streams. In Table 1, "%" represents (total frames –False Alarm – Miss)/ total frames *100(%) as a rate of the right extracted frames to the total frames. 93.75% among the total 11,529 frames in this experiment were rightly recognized as shown in Table 1.

For evaluate the accuracy of the estimated parameters by the proposed method, we have constructed mosaic images. Seamless mosaic depends on the accuracy of the estimated parameters of camera operation [13]. Fig. 7 shows the mosaic images that are achieved by the parameters extracted from the baseball sequence with the pan right for 130 frames and the sports new sequence with the pan right and caption.

Fig. 7. Mosaic of baseball and sports news sequence

5. Conclusion

This paper proposes a method for finding the sequential OF using only the MVs in the compressed domain as MPEG1 or MPEG2. Also, the generalized Hough transform technique for the estimation of parameters for camera operation is suggested. This method is based on the facts that the camera motion occurs globally through the whole frame, and the local object motions can be treated as outliers. The camera motion assumed in this paper is pan-tilt-zoom model, and corresponding parameters are Δx_0, Δy_0, and α. The proposed Hough transform method is robust to the error-prone object motions compared to the conventional least square method. By this reason, preprocessing step removing error-prone blocks for overcoming the error can be omitted. As a result, 93.75% accuracy of interpretation was obtained for some video streams in spite of using only compressed information. The accuracy of the estimated parameters is good as one can construct mosaic images based on them.

References

1. V. Kobla, D. Doermann, "Compressed domain video indexing techniques using DCT and motion vector information in MPEG video," *SRIVD V*, SPIE vol.3022, pp.200-211, Jan 1997.
2. O.N. Gerek, Y. Altunbasak, "Key Frame Selection from MPEG Video Data," *VCIP*, SPIE Vol. 3024, pp.920-925, 1997.
3. J. Meng, Y. Juan, S-F Chang, "Scene Change Detection in a MPEG Compressed Video Sequence," Digital Video Compression, SPIE Vol. 2419, pp.14-25, 1995.
4. Y. Ariki, Y. Saito, "Extraction of TV News Articles Based on Scene Cut Detection Using DCT Clustering," *ICIP 96*, Vol. 3, pp.847-850, 1996.
5. Marco la Cascia, Edoardo Ardizzone, "JACOB: Just a Content-Based Query System for Video Databases," *ICASSP '96*, Vol. 2, pp.1216-1219, May 1996
6. Ramesh Jain, Rangachar Kasturi and Brian G. Schunck, 'Machine Vision', McGraw-Hill, 1995.
7. Saur Drew D, Tan Yap-Peng, Kulkarni Sanjeev R, Ramadge Peter J, "Automated Analysis and Annotation of Basketball Video," *Storage and Retrieval for Image and Video Databases V*, SPIE Vol 3022, pp.176-187, Jan 1997.
8. ISO-IEC13812-1/2 International Standards, 1st Ed., 1996.
9. Keith Jack, 'Video Demystified A Handbook for the Digital Engineer,' 2nd Ed., Hightext Interactive, 1996.
10. R. Milanese, A. Jacot-Descombes, "Efficient Segmentation and Camera Motion Indexing of Compressed Video," *Real-Time Imaging*, Vol. 5, No. 4, pp. 231-241, Aug 1999.
11. M. Pilu, "On using raw MPEG motion vectors to determine global camera motion," *Visual Communications and Image Processing '98*, SPIE vol.3309 p.448-459, Jan 1998.
12. P. Sobey, M. V. Srinvansan, "Measurement of Optical Flow by Generalized Gradient Scheme." *J.Opt.Soc.Am.A*, Vol. 8, No. 9, pp. 1488-1498, 1991.
13. M. Pilu, "On using raw MPEG motion vectors to determine global camera motion," *Visual Communications & Image Processing'98*, SPIE vol. 3309 pp. 448-459, Jan. 1998.

Speech Driven MPEG-4 Based Face Animation via Neural Network

Yiqiang Chen[1], Wen Gao[1,2], Zhaoqi Wang[1] and Li Zuo[1]

[1](Institute of Computing Technology, Chinese Academy of Sciences, 100080)
[2](Department of Computer Science, Harbin Institute of Technology, 150001)
{Yqchen, Wgao, Zqwang, Lzuo}@ict.ac.cn

Abstract. In this paper, some clustering and machine learning methods are combined together to learn the correspondence between speech acoustic and MPEG-4 based face animation parameters. The features of audio and image sequences can be extracted from the large recorded audio-visual database. The face animation parameter (FAP) sequences can be computed and then clustered to FAP patterns. An artificial neural network (ANN) was trained to map the linear predictive coefficients (LPC) and some prosodic features of an individual's natural speech to FAP patterns. The performance of our system shows that the proposed learning algorithm is suitable, which can greatly improve the realism of real time face animation during speech.

1 Introduction

As the realistic-looking scenes and facial can be generated by some images with rendering or other techniques, people are beginning to expect realistic-looking behavior. More challenge task in human's behavior simulation is to synthesize virtual human's lip motion facial animation during speech. Hani Yehia [1] presents the method to estimate face motion from speech acoustic by training nonlinear estimators whose inputs are LSP coefficients and whose output are face marker positions. Massaro and Beskow [2] presents an implementation that synthesized visual speech directly from the acoustic waveform based on artificial neural network. Based on a set of rules [3], they define the properties of the synthesis parameters for each speech segment. Though they can obtain a good result, to assign each training segments of audio some control parameters via defined rules is a hard work and less precise. Matthew brand [4] introduce and apply the HMM to voice puppetry, the voice puppet learns a facial control model from computer vision of real facial behavior, automatically incorporating vocal and facial dynamics such as co-articulation. But this method cannot be real time and the problem of error beyond retrieve in HMM viterbi decoding is inherent.

In this paper, some clustering and machine learning methods are combined together for generating new facial animation sequences during speech more precisely that can be incorporated into existing face synthesis system to improve the naturalness and intelligibility. The rest part of this paper is organized as follows: Section 2 overviews our speech driven system. Section 3 presents the data preprocessing methods. The clustering algorithm and ANN are introduced in section 4. The experiments are presented in section 5. And then we conclude a summary in section 6.

2 System Overview

The face animation controlled by speech is very complex research work. There are two ways for implementing the animated talking head with original speech: via speech recognition [5] or not via speech recognition. A potential limitation of the fore approach is that automatic speech recognition is not accurate enough to provide a reliable transcription of the utterance. In this paper, we try to map the acoustics directly to face animation parameter (FAP) patterns including upper facial expressions. The FAP patterns are not clustered regard to hypothesized categories of speech perception, but classified from large recorded image sequence only. We assume that adjusting these basic FAP patterns can simulate the facial behavior.

Figure 1 Schematically outlines the main phases of our learning framework. The feature points according to face defined parameter (FDP) and FAP defined by MPEG4 are auto-tracked and extracted from the image sequences.

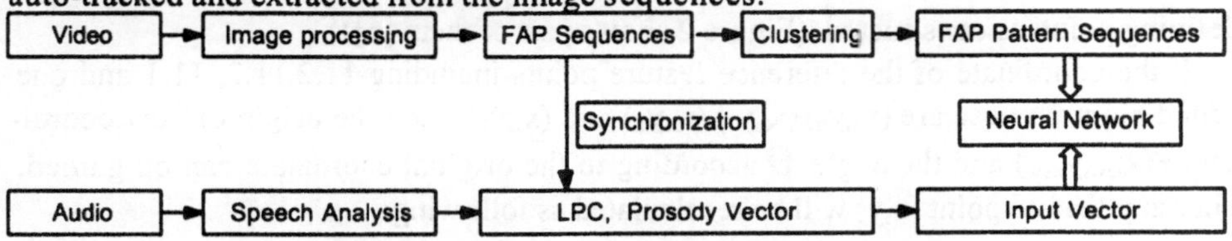

Fig. 1. The main phases of learning framework

The FAP sequences can be clustered. In the mean time, the acoustic speech is analyzed to LPC cestrum coefficients and some prosodic features such as formant frequencies and the energy. An artificial neural network was trained to map the cepstral coefficients including forward and backward of an individual's natural speech to FAP pattern in frame level.

3 Data Preprocess

3.1 Audio Signal Analysis

All the audio features are designed for phonemic analysis and always successfully used in speech recognition, however it's not necessarily good at indicating the facial behavior. The relationship between facial and speech may be more complex but in-compact than phoneme and speech. To obtain a useful vocal representation, we calculate LPC and some prosody parameters such as the formant frequencies and the energy to represent the audio features.

3.2 Video Signal Analysis

To obtain facial articulation data and the FAP defined by MPEG4, we put some color marks on the face of actor. A computer image processing system was developed to obtain the exact coordinate of each feature points in the image sequences (Fig.2).

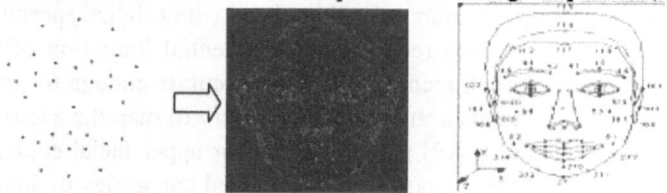

Fig.2. Tracking result and the reference coordinate

Thought we asked subjects to reduce head motion, there inevitably existing noise in our tracking data. To make the data more accurate, a filter according to some facial defining points is constructed. (Figure 2 shows part of them [6]).

If the coordinate of the reference feature points including 11.2,11.3, 11.1 and one added point on nose are (x_0,y_0),(x_1,y_1),(x_2,y_2) and (x_3,y_3), then the origin of new coordinate $P(x_{new},y_{new})$ and the angle θ according to the original coordinate can be gained. Thus any feature point (x,y) will be recalculated as following:

$$x' = x \times \cos(\theta) - x \times \sin(\theta) + P(x_{new}) \tag{1}$$

$$y' = y \times \sin(\theta) - y \times \cos(\theta) + P(y_{new}) \tag{2}$$

To avoid the effect of different scale, the relative coordinate should be obtained by calculating relative location of each point. After filtering, the relative coordinate can be calculated to the FAP according to face animation parameter unit (FAPU)[6].

4 Clustering and Learning

4.1 Clustering

Due to the number of basic units for facial is not known at all, the unsupervised cluster method was applied in this work. The ISODATA [7](Iterative Self-organizing

Data) algorithm is chosen for our clustering. After clustering, there are 16 FAP patterns are classified (Figure 3 shows them).

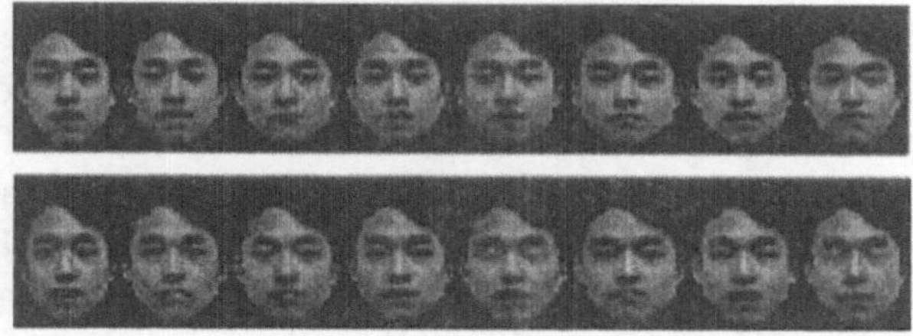

Fig. 3. FAP patterns

4.2 Artificial Neural Network

We can view the mapping from acoustic speech to FAP patterns as a pattern recognition task. There are many learning machines can be choose for this task, such as HMM, SVM and Neural Network. Since neural network have been shown to be efficient and robust learning machine, which solve an input-output mapping. We train the network against many recorded sentences. The feed-forward artificial neural network (ANN) with three layers, as shown in Figure 4, was constructed.

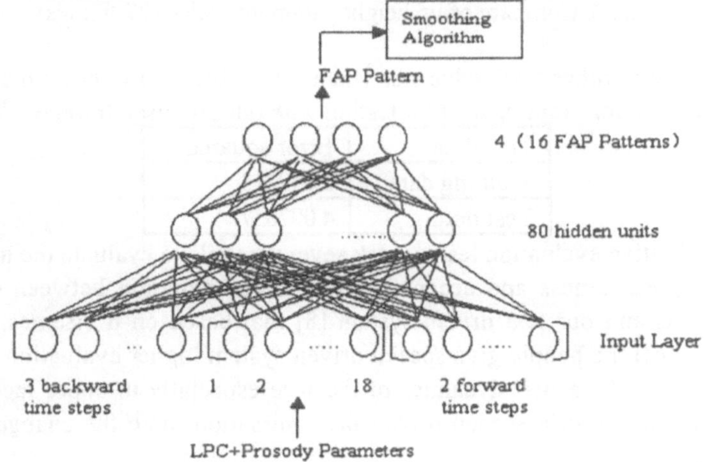

Fig. 4. The model architecture of our ANN

The acoustic input is streamed at 60 frames a second. At every frame, 16 LPC and 2 prosody parameters serve as the input to 18 input units. All of the 18 input parameters were taken at 6 consecutive time frames (3 frames back and two frames forward) yielding a total of 108 input nodes. There are 16 FAP patterns, thus the output of neural network consists of 4 units, which can code these 16 classes. Network with 80 hidden units were trained using the back-propagation algorithm with learning rate of 0.001 and the network sum-squared error rate is 0.001.

5 Experiment

To cover most pronunciation of one people in small dataset, the text information of Chinese speech synthesis database called CoSS-1 was selected for the pronounce material. We Record Audio-Visual database, about 200 sentences, different from other record the phoneme. Face motion was measured via color marks and tracked at 25 frames/s. The tracking result can be calculated and clustered to FAP pattern. The speech waveform was sampled at 8040Hz, and analyzed using frame length of 256 samples and a frame shift of 65 samples. A Hamming window was applied and LPC analysis of order P=16 was carried out for each frame. One ANN is trained for mapping from acoustic vector to FAP pattern.

Two approaches for evaluation tests have been proposed in our work: quantitative evaluation test and qualitative evaluation test. In our quantitative evaluation, we compare computed values with real values. Figure 5 shows the example of values of the lip height parameter (2.2 in Figure 2) of the synthetic face compared with the same values obtained from the analysis of real motion capture data.

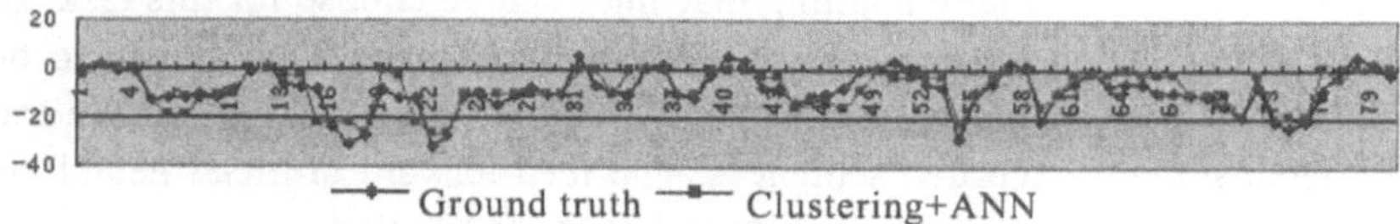

Fig. 5. Compare of lip height parameter value (77 frames)

The compare of other FAP value was taken. The table below shows mean errors of training data and non-training data for testing with our proposed framework.

Test data	Error squared
Training data	2.859213
Test data	4.097657

In our qualitative evaluation test, we ask several people to evaluate the intelligibility, naturalness, pleasantness and acceptability of face animation between our speech driven systems and our text driven system [8] that based on 6 visemes. The result sounds good, All the people give speech driven system higher evaluation since it not only can address the actual dynamics of the face especially in upper face. Figure 6 shows the frames from a speech driven face animation, note the changes in upper facial expression.

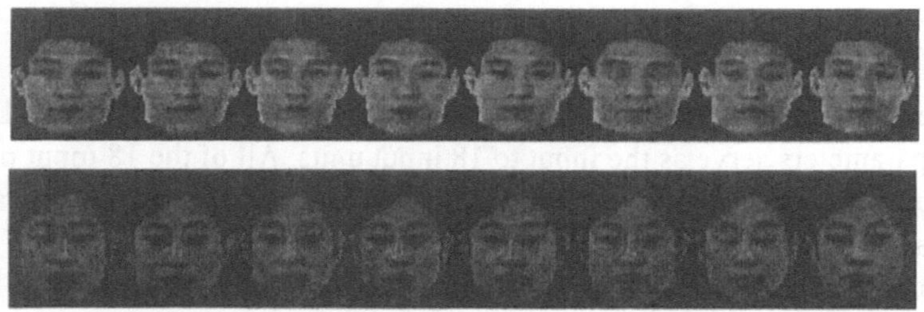

Fig. 6. Some frames from our speech driven face animation

6 Conclusions and Future Work

In this paper, Some Clustering and Machine Learning methods are combined together to learn the correspondence between speech acoustic and MPEG-4 based face animation parameters. Our learning technical is useful because it is a good compromise between the two opposing extremes: rule based method and performance based method. And this MPEG-4 based model are suitable for driving many different kinds of animation ranging from video-realistic image wraps to 3D cartoon characters. Experiment shows that the proposed learning algorithm is good, which greatly improves the realism of face animation during speech. The future work includes making the system more robust to variations between speakers and recording conditions, and more powerful clustering and learning algorithm.

7 Acknowledgement

This research is sponsored partly by Natural Science Foundation of China (No.69789301), National Hi-Tech Program of China (No.863-306-ZD03-01-2), and 100 Talents Foundation of Chinese Academy of Sciences.

8 Reference

1. Hani Yehia, Takaaki Kuratate and Eric Vatikiotis-Bateson. Using speech acoustics to drive facial motion. In Proc. 14th international congress of phonetic sciences (ICPhS'99), vol.1, (1999), 631-634.
2. Dominic W.Massaro , Jonas Beskow and Michael M. Cohen. Picture My Voice: Audio to Visual Speech Synthesis using Artificial Neural Networks. In: The fourth annual Auditory-Visual Speech Processing conference (AVSP'99). Santa Cruz, (1999).
3. J.Beskow. Rule-based visual speech synthesis. In ESCA-EUROSPEECH'95. 4th European Conference on Speech Communication and Technology, Madrid, September (1995).
4. Matthew Brand. Voice Puppetry. In: Proceedings of SIGGRAPH 99. (1999), 21-28.
5. T.Chen and R. Rao. Audio-Visual integration in multimodal communication. In Proc. IEEE Special Issue on Multimedia signal processing, (1998), 837-852.
6. J.Ostermann, Animation of Synthetic Faces in MPEG-4, Computer Animation, (1998), 49-51.
7. Yiqang Chen, Wen Gao, Tingshao Zhu, Jiyong Ma, Multi-stragy Data mining framework for mandarin prosodic pattern, ICSLP2000 , Vol2 , (2000), 59-62.
8. Shiguang Shan, WenGao, Jie Yan, Individual 3d face synthesis based on orthogonal photos and speech-driven facial animation, ICIP'2000, Vol. 3, (2000), 238-242.

Mesh Simplification by Vertex Cluster Contraction

Kam-Fai Chan and Chi-Wah Kok

Department of Electrical and Electronic Engineering, Hong Kong University of Science and Technology, Clear Water Bay, HONG KONG

Abstract. A novel 3D mesh model simplification algorithm that makes use of vertex cluster contraction is proposed. The proposed algorithm computes a distortion metrics that satisfy the volume preservation and shape preservation criterion. The simplification results are shown to have better visual quality than other algorithms in literature. Furthermore, the proposed algorithm can generate progressive mesh models.

1 Introduction

3D models constructed by free-form modelling using triangular meshes have found applications in computer graphics and visualizations. In order to accommodate the growing complexity of 3D models, streamability, scalability, and compression of 3D meshes are essential. This can be archived by multiresolution mesh representation which represents the 3D model by a low resolution model and a series of corrections at increasing level-of-details (LODs). The idea was first demonstrated by rossignac [6] for geometric models and later extended by chen [7] to include vertex attributes, such as color and texture. To support multiresolution mesh representation, an efficient algorithm that generates a series of approximating meshes known as mesh simplification is required. Most of the existing simplification algorithms are heuristic in nature, therefore, the visual appearance of the simplified mesh depends heavily on the order of the visited vertices. A geometric error metric was proposed by Garland [1] to measure the geometric error induced by edge contraction, as a result, better visual quality simplification results can be obtained. A novel simplification algorithm is proposed based on vertex cluster contraction. Both the geometric model and the associated attribute are jointly simplified and can be used to generate multiresolution mesh models with different level of details.

Notation A vertex V defined by coordinate $\{x, y, z\}$ is denoted by the vector $[x \;\; y \;\; z \;\; 1]^T$. A triangle T is defined by a collection of three vertices, $\{V_1, V_2, V_3\}$. $T_i : \{V_{i1}, V_{i2}, V_{i3}\}$ is a neighbor of $T_0 : \{V_{01}, V_{02}, V_{03}\}$ iff there exist $j, k \in [1, 3]$ such that $V_{ij} = V_{0k}$. A normalized plane p defined by $ax + by + cz + d = 0$ with $a^2 + b^2 + c^2 = 1$ is denoted by the vector $[a \;\; b \;\; c \;\; d]^T$.

2 Vertex Cluster Contraction

The proposed algorithm reduces the number of vertices and faces by contracting a collection of connected vertices that form a face to a single vertex. To simplify our discussion, we concentrated on triangular vertex cluster contraction. Figure 1 illustrates the triangle contraction process where the triangle $T_0 : \{V_1, V_2, V_3\}$ is contracted to V_0. The presented algorithm can be applied to other forms of vertex clusters that form a coplanar surface. A geometric error metric that consists of distance metric, angle metric, and attribute metric, is defined to quantify the simplification error induced by vertex cluster contraction.

2.1 Distance Metric

The volume preservation criteria discussed by Kalvin [10] and the distance metric defined by Garland [1] are shown to be equivalent by Kim [8]. As a result, we concentrated on the distance metric, as it is easy to formulate. Assume S is the set of planes that contains all neighbors of T_0. The distance metric $D(V_0, T_0)$ for contracting T_0 to V_0 is given by

$$D(V_0, T_0) = \sum_{p_i \in S} \|p_i^T V_0\| + \|p_0^T V_0\| = \sum_{p_i \in S, p_0} (V_0^T p_i)(p_i^T V_0) \tag{1}$$

$$= V_0^T \Big(\sum_{p_i \in S, p_0} p_i p_i^T \Big) V_0 = V_0^T Q V_0, \tag{2}$$

where p_i is the normalized plane containing T_i, the i-th neighbors of T_0, and $\|p_i^T V_0\|$ is the normal distance between the plane p_i and V_0. Since eq.(2) is quadratic, the optimal contraction point can be obtained by equating the derivative of $D(V_0, T_0)$ to zero.

$$\frac{\partial D(V_0, T_0)}{\partial V_{0,x}} = \frac{\partial D(V_0, T_0)}{\partial V_{0,y}} = \frac{\partial D(V_0, T_0)}{\partial V_{0,z}} = 0. \tag{3}$$

The above system of equation can be written in vector matrix form as

$$V_0 = \begin{bmatrix} q_{11} & q_{12} & q_{13} & q_{14} \\ q_{21} & q_{22} & q_{23} & q_{24} \\ q_{31} & q_{32} & q_{33} & q_{34} \\ 0 & 0 & 0 & 1 \end{bmatrix}^{-1} \begin{bmatrix} 0 \\ 0 \\ 0 \\ 1 \end{bmatrix}. \tag{4}$$

where q_{ij} is the (i,j)-th component of Q. There may be cases when the matrix in eq.(4) is singular, such as (i) when T_0 and it's neighbors lies on the same plane, or (ii) when T_0 and it's neighbors lies on two connect planes, or (iii) when T_0 are regular, i.e. equilateral. In that case, seven vertices are selected as candidates for the optimal vertex: (i) centroid (ii) the midpoints on each edge and and (iii) three vertices of T_0. The candidate with the smallest $D(V_0, T_0)$ will be selected as the optimal contraction vertex.

The distance metric in eq.(2) is similar to that defined by Garland [1], and with the following two improvements. First, eq.(2) is generalized for arbitrary coplanar vertex cluster contraction, compared to edge contraction in [1]. Freeform model with topological configurations other than triangluar, such as quadrilateral, or hexagonal meshes etc., have been used in various applications because of the file size required to store the face description in mesh model with large number of vertex topological configuration is lower than triangular mesh. Since the algorithm in [1] requires a triangulation step (no matter implicit or explicit) thus increases the storage size. Secondly, the distance metric in eq.(1) only consider the sum of normal distance between the contraction vertex V_0 to neighbors of T_0, i.e. the summation term in eq.(1). While eq.(1) also considered the normal distance between V_0 to T_0. As a result, the simplified mesh from [1] when compared to that generated from the proposed algorithm may be too sharp or too blunt when visually compared to the original mesh.

2.2 Angle Metric

Eq.(4) does not consider the spatial location of V_0. As a result, the "global" direction of the simplified mesh may be very different from that of the original model. The angle metric computes the difference between the global directions of T_0 and that of V_0 formed by it's neigboring triangles can be computed as

$$A(V_0, T_0) = \sum_{p_i \in S, p_0} \angle \mathcal{N}(p_i) - \sum_{p_j \in U} \angle \mathcal{N}(p_j), \tag{5}$$

where $\mathcal{N}(p_i)$ is the unit normal to the plane p_i, and $\angle(\cdot)$ is the angle operator. S is the set of planes containing triangle T_k that are neighbors of T_0. U is the set of planes containing triangle T_m which has V_0 as one of it's vertex after contraction. The arrows showing in Figure 1 is a normal vector $\mathcal{N}(p_i)$ for the i-th triangle. The angle metric is similar to a measure of "curvature" in a localized area associated with the vertex cluster to be contracted.

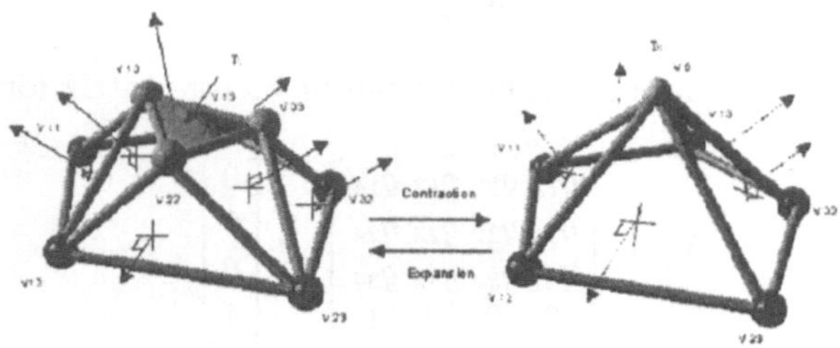

Fig. 1. The contraction and expansion of triangle T_0 formed by V_{13}, V_{22} and V_{33} to contraction vertex V_0. Notice the T_0 is contacted and it's neighbour, $\{V_{32}, V_{13}, V_{33}\}$, $\{V_{13}, V_{22}, V_{12}\}$, and $\{V_{33}, V_{22}, V_{23}\}$, are eliminated in the contraction process. Their connection are required to be stored for expansion.

2.3 Attribute Metrics

After vertex cluster contraction, the surface attribute is re-mapped to the new triangles after contraction. The re-mapped attribute can be computed as the mean attribute value, which can be texture coordinates, vertex color etc.

$$C(V_0) = \frac{\sum_{i=1}^{3} C(V_i)}{3}, \tag{6}$$

where $C(V_i)$ is the attribute of vertex V_i, the vertices of T_0. Other vertices' surface attribute is not required to be re-mapped. As a result, an attribute metrics $G(T_0)$ that quantify the texture similarity is given by

$$G(T_0) = \sum_{i,j\in[1,3];\ i>j} \|C(V_j) - C(V_i)\|, \tag{7}$$

where $\|\cdot\|$ is the norm for texture, which is defined as L_2 norm in our simulation. Such that T_0 with smallest $G(T_0)$ should be contracted in order to minimize the visual artifacts due to texture re-mapping.

2.4 Memory Simplification

The proposed simplification computes the contraction vertex V_0, and the associated metrics, $D(V_0, T_0)$, $A(V_0, T_0)$, $G(T_0)$, for every triangles T_0 in the mesh. The simplification error for contracting a particular triangle T_0 to V_0 is given by

$$E(V_0, T_0) = (1 - \alpha - \beta)D(V_0, T_0) + \alpha A(V_0, T_0) + \beta G(T_0),$$

where $\alpha + \beta \leq 1$ and $\alpha, \beta \geq 0$. The simplification algorithm iteratively contract triangles in the mesh. Unlike edge collapse [1] or vertex decimation [7, 12], the topological configuration of the mesh model is preserved in vertex cluster contraction until there are less triangles available to maintain the original topological configuration. As a result, no re-triangulations are required to maintain the mesh topology. The simplification error $E(V_0, T_0)$ is computed after each contraction which imposes a huge computational complexity. However, it is found that only the simplification errors of the neighbors of T_0 and their associated neighbors are required to be updated without losing any performance [5]. By maintaining a sorted list of $E(V_0, T_0)$, and the associated V_0, an efficient local update algorithm is developed. Such that only $E(V_0, T_0)$ and that of neighbors of T_0 and their associated neighbors are updated in the sorted list.

3 Simulation Results

Showing in Figure 2, and 3 are the simplification results of various mesh models which shown that the proposed algorithm can preserve *distinct features*, such as the horn, breast and tail of the cow model even under severe simplification (89%). While such features are subjected to smoothing effect and vanished in similar simplification ratio for algorithms in [1, 4–7, 10–12, 15]. The *symmetrical shape* of the toup model in Figure 3 is well preserved in the simplified meshes generated by the proposed algorithm, while distorted in simplified mesh by other algorithms. This is because of the lack of shape preservation in the geometric error metrics in other algorithms. The importance of the angle metric in preserving the symmetric shape of the toup mesh model is clearly shown in Figure 3 with $\alpha = 0$. Figure 3 also showed that other distinct features, such as the sharp pointer in the toup model are smoothed in the simplification results generated by other algorithms. With an effective local update computation, memoryless simplification can achieve 98% simplification for most objects (e.g. cow model from (2904,5804) to (54,104) vertices and faces respectively) in less than 1 mins and 30 secs on a P-II 300MHz PC which is comparable to that obtained by other algorithms.

4 Conclusions

We have presented a novel vertex cluster contraction has been presented which support on-the-fly generation of multiresolution meshes at high accuracy with different level of details. Simulation results have shown that the proposed simplification algorithm can produce simplified mesh with better visual quality.

References

1. M.Garland and P.Heckbert, "Surface simplification using quadric error metrics," *Proc. SIGGRAPH'97*, pp.115-122, 1997.
2. M.Garland and P.Heckbert, "Simplifying surfaces with color and texture using quadric error metrics," *Proc. Visualization'98*, pp.263-269, 1998.
3. P.Heckbert and M.Garland, "Survey of polygonal surface simplification algorithms," *SIGGRAPH'97 Course note # 25*, ACM SIGGRAPH, 1997.
4. H.Hoppe, "Efficient implementation of progressive meshes," *Computers and Graphics*, pp.27-36, 1998.
5. H.Hoppe, "New quadric metric for simplifying meshes with appearance attributes," *Proc. Visualization'99*, pp.59-66, 1999.
6. J.Rossignac and P.Borrel "Multiresolution 3D approximations for rendering complex scenes," *Modeling in Computer Graphics: Methods and Applications*, pp. 455-465, 1993.
7. M.Okuda and T.Chen, "Joint geometry/texture progressive coding of 3D models," *Proc. ICIP-2000*, 2000.
8. D.Kim, J.Kim and H.Ko, "Unification of Distance and volume Optimization in Surface Simplification," *The Journal of Graphical Models and Image Processing*, vol. 61, no.363-367, 1999.
9. G.Taubin and J.Rossignac, "Geometric compression through topological surgery", *ACM Trans. on Graphics*, Vol.17, no.2, pp.84-115, 1998.
10. A.Kalvin and R.H.Taylor, "Polygonal mesh simplification with bounded error," *IEEE Computer Graph. Appl.*, pp.64-77, 1996.
11. S.Melax, "A Simple, Fast, and Effective Polygon Reduction Algorithm," *Game Developer*, pp.44-49, 1997.

12. W.J.Shroeder, A.Zerge and W.E.Lorensen, "Decimation of triangle meshes", *Proc. SIGGRAPH*, pp.65-70, 1992.
13. V.Abadjev, M.del Rosario, A.Lebedev, A.Migdal and V.Paskhaver. "MetaStream," *Proc. VRML'99*, pp.53-62, 1999.
14. MPEG-4 SNHC, G.Taubin Ed. "SNHC verification model 9.0 [3D mesh encoding]," W2301, July 1998.
15. C.F.Lee, K.H.Wu and L.H.Wong, "Multiresolution mesh representation," *Final Year Project Report*, Depart. EEE, HKUST, 2000.

Fig. 2. From upper left to lower right : Original mesh model of cow (2904 vertices and 5804 faces); simplification results obtained by the proposed algorithm with (α = 0.4, $\beta = 0$) at 20% (vertices and faces), 83% (494 vertices and 980 faces) and 91% (260 vertices and 512 faces) simplification ratios; simplification results obtained by the proposed algorithm with ($\alpha = 0$, $\beta = 0$) at 20%, 83% and 91% simplification ratios.

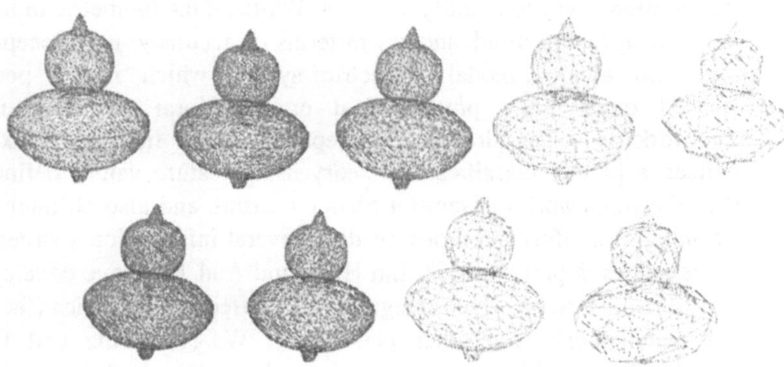

Fig. 3. From upper left to lower right : Original mesh model of toup (5055 vertices and 10008 faces); simplification results obtained by the proposed algorithm with (α = 0.6, $\beta = 0$) at 10% (4549 vertices and 9052 faces), 50% (2527 vertices and 5022 faces), 90% (505 vertices and 993 faces) and 99% (75 vertices and 134 faces) simplification ratios; simplification results obtained by the proposed algorithm with ($\alpha = 0$, $\beta = 0$) at 10%, 50%, 90% and 99% simplification ratios.

Fusion of Biometrics Based on D-S Theory

Xiujuan Gao [1], Hongxun Yao [1], Wen Gao [2], Wei Zeng [1]

[1] Department of Computer Science, Harbin Institute of Technology, 150001, China
{gxj, yhx,wzeng}@vilab.hit.edu.cn
[2] Institute of Computing Technology, Chinese Academy of Sciences, 100080, China
wgao@ict.ac.cn

Abstract. Human face and voice are often used biometric characteristics to establish personal identity. While an automatic personal identification system based sorely on faces or voices is often not able to meet the system performance requirements when the environment light changes or there exists environment noises. We have developed a personal identification system integrating human faces and voices. Experimental results show that the recognition accuracy of the fusion system is much higher than the single channel. D-S theory is one of the often used method in integrating multiple clues. It's essence is to undraw the basic probability of each class after fusion.

1 Introduction

Biometrics, which refers to the identification of a person based on her physiological or behavioral characteristics [1], is reported more often than ever before, since it is more reliable than the traditional way to identify a person. While all the biometric indicators have their own advantages and disadvantages in terms of accuracy, user acceptance, and applicability. So a multi-modal biometric system which makes personal identification based on multiple physiological or behavioral characteristics is preferred. Some work on it has already been reported in the literature. Takahiko Horiuchi formalized a pattern classification theory using feature values defined on closed interval in the framework of Demster-Shafer measure and also an integration algorithm which integrates information observed by several information sources with considering source values is proposed [2]. Lin Hong and Anil Jain have developed a multi-modal identification system which integrates two different biometrics (face and fingerprint) that complement each other [1]. Robert W. Frischholz and Ulrich Dieckmann have developed a biometric system named BioID, which integrates lip movement, face and voice based on the principle that a human uses multiple clues to identify a person [3].

The purpose of this paper is to push forward a multi-modal biometric system based on Dempser-Shafer evidence inference theory (often called D-S theory), which integrates human face recognition and voice speaker recognition. For convenience we use the same definitions and symbols as reference [2]. In section 2 application of D-S theory in the biometric fusion system is discussed; and in section 3, four experiments for different purposes are taken and then in section 4 conclusions are drawn.

2 D-S Theory In Biometric System

For the specific biometric system of this paper, discernment frame Θ is all the identities of personal identification system. And the following definition of basic probability distribution function is used in this paper [4]:

$$m_i(j) = \frac{C_i(j)}{\sum_j C_i(j) + N(1-R_i)(1-\alpha_i\beta_i\omega_i)} \tag{1}$$

$$m_i(\Theta) = \frac{N(1-R_i)(1-\alpha_i\beta_i\omega_i)}{\sum_j C_i(j) + N(1-R_i)(1-\alpha_i\beta_i\omega_i)} \tag{2}$$

$$\alpha_i = \max_j\{C_i(j)\} \qquad \beta_i = \frac{\alpha_i}{\sum_j C_i(j)} \qquad R_i = \frac{\alpha_i\beta_i\omega_i}{\sum_i \alpha_i\beta_i\omega_i} \tag{3}$$

The identity recognition classification rule used in this paper is the very classical one as used in reference [5].

3 Experimental Results And Analysis

Based on D-S theory, an identity recognition system integrating human face and voice is developed. First, the system gets the human face image and voice data respectively using CCD and microphone, then both channels take their pattern recognition pre-judging according to their own recognition model, and the quality information of each channel is recorded when pre-judging, then the pre-judging results and quality information are sent to the fusion module at the same time. The fusion module uses D-S theory to integrate information from both channels and give the final recognition results according to the identity recognition classification rule.

3.1 Experiment 1 - System Recognition Accuracy

In this experiment we try to see if the fusion system recognition accuracy is higher than the sub-systems. From Table 1 we can see that when qualities of both channels become worse, recognition accuracy of the fusion system will get lower too, but the decrease scope is less than that of either channel; When one of the two channels is in good quality, fusion system has high recognition accuracy too, and it is still greater than that of the single channel; And when both channels are in good quality, recognition accuracy of the fusion system reaches the fusion peak.

Table 1. System Recognition Accuracy

Serial Number	Human Face Recognition Channel	Voice Speaker Recognition Channel	Fusion System	Recognition Accuracy Added
1	71.5%	90.4%	97.0%	6.6%
2	71.5%	80.0%	88.1%	8.5%
3	71.5%	73.0%	84.1%	11.8%
4	71.5%	65.9%	79.6%	8.1%
5	72.2%	91.9%	97.0%	6.1%
6	72.2%	73.0%	79.3%	5.2%

3.2 Experiment 2– Relationship Between Fusion Weight and System Accuracy

Figure 1.gives the relationship between changes of fusion weight and fusion system recognition accuracy.

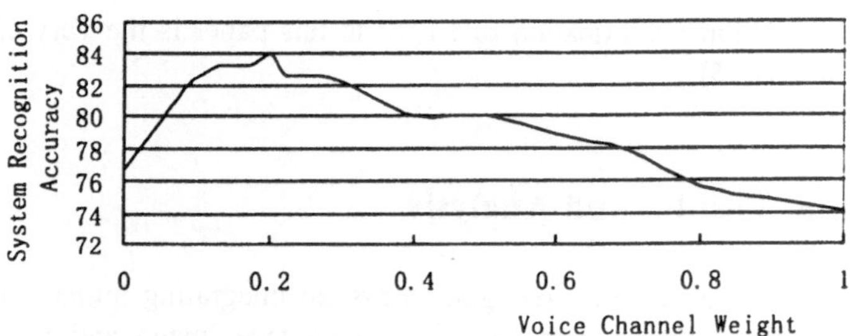

Fig. 1. The Relationship Between Fusion Weight and Fusion System Recognition Accuracy

The horizontal axis is weight value of voice speaker channel, while that of human face channel is the difference between 1 and the weight of voice speaker channel, the vertical axis is the system recognition accuracy. The number of samples used in this system is 270, and the human face recognition accuracy is 71.5%, while that of the voice speaker channel is 73.0%. It can be obviously seen from the figure that the system recognition accuracy curve is a process from ascending to descending, with the increasing of the voice speaker channel weight, i.e., the decreasing of the human face channel weight, and the fusion system recognition accuracy changes from 76.7% to 74.1%. It reaches the peak value when the voice channel weight is about 0.2, the reason for which is that the recognition accuracy of the fusion system is higher than the single channel and the first ascending and then descending process reflects the changing process of the contribution done by both channels to improve the fusion system's recognition accuracy, and in this process there exists fusion peak. In each fusion process, under some channel quality, there do exist fusion peak, i.e., when each channel has the appropriate fusion weight value, the fusion system recognition accuracy can reach it's peak value.

3.3 Experiment 3 – Relationship Between Channel Quality and Fusion Peak

Figure 2. depicts the situations of fusion peak under different channel qualities.

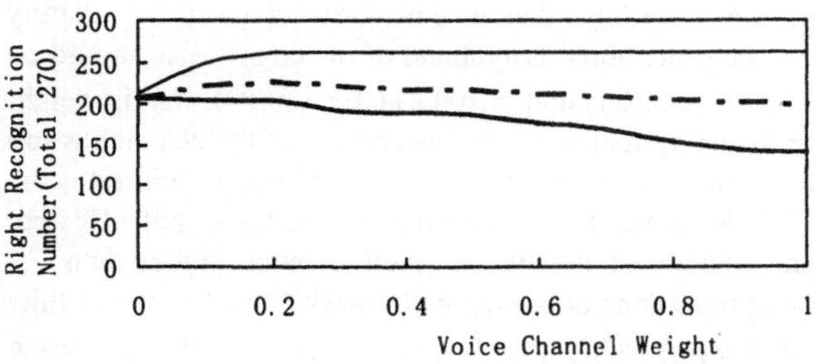

Fig. 2. The Distribution of Fusion Peak

The horizontal axis is the fusion weight of the voice speaker channel, the vertical axis is the system right recognition number (total 270 images and 270 segments of voice data). The corresponding recognition accuracy of the voice speaker channel for the three curves from low to high are respectively 51.9%, 73.0% and 91.9%, and the human face channel recognition is the same 71.5% for all. It can be seen from the figure that the fusion peak of each curve moves forward with the ascending of the voice speaker channel recognition accuracy, i.e., moves to the direction of greater voice speaker channel weight, and the moving scope is relevant to recognition accuracy of the human face channel and voice speaker channel. When the recognition accuracy of the voice speaker channel is lower, the fusion peak is where the weight of the human face channel is greater and that of the voice speaker channel is lower. With the voice speaker channel recognition accuracy ascending, the system fusion peak moves to the direction where weight of the human face channel is lower while that of the voice speaker is higher. However the improvement of the fusion system recognition accuracy is limited, which can be obviously seen from the figure that when the recognition accuracy of the voice speaker is higher than 91.9%, the fusion system recognition accuracy is steady after reaching fusion peak where weight of voice speaker channel is 0.3.

3.4 Experiment 4 - About Construction Function

Table 1 shows that the fusion system based on D-S theory operates very well. While it's essence is to reduce the uncertainty $m(\Theta)$ and undraws the basic probability of each class after fusion, which can be verified that $m(\Theta)$ of the fusion system is less than that of original single channel. The following will discuss two extreme situations and the usual situation of it.

Consider a fusion system C_F composed of two biometric channels C_1 and C_2, let ω_1 and ω_2 be the fusion weight of C_1 and C_2 respectively, m_1, m_2, m_F be the basic probability distribution function of C_1, C_2 and C_F respectively, I_1, I_2, I_F be the class which has the maximum basic probability assignment for C_1, C_2 and C_F respectively, then we have:

(1) If ω_1=0, ω_2=1, then $m_1(I_1) < m_1(\Theta)$, that is this does not meet the identity recognition rule that the basic probability assignment of the target class should be greater than the uncertainty value $m(\Theta)$; and $m_2(\Theta) < m_F(\Theta) < m_1(\Theta)$, that is weight of C_1 is too little, and the fusion system takes the uncertainty of the channel as too high, so reduces its uncertainty, and doesn't reduce that of C_2, as this rate, the recognition accuracy of C_1 is turned to 0 while that of the C_2 is not affected, however, the recognition accuracy of the fusion result is much higher than C_2, which is because that the system does not completely mask C_1 and only set this: $m_1(j) = C_1(j)/3$, $m_1(\Theta) = 2/3$ $m_2(j) = C_2(j)$, and $m_2(\Theta) = 0$, so C_1 still have some effects on the system, and was not completely abandoned, that is why the recognition accuracy of C_F is still higher than C_2.

(2) If ω_1=1, ω_2=0, everything is opposite to the situation described above.

(3) If $0 < \omega_1, \omega_2 < 1$, then $m_F(\Theta) < m_1(\Theta)$ and $m_F(\Theta) < m_2(\Theta)$ i.e., the fusion system thinks both channels have their certainty and uncertainty, and reduces the uncertainty of both channels, recognition accuracy of fusion system is higher than either of the two channels. The following table 2 shows the specific data of the system we developed.

In table 2, WI indicates weight of human face image channel, WV - weight of voice speaker, I - Human face image channel, V - Voice speaker channel, F - Fusion system, and the item ' m(result) > m(Θ)' means the number of tests meeting rule that the basic probability assignment of the target class must be greater than the uncertainty probability value $m_i(\Theta)$ respectively for the human face recognition, voice speaker recognition and fusion system; and the item 'NDU' means 'Number of Decrease in Uncertainty', that is the number of tests in which m(Θ) of the fusion system is less than the subsystems including human face recognition and voice speaker recognition. The table can verify the conclusion described above about D-S theory's essence.

Table 2. Data About m(Θ)

WI	WV	Recognition Rate			m(result) > m(Θ)			NDU	
		I	V	F	I	V	F	I	V
0.0	1.0	0	91.1	97.0	0	270	270	270	0
0.2	0.8	0	25.2	30.7	0	68	83	270	270
0.4	0.6	0	0.7	1.1	0	2	3	270	270
0.6	0.4	0	0	0	0	0	0	270	270
0.8	0.2	0	0	0	0	0	0	270	270
1.0	0.0	72.2	0	78.1	270	0	270	0	270

4 Conclusions And Future Work

We have developed a specific biometric fusion system, which integrates human face and voice in authenticating a personal identification. The proposed system based on D-S theory operates in the identification mode. The basic probability distribution function and decision rule used in this system enables performance improvement by integrating multiple clues with different confidence measures and different quality evaluations. The quality information makes the fusion system recognition accuracy reach it's fusion peak. Experimental results show the system works well. Essential feature of D-S evidence inference theory is to reduce the uncertainty of evidence.

However, there still remain some future researches. For example, the test set isn't big enough, and the construction function of basic probability distribution used in this paper is not the best for this fusion system, then how to find the best function for a specific biometric system is a research topic for us.

5 Acknowledgement

This work has been supported by National Science Foundation of China (contract number 69789301), National Hi-Tech Development Programme of China (contract number 863-306-ZD03-01-2), and 100 Outstanding Scientist Foundation of Chinese Academy of Sciences.

References

1. Lin Hong and Anil Jain.: Integrating Faces and Fingerprints for Personal Identification. IEEE Transactions on Pattern Analysis and Machine Intelligence, Vol. 20, no.12, (1998) 1295-1306.
2. Takahiko Horiuchi.: Decision Rule for Pattern Classification by Integrating Interval Feature Values. IEEE Transactions on Pattern Analysis and Machine Intelligence, Vol. 20, no.4, (1998) 440-448.
3. Robert W. Frischholz and Ulrich Dieckmann.: BioID: A Multimodal Biometric Identification System. Membership Magazine of IEEE Computer Society, Vol.33, no.2, Feb. 2000.
4. Yanping Wang, Jie Yuan, Yuan Liao and Xiangfang Su.: Pattern Recognition of Occluded Objects Using Information Fusion. Journal of Image and Graphics, Vol. 5 no.3, (Mar.2000) 237-241.
5. Shafer, G.A., "A Mathematical Theory of Evidence," Princeton, NJ. , Princeton University Press, 1976.

Eyeglasses Verification by Support Vector Machine

Chenyu Wu, Ce Liu, and Jie Zhou

Institution of Information Processing, Department of Automation
Tsinghua University, 100084 Beijing, China
{wuchenyu00,liuce99}@mails.tsinghua.edu.cn

Abstract. In this paper we propose a method to verify the existence of eyeglasses in the frontal face images by support vector machine. The difficulty of such task comes from the unpredictable illumination and the complex composition of facial appearance and eyeglasses. The lighting uncertainty is eliminated by feature selection, where the orientation and anisotropic measure is chosen as the feature space. Due to the nonlinear composition of glasses to face and the small quantity of examples, support vector machine(SVM) is utilized to give a nonlinear decision surface. By carefully choosing kernel functions, an optimal classifier is achieved from training. The experiments illustrate that our model performs well in eyeglasses verification.

1 Introduction

In literature, the designing of face detection and recognition models is always focused on the faces without eyeglasses. It is always the case that the detection algorithms miss the existance of the faces wearing eyeglasses. A face recognition system would probably not verify a person if he wears eyeglasses, who in fact has already been recorded in the database without eyeglasses. The appearance of eyeglasses heavily affects face detection and recognition, but it does not gain appropriate attentions. There might be two reasons: in some applications the eyeglasses can be assumed not exist; the problem itself is too hard.

There are a variety of eyeglasses in the world, circular, oval, rectangular in shape, transparent, dark, even red in color, and different transmissible, refractive and reflective glass properties. The substance of the frame might be metal or plastic. Such variations make it very difficult to build a sophisticated and accurate appearance model for eyeglasses.

Although rather difficult, eyeglasses analysis is needed in many applications. In face detection, we can train a detector using the facial images with eyeglasses to reduce the miss ratio. In face recognition, the eyeglasses analysis is inevitable needed because the visual appearance changes a lot if a person wearing eyeglasses. Current face recognition systems might report different individuals, when input two images of the identical person with and without eyeglasses respectively. Suppose an eyeglasses verification and removal subsystem is anteceded the recognition module, such problem will be well solved after the eyeglasses are verified and removed. In literature, there has been some works on eyeglasses analysis.

[2] gives a method to detect eyeglasses by deformable contour. [9] removes the eyeglasses based on the correspondence between eyeglasses and non-eyeglasses images by PCA. However, both of them assume the input image already verified to be eyeglasses one. It is obvious that eyeglasses verification is the first step. But how to automatically verify eyeglasses on face image? We shall illustrate it in this paper.

Since eyeglasses introduce too much lighting variation to the intensity face image, transformed or filtered image insensitive to illumination should be selected as feature. We chose the orientation image as feature considering its capability of distinguishing eyeglasses and non-eyeglasses patterns, as well as its stability to illumination and shadowing. Further we find in linear subspace these two patterns are nonlinearly classifiable. Support vector machine (SVM) is then utilized in classification because of its great success on nonlinear classifications with only a few examples. By carefully choosing kernel functions, the recognizing rate by our classifier achieves no less than 95%, based on merely 14 positive and 12 negative examples in a leave-one-out experiment.

This article is formulated as follows. The feature selection is discussed in section 2. Section 3 introduces in details how to design and train the classifier, in particular Gaussian and SVM models. Some experiments are shown in section 4. Section 5 gives the conclusion and future work.

2 Feature Selection

Compared with other facial parts, e.g. eyes, nose, mouth, the eyeglasses pattern looks more regular with respect to orientation and symmetry. In most cases (the illumination is smooth and gentle), the eyeglass is transparent such that the frame and its shadow are the main part in image. We employ the orientation image as the feature such that the main information of eyeglass is kept.

The orientation in [5] is used for reference in our model, computed as

$$\theta(u,v) = \frac{1}{2}\arctan\frac{\iint_{\Omega(u,v)} 2I'_x I'_y dxdy}{\iint_{\Omega(u,v)} (I'^2_x - I'^2_y)dxdy} + \frac{\pi}{2}, \tag{1}$$

$$\chi(u,v) = \frac{(\iint_{\Omega(u,v)} (I'^2_x - I'^2_y)dxdy)^2 + (\iint_{\Omega(u,v)} 2I'_x I'_y dxdy)^2}{(\iint_{\Omega(u,v)} (I'^2_x + I'^2_y)dxdy)^2}, \tag{2}$$

where I'_x and I'_y are the partial derivatives of the intensity image $I(x,y)$ with respect to x and y, and $\Omega(u,v)$ is the local neighborhood of (u,v). Note in above equations, not only the orientation $\theta(u,v)$, but also an anisotropic measure $\chi(u,v)$ is obtained for each pixel. Such measure counts the ratio of the pixels with nearly the same orientation in a local area. The more pixels share the same orientation, the larger the anisotropic measure would be.

The orientation images of both eyeglasses and non-eyeglasses faces are displayed in Figure 1. It is obvious that such features around eyes in eyeglasses images are much more intense than those in non-eyeglasses images. The face in (c) has thin eyebrows, which make the feature around eyes inconspicuous. The face in (d) however has thick eyebrows which form very strong feature on the top of eyes, but it is still very weak on the bottom for no eyeglasses on it. The faces in both (a) and (b) have strong features all around eyes. On the other hand, although the illumination and quality of the four images vary a lot, the feature images remain stable to them. Moreover, the orientation has been widely used in many applications [6].

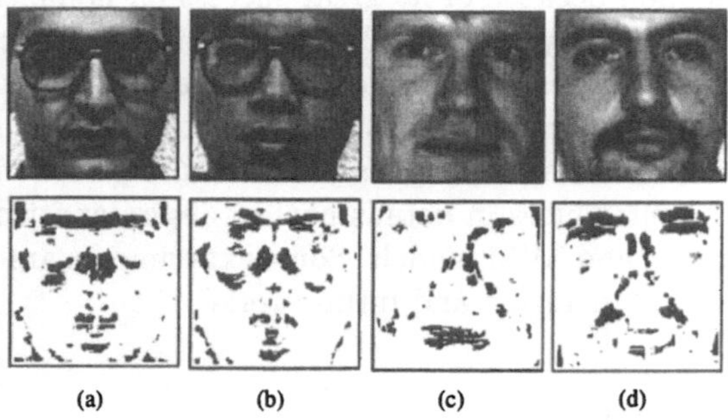

Fig. 1. The orientation image of face. Above: intensity images; below: orientation images. The 2/3 upper part of the orientation image is chosen as the feature.

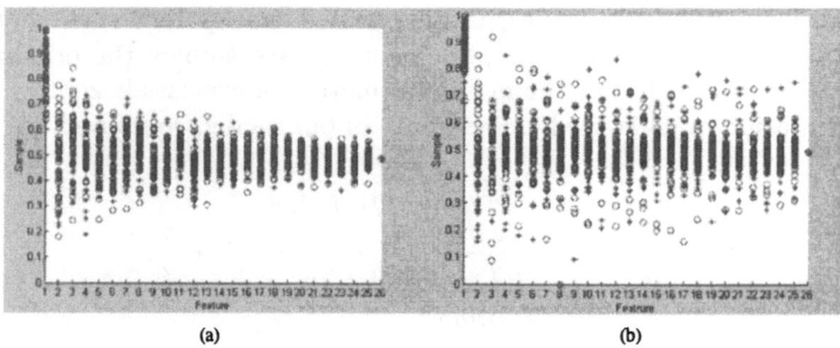

Fig. 2. The illustration of why the orientation image rather than the intensity one is chosen as feature space. (a) and (b) are the marginal distributions of observed examples projected on the 26 eigenvectors of the intensity and orientation image, respectively. * and o indicate positive and negative examples, respectively.

Furthermore PCA is utilized to compare the intensity and the orientation image. Since the whole face will bring much redundant information to the original problem, we use 2/3 upper part of the face. We regularize each face image to 64×64, thus the dimensionality of feature space is $64 \times 43 = 2752$. We only have 26 examples (12 positive and 14 negative) on hand, composing a 26-dimensional subspace without loose of any information (the detail is discussed in section 3.1). The marginal distributions of the observed examples along each eigenvectors are shown in Figure 2, with (a) the intensity image and (b) the orientation image. The positive and negative examples are marked by * and o respectively. It is obvious that all the samples in (a) crowd together but those in (b) are more separable, which leads us to choose the orientation image as the feature.

3 Classifier Designing

3.1 Gaussian Model

Based on Bayesian rule, the classification can be easily drawn if the probability density functions (*pdf*) of the likelihood and prior are known. Suppose the *pdf* of eyeglass and non-eyeglass face image is $g_e(x)$ and $g_n(x)$ respectively, where x is the variable in the d=2752 dimensional feature space. It is natural to presume that the prior of eyeglass and non-eyeglass face is equal. Therefore the Bayesian rule can be written as

$$\text{if } g_e(x) > g_n(x), x \text{ is eyeglass face image.} \tag{3}$$

What we shall do is to model $g_e(x)$ and $g_n(x)$. Since the observed example is so rare (totally 26), we can simply estimate the distribution in a Gaussian form. Note the distribution only occupies a 26-dimensional subspace spanned by 26 eigenvectors of the covariance matrix.

However, the performance of the Gaussian model based on (3) is poor. In the leave-one-out experiment, the recognition ratio is only 46.2%. This demonstrates that the two classes are not linearly classifiable. Further we use some combination (not all) of the eigenvectors to constitute the subspace in which the Gaussian model is estimated, but no obvious improvement appears. These facts indicate that the addition of eyeglasses to face does not affect the image value in a linear way. We have to seek for a nonlinear classifier.

3.2 Support Vector Machine

The most popular nonlinear classifier must be the nearest neighborhood method, namely a segmental linear one. If the quantity of samples goes infinite, the lower limit of the recognition error will touch the error of Bayesian model. However, we have only 26 examples on hand, too insufficient to label a test one by the class which the nearest example belongs to. In the leave-one-out experiment, the recognition ratio is as poor as 27.8%. Other probability density model like mixture of Gaussians can be utilized in *pdf* estimation. However, the small quantity of examples makes them too complex to be unbias.

Support vector machine (SVM) [1, 10] is a general method of designing a nonlinear classifier with small quantity of examples. While most of the methods used to train classifiers are based on minimizing the training error, also called the empirical risk minimization(ERM), SVM deals with another induction principle called ***structural risk minimization***(SRM) which minimizes an upper bound on the generalization error. It has been successfully used in many applications such as face detection [7] and text categorization [3].

We have l labelled examples $\{(x_i, y_i)_{i=1}^{l}\}$, where $y_i \in \{-1, 1\}$ indicates negative and positive class respectively. In SVM, the nonlinear decision surface in the low (original)-dimensional space can be mapped to a linear decision surface in a high-dimensional space. This is easily done by projecting the original set of variables x to a higher dimensional space: $x \in \mathbf{R}^d \Longrightarrow z(x) = (\phi_1(x), \phi_2(x), \cdots, \phi_n(x)) \in \mathbf{R}^n$ and by formulating the linear classification problem in that higher dimensional space. The solution has the form

$$f(x) = \text{sign}(\sum_{i=1}^{l} \lambda_i y_i z^T(x) z(x_i) + b) \tag{4}$$

where coefficients vector $\Lambda = (\lambda_1, \cdots, \lambda_l)^T$ is the solution of the following QP problem:

$$\Lambda^* = \arg\min_{\Lambda} W(\Lambda) = \arg\min_{\Lambda}(-\Lambda^T \mathbf{1} + \frac{1}{2}\Lambda^T D \Lambda) \tag{5}$$

subjected to

$$\Lambda^T y = 0, \quad \Lambda - C\mathbf{1} \leq 0 \quad \text{and} \quad -\Lambda \leq 0$$

where $\mathbf{1}$ is a vector with all element 1, C is a positive constant as trade off between the margin of two classes and the misclassification error, and $D_{ij} = y_i y_j z^T(x) z(x_i)$. It turns out that only a small number of coefficients λ_i are different from zero, associated with which are data points called ***support vectors.*** The ***support vectors***, intuitively the data points that lie at the border between the two classes, are the only ones to be relevant with the solution of the problem.

In Hilbert space, the computation of scalar product $z^T(x)z(x_i)$ in the higher dimensional space can be simplified to that in the original space by:

$$z^T(x)z(y) = K(x, y) \tag{6}$$

where $K(x, y)$ is called ***kernel function***, which must be positive definite symmetric and subjected to the Mercer-Hilbert-Schmidt theorem. As a result, the SVM classifier has the form: $f(x) = \text{sign}(\sum_{i=1}^{l} \lambda_i K(x, x_i) + b)$. Some possible kernel functions are listed in [7], such as Polynomial, Gaussian RBF, Multi-layer Perception etc. We choose SVM^{light}[4] as our training algorithm by comparing it with SMO[8]. The optimal kernel function is chosen to minimize the classification error.

4 Experiments

We collect 26 facial images (14 contain eyeglasses and 12 non-eyeglasses) from MIT and Yale face library as training set. They are mainly westerns. Another 37 images of Chinese captured in our lab are used to test the classifier. Before training the classifier, we normalize the original image to the same scale and orientation by constellating two eyes in horizontality and with similar distance. Each face image is thus regularized to 64×64. The $2/3$ upper part of the face, *i.e.* 64×43 image patch is defined to be the original input. The threshold of anisotropic measure is empirically chosen as 0.8. The radius of neighborhood in equation (1) is 3. Standard principal component analysis (PCA) technique is employed to find the subspace where lie the examples. To train the SVM classifier, we use the SVM^{light} program (version 2.01) [4]. The parameters are all set default.

In the leave-one-out experiment, we find the polynomial kernel function with degree 2 is the optimal one, with the recognition ratio 96%. While in the test by another 37 images, the recognition ratio is 81%. Such results convince us that the SVM classifier performs well in eyeglasses verification.

5 Conclusion and Future Work

In eyeglasses pattern analysis, although the feature selection is difficult, the orientation image has been proven to be a good feature to represent the eyeglasses. The result of simple Gaussian model demonstrates that the eyeglasses and non-eyeglasses patterns are nonlinearly classifiable indeed. Considering the small quantity of samples, a SVM classifier with two-degree polynomial kernel function is trained, which is robust and effective revealed by the experiment.

In our future work, we shall integrate the eyeglasses verification module with the removal module to automatically remove eyeglasses from face images.

References

1. C.J.C.Burges: A Tutorial on Support Vector Machines for Pattern Rrecognition. Data Mining and Knowledge Discovery, Vol. 2, No. 2, 1998, pp.121–167.
2. Z. Jing and R. Mariani: Glasses Detection and Extraction By Deformable Contour. ICPR'2000 Barcelona. September 2000, pp.3–9.
3. T. Joachims: Text Categorization With Support Vector Machines: Learning with Many Relevant Features, in Proc. of 10th European Conference on Machine Learning, Springer Verlag, 1998.
4. T. Joachims: Making Large-scale SVM Learning Practical, in Advances in Kernel Methods - Support Vector Learning, MIT Press, 1998.
5. M. Kass and A. Witkin: Analyzing orientated pattern, Computer Vision, Graphics and Image Processing, Vol.37, 1987, pp.362–397.
6. X.G. Lv, J. Zhou and C.S. Zhang: A Novel Algorithm for Rotated Human Face Detection, Proc. of CVPR, 2000, pp. 760–765.
7. E. Osuna, R. Freund and F. Girosi: Training Support Vector machines: An Application to Face Detection, Proc. of CVPR, 1997, pp.130–136.
8. J. Platt: Fast Training of Support Vector Machines Using Sequential Minimal Optimization, in Advances in Kernel Methods - Support Vector Learning, MIT Press, 1998.
9. Y. Saito, Y. Kenmochi and K. Kotani: Estimation of Eyeglassless Facial Images Using Principal Component Analysis, Proc. of ICIP, 1999, pp.197–201.
10. V. Vapnik: Statistical Learning Theory, J. Wiley, New York, 1998.

A GMM-Based Handset Selector for Channel Mismatch Compensation with Applications to Speaker Identification

K.K. Yiu, M.W. Mak, and S.Y. Kung

Center for Multimedia Signal Processing,
Dept. of Electronic and Information Engineering,
The Hong Kong Polytechnic University, Hong Kong. **
Email: enmwmak@polyu.edu.hk
http://www.en.polyu.edu.hk/~ mwmak/mypage.htm

Abstract. In telephone-based speaker identification, variation in handset characteristics can introduce severe speech variability even for speech uttered by the same speaker. This paper proposes a method to compensate the variation in handset characteristics. In the method, a number of Gaussian mixture models are independently trained to identify the most likely handset given a test utterance. The identified handset is used to select a compensation vector from a set of pre-computed vectors, where the pre-computed vectors are the average frame-by-frame differences between the clean and distorted utterances. The clean features are then recovered by subtracting the selected compensation vector from the distorted vectors. Experimental results based on 138 speakers of the YOHO and telephone YOHO corpora show that the proposed approach is computationally efficient and is able to increase the accuracy from 17% (without compensation) to 85% (with compensation).

1 Introduction

Although speaker recognition based on clean speech has reached a high level of performance [1], severe performance degradation is still very common in practical, mismatched conditions. This presents one of the major obstacles to the commercialization of speaker recognition technologies. One example of "mismatched conditions" is handset mismatch (or transducer mismatch). For automatic speaker recognition over the telephone, handset mismatch occurs when the recognizer is trained with speech recorded from one type of handsets and tested with speech recorded from another type of handsets.

Several successful compensation techniques, including cepstral mean subtraction [2] and signal bias removal [3], have been proposed to compensate the channel and handset mismatches. In CMS, the channel is represented by the mean

** S. Y. Kung is on sabbatical from the Princeton University, USA. He is currently a distinguished chair professor of the Department of Electronic and Information Engineering, The Hong Kong Polytechnic University. This project was supported by the Hong Kong Polytechnic University Grant No. 1.42.37.A410.

cepstral vector of the distorted utterance. Although CMS has been widely used in speech and speaker recognition, it assumes that the mean cepstrum of clean speech is zero, which is not always correct (see [4]). In SBR, channel distortion is considered as an additive bias to the clean speech cepstrum. The bias is estimated from the distorted speech using a maximum likelihood formulation which results in a two-step iterative procedure. Although SBR is a promising approach to compensating the channel effect, its iterative procedure is computationally intensive and therefore not practical for real-time applications.

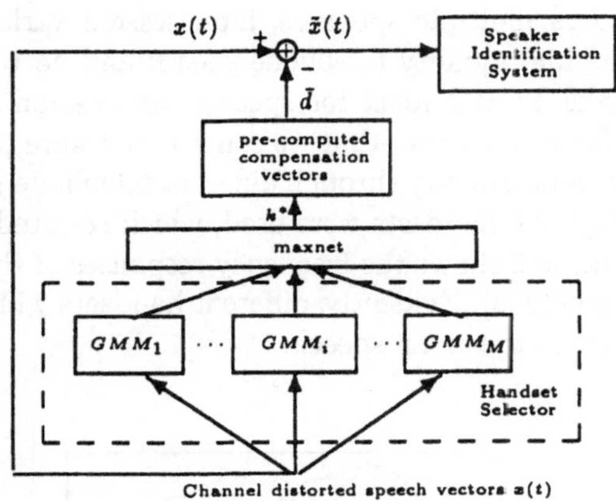

Fig. 1. A GMM-based Handset Selector for channel mismatch compensation.

To overcome the drawbacks of CMS and SBR, we have recently proposed to subtract the cepstral mean of a target handset from the CMS-cepstrum [4] and to estimate the channel cepstrum directly by measuring the frequency response of the corresponding telephone handset [5]. Although the results showed that these approach achieves a lower error rate than CMS and is faster than SBR, their operation relies on the a priori knowledge of handset types (for selecting the target cepstral mean in [4] and channel cepstrum in [5]), which means that these approaches may not be practical in real situation. This paper proposes an approach to overcome this problem. In this approach, a GMM-based handset selector as shown in Fig. 1 is trained to identify the most likely handset given a test utterance. The identity, k^*, of the most likely handset is used to select a compensation vector from a set of pre-computed vectors (also referred to as the channel cepstra). The pre-computed vectors are the average frame-by-frame differences between the clean and distorted utterances, and each handset is associated with one pre-computed vector. Similar to CMS and SBR, the clean cepstra are recovered by subtracting the selected channel cepstrum from the distorted ones.

This approach makes our previous proposals [4], [5] more practical because it provides a handset selector to select the best compensation vector for each test utterance. It is also faster than SBR because it does not require any iterative procedure during recognition. Experimental results demonstrate that to identify a speaker from 138 speakers, the proposed approach is thousand times faster than SBR. While SBR achieves the highest recognition accuracy, its accuracy is only 5% higher than that of our proposed approach.

2 TYOHO Corpus

The YOHO corpus [6] was collected by ITT for government secure access applications. It features multiple speakers, inter-session variability, combination lock phrase syntax, high-quality telephone speech and no telephone line effect. These features make YOHO ideal for speaker verification research. The telephone YOHO (TYOHO) corpora that we constructed were produced by playing the clean YOHO corpus directly through different telephone handsets (see [5] for details). Three telephone handsets were used, which resulted in three telephone YOHO corpora. Figure 2 shows the frequency responses of three handsets based on actual measurements [5]. Evidently, different handsets will introduce different degrees of distortion to the clean speech.

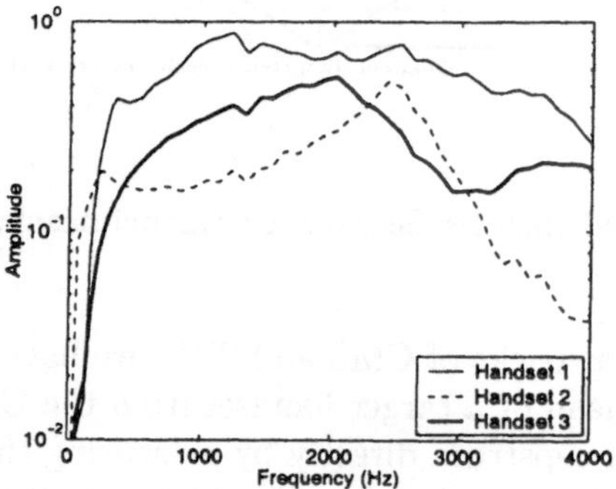

Fig. 2. Frequency responses of three handsets at 85dB sound pressure level.

3 Handset Selector

Research has shown that the handsets are the major source of recognition errors [7] and that different handsets cause different degree of distortion on speech signals [8]. As a result, the probability density functions of distorted cepstra caused by different handsets are different, and we can use a set of GMMs to estimate the probability that the observed speech is come from a particular handset.

In this work, M Gaussian mixture models (GMMs), $\{\Lambda_k\}_{k=1}^{M}$, were independently trained using the distorted speech produced by the corresponding handset. More specifically, model Λ_k was trained to maximize the log-likelihood function

$$\log \prod_{t=1}^{T} p(x(t)|\Lambda_k) = \sum_{t=1}^{T} \log p(x(t)|\Lambda_k) \quad k = 1, ..., M \tag{1}$$

where for notation convince we denote the distorted cepstra by $x(t)$, T is the number of speech patterns in the utterance and M is the total number of handset under tested. During identification, an unknown utterance was fed to the GMMs. The most likely handset is selected according to

$$k^* = \arg\max_{k=1}^{M} \sum_{t=1}^{T} \log p(x(t)|\Lambda_k). \tag{2}$$

Then, the clean cepstra $\tilde{x}(t)$ are recovered by subtracting the k^*-th compensating cepstrum from the distorted cepstra $x(t)$.

In this study, three telephone YOHO corpora were used to train three GMMs. Each GMM, consisted of 128 component mixtures with diagonal covariance matrices, was trained with the training sessions of all speakers in the corresponding TYOHO corpus. The GMM parameters were estimated by using the expectation maximization (EM) algorithm [9]. Table 1 shows the recognition accuracy of the handset selector, which was obtained by using the verification sessions of the TYOHO corpora. The results suggest that the handset selector can correctly label more than 95% of the test utterances.

Testing sessions from	Recognized by Handset Selector		
	T1 Yoho	T2 Yoho	T3 Yoho
T1 Yoho	95.00%	1.63%	3.37%
T2 Yoho	0.89%	98.86%	0.25%
T3 Yoho	3.88%	0.87%	95.25%

Table 1. Recognition accuracy of the handset selector.

4 Speaker Identification Experiments

4.1 Speaker Models and Performance Index

A GMM-based speaker identification system was used in the evaluation. Specifically, each speaker in the system was modeled by a 128-mixture GMM with diagonal covariance matrices, and the GMMs were trained using the enrollment sessions of the clean YOHO corpus. Specifically, for each registered speaker, their corresponding GMM was generated by clustering his/her voice patterns by means of the expectation maximization algorithm [9].

Identification was performed using the testing sessions of the clean YOHO corpus and the telephone YOHO corpora. The aim was to compare the speaker identification performance under "matched" and "mismatched" conditions.

The recognition accuracy was used as the performance index to compare the performance of different channel compensation techniques. As the speaker models remain fixed after the training (excluding the case of CMS), the recognition accuracies can be used to indicate the capability of different compensation methods.

In the case of CMS, another set of speaker models, each with the same number of free parameter (128 mixtures with diagonal covariance matrices), was trained using the mean removed cepstra of the clean YOHO corpus.

4.2 Stereo Corpus Based Compensation Cepstra

In this approach, the compensation cepstrum is computed as the average of the frame-by-frame difference between the clean cepstrum and distorted cepstrum:

$$\bar{d}_k = \frac{1}{N}\sum_{t=1}^{N}(y_t - x_t) \quad k = 1, \dots, M \tag{3}$$

where x_t and y_t are the cepstral vectors at frame t for the YOHO and the k-th TYOHO corpora respectively, and N is the total number of speech frames in the corpora.

The clean cepstra are recovered by subtracting the average from the distorted cepstra, i.e., $\tilde{x}_t = y_t - \bar{d}_{k^*}$ where k^* is computed according to (2). As the compensation cepstra are handset specific, an automatic handset selector as described in Section 3 is required to label each of the testing utterances.

4.3 Speaker Identification Results

Table 2 compares the recognition accuracies obtained by different channel compensation techniques. The low recognition accuracies corresponding to the telephone speech evidence the mismatched conditions created by the handsets. The results show that the performance of the compensation cepstra is comparable to CMS and is slightly better than CMS in the case of T3YOHO. Although the SBR achieves the highest recognition accuracy, its two-step iterative procedure is computational intensive.

In order to measure the computational complexity, we measured the average processing time required to extract the features and to perform the compensation, and the results are shown in the last column of Table 2. The results reveal that SBR takes a significantly longer time than the other methods for pre-processing. Our compensation cepstrum takes less time as compared to SBR, but it is slightly slower than CMS. Although SBR achieves the best performance in terms of error rate, its computational requirement makes it unsuitable for real-time applications. Our compensation cepstra, on the other hand, strike a good balance between identification accuracy and computational efficiency.

Channel Normalization Method	Recognition Accuracy (%)				Processing Time (sec.)
	Clean Yoho	T1 Yoho	T2 Yoho	T3 Yoho	
No compensation	93.29	25.49	11.76	14.29	0.8
CMS	93.02	88.96	79.24	86.64	0.8
Compensation cepstrum	–	88.63	79.19	88.34	1.2
SBR	96.85	94.14	85.24	91.79	1576.0

Table 2. Recognition accuracies and processing time.

5 Conclusion

In this paper, we propose to estimate the compensation cepstra by computing the average of the frame-by-frame differences between the clean cepstra and distorted cepstra based on clean and distorted corpora. Experimental evaluations indicate that the performance of our compensation cepstra are comparable to that of the cepstral mean subtraction. Although the proposed compensation cepstra are inferior to signal bias removal (SBR) in terms of their ability to reduce channel distortion, they do not have the computational burden of SBR.

References

1. M. W. Mak and S. Y. Kung. Estimation of elliptical basis function parameters by the EM algorithms with application to speaker verification. In *IEEE Trans. on Neural Networks*, volume 11, pages 961–969, 2000.
2. S. Furui. Cepstral analysis technique for automatic speaker verification. *IEEE Trans. on Acoustics, Speech and Signal Processing*, ASSP-29(2):254–272, April 1981.
3. M. G. Rahim and B. H. Juang. Signal bias removal by maximum likelihood estimation for robust telephone speech recognition. *IEEE Transactions on Speech and Audio Processing*, 4(1):19–30, Jan 1996.
4. T. F. Lo, K. K. Yiu, and M. W. Mak. A new cepstrum-based channel compensation method for speaker verification. In *Proc. Eurospeech'99*, volume 2, pages 775–778, Sept. 1999.
5. K. K. Yiu, M. W. Mak, and S. Y. Kung. Channel distortion compensation based on the measurement of handset's frequency responses. In *International Symposium on Intelligent Multimedia, Video and Speech Processing*, 2001.
6. J. P. Campbell. Testing with the YOHO CD-ROM voice verification corpus. In *ICASSP'95*, volume 1, pages 341–344, 1995.
7. L. P. Heck and M. Weintraub. Handset dependent background models for robust text-independent speaker recognition. In *ICASSP97*, volume 2, pages 1071–1074, 1997.
8. C. Mokbel, D. Jouvet, and J. Monné. Deconvolution of telephone line effects for speech recognition. *Speech Communication*, 19:185–196, 1996.
9. A. P. Dempster, N. M. Laird, and D. B. Rubin. Maximum likelihood from incomplete data via the EM algorithm. *J. of Royal Statistical Soc., Ser. B.*, 39(1):1–38, 1977.

Performance Evaluation of 2D Feature Tracking Based on Bayesian Estimation

Yan Li Liu Wenyin Heung-Yeung Shum

Microsoft Research China, 49 Zhichun Road, Beijing 100080, PR China
{yli, wyliu, hshum}@microsoft.com

Abstract. Feature tracking methods based on Bayesian estimation are widely studied in computer vision systems. The performance of Bayesian decision, however, remains an open problem because an implementation of Bayesian estimation is significantly affected by many parameters in modeling the prior and observation probabilities. In this paper, we evaluate the performance of our MAP based feature tracking algorithm with various parameter settings for many features. For most 2D feature points in our experiments, we found that the uniform distribution model (or Gaussian model with a very large variance) with linear prediction yields the best feature tracking performance.

1 Introduction

Bayesian estimation or its most common form—maximum a posteriori probability (MAP) estimation—has been widely used in many applications of computer vision and pattern recognition [1][4]. However, its performance is seldom evaluated objectively and quantitatively, despite that many applications are claimed successful. Usually, the probability densities involved in the MAP-based solutions have to be modeled differently for different applications. At the very least, several parameters should be decided/set differently for different applications on different test (input) data. Although the Bayesian estimation method (and its basis—the Bayes' Theorem and Bayes' decision rule) is rational in theory, it is generally hard to find a common set of parameter values that make the method work at the same level of performance on all test data. It makes all application-specific solutions ad hoc. The reason is probably that the real world is hard to model uniformly (in the sense of fixed parameter values). In this paper, we empirically evaluate the performance of the MAP estimation applied to 2D feature tracking. We have tested 40 feature points in two image sequences and calculated the mean and variance of the differences between the tracking results and the ground truth. Experiments show that the prior probability within the predicted searching window makes less contribution to the overall posterior probability estimation than the observation density in MAP based 2D feature tracking problems. We further conclude that when the searching window is not very large, the prior probability density function of a feature becomes nearly a uniform distribution.

2 Bayesian Feature Tracking Method

Generally speaking, the task of tracking is to trace an object in motion. Specifically, in computer vision, a tracking system is to obtain an object's motion parameters, including translations and rotations, in a temporal image sequence frame by frame. Visual object tracking can utilize dynamic information, e.g., information of previous frames. The information obtained about the object from previous frames provides some prior knowledge about the object's current state. Combining the prior knowledge with the likelihood between the hypothetical object and the current frame image, a posteriori estimate (probability) is obtained. Hence, maximum a posteriori probability (MAP) estimation, which is the most common form of the Bayesian method, is frequently used in tracking.

2.1 The Feature Tracking Problem

The 2D feature tracking problem is to find the motion (or simply, location since a point has no rotation or in-depth translation) of a feature point, e.g., a nostril of a face, in a temporal image sequence, as formally defined as follows.

Given an image sequence $I = \{I_0, I_1 ......, I_{n-1}\}$ and a feature point $X_k(u_k, v_k)$ (k=0…i-1) in the previous i frame images, the tracking problem can be described as finding a motion vector $D_i = (d_u, d_v)$ to locate its position $X_i(u_i, v_i)$ in the successive image, that is:

$$X_i = X_{i-1} + D_i$$

Like in other tracking tasks, MAP based method is employed in many feature tracking methods, as defined by

$$X_i = \arg\max_X (p_t(X) = p_r(X) \cdot p_z(X)) \qquad (1)$$

where, pr(X) is the prior density of X learned from the information from previous frames, pz(X) is the observation density that characterizes the statistical variability (which is also referred to as the observation model) of frame image z and an object state X. pt(X) is the posterior density computed from the prior pr(X) and the observation pz(X) by the Bayes' Theorem.

2.2 The Modeling of Probability Densities

As can be seen from Eq. (1), two probabilities (the prior and the observation) should be modeled in the MAP approach in order to calculate the posterior probability. Radial basis functions, e.g., Gaussian functions, are usually used.

The prior density $p_r(X)$ for the state X_i (e.g., in our case, location of a feature point) is usually predicted from state X_{i-1} according to a dynamic model. We use a simple constant velocity predictor in this model, which means that the feature point moves at a constant velocity in the image plane. The feature point being tracked will most likely appear within a region $\Re$ centered at $X_{i-1} + D_{i-1}$,

$$X_i \in \Re(X_{i-1} + D_{i-1}), \text{ where } D_{i-1} = X_{i-1} - X_{i-2}.$$

Furthermore, it is expected that, the smaller the distance between a point and the region center, the higher probability with which the point is the real feature point. The prior probability has the form of Eq. (2) when expressed in a Gaussian function.

$$p_r = p(\|(X_i - (X_{i-1} + D_{i-1})\| = d) = e^{-d/\sigma_1} \quad (2)$$

where d is the distance between X_i and region center, and σ_1 is the variance that has to be set in the experiments.
The observation density is used to characterize the statistical variability of an object state *X* and its observation (the frame image). It is usually expressed using the difference between the expected observation and the real observation of *X*. Similar to the prior probability, the observation probability is usually modeled as a Gaussian function in Eq (3).

$$p_z = e^{-r/\sigma_2} \quad (3)$$

where *r* is the difference between the expected observation and the real observation of *X*, and σ_2 is the variance.
A feature point in an image is usually represented by its template. A template is a small window of pixels centered at the feature point, e.g., a nostril is usually a small black area. In this case, *r* in Eq. (3) is the residual of the template matching. Generally, any correlation method, including the maximum cross-correlation, the minimum mean square error (MSE), the minimum mean absolute difference (MAD), and maximum matching pixel count (MPC) [7] can be used to calculate the residual. We use in our experiments the sum of squared distance (SSD) as the residual *r*.

In Eqs (2) and (3), σ_1 and σ_2 are two scale factors to balance the contributions of the prior probability density and observation probability density to the a posteriori probability density. They should take some predefined values in order to do the calculation of the a posteriori probability. However, we do not know what values they should take for each application before experiments in order to get the best performance. In other words, we are not sure if there exist two optimal values for parameter σ_1 and σ_2 which can output the best tracking results for any features. Instead, we need to adjust the values during experiments. In next sections, we first discuss the performance definition and the experiments.

3 Performance Evaluation of the Feature Tracking Algorithm

As Liu and Dori [3] mentioned, the performance is a set of metrics of interest on the output data that a system/algorithm produces with respect to the expected, ground truth data. Usually, the metrics are expressed in terms of the difference between the expected output and the actual output of the system. The smaller the difference, the better the performance.
The three elements to construct a performance evaluation protocol for graphics recognition systems proposed by Liu and Dori [3] are also applicable to evaluate the performance of feature tracking algorithms. In order to evaluate the performance of feature tracking algorithms, we define the three evaluation elements respectively.

(1) Ground truth acquisition is the process that generates the expected output (ground truth) for comparison with the actual output. To comprehensively and thoroughly evaluate an algorithm on a feature tracking algorithm, the correct feature positions in each frame are highly desirable. However, this type of ground truth is hard to obtain, as it requires manual measurements, which are labor intensive and error-prone. However, this seems to be the only method to acquire the ground truth for feature tracking systems. This is so since if we would have been able to find an automatic way to obtain the ground truth of feature positions in each frames, it would be the ultimate feature tracking algorithm, making any other algorithm useless.
In our experiments, we manually label the positions of each feature in the image sequence. As verified by human vision, they are good enough as the ground truth.

(2) To measure the difference between actual and tracking features, ground truth should be matched with the tracking results. Concerns in this procedure are how to match and what can be considered as a match (or match acceptance). There is no universal way to define the matching criteria. People may define them from different aspects of performance, some of which may be controversial. For purpose of simplicity, in our experiments, each feature is tracked individually and so the matching procedure can be ignored.

(3) The performance metrics definition is another controversial issue in performance evaluation. Liu and Dori [3] propose that three principles should be followed in metrics definition: 1. The metrics should be objective-driven; 2. The performance evaluation should be comprehensive; 3. The metrics definition should be quantitative, normative, objective, and compatible with the human vision evaluation. Huwer and Niemann use local overlap, tracking length, and computation time to measure the quality of tracking results [2].
In our experiment, we do not care the efficiency of the algorithm. The performance metrics for a single feature point in one frame is defined as the Euclidean distance between the ground truth feature and the tracking result. The overall performance of the Bayesian feature tracking method on a single feature point tracked in an image sequence is defined as the mean and the variance of such distances for all frames. The smaller the mean and the variance, the better is the algorithm. Since the performance of the algorithm is affected also by the parameter setting. We usually choose the parameter setting so that it makes the algorithm reach the best performance, i.e., the smallest mean (and the variance). By doing so, in the experiments, we obtain for each feature point the best parameter set.

4 Experiment and Discussion

How to select features that can be tracked well and correspond to physically distinguishable points in the physical world is a very important but difficult problem. Since most tracking methods are based on gray level correlation, good features should be corners [6] or windows with high spatial frequency textures. But the occluded edges or deformable regions should be avoided because they do not keep the invariance property for correlation computation [5]. As for the face feature tracking application, we select the corners of the mouth, canthus, and nostril as good features to track.

We use in our experiments two video sequences as the testing data, each containing 100 frames of gray images. For each video sequence, 20 "good" feature points are selected and their positions in each frame are manually labeled. As verified by human vision evaluation, they are good enough to be used as the ground truth.
We then track these selected feature points individually using the Bayesian (MAP) method with varying values of the two parameters σ_1 in Eq (2) and σ_2 in Eq (3). For each feature points we obtained the optimal parameter pair σ_1 and σ_2 to yield the best performance defined in Section 3.
Given the parameter space R and the average distance $\bar{d}_{I,P}(\sigma_1,\sigma_2)$ between the ground truth and tracking result for feature P in video sequence I using the parameter pair (σ_1,σ_2), the optimal parameter pair $(\sigma_{1optimal},\sigma_{2optimal})$ is defined by

$$(\sigma_{1optimal},\sigma_{2optimal}) = \arg\min_{(\sigma_1,\sigma_2)\in R} \bar{d}_{I,P}(\sigma_1,\sigma_2), \tag{4}$$

The following parameter values are also used for the experiments on the video sequences:

- The template size for all features is 9x9 pixels.
- The searching window for the feature template matching is 21x21 pixels

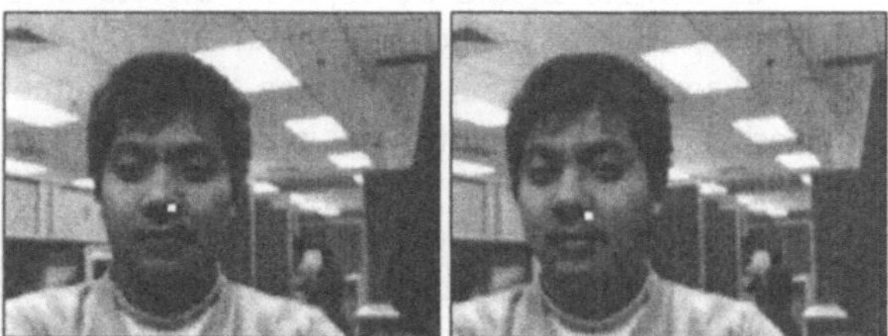

Figure 1. Feature tracking result using the MAP based method

Figure 1 shows the 1st and 50th image frames of the first video sequence. The left image is the first frame of the sequence, on which the small white square at the man's left nostril is manually labeled. The small square on the right image denotes the tracking result on the 50th frame for this feature using a specific parameter pair in the MAP based method. We have tracked this feature using 950x2000 different parameter pairs (formed with 950 different σ_1 values and 2000 σ_2 different values combinatorially). For each parameter pair, we calculate the mean and variance of the distances the tracking results deviate from their ground truth over all frames in the sequence. Figure 2 shows the best means and variances of such average distances for each σ_1 value.

As shown in Fig.2, the tracking performance improves as σ_1 increases, meaning that the first item (p_r) in the MAP function (Eq. 1) makes a less contribution to the tracking result than the second item p_z. Experiments on the other feature points show very similar results. This can be explained as following: in Section 2 we model the prior probability by a Gaussian function. For most 2D feature tracking problem, the optimal value of parameter σ_1 is a very large value comparable to the local searching window size. So p_r is nearly a uniform distribution within the predicted searching window. But for a specific feature point, we do not know the lower bound of $\sigma_{1optimal}$ and its corresponding $\sigma_{2optimal}$.

5 Conclusion

In this paper, we have empirically evaluated the performance of the MAP estimation based 2D feature tracking algorithm. Three evaluation elements are defined specifically in our evaluation protocol. Experiments show that for MAP based 2D feature point tracking problem, the prior probability makes less contribution to the posterior probability estimation than the observation density. We have also found that when the searching window is not very large, the prior probability density function of a feature is nearly a uniform distribution. Extensive experiments are planned for our future work.

References

[1] C.L. Chan and A.K. Katsaggelos. Iterative maximum likelihood displacement field estimation in quantum-limited image sequences. IEEE Transactions on Image Processing, 4(6), June 1995, pp. 743-751.

[2] S. Huwer and H. Niemann. 2D-object tracking based on projection-histograms. In: Proc. ECCV98, Vol. I, pp. 861-876.

[3] W. Liu and D. Dori. Performance Evaluation of Graphics Recognition Algorithms: Principles and Applications. In: Proc. of 14th ICPR, Sydney, August, 1998.

[4] M.I. Miller, A. Srivastava and U. Grenander. Conditional-mean estimation via jump-diffusion processes in multiple target tracking/recognition. IEEE Transactions on Signal Processing, 43(1), Nov, 1995, pp.2678-2690.

[5] J. Shi and C. Tomasi. Good features to track. In: Proc. CVPR94, pp. 593-600.

[6] S.M. Smith and J.M. Brady. SUSAN - a new approach to low level image processing. International Journal of Computer Vision, 23(1), May 1997, pp. 45-78.

[7] A.M. Tekalp. Digital video processing. Prentice Hall, 1995.

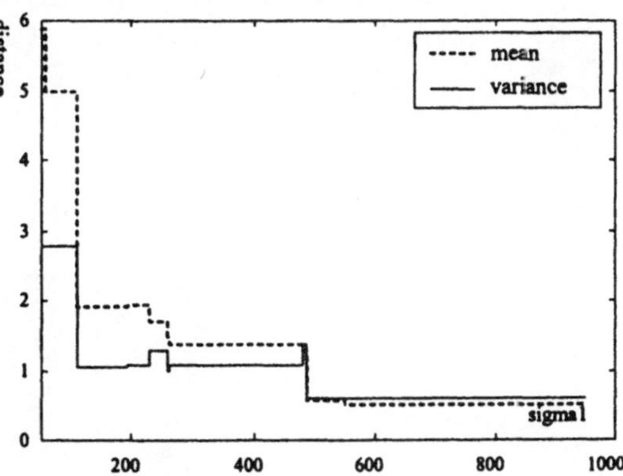

Figure 1. optimal parameters determination

Author Index

E

F

G

H

I

J

K

L

M

N

O

P

Q

Y

Z

Lecture Notes in Computer Science

For information about Vols. 1–2118
please contact your bookseller or Springer-Verlag

Vol. 1962: Y. Frankel (Ed.), Financial Cryptography. Proceedings, 2000. XI, 379 pages. 2001.

Vol. 2119: V. Varadharajan, Y. Mu (Eds.), Information Security and Privacy. Proceedings, 2001. XI, 522 pages. 2001.

Vol. 2120: H.S. Delugach, G. Stumme (Eds.), Conceptual Structures: Broadening the Base. Proceedings, 2001. X, 377 pages. 2001. (Subseries LNAI).

Vol. 2121: C.S. Jensen, M. Schneider, B. Seeger, V.J. Tsotras (Eds.), Advances in Spatial and Temporal Databases. Proceedings, 2001. XI, 543 pages. 2001.

Vol. 2123: P. Perner (Ed.), Machine Learning and Data Mining in Pattern Recognition. Proceedings, 2001. XI, 363 pages. 2001. (Subseries LNAI).

Vol. 2124: W. Skarbek (Ed.), Computer Analysis of Images and Patterns. Proceedings, 2001. XV, 743 pages. 2001.

Vol. 2125: F. Dehne, J.-R. Sack, R. Tamassia (Eds.), Algorithms and Data Structures. Proceedings, 2001. XII, 484 pages. 2001.

Vol. 2126: P. Cousot (Ed.), Static Analysis. Proceedings, 2001. XI, 439 pages. 2001.

Vol. 2127: V. Malyshkin (Ed.), Parallel Computing Technologies. Proceedings, 2001. XII, 516 pages. 2001.

Vol. 2129: M. Goemans, K. Jansen, J.D.P. Rolim, L. Trevisan (Eds.), Approximation, Randomization, and Combinatorial Optimization. Proceedings, 2001. IX, 297 pages. 2001.

Vol. 2130: G. Dorffner, H. Bischof, K. Hornik (Eds.), Artificial Neural Networks – ICANN 2001. Proceedings, 2001. XXII, 1259 pages. 2001.

Vol. 2131: Y. Cotronis, J. Dongarra (Eds.), Recent Advances in Parallel Virtual Machine and Message Passing Interface. Proceedings, 2001. XV, 438 pages. 2001.

Vol. 2132: S.-T. Yuan, M. Yokoo (Eds.), Intelligent Agents. Specification. Modeling, and Application. Proceedings, 2001. X, 237 pages. 2001. (Subseries LNAI).

Vol. 2133: B. Christianson, B. Crispo, J.A. Malcolm, M. Roe (Eds.), Security Protocols. Proceedings, 2001. VIII, 257 pages. 2001.

Vol. 2134: M. Figueiredo, J. Zerubia, A.K. Jain (Eds.), Energy Minimization Methods in Computer Vision and Pattern Recognition. Proceedings, 2001. X, 652 pages. 2001.

Vol. 2136: J. Sgall, A. Pultr, P. Kolman (Eds.), Mathematical Foundations of Computer Science 2001. Proceedings, 2001. XII, 716 pages. 2001.

Vol. 2138: R. Freivalds (Ed.), Fundamentals of Computation Theory. Proceedings, 2001. XIII, 542 pages. 2001.

Vol. 2139: J. Kilian (Ed.), Advances in Cryptology – CRYPTO 2001. Proceedings, 2001. XI, 599 pages. 2001.

Vol. 2140: I. Attali, T. Jensen (Eds.), Java on Smart Cards: Programming and Security. Proceedings, 2001. VIII, 255 pages. 2001.

Vol. 2141: G.S. Brodal, D. Frigioni, A. Marchetti-Spaccamela (Eds.), Algorithm Engineering. Proceedings, 2001. X, 199 pages. 2001.

Vol. 2142: L. Fribourg (Ed.), Computer Science Logic. Proceedings, 2001. XII, 615 pages. 2001.

Vol. 2143: S. Benferhat, P. Besnard (Eds.), Symbolic and Quantitative Approaches to Reasoning with Uncertainty. Proceedings, 2001. XIV, 818 pages. 2001. (Subseries LNAI).

Vol. 2144: T. Margaria, T. Melham (Eds.), Correct Hardware Design and Verification Methods. Proceedings, 2001. XII, 482 pages. 2001.

Vol. 2145: M. Leyton, A Generative Theory of Shape. XVI, 554 pages. 2001.

Vol. 2146: J.H. Silverman (Eds.), Cryptography and Lattices. Proceedings, 2001. VII, 219 pages. 2001.

Vol. 2147: G. Brebner, R. Woods (Eds.), Field-Programmable Logic and Applications. Proceedings, 2001. XV, 665 pages. 2001.

Vol. 2149: O. Gascuel, B.M.E. Moret (Eds.), Algorithms in Bioinformatics. Proceedings, 2001. X, 307 pages. 2001.

Vol. 2150: R. Sakellariou, J. Keane, J. Gurd, L. Freeman (Eds.), Euro-Par 2001 Parallel Processing. Proceedings, 2001. XXX, 943 pages. 2001.

Vol. 2151: A. Caplinskas, J. Eder (Eds.), Advances in Databases and Information Systems. Proceedings, 2001. XIII, 381 pages. 2001.

Vol. 2152: R.J. Boulton, P.B. Jackson (Eds.), Theorem Proving in Higher Order Logics. Proceedings, 2001. X, 395 pages. 2001.

Vol. 2153: A.L. Buchsbaum, J. Snoeyink (Eds.), Algorithm Engineering and Experimentation. Proceedings, 2001. VIII, 231 pages. 2001.

Vol. 2154: K.G. Larsen, M. Nielsen (Eds.), CONCUR 2001 – Concurrency Theory. Proceedings, 2001. XI, 583 pages. 2001.

Vol. 2156: M.I. Smirnov, J. Crowcroft, J. Roberts, F. Boavida (Eds.), Quality of Future Internet Services. Proceedings, 2001. XI, 333 pages. 2001.

Vol. 2157: C. Rouveirol, M. Sebag (Eds.), Inductive Logic Programming. Proceedings, 2001. X, 261 pages. 2001. (Subseries LNAI).

Vol. 2158: D. Shepherd, J. Finney, L. Mathy, N. Race (Eds.), Interactive Distributed Multimedia Systems. Proceedings, 2001. XIII, 258 pages. 2001.

Vol. 2159: J. Kelemen, P. Sosík (Eds.), Advances in Artificial Life. Proceedings, 2001. XIX, 724 pages. 2001. (Subseries LNAI).

Vol. 2161: F. Meyer auf der Heide (Ed.), Algorithms – ESA 2001. Proceedings, 2001. XII, 538 pages. 2001.

Vol. 2162: Ç. K. Koç, D. Naccache, C. Paar (Eds.), Cryptographic Hardware and Embedded Systems – CHES 2001. Proceedings, 2001. XIV, 411 pages. 2001.

Vol. 2163: P. Constantopoulos, I.T. Sølvberg (Eds.), Research and Advanced Technology for Digital Libraries. Proceedings, 2001. XII, 462 pages. 2001.

Vol. 2164: S. Pierre, R. Glitho (Eds.), Mobile Agents for Telecommunication Applications. Proceedings, 2001. XI, 292 pages. 2001.

Vol. 2165: L. de Alfaro, S. Gilmore (Eds.), Process Algebra and Probabilistic Methods. Proceedings, 2001. XII, 217 pages. 2001.

Vol. 2166: V. Matoušek, P. Mautner, R. Mouček, K. Taušer (Eds.), Text, Speech and Dialogue. Proceedings, 2001. XIII, 452 pages. 2001. (Subseries LNAI).

Vol. 2167: L. De Raedt, P. Flach (Eds.), Machine Learning: ECML 2001. Proceedings, 2001. XVII, 618 pages. 2001. (Subseries LNAI).

Vol. 2168: L. De Raedt, A. Siebes (Eds.), Principles of Data Mining and Knowledge Discovery. Proceedings, 2001. XVII, 510 pages. 2001. (Subseries LNAI).

Vol. 2170: S. Palazzo (Ed.), Evolutionary Trends of the Internet. Proceedings, 2001. XIII, 722 pages. 2001.

Vol. 2172: C. Batini, F. Giunchiglia, P. Giorgini, M. Mecella (Eds.), Cooperative Information Systems. Proceedings, 2001. XI, 450 pages. 2001.

Vol. 2173: T. Eiter, W. Faber, M. Truszczynski (Eds.), Logic Programming and Nonmonotonic Reasoning. Proceedings, 2001. XI, 444 pages. 2001. (Subseries LNAI).

Vol. 2174: F. Baader, G. Brewka, T. Eiter (Eds.), KI 2001: Advances in Artificial Intelligence. Proceedings, 2001. XIII, 471 pages. 2001. (Subseries LNAI).

Vol. 2175: F. Esposito (Ed.), AI*IA 2001: Advances in Artificial Intelligence. Proceedings, 2001. XII, 396 pages. 2001. (Subseries LNAI).

Vol. 2176: K.-D. Althoff, R.L. Feldmann, W. Müller (Eds.), Advances in Learning Software Organizations. Proceedings, 2001. XI, 241 pages. 2001.

Vol. 2177: G. Butler, S. Jarzabek (Eds.), Generative and Component-Based Software Engineering. Proceedings, 2001. X, 203 pages. 2001.

Vol. 2180: J. Welch (Ed.), Distributed Computing. Proceedings, 2001. X, 343 pages. 2001.

Vol. 2181: C. Y. Westort (Ed.), Digital Earth Moving. Proceedings, 2001. XII, 117 pages. 2001.

Vol. 2182: M. Klusch, F. Zambonelli (Eds.), Cooperative Information Agents V. Proceedings, 2001. XII, 288 pages. 2001. (Subseries LNAI).

Vol. 2184: M. Tucci (Ed.), Multimedia Databases and Image Communication. Proceedings, 2001. X, 225 pages. 2001.

Vol. 2185: M. Gogolla, C. Kobryn (Eds.), «UML» 2001 – The Unified Modeling Language. Proceedings, 2001. XIV, 510 pages. 2001.

Vol. 2186: J. Bosch (Ed.), Generative and Component-Based Software Engineering. Proceedings, 2001. VIII, 177 pages. 2001.

Vol. 2187: U. Voges (Ed.), Computer Safety, Reliability and Security. Proceedings, 2001. XVI, 261 pages. 2001.

Vol. 2188: F. Bomarius, S. Komi-Sirviö (Eds.), Product Focused Software Process Improvement. Proceedings, 2001. XI, 382 pages. 2001.

Vol. 2189: F. Hoffmann, D.J. Hand, N. Adams, D. Fisher, G. Guimaraes (Eds.), Advances in Intelligent Data Analysis. Proceedings, 2001. XII, 384 pages. 2001.

Vol. 2190: A. de Antonio, R. Aylett, D. Ballin (Eds.), Intelligent Virtual Agents. Proceedings, 2001. VIII, 245 pages. 2001. (Subseries LNAI).

Vol. 2191: B. Radig, S. Florczyk (Eds.), Pattern Recognition. Proceedings, 2001. XVI, 452 pages. 2001.

Vol. 2192: A. Yonezawa, S. Matsuoka (Eds.), Metalevel Architectures and Separation of Crosscutting Concerns. Proceedings, 2001. XI, 283 pages. 2001.

Vol. 2193: F. Casati, D. Georgakopoulos, M.-C. Shan (Eds.), Technologies for E-Services. Proceedings, 2001. X, 213 pages. 2001.

Vol. 2194: A.K. Datta, T. Herman (Eds.), Self-Stabilizing Systems. Proceedings, 2001. VII, 229 pages. 2001.

Vol. 2195: H.-Y. Shum, M. Liao, S.-F. Chang (Eds.), Advances in Multimedia Information Processing – PCM 2001. Proceedings, 2001. XX, 1149 pages. 2001.

Vol. 2196: W. Taha (Ed.), Semantics, Applications, and Implementation of Program Generation. Proceedings, 2001. X, 219 pages. 2001.

Vol. 2197: O. Balet, G. Subsol, P. Torguet (Eds.), Virtual Storytelling. Proceedings, 2001. XI, 213 pages. 2001.

Vol. 2200: G.I. Davida, Y. Frankel (Eds.), Information Security. Proceedings, 2001. XIII, 554 pages. 2001.

Vol. 2201: G.D. Abowd, B. Brumitt, S. Shafer (Eds.), Ubicomp 2001: Ubiquitous Computing. Proceedings, 2001. XIII, 372 pages. 2001.

Vol. 2202: A. Restivo, S. Ronchi Della Rocca, L. Roversi (Eds.), Theoretical Computer Science. Proceedings, 2001. XI, 440 pages. 2001.

Vol. 2205: D.R. Montello (Ed.), Spatial Information Theory. Proceedings, 2001. XIV, 503 pages. 2001.

Vol. 2206: B. Reusch (Ed.), Computational Intelligence. Proceedings, 2001. XVII, 1003 pages. 2001.

Vol. 2207: I.W. Marshall, S. Nettles, N. Wakamiya (Eds.), Active Networks. Proceedings, 2001. IX, 165 pages. 2001.

Vol. 2208: W.J. Niessen, M.A. Viergever (Eds.), Medical Image Computing and Computer-Assisted Intervention – MICCAI 2001. Proceedings, 2001. XXXV, 1446 pages. 2001.

Vol. 2209: W. Jonker (Ed.), Databases in Telecommunications II. Proceedings, 2001. VII, 179 pages. 2001.

Vol. 2210: Y. Liu, K. Tanaka, M. Iwata, T. Higuchi, M. Yasunaga (Eds.), Evolvable Systems: From Biology to Hardware. Proceedings, 2001. XI, 341 pages. 2001.

Vol. 2211: T.A. Henzinger, C.M. Kirsch (Eds.), Embedded Software. Proceedings, 2001. IX, 504 pages. 2001.

Vol. 2212: W. Lee, L. Mé, A. Wespi (Eds.), Recent Advances in Intrusion Detection. Proceedings, 2001. X, 205 pages. 2001.

Vol. 2213: M.J. van Sinderen, L.J.M. Nieuwenhuis (Eds.), Protocols for Multimedia Systems. Proceedings, 2001. XII, 239 pages. 2001.